Cedar Antique Centre

Opened in March of 1998 in fully renovated premises, the new up-market centre is managed by Derek and Sally Green. It complements the other 12 long established dealers in Hartley Wintney who make the village such an excellent trade and private buyers call. It is situated in the same building, but separated from Cedar Antiques which will continue to operate in the same way as it has done for the last 30 years dealing in fine country furniture.

The centre houses some 40 dealers carefully chosen for their high quality and wide range of interesting stock.

You will find everything here from fine furniture through Teddy Bears to Treen

Open 7 days a week Monday to Saturday 10am to 5.30pm Sunday 10am to 4pm

Shipping : Transport : Accommodation all arranged

High Street - Hartley Wintney - Hook - Hampshire - RG27 8NY

Tel 01252 843222 Fax 01252 842111 e-mail cac@cedar-ltd.demon.co.uk

ANTIQUE COLLECTORS' CLUB
NEW CHILDREN'S TITLES

MISTRESS MASHAM'S REPOSE

T. H. White
Illustrated by Martin Hargreaves
Introduction by Anne Fine

This is a beautiful new edition of T. H. White's highly-imaginative tale of a young girl who discovers a colony of tiny people living in secrecy on an overgrown island.

7½ x 9½ in./190 x 240mm., 160 pp., colour illustrations.
ISBN 1 85149 700 5. **£12.99**

THE PRINCESS AND THE GOBLIN

George MacDonald
Illustrated by Nick Walton Introduction by Joan Aiken

This is the story of a young princess and a miner boy who outwit a colony of scheming goblins in an exciting adventure set in a maze of underground caverns.

7½ 9½ in./190 x 240mm., 160 pp., colour illustrations.
ISBN 1 85149 701 3.
£12.99

PETER PAN

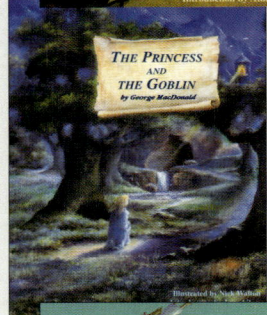

J. M. Barrie
Illustrated by Greg Becker

This is a delightful new edition of one of the greatest children's stories ever written.

When Peter Pan flies through the nursery window one evening, he entices Wendy, Michael and John to follow him to the magical island of Neverland. They soon learn how to fly and encounter the Lost Boys, mermaids and fairies.

7½ x 9½ in./190 x 240mm., 144 pp., colour illustrations.
ISBN 1 85149 702 1. **£12.99**

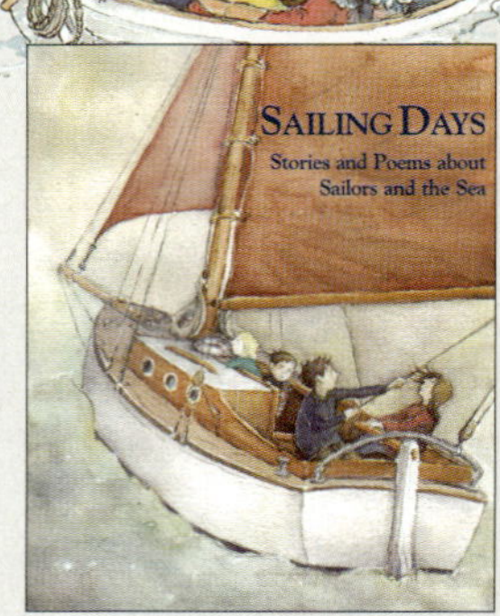

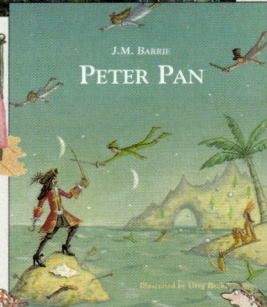

SAILING DAYS
Stories and Poems about Sailors and the Sea

Edited by Amy McKay

There are accounts of shipwreck and of sea-sickness; building a boat and learning to row; climbing the rigging to earn a place in the crew; and being thrown overboard.

It includes extracts from *Treasure Island, We didn't Mean to go to Sea, The Coral Island, 20,000 Leagues Under the Sea, Robinson Crusoe, The Voyages of Doctor Dolittle* and many other classics.

7½ x 9½in./190 x 240mm., 120 pp., colour illustrations.
ISBN 1 85149 703 X. **£12.99**

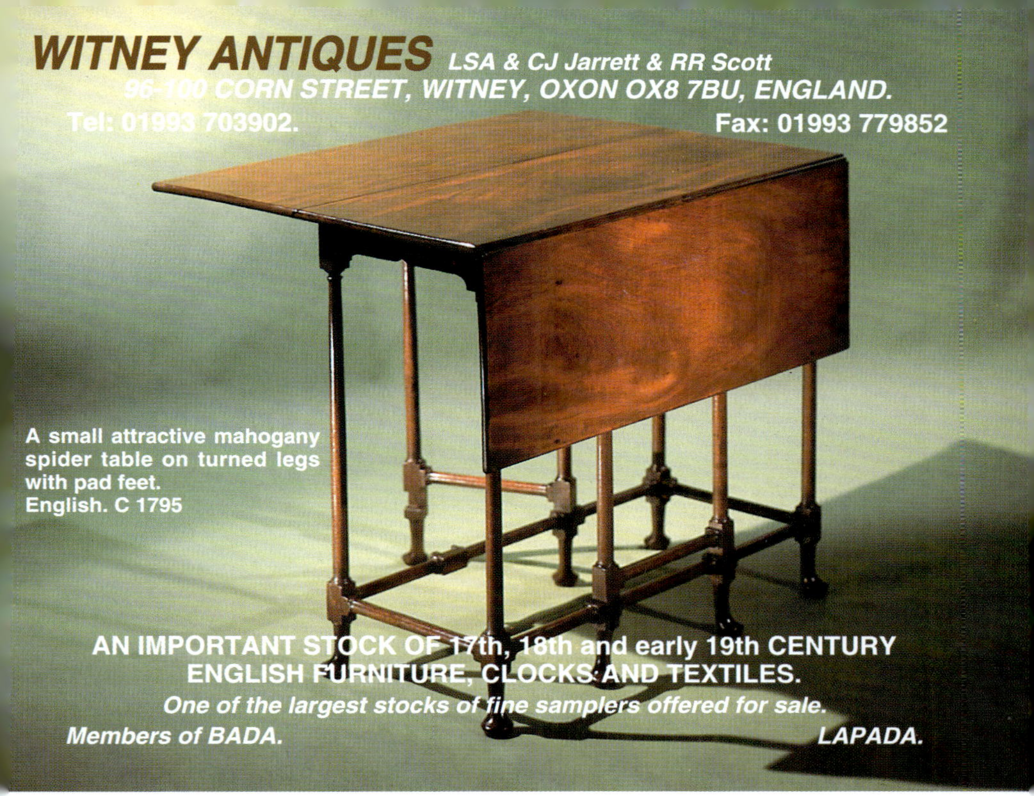

WITNEY ANTIQUES LSA & CJ Jarrett & RR Scott

96-100 CORN STREET, WITNEY, OXON OX8 7BU, ENGLAND.

Tel: 01993 703902. Fax: 01993 779852

A small attractive mahogany spider table on turned legs with pad feet. English. C 1795

AN IMPORTANT STOCK OF 17th, 18th and early 19th CENTURY ENGLISH FURNITURE, CLOCKS AND TEXTILES.

One of the largest stocks of fine samplers offered for sale.

Members of BADA. *LAPADA.*

Kuwahara Ltd.

We are Fine Art Packers & Shippers.

桑原運輸は美術品輸送のスペシャリストです。経験豊富な日本人スタッフが、全ての輸送に関するお手伝いをさせていただきます。

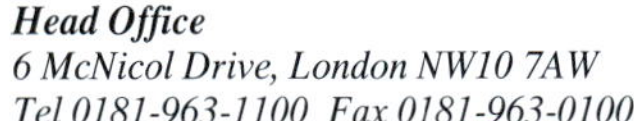

Head Office
6 McNicol Drive, London NW10 7AW
Tel 0181-963-1100 Fax 0181-963-0100

Tokyo Office
c/o Japan Express Co. Ltd.
5-5-6 Konan, Minato-ku, Tokyo 108
Tel 03-5463-4541 Fax 03-5463-4548

- Specialist for Japanese and far east market.
- Bi-lingual courier service.
- 24 hour security bonded, purpose built warehouse.
- Clients assured of a personal service from a well established company.

CONTENTS

ACKNOWLEDGEMENTS

Our main sources of information are still the trade magazines but we would like to thank those dealers who provide information about new shops and closures in their area. Without their assistance our job would be far more difficult.

We would also like to thank those dealers who supported us with advertising - without this revenue each copy would cost £30, instead of £14.95 - and those who up-date their entry when we send them the first reminder. Each year we include a form at the end of the Guide which dealers can use to up-date details about their own business. In anticipation of next year's Guide, we are grateful to those dealers who make use of this form.

Finally, thanks must go to the editorial team who carry out the mammoth task of up-dating, compiling and indexing the entries.

C.A.

Editor **Carol Adams**
Advertising Sales **Jean Johnson**
Editorial Team **Judith Neal, Diana Dutson**

INTRODUCTION

This is the 27th edition of the **Guide to the Antique Shops of Britain** which is universally accepted as *the* guide for anybody who wishes to buy antiques in Britain.

This year we have listed nearly 6,000 establishments and, as usual, every one has been confirmed before reprinting. Please help to keep our costs down by returning the first reminder.

We appreciate that quantity without quality is meaningless and the range of information we provide is more detailed and up-to-date than is available in any other publication. We state the obvious facts - name of proprietor, address, telephone number, opening hours and stock and also size of showroom and price ranges (where supplied). Additional information gives details of major trade association members, the date the business was established, the location and also the parking situation. Whilst none of these points are decisive in themselves, we feel that they build up to a useful picture of the sort of establishment likely to be found and may well influence a prospective buyer's decision as to whether or not to visit a particular shop. As always, we advise a prior telephone call before making a long trip.

We start preparing the next edition in early 1999. Please let us know if there are any alterations to your entry and, if possible, any changes in your area - openings and closures. We do not print any information given about other dealers without first contacting them, but obviously the more shops in a particular town or village, the more attractive it is to prospective buyers on trips around the country. We would also be grateful for your comments on the Guide and, if you find any information given in the Guide to be incorrect, we would be grateful for your input. We have occasionally had dealers telephoning to say that the stock listed is not what they found when visiting a particular establishment but then refuse to tell us the name of the shop which means we can do nothing about the complaint. Any constructive criticism is welcomed and we look forward to your comments.

HOW TO USE THIS GUIDE

The Guide is set out under six main headings; London, England, Channel Islands, Northern Ireland, Scotland and Wales. Counties are listed alphabetically and within counties the towns are listed alphabetically and within towns the shops are listed, again alphabetically. London is divided into postal districts.

To make route planning easier there is a map at the beginning of each county, coded to show the number of shops in any one town or village. The roads indicated on the map are only a broad intimation of the routes available and it is advisable to use an up-to-date map showing the latest improvements in the road system.

Apart from the six main headings above, there are further helpful lists - an alphabetical list of towns, showing the counties in which they will be found for those not familiar with the location of towns within counties, e.g. Woodbridge is shown in the county of Suffolk. One therefore turns to the Suffolk section to look up Woodbridge. This listing is a valuable aid to the overseas visitor. The second is particularly important to British dealers and collectors - giving an alphabetical list of the name of every shop, proprietor and company director known to be connected with a shop or gallery. Thus, if A. Bloggs and B. Brown own an antique shop called Castle Antiques, there will be entries under Bloggs, A., Brown, B., and Castle Antiques. Listings of specialist dealers, auctioneers, shippers and packers, services, and fairs organisers are also included.

2

One point that both dealers and collectors constantly seem to miss is that the telephone offers great savings of time and money. Nearly all dealers have to make unscheduled calls during opening hours and the "Back in 5 minutes" notice which has been in the window of a small shop for 20 minutes is a cause of great irritation to the potential buyer. If you have to be a hundred miles along the road in two hours, but there is something at the back of the shop which looks interesting, then the decision to wait or not wait is even more frustrating. A prior telephone call can forstall this. When you telephone, it is usually quite acceptable to describe what you are looking for in terms of Antique Collectors' Club books. Increasingly one sees advertisements referring to page numbers. Most dealers have at least some of the books and use them as a basis for communicating information.

In the main, dealers are factual and accurate in describing their stock to us but there are probably a few who list what they would like to stock rather than as it is. We would appreciate you letting us know of any such anomalies. Please telephone (01394) 385501 or drop us a postcard and help us to ensure that the Guide remains Britain's premier listing of antique shops and galleries.

ABBREVIATIONS IN ENTRIES

In order to cut the bulk of this book as much as possible without curtailing the amount of information, we have made some very simple contractions in the entries.

BADA and LAPADA: Members are indicated by using a bold type face.

BABADA: Bath and Bradford on Avon Antique Dealers Association.

EADA: Essex Antique Dealers Association.

HADA: Highlands Antique Dealers Association.

TADA: Tetbury Antique Dealers Association.

TVADA: Thames Valley Antique Dealers Association.

CADA: Cotswold Antique Dealers Association.

EST: Shows the year in which the shop was established or the number of years the dealer or firm has been trading.

CL: Days when the business is normally closed. It follows the hours of opening. In some small businesses these may prove erratic, as it is often necessary for the dealer to go out at short notice. Unless otherwise stated shops are closed on Sundays. If making a long journey, it is advisable to telephone and make an appointment.

SIZE: A guide to the size of the showrooms is given to indicate the quantity of stock likely to be seen. Small is under 600 sq. ft. (60 sq. metres), medium between 600 and 1,500 sq. ft. (60 and 150 sq. metres) and large over 1,500 sq. ft. (150 sq.metres).

STOCK: Dealers are asked to list their stock in order of importance, so that the items listed can be expected to comprise a significant part of the stock. The price range is of very general application and is designed to give some idea to prospective buyers of the type of items to be seen. Not stocked items are indicated after those which are stocked, the items listed are not normally to be found in this shop. Advertisements often give extra information on the size of showrooms, etc.

LOC: Location of shop. This is a description given by the owner designed to help the would-be caller. Road numbers in the entries are not necessarily shown on the county maps of the Guide, which are merely general aids to direction.

PARK: This indicates how easy it is for a car to park for 15 minutes outside the shop. Where parking is not easy, alternative suggestions for parking are often given.

TEL: In addition to their business numbers, some dealers have listed their home telephone numbers so customers can ring for an appointment outside business hours. Clearly callers should use discretion and only make calls out of business hours when they are seriously interested, and in any event not late at night or early in the morning.

SER: Additional services which the dealer offers. Where "buys at auction" is shown in this section it indicates that if an auction is one which a dealer might normally attend, he may be approached to act as bidder on behalf of someone else. Check the cost of this service, and any others offered, beforehand.

VAT: Indicates which of the VAT schemes are in operation.

London

HERTFORDS
N.14
N.20
N.W.7
N.12
N.11
N.3
N.10
N.2
N.W.4
N.W.9
N.W.11
N.6
N.19
N.W.2
N.W.3
BUCKINGHAMSHIRE
N.W.5
N.W.10
N.W.6
N.W.8
N.W.1
W.9
W.10
W.13
W.5
W.7
W.3
W.12
W.11
W.2
W.1
W.8
W.14
S.W.7
S.W.1
W.6
S.W.5
S.W.3
W.4
S.W.10
S.W.8
S.W.13
S.W.6
S.W.11
S.W.14
S.W.4
S.W.15
S.W.18
S.W.12
S.W.17
S.W.19
S.W.20
SURREY

London postal districts

LONDON LISTING

London shops are listed by postal districts in the following order:

W.1	and numerically through to			W.14
S.W.1	"	"	"	" S.W.20
S.E.1	"	"	"	" S.E.26
E.1	"	"	"	" E.18
E.C.1	"	"	"	" E.C.4
N.1	"	"	"	" N.21
N.W.1	"	"	"	" N.W.11
W.C.1	"	"	"	" W.C.2

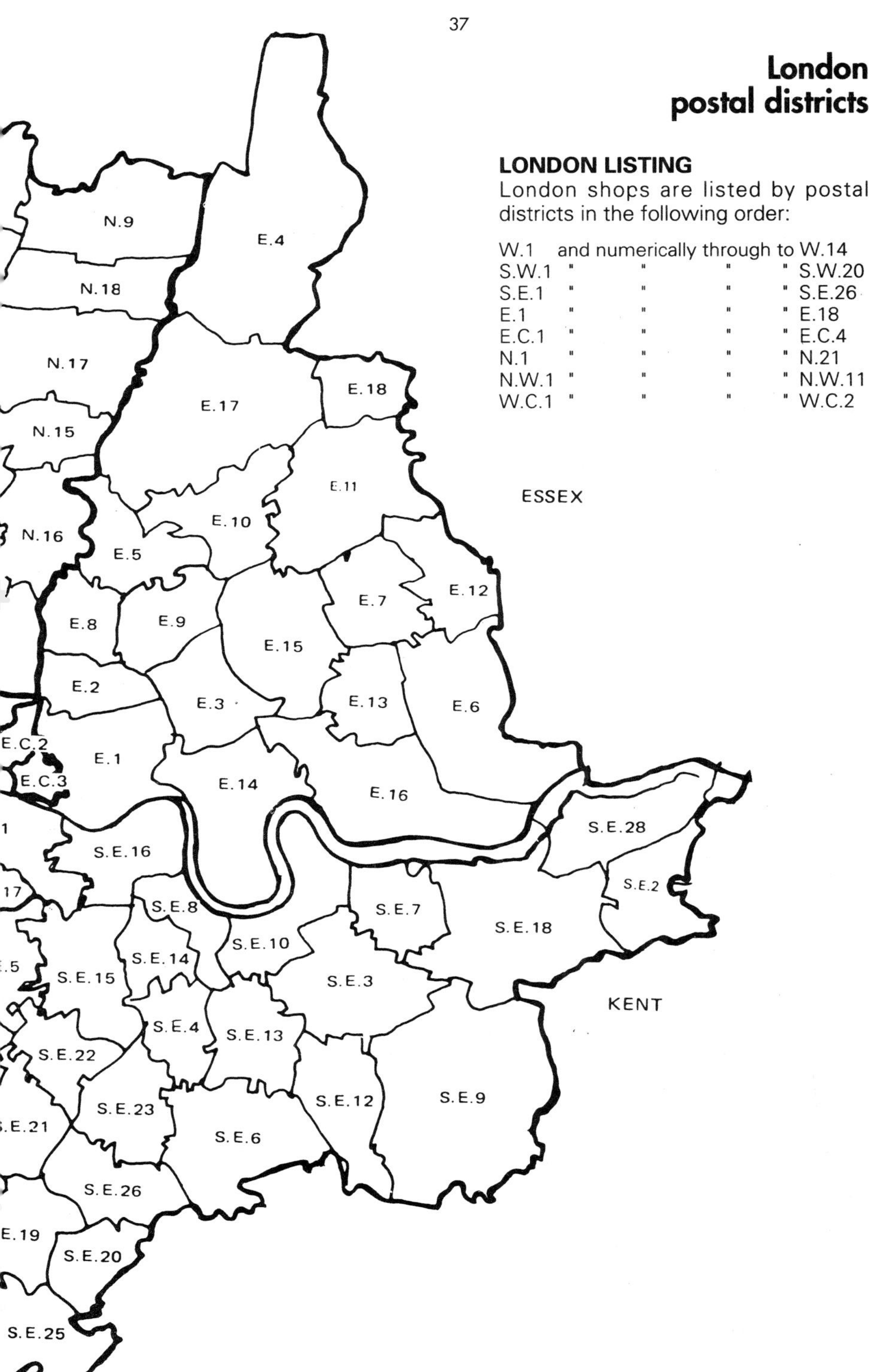

LONDON W1

Aaron Gallery
34 Bruton St. W1X 7DD. (M. and D. Aaron). Est. 1910. Open 10-6, Sat. by appointment. *STOCK: Islamic and ancient art, Oriental carpets.* TEL: 0171 499 9434/5; fax - 0171 499 0072.

Agnew's BADA
43 Old Bond St. and 3 Albemarle St. W1X 4BA. SLAD. Est. 1817. Open 9.30-5.30, Thurs. 9.30-6.30. CL: Sat. SIZE: Large. *STOCK: Paintings, drawings, watercolours, engravings and sculptures of all schools.* TEL: 0171 629 6176; fax - 0171 629 4359. VAT: Spec.

Adrian Alan Ltd BADA LAPADA
66/67 South Audley St. W1Y 5FE. Est. 1963. Open 10-6. CL: Sat. SIZE: Large. *STOCK: English and Continental furniture, especially fine 19th C; sculpture and works of art.* TEL: 0171 495 2324; fax - 0171 495 0204. VAT: Stan/Spec.

Philip Antrobus Ltd
11 New Bond St. W1Y 0SE. Est. 1815. *STOCK: Jewellery.* TEL: 0171 493 4557; fax - 0171 495 2120.

Argyll Etkin Gallery
48 Conduit St. W1R 9FB. (Argyll Etkin Ltd). Est. 1954. Open 9-5.30. CL: Sat. SIZE: Medium. *STOCK: Classic postage stamps, postal history and covers, historical documents and antique letters, 1400-1950, £50-£25,000; stamp boxes and associated writing equipment, 1700-1930, £50-£500.* LOC: Near Oxford Circus. PARK: Savile Row. TEL: 0171 437 7800 (6 lines). SER: Valuations; collections purchased. FAIRS: Major stamp exhibitions worldwide. VAT: Stan.

Armour-Winston Ltd
43 Burlington Arcade. W1V 9AE. Est. 1952. Open 9-5. Sat. 9.30-2. SIZE: Small. *STOCK: Jewellery, especially Victorian; gentlemen's cufflinks.* LOC: Off Piccadilly. Between Green Park and Piccadilly tube stations. PARK: Savile Row. TEL: 0171 493 8937. SER: Valuations; restorations. VAT: Stan/Spec.

W1 continued

Asprey plc BADA
165-169 New Bond St. W1Y 0AR. Est. 1781. Open 9.30-5.30, Sat. 10-5. SIZE: Large. *STOCK: Furniture, works of art, clocks, silver, jewellery, Fabergé and objets de vertu, glass.* PARK: Albemarle St., entrance No.22. TEL: 0171 493 6767; fax - 0171 491 0384. SER: Valuations; restorations (furniture, jewellery, clocks, silver). VAT: Stan/Spec.

Atlantic Bay Carpets BADA
5 Sedley Place. W1R 1HH. (W. Grodzinski and Z. Golebiowski). Est. 1945. Open 9-5, Sat. 9-1. SIZE: Medium. *STOCK: Antique Oriental and European carpets and textiles.* LOC: Near Bond/Oxford St. PARK: Easy. TEL: 0171 355 3301; fax - 0171 355 3760. SER: Valuations; restorations; buys at auction (as stock). VAT: Stan/Spec.

John and Arthur Beare BADA
7 Broadwick St. W1V 1FJ. (J. and A. Beare Ltd). Est. 1892. Open 9-12.15 and 1.30-5. CL: Sat. *STOCK: Violins, violas, cellos, bows and accessories.* TEL: 0171 437 1449. SER: Valuations. VAT: Stan/Spec.

Paul Bennett LAPADA
48A George St. W1H 5RF. (M.J. Dubiner). Open 9.30-6. CL: Sat. SIZE: Large. *STOCK: Silver, 1740-1963, £10-£10,000; Sheffield plate.* PARK: Meters. TEL: 0171 935 1555/486 8836. VAT: Stan/Spec.

Bentley & Co Ltd LAPADA
8 New Bond St. W1Y 9PE. Open 10-5.30. *STOCK: Jewellery, Fabergé, objets d'art.* PARK: Meters. TEL: 0171 629 0651. SER: Valuations; repairs. VAT: Stan/Spec.

Konrad O. Bernheimer Ltd BADA
1 Mount St., Mayfair. W1Y 5AA. CINOA SLAD. Est. 1985. Open by appointment only. *STOCK: Old Master paintings, Continental furniture and Chinese ceramics.* TEL: 0171 495 7028; fax - 0171 495 7027.

W1 continued

Peter Biddulph
34 St George St., Hanover Sq. W1R 0ND. Open 10-6. CL: Sat. *STOCK: Violins, violas, cellos and bows.* TEL: 0171 491 8621; fax - 0171 495 1428.

H. Blairman and Sons Ltd. BADA
119 Mount St. W1Y 5HB. (M.P. and W.Y. Levy and L.G. Hannen). Est. 1884. Open daily. CL: Sat. SIZE: Medium. *STOCK: English and French antiques, mid-18th to early 19th C; works of art, mounted porcelain, Chinese mirror pictures; architect designed furniture, 19th C.* TEL: 0171 493 0444; fax - 0171 495 0766. FAIRS: Grosvenor House; Fine Art & Antique Dealers, New York. VAT: Spec.

Blunderbuss Antiques
29 Thayer St. W1M 5LJ. (T. Greenaway). Open 9.30-4.30. *STOCK: Arms and armour, militaria.* TEL: 0171 486 2444.

Bond Street Antiques Centre
124 New Bond St. W1. (Atlantic Antique Centres Ltd). Est. 1970. Open 10-5.30, Sat. 11-5.30. SIZE: Large - 27 dealers. *STOCK: Wide range of general antiques especially jewellery.* LOC: Bond St., Oxford St. or Green Park tube stations. TEL: Enquiries - 0171 351 5353; fax - 0171 351 5350; e-mail - atlan@globalnet.co.uk. Below are listed some of the dealers at this market.

Emmy Abe
Stand 33. *Jewellery and silver.* TEL: 0171 629 1826.

Accurate Trading Co
Stand 1D. (E. Fahimian). *Jewellery.* TEL: 0171 629 0277.

Anita's Antiques
Stand 40. *Jewellery.* TEL: 0171 409 2107.

Anne Bloom Jewellers Ltd
Stand 15. Open 11-5. *Period and contemporary jewellery and objet d'art.* TEL: 0171 491 1213. VAT: Stan/Margin

Clayre Armitage & Ann Music
Stand 31. *Jewellery and objects.* TEL: 0171 493 5830.

Ertan Balkir
Stand 10/11. *Prints, maps, drawings.*

Daniel Bexfield Antiques
Stand 34/35. *Fine silver and objects of virtue, 18th-20th C.* TEL: 0171 491 1720; fax - 0171 491 1730; mobile - 0820 681150; e-mail - antiques@bexfield.co.uk; internet - http://www.bexfield.co.uk.

N. Bloom & Son (1912) Ltd LAPADA
Stand 7-9 & 19-20. (I. Harris). *Jewellery, mainly 1860-1960; small silver items, objets d'art and vertu, paintings.* TEL: 0171 629 5060; fax - 0171 493 2528; mobile - 0973 149363; e-mail - nbloom@nbloom.co.uk; internet - http://www.nbloom.co.uk. SER: Valuations; restorations; repairs; buys at auction. VAT: Stan/Spec.

W1 continued

Mr. Cyrlin
Stand 32. *Watches.* TEL: 0171 629 0133.

Adele de Havilland
Stand 18. *Oriental porcelain, netsuke, jade.* TEL: 0171 499 7127.

Mr. Downing
Stand 17. *Jewellery and gemstones.* TEL: 0171 499 4346.

David Duggan LAPADA
Stands 1A, 1B. *Vintage watches.* TEL: 0171 491 1362; fax - 0171 408 1727.

Elisabeth's Antiques LAPADA
Stands 42-44. (Mrs E. Hage). *Jewellery.* TEL: 0171 491 1723; mobile - 0860 550300.

Matthew Foster
Stand 16. *Jewellery.* TEL: 0171 629 4977.

Anthony Green Antiques
Stand 39. *Watches and objects.* TEL: 0171 409 2854; fax - 0171 408 0010.

Massada Antiques LAPADA
Stand 2. (C.B. and C. Yacobi). Est. 1970. Open Mon.-Fri. 10-5.30. *Jewellery and silver.* TEL: 0171 493 4792/629 3402.

Myra Antiques
Stands 4. *Jewellery, glass, paintings and objects.* TEL: 0171 408 1508.

Nonesuch Antiques LAPADA
Stand 3. (Mrs E. Michelson). *Jewellery and objects.* TEL: 0171 629 6783.

P.M.R. Antiques
Stand 25/26. (Peter Rosen). *Jewellery.* TEL: 0171 495 4406.

Resner's BADA LAPADA
Stands 5/6. (S. and G.R. Resner, M.P. Daniels). Est. 1918. *Jewellery, £250-£10,000; objets d'art, £200-£1,000; silver, £100-£2,500; all 18th-19th C.* TEL: 0171 629 1413; fax - same; mobile - 0860 704251. SER: Valuations; restorations (jewellery). VAT: Stan/Spec.

Sadi & Sahar
Stand 29/30 & 36/37. (Mrs S. Noorani). *Jewellery, glass and porcelain.* TEL: 0171 491 2081.

Nino Santi
Stand 38. *Jewellery and watches.* TEL: 0171 629 3008.

Sergio Tencati
Stand 12. *Jewellery and silver.*

Trianon Antiques and Michael Longmore LAPADA
Stand 1C. *Jewellery.* TEL: 0171 629 6678.

W1 continued

Matsuko Yamamoto
Stand 23. *Jewellery and porcelain.* TEL: 0171 491 0983.

Bond Street Silver Galleries
111-112 New Bond St. W1. Open 9-5.30. CL: Sat. PARK: Meters. TEL: 0171 493 6180; fax - 0171 495 3493. Below are listed the dealers at these galleries.

Barnes Jewellers
Fine jewellery. TEL: 0171 495 7554; fax - 0171 495 7556.

Brian Beet
Silver and works of art. TEL: 0171 437 4975; fax - 0171 495 8635.

A. and B. Bloomstein Ltd BADA LAPADA
***Silver, Sheffield plate.* TEL: 0171 493 6180; fax - 0171 495 3493. SER:Valuations; restorations.**

Bruford and Heming LAPADA
NAG. *Domestic silver especially flatware, jewellery.,* TEL: 0171 499 7644/629 4289; fax - 0171 493 5879. SER: Valuations; restorations. Stan/Spec.

R. Close Jewellery Restoration
TEL: 0171 495 0287.

Phillip Cull
Silver and Sheffield plate. TEL: 0171 493 2047.

Adrian Ewart (Gavina Ewart Antiques) BADA
***Silver, porcelain, bronze and ormulu.* TEL: 0171 491 7266; 01242 526994.**

O. Frydman
Silver, Sheffield and Victorian plate. TEL: 0171 493 4895. VAT: Stan/Spec.

Graus Antiques
Objets d'art, jewellery and silver. TEL: 0171 629 6680/6651; fax - 0171 629 3361.

A. Lee & Co
Watch and clock makers and repairers. TEL: 0171 629 3067; fax - 0171 629 4221.

M & L Silver Partnership
Silver, old Sheffield and silver plate. TEL: 0171 499 5170; fax - same.

A. Pash & Son
Silver and old Sheffield plate. TEL: 0171 493 5176; fax - 0171 355 3676.

Harry Perovetz
Silver, old Sheffield and Victorian plate. TEL: 0171 954 7780/0181 954 6317; fax - 0181 954 6902.

M. Sedler
Silver and plate. TEL: 0171 839 3131.

W1 continued

D. P. Stern Jewellery and Silver Restoration
TEL: 0171 629 6292; fax - 0171 355 1427.

E. Swonnell (Silverware) Ltd
Silver, Sheffield plate. TEL: 0171 629 9649; fax - same. VAT: Stan/Spec.

David Webb
Old silver, plated ware, decorative objects. TEL: 0171 493 1849; fax - 0171 491 7211.

Boodle and Dunthorne Ltd
128-130 Regent St. W1. Open 9-6. *STOCK: Fine English and French jewellery, 19th-20th C, £100-£30,000.* TEL: 0171 437 5050; 0171 584 6363.

Brandt Oriental Art BADA
First Floor, 29 New Bond St. W1Y 9HD. (R. Brandt). Est. 1981. Open by appointment. *STOCK: Oriental works of art, £500-£10,000.* TEL: 0171 499 8835; mobile - 0374 989661. VAT: Spec.

Browse and Darby Ltd
19 Cork St. W1X 2LP. SLAD. Est. 1977. *STOCK: French and British paintings, drawings and sculpture, 19th-20th C.* TEL: 0171 734 7984. VAT: Spec.

John Bull (Antiques) Ltd

JB Silverware LAPADA
139A New Bond St. W1Y 9FB. Open 9-5. CL: Sat. *STOCK: Silver and plate; reproduction silver photo-frames.* TEL: 0171 629 1251; fax - 0171 495 3001. VAT: Global/Margin.

Burlington Paintings Ltd BADA
12 Burlington Gardens. W1X 1LG. (A. Lloyd, M. Day and J. Lloyd). Est. 1981. Open 9.30-5.30, Sat. 10-5. SIZE: Small. *STOCK: British and European oil paintings, 19th-20th C, from £1,000.* LOC: Between Old Bond St. and Regent St., facing Savile Row. PARK: NCP Brewer St. TEL: 0171 734 9984. SER: Valuations; restorations (lining, cleaning, reframing oils and watercolours); buys at auction (pictures). VAT: Stan/Spec.

The Button Queen
19 Marylebone Lane. W1M 5FE. (T. and M. Frith). Est. 1953. Open 10-5, Thurs. and Fri. 10-6, Sat. 10-4. SIZE: Large. *STOCK: Antique, old and modern buttons.* LOC: Off Wigmore St. TEL: 0171 935 1505. VAT: Stan.

Carrington and Co. Ltd
170 Regent St. W1R 6BQ. Open 9-5.30. *STOCK: Regimental jewellery and silver, trophies, watches, clocks.* TEL: 0171 734 3727.

Lumley Cazalet Ltd
33 Davies St. W1Y 1FN. SLAD. Est. 1967. Open 10-6. CL: Sat. *STOCK: Late 19th and 20th C original prints including Braque, Chagall, Miro, Matisse, Picasso; drawings by Matisse; drawings and sculpture by Elisabeth Frink.* TEL: 0171 491 4767; fax - 0171 493 8644.

W1 continued

Antoine Cheneviere Fine Arts BADA
27 Bruton St. W1. Open 9.30-6. CL: Sat. *STOCK: 18th-19th C furniture and paintings, objets d'art from Russia, Italy, Austria, Sweden and Germany.* TEL: 0171 491 1007.

Andrew Clayton-Payne
2nd Floor, 14 Old Bond St. W1 3BD. Open by appointment. SIZE: Small. *STOCK: English watercolours, £500-£10,000.* PARK: Easy. TEL: 0171 493 6980; fax - same. SER: Valuations; buys at auction (pictures). FAIRS: World of Watercolours & Drawings. VAT: Spec.

Colefax and Fowler
39 Brook St. W1Y 2JE. Est. 1933. Open 9.30-5.30. CL: Sat. SIZE: Large. *STOCK: Decorative furniture, pictures, lamps and carpets, 18th-19th C.* PARK: Meters. TEL: 0171 493 2231. VAT: Stan/Spec.

P. and D. Colnaghi & Co Ltd BADA
15 Old Bond St. W1X 4JL. Est. 1760. Open 9.30-6. SIZE: Large. *STOCK: Master paintings and drawings, 14th-19th C; English paintings.* TEL: 0171 491 7408. SER: Experts and appraisers. VAT: Spec.

Connaught Brown plc
2 Albemarle St. W1X 3HF. (A. Brown). SLAD. Est. 1980. Open 10-6, Sat. 10-12.30. SIZE: Medium. *STOCK: Post Impressionist, Scandinavian and modern works, from £5,000+; contemporary, from £500+.* LOC: Off Piccadilly and parallel to Bond St. PARK: Berkeley Sq. TEL: 0171 408 0362. SER: Valuations; restorations (paintings, drawings, watercolours and sculpture). FAIRS: Chicago New Pier Art; Islington. VAT: Stan/Spec.

Sandra Cronan Ltd BADA LAPADA
18 Burlington Arcade. W1V 9AB. Est. 1975. Open 10-5. *STOCK: Fine and unusual jewels, 18th to early 20th C, £500-£50,000.* LOC: Off Bond St. TEL: 0171 491 4851; fax - 0171 493 2758. SER: Valuations; design commissions. FAIRS: Fine Art & Antiques, Olympia (June); BADA (March). VAT: Stan/Spec.

Barry Davies Oriental Art BADA
1 Davies St. W1Y 1LL. Open 10-6. CL: Sat. *STOCK: Japanese works of art, netsuke, lacquer and bronzes.* TEL: 0171 408 0207.

A. B. Davis Ltd
18 Brook St., (Corner of New Bond St). W1Y 1AA. Est. 1920. Open 10-5. CL: Sat. *STOCK: Antique and secondhand jewellery, small silver items and objets d'art.* TEL: 0171 629 1053; 0171 242 7357 (ansaphone).; fax and ansaphone - 0171 499 6454. SER: Valuations; repairs (jewellery and silver). VAT: Stan/Spec.

W1 continued

Richard Day Ltd
173 New Bond St. W1Y 9PB. Open 10-5. CL: Sat. *STOCK: Old Master drawings.* TEL: 0171 629 2991; fax - 0171 493 7569. VAT: Stan.

Demas
31 Burlington Arcade. W1V 9AD. Est. 1953. Open 10-5. CL: Sat. pm. *STOCK: Georgian, Victorian and Art Deco jewellery.* TEL: 0171 493 9496. VAT: Stan.

Charles Ede Ltd
20 Brook St. W1Y 1AD. Est. 1970. Open 12.30-4.30 or by appointment. CL: Mon and Sat. *STOCK: Greek, Roman and Egyptian antiquities, £50-£50,000.* PARK: Meters. TEL: 0171 493 4944; fax - 0171 491 2548. SER: Valuations; buys at auction. VAT: Spec.

Editions Graphiques Gallery
3 Clifford St. W1. (V. Arwas). Est. 1966. Open 10-6, Sat. 10-2. SIZE: Large. *STOCK: Art Nouveau and Art Deco, glass, ceramics, bronzes, sculpture, furniture, jewellery, silver, pewter, books and posters 1880-1940, £25-£50,000; paintings, watercolours and drawings, 1880 to date, £100-£20,000; original graphics, lithographs, etchings, woodcuts, 1890 to date, £5-£10,000.* LOC: Between New Bond St and Savile Row. PARK: 50yds. TEL: 0171 734 3944. SER: Valuations; buys at auction. VAT: Stan/Spec.

Andrew Edmunds
44 Lexington St. W1R 3LH. Open 10-6. CL: Sat. *STOCK: 18th and early 19th C caricature and decorative prints and drawings.* TEL: 0171 437 8594; fax - 0171 439 2551. VAT: Stan/Spec.

Emanouel Corporation (UK) Ltd
LAPADA

64 & 64a South Audley St. W1Y 5FD. (E. Haghi). Est. 1974. Open 10-6, Sat. by appointment only. *STOCK: Important antiques and fine works of art, 18th-19th C; Islamic works of art.* TEL: 0171 493 4350; fax - 0171 629 3125; e-mail - emanouel@emanouel demon.co.uk VAT: Stan/Spec.

Eskenazi Ltd
BADA

10 Clifford St. W1X 1RB. (J.E. Eskenazi and P. Constantinidi). Est. 1960. Open 9.30-6, Sat. by appointment. SIZE: Large. *STOCK: Early Chinese ceramics; bronzes, sculpture, works of art; Japanese netsuke and lacquer.* TEL: 0171 493 5464; fax - 0171 499 3136. VAT: Spec.

John Eskenazi Ltd
BADA

15 Old Bond St. W1X 4JL. Open 9-1 and 2-6, Sat. and Sun. by appointment. SIZE: Medium. *STOCK: Oriental art, rugs and textiles; Indian, Himalayan and South East Asian art.* PARK: Meters. TEL: 0171 409 3001; fax - 0171 629 2146. SER: Rug conservation. FAIRS: International Asian Art, New York (March); Basel. VAT: Spec.

W1 continued

Essie Carpets
62 Piccadilly. W1V 9HL. (E. Sakhai). Est. 1766. Open 9.30-6.30, Sun. 10.30-6.30. CL: Sat. SIZE: Large. *STOCK: Persian and Oriental carpets and rugs.* LOC: Opposite St. James St. and Ritz Hotel. PARK: Easy. TEL: 0171 493 7766; home - 0171 586 3388. SER: Valuations; restorations; commissions undertaken. VAT: Stan/Spec.

Brian Fielden
BADA

3 New Cavendish St. W1M 7RP. Open 9.30-1 and 2-5.30, Sat. 9.30-1. SIZE: Medium. *STOCK: English walnut and mahogany furniture, 18th to early 19th C; mirrors and barometers.* LOC: 5 minutes walk north of Bond St. PARK: Meters. TEL: 0171 935 6912; fax - 0171 722 9192. VAT: Spec.

The Fine Art Society plc
148 New Bond St. W1Y 0JT. SLAD. Est. 1876. Open 9.30-5.30, Sat. 10-1. SIZE: Large. *STOCK: British fine and decorative arts, 19th-20th C.* PARK: 300yds. TEL: 0171 629 5116. SER: Buys at auction. VAT: Stan/Spec.

Sam Fogg
35 St. George St. W1R 9FA. Est. 1971. Open by appointment. *STOCK: Manuscripts, all periods.* TEL: 0171 495 2333; fax - 0171 409 3326. SER: Valuations; buys at auction.

Fortnum and Mason plc
Piccadilly. W1A 1ER. Open 9.30-6. SIZE: Medium. *STOCK: English furniture, 18th-19th C; objects of art, porcelain and decorative paste jewellery.* PARK: Meters. TEL: 0171 734 8040.

J.A. Fredericks and Son
Correspondence only to: 31 Watling Court, High St., Elstree, Herts. (J.A. and C.J. Fredericks). Est. 1938. Open by appointment. *STOCK: English furniture.* TEL: 0181 953 5859. *Trade Only.*

H. Fritz-Denneville Fine Arts Ltd
31 New Bond St. W1Y 9HD. SLAD. *STOCK: Paintings, drawings and prints, especially German Romantics, Nazarenes and Expressionists.* TEL: 0171 629 2466; fax - 0171 408 0604. SER: Valuations; restorations; buys at auction.

Deborah Gage (Works of Art) Ltd
38 Old Bond St. W1X 3AE. Est. 1982. Open 9.30-5.30. CL: Sat. *STOCK: European decorative arts and paintings, 17th-18th C; French and British pictures, late 19th to early 20th C, from £5,000.* TEL: 0171 493 3249; fax - 0171 495 1352. SER: Valuations; cataloguing; buys at auction. VAT: Stan/Spec.

Garrard & Co Ltd (The Crown Jewellers)
BADA

112 Regent St. W1A 2JJ. (Richard Jarvis). Est. 1735. Open 9.30-5.30, Sat. 10.30-5.30. SIZE: Large. *STOCK: Jewellery, silver, clocks and*

W1 continued

***watches.* TEL: 0171 734 7020; fax - 0171 734 0711. SER: Valuations; restorations (antique silver and clocks). FAIRS: Maastricht. VAT: Stan.**

Christopher Gibbs Ltd
8 Vigo St. W1X 1LG. Est. 1960. Open 9.30-5.30. CL: Sat. SIZE: Large. *STOCK: Unusual and decorative paintings, furniture, works of art and sculpture.* TEL: 0171 439 4557. VAT: Spec.

Thomas Gibson Fine Art Ltd
44 Old Bond St. W1X 4HQ. SLAD. Open 10-5. CL: Sat. *STOCK: 19th-20th C Masters and selected Old Masters.* TEL: 0171 499 8572; fax - 0171 495 1924.

Thomas Goode and Co (London) Ltd
19 South Audley St. W1. Est. 1827. Open 10-6. SIZE: Large. *STOCK: China, glass, silver, tableware, ornamental.* TEL: 0171 499 2823; fax - 0171 629 4230. SER: Restorations. VAT: Spec.

Grays Antique Market
South Molton Lane. W1Y 2LP. Open 10-6. CL: Sat. TEL: 0171 629 7034. Below are listed the dealers at this market.

2nd Time Around Ltd
Stand 105/168/9. (Waite/Kushner). TEL: 0171 499 7442.

AG Antiques LAPADA
Stand 154/5. (Anthea Geshua). TEL: 0171 493 7564.

Alexanders Cafe
Stand 117 (Elizabeth Anastos). TEL: 0171 629 3223.

Antique Medical Instruments
Stand 374. (Elizabeth Bennion). TEL: 0171 499 5334.

Arca
Stand 351/2/3. (R & E Innocentini). TEL: 0171 629 2729.

Sean Arnold
Stand 316/7/8/28. TEL: 0171 409 7358.

Asian Gallery plc
Stand 107. (Catherine Farrell and David Barrymore). TEL: 0171 629 2935.

Elias Assad
Stand A16/7. *Middle Eastern art.* TEL: 0171 499 4778.

Osman Aytac
Stand 331/2. TEL: 0171 629 7380.

Colin Baddiel
Stand B24/5/C12/3. TEL: 0171 408 1239.

David Baker
Stand H23. TEL: 0171 629 3788.

W1 continued

Rosemary Barnes
Stand 153. *Jewellery.* TEL: 0171 408 0909.

Don Bayney
Stand C24/5. TEL: 0171 629 3644.

Linda Bee
Stand M20/1. *Art Deco.* TEL: 0171 629 5921.

W. Bennett & Co
Stand C31/2. (William Bennett). TEL: 0171 408 1880.

Barbara Berg
Stand 333. TEL: 0171 499 0560.

David Bowden
Stand 319. TEL: 0171 495 1773.

Pauline Boxsey
Stand 136. TEL: 0171 495 0592.

Patrick Boyd-Carpenter
Stand 129/130. TEL: 0171 491 7623.

Sue Brown
Stand M14/5/6. TEL: 0171 491 4287.

Helen Buxton Ltd
Stand J23/4/5. (Barbara Crowell). TEL: 0171 409 2685.

Byblos Antiques
Stand K36/7/8. (Ghassan el Haddad). TEL: 0171 495 1327.

Christopher Cavey
Stand 177/8. TEL: 0171 495 1743.

Cekay
Stand 172. (F B L Kay). TEL: 0171 629 5130.

D & J Church
Stand 163. TEL: 0171 499 7936.

Classic Frames
Stand 360/1/322. (Paul Dowling). TEL: 0171 629 4533.

Coins
Stand J30/1. (L. di Lauro). TEL: 0171 355 1565.

Coleman/Sharpe
Stand J12. TEL: 0171 409 2388.

Collections
Stand 329/330. (S. Byron). TEL: 0171 493 2654.

Olivia Collings
Stand 327. TEL: 0171 499 5478.

Continium
Stand 124. (F. and E. Joy). TEL: 0171 493 4909.

Vincente Cortez Llopis
Stand 342. TEL: 0171 629 5011.

W1 continued

Croesus
Stand 323/4. (Phil and Lindy Conyngham-Hynes and A.M. Davies). *Jewellery.* TEL: 0171 493 0624.

Crystalware
Stand L16. (Patricia Angeli). *Jewellery.* TEL: 0171 493 3098.

Beverley Cunningham
Stand 343/4. TEL: 0171 408 1129.

Alan Darer
Stand A22. TEL: 0171 629 3644.

Double Bett
Stand 104. (Dave Bett). TEL: 0171 493 1530.

David Eisler
Stand C22. TEL: 0171 629 2526.

Joanna Elton
Stand 175. TEL: 0171 629 4769.

Rosemary Erbrich
Stand C26. TEL: 0171 629 2526.

Jack First
Stand 310/1. TEL: 0171 409 2722.

Nicola Franks
Stand 343/4. TEL: 0171 408 1129.

French Decorative Art
Stand 367. (Mrs Jain). TEL: 0171 491 0407.

Gallery Diem
Stand 131/143. (Andrew Day). TEL: 0171 629 3206.

Peter Gaunt
Stand 120/1/141/2. TEL: 0171 629 1072.

Trevor Gilbert **LAPADA**
Stand G10/1. TEL: 0171 408 0028.

The Gilded Lily **LAPADA**
Stand 132/144/5. (Korin Harvey). TEL: 0171 499 6260.

Golfania
Stand N47. (Sarah Fabian Baddiel). TEL: 0171 408 1239; 01223 357958/445096.

Ora Gordon
Stand J27/K14.

Patrick & Susan Gould
Stand L17. TEL: 0171 408 0129.

R.G. Graham
Stand 112/3/217. TEL: 0171 629 3223.

Peter Greenhalgh
Stand 137. TEL: 0171 491 9178.

W1 continued

Sarah Groombridge **LAPADA**
Stand 335/6/7. TEL: 0171 629 0225.

Linda Groppi
Stand M20/1. TEL: 0171 629 5921.

Guest & Gray
Stand H25/6/7/8/J10/3. (Anthony Gray). TEL: 0171 408 1252.

Alice Gullersarian
Stand K33. TEL: 0171 629 3788.

Brian Harkins
Stand 126. TEL: 0171 409 2530.

Harrison's Books
Stand J19/20. (Leo Harrison). TEL: 0171 629 1374.

Satoe Hatrell
Stand 156/166. TEL: 0171 629 4296.

Hoffman Antiques
Stand 133. TEL: 0171 499 4340.

David Hogg
Stand 109. TEL: 0171 493 0208.

Lynn and Brian Holmes **LAPADA**
Stand 304/5/6. *Jewellery.* TEL: 0171 629 7327.

J.L.A. **LAPADA**
Stand 123. (Alan Jacobs). TEL: 0171 499 1681.

Jafar
Stand H24/J14. (Jafar Hashtrudi). TEL: 0171 409 7919.

Mohammed Jawad
Stand C33/4. TEL: 0171 629 5270.

Ali Jazi
Stand A30. TEL: 0171 629 6813.

Katie Jones
Stand 126. TEL: 0171 409 2530.

Judson Ltd
Stand 321. (Alpani Kothari). TEL: 0171 493 0804/495 7327.

Junegrove Ltd
Stand 362. (Fiona Williamson). TEL: 0171 495 4889.

K & M Antiques
Stand 340/1. (Martin Harris). TEL: 0171 491 4310.

Andre and Minoo Kaae **LAPADA**
Stand G22/3. *Jewellery.* TEL: 0171 629 1200.

A.M. Khoei
Stand C33/34. TEL: 0171 629 5270.

Kikuchi Trading Co Ltd **LAPADA**
Stand 357/8/368. (Konio Kikuchi). TEL: 0171 629 6808.

W1 continued

Louis Laurence
(Ann Howard). TEL: 0171 493 0043.

Lees de Smet - Aurum
Stand 313. (Paul Lebbitel). TEL: 0171 409 0215.

Monditurn Ltd LAPADA
Stand 345/6/7. (John Joseph). TEL: 0171 629 1140.

Oasis
Stand E14/5/6/7. (Salim Hassbani). TEL: 0171 493 1202.

Oriental Works of Art
Stand K24/5/6/7+s/c. (Robert Bouita). TEL: 0171 629 5476.

Paris Smith
Stand K19. (Jackie Hopkins). TEL: 0171 629 3112.

Pars Antiques
Stand A14/5. (Kathy Williams). TEL: 0171 491 9889.

Phoenix
Stand 108. (E. and J. Edwards). TEL: 0171 495 1123.

Pieces of Time LAPADA
Stand M17/8/9. (Johnny Wachsman). TEL: 0171 629 3272.

Pillows of Bond St
Stand 301. (Robin Kumar), TEL: 0171 495 8853.

RBR
Stand 176. (D. Edmunds Brazell). TEL: 0171 495 5635.

RBR Grp
Stand 175. (Olivia Gerrish). TEL: 0171 629 4769.

M. Ritchfield Export Ltd
Stand 385. (Musako Kikuchi). TEL: 0171 629 6808.

River Cafe
Stand D17. (Maurizio Businaro). TEL: 0171 408 1831/0181 444 2932.

Rocco
Stand 363. (Jill Barnes). TEL: 0171 409 2743.

Samirami's LAPADA
Stand E18/9/20. (Hamid Ismail). TEL: 0171 629 1161.

Shadad Antiques
Stand B14. (Farah Hakemi). TEL: 0171 499 0572.

Shiraz Antiques
Stand H10/1. (R.P. Kiadah). TEL: 0171 495 0635.

John Sleight
Stand MF45 41 s/c.

W1 continued

Solimani's
Stand A20/1.(Helen Zoakee). TEL: 0171 491 2562.

Solveig & Anita LAPADA
Stand 307/8/9. (Anita Gray). TEL: 0171 408 1638.

Spa Antiques
Stand 127. (Peter Benjamin). *Oriental items.* TEL: 0171 493 2180.

Spa Antiques
Stand 127. (Ian Conn). TEL: 0171 493 2180.

Spectrum
Stand 372/3. (Sylvia Bedwell). TEL: 0171 629 3501.

Jane Stewart
Stand L26/27. *Pewter, early 17th C to 19th C, £50-£1,000; oak, £500-£1,000; writing slopes, 19th C, £80-£150.* TEL: 0171 355 3333. SER: Valuations; restorations (pewter and oak). VAT: Spec.

Tagore Ltd
Stand 302/3. (Ronald Falloon). TEL: 0171 499 0158.

Tapestries
Stand M108/9. (Kilim Akman). TEL: 0171 491 8806.

Tradewinds
Stand 148/9. (Diane Harby). TEL: 0171 629 5130.

Trianon Ltd LAPADA
Stand 334/378. (Lilliane Flowerdew). TEL: 0171 491 2764.

Trio
Stand L24. (Theresa Clayton). TEL: 0171 629 1184.

Vogue
Stand D15/6. (Danny Anderson). TEL: 0171 629 3668.

Warwick Antiques
Stand 152. (Diane Friedman). TEL: 0171 629 5130.

Watches
Stand 374. (Robert Barany). TEL: 0171 493 7497.

Mary Wellard
Stand 165. TEL: 0171 629 5130.

Westminster Grp LAPADA
Stand 138/150. (Paulette Bates and Richard Harrison). TEL: 0171 493 8672.

John Weysom
Stand M14/5/6. TEL: 0171 491 4287.

David Wheatley LAPADA
Stand 106. TEL: 0171 629 1352.

W1 continued

Wheels of Steel
Stand B10. (Jeff Williams). TEL: 0171 629 2813.

Whitehead & Graves
Stand 158. (Robert Barany). TEL: 0171 493 7497.

Aura Williamson
Stand L10/1. TEL: 0171 495 6083.

Wimpole Antiques LAPADA
Stand 348/9. (Freda Hacker). TEL: 0171 499 2889.

Craig Wyncoll
Stand 125. TEL: 0171 409 1498.

Yang
Stand 129/130. TEL: 0171 495 6068.

Yosir
Stand K24/25. TEL: 0171 491 0264.

Richard Green BADA

44 and 39 Dover St. and 33 New Bond St. W1X 4JQ. SLAD. Open 9.30-6, Sat. 10-12.30. *STOCK: Paintings - Old Master and British; French impressionist and modern British; Victorian sporting and British marine.* PARK: Meters. TEL: 0171 493 3939; fax - 0171 629 2609. VAT: Stan/Spec.

Simon Griffin Antiques Ltd

3 Royal Arcade, 28 Old Bond St. W1. (S.J. Griffin). Est. 1979. Open 10-5, Sat. 10-5.30. *STOCK: Silver, old Sheffield plate.* TEL: 0171 491 7367; fax - same. VAT: Stan/Spec.

Hadji Baba Ancient Art

34a Davies St. W1Y 1LG. (R.R. Soleimani). Est. 1939. Open 9.30-6, Sat. and Sun. by appointment. SIZE: Medium. *STOCK: Antiquities and Islamic art.* LOC: Next to Claridges Hotel. PARK: Meters. TEL: 0171 499 9363/9384; fax - 0171 493 5504. SER: Valuations.

Hadleigh Jewellers

30A Marylebone High St. W1M 3PF. Open 9.30-5.30. *STOCK: Jewellery, some silver.* TEL: 0171 935 4074. SER: Valuations; repairs; hand-made jewellery. VAT: Stan/Spec.

W1 continued

Hahn and Son Fine Art Dealers

47 Albemarle St. W1. (P. Hahn). Est. 1870. Open 9.45-5.30. CL: Sat. *STOCK: English oil paintings, 18th-19th C.* TEL: 0171 493 9196. VAT: Stan.

Halcyon Days BADA

14 Brook St. W1Y 1AA. (S. Benjamin). Est. 1950. Open 9.15-5.30. *STOCK: 18th to early 19th C enamels, treen, papier mâché, tôle, objects of vertu, Georgian and Victorian scent bottles.* LOC: Hanover Sq. end of Brook St. PARK: Meters and in Hanover Sq. TEL: 0171 629 8811; fax - 0171 409 0280. FAIRS: Grosvenor House; BADA. VAT: Stan/Spec.

Robert Hall BADA

15c Clifford St. W1X 1RF. Est. 1976. *STOCK: Chinese snuff bottles, Ching dynasty; Oriental works of art, jade carvings, 17th-19th C; all £300-£20,000. Chinese contemporary paintings.* TEL: 0171 734 4008; fax - 0171 734 4408. SER: Valuations; buys at auction. VAT: Stan/Spec.

Hancocks and Co BADA

1 Burlington Gardens. W1X 2HP. Est. 1849. Open 9.30-5.30, Sat. 10.30-3.30. SIZE: Medium. *STOCK: Fine estate jewellery and silver.* LOC: Opposite top of Burlington Arcade. TEL: 0171 493 8904; fax - 0171 493 8905. VAT: Stan/Spec.

Harcourt Antiques

5 Harcourt St. W1 1DS. (J. Christophe). Est. 1961. Open by appointment only. *STOCK: English, Continental and Oriental porcelain, pre-1830.* PARK: Easy. TEL: 0171 723 5919/727 6936. VAT: Stan. *Trade Only.*

Brian Haughton Antiques

3B Burlington Gardens, Old Bond St. W1X 1LE. Est. 1965. Open 10-5.30. SIZE: Large. *STOCK: British and European ceramics, porcelain and pottery, 18th-19th C, £100-£50,000.* PARK: Nearby, Savile Row N.C.P. TEL: 0171 734 5491. SER: Buys at auction (porcelain and pottery). FAIRS: Organiser - International Ceramics and Seminar, Park Lane Hotel; International Fine Art & Antique Dealers Show, International Fine Art and International Asian Art, New York. VAT: Spec.

W1 continued

Gerard Hawthorn Ltd BADA

104 Mount St., Mayfair. W1Y 5HE. Open 10-6, Sat. by appointment. *STOCK: Oriental art - Chinese ceramics, porcelain and pottery; cloisonné and painted enamels, jade, hardstones, lacquer, bronzes, metalwork, paintings, textiles, ivory, works of art including Tibetan and Japanese, 2000BC to 1916.* LOC: Opposite Connaught Hotel. PARK: Easy. TEL: 0171 409 2888; fax - 0171 409 2777. SER: Valuations; restorations; buys at auction; exhibition yearly. FAIRS: New York.

Hennell of Bond Street Ltd. Founded 1736 (incorporating Frazer and Haws (1868) and E. Lloyd Lawrence (1830))

12 New Bond St. W1Y 0HE. Open 9-5.30, Sat. 10-4. SIZE: Medium. *STOCK: Fine jewellery, silver and watches.* PARK: Meters. TEL: 0171 629 6888. SER: Valuations; restorations (silver, jewellery). VAT: Stan/Spec.

G. Heywood Hill Ltd

10 Curzon St. W1Y 7FJ. (J. Saumarez Smith). Open 9-5.30, Sat. 9-12.30. *STOCK: Books, Victorian illustrated, children's and natural history.* TEL: 0171 629 0647; fax - 0171 408 0286.

Holland & Holland

31-33 Bruton St. W1X 8JS. Est. 1835. Open 9.30-5.30, Sat. 10-4. SIZE: Medium. *STOCK: Modern and antique guns, rifles, associated items; sporting prints, pictures and antiquarian books; antique sporting objects.* PARK: Meters in Bruton St. TEL: 0171 499 4411; fax - 0171 499 4544.

Holmes Ltd BADA

24 Burlington Arcade. W1V 9AD. (A.N., B.J. and I.J. Neale). Open 9.30-5. *STOCK: Jewels and silver.* TEL: 0171 493 1396. SER: Valuations; restorations. VAT: Stan.

Howard Antiques

8 Davies St., Berkeley Sq. W1Y 1LJ. Est. 1955. Open 10-6, Sat. by appointment. SIZE: Medium. *STOCK: English and Continental furniture, objects.* PARK: N.C.P. nearby. TEL: 0171 629 2628. SER: Valuations. VAT: Stan/Spec.

Brand Inglis BADA

4th Floor, 5 Vigo St. W1X 1AH. Est. 1960. Open by appointment. SIZE: Small. *STOCK: Silver, 16th-20th C, £1,000-£5,000.* TEL: 0171 439 6604; fax - 0171 439 6605. SER: Valuations; restorations (silver and metalwork); buys at auction (silver). VAT: Spec.

Patrick Jefferson Ltd

94 Mount St., Mayfair. W1Y 5HG. Est. 1978. Open 9.30-6, Sat. 10-5. SIZE: Large. *STOCK: British furniture, 1700-1830, £5,000-£100,000; works of art and sculpture, 17th-19th C, £500-£25,000.* LOC: Between Berkeley Square and Park Lane, opposite Scotts. PARK: Easy. TEL: 0171 491 4931; fax - 0171 491 4932. SER: Buys at auction.

W1 continued

C. John (Rare Rugs) Ltd BADA

70 South Audley St., Mayfair. W1Y 5FE. Est. 1947. Open 9-5. CL: Sat. *STOCK: Textiles, pre-1800, carpets, tapestries, embroideries.* TEL: 0171 493 5288; fax - 0171 409 7030. VAT: Stan/Spec.

Johnson Walker & Tolhurst Ltd BADA

64 Burlington Arcade. W1V 9AF. Est. 1849. Open 9.30-5.30. *STOCK: Antique and second-hand jewellery, objets d'art, silver.* TEL: 0171 629 2615. SER: Restorations (jewellery, pearl-stringing). VAT: Stan/Spec.

Alexander Juran and Co BADA

74 New Bond St. W1Y 9DD. Est. 1951. Open 9.15-5.30. CL: Sat. *STOCK: Caucasian rugs, nomadic and tribal; carpets, rugs, tapestries.* TEL: 0171 629 2550/493 4484. SER: Valuations; repairs. VAT: Stan/Spec.

Kennedy Carpets LAPADA

9A Vigo St. W1X 1AL. (M. Kennedy). Est. 1974. Open 9.30-6. SIZE: Large. *STOCK: Decorative carpets, collectable rugs and kelims, mid-19th C to new, £500-£50,000.* LOC: Off Regent St., up Sackville St. from Piccadilly, left into Vigo St., shop on left-hand side. PARK: Sackville St. TEL: 0171 439 8873; fax - 0171 437 1201. SER: Valuations; making to order. VAT: Stan.

Roger Keverne BADA

120 Mount St. W1Y 5HB. Est. 1966. Open Mon.-Fri. 9-5.30. Large. *STOCK: Oriental art - Chinese, Japanese jade, lacquer, pottery and porcelain, bronzes, ivories and enamels; all Chinese art from 2500 BC to 1916.* PARK: Meters. TEL: 0171 355 1711; fax - 0171 409 7717. SER: Valuations; restorations; buys at auction. FAIRS: New York (Winter and March Oriental); Hong Kong. VAT: Stan/Spec.

Lacloche Freres LAPADA

1 Three Kings Yard. W1Y 1FL. Open by appointment only. SIZE: Medium. *STOCK: Fine jewellery.* LOC: Off Davies St. TEL: 0171 355 3471; fax - 0171 355 3473. SER: Valuations; restorations. VAT: Stan/Spec.

D.S. Lavender (Antiques) Ltd BADA

26 Conduit St. W1R 9TA. Est. 1945. Open 9.30-5. CL: Sat. *STOCK: Jewels, miniatures, works of art.* PARK: Meters. TEL: 0171 629 1782; fax - 0171 629 3106. SER: Valuations. VAT: Stan/Spec.

W1 continued

The Lefevre Gallery
30 Bruton St. W1X 8JD. (Alex Reid and Lefevre Ltd). SLAD. Est. 1871. Open 10-5. CL: Sat. SIZE: Medium. *STOCK: Impressionist paintings, 19th-20th C.* LOC: Between Berkeley Sq. and Bond St. PARK: Meters, Berkeley Sq. TEL: 0171 493 2107; fax - 0171 499 9088. SER: Valuations. VAT: Spec.

Leuchars and Jefferson
94 Mount St., Mayfair. W1Y 5HG. (Patrick Jefferson and Hugh Leuchars). Est. 1978. Open 9.30-6, Sat. 10-5. SIZE: Large. *STOCK: English 18th C furniture and works of art.* LOC: Between Berkeley Square and Park Lane, opposite Scotts. PARK: Easy. TEL: 0171 491 4931; fax - 0171 491 4932. VAT: Spec.

Liberty
Regent St. W1R 6AH. Est. 1875. Open 10-6.30, Thurs. till 7.30. SIZE: Large. *STOCK: British furniture, ceramics, glass and metalware, 1860-1930, Gothic Revival, Aesthetic Movement and Arts & Crafts.* LOC: Regent St. joins Piccadilly and Oxford Circus. PARK: Meters and underground in Cavendish Sq. TEL: 0171 734 1234. VAT: Stan.

Maas Gallery
15a Clifford St. W1X 1RF. (R.N. Maas). SLAD. Est. 1960. Open 10-5.30. CL: Sat. SIZE: Medium. *STOCK: Victorian and Pre-Raphaelite paintings, drawings, watercolours and illustrations.* LOC: Between New Bond St. and Cork St. PARK: Easy. TEL: 0171 734 2302; fax - 0171 287 4836. SER: Valuations; buys at auction. VAT: Spec.

Maggs Bros Ltd — BADA
50 Berkeley Sq. W1X 6EL. (J.F., B.D. and E.F. Maggs, P. Harcourt, R. Harding and H. Bett and J. Collins). ABA. Est. 1853. Open 9.30-5. CL: Sat. SIZE: Large. *STOCK: Rare books, manuscripts, autograph letters, and western miniatures.* PARK: Meters. TEL: 0171 493 7160 (6 lines); fax - 0171 499 2007. VAT: Stan/Spec.

Mahboubian Gallery
65 Grosvenor St. W1X 9DB. (H. Mahboubian). Open 10-6. CL: Sat. TEL: 0171 493 9112.

Mallett and Son (Antiques) Ltd — BADA
141 New Bond St. W1Y 0BS. Est. 1865. Open 9.15-6, Sat. 11-4. SIZE: Large. *STOCK: English furniture, 1690-1835; clocks, 17th-18th C; china, needlework, decorative pictures, objects and glass.* PARK: Meters in Berkeley Sq. TEL: 0171 499 7411; fax - 0171 495 3179.

Mallett at Bourdon House Ltd
2 Davies St., Berkeley Sq. W1Y 1LJ. Open 9.15-5.30. SIZE: Large. *STOCK: Continental furniture, clocks, objets d'art; garden statuary and ornaments.* PARK: Meters, Berkeley Sq. TEL: 0171 629 2444; fax - 0171 499 2670. VAT: Stan/Spec.

W1 continued

Mallett Gallery — BADA
141 New Bond St. W1Y 0BS. SLAD. Open 9.30-6, Sat. 11-4. *STOCK: 18th to early 20th C paintings, watercolours and drawings.* TEL: 0171 499 7411; fax - 0171 495 3179. VAT: Spec.

Mansour Gallery
46-48 Davies St. W1Y 1LD. (M. Mokhtarzadeh). Open 9.30-5.30, Sat. by appointment. *STOCK: Islamic works of art, miniatures; ancient glass and glazed wares; Greek, Roman and Egyptian antiquities.* TEL: 0171 491 7444/499 0510. VAT: Stan.

Marks Antiques — LAPADA
49 Curzon St. W1. (Anthony Marks). Est. 1945. Open 9.30-6 including bank holidays. SIZE: Large. *STOCK: Silver, Sheffield plate.* LOC: Green Park tube, opposite Washington Hotel. PARK: Meters. TEL: 0171 499 1788; fax - 0171 409 3183. SER: Valuations; buys at auction. VAT: Stan/Spec.

Marlborough Fine Art (London) Ltd
6 Albemarle St. W1. SLAD. Est. 1946. Open 10-5.30, Sat. 10-12.30. *STOCK: Masters, 19th-20th C.* PARK: Meters or near Cork St. TEL: 0171 629 5161.

Marlborough Rare Books Ltd
144-146 New Bond St. W1Y 9FD. Est. 1946. Open 9.30-5.30. CL: Sat. SIZE: Medium. *STOCK: Illustrated books of all periods; rare books on fine and applied arts and architecture; English literature.* PARK: Meters. TEL: 0171 493 6993. SER: Buys at auction; valuations; catalogues available.

Mayfair Carpet Gallery Ltd
3 Old Bond St. W1X 3TD. *STOCK: Persian, Oriental rugs and carpets.* TEL: 0171 493 0126.

Mayfair Gallery
39 South Audley St. W1Y 5DH. (M. Sinai). Open 9.30-6, Sat. by appointment. *STOCK: 19th-20th C decorative Continental furniture, clocks, chandeliers, ivories and objets d'art.* TEL: 0171 491 3435/6; fax - 0171 491 3437.

Melton's
27 Bruton Place. W1X 7AB. (C. Neal). Open 9.30-5.30. CL: Sat. *STOCK: Small antiques and decorative accessories: lamps, prints, textiles, English and Continental.* TEL: 0171 409 2938/629 3612.

David Messum — BADA LAPADA
8 Cork St. W1X 1PD. SLAD. Open 10-6, Sat. 10-4, other times by appointment. *STOCK:*

W1 continued

***British Impressionism, fine English and contemporary paintings.* TEL: 0171 437 5545. SER: Valuations; restorations; framing. VAT: Stan/Spec.**

Roy Miles Gallery

29 Bruton St. W1. Open Mon.-Fri. 9.30-5.30. *STOCK: Major art from Russia, also British works.*TEL: 0171 495 4747; fax - 0171 495 6232.

John Mitchell and Son BADA

1st Floor, 160 New Bond St. W1Y 9PA. SLAD. Est. 1931. Open 9.30-5, Sat. by appointment. SIZE: Small. *STOCK: Old Master paintings, drawings and watercolours, especially flower paintings, 17th C Dutch, 18th C English and 19th C French.* LOC: Nearest tube Green Park. PARK: Meters. TEL: 0171 493 7567. SER: Valuations; restorations (pictures); buys at auction.

Paul Mitchell Ltd BADA

99 New Bond St. W1Y 9LF. Open 9.30-5.30. CL: Sat. SIZE: Large. *STOCK: Picture frames.* PARK: Meters. TEL: 0171 493 8732/0860. VAT: Stan.

Bashir Mohamed Ltd

8 Broadbent St. W1X 9HH. Open 10-5 by appointment only. CL: Sat. *STOCK: Islamic art, Moghul and south east Asian manuscripts and objects.* TEL: 0171 723 1844. VAT: Spec.

Moira

22-23 New Bond St. W1. Open 9-6. *STOCK: Fine antique and Art Deco jewellery.* TEL: 0171 629 0160. SER: Valuations.

Sydney L. Moss Ltd BADA

51 Brook St. W1Y 1AU. (P.G. and E.M. Moss). Est. 1910. Open Mon.-Fri. 10-6. SIZE: Large. *STOCK: Chinese and Japanese paintings and works of art; Japanese netsuke and lacquer, 17th-20th C; reference books. (as stock).* LOC: From Grosvenor Sq., up Brook St. to Claridges. PARK: Meters. TEL: 0171 629 4670/493 7374; fax - 0171 491 9278. SER: Valuations and advice; buys at auction. FAIRS: Asian Art, New York (March). VAT: Spec.

Paul Nels Ltd LAPADA

6-8 Sedley Place. W1R 1HG. (P.J. Nels). Open 8.30-5. CL: Sat. pm. *STOCK: Rugs, carpets, tapestries and textiles.* TEL: 0171 629 1909.

Noortman

40-41 Old Bond St. W1X 4HP. SLAD. Open 9.30-5.30. *STOCK: Old Masters, French 19th-20th C.* TEL: 0171 491 7284.

Hal O'Nians

44 Grosvenor Hill. W1X 9JE. Open by appointment only. *STOCK: Paintings and watercolours, 16th-20th C.* TEL: 0171 724 3799; fax - same.

W1 continued

The O'Shea Gallery BADA

120a Mount St., Mayfair. W1Y 5HB. ABA. Open 9.30-6, Sat. 9.30-1. *STOCK: Maps, topographical, decorative, natural history, sporting and marine prints; rare atlases, illustrated books, 15th-19th C, £5-£25,000.* LOC: Near Berkeley Sq. TEL: 0171 629 1122; fax - 0171 629 1116. SER: Decorative framing; restorations. VAT: Stan/Spec.

Richard Ogden Ltd BADA

28 and 29 Burlington Arcade, Piccadilly. W1V 0NX. Est. 1948. Open 9.30-5.15, Sat. 9.30-5. SIZE: Medium. *STOCK: Antique jewellery, rings.* LOC: Near Piccadilly Circus. PARK: Meters. TEL: 0171 493 9136/7. SER: Valuations; repairs. VAT: Spec.

Paralos Ltd

4th Floor, 23/24 Margaret St. W1N 7LB. (Panagiotis Chantziaras and Louise Sturrock). Open by appointment. SIZE: Medium. *STOCK: Antiquarian books, atlases, maps and prints, illustrated travels, natural history, decorative Greek classics, decorative and topographical prints, early cartography, from 16th C, £10-£20,000.* LOC: From Oxford Circus, north up Regent St., second road on right. PARK: Cavendish Sq. TEL: 0171 637 0796; home - 0171 637 0819. SER: Valuations. FAIRS: Map & Print (2nd Mon. monthly), Bonnington Hotel. VAT: Stan. *Trade Only.*

Partridge Fine Arts plc

144-146 New Bond St. W1Y 0LY. SLAD. Est. 1911. Open 9-5.30. CL: Sat. SIZE: Large. *STOCK: English and French furniture, objets d'art and silver, 18th-19th C; English, French and Italian paintings, 18th C.* LOC: North of Bruton St., opposite Sotheby's. PARK: Meters. TEL: 0171 629 0834; fax - 0171 495 6266. SER: Buys at auction. VAT: Spec.

W.H. Patterson Fine Arts Ltd BADA

19 Albemarle St. W1X 3LA. (W.H. and Mrs. P.M. Patterson and J. White). SLAD. Open 9.30-6. SIZE: Large. *STOCK: 19th C and regular exhibitions for contemporary artists, the New English Art Club, Andrew Coates, Willem Dolphyn and Peter Kuhfeld.* LOC: Near Green Park tube station. PARK: Meters. TEL: 0171 629 4119. SER: Valuations; restorations. VAT: Spec.

Pelham Galleries Ltd BADA

24/25 Mount St., Mayfair. W1Y 5RB. (A. and L.J. Rubin). Est. 1928. *STOCK: Furniture, English and Continental; tapestries, decorative works of art and musical instruments.* TEL: 0171 629 0905; fax - 0171 495 4511. VAT: Spec.

W1 continued

Pendulum of Mayfair Ltd
King House, 51 Maddox St. W1. (K. R. Clements and Dr. H. Specht). Open 10-6. *STOCK: Clocks, mainly longcase, also bracket, mantle and wall; Georgian mahogany furniture.* TEL: 0171 629 6606; fax - 0171 629 6616. SER: Valuations. FAIRS: Buxton. VAT: Spec.

Ronald Phillips Ltd BADA
26 Bruton St. W1X 8LH. Est. 1952. *STOCK: English furniture, objets d'art, glass, clocks and barometers.* TEL: 0171 493 2341; fax - 0171 495 0843. VAT: Mainly Spec.

S.J. Phillips Ltd BADA
139 New Bond St. W1A 3DL. (M.S., N.E.L., J.P. and F.E. Norton). Est. 1869. Open 10-5. CL: Sat. SIZE: Large. *STOCK: Silver, jewellery, gold boxes, miniatures.* LOC: Near Bond St. tube station. PARK: Meters. TEL: 0171 629 6261; fax - 0171 495 6180. SER: Restorations; buys at auction. FAIRS: Grosvenor House; Maastricht. VAT: Stan/Spec.

Piccadilly Gallery
43 Dover St. W1X 3RE. SLAD. Est. 1952. Open 10-5.30: Sat. times vary, prior 'phone call advisable. CL: Sat. (Aug. and Sept.). *STOCK: Symbolist and Art Nouveau works, 20th C; drawings and watercolours.* PARK: Meters. TEL: 0171 629 2875; fax - 0171 499 0431. VAT: Spec.

W1 continued

Pickering and Chatto
1st Floor, 36 St George St. W1R 9FA. Est. 1820. Open Mon.-Fri. 9.30-5.30, or by appointment. SIZE: Medium. *STOCK: English literature, economics, politics, philosophy, science, medicine, general antiquarian.* PARK: Meters. TEL: 0171 491 2656; fax - 0171 491 9161; e-mail - rarebook@pandcltd. demon.co.uk.

Nicholas S. Pitcher Oriental Art
1st Floor, 29 New Bond St. W1Y 9HD. Open 10.30-5 by appointment. CL: Sat. except by appointment. SIZE: Small. *STOCK: Chinese and Japanese ceramics and works of art, early pottery, to 18th C, £200-£5,000.* LOC: Four doors from Sotheby's, above Gordon Scott shoe shop. PARK: Nearby. TEL: 0171 499 6621; home - 0171 610 0301. SER: Valuations; buys at auction. VAT: Spec.

Portal Gallery
16a Grafton St/Bond St. W1X 3LF. (Lionel Levy and Jess Wilder). Est. 1959. Open 10-5.30, Sat. 10-4. SIZE: Medium. *STOCK: Curios, bygones, artefacts, country pieces and objects of virtue, 19th C, £50-£500; contemporary British idiosyncratic paintings, including Beryl Cook.* LOC: Junction of New and Old Bond St. PARK: Easy. TEL: 0171 493 0706; fax - 0171 629 3506.

Jonathan Potter Ltd BADA LAPADA
125 New Bond St. W1Y 9AF. ABA. Est. 1975. Open 10-6, Sat. by appointment. *STOCK: British and World maps, atlases and travel books, 16th-19th C, £50-£10,000.* PARK: Meters nearby. TEL: 0171 491 3520; fax - 0171 491 9754. SER: Valuations; restorations; colouring, framing; buys at auction (maps and prints); catalogue available. VAT: Stan.

Pyms Gallery BADA
9 Mount St., Mayfair. W1Y 5AD. (A. and M. Hobart). Est. 1975. Open 10-6. CL: Sat. *STOCK: British, Irish and French paintings, 19th-20th C.* TEL: 0171 629 2020; fax - 0171 629 2060. SER: Valuations; restorations; buys at auction. VAT: Spec.

Bernard Quaritch Ltd. (Booksellers) BADA
5-8 Lower John St., Golden Sq. W1R 4AU. Est. 1847. Open 9.30-5.30. CL: Sat. SIZE: Large. *STOCK: Rare books and manuscripts.* PARK: Meters, 50yds. TEL: 0171 734 2983; fax - 0171 437 0967; e-mail - rarebooks@quaritch.com. SER: Buys at auction. VAT: Stan.

Rabi Gallery Ltd
82 Portland Place. W1. (R. and V. Soleymani). Est. 1978. Open 10-6. CL: Sat. *STOCK: Ancient art, antique carpets and works of art.* TEL: 0171 580 9064; fax - 0171 436 0772.

W1 continued

William Redford BADA

99 Mount St. W1Y 5HF. Open 10-5. CL: Sat. SIZE: Small. ***STOCK: French furniture, works of art, bronzes, some porcelain.*** **TEL: 0171 629 1165.**

David Richards and Sons LAPADA

12 New Cavendish St. W1M 7LJ. (M., H. and E. Richards). Open 9.30-5.30. CL: Sat. SIZE: Large. ***STOCK: Silver and plate.*** **LOC: Off Harley St., at corner of Marylebone High St. PARK: Easy. TEL: 0171 935 3206/0322; fax - 0171 224 4423. SER: Valuations; restorations. VAT: Stan/Spec.**

Jonathan Robinson

1st Floor, 29 New Bond St. W1Y 9HD. Est. 1984. Open by appointment. SIZE: Small. *STOCK: Chinese porcelain and works of art, from B.C. to 19th C, £200-£5,000.* LOC: Four doors from Sothebys. PARK: Meters. TEL: 0171 493 0592. SER: Valuations; consultancy; buys at auction. (Oriental items). FAIRS: International Ceramics, Park Lane Hotel. VAT: Spec.

Michael Rose - Source of the Unusual

3, 15, 44-45 Burlington Arcade, Piccadilly. W1V 9AB. *STOCK: Victorian, antique and period diamonds, jewellery, watches and Fabergé.* TEL: 0171 493 0714.

The Royal Arcade Watch Shop

4 Royal Arcade - at 28 Old Bond St. W1. Open 10-5.30. SIZE: Small. *STOCK: Modern and vintage Rolex, Cartier, Patek Phillipe.* PARK: Easy. TEL: 0171 495 4882. SER: Valuations.

Russell Rare Books

1st Floor, 81 Grosvenor St. W1X 9DE. (C. Russell). Open 10-5.30. *STOCK: Antiquarian books.* TEL: 0171 629 0532; fax - 0171 499 2983.

Frank T. Sabin Ltd BADA

13 Royal Arcade, Old Bond St. W1X 3HB. (John Sabin). Open 9.30-5.30, Sat. by appointment only. ***STOCK: English sporting and decorative prints, 18th-19th C.*** **TEL: 0171 493 3288; fax - 0171 499 3593.**

Alistair Sampson Antiques Ltd BADA

120 Mount St., Mayfair. (Formerly of 156 Brompton Rd). W1Y 5HB. Open 9.30-5.30. SIZE: Large. ***STOCK: English pottery, oak and country furniture, metalwork, needlework, primitive pictures, decorative and interesting items,17th-18th C; Chinese works of art.*** **PARK: Meters. TEL: 0171 409 1799; fax - 0171 409 7717. VAT: Spec.**

Robert G. Sawers

PO Box 4QA. W1A 4QA. Open by appointment. *STOCK: Books on the Orient, Japanese prints, screens, paintings.* TEL: 0171 409 0863; fax - 0171 409 0817.

W1 continued

Scarisbrick and Bate Ltd

111 Mount St. W1Y 5HE. (A.C. Bate). Est. 1958. Open 9.30-5.30. CL: Sat. SIZE: Medium. *STOCK: Furniture, decorative items, mid-18th C to early 19th C.* Not Stocked: Glass and china. LOC: By Connaught Hotel (off Park Lane). PARK: Meters. TEL: 0171 499 2043/4/5; fax - 0171 499 2897. SER: Restorations (furniture); buys at auction. VAT: Stan.

Seaby Antiquities

14 Old Bond St. W1X 4JL. Est. 1926. Open 10-5. CL: Sat. SIZE: Medium. *STOCK: Antiquities, ancient coins; books on coins, archaeology and history.* LOC: Just off Piccadilly, nearest tube Green Park. TEL: 0171 495 2590; fax - 0171 491 1595.

Shaikh and Son (Oriental Rugs) Ltd

16 Brook St. W1. (M. Shaikh). Open 10-6. CL: Sat. pm. *STOCK: Persian carpets, rugs, £100-£10,000.* TEL: 0171 629 3430. SER: Repairing and cleaning.

Bernard J. Shapero Rare Books

32 St George St. W1R 0EA. Est. 1979. Open 9.30-6.30, Sat. 11-5. SIZE: Large. *STOCK: Antiquarian books - travel, natural history and literature (old and modern); antiquarian prints and engravings.* LOC: Near Hanover Sq. and Bond St. TEL: 0171 493 0876. SER: Valuations; restorations (antiquarian books); buys at auction. FAIRS: Book - London, Paris, New York, San Francisco.

W. Sitch and Co. Ltd.

48 Berwick St. W1V 4JD. (R. Sitch). Est. 1776. Open 8-5, Sat. 8-1. SIZE: Large. *STOCK: Edwardian and Victorian lighting fixtures and floor standards.* LOC: Off Oxford St. TEL: 0171 437 3776. SER: Valuations; restorations; repairs. VAT: Stan.

The Sladmore Gallery of Sculpture

BADA

32 Bruton Place, Berkeley Sq. W1X 7AA. (E.F. Horswell). Open 10-6. CL: Sat. SIZE: Large. ***STOCK: Bronze sculptures, 19th C - Mene, Barye, Fremiet, Bonheur; Impressionist, Bugatti, Troubetzkoy, Pompon; contemporary, Geoffrey Dashwood birds, Mark Coreth African wildlife; sporting, polo.*** **TEL: 0171 499 0365. SER: Valuations; restorations. VAT: Stan/Spec.**

Stephen Somerville Ltd

14 Old Bond St. W1X 3DB. SLAD. Est. 1987. By appointment only. SIZE: Small. *STOCK: Old Master prints and drawings; English paintings, watercolours, prints and drawings, 17th-20th C, £50-£50,000.* LOC: Piccadilly end of Old Bond St. TEL: 0171 493 8363. SER: Buys at auction (as stock). VAT: Spec.

W1 continued

Henry Sotheran Ltd

2/5 Sackville St., Piccadilly. W1X 2DP. Est. 1761. Open 9.30-6, Sat. 10-4. *STOCK: Antiquarian books and prints, including John Gould prints.* TEL: 0171 439 6151. SER: Restorations and binding (books, prints); buys at auction. VAT: Stan.

A & J Speelman Ltd BADA

129 Mount St. W1Y 5HA. Est. 1931. Open 9-5.30. SIZE: Large. *STOCK: Chinese and Japanese works of art, Shang era to 19th C.* TEL: 0171 499 5126. SER: Valuations; buys at auction. VAT: Spec.

Spink Leger Pictures BADA

13 Old Bond St. W1X 4HU. (D.W. Posnett and L.J. Libson). SLAD. Est. 1892. Open 9-5.30, Sat. by appointment. SIZE: Large. *STOCK: Old Masters, English paintings, early English watercolours.* PARK: Meters. TEL: 0171 629 3538; fax - 0171 493 8681. SER: Valuations; restorations.

Stair and Company Ltd BADA

14 Mount St. W1Y 5RA. CINOA. Est. 1911. Open 9.30-5.30, Sat. by appointment. SIZE: Large. *STOCK: 18th C English furniture, works of art, mirrors, chandeliers, barometers, needlework, lamps, clocks, prints.* LOC: Past Connaught Hotel, towards South Audley St. PARK: Meters and Adam's Row. TEL: 0171 499 1784; fax - 0171 629 1050. SER: Restorations; decorations. VAT: Spec.

Stoppenbach and Delestre Ltd

25 Cork St. W1X 1HB. SLAD. Open 10-5.30, Sat. 10-1. *STOCK: French paintings, drawings and sculpture, 19th-20th C.* TEL: 0171 734 3534.

Tessiers Ltd BADA

26 New Bond St. W1Y 0JY. Open 10-5. *STOCK: Jewellery, silver, objets d'art.* TEL: 0171 629 0458; fax - 0171 629 1857. SER: Valuations; restorations. VAT: Spec.

William Thuillier

180 New Bond St. W1Y 9PD. Open by appointment only. *STOCK: Old Master paintings and drawings.* TEL: 0171 499 0106.

Toynbee-Clarke Interiors Ltd

95 Mount St. W1Y 5HG. (G. and D. Toynbee-Clarke). Est. 1953. Open 9-5.30. CL: Sat. SIZE: Medium. *STOCK: Decorative English and Continental furniture and objects, 17th-18th C; Chinese hand painted wallpapers, 18th C; French scenic wallpapers, early 19th C; Chinese and Japanese paintings and screens, 17th-19th C.* LOC: Between north-west corner of Berkeley Sq. and Park Lane. PARK: Meters. TEL: 0171 499 4472; fax - 0171 495 1204. SER: Buys at auction. VAT: Stan/Spec.

W1 continued

Tryon & Swann Gallery

23 Cork St. W1X 1HB. Open 10-6, Sat. by appointment. *STOCK: Sporting, wildlife and marine paintings, bronzes, books, 1900 to contemporary artists, £150-£50,000.* TEL: 0171 734 6961/2256; fax - 0171 287 2480. SER: Valuations; framing; advising; commission buying

M. Turpin Ltd LAPADA

27 Bruton St. W1X 7DB. Open 10-6 or by appointment. CL: Sat. SIZE: Large. *STOCK: English and Continental furniture, mirrors, chandeliers and objets d'art, 18th C.* LOC: Between Berkeley Sq. and Bond St. PARK: Limited and meters. TEL: 0171 493 3275; fax - 0171 408 1869.

Under Two Flags

4 St Christopher's Place. W1M 5HB. (A.C. Coutts). Est. 1973. Open 10-5. CL: Mon. SIZE: Small. *STOCK: Toy soldiers, old and new military prints, books, finely detailed painted models of all periods.* LOC: Off Oxford St. TEL: 0171 935 6934.

Jan van Beers Oriental Art BADA

34 Davies St. W1Y 1LG. Est. 1978. Open 10-6. CL: Sat. SIZE: Medium. *STOCK: Chinese and Japanese ceramics and works of art, 200BC to 1800 AD.* LOC: Between Berkeley Sq. and Oxford St. PARK: Easy. TEL: 0171 408 0434. SER: Valuations. FAIRS: Cologne. VAT: Spec.

Venners Antiques

7 New Cavendish St. W1M 7RP. (Mrs S. Davis). Open 10.15-4.15, Sat. 10-1. CL: Mon. *STOCK: 18th-19th C English porcelain and pottery.* PARK: Meters. TEL: 0171 935 0184. SER: Valuations; buys at auction. VAT: Spec.

Vigo Carpet Gallery LAPADA

6a Vigo St. W1X 1AH. Open 9-5.30, Fri. 9-5. CL: Sat. *STOCK: Oriental and European rugs and carpets, tapestries and needlework.* TEL: 0171 439 6971; fax - 0171 439 2353. SER: Design.

Rupert Wace Ancient Art Ltd

14 Old Bond St. W1X 3DB. Open Mon.-Fri. 10-5. *STOCK: Egyptian, Classical and near Eastern antiquities.* TEL: 0171 495 1623.

Walpole Gallery

38 Dover St. W1X 3RB. SLAD. Open 9.30-5.30. CL: Sat. except when exhibitions held. *STOCK: Italian Old Master paintings.* TEL: 0171 499 6626.

Wartski Ltd BADA

14 Grafton St. W1X 4DE. Est. 1865. Open 9.30-5. CL: Sat. SIZE: Medium. *STOCK: Jewellery, 18th C gold boxes, Fabergé, Russian works of art, silver.* PARK: Meters. TEL: 0171 493 1141. SER: Restorations; buys at auction. FAIRS: International Fine Art and Antique Dealers' Show, New York; Tresors; International Fine Art and Antiques for Asia, Singapore. VAT: Stan/Spec.

W1 continued

Waterhouse and Dodd BADA

1st Floor, 110 New Bond St. W1Y 9AA. (R. Waterhouse and J. Dodd). Est. 1987. Open 10-6, Sat. and Sun. by appointment. SIZE: Medium. *STOCK: British and European oil paintings, watercolours and drawings, 1850-1950, £2,000-£50,000.* LOC: Corner of Brook St. and Bond St. - entrance on Brook St. TEL: 0171 491 9293. SER: Valuations; restorations; buys at auction (paintings). FAIRS: City of London Antiques and Fine Art; Olympia. VAT: Spec.

Captain O.M. Watts

7 Dover St., Piccadilly. W1X 3PJ. Open 9-6. SIZE: Small. *STOCK: Nautical antiques and collectables, £30-£2,000.* LOC: Near Green Park. PARK: Meters. TEL: 0171 493 4633; fax - 0171 495 0755. SER: Restorations (scientific instruments); buys at auction (nautical and scientific instruments); hire. VAT: Stan.

The Weiss Gallery

1B Albemarle St. W1. Open 10-6. CL: Sat. *STOCK: Elizabethan, Jacobean and early European portraits.* TEL: 0171 409 0035. SER: Valuations; restorations.

William Weston Gallery

7 Royal Arcade, Albemarle St. W1X 3HD. SLAD. Est. 1964. Open 9.30-5.30, some Sats. 10.30-2. SIZE: Small. *STOCK: Etchings, lithographs, 1800-1970.* LOC: Off Piccadilly. TEL: 0171 493 0722; fax - 0171 491 9240. VAT: Spec.

Rollo Whately Ltd

1st Floor, 9 Old Bond St. W1X 3TA. Est. 1995. Open 9-6. CL: Sat. SIZE: Small. *STOCK: Picture frames, 16th-19th C, £500-£2,000.* LOC: Piccadilly end of Old Bond St. TEL: 0171 629 7861. SER: Valuations; restorations (frames); search; buys at auction. VAT: Stan.

Wilkins and Wilkins

1 Barrett St., St Christophers Pl. W1M 6DN. (M. Wilkins). Est. 1981. Open 10-5. CL: Sat. SIZE: Small. *STOCK: English 17th and 18th C portraits and decorative paintings, £700-£20,000.* LOC: Near Selfridges. TEL: 0171 935 9613; fax - 0171 935 4696. VAT: Stan/Spec.

Wilkinson plc

1 Grafton St. W1X 3LB. Est. 1947. Open 9.30-5. CL: Sat. *STOCK: Glass, especially chandeliers, 18th C and reproduction; art metal work.* LOC: Nearest underground - Green Park. TEL: 0171 495 2477. SER: Restorations and repairs (glass and metalwork).

Williams and Son

2 Grafton St. W1X 3LB. (J.R. Williams). Est. 1931. Open 9.30-6. CL: Sat. SIZE: Large. *STOCK: British and European paintings, 19th C.*

W1 continued

LOC: Between Bond St. and Berkeley Sq. TEL: 0171 493 4985/5751; fax - 0171 409 7363. VAT: Stan/Spec.

Linda Wrigglesworth BADA LAPADA

34 Brook St. W1Y 1YA. Est. 1978. Open 10-6. CL: Sat. *STOCK: Chinese costume and textiles of the Qing and Ming dynasty, 1398-1911, £200+.* LOC: Corner of South Molton St. PARK: Grosvenor Square. TEL: 0171 408 0177. SER: Valuations; restorations; mounting, framing; buys on commission (Oriental). FAIRS: Maastricht; Olympia; Arts of Pacific Asia, New York and San Francisco.

Alex Zadah Fine Oriental & European Carpets LAPADA

35 Bruton Place. W1X 7AB. Est. 1976. Open 9.30-6. *STOCK: Oriental and European carpets, rugs, tapestries and textiles.* TEL: 0171 493 2622/2673.

LONDON W2

Sean Arnold Sporting Antiques

21-22 Chepstow Corner, off Westbourne Grove. W2 4XE. Open 10-6. *STOCK: Sporting antiques and decorative items; golf clubs, 1840-1915, £30-£6,000; tennis racquets, £10-£3,000; vintage luggage.* TEL: 0171 221 2267; fax - 0171 221 5464.

Bayswater Books

27a Craven Terrace, Lancaster Gate. W2 3EL. Est. 1984. Open 11-7. SIZE: Small. *STOCK: Antiquarian books, maps and prints, £5-£500; secondhand books, photographica, ephemera, £1-£500.* LOC: One-way street running south from Craven Rd. to Bayswater Rd. PARK: Meters. TEL: 0171 402 7398. SER: Book search and mail order.

Claude Bornoff BADA

20 Chepstow Corner, Pembridge Villas. W2 4XE. Est. 1949. Open 9.30-5. CL: Sat. SIZE: Medium. *STOCK: English and Continental furniture, china, metalware and unusual items.* PARK: Meters. TEL: 0171 229 8947. VAT: Stan/Spec.

Ruby Buckle (Antique Fireplaces)

18 Chepstow Corner, Pembridge Villas. W2 4XE. Open 10-6. *STOCK: Fireplaces.* TEL: 0171 229 8843; fax - 0171 229 8864.

Connaught Galleries

44 Connaught St. W2 2AA. (M. Hollamby). Est. 1966. Open 10-6.30, Sat. 10-1. SIZE: Medium. *STOCK: Antique and reproduction sporting, historical, geographical and decorative prints.* LOC: Near Marble Arch. PARK: Meters. TEL: 0171 723 1660. SER: Picture framing. VAT: Spec.

W1 continued

Craven Gallery

30 Craven Terrace. W2. (C. and A. Quaradeghini). Est. 1974. Open 11-6, Sat. 3-7, other times by appointment. SIZE: Large and warehouse. *STOCK: Silver and plate, 19th-20th C; furniture, china and glass, Victorian.* LOC: Off Bayswater Rd. PARK: Easy. TEL: 0171 402 2802; home - 0181 998 0769. VAT: Stan. *Trade Only.*

Jacqueline Edge

1 Courtnell St. W2 5BU. Est. 1993. Open Sat. 11-6, other days by appointment. SIZE: Medium. *STOCK: Colonial furniture, early 20th C, £500-£1,000; lacquerware, late 19th to early 20th C; ethnic textiles; urns, pots, ceramics.* LOC: Off Westbourne Grove/Ledbury Rd., on corner with Artesian Rd. PARK: Meters. TEL: 0171 229 1172. SER: Interior/exterior design. VAT: Stan.

Hosains Books and Antiques

25 Connaught St. W2 2AY. Est. 1979. Open by appointment only. *STOCK: Secondhand and antiquarian books on India, Middle East, Central Asia; miniatures; prints of India and Middle East.* TEL: 0171 262 7900; fax - 0171 433 3126.

Manya Igel Fine Arts Ltd LAPADA

21/22 Peters Court, Porchester Rd. W2 5DR. (M. Igel and B.S. Prydal). Est. 1977. Open 10-5 by appointment only. SIZE: Large. *STOCK: Mainly modern and contemporary British works, £250-£25,000.* LOC: Off Queensway. PARK: Nearby. TEL: 0171 229 1669/8429; fax - 0171 229 6770. VAT: Spec.

Ian Lieber

The Shop, 29 Craven Terrace, Lancaster Gate. W2 3EL. Est. 1965. Open by appointment. SIZE: Medium. *STOCK: Furniture, early 19th C and decorative; porcelain, objets d'art, paintings, costume jewellery.* LOC: Near Bayswater Rd. TEL: 0171 262 5505; fax - 0171 402 4445. SER: Buys at auction. FAIRS: Olympia. VAT: Stan/Spec.

The Mark Gallery BADA

9 Porchester Place, Marble Arch. W2 2BS. (H. Mark). CINOA. Est. 1969. Open 10-1 and 2-6, Sat. 11-1. SIZE: Medium. *STOCK: Russian icons, 16th-19th C; modern graphics - French school.* LOC: Near Marble Arch. TEL: 0171 262 4906; fax - 0171 224 9416. SER: Valuations; restorations; buys at auction. VAT: Stan/Spec.

M. McAleer

W2 4SN. (Mrs M. McAleer and M.J. McAleer). Est. 1969. Open by appointment. SIZE: Small. *STOCK: Scottish provincial, Irish and small collectable silver.* TEL: 0171 727 7979. SER: Buys at auction (silver).

LONDON W4

The Chiswick Fireplace Co.

68 Southfield Rd., Chiswick. W4 1BD. (Mr Bee). Open 9.30-5.30. SIZE: Medium. *STOCK: Original cast iron fireplaces, late Victorian to early 1900's, £200-£1,000.* LOC: 8 minutes walk from Turnham Green underground. PARK: Easy. TEL: 0181 995 4011. SER: Restorations. VAT: Stan.

J. D. Marshall

38 Chiswick Lane, Chiswick. W4 2JQ. Est. 1985. Open 10-6, Sat. 10-5. CL: Mon. SIZE: Medium. *STOCK: Decorative and unusual objects, furniture, bronzes and chandeliers, £100-£50,000; some garden statuary and furniture, to £10,000.* LOC: Off A4/M4 at the Hogarth roundabout or Chiswick High Rd. PARK: Easy. TEL: 0181 742 8089; fax - same. SER: Valuations; restorations (oil and water gilding; metal patination and non-ferrous casting). VAT: Spec.

The Old Cinema Antique Department Store LAPADA

160 Chiswick High Rd. W4 1PR. Est. 1977. Open 10-6, Sun. 12-5. SIZE: Large. *STOCK: General antiques including furniture, gardenalia, decorative and architectural items, 1800-1940, £100-£6,000.* PARK: Easy. TEL: 0181 995 4166; e-mail - antique@antique.u-net.com; website - www.antiques-uk.co.uk. SER: Restorations. VAT: Stan/Spec.

The Old Dairy

164 Thames Rd., Strand-on-the-Green, Chiswick. W4 3QS. (N.J. Quinn). Est. 1980. Open Tues.-Sun. 10.30-6 and by appointment. SIZE: Medium. *STOCK: 19th C furniture and decorative items including pine, painted and fruitwood armoires, sleighbeds and dressers, £25-£950.* LOC: North side of Thames, east of Kew Bridge, near junction of north and south circulars. PARK: Easy. TEL: 0181 994 3140; home - 0181 742 2395.

Portray Antiques

136 Chiswick High Rd. W4 1PU. (Hratch Bastajian). Est. 1993. Open 8.30-6, Sat. 10-4. SIZE: Medium. *STOCK: Furniture.* PARK: Side streets. TEL: 0181 994 6549; fax - 0181 994 6589. SER: Restorations (repairs, polishing and upholstery); buys at auction (furniture). VAT: Stan/Spec.

Strand Antiques

166 Thames Rd., Strand-on-the-Green, Chiswick. W4 3QS. Est. 1977. Open 12-5 including Sun. or by appointment. SIZE: Large. *STOCK: Books, kitchen items, glass, furniture, jewellery, paintings, prints, fabrics, china, silver, clothes, and collectors' items, £1-£500.* LOC: Behind Bull's Head Public House, about 400yds. from Kew Bridge. PARK: Easy. TEL: 0181 994 1912.

LONDON W5

Aberdeen House Antiques LAPADA

75 St. Mary's Rd. W5 5RH. (N. Schwartz). CINOA. Est. 1971. Open 10-5.30. SIZE: Medium. *STOCK: Furniture and pictures, £50-£2,000; decorative items and textiles, £25-£2,000; china, glass and silver, £25-£1,000; all 18th-20th C.* LOC: On B455 1 mile north of A4. PARK: Easy and at rear. TEL: 0181 567 5194/1223. SER: Valuations. FAIRS: Olympia. VAT: Stan.

Antique Pine Ltd

16 South Ealing Rd., Ealing. W5 5EX. (L. A. and K. Denwood). Est. 1971. Open 10-6. SIZE: Large. *STOCK: Victorian and Edwardian pine furniture, £50-£1,000.* TEL: 0181 932 0168. SER: Pine stripping and repair; valuations. VAT: Stan.

The Badger

12 St. Mary's Rd. W5 5ES. (M. and E. Aalders). Est. 1967. Open 9.30-6. SIZE: Medium. *STOCK: Furniture, £100-£2,000; clocks, £1,000-£3,000; both 18th-19th C; ceramics, 19th C, £50-£1,000.* PARK: Easy. TEL: 0181 567 5601. SER: Valuations; restorations (furniture and clocks); buys at auction (clocks and watches). VAT: Stan/Spec.

Ealing Gallery

78 St. Mary's Rd., Ealing. W5 5EX. (Mrs N. Lane). Open 10.30-5.30. CL: Mon. and Wed. *STOCK: Oil paintings, £100-£5,000; watercolours, £50-£3,000; both 19th to early 20th C; contemporary paintings, £30-£250.* LOC: Piccadilly Line underground, South Ealing. PARK: Nearby. TEL: 0181 840 7883; fax - same. SER: Valuations; restorations (oils and watercolours); framing. VAT: Spec.

Harold's Place

148 South Ealing Rd. W5 4QJ. (H. Bowman). Est. 1977. Open 10-6. CL: Wed. SIZE: Medium. *STOCK: Wall plates, commemoratives, porcelain, 19th to early 20th C, £5-£100.* LOC: 1/2 mile north of A4/M4 at Ealing. TEL: 0181 579 4825.

Terrace Antiques

10-12 South Ealing Rd. W5 4QA. (N. Schwartz). Est. 1971. Open 10-5.30. SIZE: Medium. *STOCK: Georgian, Victorian and Edwardian furniture, 1780-1920, £50-£1,000; china, glass and pictures, silver and plate, 1850-1950, £10-£200.* LOC: 1 mile north of A4 on B455. PARK: Easy and opposite. TEL: 0181 567 5194/1223. SER: Valuations. FAIRS: Olympia. VAT: Stan.

LONDON W6

Architectural Antiques

324A & 351 King St. W6 9NH. (G.P.A. Duc). Est. 1985. Open 9-5, Sat. 10-4. SIZE: Medium. *STOCK: Marble/stone chimney pieces, 18th-19th C, £500-£8,000; gilt/painted overmantles, 19th C,*

W6 continued

£300-£1,500. PARK: Easy and Black Lion Lane. TEL: 0181 741 7883; fax - 0181 741 1109. SER: Valuations; cleaning and polishing (marble chimney pieces on site); repair. VAT: Stan. *Trade Only.*

R. Davighi

117 Shepherd's Bush Rd. W6. Est. 1950. Open 9-6. SIZE: Medium. *STOCK: Chandeliers and light fittings, Victorian to early 20th C.* PARK: Easy. TEL: 0171 603 5357. SER: Valuations; restorations (chandeliers and lighting); glass and brass fittings.

Tony Dixon

121 Shepherds Bush Rd., Hammersmith. W6 7LP. *STOCK: Antiques and objects of desire, English, European and Oriental ceramics and works of art; tribal art, unusual items, £10-£10,000.* TEL: 0171 603 8300; fax - 0171 603 8022.

Paravent

Flat 10, Ranelagh Gardens, Stamford Brook Ave. W6 0YE. (M. Aldbrook). Open by appointment only. *STOCK: Screens, 17th-20th C, £500-£10,000.* TEL: 0181 748 6323; fax - 0181 563 2912. SER: Restorations. VAT: Stan/Spec.

Murray Thomson Ltd

89 Richford St., Shepherds Bush. W6. 7HJ Est. 1966. Open 10-6. SIZE: Large. *STOCK: English furniture, 18th-19th C.* TEL: 0171 727 1727; fax - 0171 727 1825. VAT: Stan/Spec.

LONDON W8

Adrian Alan Ltd BADA LAPADA

219 Kensington Church St. W8 7LX. Open 10-6, Sat. 11-4. *STOCK: English and Continental furniture especially fine 19th C; sculpture and works of art.* TEL: 0171 727 4783; fax - 0171 727 7353. VAT: Stan/Spec.

AntikWest AB

140-142 Kensington Church St. W8 4BN. (Bjorn Gremner). CINOA. Est. 1979. Open 10-6, Sat. 10-4. SIZE: Small. *STOCK: Chinese pottery and porcelain, Tang to late 19th C, £200-£35,000; Chinese furniture, £200-£2,000.* LOC: 100 yards south of Notting Hill Gate. PARK: Meters. TEL: 0171 229 4115. FAIRS: Olympia (June); Eurantica, Brussels; Stockholm, Alvsjo; Helsingborg, Sweden; Singapore Tresors; Hong Kong International. VAT: Spec.

Valerie Arieta

97b Kensington Church St. W8 7LN. Open 10.30-5, Sat. and other times by appointment. *STOCK: American Indian and Eskimo art; English and Continental antiques.* TEL: 0171 243 1074/794 7613.

W8 continued

Garry Atkins

107 Kensington Church St. W8 7LN. (Garry and Julie Atkins). Est. 1986. Open 10-5.30 and Sat. am. SIZE: Small. *STOCK: English and Continental pottery, to 18th C, £100-£10,000; small furniture, to 19th C, £300-£3,000.* LOC: Between Kensington High St. and Notting Hill Gate. PARK: Meters. TEL: 0171 727 8737; fax - 0171 792 9010. SER: Valuations; buys at auction (English and Continental pottery); annual exhibition (March), catalogues available. FAIRS: International Ceramic. VAT: Spec.

Gregg Baker Oriental Art BADA LAPADA

132 Kensington Church St. W8 4BH. Est. 1985. Open 10-6, weekends by appointment. SIZE: Small. *STOCK: Japanese and Chinese works of art and screens, mainly 18th-19th C, £500-£100,000.* PARK: Meters. TEL: 0171 221 3533; fax - 0171 221 4410. SER: Valuations. VAT: Stan/Spec.

Eddy Bardawil BADA

106 Kensington Church St. W8 4BH. (E.S. Bardawil). Est. 1979. Open 10-1 and 2-5.30, Sat. 10-1.30. SIZE: Medium. *STOCK: English furniture - mahogany, satinwood, walnut; mirrors, brassware, tea-caddies, all pre-1830, £500-£50,000; prints, 18th C.* LOC: Corner premises, Berkeley Gardens/Church St. PARK: Easy. TEL: 0171 221 3967; fax - 0171 221 5124. SER: Valuations; restorations (furniture); polishing. VAT: Stan/Spec.

Barnet Antiques BADA

79 Kensington Church St. W8 4BG. *STOCK: 18th to early 19th C English furniture.* TEL: 0171 376 2817.

Baumkotter Gallery LAPADA

63a Kensington Church St. W8 4BA. (Mrs L. Baumkotter). Est. 1968. Open 9.30-6. CL: Sat. SIZE: Large. *STOCK: 17th-19th C oil paintings.* TEL: 0171 937 5171; fax - 0171 938 2312. VAT: Spec.

Berwald Oriental Art BADA

101 Kensington Church St. W8 7LN. (John R. Berwald). Est. 1986. Open 10-6, Sat. and Sun and other times by appointment. SIZE: Medium. *STOCK: Chinese porcelain, 16th to early 18th C; Chinese pottery, 200BC to 15th C; Oriental works of art; all £1,000-£100,000.* PARK: Meters and nearby. TEL: 0171 229 0800; fax - 0171 229 1101. SER: Valuations; restorations; buys at auction (Oriental). FAIRS: International Asian Arts, New York; International Ceramics, London. VAT: Spec.

W8 continued

David Brower Antiques

113 Kensington Church St. W8 7LN. Est. 1965. Open 10-6. CL: Sat. SIZE: Large. *STOCK: Oriental and Continental decorative porcelain, £100-£5,000; French and Oriental furniture, bronzes and clocks.* PARK: Meters nearby. TEL: 0171 221 4155. SER: Buys at auction. VAT: Stan/Spec.

The Lucy B. Campbell Gallery BADA

123 Kensington Church St. W8 7LP. Est. 1983. Open 10-6, Sat. 10-4. SIZE: Medium. *STOCK: Fine decorative prints, 17th-19th C; contemporary originals.* Not Stocked: Maps and sporting prints. PARK: Meters. TEL: 0171 727 2205; fax - 0171 229 4252; e-mail - lucy.b.campbell@dial.pipex.com. SER: Framing. VAT: Stan.

Anne-Marie Cattanach LAPADA

79 Kensington Church St. W8 4BG. Est. 1977. Open 10-1 and 2-5.30. SIZE: Medium. *STOCK: Furniture, £500-£20,000; boxes and candlesticks, caddies and Oriental porcelain; all 17th-19th C.* PARK: Meters. TEL: 0171 376 2817; home - 0171 727 0460. SER: Valuations; restorations (furniture). FAIRS: Olympia. VAT: Spec.

Church Gallery

77 Kensington Church St. W8 4BG. (A. Spigard). Open 9-6. *STOCK: General antiques and furniture.* TEL: 0171 937 2461; fax - 0171 938 3286. SER: Restorations. VAT: Spec.

Coats Oriental Carpets

4 Kensington Church Walk, (off Holland St). W8 4NB. (A. Coats). Est. 1973. Open 11-5, Sat. 11-3 or by appointment. SIZE: Medium. *STOCK: Oriental carpets and rugs, kelims, £50-£2,000; Oriental textiles and embroideries, £10-£100; all 19th C.* LOC: Small pedestrian alleyway just off Holland St., off south end of Kensington Church St. PARK: Easy. TEL: 0171 937 0983; home - 0171 370 2355. SER: Valuations; restorations (reweaving); buys at auction. VAT: Stan/Spec.

Cohen & Cohen BADA

101B Kensington Church St. W8 7LN. Open 10-6, Sat. 10-4. *STOCK: Chinese export porcelain and works of art.* TEL: 0171 727 7677; fax - 0171 229 9653. SER: Valuations; buys at auction. VAT: Stan/Spec.

Garrick D. Coleman

5 Kensington Court. W8 5DL. (G.D. and G.E. Coleman). Est. 1944. Open strictly by appointment only. SIZE: Medium. *STOCK: Chess sets, 1750-1880, £100-£4,000; decorative items, £50-£2,000; glass paperweights, £200-£3,000; conjuring and magic items.* PARK: Easy. TEL: 0171 937 5524; fax - 0171 937 5530. VAT: Stan/Spec.

W8 continued

Mary Cooke Antiques Ltd BADA LAPADA

121A Kensington Church St. W8 7LP. Open 9.30-5.30, Sat. am. by appointment. *STOCK: Silver.* TEL: 0171 792 8077. SER: Valuations; restorations; buys at auction. FAIRS: Chelsea Spring and Autumn; NEC; LAPADA; International; Northern. VAT: Stan/Spec.

Crawley and Asquith Ltd BADA

20 Upper Phillimore Gardens. W8 7HA. Open by appointment. *STOCK: 18th-19th C paintings, watercolours, prints, books.* TEL: 0171 937 9523; fax - 0171 937 2159.

Mrs. M.E. Crick Chandeliers

166 Kensington Church St. W8 4BN. Est. 1897. CL: Sat. *STOCK: English and Continental crystal, glass and ormulu chandeliers, 18th-19th C.* PARK: Meters. TEL: 0171 229 1338; fax - 0171 792 1073.

George Dare

9 Launceston Place, Kensington. W8 5RL. Est. 1980. Open anytime by appointment. SIZE: Medium. *STOCK: English watercolours and oil paintings, mainly 18th-19th C, £100-£2,500.* LOC: Turn left off London bound section of Cromwell Rd., opposite the Forum Hotel. PARK: Easy. TEL: 0171 937 7072; home - same. SER: Restorations; framing; buys at auction (as stock). VAT: Stan.

Davies Antiques LAPADA

40 Kensington Church St. W8 4BX. (H.Q.V. Davies). Est. 1976. Open 10-5.30, Sat. 10-3. *STOCK: Continental porcelain especially Meissen, 1710-1930.* TEL: 0171 937 9216; fax - 0171 938 2032.

Richard Dennis

144 Kensington Church St. W8. Est. 1967. Open 10-5.30, Sat. 10-2. SIZE: Medium. *STOCK: British studio pottery especially Martin, Doulton, Pilkington and Parian, 1870-1950, and contemporary.* LOC: Near Notting Hill Gate tube. TEL: 0171 727 2061. VAT: Stan/Spec.

Denton Antiques

156 Kensington Church St. W8 4BN. (M.T. and M.E. Denton). Open 9.30-5.30. CL: Sat. *STOCK: Glass, chandeliers, candelabra, 18th-19th C.* TEL: 0171 229 5866; fax - 0171 792 1073.

H. and W. Deutsch Antiques LAPADA

111 Kensington Church St. W8 7LN. Est. 1897. Open 10-5. CL: Tues., Wed. and Sat. SIZE: Large. *STOCK: 18th-19th C Continental and English porcelain and glassware; silver, plate and enamel ware, miniature portraits; Oriental porcelain, cloisonné, bronzes, £300-£5,000.* TEL: 0171 727 5984. VAT: Stan/Spec.

W8 continued

Michael C. German BADA LAPADA

38B Kensington Church St. W8 4BX. Est. 1954. Open 10-5, Sat. 10-3. *STOCK: European and Oriental arms and armour; walking stick specialist.* TEL: 0171 937 2771.

Green's Antique Galleries

117 Kensington Church St. W8 7LN. (S. Green). Open 9-5. SIZE: Medium. *STOCK: Jewellery, 18th C to date; pre-1930 clothes and lace; dolls, china, silver, furniture, paintings, masonic, crocodile and leather items.* PARK: Easy. TEL: 0171 229 9618. VAT: Stan/Spec.

Grosvenor Antiques Ltd BADA

27 Holland St., Kensington. W8 4NA. (S.C. and E. Lorie). Est. 1950. *STOCK: English and Continental porcelain, bronzes and works of art.* TEL: 0171 937 8649; fax - 0171 937 7179. VAT: Spec.

Robert Hales Antiques Ltd

131 Kensington Church St. W8 7LP. Est. 1967. Open 9.30-5.30. CL: Mon. and Sat. SIZE: Small. *STOCK: Islamic, Oriental and ethnographic arms and armour; oceanic art, 16th-19th C.* PARK: Easy. TEL: 0171 229 3887. SER: Valuations; buys at auction. VAT: Spec.

Hampson and Lewis

131E Kensington Church St. (entrance in Peel St). W8 7LP. (Peter Hampson and Sue Lewis). Est. 1981. Open Tues.-Sat. from 11.15. SIZE: Small. *STOCK: Silver and jewellery, Arts and Crafts to date, £50-£3,000.* TEL: 0171 229 8173. SER: Restorations (jewellery and silver); buys at auction (silver and jewellery). VAT: Stan/Spec.

Adrian Harrington

64A Kensington Church St., W8 4DB. ABA, ILAB, PBFA. Est. 1970. Open 10-6. Medium. *STOCK: Antiquarian books, maps and prints, 15th-20th C, especially bound library sets, English literature plate books, maps and decorative engravings.* LOC: Half-way up Kensington Church St. PARK: Meters. TEL: 0171 937 1465; fax - 0171 368 0912; e-mail - rare@harringtonbooks.co.uk. SER: Valuations; restorations (bookbinding, prints); framing; buys at auction (antiquarian books). FAIRS: Olympia Book (June); Chelsea Book (Nov). VAT: Stan.

Jonathan Harris BADA

Previously at 54 Kensington Church St. W8. CINOA. Open temporarily by appointment only, before moving to new permanent premises. *STOCK: English, Continental, Oriental furniture; works of art.* TEL: 0171 602 6255; fax - 0171 602 0488. VAT: Spec.

Haslam and Whiteway

105 Kensington Church St. W8 7LN. (T.M. Whiteway). Est. 1969. Open 10-6, Sat. 10-2. SIZE: Small. *STOCK: British furniture, £100-£10,000; British decorative arts, £50-£5,000;*

W8 continued

Continental and American decorative arts, £50-£500; all 1850-1930. Not Stocked: Pre-Victorian items. LOC: From Notting Hill Gate tube station, down Kensington Church St. Shop is approx. 300yds. down on right. PARK: Meters. TEL: 0171 229 1145. SER: Valuations; buys at auction. VAT: Stan.

Jeanette Hayhurst Fine Glass BADA

32A Kensington Church St. W8. Open 12-5, Sat. 11-4. *STOCK: Glass - 18th C English drinking, fine 19th C engraved, table decanters, contemporary art, scent bottles, Roman and Continental.* TEL: 0171 938 1539.

D. Holmes

47c Earls Court Rd. (in Abingdon Villas), Kensington. W8 6EE. Est. 1965. Open Fri. 2-7, Sat. 10-2 or by appointment. *STOCK: Decorative items and furniture, 18th-19th C.* TEL: 0171 937 6961 or 01208 880254. SER: Restorations (furniture). VAT: Stan/Spec.

Hope and Glory

(Royal Commemorative Specialists) 131a Kensington Church St. W8 7LP. Open 10-5. *STOCK: Commemorative china.* TEL: 0171 727 8424.

Jonathan Horne BADA

66b & 66c Kensington Church St. W8 4BY. Est. 1968. Open 9.30-5.30. CL: Sat. and Sun. except by appointment. SIZE: Medium. *STOCK: Early English pottery, needlework and works of art.* TEL: 0171 221 5658; fax - 0171 792 3090. VAT: Stan/Spec.

Valerie Howard LAPADA

2 Campden St., Off Kensington Church St. W8 7EP. Open 10-5.30, Sat. 10-4.30. *STOCK: Mason's and English Ironstone china, 1810-1860, £50-£10,000; French faience especially from Quimper and Rouen regions, 1750-1920, £20-£3,000; mirrors, 19th C, £500-£2,000.* TEL: 0171 792 9702 (ansaphone at night); fax - 0171 221 7008. SER: Valuations; restorations (ceramics); buys at auction (as stock). FAIRS: Olympia (June). VAT: Spec.

W8 continued

Iona Antiques BADA

PO Box 285. W8 6HZ. Est. 1974. Open by appointment only. SIZE: Large. *STOCK: 19th C animal paintings, £1,000-£30,000.* LOC: 3 minutes walk from Odeon Cinema, Kensington High St. PARK: Nearby. TEL: 0171 602 1193; fax - 0171 371 2843. FAIRS: Grosvenor House, Olympia.

W8 continued

J.A.N. Fine Art

134 Kensington Church St. W8. (Mrs F.K. Shimizu). Est. 1976. Open 10-6, Sat. by appointment. SIZE: Medium. *STOCK: Japanese and Chinese porcelain, 1st to 20th C, from £150; Japanese bronzes and works of art, 15th-20th C, from £150; Japanese paintings and screens, 16th-20th C, from £250; Tibetan thankas and ritual objects, 12th-18th C, from £250.*. PARK: Meters. TEL: 0171 792 0736; fax - 0171 221 1380. VAT: Spec.

Japanese Gallery

66d Kensington Church St. W8 4BY. (Mr. and Mrs C.D. Wertheim). Est. 1977. Open 10-6. *STOCK: Japanese wood-cut prints; books, porcelain, netsuke.* TEL: 0171 229 2934; fax - same. SER: Free authentification; on-the-spot framing for Japanese prints; exhibitions.

Roderick Jellicoe

at Stockspring Antiques, 114 Kensington Church St. W8 4BH. Est. 1974. Open 10-5.30, Sat. 10-1. SIZE: Medium. *STOCK: English porcelain, 18th-19th C, £5-£5,000+.* PARK: Meters. TEL: 0171 727 7995. SER: Valuations; buys at auction (18th C English porcelain). FAIRS: Olympia; London Ceramic. VAT: Spec.

John Jesse

160 Kensington Church St. W8 4BN. Open 10-6, Sat. 11-4. *STOCK: Decorative arts, 1880-1980, especially Art Nouveau and Art Deco silver, glass, bronzes and jewellery.* TEL: 0171 229 0312; fax - 0171 229 4732.

Howard Jones LAPADA

43 Kensington Church St. W8 4BA. (H. Howard-Jones). Est. 1971. Open 10-5. SIZE: Small. *STOCK: Silver, porcelain, bronzes, £20-£5,000.* Not Stocked: Furniture. PARK: Nearby. TEL: 0171 937 4359. VAT: Stan/Spec.

Peter Kemp

170 Kensington Church St. W8 4BN. Est. 1975. Open 10-5. CL: Sat. SIZE: Medium. *STOCK: Porcelain - 10th-19th C Chinese, 17th-19th C Japanese, 18th C Continental; Oriental works of art and porcelain, 18th-19th C.* LOC: 200yds. from Notting Hill tube station. PARK: Meters nearby. TEL: 0171 229 2988. SER: Valuations; restorations (porcelain); buys at auction (Oriental and Continental porcelain). VAT: Spec.

Kensington Church Street Antiques Centre

58-60 Kensington Church St. W8 4DB. Open 10-6. Below are listed some of the dealers at this Centre.

Nic Boston

Units 10, 14 & 15. *Majolica (Minton, Wedgwood, George Jones).* TEL: 0171 376 0425; fax - 0171 937 3400. VAT: Stan/Spec.

W8 continued

Didier Antiques

Unit 2. *Jewellery and silver, objets d'art, 1860-1960, £50-£7,000.* TEL: 0171 938 2537. VAT: Stan/Spec.

Freeforms

Unit 6. *20th C decorative arts including post-war design.* TEL: 0171 376 0425.

Gallery 8

Unit 8.

Glass Pyramid

Unit 5.

Graven Images

Unit 7.

Jag

Units 9 & 11. *Art glass, including Loetz, Murano, 1880-1960, pewter, WMF, Liberty; ceramics, bronzes and ivories.* TEL: 0171 938 4404; fax - 0171 937 3400.

M. Lorenzo

Unit 4.

C. Monk

Unit 12.

Noonstar LAPADA

Unit 1. *Cameo glass and decorative items, both 20th C.* TEL: 0171 376 2652. VAT: Stan/Spec.

Zeitgeist

Unit 3. *Liberty metalwork, ceramics and furniture.* TEL: 0171 938 4817; fax - 0171 937 3400.

The Lacquer Chest

71 and 75 Kensington Church St. W8 4BG. (G. and V. Andersen). Est. 1959. Open 9.30-5.30, Sat. 10.30-3. SIZE: Large. *STOCK: Furniture - pine, painted, oak, mahogany; blue and white, Staffordshire, lamps, candlesticks, samplers, prints, paintings, brass, mirrors, garden furniture, unusual items.* LOC: Half-way up left-hand side from High St. PARK: Meters. TEL: 0171 937 1306; fax - 0171 376 0223. VAT: Stan/Spec.

Lev (Antiques) Ltd

97A&B Kensington Church St. W8 7LN. (Mrs Lev). Est. 1882. Open 10.30-5.30. SIZE: Medium. *STOCK: Jewellery, silver, plate, curios.* PARK: Meters. TEL: 0171 727 9248. SER: Restorations (pictures); repairs (jewellery, silver).

Lewis and Lloyd BADA

65 Kensington Church St. W8 4BA. Est. 1968. Open 10.15-5.30. SIZE: Medium. *STOCK: Furniture and works of art, 18th-19th C, £2,000-£50,000.* PARK: Easy. TEL: 0171 938 3323; fax - 0171 361 0086. VAT: Spec.

W8 continued

Libra Antiques
131d Kensington Church St. W8. *STOCK: Blue and white pottery, lustre ware.* TEL: 0171 727 2990.

London Antique Gallery
66E Kensington Church St. W8 4BY. (Mr. and Mrs. C.D. Wertheim). Open 10-6. *STOCK: London prints; Meissen, Royal Worcester, collectable porcelain.* TEL: 0171 229 2934; fax - same. SER: Restorations (prints, porcelain and dolls).

Fay Lucas Gallery LAPADA
50 Kensington Church St. W8 4DA. Est. 1977. Medium. *STOCK: Signed silver holloware, 20th C, £200-£50,000; signed furniture, 20th C, £5,000-£50,000; antique military and sporting jewellery, £100-£3,000.* LOC: Off Kensington High St. PARK: Kensington Town Hall. TEL: 0171 938 3763; fax - 0171 376 1005. SER: Valuations; restorations; buys at auction. FAIRS: Olympia (Feb., June, Nov). VAT: Stan/Spec.

C.H. Major (Antiques) Ltd
154 Kensington Church St. W8 4BN. (A.H. Major). Est. 1905. Open 10-6. SIZE: Large. *STOCK: English furniture, from 1760, £200-£25,000.* Not Stocked: China, glass. PARK: Easy. TEL: 0171 229 1162; fax - 0171 221 9676; home - 0181 997 9018. VAT: Stan/Spec.

E. and H. Manners BADA
66a Kensington Church St. W8 4BY. Est. 1986. Open 10-5.30, Sat. and Sun. by appointment. *STOCK: European ceramics, pre-19th C, £100-£20,000.* TEL: 0171 229 5516; fax - same; home - 0181 741 7084. FAIRS: International Ceramic. VAT: Spec.

S. Marchant & Son BADA
120 Kensington Church St. W8 4BH. (R.P. Marchant). Est. 1925. Open 9.30-5.30. CL: Sat. *STOCK: Chinese and Japanese pottery and porcelain, jades, cloisonné, Chinese furniture and paintings.* PARK: Easy. TEL: 0171 229 5319/3770; fax - 0171 792 8979. SER: Valuations; restorations (porcelain); buys at auction. VAT: Stan/Spec.

Robert McPherson
at Stockspring Antiques, 114 Kensington Church St. W8 4BH. Est. 1985. Open 10-5.30, Sat. 10-1. *STOCK: Chinese ceramics, 2500 BC to 1800, £5-£4,000.* TEL: 0171 727 7995. FAIRS: Olympia (June). VAT: Spec.

Michael Coins
6 Hillgate St., (off Notting Hill Gate). W8 7SR. (M. Gouby). Est. 1966. Open 10-5. CL: Sat. SIZE: Small. *STOCK: Coins, English and foreign, 1066 A.D. to date; stamps, banknotes and collectors' items.* LOC: From Marble Arch to Notting Hill Gate, turn left at corner of Coronet

W8 continued

Cinema. PARK: Easy. TEL: 0171 727 1518; fax - 0171 727 1518. SER: Valuations; buys at auction. VAT: Stan/Spec.

New Century
69 Kensington Church St. W8 4BG. (H.S. Lyons). Est. 1988. *STOCK: Arts and Crafts, aesthetic and Art Nouveau furniture, metal and ceramics, 1870-1920, £20-£3,000.* TEL: 0171 937 2410. SER: Valuations; restorations; buys at auction. VAT: Stan/Spec.

Oliver-Sutton Antiques BADA
34c Kensington Church St. W8 4HA. (P. Sutton). Est. 1967. Open Mon.-Fri. 10-5. CL: Aug. *STOCK: Staffordshire, Walton, Sherratt pottery; 19th C portrait figures, animals, cottages.* TEL: 0171 937 0633. VAT: Spec.

Pruskin Gallery
73 Kensington Church St. W8 4BG. *STOCK: Fine Art Nouveau and Art Deco glass, bronzes, silver, furniture, ceramics, paintings, posters and prints.* TEL: 0171 937 1994; evenings - 0171 938 2892.

Raffety BADA LAPADA
34 Kensington Church St. W8 4HA. Open 10.30-5.30, Sat. 10.30-1.30. *STOCK: Fine English longcase and bracket clocks, 17th-18th C; carriage clocks and barometers.* TEL: 0171 938 1100; fax - 0171 938 1100; mobile - 0831 514216. SER: Valuations; buys at auction. VAT: Stan/Spec.

W8 continued

Paul Reeves

32B Kensington Church St. W8 4HA. Est. 1976. Open 10-6. *STOCK: Architect designed furniture and artifacts, 1860-1960.* TEL: 0171 937 1594.

Reindeer Antiques Ltd BADA LAPADA

81 Kensington Church St. W8 4BG. (J.W. Butterworth). Open 9.30-6. *STOCK: Period English and Continental furniture and works of art.* PARK: Meters. TEL: 0171 937 3754; fax - 0171 937 7199. VAT: Stan/Spec.

Roderick Antique Clocks LAPADA

23 Vicarage Gate, Kensington. W8 4AA. (R. Mee). Est. 1975. Open 10-5.15, Sat. 10-3. *STOCK: Clocks - French decorative and carriage, 19th C, £250-£2,000; English longcase and bracket, 18th-19th C, £2,000-£7,500.* LOC: At junction of Kensington Church St. PARK: Easy. TEL: 0171 937 8517. SER: Valuations; restorations (English and French movements and cases). VAT: Spec.

Brian Rolleston Antiques Ltd BADA

104A Kensington Church St. W8 4BU. Est. 1950. Open 10-1 and 2-5.30, Sat. by appointment. SIZE: Large. *STOCK: English furniture, 18th C, £1,500-£50,000.* PARK: Easy. TEL: 0171 229 5892; fax - same. VAT: Spec.

W8 continued

Sabin Galleries Ltd BADA

Campden Lodge, 82 Campden Hill Rd. W8 7AA. (S.F, E.P. and P.G. Sabin). SLAD. Open by appointment only. *STOCK: English paintings and drawings, pre-1830.* TEL: 0171 937 0471.

Patrick Sandberg Antiques BADA

140-142 and 150-152 Kensington Church St. W8 4BN. (P.C.F. Sandberg). Est. 1983. Open 10-6, Sat. 10-4. SIZE: Large. *STOCK: 18th to early 19th C English furniture and accessories - candlesticks, tea caddies, clocks and prints.* TEL: 0171 229 0373; fax - 0171 792 3467. FAIRS: Olympia (Feb., June, Nov). VAT: Spec.

A.V. Santos BADA

1 Campden St. W8 7EP. Open 10-1 and 2-6. CL: Sat. *STOCK: Chinese export porcelain, 17th-18th C.* TEL: 0171 727 4872; fax - 0171 229 4801. VAT: Spec.

M. and D. Seligmann BADA

37 Kensington Church St. W8 4LL. Est. 1948. Open Mon.-Fri. 10.30-5.30 or by appointment. SIZE: Medium. *STOCK: 17th-18th C English country furniture, pottery, treen, objets d'art.* LOC: Nearest underground Kensington High St. TEL: 0171 937 0400; home - 0171 722 4315; fax - same. FAIRS: Olympia (June and Nov.); Chelsea (Autumn). VAT: Stan/Spec.

Jean Sewell (Antiques) Ltd BADA

3 Campden St. W8 7EP. (E. and B. Sewell). Est. 1956. Open 10-5.30. SIZE: Medium. *STOCK: Pottery and porcelain, 18th-19th C, £1-£10,000.* Not Stocked: Silver, furniture and china after 1880. LOC: From Notting Hill Gate down Kensington Church St., fourth street on right at Churchill public house. PARK: Easy. TEL: 0171 727 3122; fax - 0171 229 1053. VAT: Stan/Spec.

Sinai Antiques Ltd

221 Kensington Church St. W8 7LX. (E. and M. Sinai). Open 9.30-6. CL: Sat. *STOCK: Carpets, Oriental and fine arts, silver, fine arts.* TEL: 0171 229 6190.

Simon Spero

109 Kensington Church St. W8 7LN. Author of 'The Price Guide to 18th C English Porcelain' and three other standard reference books. Est. 1964. Open 10-5, Sat. 10-1. SIZE: Medium. *STOCK: 18th C English ceramics, enamels and water-colours.* PARK: Meters. TEL: 0171 727 7413; fax - 0171 727 7414. SER: Valuations; buys at auction; lecturer. VAT: Spec.

Constance Stobo

31 Holland St., (off Kensington Church St.). W8 4NA. *STOCK: English lustreware, Staffordshire animals, Wemyss, 18th-19th C pottery.* TEL: 0171 937 6282.

W8 continued

Stockspring Antiques LAPADA
114 Kensington Church St. W8 4BH. (A. Agnew and F. Marno). Open 10-5.30, Sat. 10-1. *STOCK: English, European and Oriental pottery and porcelain.* TEL: 0171 727 7995. VAT: Spec.

Jacob Stodel BADA
116A Kensington Church St. W8 4BH. Est. 1949. *STOCK: Continental furniture, objets d'art, ceramics, English furniture.* TEL: 0171 221 2652; fax - 0171 229 1293. VAT: Spec.

Pamela Teignmouth and Son
108 Kensington Church St. W8 4BH. (Lady Teignmouth and Mr T. Meyer). Est. 1982. Open 10-6, incl. Sat. in winter only. SIZE: Medium. *STOCK: English and Continental furniture, 18th-19th C, decorative items, £100-£10,000.* TEL: 0171 229 1602; fax - 0171 792 5042. FAIRS: Olympia (June). VAT: Spec.

Through the Looking Glass Ltd
137 Kensington Church St. W8 7LP. (J.J.A. and D.A. Pulton). Est. 1958. Open 10-5.30. SIZE: Large. *STOCK: Mirrors, 19th C, £500-£10,000.* LOC: 200yds. from Notting Hill Gate. PARK: Side roads. TEL: 0171 221 4026. SER: Gilding. VAT: Spec.

Jorge Welsh Oriental Porcelain & Works of Art
116 Kensington Church St. W8 4BH. Est. 1987. Open 11-5.30. CL: Sat. SIZE: Medium. *STOCK: Chinese export porcelain and Oriental works of art.* LOC: Off Kensington High St. PARK: NCP Bayswater Rd. TEL: 0171 229 2140; fax - 0171 792 3535. SER: Valuations; restorations; buys at auction. FAIRS: International Ceramic. VAT: Spec.

Mary Wise BADA
27 Holland St., Kensington. W8 4NA. Est. 1959. *STOCK: English porcelain, works of art, bronzes.* Not Stocked: English pottery, jewellery. TEL: 0171 937 8649; fax - 0171 937 7179. SER: Buys at auction (Chinese and English porcelain). VAT: Spec.

LONDON W9

Clifton Little Venice
3 Warwick Place. W9 2PH. (Clifton Nurseries). *STOCK: Garden antiques, furniture and reproductions, water features.*TEL: 0171 289 7894.

Fluss and Charlesworth Ltd LAPADA
1 Lauderdale Rd. W9 1LT. (E. Fluss and J. Charlesworth). Est. 1970. Open by appointment. *STOCK: 18th to early 19th C furniture and works of art.* TEL: 0171 286 8339; mobile - 0831 830323. SER: Interior decor. FAIRS: Olympia; LAPADA.

W9 continued

Beryl Kendall, The English Watercolour Gallery
2 Warwick Place, Little Venice. W9 2PX. Est. 1953. Open 2-6, Sat. 11-3.30. CL: Mon. *STOCK: English watercolours, 19th C.* TEL: 0171 286 9902.

Vale Antiques
245 Elgin Ave., Maida Vale. W9 1NJ. (P. Gooley). *STOCK: General antiques.* TEL: 0171 328 4796.

LONDON W11

Michael Aalders
181 Westbourne Grove. W11. Open 10-6. *STOCK: Unusual furniture and furnishings, 17th-18th C; paintings, 19th-20th C.* TEL: 0171 221 4391.

Addison Fine Art
57 Addison Avenue. W11 4ZU. (Mrs D. Geddes). Est. 1978. Open by appointment. SIZE: Small. *STOCK: British and Continental post-impressionist paintings.* TEL: 0171 603 2374. SER: Valuations; restorations; buys at auction (paintings). FAIRS: 20th C British Art (Sept.); Olympia (June). VAT: Spec.

Alice's
86 Portobello Rd. W11 2QD. (D. Carter). Est. 1960. Open 9-5. SIZE: Large. *STOCK: General antiques and decorative items.* TEL: 0171 229 8187; fax - 0171 792 2456.

Arbras Gallery
292 Westbourne Grove. W11 2PS. Est. 1972. Open Fri. 10-4, Sat. 7-5. SIZE: 2 floors. *STOCK: General antiques - silver, boxes, jewellery, paintings, furniture, books, prints and decorative items.* LOC: 50 yards from Portobello Road. TEL: 0171 229 6772. VAT: Stan/Spec.

Arenski BADA LAPADA
185 Westbourne Grove. W11 2SB. (Jay Arenski). Open 10-5.30. SIZE: Large. *STOCK: Furniture, glass, objects, bronzes and paintings, from 1820, £25-£50,000.* PARK: Easy. TEL: 0171 727 8599. SER: Buys at auction. FAIRS: Olympia, LAPADA. VAT: Stan/Spec.

Axia Art Consultants Ltd
121 Ledbury Rd. W11 2AQ. Est. 1974. *STOCK: Works of art, icons, textiles, metalwork, woodwork and ceramics, Islamic and Byzantine.* TEL: 0171 727 9724.

B. and T. Antiques LAPADA
79/81 Ledbury Rd. W11 2AG. (Mrs B. Lewis). Open 10-6. *STOCK: Furniture, silver, objets d'art, paintings, 18th C to Art Deco.* TEL: 0171 229 7001; fax - 0171 229 2033.

W11 continued

P.R. Barham

111 Portobello Rd. W11 2QB. Est. 1951. Open 9-5. SIZE: Large. *STOCK: Victorian, Edwardian, Continental furniture, Oriental porcelain, objets d'art, silver, plate and clocks.* TEL: 0171 727 3397. SER: Valuations; buys at auction.

Barham Antiques

83 Portobello Rd. W11. Est. 1954. Open 9.30-5, Sat. 7-5. SIZE: Large. *STOCK: Victorian walnut and inlaid Continental furniture, writing boxes, tea caddies, inkwells and inkstands, glass epergnes, silver plate, clocks, paintings.* TEL: 0171 727 3845; fax - same. SER: Valuations; buys at auction.

Benchmark Art Furniture Ltd

184 Westbourne Grove. W11 2RH. (Ben Brierley and Sandra Keenan Kamen). Est. 1984. Open 10-6, Sun. and Mon. by appointment. SIZE: Medium. *STOCK: 19th C Art furniture and artifacts - Pugin, Godwin, Talbert, Dresser, some early Heals and Cotswold; 1940's Whitefriars glass, £50-£50,000.* LOC: Near Portobello Rd. PARK: Easy. TEL: 0171 229 4179; home - 0181 968 6625/0161 477 7953; mobile - 0468 058632/058240. SER: Buys at auction.

David Black Oriental Carpets BADA

96 Portland Rd., Holland Park. W11 4LN. Est. 1966. Open 11-6. SIZE: Large. *STOCK: Antique and new Oriental room size decorative carpets; tribal rugs, kilims, dhurries, embroideries, £500-£25,000.* LOC: From Notting Hill Gate, second right after Holland Park tube station. PARK: Meters. TEL: 0171 727 2566; fax - 0171 229 4599. SER: Valuations; restorations; cleaning underfelt. VAT: Spec.

Norman Blackburn

32 Ledbury Rd. W11 2AB. Est. 1974. Open 10-6, Sat. 10-5. CL: Mon. *STOCK: Framed prints - decorative, stipple and mezzotints, botanical, sporting, marine, portraits and views, pre-1860.* LOC: Two roads east of Portobello. TEL: 0171 229 5316; fax - 0171 229 2269. VAT: Spec.

Books & Things

Arbras Gallery, 292 Westbourne Grove. W11 2PS. (M. Steenson). ABA, PBFA. Est. 1972. Open Sat. 7-4, Fri. by appointment. SIZE: Small. *STOCK: Antiquarian books, £25-£500; posters, £50-£500; both 20th C.* PARK: Meters. TEL: 0171 370 5593 (anytime); fax - 0171 370 5593. SER: Valuations; buys at auction; catalogues issued. FAIRS: PBFA London, Oxford, Bath; ABA, Chelsea.

Britannia Export Antiques

186 Westbourne Grove. W11 2RH. (G. Fiumano). Est. 1973. Open 9.30-6, Sat. 10.30-4. SIZE: Large. *STOCK: Silver and ivory, £300-£10,000; furniture, £500-£20,000; all 18th-20th C.* PARK: Meters. TEL: 0171 221 2011. SER: Valuations; restorations (silver, porcelain, ivory, furniture and pictures); buys at auction (as restorations). VAT: Stan/Spec.

W11 continued

Butchoff Antiques LAPADA

229 and 233 Westbourne Grove. W11 2SE. Est. 1962. Open 10-6, Sat. 10-3.30. SIZE: Large. *STOCK: Fine 18th-19th C English and Continental furniture, decorative smalls and paintings, £500-£50,000.* TEL: 0171 221 8174; fax - 0171 792 8923.

Caelt Gallery

182 Westbourne Grove. W11 2RH. Est. 1967. Open 9.30-6, Sun. 10.30-6. SIZE: Large. *STOCK: Oil paintings, 17th-20th C, £200-£10,000 but mainly £300-£700.* PARK: Easy. TEL: 0171 229 9309; fax - 0171 727 8746. VAT: Spec.

Canonbury

174 Westbourne Grove. W11 2RW. (M. Worster). Est. 1965. Open 10-6, Sat. 10-4.30. SIZE: Large. *STOCK: Dutch, English and French furniture; some porcelain.* LOC: Off Portobello Road. PARK: Easy. TEL: 0171 727 4268; fax - 0171 229 5840. SER: Valuations; restorations. VAT: Stan/Spec.

Jack Casimir Ltd BADA LAPADA

23 Pembridge Rd. W11 3HG. Est. 1933. Open 10-5.30 and by appointment. SIZE: Large. *STOCK: Brass, copper, pewter.* Not Stocked: Silver, china, jewellery. LOC: 2 mins. walk from Notting Hill Gate station. PARK: 100yds. TEL: 0171 727 8643. SER: Exports. VAT: Stan/Spec.

Central Gallery (Portobello)

125 Portobello Rd. W11 2DY. Open Saturdays only 6-3. SIZE: 32+ dealers. *STOCK: Jewellery, Georgian to 1950's, cameos, hardstone, shell, lava, coral, amber, ivory, jet, tortoiseshell, piqué, micro-mosaics, pietra-dura, Art Nouveau, plique é jour, horn pendants, Arts & Crafts, Art Deco, enamels, Austro-Hungarian cut-steel, Berlin iron, Scottish, Victorian silver and gold, Alberts, Albertines, longuards, curbs, gates, fobs, seals, intaglios, pocket watches, vintage wristwatches, cufflinks, fine diamonds, rare gemstones, signed pieces, £50-£5,000+.* TEL: 0171 243 8027; fax - same. FAIRS: Olympia; Park Lane Hotel; Miami Beach. VAT: Stan/Spec/Global.

The Coach House

189 Westbourne Grove. W11 2SB. (Jay Arenski, Peter Farlow, Peter Petrou and Graham Walpole). Open 9-6. *STOCK: Fine furniture - Regency, Gothic Revival, Arts & Crafts, Aesthetic, Colonial and Campaign, Islamic and Egyptian Revival; oil paintings including maritime, Old Masters and modern, naïve portraits including animal, watercolours and prints; classical and Vienna*

W11 continued

bronzes, Grand Tour items, ormolu, metalware and treen; decorative glass, silver and plate, pottery including majolica, equestrian objects and tribal art, £200-£200,000. Not Stocked: Shipping goods and jewellery. PARK: Easy. TEL: 0171 229 8306; fax - 0171 229 4297. SER: Interior decor; shipping arranged. FAIRS: Olympia (June); BADA (May). VAT: Stan/Spec.

Cohen and Pearce (Oriental Porcelain)

BADA

84 Portobello Rd. W11 2QD. (M. Cohen). Est. 1974. Open Fri. 10-4, Sat. 8-4 or by appointment. *STOCK: Chinese porcelain, bronzes, works of art; Japanese prints.* TEL: 0171 229 9458; fax - 0171 229 9653. SER: Valuations; buys at auction. VAT: Spec.

Garrick D. Coleman

75 Portobello Rd. W11. Est. 1944. Open 10-4, Sat. 7-5. CL: Mon. *STOCK: Chess sets, 1750-1880, £100-£5,000; works of art £50-£3,000; glass paperweights, £200-£3,000; also conjuring and magic items.* TEL: 0171 937 5524; fax - 0171 937 5530. VAT: Stan/Spec.

Sheila Cook

42 Ledbury Rd. W11 2AB. Est. 1970. SIZE: Medium. *STOCK: Textiles and decorative antiques, 1800-1960, £50-£5,000.* PARK: Easy. TEL: 0171 792 8001. SER: Valuations; buys at auction. VAT: Global.

The Corner Portobello Antiques Supermarket

282-290 Westbourne Grove. W11. (B. Lipka & Son Ltd). Open Fri. 12-4, Sat. 7-5. SIZE: 150 dealers. *STOCK: General miniature antiques, silver and jewellery.* TEL: 0171 727 2027. SER: Valuations; restorations.

Crown Arcade

119 Portobello Rd. W11. (Angelo Soteriades). Est. 1986. Open Sat. 7-5.30. SIZE: Medium. LOC: Near Westbourne Grove. TEL: 0171 221 7638/436 9416/792 3619; mobile - 0956 277077.

Curá Antiques

34 Ledbury Rd. W11 2AB. (G. Antichi). Open 11-6, Sat. 10.30-1. *STOCK: Continental furniture, sculptures, majolica and paintings.* TEL: 0171 229 6880.

Daggett Gallery LAPADA

1st and 2nd Floors, 153 Portobello Rd. W11 2DY. (Caroline Daggett). Est. 1992. Open 10-5 (prior telephone call advisable) and Sat. 9-3.30. SIZE: Medium. *STOCK: Frames, 18th-20th C, from £1.* LOC: 200 yards from Westbourne Grove towards Elgin Crescent. PARK: Meters. TEL: 0171 229 2248. SER: Restorations (frames); gilding; picture plaques; framing; special paint effects. VAT: Stan/Spec.

W11 continued

Charles Daggett Gallery LAPADA

1st and 2nd Floors, 153 Portobello Rd. W11 2DY. (Charles and Caroline Daggett). Est. 1977. Open 10-4, prior telephone call advisable, and Sat. 9-3.30. SIZE: Medium. *STOCK: British pictures, 1740-1840.* LOC: 200 yards from Westbourne Grove, towards Elgin Crescent. PARK: Meters. TEL: 0171 229 2248; fax - 0171 229 0193. SER: Restorations (pictures and frames); framing. VAT: Stan/Spec.

John Dale

87 Portobello Rd. W11 2QB. Est. 1950. Open 11-3, Sat. 7-5. SIZE: Medium. *STOCK: General antiques.* TEL: 0171 727 1304. VAT: Stan.

Michael Davidson

54 Ledbury Rd., Westbourne Grove. W11 2AJ. Est. 1961. Open 9.45-12.45 and 1.15-5. CL: Sat. pm. in winter. *STOCK: Regency and period furniture, objets d'art.* TEL: 0171 229 6088. SER: Valuations. VAT: Stan/Spec.

Delehar

146 Portobello Rd. W11 2DZ. Est. 1919. Open Sat. 9-4. SIZE: Medium. *STOCK: General antiques, works of art.* Not Stocked: Furniture. TEL: 0171 727 9860. VAT: Stan/Spec.

Peter Delehar

146 Portobello Rd. W11 2DZ. Est. 1919. Open Sat. 10-4. SIZE: Medium. *STOCK: Unusual scientific/medical instruments.* TEL: 0171 727 9860 (Sat.) or 0181 866 8659; fax - same; internet - http:www.mikronet.demon.co.uk /pdelehar/. FAIRS: International Scientific and Medical Instrument (Organiser). VAT: Stan/Spec.

Demetzy Books

113 Portobello Rd. W11. (P. and M. Hutchinson). ABA, PBFA. Est. 1972. Open Sat. 7.30-3.30. SIZE: Medium. *STOCK: Antiquarian leather bound books, 18th-19th C, £5-£1,000; Dickens' first editions and children's and illustrated books, 18th-20th C, £5-£200.* LOC: 20yds. from junction with Westbourne Grove, opposite Earl of Lonsdale public house. PARK: Meters. TEL: 01993 702209. SER: Valuations; buys at auction (books). FAIRS: ABA Chelsea; PBFA Russell Hotel, London (monthly); Randolph Hotel, Oxford; ABAA Los Angeles, San Francisco.

Dodo

288 Westbourne Grove. W11 2PS. (Liz Farrow). Est. 1960. Open Sat. only 8-4. *STOCK: British and Continental posters, signs and tins; display figures, showcards, packaging, £2-£1,000.* LOC: Near Portobello Rd. TEL: Home - 0171 229 3132.

Dolphin Arcade

155-157 Portobello Rd. W11. Open Sat. 7-5.30. SIZE: Large - 34 stalls. *STOCK: Jewellery, silver, Oriental porcelain, English pottery, general antiques.* TEL: 0171 727 4883. VAT: Stan/Spec.

W11 continued

The Facade

196 Westbourne Grove. W11 2RH. Est. 1973. Open Tues.-Sat. 10.30-5. *STOCK: French decorative items and lighting, 1900-1940.* PARK: Easy. TEL: 0171 727 2159. VAT: Stan.

Fairman Carpets Ltd

218 Westbourne Grove. W11 2RH. (D.R.J., S.J. and H. Page). Open 10-6. *STOCK: Persian and Oriental carpets and rugs; tapestries.* TEL: 0171 229 2262; fax - 0171 229 2263. SER: Valuations; repairs; cleaning. VAT: Stan.

Peter Farlow BADA LAPADA

189 Westbourne Grove. W11 2SB. Est. 1986. Open 9-5.30, Mon. 9-5, evenings by appointment. SIZE: Large. *STOCK: Gothic Revival, 1830-1880, £1,000-£20,000; Arts and Crafts, Aesthetic Movement.* LOC: Near junction with Ledbury Rd. TEL: 0171 229 8306; fax 0171 229 4297. FAIRS: Olympia (June). VAT: Stan/Spec.

Fleur de Lys Gallery

227a Westbourne Grove. W11 2SE. (H.S. Coronel). Est. 1967. Open 10.30-5.30. SIZE: Medium. *STOCK: Oil paintings, 19th C, £1,000-£5,000.* PARK: Easy, but limited. TEL: 0171 727 8595; fax - same; home - 01372 467934; e-mail - fleur@art-connection.com; internet - http:www.fleur-de-lys.com.

Judy Fox LAPADA

81 Portobello Rd. and 176 Westbourne Grove. W11. Est. 1970. Open 10-5. SIZE: Large. *STOCK: Furniture and decorative items, 18th-20th C; inlaid furniture, mainly 19th C; pottery and porcelain.* TEL: 0171 229 8130; fax - 0171 229 6998.

J. Freeman LAPADA

85a Portobello Rd. W11 2QB. Est. 1962. Open 9.30-1 and 2-5.30, Sat. 9-6. SIZE: Medium. *STOCK: Victorian silver plate, 1830-1870, £10-£150; Sheffield plate, 1790-1830, £20-£100; Victorian and later silver, £5-£200.* LOC: Nearest tube station Notting Hill Gate. PARK: Easy. TEL: 0171 221 5076; fax - 0171 221 5329. VAT: Stan.

Graham and Green

4 Elgin Crescent. W11 2JA. (A. Graham and R. Harrison). Est. 1974. Open 10-6, Sat. 9.30-6, Sun. 11-5. SIZE: Medium. *STOCK: Turkish kelim rugs, pine and other furniture, re-upholstered Victorian chairs and decorative objects.* LOC: Near Portobello Rd. PARK: Meters nearby. TEL: 0171 727 4594. VAT: Stan.

Gavin Graham Gallery

47 Ledbury Rd. W11 2AA. Est. 1973. *STOCK: Oil paintings.* TEL: 0171 229 4848; fax - 0171 792 9697. VAT: Spec.

W11 continued

Grays Portobello

138 Portobello Rd. W11. Open Sat. 7-4. SIZE: Large. *STOCK: Wide range of general small antiques especially porcelain including Oriental.* TEL: 0171 221 3069; fax - 0171 724 0999.

Henry Gregory

82 Portobello Rd. W11 2QD. (H. and C. Gregory). Est. 1969. Open 10-4, Sat. 8-5. SIZE: Medium. *STOCK: Victorian decorative objects, silver, plate, jewellery, small furniture and sporting items, £2-£2,000.* LOC: Between Westbourne Grove and Chepstow Villas. PARK: Easy. TEL: 0171 792 9221. SER: Export packing and shipping. VAT: Stan/Spec.

Patricia Harbottle

Stand 16, Geoffrey Van Arcade, 107 Portobello Rd. W11 2QB. (Mrs P. Harbottle). Est. 1989. Open Sat. 6.45-3. SIZE: Small. *STOCK: Glass, corkscrews, wine and drink related items, 18th-20th C, £5-£500.* TEL: Home - 0171 731 1972; fax - 0171 731 3663. SER: Valuations; restorations; buys at auction. FAIRS: West London (Jan.); Snape; NEC (April, Aug.); Kensington Antiques (Nov.); Wilton House; Little Chelsea. VAT: Stan/Spec.

Hirst Antiques

59 Pembridge Rd. W11 3HG. Est. 1963. Open 10-6. SIZE: Medium. *STOCK: Four poster and half-tester beds; decorative furniture and articles; bronze and marble sculpture.* LOC: End of Portobello Rd., near Notting Hill Gate tube station. TEL: 0171 727 9364. SER: Valuations.

David Ireland

283 Westbourne Grove. W11. Est. 1986. Open Sat. 7-4.30. *STOCK: European and Asian costume and textiles, Paisley shawls, period costume, Chinese court and informal robes.* Not Stocked: Tapestries, cushions and upholstery. TEL: Home - 0181 968 8887. SER: Valuations. FAIRS: Antique Textile Society.

J. and B. Antiques LAPADA

at Geoffrey Van Arcade, 107 Portobello Rd. W11 2QB. (J.E. and C.A. Finch). Est. 1978. Open Sat. 7-4 or by appointment. SIZE: Medium. *STOCK: European works of art, 16th-20th C, £100-£5,000; antiquities, tribal art, £100-£10,000.* TEL: 01295 711689; mobile - 0836 684133. SER: Valuations; buys at auction. VAT: Stan/Spec.

Jones Antique Lighting

194 Westbourne Grove. W11. (Judy Jones). Est. 1978. Open 9.30-6 or by appointment. SIZE: Large. *STOCK: Original decorative lighting, 1860-1960.* Not Stocked: Reproductions. TEL: 0171 229 6866; fax - same. SER: Valuations; repairs; prop hire. VAT: Stan.

W11 continued

Lacy Gallery

203 Westbourne Grove.W11 2AB. Est. 1960. Open Tues.-Fri.10-5, Sat. 10-4. SIZE: Large. *STOCK: Period frames, 1700-1940; decorative paintings and decorative art.* LOC: Two roads east of Portobello Rd. PARK: Easy. TEL: 0171 229 6340; fax - 0171 229 9105. VAT: Stan/Spec.

Patrick Lassalle

139 Portobello Rd. W11. Open Sat. 8-5.30. *STOCK: Prints and maps, 17th to early 20th C, £3-£350.* PARK: Meters nearby. TEL: 0171 607 7121.

Joan Leigh

153 Portobello Rd. W11. Est. 1959. *STOCK: Art Nouveau, Art Deco.* TEL: 0171 727 6848.

M. and D. Lewis

1 Lonsdale Rd., 172 and 193 Westbourne Grove, 83-85 Ledbury Rd. W11. Est. 1960. Open 9.30-5.30, Sat. 9.30-4. *STOCK: Continental and Victorian furniture, porcelain, bronzes.* TEL: 0171 727 3908. VAT: Stan/Spec.

J. Lipitch Ltd BADA

177 Westbourne Grove. W11 2SB. Est. 1955. Open 10-1 and 2-5.30, Sat. 10-1.30. *STOCK: English and Continental furniture, 17th-18th C; bronze, ormolu and porcelain.* TEL: 0171 229 0783. VAT: Spec.

M.C.N. Antiques

183 Westbourne Grove. W11 2SB. Open 9.30-6 or by appointment. *STOCK: Japanese porcelain, cloisonné, Satsuma, bronze, lacquer, ivory.* LOC: Near Portobello Rd. market. PARK: Easy. TEL: 0171 727 3796; fax - 0171 229 8839. SER: Buys at auction. VAT: Stan.

Daniel Mankowitz

208a Westbourne Grove. W11 2RH. Est. 1970. Open 10-6. SIZE: Medium. *STOCK: Furniture, English and Continental, 16th-18th C, £100-£10,000; works of art, English and Continental, 15th-19th C, £50-£5,000; tapestries, 16th-18th C, £200-£3,000.* LOC: Nr. Portobello Road. PARK: Easy. TEL: 0171 229 9270; fax - 0171 229 4687. FAIRS: Olympia. VAT: Spec.

Robin Martin Antiques

44 Ledbury Rd. W11 2AB. (Paul Martin). Est. 1972. Open 10-6. SIZE: Medium. *STOCK: English and Continental furniture and works of art, 17th-19th C.* LOC: Westbourne Grove area. TEL: 0171 727 1301; fax - same; mobile - 0831 544055. VAT: Spec.

Mayflower Antiques

117 Portobello Rd. W11. (J.W. Odgers). Est. 1970. Open Sat. 7-5. SIZE: Medium. *STOCK: Clocks, mechanical music, scientific and marine*

W11 continued

instruments, general antiques. TEL: Sat. - 0171 727 0381; office - 01255 504079; fax - same; mobile - 0860 843569; e-mail - mayflower @anglianet.co.uk. VAT: Stan/Spec.

Mercury Antiques BADA

1 Ladbroke Rd. W11 3PA. (L. Richards). Est. 1963. Open 10-5.30. SIZE: Medium. *STOCK: English porcelain, 1745-1840; English pottery and Delft, 1700-1850; glass, 1780-1850.* Not Stocked: Jewellery, silver, plate, Art Nouveau. LOC: Half minute from Notting Hill Gate underground station, turn into Pembridge Rd. and bear left. TEL: 0171 727 5106; fax - 0171 229 3738. VAT: Spec.

Milne and Moller LAPADA

W11 2BU. (Mr and Mrs C. Moller). Est. 1976. Open by appointment. SIZE: Small. *STOCK: Watercolours, oils, ceramics and sculpture, 19th C to contemporary.* LOC: Near junction of Westbourne Grove and Ledbury Rd. PARK: Easy. TEL: 0171 727 1679; home - same. SER: Portrait commissioning. FAIRS: Olympia; Chelsea Art. VAT: Spec.

Terence Morse and Son Ltd

197 and 237 Westbourne Grove. W11 2SE. Est. 1947. Open 10-6, Sat. 11-2. SIZE: Large. *STOCK: Furniture, 18th-19th C, £1,000+.* LOC: 200yds. from Portobello Rd. PARK: Easy. TEL: 0171 229 9380/229 4059; fax - 0171 792 3284. VAT: Stan/Spec.

Myriad Antiques

131 Portland Rd., Holland Park Ave. W11 4LW. (S. Nickerson). Est. 1970. Open 11-6. SIZE: Medium. *STOCK: Decorative and unusual furniture. (including garden) and objects, mainly 19th C, £10-£1,500.* LOC: Between Notting Hill Gate and Shepherds Bush roundabout. TEL: 0171 229 1709. VAT: Stan.

The Nanking Porcelain Co

Admiral Vernon Antiques Market, 141-149 Portobello Road. W11 2DY. (M. Hyams and E. Porter). Est. 1967. Open Sat. 8.30-3.30. *STOCK: Fine Chinese export porcelain, 18th-19th C, £250-£20,000; Orientalia, 18th-19th C, £100-£5,000.* TEL: 0171 924 2349. VAT: Spec.

Oakstar Ltd LAPADA

Clarendon Rd. W11. (Mrs P. Bromage). Est. 1982. Open by appointment only. SIZE: Small. *STOCK: French and English furniture, 18th-19th C, £200-£10,000; papier mâché trays, £750-£4,000; mirrors, prints and objets d'art, £200-£5,000.* TEL: 0171 630 1822. SER: Restorations (lacquer). FAIRS: Decorative Antiques and Textiles; Olympia Fine Art and Antiques. VAT: Stan/Spec.

W11 continued

Old Father Time Clock Centre

Portobello Studios, 1st Floor, 101 Portobello Rd. W11 2BQ. (John Denvir). Open Fri. 9-2, Sat. 6-4, other times by appointment. *STOCK: Clocks - all types, especially electric. (eg. Eureka), mystery, Atmos, novelty, skeleton, carriage, dial and bracket; also spares, books, barometers and glass domes.* TEL: 0181 546 6299; fax - same; 0171 229 2796; mobile - 0836 712088.

E.S. Phillips and Sons LAPADA

99 Portobello Rd. W11 2QB. Est. 1962. Open 10-5. *STOCK: Ecclesiastical antiques and stained glass.* TEL: 0171 229 2113; fax - 0171 229 1963.

Philp BADA

59 Ledbury Rd. W11 2AA. (R. Philp). SLAD. Est. 1961. Open by appointment. *STOCK: Old Master drawings, 16th-17th C English portraiture and Old Master paintings, medieval sculpture, early furniture and 20th C drawings, £50-£40,000.* PARK: Easy. TEL: 0171 727 7915. VAT: Spec.

Piano Nobile Fine Paintings

129 Portland Rd., Holland Park. W11 4LW. (Dr. Robert A. Travers). Est. 1986. Open Tues.-Sat. 10-5.30. SIZE: Medium. *STOCK: Fine 19th C Impressionist and 20th C Post-Impressionist and Modernist British and Continental oil paintings and sculpture, especially Les Petit Maitres of the Paris Schools, £500-£50,000.* PARK: Easy. TEL: 0171 229 1099; fax - same. SER: Valuations; restorations (paintings and sculptures); framing; buys at auction (19th-20th C oil paintings). FAIRS: Grosvenor; 20th C British Art and London Contemporary.

Portobello Antique Co

133 Portobello Rd. W11 2DY. (L. Meltzer and A. Goldsmith). Open Fri. 11-4.30, Sat. 8-4.30, other times by appointment. *STOCK: Porcelain, small furniture, reproduction silver plate and cutlery.* LOC: Off Westbourne Grove. PARK: Easy. TEL: 0171 221 0344; home - 0181 959 8886. VAT: Stan/Spec.

Portobello Antique Store

79 Portobello Rd. W11 2QB. (J.F. Ewing). Est. 1971. Open 10-4, Sat. 8-4.30. SIZE: Large. *STOCK: Silver and plate, £2-£3,000.* LOC: Notting Hill end of Portobello Rd. PARK: Easy weekdays. TEL: 0171 221 1994. SER: Export. VAT: Stan.

Quadrille

146 Portobello Rd.W11 2DZ. (Valerie Jackson-Harris). Open Sat. 9-4. *STOCK: Ephemera.* TEL: 0171 727 9860.

W11 continued

The Red Lion Market (Portobello Antiques Market)

165/169 Portobello Rd. W11. (Angelo Soteriades). Est. 1951. Open 5.30-5. SIZE: 200 dealers. *STOCK: General antiques including ethnic antiquities, bronzes, ivory statues, jade, precious metals, dolls, silver and plate, drinking vessels, costumes, Oriental and Western porcelain, furniture, collectables, prints, lace, linen, books, manuscripts, stamps, coins, banknotes, paintings, etchings, sporting memorabilia and curios.* TEL: 0171 221 7638/436 9416; mobile - 0956 277077. SER: Valuations; shipping.

A. Rezai Persian Carpets

123 Portobello Rd. W11. Open 9-5. *STOCK: Oriental carpets, kilims, tribal rugs and silk embroideries.* TEL: 0171 221 5012.

Roger's Antiques Gallery

65 Portobello Rd. W11. (Bath Antiques Market Ltd). Open Sat. 7-4.30. SIZE: 65 dealers. *STOCK: Wide range of general antiques and collectables with specialist dealers in most fields, especially jewellery.* TEL: Enquiries - 0171 351 5353; fax - 0171 351 5350. SER: Valuations.

Rostrum Antiques

115 Portobello Rd. W11 2DY. (Peter Skupien). Est. 1988. Open Sat. 8.30-5.30, other days by appointment. SIZE: Medium. *STOCK: English and Continental furniture, objets d'art, clocks and paintings, 18th-19th C, £100-£20,000.* LOC: Corner of Westbourne Grove. TEL: 0171 243 0420. SER: Valuations; restorations (quality antique furniture only). VAT: Spec.

Schredds of Portobello LAPADA

107 Portobello Rd. W11 2QB. (H.J. and G.R. Schrager). Est. 1969. Open Sat. 7.30-3.30. SIZE: Small. *STOCK: Collectors' silver, 17th-19th C, £10-£1,000; Wedgwood, 18th-19th C.* TEL: 0181 348 3314; home - same; fax - 0181 341 5971; internet - www.schredds.com/schredds. SER: Valuations; buys at auction. FAIRS: Kensington (Jan. and Nov.); Earls Court (Aug.). VAT: Stan/Spec.

The Silver Fox Gallery

121 Portobello Rd. W11 2DY. Open Sat. only 6-3. SIZE: 32+ dealers. *STOCK: Antique jewellery - cameos, hardstone, shell, lava, coral, amber, ivory, jet, tortoiseshell, piqué, micro-mosaics, pietra-dura, Art Nouveau, plique é jour, horn pendants, Arts and Crafts, Art Deco, enamels, Austro-Hungarian, cut-steel, Berlin iron, Scottish, Victorian silver and gold, Alberts, Albertines, longuards, curbs, gates, fobs, seals, intaglios, pocket and vintage wrist watches, cufflinks, fine diamonds, rare gemstones, 18th C to Art Deco, from under £50-£5,000+.* TEL: 0171 243 8027; fax - same. FAIRS: Olympia; Park Lane Hotel. VAT: Stan/Spec/Global.

W11 continued

Justin F. Skrebowski Prints

2nd Floor, 288 Westbourne Grove. W11 2PS. Est. 1985. Open Sat. 9-4, otherwise by appointment. SIZE: Small. *STOCK: Prints, engravings and lithographs, 1700-1850, £50-£500; oil paintings, 1700-1900, £200-£1,500; watercolours, drawings including Old Masters, 1600-1900, £50-£1,000; modern mahogany folio stands and easels; frames - gilt, rosewood, maple, carved, 18th-19th C.* PARK: Meters. TEL: 0171 792 9742; mobile - 0374 612474. SER: Valuations. VAT: Stan/Spec.

David Slater

170 Westbourne Grove. W11 2RW. Est. 1961. Open 9.30-1 and 2-5.30, Sat. 10-1. SIZE: Large. *STOCK: General antiques, decorative items.* PARK: Easy. TEL: 0171 727 3336. VAT: Stan.

Colin Smith and Gerald Robinson Antiques

105 Portobello Rd. W11 2QB. Est. 1979. Open Sat., and Fri. by appointment. SIZE: Large. *STOCK: Tortoiseshell, £100-£2,000; silver, ivory and crocodile items.* TEL: 0181 994 3783/0171 225 1163. FAIRS: Olympia. VAT: Stan.

Spectus Gallery

298 Westbourne Grove. W11. (Angelo Soteriades). Open Sat. 6.30-5. TEL: 0171 221 7638/436 9416; mobile - 0956 277077.

Louis Stanton BADA

299 and 301 Westbourne Grove. W11 2QA. (L.R. and S.A. Stanton). CINOA. Est. 1965. Open 10-1 and 2-6. SIZE: Medium. *STOCK: Early English oak and walnut furniture, tapestries, sculpture, metalware, objets d'art, pre-1750, £20-£35,000.* PARK: Easy. TEL: 0171 727 9336; fax - 0171 727 5424. SER: Valuations; buys at auction. VAT: Stan/Spec.

Stern Art Dealers LAPADA

46 Ledbury Rd. W11 2AB. (David Stern). Est. 1963. Open 10-6. SIZE: Medium. *STOCK: Oil paintings, 19th-20th C, £500-£6,000.* LOC: Off Westbourne Grove near Portobello. PARK: Easy. TEL: 0171 229 6187. SER: Valuations; restorations. VAT: Stan.

June and Tony Stone Fine Antique Boxes LAPADA

75 Portobello Rd. W11 2BQ. Open 10.30-4.30, Sat. 7-5. CL: Mon. *STOCK: Fine boxes especially tea caddies, 18th-19th C, £200-£10,000.* TEL: 0171 221 1121; office - 01273 500212; mobile - 0468 382424; fax - 01273 500024. FAIRS: Olympia (June, Nov. and Feb). VAT: Stan/Spec.

Stouts Antiques Market

144 Portobello Rd. W11 2DZ. Open Sat. only 6.30-4. TEL: 0171 727 3649; fax - 01923 897618; mobile - 0850 375501. Below are listed some of the dealers at this market.

W11 continued

James Forbes Fine Art

Est. 1982. *English works of art, jewellery and silver, from 1700, £50-£5,000.* TEL: 01562 730976; mobile - 0802 291804. VAT: Stan/Spec.

Kleanthous Antiques Ltd LAPADA

Est. 1969. Open Sat. 6.30-4 and by appointment. *Specially selected pieces of jewellery - Georgian, Victorian, Art Nouveau, Art Deco, to 1950; vintage pocket and wrist watches by Rolex, Cartier, Patek Phillipe, Vacheron and Constantin, Jaeger le Coultre, Longines, I.W.C., Universal and Omega; English and Continental silver, 18th-20th C; boudoir, desk, carriage and mantel clocks; objects of vertu; furniture. Full guarantee with all purchases.* TEL: 0171 727 3649; fax - 0181 980 1199 and 01923 897618; mobile - 0850 375501/375502. VAT: Stan/Spec.

B.G.L. Lenisa

Toys, jewellery and cameras. TEL: 0171 603 3706.

Leon

Pocket, fob and wrist watches, 1700-1950.

S. and G. Antiques

(G. Sirett). *Specialist in miniature porcelain cups and saucers, teasets and vases, £25-£500; English and Continental glass, £25-£1,000; Meissen porcelain and objets d'art, £20-£5,000.,* TEL: 0171 229 2178 (Sat.); 0181 907 7140; fax - 0181 909 3277; mobile - 0860 863360. VAT: Stan/Spec.

Temple Gallery

6 Clarendon Cross. W11 4AP. (R.C.C. Temple). Est. 1959. Open 10-6, weekends and evenings by appointment. SIZE: Large. *STOCK: Icons, Russian and Greek, 12th-16th C, £1,000-£50,000.* PARK: Easy. TEL: 0171 727 3809; fax - 0171 727 1546. SER: Valuations; restorations; buys at auction (icons). VAT: Spec.

Themes and Variations

231 Westbourne Grove. W11 2SE. (L. Fawcett). Open 10-1 and 2-6, Sat 10-6. *STOCK: Post war and contemporary decorative items, furniture, glass, ceramics, carpets, lamps, jewellery.* TEL: 0171 727 5531; fax - 0171 221 6378.

Tomkinson Stained Glass

87 Portobello Rd. W11 2QB. (S. Tomkinson). Open 10-5, Sat. 7-5. SIZE: Medium. *STOCK: Stained glass windows.* LOC: 5 minutes from Notting Hill Gate underground. PARK: Easy. TEL: 0171 267 1669; mobile - 0831 861641. SER: Valuations; restorations (as stock). VAT: Stan.

Christina Truscott

Geoffrey Van Arcade, 105-107 Portobello Rd. W11 2QB. Est. 1967. Open Sat. 6.45-3.30. *STOCK: Lacquer, papier-mâché, tortoiseshell, fans.* TEL: 01403 730554.

W11 continued

Edric Van Vredenburgh Ltd

105 Portobello Rd. W11 2QB. Est. 1961. Open by appointment only. SIZE: Small. *STOCK: European decorative arts, 1500-1800; sculpture, early objects; Oriental decorative arts, 18th-19th C.* TEL: 0171 727 2739; fax - 0171 792 2092. SER: Valuations; buys at auction. VAT: Stan/Spec.

Victoriana Dolls

101 Portobello Rd. W11 2BQ. (Mrs C. Bond). Open Sat. 8-3 or by appointment. *STOCK: Dolls, toys and accessories.* TEL: Home - 01737 249525.

Virginia

98 Portland Rd., Holland Park. W11 4LQ. (V. Bates). Est. 1971. Open 11-6. SIZE: Medium. *STOCK: Decorative items, £50-£2,000; textiles, clothes and lace, £25-£500; bathroom fittings, £15-£600; all 19th-20th C.* LOC: Holland Park Ave. PARK: Easy. TEL: 0171 727 9908; fax - 0171 229 2198. VAT: Stan.

Johnny Von Pflugh Antiques

286 Westbourne Grove. W11. Est. 1985. Open Sat. 8-5 at Portobello Market or by appointment. SIZE: Small. *STOCK: European works of art, Italian oil paintings, gouaches, 17th-19th C, £300-£1,500; fine ironware, 17th-18th C, £300-£800; medical and scientific instruments, 18th-19th C, £200-£1,000.* LOC: Off Portobello Rd. PARK: Easy. TEL: 0181 740 5306. SER: Valuations; buys at auction (keys, caskets, medical instruments, Italian oil paintings, and gouaches). FAIRS: Olympia (June); Little Chelsea (Scientific and Medical). VAT: Spec.

David and Charles Wainwright

251 Portobello Rd. W11 1LT. Est. 1989. Open 10-6.30, Sun. 11-5. SIZE: Large. *STOCK: Furniture, 15th-20th C including 18th-19th C cupboards, dining tables and architectural pieces, £5-£2000; stonework - urns, mortars, water containers, to 19th C; contemporary wrought iron.* LOC: Corner of Lancaster Rd. PARK: Easy. TEL: 0171 792 1988. FAIRS: Olympia. VAT: Stan.

Graham Walpole LAPADA

187 Westbourne Grove. W11 2RS. Est. 1973. Open 10-5.30. SIZE: Medium. *STOCK: Metalware including brass, bronze, Vienna bronzes, and ormolu; pictures, folk art, lighting, furniture and collectables, £100-£15,000.* LOC: 300 yards off Portobello Rd. PARK: Easy. TEL: 0171 229 0267. FAIRS: Olympia (June). VAT: Stan.

Trude Weaver LAPADA

71 Portobello Rd. W11. Est. 1968. Open 9-5. CL: Mon. and Tues. SIZE: Medium. *STOCK: 18th-19th C furniture, selected objects, textiles.* PARK: Easy. TEL: 0171 229 8738; fax - same. SER: Valuations.

W11 continued

Wolseley Fine Arts Ltd

12 Needham Rd. W11 2RP. (Rupert Otten and Hanneke van der Werf). *STOCK: British and European 20th C drawings and sculpture, works of all description by David Jones, Eric Gill and Edgar Holloway.* TEL: 0171 792 2788; fax - 0171 792 2988. SER: Regular catalogues on subscription.

World Famous Portobello Market

177 Portobello Rd. W11. (Angelo Soteriades). Est. 1951. Open Sat. 5-6. SIZE: 200 dealers. *STOCK: General antiques including ethnic antiquities, bronzes, ivory statues, jade, precious metals, dolls, silver and plate, drinking vessels and costumes; also specialist golf shop.* TEL: 0171 221 7638/436 9416; mobile - 0956 277077. SER: Valuations; restorations; shipping.

LONDON W13

Rupert's

151 Northfield Ave., Ealing. W13 9QT. (R. Loftus Brigham). Open 10-6 or by appointment. CL: Sat. *STOCK: Early wireless equipment.* TEL: 0181 567 1368.

W.13 Antiques

10 The Avenue, Ealing. W13 8PH. Open Tues., Thurs. and Sat. 10-5 or by appointment. SIZE: Medium. *STOCK: Furniture, china and general antiques, 18th-20th C.* LOC: Off Uxbridge Rd., West Ealing. PARK: Easy. TEL: 0181 998 0390. SER: Valuations. VAT: Stan.

LONDON W14

Andy's All Pine

OBQ, 70 Russell Rd., Kensington. W14 8YL. (A. Gibb). Open 9-5, weekends by appointment. *STOCK: Victorian pine.* TEL: 0171 371 1969; fax - 0171 602 8655.

Stephen Garratt (Fine Paintings)

60 Addison Rd. W14 8JJ. Open by appointment only. *STOCK: Oils and watercolours, 18th-20th C.* TEL: 0171 603 0681.

Marshall Gallery

67 Masbro Rd. W14 0LS. (D. A. and J. Marshall). Resident. Est. 1978. Open 10-6, Sat. 10-5. CL: Mon. SIZE: Medium. *STOCK: French and decorative furniture, £500-£20,000; objects and lighting, £200-£12,000; pictures, from £100; all 18th-20th C.* LOC: Just behind Olympia, off Hammersmith Rd. PARK: Easy. TEL: 0171 602 3317. SER: Restorations (furniture, re-gilding, rewiring). VAT: Spec.

D. Parikian

3 Caithness Rd. W14 0JB. Open by appointment. *STOCK: Antiquarian books, mythology, iconography, emblemata, Continental books pre-1800.* TEL: 0171 603 8375; fax - 0171 602 1178.

W14 continued

J. Roger (Antiques) Ltd BADA
W14. (J. Roger and C. Bayley). Open by appointment only. ***STOCK: Late 18th to early 19th C small elegant pieces furniture, mirrors, prints, porcelain and boxes.*** **TEL: 0171 381 2884/603 7627.**

LONDON SW1

A.D.C. Heritage Ltd BADA
SW1V 4PB. (F. and T. Raeymaekers and E. Bellord). Open by appointment only. ***STOCK: Silver, old Sheffield plate.*** **TEL: 0171 976 5271; fax - 0171 976 5898. SER: Valuations; restorations; buys at auction.**

Didier Aaron (London)Ltd BADA
21 Ryder St., St. James's. SW1Y 6PX. Open 10-6. CL: Sat. SIZE: Large. ***STOCK: French furniture, 18th C, £5,000-£500,000; Old Master and 19th C pictures, £5,000-£500,000; objets d'art, £1,000-£50,000.*** **LOC: 20 yds. from Christie's. TEL: 0171 839 4716. FAIRS: Paris Biennale. VAT: Stan/Spec.**

Ackermann & Johnson BADA
27 Lowndes St. SW1X 9HY. Est. 1963. Open 9-5.30, Sat. by appointment. SIZE: Medium. ***STOCK: English paintings especially sporting,***

SW1 continued

18th-20th C. **PARK: Meters. TEL: 0171 235 6464. SER: Valuations; restorations. VAT: Spec.**

Addison-Ross Gallery
40 Eaton Terrace, Belgravia. SW1. (T.C.A. and D.A.A. Ross). *STOCK: Paintings and prints especially sporting and natural history.* TEL: 0171 730 1536. SER: Interior design (pictures).

J. A. Allen & Co (The Horseman's Bookshop) Ltd
1 & 4 Lower Grosvenor Pl. SW1W 0EL. Est. 1926. Open 9-5.30. CL: Sat. pm. *STOCK: Horse books, from 1600.* PARK: Meters. TEL: 0171 834 5606; fax - 0171 233 8001. VAT: Stan.

Verner Åmell Ltd
4 Ryder St., St. James's. SW1Y 6QB Open 10-5.30. CL: Sat. *STOCK: Dutch and Flemish Old Masters, 16th-17th C; 18th C French and 19th C Scandinavian paintings.* TEL: 0171 925 2759.

Albert Amor Ltd
37 Bury St., St. James's. SW1Y 6AU. Est. 1837. Open 9.30-4.30. CL: Sat. SIZE: Small. *STOCK: 18th C English ceramics, especially first period Worcester and blue and white porcelain.* PARK: Meters. TEL: 0171 930 2444; fax - 0171 930 9067. SER: Valuations; buys at auction. VAT: Spec.

SW1 continued

Anno Domini Antiques BADA

66 Pimlico Rd. SW1W 8LS. (F. Bartman). Est. 1960. Open 10-1 and 2.15-6. CL: Sat. pm. SIZE: Large. *STOCK: Furniture, 17th to early 19th C, £500-£20,000; mirrors, 17th-19th C, £300-£3,000; glass, screens, decorative items and tapestries, £15-£10,000.* Not Stocked: Silver, jewellery, arms, coins. LOC: From Sloane Sq. go down Lower Sloane St., turn left at traffic lights. PARK: Easy. TEL: 0171 730 5496; home - 0171 352 3084. SER: Buys at auction. VAT: Stan/Spec.

Antiquités

227 Ebury St. SW1 8UT. (A. De Cacqueray). Open 10-6, Sat. 11-4. *STOCK: French and Continental furniture, objets d'art.* TEL: 0171 730 5000; fax - 0171 730 0005.

Antiquus

90-92 Pimlico Rd. SW1W 8PL. (E. Amati). Open 9.30-5.30. SIZE: Large. *STOCK: Classical, medieval and Renaissance works of art, paintings, textiles and glass.* LOC: Near Sloane Sq. underground station. PARK: Meters in Holbein Place. TEL: 0171 730 8681; fax - 0171 823 6409.

The Armoury of St. James's Military Antiquarians

17 Piccadilly Arcade, Piccadilly. SW1Y 6NH. Open 9.30-6. SIZE: Small. *STOCK: British and foreign orders, decorations and medals, 18th C to date, £1-£50,000; militaria; toy and hand-painted collectors model soldiers, £4-£4,000.* LOC: Between Piccadilly and Jermyn St. TEL: 0171 493 5082. SER: Valuations. VAT: Stan/Spec.

Astleys

16 Piccadilly Arcade. SW1. Est. 1862. CL: Sat. pm. *STOCK: Meerschaum pipes, 19th C, £30-£1,500; pottery, porcelain, primitive and Oriental pipes, £30-£1,500; smoking accessories, cigar boxes, smoking cabinets, tobacco jars, 19th C, £20-£200.* PARK: Meters. TEL: 0171 499 9950. SER: Valuations; restorations (pipes). VAT: Stan.

Hilary Batstone Decorative Antiques LAPADA

51 Kinnerton St. SW1. Est. 1983. Open 10-5, Sat. by appointment. SIZE: Small. *STOCK: Textiles including antique curtains, tassels and tie-backs. Painted furniture, £500-£5,000; decorative objects, £50-£1,000; lighting, £50-£3,000; garden statuary, £200-£5,000, both 19th-20th C.* LOC: From Knightsbridge, left into Wilton Place, then right. PARK: Motcomb Street garage. TEL: 0171 259 6070. SER: Restorations (lighting including conversions); shades made to order. FAIRS: Decorative Antiques and Textiles, Chelsea, LAPADA. VAT: Spec.

SW1 continued

Chris Beetles Ltd

10 Ryder St., St. James's. SW1Y 6QB. Open 10-5.30, by appointment at weekends. SIZE: Large. *STOCK: English watercolours, paintings and illustrations, 18th-20th C, £500-£50,000.* LOC: 100yds. from Royal Academy. PARK: Meters. TEL: 0171 839 7551. SER: Valuations; framing. VAT: Spec.

Belgrave Carpet Gallery Ltd

91 Knightsbridge. SW1. (A.H. Khawaja). Open 9.30-6.30. *STOCK: Hand knotted Oriental carpets and rugs.* TEL: 0171 235 2541/245 9749.

Blanchard (London) Ltd

86/88 Pimlico Rd. SW1W 8PL. Est. 1990. Open 10-6, Sat. 10-3. SIZE: Medium. *STOCK: English and Continental furniture, lighting and objets d'art.* LOC: Near Sloane Sq. underground station. TEL: 0171 823 6310; fax - 0171 823 6303. SER: Valuations; restorations; buys at auction. VAT: Stan/Spec.

John Bly BADA LAPADA

27 Bury St., St. James's. SW1Y 6AL. (N., J. and V. Bly). CINOA Est. 1891. Open 9.30-5, Sat. by appointment. *STOCK: English furniture, silver, glass, porcelain and fine paintings, 18th-19th C.* TEL: 0171 930 1292; fax - 0171 839 4775.

J.H. Bourdon-Smith Ltd BADA

24 Mason's Yard, Duke St., St. James's. SW1Y 6BU. Est. 1954. Open 9.30-6. CL: Sat. SIZE: Medium. *STOCK: Silver, 1680-1830, £50-£15,000; Victorian and modern silver, 1830 to date, £25-£10,000.* PARK: Meters. TEL: 0171 839 4714. SER: Valuations; restorations (silver); buys at auction. FAIRS: Olympia (Nov); Harrogate; Grosvenor House; BADA; New York; San Francisco; Hong Kong. VAT: Stan/Spec.

Robert Bowman BADA

Est. 1992. Strictly by appointment. SIZE: Medium. *STOCK: Sculpture in bronze, marble and terracotta, early 19th C to early 20th C, £1,000-£200,000.* LOC: Close to Sloane Square. PARK: Metered bays. TEL: 0171 730 8057; fax - 0171 259 9195. SER: Valuations; restorations (bronze, marble and terracotta). FAIRS: Olympia, Maastricht, Singapore, New York. VAT: Spec.

Brisigotti Antiques Ltd

44 Duke St., St. James's. SW1Y 6DD. Open 9.30-6. *STOCK: European works of art, Old Master paintings.* TEL: 0171 839 4441; fax - 0171 976 1663.

Anno Domini

Antiques

66 Pimlico Road, London S.W.1
0171-730 5496

Fine small Regency rosewood brass inlaid sofa table, c.1820. 30 in. x 12 in. x 28½in. (high)

SW1 continued

Camerer Cuss and Co
17 Ryder St., St. James's. SW1Y 6PY. Est. 1788. Open 9.30-5. CL: Sat. SIZE: Medium. *STOCK: Clocks, 1600-1910, £250-£30,000; watches, 1600-1930, £100-£35,000.* TEL: 0171 930 1941. SER: Valuations; restorations (clocks and watches); buys at auction. VAT: Stan/Spec.

John Carlton-Smith BADA
17 Ryder St., St. James's. SW1Y 6PY. Open 9.30-5.30. CL: Sat. *STOCK: Clocks, barometers, chronometers, 17th-19th C.* TEL: 0171 930 6622. SER: Valuations. VAT: Spec.

David Carritt Limited
15 Duke St., St. James's. SW1Y 6DB. (Timothy Bathurst, Sebastian Goetz and Adrian Eeles). Open 9.30-5.30. CL: Sat. *STOCK: Old Master, 19th C and modern paintings, drawings and prints.* TEL: 0171 930 8733.

Miles Wynn Cato
60 Lower Sloane St. SW1W 8BP. Open Mon.-Fri. 9.30-5.30 and by appointment. *STOCK: English and Welsh pictures and works of art, 1550-1950.* TEL: 0171 259 0306; fax - 0171 259 0305.

Chaucer Fine Arts Ltd
45 Pimlico Rd. SW1W 8NE. Open Mon.-Fri. 10-6, and by appointment. *STOCK: Old Master paintings, sculpture and works of art.* TEL: 0171 730 2972/5872.

Ciancimino Ltd
99 Pimlico Rd. SW1W 8PH. Open 10-6, Sat. 11-4. *STOCK: English and European fine furniture and decorative works of art, 19th to early 20th C.* TEL: 0171 730 9950/9959; fax - 0171 730 5365.

Classic Bindings
61 Cambridge St. SW1V 4PS. (Sasha Koziell). Est. 1989. Open 9.30-1 and 2-5.30, Sat. 10.30-1. SIZE: Medium. *STOCK: Bindings, 18th to early 20th C, £8-£150.* LOC: Off Warwick Way, Pimlico. PARK: Easy. TEL: 0171 735 1872; fax - 0171 630 6632. SER: Valuations; restorations (rebinding); buys at auction. VAT: Stan.

Cobra and Bellamy
149 Sloane St. SW1X 9BZ. (V. Manussis and T. Hunter). Est. 1976. Open 10.30-6. SIZE: Medium. *STOCK: Jewellery and designer jewellery, 20th C, £50-£1,000.* TEL: 0171 730 2823. VAT: Stan.

Cornucopia
12 Upper Tachbrook St. SW1V 1SH. Est. 1967. Open 11-6. SIZE: Large. *STOCK: Jewellery, 20th C clothing and accessories.* PARK: Meters. TEL: 0171 828 5752.

Cox and Company
37 Duke St., St. James's. SW1Y 6DF. (Mr and Mrs R. Cox). Est. 1972. Open 10-5.30, Sat. by appointment. SIZE: Small. *STOCK: European paintings, 19th-20th C, £1,000-£20,000.* LOC: Off Piccadilly. TEL: 0171 930 1987. SER: Valuations; restorations; buys at auction. VAT: Spec.

SW1 continued

Peter Dale Ltd LAPADA
11/12 Royal Opera Arcade, Pall Mall. SW1Y 4UY. Est. 1955. Open 9.30-5. CL: Sat. SIZE: Medium. *STOCK: Firearms, 16th-19th C; edged weapons, armour, 14th-19th C; militaria.* LOC: Arcade behind Her Majesty's Theatre and New Zealand House. PARK: 350yds. Whitcomb St., Public Garage. TEL: 0171 930 3695. SER: Valuations; buys at auction. FAIRS: Arms, spring and autumn. VAT: Spec.

Kenneth Davis (Works of Art) Ltd
15 King St., St. James's. SW1Y 6QU. Open 9-5. CL: Sat. *STOCK: Antique silver and works of art.* TEL: 0171 930 0313; fax - 0171 976 1306.

Shirley Day Ltd BADA
91b Jermyn St. SW1Y 6JB. Est. 1967. *STOCK: Indian, Himalayan and South East Asian sculpture; Japanese screens and paintings.* TEL: 0171 839 2804; fax - 0171 839 3334. VAT: Spec.

Alastair Dickenson Fine Silver Ltd
90 Jermyn St. SW1Y 6JD.. Open 9.30-5.30. CL: Sat. SIZE: Small. *STOCK: Fine English, Irish and Scottish silver, 16th to early 19th C; unusual collectable silver - vinaigrettes, wine labels, card cases, caddy spoons, snuff boxes; Arts and Crafts silver including Omar Ramsden.* LOC: Off Duke St. PARK: Meters. TEL: 0171 839 2808; fax - 0171 839 2809; mobile - 0976 283530. SER: Valuations; restorations (repairs, gilding, re-plating), replacement cruet and ink bottles; buys at auction. VAT: Spec.

Simon Dickinson Ltd
58 Jermyn St. SW1Y 6LX. (Simon Dickinson and David Ker). SLAD. Open 10-5.30, Fri. 10-4.30. CL: Sat. SIZE: Large. *STOCK: Important Old Master and Modern Master paintings.* LOC: 2 mins. from Piccadilly. TEL: 0171 493 0340; fax - 0171 493 0796. SER: Valuations; restorations; buys at auction. VAT: Spec.

Douwes Fine Art Ltd
38 Duke St., St. James's. SW1Y 6DF. SLAD. Est. 1805. Open 9.30-5.30. CL: Sat. SIZE: Medium. *STOCK: Old Master paintings, drawings, watercolours.* PARK: Meters. TEL: 0171 839 5795. SER: Valuations; restorations. VAT: Spec.

Eaton Gallery LAPADA
34 Duke St., St. James's and 9 and 12a Princes Arcade, Jermyn St. SW1Y 6DF. (D. George). Open 10-5.30. *STOCK: English and European paintings, 19th-20th C and contemporary.* TEL: 0171 930 5950; fax - 0171 839 8076.

SW1 continued

Christopher Edwards

63 Jermyn St., St. James's. SW1Y 6LX. Appointment preferred. *STOCK: English literature, to 1900; early Continental books, all subjects.* TEL: 0171 495 4263; fax - 0171 495 4264.

N. and I. Franklin BADA

11 Bury St., St. James's. SW1Y 6AB. Open 9.30-5.30. CL: Sat. *STOCK: Fine silver and works of art.* TEL: 0171 839 3131; fax - 0171 839 3132.

Victor Franses Gallery BADA

57 Jermyn St., St. James's. SW1Y 6LX. Est. 1948. Open 10-5, Sat. by appointment. *STOCK: 19th C animalier bronzes, rare carpets and rugs.* TEL: 0171 493 6284/629 1144; fax - 0171 495 3668. SER: Valuations; restorations.

S. Franses Ltd

Jermyn St. at Duke St., St. James's. SW1Y 6JD. Est. 1909. Open 9-5. CL: Sat. SIZE: Large. *STOCK: Historic and decorative tapestries, carpets, fabrics and textiles.* TEL: 0171 976 1234. SER: Valuations; restorations; cleaning. VAT: Spec.

Charles Frodsham & Co Ltd

32 Bury St., St. James's. SW1Y 6AU. Open Mon.-Fri. 10-5.30, other times by appointment. SIZE: Medium. *STOCK: Clocks, watches, marine chronometers and other horological items.* LOC: Between Jermyn St. and St. James's St. PARK: Meters. TEL: 0171 839 1234; fax - 0171 839 2000. VAT: Stan/Spec.

Frost and Reed Ltd (Est.1808) BADA

2-4 King St., St James's. SW1Y 6QP SLAD. Open 9-5.30. CL: Sat. *STOCK: Fine 19th C British and Continental paintings, marine and sporting pictures, Impressionist drawings and watercolours; works by Sir Alfred Munnings, Montague Dawson, Sir William Russell Flint and Marcel Dyf.* PARK: Meters. TEL: 0171 839 4645. VAT: Stan/Spec.

Galerie Moderne Ltd

10 Halkin Arcade, Motcomb St. SW1X 8JT. Open 9.30-6, Sat. by appointment. *STOCK: René Lalique glass; Sèvres porcelain, 1850-1950; vintage cocktail shakers; antique automobile posters.* TEL: 0171 245 6907.

Gallery '25

6 Halkin Arcade, West Halkin St., Belgravia. SW1. (D. Iglesis). Est. 1969. Open 9.30-5.30, Sat. 10-2. SIZE: Medium. *STOCK: Art glass, £100-£5,000; signed furniture, £1,000-£10,000; decorative fine art, £500-£5,000; all 1900-1930.* LOC: Arcade between Motcomb St and West Halkin St. PARK: Easy. Cadogan Sq. TEL: 0171 235 5178. SER: Valuations; buys at auction (as stock). FAIRS: Park Lane; Olympia. VAT: Stan/Spec.

SW1 continued

General Trading Co Ltd LAPADA

144 Sloane St. SW1X 9BL. (Julian Geach). Est. 1920. Open 9.30-6. SIZE: Medium. *STOCK: English furniture, £100-£6,000; china, prints, £20-£500; all 18th-19th C.* PARK: 50yds., underground garage (Cadogan Place). TEL: 0171 730 0411. VAT: Stan/Spec.

Nicholas Gifford-Mead BADA LAPADA

68 Pimlico Rd. SW1W 8LS. Est. 1972. Open 9.30-5.30, Sat. 9.30-1.30. SIZE: Medium. *STOCK: Chimney pieces and sculpture, 18th-19th C, from £1,000.* LOC: 3 minutes from Sloane Sq. TEL: 0171 730 6233; fax - 0171 730 6239. SER: Valuations. VAT: Stan/Spec.

Joss Graham

10 Eccleston St. SW1W 9LT Open 10-6. *STOCK: Textiles including rugs, kelims, embroideries, tribal costume and shawls; jewellery, metalwork, furniture, masks and primitive art - Indian, Middle Eastern, Central Asian and African.* TEL: 0171 730 4370; fax - same; e-mail - joss.graham @btinternet.com.

Martyn Gregory Gallery BADA

34 Bury St., St. James's. SW1Y 6AU. SLAD. Open 10-6. CL: Sat. SIZE: Medium. *STOCK: Early English watercolours, 18th-20th C; British paintings, both £500-£100,000; specialists in pictures relating to China and the Far East.* TEL: 0171 839 3731. SER: Valuations. VAT: Spec.

Ross Hamilton Ltd LAPADA

95 Pimlico Rd. SW1W 8PH. (Mark Boyce). Est. 1971. Open 9.30-1 and 2-6, Sat. 11-4. SIZE: Large. *STOCK: English and Continental furniture, 17th-19th C, £1,000-£100,000; porcelain and objects, 18th-19th C, £1,000-£3,000; paintings, 17th-19th C, £1,000-£10,000+.* LOC: 2 minutes walk from Sloane Square. PARK: Side streets. TEL: 0171 730 3015. VAT: Stan/Spec.

Harrods Ltd

Brompton Rd., Knightsbridge. SW1X 7XL. Open 10-6, Wed., Thurs. and Fri. 10-7. SIZE: Large. *STOCK: Fine Victorian, Edwardian and period furniture; clocks, oil paintings and objets d'art.* PARK: Own. TEL: 0171 730 1234, ext. 5940/2759.

Julian Hartnoll

2nd. Floor, 14 Mason's Yard, Duke St., St. James's. SW1Y 6BU Est. 1968. Open 2.30-5. *STOCK: 19th-20th C British paintings, drawings and prints especially pre-Raphaelite and works by the kitchen sink artists, including Bratby.* TEL: 0171 839 3842. VAT: Spec.

SW1 continued

Harvey and Gore BADA
41 Duke St., St. James's. SW1Y 6DF. (B.E. Norman). Est. 1723. Open 9.30-5. CL: Sat. SIZE: Small. *STOCK: Jewellery, £150-£50,000; silver, £50-£15,000; old Sheffield plate, £65-£6,000; antique paste.* TEL: 0171 839 4033; fax - 0171 839 3313. SER: Valuations; restorations (jewellery and silver); buys at auction. VAT: Stan/Spec.

Hawksmoor
9 West Halkin St. SW1X 8JL. (S. Hunter). Est. 1962. Open 9.30-5.30. SIZE: Large. *STOCK: Furniture, 18th-19th C; pictures, 16th-20th; works of art.* LOC: Just off Sloane St., near Harvey Nicholls. PARK: Nearby. TEL: 0171 235 8989. SER: Valuations; restorations (furniture and paintings); buys at auction. VAT: Spec.

Hazlitt, Gooden and Fox Ltd
38 Bury St., St. James's. SW1Y 6BB. SLAD. Open 9.30-5.30. CL: Sat. SIZE: Large. *STOCK: Paintings, drawings and sculpture.* PARK: Meters. TEL: 0171 930 6422; fax - 0171 839 5984. SER: Valuations; restorations. VAT: Spec.

Thomas Heneage Art Books LAPADA
42 Duke St., St. James's. SW1Y 6DJ. Est. 1975. Open 9.30-6 or by appointment. CL: Sat. *STOCK: Art reference books.* TEL: 0171 930 9223; fax - 0171 839 9223; e-mail - shop@ heneage.com.

Heraz (David Hartwright Ltd)
2 Halkin Arcade, Motcomb St., Belgravia. SW1X 8JT. Est. 1978. Open 10-6, Sat. by appointment. SIZE: Small. *STOCK: Cushions, 17th-19th C; antique Oriental and European carpets and tapestries.* PARK: Easy.TEL: 0171 245 9497. SER: Valuations; restorations (antique textiles and carpets including cleaning). VAT: Stan.

Hermitage Antiques plc
97 Pimlico Rd. SW1W 8PH. (B. Vieux-Pernon). Est. 1967. Open 10-6, Sat. 10-5, Sun. by appointment. SIZE: Large. *STOCK: Biedermeier, Empire and Russian furniture; oil paintings; decorative arts; chandeliers; bronzes.* Not Stocked: Silver and jewellery. LOC: Off Sloane Square. PARK: Easy. TEL: 0171 730 1973; fax - 0171 730 6586. VAT: Stan/Spec.

Carlton Hobbs BADA
46 Pimlico Rd. SW1W 8LP. Est. 1975. Open 9-6, Sat. 10-5, or by appointment. *STOCK: English and Continental furniture, paintings, chandeliers, works of art, £4,000-£850,000.* TEL: 0171 730 3640/3517; fax - 0171 730 6080.

Christopher Hodsoll Ltd BADA
Bennison, 89-91 Pimlico Rd. SW1W 8PH. Open 9-7, Sat. and Sun. by appointment. *STOCK: Furniture, sculpture, pictures and objects.* PARK: Meters. TEL: 0171 730 3370; fax - 0171 730 1516. VAT: Stan/Spec.

SW1 continued

William Hotopf Antiques LAPADA
24 Pimlico Rd. SW1. Open 10-6, Sat. and Sun. by appointment. SIZE: Medium. *STOCK: Furniture, 19th C; Anglo-Irish glass, 18th-19th C.* PARK: Multi-storey or meters. TEL: 0171 730 3971; fax - 0171 730 8703. VAT: Stan/Spec.

Hotspur Ltd BADA
14 Lowndes St. SW1X 9EX. (R.A.B. and B.S. Kern). Est. 1924. Open 8.30-6, Sat. 9.30-1. SIZE: Large. *STOCK: English furniture, 1690-1800.* LOC: Between Belgrave Sq. and Lowndes Sq. PARK: 2 underground within 100yds. TEL: 0171 235 1918. VAT: Spec.

How of Edinburgh
41 St. James's Place. SW1A 1NS. (Mrs G.E.P. How). Est. 1930. Open by appointment only. TEL: 0171 495 5481. VAT: Stan/Spec.

Christopher Howe
93 Pimlico Rd. SW1W 8PH. and 36 Bourne St. SW1W 8JA. Est. 1982. Open 9-5.30, Sat. 10-2.30. SIZE: Large + warehouse nearby. *STOCK: English and European furniture, 16th-20th C, £100-£50,000; decorative objects and lighting.* LOC: Near Sloane Square. PARK: Easy. TEL: 0171 730 7987; fax - 0171 730 0157. SER: Valuations. VAT: Stan/Spec.

Christopher Hull Gallery
17 Motcomb St. SW1X 8LB. Open 10-6, Sat. 10-1. *STOCK: Modern British paintings and young artists of promise.* TEL: 0171 235 0500.

Humphrey-Carrasco
43 Pimlico Rd. SW1W 8LP (David Humphrey and Marylise Carrasco). Est. 1987. Open 10-6, Sat. 10-5. *STOCK: English furniture and lighting, architectural objects, 18th-19th C.* LOC: 10 minute walk from Sloane Sq. PARK: Easy. TEL: 0171 730 9911; fax - same. SER: Buys at auction. FAIRS: Olympia. VAT: Stan/Spec.

Sally Hunter Fine Art
11/12 Halkin Arcade, Motcomb St. SW1X 8JT. Open 10-6. CL: Sat. *STOCK: British art, 1920 to date.* TEL: 0171 235 0934.

Malcolm Innes Gallery
7 Bury St.,St. James's. SW1Y 6AL. SLAD. Est. 1973. Open 9.30-6 and some Sats. 10-1. *STOCK: Scottish, landscape, sporting and military pictures.* TEL: 0171 839 8083/4; fax - 0171 839 8085. SER: Restorations; framing. VAT: Spec.

Jeremy Ltd BADA
29 Lowndes St. SW1X 9HX. (G.M. and J. Hill). Est. 1946. Open 8.30-6. SIZE: Large. *STOCK: English and French furniture, objets d'art, glass chandeliers, 18th to early 19th C.* PARK: Easy. TEL: 0171 823 2923. FAIRS: Grosvenor House; IAD New York. VAT: Spec.

SW1 continued

Jillings of Belgravia LAPADA

8 Halkin Arcade, Motcomb St. SW1X 8JT. (Doro and John Jillings). Est. 1986. Open 10-6, Sat. 10-3. CL: Mon. SIZE: Small. *STOCK: Clocks including restored longcase, bracket, bronze, ormolu and wall; barometers and small scientific instruments, all 18th-19th C, £500-£25,000.* LOC: 5 minutes from Harrods - Sloane St., left into Cadogan Place, over Lowndes St. into West Halkin St., left into Halkin Arcade. PARK: Meters or Motcomb St. Garage. TEL: 0171 235 8600; fax - 0171 235 9898. SER: Valuations; restorations (hand cleaning and over-hauling of English and French antique clocks and barometers; repairs and case restoration including gilding). Shipping arranged. FAIRS: LAPADA. VAT: Spec.

Derek Johns Ltd

12 Duke St., St. James's. SW1Y 6BN. SLAD. Open 9.30-6. *STOCK: Old Master paintings.* TEL: 0171 839 7671; fax - 0171 930 0986.

Lucy Johnson BADA LAPADA

SW1. CINOA. Est. 1982. Open by appointment. SIZE: Medium. *STOCK: Fine furniture; English delftware; period interiors, 1660-1714.* PARK: Easy. TEL: 0171 235 2088; fax - 0171 235 2098. FAIRS: Olympia. VAT: Stan/Spec.

The Hugh Johnson Collection

68 St. James's St. SW1A 1PH. Open 9.30-5.30. CL: Sat. *STOCK: Antique and modern wine accessories including decanters, glasses, funnels, port tongs.* TEL: 0171 491 4912; fax - 0171 493 0602.

Peter Jones

Sloane Sq. SW1W 8EL. (John Lewis plc). Est. 1945. Open 9.30-6, Wed. 10-7. SIZE: Large. *STOCK: 18th and 19th C furniture and pictures.* LOC: Fourth floor. TEL: 0171 730 3434.

Keshishian BADA

73 Pimlico Rd. SW1W 8NE. Est. 1978. Open 9.30-6, Sat. 10-5. SIZE: Large. *STOCK: European and Oriental carpets, to late 19th C; Aubussons, mid 19th C; European tapestries, 16th-18th C; Arts and Crafts and Art Deco carpet specialists.* LOC: Off Lower Sloane St. PARK: Easy. TEL: 0171 730 8810; fax - 0171 730 8803. SER: Valuations; restorations. VAT: Stan/Spec.

Knightsbridge Coins

43 Duke St., St. James's. SW1. Open 10-6. CL: Sat. *STOCK: Coins - British, American and South African; medals.* TEL: 0171 930 7597/930 8215.

Kojis Antique Jewellery Ltd

Harrods Fine Jewellery Room, Harrods Ltd., Brompton Rd., Knightsbridge. SW1X 7XL. Open 10-6, Wed., Thurs. and Fri. 10-7. *STOCK: Antique and contemporary jewellery and objects; jade.* TEL: 0171 730 1234 ext. 4062/4072. SER: Valuations; repairs; re-stringing (pearls); designs.

SW1 continued

Bob Lawrence Gallery

93 Lower Sloane St. SW1. Est. 1972. Open 10-6. Small. *STOCK: Decorative arts to Art Deco - furniture, paintings, objects and furnishings, £50-£10,000.* LOC: 2 minutes Sloane Sq., adjacent Pimlico Rd. PARK: Easy. TEL: 0170 730 5900; fax - 0171 730 5902. SER: Valuations; restorations; buys at auction. VAT: Stan/Spec.

Clare Lawrence Ltd

3 Bury St., St James's. SW1Y 6AB. Est. 1986. Open 11-5. CL: Sat. SIZE: Medium. *STOCK: Chinese snuff bottles and Chinese glass, 18th-19th C.* LOC: Off King St. and Jermyn St., St James's. PARK: St James Sq. TEL: 0171 930 2778. SER: Valuations; publishing; restorations; buys at auction. FAIRS: Arts of Pacific Asia - New York, San Francisco; Snuff Bottle Convention. VAT: Spec.

Le Pavillon de Sèvres Ltd

9 Halkin Arcade, Motcomb St. SW1X 8JT. Open 9.30-6, Sat. by appointment. *STOCK: 20th C Sèvres porcelain.* TEL: 0171 235 0937.

SW1 continued

Lennox Money (Antiques) Ltd

93 Pimlico Rd. SW1W 8PH. (L.B. Money). Est. 1964. Open 9.45-6. CL: Sat. pm. SIZE: Large. *STOCK: Indian colonial and furniture made of unusual woods; chandeliers and textiles.* LOC: 200yds. south of Sloane Sq. TEL: 0171 730 3070. VAT: Spec.

M. and D. Lewis

84 Pimlico Rd. SW1. Open 9.30-5.30, Sat. 9.30-12, Sun. by appointment. *STOCK: Continental and Victorian furniture, porcelain, bronzes.* TEL: 0171 730 1015; fax - 0171 727 3908 (after 6). VAT: Stan.

Lion, Witch and Lampshade

c/o Muriel Michalos Ltd., 57 Elizabeth St. SW1W 9PP. (Mr. and Mrs N. Dixon). Est. 1984. Open by appointment. *STOCK: Unusual decorative objects, 18th to early 20th C, £5-£150; lamps, wall brackets, chandeliers and candlesticks, £50-£1,000; rocking horses.* PARK: Easy. TEL: 0171 730 1774. SER: Restorations (porcelain and glass). VAT: Stan/Spec.

Longmire Ltd (Three Royal Warrants)

12 Bury St., St. James's. SW1Y 6AB. Open 9.30-5.30, Sat. in Nov. and Dec. only. *STOCK: Individual antique jewellery, cufflink and dress sets: antique, signed, platinum, gold, gem set, hardstone, pearl, carved crystal or enamel - four vices, fishing, polo, golfing, shooting, big game, ladybird and pigs.* LOC: Coming from Piccadilly, down Duke St., right into King St. past Christies, first right into Bury St. PARK: Easy. TEL: 0171 930 8720; fax - 0171 930 1898. SER: Custom hand engraving or enamelling in colour - any corporate logo, initials, crest, coats of arms or tartan, any animal (cat, dog etc.), racing silks, sailing burgees, favourite hobbies or own automobiles.

MacConnal-Mason Gallery

14 and 17 Duke St., St. James's. SW1Y 6DB. Est. 1893. Open 9-6, Sat. 10-2. SIZE: Large. *STOCK: Pictures, 19th-20th C.* PARK: Meters. TEL: 0171 839 7693/409 7323; fax - 0171 839 6797. SER: Valuations; restorations. VAT: Spec.

The Mall Galleries

The Mall. SW1Y 5BD. Open 10-5 seven days. *STOCK: Paintings.* LOC: Near Trafalgar Sq. TEL: 0171 930 6844; fax - 0171 839 7830. SER: Contemporary art exhibitions held.

Paul Mason Gallery BADA

149 Sloane St. SW1X 9BZ. Est. 1969. Open 9-6, Wed. 9-7, Sat. 9-1. *STOCK: Marine, sporting and decorative paintings and prints, 18th-19th C; period and old frames, portfolio stands, ship models.* LOC: Sloane Sq. end of Sloane St. PARK: Easy. TEL: 0171 730 3683/7359. SER:

SW1 continued

Valuations; restorations (prints, paintings); buys at auction. FAIRS: England and Europe. VAT: Stan/Spec.

Mathaf Gallery Ltd LAPADA

24 Motcomb St. SW1X 8JU. SLAD. Est. 1975. Open 9.30-5.30. *STOCK: Paintings, Middle East subjects, 19th C.* TEL: 0171 235 0010. SER: Valuations.

Matthiesen Fine Art Ltd.

7-8 Mason's Yard, Duke St., St. James's. SW1Y 6BU. Est. 1978. Open by appointment only. *STOCK: Fine Italian Old Master paintings, 1300-1800; French and Spanish Old Master paintings.* TEL: 0171 930 2437; fax - 0171 930 1387. SER: Valuations; buys at auction.

Mayorcas Ltd BADA

8 Duke St., St. James's. SW1Y 6BN. (J.D. and S.M. Mayorcas). Est. 1930. Open 9.30-5.30, Sat. by appointment. SIZE: Medium. *STOCK: Tapestries, textiles, embroideries, needlework, church vestments, European carpets and rugs.* TEL: 0171 839 3100; fax - 0171 839 3223. SER: Valuations; restorations. VAT: Spec.

McCEd

8 Holbein Place. SW1W 8NL. Open 10-6, Sat. 10.30-4.30. *STOCK: Architecturally inspired furniture, objects and hall lanterns.* LOC: 50 yards from Pimlico Road. TEL: 0171 730 4025; fax - same. VAT: Stan/Spec/Export.

McClenaghan

69 Pimlico Rd. SW1W 8NE. Open 10-6, Sat. 10.30-4.30. SIZE: Medium. *STOCK: English furniture, objects and period lighting.* LOC: Opp. Carlton Hobbs. TEL: 0171 730 4187; fax - same. VAT: Stan/Spec/Export.

Christopher Mendez incorporating Craddock and Barnard

58 Jermyn St. SW1Y 6LP. Est. 1966. Open 10-5.30. CL: Sat. SIZE: Small. *STOCK: Old Master prints.* TEL: 0171 491 0015; fax - 0171 495 4949. SER: Valuations; buys at auction. VAT: Stan.

Thomas Mercer (Chronometers) Ltd

32 Bury St., St. James's. SW1Y 6AU. Open Mon.-Fri. 10-5.30, other times by appointment. SIZE: Medium. *STOCK: Marine chronometers.* LOC: Between Jermyn St. and St. James's St. PARK: Meters. TEL: 0171 930 9300; fax - 0171 321 0350. VAT: Stan/Spec.

Nigel Milne Ltd

38 Jermyn St. SW1Y 6DN. Est. 1979. Open 9.30-5.30. SIZE: Small. *STOCK: Jewellery, silver frames and objects.* TEL: 0171 434 9343. SER: Valuations. VAT: Stan/Spec.

◆ McCEd ◆

8 Holbein Place
London SW1 W8NL
Tel/Fax: 0171-730 4025

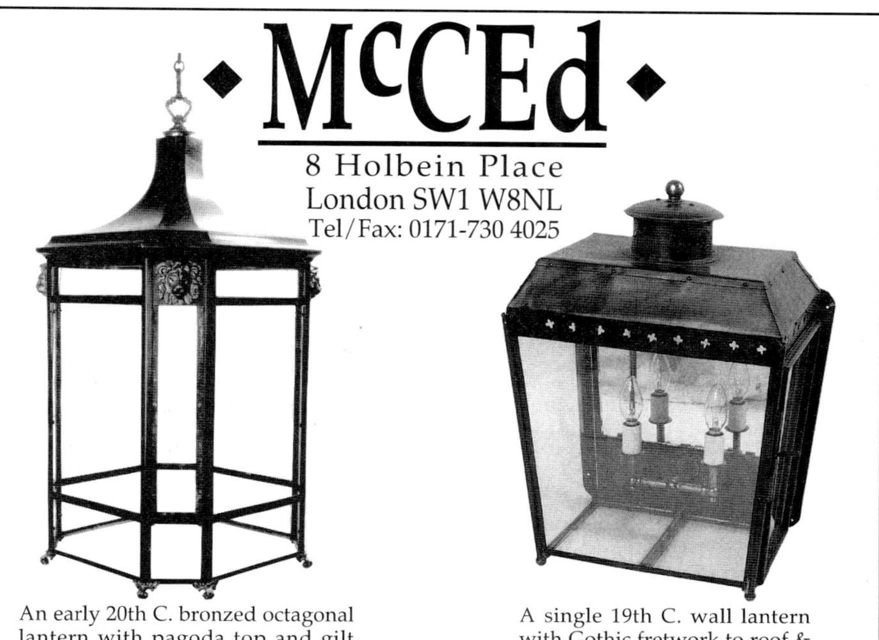

An early 20th C. bronzed octagonal lantern with pagoda top and gilt lions masks to four corners.

A single 19th C. wall lantern with Gothic fretwork to roof & chimney.

McCLENAGHAN

69 Pimlico Road London SW1W 8NE Telephone/Fax 0171 730 4187

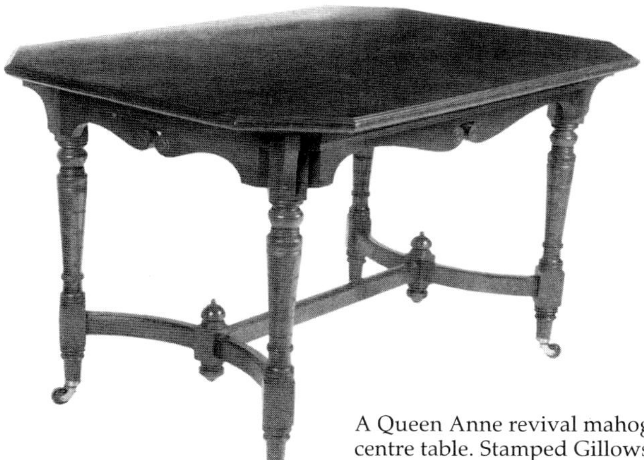

A Queen Anne revival mahogany centre table. Stamped Gillows. English c.1875.

SW1 continued

Mrs Monro Ltd

16 Motcomb St. SW1X 8LB. Est. 1929. Open 9.30-5.30, Fri. 9.30-5. CL: Sat. SIZE: Medium. *STOCK: Small decorative furniture, £500-£1,000+; china, £50-£500+; rugs; prints; pictures and general decorative items, from £50; all 18th-19th C.* LOC: Between Lowndes Sq. and Belgrave Sq. PARK: Garage nearby. TEL: 0171 235 0326; fax - 0171 259 6305. SER: Restorations (furniture and china). VAT: Stan/Spec.

Moreton Street Gallery

40 Moreton St. SW1V 2PB. (W.M. Pearson - Frasco International Ltd). Est. 1972. Open 9-1 and 2-6. CL: Sat. SIZE: Medium. *STOCK: Contemporary oils, watercolours, limited editions, posters; early engravings - Bunbury, Rowlandson, Hogarth, Gilray and Heath.* LOC: Off Belgrave Rd. PARK: Easy. TEL: 0171 834 7773/5; fax - 0171 834 7834. SER: Valuations; restorations; buys at auction (originals and engravings). VAT: Stan.

Guy Morrison

91a Jermyn St. SW1Y 6JB. SLAD. Open 9.30-5.30. CL: Sat. *STOCK: British paintings from 1900.* TEL: 0171 839 1454.

Peter Nahum at The Leicester Galleries LAPADA

5 Ryder St. SW1Y 6PY. Open 9.30-5.30. CL: Sat. and Sun. except by appointment. SIZE: Large. *STOCK: British and European paintings, works on paper and bronzes, including the Pre-Raphaelites and Modern British, 19th-20th C, £1,000-£100,000+.* LOC: 100yds. from Royal Academy. PARK: Meters. TEL: 0171 930 6059; fax - 0171 930 4678. SER: Valuations. VAT: Spec.

Old Maps and Prints

3rd Floor, Harrods, Knightsbridge. SW1X 7XL. Est. 1976. *STOCK: Maps, 16th C to 1890; engravings (all subjects); watercolours.* TEL: 0171 730 1234, ext. 2124.

Ossowski BADA

83 Pimlico Rd. SW1W 8PH. Est. 1960. Open 9-6. CL: Sat. pm. SIZE: Medium. *STOCK: Carved gilt, 18th C; mirrors, consoles, wood carvings.* TEL: 0171 730 3256. SER: Valuations; restorations (gilt furniture). VAT: Stan/Spec.

Pairs Antiques Ltd

202 Ebury St. SW1W 8UN. (Iain M. Brunt). Est. 1994. Open 10-6, Sat. 10-4, or by appointment. SIZE: Medium. *STOCK: Pairs only - 18th-19th C furniture, £500-£10,000; 18th-20th C decorative objects; 19th C paintings, £3,000-£10,000.* PARK: Meters. TEL: 0171 730 1771; fax - 0171 730 1661. SER: Valuations; restorations; buys at auction. VAT: Stan/Spec.

SW1 continued

Paisnel Gallery

22 Mason's Yard, Duke St., St James's. SW1Y 6BU. (Stephen Paisnel). Est. 1977. Open 11-6. CL: Sat. SIZE: Small. *STOCK: Modern British paintings, especially Newlyn and St. Ives Schools, £1,000-£15,000.* LOC: Duke St. runs between Piccadilly and King St. 1 minute from Christies. PARK: St. James Sq. TEL: 0171 930 9293. VAT: Spec.

The Parker Gallery BADA

28 Pimlico Rd. SW1W 8LJ. (Thomas H. Parker Ltd). SLAD. Est. 1750. Open 9.30-5.30, Sat. by appointment. SIZE: Medium. *STOCK: Historical prints, £45-£1,200; English paintings, £1,000-£30,000; ship models, £95-£30,000.* LOC: 5 minutes from Sloane Sq. TEL: 0171 730 6768; fax - 0171 259 9180. SER: Restorations (as stock); mounting; framing. VAT: Stan/Spec.

Michael Parkin Fine Art Ltd

11 Motcomb St. SW1X 8LB. SLAD. Open 10-6. *STOCK: British paintings, watercolours, drawings and prints, 1860-1960, £50-£10,000.* PARK: Easy. TEL: 0171 235 8144/1845; fax - 0171 245 9846. VAT: Spec.

Trevor Philip and Sons Ltd BADA

75a Jermyn St., St. James's. SW1Y 6NP. (T. and R. Waterman). Est. 1972. Open 9-6, Sat. 10-4. SIZE: Medium. *STOCK: Early scientific instruments, globes, barometers and ships models; silver and vertu.* PARK: At rear. TEL: 0171 930 2954; fax - 0171 321 0212. SER: Valuations; restorations (clocks and scientific instruments); buys at auction. VAT: Stan/Spec.

Polak Gallery BADA

21 King St., St. James's. SW1Y 6QY. Est. 1854. Open 9.30-5.30. CL: Sat. SIZE: Medium. *STOCK: English and Continental oils and watercolours, 19th-20th C.* PARK: Meters. TEL: 0171 839 2871. SER: Valuations; restorations. VAT: Spec.

Portland Gallery

9 Bury St., St. James's. SW1Y 6AB. SLAD. Est. 1985. Open 10-6. CL: Sat. SIZE: Medium. *STOCK: Scottish pictures, 20th C, £200-£100,000.* TEL: 0171 321 0422. SER: Valuations; buys at auction. VAT: Spec.

Steven Rich & Michael Rich

39 Duke St., St. James's. SW1Y 6DF. Open daily, Sat. by appointment. SIZE: Medium. *STOCK: Master paintings, 16th-19th C; collectors items.* LOC: Just off Piccadilly. PARK: St. James's Sq. TEL: 0171 930 9308; fax - 0171 930 2088. SER: Valuations. VAT: Spec. *Trade Only.*

THE PARKER GALLERY

(ESTABLISHED 1750)

28, PIMLICO ROAD, LONDON SW1W 8LJ

TEL: 0171-730 6768 FAX: 0171-259 9180

Changing Horses
Coloured aquatint by J. Harris after Charles Cooper Henderson.
Published Fores 1842. Size 17½ x 26¼ inches (44.5 x 68 cms).

H.M. Frigate *Firebrand* and the Experimental Squadron
Coloured lithograph by and after H.J. Vernon. Published 1845.
Size 10¼ x 14¾ inches (26 x 37.5 cms).

DEALERS IN PRINTS, PAINTINGS AND WATERCOLOURS OF THE 18th, 19th & 20th CENTURY, COVERING MARINE, MILITARY, TOPOGRAPHICAL AND SPORTING SUBJECTS, MAPS & SHIP MODELS

BADA SLAD

SW1 continued

Rogier Antiques

20A Pimlico Rd. SW1W 8LJ. (Miss Lauriance Rogier). Est. 1980. Open 10-6, Sat. 11-4. SIZE: Small. *STOCK: French and Continental painted and country furniture, 18th-19th C, £1,000-£5,000; lamps and wall sconces, 19th C, from £500; decorative antique and reproduction items, from £300.* LOC: 5 minutes walk from Sloane Sq. PARK: Meters. TEL: 0171 823 4780. SER: Restorations (furniture - polishing, painting, lacquering, gilding, copies, decoration, painted effects, murals, trompe l'oeil). VAT: Spec.

Sainsbury & Mason

145 Ebury St. SW1. Est. 1968. Open 10-1 and 2-5.30. *STOCK: Period Oriental and European works of art, especially Chinese and Japanese, bronzes, lacquer, porcelain, glass and pictures.* TEL: 0171 730 3393/8331; home - 0181 874 4173; fax - 0171 730 8334. VAT: Spec.

Gerald Sattin Ltd BADA

14 King St., St. James's. SW1Y 6QU. (G. and M. Sattin). Est. 1966. Open 9.30-5.30, Sat. by appointment. SIZE: Medium. *STOCK: English and Continental porcelain, 1720-1900; English glass, 1700-1900; both £55-£2,500; English silver, 1680-1920, £55-£5,000.* Not Stocked: Oriental and post 1920 items. LOC: Close to Christie's. PARK: Meters. TEL: 0171 493 6557; fax - same. SER: Buys at auction. VAT: Stan/Spec.

Seago BADA

22 Pimlico Rd. SW1W 8LJ. (T.P. and L.G. Seago). Open Mon.-Fri. 9.30-5.30 or by appointment. *STOCK: Fine 17th-19th C garden sculpture and ornaments in marble, stone, bronze, lead, terracotta, cast and wrought iron.* TEL: 0171 730 7502; fax - 0171 730 9179.

Sensation Ltd

17 Lennox Gardens. SW1. (M. Fenwick). Est. 1958. Open by appointment only. *STOCK: Porcelain, decorative objects, painted furniture.* TEL: 0171 581 1533; fax - same.

The Silver Fund Ltd

40 Bury St. SW1Y 6AU. (Alastair Crawford and Michael James). Est. 1977. Open daily, Sat. and Sun. by appointment. SIZE: Large. *STOCK: Silver - English, £200-£20,000; Jensen and Tiffany, £100-£50,000; American, £100-£5,000.* LOC: Opposite Sotheby's. PARK: NCP Mayfair. TEL: 0171 839 7664; fax - 0171 839 8935. SER: Valuations; restorations. FAIRS: Decorative Antiques, London; NEC; Olympia. VAT: Stan/Spec.

Julian Simon Fine Art Ltd BADA

70 Pimlico Rd. SW1W 8LS. (M. and J. Brookstone). Open 10-6, Sat. 10-4 or by appointment. *STOCK: Fine English and Continental pictures, 18th-20th C.* TEL: 0171 730 8673; fax - 0171 823 6116.

SW1 continued

Sims, Reed Ltd

43a Duke St., St James's. SW1Y 6DD. Open 10-6, Sat. 10-4. *STOCK: Illustrated rare and in-print books on the fine and applied arts; leather-bound literary sets; contemporary books.* TEL: 0171 493 5660; fax - 0171 493 8468.

Peta Smyth - Antique Textiles LAPADA

42 Moreton St., Pimlico. SW1V 2PB. GMC. Est. 1977. Open 9.30-5.30. CL: Sat. *STOCK: European textiles and needlework, 17th-19th C, £10-£5,000; tapestries and cushions.* PARK: Easy. TEL: 0171 630 9898; fax - 0171 630 5398. SER: Restorations (needlework, tapestries, textiles). FAIRS: Olympia. VAT: Spec.

Somlo Antiques BADA

7 Piccadilly Arcade. SW1Y 6NH. Est. 1972. Open 10-5.30, Sat. 10.30-5. SIZE: Medium. *STOCK: Vintage wrist and antique pocket watches, from £1,000.* LOC: Between Piccadilly and Jermyn St. PARK: Meters. TEL: 0171 499 6526. SER: Restorations.

Henry Sotheran Ltd

80 Pimlico Rd. SW1W 8PL. Open 10-6, Sat. 10-4. *STOCK: Fine and rare antique prints of architecture, decorative, natural history, travel and topography.* TEL: 0171 730 8756; fax - 0171 823 6090.

Spink and Son Ltd BADA

5 King St., St. James's. SW1Y 6QS. SLAD. Est. 1666. Open 9-5.30. CL: Sat. SIZE: Large. *STOCK: English paintings and watercolours; jewellery; furniture; Chinese, Japanese, Indian, South East Asian, Himalayan and Islamic works of art; textiles; Greek and Roman to present day coins, banknotes, bullion, orders, medals and decorations, militaria, numismatic books, stamps.* PARK: Meters. TEL: 0171 930 7888. SER: Valuations; buys at auction; commission sales on behalf of private collectors; coin auctions. VAT: Stan/Spec.

Robin Symes Ltd

3 Ormond Yard, Duke of York St., St. James's. SW1. Open by appointment only. SIZE: Large. *STOCK: Antiquities, ancient art.* PARK: Meters. TEL: 0171 930 9856/7; 0171 930 5300.

Bill Thomson - Albany Gallery BADA

1 Bury St., St. James's. SW1Y 6AB. (W.B. Thomson). Open 8.30-6, Sat. by appointment. *STOCK: British drawings, watercolours and paintings, 1700-1850 and some 20th C.* TEL: 0171 839 6119; fax - 0171 930 4211.

William Tillman Ltd BADA

30 St. James's St. SW1A 1HB. Open 9.30-5.30, Sat. by appointment. *STOCK: English furniture, 18th C.* TEL: 0171 839 2500.

SW1 continued

Trafalgar Galleries BADA
35 Bury St., St. James's. SW1Y 6AY Open 9.30-6. CL: Sat. *STOCK: Old Master paintings.* LOC: Just south of Piccadilly. TEL: 0171 839 6466.

Rafael Valls Ltd BADA
11 Duke St., St. James's. SW1Y 6BN. SLAD. Est. 1976. Open Mon.-Fri. 9.30-6. *STOCK: Old Master pictures, Dutch and Flemish, 16th-18th C.* TEL: 0171 930 1144; fax - 0171 976 1596. VAT: Spec.

Rafael Valls Ltd BADA
6 Ryder St., St. James's. SW1Y 6QB. SLAD. Open Mon.-Fri. 9.30-6. *STOCK: Decorative European pictures, 18th-19th C.* TEL: 0171 930 0029; fax - 0171 976 1596. VAT: Spec.

Johnny Van Haeften Ltd BADA
13 Duke St., St. James's. SW1Y 6DB. (J. and S. Van Haeften). SLAD, TEFAF. Est. 1978. Open 10-6, Sat. and Sun. by appointment. SIZE: Medium. *STOCK: Dutch and Flemish Old Master paintings, 16th-17th C, £5,000-£5m.* LOC: Middle of Duke St. TEL: 0171 930 3062/3; fax - 0171 839 6303. SER: Valuations; restorations (Old Masters); buys at auction (paintings including Old Masters). VAT: Spec.

Waterman Fine Art Ltd
74A Jermyn St., St. James's. SW1Y 6NP. Open 9-6, Sat. 10-4. *STOCK: 20th C paintings and watercolours.* TEL: 0171 839 5203; fax - 0171 321 0212.

Westenholz Antiques Ltd
76-78 Pimlico Rd. SW1W 8LP. Open 10-6, Sat. by appointment. *STOCK: 18th-19th C furniture, pictures, objects, lamps, mirrors.* TEL: 0171 824 8090.

Whitford Fine Art
6 Duke St., St. James's. SW1Y 6BN. (Adrian Mibus). Open 10-6. CL: Sat. *STOCK: Oil paintings and sculpture, late 19th to 20th C; Post War abstract and pop art.* TEL: 0171 930 9332; fax - 0171 930 5577.

Arnold Wiggins and Sons Ltd BADA
4 Bury St., St. James's. SW1Y 6AB. (M. Gregory). Open Mon.-Fri 9-5.30. *STOCK: Picture frames, 16th-19th C.* TEL: 0171 925 0195.

Wildenstein and Co Ltd
46 St. James's Place. SW1A 1NS. SLAD. Est. 1934. By appointment only. *STOCK: Impressionist and Old Master paintings and drawings.* TEL: 0171 629 0602; fax - 0171 493 3924.

Thomas Williams (Fine Art) Ltd
SW1. Open by appointment only. *STOCK: Old and modern Master drawings, £300-£150,000.* TEL: 0171 930 7818; fax - 0171 930 7815. SER: Valuations; buys at auction (paintings and drawings).

LONDON SW3

Norman Adams Ltd BADA
8/10 Hans Rd., Knightsbridge. SW3 1RX. Est. 1923. Open 9-5.30, Sat. and Sun. by appointment. SIZE: Large. *STOCK: English furniture, 18th C, £650-£250,000; objets d'art (English and French) £500-£50,000; mirrors, glass pictures, 18th C; clocks and barometers.* LOC: 30yds. off the Brompton Rd., opposite west side entrance to Harrods. TEL: 0171 589 5266; fax - 0171 589 1968. FAIRS: Grosvenor House; BADA. VAT: Spec.

After Noah
261 King's Rd. SW3 5EL. (M. Crawford and Z. Candlin). *STOCK: Arts and Craft oak and similar furniture, 1880's to 1950's, £1-£1,000; iron, iron and brass beds; decorative items, bric-a-brac including candlesticks, mirrors, lighting, kitchenalia and jewellery.* TEL: 0171 351 2610. SER: Restorations. VAT: Stan.

The Andipa Gallery LAPADA
162 Walton St. SW3 2JL. Est. 1969. Open Tues.-Sat. 11-6. *STOCK: Icons from Byzantium, Greece, Russia, Eastern Europe, Asia Minor and North Africa; Italian Masters and Old Masters, all from 14th-19th C.* TEL: 0171 589 2371. SER: Valuations; restorations; research; collections.

A cream jug, c.1790, pattern 172, £70-£90.

From an article entitled "Factory Fact File: New Hall" by David Battie which appeared in the May 1998 issue of **Antique Collecting**

SW3 continued

Antiquarius

131/141 King's Rd. SW3. (Atlantic Antiques Centres Ltd). Est. 1970. Open 10-6. LOC: On the corner of King's Rd. and Flood St., next to Chelsea Town Hall. TEL: Enquiries - 0171 351 5353; fax - 0171 351 5350. Below are listed some of the many specialist dealers at this market.

225 Jewellery Exchange LAPADA
Stand V38. (Mrs Michelle Rowan). *Jewellery and silver.* TEL: 0171 352 8744.

Jaki Abbott
Stand M12. *Jewellery.* TEL: 0171 352 7989; mobile - 0374 864442.

Trevor Allen
Stand V36. *Jewellery.* TEL: 0171 352 7061.

AM-PM
Stands V35. (L. Ghini). *Vintage watches.* TEL: 0171 351 5654.

Amato Antiques LAPADA
Stand V9. *Decorative antiques.* TEL: 0171 352 3666.

S. Arena
Stand E5. *General antiques, silver plate, ivory.* TEL: 0171 352 7989.

Baptista Arts LAPADA
Stand V10. (John Cox). *Decorative antiques, silver.* TEL: 0171 352 5793.

Beauty & The Beast
Stand Q9-10. (J. Rothman). *Costume jewellery, BP Austrian bronzes, handbags.* TEL: 0171 351 5149.

Alexandra Bolla
Stand J1. *Jewellery.* TEL: 0171 352 7989.

Miss E. Bradwin
Stand T5/6. *Jewellery, Art Deco and bronze animals.* TEL: 0171 351 5149.

Margaret Bristow
Stand T1/2. *Silver and plate.* TEL: 0171 352 1285.

SW3 continued

Brown & Kingston
Stand V5/V6. *Staffordshire porcelain, Imari, blue and white.* TEL: 0171 376 8881.

Derek Brunwin
Stand V25. *Jewellery and silver.* TEL: 0171 352 4690.

Miss T. Buchinger
Stand Q2. *Jewellery.* TEL: 0171 352 8734.

Mrs V. Carroll
Stand N1. *General antiques.* TEL: 0171 352 8734.

Chelsea Antiques Rug Gallery
Stand V15. (N. Somnez). *Oriental carpets and Persian rugs.* TEL: 0171 351 6611.

Chelsea Clocks
Stand H3-4, R1-2. (P. Dixon). *Clocks and general.* TEL: 0171 352 8646.

Chelsea Military Antiques
Stand N13/14. (Dominic Abbott and Richard Black). *Militaria, swords, revolvers, uniforms, medals (WWII and British Empire).* TEL: 0171 352 0308; mobile - 0589 600844.

Claude & Martine
Stand V16. (C. and M. Latreville). *Fine silver and jewellery.* TEL: 0171 352 5964.

Eli Cohen
Stand Q5. *Jade, netsuke, Oriental art.* TEL: 0171 351 7038.

John Cowan
Stand N12. *Silver, plate.* TEL: 0171 351 1750.

Glen Dewart
Stand P7/8. *Prints and paintings.* TEL: 0171 352 4777.

Edge LAPADA
Stand V17. (D.M. Edge). *Decorative items, furniture, pictures, jewellery.* TEL: 0171 352 2660.

Mrs. Patricia Evans
Stand N6/7. *Dolls, toys and accessories.* TEL: 0171 376 4419.

SW3 continued

Makiko Featherstone
Stand V22. *Silver jewellery, small objets d'art.* TEL: 0171 376 8845.

Ferguson Fine Art
Stands V30/33. (Serena Ferguson). *Fine art and sporting collectables.* TEL: 0171 352 5272.

Flight of Fancy
Stand A9-A11. (Jesse Davis). *Majolica, china, objects, silver.* TEL: 0171 352 4314.

Fothergill & Crowley
Stand L1/10. *Period clothing and textiles.* TEL: 0171 351 0011.

French Glass House
Stand P14/15 N4/5. (M. Aboudara). *Art Deco and Art Nouveau glass.* TEL: 0171 376 5394.

Mrs E. Gibbons
Stand N15/16. *Textiles and lace.* TEL: 0171 352 8734.

C. Gibson
Stand M10. *Silver and plate, general antiques.* TEL: 0171 352 4690.

Brian Gordon LAPADA
Stand G1. *Silver and plate.* TEL: 0171 352 5808.

Mrs B. Gunn
Stand M3-4. *Fans,porcelain and frames.* TEL: 0171 352 4690.

Hayman & Hayman
Stands K2/3/4/5. *Photo frames/scent bottles.* TEL: 0171 351 6568.

Mr and Mrs I Howard
Stand P12. *Jewellery, silver, watches, porcelain, buttons.* TEL: 0171 351 6140; mobile - 0381 447428.

Peter & Philip Jeffs - Aesthetics BADA LAPADA
Stand V2/3. *Silver, ceramics and decorative arts, 1860-1960.* TEL: 0171 352 0395.

Mrs P.A. Kaskimo
Stand D6. *Paintings and general antiques.* TEL: 0171 352 7989.

Martin Kaye
Stands V27/28. (Mr Kushner) *Watches, jewellery and silver.* TEL: 0171 351 3051.

D. Kelly
Stand L3, M13. *Books, including reference.* TEL: 0171 352 4690.

Miss Kukielska
Stand P1. *Jewellery, china, Art Deco objects.* TEL: 0171 352 8734.

The Lace Shop
Stand Q7/8. (Mrs Williamson) *Lace, textiles and decorative antiques.* TEL: Mobile - 0378 659783.

SW3 continued

Mrs Larpari
Stand L2. *Jewellery.* TEL: 0171 352 5592.

Mr. E. Lehane
Stand V11. *Tortoiseshell and collectables.* TEL: 0171 349 8638.

Michael Lexton
Stand N8-11. *Silver.* TEL: 0171 351 5980.

Little River
Stand D1/D2. (D. Dykes). *Asian prints, Oriental china, porcelain.* TEL: 0171 376 7348. SER: Restorations (Oriental furniture).

Peggy Malone
Stand V8. *Jewellery.* TEL: 0171 352 7720.

W.D.K. Mandozai
Stand D3. *Oil paintings.* TEL: 0171 352 0518.

Henry Mann
Stand V14. *Art Deco/Art Nouveau.* TEL: 0171 352 4690.

Mr M. Marino
Stand V7. *19th and 20th C glass.*

Mrs D. Martin & Miss Jasmin Cameron
Stand M1/14/15/16. *Silver and plate, inkpots and pens, artists materials, glass,* TEL: 0171 351 4154; mobile - 0973 222520.

Mr Martinez-Negrillo
Stand Q1/16. *Objets d'art, bronzes, porcelain and general antiques.* TEL: 0171 349 0038; mobile - 0956 406954.

Mr. Martinez-Negrilo
Stand P2/3. *Jewellery, porcelain, glass and paintings de vertus.* TEL: 0171 349 0038; mobile - 0956 406954.

Gerald Mathias
Stand R3-6. *Victorian, Edwardian furniture, clocks, boxes.* TEL: 0171 351 0484.

Mrs Sue Mautner
Stand P13. *40s' and 50's costume jewellery.* TEL: 0171 376 4419.

May Avenue
Stand V13. (Zoe Bajcer). *Art Deco ceramics, including Clarice Cliff, Keith Murray.* TEL: 0171 351 5757; mobile - 0410 424033.

Stella McDonald
Stand G4-6. *Furniture.* TEL: 0171 352 8734; 0181 788 4981.

Mrs N. McDonald-Hobley
Stand A4. *Jewellery.* TEL: 0171 351 0154.

William McLeod-Brown
Stand L5-8. *Prints especially botanicals, books.* TEL: 0171 352 4690; workshop - 0171 730 3547.

SW3 continued

Mrs Teresa Molloy
Stand E6. *Oil paintings.* TEL: 0171 352 7989.

Moneta
Stand V21. (Sam Lindsey). *Jewellery.* TEL: 0171 351 7378.

Mrs. D. Mousavi
Stand D4. *Gold and silver, jade, netsuke.* TEL: 0171 352 8734.

R.S. and S. Necus
Stand A18-19, H1/2. *Silver, plate, objets de vertu.* TEL: 0171 352 2405.

Sue Norman
Stand L4. (Mr and Mrs Alloway) *Blue and white transfer ware.* TEL: 0171 352 7217.

Miss J. Palmer
Stand M8/9. *Jewellery and silver.* TEL: 0171 352 0431.

Maria Perez
Stand V23/24. *Jewellery.* TEL: 0171 351 1986.

Phillipa & John
Stand J4/5. *Jewellery.* TEL: 0171 352 4690/351 0294.

The Purple Shop
Stand J9-11. (Gardner and Becker). *Antique, period, Art Nouveau and Art Deco jewellery..* TEL: 0171 352 1127.

Mrs Victoria Quiroz
Stand Q14/15. *General antiques.* TEL: 0171 351 5141; mobile - 0705 143837.

Abdul Rabi
Stand P4. *Jewellery and watch repairs.* TEL: 0171 352 8734.

Robert Raymond **LAPADA**
Stand V19. *Jewellery.* TEL: 0171 349 0809.

K. Reilly
Stand V4. *Art Nouveau, Art Deco.* TEL: 0171 352 2099.

Alex Ronco
Stand V1. *Bronzes.* TEL: 0171 376 8116.

Miss Jerri Scott
Stand P9-P11. *General antiques and jewellery.* TEL: 0171 352 9471.

Seraphim Antiques
Stand Q3/4. (Mrs A. Martin). *Jewellery, decorative antiques.* TEL: Mobile - 0370 798186.

Simar Antiques
Stand B2/3. (A. Cohen). *Silver.* TEL: 0171 352 7155.

M. Simpson
Stand E1. *Ivory.* TEL: 0171 352 7989.

SW3 continued

Mr A. Sultani
Stand A7/8. *Antiquities, jewellery, beads.* TEL: Mobile - 0956 814541.

John Szwarc
Stand G2/3. *Jewellery and cuff-links.* TEL: 0171 352 8201.

S & A Thompson **LAPADA**
Stand V12. *Silver, small furniture.* TEL: 0171 352 8680.

Simon Thorpe **LAPADA**
Stand T3-4. *Silver and jewellery.* TEL: 0171 351 2911.

Trio Antiques
Stand P5/6. (Jackie Harrison). *Country style antiques.* TEL: 0171 352 8734.

Mr. Vidich
Stand A14-17. *Prints, etchings and maps.* TEL: 0171 376 4252.

Geoffrey Waters **LAPADA**
Stand F1-6. *Oriental porcelain and silver.* TEL: 0171 376 5467.

West Country Jewellery
Stand M5/6/7. (David Billing). *Jewellery, objects, silver.* TEL: 0171 376 8252.

Whyte-Donovan
Stand V18/29. (Miss Amber Donovan). *Vintage watches, gold jewellery.* TEL: 0171 376 7808; fax - 0171 349 9746; mobile - 0370 367703.

XS Baggage
Stand A1,2,3 & 6, B1/4-6, C2. (Mr and Mrs Lehane) *Antique luggage and travel requisites including Louis Vuitton and Asprey; sporting memorabilia.* TEL: 0171 352 7989/376 8781.

Miss Etsuko Zakoji
Stand V20. *Jewellery and small decorative objects.* TEL: 0171 352 2329.

Ms Basia Zarzycka
Stand W3. *Couture masks/wedding dresses and accessories.* TEL: 0171 351 7276.

Ziggy
Stand E3/4. (S. Aritake). *General antique watches and lighters.* TEL: 0171 376 5628.

Apter Fredericks Ltd **BADA**
265-267 Fulham Rd. SW3 6HY. (B. and Mrs. C Apter and H. Apter). Open 9.30-5.30, Sat. and evenings by appointment. *STOCK: English furniture, 17th to early 19th C.* TEL: 0171 352 2188; fax - 0171 376 5619. VAT: Stan/Spec.

SW3 continued

Joanna Booth BADA

247 King's Rd., Chelsea. SW3 5EL. Est. 1963. Open 10-6. SIZE: Medium. *STOCK: Wood carvings, oak furniture, 17th C, £50-£5,000; Old Master drawings, textiles, tapestry.* Not Stocked: Silver, glass, pottery, clocks. PARK: Meters. TEL: 0171 352 8998; fax - 0171 376 7350. SER: Buys at auction. VAT: Spec.

Bourbon-Hanby Antiques Centre

151 Sydney Street, Chelsea. SW3 6NT. Open 10-6, Sun. 11-4. LOC: Just off Kings Road, opposite town hall. TEL: 0171 352 2106.

Butler and Wilson

189 Fulham Rd. SW3 6JN. *STOCK: Jewellery, Art Deco, bags, objects and accessories.* TEL: 0171 352 3045.

Campbell's of Walton Street

164 Walton St. SW3 2JL. Open 9.30-5.30. *STOCK: 20th C impressionist and modern British oils and watercolours.* TEL: 0171 584 9268; fax - 0171 581 3499. SER: Master framing, carving, gilding and restorations.

Richard Courtney Ltd BADA

112-114 Fulham Rd. SW3 6HU. Est. 1959. Open 9.30-1 and 2-6. CL: Sat. SIZE: Large. *STOCK: English furniture, 18th C, £500-£20,000.* PARK: Easy. TEL: 0171 370 4020. VAT: Spec.

Colin Denny Ltd

18 Cale St. SW3 3QU. Est. 1968. Open 10-6. *STOCK: Marine works of art, 19th C.* TEL: 0171 584 0240. VAT: Stan/Spec.

Robert Dickson and Lesley Rendall Antiques BADA

263 Fulham Rd. SW3 6HY. Est. 1969. Open 10-6, Sat. 10.30-4. SIZE: Medium. *STOCK: Late 18th to early 19th C furniture and works of art, £500-£100,000.* PARK: Easy. TEL: 0171 351 0330. VAT: Spec.

Dragons of Walton St. Ltd

23 Walton St. SW3 2HX. (R. Fisher). *STOCK: Mainly painted and decorated furniture; hand decorated children's furniture, decorative items.* LOC: Close to Harrods. PARK: Hasker St. or First St. TEL: 0171 589 3795; fax - 0171 584 4570.

Michael Foster BADA

118 Fulham Rd., Chelsea. SW3 6HU. Open 9.30-5.30, Sat. by appointment. *STOCK: 18th C English furniture and works of art.* TEL: 0171 373 3636/3040. SER: Valuations.

C. Fredericks and Son BADA

92 Fulham Rd. SW3 6HR. (R.F. Fredericks). Open 9.30-5.30, Sat. by appointment. SIZE:

SW3 continued

Large. *STOCK: Furniture, 18th C, £500-£15,000.* LOC: Near to South Kensington underground station. PARK: Easy. TEL: 0171 589 5847. VAT: Stan/Spec.

Gallery Lingard

Walpole House, 35 Walpole St. SW3 4QS. SLAD. Open by appointment only. *STOCK: Architectural drawings, watercolours, paintings and prints.* TEL: 0171 730 9233; fax - 0171 730 9152.

Gallery Yacou LAPADA

127 Fulham Rd. SW3 6RT. Open 10.30-6, Sat. 11-6. *STOCK: Decorative and antique Oriental and European carpets (room-size and over-size).* LOC: Walking distance from Bibendum. TEL: 0171 584 2929; fax - 0171 584 3535.

David Gill LAPADA

60 Fulham Rd. SW3 6HH. Est. 1986. Open 10-6. SIZE: Medium. *STOCK: Decorative and fine arts, Picasso, Cocteau ceramics and drawings, 1900 to present day.* PARK: Onslow Sq. TEL: 0171 589 5946; fax - 0171 584 9184. VAT: Stan.

Godson and Coles BADA

310 King's Rd. SW3 5UH Est. 1978. Open 9.30-5.30 and by appointment. CL: Sat. *STOCK: Fine 18th to early 19th C English furniture and works of art.* TEL: 0171 352 8509: fax - 0171 351 9947.

Green and Stone

259 Kings Rd. SW3 5EL. (R.J.S. Baldwin). Est. 1927. Open 9-5.30, Sat. 9.30-6. *STOCK: Writing and artists' materials, watercolours, 18th-19th C; drawings, 19th C.* LOC: At junction of King's Rd. and Old Church St. PARK: Meters. TEL: 0171 352 0837/6521. SER: Restorations (pictures). VAT: Stan.

James Hardy and Co

235 Brompton Rd. SW3 2EP. Open 10-5.30. *STOCK: Silver including tableware, and jewellery.* PARK: Meters. TEL: 0171 589 5050; fax - 0171 589 9009. SER: Valuations; repairs.

Stephanie Hoppen Ltd

17 Walton St. SW3 2HX. Est. 1962. Open 10-6, Sat. 12-5. *STOCK: Decorative picture specialist - watercolours, oils, drawings and prints, antique and modern.* TEL: 0171 589 3678.

Anthony James and Son Ltd BADA

88 Fulham Rd. SW3 6HR. Est. 1949. Open 9.30-5.45, Sat. by appointment. SIZE: Large. *STOCK: Furniture, 1700-1880, £200-£50,000; mirrors, bronzes, ormolu and decorative items, £200-£20,000.* PARK: Easy. TEL: 0171 584 1120; fax - 0171 823 7618. SER: Valuations; buys at auction. VAT: Spec.

SW3 continued

John Keil Ltd BADA
1st Floor, 154 Brompton Rd. SW3 1HX. Est. 1959. Open 9-6. CL: Sat. except by appointment. SIZE: Large. *STOCK: English furniture, 18th to early 19th C, from £500.* LOC: Near Knightsbridge underground station. PARK: 200 yds. TEL: 0171 589 6454; fax - 0171 823 8235. VAT: Spec.

Stanley Leslie
15 Beauchamp Place. SW3 1NQ. Open 9-5. *STOCK: Silver and Sheffield plate.* PARK: Meters. TEL: 0171 589 2333.

Michael Lipitch Ltd BADA
98 Fulham Rd. SW3 6HS. *STOCK: 18th to early 19th C English furniture, decoration and works of art.* TEL: 0171 589 7327; fax - 0171 823 9106.

Peter Lipitch Ltd BADA
120/124 Fulham Rd. SW3 6HU. Est. 1954. Open 9.30-5.30. SIZE: Large. *STOCK: Fine English furniture and mirrors.* TEL: 0171 373 3328; fax - 0171 373 8888. VAT: Spec.

Sylvanna Llewelyn
Unit 5, Bourbon-Hanby Antiques Centre, 151 Sydney St., Chelsea, SW3. (Sylvia H. Llewelyn). Est. 1982. Open 10-6 including Sun. SIZE: Small.

SW3 continued

STOCK: Costume jewellery, 19th-20th C, £5-£100; buttons, 450 BC to 20th C, £5-£1,000; ceramics, 19th C, £50-£1,000. LOC: Just off King's Rd., opposite town hall. TEL: 0171 351 4981. SER: Valuations; buys at auction.

The Map House
54 Beauchamp Place. SW3 1NY. (P. Curtis and P. Stuchlik). Est. 1907. Open 9.45-5.45, Sat. 10.30-5 or by appointment. *STOCK: Antique and rare maps, atlases, engravings and globes.* TEL: 0171 589 4325/584 8559; fax - 0171 589 1041. VAT: Stan.

McKenna and Co LAPADA
28 Beauchamp Place. SW3 1NJ. (C. Macmillan and M. McKenna). Est. 1982. Open 10-6. SIZE: Medium. *STOCK: Fine jewellery, Georgian to post war, £50-£10,000; some silver and objects.* Not Stocked: Pictures and furniture. LOC: Off Brompton Rd., near Harrods. PARK: Meters. TEL: 0171 584 1966; fax - 0171 225 2893. SER: Valuations; restorations. FAIRS: Olympia. VAT: Stan/Spec.

Merola
178 Walton St. SW3 2JL. (M. Merola). Open 10-6. *STOCK: Jewellery, handbags, hats and accessories, 1900-1960.* TEL: 0171 589 0365; fax - 0171 373 4297.

No. 12
12 Cale St., Chelsea Green. SW3 3QU. Open 10-6. *STOCK: French country furniture and accessories.* TEL: 0171 581 5022; fax - 0171 581 3966.

Old Church Galleries
320 King's Rd., Chelsea. SW3 5UH. (Mrs M. Harrington). Open 10-6. *STOCK: Maps and engravings, from 16th C; sporting and decorative prints.* TEL: 0171 351 4649; fax - 0171 351 4449. SER: Framing.

Jacqueline Oosthuizen LAPADA
23 Cale St., (Off Sydney St.), Chelsea Green. SW3 3QR. Est. 1960. Open 10-6, Sat. and Sun. by appointment. SIZE: Medium. *STOCK: Staffordshire figures, animals, cottages and toby jugs, 18th-19th C; jewellery, 19th-20th C, £15-£5,000; decorative ceramics including Poole pottery, 19th-20th C, £20-£1,000.* LOC: Near King's Rd. and Fulham Rd. PARK: Easy. TEL: 0171 352 6071. VAT: Stan/Spec.

Jacqueline & Pieter Oosthuizen
at Bourbon-Hanby Antiques Centre, 151 Sydney St. SW3. Open 10-4.30. *STOCK: Staffordshire figures, animals, cottages and tobies, Dutch Art Nouveau pottery.* LOC: Just off King's Rd. opposite town hall. TEL: 0171 352 6071/460 3078.

Rogers de Rin Antiques
76
Specialists in
WEMYSS WARE
76 Royal Hospital Road
Tel: 0171 352 9007 Fax: 0171 351 9407
London SW3 4HN

SW3 continued

Perez LAPADA

199 Brompton Rd. SW3 1LA. (Mr Tyran). Est. 1983. Open 10-6. SIZE: Large. *STOCK: Antique carpets, rugs, tapestries and Aubussons.* LOC: 50 yards from Harrods. PARK: Easy. TEL: 0171 589 2199 (ansaphone). SER: Valuations; restorations; buys at auction. VAT: Stan/Spec.

Prides of London

15 Paultons House, Paultons Sq. SW3 5DU. Open by appointment only. *STOCK: Fine 18th-19th C English and Continental furniture; objets d'art.* TEL: 0171 586 1227. SER: Interior design.

The Purple Shop

15 Flood St., Chelsea. SW3 5ST. (A.J. Gardner and O.M. Becker). Est. 1967. Open 10-6. *STOCK: Antique and period jewellery especially Art Nouveau and Art Deco; studio pottery.* LOC: Near Chelsea Town Hall. PARK: Meters and nearby. TEL: 0171 352 1127. SER: Valuations. VAT: Stan.

Rogers de Rin LAPADA

76 Royal Hospital Rd., Chelsea. SW3 4HN. (V. de Rin). Est. 1950. Open 10-5.30, Sat. 10-1, Sun. by appointment. SIZE: Small. *STOCK: Wemyss pottery, objets d'art, decorative furnishings (Regency taste), collectors' specialities,*

SW3 continued

***18th-19th C, £50-£10,000.* LOC: Just beyond Royal Hospital, corner of Paradise Walk. PARK: Easy. TEL: 0171 352 9007; fax - 0171 351 9407. SER: Buys at auction; free catalogue on request. VAT: Stan/Spec.**

Charles Saunders Antiques

255 Fulham Rd. SW3 6JA. Open 9.30-5.30, Sat. 10-5. *STOCK: Decorative furniture, objects and lamps, 18th-19th C.* TEL: 0171 351 5242. VAT: Spec.

Christine Schell LAPADA

15 Cale St. SW3 3QS. (B. King and C. Davies). Est. 1971. Open 10-5.30. SIZE: Small. *STOCK: Unusual tortoiseshell, silver and enamel objects, late 19th to early 20th C, £150-£2,500.* LOC: North of King's Rd., between Sloane Ave. and Sydney St. PARK: Easy. TEL: 0171 352 5563. SER: Valuations; restorations (tortoiseshell, ivory, shagreen, crocodile, leather, enamels, silver and hairbrush re-bristling). FAIRS: Olympia. VAT: Stan/Spec.

Robert Stephenson

1 Elystan St., Chelsea Green. SW3 3NT. Open 9.30-5.30, Sat. 10.30-2. *STOCK: Antique and decorative room-sized carpets and kilims; antique Oriental rugs, European tapestries and Aubussons, textiles, needlepoints and cushions.* TEL: 0171 225 2343; fax - same.

SW3 continued

Gordon Watson Ltd LAPADA
50 Fulham Rd. SW3 6HH. Est. 1977. Open 11-6. *STOCK: Art Deco and 1940's glass, jewellery and furniture, £500-£10,000; silver by Jensen and Jean E. Puiforcat, 1920's, £500-£30,000.* LOC: At junction with Sydney St. PARK: Sydney St. TEL: 0171 589 3108/584 6328. SER: Valuations; buys at auction (Art Nouveau and Art Deco). VAT: Stan/Spec.

O.F. Wilson Ltd BADA LAPADA
Queens Elm Parade, Old Church St. (corner Fulham Rd.), Chelsea. SW3 6EJ. (P. and V.E. Jackson, M.E. Briscoe-Knight and R.G. White). Est. 1935. Open 9.30-5.30, Sat. 10.30-1. *STOCK: English and French furniture, mantelpieces, objets d'art.* TEL: 0171 352 9554; fax - 0171 351 0765. SER: Valuations. VAT: Spec.

Clifford Wright Antiques Ltd BADA
104-106 Fulham Rd. SW3 6HS. Est. 1964. Open Mon.-Fri. 9-5.30, or by appointment. *STOCK: Furniture, period giltwood, looking glasses and consoles, 18th to early 19th C.* TEL: 0171 589 0986; fax - 0171 589 3565. VAT: Spec.

LONDON SW5

Antique and Modern Furniture Ltd
160 Earls Court Rd. SW5 9QQ. Est. 1941. Open 9.30-1 and 2.30-6. CL: Thurs. *STOCK: Furniture, mainly 18th-19th C.* TEL: 0171 373 2935.

Beaver Coin Room
Beaver Hotel, 57 Philbeach Gdns. SW5 9ED. (J. Lis). Est. 1971. Open by appointment. SIZE: Small. *STOCK: European coins, 10th-18th C; commemorative medals, 15th-20th C; all £5-£5,000.* LOC: 2 mins. walk from Earls Court Rd. PARK: Easy. TEL: 0171 373 4553; fax - 0171 373 4555. SER: Valuations; buys at auction (coins and medals). FAIRS: London Coin and Coinex. VAT: Stan.

LONDON SW6

20th Century Gallery
821 Fulham Rd. SW6 5HG. (E. Brandl and H. Chapman). Open 10-6, Sat. 10-1. SIZE: Small. *STOCK: Post impressionist and modern British oils and watercolours; original prints.* LOC: Near Munster Rd. junction. PARK: Easy. TEL: 0171 731 5888. SER: Restorations (paintings); framing. VAT: Spec.

SW6 continued

275 Antiques

275 Lillie Rd., Fulham. SW6. (David Fisher). Open 10-5.30. SIZE: Medium. *STOCK: English and Continental decorative furniture, £200-£1,500; decorative objects, £25-£300; unique table lamps, £100-£700; mirrors, £400-£1,500; garden furniture, £50-£800.* PARK: Easy. TEL: 0171 386 7382; home - 0171 381 5094.

313 Antiques

313 Lillie Rd., Fulham. SW6 7LL. (Murray France Brown and Marcelline Herald). Est. 1986. Open 11-5.30. *STOCK: Furniture, 18th-19th C, £150-£2,500; decorative smalls, candlesticks, lamps and chandeliers, £50-£1,000; pictures and mirrors, 18th-20th C, £50-£1,250. Textiles, costumes, curtains, table and bed covers, tie backs, £40-£500; French and English decorative furniture, £100-£10,000; decorative smalls and prints, plant holders, photo frames, £20-£300.* LOC: From Old Brompton Rd., west for half a mile after crossing Northend Rd. PARK: Easy and nearby. TEL: 0171 610 2380; fax - same;. SER: Shipping arranged. FAIRS: Vincent Sq.; Kensington Town Hall, Brocante; Mainwarings; Newark; Ardingly; NEC.

(55) For Decorative Living

55 New King's Rd., Chelsea. SW6 4SE. (Mrs J. Rhodes). Open 10.30-5.30. *STOCK: Furniture, lighting and decorative items.* TEL: 0171 736 5623. SER: Design.

And So To Bed Limited

638/640 King's Rd. SW6 Est. 1970. Open 10-6. SIZE: Large. *STOCK: Brass, lacquered and wooded beds.* LOC: End of King's Rd., towards Fulham. PARK: Easy. TEL: 0171 731 3593/4/5. SER: Restorations; spares; interior design. VAT: Stan.

Christopher Bangs BADA LAPADA

P O Box 6077. SW6 7XS. CINOA. Est. 1971. Open by appointment only. *STOCK: Domestic metalwork and metalware, works of art, decorative objects.* TEL: 0171 381 3532 (24 hrs); fax - 0171 381 2192 (24 hrs); mobile - 0836 333532. SER: Valuations; research; commission buys at auction; finder. VAT: Stan/Spec.

Barclay Samson Ltd

65 Finlay St. SW6 6HF. Open by appointment only. *STOCK: Pre 1950 original lithographic posters: French, German, Swiss, American, British and Russian Constructivist schools.* TEL: 0171 731 8012; fax - 0171 731 8013; mobile - 0385 306401. VAT: Spec.

Robert Barley Antiques

48 Fulham High St. SW6 3LQ. (R.A. Barley). Est. 1965. Open 9.30-5.30, Sat. 10-1. SIZE: Medium. *STOCK: Unusual decorative objects, furniture, lighting.* LOC: Near Putney Bridge. PARK: Easy. TEL: 0171 736 4429; fax - same. VAT: Stan/Spec.

SW6 continued

Baroque 'n' Roll

291 Lillie Rd., Fulham. SW6 7LL. SIZE: Large. *STOCK: Highly decorative antiques, Gothic style and 18th C splendour; mirrors, garden statuary and textiles.* TEL: 0171 381 5008. SER: Lavish interior design.

Big Ben Antique Clocks

5 Broxholme House, New King's Rd. SW6 4AA. (R. Lascelles). Est. 1978. Open 10-4. *STOCK: Longcase painted dial clocks, from £1,500; also decorative antiques and accessories.* LOC: At junction of Wandsworth Bridge Rd. and New King's Rd. TEL: 0171 736 1770; fax - 0171 384 1957. SER: Buys at auction.

Bishops Park Antiques

53-55 Fulham High St. SW6 3JJ. Open 10-6. *STOCK: Pine especially English and Continental, 18th-19th C.* TEL: 0171 736 4573.

Bookham Galleries

164 Wandsworth Bridge Rd. SW6. (J.H. and J. Rowe). Est. 1969. Open 10-5.30. CL: Mon. and Thurs. *STOCK: Furniture, 18th-19th C; Oriental rugs.* TEL: 0171 736 5125.

Julia Boston LAPADA

The Old Stores, The Gasworks, 2 Michael Rd. SW6 2AD. CINOA. Est. 1976. Open Mon.-Fri. 10-6, other times by appointment. SIZE: Large. *STOCK: Tapestry cartoons, 18th-19th C; prints and works of art, 16th-19th C; furniture, 18th-19th C.* LOC: King's Rd. towards Fulham, left Waterford Rd., straight over roundabout, through industrial gates. PARK: Own. TEL: 0171 610 6783; fax - 0171 610 6784. SER: Restorations (pictures and prints). FAIRS: Olympia (June); Decorative (Jan., April, Sept.). VAT: Spec.

CHARLES EDWARDS
582 KINGS ROAD, LONDON, SW6 2DY TEL. 0171 736 8490 FAX. 0171 371 5436

SW6 continued

I. and J.L. Brown Ltd
632-636 King's Rd. SW6 2DU. Open 9-5.30. *STOCK: English country and French provincial furniture including tables and country chairs; metalware and decorative items.* TEL: 0171 736 4141; fax - 0171 736 9164. SER: Restorations.

Rupert Cavendish Antiques
610 King's Rd. SW6 2DX. Est. 1980. Open 10-6. SIZE: Large. *STOCK: Empire, Biedermeier and Art Deco furniture; 20th C oil paintings.* LOC: Just before New King's Rd. PARK: Easy. TEL: 0171 731 7041; fax - 0171 731 8302. SER: Valuations. VAT: Spec.

John Clay
263 New King's Rd., Fulham. SW6 4RB. Est. 1974. Open 8.30-6, Sat. 10-6. SIZE: Medium. *STOCK: Furniture, £50-£10,000; objets d'art and animal objects, silver and clocks, £10-£5,000; all 18th-19th C.* Not Stocked: Pine. LOC: Close to Parsons Green, A3. PARK: Easy. TEL: 0171 731 5677. SER: Restorations (furniture, objets d'art). VAT: Stan/Spec.

Fergus Cochrane Antiques
570 King's Rd. SW6 2DY. (F.V. Cochrane and L. Warren). Est. 1981. Open 10-5. SIZE: Medium. *STOCK: Decorative lighting, furniture and objects, 1700-1930, £100-£3,000.* PARK: Easy. TEL: 0171 736 9166.

SW6 continued

J. Crotty and Son Ltd
74 New King's Rd., Parsons Green. SW6 4LT. Est. 1945. Open 9.30-5. CL: Sat. pm. SIZE: Medium. *STOCK: Fire grates, fenders, 18th-19th C; marble and pine mantelpieces, fire irons and screens, period lighting.* PARK: In adjacent side street. TEL: 0171 731 4209. SER: Restorations (antique metal fireplace equipment); buys at auction. VAT: Stan.

Charles Edwards — BADA
582 King's Rd. SW6 2DY. Open 9.30-6. *STOCK: Antique and reproduction light fixtures; furniture, 18th-19th C; architectural and decorative items, mirrors, British oil paintings, garden furniture and statuary.* TEL: 0171 736 8490; fax - 0171 371 5436.

Christopher Edwards
The Old Stores, The Gasworks, 2 Michael Rd. SW6 2AD. Est. 1982. Open Tues., Wed. and Thurs. 10-6 or by appointment. SIZE: Large. *STOCK: Architecturally inspired furniture, works of art, lighting, 19th C, £100-£10,000.* LOC: King's Rd. towards Fulham, left Waterford Rd., straight over roundabout, through industrial gates. PARK: Own. TEL: 0171 610 6836; fax - 0171 610 6847; mobile - 0831 707043. SER: Valuations; buys at auction. FAIRS: Olympia (June and Nov). VAT: Stan/Spec.

SW6 continued

Nicole Fabre

592 King's Rd. SW6 2DX. CINOA Est. 1989. Open 10.30-6, Sat. 11-6, Sun. by appointment only. SIZE: Medium. *STOCK: French furniture, provincial style, French textiles, decorative objects, some English country furniture, to 1870.* PARK: Meters. TEL: 0171 384 3112; fax - 0171 610 6410. FAIRS: Olympia. VAT: Spec.

Fairfax Antiques and Fireplaces

568 King's Rd. SW6 2DY. Open 11-5.30. *STOCK: Cast iron and pine fireplaces, architectural items, decorative furniture.* TEL: 0171 736 5023.

George Floyd Ltd

592 Fulham Rd. SW6 5UA Open 8.30-5.30. SIZE: Large. *STOCK: 18th to early 19th C furniture and accessories.* TEL: 0171 736 1649. VAT: Stan/Spec.

Birdie Fortescue Antiques LAPADA

Studio 3T, Cooper House, 2 Michael Rd. SW6 2AD. Open by appointment only. SIZE: Medium. *STOCK: French fruitwood furniture, 18th to early 19th C, £500-£5,000.* LOC: Off King's Rd. TEL: 0171 371 8600; fax - same; mobile - 0378 263467. FAIRS: Olympia (June): Decorative (Jan., Mar. and Sept). VAT: Spec.

Fulham Cross Antiques

318-320 Munster Rd., Fulham. SW6 6BH. SIZE: Large. *STOCK: English, Continental and decorative antique furniture, mirrors and lighting.* TEL: 0171 610 3644.

George d'Epinois

793 Fulham Rd. SW6. (A. George). Est. 1979. Open 9.30-5.30. *STOCK: English furniture, 1690-1820, £250-£30,000.* PARK: Easy. TEL: 0171 736 2387. SER: Valuations; restorations. FAIRS: Harrogate; Olympia; Brugge, Belgium. VAT: Spec.

Judy Greenwood

657 Fulham Rd. SW6 5PY. Est. 1978. Open 10-5. *STOCK: French decorative furniture, lighting, quilts and textiles.* TEL: 0171 736 6037.

Robin Greer

434 Fulham Palace Rd. SW6 6HX Est. 1965. Open by appointment. *STOCK: Children's and illustrated books, original illustrations.* TEL: 0171 381 9113; fax - 0171 381 6499. SER: Catalogues issued.

Gregory, Bottley and Lloyd

13 Seagrave Rd. SW6 1RP. Est. 1858. SIZE: Medium. *STOCK: Mineral specimens, £1-£5,000; fossils, £5-£500.* PARK: Easy. TEL: 0171 381 5522; fax - 0171 381 5512. SER: Valuations. VAT: Stan.

SW6 continued

Guinevere Antiques

574/580 King's Rd. SW6 2DY. Open 9.30-6, Sat. 10-5.30. SIZE: Large. *STOCK: Period and decorative antiques and accessories.* TEL: 0171 736 2917; fax - 0171 736 8267.

Gutlin Clocks and Antiques

616 King's Rd. SW6. Est. 1990. Open 9.30-7. SIZE: Medium. *STOCK: Longcase clocks, £2,000-£8,000; mantle clocks, £300-£6,000; furniture and lighting, £500-£3,000; all 18th-19th C.* LOC: 200 yards from beginning of New King's Rd. PARK: Maxwell Rd. TEL: 0171 384 2439; fax - same; home - 0181 740 6830. SER: Valuations; restorations (clocks and clock cases); buys at auction (clocks).

Nicholas Harris BADA

PO Box 14430. SW6 2WG. Est. 1971. Open only by appointment. *STOCK: Fine and estate jewellery; silver and decorative arts, 19th-20th C.* TEL: 0171 371 9711; fax - 0171 371 9537. VAT: Stan/Spec.

Hollingshead and Co

56 Tasso Rd., Fulham. SW6. (D. Hollingshead). Est. 1946. Open 8.30-5, Sat. 9-1. SIZE: Medium. *STOCK: Marble and wood mantelpieces, grates, fenders, fire irons, chandeliers, £50-£20,000.* Not Stocked: Furniture. TEL: 0171 385 8519. SER: Valuations; restorations (marblework and wood mantelpieces). VAT: Stan.

House of Mirrors

597 King's Rd. SW6 2EL. (G. Witek). Est. 1960. Open 10-6. *STOCK: Mirrors.* TEL: 0171 736 5885.

HRW Antiques (London) Ltd LAPADA

26 Sulivan Rd. SW6 3DT. Open 9-5, Sat. 10-1. SIZE: Large. *STOCK: Furniture and objects of art, 18th-19th C.* TEL: 0171 371 7995; fax - 0171 371 9522.

Peter Hurford Antiques

618-620 King's Rd. SW6 2DU Open 10-5.30. *STOCK: Continental and British decorative objects and furniture, screens and mirrors, 18th-19th C, £500-£10,000.* TEL: 0171 731 4655. VAT: Spec.

P.L. James

590 Fulham Rd. SW6 5NT. Open 7-5. CL: Sat. *STOCK: Gilded mirrors, English and Oriental lacquer, period objects and furniture.* TEL: 0171 736 0183. SER: Restorations (painted and lacquer furniture, gilding, carving). VAT: Stan/Spec.

Ki

594 King's Rd. SW6 2DX. (Henry Money-Coutts). Open 10-6. *STOCK: Japanese furniture.* TEL: 0171 736 5999.

SW6 continued

Eric King Antiques

11 Crondace Rd. SW6 4BB. Est. 1966. Open by appointment. *STOCK: Decorative furniture and accessories, 18th-20th C.* PARK: Easy. TEL: 0171 731 2554.

King's Court Galleries

949/953 Fulham Rd. SW6 5HY. (Mrs J. Joel). Open 9.30-5.30. *STOCK: Antique maps, engravings, decorative and sporting prints.* TEL: 0171 610 6939. SER: Framing (on site).

L. and E. Kreckovic

559 King's Rd. SW6. Open 10-6. *STOCK: 18th-19th C furniture.* TEL: 0171 736 0753; fax - 0171 731 5904.

The Lamp Gallery

355 New King's Rd. SW6 4RJ. (G. Jones). Est. 1986. Open 10-5.30. SIZE: Medium. *STOCK: Interior lighting including Art Nouveau and Art Deco lamps, 1840-1940, £10-£5,000+.* LOC: 400yds. from Putney Bridge. PARK: Easy - pay and display. TEL: 0171 736 6188; fax - 0171 731 2632. SER: Valuations; restorations (metal polishing, re-wiring). VAT: Stan/Spec.

Lewin

638 Fulham Rd. SW6 5RT. (David and Harriett Lewin). Open 10-5.30, Sun. 11-4.30. SIZE: Medium. *STOCK: Dutch colonial furniture, 1900-1930; textiles and gifts.* TEL: 0171 731 1616. VAT: Stan.

Michael Luther Antiques

590 King's Rd., Chelsea. SW6 2DX. (Michael Luther and Peter Goodwin). Est. 1967. Open 10-6, Sat. 10-5.30. SIZE: Large. *STOCK: Furniture - 18th-19th C, £500-£10,000; early 20th C, £300-£3,000. Lighting, 19th-20th C, £300-£5,000.* LOC: Between Lots Rd. and Wandsworth Bridge Rd. PARK: Nearby. TEL: 0171 371 8492; fax - same. SER: Valuations; buys at auction (furniture). VAT: Spec.

Magpies

152 Wandsworth Bridge Rd., Fulham. SW6 2UH. Open 10-5. SIZE: 4 dealers. *STOCK: China, glass, kitchenalia, collectables, cutlery, door furniture, lighting, silver plate, fireplace accessories and small furniture.* TEL: 0171 736 3738.

Michael Marriott Ltd

588 Fulham Rd. SW6 5NT. Est. 1979. Open 10-5.30. CL: Sat. pm. and Sun. except by appointment. SIZE: Large. *STOCK: English furniture, 1700-1850, £400-£15,000; leather upholstery, £250-£4,500; framed prints, £45-£800.* LOC: Junction of Fulham Rd. and Parsons Green Lane. PARK: Easy. TEL: 0171 736 3110/736 0568. SER: Valuations; restorations. VAT: Stan/Spec.

SW6 continued

David Martin-Taylor Antiques LAPADA

558 King's Rd. SW6 2DZ. Open 10-6, Sat. 11-5. SIZE: Medium. *STOCK: Classic and decorative furniture and unusual objects, 18th-19th C; 19th C American wickers.* PARK: Easy. TEL: 0171 731 4135; fax - 0171 371 0029; internet - Http://www.all-about-antiques.co.uk. SER: Hire. VAT: Stan/Spec.

Megan Mathers Antiques LAPADA

571 Kings Rd. SW6 2EB. Open 10-6. *STOCK: 18th-19th C English and Continental furniture and decorative objects.* TEL: 0171 371 7837.

Mark Maynard Antiques

651 Fulham Rd. SW6 5PU. Est. 1977. Open 10-5, Sun. by appointment. SIZE: Medium. *STOCK: Decorative items, £25-£300.* LOC: Near Fulham Broadway underground. PARK: Easy. TEL: 0171 731 3533; home - 0171 373 4681. VAT: Stan/Spec.

Mora & Upham Antiques

584 King's Rd. SW6 2DX. (Matthew Upham). Est. 1976. Open 10-6. SIZE: Medium. *STOCK: Furniture, pictures and decorative objects, 18th-19th C.* LOC: Corner premises. PARK: Easy. TEL: 0171 731 4444; fax - 0171 736 0440. SER: Valuations; restorations (pictures, china and furniture); buys at auction (furniture and jewellery). VAT: Spec.

Sylvia Napier Ltd

554 King's Rd. SW6 2DZ. Est. 1972. Open 10-6. SIZE: Large. *STOCK: Furniture - decorative European, 18th-19th C, £100-£15,000; decorative Oriental, 17th-19th C, £200-£7,000; garden, 19th C, £150-£7,000; objets d'art; unusual chandeliers.* LOC: Near junction with Lots Rd. PARK: Easy. TEL: 0171 371 5881. SER: Restorations. VAT: Spec.

Old World Trading Co

565 King's Rd. SW6. (R.J. Campion). Est. 1970. Open 9.30-6. *STOCK: Fireplaces, chimney pieces and accessories, chandeliers, mirrors, furniture including decorative, works of art.* TEL: 0171 731 4708; fax - 0171 731 1291.

Orrell & Brown Interiors

5 Broxholme House, New King's Rd. SW6 4AA. *STOCK: 19th C decorative items, French Empire, Louis XV and Regency, specialising in US market.* LOC: Junction of Harwood Rd. TEL: 0171 736 1770; fax - 0171 731 7017; e-mail - angela@mailbox.co.uk SER: Furniture and curtain design, upholstery, trompe l'oeil; restorations.

Ossowski

595 King's Rd. SW6 2EL. Est. 1960. Open 9.30-5.30. SIZE: Large. *STOCK: Furniture, 18th C.* TEL: 0171 731 0334. SER: Valuations; restorations. VAT: Stan/Spec.

SW6 continued

M. Pauw Antiques

561 King's Rd. SW6 2EB. Est. 1985. SIZE: Medium. *STOCK: English and Continental furniture, 18th-19th C; decorative items, lighting fixtures, cast iron and lead planters, £500-£20,000.* PARK: Easy. TEL: 0171 731 4022; fax - 0171 731 7356. VAT: Stan/Spec.

Perez Antique Carpets Gallery

150 Wandsworth Bridge Rd., Fulham. SW6 2UH. (R. Tyran). Est. 1984. Open 10-6.30, Wed. 10-7.30. SIZE: Large. *STOCK: Carpets, 19th C, £400-£40,000; rugs, 18th-20th C, £300-£3,000; textiles, 19th C, £70-£1,500.* PARK: Easy. TEL: 0171 371 9619/9620. SER: Valuations; restorations; buys at auction (Oriental and European carpets, rugs and textiles, tapestries). VAT: Stan/Spec.

The Pine Mine (Crewe-Read Antiques)

100 Wandsworth Bridge Rd., Fulham. SW6 2TF. (D. Crewe-Read). Est. 1971. Open 9.45-5.45, Sat. till 4.30. SIZE: Large. *STOCK: Georgian and Victorian pine, Welsh dressers, farmhouse tables, chests of drawers, boxes and some architectural items.* LOC: From Sloane Sq., down King's Rd., into New King's Rd., left into Wandsworth Bridge Rd. PARK: Outside. TEL: 0171 736 1092. SER: Furniture made from old wood; stripping; export.

Peter Place Antiques

632-636 King's Rd. SW6. Usually open 9.30-5.30. *STOCK: 18th-19th C metalware, decorative items, paintings, folk art.* TEL: 0171 736 9945.

Daphne Rankin and Ian Conn LAPADA

608 King's Rd. SW6 2DX. Est. 1979. Open 10.30-6. SIZE: Medium. *STOCK: Oriental porcelain including Chinese, Japanese, Imari, Cantonese, Satsuma, Nanking, Famille Rose, £500-£25,000.* PARK: Maxwell Rd. adjacent to shop. TEL: 0171 384 1847; fax - 0171 352 0218. SER: Valuations; buys at auction (as stock). FAIRS: Olympia (June). VAT: Stan/Spec.

Reffold

572 King's Rd. SW6 2DY. (K. Jackson Shield & Allen). Est. 1968. Open Mon.-Fri. 10-5. SIZE: Medium. *STOCK: Early furniture, works of art and paintings.* PARK: Easy. TEL: 0171 736 7145; fax - 0171 736 0029. VAT: Spec.

Richardson and Kailas Icons BADA LAPADA

65 Rivermead Court, Ranelagh Gardens. SW6 3RY. (C. Richardson and M. Kailas). Open by appointment. *STOCK: Icons and frescoes.* TEL: 0171 371 0491.

Rogers & Co LAPADA

604 Fulham Rd. SW6 5RP. (M. and C. Rogers). Est. 1971. Open 10-5.30. SIZE: Large. *STOCK: Furniture, 18th-19th C, £100-£3,000; upholstered and boardroom furniture, Tillman dining tables.* LOC: Near Fulham library, Parsons Green Lane. PARK: Side streets. TEL: 0171 731 8504; fax - 0171 610 6040. SER: Valuations; interior design. VAT: Stan/Spec.

George Sherlock Antiques

588 King's Rd. SW6 2DX. Est. 1968. Open 9.30-5.30. SIZE: Large. *STOCK: General antiques, decorative furniture and upholstery, 1650-1900, £20-£15,000.* PARK: Easy. TEL: 0171 736 3955; fax - 0171 371 5179. VAT: Stan/Spec.

Simon Horn Furniture Ltd

117-121 Wandsworth Bridge Rd. SW6 2TP. IDDA. Est. 1981. Open 9.30-5.30, Sun. by appointment. SIZE: Large. *STOCK: Wooden classical style bedframes, £500-£5,000; bedside tables, £150-£650; all 1790-1910 or recent larger copies.* LOC: South from New King's Rd., towards river down Wandsworth Bridge Rd., premises on left at first zebra crossing. PARK: Easy. TEL: 0171 731 1279; fax - 0171 736 3522. SER: Restorations (as stock). FAIRS: Decorex; House & Garden. VAT: Stan.

John Spink BADA

14 Darlan Rd., Fulham. SW6 5BT. Open by appointment. *STOCK: Fine English water-colours and selected oils, 1720-1920.* TEL: 0171 731 8292; fax - 0171 731 6955.

Thornhill Galleries Ltd

76 New King's Rd. SW6 4LT. Est. 1880. Open 10-5, Sat. 10-3. SIZE: Large. *STOCK: English and French marble, stone and wood chimney-pieces, panelled rooms, architectural features and wood carvings, fire grates and fenders, all 17th-19th C; decorative iron interiors and other fire accessories, 17th-20th C.* LOC: Continuation of King's Rd. Coming from Sloane Sq. shop is on right-hand side. PARK: Easy. TEL: 0171 736 5830. SER: Valuations; restorations (architectural items); buys at auction (architectural items). VAT: Stan/Spec.

Through the Looking Glass Ltd

563 King's Rd. SW6 2EB. (J.J.A. and D.A. Pulton). Est. 1966. Open 10-5.30. SIZE: Large. *STOCK: Mirrors, 18th-19th C.* TEL: 0171 736 7799. SER: Restorations. VAT: Spec.

Ferenc Toth

598A King's Rd. SW6 2DX. (F.I. Toth). Est. 1978. Open 9.30-5.30. SIZE: Medium. *STOCK: Mirrors, furniture and decorative items, 18th-19th C.* LOC: Fulham end of King's Rd., Chelsea. PARK: Easy. TEL: 0171 731 2063; fax - same; home - 0171 602 1771. SER: Valuations; buys at auction. VAT: Spec.

Trowbridge Gallery LAPADA

555 King's Rd. SW6 2EB. (M. Trowbridge). Est. 1980. Open 9.30-6, Sat. 10-5.30. SIZE: Large. *STOCK: Decorative prints, 17th-19th C, £35-£3,000.* LOC: Near Christopher Wray

SW6 continued

Lighting. PARK: Easy. TEL: 0171 371 8733. SER: Valuations; restorations; buys at auction (antiquarian books and prints); hand-made frames; decorative mounting. FAIRS: Decorative Antiques and Textiles, Olympia, LAPADA, City of London. VAT: Stan.

Tulissio De Beaumont LAPADA

283 Lillie Rd. SW6 7LL. (David Tulissio and Dominic De Beaumont). Est. 1987. Open 10-6. SIZE: Medium. *STOCK: Chandeliers, wall lights and lamps, 18th-20th C, £100-£1,500; bronzes and sculpture, 19th C, £50-£1,500; general decorative antiques, 18th-20th C, £50-£2,500; furniture, 18th-19th C, £50-£5,000.* LOC: 10 minutes from New King's Road, next to Fulham Cross. PARK: Easy. TEL: 0171 385 0156; fax - 0171 610 0455; mobiles - 0973 186305/176047. VAT: Stan/Spec.

Vaughan

156-160 Wandsworth Bridge Rd. SW6 2UH. (Vaughan Ltd). Est. 1980. Open 10-5. CL: Sat. SIZE: Large. *STOCK: Decorative furniture and objects, 18th-19th C; lamps and light fittings.* PARK: Easy. TEL: 0171 731 3133. VAT: Stan/Spec.

Whiteway and Waldron Ltd

305 Munster Rd., Fulham. SW6 6BJ. (M. Whiteway and G. Kirkland). Est. 1976. Open 10-6, Sat. 11-4. SIZE: Large. *STOCK: Religious antiques including candlesticks, statuary, gothic and carved church woodwork.* LOC: At junction with Lillie Rd. PARK: On forecourt for loading, or Strode Rd. TEL: 0171 381 3195; fax - same. SER: Buys at auction (religious items). VAT: Stan.

Christopher Wray's Lighting Emporium

600 King's Rd. SW6 2DX Est. 1964. Open 10-6. SIZE: Large. *STOCK: Decorative light fittings of 1880s, brass, antiques, decorative objects.* LOC: From Sloane Sq. over Stanley Bridge. PARK: Own. TEL: 0171 736 8434; fax - 0171 731 3507. VAT: Stan.

LONDON SW7

Anglo Persian Carpet Co

6 South Kensington Station Arcade. SW7 2NA. Est. 1910. Open 9.30-6. *STOCK: Carpets and rugs.* TEL: 0171 589 5457. SER: Valuations; restorations (carpets and rugs); cleaning.

Aubrey Brocklehurst BADA

124 Cromwell Rd. SW7 4ET. Est. 1946. Open 9-1 and 2-5.30 (or later by arrangement), Sat. 10-1. SIZE: Medium. *STOCK: English clocks and barometers.* TEL: 0171 373 0319. SER: Valuations; restorations; furniture and clock repairs; buys at auction. VAT: Spec.

SW7 continued

Julie Collino

15 Glendower Place, South Kensington. SW7 3DR. Est. 1971. Open 11-6, Sat. 2-6, Sun. by appointment. *STOCK: Watercolours, oils, etchings, £25-£1,000; china, £25-£500; both 19th-20th C; furniture, £50-£2,000.* LOC: Off Harrington Rd. TEL: 0171 584 4733; home - 0181 568 7440.

M.P. Levene Ltd BADA

5 Thurloe Place. SW7 2RR. Est. 1926. Open 9.30-6. CL: Sat. pm. *STOCK: Silver, old Sheffield plate, scale silver models, various, all prices.* LOC: Few minutes past Harrods near South Kensington station. PARK: Easy. TEL: 0171 589 3755. SER: Valuations; buys at auction. VAT: Stan/Spec.

A. & H. Page

66 Gloucester Rd. SW7 4QT. Est. 1840. Open 9-5.45, Sat. 10-2. *STOCK: Silver, jewellery, watches.* TEL: 0171 584 7349. SER: Valuations; repairs; silversmith.

Period Brass Lights

9a Thurloe Place, Brompton Rd. SW7. (M. Beattie). Est. 1967. *STOCK: Brass reproduction and antique light fittings; suits of armour.* PARK: Meters. TEL: 0171 589 8305.

Christopher Sheppard

No. 302, 3 Sussex Mansions. SW7 3LB. Open by appointment only. *STOCK: Ancient and antique glass.* TEL: 0171 589 2565; fax - 0171 225 1697.

The Taylor Gallery

1 Bolney Gate. SW7 1QW. (J. Taylor). Est. 1986. Open by appointment only. *STOCK: Irish, British and marine paintings, 19th-20th C.* TEL: 0171 581 0253.

The Wyllie Gallery

44 Elvaston Place. SW7 5NP. (J.G. Wyllie). Open by appointment. *STOCK: 19th-20th C marine paintings and etchings, especially works by the Wyllie family.* TEL: 0171 584 6024.

LONDON SW8

Heskia BADA

SW8 5BP. Est. 1877. Open by appointment only. *STOCK: Oriental carpets, rugs and tapestries.* TEL: 0171 373 4489. SER: Valuations; cleaning and repairs.

H.W. Newby (A.J. & M.V. Waller)

SW8 5BP. Est. 1949. Open by appointment. SIZE: Small. *STOCK: Porcelain, faience, pottery, pre-1830, £50-£5,000; English and Continental glass.* Not Stocked: Silver, jewellery. PARK: Easy. TEL: 0181 974 8659; mobile - 0836 294523. SER: Valuations; buys at auction.

SW8 continued

Paul Orssich
2 St. Stephen's Terrace, South Lambeth. SW8 1DH. Open by appointment only. *STOCK: Old, rare and out of print books on Spain and Hispanic studies; old maps of all parts of the world, from £20.* TEL: 0171 787 0030; fax - 0171 735 9612; e-mail - paulo@orsich.com; internet - www.orrssich.com.

LONDON SW10

Alasdair Brown Antiques
24 Chelsea Wharf, 15 Lots Road. SW10 0QJ. Est. 1986. Open 10-6, Sat. and Sun. by appointment. SIZE: Large. *STOCK: Furniture, to £10,000; decorative items, to £5,000; upholstery, lighting and unusual items.* LOC: On the river close to Chelsea Harbour. PARK: Easy. TEL: 0171 351 1477; fax - 0171 351 1577; e-mail - AJCB@alasdair-Brown.Demon.Co.UK. SER: Valuations; restorations; finder service. FAIRS: Olympia (Feb., June and Nov). VAT: Stan/Spec.

Jonathan Clark & Co
18 Park Walk, Chelsea. SW10 0AQ. Open 10-6.30, Sat. by appointment. *STOCK: Modern British and European paintings and sculpture.* TEL: 0171 351 3555; fax - 0171 823 3187.

Collins and Hastie Ltd
5 Park Walk, Chelsea. SW10 0AJ. (Caroline Hastie and Diana Collins). Open 10-6, Sat. by appointment only. SIZE: Medium. *STOCK: British oils - sporting, animal and country scenes, 19th C, £500-£30,000; watercolours - sporting, animal including dogs, 19th-20th C.* LOC: Park Walk runs between King's Rd. and Fulham Rd. PARK: Easy. TEL: 0171 351 4292. SER: Restorations (pictures); buys at auction.VAT: Spec.

The Furniture Cave
533 King's Rd. SW10 0TZ. Est. 1967. Open 10-6 Sun. 11-4. SIZE: Large. LOC: Corner of Lots Rd. PARK: Meters. TEL: 0171 352 4229/5478. SER: Shipping; forwarding. VAT: Stan/Spec. All dealers specialise in antique furniture and decorative objects.

Paul Andrews Antiques
Basement. *English and Continental decorative furniture; sculpture, Old Master paintings, prints and drawings.* TEL: 0171 352 4584; fax - 0171 351 78165.

Brown's Antique Furniture
First Floor. *Library and dining, and decorative objects, from early 18th C.* TEL: 0171 352 2046; fax - 0171 352 3654.

Stuart Duggan
First Floor. *Georgian and Victorian furniture especially 19th-20th C pianos.* TEL: 0171 352 2046; fax - 0171 352 3654.

SW10 continued

Ronald Harman
Ground Floor. *Early 19th C and Regency furniture.* TEL: 0171 352 3775; fax - 0171 352 3759.

Kenneth Harvey **LAPADA**
Ground Floor. *Decorative furniture, mirrors, chandeliers, light fittings.* TEL: 0171 352 8645; fax - 0171 376 3225.

Simon Hatchwell Antiques
Ground Floor. Est. 1961. *English and Continental decorative furniture and objets d'art.* TEL: 0171 351 2344; fax - 0171 351 3520.

MSM Antiques
Basement. *Town and country furniture.* TEL: 0171 352 7305; fax - 0171 351 0480.

Anthony Outred **BADA**
Ground Floor. *English and Continental furniture, 18th-19th C; works of art.* TEL: 0171 352 8840; fax - 0171 376 3627.

Phoenix Trading Company
Furniture including Indian, porcelain, bronzes. TEL: 0171 351 6543; fax - 0171 352 9803.

Mark Ransom Limited
First Floor. *Continental furniture specialising French Empire; antiquarian books, maps and prints.* TEL: 0171 376 7653; fax - 0171 352 3654.

Anthony Redmile
Basement. *Marble resin neo-classical Grand Tour objects.* TEL: 0171 351 3813; fax - 0171 352 8131.

Steve Thomas
First Floor. *Georgian and Victorian furniture: pedestal desks, writing tables, library, bureaux.* TEL: 0171 352 2046; fax - 0171 352 3654.

York Whiting **LAPADA**
Ground Floor. *17th-20th C furniture, English and Continental, paintings, carpets and textiles.* TEL: 0171 376 8530; fax - 0171 352 7994.

Rupert Hastie
5 Park Walk, Chelsea. SW10 0AJ. Open 10-6, Sat. 11-4. *STOCK: Continental and English furniture and works of art, 18th-19th C.* TEL: 0171 351 6820; fax - 0171 351 7929. VAT: Spec.

Hollywood Road Gallery
12 Hollywood Rd., Chelsea. SW10 9HY. (P. and C. Kennaugh). Open 10.30-7, Fri. and Sat. 10.30-3. *STOCK: Oils, watercolours, prints, 19th-20th C, £200-£3,000.* TEL: 0171 351 1973.

Hünersdorff Rare Books
P.O. Box 582. SW10 9RU. ABA. Est. 1969. Open by appointment only. *STOCK: Continental books in rare editions, early printing, science and medicine, illustrated books, Latin America, natural history.* TEL: 0171 373 3899; fax - 0171 370 1244.

SW10 continued

Thomas Kerr Antiques Ltd

at L'Encoignure, 517 King's Rd. SW10 0TX. Est. 1977. Open 10-6. SIZE: Large. *STOCK: French country furniture, paintings, mirrors and decorative items.* TEL: 0171 351 6465; fax - 0171 351 4744. VAT: Stan/Spec.

Lane Fine Art Ltd

8 Drayton Gardens. SW10 9SA. (C. Foley). Open by appointment only. *STOCK: Oil paintings, 1500-1850, principally English, major works by the main artists of the period, £10,000-£1million+.* TEL: 0171 373 3130. VAT: Stan/Spec.

Langford's Marine Antiques BADA LAPADA

The Plaza, 535 King's Rd. SW10 0SZ. (L.L. Langford). Est. 1941. *STOCK: Ships models, antique and marine objects, stationary steam engine models.* TEL: 0171 351 4881; fax - 0171 352 0763; e-mail - Langford@dircon.co.uk. SER: Valuations; restorations. VAT: Stan/Spec.

Stephen Long

348 Fulham Rd. SW10 9UH. Est. 1966. Open 9-1 and 2.15-5.30. CL: Sat. pm. and Sun. except by appointment. SIZE: Small. *STOCK: English pottery, 18th-19th C, to £400; English painted furniture, 18th to early 19th C; toys and games, household and kitchen items, chintz, materials and patchwork, to £500.* Not Stocked: Stripped pine, large brown furniture, fashionable antiques. LOC: From South Kensington along road on right between Ifield Rd. and Billing Rd. PARK: Easy. TEL: 0171 352 8226. VAT: Stan/Spec.

Mallord Street Antiques

Lower Floor, 498 King's Rd. SW10. (Ginny Mejia). Est. 1987. Open 10-5. SIZE: Small. *STOCK: Decorative furniture and objets d'art, 18th-19th C.* LOC: Near World's End. PARK: Easy. TEL: 0171 351 1442; home/fax - 0171 352 9659. SER: Valuations; buys at auction (furniture). FAIRS: Decorative (Mar. and Sept.). VAT: Stan/Spec.

McVeigh & Charpentier

498 King's Rd. SW10. (Maggie Charpentier and Pam McVeigh). Est. 1979. Open 10.30-5.30, Sat. 11-3. SIZE: Medium. *STOCK: Continental furniture, £600-£6,000; objets d'art, £200-£2,000, all 17th-19th C.* LOC: Two blocks down from Earls Court. PARK: In cul de sac adjacent. TEL: 0171 351 1442/352 6084; home - 0171 937 6459. SER: Restorations. FAIRS: Olympia (Nov. and June); Harvey (Sept., Jan. and Mar.). VAT: Spec.

McWhirter

22 Park Walk, Chelsea. SW10 0AQ. (A.J.K. McWhirter). Open 10-6, Sat. by appointment. SIZE: Medium. *STOCK: Unusual furniture,*

SW10 continued

objects and works of art. LOC: Near Fulham Road Cinema. PARK: Easy. TEL: 0171 351 5399; fax - 0171 352 9821. SER: Valuations; buys at auction. VAT: Spec.

Offer Waterman and Co. Fine Art

20 Park Walk. SW10 0AQ. Est. 1986. Open 9-6.30, Sat. 10-4, Sun. by appointment. SIZE: Small. *STOCK: Modern and Contemporary British paintings, 1900-1996, £500-£5,000.* LOC: Off Fulham Rd. PARK: Easy. TEL: 0171 351 0068; fax - 0171 351 2269. SER: Valuations; restorations (as stock); framing; buys at auction (Modern British paintings). FAIRS: Art '98; 20th C British Art; Olympia. VAT: Stan/Spec.

Park Walk Gallery

20 Park Walk, Chelsea. SW10 0AQ. (J. Cooper). Est. 1988. Open 10-6.30, Sat. 11-4. SIZE: Medium. *STOCK: Paintings, £250-£100,000; watercolours, £250-£20,000; drawings, £200-£15,000; all 19th-20th C English and Continental.* LOC: Off Fulham Rd. PARK: Easy. TEL: 0171 351 0410; fax - same. SER: Valuations; restorations. FAIRS: 20th C British, Olympia. VAT: Spec.

Pawsey and Payne BADA

PO Box No. 11830 SW10 9FE. (Hon. N.V.B. and L.N.J. Wallop). Est. 1910. Open by appointment. *STOCK: English oils and watercolours, 18th-19th C.* TEL: 0171 930 4221; fax - 0171 370 0959. SER: Valuations; restorations. VAT: Stan/Spec.

H.W. Poulter and Son

279 Fulham Rd. SW10 9PZ. Est. 1946. Open 9.30-5. CL: Sat. pm. SIZE: Large. *STOCK: English and French marble chimney pieces, grates, fenders, fire-irons, brass, chandeliers.* PARK: Meters. TEL: 0171 352 7268. SER: Restorations (marble work). VAT: Stan/Spec.

Rare Carpets Gallery

496 King's Rd., Chelsea. SW10. Est. 1963. Open 10-6. SIZE: Large. *STOCK: European and Oriental decorative carpets, tapestries.* TEL: 0171 351 3296; fax - 0171 376 4876. SER: Valuations; restorations; cleaning; part exchange. VAT: Stan.

Rendlesham Antiques

498 King's Rd. SW10. Est. 1970. Open 10-6, Sat. 11-2. SIZE: Medium. *STOCK: English and Continental furniture, objets d'art.* TEL: 0171 351 1442.

John Thornton

455 Fulham Rd. SW10 9UZ. Open 10-5.30. *STOCK: Antiquarian books especially theology.* TEL: 0171 352 8810.

LONDON SW11

Antiques and Things

91 Eccles Rd. SW11 1LX. (Mrs V. Crowther). Est. 1986. Open 10-5, Sat. 10-6. SIZE: Medium. *STOCK: Decorative curtain furniture and fittings; linen, lace, textiles, Victorian to Edwardian, £1-£500; china, glass, kitchenalia, 18th-19th C, £5-£500; English and French furniture, decorative items, 19th C, £20-£2,000.* LOC: Off Lavender Hill, near Clapham junction. TEL: 0171 350 0597.

John Bloxham (Fine Art) Ltd

117 St John's Hill, Battersea. SW11 1SZ. Est. 1978. Open Tues.-Sat. 10-5, other times by appointment. SIZE: Medium. *STOCK: Watercolours and oils, 19th-20th C, £200-£3,000; decorative and antiquarian prints, 18th-20th C, £20-£500.* LOC: Just off South Circular, near Wandsworth Common. PARK: Easy. TEL: 0171 924 7500 (ansaphone). SER: Valuations; restorations (works on paper and oils, frames); buys at auction (as stock); conservation mounting and framing. VAT: Stan.

Eccles Road Antiques

60 Eccles Rd., Battersea. SW11. (H. Rix). Open 10-5. *STOCK: General antiques, pine furniture and smalls.* TEL: 0171 228 1638.

SW11 continued

Keith Gretton Old Advertising

Unit 14, Northcote Rd. Antiques Market, 155A Northcote Rd., Battersea. SW11 6QB. Open 10-6, Sun. 12-5. *STOCK: Advertising, signs, bottles, packaging and display.* LOC: Near Clapham Junction. PARK: Easy. TEL: 0171 228 6850; home - 0171 228 0741. SER: Valuations.

Northcote Road Antiques Market

155A Northcote Rd., Battersea. SW11 6QB. (H. Rix). Open 10-6, Sun. 12-5. SIZE: 30 dealers. *STOCK: Victoriana and Art Deco collectables, silver, glass, furniture, lighting, textiles, jewellery, old advertising.* TEL: 0171 228 6850.

Overmantels

66 Battersea Bridge Rd. SW11 3AG. (Seth Taylor). BCFA. Est. 1980. Open 9.30-5.30. SIZE: Medium. *STOCK: English giltwood mirrors, £400-£3,000; French giltwood mirrors, £700-£3,000; both 18th-19th C. Furniture, 19th C, £200-£2,000.* LOC: 200m south of Battersea Bridge. PARK: Nearby. TEL: 0171 223 8151; fax - 0171 924 2283. SER: Valuations; restorations (gesso work and gilding). VAT: Stan/Spec.

SW11 continued

Robert Young Antiques

68 Battersea Bridge Rd. SW11 3AE. Est. 1974. Open 10-6, Sat. 10-5. CL: Mon. SIZE: Medium. *STOCK: English oak and country furniture, 17th-18th C, £500-£20,000; English and European treen and objects of folk art, £20-£10,000; English and European provincial pottery and metalwork, £20-£2,500.* LOC: Turn off King's Rd. or Chelsea Embankment into Beaufort St., cross over Battersea Bridge Rd., 9th shop on right. PARK: Opposite in side street. TEL: 0171 228 7847; fax - 0171 585 0489. SER: Valuations; buys at auction (treen and country furniture). FAIRS: Olympia, Chelsea. VAT: Stan/Spec.

LONDON SW12

The Kilim Warehouse Ltd

28A Pickets St. SW12 8QB.(J. Luczyc-Wyhowska). Est. 1982. Open 10-5.30, Sat. 10-4. SIZE: Medium. *STOCK: Kilims from Eastern Europe, Asia Minor and beyond, £50-£8,000.* LOC: Near Clapham South tube station and Nightingale Lane. PARK: Easy. TEL: 0181 675 3122; fax - 0181 675 8494; internet - http://www.kilim-warehouse.co.uk/kilim/; e-mail - info@kilim-warehouse.co.uk. SER: Restorations; cleaning. VAT: Stan.

Twentieth Century

SW12 2HW. (M. Taylor). Est. 1986. By appointment only. *STOCK: Art Deco, Art Nouveau, Arts and Crafts, decorative arts items, £50-£500.* PARK: Easy. TEL: 0181 675 6351; fax - same; e-mail - nbserve@dircon.co.uk. FAIRS: Battersea Art Deco; Kensington Decorative Arts; Loughborough Art Deco; Manchester; Birmingham. VAT: Stan.

LONDON SW13

Alton Gallery

2a Suffolk Rd., Barnes. SW13 9PH. Open by appointment only. *STOCK: 19th-20th C British art.* TEL: 0181 748 0606. SER: Framing.

Christine Bridge LAPADA

78 Castelnau, Barnes. SW13 9EX. Est. 1972. Open anytime by appointment only. SIZE: Medium. *STOCK: Glass - 18th C collectors and 19th C coloured, engraved and decorative, £50-£15,000; small decorative items - papier mâché, bronzes, needlework, ceramics.* LOC: Main road from Hammersmith Bridge. PARK: Easy. TEL: 0181 741 5501; fax - same; mobile - 0831 126668; e-mail - christine@bridge-antiques.com; internet - http://www.bridge-antiques.com/4GLASS/. SER: Valuations; restorations (glass - cutting, polishing, declouding); buys at auction; shipping. FAIRS: Olympia; LAPADA; Chelsea; West London; Brussels; Tokyo; Melbourne; Sydney; Singapore; Santa Monica. VAT: Stan/Spec.

SW13 continued

Campion

71 White Hart Lane, Barnes. SW13 0PP. (J. Richards). Est. 1983. Open 10-1 and 2-5.30. SIZE: Small. *STOCK: Interesting lights, kilims, small furniture, coffee tables.* LOC: Along river from Barnes High St., turn left at White Hart public house. PARK: Easy. TEL: 0181 878 6688; home - same.

Classic Fabrics with Robin Haydock

6 The Broadway, White Hart Lane, Barnes. SW13 0NY. Open by appointment. *STOCK: Decorative antiques and 18th C textiles.* TEL: 0181 392 1655.

Simon Coleman Antiques

40 White Hart Lane, Barnes. SW13. Est. 1974. SIZE: Large. *STOCK: Country furniture, oak, fruitwood, pine, French and English farm tables, 18th-19th C.* PARK: Easy. TEL: 0181 878 5037. VAT: Stan/Spec.

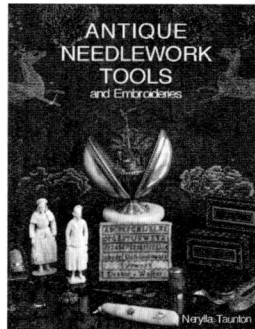

SW13 continued

The Dining Room Shop

62/64 White Hart Lane, Barnes. SW13 0PZ. (K. Dyson). Est. 1985. Open 10-5.30, Sun. by appointment. SIZE: Medium. *STOCK: Formal and country dining room furniture, 18th-19th C; glasses, china especially dinner services; cutlery, damask and lace table linen, 19th C; associated small and decorative items.* LOC: Near Barnes railway bridge, turning opposite White Hart public house. PARK: Easy. TEL: 0181 878 1020; home - 0181 876 5212. SER: Valuations; restorations; finder; interior decorating. VAT: Stan/Spec.

Joy McDonald

50 Station Rd., Barnes. SW13 0LP. Resident. Est. 1966. SIZE: Small. *STOCK: Mirrors, especially 19th C French gilt; furniture, 18th-19th C fruitwood, oak; decorative items; some china and glass.* PARK: Easy. TEL: 0181 876 6184.

New Grafton Gallery

49 Church Rd., Barnes. SW13 9HH. (D. Wolfers). Est. 1968. Open 10-5.30. CL: Mon. SIZE: Medium. *STOCK: British paintings and drawings, £150-£3,000.* LOC: Off Castelnau which runs from Hammersmith Bridge. PARK: Easy. TEL: 0181 748 8850; home - 0181 876 6294. SER: Valuations; restorations; buys at auction. VAT: Stan/Spec.

SW13 continued

Remember When

6 and 7 Rocks Lane, Barnes. SW13 0DB. Est. 1973. Open 9.30-7 including Sun. *STOCK: Pine furniture.* TEL: 0181 878 2817; fax - 0181 876 6934.

Jeremy Seale Antiques

56 White Hart Lane, Barnes. SW13 0PZ. Est. 1988. Open 10-1 and 2-5.30, Sat. 10-5.30, evenings by appointment. SIZE: Medium. *STOCK: Furniture, 18th-19th C, £300-£6,000; decorative items, 19th C; pictures and prints, 18th-19th C; both £50-£500.* LOC: From M3 into London, just off A316 (sign to Mortlake and Barnes), White Hart Lane on right on Barnes approach. PARK: Easy. TEL: 0181 876 1041; fax - 0181 296 0717; mobile - 0956 457795. SER: Finder; valuations; interior design consultant. VAT: Stan/Spec.

Tobias and The Angel

68 White Hart Lane, Barnes. SW13 0PZ. (A. Hughes). Est. 1985. Open 10-6. SIZE: Large. *STOCK: Quilts, textiles, furniture, country and painted beds, decorative objects, from 1800.* LOC: Parallel to Barnes High St. PARK: Easy. TEL: 0181 878 8902; home - 01206 391003. SER: Interior design. VAT: Stan/Spec.

LONDON SW14

The Arts & Crafts Furniture Co Ltd

49 Sheen Lane, East Sheen. SW14 4AB. (Patrick Rogers). Est. 1985. Medium. *STOCK: Arts and Crafts furniture and effects, Gothic and Aesthetic movement, 1850-1950, £500-£5,000.* LOC: Sheen Lane is off Upper Richmond Road (South Circular A205). PARK: Nearby. TEL: 0181 876 6544; fax - same. SER: Valuations; restorations including French polishing and upholstery; buys at auction. VAT: Spec.

Paul Foster's Bookshop

119 Sheen Lane, East Sheen. SW14 8AE. ABA, PBFA. Est. 1983. Open 10.30-6. SIZE: Medium. *STOCK: Books - antiquarian, 17th-19th C, £100-£1,000; out of print, 19th-20th C, £1-£500; general, 50p-£100.* LOC: 20 yards from South Circular. PARK: Easy. TEL: 0181 876 7424; fax - same. FAIRS: Hotel Russell, PBFA monthly.

Yesterday's Antiques

315 Upper Richmond Rd. West. SW14 8QR. (H. Rau). Open 9.30-6, Sun. 9.30-5. *STOCK: Old pine and country furniture.* TEL: 0181 876 7536.

LONDON SW15

R.A. Barnes Antiques LAPADA

26 Lower Richmond Rd., Putney. SW15. Open 10-5. CL: Sat. SIZE: Large. *STOCK: English, Oriental and Continental porcelain, antiques and collectables; Wedgwood, ironstone, china, brass, copper, 19th C; Bohemian and art glass, Regency, Victorian and some 18th C small furniture, primitive paintings.* TEL: 0181 789 3371. VAT: Stan/Spec.

The Clock Clinic Ltd LAPADA

85 Lower Richmond Rd., Putney. SW15 1EU. (R.S. Pedler). FBHI. Est. 1971. Open 9-6, Sat. 9-1. CL: Mon. *STOCK: Clocks and barometers.* TEL: 0181 788 1407; fax - 0181 780 2838. SER: Valuations; restorations (as stock); buys at auction. VAT: Stan/Spec.

Han-Shan Tang Books

Unit 3 Ashburton Centre, 276 Cortis Rd. SW15 3AY. ABA. Open by appointment only. *STOCK: Second-hand and antiquarian books and periodicals on Chinese, Japanese, Korean and Central Asian art and culture.* TEL: 0181 788 4464; fax - 0181 780 1565; e-mail - hst@hanshan.com; internet - http://www. hanshan.com/.

Harwood Antiques

24 Lower Richmond Rd., Putney. SW15 1JP. (G. M. Harwood). Est. 1962. SIZE: Medium. *STOCK: Decorative items and furniture, £150-£1,500; textiles, £30-£500; mirrors, oils, watercolours and prints, £100-£550; all 18th-19th C.* LOC: Continuation of King's Rd., over Putney Bridge. PARK: Nearby. TEL: 0181 788 7444.

SW15 continued

Jorgen Antiques

40 Lower Richmond Rd., Putney. SW15 1JP. (A.J. Dolleris). Est. 1960. Open 11-5. CL: Mon. and Sat. SIZE: Large. *STOCK: English and Continental furniture, 18th to early 19th C, £50-£5,000.* LOC: Between Putney Bridge and Putney Common. PARK: Easy. TEL: 0181 789 7329. VAT: Spec.

Thornhill Galleries Ltd. in association with A. & R. Dockerill Ltd

Rear of 78 Deodar Rd., Putney. SW15 2NJ. Est. 1880. Open 9-5.15, Sat. 10-12.30. SIZE: Large. *STOCK: English and French period panelling, chimneypieces in wood, marble and stone; architectural items, wood carvings, 17th-19th C firegrates and fenders, fireplace accessories and iron interiors.* LOC: Off Putney Bridge Rd. PARK: Easy. TEL: 0181 874 2101/5669. SER: Valuations; restorations (architectural items); buys at auction (architectural items). VAT: Stan/Spec.

LONDON SW16

H.C. Baxter and Sons BADA LAPADA

40 Drewstead Rd. SW16 1AB. (T.J., J. and G.J Baxter). Est. 1928. Open Wed. and Thurs. 8.30-5.15, or by appointment. SIZE: Medium. *STOCK: English furniture, 1730-1830, £1,000-£35,000.* LOC: Near Streatham Hill station. PARK: Easy. TEL: 0181 769 5869/5969; fax - 0181 769 0898.

A. and J. Fowle

542 Streatham High Rd. SW16 3QF. Est. 1962. Open 9.30-7. SIZE: Large. *STOCK: General antiques, Victorian and Edwardian furniture.* LOC: From London take A23 towards Brighton. PARK: Easy. TEL: 0181 764 2896.

Rapscallion Antiques Ltd

25 Shrubbery Rd., Streatham. SW16 2AS. (Mrs P. Barry). Open 10-5. CL: Mon. and Thurs. *STOCK: General antiques and bric-a-brac.* TEL: 0181 769 8078.

William Reeves Bookseller Ltd

1a Norbury Crescent. SW16 4JR Est. 1871. Open by appointment. SIZE: Medium. *STOCK: Books about music, 1800-1970, £1-£100.* LOC: From station under railway bridge, first left. PARK: Easy. TEL: 0181 764 2108.

LONDON SW17

A & C International

Knapton Mews, 1F Seely Rd. SW17 9RJ. Open 9-6. CL: All day Mon. and Wed. pm. except by appointment. *STOCK: Oils, watercolours, etchings, limited edition prints, 19th-20th C.* TEL: 0181 672 8749/682 3361; fax - 0181 682 2858.

SW17 continued

Ted Few
97 Drakefield Rd. SW17 8RS. Resident. Est. 1975. Open by appointment. SIZE: Medium. *STOCK: Paintings and sculpture, 1700-1940, £500-£5,000.* LOC: 5 mins. walk from Tooting Bec underground station. TEL: 0181 767 2314. SER: Valuations; buys at auction. VAT: Spec.

LONDON SW18

Mr Wandle's Workshop
202 Garratt Lane, Wandsworth. SW18 4ED. (S. Zoil). Open 9-5.30. *STOCK: Victorian and Edwardian fireplaces and surrounds especially cast iron.* TEL: 0181 870 5873. SER: Shot-blasting.

Woodentops Country Furniture
537/539 Garratt Lane, Earlsfield. SW18 4SR. (C. R. Smith). Est. 1987. Open 10-7, Sun. 10.30-5. SIZE: Large. *STOCK: Pine furniture, mainly reproduction.* LOC: Main road between Wandsworth and Tooting. PARK: Easy. TEL: 0181 947 6124. SER: Restorations (pine). VAT: Stan.

LONDON SW19

Acanthus Antiques
3 The Brambles, Woodside, Wimbledon. SW19 7AY. (Isabella von Lobkowitz and Jerry Pol). Est. 1983. Open by appointment. SIZE: Small. *STOCK: Small furniture and general antiques, Arts and Crafts, Art Nouveau, £20-£2,000.* TEL: 0181 946 1943.

Adams Room Antiques LAPADA
18-20 Ridgway, Wimbledon Village. SW19 4LN. Est. 1971. Open 10-5. SIZE: Large. *STOCK: 18th-19th C English and French furniture especially dining; decorative Regency chairs, silver.* LOC: 4 miles from King's Rd., Chelsea; 1 mile off Kingston by-pass, M3. TEL: 0181 946 7047/947 4784; fax - 0181 946 7476. SER: Export orders arranged. VAT: Spec.

Allegra's Lighthouse Antiques LAPADA
75-77 Ridgway, Wimbledon Village. SW19 4ST. (Mrs E. Kingston). Est. 1969. Open 12-5.30, Sat. 10-5.30. *STOCK: Antique lighting, brass and glass chandeliers, sets of wall lights, table lights; period mirrors; 19th C furniture, £600-£6,000.* PARK: Easy. TEL: 0181 946 2050.

Chelsea Bric-a-Brac Shop Ltd
16 Hartfield Rd., Wimbledon. SW19 3TA. (P. and C. Wirth). Est. 1960. Open 10-5 or by appointment. CL: Wed. SIZE: Medium. *STOCK: Furniture - antique, Victorian, pine and shipping, 1800-1930, £20-£5,000; brass, copper, steel, £1-£500; bric-a-brac, £1-£250; all from Victorian.* Not Stocked: Jewellery, weapons. LOC: Left from Wimbledon station, first turning on right, shop 100yds. on left. PARK: 100yds. TEL: 0181 946 6894; home - 0181 542 5509. SER: Restorations (wood and upholstery); Continental export. VAT: Stan.

SW19 continued

Clunes Antiques
9 West Place, Wimbledon Common. SW19 4UH. Est. 1973. Open 10-4.30. CL: Mon. *STOCK: General small and country antiques, Staffordshire figures, theatrical ephemera.* TEL: 0181 946 1643.

Coromandel
P.O Box 9772. SW19 3ZG. (P. Lang and B. Leigh). Resident. Open at any time by appointment. SIZE: Small. *STOCK: Boxes and table cabinets veneered in ivory, horn or tortoiseshell, sadeli (micro-mosaic work) or from solid exotic woods (sandalwood, amboyna, ebony, coromandel, etc) - Anglo-Indian, Vizagapatam, Indo-Portuguese, Dutch East Indies, Sri Lanka, 17th-19th C, £250-£5,000.* PARK: Easy. TEL: 0181 543 9115; fax - 0181 543 6255.

The David Curzon Gallery
35 Church Rd., Wimbledon Village. SW19. Open 10-6. CL: Mon. SIZE: Medium. *STOCK: Paintings and watercolours, from 1900, £350-£10,000.* LOC: 7 min. walk from Wimbledon Underground/BR. PARK: Reasonable. TEL: 0181 944 6098. VAT: Spec.

Richard Maryan and Daughters
177 Merton Rd. SW19 1EE. Est. 1966. Open 10-5. CL: Wed. pm. and Mon. SIZE: Large. *STOCK: General antiques.* PARK: Reasonable. TEL: 0181 542 5846.

Mark J. West - Cobb Antiques Ltd
BADA

39B High St., Wimbledon Village. SW19 5BY. Open 10-5.30, other times by appointment. SIZE: Large. *STOCK: Antique glass, £5-£5,000.* PARK: Easy. TEL: 0181 946 2811/540 7982. SER: Valuations; buys at auction. FAIRS: Olympia; Grosvenor House.

LONDON SW20

W.G.T. Burne (Antique Glass) Ltd
BADA

PO Box 9465. (Formerly of Elystan St.) SW20 9ZD. (Mrs G. and A.T.G. Burne). Est. 1936. *STOCK: English and Irish glassware, Georgian and Victorian decanters; chandeliers, candelabra and lustres.* TEL: 0181 543 6319 (answerphone); fax - same; mobile - 0374 725834. SER: Valuations; restorations. VAT: Stan/Spec.

SW20 continued

Hamilton's Corner
407A Kingston Rd. SW20 8JS. (P. and W Hamilton). Est. 1972. Open 9.30-5.30. CL: Wed. SIZE: Medium. *STOCK: Edwardian furniture; stripped pine, shipping goods, £25-£500.* LOC: From A3 at New Malden follow A298 Merton for 1 mile. PARK: Easy. TEL: 0181 540 1744. VAT: Stan.

Kensington Sporting Paintings Ltd
2 The Downs, Wimbledon. SW20 8HN. (J.S. Bates). Open by appointment only. *STOCK: Oil paintings especially sporting; animalier bronzes, 19th C.* TEL: 0181 947 7772. SER: Valuations; restorations.

LONDON SE1

Antique Trade Warehouse
155 Tower Bridge Rd., Bermondsey. SE1 3LW. (Margaret McCarthy). Est. 1983. Open 9.30-5. SIZE: Warehouse. *STOCK: General antiques and shipping goods.* PARK: Easy. SER: Valuations.

Antique Warehouse
175D Bermondsey St., Newhams Row. SE1 3UW. (Waterloo Trading Co. and Micallef Antiques). Open Mon.-Fri. 8-6. SIZE: Large. *STOCK: Victorian, Edwardian and shipping furniture.* TEL: 0171 357 7168; fax - 0171 357 7179. SER: Robert Boys Shipping; packing.

The Antiques Pavilion
175 Bermondsey St. SE1 3UW. (Capital City Investments Ltd). Est. 1966. Open 9.30-6, Fri. 7-6, Sat. 9-2. SIZE: Large. *STOCK: Furniture, Georgian to 1930's, £25-£25,000.* LOC: Near Bermondsey Market, close to Tower Bridge. PARK: Easy. TEL: 0171 403 2021. SER: Restorations (re-leathering, French polishing); buys at auction. VAT: Stan.

Nigel A. Bartlett
63 St. Thomas St. SE1 3QX. Open 9.30-5.30. CL: Sat. *STOCK: Marble, pine and stone chimney pieces.* TEL: 0171 378 7895/6; fax - 0171 378 0388.

Bermondsey Antique Traders LAPADA
158 Bermondsey St. SE1. (R. Bush and B. Hawkins). Open 9.30-5. SIZE: Large. *STOCK: Furniture.* TEL: 0171 378 1000; fax - same.

Bermondsey Antiques Market
Corner of Long Lane and Bermondsey St. SE1. (Atlantic Antiques Centres Ltd). Est. 1959. Open Fri. 5 am-2 pm. *STOCK: Wide range of general antiques and collectables including specialist dealers in most fields especially silver.* LOC: Borough, Tower Hill or London Bridge tube stations. TEL: Enquiries - 0171 351 5353; fax - 0171 351 5350. SER: Valuations; book binding.

SE1 continued

Victor Burness Antiques and Scientific Instruments
241 Long Lane, Bermondsey. SE1 4PR. (V.G. Burness). Est. 1975. Open Fri. 6am-1pm or by appointment. SIZE: Small. *STOCK: Scientific instruments, marine items, 19th C, £20-£1,500.* PARK: Easy. TEL: Home - 01732 454591. SER: Valuations. FAIRS: Portman Hotel.

Euro Antiques Warehouse
Royal Oak Yard, Bermondsey St. SE1. (Ian Wilson). Est. 1975. Open 9-6, Fri. 7-6. SIZE: Warehouse. *STOCK: Furniture including antique, Victorian, Edwardian and 1930's, £60-£6,000.* PARK: Own. TEL: 0171 403 0765; home - 01732 885527. VAT: Stan.

The Old Cinema Antique Warehouse
LAPADA

157 Tower Bridge Rd., Bermondsey. SE1 3LW. Open 10-6, Sun. 12-5. SIZE: Very large. *STOCK: Furniture - antique, architectural, garden and shop including replica, £100-£20,000.* PARK: Easy. TEL: 0171 407 5371; fax - 0171 403 0359; internet - www.antiques-uk.co.uk. VAT: Stan/Spec.

Oola Boola Antiques London
166 Tower Bridge Rd. SE1 3LS. (R. and S. Scales). Est. 1968. Open 9-5.30, Sat.10-5. SIZE: Large. *STOCK: Furniture, £5-£3,000; mahogany, oak, some walnut, Victorian, Arts & Crafts, Art Nouveau, Edwardian, Art Deco and shipping goods.* TEL: 0171 403 0794; home - 0181 693 5050; fax - 0171 403 8405.

Penny Farthing Antiques
177 Bermondsey St. SE1. Est. 1976. Open 10-5. CL: Sat. SIZE: Medium. *STOCK: Furniture including shipping, £25-£1,000; longcase clocks, £200-£1,000; general small antiques and shipping items, £5-£200.* LOC: 5 mins. from Tower Bridge. PARK: Usually easy. TEL: 0171 407 5171. VAT: Stan.

Tower Bridge Antiques
159/161 Tower Bridge Rd. SE1 3LW. Open 9-5.30, Sat. 10.30-6, Sun. 11-5. SIZE: Large. *STOCK: Victorian, Georgian and Edwardian furniture, shipping goods.* TEL: 0171 403 3660. VAT: Stan.

Giovanni Viventi
173 Bermondsey St. SE1 3UW. Est. 1976. Open 9.30-6.30. CL: Sat. and Sun. except by appointment. SIZE: Large. *STOCK: Furniture and general antiques.* TEL: 0171 407 2566/403 0022; fax - 0171 403 6808.

George S. Wissinger Antiques
166 Bermondsey St. SE1 3TQ. Open 7-5.30. CL: Sat. SIZE: Large. *STOCK: Furniture and paintings.* TEL: 0171 407 5795; fax - same.

LONDON SE3

Michael Silverman

PO Box 350. SE3 0LZ. *STOCK: Manuscripts, autograph letters, historical documents.* TEL: 0181 319 4452; fax - 0181 856 6006. SER: Catalogue available. *Postal Only.*

Vale Stamps and Antiques

21 Tranquil Vale, Blackheath. SE3 0BU. (H.J. and R.P. Varnham). Est. 1952. Open 10-5.30. CL: Thurs. SIZE: Small. *STOCK: Georgian and Victorian jewellery, £25-£500.* LOC: Village centre, 100yds. from station. PARK: Nearby. TEL: 0181 852 9817. SER: Valuations. VAT: Stan/Spec.

Wallace Antiques Ltd

56 Tranquil Vale, Blackheath. SE3 0BD. Open 9.30-5.30. *STOCK: Furniture including reproduction.* TEL: 0181 852 2647.

LONDON SE5

Franklin's Camberwell Antiques Market

161 Camberwell Rd. SE5. (R. Franklin). Est. 1968. Open 10-6, Sun. 1-6. SIZE: Large - five floors. *STOCK: French and English mirrors and beds, furniture, lighting, prints, architectural and garden items.* LOC: 1 mile from Elephant and Castle via Walworth Rd. PARK: 50yds. behind building, outside premises on Sunday. TEL: 0171 703 8089. VAT: Stan/Spec.

Robert E. Hirschhorn BADA

SE5 8JA. Est. 1979. Open by appointment. *STOCK: Unusual English and Continental Country furniture, mainly oak, walnut and fruitwood, and interesting objects, 18th C and earlier.* TEL: 0171 703 7443; mobile - 0831 405937. FAIRS: BADA (March); Olympia (June and Nov.); Chelsea (Sept.); Grosvenor House (June).

LONDON SE6

Wilkinson plc

5 Catford Hill. SE6 4NU. Est. 1947. Open 9-5. CL: Sat. SIZE: Medium. *STOCK: Glass especially chandeliers, 18th C and reproduction, art metal work.* LOC: Opposite Catford Bridge railway station. Entrance through Wickes D.I.Y. car park. PARK: Easy. TEL: 0181 314 1080. SER: Restorations and repairs (glass, metalwork).

LONDON SE7

Ward Antiques

267 Woolwich Rd., Charlton. SE7. (T. and M. Ward). Est. 1981. Open 9.30-5.30, Sun. 10-2. SIZE: Medium. *STOCK: Victorian fireplaces, Victorian and Edwardian furniture, £50-£1,000.* LOC: From A102 M take Woolwich/Woolwich ferry turn, 100yds. from roundabout, immediately under railway bridge across the road. PARK: Easy. TEL: 0181 305 0963; home - 0181 698 0771.

SE7 continued

LONDON SE8

Antique Warehouse

9-14 Deptford Broadway. SE8 4PA. Est. 1986. Open 10-6, Sun. 11-4. SIZE: Large. *STOCK: Fine furniture, 1750 to 20th C; sofas, chairs, mirrors and oleographs.* TEL: 0181 691 3062. VAT: Stan.

LONDON SE9

Cobwebs

73 Avery Hill Rd., New Eltham. SE9 2BJ. (Martin Baker). Est. 1991. Open 10-5.30, Sun. 10-2. SIZE: Medium - 6 dealers. *STOCK: Furniture, smalls books, Oriental items, clocks.* LOC: Between A20 and A2 and 5 minutes from New Eltham BR station. PARK: Easy. TEL: 0181 850 5611. SER: Valuations; restorations (china).

The Fireplace

257 High St., Eltham. SE9 1TY. (A. Clark). Est. 1978. Open daily. SIZE: Medium. *STOCK: Fireplaces, 19th-20th C, £100-£1,000.* PARK: Adjacent side streets. TEL: 0181 850 4887. SER: Restorations (fireplaces). VAT: Stan.

R.E. Rose FBHI

731 Sidcup Rd., Eltham. SE9 3SA. Est. 1976. Open 9-5. CL: Thurs. SIZE: Small. *STOCK: Clocks and barometers, 1750-1930, £50-£5,000.* LOC: A20 from London, shop on left just past fiveways traffic lights at Green Lane. PARK: Easy. TEL: 0181 859 4754. SER: Restorations (clocks and barometers); spare parts for antique clocks and barometers. VAT: Stan/Spec.

LONDON SE10

Creek Antiques

23 South St., Greenwich. SE10 8NW. Est. 1986. Open 11-5, appointment advisable Mon. and Tues. SIZE: Small. *STOCK: Jewellery and silver, from Victorian, £5-£500.* LOC: 200 yards from British Rail station. PARK: Easy. TEL: 0181 293 5721; mobile - 0378 427521.

Greenwich Antiques Market

Greenwich High Rd. SE10. Est. 1972. Open Sun. 7.30-4.30, and Sat. (June-Sept.). SIZE: 80 stalls. *STOCK: General antiques and bric-a-brac.* LOC: Almost opposite railway station. PARK: Adjacent.

The Greenwich Gallery

9 Nevada St. SE10 9JL. (R.F. Moy). Est. 1965. Open 10-5.30 including Sun. *STOCK: Mainly English oil paintings and watercolours, 18th C to 1950.* TEL: 0181 305 1666. SER: Restorations; framing; exhibitions. VAT: Spec.

SE10 continued

The Junk Shop

9 Greenwich South St. SE10 8NW. (T.B. de C. Moy). Est. 1985. Open 10-5.30 including Sun. SIZE: Large. *STOCK: Larger antique and decorative items, 18th C to 1950s; furniture, architectural antiques, bric-a-brac.* LOC: A202. From London follow A2, then turn left at Deptford - or follow riverside road from Tower Bridge. PARK: Meters. TEL: 0181 305 1666, ext. 25. SER: Restorations (furniture). VAT: Stan/Spec.

Lamont Antiques Ltd LAPADA

Tunnel Avenue Antique Warehouse, Tunnel Avenue Trading Estate, Greenwich. SE10. (N. Lamont and F. Llewellyn). Open 9-5.30. CL: Sat. SIZE: Large. *STOCK: Architectural fixtures and fittings, bars, stained glass, pub mirrors and signs, shipping furniture, £5-£25,000.* PARK: Own. TEL: 0181 305 2230; fax - 0181 305 1805. SER: Container packing.

Peter Laurie Antiques

28 Greenwich Church St. SE10 9BQ. Open 10-5 including Sun. CL: Fri. am. *STOCK: Nautical items, navigational instruments, maritime curiosities, weapons and photographic items.* TEL: 0181 853 5777.

SE10 continued

The Warwick Leadlay Gallery

5 Nelson Rd., Greenwich. SE10 9JB. Est. 1974. Open 9.30-5.30, Sun. and Bank Holidays 11-5.30. SIZE: Large. *STOCK: Antiquarian prints, maps, illustrated books and Nelsoniana, 17th-20th C.* LOC: 2 mins. walk from Cutty Sark. PARK: Nearby. TEL: 0181 858 0317; fax - 0181 853 1773; home - 0181 293 5032. SER: Valuations; restorations, cleaning, colouring, mounting, framing. VAT: Stan.

Main Street Antiques

24 Woolwich Rd. SE10 0JU. (B. Sessacar). Open 10-6 including Sun. CL: Thurs. *STOCK: Victorian pine and fireplaces.* TEL: 0181 305 1971.

Relcy Antiques

9 Nelson Rd., Greenwich. SE10. (R. Challis). Est. 1958. Open 10-6. CL: Sun. except by appointment. SIZE: Large. *STOCK: English furniture, especially bureaux and bookcases, £50-£15,000; English and Continental pictures, especially marine and sporting, £20-£5,000; instruments and marine items, ships' heads, sextants, telescopes, models, £20-£15,000; all 18th-19th C.* Not Stocked: Reproduction and Art Deco. LOC: 3/4 mile off A2 towards River Thames. TEL: 0181 858 2812. SER: Valuations, restorations (furniture and pictures); buys at auction (Georgian and Victorian furniture, pictures). VAT: Stan/Spec.

SE10 continued

Rogers Turner Books
22 Nelson Rd., Greenwich. SE10 9JB. Est. 1975. Open Thurs.-Sun. 10-6. *STOCK: Antiquarian books especially on clocks and scientific instruments.* TEL: 0181 853 5271; fax - same; Paris - 0033 13912 1191. SER: Buys at auction (British and European); catalogues available.

Spread Eagle Antiques
8 Nevada St. SE10 9JL. (R.F. Moy). Est. 1954. Open 10-5.30 including Sun. SIZE: Large. *STOCK: Books, period costume, curios, china, bric-a-brac, prints, postcards.* Not Stocked: Furniture. LOC: A202. From London follow A2, then turn left at Deptford - or follow riverside road from Tower Bridge. PARK: Easy. TEL: 0181 305 1666. SER: Valuations; restorations (furniture, china, pictures). VAT: Stan/Spec.

Spread Eagle Antiques
1 Stockwell St. SE10 9JL. (R.F. Moy). Est. 1954. Open 10-5.30 including Sun. SIZE: Large. *STOCK: Furniture, pictures and decorative items, 18th-19th C.* PARK: Easy. TEL: 0181 305 1666; home - 0181 692 1618. SER: Valuations; restorations (pictures, furniture). VAT: Stan/Spec.

Robert Whitfield Antiques LAPADA
Tunnel Avenue Antique Warehouse, Tunnel Avenue Trading Estate, Greenwich. SE10 0QH. Open 10-5. CL: Sat. *STOCK: Edwardian, Victorian and secondhand furniture, especially bentwood chairs.* TEL: 0181 305 2230; fax - 0181 305 1805. SER: Container packing.

LONDON SE13

Robert Morley and Co Ltd BADA
34 Engate St. SE13 7HA. Est. 1881. Open 9-5. *STOCK: Pianos, harpsichords, clavichords, spinets, virginals.* PARK: Own. TEL: 0181 318 5838; fax - 0181 297 0720. SER: Restorations (musical instruments). VAT: Stan.

LONDON SE15

Peter Allen Antiques Ltd. World Wide Antique Exporters LAPADA
17-17a Nunhead Green, Peckham. SE15 3QQ. Est. 1966. Open 8-4. CL: Sat. SIZE: Large. *STOCK: Fine Victorian furniture.* TEL: 0171 732 1968.

A. Fagiani
30 Wagner St. SE15. Est. 1965. Open 8-1 and 2-6, Sat. 8-1. *STOCK: Bookcases, pedestal desks.* LOC: Off Kent Rd. and Ilderton Rd. TEL: 0171 732 7188. SER: Valuations; restorations (furniture); French polishing. VAT: Stan.

LONDON SE20

Bearly Trading Co
202 High St., Penge. SE20 7QB. (Brian Aust). Open 9-5.30. CL: Mon. *STOCK: Old bears and toys, artists' bears, furniture, decorative items.* LOC: Opposite Kent House Rd., Beckenham, Kent. TEL: 0181 659 0500; fax - 0181 460 3166.

LONDON SE21

Acorn Antiques
111 Rosendale Rd., West Dulwich. SE21 8EZ. (Mrs G. Kingham). Open 10-6, Sat. 10-5.30. *STOCK: Jewellery, china, glass, silver and plate, fire irons and fenders.* TEL: 0181 761 3349.

LONDON SE23

Oddiquities
61 Waldram Park Rd. and 20 Sunderland Rd., Forest Hill. SE23 2PW. (Mrs S.A. Butler). Est. 1966. Open 10-6, Sat. 10-4. CL: Sun. except by appointment and Thurs. SIZE: Medium. *STOCK: Oil lamps, gas and electric light fitments, 1800-1930; fire furnishings, 1780-1920; all £20-£500; general antiques, 1800-1920, £15-£1,000.* Not Stocked: Coins, stamps, medals, jewellery. LOC: On South Circular Rd., between Catford and Forest Hill. PARK: Opposite. TEL: 0181 699 9574.

LONDON SE24

Under Milkwood
379-381 Milkwood Rd., Herne Hill. SE24 0HA. (Nick and Sue Williams). Est. 1988. Open 9-5.30. SIZE: Small. *STOCK: Victorian, Edwardian and reproduction mantelpieces, £200-£2,000.* LOC: At rear of Herne Hill station. PARK: Easy. TEL: 0171 733 3921; home - 0181 244 8562. SER: Valuations; restorations; installations; gas fires; slate hearths. FAIRS: Ardingly, Newark.

LONDON SE25

Engine 'n' Tender
19 Spring Lane, Woodside Green. SE25 4SP. (Mrs Joyce M. Buttigieg). Est. 1957. Open Thurs. 12-6, Fri. 12-6.30, Sat. 10-6. SIZE: Small. *STOCK: Model railways, mainly pre 1939; Dinky toys, to 1968; old toys, mainly tinplate.* LOC: Near Woodside station. PARK: Easy. TEL: 0181 654 0386. FAIRS: Local toy.

North London Clock Shop Ltd
Rear of 60 Saxon Rd. SE25 5EH. (D.S. Tomlin). Est. 1960. Open 9-6. CL: Sat. SIZE: Medium. *STOCK: Clocks, longcase, bracket, carriage, skeleton, 18th-19th C.* PARK: Easy. TEL: 0181 664 8089. SER: Restorations (clocks and barometer); wheel cutting, hand engraving, dial painting, clock reconversions. FAIRS: Olympia. VAT: Stan.

LONDON SE26

Abbott Antiques and Country Pine
109 Kirkdale, Sydenham. SE26 4QJ. Est. 1972. Open 10-5.30, Sat. 10-5, Sun. 11-3. *STOCK: Victorian and Edwardian furniture including pine, and bric-a-brac.* LOC: 1/2 mile from South Circular Rd. at Forest Hill. TEL: 0181 699 1363.

Behind the Boxes - Art Deco
98 Kirkdale, Sydenham. SE26 4BG. (Ray Owen). Est. 1987. Open 10.30-5, Sun. and Mon. by appointment. SIZE: Large. *STOCK: Furniture, lighting and costume jewellery, 1930's, from £25.* LOC: 1 mile from Crystal Palace. BR station Forest Hill. PARK: Loading, otherwise Fransfield Rd. TEL: 0181 291 6116. SER: Valuations; buys at auction. FAIRS: Decorama and Deco.

T.A. Hillyer Antiques
301 Sydenham Rd., Sydenham. SE26 5EW. Est. 1952. Open 9.30-4, Sat. 9.30-2. CL: Wed. SIZE: Small. *STOCK: Furniture, silver, plate, porcelain, glass, books, bric-a-brac.* PARK: Easy. TEL: 0181 778 6361; home - 0181 777 2506.

Sydenham Antiques Centre
48 Sydenham Rd., Sydenham. SE26 5QF. (Mrs L. Cockton). Est. 1996. Open 10-5. SIZE: Medium. *STOCK: China, glass, silver, collectables, furniture and jewellery, 19th-20th C, £5-£500.* LOC: 2 doors down from Post Office in High St. PARK: Easy and nearby. TEL: 0181 778 1706. SER: Valuations; restorations (china).

Vintage Cameras Ltd
256 Kirkdale, Sydenham. SE26 4NL. (J. Jenkins). Est. 1968. Open 9-5. SIZE: Large. *STOCK: Vintage cameras, 1840-1950, £50-£5,000; general photographica, 1840-1950, £5-£500.* LOC: Near South Circular Rd. PARK: Nearby. TEL: 0181 778 5416; fax - 0181 778 5841. SER: Valuations. VAT: Stan.

LONDON E2

John Jackson LAPADA
124 Columbia Rd. E2 7RG. Open Sunday mornings or by appointment. *STOCK: Formal and decorative furniture, 17th-19th C.* TEL: 0411 319237. FAIRS: London.

George Rankin Coin Co. Ltd
325 Bethnal Green Rd. E2. Open 10-5. *STOCK: Coins, medals, medallions and jewellery.* TEL: 0171 739 1840/729 1280; fax - 0171 729 5023.

LONDON E4

Record Detector
3 & 4 Station Approach, Station Rd., Chingford. E4 6AL. (N. Salter). Est. 1992. Open 10-6. CL: Thurs. SIZE: Small (2 shops). *STOCK: Second*

E4 continued

hand and collectable records, L.P's, E.P's, singles and CD's. LOC: In forecourt of North Chingford railway station. PARK: Easy. TEL: 0181 529 6361/2938.

LONDON E8

Boxes and Musical Instruments
2 Middleton Rd., Hackney. E8 4BL. (A. and J. O'Kelly). Est. 1974. Open any time by appointment. SIZE: Medium. *STOCK: Boxes - caddies, sewing, writing, snuff, vanity, jewellery and desk, £50-£3,000; musical instruments, plucked string, £250-£1,500; all 18th-19th C.* LOC: Off Kingsland Rd., continuation of Bishopsgate. PARK: Easy. TEL: 0171 254 7074; home - same; e-mail - boxes@globalnet.co.uk. SER: Valuations; restorations (exceptional instruments only). Registered with the Conservation Unit of the Museums and Galleries Commission.

LONDON E11

P. Blake - Old Cottage Antiques
8 High St., Wanstead. E11 2AJ. Est. 1920. Open Thurs. and Fri. 10.30-5.30. SIZE: Medium. *STOCK: Furniture, paintings, 19th-20th C.* LOC: Near Wanstead station and Snaresbrook. TEL: 0181 989 2317/504 9264. SER: Valuations; buys at auction. VAT: Stan/Spec.

LONDON E17

Collectors Centre - Antique City
98 Wood St. E17. Est. 1978. Open 9.30-5.30. CL: Thurs. SIZE: Large. *STOCK: Antiques, collectables, 40's, 50's, 60's, £1-£500.* PARK: Opposite. TEL: 0181 520 4032. *Trade Only.*

Georgian Village Antiques Market
100 Wood St., Walthamstow. E17 3HX. Est. 1972. Open 10-5. CL: Thurs. SIZE: 10 shops. *STOCK: Clocks, barometers, postcards, collectables, jewellery, brass, copper, stamps, silver, silver plate, crafts.* LOC: 50yds. from Dukes Head. PARK: Adjacent. TEL: 0181 520 6638.

LONDON EC1

Bookal's
412 St John St. EC1V 4NJ. (Everton and Marilyn Bookal). Est. 1977. Open 10.30-6, Sun. by appointment. SIZE: Medium. *STOCK: 19th C decorative furniture, £1,000-£5,000; 18th C furniture, £1,500-£4,000; 19th C bric-a-brac, £250-£2,000.* LOC: 5 minutes from Camden Passage towards city. PARK: Easy. TEL: 0171 837 3900; fax - same. SER: Valuations; restorations; buys at auction. FAIRS: Decorative Antiques & Textiles. VAT: Stan/Spec.

EC1 continued

City Clocks

31 Amwell St. EC1R 1UN. (J. Rosson). FBHI. Est. 1960. Open 9-5, Sat. 9.30-1.30 or by appointment. CL: Mon. SIZE: Medium. *STOCK: Clocks, watches, some furniture, 18th-19th C, £100-£7,000.* PARK: Easy. TEL: 0171 278 1154. SER: Valuations; restorations (clocks and watches); buys at auction. VAT: Stan.

Eldridge London

99-101 Farringdon Rd. EC1R 3DT. (B Eldridge). Est. 1953. Open 10-5, Sat. 10-1. SIZE: Large. *STOCK: Furniture and items of social and historical importance.* PARK: Easy. TEL: 0171 837 0379. VAT: Spec.

Finecraft Workshop Ltd

10 Greville St. EC1 8SB. (Martyn J. Pummell). NAG. Est. 1955. Open 10.15-5, Sat. 10.15-4.30, Sun. 10.15-2. SIZE: Medium. *STOCK: Jewellery, 19th-20th C, £100-£8,000+.* LOC: Between Farringdon Rd. and Hatton Garden. PARK: Nearby. TEL: 0171 242 3825; fax - 0171 404 0170. SER: Valuations; restorations; re-making and repairing; insurance claims undertaken; buys at auction. FAIRS: Europe and USA. VAT: Stan.

EC1 continued

C.R. Frost and Son Ltd

60-62 Clerkenwell Rd. EC1M 5PX. BCWMG; BHI. *STOCK: Quality vintage watches, clocks and barometers.* TEL: 0171 253 0315; fax - 0171 253 7454. SER: Repairs; clock and watch materials; batteries; clock glasses and bevelling to order.

Jonathan Harris (Jewellery) Ltd

63-66 Hatton Garden (office). EC1N 8LE. (E.C. and D. Harris). Est. 1958. Open 9.30-4.30. CL: Sat. *STOCK: Antique and secondhand rings, brooches, pendants, bracelets and other jewellery, from £100.* PARK: Nearby. TEL: 0171 242 9115/242 1558; fax - 0171 831 4417. SER: Valuations; export. FAIRS: Basle, Switzerland and Munich, Germany. VAT: Stan/Spec.

Hirsh Ltd

10 Hatton Garden. EC1N 8AH. (A. Hirsh). Open 10-5.30. *STOCK: Fine jewellery, silver and objets d'art.* TEL: 0171 405 6080; fax - 0171 430 0107; e-mail - enquiries@hirsh.co.uk. SER: Valuations; jewellery designed and re-modelled.

R. Holt and Co. Ltd

98 Hatton Garden. EC1N 8NX. Est. 1948. Open 9.30-5.30. CL: Sat. *STOCK: Gemstone specialists.* TEL: 0171 405 5286/0197; fax - 0171 430 1279. SER: Valuations; restorations (gem stone cutting and testing; bead stringing; inlaid work).

Joseph and Pearce Ltd LAPADA

63-66 Hatton Garden. EC1. Est. 1896. Open by appointment. *STOCK: Jewellery, 1800-1960, £100-£2,500.* TEL: 0171 405 4604/7; fax - 0171 242 1902. VAT: Stan/Spec. *Trade Only.*

A.R. Ullmann Ltd

10 Hatton Garden. EC1N 8AH. (J.S. Ullmann). Est. 1939. Open 9-5, Sat. 9.30-5. SIZE: Small. *STOCK: Jewellery, gold, silver and diamond; silver and objets d'art.* LOC: Very close to Farringdon and Chancery Lane tube stations. PARK: Multi-storey in St. Cross St. TEL: 0171 405 1877; fax - 0171 404 7071; home - 0181 346 2546. SER: Valuations; restorations. VAT: Stan/Spec.

LONDON EC2

The London Architectural Salvage & Supply Co. (LASSCo) LAPADA

St. Michael's Church, Mark St. (off Paul St.). EC2A 4ER. Est. 1977. Open 10-5 including Sun. *STOCK: Architectural antiques including panelled rooms, chimney pieces, lighting, statuary, garden ornaments, fountains, church and door furniture, stained glass, nautical salvage, columns and capitals, architectural stonework, relics and curiosities.* TEL: 0171 739 0448; fax - 0171 729 6853.

EC2 continued

Westland & Company

St. Michael's Church, Leonard St. EC2A 4ER Est. 1969. Open 9-6 including Sun. SIZE: Large. *STOCK: Period chimneypieces, architectural elements, panelled rooms, light fittings, statuary, paintings and furniture, £100-£100,000.* LOC: Off Gt. Eastern St. PARK: Easy. TEL: 0171 739 8094; fax - 0171 729 3620.

LONDON EC3

Ash Rare Books

25 Royal Exchange. EC3V 3LP. (L. Worms). Est. 1946. Open 10-5.30. CL: Sat. SIZE: Small. *STOCK: Books, 1550-1980, £20-£10,000; maps, 1550-1850, £25-£2,000; prints, 1650-1900, £20-£1,000.* LOC: On the Threadneedle St. side of the Royal Exchange, opposite Bank of England. TEL: 0171 626 2665; fax - 0171 623 9052. SER: Buys at auction (books and maps); picture framing and mount cutting. VAT: Stan.

Halcyon Days BADA

4 Royal Exchange. EC3V 3LL. (S. Benjamin). Est. 1950. Open 10-5.30. *STOCK: 18th to early 19th C enamels, Georgian and Victorian scent bottles, papier mâché, tôle, objects of vertu, treen, unusual small Georgian furniture.* TEL: 0171 626 1120; fax - 0171 283 1876. FAIRS: Grosvenor House; BADA. VAT: Stan/Spec.

Nanwani and Co

2 Shopping Arcade, Bank Station, Cornhill. EC3V 3LA. Est. 1958. CL: Sat. *STOCK: Precious and semi-precious stones, Oriental items, objets d'art.* TEL: 0171 623 8232; fax - 0171 283 2548. VAT: Stan.

Royal Exchange Art Gallery

14 Royal Exchange. EC3V 3LL. Est. 1974. Open 10.30-5.15. CL: Sat. *STOCK: Oil paintings, watercolours and etchings, especially marine and landscape, 18th-20th C.* TEL: 0171 283 4400.

Searle and Co Ltd

1 Royal Exchange, Cornhill. EC3V 3LL. Est. 1893. Open 9-5.30. SIZE: Medium. *STOCK: Georgian, Victorian and secondhand silver; Victorian, Edwardian and secondhand jewellery.* LOC: Near Bank underground. PARK: Meters. TEL: 0171 626 2456. SER: Valuations; restorations; repairs; engraving. VAT: Stan/Spec.

LONDON EC4

J. Clarke-Hall Ltd

22 Bride Lane. EC4Y 8DX. ABA. Est. 1934. Open Mon.-Fri. 12-4. SIZE: Small. *STOCK: Victorian maps, prints and greetings cards.* LOC: Off bottom of Fleet St., near Ludgate Hill. PARK: Meters. TEL: 0171 353 5483/4116. SER: Bookbinding; framing. VAT: Stan.

EC4 continued

J. Clarke-Hall Ltd

5 Bride Court, Fleet St. EC4Y 8DX. ABA. Est. 1934. Open Mon.-Fri. 10.30-6. SIZE: Small. *STOCK: English literature, specialising in Samuel Johnson, Lewis Carroll; illustrated books, modern first editions, £5-£750.* TEL: 0171 353 4116/5483. SER: Bookbinding; framing; quarterly catalogue.

LONDON N1

After Noah

121 Upper St., Islington. N1 1QP. (M. Crawford and Z. Candlin). Est. 1990. Open 10-6, Sun. 12-5. SIZE: Medium. *STOCK: Arts and Craft oak and similar furniture, 1880's to 1950's, £1-£1,000; iron, iron and brass beds; decorative items, bric-a-brac including candlesticks, mirrors, lighting, kitchenalia and jewellery.* PARK: Side streets. TEL: 0171 359 4281; fax - same. SER: Restorations. VAT: Stan.

Angel Arcade

116-118 Islington High St., Camden Passage. N1 8EG. Open Wed. and Sat. Other days access available to the shops. SIZE: Large. *STOCK: General antiques.*

Annie's Vintage Costume & Textiles

10 Camden Passage, Islington. N1 8ED. (A. Moss). Open 11-5. CL: Mon. TEL: 0171 359 0796.

The Antique Trader

The Millinery Works, 85/87 Southgate Rd. N1 3JS. (B. Thompson and D. Rothera). Est. 1968. Open at any time by appointment. SIZE: Large. *STOCK: Arts & Crafts and art furniture, £100-£15,000.* LOC: Close to Camden Passage Antiques Centre. PARK: Free. TEL: 0171 359 2019; fax - 0171 226 9446. VAT: Stan/Spec.

At the Sign of the Chest of Drawers

281 Upper St., Islington. N1 2TZ. (A. Harms). Open 10-6 including Sun. *STOCK: Pine, country furniture.* TEL: 0171 359 5909.

Ian Auld

1 Gateway Arcade, Camden Passage, Islington. N1 0PG. Est. 1968. Open Wed. and Sat. 10-5. SIZE: Small. *STOCK: Tribal art, mainly African; antiquities, mainly pottery, some Pre-Colombian, £25-£1,000.* Not Stocked: Victoriana. LOC: Near Angel tube station. PARK: Easy. TEL: 0171 359 1440.

Banbury Fayre

6 Pierrepont Arcade, Camden Passage, Islington. N1. (N. Steel). Est. 1984. Open Wed., Fri. and Sat. SIZE: Small. *STOCK: Collectables including commemoratives, shipping, Boy Scout movement, Boer War, air line travel.* PARK: 200yds. TEL: Home - 0181 852 5675.

N1 continued

Boutique Fantasque

13 Pierrepont Row, Camden Passage, Islington. N1. (Mrs M.A.B. Gates). Est. 1962. Open Wed. and Sat. SIZE: Small. *STOCK: Watercolours and prints, general antiques, porcelain, jewellery, small collectors' items.* LOC: From Piccadilly, No.19 bus. Tube to Angel station. PARK: 200yds.

Camden Passage Antiques Centre

12 Camden Passage. N1 8ED. (S. Lemkow). Est. 1960. Open weekdays 10.30-5.30. Also 100 stalls open Wed. 8-3 and Sat. 9-5 - general antiques; Thurs. 9-4 - books. SIZE: 400 shops and boutiques some of which are listed in this section. LOC: Behind the Angel, Islington. TEL: 0171 359 0190.

Patric Capon BADA

350 Upper St., Islington. N1 0PD. Est. 1970. Open Wed. and Sat. or by appointment. SIZE: Medium. *STOCK: Unusual carriage clocks, 19th C, £450-£6,000; 8-day and 2-day marine chronometers, 19th C, £850-£4,500; clocks and barometers, 18th-19th C, £400-£6,500.* LOC: Adjacent Camden Passage. PARK: Easy. TEL: 0171 354 0487; fax - 0181 295 1475; home - 0181 467 5722. SER: Valuations; restorations. FAIRS: Olympia. VAT: Stan/Spec.

Chancery Antiques Ltd

357a Upper St., Islington. N1 0PD. (R. and D. Rote). Est. 1950. Open 10.30-5 or by appointment. CL: Mon. and Thurs. SIZE: Medium. *STOCK: Oriental works of art especially Japanese Meiji period.* TEL: 0171 359 9035. VAT: Stan/Spec.

Peter Chapman Antiques LAPADA

10 Theberton St., Islington. N1 0QX. (P.J. Chapman). CPTA. Est. 1971. Open 9.30-1 and 2-6. CL: Sun. and public holidays except by appointment. SIZE: Medium. *STOCK: Furniture and decorative objects, 1700-1900; paintings, drawings and prints, 17th to early 20th C; stained glass.* LOC: 5 mins. walk from Camden Passage down Upper St. PARK: Easy. TEL: 0171 226 5565; mobile - 0831 093662; fax - 0181 348 4846. SER: Valuations; restorations (furniture and period objects); buys at auction. VAT: Stan/Spec.

Chapter One

2 Pierrepont Arcade, Camden Passage. N1 9EG. (Yvonne Gill). Est. 1993. Open Wed. 9-3, Sat. 9-5 or by appointment. SIZE: Small. *STOCK: Handbags, costume jewellery, vintage accessories, fabrics, bric-a-brac, 1880-1960, £5-£300.* TEL: 0171 359 1185. SER: Jewellery repairs.

Charlton House Antiques

7 Charlton Place, Camden Passage, Islington. N1 8AQ. Open Wed. and Sat. 8-5, Tue. and Fri. 10-4. SIZE: Large. *STOCK: European and Scandinavian furniture, 1840-1930, £100-£5,000; general antiques.* LOC: Near Angel underground station. PARK: Easy. TEL: 0171 226 3141; fax - same. VAT: Stan/Spec.

Carlton Davidson Antiques

33 Camden Passage, Islington. N1 8EA. Est. 1981. Open Wed.-Sat. 10-4. SIZE: Medium. *STOCK: Lamps, chandeliers, mirrors and decorative items, £100-£3,000.* LOC: Near Charlton Place. PARK: Meters. TEL: 0171 226 7491. FAIRS: Decorative Antiques, Chelsea. VAT: Stan.

Dean's Antiques

25 Camden Passage, Islington. N1. Open Wed. and Sat. 9.30-5. *STOCK: Decorative items.* TEL: 0171 354 9940.

Dome Antiques (Exports) Ltd LAPADA

75 Upper St., Islington. N1 0NU. (A.D. Woolf). Est. 1961. Open 9.30-5.30. SIZE: Large. *STOCK: English furniture, 1700-1900, £500-£10,000; desks, library and dining tables, sets of chairs.* LOC: Opposite Islington Green. PARK: At rear. TEL: 0171 226 7227; mobile - 0831 805888; fax - 0171 704 2960. SER: Valuations. VAT: Stan/Spec.

Donay Antiques

35 Camden Passage, Islington. N1 8EA. (D.C. and C.E. Goddard). Est. 1980. Open Wed. and Sat. 9-5. SIZE: Large. *STOCK: Games and puzzles, £10-£2,000; chess sets, £50-£2,000; artists' colour boxes, £200-£800; stationery and letter boxes; amusement arcade machines.* LOC: Near Angel tube station. PARK: Charlton Place nearby. TEL: 0171 359 1880; fax - 0171 704 0488.

Eclectica

2 Charlton Place. N1. (Liz Wilson). Open 11-5.30, Wed. and Sat. 9-5.30. *STOCK: Vintage costume jewellery.* TEL: 0171 226 5625; fax - same.

Feljoy Antiques

Shop 3, Angel Arcade, Camden Passage. N1 8EA. Open Wed. and Sat. 8-4. *STOCK: Chintzware, decorative antiques and textiles.* TEL: 0171 354 5336.

Michael Finney Antique Prints and Books

11 Camden Passage, Islington. N1 8EA. Open 10-5. CL: Mon. *STOCK: Prints, 17th-19th C; plate books, watercolours especially David Roberts, Egypt, Holy Land and Spain, £1-£1,000.* PARK: Meters. TEL: 0171 226 9280; fax - 0171 359 0321.

The Fleamarket

7 Pierrepont Row, Camden Passage, Islington. N1 8EE. Open 9.30-6. CL: Mon. SIZE: Large. 26 stand-holders. *STOCK: Jewellery, furniture,*

N1 continued

objets d'art, militaria, guns, swords, pistols, porcelain, coins, medals, stamps, 18th-19th C, £1-£500; antiquarian books, prints, fine art, china, silver, glass and general antiques. PARK: Easy. TEL: 0171 226 8211. SER: Valuations; buys at auction; weapon repairs.

Vincent Freeman

1 Camden Passage, Islington. N1 2UD. Est. 1966. Open 10-5. CL: Mon. and Thurs. SIZE: Large. *STOCK: Music boxes, furniture and decorative items, from £100.* TEL: 0171 226 6178; fax - 0171 226 7231. VAT: Stan/Spec.

Furniture Vault

50 Camden Passage, Islington. N1 8AE. Open Tues.-Sat. 9.30-4.30. *STOCK: Furniture, 18th-20th C; decorative bronzes.* TEL: 0171 354 1047.

Georgian Village

30-31 Islington Green. N1. Open 10-4, Wed. and Sat. 7-5. PARK: Nearby. TEL: 0171 226 1571.

"Get Stuffed"

105 Essex Rd., Islington. N1 2SL. Est. 1975. Open 12-5, Mon. 1-5, Sat. 12-3. CL: Thurs. *STOCK: Stuffed birds, fish, animals, trophy heads; rugs; butterflies, insects.* TEL: 0171 226 1364; fax - 0171 359 8253. SER: Restorations; taxidermy; glass domes and cases supplied.

The Graham Gallery LAPADA

104 Islington High St., Camden Passage, Islington. N1 8EG. Est. 1973. Open 10-5. SIZE: Large. *STOCK: Silver, 1750-1930, £250-£50,000; Victorian silver plate, £250-£50,000; Sheffield plate, £250-£25,000; Victorian oil paintings, £2,000-£50,000; late Victorian fine marquetry and painted furniture, £1,000-£50,000.* LOC: 2 mins. from Angel Underground. PARK: Easy. TEL: 0171 354 2112; fax - 0171 704 0728. VAT: Stan.

Gordon Gridley

28 & 41 Camden Passage, Islington. N1 8EA. Est. 1968. CL: Mon. SIZE: Large + warehouse at rear. *STOCK: English and Continental furniture, paintings, decorative objects, metalwork, glass and ceramics, statuary and garden furniture, 17th-19th C, £50-£20,000.* PARK: Business Design Centre or Charlton Place. TEL: 0171 226 0643. SER: Valuations; restorations. VAT: Stan/Spec.

Linda Gumb LAPADA

9 Camden Passage, Islington. N1. Est. 1981. Open 9.30-4.30, Wed. 7.30-5, Sat. 9-5. SIZE: Medium. *STOCK: Textiles, 18th-19th C; decorative objects, 19th C; all £10-£5,000.* PARK: Easy. TEL: 0171 354 1184. SER: Buys at auction. FAIRS: Olympia. VAT: Stan.

N1 continued

Rosemary Hart

4 Gateway Arcade, 355 Upper St., Camden Passage. N1 0PG. Est. 1980. Open Wed. and Sat. 9-5, Tues. and Fri. 11-4. SIZE: Small. *STOCK: Silver plated tableware and decorative serving pieces, £5-£500; small silver gifts, from £50.* LOC: Near Angel tube station. TEL: 0171 359 6839; fax - same.

Hart and Rosenberg

2 and 3 Gateway Arcade, Camden Passage, Islington. N1 0PG. (E. Hart and H. Rosenberg). Est. 1968. Open 10-5, Wed. 9-5. CL: Mon. and Thurs. SIZE: Medium. *STOCK: Chinese, Japanese and European porcelain, works of art, decorative items, some furniture, £25-£5,000.* LOC: Near Angel tube station. PARK: Nearby. TEL: 0171 359 6839; fax - same. SER: Valuations; buys at auction. VAT: Stan/Spec.

Sherry Hatcher

5 Gateway Arcade, Camden Passage, Upper St., Islington. N1 0PG. Est. 1966. Open 10-5. SIZE: Small. *STOCK: Perfume bottles, sugar shakers, silver, boxes and interesting silver items.* LOC: Near Angel tube station. PARK: Easy. TEL: 0171 226 5679.

Heritage Antiques

112 Islington High St., Camden Passage. N1 8EG. (A. Daniel). Est. 1975. Open Wed. 8.30-5 and Sat. 9.30-5 or by appointment. SIZE: Large. *STOCK: Metalware, £25-£3,000; some furniture and decorative items.* TEL: 0171 226 7789 or 01273 326850; fax - 01273 326850. VAT: Stan/Spec.

House of Steel Antiques

400 Caledonian Rd. N1 1DN. (J. Cole). Est. 1974. Open 10.30-5.30, Sat. by appointment. SIZE: Warehouse. *STOCK: Metal items - fireplaces, 18th-19th C, £50-£1,000; spiral staircases, £300-£1,000; balconies, railings, garden furniture, £50-£500; all 19th C.* LOC: Near King's Cross. PARK: Own. TEL: 0171 607 5889. SER: Valuations; restorations (welding, polishing, sand-blasting); steel furniture manufactured, items made to order. VAT: Stan.

Diana Huntley LAPADA

8 Camden Passage, Islington. N1 3ED. Est. 1970. Open Tues. and Fri. 10-4, Wed. 7.30-5, Thurs. by appointment, Sat. 9-5. *STOCK: European porcelain, £50-£10,000; objets d'art; all 19th C.* TEL: 0171 226 4605; fax - 0171 359 0240. SER: Valuations. VAT: Stan/Spec.

Inheritance

8-10 Gateway Arcade, Camden Passage, Islington. N1 8EG. (A. Pantelli). Est. 1969. Open 10.30-5. CL: Mon. SIZE: Small. *STOCK: Victorian paintings, Old Masters, 18th-19th C furniture, clocks, Oriental porcelain, silver.* TEL: 0171 226 8305. SER: Valuations. VAT: Stan/Spec.

N1 continued

Intercol London

Gallery, 114 Islington High St. (within Camden Passage). Correspondence - 43 Templars Crescent, N3 3QR. (Y. Beresiner). Est. 1977. Open Wed.-Sat. 9-5, other times by appointment. SIZE: Large. *STOCK: Playing cards, maps and banknotes and related literature, £5-£1,000+.* PARK: Easy. TEL: 0181 349 2207; fax - 0181 346 9539. SER: Valuations; restorations (maps including colouring); buys at auction (playing cards, maps, banknotes and books). FAIRS: Major specialist European, U.S.A. and Far Eastern. VAT: Stan/Spec.

Islington Antiques

12-14 Essex Rd. N1 8LN. (R.A. Bent). Est. 1984. Open 9-6. SIZE: Large. *STOCK: Original pine furniture, English and Continental.* TEL: 0171 226 6867.

Japanese Gallery

23 Camden Passage, Islington. N1 8EA. Open 9.30-4.30. *STOCK: Japanese woodcut prints; books, porcelain, screens, kimonos, scrolls, furniture.* TEL: 0171 226 3347; fax - 0171 229 2934. SER: Framing; free authentification.

Jubilee Photographica

10 Pierrepont Row, Camden Passage, Islington. N1 8E. (Beryl Vosburgh). Est. 1970. Open Wed. and Sat. 10.30-4 or by appointment. SIZE: Small. *STOCK: Photographica - apparatus, images, daguerreotypes, ambrotypes, tintypes, vintage paper prints, stereoscopic cards and viewers, magic lanterns and slides, topographical and family-albums, cabinet cards and cartes de visite, 10p-£1,000.* LOC: From Piccadilly Circus, take 19 bus to Angel, Islington. PARK: Meters. TEL: Home - 0171 607 5462. SER: Buys at auction.

Julian Antiques LAPADA

54 Duncan St. N1. Est. 1964. Open by appointment only. *STOCK: French clocks, fireplaces, bronzes, fenders, mirrors.* TEL: 0171 833 0835.

Carol Ketley Antiques LAPADA

PO Box 16199. N1 7WD. Est. 1979. Open by appointment. SIZE: Medium. *STOCK: Mirrors, decanters, drinking glasses, blue and white pottery and decorative objects, 1780-1900, £10-£2,000.* LOC: Showroom close to Camden Passage. PARK: Easy. TEL: 0171 359 5529; mobile - 0831 827284; fax - 0171 226 4589. FAIRS: Olympia; Little Chelsea; Decorative Antiques and Textile. VAT: Global.

Judith Lassalle

7 Pierrepont Arcade, Camden Passage, Islington. N1 8EF. Est. 1765 Cornhill. Open Wed. 7.30-4, Sat. 9.30-4, other times by appointment. *STOCK: Books, maps, children's games, optical toys and rocking horses, 17th C to 1914, £25-£5,000.* PARK: Nearby. TEL: 0171 607 7121; shop - 0171 354 9344. SER: Valuations; restorations; buys at auction. FAIRS: Ephemera.

N1 continued

John Laurie (Antiques) Ltd LAPADA

351/352 Upper St., Islington. N1 0PD. (J. Gewirtz). Est. 1962. Open 9.30-5. SIZE: Large. *STOCK: Silver, Sheffield plate.* TEL: 0171 226 0913/6969; fax - 0171 226 4599. SER: Restorations; packing; shipping. VAT: Stan.

Sara Lemkow

12 Camden Passage. N1. Open 10-5. *STOCK: Oil lamps, brass, iron, copper, kitchen utensils.* TEL: 0171 359 0190.

Michael Lewis Antiques LAPADA

16 Essex Rd., Islington. N1 8LN. Est. 1977. Open 9-6, Sun. by appointment. SIZE: Large. *STOCK: Pine and country furniture, British and Irish, 18th-19th C, £100-£6,500.* LOC: 100yds. north of Camden Passage. PARK: Easy. TEL: 0171 359 7733. VAT: Stan/Spec.

Wan Li

7 Gateway Arcade, 355 Upper St., Camden Passage, Islington. N1 0PD. Est. 1969. *STOCK: Mainly Chinese ceramics, works of art and silver; English ceramics, glass, small objects and paintings.* VAT: Stan/Spec.

London Militaria Market

Angel Arcade, Camden Passage, Islington. N1. (S. Bosley and M. Warren). Est. 1987. Open Sat. 8-2. SIZE: Large. 35 dealers. *STOCK: Militaria, 1800 to date.* LOC: Near Angel tube station. PARK: Meters and nearby. TEL: 01628 822503 or 01455 556971.

Janet Love Interiors

Camden Passage, 110 Islington High St. N1 8ED. IDDA. Open Wed. 9-5, Sat. 10-5, other times by appointment. SIZE: Small. *STOCK: French and English decorative furniture, 18th-20th C, £500-£5,000; prints, £100-£2,000; objets d'art, £50-£500; both 18th-19th C.* TEL: Mobile - 0468 781573. SER: Valuations.

Finbar MacDonnell

17 Camden Passage, Islington. N1 8EA. Open 10-6. *STOCK: Decorative prints, mainly pre-1850.* TEL: 0171 226 0537.

N1 continued

The Mall Antiques Arcade

359 Upper St., Islington. N1. (Atlantic Antiques Centres Ltd). Est. 1979. Open 10-5, Wed. 7.30-5, Sat. 9-6. CL: Mon. LOC: 5 mins. from Angel tube station. PARK: Meters. TEL: 0171 354 2839; enquiries - 0171 351 5353. Below are listed the dealers at this Arcade.

Alexandra Alfandary LAPADA

Stand G9. *Meissen porcelain.* TEL: 0171 354 9762.

Alma Antiques

Stand G17. (T. and A. Goldstrom). *Miniatures, objects, watercolours and jewellery.* TEL: 0171 359 9045.

Antique Clocks - Terence Plank

Stand G23. *Clocks.* TEL: 0171 226 2426.

Audley Art Ltd

Stand G20. (A. Singer). *Meissen porcelain and oil paintings.* TEL: 0171 704 9507.

Louise Bannister

Stand G27. *Decorative items.* TEL: 0171 226 6665.

David Bowden

Stand G12. *Oriental and European works of art, watches.* TEL: 0171 226 3033.

Tony Coakley

Stand G2. *Art Deco and Art Nouveau,* TEL: 0171 354 3349.

P. Collingridge

Stand G6. *Lighting, brass and furniture.* TEL: 0171 354 9189.

Coperffelde

Stand G21. (Frank Bench). *Small furniture, porcelain.* TEL: 0171 226 0779; mobile - 0850 457261.

Chris Dunn St. James

Stand G7. *Vintage jewellery.* TEL: 0171 704 0127.

N1 continued

Hallmark Antiques
Stand G15. (Ralph Heller and Raymond Karpelowsky). *Jewellery and objets de vertu.* TEL: 0171 354 1616; fax - 0171 266 3587.

Heather Antiques
Stand G25. (Mrs. Cohen) *Silver and plate.* TEL: 0171 226 2412.

Patricia Kleinman LAPADA
Stand G3. *English watercolours, 19th to early 20th C.* TEL: 0171 704 0798.

Andrew Lineham BADA
Stand G19. *Glass and porcelain.* TEL: 0171 704 0195.

The London Barometer Co
Stand B5. (John Carnie and Ms Carolyn Grummit). *Barometers, scientific instruments, related accessories and small furniture, medical.* TEL: 0171 226 4992.

Monika
Stand G16. (M. Jartelius). *Fine period costume jewellery and accessories, 1920's-1950's.* TEL: 0171 354 3125.

Linda Morgan Antiques
Stand G26. *Jewellery.* TEL: 0171 359 0654.

D. L. Murphy
Stand G4/5. *Silver.* TEL: 0171 345 1204.

Number One The Mall
Stand G1. (Sonia Shea). *Silver, glass and jewellery.* TEL: 0171 354 2839.

Nadine Okker LAPADA
Stand G8. *Porcelain, glass and bronzes.* TEL: 0171 354 9496.

Original Photgraphic Prints
Stand G14. (Ed Pritchard and Manuela Höfer). *Photographs and prints.* TEL: 0171 930 1904; fax - 0171 839 7509.

John Pearman
Stand G24. *Glass and porcelain.* TEL: 0171 359 0591.

Phoenix
Stand B6. (Mr Edwards) *Oriental works of art.* TEL: 0171 226 4474; mobile - 0802 763518.

Mrs Sylvia Powell LAPADA
Stand G18. *Decorative arts, art pottery, 1870-1894.* TEL: 0171 354 2977.

Robin Quy
Stand G11. *Silver and Georgian glass.* TEL: 0171 359 8671.

Rumours
Stand G10. (J. Donovan). *Art Nouveau and Art Deco china and objets d'art.* TEL: 0171 359 8416.

N1 continued

Gad Sassower
Stand G13. *Bakelite items, gramophones, radios.* TEL: 0171 354 4473; mobile - 0831 326326.

Templar Antiques
Stand G28. (Mrs Pamela Wilson). *Glass.* TEL: 0171 704 9448; mobile - 0467 387869.

Michael Young
Stand G22. *Decorative items, model boats.* TEL: 0171 226 2225.

Lower Mall

The Clock Studio
Stand B1. (George Riley). *Clocks and collectables.* TEL: 0171 354 1719.

Peter Lehmann
Stand B8. *Furniture and silver.* TEL: 0171 704 0701.

Mrs C. Sidoli
Stand B4. *18th-19th C furniture, paintings and decorative accessories.* TEL: 0171 359 9533.

Malcolm D. Stevens LAPADA
Stand B2/3. *Furniture.* TEL: 0171 359 1020.

Alex Woodage
Stand B7. *Furniture.* TEL: 0171 226 4173.

Turner Brown Antiques
Stand B9/10. (D. Aron and V Brown). *Furniture, watches and general antiques.*

Laurence Mitchell Antiques Ltd
LAPADA

13 and 27 Camden Passage, Islington. N1 8EA. (L.P.J. Mitchell). Est. 1972. Open 10-5, Wed. 8-5, Mon. by appointment. *STOCK: Meissen, European and English porcelain; Oriental works of art, Chinese export and Japanese porcelain.* TEL: 0171 359 7579; fax - 0171 226 1738; e-mail - laurence.mitchell@virgin.net; internet - http://business.virgin.net/laurence.mitchell and http://www.thesaurus.co.uk/laurence-mitchell. VAT: Stan/Spec.

Chris Newland Antiques
357 Upper St., Islington. N1. Est. 1964. Open 10-6. SIZE: Large. *STOCK: Mahogany furniture, 19th C, £300-£1,000; office furniture, 19th-20th C; shipping furniture, marble, works of art.* PARK: NCP 100 yards. TEL: 0171 359 9805. SER: Valuations; restorations (furniture, French polishing). VAT: Stan/Spec.

Number Nineteen
19 Camden Passage, Islington. N1 8EA. (D. Griffith and J. Wright). Open 10-5. *STOCK: Decorative antiques including military and campaign furniture, leather chairs, pub accessories, club fenders and other fittings from hotels and gentlemen's clubs; quality vintage luggage.* TEL: 0171 226 1126.

N1 continued

The Old Tool Chest
41 Cross St., Islington. N1 2BB. (E.J. Maskell). Open 10-6. *STOCK: Woodworking tools.* TEL: 0171 359 9313.

Jacqueline Oosthuizen
1st Floor, Georgian Village, Camden Passage, Islington. N1. Est. 1960. Open Wed. and Sat. 8-4. SIZE: Medium. *STOCK: Staffordshire figures, 18th-19th C; jewellery, European and English ceramics, 18th-20th C.* PARK: Nearby. TEL: 0171 226 5393/352 6071. VAT: Stan/Spec.

Pieter Oosthuizen t/a de Verzamelaar
1st Floor, Georgian Village, Camden Passage. N1. Est. 1992. Open Wed. and Sat. 8-4. SIZE: Medium. *STOCK: Dutch Art Nouveau ceramics, 1880-1930, £30-£8,000; Boer War memorabilia, 1899-1902, £5-£2,000.* PARK: Nearby. TEL: 0171 359 3322; tel/fax - 0171 376 3852. SER: Buys at auction. VAT: Spec.

Kevin Page Oriental Art LAPADA
2, 4 and 6 Camden Passage, Islington. N1 8ED. Est. 1968. Open 10-4. CL: Mon. SIZE: Large. *STOCK: Oriental porcelain and furniture, cloisonné, bronzes, ivories.* LOC: 1 min. from Angel tube station. PARK: Easy. TEL: 0171 226 8558. SER: Valuations. VAT: Stan.

Sue Pottle
9 Georgian Village, 30-31 Islington Green, Islington. N1. Open Wed. and Sat. 7-3. SIZE: Small. *STOCK: Pine, majolica, decorative items.* LOC: Junction of Upper St. and Essex Rd. PARK: Nearby. TEL: 0171 226 9907 and 0181 348 5801.

Regent Antiques
Barpart House, North London Freight Depot, York Way. N1 0UZ. (T. Quaradeghini). Est. 1983. Open 9-5.30, other times by appointment. SIZE: Large. *STOCK: Furniture, 18th C to Edwardian.* LOC: 1/4 mile from Kings Cross Station. PARK: Own. TEL: 0171 833 5545; fax - 0171 278 2236. SER: Restorations (furniture). VAT: Stan. *Trade Only.*

N1 continued

Relic Antiques
21 Camden Passage, Islington. N1. (Malcolm Gliksten). Est. 1968. Open 10-5. CL: Mon., Tues., and Thurs. *STOCK: Näive art, figureheads and trade signs; fairground art; boat and plane models; toys and games; decorative items; French country furniture and carved framed mirrors; original tea canisters and period shopfittings, £40-£3,000.* PARK: Meters. TEL: 0171 388 2691; fax - same; 0171 359 2597; mobile - 0831 785059. FAIRS: Chelsea Decorative. VAT: Stan.

Restall Brown and Clennell Ltd
Adelaide Wharf, 120 Queensbridge Rd., E2 8PD. (S. Brown). Open Mon.-Fri. 9-5.30 appointment advisable. *STOCK: English furniture, 17th-19th C.* TEL: 0171 739 6626; fax - 0171 739 6123. VAT: Stan/Spec.

Rookery Farm Antiques
12 Camden Passage, Islington. N1 8ED. *STOCK: Pine and country furniture and bamboo.* TEL: 0171 359 0190.

Marcus Ross Antiques
16 Pierrepont Row, Camden Passage, Islington. N1 8EF. Est. 1972. Open 10.30-4.30. CL: Mon. *STOCK: Oriental porcelain, general antiques, Victorian walnut furniture.* TEL: 0171 359 8494.

Keith Skeel Antique Warehouse LAPADA
46 Essex Rd. N1. SIZE: Large. *STOCK: Interesting and unusual furniture.* TEL: 0171 359 5633. *Trade Only.*

Keith Skeel Antiques and Eccentricities LAPADA
94/98 Islington High St. N1 8EG. Est. 1969. Open 9-6. SIZE: Large. *STOCK: Interesting and unusual decorative items.* LOC: 1 min. from the Angel underground station. TEL: 0171 359 9894/226 7012. VAT: Stan. *Trade and Export Only.*

N1 continued

Style
1 Ground Floor, Georgian Village, Camden Passage. N1. (M. Webb and P. Coakley). Open Wed. and Sat. 9.30-4 or by appointment. *STOCK: Art Nouveau, WMF and Liberty pewter, Art Deco bronzes, ceramics and glass.* TEL: 0171 359 7867; private - 0181 449 2588; fax - same; mobile - 0831 229640.

Sugar Antiques
8-9 Pierrepont Arcade, Camden Passage, Islington. N1 8EF. (Elayne and Tony Sugarman). Est. 1980. Open Wed. 6.30-4, Sat. 9-4, other times by appointment. SIZE: Medium. *STOCK: Wrist and pocket watches, 19th-20th C, £25-£2,000; fountain pens and lighters, early 20th C to 1960's, £15-£1,000; costume jewellery and collectables, 19th-20th C, £5-£500.* PARK: Meters. TEL: 0171 354 9896 (answerphone). SER: Repairs (as stock); buys at auction (as stock). VAT: Stan.

Swan Fine Art
120 Islington High St., Camden Passage. N1 8EG. (P. Child). Open 10-5, Wed. and Sat. 9-5 or by appointment. SIZE: Medium. *STOCK: Paintings, fine and decorative sporting and animal, portraits, 17th-19th C, £500-£25,000+.* PARK: Easy, except Wed. and Sat.. TEL: 0171 226 5335; fax - 0171 359 2225; mobile - 0860 795336. VAT: Spec.

Tadema Gallery — BADA LAPADA
10 Charlton Place, Camden Passage, Islington. N1. (S. and D. Newell-Smith). Est. 1978. Open Wed. and Sat. 10-5, or by appointment. SIZE: Medium. *STOCK: 20th C abstract art and jewellery, from Art Nouveau to 1960's artist designed pieces.* PARK: Reasonable. TEL: 0171 359 1055; fax - same. SER: Valuations. VAT: Spec.

Tapsell Antiques
at Christopher House, 5 Camden Passage, Islington. N1 8EH. (Christopher Tapsell). Est. 1969. Open 10.30-5.30, Wed. and Sat. 9-5.30, Mon. by appointment. SIZE: Medium. *STOCK: English and Continental furniture, mid 18th C to 1900, £400-£15,000; Oriental porcelain, 17th C to 1900, £50-£10,000; decorative bronzes, mirrors and lighting, 17th C to 1900, £300-£4,000.* PARK: Opposite. TEL: 0171 354 3603; fax - 0171 226 4326. SER: Valuations; restorations; buys at auction (European furniture and Oriental porcelain). FAIRS: Olympia. VAT: Stan/Spec.

The Textile Company
P.O Box 2800, London N1 4DQ. (Judy Wentworth). Est. 1982. Open by appointment only. *STOCK: 18th C silks, British and French printed cottons, patchworks, lace, 1600-1850; Paisley and Kashmir shawls, period costume and accessories.* Not Stocked: Tapestries, upholstery and cushions. TEL: 0171 254 3256. SER: Buys at auction; hire; photographic archive.

N1 continued

Titus Omega
Shop 18, Ground Floor, Georgian Village, Camden Passage. N1. (John Featherstone-Harvey). Est. 1986. Open Wed. 8-3, Sat. 9-4. SIZE: Small. *STOCK: Art Nouveau, 1890-1910, £100-£3,000.* LOC: Islington Green. TEL: 0171 704 8003; home - 0171 607 8996. SER: Valuations.

Turn On Lighting
116/118 Islington High St., Camden Passage. N1 8EG. Est. 1976. *STOCK: Lighting, 1840-1940.* TEL: 0171 359 7616; fax - same.

Vane House Antiques
15 Camden Passage, Islington. N1 8EH. (M. Till and B. Snyder). Est. 1950. Open 10-5. *STOCK: 18th to early 19th C furniture.* TEL: 0171 359 1343. VAT: Stan/Spec.

Yesterday Child — LAPADA
Angel Arcade, 118 Islington High St. N1. (D. and G. Barrington). Est. 1970. Open Wed. and Sat. 8.30-3. SIZE: Small. *STOCK: Dolls, 1800-1925, £25-£5,000.* PARK: Easy. TEL: 0171 354 1601; home and fax - 01908 583403. SER: Valuations; restorations. VAT: Stan/Spec.

LONDON N2

Amazing Grates - Fireplaces Ltd
61-63 High Rd., East Finchley. N2. (T. Tew). Resident. Est. 1971. Open 10-6. SIZE: Large. *STOCK: Mantelpieces, grates and fireside items, £200-£5,000; Victorian tiling, £2-£20; early ironwork, all 19th C.* LOC: 100yds. north of East Finchley tube station. PARK: Own. TEL: 0181 883 9590/6017. SER: Valuations; restorations (ironwork, welding of cast iron and brazing, polishing); installations. VAT: Stan.

The Antique Shop (Valantique)
9 Fortis Green. N2 9JR. (Mrs V. Steel). Open Tues.-Sat. 11-6. SIZE: Medium. *STOCK: General antiques especially original lighting and fenders; small furniture, pottery, porcelain, glass, oil paintings, watercolours, prints, mirrors, copper, brass, unusual items, £5-£500.* LOC: 2 mins. from East Finchley tube station. PARK: Side street. TEL: 0181 883 7651. SER: Buys at auction.

Martin Henham (Antiques)
218 High Rd., East Finchley. N2 9AY. Open 10-6. SIZE: Medium. *STOCK: Furniture and porcelain, 1710-1920, £5-£1,700; paintings, 1650-1900, £10-£1,000.* PARK: Easy. TEL: 0181 444 5274. SER: Valuations; restorations (furniture and paintings); buys at auction.

Lauri Stewart - Fine Art
36 Church Lane. N2 8DT. Open 10-5. CL: Mon. *STOCK: Modern British oils and watercolours.* TEL: 0181 883 7719.

LONDON N4

Joseph Lavian LAPADA

Building E, Ground Floor, 105 Eade Rd. N4 1TJ. Est. 1950. Open 9.30-5.30. SIZE: Large. *STOCK: Oriental carpets, rugs, kelims, tapestries and needlework, Aubusson, Savonnerie and textiles, 17th-19th C.* TEL: 0181 800 0707; fax - 0181 800 0404. SER: Valuations; restorations.

Teger Trading and Bushe Antiques

318 Green Lanes. N4 1BX. *STOCK: Reproduction garden statuary, lamps, Art Deco, Art Nouveau, animalier, Oriental and classical style figures.* TEL: 0181 802 0156; fax - 0181 802 4110. SER: Restorations; film hire. *Trade Only.*

LONDON N5

Strike One (Islington) Ltd BADA

48a Highbury Hill. N5 1AP. (J. Mighell). Est. 1968. Open by appointment. SIZE: Medium. *STOCK: Clocks, pre-1870, especially early English wall and Act of Parliament, £2,000-£15,000; English longcase, 1675-1820, £3,000-£40,000; English bracket, lantern, skeleton and French carriage; Vienna regulators; barometers, music boxes, horological books.* PARK: Easy. TEL: 0171 354 2790; fax - same. SER: Valuations; restorations (clocks, barometers); catalogue available. VAT: Stan/Spec.

Walford's - Nicholas Goodyer

15 Calabria Rd., Highbury Fields. N5 1JB. Est. 1951. Open 9.30-5, but prior telephone call advisable. CL: Sat. *STOCK: Antiquarian books especially illustrated.* TEL: 0171 226 5682; fax - 0171 354 4716.

LONDON N6

Centaur Gallery

82 Highgate High St., Highgate Village. N6. (J. and D. Wieliczko). Est. 1960. Open 11-6. *STOCK: 18th to early 19th C oil paintings, watercolours, prints, sculpture, ethnic and folk art, unusual items.* TEL: 0181 340 0087.

Fisher and Sperr

46 Highgate High St. N6 5JB. (J.R. Sperr). Est. 1945. Open daily 10.30-6. SIZE: Large. *STOCK: Books, 15th C to date.* LOC: From centre of Highgate Village, nearest underground stations Archway (Highgate), Highgate. PARK: Easy. TEL: 0181 340 7244; fax - 0181 348 4293. SER: Valuations; restorations (books); buys at auction. VAT: Stan.

Betty Gould and Julian Gonnermann Antiques

408-410 Archway Rd., Highgate. N6 5AT. Est. 1964. Open 10-5.30, Sat. 9.30-5.30. CL: Mon. and Thurs. SIZE: Medium. *STOCK: Furniture, 18th-20th C, £50-£5,000.* LOC: On A1, just below

N6 continued

Highgate tube station (corner of Shepherds Hill). TEL: 0181 340 4987. SER: Restorations; French polishing; upholstery.

Highgate Antiques BADA LAPADA

P O Box 10060, Highgate. N6 5JH. (Jean Horsman and Enid Thomas). Est. 1984. *STOCK: English and Welsh porcelain and glass, 18th to early 19th C, £100-£4,000.* TEL: 0181 340 9872/348 3016; fax - 0181 340 1621/348 3016. SER: Valuations. FAIRS: Olympia, BADA, NEC, Cumberland Ceramic. VAT: Spec.

Home to Home

355c Archway Rd. N6 4EJ. Open 9.30-6.30, Sat. 10-5. *STOCK: Mainly Victorian, Edwardian and some Georgian furniture; Victorian pine.* TEL: 0181 340 8354.

D.M. and P. Manheim (Peter Manheim) Ltd

P.O. Box 1259. N6 4TR. (P. Manheim). Est. 1926. Open by appointment only. *STOCK: English porcelain, pottery and enamels, 1680-1820.* TEL: 0181 340 9211. VAT: Spec.

LONDON N7

Tsar Architectural

487 Liverpool Rd. N7. (R. Quinn). Open 9.30-7. *STOCK: Fireplaces and associated items.* TEL: 0171 609 4238. SER: Restorations.

LONDON N8

Crouch End Antiques

47 Park Rd., Crouch End. N8 8TE. (M.V. Kairis). Est. 1979. Open 10-6. SIZE: Medium. *STOCK: Furniture, 19th C, £100-£1,000.* LOC: Corner of Shanklin Rd. TEL: 0181 348 7652. SER: Valuations; restorations; renovation materials supplied. FAIRS: Alexandra Palace. VAT: Stan/Spec.

Sandra Lummis Fine Art

Flat 7, 17 Haslemere Rd. N8 9QP. (Mrs. S. Lummis and Dr T. Lummis). Est. 1985. Viewing by appointment. CL: Aug. *STOCK: British art (Modernist school), 20th C from Sickert to contemporary, especially Bloomsbury painters, £500-£50,000.* LOC: From Highgate Hill, along Hornsey Lane, left at 'T' junction, then 1st right. PARK: Easy. TEL: 0181 340 2293; home - same. SER: Commissions; valuations; advice on restoration and framing. VAT: Spec.

Solomon

49 Park Rd., Crouch End. N8 8SY. (Solomon Salim). Est. 1984. Open 9.30-6. SIZE: Medium. *STOCK: Furniture including upholstered, £200-£2,000; decorative items, £100-£500; all 1800-1920.* LOC: 2 minutes off North Circular at Muswell Hill turn-off. PARK: Easy. TEL: 0181 341 1817. SER: Valuations; restorations (furniture including upholstery); buys at auction (furniture). VAT: Spec.

LONDON N10

M.E. Korn

47 Tetherdown, Muswell Hill. N10 1NH. (E. Korn). ABA, PBFA. Est. 1971. Open by appointment. *STOCK: Books - natural history, medical, science, art and literature, 16th-19th C, £10-£1,000.* TEL: 0181 883 5251 (answerphone); fax - same. SER: Valuations; buys at auction (antiquarian books). FAIRS: PBFA, Russell Hotel monthly; York, Oxford, Cambridge; ABAA in California, Boston, New York and Toronto.

LONDON N12

Finchley Fine Art Galleries

983 High Rd., North Finchley. N12 8QR. (S. Greenman). Est. 1972. Open 1-7, including Sun., Wed. by appointment. SIZE: Large. *STOCK: 18th-20th C watercolours, paintings, etchings, prints, mostly English, £25-£10,000; Georgian, Victorian, Edwardian furniture, to £4,000; china and porcelain - Moorcroft, Doulton, Worcester, Clarice Cliff, £5-£2,000; musical and scientific instruments, bronzes, early photographic apparatus, fire-arms, shotguns.* LOC: Off M25, junction 23, take Barnet road. Gallery on right 3 miles south of Barnet church, opposite Britannia Road. PARK: Easy. TEL: 0181 446 4848. SER: Valuations; restorations; picture re-lining, cleaning and framing.

LONDON N13

Palmers Green Antiques Centre

472 Green Lanes, Palmers Green. N13 5PA. (Michael Webb). Est. 1976. Open 10-5.30, Sun. 11-5. CL: Tues. SIZE: Medium. *STOCK: General antiques and collectables.* PARK: Nearby. TEL: 0181 350 0878. SER: Valuations; restorations. FAIRS: Alexandra Palace; Kempton Park.

LONDON N14

C.J. Martin (Coins) Ltd — LAPADA

85 The Vale, Southgate. N14 6AT. Open by appointment. *STOCK: Ancient and medieval coins and ancient artefacts.* TEL: 0181 882 1509/4359.

Southgate Antiques & Collectables

46 Chase Side, Southgate. N14 5PA. Open 10-5.30. SIZE: Medium - 10 dealers. *STOCK: Gramophones, radios, records, sci-fi, militaria, wide range of general small antique and collector's items, including named porcelain and glass, china tableware, silver and jewelery; period furniture.* LOC: Near Southgate underground station. TEL: 0181 447 8017. VAT: Stan.

LONDON N16

W. Forster

83a Stamford Hill. N16 5TP. Est. 1952. Open by appointment. *STOCK: Bibliography and books about books.* LOC: Nearest station Manor House (Piccadilly Line) or 253 bus to Stamford Hill Broadway. PARK: Easy. TEL: 0181 800 3919.

LONDON N19

Curios

130c Junction Rd., Archway. N19. Open 12-7 including Sun. *STOCK: Decorative objects especially unusual items; general antiques, pictures, taxidermy and fireplaces.* TEL: 0171 272 5603.

LONDON N20

The Totteridge Gallery

61 Totteridge Lane. N20 0HD. Est. 1979. Open daily, Sun. by appointment. SIZE: Small. *STOCK:*

N20 continued

Oil paintings, £1,000-£25,000; watercolours, £300-£10,000; both 18th to early 20th C. Limited edition Russell Flint prints, 20th C, £500-£3,000. LOC: Opposite Totteridge and Whetstone tube station. PARK: Easy. TEL: 0181 446 7896. SER: Valuations; restorations; frame repairs. VAT: Stan/Spec.

LONDON N21

Dolly Land

864 Green Lanes, Winchmore Hill. N21 2RS. Est. 1987. Open 9.30-4.30. CL: Mon. and Wed. *STOCK: Dolls, teddies, trains, die-cast limited editions.* PARK: Easy. TEL: 0181 360 1053; fax - 0181 364 1370. SER: Restorations; part exchange; dolls' hospital. FAIRS: Doll and Bear.

The Little Curiosity Shop

24 The Green, Winchmore Hill. N21. (Mrs H. Freedman). Est. 1967. Open 1-5. CL: Wed. *STOCK: Clocks, porcelain, general antiques, mostly Victorian, bronzes, silver, music boxes, jewellery and diamond items.* LOC: Nearest stations - Winchmore Hill (Eastern Region), and Southgate (Piccadilly Line underground). PARK: Easy. TEL: 0181 886 0925. VAT: Stan.

Winchmore Antiques

14 The Green, Winchmore Hill. N21 1AY. (David Hicks and Stewart Christian). Open 10-6. SIZE: Medium. *STOCK: General antiques, £1-£500; architectural brass fittings, vintage lamps and spare parts; all 18th-20th C.* LOC: Junction of 5 roads, at east end of Broad Walk. PARK: Easy. TEL: 0181 882 4800. SER: Valuations; restorations (metal polishing, silver plating, oil lamps).

LONDON NW1

Art Furniture

158 Camden St. NW1 9PA. Open 12-5 including Sun. SIZE: Warehouse. *STOCK: Decorative arts 1851-1951, Arts & Crafts furniture by Heal's, Liberty and others; Art Deco furniture including Aalto, P.E.L.* LOC: Under railway bridge on Camden St. going south. PARK: Easy. TEL: 0171 267 4324; fax - 0171 267 5199. SER: Export; hire. VAT: Stan.

Barkes and Barkes

76 Parkway. NW1 7AH. (J.N. and P. R. Barkes). Est. 1976. Open Thurs. 12-7.30, Fri. and Sat. 12-6, and every day during exhibitions. *STOCK: Post-war Russian paintings; British artists - Nick Botting and Mark Pearson.* LOC: Just north of Regents Park. PARK: Next street. TEL: 0171 284 1550. VAT: Spec.

Madeline Crispin Antiques

95 Lisson Grove. NW1 6UP. Est. 1971. Open 10-5. *STOCK: General antiques and shipping goods.* TEL: 0171 402 6845. VAT: Stan. *Trade Only.*

NW1 continued

East-Asia Co

101-105 Camden High St. NW1. Est. 1972. Open 10-6. *STOCK: Oriental antiquarian books on history and culture; Japanese and Chinese paintings and prints; jade, netsuke, objets d'art; books on Oriental art.* TEL: 0171 388 5783; fax - 0171 387 5766.

W.R. Harvey & Co (Antiques) Ltd

BADA

70 Chalk Farm Rd. NW1 8AN. GMC. Open by appointment only. SIZE: Medium. *STOCK: Fine English furniture, £500-£50,000; clocks, mirrors, objets d'art, £250-£20,000; all 1680-1830.* LOC: 100 yds from The Roundhouse Theatre; 300 yds from Camden High St. PARK: Easy. TEL: 01993 706501; fax - 01993 906601. SER: Valuations; restorations. FAIRS: BADA, Chelsea (March, Sept). VAT: Stan/Spec.

Laurence Corner

62-64 Hampstead Rd. NW1 2NU. Est. 1955. Open 9.30-6. SIZE: Large. *STOCK: Uniforms, helmets, militaria, theatrical costumes, props, fancy dress, flags.* LOC: From Tottenham Court Rd. - Warren St. end - continue into Hampstead Rd., then Drummond St. is first turning on right by traffic lights. PARK: Easy. TEL: 0171 813 1010; fax - 0171 813 1413. SER: Hire.

Relic Antiques Trade Warehouse

127 Pancras Rd. NW1 1UN. (Malcolm Gliksten). Est. 1968. Open 10-5.30, Sat. 11-5. *STOCK: Original pond yacht models; ornate French mirrors; small decorative items and brocante; French posters.* PARK: Meters. TEL: 0171 387 6039; fax - 0171 388 2691; mobile - 0831 785059. FAIRS: Chelsea Decorative. VAT: Stan.

This and That (Furniture)

50 and 51 Chalk Farm Rd. NW1 8AN. (R.P. Schanzer). Est. 1974. Open 10.30-6 including Sun. SIZE: Medium. *STOCK: Country furniture, stripped pine, oak and walnut, 1890-1930.* LOC: Between Roundhouse and Camden Lock. PARK: Easy. TEL: 0171 267 5433. VAT: Stan.

David J. Wilkins

27 Princess Rd., Regents Park. NW1 8JR. Est. 1974. Open 9.15-5. CL: Sat. SIZE: Large. *STOCK: Oriental rugs.* LOC: Off Regent's Park Rd., near St Mark's church. PARK: Easy. TEL: 0171 722 7608; home - 01279 771368. SER: Valuations; restorations; Oriental rug broker. VAT: Stan.

LONDON NW2

The Corner Cupboard

679 Finchley Rd. NW2 2JP. (R. Fischelis). Est. 1950. Open 9.30-5.30. SIZE: Small. *STOCK: Jewellery, 18th-19th C, from £5; silver, china, glass.* LOC: Number 2 or 13 bus from Central London. PARK: Easy. TEL: 0171 435 4870. VAT: Stan.

NW2 continued

G. and F. Gillingham Ltd LAPADA

62 Menelik Rd. NW2 3RH. Est. 1960. Open by appointment. *STOCK: Furniture, 1750-1950.* TEL: 0171 435 5644; fax - same. *Export Trade Only.*

Gunter Fine Art

4 Randall Ave. NW2 7RN. (G.A. and A.M. Goodwin). Est. 1977. Open by appointment only. SIZE: Small. *STOCK: Watercolours, 18th-20th C, £150-£3,000; oil paintings, 19th-20th C £200-£3,000.* LOC: North Circular Rd., near Brent Cross shopping centre. PARK: Easy. TEL: 0181 452 3997. SER: Buys at auction.

The Schuster Gallery

PO Box 14849. NW2 5WU. ABA. Est. 1973. Open by appointment only. *STOCK: Antique prints, maps, medieval manuscripts, fine and rare colour plate books, atlases, Beatrix Potter, Kate Greenaway and Alice in Wonderland.* TEL: 0181 830 1311; fax - 0181 830 1313; e-mail - tschuster @easynet.co.uk; internet - hppt://www. acid.co. uk/acid/schus.htm.

Soviet Carpet and Art Centre

303-305 Cricklewood Broadway. NW2 6PG. (R. Rabilizirov). Est. 1983. Open 10.30-5, Sun. 10.30-5.30. CL: Sat. SIZE: Large. *STOCK: Hand-made rugs, 19th-20th C, £500-£1,000; fine and applied art, 20th C, £100-£500.* LOC: A5. PARK: Side road. TEL: 0181 452 2445. SER: Valuations; restorations (hand-made rugs). VAT: Stan.

LONDON NW3

Patricia Beckman Antiques LAPADA

NW3 7SN. (Patricia Beckman and Peter Beckman). Est. 1968. Open by appointment. *STOCK: Furniture, 18th-19th C.* TEL: 0171 435 5050/0500. VAT: Spec.

Tony Bingham LAPADA

11 Pond St. NW3 2PN. Est. 1964. *STOCK: Musical instruments, books, music, oil paintings, engravings of musical interest.* TEL: 0171 794 1596; fax - 0171 433 3662. VAT: Stan/Spec.

P.G. de Lotz

20 Downside Cres., Hampstead. NW3 2AP. Est. 1967. *STOCK: Antiquarian books on history warfare - naval, military and aviation.* TEL: 0171 794 5709; fax - 0171 284 3058. SER: Catalogue available; search. *Mail Order only.*

Dolphin Coins

2c England's Lane, Hampstead. NW3 4TG. (R. Ilsley). BNTA. Est. 1966. Open 9.30-5. SIZE: Medium. *STOCK: British and world coins, early and medieval, from 100BC, £20-£50,000.* LOC: Off Haverstock Hill. PARK: Easy. TEL: 0171 722 4116; fax - 0171 483 2000. SER: Valuations; catalogues; buys at auction (coins). VAT: Spec.

NW3 continued

Brigitte Farrelly Antiques

152 Fleet Rd., Hampstead. NW3 2QX. Est. 1948. Open 10-5. *STOCK: Furniture, pictures, porcelain, general antiques.* TEL: 0171 485 2089.

Keith Fawkes

1-3 Flask Walk, Hampstead. NW3 1HJ. Est. 1970. Open 10-5.30. *STOCK: Antiquarian and general books.* TEL: 0171 435 0614.

Otto Haas (A. and M. Rosenthal)

49 Belsize Park Gardens. NW3 4JL. Est. 1866. By appointment only. CL: Sat. *STOCK: Manuscripts, printed music, autographs, rare books on music.* TEL: 0171 722 1488; fax - 0171 722 2364.

Hampstead Antique and Craft Market

12 Heath St., Hampstead. NW3 6TE. Est. 1967. Open 10.30-5, Sat. 10-6, Sun. 11.30-5.30 (Courtyard only). CL: Mon. SIZE: 24 units. *STOCK: General antiques.* LOC: 2 mins. walk from Hampstead underground. TEL: 0171 794 3297.

Klaber and Klaber BADA

PO Box 9445. NW3 1WD. (Mrs B. Klaber and Miss P. Klaber). Est. 1968. Open by appointment. *STOCK: English and Continental porcelain and enamels, 18th-19th C.* TEL: 0171 435 6537; fax - 0171 435 9459. SER: Buys at auction (porcelain, enamels). FAIRS: Grosvenor House. VAT: Spec.

Leask Ward LAPADA

NW3 2SS. Open by appointment. *STOCK: Oriental and European antiques and paintings.* TEL: 0171 435 9781; fax - same. SER: Consultancy. VAT: Spec.

Duncan R. Miller Fine Arts BADA

17 Flask Walk, Hampstead. NW3 1HJ. SLAD. Open 10-6, Sat. 11-5, Sun. 2-5. SIZE: Small. *STOCK: Modern British and European paintings, drawings and sculpture, especially Scottish Colourist paintings.* LOC: Off Hampstead High St., near underground station. PARK: Nearby. TEL: 0171 435 5462. SER: Valuations; conservation and restoration (oils, works on paper and Oriental rugs); buys at auction. FAIRS: Grosvenor House; BADA. VAT: Spec.

Newhart (Pictures) Ltd

PO Box 1608. NW3 3LB. (Ann and Bernard Hart). Open by appointment only. *STOCK: Oil paintings and watercolours, 1850-1930, from £500.* TEL: 0171 722 2537; fax - 0171 722 4335. SER: Valuations; restorations; framing. VAT: Spec.

Malcolm Rushton - Early Oriental Art

13 Belsize Grove. NW3 4UX. (Dr Malcolm Rushton). Est. 1997. By appointment only, mainly

NW3 continued

evenings and weekends. SIZE: Small. *STOCK: Fine early Oriental art including Tang dynasty, to £15,000.* LOC: Near Belsize Park tube station, off Haverstock Hill. PARK: Easy. TEL: 0171 722 1989. SER: Valuations; restorations (ceramics, sculpture mounting); buys at auction (early Chinese and Asian art). VAT: Stan.

David and Charles Wainwright

28 Rosslyn Hill. NW3 1NH. Est. 1989. Open 10-6, Sun. 11-5. SIZE: Large. *STOCK: Furniture, 15th-20th C including 18th-19th C cupboards, dining tables and architectural pieces, £5-£2,000; stonework - urns, mortars and water containers, to 19th C; contemporary ironwork.* LOC: Hampstead, on corner of Downshire Hill. PARK: Easy. TEL: 0171 431 5900. FAIRS: Olympia. VAT: Stan.

LONDON NW4

Talking Machine

30 Watford Way, Hendon. NW4 3AL. Open 10-5, Sat. 9.30-1.30. *STOCK: Mechanical music, old gramophones, phonographs, vintage records and 78's, needles and spare parts, early radios and televisions, typewriters, sewing machines, juke boxes, early telephones.* TEL: 0181 202 3473; fax - same; mobile - 0374 103139. SER: Buys at auction. VAT: Stan.

LONDON NW5

Acquisitions (Fireplaces) Ltd

24-26 Holmes Rd., Kentish Town. NW5. (K. Kennedy). Est. 1970. Open 9-5. SIZE: Large. *STOCK: Fireplaces, Georgian, Victorian, Edwardian reproduction, fire-side accessories, £195-£595.* LOC: 3 mins. walk from Kentish Town tube station. PARK: Easy. TEL: 0171 485 4955. VAT: Stan.

Barrie Marks Ltd

11 Laurier Rd. NW5 1SD ABA. Open by appointment only. *STOCK: Antiquarian books - illustrated, private press, colourplate, colour printing; modern first editions.* TEL: 0171 482 5684; fax - 0171 284 3149.

Oriental Bronzes Ltd BADA

24a Ryland Rd. NW5 3EH. Open 10-5.30. CL: Sat. SIZE: Medium. *STOCK: Chinese archaeology, Neolithic to Ming.*

Orientalist LAPADA

74 Highgate Rd. NW5 1PB. (E. and H. Sakhai). Est. 1885. SIZE: Large. *STOCK: Rugs and carpets including reproduction.* PARK: Easy and nearby. TEL: 0171 482 0555; fax - 0171 267 9603. SER: Valuations; restorations (cleaning and repairing rugs, carpets and tapestries); buys at auction (Oriental carpets, rugs and textiles). VAT: Stan/Spec.

LONDON NW6

H. Baron

76 Fortune Green Rd. NW6 1DS. Open Fri. and Sat. 1-6. *STOCK: Antiquarian music, books on music and iconography, autograph music and letters.* TEL: 0171 794 4041; office and fax - 0181 459 2035.

John Denham Gallery

50 Mill Lane, West Hampstead. NW6 1NJ. Open 10-5. CL: Sat. *STOCK: Paintings, drawings and prints, 17th-20th C, £5-£5,000.* TEL: 0171 794 2635. SER: Restorations; conservation; re-framing. VAT: Spec.

Gallery Kaleidoscope

66 Willesden Lane. NW6 7SX. (K. Barrie). Est. 1965. Open 10-6. SIZE: Medium. *STOCK: Oils, watercolours, prints, pottery and sculpture, 19th-20th C.* LOC: 10 mins. from Marble Arch. PARK: Easy. TEL: 0171 328 5833. SER: Restorations; framing. VAT: Stan/Spec.

Milne Henderson BADA

15 Greville Place. NW6 5JE. (S. Milne Henderson). Est. 1970. Open by appointment. *STOCK: Japanese, Chinese and Korean paintings and screens.* TEL: 0171 328 2171; fax - 0171 624 7274. SER: Valuations; buys at auction. VAT: Stan.

Scope Antiques

64-66 Willesden Lane. NW6 7SX. (K. Barrie). Est. 1966. Open 10-6. SIZE: Large. *STOCK: Furniture, general antiques, decorative items, silver, bric-a-brac.* PARK: Easy. TEL: 0171 328 5833. SER: Restorations (silver). VAT: Stan/Spec.

LONDON NW8

Alfies Antique Market

13-25 Church St. NW8. (B. Gray). Open Tues.-Sat. 10-6. SIZE: 300 stands with 180+ dealers on 4 floors. TEL: 0171 723 6066; fax - 0171 724 0999; e-mail - postbox@alfies-uk.com.

20th Century Design

Stand G56/57. (Simon Alderson). *20th C furniture.* TEL: 0171 723 5613.

Michael Abrahams

Stand F117. *Oils and watercolours, 19th-20th C, from £30.* TEL: 0171 724 4041.

Beth Adams

Stand G43/44. *Decorative arts, 1860-1950's, £8-£750.* TEL: 0171 723 5613; fax - 0171 262 1576.

Mike Amey

Stand F21. *Paintings, furniture and objets d'art.* TEL: 0171 723 0678

Mavis Axe

Stand G112. *Gold, glass, costume jewellery and bric-a-brac, 1920's to 1960's, £15-£500.*

NW8 continued

Louise Ayre
Stand S11. *Objets d'art, collectables, 19th-20th C.* TEL: 0171 723 6105.

Bébé
Stand S12. (Sue Evans). *Vintage clothing.*

David Bennett Antiques
Stand G104/5. *Boxes, scent bottles, small furniture, silver inkwells, fish servers, clocks, brass scales, glasses, decanters, wooden watch stands, 1800-1900, £20-£300.* TEL: 0171 723 0564.

Bibliopola
Stand F17. (Jo Del-Grosso). *Antiquarian illustrated, childrens books; modern first editions, 1600-1940.* TEL: 0171 724 7231.

M. J. Black
Stand F59/61. *Decorative and unusual objects.* TEL: 0171 723 0687.

Maryam Bonar
Stand S111/2/9/20. *French furniture and decorative objects.* TEL: 0171 723 5731.

P. Brooks
Stand G103. *Jewellery, figures, mugs and objets d'art, Georgian to 1960, £25-£1,500.* TEL: 0171 723 0564; mobile - 0385 786395.

Jackie Brown
Stand S113-118. *Decorative items, 19th to early 20th C.* TEL: 0171 723 5731; mobile - 0589 540789.

Bernie Bruno
Stand G115. *Clocks and watches.* TEL: 0171 723 0564

Sandra Brunswick
Stand F1-12. *House and garden furnishings, from 18th C.* TEL: 0171 724 9097; fax - 0181 902 5656.

Ursula Burnstock
Stand S121/133/134. *French and English chandeliers, wall lights, mirrors, small furniture, decorative items, 19th C.*

D. Burrows
Stand G90. *Mirrors and lighting, 18th to early 20th C.* TEL: 0171 723 0449.

Vincenzo Cafferella
Stand G108/9, G118/9. *Oil paintings.,* TEL: 0171 723 0564.

William Campbell
Stand B28-32. *Period picture framer, original frames cut to size, 18th-20th C, £20-£1,000.* TEL: 0171 724 3437.

Wendy Carmichael
Stand S126-129. *Country furniture and decorative antiques, 18th-20th C.* TEL: 0171 723 0449.

NW8 continued

David Casolani
Stand F107/8. *Oil paintings and watercolours, 19th-20th C, from £30.* TEL: 0171 724 4041.

Castaside
Stand B037-42. (David Smith). *Theatre memorabilia.* TEL: 0171 723 7686.

Marsia Cavicchio
Stand G132. *Art Deco.* TEL: 0171 723 0564.

Richard Chamberlin - Target
Stand S1. *Post-war design.* TEL: 0171 723 6105.

Linda Chan
Stand G120. *Jewellery.* TEL: 0171 723 0564.

Classical Casts
Stand G49. (Tina Art). *Greek and Roman plaster casts of mythological figures and scenes, copied from originals, £8-£160.* TEL: 0171 723 5613; mobile - 0956 243784.

Collectors World
Stand G101, G130/143. (Jo Khan). *Toys including tin plate, Dinky, Meccano, lead soldiers; clocks, watches, cameras, film and TV memorabilia.* TEL: 0171 723 0564; mobile - 0860 791588.

Susie Cooper Ceramics
Stand G70-4, G93-5. (Nick Jones). *Susie Cooper ceramics, from £10.* TEL: 0171 723 0449; fax - 01634 405325.

Cristobal
Stand G125-7. (Steve Miners). *Period costume, jewellery and accessories, 1920's to 1960's, £14-£2,000.* TEL: 0171 724 7789; fax - same; mobile 0956 388194.

Dalmoak Fine Art
Stand F46/7. (W. Simpson). *Decorative items, 18th-20th C, £50-£2,000.* TEL: 0171 723 0678.

Annick Dauchy
Stand F109-111/114-116. *18th-19th C French furniture and decorative items.* TEL: 0171 723 1370.

Dodo
Stand F73, F83/84. (Liz Farrow). *Posters, tins and advertising signs, 1890-1940.* TEL: 0171 706 1545.

Gerald Dougall
Stand F16. *Decorative antiques, 18th-20th C, £20-£1,000.* TEL: 0171 723 0678.

Michael Druks
Stand 050/51. *Collectables, unusual and curious items, 19th-20th C, £5-£250.* TEL: 0171 723 2548; fax - 0171 209 2764.

East-West Antiques
Stand G113/4, G117. (Colin Thompson). *Books and Oriental objects, from 1800, £5-£500.* TEL: 0171 723 0564.

NW8 continued

Eastgates Antiques
Stand 7/9. (Joan Latford). *China teasets, wall plates, cups and saucers; Victorian coloured and Art Deco pressed glass; oil lamps and silver, 19th-20th C, £15-£1,500.* TEL: 0171 258 0312.

Paul Evans
Stand G54/55. *20th C design, art jewellery, books, £50-£1,000.* TEL: Mobile - 0378 791216.

Fashion in Print
Stand G5. (Katie Tilleke). *Fashion engravings and prints, 17th-20th C, £5-£500.* TEL: 0171 724 3722.

Julia Foster
Stand F56. (J. Foster Fogle). *19th C decorative antiques.* TEL: 0171 723 0678; mobile - 0973 146610.

Furniture and Design
Stand B3-8, B13-15. (Fiona Wicks). *English Arts and Crafts furniture, 1860-1960, £20-£2,000.* TEL: 0171 724 9761.

Robin Gardiner
Stand G45/6. *Prints.* TEL: 0171 723 0449.

Gardiner and Gardiner
Stand F13/24. (Helen Gardiner). *Ornamental antiques, 18th-19th C.* TEL: 0171 723 5595.

Gatti's Works of Art
Stand F105. *Carvings, objects and paintings, 15th-18th C, £300+.* TEL: 0171 724 2892.

Genie
Stand S57/58. (E. Deimbacher). *Collectables and cutlery, 1900-1970, £2-£100.* TEL: 0171 723 2548.

Brenda Gerwat-Clark
Stand G2/4. *Dolls and teddy bears.* TEL: 0171 724 5650.

Richard Gibbon
Stand G66-68/85/86. *Costume jewellery, 20th C decorative arts, lighting, £10-£2,000.* TEL: 0171 723 0449.

Jocelyn Glenn Antiques
Stand F22. *Furniture and objects, Edwardian and Victorian.* TEL: 0171 723 0678.

Goldsmith and Perris **LAPADA**
Stand G59-62. *Silver and plate.* TEL: 0171 724 7051.

Anne Gormley-Greene
Stand S104. *Pictures, prints, samplers, English porcelain, small decorative furniture, 18th-19th C, £5-£1,000.* TEL: 0171 723 5731.

Patricia Gould
Stand F70. *Textiles, 1400-1900, £5-£1,500.* TEL: 0171 723 0429.

NW8 continued

Guillou-Emary
Stand G40/1. (Jean Gillou). *General decorative antiques, 18th-20th C, £25-£800.* TEL: 0171 723 5613.

Annie Hartnett and Ann Davey
Stand G35/6. *Textiles, beaded bags, embroidery, period costume, quilts, linen and lace, wedding veils, stoles and collars, 18th C to 1940's, £3-£500.* TEL: 0171 706 4123; fax - 01273 749860.

Victoria Harvey
Stand F74-76. *General decorative antiques.* TEL: 0171 723 0429.

Henry Hay
Stand S54. *Art Deco, chrome and brass lamps, bakelite telephones, 20th C, £25-£500.* TEL: 0171 723 2548.

George Hepburn
Stand B43/4. *Paintings, 18th-20th C, £50-£2,000.* TEL: 0171 723 3437; mobile - 0421 598487.

Noel Hickey
Stand F54/5. *Decorative antiques.* TEL: 0171 723 0678.

Edward Holden - Old Paintings & Drawings
Stand F122-5, F130. (Holden & Li). *Oils and watercolours, drawings, 17th to early 20th C, £10-£2,000.* TEL: 0171 723 1370; fax - 0171 609 0864.

Frances Houlding
Stand G121-4. *Silver and jewellery.* TEL: 0171 723 1513.

Dudley R. Howe
Stand S55/6, S67. *Collectables, 1900-1970, £5-£50.* TEL: 0171 723 2548.

V. Hoyer-Millar
Stand F57/8. *Decorative antiques.* TEL: 0171 723 0678.

Huxtable's Old Advertising
Stand S3/5. (David Huxtable). *Advertising, collectables, tins, signs, bottles, commemoratives, old packaging, from late Victorian, 50p to £1,000.* TEL: 0171 724 2200; fax - 01727 833445.

Peter Jacques
Stand S59/60. *Brass and architectural fittings.* TEL: 0171 723 6105.

Jay and Gee
Stand B35/6. (Ms and Jacob Fefer). *Bronzes, glass and collectables, Victorian to Art Deco, £10-£2,000.* TEL: 0171 724 3437.

Jeremiah Fine Art
Stand G12/13, G145. (Jeremy Sewell). *Prints, 17th-20th C.* TEL: 0171 723 1513.

NW8 continued

Jaydev Judeo
Stand G118. *Scientific and nautical instruments.* TEL: 0171 723 0564.

Mrs Khawaja
Stand G31. *Gold jewellery, 1940's to 1960's, £50-£1,200.* TEL: 0171 723 1513; mobile - 0956 272490.

Kitchen Bygones
Stand B51-53. (N. Oakley). *Kitchen antiques - working and decorative, 1800-1940's, £1.50-£500.* TEL: 0171 258 3045; fax - 01923 260453.

Bea Kornicky
Stand G64/65a. *General antiques and Oriental items, 19th C.* TEL: 0171 723 0449.

Barry Landsman
Stand F103/4. *Watercolours, 18th-19th C, £50-£1,000.* TEL: 0171 723 1370.

Michael Lassere
Stand F40-45. *19th C general antiques, £20-£1,000.* TEL: 0171 723 2688.

Legacy
Stand G50/1. (J. Rosser and W. Garraway). *Postcards, old tins, ephemera, commemoratives, decorative and miniature objects.* TEL: 0171 723 0449.

Diane Levitt
Stand G102. TEL: 0171 723 0564. SER: Jewellery repair.

Sarah Lewis
Stand S40. *Textiles - cushions, curtains, tapestries and embroideries; trims, tassels, prints, linen and lace, silk, shawls and clothes, 19th-20th C, £10-£10,000.* TEL: 0171 723 6105.

Libra Designs
Stand B37/9, B45/6. (Marie Gottlieb). *Art Deco furniture, 20th C, £50-£5,000.* TEL: 0171 402 1976; fax - 0171 637 5210.

Aidan Lindsay
Stand B58/9. *Upholstery.* TEL: 0171 784 3439.

Marie-Louise Lowcock
Stand S52. *Millinery, using antique fabrics.* TEL: 0171 723 6105.

Connie Margrie
Stand F50/1. *Soft furnishings and decorative objects, 1830-1930.* TEL: 0171 723 0678.

Marie Antiques
Stand G107, G136/9. (Marie Warner). *Victorian jewellery, Glens silver plate, small furniture, 18th-19th C.* TEL: 0171 723 0564.

Nigel Martin
Stand S44/45. *Textiles.* TEL: 0171 723 1370.

NW8 continued

Francesca Martire
Stand F131-7. *Arts and Crafts, 20th C paintings costume jewellery, decorative arts.* TEL: 0171 723 1370.

Maryam
Stand G25. (R. Fatemi). *Jewellery, 1920- 1960's, £35-1,000.* TEL: 0171 723 1513.

The Maze
Stand G133/4. (S. Thammachote). *Costume jewellery and accessories, 1920's to 1960's, £14-£2,000.* TEL: 0171 724 7789; fax - same; mobile - 0956 388194.

Robert McCoy
Stand F20. *Paintings, 19th-20th C, £50-£500.* TEL: 0171 723 0678.

Nigel McDonald
Stand F23. *Decorative antiques.* TEL: 0171 723 0678.

Peter McGee
Stand G100. *Cameras.* TEL: 0171 723 0564.

Margaret Miall
Stand G19. *English and Continental porcelain, glass and furniture, to mid 20th C.*

Mike Miller
Stand G37. *Art Nouveau, Art Deco fittings and lighting, £25-£500.* TEL: 0171 723 5613.

Modus Vivendi
Stand G79/80. (Helga Wellingham). *Antique and decorative prints.* TEL: 0171 723 0449.

Murray
S48/49. (John Beck). *Pottery - Torquay, North Devon, Honiton and Elton.* TEL: 0171 723 6105.

Bruna Naufal
Stand B1/2. *Modernist furniture, from 1920.* TEL: 0171 724 3437.

Dean Nicholson
Stand S13. *General antiques.* TEL: 0171 723 6105.

Noe & Chiesa
Stand G87-8. *Art Deco and bakelite, 20th C, from £4.* TEL: 0171 723 0449.

Teresa Norton-Gore
Stand S10. *Buttons.* TEL: 0171 723 6105.

K. Norton-Grant
Stand F113/126. *Brass, pewter, pottery and china, 16th-20th C, £1-£250.* TEL: 0171 723 1370.

NS Watches
Stand G1. (M. Heidarieh). *Watches, clocks, prints, pens and silver, from 1850, from £10.* TEL: 0171 724 5650.

NW8 continued

Pandora Antiques
Stand G16-18/20/22. *Decorative lamps, ceiling light bowls, furniture, late 18th C.* TEL: 0171 706 3254.

G. Payder
Stand G24. TEL: 0171 723 1513.

M. Payne
Stand S53. *Jewellery, collectables.* TEL: 0171 723 6105.

Gary Pe
Stand S2/4. *Decorative arts.* TEL: 0171 723 6105.

Stevie Pearce
Stand G144, T105. *Costume jewellery, fashion accessories, 1900-1970, from £10.* TEL: 0171 723 1513.

Sam Peters
Stand S14. *Cushion repair/making.* TEL: 0171 723 4990.

Mateo Picasso
Stand B47/8, B50. *Silver and plate, furniture.* TEL: 0171 724 3439.

Pinnington & Verrinder
Stand G116/129. *Antique luggage, ceramics.* TEL: 0171 723 0564.

Laraine Plummer Antiques
Stand S131/2. *Country furniture and decorative antiques, 18th-19th C, £10-£500.* TEL: 0171 723 5731.

Katharine Pole
Stand S105. *Textiles and decorative antiques, 18th-19th C, £5-£500.* TEL: 0171 723 5731.

Shoshi Preiss
Stand F48, F71/2. *Fine arts.* TEL: 0171 723 0678.

Angela Pullan-Wells
Stand G140/2. (A. J. Futerman and D. Partleton). *Decorative furniture, art, glass, porcelain and cushions, jewellery, perfume bottles, collectables, 1780-1950, £20-£4,000.* TEL: 0171 723 0564.

Quality Artefacts
Stand F127-9/138-140. (Frank Ainsworth). *Fine glass, ceramics, collectables, Royal Lancastrian glazes, fine silver, 18th-20th C, £30-£1,800.* TEL: 0171 723 1370.

John Rastall
Stand G47/8. *20th C ceramics.* TEL: 0171 723 0449.

Angela Regana
Stand S110. TEL: 0171 723 5731.SER: Restorations.

Geoffrey Robinson
Stand G77/78/91/92. *Glass, lighting, chrome, Art Deco, 1925-1960's.* TEL: 0171 723 0449; fax - 0171 706 3254.

NW8 continued

Albert Rockman
Stand G28/9. *China.* TEL: 0171 723 1513.

Rojeh Antiques
Stand B22-27, B33/4. (I. Fayez). *Art Deco furniture, £20-£7,000.* TEL: 0171 724 6960; mobile - 0860 156390; fax - 0181 964 5959.

Alvin Ross
Stand G9/11. *Toys, games, dolls, teddy bears, miniatures, ephemera, collectables, Victorian to 1980.* TEL: 0171 723 1513.

J. Rothenberg
Stand F19. *Pottery and collectable items.* TEL: 0171 723 0678.

Hoshang Samii
Stand S102/103. *French decorative antiques, 18th-19th C, £10-£600.* TEL: 0171 723 5731.

Patrick Scola
Stand G63. *Collectables and memorabilia.* TEL: 0171 723 0449.

Michael Scott
Stand G38/9. *Furniture.* TEL: 0171 723 5613.

Scott & Lane
Stand G142. *Antiques and collectables.* TEL: 0171 723 0564.

Gloria Sinclair
Stand F118/21. *Porcelain and jewellery, 18th-19th C.* TEL: 0171 724 7118.

Derek Smith
Stand G52/3. *Lamps, china, bakelite and glass, 1920's to 1930's, £60-£350.* TEL: 0171 723 0449.

Kelvin Spooner
Stand S107. *Prints.* TEL: 0171 723 5731.

Elise Taylor
Stand G135. *Jewellery and handbags, 1860-1930.* TEL: 0171 723 0564.

Eugene Tiernan
Stand F14. *Decorative antiques, 19th-20th C, £50-£1,500.* TEL: 0171 723 8964; fax - same.

David Tileke - Antique Prints & Engravings
Stand G6-8. *Prints and engravings, 17th-20th C, £5-£500.* TEL: 0171 724 3722.

The Toy Boy
Stand G23. (Paul Mulvey). *TV and film related dolls, toys and autographs, 1960's to 1980's, £1-£2,000.*, TEL: 0171 723 1513; mobile - 0973 135906.

Travers Antiques
Stand G33/4. (Paula and S. Kluth). *Furniture and decorative objects, mainly 19th C, £250-£2,000.* TEL: 0171 258 0662.

NW8 continued

Doris Urquhart
Stand F79. *Primitive and country objects, 19th C.* TEL: 0171 723 0429.

June Victor
Stand S42-47. *Decorative textiles and antique linen, 17th-20th C, £5-£500.* TEL: 0171 723 6105.

Catherine Wallis
Stand F52/3. *Decorative items, French furniture.* TEL: 0171 723 0429.

D. F. Wallis
Stand F15. *Medical and scientific items, corkscrews, 19th C, £1-£500.* TEL: 0171 402 1038; fax - same.

Martin Wallis
Stand S106. *Paintings, prints and frames, 18th-20th C, £50-£2,000.* TEL: 0171 723 5731; fax - 01322 446443.

Jessica Ward
Stand S100/1. *Decorative antiques, 18th-20th C, £5-£1,000.* TEL: 0171 723 5731.

Stephen Watson
Stand G69. *Decorative glass including Lalique.* TEL: 0171 723 0449.

J. Zanotti
Stand F80-82. *Decorative furniture.* TEL: 0171 723 0429.

All In One Antiques
1 Church St. NW8 8EE. (H. Freeman). Open 9.30-5, Mon. 10-3. *STOCK: General antiques including upholstered items.* TEL: 0171 724 3746. SER: Restorations; upholstery.

Beverley
30 Church St., Marylebone. NW8 8EP. Open 11-7 or by appointment. *STOCK: Art Nouveau, Art Deco, decorative objects.* TEL: 0171 262 1576.

D. and A. Binder
34 Church St. NW8 8EP. Open 10-6. *STOCK: Traditional shop-fittings, counters, cabinets, vitrines and display stands.* LOC: Near Lisson Grove. TEL: 0171 723 0542; fax - 0171 724 0837.

Bizarre
24 Church St., Marylebone. NW8 8EP. (A. Taramasco and V. Conti). Open 10-5. *STOCK: Art Deco and Art Nouveau.* TEL: 0171 724 1305; fax - 0171 724 1316.

Camden Art Gallery
22 Church St. NW8 8EP. (Allen and Anne Silver). Est. 1968. Open 10-5. SIZE: Medium. *STOCK: Oil paintings and furniture, 18th-19th C, £300-£10,000.* LOC: Off Edgware Rd. PARK: Easy. TEL: 0171 262 3613; fax - 0171 723 2333. SER: Valuations; restorations (furniture, picture framing and cleaning). FAIRS: Barbican. VAT: Spec.

NW8 continued

The Collector
9 Church St., Marylebone. NW8 8EE. (Tom Power). Est. 1973. Open 9.30-5.30, Sun. 10-2. SIZE: Large. *STOCK: Royal Doulton, from 1900, £50-£3,000; Beswick, from 1920, £40-£1,000; Moorcroft, £150-£750.* LOC: 500 yards from Edgware Road underground station, 1/2 mile from Marble Arch. PARK: Easy (Not Sat.). TEL: 0171 706 4586; fax - 0171 706 2948. SER: Valuations. FAIRS: Specialist Decorative Art, mainly Royal Doulton. VAT: Stan.

Nicholas Drummond/Wrawby Moor Art Gallery Ltd
6 St. John's Wood Rd. NW8 8RE. (J.N. Drummond). Est. 1972. Open by appointment only. *STOCK: English and European oils, £250-£30,000; works on paper.* LOC: Pass Lords entrance and next lights, house last bow front on left, facing down Hamilton Terrace. TEL: 0171 286 6452; home - same; fax - 0171 266 9070. SER: Valuations; restorations (oils); buys at auction. VAT: Spec.

Robert Franses and Sons
NW8. Est. 1969. Open by appointment only. *STOCK: European and Oriental carpets, tapestries, needlework, Turkish village and early Chinese rugs.* TEL: 0171 328 0949. SER: Restorations. VAT: Stan/Spec.

Gallery of Antique Costume and Textiles
2 Church St., Marylebone. NW8 8ED. Open 10-5.30. *STOCK: Curtains, needleworks, paisley shawls, original clothing up to 1940's and English quilts, 19th-20th C; tassles, decorative borders, silk panels, velvets and brocades, £5-£20,000.* LOC: 500yds. from Marylebone tube and 1/2 mile from Marble Arch. PARK: Easy. TEL: 0171 723 9981 (ansaphone).

The Gallery on Church Street
12 Church St. NW8 8EP. (E. Phillips). Open 10-5.30. SIZE: Small. *STOCK: Posters, Art Nouveau and Art Deco, watercolours, oils and decorative prints.* PARK: Easy. TEL: 0171 723 3389; fax - 0171 723 3389.

Patricia Harvey Antiques and Decoration LAPADA
42 Church St., Marylebone. NW8 8EP. Est. 1961. Open 10-6, Sat. 11-4. SIZE: Medium. *STOCK: Decorative furniture, objets, accessories and paintings, £100-£20,000.* LOC: Between Lisson Grove and Edgware Rd., shop is near Alfies Antique Market. TEL: 0171 262 8989; home - 0171 624 1787; fax - 0171 262 9090. SER: Valuations; buys at auction; interior decoration. FAIRS: Decorative Antiques and Textiles. VAT: Stan.

NW8 continued

Just Desks
20 Church St. NW8 8EP. (G. Gordon and N. Finch). Est. 1967. Open 9.30-6 or by appointment. *STOCK: Victorian, Edwardian and reproduction desks, writing tables, davenports, bureaux, chairs, filing cabinets and roll tops.* PARK: Meters. TEL: 0171 723 7976; fax - 0171 402 6416. VAT: Stan.

Lenson Smith LAPADA
11 Church St., Lisson Grove, NW8. *STOCK: Decorative items, Vienna bronzes, early brass, animalia, French furniture.* TEL: 0171 724 7763.

Risky Business
44 Church St. NW8 8EP. (P.R. John and Mrs C.M. Dobson). Est. 1976. Open Tues.-Sat. 10-5.30. SIZE: Medium. *STOCK: Decorative furnishings, 1900-1950; vintage sporting paraphernalia, luggage; cane, rattan, club style furniture and one-off original pieces.* LOC: Near Lisson Grove. PARK: Easy. TEL: 0171 724 2194. VAT: Stan.

Silver Belle
48 Church St. NW8 8EP. Est. 1986. Open 9.30-5.30, Sun. and Mon. by appointment. SIZE: Medium. *STOCK: Silver and Sheffield plate, china including tea sets.* PARK: Easy. TEL: 0171 723 2908; fax - same. SER: Valuations; restorations (re-plating).

The Studio
NW8. (John Beer). Open by appointment only. *STOCK: British Arts and Crafts, Gothic and Art Deco, especially furniture, 1830-1960's.* TEL: 0976 704306. SER: Valuations; buys at auction.

Tara Antiques
6 Church St. NW8 8ED. (G. Robinson). Est. 1971. Open 10-6. CL: Mon. SIZE: Medium. *STOCK: Unusual marble and bronze statuary; Vienna bronzes, silver, furniture, paintings, ivory and tortoiseshell.* PARK: Easy. TEL: 0171 724 2405. SER: Buys at auction. VAT: Stan.

NW8 continued

Townsends
81 Abbey Rd., St. John's Wood and 106 Boundary Rd. NW8 0AE. (M. Townsend). Est. 1972. Open 10-6. SIZE: Large. *STOCK: Fireplaces, £100-£3,000; stained glass, £30-£200; architectural items, £10-£300; all mainly 19th C.* LOC: Corner of Abbey Rd. and Boundary Rd. PARK: Easy. TEL: 0171 624 4756; fax - 0171 372 3005. SER: Valuations. VAT: Stan.

Wellington Gallery LAPADA
1 St John's Wood High St. NW8 7NG. (Mrs K. Barclay). Open 10.30-6. *STOCK: Fine furniture, 18th-19th C; paintings, Georgian glass, porcelain, silver and Sheffield plate, general antiques.* TEL: 0171 586 2620; fax - 0171 722 4242. SER: Valuations; restorations; curtain making, upholstery.

LONDON NW9

B.C. Metalcrafts Ltd LAPADA
69 Tewkesbury Gardens. NW9 0QU. Est. 1946. Open by appointment only. *STOCK: Lighting, ormolu and marble lamps; Oriental and European vases; clocks, pre-1900, £5-£500.* Not Stocked: Silver. TEL: 0181 204 2446; fax - 0181 206 2871. SER: Restorations and conversions; buys at auction. VAT: Stan/Spec. *Trade Only.*

LONDON NW10

David Malik and Son Ltd
5 Metro Centre, Britannia Way, Park Royal. NW10 7PA. Open 9-5. CL: Sat. *STOCK: Chandeliers, wall lights.* PARK: Easy. TEL: 0181 965 4232; fax - 0181 965 2401. VAT: Stan.

LONDON NW11

Delieb Antiques
31 Woodville Rd. NW11 9TP. (E. Delieb). Est. 1953. Open by appointment only. CL: Sat. *STOCK: Collectors' silver and rarities.* TEL: 0181 458 2083. SER: Valuations.

NW11 continued

Christopher Eimer
P.O. Box 352. NW11 7RF. *STOCK: Commemorative and historical medals.* TEL: 0181 458 9933; fax - 0181 455 3535.

LONDON WC1

Abbott and Holder
30 Museum St. WC1A 1LH. Est. 1938. Open 9.30-6, Thurs. till 7. *STOCK: Pictures, especially watercolours.* TEL: 0171 637 3981. VAT: Spec

Atlantis Bookshop
49a Museum St. WC1 1LY. Open 10.30-6, Sat. 11-6. *STOCK: Antiquarian books on the occult and paranormal.* TEL: 0171 405 2120

Austin/Desmond Fine Art
Pied Bull Yard, 68/69 Great Russell St. WC1B 3BN. (J. Austin). SLAD. Open 10.30-5.30. *STOCK: Modern and contemporary British paintings and prints.* TEL: 0171 242 4443; fax - 0171 404 4480.

Cinema Bookshop
13-14 Great Russell St. WC1B 3NH. (F. Zentner). Est. 1969. Open 10.30-5.30. SIZE: Small. *STOCK: Books, magazines, posters and stills.* LOC: First right off Tottenham Court Rd. PARK: Easy. TEL: 0171 637 0206. SER: Mail order. VAT: Stan.

Classic Collection
2 Pied Bull Yard, Bury Place. WC1A 2JR. Open 9-5.30. SIZE: Medium. *STOCK: Classic and collectors' cameras, 1850-1960, from £10; daguerreotypes, optical toys and steroscopes.* LOC: Near Great Russell St. and Bloomsbury. PARK: Easy. TEL: 0171 831 6000; fax - 0171 831 5424; internet - www.classiccollection.com. SER: Valuations; restorations. FAIRS: Camera Collectors, U.K. and Europe. VAT: Stan.

George and Peter Cohn
Unit 21, 21 Wren St. WC1X 0HF. Est. 1947. Open 9-5, Sat. and Fri. pm. by appointment. *STOCK: Decorative lights.* PARK: Forecourt. TEL: 0171 278 3749. SER: Restorations (chandeliers and wall-lights). *Trade Only.*

Sebastian D'Orsai Ltd
39 Theobalds Rd. WC1X 8NW. (A. Brooks). Open 9-5. CL: Sat. *STOCK: Framed watercolours.* TEL: 0171 405 6663. SER: Restorations (paintings and prints); framing; gilding. VAT: Stan.

J.A.L. Franks & Co
7 New Oxford St. WC1A 1BA. Est. 1947. *STOCK: Stamps and maps.* TEL: 0171 405 0274; fax - 0171 430 1259.

WC1 continued

Robert Frew Ltd
106 Gt. Russell St. WC1B 3NA. ABA, PBFA. Open 10-6, Sat. 10-2. *STOCK: Books, 15th-20th C, £5-£25,000; maps and prints, 15th-19th C, £5-£5,000.* LOC: Turn right off Tottenham Court Rd. to British Museum, shop on left past YMCA. PARK: Easy. TEL: 0171 580 2311. FAIRS: ABA Grosvenor House, Chelsea; PBFA, Hotel Russell; various USA. VAT: Stan.

Jessop Classic Photographica
67 Great Russell St. WC1 3BN. Open 9-5.30. *STOCK: Classic photographic equipment, cameras and optical toys.* TEL: 0171 831 3640; fax - 0171 831 3956.

London Antiquarian Book Arcade
37 Great Russell St. WC1. (Ronald Morris and Myrna Adolph-Morris). ABA. Open 10-6, Thurs. 10-8, Sun. 12-5. SIZE: Large. *STOCK: Antiquarian books, 17th-19th C, £30-£2,000; modern first editions, £10-£6,000; maps and prints, 18th-19th C, £10-£500; modern prints, £10-£500.* LOC: Near British Museum. TEL: 0171 436 2054; home - same; fax - 0171 436 2057; e-mail - antiqarc@easynet.co.uk. SER: Valuations; book search. VAT: Stan.

Marchmont Bookshop
39 Burton St. WC1H 9AL. (D. Holder). Open 11-6.30. CL: Sat. *STOCK: Literature, including modern first editions.* TEL: 0171 387 7989.

The Museum Bookshop
36 Gt. Russell St. WC1B 3PP. (Ashley Jones). Est. 1982. Open 10-5.30. *STOCK: Books on antiquities - Egyptian, Middle Eastern, classical; glass, ceramics, conservation.* LOC: 3 minutes from Tottenham Court Rd. underground station. PARK: Easy. TEL: 0171 580 4086; fax - 0171 436 4361.

Nortonbury Antiques LAPADA
BCM Box 5345. WC1N 3XX. Open by appointment. *STOCK: Silver, 17th-19th C.* TEL: 01984 631668; fax - same; mobile - 0374 174092.

The Print Room
37 Museum St. WC1A 1LP. (A. Balfour-Lynn and K. Surya). Est. 1984. Open 10-6, Sat. 10-4, other times by appointment. *STOCK: Prints including natural history, views of London, costume plates and caricatures, 1580-1850, £10-£3,000.* LOC: Off Gt. Russell St., opposite British Museum. PARK: N.C.P. Bloomsbury Sq. TEL: 0171 430 0159; fax - 0171 831 2874. SER: Valuations; buys at auction (antiquarian books and prints).

WC1 continued

Rennies

13 Rugby St. WC1.(Paul and Karen Rennie). Open Tues.-Sat. *STOCK: Decorative arts, 1880-1960; vintage posters, mainly British.* TEL: 0171 405 0220.

Skoob Books Ltd

11a-15 Sicilian Ave., Southampton Row, Holborn. WC1A 2QH. Est. 1978. Open 10.30-6.30. SIZE: Large. *STOCK: Secondhand books specialising in philosophy, cultural strudies, literature, science and technology.* LOC: In pedestrian arcade, near Holborn Underground. PARK: Easy. TEL: 0171 404 3063; fax - 0171 404 4398. SER: Publishers of Skoob Seriph and Skoob Pacifica series; catalogue for philosophy.

Skoob Two

17 Sicilian Ave., Southampton Row. WC1A 2QH. Open 10.30-6.30. SIZE: Medium. *STOCK: Secondhand books on anthropology, the sciences, classics, psychology, esoterica and new age; used classical and jazz CDs.* TEL: 0171 405 0030; fax - 0171 404 4398. SER: Publishers of Skoob Esoterica.

LONDON WC2

Anchor Antiques Ltd

26 Charing Cross Rd. WC2H 0DG. (K.B. Embden and H. Samne). Est. 1964. Open by appointment. *STOCK: Continental and Oriental ceramics, European works of art and objets de vertu.* TEL: 0171 836 5686. VAT: Spec. *Trade Only.*

Apple Market Stalls

Covent Garden Market. WC2E 8RF. Open every Monday. SIZE: 48 stalls. *STOCK: General antiques and quality collectables.* TEL: 0171 836 9136.

A.H. Baldwin and Sons Ltd BADA

11 Adelphi Terrace. WC2N 6BJ. IAPN, BNTA. Est. 1872. Open 9-5. CL: Sat. SIZE: Medium. *STOCK: Coins, 600 BC to present; commemorative medals, 16th C to present, numismatic literature.* LOC: Off Robert St., near Charing Cross. TEL: 0171 930 6879/839 1310; fax - 0171 930 9450. SER: Valuations; auction agents for selling and purchasing. VAT: Stan/Spec.

Bell, Book and Radmall

4 Cecil Court. WC2N 4HE. Est. 1974. Open 10-5.30, Sat. 11-4. *STOCK: First editions of 19th-20th C English and American literature including detective fiction.* TEL: 0171 240 2161.

Blackwell's

100 Charing Cross Rd. WC2. SIZE: Small. *STOCK: Antiquarian and rare modern books.*

WC2 continued

M. Bord (Gold Coin Exchange)

16 Charing Cross Rd. WC2H 0HR. Est. 1969. Open 9.30-6. SIZE: Small. *STOCK: Gold, silver and copper coins, Roman to Elizabeth II, all prices.* LOC: Near Leicester Sq. underground station. TEL: 0171 836 0631/240 0479. SER: Valuations; buys at auction. FAIRS: All major coin. VAT: Stan/Spec.

Covent Garden Flea Market

Jubilee Market, Covent Garden. WC2E 8RB. (Sherman and Waterman Associates Ltd). Est. 1975. Open Mon. and Bank Holidays 5-5. SIZE: 200 stalls. *STOCK: General antiques.* LOC: South side of piazza, just off The Strand, via Southampton St. PARK: Easy and N.C.P. Drury Lane. TEL: 0171 836 2139/240 7405.

Deco Inspired

67 Monmouth St. WC2H 9DG. (Stanley and Nicole Chaman). Est. 1984. Open 11-7. SIZE: Small. *STOCK: American furniture, lighting and objets, 1930-1970.* PARK: Easy. TEL: 0171 240 5719. VAT: Stan.

David Drummond at Pleasures of Past Times

11 Cecil Court, Charing Cross Rd. WC2N 4EZ. Est. 1962. Open 11-2.30 and 3.30-5.45 and usually 1st Sat. monthly, other times by appointment. SIZE: Medium. *STOCK: Scarce and out-of-print books of the performing arts; early juvenile and illustrated books; vintage postcards, valentines, entertainment ephemera.* Not Stocked: Coins, stamps, medals, jewellery, maps, cigarette cards. LOC: In pedestrian court between Charing Cross Rd. and St. Martin's Lane. TEL: 0171 836 1142. VAT: Stan.

W. and G. Foyle Ltd

113-119 Charing Cross Rd. WC2. Est. 1904. *STOCK: Antiquarian books.*

Stanley Gibbons

399 Strand. WC2R 0LX. Est. 1856. Open 8.30-6, Sat. 9.30-5.30. SIZE: Large. *STOCK: Popular and specialised stamps, postal history, catalogues, albums, accessories; autographs and memorabilia.* LOC: Opposite Savoy Hotel. TEL: 0171 836 8444; fax - 0171 836 7342. SER: Valuations. VAT: Stan/Spec.

Gillian Gould at Ocean Leisure

Embankment Place, 11-14 Northumberland Avenue. WC2N 5AQ. Est. 1988. Open 9.30-6, Thurs. 9.30-7, Sat. 9.30-5.30 or by appointment. SIZE: Small. *STOCK: Marine antiques and collectables, scientific instruments, £30-£1,000.* PARK: Meters. TEL: 0171 930 5050; fax - 0171 930 3032; home - 0171 419 0500; fax - 0171 419 0400; mobile - 0831 150060. SER: Valuations; restorations; hire; sources gifts for personal and corporate presentation; buys at auction. VAT: Stan.

WC2 continued

Grosvenor Prints
28/32 Shelton St., Covent Garden. WC2H 9HP. Est. 1975. Open 10-6, Sat. 11-4. SIZE: Large. *STOCK: 18th-19th C topographical and decorative prints, specialising in portraits, dogs and British field sports.* LOC: One street north of Covent Garden tube. PARK: Easy. TEL: 0171 836 1979; fax - 0171 379 6695. SER: Valuations; restorations; buys at auction. VAT: Stan/Spec.

Lee Jackson
2 Southampton St., Covent Garden. WC2E 7HA. PBFA. Est. 1996. Open 10-5.30. SIZE: Large. *STOCK: Maps and views of the world, 16th-19th C, £10-£3,000.* LOC: Off the Strand, opposite the Savoy Hotel. PARK: Meters. TEL: 0171 240 1970. VAT: Stan.

S. and H. Jewell Ltd
26 Parker St. WC2B 5PH. Est. 1830. Open 9-5.30, Sat. by appointment. SIZE: Large. *STOCK: Furniture.* TEL: 0171 405 8520. SER: Valuations; restorations. VAT: Stan/Spec.

Thomas Kettle Ltd
53a Neal St. WC2. Est. 1974. Open 10-7. SIZE: Medium. *STOCK: Wrist watches, 1910-1950, £350-£5,000; contemporary designer jewellery, £40-£2,000.* LOC: Near Covent Garden tube. PARK: Leicester Sq. TEL: 0171 379 3579. SER: Valuations; restorations (wrist watches). VAT: Stan.

The London Silver Vaults
Chancery House, 53-65 Chancery Lane. WC2. Est. 1892. Open 9-5.30, Sat. 9-1. SIZE: 34 shops. *STOCK: Antique and modern silver, plate, jewellery, objets d'art, clocks, watches, collectors' items.* TEL: 0171 242 3844. The following are some of the dealers at these vaults.

A. M. W. Silverware
Vault 52. TEL: 0171 242 3620; fax - 0171 831 3923.

Argenteus Ltd — LAPADA
Vault 2. TEL: 0171 831 3637; fax - 0171 430 0126. VAT: Stan/Spec.

Benjamin Jewellery Ltd — LAPADA
Vault 46. TEL: 0171 831 1380; fax - 0171 831 4629.

Lawrence Block
Vault 28 and 65. Est. 1959. *Silver especially flatware; jewellery.* TEL: 0171 242 0749. SER: Valuations; restorations; buys at auction.

A. Bloom
Vault 27. TEL: 0171 242 6189.

Luigi Brian Antiques
Vault 17. TEL: 0171 405 2484; fax - same.

WC2 continued

B.L. Collins
Vault 20. TEL: 0171 404 0628; fax - 0171 404 1451.

P. Daniels
Vault 51. TEL: 0171 430 1327.

B. Douglas — LAPADA
Vault 12/14. TEL: 0171 242 7073.

M.J. Dubiner
Vault 38.

R. Feldman Ltd — LAPADA
Vault 4/6. TEL: 0171 405 6111; fax - 0171 430 0126.

I. Franks — LAPADA
Vault 9/11. Est. 1926. TEL: 0171 242 4035.

Hamilton
Vault 25. TEL: 0171 831 7030; fax - 0171 831 5483.

S. Kalms — LAPADA
Vault 31/32. TEL: 0171 430 1254; fax - 0171 405 6206.

B. Lampert
Vault 19. TEL: 0171 242 4121.

Langfords — LAPADA
Vault 8/10. Est. 1940. *Silver and plate especially cutlery.* TEL: 0171 242 5506; fax - 0171 405 0431. SER:Valuations. VAT: Stan/Spec.

Nat Leslie Ltd
Vault 21/22/23. Est. 1940. *Silver and plate, especially cutlery.* TEL: 0171 242 4787; fax - 0171 242 4504. VAT: Stan/Spec.

Linden and Co. (Antiques) Ltd
Vault 7. (H, F, H.M. and S. C. Linden). TEL: 0171 242 4863; fax - 0171 405 9946. VAT: Stan/Spec.

C. and T. Mammon
Vault 31 & 64. TEL: 0171 405 2397.

I. Nagioff (Jewellery)
Vault 63 and 69. (I. and R. Nagioff). Est. 1955. *Jewellery, 18th-20th C, £5-£2,000+; objets d'art, 19th C, to £200.* TEL: 0171 405 3766. SER: Valuations; restorations (jewellery). VAT: Stan.

Percy's — LAPADA
Vault 16. *Candelabra, candlesticks, flatware and collectables.* TEL: 0171 242 3618.

Rare Art
Vault 15. TEL: 0171 405 9968.

Saunders
Vault 60.

WC2 continued

David S. Shure and Co
Vault 1. (S. Bulka). Est. 1900. Author. *Silver and plate.* TEL: 0171 405 0011; fax - same. SER: Valuations. VAT: Stan.

Silstar
Vault 29. (B. Stern). Est. 1955. TEL: 0171 242 6740. VAT: Stan/Spec.

B. Silverman BADA
Vault 26/33. (S. and R. Silverman). Est. 1927. TEL: 0171 242 3269. SER:Valuations; buys at auction. VAT: Stan/Spec.

Jack Simons (Antiques) Ltd LAPADA
Vault 35 and 37. Est. 1955. TEL: 0171 242 3221. VAT: Stan/Spec.

S. and J. Stodel
Vault 24. TEL: 0171 405 7009; fax - 0171 242 6366.

A. Urbach
Vault 50.

William Walter Antiques Ltd BADA LAPADA
Vault 3/5. (R.W. Walter). Est. 1927. TEL: 0171 242 3248; fax - 0171 404 1280. SER:Valuations; restorations (silver, plate).

A. and G. Weiss
Vault 42/44. TEL: 0171 242 8100. VAT: Stan.

Peter K. Weiss
Vault 18. Est. 1955. *Watches, clocks.* TEL: 0171 242 8100; fax - 0171 242 7310. VAT: Stan.

Wolfe (Jewellery)
Vault 41. TEL: 0171 405 2101; fax - same. VAT: Stan/Spec.

Lunn Antiques
22 Cucumber Alley, Thomas Neal's, Shorts Gardens. WC2. (S. Lunn). Est. 1975. Open 10-6. *STOCK: Victorian and Edwardian hand worked linens, sheets, bedspreads, pillowcases, tablecloths, Oriental embroidery, pre-war clothing, some early lace and costume.* TEL: 0171 379 1974. VAT: Stan.

Arthur Middleton
12 New Row, Covent Garden. WC2N 4LF. Est. 1968. Open 10-6, Sat. by appointment only. SIZE: Medium. *STOCK: Globes, 1720-1950, from miniatures to large library pairs; scientific instruments - navigation, astronomy, surveying, microscopes, 18th-19th C, £100-£50,000.* LOC: New Row runs between Leicester Sq. and Covent Garden. Shop 300yds. east from Leicester Sq. TEL: 0171 836 7042/7062; fax - 0171 497 2486. SER: Valuations; buys at auction; prop hire. VAT: Stan.

WC2 continued

Pearl Cross Ltd
35 St. Martin's Court. WC2N 4AL. Est. 1897. Open 9.30-4.45. CL: Sat. *STOCK: Jewellery, silver, clocks, watches.* PARK: Meters. TEL: 0171 836 2814/240 0795; fax - 0171 240 2733. SER: Valuations; restorations (jewellery, silver). VAT: Stan/Spec.

Henry Pordes Books Ltd
58-60 Charing Cross Rd. WC2H 0BB. Open 10-7. *STOCK: Secondhand and remainder books on most subjects including antiques.* TEL: 0171 836 9031; fax - 0181 886 2201.

Reg and Philip Remington
18 Cecil Court, Charing Cross Rd. WC2N 4HE. ABA. Est. 1979. Open 10-5, Sat. by appointment. SIZE: Medium. *STOCK: Voyages and travels, 17th-20th C, £5-£1,000.* LOC: Near Trafalgar Sq. TEL: 0171 836 9771. SER: Buys at auction. FAIRS: London Book, Grosvenor House. VAT: Stan.

Bertram Rota Ltd
1st Floor, 31 Long Acre. WC2E 9LT. Est. 1923. Open 9.30-5.30. CL: Sat. *STOCK: Antiquarian and secondhand books, especially first editions, private presses, English literature, and literary autographs.* TEL: 0171 836 0723.

The Silver Mouse Trap
56 Carey St. WC2A 2JB. (A. Woodhouse). Est. 1690. Open 10-5. CL: Sat. SIZE: Medium. *STOCK: Jewellery, silver.* LOC: South of Lincoln's Inn Fields. TEL: 0171 405 2578. SER: Valuations; restorations. VAT: Spec.

Stage Door Prints
9 Cecil Court, Charing Cross Rd. WC2N 4EZ. (A. Reynold). Open 11-6. *STOCK: Prints of performing arts, sports and topographical; signed photographs, maps, Victorian cards, valentines; film shop - posters, stills, books, memorabilia; performing arts book room and bargain basement.* TEL: 0171 240 1683.

Storey's Ltd
3 Cecil Court, Charing Cross Rd. WC2 4EZ. (T. Kingswood). Est. 1929. Open 10-6. *STOCK: Prints, especially naval and military, topography, antiquarian books.* LOC: Between Charing Cross Rd. and St. Martin's Lane. PARK: Trafalgar Square garage. TEL: 0171 836 3777; fax - same.

Tooley Adams & Co.
13 Cecil Court, Charing Cross Rd. WC2N 4EZ. (D. Adams and S. Luck). ABA. Est. 1964. Open 9-5. SIZE: Large. *STOCK: Antiquarian maps, atlases; travel and map related reference books.* LOC: Between St. Martin's Lane and Charing Cross Rd. PARK: St. Martin's Lane. TEL: 0171 240 4406; fax - 0171 240 8058; e-mail - tooley-adams@compuserve.com. SER: Valuations; restorations. FAIRS: Bonnington Map; Imcos Map. VAT: Stan.

WC2 continued

Trafalgar Square Collectors Centre

7 Whitcomb St. WC2H 7HA. (D.C. Pratchett and R.D. Holdich). Est. 1979. Open 10-5. CL: Sat. *STOCK: Coins and military medals, bonds, banknotes, badges and militaria, 18th-20th C, £5-£10,000.* LOC: Next to National Gallery. PARK: NCP. TEL: 0171 930 1979; fax - 0171 930 1152. SER: Valuations; buys at auction (coins and military medals). VAT: Stan/Spec.

Travis and Emery

17 Cecil Court, Charing Cross Rd. WC2N 4EZ. (V. Emery). ABA. Est. 1960. Open 10-6. SIZE: Medium. *STOCK: Musical literature, music and prints.* LOC: Between Charing Cross Rd. and St. Martin's Lane. PARK: Meters. TEL: 0171 240 2129; fax - 0171 497 0790. VAT: Stan.

Watkins Books Ltd

19 Cecil Court, Charing Cross Rd. WC2N 4EZ. Est. 1880. Open 10-6, Thurs. 10-8, Sat. 10.30-6. *STOCK: Mysticism, occultism, Oriental religions, astrology, psychology, complementary medicine and a wide selection of books in the field of mind, body and spirit - both new and secondhand.* TEL: 0171 836 2182; fax - 0171 836 6700.

WC2 continued

The Witch Ball

2 Cecil Court, Charing Cross Rd. WC2. (R. Glassman). Resident. Est. 1969. Open 10.30-6. SIZE: Small. *STOCK: Prints relating to the performing arts, from 17th C, 20th C posters.* LOC: 2 mins. from Leicester Sq. tube station. PARK: NCP nearby. TEL: 0171 836 2922. VAT: Stan.

Zeno Booksellers and Publishers

6 Denmark St. WC2H 8LP. Est. 1944. Open 9.30-6, Sat. till 5. SIZE: Medium. *STOCK: Antiquarian books on Greece, Cyprus, Byzantium, Turkey, Middle East and the Balkans.* LOC: From Tottenham Court Rd., into Charing Cross Rd., first turning on left. TEL: 0171 240 1968; 0171 836 2522; fax - same; e-mail - L4books@AOL.com.

Zwemmer

24 Litchfield St. WC2H 9NJ. Est. 1921. Open 10-6.30, Sat. 10-6. SIZE: Large. *STOCK: Books on art and fine art; rare and out-of-print catalogue raisonnés.* LOC: Just south of Cambridge Circus, Leicester Sq. underground. TEL: 0171 379 7886.

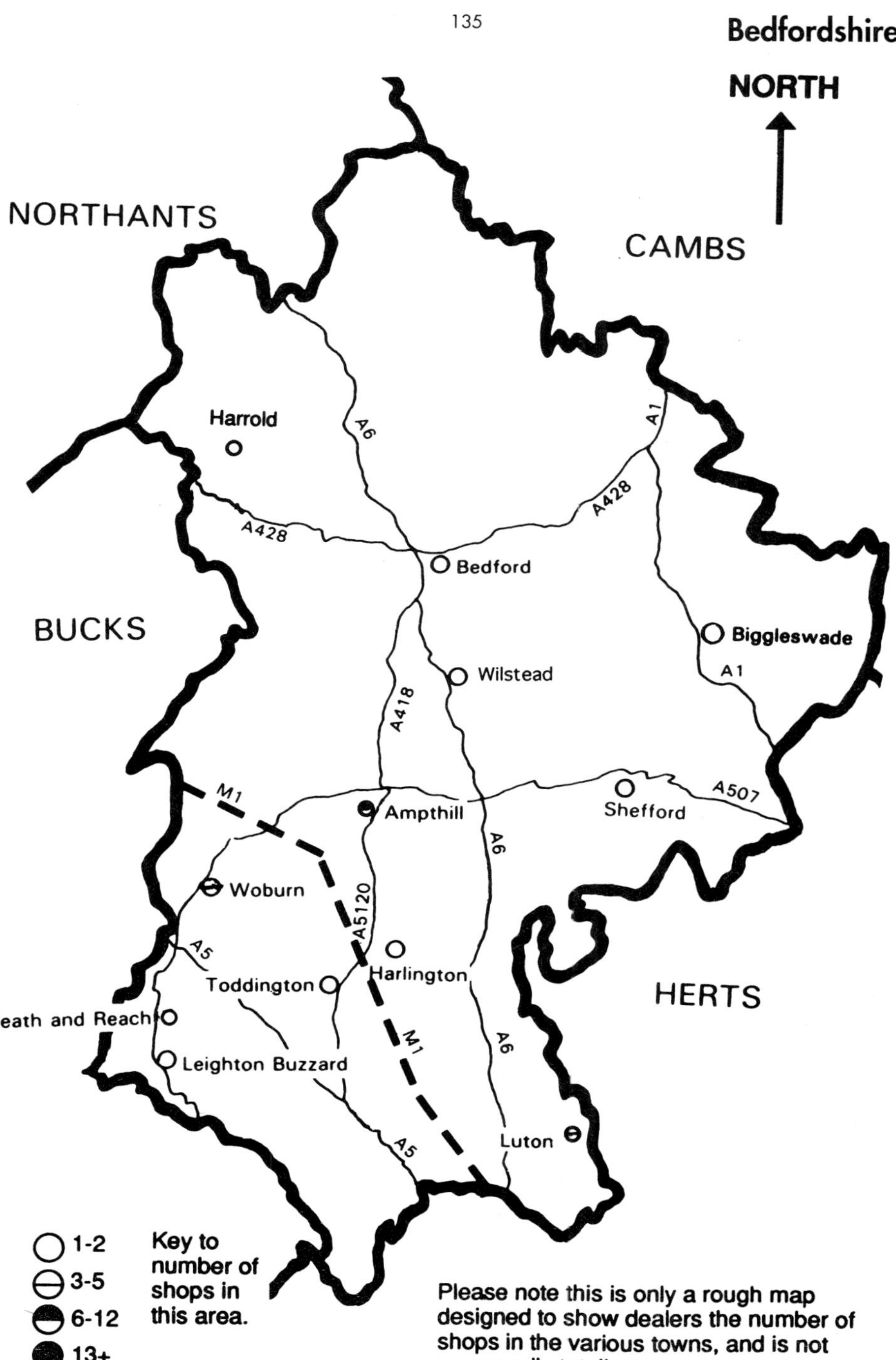

Please note this is only a rough map designed to show dealers the number of shops in the various towns, and is not necessarily totally accurate.

AMPTHILL

Ampthill Antiques
Market Sq. MK45 5ZP. (A. Olney). Est. 1980. Open 10-5, Sun. 2-5. CL: Mon. SIZE: Large. *STOCK: Furniture, collectables, jewellery, Clarice Cliff, clocks.* LOC: Town centre. PARK: Easy and at rear. TEL: 01525 403344.

Ampthill Emporium
6 Bedford St. MK45 2NB. Est. 1979. Open 10-5.30 including Sun. SIZE: Large - 25 dealers. *STOCK: Antique and secondhand furniture.* LOC: 5 mins. from junction 13, M1. PARK: Easy. TEL: 01525 402131.

Robert Harman Antiques
Church St. MK45. (Robert Harman Cannell). Est. 1979. Open by appointment only. SIZE: Medium. *STOCK: Furniture, £1,000-£30,000; tea caddies, £200-£10,000; works of art, £200-£20,000, all 18th to early 19th C.* TEL: 01525 402322. SER: Valuations; restorations (furniture); buys at auction. FAIRS: Olympia; Chelsea; BADA. VAT: Spec.

House of Clocks
106 Dunstable St. Resident. (John Ginty). Est. 1957. Open 9-5, Sun. 1-5. SIZE: Medium. *STOCK: Clocks including longcase, bracket, carriage and wall, £150-£12,000.* PARK: Behind Market Sq. TEL: 01525 403136; fax - same. SER: Valuations; restorations (clocks). FAIRS: Manchester; Birmingham: Uxbridge: Kettering: Luton. VAT: Stan/Spec.

Paris Antiques
97B Dunstable St. MK45 2NG. (Paul and Elizabeth Northwood). Est. 1985. Open 9.30-5. CL: Mon. SIZE: Medium. *STOCK: Furniture, 18th to early 20th C, £250-£4,000; brass and copper, silver and plate, pictures and smalls.* LOC: Off junction 12, M1. PARK: Opposite. TEL: 01525 840488; home - 01525 861420; mobile - 0802 535059. SER: Valuations; restorations (mainly furniture, some metal); buys at auction.

Pilgrim Antiques
11 Dunstable St. MK45 1BY. (Gary Lester). Est. 1982. Open 10-5.30, including Sun. SIZE: Large. *STOCK: Furniture including dining tables, bookcases, chairs and upholstery, 18th-20th C, £500-£5,000.* LOC: Town centre. PARK: Rear of premises. TEL: 01525 633023; home - 01525 752460. SER: Restorations.

The Pine Parlour
82a Dunstable St. MK45 2LF. (Lynn Barker). Est. 1989. Open 10-5 including Sun. CL: Mon. SIZE: Small. *STOCK: Pine furniture, 19th C, £200-£800; kitchenalia, £5-£60.* PARK: Easy. TEL: 01525 403030; home - same. SER: Valuations.

Ampthill continued

Guy Roe Antiques
20 Dunstable St. MK45 2JT. Est. 1990. Open 9.30-5, appointment preferred. CL: Sat. and Sun. except by appointment. SIZE: Small. *STOCK: Fine furniture, 18th to early 19th C, £500-£5,000; tea caddies, associated objects.* LOC: Near council offices on Flitwick road. PARK: Easy, opposite. TEL: 01525 404795; fax - same; mobile - 0374 808347. VAT: Stan/Spec. *Mainly Trade.*

S. and S. Timms Antiques Ltd LAPADA
Rear of 20 Dunstable St. MK45 2JT. Est. 1976. Open Fri., Sat. and Sun. 11-5; Mon.-Fri. 9.30-5 (trade only) or any time by appointment. SIZE: Large. *STOCK: Furniture, 1700-1900, £100-£10,000; copper, brass.* LOC: A5120. PARK: Easy. TEL: 01525 403067; home - 01525 718829; mobile - 0860 482995 and 0585 458541. FAIRS: LAPADA, Guildford and provincial; Chelsea Decorative. VAT: Stan/Spec.

Transatlantic Antiques & Fine Art
101 Dunstable St. MK45. (I.J. and D. M. Higgins). Est. 1995. Open 10.30-5 including Sun. CL: Mon. SIZE: Large. *STOCK: 19th C furniture, £150-£4,000; glass, ceramics, silver and metalware, 19th C, £5-£3,000; pictures and interesting objects, 18th-19th C, £50-£1,000.* LOC: Main street. PARK: Off Market Square. TEL: 01525 403346; fax - same. SER: Restorations; buys at auction. FAIRS: NEC. VAT: Spec.

BEDFORD

Architectural Antiques - Bedford
70 Pembroke St. MK40 3RQ. (Paul and Linda Hoare). Est. 1989. Open 12-5, Sat. 10-5. SIZE: Medium. *STOCK: Early Georgian to early 20th C fireplaces, £500-£1,000; sanitary ware, from late Victorian, £100-£500; doors, panelling, pews, chimney pots and other architectural items, Georgian and Victorian, £50-£100.* LOC: Follow signs to town centre, turn on The Embankment or Castle Rd., shop is off Castle Rd., near Post Office. PARK: Easy. TEL: 01234 213131/ 343421. SER: Valuations; restorations; installations, particularly period fireplaces.

BIGGLESWADE

Shortmead Antiques
46 Shortmead St. SG18 0AP. (S.E. Sinfield). Open 10.30-4. CL: Thurs. SIZE: Small. *STOCK: Furniture, £50-£1,000; boxes, porcelain, silver, bronzes, copper and brass, all pre-1930.* LOC: 1/2 mile from A1. TEL: 01767 601780 (ansaphone).

HARLINGTON

Willow Farm Pine Centre

Willow Farm. LU5 6LJ. (M. and A. Price). Est. 1974. Open 10-5 daily. SIZE: Large. *STOCK: Good reclaimed and antique pine.* LOC: Off Barton Rd., near kennels. PARK: Easy. TEL: 01525 872052; home - same.

HEATH AND REACH, Nr. Leighton Buzzard

Baroq at Brindleys

Woburn Rd. LU7 0AR. (Brian Dawson). Open 10-5, Sun. 12-4. SIZE: 20 dealers. *STOCK: Pottery and porcelain, £10-£500; paintings and watercolours, 18th-20th C, £100-£1,000; furniture, £100-£2,500.* LOC: A418, off A5. PARK: Easy and Red Lion. TEL: 01525 237750; restoration - 01525 237831; home - 01234 240448.

Charterhouse Gallery Ltd

26 Birds Hill. LU7 0AQ. Open by appointment only. *STOCK: 19th to early 20th C watercolours.* PARK: Easy - next door. TEL: 01525 237379. SER: Restoration (pictures and frames).

LEIGHTON BUZZARD

David Ball Antique Furnisher LAPADA

59 North St. LU7 7EQ. (D. and J. Ball). Est. 1968. Open Mon. 10-5 or by appointment. *STOCK: Furniture, general antiques and watercolours, 17th-20th C, £3-£2,000.* LOC: A418 to Woburn. PARK: Easy. TEL: 01525 382954; home - 01525 210753. SER: Valuations; restorations. FAIRS: Luton. VAT: Stan/Spec.

LUTON

Bargain Box

4 & 6a Adelaide St. LU1 5BB. Open 9-6, Wed. 9-1. *STOCK: General antiques and collectables.* TEL: 01582 423809.

Bernadette's Antiques & Collectables

19a Adelaide St. LU1 5BB. Open 9-6, Wed. 9-1. *STOCK: General antiques.* TEL: 01582 423809.

J. Denton (Antiques)

Rear of 440 Dunstable Rd. LU4 8DJ. Est. 1979. Open 10.15-4 or by appointment. CL: Sat. SIZE: Medium. *STOCK: Furniture and small items, Victorian and Edwardian; shipping goods, bric-a-brac.* LOC: Corner of Arundel Rd. and Dunstable Rd. PARK: Easy. TEL: 01582 582726; home - 01296 661471.

Foye Gallery

15 Stanley St. LU1 5AL. Est. 1960. Open 9.30-5 or by appointment. *STOCK: Engravings, etchings, drawings, watercolours, paintings, maps, books.* TEL: 01582 738487. VAT: Stan.

Luton continued

Knight's Gallery

41 Mill St. LU1 2NA. (J.C. Knight). Est. 1973. Open 9-5, Sat. 10-1. SIZE: Small. *STOCK: Watercolours, 19th-20th C, £50-£2,000.* PARK: Easy. TEL: 01582 736266; home - 01582 615495. SER: Valuations; restorations; framing; buys at auction (watercolours).

Luton Antiques Centre

Auction House, Crescent Rd. LU2 0AH. (Frank and Shirley Horn). Est. 1977. Open 10-5, Wed. and Thurs. 10-8. SIZE: Large. *STOCK: Furniture, Victorian to 1930's, £50-£500; china and glass, Victorian to 1950's, £5-£150.* LOC: Near rail and bus stations. PARK: Easy. TEL: 01582 405281/738624; fax - 01582 454080. SER: Valuations. FAIRS: Major.

S & J Acquisitions

28 Hitchin Rd. (Syliva and Jo Holdstock). Est. 1992. Open 12-3, Sat. 11-4. CL: Wed., Fri. and Sun. except by appointment. SIZE: Medium. *STOCK: Antiques for the garden, 18th-19th C; decorative artefacts for pubs etc, farming bygones and kitchenalia; all £5-£400.* LOC: From M1, junction 10 (Luton Airport), follow town centre signs, Hitchin Rd., adjacent to railway station. PARK: Easy. TEL: 01582 451507; home - 01582 415834.

The classical early floral engraved key wound 30-hour clock. One engraver would work for several clockmakers. Notice that the engraving was done before the winding holes were drilled and so they go through the pattern - this frequently happens.

From an article entitled "The 30-Hour Longcase Clock" by Edward Manson which appeared in the April 1998 issue of **Antique Collecting**

SHEFFORD

Secondhand Alley

2-4 High St. SG17 5DG. Open Mon., Fri. and Sat. 9-5, Sun. and Bank Holidays 12-5. *STOCK: Shipping furniture, bric-a-brac.* PARK: Easy. TEL: 01462 814747. VAT: Spec.

TODDINGTON, Nr. Dunstable

Cobblers Hall Antiques

119/121 Leighton Rd. LU5 6AR. (A.G. Huckett). Est. 1974. Open by appointment only. *STOCK: English porcelain, mid-18th to mid-19th C, £25-£1,000. Georgian and early Victorian writing boxes and slopes, treen, Tunbridgeware, period brass and copper.* PARK: Easy. TEL: 01525 872890. FAIRS: Worcester; Petersfield; Derby; Felbridge; Oatland Park; NEC; Luton; Solihull; Wilton; Chepstow; Burford.

WILSTEAD (WILSHAMSTEAD) Nr. Bedford

Manor Antiques

The Manor House, Cottonend Rd. MK45 3BT. (Mrs S. Bowen). Est. 1976. Open 10-5, Sun. by appointment. SIZE: Large. *STOCK: Furniture, especially dining, 19thC to Edwardian, £100-£5,000; lighting and oil lamps, Victorian to 1940's; general antiques.* LOC: Just off A6, 4 miles south of Bedford. PARK: Own. TEL:

Wilstead continued

01234 740262; home - same. SER: Restorations (furniture); buys at auction. FAIRS: London Decorative. VAT: Stan/Spec.

WOBURN

Questor

13/14 Market Place. MK17 9PZ. (P. Parkinson-Large). Open 10-1 and 2-5.30, Sun. 11-1 and 2-5. *STOCK: Furniture including painted, £50-£1,000; porcelain, jewellery, small antiques, original works of art.* TEL: 01525 290658.

Christopher Sykes Antiques

The Old Parsonage. MK17 9QL. (C. and M. Sykes). Est. 1949. Open 9-5. SIZE: Large. *STOCK: Collectors' items - attractive, early brass, copper and pewter; scientific and medical instruments; specialist in rare corkscrews, £10-£800; silver decanter labels, tastvins and funnels, pottery barrels and bin labels, glass decanters and tantalus.* LOC: In main street opposite Post Office on A50. PARK: Easy. TEL: 01525 290259/290467; fax - 01525 290061. SER: 130 page illustrated mail order catalogue on corkscrews and wine related antiques available £7 each. VAT: Stan/Spec.

Town Hall Antiques

Market Place. MK17 9PZ. Open 10-5.30, Sun. 11-5.30. SIZE: Medium. *STOCK: Furniture, £50-£5,000; lighting, clocks, ceramics, glass, silver and plate, £10-£2,000; prints and pictures, £5-£2,000; all 18th to early 20th C; mirrors, 17th-20th C; domestic metalware; antiquities - Bronze Age, Iron Age, Egyptian and Roman; cigarette cards, books, tools, sporting memorabilia, kitchenalia.* LOC: Off A5 and off junction 12 or 13, M1. PARK: Easy. TEL: 01525 290950. SER: Valuations; framing.

The Woburn Abbey Antiques Centre

MK43 0TP. Est. 1967. Open every day (including Bank Holidays) 11-5 Nov. to Easter; 10-6 Easter to Oct. CL: 24th-26th Dec. 1998. SIZE: Over 50 shops and showcases on two floors. *STOCK: English and Continental furniture, porcelain, mirrors, clocks, engravings, silver, oils and watercolours.* LOC: Exits 12 and 13, M1. On A5 follow signs to Woburn Abbey and after entering grounds, follow signs, The Antiques Centre is in the South Courtyard. PARK: Easy. TEL: 01525 290350; fax - 01525 290271. SER: Carriage for large items; worldwide shipping.

Woburn Fine Arts

12 Market Place. MK17 9PZ. (Z. Bieganski). Est. 1983. Open 2-5.30, Sat. and Sun. 11-1 and 2-5.30 or by appointment. CL: Thurs. SIZE: Medium. *STOCK: Post-impressionist paintings, 1880-1940; European paintings, 17th-18th C; British paintings, 20th C.* PARK: Easy. TEL: 01525 290624. SER: Restorations (oils and water-colours); framing.

Woburn Abbey Antiques Centre

One of the streets on the ground floor

One of the largest Antiques Centres under one roof in Great Britain and the most original — with 40 independent shops and 12 showcases comprising 50 established dealers, some of whom are members of L.A.P.A.D.A. and B.A.D.A. — is situated in the magnificent South Court of Woburn Abbey.

We are pleased to offer the dealer and private collector a wide range of Antiques: Clocks, Lamps, Porcelain and Glass, Paintings, Prints, Georgian and Victorian Furniture, Jewellery, Georgian Silver, Painted Furniture, Works of Art, etc., at competitive prices.

Within one hour's drive of Oxford, Cambridge, Birmingham and London (via M1, Exit 12 or 13 signposted Woburn Abbey). Trains from St. Pancras to Flitwick or Euston to Bletchley can be met by prior arrangement. Dealers admitted free and their park entrance refunded at the Antiques Centre. Visiting dealers' car park adjacent to the Antiques Centre.

One of the streets on the ground floor

OPEN EVERY DAY OF THE YEAR EXCEPT
24th-26th DECEMBER 1998

Easter Sunday to October 10-6 p.m. November to Easter 11-5 p.m.

WOBURN ABBEY ANTIQUES CENTRE, WOBURN ABBEY
BEDFORDSHIRE MK43 0TP

Telephone Woburn (01525) 290350 Fax (01525) 290271

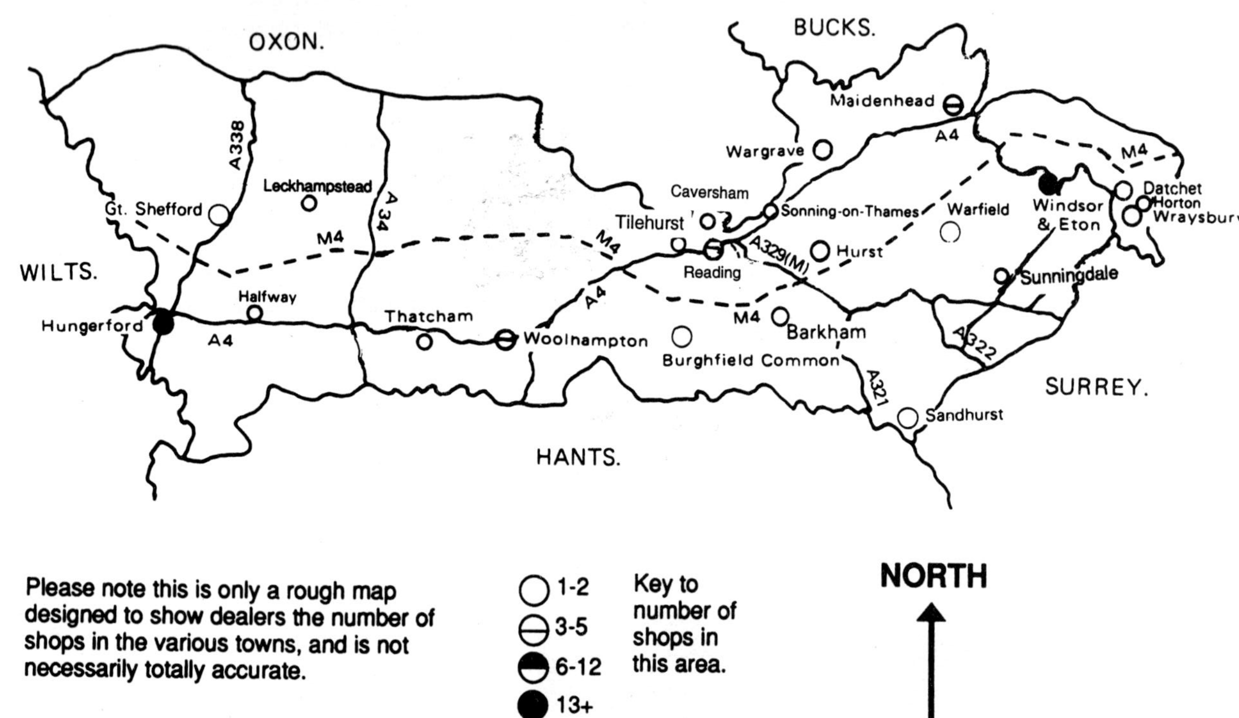

Please note this is only a rough map designed to show dealers the number of shops in the various towns, and is not necessarily totally accurate.

BARKHAM, Nr. Wokingham

Barkham Antique Centre

Barkham St. RG40 4PJ. (Eileen and Ken Lowes). Open 10.30-5 including Sun. SIZE: Large - 50+ dealers. *STOCK: Tables, chairs, chests, 18th-20th C, £100-£3,500; sofas, Victorian lady's chairs, collectables, kitchenalia, Dinky toys, model cars, porcelain, stamps, badges, metalware, lamps and bric-a-brac.* LOC: Off M4 junction 10, A329M to Wokingham, over station crossing to Barkham (B3349), left at Bull public house. PARK: Easy. TEL: 0118 9761355; fax - same; home - 0118 9783705; mobile - 0370 606279. SER: Valuations; restorations (china, French polishing, upholstery, cabinet making); china search; courtesy car from Wokingham station on request.

BURGHFIELD COMMON Nr. Reading

Graham Gallery

Highwoods. RG7 3BG. (J. Steeds). Est. 1976. Open by appointment at any time. SIZE: Medium. *STOCK: English watercolours, £50-£1,500; English oil paintings, £200-£8,000; English prints, £25-£200; all 19th to early 20th C.* LOC: 4 miles from Reading on Burghfield road. PARK: Easy. TEL: 0118 9832320; fax - 0118 9831070. SER: Valuations; restorations (cleaning, framing).

CAVERSHAM, Nr. Reading

The Clock Workshop LAPADA

17 Prospect St. RG4 8JB. FBHI, TVADA. (J. M. Yealland). Est. 1980. Open 9.30-5.30, Sat. 10-1. SIZE: Small. *STOCK: Clocks, late 17th to late 19th C, £350-£60,000; barometers, 18th-19th C, £500-£8,000.* LOC: Prospect St. is the beginning of main Reading to Henley road. PARK: North St. TEL: 01734 470741. SER: Valuations; restorations (clocks and barometers); buys at auction. FAIRS: TVADA; LAPADA; Olympia. VAT: Stan/Spec.

DATCHET

The Studio Gallery

The Old Bank, The Green, SL3 9JH. (Julian Bettney). Open 11-7, until 6 Sun. CL: Tues. am. and Fri. *STOCK: Fine paintings and prints, 1740-1940; architectural fittings; decorative furniture and fittings, garden items.* LOC: Off junction 5, M4, opposite Manor Hotel. TEL: 01753 544100; mobile - 0836 330566. SER: New age furniture designed and manufactured; framing; restorations (oil paintings and frames) ; garden design.

GREAT SHEFFORD, Nr. Hungerford

Alan Hodgson

No 2 Ivy House, Wantage Rd. RG16 7DA. *STOCK: Country and pine furniture, boxes, collectors' items.* LOC: A338, 10 minutes from Hungerford towards Wantage. TEL: 01488 648172.

HALFWAY, Nr. Newbury

Alan Walker BADA

Halfway Manor. RG20 8NR. TVADA. Open by appointment. *STOCK: Fine barometers and weather instruments.* TEL: 01488 657670; mobile - 0831 147480. SER: Restorations.

HORTON, Nr. Windsor

John A. Pearson Antiques BADA

Horton Lodge, Horton Rd. SL3 9NU. (Mrs J.C. Sinclair Hill). Est. 1902. Open by appointment only. SIZE: Large. *STOCK: English and Continental furniture, 1700-1850, £50-£30,000; oil paintings, 17th-19th C, £50-£50,000; decorative objects.* Not Stocked: Items after 19th C. LOC: From London turn off M4, exit 5, past London Airport; from M25 take exit 14. 10 mins from Heathrow. PARK: Easy. TEL: 01753 682136.

HUNGERFORD

Beedham Antiques Ltd BADA

Charnham Close. RG17 0EJ. Open 10-5 or by appointment. *STOCK: English oak furniture, 16th-18th C; objects and works of art.* TEL: 01488 684141. VAT: Spec.

Below Stairs of Hungerford

103 High St. RG17 0NB. (S. Hofgartner). Est. 1974. Open 10-6, including Sun. SIZE: Large. *STOCK: Kitchen and decorative garden items, bedroom furniture, lighting, collectables, sporting items and memorabilia, interior fittings and taxidermy, mainly 19th C English, £20-£2,500.* Not Stocked: Reproductions. LOC: Main street. PARK: Easy. TEL: 01488 682317. SER: Valuations. VAT: Stan.

Sir William Bentley Billiards (Antique Billiard Table Specialist Company)

Standen Manor Farm. RG17 0RB. Open by appointment seven days a week. SIZE: Large. *STOCK: Billiard tables, billiard/dining tables; antique and modern accessories including panelling and brass lights.* TEL: 01488 681711; 0181 9401152; fax - 01488 685197. SER: Restorations; removals and storage.

Bow House Antiques

3-4 Faulkner Sq., Charnham St. RG17 0ER. (L.R. Herrington). Open 10.30-4. CL: Mon. SIZE: Medium. *STOCK: Small period and Victorian furniture.* LOC: A4. PARK: Easy, own. TEL: 01488 683198; home - 01488 684319.

Hungerford continued

Dolls and Toys of Yesteryear at Bow House Antiques

3-4 Faulkner Sq., Charnham St. RG17 0HH. (D.M.Herrington). Open 10.30-4. CL: Mon. SIZE: Medium. *STOCK: Dolls' houses, £150-£3,000; dolls' house furniture and accessories, £1-£300; rocking horses, £500-£1,500; all 19th to early 20th.* PARK: Easy. TEL: 01488 683198; home - 01488 684319. FAIRS: Toy and Doll, Kensington Town Hall; London Victoria International Doll Shows.

The Fire Place (Hungerford) Ltd

Hungerford Old Fire Station, Charnham St. RG17 0EP. (E.B. and E.M. Smith). Est. 1976. Open 10-1.30 and 2.15-5. SIZE: Large. *STOCK: Fireplace furnishings and metalware especially fenders; paintings.* LOC: On A4. PARK: Opposite. TEL: 01488 683420. VAT: Stan/Spec.

Robert and Georgina Hastie LAPADA

35a High St. RG17 0NF. Est. 1987. Open 9.30-5, Sun. by appointment. SIZE: Medium. *STOCK: Decorative items, 1750-1920, £50-£6,000; furniture and clocks, 18th-19th C, £200-£6,000; textiles, 19th C, £50-£1,000.* Not Stocked: Silver, porcelain and dolls. LOC: A338. PARK: Easy. TEL: 01488 682873; fax - 01264 731289; mobile - 0410 244894. VAT: Stan/Spec.

Hungerford continued

Hungerford Arcade

High St. RG17 0NF. (Wynsave Investments Ltd). Est. 1972. Open 9.30-5.30, Sun. 11-5. SIZE: Over 80 stallholders. *STOCK: General antiques and period furniture.* PARK: Easy. TEL: 01488 683701.

Roger King Antiques

111 High St. RG17 0NB. (Mr and Mrs R.F. King). Est. 1974. Open 9.30-5. SIZE: Large. *STOCK: Furniture, 1750-1910, £100-£2,000; china, 19th C; oil paintings.* Not Stocked: Silver, jewellery. LOC: Opposite Hungerford Arcade. PARK: Easy. TEL: 01488 682256. VAT: Spec.

Marlborough Sporting Gallery and Bookshop

127a High St. RG17 0EY. Est. 1977. Open 10-6, Sun. 11-5. SIZE: Medium. *STOCK: Sporting oils, watercolours, £100-£10,000; sporting prints, £20-£5000; all 1800-1975; books, 1750 to date, £10-£500.* PARK: Easy. TEL: 01488 686921; fax - 01488 686143. SER: Valuations; restorations (oils, watercolours, prints); buys at auction. FAIRS: Major equestrian events. VAT: Spec.

Medalcrest Ltd

Charnham House, 29/30 Charnham St. RG17 0EJ. (D.H. Farrow). Est. 1981. Open 9.30-5.30, Sat. 10-6, Sun. by appointment. SIZE: Large. *STOCK: 18th-19th C furniture; barometers, metalware, small items.* TEL: 01488 684157; fax - same. VAT: Spec.

The Old Malthouse BADA

15 Bridge St. RG17 0EG. CINOA. (P.F. Hunwick). Est. 1963. Open 10-5.30. SIZE: Large. *STOCK: 18th to early 19th C walnut and mahogany furniture - dining tables, sets of chairs, mirrors, chests of drawers; clocks, barometers, decorative items and glass.* Not Stocked: Orientalia. LOC: A338, left at Bear Hotel, shop is approx. 120 yds. on left, just before bridge. PARK: In front of shop. TEL: 01488 682209; fax - same. SER: Valuations. VAT: Spec.

Riverside Antiques LAPADA

Charnham St. RG17 0EP. (M. Stockland). Est. 1976. Open 10-5.30. SIZE: Large. *STOCK: General antiques including furniture and decorative items.* LOC: On A4 just before The Bear Hotel. PARK: Easy. TEL: 01488 682314. VAT: Stan/Spec.

Styles Silver LAPADA

12 Bridge St. RG17 0EH. (P. and D. Styles). Est. 1974. Open Sat. and any time by appointment. SIZE: Medium. *STOCK: Antique, Victorian and secondhand silver including cutlery.* PARK: Easy. TEL: 01488 683922; home - same; fax - 01488 683488; mobile - 0378 769559. SER: Repairs; finder.

Hungerford continued

Turpins Antiques BADA

17 Bridge St. RG17 0EG. Open Fri., Sat., and Mon. or by appointment. SIZE: Large. *STOCK: 17th-18th C walnut and mahogany furniture, early metalware.* TEL: 01488 681886; home - 01672 870727. VAT: Spec.

Youll's Antiques

27 and 28 Charnham St. RG17 0EJ. (B. Youll). Open 10.30-5.30 including Sun. *STOCK: French and English furniture and decorative items.*

HURST, Nr. Reading

Peter Shepherd Antiques

Penfold, Lodge Rd. RG10 0EG. Est. 1962. Open by appointment only. *STOCK: Glass, rarities and books.* TEL: 01734 340755.

LECKHAMPSTEAD, Nr. Newbury

Hill Farm Antiques

Hill Farm, Shop Lane. RG20 8QG. (Mike Beesley). Open 9-5, Sun. by appointment. *STOCK: 19th C dining tables, chairs and library furniture.* LOC: Off B4494 between Stag public house and church. PARK: Own at rear. TEL: 01488 638541/638361. SER: Restorations; shipping arranged; buys at auction.

MAIDENHEAD

Jaspers Fine Arts Ltd

36 Queen St. SL6 1HZ. (D. N. Johnson). Open 9-6. *STOCK: Victorian watercolours and paintings; maps and prints.* TEL: 01628 636459. SER: Restorations; framing.

Miscellanea

71 St. Marks Rd. SL6 2DP. (J. Davidson). Open 10-5.30. SIZE: Large. *STOCK: Furniture, books, bric-a-brac, collectors' items.* LOC: 1/2 mile off A4. PARK: Easy. TEL: 01628 623058.

Widmerpool House Antiques

Boulters Lock. Open by appointment only. *STOCK: English furniture, 18th-19th C; oil paintings, watercolours, prints; porcelain, glass, silver, 19th C.* TEL: 01628 623752.

READING

Blond Fine Art

Barnat Works, 1a Upper Redlands Rd. RG1 5JJ. TVADA. (Simon Blond). Open by appointment only. *STOCK: British original prints, 1920-1980; Art Deco ceramics.* TEL: 0118 9260880.

P.D. Leatherland Antiques

68 London St. RG1 4SQ. TVADA. Est. 1970. Open 9-5. *STOCK: Furniture, 18th C to 1920's; decorative china, clocks, metalware, mirrors and pictures, £5-£4,000.* PARK: Easy. TEL: 0118 9581960. VAT: Stan/Spec.

Reading continued

Stables Antique Centre

1a Merchants Place (off Friar St). RG1 1DT. Est. 1972. Open 10-5. SIZE: 2 Floors. *STOCK: General antiques including Victoriana, advertising items, jewellery and bottles.* TEL: 0118 959 0290.

SANDHURST

Antiques - Sheila White

Sandhurst Farmhouse, 207 Yorktown Rd., College Town. GU47 0RT. *STOCK: General antiques.* LOC: Barn at rear of premises. TEL: 01252 873290.

Berkshire Metal Finishers Ltd

Swan Lane Trading Estate. GU47 9DD. (J.A. and Mrs. J. Sturgeon). Est. 1957. Open 8-1 and 2-6, Sat. 8-1 and 2-4, Sun. 9-1. SIZE: Large. *STOCK: Brass, copper and steel metalware; silver plate.* LOC: Off A30 towards Wokingham on A321, after 1.25 miles turn left into Swan Lane, estate 1st turning right, last factory near car park. PARK: Easy. TEL: 01252 873475; fax - 01252 875434. SER: Restorations (metalware polishing and lacquering).

SONNING-ON-THAMES

Cavendish Fine Arts LAPADA

The Dower House. RG4 6UL. TVADA. (Janet Middlemiss and Guy Hazel). Open by appointment only. *STOCK: Fine Queen Anne and English Georgian furniture, glass and porcelain.* TEL: 01189 691904; mobile - 0831 295575. VAT: Stan/Spec.

Csaky's Antiques

RG4 0TW. Open by appointment only. *STOCK: Early English and Continental furniture; carvings, works of art; Modern art and sculpture, specialising in Guy Taplin.* TEL: 0118 9697608.

SUNNINGDALE

The Coworth Gallery

9 Coworth Rd. SL5 0NX. (Stephen Paddon). Est. 1985. Open most times, subject to a 'phone call. SIZE: Small. *STOCK: 19th C English and French country furniture, paintings, carpets, decorative items.* LOC: Turn right into Bedford Lane off A30 from London, after I Gladiatori. PARK: Easy. TEL: 01344 26532; mobile - 0831 182076. SER: Restorations.

THATCHAM, Nr. Newbury

Farmhouse Antiques

Bluecoat School. (D. Johnson). Open 10-4.30. CL: Mon. and Tues. *STOCK: General antiques.* PARK: Easy. TEL: 01635 865901.

TILEHURST, Nr. Reading

Hall's Corner Antiques

207 Hall's Rd. RG30 4PT. (Jane Boyes and John Vanstone). Est. 1994. Open 10.30-6 including Sun. SIZE: Medium - several dealers. *STOCK: Wide variety of general antiques, mainly 19th-20th C, £5-£1,500.* LOC: Opposite The Bear public house. PARK: Easy. TEL: 01189 423700. SER: Restorations (furniture); buys at auction (furniture). FAIRS: Goodwood, Shepton Mallet, Newbury.

WARFIELD

Moss End Antique Centre

Moss End Garden Centre. RG12 6EJ. TVADA. Open 10.30-5. CL: Mon. SIZE: Large - 25 dealers. *STOCK: General antiques and collectables.* LOC: A3095. PARK: Own. TEL: 01344 861942.

WARGRAVE

John Connell - Wargrave Antiques

66 High St. RG10 8BY. Open Wed.-Sun. other times by appointment. SIZE: Large - several dealers. *STOCK: Furniture, Georgian-Edwardian; small items, china, glass, metal.* PARK: Nearby. TEL: 01734 402914. SER: Restorations (furniture); silver plating; metal polishing.

WINDSOR & ETON

The Ancient Art Shop

8 Windsor Royal Station. *STOCK: Antiquities.*

Roger Barnett Antiques

91 High St., Eton. SL4 6AF. Est. 1975. TEL: 01753 867785.

Berkshire Antiques Co Ltd

42 Thames St., Windsor. SL4 1YY. Open 10.30-5.30, Sun. by appointment. SIZE: Large. *STOCK: Antique and modern designer jewellery; general antiques, china, porcelain and glass, silver and silverplate, Royal commemoratives, toys and dolls, £10-£25,000.* TEL: 01753 830100; fax - 01753 832278; internet - hhp://www.users.dircon.co.uk/~jewels; e-mail - jewels@dircon.co.uk. SER: Valuations; repairs.

Claudia Casuis

17 High St., Eton. Open 10-5. *STOCK: Furniture, objets d'art, porcelain and textiles.* TEL: 01753 831039; home - 01753 840848.

Country Furniture

79 St. Leonards Rd., Windsor. SL4 3BZ. TVADA. (Jan Hicks and Austin Maude). Open 9.30-5.30. *STOCK: French provincial furniture and unusual decorative items.* TEL: 01753 830154; fax - same.

Dee's Antique Pine

89 Grove Rd. SL4 1HT. TVADA. (Dee Waghorn). Open 10.30-6, other times by appointment. *STOCK: 19th C pine furniture.* TEL: 01753 865627; fax - 01753 850926.

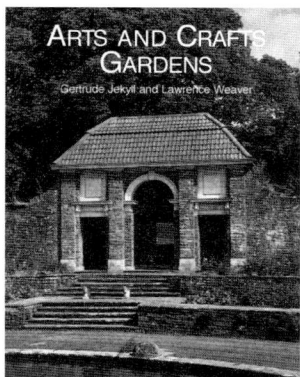

Windsor & Eton continued

Eton Antique Bookshop
88 High St., Eton. SL4 6AF. TEL: 01753 855534.

Eton Antiques Partnership
80 High St., Eton. SL4 6AF. (Mark Procter). Est. 1967. Open 10-5, Sun. 11-5.30. SIZE: Large. *STOCK: Mahogany and rosewood furniture, 18th-19th C.* LOC: Slough East exit from M4 westbound. PARK: Nearby. TEL: 01753 860752; home - same. SER: Exporting; interior design consultants. VAT: Stan/Spec.

Eton Gallery LAPADA
TVADA. (Josephine Smith). Open by appointment only. *STOCK: 18th to early 19th C furniture, specialising in dining tables and sets of chairs.* TEL: 01753 860963.

Grove Gallery
89 Grove Rd., Windsor. *STOCK: Oils, watercolours, prints.* TEL: 01753 865954/853658.

Shirley Hayden Antiques
79 High St., Eton. SL4 6AF. TVADA. Est. 1980. Open 10-5.30, Sun. 11.30-5. SIZE: Small. *STOCK: English mahogany furniture, 18th-19th C, £350-*

Windsor & Eton continued

£4,500; decorative items - pictures, mirrors, lamps and porcelain. LOC: First antiques shop on left over the bridge from Windsor. PARK: Meadow Lane. TEL: 01753 833085; home - 01753 540203. FAIRS: TVADA. VAT: Spec.

J. Manley
27 High St., Eton. SL4 6AX. Est. 1891. Open 9-5. *STOCK: Watercolours, old prints.* TEL: 01753 865647. SER: Restorations; framing, mounting.

Peter J. Martin
40 High St., Eton. SL4 6BD. TVADA. Est. 1963. Open 9-1 and 2-5. CL: Sun. SIZE: Large and warehouse. *STOCK: Period, Victorian and decorative furniture and furnishings, £50-£5,000; metalware, £10-£500, all from 1800.* PARK: 50yds. opposite. TEL: 01753 864901; home - 01753 863987. SER: Restorations; shipping arranged; buys at auction. VAT: Stan/Spec.

Morgan Stobbs
17 High St., Eton. SL4 6AX. TVADA. (Glenn Morgan). Open 10.30-5.30, Sun. 1-5. *STOCK: Arts & Crafts, Art Deco furniture and objects, 1880-1940.* TEL: 01753 840631.

Windsor & Eton continued

Mostly Boxes
93 High St., Eton. SL4 6AF. (G.S. Munday). Est. 1977. Open 9.30-6.45. SIZE: Small. *STOCK: Wooden, mother of pearl, and tortoiseshell boxes.* PARK: 100 yds. TEL: 01753 858470. SER: Restorations (boxes). VAT: Spec.

O'Connor Brothers
Trinity Yard, 59 St. Leonards Rd., Windsor. SL4 3BX. *STOCK: Furniture and general antiques.* TEL: 01753 866732; freephone - 0500 030405. VAT: Stan.

Oriental Rug Gallery Ltd
115-116 High St., Eton. SL4 6AN. TVADA, BORDA. (Richard Mathias and Julian Blair). Open 10-5.30. *STOCK: Russian, Afghan, Turkish and Persian carpets, rugs and kelims; Oriental objets d'art.* PARK: Behind showroom. TEL: 01753 623000; fax - same.

Rules Antiques
62 St Leonard's Rd. SL4 3BY. TVADA. (Sue Rule and Kathryn Cale). Open 10.30-6. *STOCK: Fixtures and fittings; brass, metalwork; unusual small furniture; lighting.* TEL: 01753 833210.

Ulla Stafford Antiques BADA
41 High St., Eton. SL4 6BD. SIZE: Large. *STOCK: Georgian and Continental furniture, Chinese export porcelain, 18th C; works of art and ceramics, 17th-18th C.* PARK: Easy. TEL: 01753 859625; home - 01734 343208; fax - same. VAT: Spec.

Studio 101
101 High St., Eton. SL4 6AF. (Anthony Cove). Est. 1959. SIZE: Medium. *STOCK: Mahogany furniture, some 18th C, mainly 19th C, £50-£1,000; brass, silver plate, 19th C, £10-£200.* LOC: Walk over Windsor Bridge from Windsor and Eton Riverside railway station. PARK: Public, at rear of premises. TEL: 01753 863333.

T.L.O. Militaria
Longclose House, Common Rd., Eton Wick. SL4 6QY. (Tony L. Oliver). Est. 1959. Open 9-5 by appointment only. *STOCK: Militaria, medals, badges, insignia especially German 1914-1990; civilian and military vehicles, 1914-1955.* TEL: 01753 862637; fax - 01753 841998.

Times Past Antiques
59 High St., Eton. SL4 6BL. MBHI. (P. Jackson). Est. 1970. Open 10-6, Sun. 12-5. SIZE: Medium. *STOCK: Clocks and music boxes, £100-£3,000; furniture, all 18th-19th C; silver, 19th C, £5-£500.* PARK: Reasonable. TEL: 01753 857018; home - same. SER: Valuations; restorations (clocks and watches); buys at auction (clocks). VAT: Stan/Spec.

Windsor & Eton continued

Turks Head Antiques
98 High St., Eton. SL4 6AF. Open 10-5. CL: Mon. *STOCK: Silver and plate, porcelain, glass and interesting collectables.* TEL: 01753 863939.

Woodage Antiques
4 High St., Eton. SL4 6AS. TVADA. Open daily, prior telephone call advisable. *STOCK: Mainly 18th-19th C furniture and associated decorative items; samplers, marble, gilt mirrors.* LOC: Close to college. PARK: Easy. TEL: 01753 863016; fax - same.

WOOLHAMPTON, Nr. Reading

The Bath Chair
Woodbine Cottage, Bath Rd. RG7 5RT. (J.A. Lewzey). Est. 1980. Usually open 10-6 and by appointment. SIZE: Small. *STOCK: Furniture and decorative items, £5-£5,000.* LOC: A4. PARK: Easy. TEL: 0118 9712225. SER: Valuations; buys at auction.

The Old Bakery Antiques
Bath Rd. RG7 5RE. Resident. (S. Everard). Est. 1969. *STOCK: Furniture, objets d'art, collectors' items, general antiques.* TEL: 0118 9712116.

Old Post House Antiques
Bath Rd. RG7 5RE. (V. A. Liddiard). Est. 1975. Open 10-6. SIZE: Small. *STOCK: Furniture, 18th-19th C, £50-£300; bric-a-brac and brassware, £2-£100.* LOC: On A4. PARK: Easy. TEL: 0118 9712294; home - 0118 9713460.

WRAYSBURY

Clive Rogers Oriental Rugs
TW19 5PE. Est. 1974. Open by appointment. SIZE: Medium. *STOCK: Oriental rugs, carpets, textiles; Oriental and Islamic works of art.* LOC: On B376, 10 minutes from Heathrow Airport. PARK: Own. TEL: 01784 481177/481100; fax - 01784 481144. SER: Valuations; restorations (as stock); historical analysis commission agents; buys at auction. VAT: Stan/Spec.

Wyrardisbury Antiques
23 High St. TW19 5DA. (C. Tuffs). Est. 1978. Open 10-5. CL: Mon. and Thurs. except by appointment. SIZE: Small. *STOCK: Clocks, £25-£2,000; small furniture, tea caddies, boxes and watercolours, £10-£500.* LOC: A376 from Staines by-pass (A30) or from junction 5 M4/A4 via B470, then B376. PARK: Easy. TEL: 01784 483225. SER: Restorations (clocks).

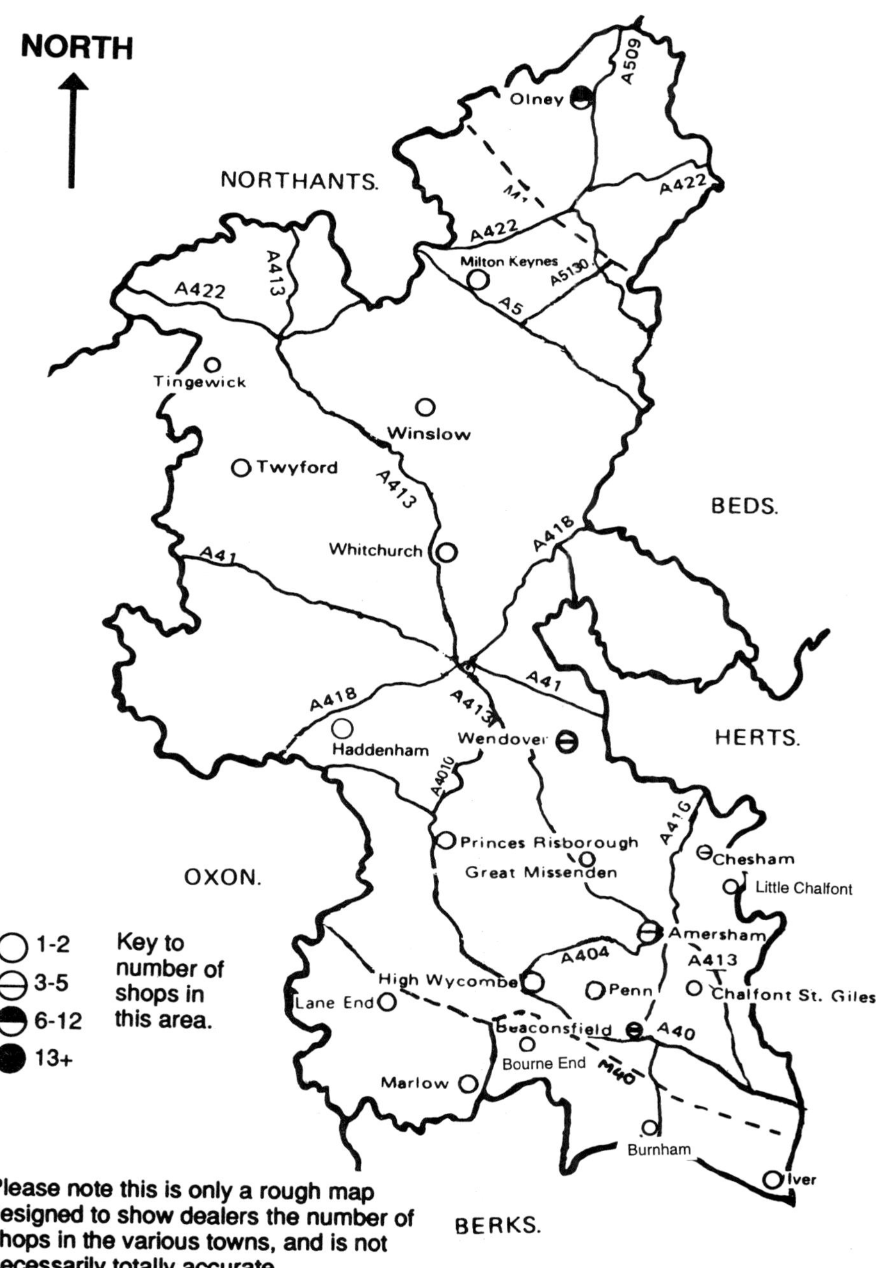

Please note this is only a rough map designed to show dealers the number of shops in the various towns, and is not necessarily totally accurate.

AMERSHAM

Amersham Antiques and Collectors Centre

20-22 Whielden St., Old Amersham. HP7 0HT. Open 9.30-5.30. SIZE: 35-40 dealers. *STOCK: Antiques and collectables.* TEL: 01494 431282.

The Cupboard Antiques LAPADA

80 High St., Old Amersham. HP7 0DS. TVADA. (N. Lucas). Open 10-5. CL: Fri. SIZE: 4 showrooms. *STOCK: Georgian, Regency and early Victorian furniture and decorative items.* PARK: Easy. TEL: 01494 722882.

Partridges

67 High St., Old Amersham. HP7 0DT. (Mrs Diana Krolle). Est. 1976. Open by appointment. *STOCK: Antique and decorative items, small furniture.* PARK: Easy. TEL: 01753 882331 (answerphone).

Michael and Jackie Quilter

38 High St. HP7 0DJ. Est. 1970. Open 10-5. *STOCK: General antiques, stripped pine, copper, brass, unusual objects.* PARK: Easy. TEL: 01494 433723. VAT: Stan.

Sundial Antiques

19 Whielden St. HP7 0HU. (A. and Mrs M. Macdonald). Est. 1970. Open 9.30-5.30. CL: Thurs. SIZE: Small. *STOCK: English and European brass, copper, metalware, fireplace furniture, 18th-19th C, £5-£500; small period furniture, 1670-1910, £25-£1,500; oil lamps, 1840-1914, £25-£500; decorative items, 1750-1910, £5-£500; pottery, porcelain, curios, pre-1914, £10-£750.* Not Stocked: Jewellery, clocks, coins, oil paintings, stamps, books, silver, firegrates. LOC: On A404, in Old Town 200yds. from High St. on right; from High Wycombe, 500yds. from hospital on left. PARK: Easy. TEL: 01494 727955.

BEACONSFIELD

Buck House Antique Centre

47 Wycombe End, Old Town. HP9 1LZ. (C. and B. Whitby). Est. 1979. Open 10-5, Sun. 12-5. CL: Wed. SIZE: Medium - 10 dealers. *STOCK: Wide variety of general antiques including English and Oriental porcelain, clocks, barometers, oak and mahogany furniture, stripped pine, boxes and beds, to 1930's, £5-£5,000.* LOC: A40. TEL: 01494 670714. SER: Valuations.

June Elsworth - Beaconsfield Ltd

Clover House, 16 London End. HP9 2JH. (Mrs J. Elsworth). Est. 1983. CL: Mon. SIZE: Small. *STOCK: Fine English furniture, 18th-19th C; decorative accessories and silver,19th C.* LOC: In old town, on A40. PARK: Easy. TEL: 01494 675611; fax - 01494 671273. VAT: Spec.

Beaconsfield continued

Grosvenor House Interiors

51 Wycombe End, Beaconsfield Old Town. HP9 1LX. (T.I. Marriott). Est. 1970. Open 9-1 and 2-5.30. CL: Wed. SIZE: Large. *STOCK: 18th-19th C furniture, especially upholstered and mid-19th C walnut; fireplaces and accessories; 19th C watercolours.* PARK: Easy. TEL: 01494 677498. SER: Interior architectural design, fireplace specialists. VAT: Stan/Spec.

Period Furniture Showrooms

49 London End. HP9 2HW. TVADA. (R.E.W. Hearne and N.J. Hearne). Est. 1965. Open 9-5.30. SIZE: Large. *STOCK: Furniture, 1700-1900, £50-£3,000.* LOC: A40 Beaconsfield Old Town. PARK: Own. TEL: 01494 674112; fax - 01494 681046. SER: Restorations (furniture). VAT: Stan/Spec.

The Spinning Wheel

86 London End. HP9 2JD. (Mrs M. Royle). Est. 1945. Open 10-5. CL: Wed. *STOCK: English furniture, 18th-19th C, mahogany and oak items, porcelain, glass.* TEL: 01494 673055; home - 01494 3294. VAT: Stan/Spec.

BOURNE END

Bourne End Antiques Centre

67 The Parade. SL8 5SB. (S. Shepheard). Est. 1995. Open 10-5.30, Sun. 1-5.30. SIZE: Large. *STOCK: Furniture - pine, £150-£900, darkwood, £200-£800; both from 19th C. China and glass, £1-£100.* LOC: A4155, 2 miles from Marlow. PARK: Easy. TEL: 01628 533298; home - 01494 525911. VAT: Stan.

BURNHAM

H. Edwards - The Treasure Chest

17 Britwell Road. SL1 8AQ. TVADA. Open by appointment only. *STOCK: Porcelain and jewellery.* TEL: 01628 603510. FAIRS: Oxford; Blue Coat School, (Reading); Thame.

CHALFONT ST. GILES

Gallery 23 Antiques

High St. HP9 4QH. (Mrs A. Vollaro). Est. 1991. Open 10-5. *STOCK: Furniture, silver, Continental and English porcelain, glass, paintings, prints and watercolours.* TEL: 01494 871512.

T. Smith

The Furniture Village, London Rd. HP8 4NN. Est. 1982. Open 10-5 including Sun. SIZE: Medium. *STOCK: Antique pine and architectural items.* LOC: Opposite Pheasant public house. PARK: Easy. TEL: 01494 873031. SER: Valuations; restorations (including upholstery); buys at auction (furniture).

CHESHAM

Chess Antiques LAPADA

85 Broad St. HP5 3EF. (M.P. Wilder). Est. 1966. Open 9-5, Sat. 10-5. SIZE: Small. *STOCK: Furniture and clocks.* PARK: Easy. TEL: 01494 783043. SER: Valuations; restorations. VAT: Stan/Spec.

For Pine

340 Berkhampstead Rd. HP5 3HF. (D. Hutchin). Open 10-5. CL: Thurs. *STOCK: Pine furniture.* Not Stocked: Reproduction. TEL: 01494 776119.

Omniphil Prints

Germains Lodge, Fullers Hill. HP5 1LR. (Ross Muddiman). Est. 1953. Open 9-5.30 or by appointment. CL: Sat. SIZE: Warehouse. *STOCK: Rare prints on all subjects and Illustrated London News from 1842.* TEL: 01494 771851.

Queen Anne House

57 Church St. HP5 1HY. (Miss A.E. Jackson). Est. 1918. Open Wed., Fri. and Sat. 9.30-5, other times by appointment. SIZE: Large. *STOCK: Furniture, decorative and furnishing pieces, porcelain figures, other china, glass, silver plate, copper, brass, Victoriana, Persian rugs.* Not Stocked: Silver, weapons, jewellery. PARK: Easy. TEL: 01494 783811. SER: Buys at auction.

M.V. Tooley, CMBHI

at Chess Antiques, 85 Broad St. HP5 3EF. Est. 1960. Open 9-6, Sat. 10-5. SIZE: Small. *STOCK: Clocks and barometers.* TEL: 01494 783043. SER: Valuations; restorations; spare parts.

GREAT MISSENDEN

The Pine Merchants

52 High St. HP16 0AU. (Mrs J. Peters). Open 10-5. CL: Mon. SIZE: Medium. *STOCK: Stripped pine and Victorian bedsteads.* TEL: 01494 862002.

Peter Wright Antiques

(Incorporating Missenden Restorations and Abbey Clocks & Repairs), 36b High St. HP16 0AU. Est. 1992. Open 10-6 or any time by appointment. SIZE: Small. *STOCK: General antiques, curios and collectors' items.* LOC: A413. TEL: 01494 891330. SER: Restorations (clocks, furniture and ceramics).

HADDENHAM

H.S. Wellby Ltd

The Malt House, Church End. HP17 8AH. (C.S. Wellby). Est. 1820. Open by appointment 9-6. *STOCK: 18th-19th C paintings.* TEL: 01844 290036. SER: Restorations. VAT: Spec.

HIGH WYCOMBE

Browns' of West Wycombe

Church Lane, West Wycombe. HP14 3AH. Est. Pre-1900. Open 8-5.30. CL: Sat. *STOCK:*

High Wycombe continued

Furniture. LOC: On A40 approximately 3 miles west of High Wycombe on Oxford Rd. PARK: Easy. TEL: 01494 524537; fax - 01494 439548. SER: Restorations and hand-made copies of period chairs.

Windmill Fine Art

Widmer End. TVADA. (Ray and Carol White). Open by appointment only. *STOCK: Fine Victorian and early 20th C watercolours.* TEL: 01494 713757; fax - same; mobile - 0585 370408. SER: Valuations; commission search. FAIRS: Most major.

IVER

"Yester-year"

12 High St. SL0 9NG. Resident. (P.J. Frost). Est. 1969. Open 10.30-6. SIZE: Small. *STOCK: Furniture, porcelain, pottery, glass, metalwork, 18th to early 20th C.* PARK: Easy. TEL: 01753 652072. SER: Valuations; restorations (furniture, pictures); framing; buys at auction.

LANE END, Nr. High Wycombe

Bach Antiques

Essex House, Finings Rd. HP14 3EY. (C. and Mrs. B. Whitby). Est. 1982. Open Thurs., Fri. and Sat. 12-4. SIZE: Small. *STOCK: Furniture including pine, general antiques, pre 1920.* LOC: B482 between Marlow and Stokenchurch, Finings Rd. is extension of High St. PARK: Easy. TEL: 01494 882683. SER: Valuations; restorations (furniture).

LITTLE CHALFONT

Nightingale Antiques

17 Nightingale's Corner. HP7 9PZ. (Lee Andreou). Est. 1995. Open 9.30-5.30. SIZE: Medium. *STOCK: Silver, 19th C, £50-£100; ceramics, 19th-20th C, £5-£25; furniture, 18th-19th C, £50-£1,000.* PARK: Easy. TEL: 01494 762163. SER: Valuations; restorations (silver plating, furniture and ceramics). FAIRS: Chiltern.

MARLOW

The Farmhouse Antiques

52 Marlow Bottom Rd. SL7 3NB. (Joan Jackson). Est. 1969. Open Tues.-Sat. 10-5, other times by appointment. SIZE: Small. *STOCK: Furniture, jewellery and silver, glass and porcelain, 19th-20th C, £25-£1,000; pre-1940's framed watercolours, £100-£800.* LOC: From A404 towards Marlow. Immediately on leaving roundabout, take first right to Marlow Bottom, then left - shop.5 mile on right. PARK: Easy. TEL: 01628 478490; fax - same; home - 01628 477145. SER: Valuations; restorations (small repairs). FAIRS: East Berkshire (3 day): Bell House Fine Arts (2 day). VAT: Stan/Spec.

Marlow continued

Glade Antiques LAPADA

CINOA, TVADA. (Sonia Garry). Open by appointment only. ***STOCK: Fine Oriental ceramics, bronzes and jades: Chinese items from Han, Tang, Song, Ming and Quing periods; Japanese items - mainly Kakiemon, Nabeshima, Kutani, Satsuma and Imari; also Korean Koryo, Yi and Choson periods.*** **TEL: 01628 487255; fax - 01628 476601; mobile - 0976 159669.**

Jack Harness Antiques

Westfield Farm, Henley Rd., Medmenham. SL7. Est. 1981. Open 9-5 or by appointment. SIZE: Large warehouse. *STOCK: Pine and country furniture, especially period pine and original painted French provincial furniture.* PARK: Easy. TEL: 01491 410691; fax - same; mobile - 0468 666833; home - 01628 471775. SER: Restorations; courier. VAT: Stan/Spec. *Mainly Trade.*

Angela Hone Watercolours LAPADA

SL7 1QB. CINOA Open by appointment only. ***STOCK: English and French watercolours and pastels, 1850-1930.*** **TEL: 01628 484170.**

Marlow Antique Centre

35 Station Rd. SL7 1NW. TVADA. (Kay Darby and Keith Hill). SIZE: 30+ dealers. *STOCK: Wide range of general antiques and collectables including Georgian, Victorian and Edwardian furniture, country pine, silver, glass, china, bedsteads, clocks, old tools and garden items, cameras, books, jewellery.* TEL: 01628 473223; fax - 01628 778834.

MILTON KEYNES

Temple Lighting (Jeanne Temple Antiques)

Stockwell House, Wavendon. MK17 8LS. Est. 1968. SIZE: Medium. *STOCK: Victorian, Edwardian and 1930's light fittings; 19th C furniture; decorative items.* LOC: Just off main Woburn Sands to Newport Pagnell road. TEL: 01908 583597.

OLNEY

Courtyard Antiques

4 Rose Court. MK46 4BY. (Trisha Sharp). Est. 1993. Open 10-4.30, Sat. 10-5, Sun. 2-5. SIZE: Medium. *STOCK: Pine and country furniture, 18th-19th C, £50-£1,000; china, glass, figures and silver, 18th C to Art Deco, £5-£300; prints, watercolours, framed cigarette cards, 18th-20th C, £10-£500+.* LOC: Off Market Sq., down alleyway. PARK: Rear access to traders car park. TEL: 01234 712200.

Fenlan

17B Stilebrook Rd.,Yardley Road Industrial Estate. Est. 1982. Open 8-5, Sat. 9-1. SIZE: Medium. *STOCK: Mahogany, rosewood, walnut, oak and pine furniture, 18th to early 20th C.* PARK: Easy. TEL: 01234 711799; fax - 01234 711799. SER: Restorations; cabinet making; restoration products and sundries; French polishing. FAIRS: Newark. VAT: Stan/Spec.

Market Square Antiques

MK46 4BA. (J.D. and H. Vella). Open 10-5, Sun. 1.30-5. *STOCK: Furniture, clocks, china, silver, glass, copper, brass, pine.* TEL: 01234 712172. SER: Restorations.

John Overland Antiques

Rose Court, Market Place. MK46 4BY. Est. 1977. Open 10-5 including Sun. SIZE: Medium. *STOCK: 18th-19th C mahogany and oak furniture, clocks, writing boxes, smalls, brass, copper.* PARK: Market Sq. TEL: 01234 712351. SER: Valuations; restorations (furniture, clocks). VAT: Stan/Spec.

Pine Antiques

10 Market Place. MK46 4EA. (Linda Wilkinson). Open 10-5, Sat. 9.30-5.30, Sun. 12-5. *STOCK: Pine furniture.* TEL: 01234 711065; 01908 510226.

Robin Unsworth Antiques

1 Weston Rd. (R. and Z. M. Unsworth). Est. 1971. Open 10-5, Sun. 1-5. SIZE: Small. *STOCK: Longcase and wall clocks, £500-£4,000; period and Victorian furniture, £200-£4,000; objects of art, £50-£1,000.* LOC: 6 miles from junction 14, M1. PARK: Easy. TEL: 01234 711210; home - 01908 617193. SER: Valuations; buys at auction (clocks).

PENN, Nr. High Wycombe

Country Furniture Shop LAPADA

3 Hazlemere Rd., Potters Cross. HP10 8AA. (M. and V. Thomas). Est. 1955. Open 9.30-1 and 2-5.30. SIZE: Large. *STOCK: Furniture, Georgian, £100-£5,000; Victoriana, £5-£2,500; large Victorian dining tables, Victorian dining chairs.* LOC: B474. PARK: Easy. TEL: 01494 812244; home - same. SER: Valuations. VAT: Stan/Spec.

Penn Barn

By the Pond, Elm Rd. HP10 8LB. ABA. (P. J. M. Hunnings). Est. 1968. Open Tues.-Sat. 9.30-1 and 2-5. SIZE: Medium. *STOCK: Antiquarian books, maps and prints, 19th C, £5-£250; watercolours and oils, 19th-20th C, £50-£1,000.* LOC: B474. PARK: Easy. TEL: 01494 815691. SER: Restorations; cleaning and repairs.

PRINCES RISBOROUGH

Well Cottage Antiques Centre

20-22 Bell St. HP27 0AD. Open 9.30-5.30, Sun. and Bank Holidays 1-5. SIZE: Medium. *STOCK: Furniture including pine; silver, jewellery, china, glass, brass, copper, silhouettes, miniatures, treen, pictures and collectables.* LOC: A4010. TEL: 01844 342002.

TINGEWICK, Nr. Buckingham

Tim Marshall Antiques

Main St. MK18 4NL. Resident. Open 9.30-6, Sun. 12-6. SIZE: Medium. *STOCK: Early oak and country furniture; longcase clocks.* TEL: 01280 848546.

Tingewick Antiques Centre

Main St. MK18 4NN. (B.J. and R. Smith). Est. 1982. Open 10-5.30, Sun. 11-4.30. CL: Fri. SIZE: Medium. *STOCK: Furniture including desks, mainly pine and oak, 19th to early 20th C, £5-£1,000; clocks, 18th-19th C, £20-£2,000; collectables, kitchenalia, Art Deco, pottery, pictures, £1-£1,500.* LOC: On A421. TEL: 01280 848219; home - same. SER: Valuations; restorations (copper, brass, spelter); upholstery; French polishing.

TWYFORD, Nr. Buckingham

Adrian Hornsey Ltd

Three Bridge Mill. MK18 4DY. Open by appointment. SIZE: Large. *STOCK: Victorian and Edwardian oak and mahogany, European and English architectural interiors (bars).* TEL: 01296 738373; fax - 01296 738322. *Trade Only.*

WENDOVER

Antiques at. . .Wendover Antiques Centre

The Old Post Office, 25 High St. HP22 6DU. (N. Gregory). Open 10.30-5.30, Sun. and Bank

Wendover continued

Holidays 11-5.30. SIZE: Large - 30 dealers. *STOCK: General antiques including town and country furniture, flatware, kitchenalia, gardenalia, pottery and porcelain, silver, lamps and lighting, clocks, barometers, telescopes, scientific and medical instruments, beds and bathroom fittings, decorative items, glass, metalware, lace and linen, artifacts including Roman and Egyptian and architectural salvage, to 1930.* PARK: Own. TEL: 01296 625335; evenings - 01296 624633.

Past Treasures Ltd

Upstairs at Antiques At Wendover, The Old Post Office, 25 High St. HP22 6DU. (S.Valledy and M. Ryan). Est. 1996. Open 10.30-5.30, Sun. and Bank Holidays 11-5.30. SIZE: Small. *STOCK: Antiquities including Roman, Egyptian, Chinese and Greek, 2000 BC to 1600 AD, £20-£500; fossils, £5-£150; breweriana, old bottles, potlids, enamel advertising signs, £1-£150; collectables, to £50.* PARK: Easy. TEL: Mobile - 0956 909466; home - 01908 227149.

Sally Turner Antiques LAPADA

Hogarth House, High St. HP22 6DU. Open 10-5. SIZE: 7 showrooms + barn. *STOCK: Decorative and period furniture, general antiques and jewellery.* PARK: At rear of shop. TEL: 01296 624402; fax - same.

Wendover Antiques LAPADA

1 South St. HP22 6EF. (R. and D. Davies). Est. 1979. Open 9-5.30, prior telephone call advisable. SIZE: Medium. *STOCK: Furniture, oils, 17th-19th C; decorative prints; 18th C silk embroideries, silhouettes, miniatures, Georgian decanters, some silver and Sheffield plate; all £50-£5,000.* LOC: Near village centre on Wendover-Amersham road. PARK: 100yds. TEL: 01296 622078. VAT: Stan/Spec.

WHITCHURCH

Deerstalker Antiques

28 High St. HP22 4JT. (R.J. and L.L. Eichler). Open 10-5.30. CL: Mon. SIZE: Small. *STOCK: General antiques.* TEL: 01296 641505.

WINSLOW

Medina Antiquarian Maps and Prints

8 High St. MK18 3HF. (P. Williams). Open 9.30-5.30. CL: Thurs. pm. *STOCK: Maps, prints and watercolours.* TEL: 01296 712468.

Winslow Antiques Centre

15 Market Sq. MK18 3AB. Est. 1992. Open 10-5 or by appointment. SIZE: 20 dealers. *STOCK: Furniture, English pottery, silver and jewellery, general antiques.* LOC: A413. TEL: 01296 714540; fax - 01296 714556.

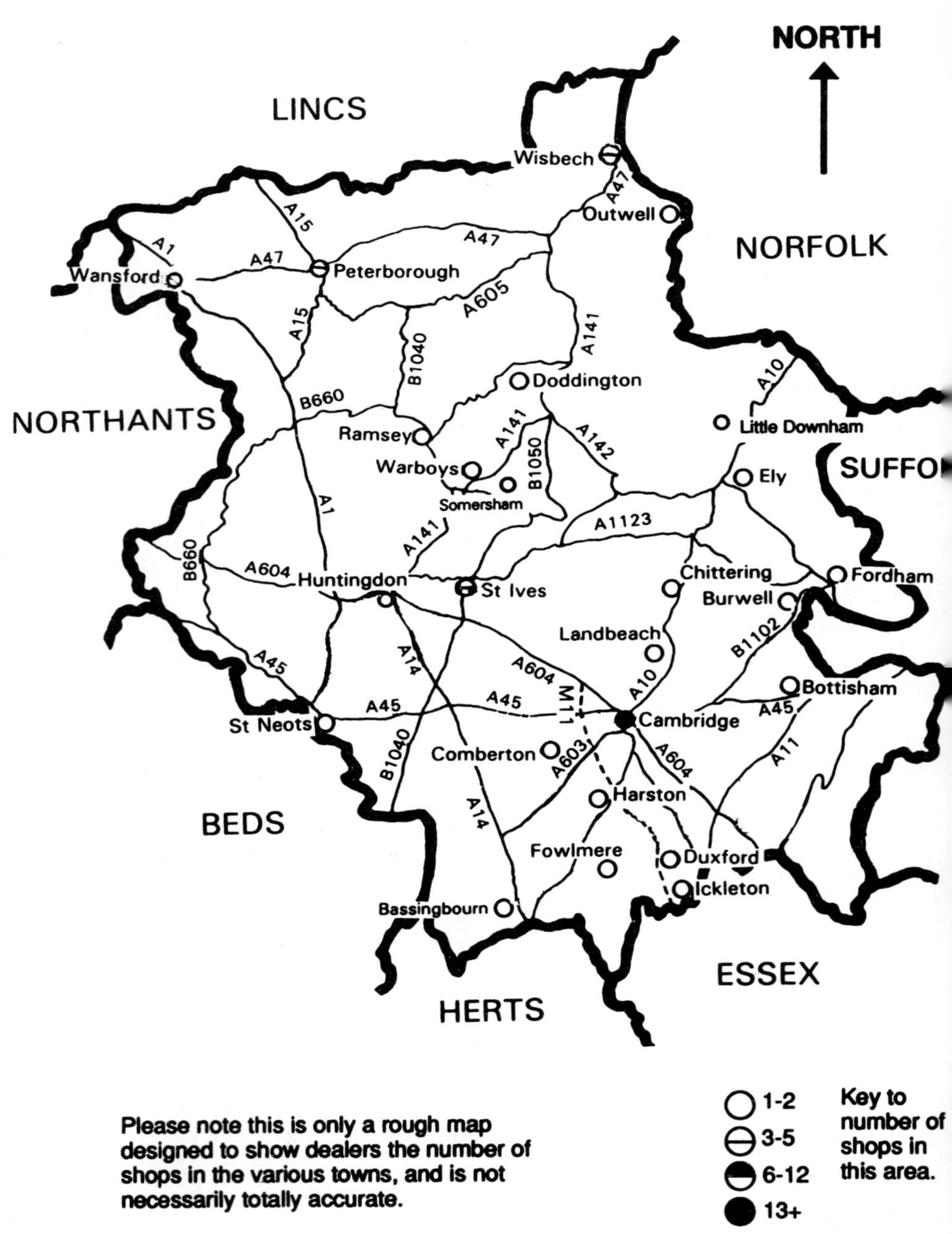

Please note this is only a rough map designed to show dealers the number of shops in the various towns, and is not necessarily totally accurate.

Key to number of shops in this area.

- 1-2
- 3-5
- 6-12
- 13+

BASSINGBOURN, Nr. Royston

David Bickersteth

4 South End. SG8 5NG. Est. 1967. Open by appointment. *STOCK: Antiquarian books.* TEL: 01763 245619; fax - 01763 242969.

BOTTISHAM, Nr. Cambridge

Cambridge Pine

Hall Farm, Lode Rd. CB5 9DN. (Mr and Mrs D. Weir). Est. 1980. Open seven days. SIZE: Large. *STOCK: Pine, 18th-19th C and reproduction, £25-£1,400.* LOC: Midway between Bottisham and Lode, near Anglesey Abbey. PARK: Easy. TEL: 01223 811208; home - same. SER: Copies made in old timber with or without painted finish.

BURWELL

Peter Norman Antiques and Restorations

Sefton House, 57 North St. CB5 0BA. (P. Norman and A. Marpole). Est. 1975. Open 9-12.30 and 2-5.30. SIZE: Medium. *STOCK: Furniture, clocks, arms and Oriental rugs, 17th-19th C, £250-£10,000.* PARK: Easy. TEL: 01638 616914. SER: Valuations; restorations (furniture, oil paintings, clocks, arms). VAT: Stan/Spec.

CAMBRIDGE

20th Century

169 Histon Rd. CB4 3JD. (S. Charles). Open Wed., Thurs., and Fri. 12-5, Sat. 10-5. *STOCK: Decorative arts, 1880-1980.* TEL: 01223 359482.

Jess Applin Antiques BADA

8 Lensfield Rd. CB2 1EG. Est. 1968. Open 10-5.30. *STOCK: Furniture, 17th-19th C; works of art.* LOC: At junction with Hills Rd., opposite church. PARK: Pay and display nearby. TEL: 01223 315168. VAT: Spec.

John Beazor and Sons Ltd BADA

78-80 Regent St. CB2 1DP. Est. 1875. Open 9.15-5, Sat. 10-4 or by appointment. *STOCK: English furniture, late 17th to early 19th C; clocks, barometers and decorative items.* TEL: 01223 355178; fax - same. SER: Valuations. VAT: Spec.

Benet Gallery

26 Long Rd. CB2 2PS. (G.H. and J. Criddle). Est. 1965. Open by appointment. SIZE: Large. *STOCK: Maps and prints of Cambridge, including college views by Ackermann, all periods.* TEL: 01223 248739. VAT: Stan.

Buckies LAPADA

31 Trinity St. CB2 1TB. NAG, GMC. (G. McClure-Buckie). Est. 1972. Open 9.45-5. CL: Mon. SIZE: Medium. *STOCK: Jewellery, silver, objets d'art.* PARK: Multi-storey, nearby. TEL: 01223 357910. SER: Valuations; restorations and repairs. VAT: Stan/Spec.

Cambridge continued

Cambridge Fine Art Ltd LAPADA

Priesthouse, 33 Church St., Little Shelford. CB2 5HG. Resident. (R. and J. Lury). Est. 1972. Open daily 10-6, Sun. by appointment. SIZE: Large. *STOCK: British and European paintings, 1780-1900; modern British paintings, 1880-1940; British prints by J.M. Kronheim to the Baxter Process.* LOC: Next to church. PARK: Easy. TEL: 01223 842866/843537. SER: Valuations; restorations; buys at auction. VAT: Stan/Spec.

Collectors' Market

Dales Brewery, Gwydir St (off Mill Rd). (Mrs E.M. Highmoor). Est. 1976. Open 10-5, Sat. 9.30-5.30. SIZE: 8 units. *STOCK: Collectors' items from £1.50-£750, including bygones, 1950's and 1960's, prints, pine, bric-a-brac, kitchenalia, sofas and chairs.* TEL: 01223 300269.

Gabor Cossa Antiques

34 Trumpington St. CB2 1QY. (M. Edgell and D. Theobaldy). Est. 1948. Open 10-5.30. *STOCK: English ceramics, Delftware, English glass, Oriental ceramics, bijouterie.* LOC: Opposite Fitzwilliam Museum. PARK: 400yds. TEL: 01223 356049. VAT: Global.

Cottage Antiques

16-18 Lensfield Rd. CB2 1EG. (Mrs A. Owen and Mrs A. Yandell). Est. 1981. Open 10-5.30, Sun. by appointment. SIZE: Medium. *STOCK: 18th-19th C pottery, porcelain, blue and white, Staffordshire figures, glass, country furniture, brass, copper; general antiques and antiquities, rugs and kitchenalia.* LOC: Opposite Catholic Church. PARK: Nearby. TEL: 01223 316698.

Peter Ian Crabbe

3 Pembroke St. CB2 3QY. Open 10-4.30. *STOCK: Furniture and porcelain.* TEL: 01223 357117. VAT: Spec.

G. David

16 St. Edward's Passage. CB2 3PJ. ABA, PBFA. Est. 1896. Open 9-5. *STOCK: Antiquarian books, fine bindings, secondhand and out of print books, selected publishers remainders.* TEL: 01223 354619.

Deighton Bell and Co

13 Trinity St. CB2 1TD. ABA, PBFA. (Heffers Booksellers). Est. 1794. Open 9-5.30. SIZE: Large. *STOCK: Antiquarian, rare and fine old books, most subjects; also bibliography, typography and illustrated books.* PARK: Multi-storey, 300yds. TEL: 01223 568585; fax - 01223 354936. SER: Buys at auction. VAT: Stan.

Galloway and Porter Ltd

30 Sidney St., and 3 Green St. CB2 3HS. ABA. Est. 1900. *STOCK: Antiquarian and secondhand books.* TEL: 01223 67876.

Cambridge continued

Gwydir Street Antiques Centre

Units 1 & 2 Dales Brewery, Gwydir St. CB1 2LJ. Open 10-5, Sat. 9.30-5.30, Sun. 11-5. *STOCK: Victorian and Edwardian furniture in mahogany, walnut, pine, satinwood and oak; upholstered arm chairs and sofas; lamps, mirrors and other decorative items.* LOC: Off Mill Rd. PARK: Opposite. TEL: 01223 356391.

W. Heffer

CB4 3EJ. Est. 1970. Open by appointment only. *STOCK: General furniture, silver, china, clocks, watches.* TEL: Home - 01223 363634. SER: Valuations; restorations (wood, metalware, silver, china, mother-of-pearl).

Sarah Key

The Haunted Bookshop, 9 St. Edward's Passage. CB2 3PJ. Est. 1987. Open 10-5. *STOCK: Children's and illustrated books, literature and antiquarian.* TEL: 01223 312913.

The Lawson Gallery

7-8 King's Parade. CB2 1SJ. Est. 1967. Open 9.30-5. SIZE: Medium. *STOCK: Local and fine art; reproduction railway posters of '30s, '40s and '50s; prints.* LOC: Opposite King's College. PARK: Lion's Yard. TEL: 01223 313970. VAT: Stan.

Sebastian Pearson Paintings Prints and Works of Art

3 Pembroke St. CB2 3QY. Est. 1989. Open 10.30-5.30. CL: Mon. SIZE: Medium. *STOCK: Oil paintings and watercolours, £300-£3,500; 20th C British prints (etchings and wood engravings), £60-£600.* LOC: City centre. PARK: Nearby. TEL: 01223 323999; home - 01438 871364. SER: Valuations; picture framing. VAT: Spec.

Pembroke Antiques

7 Pembroke St. CB2 3QY. (K.N. and R.M. Galey). Open 10-4. CL: Mon. SIZE: Small. *STOCK: Silver, furniture, 18th-19th C; jewellery, 18th-20th C.* LOC: 100 yards off Trumpington St., opposite Pembroke College. PARK: 100 yards. TEL: 01223 363246. VAT: Stan/Spec.

Solopark Plc

Station Rd., Nr. Pampisford. CB2 4HB. (R.J. Bird). Open 8-5, Fri. and Sat. 8-4, Sun. 9-1. *STOCK: Recycled and traditional building materials and period architectural items.* TEL: 01223 834663; fax - 01223 834780; e-mail - info@solopark.co.uk; internet - http://www.solopark.co.uk.

CHITTERING, Nr. Cambridge

Simon and Penny Rumble Antiques

Causeway End Farmhouse. CB5 9PW. Open by appointment. *STOCK: Early oak and country furniture, some decorative items.* LOC: 6 miles north of Cambridge, off A10. TEL: 01223 861831.

COMBERTON

Comberton Antiques

5a West St. CB3 7DS. (Mrs M. McEvoy). Est. 1980. Open Mon., Fri. and Sat. 10-5, Sun. 2-5. SIZE: Medium. *STOCK: Furniture, 1780-1920, £50-£2,000; bric-a-brac, 1830-1920, £5-£100; hand-made Turkish kelims; shipping goods.* LOC: 6 miles west of Cambridge, 2 miles west of M11. PARK: Easy. TEL: 01223 262674; home - 01223 263457.

DODDINGTON

Doddington House Antiques

2 Benwick Rd. PE15 0TG. (B.A. Frankland). Est. 1974. *STOCK: Furniture, mirrors, clocks, barometers, pictures and interesting items.* LOC: At Clocktower. PARK: Easy. TEL: 01354 740755. SER: Restorations (chair caning and rushing, barometers).

DUXFORD

Riro D. Mooney

4 Moorfield Rd. CB2 4PS. Est. 1946. Open 9-7. SIZE: Medium. *STOCK: General antiques, 1780-1920, £5-£1,200.* LOC: 1 mile from M11. PARK: Easy. TEL: 01223 832252. VAT: Stan/Spec.

ELY

Mrs Mills Antiques

1a St. Mary's St. CB7 4ER. Open 10-5. CL: Tues. *STOCK: China, jewellery, silver.* Not Stocked: Furniture. TEL: 01353 664268.

Waterside Antiques

The Wharf. CB7 4AU. (G. Peters). Est. 1986. Open 9.30-5.30 including Bank Holidays, Sun. 1-5.30. SIZE: Large. *STOCK: General antiques.* LOC: Waterside area. PARK: Easy. TEL: 01353 667066. SER: Valuations.

FORDHAM

Phoenix Antiques

1 Carter St. CB7 5NG. Est. 1966. Open by appointment only. SIZE: Medium. *STOCK: Early European furniture, domestic metalwork, pottery and delft, carpets, scientific instruments, treen and bygones.* LOC: Centre of village. PARK: Own. TEL: 01638 720363.

FOWLMERE, Nr. Royston

Mere Antiques

High St. SG8 7SU. (R.W. Smith). Est. 1979. Open 10-1 and 2-6, including Sun. SIZE: Medium. *STOCK: Furniture, porcelain and clocks, 18th-19th C, to £5,000.* PARK: Easy. TEL: 01763 208477; home - 01763 208495. SER: Valuations. VAT: Spec.

HARSTON

Antique Clocks

1 High St. CB2 5PX. (C.J. Stocker). Open every day. LOC: On A10, 5 miles south of Cambridge. PARK: Easy. TEL: 01223 870264.

HUNTINGDON

Adams Furniture Centre

The Old Post Office, George St. PE18 6AW. (Stephen Copsey). Est. 1977. Open 9.30-5.30. CL: Thurs. SIZE: Large. *STOCK: Mainly furniture.* LOC: Off Huntingdon ring road. PARK: Easy. TEL: 01480 435100; fax - 01480 454387. SER: Valuations; buys at auction. VAT: Stan/Spec.

ICKLETON

Abbey Antiques

18 Abbey St. CB10 1SS. (K. Wilson). Est. 1974. Open 10-5, Sun. 2-5. SIZE: Large. *STOCK: General antiques, 17th-20th C, £1-£1,000.* LOC: Turn off at Stumps Cross at Gt. Chesterford, 1 mile to Ickleton, shop is in main street. PARK: Easy. TEL: 01799 530637. SER: Valuations; restorations (furniture); French polishing.

LANDBEACH

P.R. Garner Antiques

104 High St. CB4 4DT. Est. 1966. Open by appointment only. SIZE: Medium. *STOCK: China, glass, brass, copper, pewter, unrestored furniture, Victorian and earlier; automobilia and collectors cars; shipping goods.* LOC: Off A10. PARK: Easy. TEL: 01223 860470. SER: Valuations. VAT: Stan/Spec.

J.V. Pianos and Cambridge Pianola Company

The Limes. CB4 4DR. (F.T. Poole). Est. 1972. Open Mon.-Fri., evenings and weekends by appointment. SIZE: Medium. *STOCK: Pianos, pianolas and pianola rolls.* LOC: First building on right in Landbeach from A10. PARK: Easy. TEL: 01223 861348/861507; home - same; fax - 01223 441276. SER: Valuations; restorations. VAT: Stan.

LITTLE DOWNHAM, Nr. Ely

The Old Bishop's Palace Antique Centre

Tower Rd. CB6 2TD. (Elaine Griffin-Singh). Est. 1992. Open every day, including Bank Holidays. SIZE: 60 dealers. *STOCK: Furniture, paintings, glass, silver, jewellery, golf clubs, fishing tackle, sporting prints, kelims, china, mainly 18th-19th C, £5-£5,000.* LOC: A10 Ely by-pass, then B1411 to Little Downham. PARK: Own. TEL: 01353 699177; home - same. SER: Restorations. VAT: Stan/Spec.

OUTWELL, Nr. Wisbech

A.P. and M.A. Haylett

Glen-Royd, 393 Wisbech Rd. PE14 8PG. Open 9-6 including Sun. *STOCK: Country furniture, pottery, treen and metalware, 1750-1900, £5-£500.* Not Stocked: Firearms. LOC: A1101. PARK: Easy. TEL: 01945 772427; home - same. SER: Buys at auction.

PETERBOROUGH

Fitzwilliam Antiques Centre

Fitzwilliam St. PE1 2RX. (Watkins and Stafford Ltd). Open 10-5, Sun. 12-5. SIZE: 50 dealers. *STOCK: General antiques.* LOC: Near city centre. PARK: Easy. TEL: 01733 565415.

Ivor and Patricia Lewis Antique and Fine Art Dealers LAPADA

Westfield, 30 Westwood Park Rd. PE3 6JL. Open by appointment. *STOCK: Furniture - fine 19th C ormolu mounted French, painted and inlaid Edwardian satinwood; bronzes and porcelain.* TEL: 01733 344567.

Old Soke Books

68 Burghley Rd. PE1 2QE. (Peter and Linda Clay). Open Tues.-Sat. 10.30-5.30. *STOCK: Antiquarian and secondhand books, paintings, prints, ephemera and postcards, some furniture and small antiques.* TEL: 01733 64147.

G. Smith and Sons (Peterborough) Ltd

1379 Lincoln Rd., Werrington. PE4 6LT. (Mike Groucott). Est. 1902. Open 9-5. SIZE: Medium. *STOCK: General antiques, furniture and clocks.* LOC: Old Lincoln Road, Werrington village. PARK: Easy. TEL: 01733 571630. SER: Restorations.

RAMSEY, Nr. Huntingdon

Abbey Antiques

63 Great Whyte. PE17 1HL. (R. and J. Smith). Est. 1977. Open 10-5 including Sun. CL: Mon. SIZE: Small. *STOCK: Furniture including pine, 1850-1930, £50-£500; porcelain, Goss and crested china, 1830-1950, £3-£500; Beswick, Wade and Fen pottery and small collectables, Mabel Lucie Attwell.* PARK: Easy. TEL: 01487 814753. SER: Museum and Collectors' Club - Memories UK (Enesco figurines sold). FAIRS: Alexandra Palace, Harrow.

SOMERSHAM, Nr. Huntingdon

T. W. Pawson - Clocks

31A High St. PE17 3JA. Est. 1981. Open 9.30-6, Sat. 10-1 but appointment advisable. SIZE: Small. *STOCK: Antique clocks, £150-£5,000; mercury barometers, mid to late 19th C.* LOC: Main road through village. PARK: Easy. TEL: 01487 841537; home - same. SER: Clock and barometer restoration, overhauls, repairs; buys at auction.

ST IVES

Hyperion Antique Centre

Station Rd. PE17 4BH. (Colin Gunter and Pat Bernard). Est. 1996. Open 9.30-5. SIZE: Medium. *STOCK: Furniture, 18th-20th C, £30-£3,000; ceramics and pictures, silver and plate, £5-£200; linen and lace, £2-£100; all 19th-20th C.* LOC: Turn right into Station Rd. at far end of car park. PARK: Nearby. TEL: 01480 464140. VAT: Stan/Spec.

B.R. Knight and Sons

Quay Court, Bull Lane, Bridge St. PE17 4AU. (M. Knight). Est. 1972. Open Mon., Wed., Fri. 11-2, Sat. 10.30-4.30 or by appointment. SIZE: Medium. *STOCK: Porcelain, pottery, jewellery, paintings, watercolours, prints, decorative arts.* LOC: Off Bridge St. PARK: Nearby. TEL: 01480 468295/300042.

Quayside Antiques

3 The Quay. PE17 4AR. (H.S. Northwood). Est. 1960. Open 10-5.30 including Sun. SIZE: Large. *STOCK: Fine English furniture, to 1820, from £1,000.* LOC: 30 yards from historic 17th C bridge over River Ouse. PARK: Easy. TEL: 01480 495181. SER: Valuations; restorations. VAT: Stan/Spec.

ST. NEOTS

Tavistock Antiques

Cross Hall Manor, Eaton Ford. PE19 4AH. Open by appointment. *STOCK: Period English furniture.* TEL: 01480 472082. *Trade Only.*

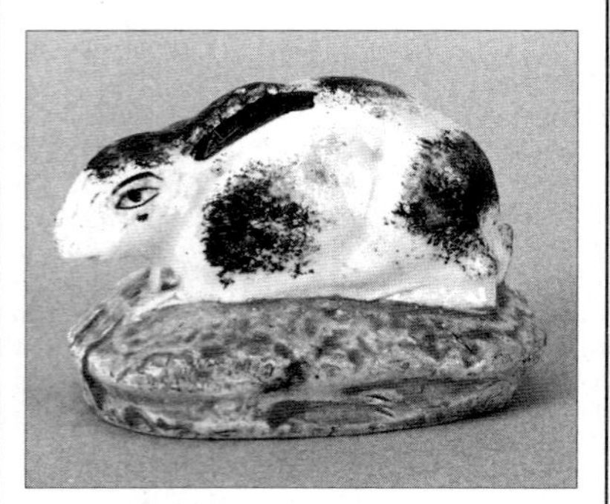

On 9th April this white rabbit, complete with black patches, will invite £200-£300 when offered in Christie's South Kensington's Staffordshire and related wares sale.

From an Auction Preview which appeared in the April 1998 issue of **Antique Collecting**

WANSFORD, Nr. Peterborough

Starlight

16 London Rd. PE8 6JB. Resident. Open Tues.-Fri. and usually Sat. 10-1 and 2-5 or by appointment. *STOCK: Period and new lighting, candles, oil lamps and parts.* LOC: On A1 near A47 junction. PARK: Easy. TEL: 01780 783999; fax - same.

Sydney House Antiques

14 Elton Rd. PE8 6JD. (G. and R. Hancox). Est. 1972. Open 10-5 including Sun., Mon. 2-5.30, other times by appointment. SIZE: Large. *STOCK: Furniture, including marquetry, 19th-20th C, £150-£2,000; Minton, 1850-1920, £100-£2,000; Doulton and Lambeth, £50-£1,000; Royal Worcester, 1860-1940, £100-£1,500.* PARK: Easy. TEL: 01780 782786. SER: Valuations; buys at auction (Minton, Doulton, Royal Worcester, 19th C furniture).

WARBOYS

Warboys Antiques

Old Church School, High St. PE17 2SX. (J. Lambden and E. Godfrey). Est. 1986. Open Tues.-Sat. 11-5. SIZE: Medium. *STOCK: Decorative smalls, 18th-20th C; sports equipment, advertising items, 19th-20th C; all £1-£1,500.* LOC: Off A141. PARK: Easy. TEL: 01487 823686; fax - 01480 496296. SER: Valuations. FAIRS: Alexandra Palace.

WISBECH

Attic Gallery

88 Elm Rd. PE13 2TB. (B.G. Ransome). Est. 1980. Open by appointment. SIZE: Small. *STOCK: Georgian and Victorian silver.* PARK: Easy. TEL: 01945 583734.

Peter A. Crofts BADA

Briar Patch, High Rd., Elm. PE14 0DN. Est. 1949. CL: Sat. *STOCK: General antiques, furniture, porcelain, silver, jewellery.* LOC: A1101. TEL: 01945 584614. VAT: Stan/Spec.

Walpole Highway Antiques Centre

Walpole Highway. PE14 7RN. (D. Bayley). Open Sat. and Sun. only, 10-5. SIZE: Large - 35 dealers. *STOCK: General antiques - furniture including pine, china and bygones. £1-£1,500.* LOC: A47 between Wisbech and King's Lynn. PARK: Own. TEL: 01945 881033.

R. Wilding

Lanes End, Gadds Lane, Leverington. PE13 5BJ. *STOCK: Walnut chests, bureau bookcases, serving tables, mahogany and gilt console tables, mahogany, walnut and gilt mirrors.* TEL: 01945 588204; fax - 01945 476558. SER: Veneering; polishing; (compo) gilding; conversions; cabinet making. *Trade Only.*

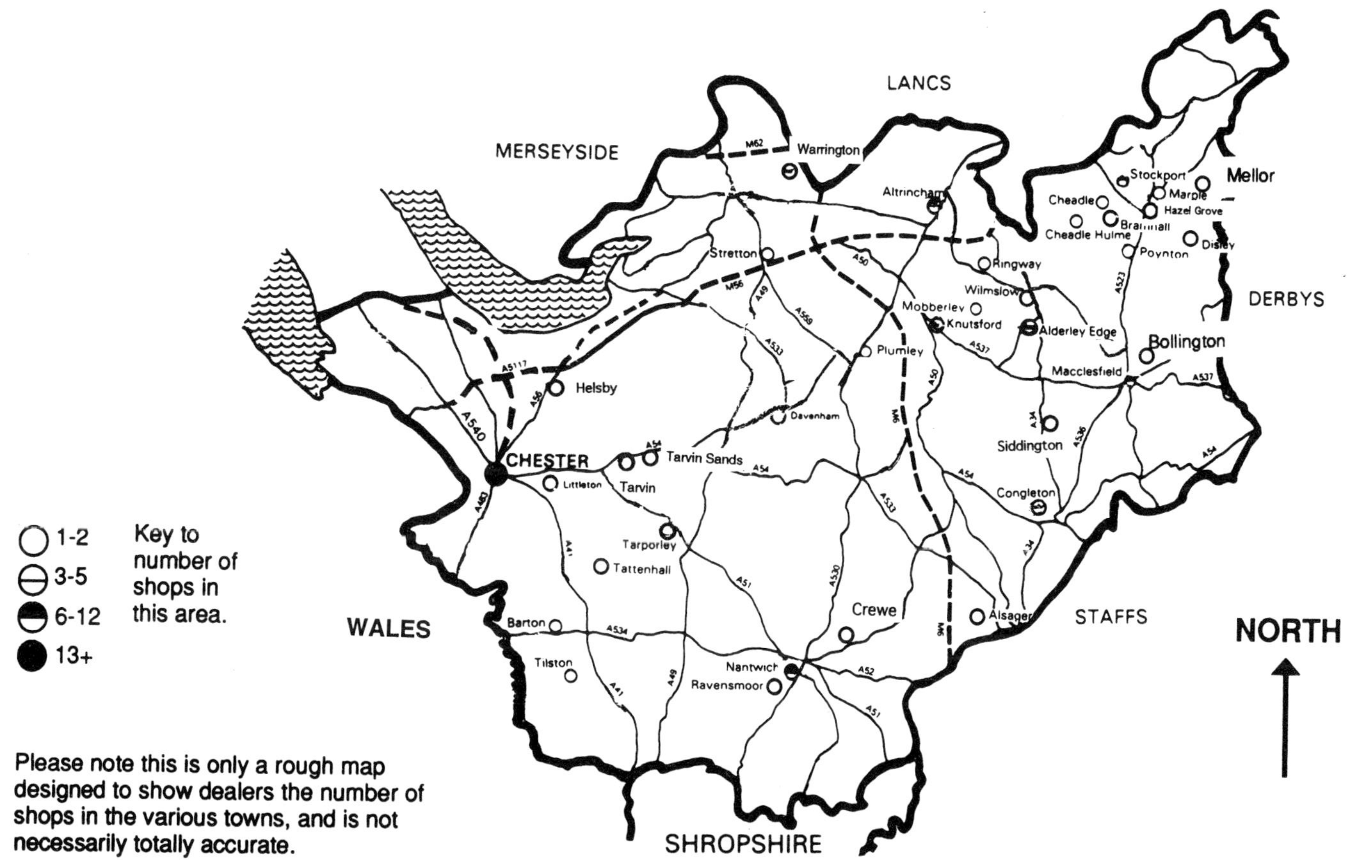

○ 1-2
⊖ 3-5
◐ 6-12
● 13+

Key to number of shops in this area.

Please note this is only a rough map designed to show dealers the number of shops in the various towns, and is not necessarily totally accurate.

ALDERLEY EDGE

Anthony Baker Antiques LAPADA

14 London Rd. SK9 7JS. (G.D.A. Price). Est. 1974. Open 11-5.30. CL: Mon. and Wed. SIZE: Medium. *STOCK: Furniture and clocks, 17th-19th C, £50-£2,000; glass, pottery and collectors items.* Not Stocked: Jewellery, weapons. LOC: A34, village centre. PARK: Easy. TEL: 01625 582674. VAT: Stan/Spec.

Brook Lane Antiques

93 Brook Lane. SK9 7SD. (G.M. Broadbridge). Est. 1983. Open 9-5. SIZE: Small. *STOCK: Furniture especially wardrobes.* TEL: 01625 584896.

The Edge Antiques

8 Trafford Rd. SK9 7HZ. (Vivienne and Andrew Smith). Est. 1977. Open 10-12.30 and 2-4.30, Sat. 10-1, Sun. and Sat. pm. by appointment. CL: Mon. and Wed. SIZE: Small. *STOCK: Victorian light fittings, gas brackets, £100-£500; Victorian pine.* LOC: Parallel to London Rd. (A34). PARK: Easy. TEL: 01625 582176; home - 01625 584089.

Sara Frances Antiques

2 West St. SK9 7EG. (Mrs. F.S. Waterworth). Est. 1990. Open Thurs.-Sat. 10-1 and 2-5. SIZE: Small. *STOCK: Furniture, 17th-19th C, £100-£3,500; silver, 19th-20th C, £50-£500; decorative items, 17th-20th C, £100-£2,500.* LOC: A34 from Congleton. Off London Rd., shop next to Barclays Bank. PARK: Easy. TEL: 01625 585549; home - 01625 861268. SER: Valuations; restorations (furniture and silver).

D.J. Massey and Son

51a London Rd. SK9 7DY. Est. 1900. Open 9-5.30, Wed. 9-5. SIZE: Large. *STOCK: Gold and diamond jewellery; silver, all periods.* LOC: On A34. PARK: Easy. TEL: 01625 583565. VAT: Stan/Spec.

ALSAGER, Nr. Crewe

Forest Books of Cheshire

The Bookshop Upstairs, 14b Lawton Rd. ST7 2AF. (Mrs E. Mann). Open Mon. and Wed.11-5, Tues. and Sat. 11-5.30, Thurs.and Fri. 11-7. *STOCK: Books including new and secondhand, antiquarian, humanities; pictures, ephemera, collectables.* TEL: 01270 882618.

Trash 'n' Treasure

48 Sandbach Rd. South. ST7 2LP. (G. and D. Ogden). Est. 1979. Open 10-12 and 1-5, Fri. and Sat. 10-12 and 1-5.30. CL: Wed. SIZE: Medium. *STOCK: Ceramics, furniture and pictures, Victorian, Edwardian and 1930's, £5-£1, 000.* LOC: 10 minutes junction 16, M6. PARK: Nearby. TEL: 01270 872972/873246. SER: Valuations.

ALTRINCHAM

Altrincham Antiques

39 Hale Rd. and 15 & 23 Tipping St. WA14 2EY. Open 10-6 including Sun. SIZE: Medium. *STOCK: General antiques, £5-£6,500.* LOC: A538 Hale road. PARK: Own. TEL: 0161 941 3554; fax - same; mobile - 0836 316366.

Bizarre Decorative Arts North West

116 Manchester Rd. WA14 4PY. Resident. (Malcolm C. and Rebecca Lamb). Est. 1986. Open 10-6, Sun. by appointment. SIZE: Large. *STOCK: Furniture and lighting, £100-£15,000; figurines, bronzes, ceramics including Clarice Cliff, and jewellery, £5-£2,000; all Art Nouveau and Art Deco.* LOC: A56. PARK: Own. TEL: 0161 926 8895; home - same; fax - 0161 929 8310. SER: Valuations; restorations (furniture and lighting; silver and chrome plating, pewter polishing). FAIRS: NEC Aug; Loughborough Art Deco; Kensington Decorative Arts. VAT: Stan/Spec.

Church Street Antiques

4/4a Old Market Place. WA14 4NP. (Alex Smalley and Nick Stanley). Open 10-5.30, Sun. 12-4. SIZE: Large. *STOCK: Furniture, 18th-19th C, £100-£10,000; silver and plate, 19th C, £50-£1,000; paintings, 19th C-Contemporary, £100-£5,000.* PARK: Easy. TEL: 0161 929 5196; fax - 0161 929 5146; mobile - 468 318661. SER: Valuations; restorations. FAIRS: Tatton; Chester; Lakes; Stafford; Newark; NEC. VAT: Spec.

Greenwood Street Antiques

18 Greenwood St. (Mrs Jane Kiel). Est. 1968. Open Tues., Thurs, Fri. and Sat. 10-4.30. SIZE: Medium. *STOCK: General antiques, specialising in chess sets, 18th to mid-20th C, £20-£2,000.* LOC: From A56 Knutsford to Manchester road, turn right at footbridge into Regent St., then third left. Shop faces rear of hospital. PARK: Nearby. TEL: 0161 941 6978; home - 0161 941 1379.

Lostock Antiques

23 Oxford Rd. WA14 2ED. (Timothy and Carol Lawlor). Est. 1988. Open 10-5. CL: Wed. SIZE: Medium. *STOCK: Furniture, 18th-19th C, £2-£1,500; beds, silver, pottery, prints, glass, bric-a-brac, luggage.* TEL: 0161 929 8696. SER: Restoration (furniture); French polishing; furniture made to order; own range of furniture products, pure beeswax, etc. FAIRS: Cheshire Show and local.

Robert Redford Antiques & Interiors

48 New St. WA14 2QS. (S. and R. Redford). Open 10-6. CL: Mon. and Wed. *STOCK: General antiques, furniture, small silver, porcelain, glass.* PARK: Easy. TEL: 0161 929 8171; home - 0161 926 8232; fax - 0161 928 4827.

Squires Antiques

25 Regent Rd. WA14 1RX. (V. Phillips). Est. 1977. Open 10-5. CL: Mon. and Wed. SIZE: Medium. *STOCK: Small furniture, 1800-1930,*

Altrincham continued

£60-£1,500; small silver, 1850-1970, £20-£400; brass, copper and bric-a-brac, 1850-1940, £10-£400; jewellery, porcelain, fire accessories, light fittings and interior design items. Not Stocked: Large furniture, coins and badges. LOC: Adjacent hospital, and large car park. PARK: Easy. TEL: 0161 928 0749. SER: Valuations.

BARTON, Nr. Malpas

Derek and Tina Rayment Antiques

BADA LAPADA

Orchard House, Barton Rd. SY14 7HT. (D.J. and K.M. Rayment). Est. 1960. Open by appointment every day. *STOCK: Barometers, 18th-20th C, from £100.* LOC: A534. PARK: Easy. TEL: 01829 270429; home - same. SER: Valuations; restorations (barometers only); buys at auction (barometers). FAIRS: NEC; LAPADA; BADA; Olympia; Chelsea. VAT: Stan/Spec.

BOLLINGTON, Nr. Macclesfield

Corner House Antiques

59/61 High St. SK10 5PH. Resident. (Mr and Mrs R. G. Wright). Est. 1988. Open Tues.-Sat. 10.30-6. SIZE: Medium. *STOCK: Decorative and unusual furniture and furnishings, 18th to early 20th C, £50-£2,500; prints, etchings and engravings, watercolours and oils, 19th-20th C, £50-£400; collectables, 18th-20th C, £50-£200.* PARK: Easy. TEL: 01625 576362; home - same. SER: Finder; courier; buys at auction. FAIRS: Local. VAT: Stan/Spec

Yesterdays

68 Palmerston St. SK10 5PW. (Mrs Olive Kershaw). Est. 1989. Open 9.30-1 and 2-5.30, Wed. 9.30-1, Sat. 10-4, Sun. 12-4. SIZE: Small. *STOCK: China and glass, Victorian to Art Deco; small mahogany and pine furniture; Victoriana, all £5-£1,000.* LOC: 4 miles from Macclesfield, through village, opposite car park. PARK: Opposite. TEL: 01625 573222; fax - 01625 576976. SER: Valuations; restorations (fine furniture); buys at auction. VAT: Stan.

BRAMHALL

David H. Dickinson **BADA**

P.O. Box 29. SK7 2EJ. Est. 1976. Open by appointment only. *STOCK: Fine antique furniture and extraordinary works of art.* TEL: 0161 440 0688. SER: Valuations.

CHEADLE

Malcolm Frazer Antiques

19 Brooklyn Crescent. SK8 1DX. Open by appointment. *STOCK: Marine, scientific and decorative antiques.* TEL: 0161 428 3781.

CHEADLE HULME

Allan's Antiques and Reproductions

10 Ravenoak Rd. SK8 7DL. (S. Allan and D. Lloyd). Est. 1979. CL: Wed. *STOCK: Furniture, general antiques, metalware, including silver, especially flatware/cutlery.* TEL: 0161 485 3132/486 6368 (ansaphone).

Andrew Foott Antiques

4 Claremont Rd. SK8 6EG. Est. 1985. Open by appointment only. SIZE: Small. *STOCK: Barometers, 18th-20th C, £200-£2,500; small furniture, 18th-20th C, £500-£3,000.* LOC: 5 minutes from new A34 by-pass. PARK: Easy. TEL: 0161 485 3559; fax - same. SER: Restorations (barometers and furniture). FAIRS: NEC Antiques for Everyone.

CHESTER

Adams Antiques **LAPADA**

65 Watergate Row. CH1 2LE. (B. and T. Adams). Est. 1973. Open 10-5. CL: Sun. except by appointment. SIZE: Medium. *STOCK: English and Continental furniture, £200-£4,000; English and French clocks, £150-£4,000; objets d'art, £10-£1,000; all 18th-19th C.* PARK: Nearby. TEL: 01244 319421. SER: Valuations; restorations (furniture and clocks). VAT: Stan/Spec.

Aldersey Hall Ltd

Town Hall Sq., 47 Northgate St. CH1 2HQ. (Kim Wilding-Welton). Est. 1990. Open 8.30-5.30. SIZE: Medium. *STOCK: Art Deco and general British ceramics, £5-£500; small furniture, £50-£200; all 1880-1940.* LOC: Between library and Odeon cinema. PARK: Own 100 yards. TEL: 01244 324885. SER: Valuations; buys at auction (Art Deco ceramics). FAIRS: Alexandra Palace, Loughborough, Ardingly, Newark and Birmingham. VAT: Stan/Spec.

Antique Exporters of Chester

CH3 7RZ. Open by appointment only. SIZE: Warehouse. *STOCK: Furniture.* TEL: 01829 741001; home - 01244 570069. SER: Packing. *Export Only.*

The Antique Shop

40 Watergate St. CH1 2LA. (Peter Thornber). Est 1985. Open 10-5.30, Sat. 10-6, Sun. (May-Dec.) 1-5, other times by appointment. SIZE: Small. *STOCK: Metalware - brass, pewter, copper, iron etc, 1700-1900, £35-£350; Doulton - character jugs, figures and series ware, 1890-1960, £35-£350; blue and white transfer printed ware; Prattware pot lids, British Army cap badges; fountain pens; boxes and treen; cranberry glass.* LOC: Off Bridge St. PARK: Nearby. TEL: 01244 316286; home - 0151 327 1725. SER: Restorations (metalwork). FAIRS: Cheshire.

Chester continued

Avalon Post Card and Stamp Shop
1 City Walls, Rufus Court, Northgate St. CH1 2JG. (G.E. Ellis). *STOCK: Postcards, stamps and collectables.* TEL: 01244 318406.

Baron Fine Art LAPADA
68 Watergate St. CH1 2LA. (S. and R. Baron). Est. 1984. Open 10-5.15. *STOCK: Watercolours and oils, some etchings, late 19th to early 20th C, some contemporary, £50-£25,000.* PARK: Easy. TEL: 01244 342520. SER: Restorations; framing. FAIRS: Tatton Park; World of Watercolours; LAPADA (Jan.); NEC (April and Aug.). VAT: Stan/Spec.

Boodle and Dunthorne Ltd
52 Eastgate St. CH1 1ES. *STOCK: Fine English and French jewellery, 19th-20th C, £100-£30,000.* TEL: 01244 326666; fax - 01244 317040.

Olwyn Boustead Antiques LAPADA
59-61 Watergate Row. CH1 2LE. (Mrs O.L. Boustead). Open 10-5.30. *STOCK: 17th-19th C town and country furniture; portraits, clocks, metalware, pottery, porcelain and lighting.* TEL: 01244 342300/350366.

Cameo Antiques
19 Watergate St. CH1 2LB. Est. 1994. Open 9-5, Sat. 9-5.30. SIZE: Small. *STOCK: Jewellery and English silver, 1800-1990, £20-£2,000; English (including Moorcroft) and Continental porcelain, 1750-1960.* LOC: Off Bridge St. PARK: Easy. TEL: 01244 311467; fax - same. SER: Valuations; restorations. VAT: Stan/Spec.

Chester Drawers Antique Centre
26 Watergate Row. CH1 2LD. (Alan Bailey). Open 10-5. SIZE: 12 rooms - 24 cabinets. *STOCK: Wide range of general antiques including furniture, pictures, ceramics, clocks, jewellery and collectables.* PARK: Under Moat House Hotel. TEL: 01244 311600. SER: Valuations; restorations; buys at auction. FAIRS: Robert Bailey (Chester Racecourse); Reg Cooper (Arley); NEC.

Farmhouse Antiques
21-23 Christleton Rd., Boughton. CH3 5UF. (K. Appleby). Est. 1973. Open 9-5. SIZE: Large. *STOCK: Farmhouse furniture, longcase clocks, Staffordshire pottery, country bygones, mechanical music.* LOC: 1 mile from City centre on A41. PARK: Easy. TEL: 01244 322478; evenings - 01244 318391. SER: Export. VAT: Stan/Spec.

Guildhall Fair - Chester
Watergate St. Open Thurs. 10-4. SIZE: 40 dealers. *STOCK: General antiques.*

J. Alan Hulme
Antique Maps & Old Prints, 52 Mount Way, Waverton. CH3 7QF. Open Mon.-Sat. by appointment. *STOCK: Maps, 16th-19th C; prints,18th-19th C.* TEL: 01244 336472.

Chester continued

Jamandic Ltd
22 Bridge St. Row. CH1 1NN. Est. 1975. Open 9.30-5, Sat. by appointment except during Nov. and Dec. SIZE: Medium. *STOCK: Decorative furniture, porcelain, pictures and prints.* TEL: 01244 312822. SER: Interior design; export. VAT: Stan/Spec.

Kayes of Chester
9 St. Michaels Row. CH1 1EF. NAG. (A.M. Austin-Kaye and N.J. Kaye). Est. 1948. Open 9-5.30. SIZE: Medium. *STOCK: Diamond rings and jewellery, 1850-1950, £20-£20,000; silver and plate, 1700-1930, £20-£8,000; small objects and ceramics, 19th to early 20th C, £50-£1,000.* PARK: Nearby. TEL: 01244 327149. SER: Valuations; restorations (silver, jewellery and plate); buys at auction. VAT: Stan/Spec.

Lowe and Sons
11 Bridge St. Row. CH1 1PD. Est. 1770. *STOCK: Jewellery and silver, Georgian, Victorian and Edwardian; unusual collectors' items.* TEL: 01244 325850. VAT: Stan/Spec.

Made of Honour
11 City Walls. CH1 1LD. (E. Jones). Open 10-5. *STOCK: General antiques, Staffordshire figures, British ceramics, books, woolworks, samplers, tapestries, beadworks and textiles.* LOC: Next to Eastgate clock, wall level. TEL: 01244 314208.

Melody's Antique Galleries LAPADA
30-32 City Rd. CH1 3AE. (M. Melody). Est. 1977. Open 10-5.30 or by appointment. SIZE: Large. *STOCK: 18th-20th C oak, mahogany, walnut and pine furniture; porcelain, silver, plate, lighting, decorative items.* LOC: 400yds. from station. TEL: 01244 328968; fax - 01244 341818. SER: Courier; container packing. VAT: Stan/Spec.

Moor Hall Antiques
27 Watergate Row. CH1 2LE. Resident. (John Murphy). Est. 1992. Open 10-5.30, Mon., Fri. and Sat. 10.30-5.30. SIZE: Large. *STOCK: Furniture, 18th-19th C, £1,000-£2,000; prints, 19th C, £50-£200; modern decorative items, £20-£100.* LOC: City centre. PARK: Easy. TEL: 01244 340095. SER: Restorations (oils, watercolours and furniture). VAT: Stan/Spec.

Richard A. Nicholson
25 Watergate St. CH1 2LB. Est. 1961. Open 10-1.30 and 2.15-5. SIZE: Large. *STOCK: Maps, 1540-1840, £1-£2,000; prints, 1650-1890, £1-£300; watercolours and drawings, £4-£200.* LOC: Town centre 100yds. from The Cross. PARK: 200yds. at bottom of street behind church. TEL: 01244 326818; home - 01244 336004; fax - 01244 336138; internet - http://www.antiquemaps.com. VAT: Stan/Spec.

Chester continued

On the Air

The Broadcasting Museum, 42 Bridge St. Row. CH1 1NN. (Steve Harris). Est. 1990. Open 10-5, Sun. 11-4.30. CL: Sun. and Mon. Christmas to Easter. SIZE: Small. *STOCK: Vintage wireless, gramophones and telephones, £50-£500.* LOC: 50 yards from The Cross. PARK: Rear of premises. TEL: 01244 348468; fax - 01244 348468. SER: Valuations; restorations (vintage wireless and gramophones). FAIRS: National Vintage Communications, NEC and Wembley.

Richmond Galleries

Watergate Building, New Crane St. CH1 4JE. (Mrs M. Armitage). Est. 1970. Open 10-5.30. SIZE: Large. *STOCK: Pine and country furniture, including Spanish and French; decorative items.* LOC: Direction of Sealand Rd. PARK: Own. TEL: 01244 317602; home - 01244 324285.

Stothert - Antiquarian Books

4 Nicholas St. CH1 8JG. GADAR. (T. and E. Stothert). Est. 1957. Open 9.30-1 and 2-5.30. SIZE: Medium. *STOCK: Books, 16th-20th C, £2-£1,000.* LOC: At junction with Watergate St. TEL: 01244 340756. VAT: Stan/Spec.

John Titchner & Sons LAPADA

67 Watergate Row. Open 10-5.30. *STOCK: Furniture, 18th-19th C.* TEL: 01244 326535.

Veevers

55 Watergate St. (Mr and Mrs A. C. Spicer). Est. 1986. Open 9.30-5. SIZE: Medium. *STOCK: Jewellery and silver, 18th-20th C, £5-£5,000; clocks, 19th-20th C, £50-£1,500.* PARK: Limited and nearby. TEL: 01244 400616. SER: Valuations; restorations (jewellery and clocks). FAIRS: Newark. VAT: Stan/Spec

Watergate Antiques

56 Watergate St. CH1 2LD. (A. Shindler). Est. 1968. Open 9.30-5.30. SIZE: Medium. *STOCK: Porcelain and pottery, jewellery; specialist in silver and silver plate to the Trade.* LOC: From Liverpool first set of traffic lights past Waterfall Roundabout, turn left. PARK: At rear. TEL: 01244 344516; fax - 01244 320350. VAT: Stan.

CONGLETON

W. Buckley Antiques Exports

35 Chelford Rd. CW12 4QA. Open 7 days by appointment. *STOCK: Mainly shipping and Victorian furniture.* TEL: 01260 275299. SER: Shipping.

Little Collectables

8/10 Little St. CW12 1AR. (L.C. and C. Turner). Est. 1989. CL: Wed. SIZE: Medium. *STOCK: Pottery and glass, Doulton, £5-£1,000.* LOC: Town centre. PARK: Nearby. TEL: 01260 299098.

Congleton continued

Pine Too

8/10 Rood Hill. CW12 1LG. (Mrs J.P. Tryon). Open 9.30-5.30. *STOCK: Antique and reproduction furniture.* LOC: Just off A34. PARK: Nearby. TEL: 01260 279228; mobile - 0467 472606.

Ann Roberts Antiques

22 Mill St. CW12 1AB. Est. 1983. Open Tues., Thurs., Fri. and Sat., 11.30-4.30. SIZE: Medium. *STOCK: Victorian and Edwardian wall and mantel clocks and barometers (all guaranteed), brass fireside fenders, coal boxes, fire irons, furniture and oil lamps.* LOC: Adjacent to pedestrian area town centre. PARK: Opposite. TEL: 01260 298942.

CREWE

Steven Blackhurst

102 Edleston Rd. CW2 7HD. Est. 1988. Open 9.30-5, Sat. 10-5, Sun. by appointment. CL: Wed. SIZE: Small. *STOCK: Stripped pine, 19th to early 20th C, £25-£600; satinwood furniture, 1900, £100-£500.* LOC: Turn off Nantwich Rd. (A534), shop 250 yards on left. TEL: 01270 258617; home - 01270 665991.

DAVENHAM, Nr. Northwich

Davenham Antiques Centre & Tea Room

461 London Rd. CW9 8NA. Est. 1985. Open 10-5. CL: Wed. SIZE: 9 dealers. *STOCK: General antiques including furniture, china, pictures, silver, clocks, books and collectables.* LOC: Village centre, off A556. TEL: 01606 44350.

DISLEY

Mill Farm Antiques

50 Market St. SK12 2DT. (F.E. Berry). Est. 1968. Open every day. SIZE: Medium. *STOCK: Pianos, clocks, mechanical music, shipping goods, general antiques, £50-£5,000.* LOC: A6 7 miles south of Stockport. PARK: Easy. TEL: 01663 764045 (24hrs). SER: Valuations; restorations (clocks, watches, barometers, music boxes). VAT: Stan/Spec.

HAZEL GROVE

The Clock House

14 Buxton Rd. SK7 6AD. LBHI. Resident. (A.W. Thom). Est. 1975. Open 10-6 including Sun. SIZE: Small. *STOCK: Prestige wrist and pocket watches including Rolex, clocks, barometers, jewellery.* LOC: On main A6 at Rising Sun junction. PARK: Easy. TEL: 0161 456 5752; fax - same; e-mail - clockhse@aol.com. SER: Restorations and repairs; producer of instructional horology videos.

HELSBY

Sweetbriar Gallery

Robin Hood Lane. WA6 9NH. (Mrs A. Metcalfe). Est. 1986. Open 9-5.30, or by appointment to see full stock. *STOCK: Antique and modern paperweights, £5-£5,000.* LOC: Off M56, junction 14. First left at traffic lights, first right after Elf Garage, past three right turns. Premises on hillside with long, low sandstone wall in front. PARK: Easy. TEL: 01928 723851; home - same; fax - 01928 724153; mobile - 0860 907532; e-mail - sweetbr@globalnet.co.uk; internet - http://www.sweetbriar.co.uk. SER: Valuations; buys at auction (paperweights). FAIRS: Glass (May and Nov.); National Motorcycle Museum (Birmingham); NEC (Aug.), Shepton Mallet; Newark; Ardingly. VAT: Stan/Spec.

KNUTSFORD

Arts and Antiques Centre

113 King St. WA16 6EH. (David and Patricia McLeod). Est. 1995. Open 10-5, Sun. 12-5. CL: Mon. SIZE: 20+ dealers plus contemporary art gallery. *STOCK: Furniture, 18th C, £100-£2,000; pine, £200-£600; ceramics and collectables, £10-£300; clocks, 18th C, £300-£2,000.* LOC: Main street, 5 minutes from junction 19, M6. PARK: Easy. TEL: 01565 654092. SER: Valuations; restorations (ceramics and clocks).

B.R.M. Coins

3 Minshull St. WA16 6HG. (Brian Butterworth). Est. 1968. Open 11-4, Sat. 11-1, or by appointment. SIZE: Small. *STOCK: Coins, medals and banknotes, worldwide, BC to date, from 5p; money boxes, scales and weights.* LOC: A50. PARK: Nearby. TEL: 01565 651480; home - 01606 74522. SER: Valuations; buys at auction (as stock).

Cranford Galleries

10 King St. WA16 6DL. (M.R. Bentley). Est. 1964. Open 11-5. CL: Wed. SIZE: Small. *STOCK: Pictures, prints and Victoriana.* Not Stocked: Glass. LOC: Main St. PARK: Easy. TEL: 01565 633646. SER: Framing and mounting. VAT: Stan.

Glynn Interiors

92 King St. WA16 6ED. Est. 1963. Open 9-1 and 2-5. CL: Wed. SIZE: Large. *STOCK: Furniture, 1750-1900, £50-£2,000; Victorian chairs, £50-£650.* Not Stocked: Porcelain. LOC: 10 mins. drive after leaving M6 at Exit 19. PARK: Own. TEL: 01565 634418. SER: Restorations (re-upholstery) and cabinet repairs. VAT: Stan/Spec.

Lion Gallery and Bookshop

15a Minshull St. WA16 6HG. (R.P. Hepner). Est. 1964. Open Fri. 10.30-4.30, Sat. 10-4.30. *STOCK: Antiquarian maps, prints and books, watercolours and oils, 16th-20th C; O.S. maps and early directories.* LOC: King St. 3 mins. M6. PARK: Nearby. TEL: 01565 652915; mobile - 0850 270796; fax - 01565 750142. SER: Restorations; binding, cleaning, framing and mounting. VAT: Stan.

LITTLETON, Nr. Chester

John Titchner and Sons — LAPADA

Littleton Old Hall, Little Heath Rd. CH3 7DW. Open 9-5. CL: Sat. *STOCK: Furniture, 18th-19th C.* TEL: 01244 336986.

MACCLESFIELD

Gatehouse Antiques

72 Chestergate. (W.H. Livesley). Est. 1973. Open 9-5. CL: Sun. except by appointment and Wed. pm. *STOCK: Small furniture, silver and plate, glass, brass, copper, pewter, jewellery, 1650-1880.* PARK: At rear. TEL: 01625 426476; home - 01625 612841.

Hidden Gem

1,3,5 and 7 Chester Rd. SK10 5SY. (Mrs P. Tilley). Usually open 11-5 or by appointment. *STOCK: Victorian paintings and general antiques.* TEL: Home - 01625 828348.

Hills Antiques

Indoor Market, Grosvenor Centre. SK11 6SY. (D. Hill). Est. 1968. Open 9.30-5.30. *STOCK: Small furniture, jewellery, collectors' items, stamps, coins, postcards.* LOC: Town Centre. PARK: Easy. TEL: 01625 420777/420467.

D.J. Massey and Son

47 Chestergate. SK11 6QQ. Est. 1900. Open 9-5.30. *STOCK: Jewellery, gold and diamonds, all periods.* TEL: 01625 616133.

MARPLE BRIDGE, Nr. Stockport

The Mulberry Bush

20 Town St. SK6 5AA. (David M. Brookes). Est. 1983. Open 9-5, Wed 9-1. SIZE: Small. *STOCK: Furniture, 18th-20th C, £50-£1,000; ceramics, collectables, 19th-20th C, £5-£500.* LOC: By the river on New Mills road, just off A626. PARK: Easy. TEL: 0161 427 8825; home - same. SER: Valuations; buys at auction.

MELLOR, Nr. Stockport

Town House Antiques

Cold Wall Farm, Cobden Edge. (Paul Buxcey). Usually open, prior telephone call essential. *STOCK: Furniture including decorative; associated items.* TEL: 0161 427 1343.

MOBBERLEY

David Bedale

WA16 7HR. Est. 1977. By appointment. SIZE: Medium. *STOCK: 18th-19th C furniture, unusual and decorative items.* TEL: 01565 872270. VAT: Stan/Spec.

NANTWICH

Adams Antiques — LAPADA

Weaver House, 57 Welsh Row. CW5 5EW. Resident. (Sandi Summers). Est. 1975. Open 10-5 or by appointment. SIZE: Large. *STOCK:*

Nantwich continued

***Mainly oak country furniture, dressers, corner cupboards, tables and chairs; bureaux, longcase clocks, paintings for investment and interior decoration; Mason's Ironstone and Staffordshire figures.* LOC: Chester road out of Nantwich. PARK: Easy. TEL: 01270 625643; fax - same; mobile - 0468 622980. SER: Valuations. FAIRS: LAPADA; NEC; Harrogate. VAT: Stan/Spec.**

Tim Armitage

99 Welsh Row. CW5 5ET. (T.J. Armitage). Est. 1967. Open by appointment. SIZE: Small. *STOCK: Tin toys, steam models and early advertising.* LOC: Main road into town from Chester. PARK: Easy. TEL: 01270 626608; home - same. SER: Valuations; buys at auction (toys and models).

Chapel Antiques

47 Hospital St. CW5 5RL. (Miss D.J. Atkin). Est. 1983. Open 9.30-5.30, Wed. 9.30-1, or by appointment. CL: Mon. SIZE: Medium. *STOCK: Oak, mahogany and pine furniture, Georgian and Victorian, £100-£3,000; longcase clocks, pre-1830, £1,000-£3,000; copper, brass, silver, glass, porcelain, pottery and small items, 19th C, £10-£500.* LOC: Enter town via Pillory St., turn right into Hospital St. PARK: Easy. TEL: 01270 629508; home - same. SER: Valuations; restorations (furniture, clocks).

Roderick Gibson

70-72 Hospital St. CW5 5RP. Open 9-5. *STOCK: Furniture and decorative collectors' pieces.* TEL: 01270 625301. VAT: Stan/Global.

Lions and Unicorns

Kiltearn House, 33 Hospital St. CW5 5RL. (J. Pearson). Open by appointment. SIZE: Small. *STOCK: Commemoratives - pottery, porcelain, textiles, glass, tins, metals, books and postcards, £5-£350.* LOC: Town centre, near church. PARK: Easy. TEL: 01270 628892/613830; fax - 01270 626646. SER: Buys at auction; catalogue issued and constantly updated; parcel post worldwide.

Love Lane Antiques

Love Lane. CW5 5BH. (M. Simon). Open 10-5. CL: Wed. SIZE: Small. *STOCK: General antiques, 19th-20th C, £5-£500.* LOC: Two minutes walk from town square. PARK: Nearby. TEL: 01270 626239.

Nantwich Art Deco and Decorative Arts

87 Welsh Row. CW5 5ET. (M. J. Poole and P. M. Savill). Est. 1987. Open Thurs.-Sat. 10-5. SIZE: Small. *STOCK: Art Deco and decorative arts, pottery, china, cabinets, £5-£250.* PARK: Easy. TEL: 01270 624876; home - 01270 811541. FAIRS: Loughborough Art Deco; Birmingham 'Wednesday' Rag Market Fair; Alexandra Palace; Warwick and Chester Art Deco.

Nantwich continued

Pillory House

18 Pillory St. CW5 5BD. (D. Roberts). Est. 1968. Open 9-5. CL: Wed. *STOCK: Hand-carved chimney pieces and oak.* TEL: 01270 623524.

Richardson Antiques

90 Hospital St. CW5 5RP. (Terry Richardson). Est. 1981. Open daily, Sun. by appointment. SIZE: Medium. *STOCK: Furniture, collectables and china.* TEL: 01270 625963; home - 01270 628348. SER: Valuations; restorations (cleaning oil paintings, cabinet making, French polishing, upholstery, clocks).

PLUMLEY

Coppelia Antiques

Holford Lodge, Plumley Moor Rd. WA16 9RS. Resident. (V. and R. Clements). Est. 1970. Open every day by appointment. SIZE: Medium. *STOCK: Over 500 clocks (mainly longcase and wall, £1,000-£30,000); tables - Georgian mahogany, wine, oak gateleg and side; bureaux, desks, chests of drawers, lowboys, coffers, Victorian suites.* LOC: 4 miles junction 19, M6. PARK: Easy. TEL: 01565 722197; fax - 01565 722744. SER: Valuations. FAIRS: Buxton (May). VAT: Spec.

POYNTON, Nr. Stockport

Harper Fine Paintings

"Overdale", Woodford Rd. SK12 1ED. (P.R. Harper). Est. 1967. Open by appointment. SIZE: Large. *STOCK: Watercolours, £100-£35,000; oils including European, £250-£60,000; prints, British, £20-£1,000; all mainly 19th-20th C.* LOC: From A523 centre of Poynton lights, turn into Chester Rd., over railway. After 1/4 mile turn right, 1st drive on left after railway bridge. PARK: Easy. TEL: 01625 879105; home - same. SER: Valuations; restorations; buys at auction (as stock). VAT: Stan/Spec.

Recollections

73 Park Lane. SK12 1RD. (Angela Smith). Open 10-5. SIZE: Medium. *STOCK: Decorative collectables, small furniture, old costume jewellery, amber and antique linens.* PARK: Easy - Civic Centre (free). TEL: 01625 859373.

RAVENSMOOR, Nr. Nantwich

Antiques and Curios

Swanley Lane. CW5 8PZ. Resident. (Mrs R.A. Booth). Est. 1971. SIZE: Small. *STOCK: Furniture including country pine and oak; copper, brass, iron and china, 18th-19th C, £50-£10,000.* PARK: Easy. TEL: 01270 624774; home - same. SER: Restorations (pine stripping). FAIRS: Nantwich.

RINGWAY, Nr. Altrincham

Cottage Antiques

Hasty Lane. WA15 8UT. (J. and J. M. Gholam). Est. 1967. SIZE: Medium. *STOCK: Furniture, metalware, ceramics, glass, early 18th-mid 19th C.* Not Stocked: Jewellery, jade and ivory. LOC: Off junction 6, M56, off A538, very close to airport. PARK: Easy. TEL: 0161 980 7961. SER: Valuations.

SIDDINGTON, Nr. Macclesfield

G. Bagshaw Antiques

The Old Smithy, Capesthorne Hall Estate Yard. SK11 9JX. Est. 1971. Open 10-5.30. SIZE: Small. *STOCK: General antiques.* LOC: On A34 Congleton Road, near Monks Heath. PARK: Easy. TEL: 01625 860909. SER: Valuations; restorations (ceramics, clock dials re-painted, paintings and prints); ceramic restoration courses (postal and residential).

STOCKPORT

Antique Furniture Warehouse

Units 3/4 Royal Oak Buildings, Cooper St. SK1 3QJ. Open 9.30-5.30. SIZE: Large. *STOCK: English and Continental furniture, paintings, bronzes, clocks, shipping goods, Art Deco, pottery, porcelain and curios, decorative items, architectural, radios and televisions, silver and silver plate.* LOC: 2 mins. off M56 towards town centre. PARK: Easy. TEL: 0161 429 8590. VAT: Stan.

Stockport continued

Antiques Import Export UK

Hole in the Wall Antique Warehouse, Hadfield House, Lancashire Hill. SK4 1RR. Open 10-5.30. SIZE: Large. *STOCK: Victorian and Edwardian mahogany, to £1,000.* PARK: Easy. TEL: 0161 476 4013; fax - 0161 477 2684. SER: Valuations; restorations. FAIRS: Newark.

E. R. Antiques Centre

122 Wellington St., off Wellington Rd. South. SK1 1YH. (E. Warburton). Est. 1979. Open 12-5.30. SIZE: Medium - 6 dealers. *STOCK: China, pottery, glass, silver, EPNS, costume jewellery, 1820-1960, £5-£200.* LOC: Turn into Edwards St. by the Town Hall, at 'T' junction turn left, shop 500yds. on left at bollards. PARK: Easy. TEL: 0161 429 6646; home - 0161 480 5598.

Flintlock Antiques

28 and 30 Bramhall Lane. SK2 6HR. (F. Tomlinson and Son). Est. 1968. SIZE: Large. *STOCK: Furniture, clocks, pictures, scientific instruments.* TEL: 0161 480 9973. VAT: Stan/Spec.

Halcyon Antiques

435/437 Buxton Rd., Great Moor. SK2 7HE. (Mrs Jill A. Coppock). Est. 1980. Open 10-5. SIZE: Large. *STOCK: Porcelain and glass, £1-£2,000; furniture, £50-£2,000; both 1750-1940: jewellery, silver and plate, linen and lace.* LOC: A6, 2 miles south of town. PARK: Easy. TEL: 0161 483 5038; home - 0161 439 3524.

Highland Antiques

67 Wellington Rd. North. SK4 2LP. (E. Todd). Est. 1970. SIZE: Medium. *STOCK: Silver and plate; Chinese and Japanese pottery, porcelain and furniture, 18th-19th C.* LOC: A6. PARK: Easy. TEL: 0161 476 6660; fax - 0161 476 6669. SER: Valuations; restorations; buys at auction. FAIRS: Manchester. VAT: Stan/Spec.

Hole in the Wall Antiques

370 Buxton Rd., Great Moor; warehouse - Hadfield House, Lancashire Hill. SK2 7BY. (M. and A. Ledger). Est. 1960. Open 10-5, Sun. by appointment. SIZE: Large. *STOCK: Furniture, 18th-20th C, pine, smalls, £50-£5,000.* LOC: A6. PARK: Easy. TEL: 0161 483 6603; fax - 0161 477 2684; warehouse - 0161 476 4013. SER: Restorations; import and export; courier.

Imperial Antiques LAPADA

295 Buxton Rd., Great Moor. SK2 7NR. (A. Todd). Est. 1972. Open 10-5.30, Sun. by appointment. SIZE: Large. *STOCK: Silver and plate, 19th-20th C; porcelain especially Japanese and Chinese, 18th-19th C; both £10-£1,000.* LOC: A6 Buxton Rd., 1.5 miles south of town centre. PARK: Easy. TEL: 0161 483 3322. SER: Buys at auction (as stock). VAT: Stan/Spec.

Stockport continued

Limited Editions

35 King St. East. SK1 1XJ. (C.W. Fogg). Est. 1978. Open 9.45-6, Sat. 9.30-5.30. SIZE: Large. *STOCK: Furniture, 19th C, especially dining tables and chairs, £100-£5,000; arm chairs and couches for re-upholstery.* LOC: Off Warren St., next to Sainsbury's. PARK: Own at rear. TEL: 0161 480 1239. SER: Valuations; restorations (furniture). VAT: Stan/Spec.

Nostalgia Architectural Antiques

Holland's Mill, Shaw Heath. SK3 8BH. (D. and E. Durrant). Est. 1975. Open 10-6, Sat. 10-5. CL: Mon. SIZE: Large. *STOCK: Fireplaces, £200-£15,000; bathroom fittings and architectural items, £50-£2,000; all 18th-19th C.* PARK: At rear. TEL: 0161 477 7706; fax - 0161 477 2267. SER: Valuations. VAT: Stan/Spec.

Oak Room

(Nigel Pitceathly). Open by appointment. *STOCK: Oak and country furniture including primitive, 16th-19th C.* TEL: 0161 432 5976; mobile - 0831 476316.

Page Antiques

424 Buxton Rd., Great Moor. SK2 7JQ. Open Mon.-Sat. SIZE: Large. *STOCK: Georgian to Edwardian furniture, brass, copper, silver, plate, stripped pine especially for Australian and German markets.* LOC: A6. TEL: 0161 483 9202; home - 01663 732358. SER: Courier. VAT: Stan/Spec.

STRETTON, Nr. Warrington

Antiques Etc.

Shepcroft House, London Rd. WA4 5PJ. (M. Clare). Est. 1978. Resident, usually available. SIZE: Medium. *STOCK: Furniture, pine, barometers, clocks, instruments and items of interest, £5-£2,000.* LOC: A49, towards Warrington, through Stretton traffic lights, next turning on left. PARK: Easy. TEL: 01925 730431; mobile - 0836 570663.

TARPORLEY

Marie José Burke

The Pavillion, High St. CW6 0DX. ADA. Est. 1959. Open 10-5, appointment advisable. CL: Sat. *STOCK: Period English furniture.* VAT: Spec.

Maria Hopwood Antiques

Hulgrave Hall, Tiverton. CW6 9UQ. Resident. Est. 1992. Open daily including Sun. SIZE: Medium. *STOCK: Pine and country furniture, rural bygones, sporting goods and architectural antiques, kitchenalia and domestic paraphernalia, from 1750, £1-£2,000.* LOC: A49 south from Tarporley, 1 mile from Beeston market. PARK: Own. TEL: 01829 732427; home - 01829 733313; mobile - 0976 539990; fax - 01829 733802. SER: Valuations; restorations (furniture).

Tarporley continued

Milestone Antiques

67 High St. CW6 0DP. (D. Perry). Open 10-5. *STOCK: General antiques and reproduction.* TEL: 01829 733026.

Tarporley Antique Centre

76 High St. Open 10-5, Sun. 11-4. SIZE: 9 dealers on two floors. *STOCK: Furniture, ceramics, commemoratives, treen, Studio pottery, glass, oils, watercolours, prints, framing.* LOC: Main road, near Crown public house. PARK: In front of premises and opposite. TEL: 01829 733919. SER: Framing; caning; buys at auction.

TARVIN, Nr. Chester

Antique Fireplaces

The Manor House, Church St. (Mrs G. O'Toole). Est. 1979. Open Fri., Sat. and Sun. 10-5 or by appointment. SIZE: Medium. *STOCK: Fireplaces and ranges, 18th-19th C, £150-£3,000.* LOC: At junction of A556 and A51. PARK: Easy. TEL: 01829 740936; home - 01606 46717. SER: Valuations; restorations; installations (fireplaces and ranges); new tiles and fenders ordered from suppliers on request. FAIRS: Tatton Park, Knutsford.

TARVIN SANDS, Nr. Chester

Cheshire Brick and Slate Co

Brook House Farm, Salters Bridge. CH3 8HL. (Malcolm Youde). Est. 1978. Open 8-5.30, Sat. 8-4.30, Sun. 10-4. SIZE: Large. *STOCK: Reclaimed conservation building materials, 16th-20th C; architectural antiques - garden statuary, stonework, lamp posts, gates, fireplaces, bathroom suites, chimney pots and ironwork, 18th-20th C, £50-£1,000; furniture, pews, leaded lights, pottery, 18th-20th C, £5-£1,000.* LOC: Directly off A54 just outside Tarvin. PARK: Own. TEL: 01829 740883. SER: Valuations; restorations (fireplaces, timber treatment); building/ construction and demolition; renovations. VAT: Stan.

TATTENHALL, Nr. Chester

The Great Northern Architectural Antique Company Ltd

New Russia Hall, Chester Rd. CH3 9AH. Open 9.30-4.30 including Sun. SIZE: Large. *STOCK: Period doors, fire surrounds, stained glass, sanitary ware, garden statuary, furniture and curios.* LOC: Off A41. PARK: Easy. TEL: 01829 770796; fax - 01829 770971. VAT: Stan.

TILSTON, Nr. Malpas

Well House Antiques

The Well House. SY14 7DP. (S. French-Greenslade). Est. 1968. Open by appointment only. SIZE: Small. *STOCK: Collectors' items,*

Tilston continued

china, glass, silver. LOC: From Whitchurch on A41, take B5395 signposted Malpas. PARK: Easy. TEL: 01829 250332.

WARRINGTON

A. Baker and Sons

10 Cairo St. WA1 1ED. NAG. (A.R. Baker). Est. 1907. Open 9.30-5, Sat. 9.30-4. SIZE: Small. *STOCK: Silver and jewellery, 18th-20th C, from £100.* LOC: Off M6, junction 9, take A50 into town. Cairo St. off Sankey St. between Co-op and Barclays Bank. PARK: Easy. TEL: 01925 633706; fax - same. SER: Valuations; restorations (as stock). VAT: Stan.

Deja Vu Antiques

Hattersrow, Horsemarket St. WA1 1XP. (I. and Mrs A. S. Jones). Open 9.30-5. SIZE: Small. *STOCK: 1920's to 1950's telephones, £50-£500; Victorian pine and walnut furniture, general antiques and reproduction items, £5-£500.* PARK: Nearby. TEL: 01925 232677. SER: Restorations (telephones). FAIRS: Art Deco - Loughborough, Chester, Leeds, Coventry Hilton.

The Rocking Chair Antiques

Unit 3, St. Peter's Way. WA2 7BL. (N., M. and J. Barratt). Est. 1971. Open 9-5.30. SIZE: Large. *STOCK: Furniture and bric-a-brac.* LOC: Off Orford Lane. PARK: Easy. TEL: 01925 652409; fax - same; mobile - 0374 492891. SER: Valuations; shipping, packing. VAT: Stan.

WILMSLOW

Peter Bosson Antiques

10B Swan St. SK9 1HE. Est. 1965. Open 10-12.45 and 2.15-5, or by appointment. CL: Mon. and Wed. SIZE: Small. *STOCK: Clocks, 1675-1900, £5-£2,000; barometers, unusual items.* Not Stocked: Porcelain, silver. LOC: On A34. PARK: 50yds. away. TEL: 01625 525250; home - 01625 527857. SER: Restorations (clock repair); buys at auction.

Wilmslow Antique Bazaar

5 Church St. SK9 1AX. (G.M. and S.M. Dale). Est. 1977. Open 10-5. SIZE: Medium - 16 dealers. *STOCK: Wide range of general antiques, 19th-20th C, £5-£1,000+.* LOC: Town centre. PARK: At rear. TEL: 01625 540472; home - 01829 751010. SER: Valuations; buys at auction (furniture).

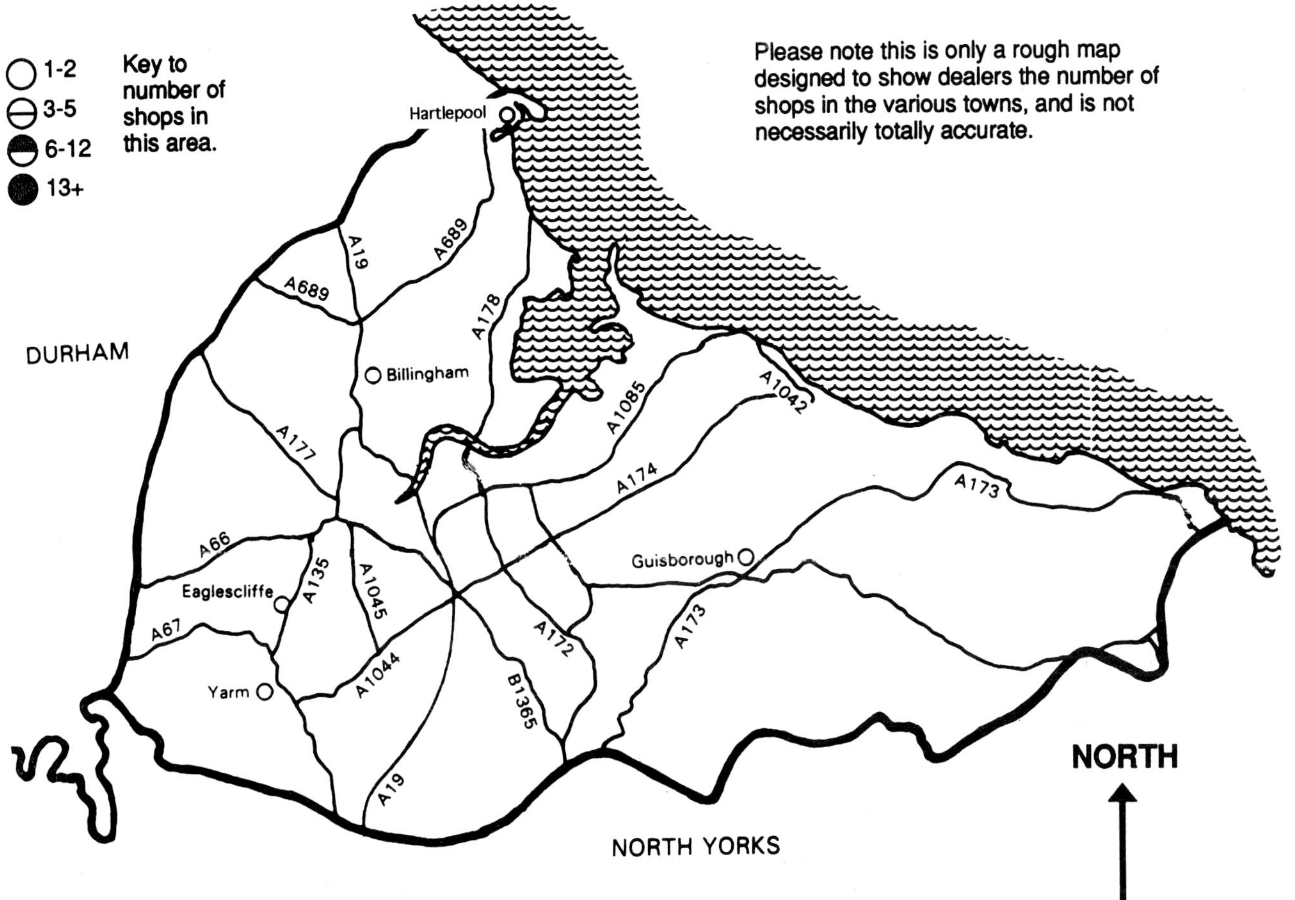
Key to number of shops in this area.
1-2
3-5
6-12
13+
Please note this is only a rough map designed to show dealers the number of shops in the various towns, and is not necessarily totally accurate.
Hartlepool
DURHAM
Billingham
Guisborough
Eaglescliffe
Yarm
NORTH YORKS
NORTH
A19
A689
A689
A178
A177
A1085
A1042
A174
A173
A66
A135
A1045
A67
A172
A173
A1044
B1365
A19

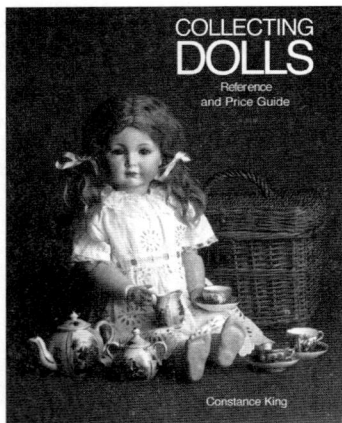

BILLINGHAM

Margaret Bedi Antiques LAPADA

5 Station Rd. TS23 1AG. Est. 1976. Open by appointment. *STOCK: Mainly English period furniture, 1720-1920; oils and watercolours, 19th-20th C.* LOC: 300yds. off A19, by village green. PARK: Easy. TEL: 01642 782346; mobile - 0860 577637. VAT: Stan/Spec.

EAGLESCLIFFE, Nr. Stockton-on-Tees

T.B. and R. Jordan (Fine Paintings) LAPADA

Aslak. TS16 0QN. Est. 1974. Open by appointment. *STOCK: Oil paintings and watercolours, 19th-20th C, £200-£5,000.* LOC: Village centre. PARK: Easy. TEL: 01642 782599; fax - 01642 780473. SER: Framing; restorations; commissions. VAT: Spec.

GUISBOROUGH

Atrium Antiques

(W.L. and M.G. Richardson). Est. 1967. Open by appointment. *STOCK: Furniture, silver, pottery, jewellery, clocks, general items.* PARK: Easy. TEL: 01287 632777.

HARTLEPOOL

Antique Fireplace Centre

Units, 6, 7 & 8 Newburn Bridge Industrial Estate. TS24 7AH. (D.J. Crowther). Est. 1983. Open 9-5. CL: Wed. SIZE: Large. *STOCK: Victorian and Edwardian fireplaces, Victorian 4-panel pine doors, architectural antiques.* TEL: 01429 279007/222433; mobile - 0374 639754.

YARM, Nr. Stockton-on-Tees

Ruby Snowden Antiques

20 High St. TS15 9AE. (R.H. Snowden). Est. 1977. Open 9-5.30, Wed. 9-5, Sun. by appointment. SIZE: Medium. *STOCK: Furniture, 1700-1930s, £50-£2,000; porcelain and Staffordshire, £5-£200; jewellery, silver, glass, copper and brass.* LOC: Opposite library. PARK: Easy. TEL: 01642 785363; home - 01642 819918. SER: Valuations. VAT: Stan/Spec.

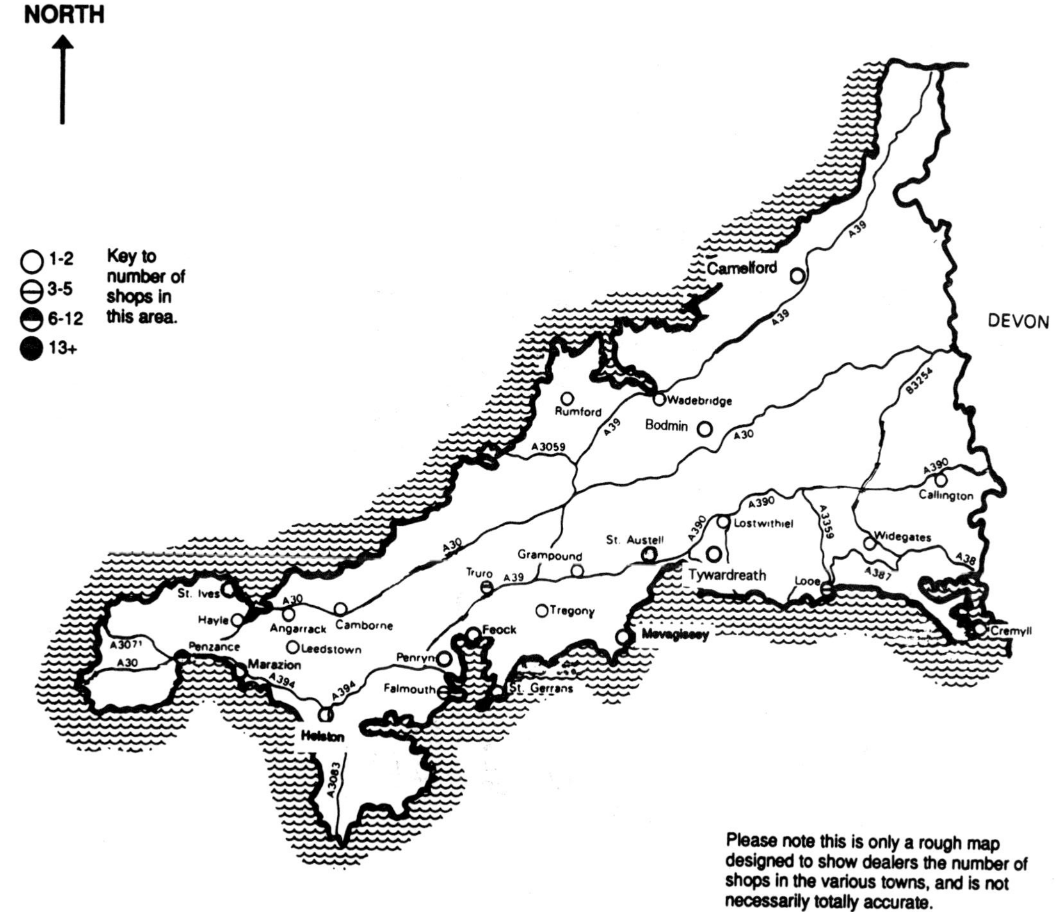
NORTH
1-2
3-5
6-12
13+
Key to number of shops in this area.
DEVON
Camelford
Wadebridge
Rumford
Bodmin
Callington
Lostwithiel
Widegates
St. Austell
Grampound
Tywardreath
Looe
Truro
Cremyll
St. Ives
Hayle
Angarrack
Camborne
Tregony
Feock
Mevagissey
Penzance
Leedstown
Penryn
Marazion
Falmouth
St. Gerrans
Helston
A39
A30
A3059
B3254
A390
A3359
A38
A387
A3071
A394
A3083
Please note this is only a rough map designed to show dealers the number of shops in the various towns, and is not necessarily totally accurate.

ANGARRACK, Nr. Hayle

Paul Jennings Antiques

Millbrook House. TR27 5HY. Est. 1974. Open by appointment. SIZE: Small. *STOCK: Clocks, furniture, £100-£3,000.* LOC: 1/2 mile from A30. TEL: 01736 754065. VAT: Stan/Spec. *Trade Only.*

BODMIN

Bodmin Antiques Centre

Town End. PL31 1LN. (Ralph and Nola Solomons). Open 10-4. SIZE: Medium - several dealers. *STOCK: Ceramics and glass, £5-£100, small furniture, £10-£350, both 19th-20th C; commemoratives, kitchenalia, toys, brass, 20th C, £5-£75.* LOC: Main road. PARK: Nearby. TEL: 01208 78661; home - 01208 74609. SER: Valuations.

BOSCASTLE

Newlyfe Antiques

The Old Mill. PL35 0AQ. (Harry Ruddy). Open seven days a week May-Sept. - prior 'phone call advisable at other times. *STOCK: Collectables, small furniture, French beds.* TEL: 01840 250230.

Old Mill Antiques & Interiors

PL35 0AQ. (B. Hedges). Open seven days a week May-Sept. - prior 'phone call advisable at other times. *STOCK: Collectables, small furniture, silver, watercolours, furnishings.* TEL: 01840 250223.

CALLINGTON

Country Living Antiques

Weston House, Haye Rd. PL17 7JJ. Resident. (Ian Baxter). Est. 1990. Open 10-6. SIZE: Large - incl. barn. *STOCK: 19th C oak and pine country furniture, general antiques, £1-£2,000.* LOC: Town centre. PARK: Own. TEL: 01579 382245; fax - same. SER: Valuations; buys at auction.

CAMBORNE

Victoria Gallery

28 Cross St. TR14 8EX. (J.P. Maker). Open Mon. 1-5.15, Tues., Wed., Fri. 11-5.15, other times by appointment. CL: Thurs. and Sat. *STOCK: Books, pictures, general antiques, furniture, silver and jewellery.* TEL: 01209 719268.

CAMELFORD

Bridge Antiques

1 Market Place. PL32 9PB. (Paul Smith). Open 10-5, Sat. 10-1. CL: Mon. SIZE: Small. *STOCK: Brown furniture, 18th-20th C, £100-£2,000; china, glass and metalware, 18th-20th C, £20-£500; watercolours and prints, 19th-20th C, £20-£200.* LOC: Town centre, on A39. PARK: Free, 1 minute walk. TEL: 01840 213701 (24 hrs). SER: Valuations; restorations (furniture); French polishing. FAIRS: Ardingly, Westpoint, Newark.

CREMYLL

Cremyll Antiques

The Cottage, Cremyll Beach, Torpoint. PL10 1HX. *STOCK: Clocks and watches, small items, jewellery.* TEL: 01752 823490. SER: Repairs (barometers, barographs, watches, clocks, jewellery).

FALMOUTH

John Maggs

54 Church St. TR11 3DS. (C.C. Nunn). Est. 1900. Open 10-5. SIZE: Medium. *STOCK: Antiquarian prints and maps, exclusive limited editions.* LOC: Main street. PARK: At rear of shop. TEL: 01326 313153; fax - same. SER: Restorations; framing; binding.

Rosina's

4 High St. TR11 2AB. (Mrs R. Gealer). Open 11-4.30. *STOCK: Old dolls, bears, including limited edition, Steiff and artist bears, toys, linen and lace, clothes; modern miniatures.* TEL: 01326 311406; home - 01326 317739. SER: Restorations.

Waterfront Antiques Market

1st Floor, 4 Quay St. Open 10-5. SIZE: 20 dealers. *STOCK: Furniture, pottery, porcelain, glass, silver, metalware, kitchenalia, pictures, books, clocks, jewellery, decorative and collectors' items.* TEL: 01326 311491.

FEOCK, Nr. Truro

Strickland and Dorling

Come-to-Good. TR3 6QS. (P. Strickland and T. Dorling). Est. 1950's. Usually open. *STOCK: Small furniture, pottery, porcelain, silver, pictures, maps of Cornwall, bijouterie and collectors' items.* TEL: 01872 862394.

GRAMPOUND, Nr. Truro

Pine and Period Furniture

Fore St. TR2 4QT. (S. Payne). Open 10-5. CL: Sat. *STOCK: Pine and period furniture.* TEL: 01726 883117.

Radnor House

Fore St. TR2 4QT. (P. and G. Hodgson). Est. 1972. Open 10-5. SIZE: Medium. *STOCK: Furniture and accessories, pre-1900.* Not Stocked: Jewellery, coins and weapons. LOC: A390. PARK: Easy. TEL: 01726 882921; home - same. SER: Valuations; buys at auction. VAT: Stan/Spec.

HAYLE

Copperhouse Gallery - W. Dyer & Sons

14 Fore St. TR27 4DX. (A.P. Dyer). Est. 1900. Open 9-1 and 2-5.30, Wed. 9-1. SIZE: Medium. *STOCK: Watercolours, some oils, including Newlyn and St. Ives Schools, 19th to early 20th C, £25-£1,000.* LOC: Main road. PARK: Easy. TEL: 01736 752787; home - 01736 753362. SER: Restorations (watercolours and oils).

HELSTON

Humphreys Antiques

45 Meneage St. TR1 38RH. (Norman Boyes). SIZE: Medium. *STOCK: General antiques.* TEL: 01326 564286.

LEEDSTOWN, Nr. Hayle

A.W. Glasby and Son Antiques

TR27 6DA. (D.E. Glasby). Est. 1936. Open 10.15-12.45 and 2.15-5. CL: Sat. and Mon. SIZE: Large. *STOCK: Furniture, porcelain and clocks, £10-£5,000.* Not Stocked: Coins, medals, scientific instruments. LOC: On main road half-way between Hayle and Helston. PARK: Easy. TEL: 01736 850303.

LOOE

Dowling and Bray

Fore St., East Looe. PL13 1AE. Est. 1920. *STOCK: General antiques, furniture and brassware.* TEL: 01503 262797.

Looe Antiques

1 Seafront Court, The Quay, East Looe. (Miss G. Jones). Est. 1986. Open daily from 10.30, Sun. from 12. CL: Sun. in winter. SIZE: Medium. *STOCK: General antiques and collectors' items, mainly 19th-20th C, £5-£1,000.* PARK: Easy in winter, otherwise nearby. TEL: 01503 265495. SER: Valuations.

Tony Martin

Fore St. PL13 1AE. Est. 1965. Open 9.30-1 and 2-5 appointment advisable. CL: Thurs. pm. SIZE: Medium. *STOCK: Porcelain, 18th C; silver, 18th-19th C, both £20-£200; glass, furniture, oils and watercolours.* LOC: Main street. TEL: 01503 262734; home - 01503 262228. VAT: Stan/Spec.

LOSTWITHIEL

John Bragg Antiques

35 Fore St. PL22 0BN. Open 10-5. *STOCK: Furniture, mainly period mahogany and Victorian.* LOC: 100yds. off A390. TEL: 01208 872827.

Old Palace Antiques

Old Palace, Quay St. PL22 0BS. (D. Bryant). Open 10-1 and 2-5. CL: Wed. pm. *STOCK: Pine, general antiques, postcards and collectors' items.* TEL: 01208 872909.

MARAZION

Antiques

The Shambles, Market Place. TR17 0AR. (Andrew S. Wood). Est. 1988. Open 10-5.30, Sun by appointment. SIZE: Medium. *STOCK: General antiques and collectors' items, especially 19th to early 20th C pottery and porcelain including Staffordshire figures; Victorian and early 20th C decorative and pressed glass; Art Deco ceramics*

Marazion continued

especially Shelley; Goss and crested china, Devon and commemorative ware, postcards and bottles. Not Stocked: Weapons and large furniture. LOC: Main street. PARK: Easy. TEL: 01736 711381; home - same.

MEVAGISSEY, Nr. St Austell

Granny's Attic

18 Church St. PL26 6SP. Resident. (Heather and David Wetzel). Est. 1988. Open April-Sept. 12-4 including Sun; Oct.-Mar. prior telephone call advisable. SIZE: Small. *STOCK: Collectables, stamps, toy cars, crested ware and militaria, 50p to £100.* LOC: A390. PARK: Adjacent. TEL: 01726 843818; fax - same. SER: Buys at auction.

PENRYN

The Antique Shop

15 Church Rd. (J.M. Gavin). Open 8.30-6. *STOCK: General antiques.* TEL: 01326 375092.

Leon Robertson Antiques

7 The Praze. TR10 8DH. (Leon Robertson). Est. 1972. *STOCK: 19th -20th C furniture, paintings and general antiques.* TEL: 01326 372767; mobile - 0860 482268.

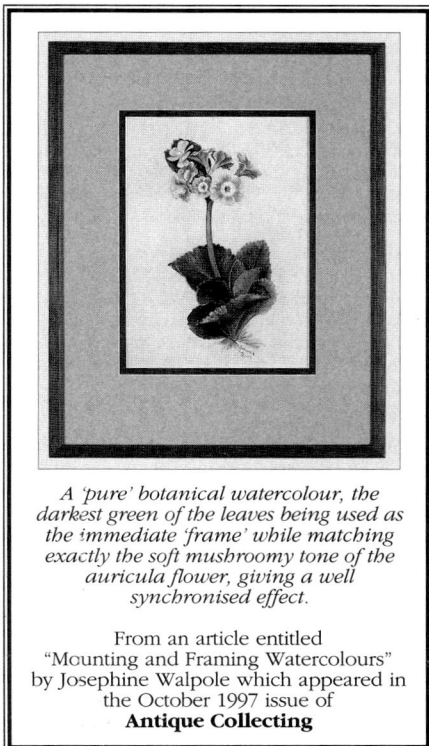

A 'pure' botanical watercolour, the darkest green of the leaves being used as the immediate 'frame' while matching exactly the soft mushroomy tone of the auricula flower, giving a well synchronised effect.

From an article entitled "Mounting and Framing Watercolours" by Josephine Walpole which appeared in the October 1997 issue of **Antique Collecting**

PENZANCE

Ken Ashbrook Antiques

Leskinnick Place. Est. 1973. Open Wed. 10-1, Thurs. and Fri. 10-1 and 2.15-5, Sat. 10.30-1, other times by appointment. SIZE: Large. *STOCK: Furniture, 18th-20th C, £100-£5,000.* LOC: 1 min. from railway station. PARK: Nearby. TEL: 01736 330914; home - 01736 365477. SER: Valuations; restorations (cabinet work); buys at auction (furniture). VAT: Stan/Spec.

James Buchanan Antiques

Captain Cutter's House, 52 Chapel St. Open 10-4.30. *STOCK: Furniture and interesting items, 1700 to modern, including town and country furniture, pictures, metalware, glass, china and rugs.* LOC: Town centre. PARK: Easy. TEL: 01736 762317; mobile - 0421 678826.

Chapel Street Antiques Market

61/62 Chapel St. Open 9.30-5. SIZE: 20 dealers. *STOCK: Furniture, pottery, porcelain, glass, silver, metalware, kitchenalia, pictures, books, clocks, jewellery, decorative and collectors' items.* TEL: 01736 363267.

Daphne's Antiques

17 Chapel St. TR18 4AW. Est. 1976. Open 9-5. SIZE: Medium. *STOCK: Early country and 18th-19th C mahogany furniture, Georgian glass, Delft, pottery and decorative objects.* TEL: 01736 361719.

Brian Humphrys Antiques

1 St. Clare St. TR18 2PB. Est. 1964. SIZE: Medium. *STOCK: Furniture, clocks, silver, jewellery, 18th-19th C, £25-£4,000.* PARK: Easy opposite. TEL: 01736 365154. SER: Valuations; buys at auction. VAT: Stan/Spec.

Little Jem's

Antron House, 55 Chapel St. TR18 5AE. (J. Lagden). Open 9.30-5. *STOCK: Antique and modern jewellery (specialising in opal and amber), gem stones, objets d'art, paintings, clocks and watches.* TEL: 01736 351400. SER: Repairs; commissions.

New Street Books

4 New St. TR18 2LZ. (B.J. Maker). Open 10-5. *STOCK: Books and pictures.* TEL: 01736 362758.

Pinewood Studios

46 Market Jew St. (R. Aby). Open 9.30-5.30. *STOCK: Pine furniture.* Not Stocked: Reproductions. TEL: 01736 368793.

Tony Sanders Penzance Gallery and Antiques

14 Chapel St. TR18 4AW. Est. 1972. Open 9-5.30. SIZE: Medium. *STOCK: Oils and watercolours specialising in Newlyn and St. Ives schools, 19th-20th C, £50-£5,000; contemporary paintings and sculpture; glass, silver, china and small furniture; specialist in Newlyn and J.F. Pool of Hayle copper.* TEL: 01736 366620/368461. VAT: Stan.

Penzance continued

RUMFORD

Henley House Antiques

PL27 7SS. (P. Neale). *STOCK: Juvenilia, small antiques, bric-a-brac.* TEL: 01841 540322.

ST. AUSTELL

Ancient and Modern

32-34 Polkyth Rd. PL25 4LW. (P.J. Watts). Est. 1965. Open 10-5. *STOCK: General antiques, paintings, clocks, jewellery, bric-a-brac.* TEL: 01726 73983.

Mrs. Margaret Chesterton

33 Pentewan Rd. PL25 5BU. Est. 1965. Open 10-5.30, appointment advisable. CL: Sat. pm. *STOCK: Victoriana, Edwardiana, 1800-1915; some furniture, porcelain, glass, £1-£500; brass, copper, pewter, jewellery, clocks, watercolours.* LOC: Coming from Plymouth, travel direct to St. Austell. Keep on main by-pass until roundabout for Mevagissey and Pentewan Rd. House is 100yds. on left down this road. PARK: Easy. TEL: 01726 72926.

ST. GERRANS, Nr. Portscatho

Turnpike Cottage Antiques and Tearooms

The Square. TR2 5EB. (T. and S. Green). Est. 1988. Open 11-1.30 and 3-6, Sun. and wintertime 3-6. CL: Thurs. SIZE: Medium. *STOCK: General antiques, furniture, porcelain, bric-a-brac, £5-£4,000.* LOC: Near church. PARK: Easy, at rear. TEL: 01872 580853; home - same. SER: Valuations; restorations (furniture, watercolours).

ST. IVES

Mike Read Antique Sciences

1 Abbey Meadow, Lelant. TR26 3LL. Est. 1974. Open by appointment. SIZE: Small. *STOCK: Scientific instruments - navigational, surveying, mining, barometers, telescopes and microscopes, medical, 18th-19th C, £10-£5,000; maritime works of art and nautical artifacts.* LOC: Turn left on hill in village, heading towards St. Ives. PARK: Easy. TEL: 01736 757237. SER: Valuations; restorations.

TREGONY, Nr. Truro

Clock Tower Antiques

57 Fore St. TR2 5RW. (The Warne Family). Open 10-6, (extended in summer), evenings and Sun. by appointment. SIZE: Medium. *STOCK: Ceramics, including Doulton stoneware, Mason's Ironstone, 19th C blue and white transferware, £10-£500; paintings and prints, 19th to early 20th C,*

Tregony continued

£1,000; furniture, 18th to early 20th C, £75-£3,000; brass, copper and treen, £10-£300. Not Stocked: Silver and jewellery. LOC: Village centre, B3287. PARK: Easy. TEL: 01872 530225; home - same.

TRURO

Alan Bennett

24 New Bridge St. TR1 2AA. Est. 1954. Open 9-5.30. SIZE: Large. *STOCK: Furniture, £50-£5,000; jewellery and porcelain, to 1900, £5-£1,000; paintings and prints, £20-£2,000.* LOC: Eastern side of cathedral. PARK: 100yds. from shop. TEL: 01872 273296. VAT: Stan/Spec.

Blackwater Pine Antiques

Blackwater. TR4 8ET. (J.S. Terrett). Open 9-6. *STOCK: Pine and country furniture.* TEL: 01872 560919. SER: Restorations; stripping; furniture made to order.

Bric-a-Brac

16A Walsingham Place. TR1 2RP. (Lynne and Richard Bonehill). Est. 1991. SIZE: Small. *STOCK: Militaria, £5-£2,000; small furniture, £20-£1,000; commemorative and crested china, £5-£150; collectors' items and bric-a-brac, 50p-£2,000; all 19th-20th C.* LOC: Town centre, just off Victoria Sq. PARK: Multi-storey nearby. TEL: 01872 225200; home - 01736 793213. SER: Buys at auction. FAIRS: Lostwithiel.

Pydar Antiques and Pine

Peoples Palace, Pydar St. TR1 2AZ. (D. Severn and J. Poole). Est. 1968. Open 10.30-5 and by appointment. SIZE: Medium. *STOCK: Furniture - English 18th and 19th C, £50-£2,500; Victorian and Edwardian, £50-£2,000; pine, £10-£1,500; silver, plate, porcelain, glass, prints and water-colours, £5-£500.* PARK: Easy. TEL: 01872 223516; home - 01872 510485 or 01637 872034.

TYWARDREATH, Nr. Par

Myles Varcoe

Treverran Barton. PL24 2TZ. Est. 1971. Open by appointment only. *STOCK: Pictures, mainly 19th and 20th C marine watercolours and oils, £50-£5,000.* LOC: Telephone for instructions. TEL: 01208 873410; fax - 01208 872956.

WADEBRIDGE

St. Breock Gallery

St. Breock Churchtown. PL27 7JS. (R.G.G. Haslam-Hopwood). Open 10-5. *STOCK: Water-colours, 19th-20th C; furniture, general antiques and objets d'art, £20-£2,000.* LOC: Near Royal Cornwall Showground. PARK: Own. TEL: 01208 812543; fax - 01208 814671. SER: Restorations; buys at auction.

Wadebridge continued

Victoria Antiques

21 Molesworth St. PL27 7DQ. (M. and S. Daly). Open Mon.-Sat. SIZE: Large. *STOCK: Furniture, 17th-19th C, £25-£10,000.* LOC: On A39 between Bude and Newquay. PARK: Nearby. TEL: 01208 814160. SER: Valuations; restorations.. VAT: Stan/Spec.

WIDEGATES, Nr. Looe

Pink Cottage Antiques

PL13 1QL. (I. and B. Barrett). Est. 1981. Open 9.30-5, Sun 2-4.30, longer hours in summer. SIZE: Medium. *STOCK: Furniture, £50-£2,500; brass and copper, £5-£250; china and glass, £2-£300; oil lamps and clocks; all mainly Victorian and Edwardian, some Georgian.* Not Stocked: Clothing, militaria, jewellery, silver. LOC: A387 from Plymouth, 4 miles before Looe. PARK: At rear. TEL: 01503 240258; home - same. SER: Restorations (furniture).

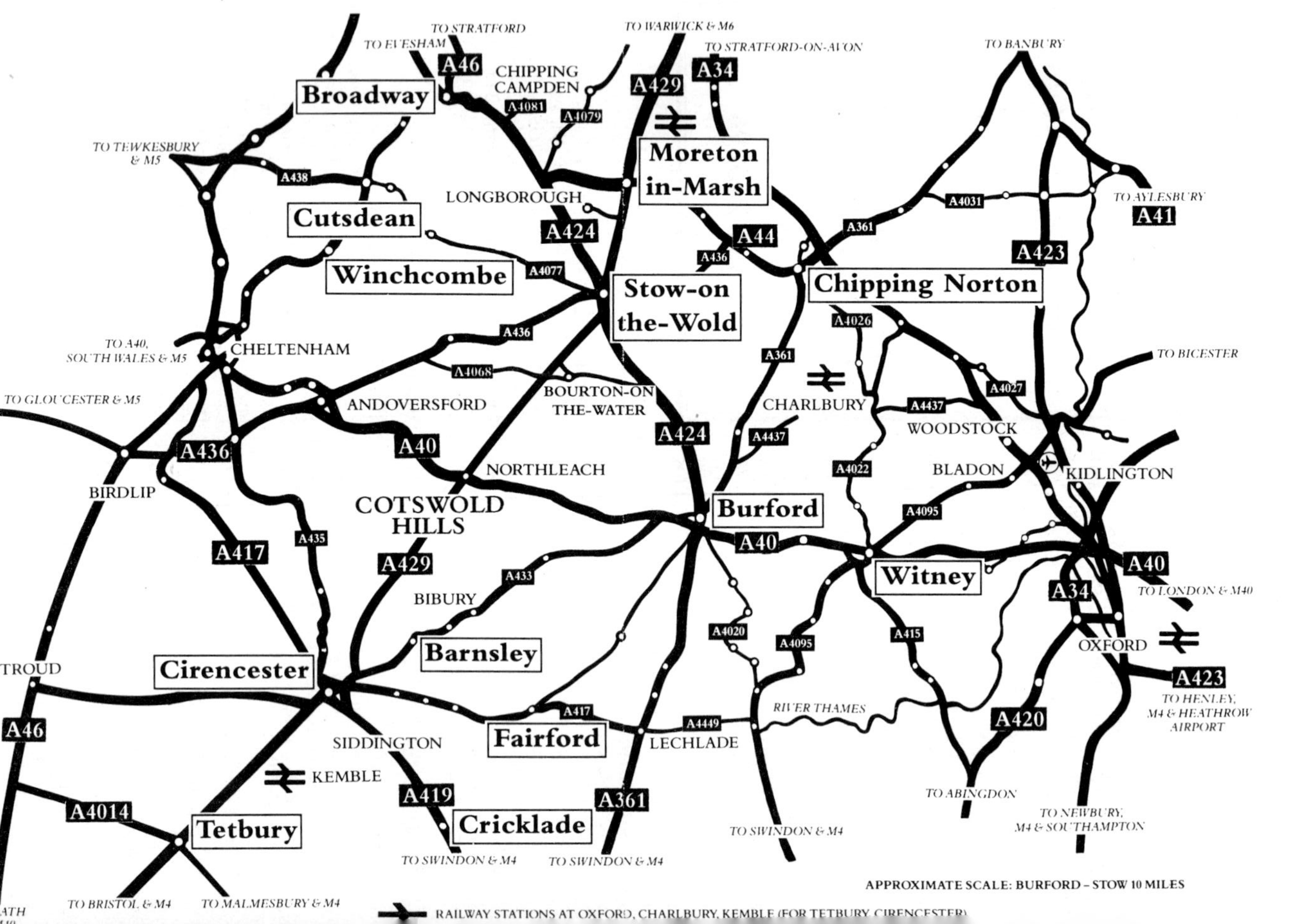
TO STRATFORD
TO EVESHAM
TO WARWICK & M6
TO STRATFORD-ON-AVON
TO BANBURY
Broadway
CHIPPING CAMPDEN
Moreton in-Marsh
TO TEWKESBURY & M5
LONGBOROUGH
Cutsdean
TO AYLESBURY
Winchcombe
Stow-on the-Wold
Chipping Norton
TO A40, SOUTH WALES & M5
CHELTENHAM
TO BICESTER
TO GLOUCESTER & M5
ANDOVERSFORD
BOURTON-ON THE-WATER
CHARLBURY
WOODSTOCK
NORTHLEACH
BLADON
KIDLINGTON
BIRDLIP
COTSWOLD HILLS
Burford
Witney
TO LONDON & M40
BIBURY
OXFORD
Barnsley
STROUD
Cirencester
TO HENLEY, M4 & HEATHROW AIRPORT
RIVER THAMES
SIDDINGTON
Fairford
LECHLADE
KEMBLE
TO ABINGDON
TO NEWBURY, M4 & SOUTHAMPTON
Tetbury
Cricklade
TO SWINDON & M4
TO SWINDON & M4
TO SWINDON & M4
TO BATH & M40
TO BRISTOL & M4
TO MALMESBURY & M4
A46
A4081
A4079
A429
A34
A438
A424
A44
A436
A361
A4031
A423
A41
A4077
A436
A4026
A361
A4068
A4027
A4437
A40
A424
A4437
A4022
A436
A4095
A435
A40
A417
A429
A40
A433
A34
A4020
A4095
A415
A423
A417
A4449
A420
A46
A419
A361
A4014
APPROXIMATE SCALE: BURFORD – STOW 10 MILES
RAILWAY STATIONS AT OXFORD, CHARLBURY, KEMBLE (FOR TETBURY, CIRENCESTER)

THE COTSWOLD ANTIQUE DEALERS' ASSOCIATION

Buy Fine Antiques and Works of Art at provincial prices in England's lovely and historic countryside

The Cotswolds, one of the finest areas of unspoilt countryside in the land, have been called "the essence and the heart of England." The region has a distinctive character created by the use of honey-coloured stone in its buildings and dry stone walls. Within the locality the towns and villages are admirably compact and close to each other and the area is well supplied with good hotels and reasonably priced inns. The Cotswolds are within easy reach of London (1½ hour by road or rail) and several major airports.

Cotswold sheep – which inspired the logo for the Cotswold Antique Dealers' Association – a quatrefoil device with a sheep in its centre – have played an important part in the region's history with much of its wealth created by the woollen industry. As for antiques, shops and warehouses of the CADA offer a selection of period furniture, pictures, porcelain, metalwork, and collectables unrivalled outside London.

With the use of the CADA directory on the following pages, which lists the names of its members, their specialities and opening times, visitors from all over the world can plan their buying visit to the Cotswolds. CADA members will assist all visiting collectors and dealers in locating antiques and works of art. They will give you advice on where to stay in the area, assistance with packing, shipping and insurance and the exchange of foreign currencies. They can advise private customers on what can realistically be bought on their available budgets, and if the first dealer does not have the piece which you are selecting he will know of several other members who will. The CADA welcomes home and overseas buyers in the certain knowledge that there are at least fifty dealers with a good and varied stock, a reputation for fair trading and an annual turnover in excess of £15,000,000.

BARNSLEY, Nr. Cirencester

Denzil Verey
Barnsley House. GL7 5EE. CADA. Resident. Est. 1980. Open 9.30-5.30, Sat. 10-5.30, other times by appointment. SIZE: Large. *STOCK: Country furniture, including pine, 18th-19th C; brass, country and kitchen bygones, unusual and decorative items.* LOC: 4 miles from Cirencester on B4425 to Burford, 1st large house in village, set back off road on the right. PARK: Easy. TEL: 01285 740402; fax - 01285 740628. VAT: Stan/Spec.

BROADWAY

Fenwick and Fenwick Antiques
88-90 High St. WR12 7AJ. CADA. Est. 1980. Open 10-6, and by appointment. SIZE: Large. *STOCK: Furniture, oak, mahogany and walnut, 17th to early 19th C; samplers, boxes, treen, Tunbridgeware, Delft, decorative items and corkscrews.* TEL: 01386 853227; after hours - 01386 841724; fax - 01386 858504.

H.W. Keil Ltd BADA
Tudor House. WR12 7DP. CADA. (V.M. Keil). Est. 1925. Open 9-5.30. CL: Thurs. pm. SIZE: Large. *STOCK: Walnut, oak, mahogany and rosewood furniture; early pewter, brass and copper, tapestry, glass and works of art, 17th-18th C.* LOC: By village clock. TEL: 01386 852408; fax - 01386 852069. VAT: Spec.

John Noott Galleries BADA LAPADA
58 High St., 14 Cotswold Court, and at The Lygon Arms, High St. WR12 7AA. CADA. Est. 1972. Open 9.30-1 and 2-5. SIZE: Large. *STOCK: Paintings, watercolours and bronzes, 19th C to Contemporary.* PARK: Easy. TEL: 01386 852787/858969; fax - 01386 858348. SER: Valuations; restorations; framing. VAT: Stan/Spec.

BURFORD

Jonathan Fyson Antiques
50 High St. OX18 4QF. CADA. (J.R. Fyson). Est. 1970. Open 9.30-1 and 2-5.30. SIZE: Medium. *STOCK: English and Continental furniture, decorative brass and steel including lighting and fireplace accessories; papier mâché, tôle, treen, porcelain, glass, jewellery.* LOC: At junction of A40/A361 between Oxford and Cheltenham. PARK: Easy. TEL: 01993 823204; fax - same; home - 01367 860223. SER: Valuations. VAT: Spec.

Burford continued

Gateway Antiques
Cheltenham Rd., Burford Roundabout. OX8 4JA. CADA. (M.C. Ford and P. Brown). Est. 1986. Open 10-5.30 and Sun. pm. SIZE: Large. *STOCK: English and Continental furniture, 18th-19th C; decorative accessories.* LOC: On roundabout (A40) Oxford/Cheltenham road. PARK: Easy. TEL: 01993 823678. SER: Valuations. VAT: Stan/Spec.

David Pickup BADA
115 High St. OX18 4RG. CADA. Est. 1977. Open 9.30-1 and 2-5.30, Sat. 10-1 and 2-4. SIZE: Medium. *STOCK: Fine furniture, works of art, from £500+; decorative objects, from £100+; all late 17th to mid 20th C, specialising in Arts & Crafts.* PARK: Easy. TEL: 01993 822555. FAIRS: BADA; Olympia. VAT: Spec.

Richard Purdon BADA
158 High St. OX18 4QY. CADA. Open 9.30-5.30. SIZE: Medium. *STOCK: Antique Eastern and European carpets, village and tribal rugs, needlework, textiles and related items.* TEL: 01993 823777; fax - 01993 823719. SER: Valuations; restorations. VAT: Stan/Spec.

Manfred Schotten Antiques
109 High St. OX18 4RH. CADA. Est. 1974. Open 9.30-5.30 or by appointment. *STOCK: Sporting antiques and library furniture.* TEL: 01993 822302; fax - 01993 822055; internet - http:/www.schotten.com. SER: Restorations.

Swan Gallery LAPADA
High St. OX18 4RE. CADA. (D. Pratt). Est. 1966. Open 9.30-5.30. SIZE: Large. *STOCK: Country furniture in oak, yew, walnut and fruitwood, 17th-19th C, £300-£9,000; oil paintings; Staffordshire figures and small decorative items, 18th-20th C, £50-£800.* PARK: Easy. TEL: 01993 822244. VAT: Mainly Spec.

CHIPPING NORTON

Bugle Antiques LAPADA
9 Horsefair. OX7 5AL. CADA. (M. and D. Harding-Hill). Est. 1971. Open 9.30-6. *STOCK: Windsor chairs including sets; English country furniture.* TEL: 01608 643322; fax - same; e-mail - bugle-windsor-chairs@dial.pipex.com. VAT: Stan/Spec.

Key Antiques BADA
11 Horse Fair. OX7 5AL. CADA. Resident. (D. and M. Robinson). Open 9.30-5.30 or by appointment. SIZE: Medium. *STOCK: Period oak and country furniture, domestic metalware including lighting and downhearth equipment, early carvings, firemarks, keys.* LOC: On main road. PARK: Easy. TEL: 01608 643777. VAT: Spec.

CIRENCESTER

William H. Stokes BADA

The Cloisters, 6/8 Dollar St. GL7 2AJ. CADA. (W.H. Stokes and P.W. Bontoft). Est. 1968. Open 9.30-5.30, Sat. 9.30-4.30. ***STOCK: Early oak furniture, £1,000-£30,000; brassware, £150-£5,000; all 16th-17th C.*** **TEL: 01285 653907; fax - same. VAT: Spec.**

Rankine Taylor Antiques LAPADA

34 Dollar St. GL7 2AN. CADA. Est. 1969. Open 9-5.30, Sun. by appointment. SIZE: Large. ***STOCK: Furniture, 17th to early 19th C, £300-£35,000; glass, 18th-20th C, £8-£350; silver, rare interesting objects and decorative items, 17th-20th C, £20-£4,000.*** **Not Stocked: Victoriana. LOC: From church, turn right into West Market Place, via Gosditch St. into Dollar St. PARK: Own - private opposite. TEL: 01285 652529. VAT: Spec.**

Bernard Weaver Antiques

28 Gloucester St. GL7 2DH. CADA. Open 9.30-6, Sat. 9.30-1. SIZE: Medium. *STOCK: Furniture, mahogany and oak, 18th-19th C; Art Nouveau and Arts and Crafts.* LOC: Continuation of Dollar St. PARK: Easy. TEL: 01285 652055; home - same. SER: Valuations.

FAIRFORD

Blenheim Antiques

Market Place. GL7 4AB. CADA. Resident. (N. Hurdle). Est. 1972. Open 9.30-6.30. *STOCK: 18th-19th C furniture.* TEL: 01285 712094. VAT: Stan/Spec.

Gloucester House Antiques Ltd

Market Place. GL7 4AB. CADA. (Mrs Scilla Chester-Master). Est. 1972. Open 9-5.30. SIZE: Large. *STOCK: English and French country furniture in oak, elm, fruitwood, pine; pottery, faïence and decorative items.* PARK: Easy. TEL: 01285 712790; home - 01285 653066; fax - 01285 713324. VAT: Spec.

MORETON-IN-MARSH

Astley House - Fine Art LAPADA

Astley House, High St. GL56 0LL. CADA. (D. and N. Glaisyer). Est. 1974. Open 9-5.30. CL: Wed. SIZE: Medium. ***STOCK: Oil paintings and botanical watercolours, 19th-20th C, £200-£10,000.*** **LOC: Main street. PARK: Easy. TEL: 01608 650601; fax - 01608 651777. SER: Restorations (oils and watercolours); framing. VAT: Spec.**

Astley House - Fine Art LAPADA

Astley House, London Rd. GL56 0LE. CADA. (D. and N. Glaisyer). Est. 1974. Open 10-1 and

Moreton-in-Marsh continued

2-5. CL: Wed. SIZE: Large. ***STOCK: Oil paintings, 19th-20th C; large decorative paintings and portraits.*** **LOC: Town centre. PARK: Easy. TEL: 01608 650601; fax - 01608 651777. SER: Restorations (oils and watercolours); porcelain framing. VAT: Spec.**

STOW-ON-THE-WOLD

Duncan J. Baggott LAPADA

Woolcomber House, Sheep St. GL54 1AA. CADA. Est. 1967. Open 9-5.30 or by appointment. SIZE: Large. ***STOCK: 17th-20th C English furniture, paintings, domestic metalwork and decorative items; garden statuary and ornaments.*** **PARK: Sheep St. or Market Sq. TEL: 01451 830662; fax - 01451 832174.**

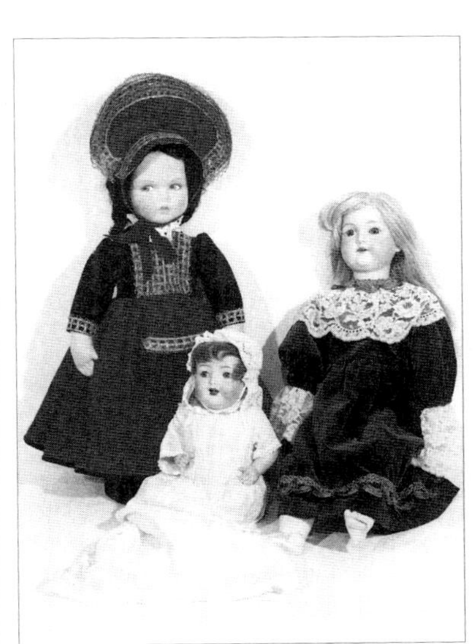

(Left) A Lenci costume girl doll with moulded and painted felt face, £820. (Centre) A Kammer and Reinhardt bisque head character doll, 15 inches high, £260. (Right) An Armand Marseille bisque head girl doll, £200. Andrew Hartley Fine Arts.

From a feature on Saleroom Prices which appeared in the November 1997 issue of **Antique Collecting**

Stow-on-the-Wold continued

Baggott Church Street Ltd BADA
Church St. GL54 1BB. CADA. (D.J. and C.M. Baggott). Est. 1978. Open 9.30-5.30 or by appointment. SIZE: Large. *STOCK: English furniture, 17th-19th C; portrait paintings, metalwork, pottery, treen and decorative items.* LOC: South-west corner of market square. PARK: In market square. TEL: 01451 830370; fax - 01451 832174.

Christopher Clarke Antiques Ltd
The Fosseway. GL54 1JS. CADA. (C.J. and I.D. Clarke). Est. 1961. Open 9.30-5.30 or by appointment. SIZE: Large. *STOCK: Furniture, 17th-19th C; works of art, metalware, treen, pictures and decorative items.* LOC: Corner of The Fosseway and Sheep St. PARK: Easy. TEL: 01451 830476; fax - 01451 830300.

Cotswold Galleries
GL54 1AB. CADA. (Richard and Cherry Glaisyer). Est. 1961. Open 9-5.30 or by appointment. SIZE: Large. *STOCK: Oil paintings, especially 19th-20th C landscape.* TEL: 01451 870567; fax - 01451 870678. SER: Restorations; framing.

The John Davies Gallery
Church St. GL54 1BB. CADA. Est. 1977. Open 9.30-1.30 and 2.30-5.30. SIZE: Large. *STOCK: Contemporary and late period paintings; limited edition bronzes.* PARK: In square. TEL: 01451 831698; fax - 01451 832477. SER: Restoration and conservation to museum standard.

Fosse Way Antiques
Ross House, The Square. GL54 1AF. CADA. (M. Beeston). Est. 1969. Open 10-5. SIZE: Large. *STOCK: Furniture and oil paintings, £300-£8,000; bronzes, Sheffield plate, caddies, boxes and decorative objects, £50-£1,000; all 18th-19th C.* LOC: East side of the Square, behind the Town Hall. PARK: Easy. TEL: 01451 830776. SER: Valuations; buys at auction. VAT: Spec.

Keith Hockin (Antiques) Ltd BADA
The Square. GL54 1AF. CADA. Est. 1968. Open Thurs., Fri., Sat., 9-6, other times by appointment. SIZE: Medium. *STOCK: Oak furniture, 1600-1750; country furniture in oak, fruitwoods, yew, 1700-1850; pewter, copper, brass, ironwork, all periods.* Not Stocked: Mahogany. PARK: Easy. TEL: 01451 831058. SER: Buys at auction (oak, pewter, metalwork). VAT: Stan/Spec.

Huntington Antiques Ltd LAPADA
The Old Forge, Church St. GL54 1BE. CADA. CINOA. TEFAF. Resident. (M.F. and S.P. Golding). Est. 1974. Open 9.30-5.30 or by appointment. *STOCK: Early period and fine country furniture, metalware, treen and textiles, tapestries and works of art.* TEL: 01451 830842; fax - 01451 832211. SER: Valuations; buys at auction. FAIRS: Maastricht; Madrid. VAT: Spec.

Stow-on-the-Wold continued

Roger Lamb Antiques & Works of Art
LAPADA

The Square. GL54 1AB. CADA. Open 10-5. *STOCK: 18th to early 19th C furniture especially small items, lighting, decorative accessories, oils and watercolours.* TEL: 01451 831371. SER: Search.

Antony Preston Antiques Ltd BADA
The Square. GL54 1AB. CADA. Est. 1965. Open 9.30-5.30 or by appointment. *STOCK: 18th-19th C English and Continental furniture and objects; barometers and period lighting.* TEL: 01451 831586; fax - 0171 581 5076. VAT: Stan/Spec.

Queens Parade Antiques Ltd BADA
The Square. GL54 1AB. CADA. (Antony Preston Antiques Ltd). Est. 1965. Open 9.30-5.30. SIZE: Large. *STOCK: 18th-19th C furniture, papier mâché, tôle peinte, needlework and period lighting.* LOC: Off Fosse Way. PARK: Easy. TEL: 01451 831586. VAT: Stan/Spec.

Ruskin Antiques
5 Talbot Court. GL54 1DP. CADA. (Anne and William Morris). Est. 1990. Open 9.30-1 and 2-5.30. SIZE: Small. *STOCK: Interesting and unusual decorative objects - Arts & Crafts movement and Art Deco glass and pottery, 1860-1940.* LOC: Between The Square and Sheep Street. PARK: Nearby. TEL: 01451 832254; home - 01993 831880. SER: Valuations.

Samarkand Galleries LAPADA
8 Brewery Yard, Sheep St. GL54 1AA. CADA. CINOA. (Brian MacDonald). Est. 1980. Open 10-5.30, Sun. by appointment. SIZE: Medium. *STOCK: Tribal and village rugs and artefacts, 19th C, £100-£10,000; fine decorative carpets, 19th-20th C, £1,000-£10,000+; kelims, 19th-20th C, £200-£2,000.* LOC: Street adjacent to Market Sq. PARK: Easy. TEL: 01451 832322; fax - same. SER: Exhibitions; valuations; restorations; cleaning. VAT: Stan/Spec.

Stow Antiques LAPADA
The Square. GL54 1AF. CADA. Resident. (Mr and Mrs J. Hutton-Clarke). Est. 1969. Open Mon.-Thurs. 2-5.30, Sat. 11-1 and 2-5.30, other times by appointment. SIZE: Large. *STOCK: Furniture, mainly Georgian, £500-£30,000; decorative items, gilded mirrors, £50-£10,000.* PARK: Easy. TEL: 01451 830377; fax - 01451 870018. SER: Shipping worldwide.

STRETTON-ON-FOSS, Nr. Moreton-in-Marsh

Astley House - Fine Art LAPADA
The Old School. GL56 9SA. CADA. (D. and N. Glaisyer). Est. 1974. Open by appointment. SIZE: Large. *STOCK: Large decorative oil paintings, 19th-20th C.* LOC: Village centre. PARK: Easy. TEL: 01608 650601; fax - 01608 651777. SER: Restorations; framing; exhibitions; mailing list. VAT: Spec.

TADDINGTON, Nr. Cutsdean

Architectural Heritage
Taddington Manor. GL54 5RY. CADA. Est. 1978. Open 9.30-5.30, Sat. 10.30-4.30. SIZE: Large. *STOCK: Period panelling, oak, mahogany and pine; chimney pieces in marble, stone, oak and mahogany; garden statuary, fountains, seats and urns.* PARK: Easy. TEL: 01386 584414; fax - 01386 584236. VAT: Stan.

TETBURY

Breakspeare Antiques LAPADA
36 and 57 Long St. GL8 8AQ. CADA. Resident. (M. and S. Breakspeare). Est. 1962. Open 10-5 or by appointment. CL: Thurs. SIZE: Medium. *STOCK: English period furniture - early walnut, 1690-1740, mahogany, 1750-1835.* PARK: Own. TEL: 01666 503122; fax - same. VAT: Stan/Spec.

Day Antiques
5 New Church St. GL8 8DS. CADA. TADA. Est. 1975. Open 9-6. SIZE: Medium. *STOCK: Oak and country furniture, early pottery, metalware, treen, some period mahogany.* TEL: 01666 502413. VAT: Stan/Spec.

WINCHCOMBE, Nr. Cheltenham

Prichard Antiques
16 High St. GL54 5LJ. CADA. (K.H. and D.Y. Prichard). Est. 1979. Open 9-5.30, Sun. by appointment. SIZE: Large. *STOCK: Period and decorative furniture, £10-£10,000; treen and metalwork, £5-£500; interesting and decorative accessories.* LOC: On B4632 Broadway to Cheltenham road. PARK: Easy. TEL: 01242 603566. VAT: Spec.

WITNEY

W.R. Harvey & Co (Antiques) Ltd BADA
86 Corn St. OX8 7BU. CADA. GMC. Open 9.30-5.30, and by appointment. SIZE: Large. *STOCK: Fine English furniture, £500-£50,000; clocks, mirrors, objets d'art, £250-£20,000; all 1680-1830.* LOC: 100 yds. from Market Place. TEL: 01993 706501; fax - 01993 706601. SER: Valuations; restorations; consultancy. FAIRS: BADA; Chelsea (March & Sept.) VAT: Stan/Spec.

Witney Antiques BADA LAPADA
96/100 Corn St. OX8 7BU. CADA. (L.S.A. and C.J. Jarrett and R.R. Jarrett-Scott). Est. 1962. Open 10-5. SIZE: Large. *STOCK: English furniture, 17th-18th C; bracket and longcase clocks, mahogany, oak and walnut, metalware, needleworks and works of art.* LOC: From Oxford on old A40 through Witney via High St., turn right at T-junction, 400yds. on right. PARK: Easy. TEL: 01993 703902/703887; fax - 01993 779852. SER: Restorations. FAIRS: BADA; Grosvenor House. VAT: Spec.

TETBURY ANTIQUE DEALERS' ASSOCIATION

Philip Adler Antiques
32 Long St. GL8 8AQ. TADA. Open 10-5 or by appointment. *STOCK: Eclectic and general decorative and period antiques.* TEL: 01666 505759.

The Antique and Interior Centre
51A Long St. TADA. Open 10-5, Sun. 11-5 and most Bank Holidays. SIZE: 8 dealers. *STOCK: Furniture, porcelain, silver and pictures; interior design items.* TEL: 01666 505083.

The Antiques Emporium
The Old Chapel, Long St. GL8 8AA. TADA. (C. and D. Sayers). Est. 1993. Open 10-5, Sun. 1-5. SIZE: Large - 38 dealers. *STOCK: Fruitwood and country furniture, fine oak and mahogany, china, porcelain, treen, copper and brass, jewellery, silver, kitchenalia, militaria, £1-£15,000.* Not Stocked: Reproductions. PARK: Nearby. TEL: 01666 505281. SER: Export. VAT: Stan/Spec.

Artique
18 Long St. GL8 8AQ. TADA. (George Bristow). Open 9-5. *STOCK: Interiors, textiles, carpets and kelims and objets d'art from the Orient.* TEL: 01666 503597.

Ball and Claw Antiques
45 Long St. GL8 8AA. TADA. (Chris and Nick Kirkland). Est. 1995. Open 10-1 and 2-5. SIZE: Medium. *STOCK: Furniture, 18th-19th C, £50-£5,000; decorative items, objects and prints, some country items.* PARK: Easy. TEL: 01666 502440; internet - http://www.all-about-antiques.co.uk/ballc.html. SER: Valuations; buys at auction. VAT: Stan/Spec.

Balmuir House Antiques **LAPADA**
14 Long St. GL8 8AQ. TADA. (P. Whittam). Est. 1946. Open 9.30-5.30, Sun. by appointment. SIZE: Large. *STOCK: Furniture, paintings, mirrors, 19th C, £500-£5,000.* LOC: Town centre. PARK: Easy. TEL: 01666 503822; home - same. SER: Valuations; restorations (furniture, upholstery, paintings). VAT: Spec.

The Chest of Drawers
24 Long St. GL8 8AQ. TADA. Resident. (A. and P. Bristow). Est. 1969. Open 9.30-6 or by appointment. CL: Thurs. am. SIZE: Medium + trade store. *STOCK: Late Georgian, Regency and Victorian furniture; country pieces, 17th-18th C; china and brass.* LOC: On A433. PARK: Easy. TEL: 01666 502105; home - same. VAT: Spec.

The Coach House Bookshop
4 The Chipping. TADA. (Philip Gibbons). Open 10-6, Sun. 11-5. *STOCK: Secondhand and antiquarian titles including A & C Black colour plate books; prints, antique furniture and small items.* TEL: 01666 504330; e-mail - bookshop@tetbury.co.uk SER: Booksearch.

Day Antiques
5 New Church St. GL8 8DS. CADA. TADA. Est. 1975. Open 9-6. SIZE: Medium. *STOCK: Oak and country furniture, early pottery, metalware, treen, some period mahogany.* TEL: 01666 502413. VAT: Stan/Spec.

The Decorator Source
39a Long St. GL8 8AA. TADA. (Colin Gee). Open 10-5 or by appointment. SIZE: Large. *STOCK: French provincial furniture - armoires, farm tables, buffets; decorative items and accessories of interest to interior decorators.* PARK: Easy. TEL: 01666 505358. VAT: Stan/Spec.

Dolphin Antiques
48 Long St. GL8 8AQ. TADA. (P. and L. Davis). Est. 1986. Open 10-5.30. CL: Thurs. SIZE: Small. *STOCK: Mainly 19th C decorative porcelain including Meissen, Dresden, Royal Worcester, Samson, Coalport and Sitzendorf; some general antiques; all 1750-1930, £20-£2,000.* Not Stocked: Furniture. PARK: Nearby. TEL: 01666 504242; home - same.

Fifty-One Antiques Et Cetera
51 Long St. TADA. (Sylvia Powell). Est. 1977. Open 10-5, Sun. by appointment. SIZE: Small. *STOCK: English and French country furniture, £50-£5,000; decorative items.* PARK: Easy. TEL: 01666 505026.

Anne Fowler
35 Long St. GL8 8AA. TADA. Est. 1971. Open 10-5.30, Sun. by appointment. SIZE: Medium. *STOCK: Mainly French painted and decorative items including garden furniture and accessories, mirrors, faience and pots, wirework, lighting and prints, £20-£2,000.* PARK: Easy. TEL: 01666 504043; home - same; fax - 01666 504900. VAT: Stan/Spec.

Gales Antiques
52 Long St. GL8 8AQ. TADA. (M.R. Mathews). Est. 1979. Open 10-5.30. SIZE: Medium. *STOCK: English and French country furniture and decorative items, 17th-19th C, £5-£5,000.* PARK: Easy. TEL: 01666 502686. VAT: Stan/Spec.

Jester Antiques
10 Church St. TADA. (Lorna Coles and Peter Bairstow). Open every day 10-5.30. *STOCK: Furniture, decorative items, lamps, lanterns, mirrors, clocks, memorabilia, curios, pictures, copper and brass, Oriental items.* TEL: 01666 505125.

Lyon Oliver Antiques

TADA. By appointment. *STOCK: English and Irish country furniture, large mirrors, upholstery and decorative sculpture.* TEL: 01666 577603; e-mail - kate.oliver@virgin.net

Bobbie Middleton

58 Long St. TADA. Open 10-1 and 2-5, Sun. by appointment. *STOCK: 18th-19th C mahogany, oak, fruitwood and painted furniture, mirrors, upholstery and decorative items.* LOC: Corner of Long St. and New Church St. TEL: 01666 502761; mobile - 0374 192660. VAT: Spec.

Morpheus - Elgin House

1 New Church St. GL8 8DT. TADA. (B. Symes). Open every day 9-5.30. *STOCK: 18th-19th C oak, mahogany and pine furniture; restored wood, brass and upholstered beds, 4-posters, half-testers and lit bateau styles.* TEL: 01666 504068; fax - 01666 503352.

Peter Norden Antiques

61 Long St. GL8 8AA. TADA. Open 10-5.30, Sun. by appointment. SIZE: Medium. *STOCK: Early oak furniture, 16th-18th C, £250-£10,000; country furniture, 15th-19th C, £75-£10,000; early carvings, metalware, pewter, pottery, 14th-19th C, £10-£2,000.* PARK: Nearby. TEL: 01666 503854; home - 01993 831607. SER: Valuations; buys at auction. FAIRS: NEC. VAT: Spec.

Old Mill Market Shop

12 Church St. GL8 8JG. TADA. (Mr and Mrs M. Green). Open 10-5.30, Thurs. 10-1. *STOCK: General antiques, collectables and bric-a-brac.* TEL: 01666 503127.

Porch House Antiques

40/42 Long St. GL8 8AQ. TADA. Open 10-5. *STOCK: 17th-20th C furniture and decorative items.* TEL: 01666 502687.

Simon Seiff Antiques

30 Long St. GL8 8AQ. TADA. Est. 1994. Open 9-5.30, Sun. by appointment. SIZE: Large. *STOCK: French and English provincial country furniture, 1780-1900, £50-£8,000.* PARK: Easy. TEL: 01666 502342. SER: Valuations; buys at auction. FAIRS: Hervey Decorative Antique & Textile. VAT: Stan/Spec.

Tetbury Gallery

18 Market Place. FATG. TADA. (Jane Maile). Open every day. *STOCK: Original and limited edition prints, from Victorian watercolours and oils to contemporary artists including Russell Flint, David Shepherd and Ben Maile.* TEL: 0166 503412.

Westwood House Antiques

29 Long St. TADA. Resident. (Richard Griffiths and Lynne Petersen). Open 10-5.30 or by appointment. *STOCK: Oak, elm and ash country furniture especially dressers, dresser bases and tables, 17th-19th C; occasional French pieces; decorative pottery, pewter and treen.* TEL: 01666 502328; fax - same.

Cumbria

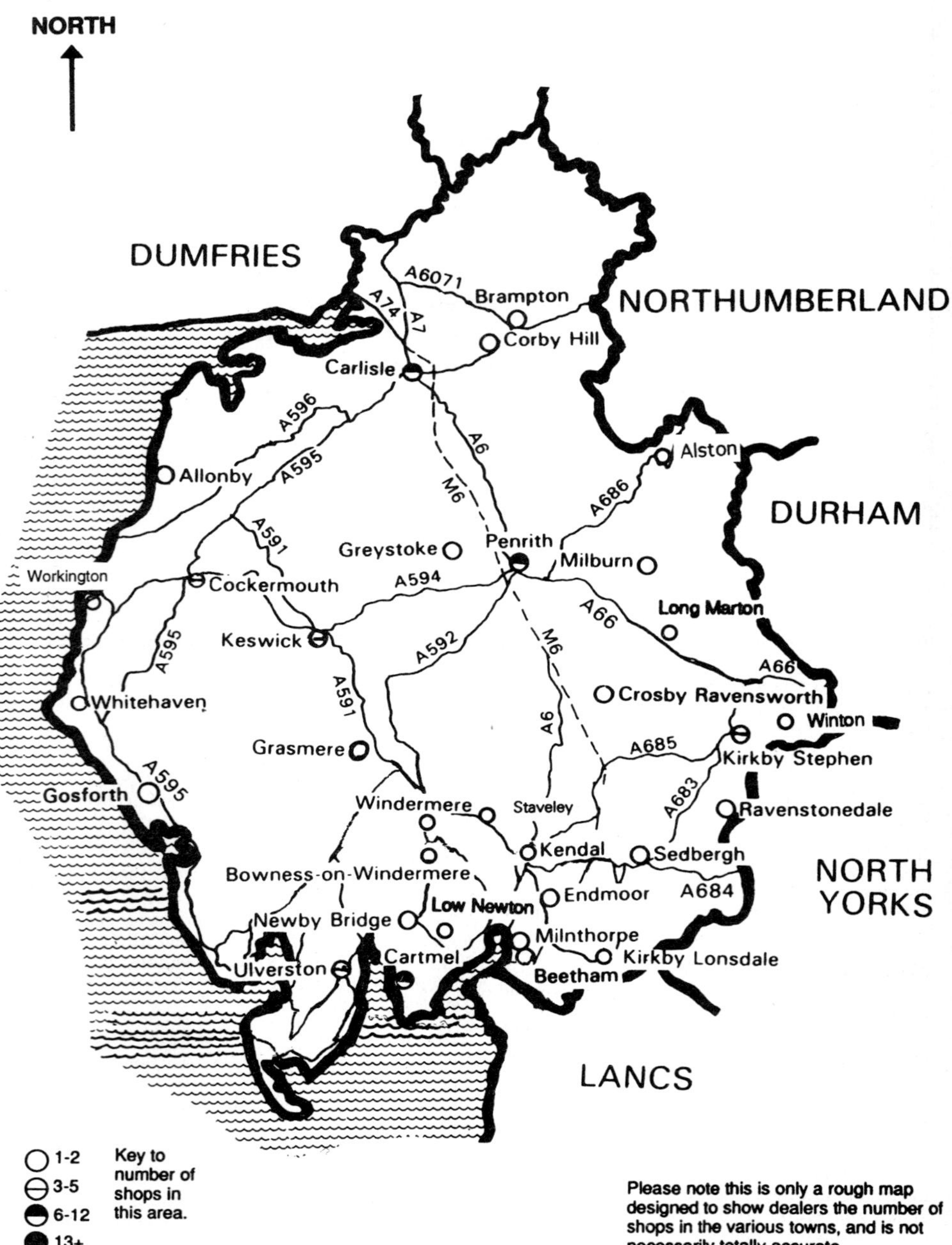

1-2
3-5
6-12
13+

Key to number of shops in this area.

Please note this is only a rough map designed to show dealers the number of shops in the various towns, and is not necessarily totally accurate.

ALLONBY

Cottage Curios

Main St. CA15 6PX. (B. Pickering). Est. 1965. Open daily from 2 pm.

ALSTON

Brownside Coach House

CA9 3BP. (M.J. Graham). Est. 1987. Open 11-5, May to end Sept. CL: Mon. and Tues. *STOCK: Glass, 1780-1920's, to £800.* LOC: 1.5 miles outside Alston on Penrith road. PARK: Easy. TEL: 01434 381263. FAIRS: Windermere; Holker Hall; Swinton Castle.

BEETHAM, Nr. Milnthorpe

Peter Haworth

Temple Bank. LA7 7AL. Open by appointment. *STOCK: English and Scottish paintings and watercolours, 1850-1950, £100-£25,000.* LOC: 2 miles south of Milnthorpe on A6 to Lancaster. PARK: Easy. TEL: 015395 62352; fax - 015395 63438. SER: Valuations; restorations; commissions.

BOWNESS-ON-WINDERMERE

J.W. Thornton Antiques Supermarket

North Terrace. LA23 3AU. SIZE: Large. *STOCK: Fine art, general antiques, furniture, shipping and architectural items, pine, bric-a-brac, paintings, decorators items.* TEL: 015394 42930/45183 or 01229 869745/580284. SER: Valuations; buys at auction. VAT: Stan/Spec.

White Elephant Antiques

66 Quarry Rigg, Lake Rd. (Mrs J.C. Barlow). Est. 1987. Open 9.30-5.30 including Sun. SIZE: Medium. *STOCK: General antiques, 18th-19th C, £50-£3,000; copper, brass, mahogany furniture, collectables and decorative art.* LOC: Far end of Quarry Rigg precinct. PARK: Easy. TEL: 015394 46962; home - 015394 88685. SER: Buys at auction.

BRAMPTON

Mary Fell Antiques

Collectors' Corner, 32-34 Main St. CA8 1RS. Est. 1960. Open Tues., Wed., Fri. and Sat. 11-6, other times by appointment. *STOCK: Sheraton and Victorian furniture, porcelain, china, glass, silver and plate, bric-a-brac, early Victorian oil paintings, pictures, prints, jewellery, pot-lids.* Not Stocked: Coins, armour and swords. LOC: Town centre, beside public car park. PARK: Easy. TEL: Home - 01228 22224. SER: Valuations; restorations (furniture); buys at auction.

CARLISLE

Carlisle Antique and Craft Centre

Cecil Hall, Cecil St. CA1 1NT. Open 9-5. SIZE: Large plus trade warehouse (Basement - Fri. and Sat. indoor market - bric-a-brac, collectibles). LOC: Off Warwick Rd. PARK: Easy. TEL: 01228 36910; fax - same. Below are listed the dealers at this centre.

AGM Antiques

(A. Mawer) *Old and new pine, mahogany and oak furniture.*

Cumbria Country Pine

(W. Kraft) *Pine furniture to order. French oak furniture.*

Fine Pine

Stripped pine furniture; mahogany and oak bedroom suites, large furniture, china, quilts.

It's About Time

(B. and W. Mitton). Est. 1985. *Longcase, bracket and carriage clocks, watches; Royal Worcester fine porcelain, jewellery, textiles.* TEL: 01228 36910.

Logwood Antiques

(Philip Dent). *Oak and mahogany furniture.*

Glenn Mitton

Paintings, prints, Art Nouveau, Art Deco, porcelain, bronzes.

Maureen Morano

Cane and rush seating. SER: Restorations (as stock).

Warwick Antiques

(J. Wardrope). CMBHI. *Period furniture, wall and bracket clocks.* SER: Valuations; restorations (clocks).

Yesterday's Pine

(J. Conway). *Pine furniture.* SER: Pine stripping.

James W. Clements

19 Fisher St. CA3 8RF. Est. 1887. Open 9.30-5. CL: Thurs. *STOCK: Silver, jewellery, porcelain and glass.* TEL: 01228 25565. VAT: Global/margin.

Maurice Dodd Books

44 Cecil St. CA1 1NT. (R.J. McRoberts). Est. 1945. CL: Sat. pm. *STOCK: Antiquarian books.* TEL: 01228 22087; fax - same. VAT: Stan/Spec.

Saint Nicholas Galleries (Antiques) Ltd

28 London Rd. CA1 2EL. (J., C. and F.E. Carruthers). Open 9.30-5. SIZE: Medium. *STOCK: General antiques, 18th C, £5-£500.* LOC: City centre. PARK: Nearby. TEL: 01228 34425.

Carlisle continued

Saint Nicholas Galleries Ltd. (Antiques and Jewellery)

39 Bank St. CA3 8HJ. (C.J. Carruthers). Open 10-5. CL: Mon. SIZE: Medium. *STOCK: Jewellery, silver, plate, Rolex and pocket watches, clocks; collectables; Royal Doulton; Dux, Oriental vases; pottery, porcelain; watercolours, oil paintings; pine furniture; brass and copper.* LOC: City centre. PARK: Nearby. TEL: 01228 44459.

Souvenir Antiques

Treasury Court, Fisher St. CA3 8RF. (J. Higham). Open 10-5. SIZE: Small. *STOCK: Porcelain and pottery, Victorian to Art Deco, £5-£500; coronation ware, crested china, local prints, maps, postcards, Roman and medieval coins, costume jewellery.* Not Stocked: Textiles. LOC: City centre between Fisher St. and Scotch St. PARK: Nearby. TEL: 01228 401281.

CARTMEL

Anthemion - The Antique Shop BADA LAPADA

LA11 6QD. (J. Wood). Est. 1982. Open 10-5 including Sun. SIZE: Large. *STOCK: English period furniture, 17th to early 19th C, £100-£30,000; decorative items, 17th-19th C, £20-£2, 000.* Not Stocked: Victoriana, bric-a-brac.

Cartmel continued

LOC: Village centre. PARK: Easy. TEL: 01539 536295; mobile - 0468 443757. FAIRS: BADA; NEC; Olympia; Chester; West London. VAT: Stan/Spec.

Anvil Antiques

Cavendish St. LA11 6PU. (J. Wood). Est. 1993. Open 10-5 including Sun. SIZE: Large. *STOCK: Oak and country furniture, brass, copper, treen and decorative items, 17th-19th C.* LOC: From the village square, under the archway and past the Cavendish Arms. PARK: Easy. TEL: 01539 536362. VAT: Stan/Spec.

Bacchus Antiques - In the Service of Wine

Longlands. LA11 6HG. (Mrs J.A. Johnson). Est. 1979. Open by appointment only. *STOCK: Fine corkscrews.* TEL: 01539 536475.

Norman Kerr - Gatehouse Bookshop

The Square. LA11 6PX. Open by appointment only. *STOCK: Antiquarian books.* TEL: 01539 536247.

Peter Bain Smith (Bookseller)

Bank Court, Market Sq. LA11 6QB. In season open every day 1.30-6. CL: Mon. and Tues. from mid Nov. to Easter. Open 1.30-4.30. *STOCK: Books including antiquarian, especially children's and local topography.* LOC: A590 from Levens Bridge, off roundabout at Lindale by-pass through Grange-over-Sands. PARK: Nearby. TEL: 01539 536369. SER: Valuations.

Maggie Tallentire Antiques

at Anvil Antiques, Cavendish St. LA11 6PU. Open 10-5 including Sun. SIZE: Small. *STOCK: Oak and country furniture, 17th-19th C; country pottery, treen, needlework and decorative accessories.* TEL: 01539 536362; mobile - 0585 764151. VAT: Stan/Spec.

COCKERMOUTH

Cockermouth Antiques

5 Station St. CA13 9QW. (E. Bell and G. Davies). Est. 1983. Open 10-5. SIZE: Large. *STOCK: General antiques especially ceramics, furniture, pictures, glass, books, metalware, quilts.* LOC: Just off A66, in town centre. PARK: Easy. TEL: 01900 826746.

Cockermouth Antiques Market

Courthouse, Main St. CA15 5XM. Est. 1979. Open 10-5. SIZE: Large - 7 stallholders. *STOCK: Victorian, Edwardian and Art Deco items, furniture, printed collectables, postcards, books, linen, china, glass, textiles, jewellery and pictures.* LOC: Town centre, just off A66. PARK: 50 yds. TEL: 01900 824346. SER: Restorations (furniture); stripping (pine). VAT: Stan/Spec.

Cockermouth continued

Holmes Antiques
1 Market Place. CA13 9NH. (C. and S. Holmes). Est. 1972. Open 10-5. CL: Thurs. SIZE: Medium. *STOCK: Furniture, paintings, prints, small antiques, collectors' items.* PARK: Rear of premises. TEL: 01900 826114; home - 017687 78364.

CORBY HILL, Nr. Carlisle

Langley Antiques
The Forge. CA4 8PL. Open 10.30-5. CL: Thurs. SIZE: Medium. *STOCK: Country oak, period and Edwardian furniture, specialising in clocks.* LOC: 5 miles from Carlisle on A69 Hexham/Newcastle road. PARK: Easy. TEL: 01228 560899. SER: Upholstery.

CROSBY RAVENSWORTH, Nr. Penrith

Jennywell Hall Antiques
CA10 3JP. Resident. (Mrs M. Macadie). Est. 1975. Open weekends 10-6, also most weekdays but phone call advisable. SIZE: Medium. *STOCK: Oak and mahogany furniture, paintings, interesting objects.* LOC: 5 miles from junction 39, M6. PARK: Easy. TEL: 01931 715288; home - same.

ENDMOOR, Nr. Kendal

Calvert Antiques
Sycamore House. LA8 0ET. (N.A. Hutchinson-Shire). Est. 1986. Open 9.30-5.30, Sun. 10.30-4, other times by appointment. SIZE: Medium. *STOCK: Furniture, 17th to early 19th C; clocks, 17th-19th C.* Not Stocked: China, silver, treen and jewellery. LOC: On A65. Leave M6 at junction 36 on to Skipton/Kirby Lonsdale road, first exit left to Endmoor. PARK: Easy. TEL: 0153 956 7597; home - same. SER: Restorations (furniture); replica furniture made to order; upholstery.

GOSFORTH

Archie Miles Bookshop
Beck Place. CA20 1AT. (Mrs C.M. Linsley). Open 10-5.30, Sun. 1-5.30, out of season opening times may vary. CL: Mon. *STOCK: Secondhand, antiquarian and out-of-print books, maps and prints.* TEL: 0194 67 25792.

GRASMERE, Nr. Ambleside

The Stables
College St. LA22 9SW. (J.A. and K.M. Saalmans). Est. 1971. Open daily 10-6 Easter-November, other times telephone call advisable. SIZE: Small. *STOCK: Brass and copper items, oil lamps, domestic bygones; pottery, silver, prints, books.* Not Stocked: Weapons, coins. LOC: By the side of Moss Grove Hotel. PARK: Easy. TEL: 015394 35453; home - same.

GREYSTOKE, Nr. Penrith

Roadside Antiques
Watsons Farm, Greystoke Gill. CA11 0UQ. Resident. (K. and R. Sealby). Est. 1988. Open 10-6 including Sun. SIZE: Medium. *STOCK: Ceramics, longcase clocks, glass, Staffordshire figures, pot-lids, furniture, small collectables, jewellery, mainly 19th C, £5-£2,000.* LOC: B5288 Penrith/Keswick road to Greystoke, through village, first left then left again, premises second on right. PARK: Easy. TEL: 01768 483279.

KENDAL

Below Stairs
125 Stricklandgate. (S. and T. Ritchie). Open 10-4. *STOCK: China, brass, copper, coloured glass, silver and collectables.* LOC: Main street on road towards Windermere. TEL: 01539 741278.

Dower House Antiques
40 Kirkland. LA9 5AD. (Brian Blakemore). Open 9.15-6, Thurs. 9.15-1. *STOCK: Pottery, porcelain, paintings, furniture.* TEL: 01539 722778.

Kendal Studios Antiques
2/3 Wildman St. LA9 6EN. (R. Aindow). Est. 1950. Open 10.30-4, prior telephone call advisable. CL: Mon. SIZE: Medium. *STOCK: Ceramics, maps and prints, paintings, oak furniture, art pottery.* LOC: Leave M6 at junction 37, follow one-way system, shop on left. PARK: Nearby. TEL: 01539 723291 (24 hrs. answering service). SER: Finder; shipping. VAT: Stan/Spec.

The Silver Thimble
39 All Hallows Lane. (V. Ritchie). Est. 1980. Open 10-4. SIZE: Large. *STOCK: Jewellery, silver, glass, linen and lace, porcelain, copper and brass.* LOC: Turn left at second set of traffic lights on main road into Kendal from south, shop 200yds. on right. PARK: Easy. TEL: 01539 731456.

KESWICK

And So To Bed
Lake Rd. CA12 5BZ. (W.I. Raw). Est. 1981. Open 9.30-5. *STOCK: Brass beds, iron and brass beds, mattress and base sets for antique beds, mirrors, linen, quilts, £150-£2,000.* LOC: Top of Main St. TEL: 0176 87 74881. VAT: Stan.

Cat in the Window
29 Station St., (Beneath Ravensworth Hotel). CA12 5HH. (E. Fell). Est. 1980. Open 10-12.30 and 1.30-4.30, Fri. 12-5, Mon. and Wed. by appointment. SIZE: Small. *STOCK: Porcelain and pottery, copper, brass and pewter, small furniture.* LOC: Near Fitz Park. PARK: Easy and nearby. TEL: 017687 71234. SER: Valuations; buys at auction. FAIRS: Colin Caygill in Cumbria.

Keswick continued

John Young and Son (Antiques) LAPADA
12-14 Main St. CA12 5JD. Est. 1890. Open 9-5.30. SIZE: Large. *STOCK: 17th-20th C. furniture, clocks and decorative items for the home and garden.* LOC: Town centre. PARK: At rear. TEL: 017687 73434. VAT: Stan/Spec.

KIRKBY LONSDALE

Architus Antiques

14 Main St. (J. Pearson and B. Rigby). Est. 1990. Open 10-4.30, Sat. 10-5.30. SIZE: Medium. *STOCK: Victorian oil lamps, £100-£250; china and glass, jewellery and silver, Victorian to early 20th C.* LOC: First antique shop on left in village from A65 towards Kendal. TEL: 015242 72409; home - 015242 71517. SER: Valuations.

KIRKBY STEPHEN

Archway Antiques

1 Walton's Yard, Market Sq. CA17 4QT. (Alan and Beatrice Stocks). Est. 1993. Open Fri., Sat., Sun. and Mon.10.30-5.30. CL: Bank Holidays and Christmas to end Jan. SIZE: Small. *STOCK: Ceramics, glass and metalware, £5-1,000; small furniture, to £1,500; all mainly 18th to early 20th C.* LOC: Town centre, behind war memorial. PARK: Easy. TEL: 017683 71905; fax - same; home - 015396 21221. SER: Buys at auction; commission sales.

Kirkby Stephen continued

Haughey Antiques LAPADA
28/30 Market St. CA17 4QW. (D.M. Haughey). Est. 1969. Open 10-5, Sun. by appointment. SIZE: Large. *STOCK: Furniture, 17th-19th C; garden furniture and statuary.* PARK: Own. TEL: 0176 83 71302; fax - 0176 83 72423. SER: Valuations. VAT: Stan/Spec.

David Hill

36 Market Sq. CA17 4QT. Est. 1965. Open 9.30-4. SIZE: Medium. *STOCK: Country clocks and furniture, £10-£1,000; both 18th-19th C; glassware, £5-£75; curios, £5-£50; shipping goods, kitchenalia, iron and brassware.* LOC: On A685. PARK: Easy. TEL: 0176 83 71598. VAT: Stan/Spec.

Mortlake Antiques

32-34 Market St. CA17 4QW. (C.J. and J.A. Bate). Est. 1946. Open 10-5, Mon.-Sat. in summer and Mon, Fri. and Sat. in winter. SIZE: Medium. *STOCK: Furniture, period, Victorian, Edwardian and country including stripped pine; treen, kitchenalia, bygones, bric-a-brac and metalware.* Not Stocked: Silver, glass, porcelain. LOC: On A685, 12 miles east of junction 38, M6. PARK: Easy. TEL: 017683 71666 (ansaphone).

LONG MARTON, Nr. Appleby

Ben Eggleston Antiques

The Dovecote. CA16 6BJ. (Ben and Kay Eggleston). Est. 1976. Open strictly by appointment. SIZE: Large. *STOCK: Pine furniture, unstripped and unrestored for the trade, £5-£2,500.* LOC: 2 miles east of A66 between Appleby and Penrith. PARK: Easy. TEL: 017683 61849; home and fax - same. SER: Valuations; buys at auction. VAT: Stan/Spec. *Strictly Trade Only.*

LOW NEWTON, Nr. Grange-over-Sands.

Utopia Antiques Ltd

Yew Tree Barn. LA11 6JP. (P.J. and Mrs J. Wilkinson). Open 10-5. *STOCK: Pine and country furniture, decorative accessories.* PARK: Easy. TEL: 015395 30065. VAT: Stan.

W.R.S. Architectural Antiques

Yew Tree Barn. LA11 6JP. (Clive Wilson). Open 10-5, Sun. 12-6 (winter 11-5). *STOCK: General architectural antiques including fireplaces; period furniture.* TEL: 01539 531498.

MILBURN, Nr. Penrith

Netherley Cottage Antiques

CA10 1TN. (J. Heelis). Est. 1970. Usually open 8.30-8 but appointment advisable. SIZE: Small. *STOCK: Country cottage pottery, porcelain and ornaments, 18th-19th C, £1-£70; kitchen and dairy items, interesting bygones, brass, watercolours, £1-£85; treen, some Oriental items.* Not Stocked: Silver and clocks. TEL: 0176 83 61403. SER: Buys at auction.

MILNTHORPE

The Antique Shop

Park Rd. LA7 7PW. Open 10-4.30. SIZE: Medium. *STOCK: General antiques, books, furniture.* LOC: From A6, left at traffic lights in village, opposite Post Office. TEL: 01524 781718.

NEWBY BRIDGE

Shire Antiques

The Post House, High Newton, Newton-in-Cartmel. LA11 6JQ. (B. and Mrs J. Shire). Open every day except Tues. SIZE: Medium. *STOCK: Early oak furniture, 16th-18th C; Georgian copper, brass, treen.* Not Stocked: Silver and jewellery. LOC: On A590 to Barrow, house is 50yds. from main road in High Newton. PARK: Easy. TEL: 0153 95 31431; home - same. SER: Valuations; restorations (furniture). VAT: Stan/Spec.

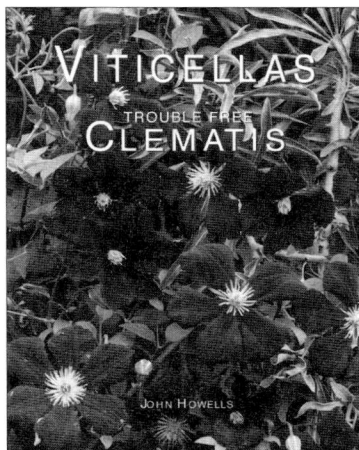

Newby Bridge continued

Townhead Antiques LAPADA

LA12 8NP. (E.M. and C.P. Townley). Est. 1960. Open 9-5, other times by appointment. SIZE: Large. *STOCK: 18th-19th C furniture, silver, porcelain, glass, decorative pieces; clocks, pictures, garden furniture.* LOC: A592. 1 mile from Newby Bridge on the Windermere road. PARK: Easy. TEL: 0153 95 31321; fax - 0153 95 30019. SER: Valuations. VAT: Stan/Spec.

PENRITH

Antiques of Penrith

4 Corney Sq. CA11 7PX. (L. Mildwurf and Partners). Est. 1964. Open 10-12 and 1.30-5, Sat. 10-12.30. CL: Wed. SIZE: Large. *STOCK: Early oak and mahogany furniture, clocks, brass, copper, glass, china, silver plate, metal, Staffordshire figures, curios.* Not Stocked: Jewellery, paintings, rugs. LOC: Near Town Hall. PARK: Easy. TEL: 01768 862801. VAT: Stan/Spec/ Global.

The Gallery

54 Castlegate. CA11 7HY. (K.G. Plant). Est. 1969. Open by appointment only. SIZE: Small. *STOCK: Paintings and watercolours, 17th-20th C, £50-£20,000.* LOC: From town centre towards the railway station. TEL: 01768 865538; home - same. SER: Valuations. VAT: Stan/Spec.

Penrith continued

Hearth and Home

6 Brunswick Rd. CA11 7LU. Open 9-5. *STOCK: Antique and reproduction furniture and decorative accessories, fireplaces, multi-fuel and gas stoves.* TEL: 01768 867200.

Joseph James Antiques

Corney Sq. CA11 7PX. (G.R. Walker). Est. 1970. Open 9-5.30. CL: Wed. SIZE: Medium. *STOCK: Furniture and upholstery, 18th C and Victorian, £10-£3,000; porcelain and pottery, £5-£1,000; silver and plate, pictures, £2-£800; all 18th-19th C.* LOC: On the one-way system in the town, 100yds. from the main shopping area (Middlegate), 50yds. from the town hall. PARK: Easy and 100yds. TEL: 01768 862065. SER: Re-upholstery; soft furnishings. VAT: Stan.

Market Place Antiques

22 Cornmarket. CA11 7HS. (R.H. and A.M. Sealby). Est. 1995. Open Tues., Thurs., Fri. and Sat. 10-4.30. *STOCK: Ceramics, clocks, glass, Staffordshire figures, pot lids, furniture and small collectables, mainly 19th C, £1-£1,500.* PARK: Gt Dockray or Southend. TEL: 01768 899579.

Penrith Coin and Stamp Centre

37 King St. CA11 7AY. Resident. (Mr and Mrs A. Gray). Est. 1974. Open 9-5.30. CL: Wed. Sept.-May. SIZE: Medium. *STOCK: Coins, B.C. to date, 1p-£500; jewellery, secondhand, £5-£500; Great Britain and Commonwealth stamps.* LOC: Just off town centre. PARK: Behind shop. TEL: 01768 864185; fax - same. SER: Valuations; jewellery repairs. FAIRS: Many coin. VAT: Stan.

Jane Pollock Antiques LAPADA

4 Castlegate. CA11 7HZ. Open 9.30-5. CL: Wed. SIZE: Medium. *STOCK: Georgian and Victorian silver, some 20th C small items; Victorian pottery, blue and white lustre; wooden boxes, some small furniture.* LOC: One-way street from town centre towards station. PARK: Easy. TEL: 01768 867211. SER: Valuations; restorations (silver, blue glass liners); buys at auction (silver, pottery). FAIRS: Olympia, Kensington, Chester and Harrogate. VAT: Global/margin.

Sandgate Antiques

21 Sandgate. CA11 7TJ. (Steve Bates). Est. 1973. Open 10-5, Wed., Thurs. and Sun. by appointment only. SIZE: Medium. *STOCK: Oak and country furniture, 17th to early 19th C; longcase clocks, Delft, 18th C; small decorative items.* LOC: Near town centre, past bus station up hill on right. PARK: Easy. TEL: 01768 899599; fax - same. SER: Buys at auction (furniture). VAT: Spec.

RAVENSTONEDALE, Nr. Kirkby Stephen

The Book House

Grey Garth. CA17 4NQ. PBFA. (C. and M. Irwin). Est. 1963. Open 9-5. CL: Tues. *STOCK: Books, mainly 19th-20th C, £1-£1,000; some postcards, 20th C, 25p-£10.* LOC: Off A685. Square house across road triangle from village school. PARK: Easy. TEL: 015396 23634; home - same; fax - 015396 - 23434. SER: Valuations. FAIRS: Northern PBFA. VAT: Stan.

SEDBERGH

R. F. G. Hollett and Son

6 Finkle St. LA10 5BZ. (R. F. G. and C. G. Hollett). Est. 1951. Open 10-12 and 1.15-5. SIZE: Large. *STOCK: Antiquarian books, 15th-20th C, £20-£20,000+; maps, prints and paintings, 17th-19th C, £10-£5,000.* LOC: Town centre. PARK: Free nearby. TEL: 015396 20298; fax - 015396 21396; e-mail - hollett@sedbergh.demon.co.uk. SER: Valuations. VAT: Stan.

Stable Antiques

Wheelwright Cottage, 15-16 Back Lane. LA10 5AQ. Est. 1970. Open 10-6 or by appointment. *STOCK: Small furniture, brass, copper, silver, china, prints, small collectors' items, treen.* LOC: 5 miles from exit 37, M6. TEL: 015396 20251.

STAVELEY

Staveley Antiques

27/29 Main St. LA8 9LU. (P. John Corry). Est. 1991. Open 10-5, Sun. by appointment. SIZE: Large. *STOCK: Brass and iron bedsteads, 1830-1930, £200-£1,200; lighting, 1880-1935, from £50; fire-irons, kerbs and metalware, from 1850, from £50.* LOC: Between Kendal and Windermere on A591 (now bypassed). PARK: Easy. TEL: 01539 821393; home - 01539 821123. SER: Valuations; restorations (brass and iron bedsteads, metalware)

ULVERSTON

A1A Antiques

59B Market St. (J.W. Thornton). Est. 1960. Open by appointment. SIZE: Large. *STOCK: Bric-a-brac, clocks, furniture, shipping items, pictures, decorators items.* PARK: Easy. TEL: 01229 869745/580284 or 015394 42930/45183. SER: Valuations; restorations; buys at auction. VAT: Stan/Spec.

Elizabeth and Son

Market Hall. (J.R. Bevins). Est. 1960. Open 9-5. CL: Wed. SIZE: Medium. *STOCK: Victorian and Edwardian glass, silver, brass and copper, gold and silver jewellery, books.* LOC: Town centre. PARK: Easy. TEL: 01229 582763.

Ulverston continued

Smith's Court Antiques

Lower Brook St. (David Wood). Est. 1988. Open Mon. and Fri. 11-4, Tues. 10-4, Thurs. and Sat. 10-4.30. SIZE: Small. *STOCK: Silver, brass and copper, china and glass, small furniture, 18th-19th C, £20-£900.* LOC: Town centre. TEL: 01229 581324; home - 01229 869252. FAIRS: Harrogate.

WHITEHAVEN

Michael Moon

41-43 Roper St. CA28 7BS. SBA, PBFA. (M. and S. Moon). Est. 1969. Open 9.30-5. SIZE: Large. *STOCK: Antiquarian books including Cumbrian topography.* PARK: Nearby. TEL: 01946 62936. FAIRS: PBFA Northern. VAT: Stan.

WINDERMERE

The Birdcage Antiques

College Rd. LA23 1BX. (Mrs T.A. Griffiths). Est. 1983. Open Wed., Fri. and Sat. 10-5, or by appointment. SIZE: Small. *STOCK: General antiques, glass, brass, copper, pre-1920's lighting, country bygones, Staffordshire, 18th C to 1920; 19th C pottery.* LOC: From A591 through village, past end of one-way system, turn right after 50yds. PARK: Alongside shop. TEL: 015394 45063; home - 015394 43041/43310. VAT: Global/Stan.

Joseph Thornton Antiques

4 Victoria St. LA23 1AB. (J.W. Thornton). Est. 1971. Open Tues.-Sat. 10-4.30 or by appointment. SIZE: Large. *STOCK: General antiques, art, architectural and decorators' items, clocks, bric-a-brac.* LOC: 50yds. from railway station. PARK: Easy. TEL: 015394 42930/45183 or 01229 869745/580284. SER: Valuations; buys at auction. VAT: Stan/Spec.

WINTON, Nr. Kirkby Stephen

Winton Hall Antiques

The Manor House. Resident. (S. Baldwick). Est. 1975. Open 9-5 including Sun. SIZE: Large. *STOCK: Oak and country furniture, 1600-1800, £100-£7,000; mahogany, 1750-1830, £100-£4,000.* LOC: One mile through Kirkby Stephen on A685, take 2nd right to Winton, approx 200yds on - large Georgian house overlooking village green. PARK: Easy. TEL: 017683 72194; home - 017683 72194. SER: Valuations; buys at auction. VAT: Stan/spec.

WORKINGTON

Castle Curios

27 Washington St. CA14 3AW. SIZE: Medium. *STOCK: Victorian and Edwardian collectables - postcards, books, bottles, jewellery and linen.* LOC: Just off A66 coming into town. PARK: Nearby. TEL: 01900 601387.

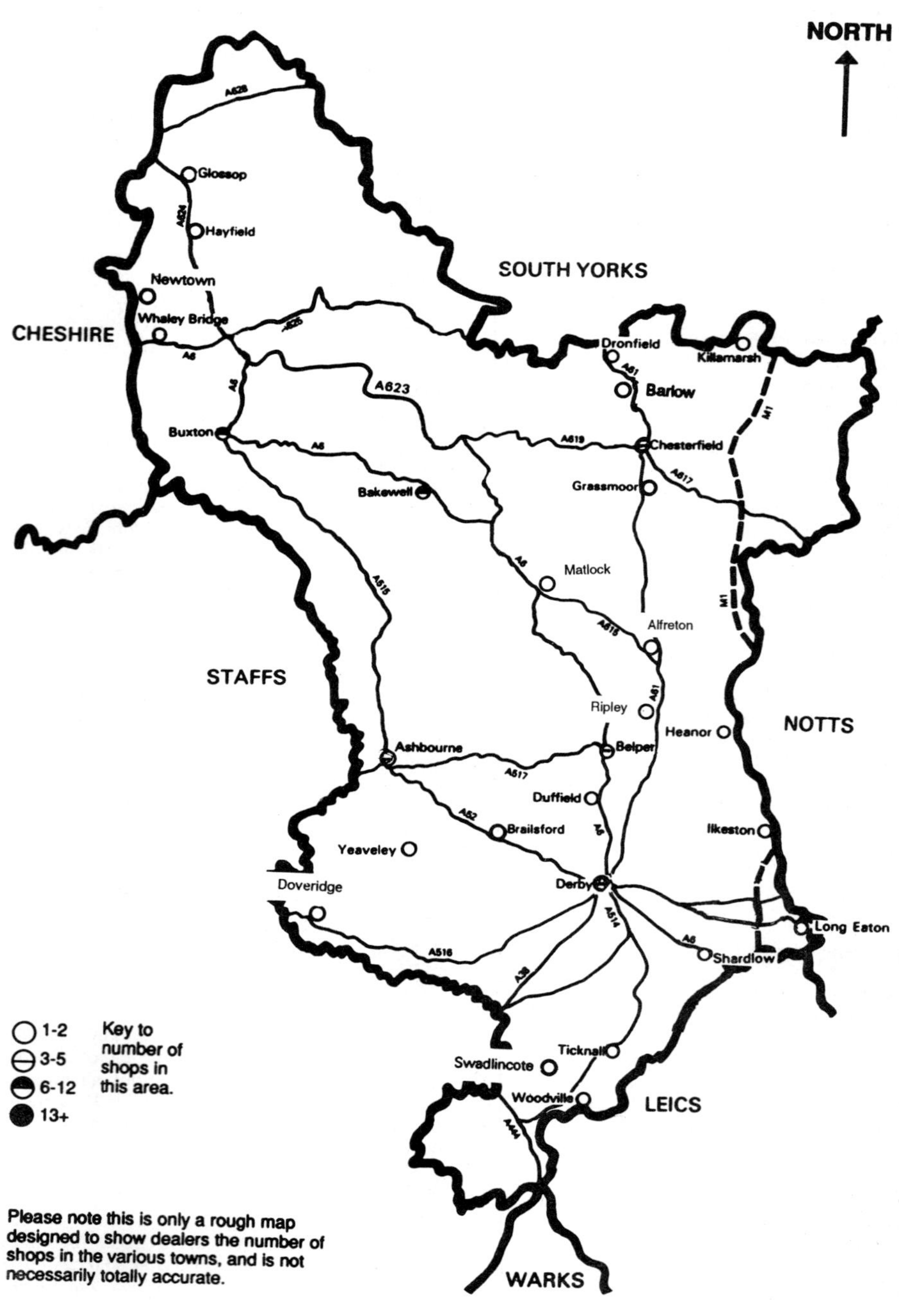

Please note this is only a rough map designed to show dealers the number of shops in the various towns, and is not necessarily totally accurate.

ALFRETON

Alfreton Antiques Centre

11 King St. DE55 7AF. (Helen Dixon). Open 10-4.30, Sun. and Bank Hols. 11-3. SIZE: Large - 40 dealers. *STOCK: Wide range of furniture, ceramics, books, postcards, lighting, metalware, glass, collectables, Deco, costume jewellery, pictures, Langley Artware pottery.* LOC: M1 J28, A38 to Alfreton, King St. is main street up to traffic lights, shop on right before the lights. PARK: Easy. TEL: 01773 520781; home - 01773 852695. SER: Valuations; Denby replacement service. FAIRS: Newark.

ASHBOURNE

Pamela Elsom - Antiques

5 Church St. DE6 1AE. Est. 1963. Open Thurs., Fri., Sat., 10-5, other days and times by appointment. SIZE: Medium. *STOCK: Furniture, £20-£5,000, metalware, both 17th-19th C; period smalls, general antiques, treen, pottery, glass, secondhand books.* Not Stocked: Coins, militaria. LOC: On A52. PARK: Easy. TEL: 01335 343468/344311. SER: Valuations. VAT: Spec.

Manion Antiques

23 Church St. DE6 1AE. (Mrs V.J. Manion). Est. 1984. Open Thurs., Fri. and Sat. 10-5, other times by appointment. SIZE: Small. *STOCK: Porcelain, silver, jewellery, small furniture, £50-£100+.* PARK: Easy. TEL: 01335 343207; home - same. SER: Valuations.

Rose Antiques

37 Church St. DE6 1AJ. Est. 1982. Open 10-5. SIZE: Medium. *STOCK: Furniture, silver, porcelain, jewellery, copper, brass and pine.* LOC: A52. PARK: Easy. TEL: 01335 343822; home - 01283 575301.

Spurrier-Smith Antiques LAPADA

28, 39 and 41 Church St. DE6 1AJ. (I. Spurrier-Smith). Est. 1973. Open 10-5, Wed. and Sun. by appointment. SIZE: Large (8 showrooms) + warehouse. *STOCK: Furniture, oils, watercolours, porcelain, pottery, metalware, instruments, Oriental bronzes, collectables, pine, decorative items. Warehouse - pine and American export goods.* TEL: 01335 343669/342198; home - 01629 822502. SER: Valuations. VAT: Stan/Spec.

Kenneth Upchurch

30B Church St. Est. 1972. *STOCK: Oil paintings and watercolours, mainly 19th C; pottery and porcelain.* TEL: 01332 754499.

BAKEWELL

Bakewell Antiques and Collectors' Centre

King St. DE45 1DZ. Est. 1992. Open 10-5, Sun. 11-5. *STOCK: General antiques and collectables.* TEL: 01629 812496; fax - 01629 814531. Below are listed the dealers at this market.

Bakewell continued

Yvonne Adams Antiques
18th and 19th C furniture, objects d'art. and treen

Alderley Antiques LAPADA
18th and 19th C furniture and decoration.

M. & G. Bassett Antiques
Antique pine and decorative items.

Rex Boyer Antiques LAPADA
18th & 19th C furniture and decorative objects.

Barbara Cattle BADA
Silver and Old Sheffield plate.

Chappell's Antiques & Fine Art BADA LAPADA
Est. 1940. *17th-19th C English furniture, oil paintings, porcelain, pottery, metalwork, clocks and decorative items.* VAT: Stan/Spec.

Cottage Antiques LAPADA
18th and 19th C furniture, glass, treen and decorative items.

De Vine Antiques LAPADA
(Mr. and Mrs. P.A. Vine) Est. 1994. *British pottery and porcelain including Moorcroft, Worcester, Wedgwood fairyland lustre, Doulton, late 19th-early 20th C, £100-£4,000.* TEL: Mobile - 0585 212684; fax - 01733 390451; home - 01733 223119. VAT: Stan/Spec.

Elizabeth Ann Antiques
Furniture and decorative items.

Vivienne Flint Antiques
Town furniture and decorative items.

G.W. Ford & Son Ltd LAPADA
(I.G.F. Thomson) Est. 1890. *Mahogany and country furniture, 18th-19th C, £50-£5,000; sculpture, 19th-early 20th C, £50-£3,000; various collectable and decorative items, 18th-19th C, £10-£1,200.* TEL: Fax - 01246 410512; home - 01246 410512. SER: Valuations; restorations (furniture, silver and EP). VAT: Stan/Spec.

P.M. & J.J. Furness
Quality books and prints, especially sporting.

Ganymede Antiques
18th and 19th C clocks, furniture, silver and plate, pewter, brass and decorative items.

Julie Goddard Antiques
19th C furniture and decorative items.

J.H.S. Antiques LAPADA
17th to early 19th C country furniture, Staffordshire, treen and metalware.

Peter Kelsey Antiques
Furniture and works of art.

Bakewell continued

Millennium Antiques
Fine English silver, silver plate, glass and bijouterie.

M.F. Morris Antiques
Fine Derby, Royal Crown Derby and Lynton porcelain.

Newton Fine Art
19th and 20th C oil paintings and watercolours.

Paraphernalia Lighting
Antique lighting and decorative arts.

Judy Portway
(Benjamin Henry & Co) *Vintage and designer costume jewelley and accessories.*

Ginny Rattenbury & Trevor Russell
Decorative ceramics and fountain pens.

Renaissance Antiques
Pottery, papier-mâché, metals, glass and objects d'art.

Lot 319, Scottish pearlware figure of a milkmaid with a churn (detachable cover), second quarter of the 19th century. Est. £250-£350, hammer £280. [Bid £500. Got it at half my bid. It's rare and mildly naughty. I think it's a bargain.].

From an article which appeared in the March 1998 issue of **Antique Collecting** entitled "Starting an English Ceramics Collection: A Fantasy" The auction was real: but how did Lars Tharp's fictional collector perform?...

Bakewell continued

Sandra Wallhead Antiques
19th and early 20th C furniture, Cranberry glass and objects d'art.

Michael Wisehall Antiques
Furniture, plate, glass, pictures, metalware and pottery.

Peter Bunting Antiques BADA LAPADA
Harthill Hall, Alport. DE45 1LH. Est. 1980. Open by appointment. SIZE: Medium. *STOCK: Early oak, country furniture, portraits and period decoration.* LOC: On B5056. PARK: Own. TEL: 01629 636203; fax - 01629 636190; mobile - 0860 540870. VAT: Stan/Spec.

Michael Goldstone BADA
Avenel Court. DE45 1DZ. Est. 1927. Open 9.30-5 or by appointment, prior telephone call advisable. SIZE: Large. *STOCK: Oak furniture, 16th-18th C, from £100; walnut furniture, brass, 18th C, from £500.* PARK: Easy. TEL: 01629 812487; home - same. VAT: Spec.

Martin and Dorothy Harper Antiques LAPADA
King St. DE45 1DZ. Est. 1973. Open 10-5.30, Sun. and other times by appointment. CL: Thurs. SIZE: Medium. *STOCK: Furniture, £100-£5,000; metalware, £30-£300; glass, £15-£150; all 17th to late 19th C; needlework, 19th C.* PARK: Easy. TEL: 01629 814757. SER: Valuations; restorations (re-upholstery); buys at auction. VAT: Stan/Spec.

Lewis Antiques
King St. Est. 1977. Open 10-5, Sun. by appointment. SIZE: Small. *STOCK: Furniture, clocks, barometers, pictures and porcelain, 17th-late 19th C, £50-£5,000.* PARK: Easy. TEL: 01629 813141. VAT: Stan/Spec.

Water Lane Antiques
Water Lane. DE45 1EU. (M. and L. Pembery). Est. 1967. Open 9.30-1 and 1.30-5.30. SIZE: Medium. *STOCK: Furniture, £500-£4,000; metalware, £100-£1,000; objets d'art, £100-£1,500; all 18th-19th C.* LOC: Off Market Sq. PARK: Nearby. TEL: 01629 814161. SER: Valuations; restorations. VAT: Stan/Spec.

BARLOW, Nr. Chesterfield

Byethorpe Furniture (Brian Yates Antiques)
Shippen Rural Business Centre, Church Farm. Est. 1977. Open 10-5. SIZE: Medium. *STOCK: Country furniture, mainly 17th-18th C, £100-£5,000; boxes, £50-£500; porcelain, copper and brass, £10-£300.* PARK: Easy. TEL: 0114 2899111; fax - same. SER: Restorations (furniture); specialist woodwork; upholstery; handmade reproductions. VAT: Stan/Spec.

BELPER

Belper Antiques Centre

2 Queen St. DE56 1NR. (R. Briggs). Est. 1973. SIZE: Medium. *STOCK: Pre 1950 smalls and 19th-20th C jewellery, £5-£500; furniture, clocks and pictures, 18th-19th C, £50-£2,000.* LOC: Turn right towards Market Place at Safeway island on A6 north of Derby. PARK: Nearby. TEL: 01773 823002. SER: Valuations; restorations (clocks, gilding, furniture); buys at auction. FAIRS: Newark, Birmingham. VAT: Stan.

Sweetings (Antiques 'n' Things)

1 & 1a The Butts. DE56 1HX. (K.J. and J.L. Sweeting). Est. 1971. Open daily. SIZE: Large. *STOCK: Pre 1940's furniture including stripped pine, oak, mahogany, satinwood, £20-£1,000.* LOC: Off A6, near Market Place. PARK: Easy. TEL: 01773 825930/822780. SER: Valuations; restorations (pine and satinwood); shipping. VAT: Stan.

Neil Wayne "The Razor Man"

The Cedars (rear of 55 Field Lane), DE56 1DD. Resident. Est. 1969. Open every day 9.30-6, prior telephone call essential. SIZE: Medium. *STOCK: Razors and shaving items, 18th to early 19th C, £20-£300.* PARK: Easy. TEL: 01773 824157; fax - 01773 825573; e-mail - neil-wayne@freedmus.demon.co.uk; internet - www.freedmus.demon.co.uk/Razor.htm.

BRAILSFORD

Antique Exporters U.K

The Estate Yard, Post Office Lane. DE6 3BT. Est. 1977. Open by appointment. SIZE: Large. *STOCK: Special orders only - English furniture, 17th-19th C and reproduction.* LOC: A52 Ashbourne/Derby. PARK: Easy. TEL: 01335 360005; fax - 01335 360121. SER: Restorations; cabinet makers; interior design; packers and shippers. VAT: Stan. *Trade Only.*

BUXTON

The Antiques Warehouse

25 Lightwood Rd. SK17 7BJ. (N.F. Thompson). Est. 1983. Open 10.30-4.30 or by appointment. SIZE: Large. *STOCK: Furniture, mainly mahogany, 17th-20th C; paintings, smalls, Victorian brass and iron beds.* LOC: Off A6. PARK: Own. TEL: 01298 72967; home - 01298 871932. SER: Valuations; restorations; buys at auction.

The Barn

Wainwright Yard, Ashwood Rd. SK17 7EL. (Roger and Lucy Judd). Est. 1986. Open 9.30-5 and by appointment Sun. pm. CL: Mon. and Sun. am. SIZE: Medium. *STOCK: Pine robes and furniture, 1840-1920, £200-£800; Victorian kitchenalia and chairs, £10-£200.* LOC: From A6 southbound, turn left after golf course - 5th turning on right. PARK: Easy. TEL: 01298 71680; home - same. SER: Valuations; restorations; pine stripping; buys at auction (country chairs).

Buxton continued

Maggie Mays

Unit 10, Cavendish Arcade. (Mrs. J. Wild). Est. 1993. Open 10.30-5. CL: Mon. *STOCK: Victorian furniture and effects, £35-£800; Art Deco glassware, mirrors, pottery, £20-£500; Edwardian furniture, £100-£800.* LOC: Opposite Turners Memorial on Terrace Road. PARK: Easy. TEL: Mobile - 0831 606003; home - 01663 733935. SER: Valuations; buys at auction.

The Penny Post Antiques

9 Cavendish Circus. SK17 6AT. (D. and R. Hammond). Est. 1978. Open 10-4.30, Sat. 10-5. SIZE: Small. *STOCK: Furniture, 18th to early 20th C, £100-£1,000; commemoratives and crested china, £5-£150; pictures, £50-£200; collectables; general antiques.* LOC: Town centre, opposite Palace Hotel. PARK: Easy. TEL: Home - 01298 25965.

West End Galleries

8 Cavendish Circus. SK17 6AT. (A. and A. Needham). Est. 1955. Open 9-5. CL: Sat. p.m. SIZE: Large. *STOCK: French, Dutch, English furniture; clocks, paintings, works of art, bronzes.* LOC: A6. PARK: Easy. TEL: 01298 24546. VAT: Stan/Spec.

What Now Antiques

Cavendish Arcade, The Crescent. SK17 9BQ. (L. Carruthers). Open 10.30-5, Sun. 2-5. CL: Mon. *STOCK: General antiques and collectables including 19th-20th C pottery, silver and plate, jewellery, die-cast toys, textiles, watercolours, Victorian and Edwardian furniture, £1-£1,000.* TEL: 01298 27178/23417. SER: Export; guided tours for foreign trade; valuations.

CHESTERFIELD

Anthony D. Goodlad

26 Fairfield Rd. Brockwell. S40 4TP. Est. 1974. Open by appointment only. *STOCK: General militaria, WWI and WWII.* LOC: Close to town centre. PARK: Easy. TEL: 01246 204004.

Hackney House Antiques

Hackney Lane, Barlow. S18 5TQ. Resident. (Mrs J.M. Gorman). Est. 1984. *STOCK: Furniture, 18th-19th C; prints, clocks, linen, silver.* TEL: 01142 890248.

Ian Morris

479 Chatsworth Rd. S40 3AD. Est. 1967. Open 9-5, Sat. 12-5. SIZE: Medium. *STOCK: Furniture, 18th-20th C, £50-£2,000; pictures, small items.* LOC: Main road A619, to Barlow and Chatsworth House. TEL: 01246 235120. VAT: Stan/Spec.

DERBY

Abbey House

115 Woods Lane. DE22 3UE. Resident. (Shirley White). Est. 1959. Open by appointment. *STOCK: Dolls, teddy bears and all things juvenile.* TEL: 01332 331426; fax - same. SER: Repairs (dolls and teddies); restorations (furniture).

Friargate Pine and Antiques Centre

The Pump House, Friargate Wharf, Stafford St. Entrance. DE1 1JL. (N. J. Marianski). Open 9-5. *STOCK: Antique and reproduction pine furniture.* TEL: 01332 341215.

Brian Matsell

DE1 1HE. Est. 1945. Open by appointment only. *STOCK: Decorative objects, works of art, Oriental and European ceramics, fine furniture.* TEL: Mobile - 0973 368590; fax - 01332 299910. SER: Consultant; client advice; buys on commission.

Tanglewood

Tanglewood Mill, Coke St. DE1 1NE. (R. Beech). Est. 1979. Open 10-5. CL: Sat. (Trade anytime). SIZE: Large + warehouse. *STOCK: British and Irish country pine, 18th-19th C.* LOC: Off A52. PARK: Own. TEL: 01332 346005; fax - same. VAT: Stan.

Charles H. Ward

12 Friar Gate. DE1 1BU. (M.G. Ward). CL: Wed. pm. *STOCK: Oil paintings, 19th-20th C; watercolours.* TEL: 01332 342893. SER: Restorations.

DOVERIDGE

Pine Antiques Workshop

Bell Farm, Yelt Lane. DE6 5JU. (M.A. and A. Groves). Open Tues.-Sat. 9-5.30, other times by appointment. *STOCK: English and Welsh pine, pottery, linen and kitchenalia.* TEL: 01889 564898; fax - same.

DRONFIELD

Bardwell Antiques

51 Chesterfield Rd. S18 6XA. (S. Bardwell). Open 9-5. *STOCK: General antiques.* TEL: 01246 412183; fax - same.

DUFFIELD, Nr. Derby

Dragon Antiques

1 Tamworth St. (J.A. Palfree). Est. 1991. Open 9.30-5.30, Sun. by appointment. SIZE: Medium. *STOCK: Furniture, late 18th to early 20th C, £350-£2,000; mantel, wall and longcase clocks, 18th-19th C, £100-£6,000; decorative pictures, porcelain and books, 19th C, £5-£500.* LOC: Just off A6 in village centre. PARK: Easy. TEL: 01332 842332. VAT: Spec.

Duffield continued

Wayside Antiques

62 Town St. DE6 4GG. (Mrs J. Harding). Est. 1975. *STOCK: Furniture, 18th-19th C, £50-£5,000; porcelain, pictures, boxes and silver.* TEL: 01332 840346. VAT: Stan/Spec.

GLOSSOP

Derbyshire Clocks

104 High St. West. SK13 8BB. (J.A. and T.P. Lees). Est. 1975. CL: Tues. *STOCK: Clocks.* TEL: 01457 862677. SER: Restorations (clocks and barometers).

GRASSMOOR, Nr. Chesterfield

N. and C.A. Haslam

220 Chesterfield Rd. S42 5EZ. Open by appointment. *STOCK: 17th-19th C furniture and decorative items.* TEL: 01246 853672 (24 hrs). SER: Buys at auction and on commission. VAT: Stan/Spec.

HAYFIELD, Nr. New Mills

Michael Allcroft Antiques

1 Church St. Open Sat. and Sun. 12-5, other times by appointment. *STOCK: Pine furniture and decorative items.* TEL: 01663 742684.

HEANOR

Bygones

23c Derby Rd. DE7 7QG. (Mrs P. Buttifant). Open 10-5. CL: Mon. and Wed. *STOCK: Furniture, porcelain, objets d'art, paintings and prints.* TEL: 01773 768503. SER: Framing.

KILLAMARSH

Havenplan's Architectural Emporium

The Old Station, Station Rd. S21 1EN. Est. 1972. Open Tues.-Sat. 10-4. SIZE: Large. *STOCK: Architectural fittings and decorative items, church interiors and furnishings, fireplaces, doors, decorative cast ironwork, masonry, bygones, garden ornaments, 18th to early 20th C.* LOC: M1, exit 30. Take A616 towards Sheffield, turn right on to B6053, turn right on to B6058 towards Killamarsh, turn right between two railway bridges. PARK: Easy. TEL: 01142 489972; fax - same; home - 01246 433315. SER: Hire.

LONG EATON

Goodacre Engraving Ltd

Thrumpton Ave. (off Chatsworth Ave.), Meadow Lane. NG10 2GB. Est. 1948. *STOCK: Longcase and bracket clock movements, parts and castings.* TEL: 01159 734387; fax - 01159 461193. SER: Hand engraving, movement repairs, silvering and dial repainting. VAT: Stan.

Long Eaton continued

Miss Elany

2 Salisbury St. NG10 1BA. (D. and Mrs Mottershead). Est. 1977. Open 9-5. SIZE: Medium. *STOCK: Pianos, 1900 to date, £50-£500; general antiques, Victorian and Edwardian, £25-£200.* PARK: Easy. TEL: 0115 9734835. VAT: Stan.

MATLOCK

Matlock Antiques, Collectables and Craft Centre

7 Dale Rd. DE4 3LT. Resident. (W. Shirley). Est. 1978. Open 10-4, including Sun., Sat. 10-5. SIZE: Large. LOC: Town centre. PARK: Easy. TEL: 01629 760808.

NEWTOWN, Nr. New Mills

Michael Allcroft Antiques

203 Buxton Rd. SIZE: Large. *STOCK: 1930's oak furniture.* TEL: 01663 742684; mobile - 0831 588613.

RIPLEY

Memory Lane Antiques Centre

Nottingham Rd. DE5 3AS. (James Cullen). Est. 1994. Open 10.30-4 including Sun. SIZE: Large. *STOCK: Victoriana and 20th C collectables, pine furniture, specialist in old Denby, £50-£100.* LOC: 200 yds from town centre - 500 yds from A610 (Sainsburys) roundabout. PARK: Easy. TEL: 01773 570184; mobile - 0585 281913. SER: Valuations; pine stripping; old Denby replacement service. FAIRS: Derby University; Newark; Sheffield; Abacus.

Taylor Robinson Antiques

6 Market Place. DE5 3FJ. (A. and B. Robinson). Est. 1973. Open 9.30-4.30. SIZE: Medium. *STOCK: Furniture, £100-£1,000; ceramics, copper, £5-£200, all 19th C.* LOC: Opposite Town Hll. PARK: Opposite - Mon.-Thurs. TEL: 01773 743597; home - 01773 603659. FAIRS: Stafford; Donnington; Edinburgh.

SHARDLOW, Nr. Derby

Shardlow Antiques Warehouse

24 The Wharf. DE7 2GH. Open 10.30-5, Sun. 12-5. CL: Fri. SIZE: Large. *STOCK: Furniture, Georgian to shipping.* LOC: Off M1, junction 24. PARK: Own. TEL: 01332 792899/662899.

SWADLINCOTE

G.K. Hadfield

Rock Farm, Chilcote. DE12 8DQ. (G.K. and J.V. Hadfield and D.W. and N.R. Hadfield-Tilly). Est. 1972. Open Tues.-Sat. 9-5. *STOCK: Clocks - longcase, dial, Act of Parliament, skeleton, Black Forest, American and carriage; unrestored antiques clocks; secondhand, new and out of print*

Swadlincote continued

horological books; secondhand workshop tools and materials. LOC: Between Ashby-de-la-Zouch and Tamworth, 3 miles from Junc. 11 A42/M42. TEL: 01827 373466; fax - 01827 373699. SER: Restoration materials (antique clocks); valuations (clocks and horological books). VAT: Stan/Spec.

TICKNALL

Sam Savage Antiques

The Old Coach House, Hayes Farm, Main St. DE73 1JZ. Resident. (S. Savage). Est. 1969. Open by appointment only. *STOCK: Early period furniture, 17th-19th C; decorative items, Oriental rugs, paintings.* LOC: Centre of Ticknall, on A514, 4 miles from Ashby-de-la-Zouch, 10 miles west from exit 24, M1 and 6 miles east of Ashby turn-off on M42. PARK: Easy. TEL: 01332 862195. SER: Valuations.

WHALEY BRIDGE

Richard Glass

Hockerley Old Hall, Hockerley Lane. Resident. Open by appointment only. SIZE: Small. *STOCK:Oak furniture, 17th-18th C, £1,000-£5,000; paintings, drawings, metal and stoneware, 17th-19th C, £200-£2,000.* LOC: From town centre towards Stockport, turn left at station car park, up hill and 2nd right into Hockerley Lane, up farm track at end of lane, house on left. PARK: Easy. TEL: 0161 236 1520; fax - 0161 236 0886. SER: Valuations. FAIRS: Kenilworth. VAT: Spec.

Nimbus Antiques

Chapel Rd. (L.M. and H.C. Brobbin). Est. 1978. Open 9-5.30, Sun. 2-5.30. SIZE: Large. *STOCK: Furniture, mainly mahogany, desks, dining tables, chairs and clocks, 18th-19th C.* LOC: A6. PARK: Easy. TEL: 01663 734248; home - 01663 733332. SER: Valuations; restorations. VAT: Stan/Spec.

WOODVILLE

Wooden Box Antiques

32 High St. DE11 7EH. (Mrs R. Bowler). Est. 1982. Open 10-5 including some Sun. SIZE: Medium. *STOCK: Furniture, Georgian-Edwardian, £75-£400; original cast-iron fireplaces, surrounds, £50-£600; Victorian tiles, country pine furniture, pine doors.* LOC: A511 (was A50), between Ashby-de-la-Zouch and Burton-on-Trent. PARK: Easy. TEL: 01283 212014; home - same.

YEAVELEY, Nr. Ashbourne

Gravelly Bank Pine Antiques

DE6 2DT. (A. Brassington). Open every day including evenings. *STOCK: Mahogany, oak and pine furniture, 18th-19th C, £50-£500.* PARK: Easy. TEL: 01335 330237; home and fax - same. SER: Valuations; restorations (pine); buys at auction.

Devon

SOMERSET
CORNWALL
Ilfracombe
Lynton
Braunton
Barnstaple
South Molton
A361
Bideford
Bampton
A386
Tiverton
A361
Merton
Cullompton
Stockland
A388
Morchard Bishop
Kentisbeare
Monkton
M5
Honiton
Axminster
Hatherleigh
A377
Whimple
Newton St. Cyres
Colyton
Okehampton
Seaton
Exeter
Topsham
Woodbury
Sidmouth
East Budleigh
Chagford
Budleigh Salterton
A386
Moretonhampstead
A30
Lydford
A382
Exmouth
Bovey Tracey
Newton Abbot
Teignmouth
A384
Shaldon
Tavistock
Ashburton
Maidencombe
A381
Torquay
South Brent
A385
Paignton
Totnes
Brixham
Plymouth
A38
Ermington
Modbury
Kingswear
Dartmouth
Yealmpton
Kingsbridge

1-2 — 3-5 — 6-12 — 13+

Key to number of shops in this area.

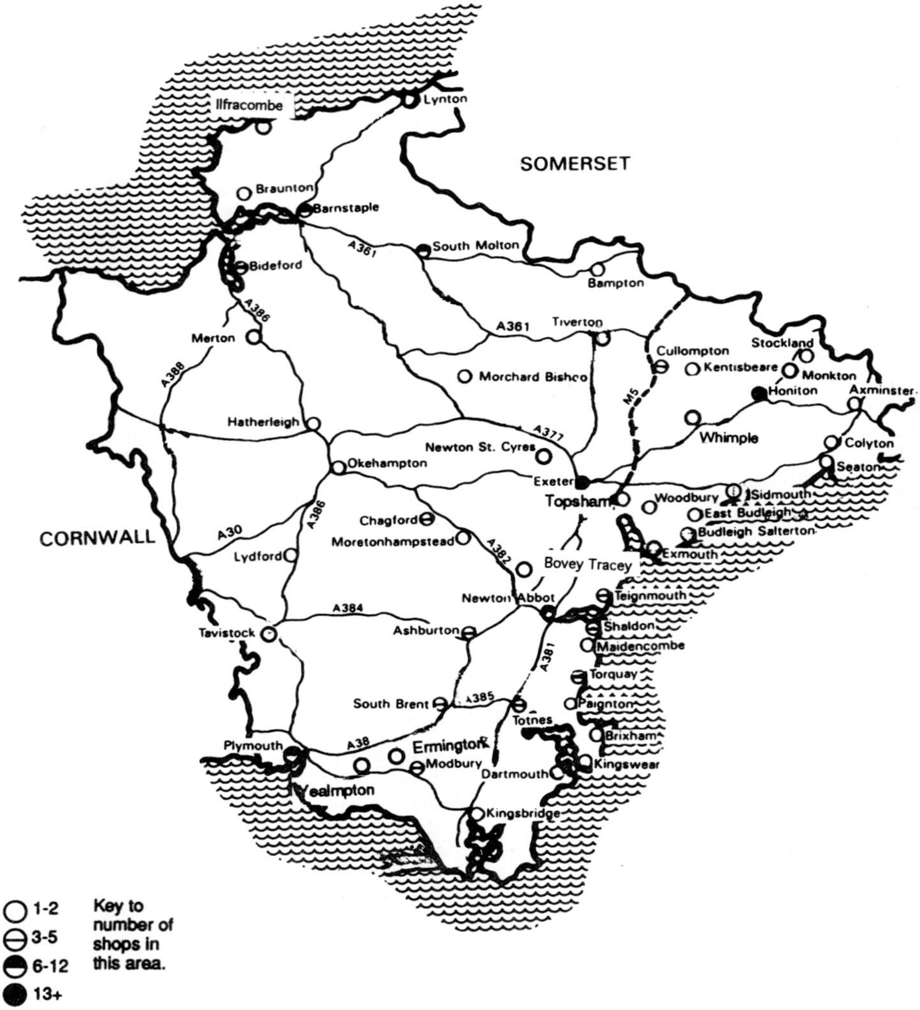

Please note this is only a rough map designed to show dealers the number of shops in the various towns, and is not necessarily totally accurate.

ASHBURTON

Ashburton Marbles

Great Hall, North St. TQ13 7DU. (Adrian Ager). Est. 1976. Open 8-5, Sat. 10-2. SIZE: Warehouse and showroom. *STOCK: Marble and wooden fire-surrounds, decorative cast iron inserts; scuttles, fenders, overmantels, 1790-1910; architectural decorative antiques, garden statuary and related items, chandeliers, soft furnishings and furniture.* PARK: Easy. TEL: 01364 653189; fax - same.

M. W. Dunscombe Antiques

6 East St. TQ13 7AA. Est. 1996. Open Thurs. and Fri. 9.30-5, Sat. 9.30-1, other times by appointment. SIZE: Large. *STOCK: Furniture, 18th C to Edwardian, £400-£4,000.* LOC: Just off A38 town centre. PARK: Easy. TEL: 01364 654144; fax - same; home - same. VAT: Spec.

Moor Antiques

19a North St. TQ13 7QH. (T. and Mrs E. Gatland). Est. 1984. CL: Wed. pm. SIZE: Small. *STOCK: Small furniture, 1780-1900, £250-£2,500; clocks, 1830-1910, £150-£2,000; silver and china, 1800-1900, £25-£500.* LOC: A38 town centre, 100 yards past town hall. PARK: Nearby. TEL: 01364 653767. SER: Valuations.

The Shambles

22 North St. TQ13 7QD. Est. 1982. Open 10-5, Sat. 10-1. SIZE: 8 dealers. *STOCK: Country and general antiques and decorative items, £5-£1,500.* LOC: Town centre. PARK: Opposite. TEL: 01364 653848. SER: Valuations. FAIRS: Little Chelsea, Sandown, Kensington Brocante, Westpoint Exeter. VAT: Stan/Spec.

AXMINSTER

W.G. Potter and Son

1 West St. EX13 5HS. Est. 1863. Open 9-5. CL: Sat. pm. SIZE: Medium. *STOCK: Pine, 19th-20th C; some mahogany and oak.* LOC: In main street (A35) opposite church. PARK: Easy. TEL: 01297 32063. SER: Restorations (furniture); buys at auction. VAT: Stan/Spec.

BAMPTON, Nr. Tiverton

Robert Byles

7 Castle St. Est. 1966. Open by chance, knocking or appointment. *STOCK: Early oak, local farm-house tables and settles, metalwork, pottery, unstripped period pine, architectural items.* TEL: 01398 331515. SER: Restoration materials. VAT: Stan/Spec.

Chattels

9 Castle St. EX16 9LN. (P. Newton and S. Byrt). Open 10-4. CL: Mon. SIZE: Medium. *STOCK: General antiques including furniture, country kitchenalia, pottery, porcelain, glass, linen, collectables.* LOC: B3227 from Taunton. PARK: Easy. TEL: 01398 331994/323405.

BARNSTAPLE

Barn Antiques

73 Newport Rd. EX32 9BG. (E. Cusack). Open 9.30-5, Wed. 9.30-1. SIZE: Large. *STOCK: General antiques.* TEL: 01271 323131.

Elizabeth Longhurst Antiques & Collectables

20a Newport Rd. EX32 9BG. Open 10-4. CL: Wed. *STOCK: General antiques.* TEL: 01271 321414.

Madeline's Emporium

74 Newport Rd. EX32 9BG. (Mrs. M. Robinson). Open 9.30-5.30, Sun. 10-4.30. *STOCK: Georgian and Victorian furniture, collectables, militaria, architectural antiques.* TEL: 01271 345156.

Medina Gallery

80 Boutport St. EX31 1SR. (R. Jennings). Est. 1972. Open 9.30-5. CL: Wed. pm. SIZE: Small. *STOCK: Maps, prints, photographs, oils and watercolours, £1-£500.* TEL: 01271 371025. SER: Picture framing, mounting. VAT: Stan.

Nick Nacks

86 Newport Rd. EX32 9BE. Open 10-5, Wed. 10-1. *STOCK: Furniture, incl. shipping.* TEL: 01271 321449.

Mark Parkhouse Antiques and Jewellery

106 High St. EX31 1HP. Est. 1976. CL: Wed. *STOCK: Jewellery, furniture, silver, paintings, clocks, glass, porcelain, small collectors' items, 18th-19th C, £100-£10,000.* PARK: Nearby. TEL: 01271 374504; fax - 01271 323499. SER: Valuations; buys at auction. VAT: Stan/Spec.

Selected Antiques & Collectables

19 Newport Rd. EX32 9BG. (Helen Chugg). Est. 1994. Open 9.45-4.30, Wed. 10.30-4.30, some Mondays (prior telephone call advisable). SIZE: Medium. *STOCK: North Devon pottery, 19th C; porcelain and ceramics, glass, collectables, 19th-20th C.* PARK: Easy. TEL: 01271 321338 (answerphone). SER: Valuations; restorations (ceramics); buys at auction.

Tudor House

115 Boutport St. (C. and D. Pilon). Est. 1980. Open 9.30-3.30,Wed. 9.30-1. SIZE: Large. *STOCK: Furniture and bric-a-brac, late 18th C and reproduction.* LOC: Off M5, Tiverton link road to town centre. PARK: Easy. TEL: 01271 375370; home - 01271 371750. SER: Valuations; restorations (furniture).

BIDEFORD

J. Collins and Son BADA LAPADA

The Studio, 28 High St. EX39 2AN. CINOA. (J. and P. Biggs). Est. 1953. Open by request. SIZE: Large. *STOCK: Georgian and Regency furniture; general antiques including framed and restored 19th-20th C oils and watercolours, £50-£50,000.* LOC: From Bideford Old Bridge turn right, then first left into the High St. PARK: Easy. TEL: 01237 473103; fax - 01237 475658; home - 01237 476485. SER: Valuations; restorations (period furniture, paintings and watercolours); cleaning and framing. FAIRS: LAPADA (NEC Jan); BADA (March); Olympia (June, Nov); Harrogate (Sept). VAT: Spec.

Medina Gallery

20 Mill St. EX39 2JR. (R. Jennings). Est. 1973. Open 9.30-5. CL: Wed. pm. SIZE: Medium. *STOCK: Maps and prints, photographs, oils, watercolours, £1-£500.* PARK: Easy. TEL: 01237 476483. SER: Picture framing, mounting. VAT: Stan.

Petticombe Manor Antiques

Petticombe Manor, Monkleigh. EX39 5JR. (O. Wilson). Est. 1971. Open daily until 7 pm. SIZE: Large. *STOCK: Furniture including dining tables and chairs, desks and bureaux, bookcases and display cabinets, Pembroke and Sutherland tables; china, glass, brass and copper, oils and watercolours, prints and mirrors, hand-stripped pine, mainly 19th to early 20th C.* LOC: Large manor house on A388 Bideford to Holsworthy road. PARK: Own. TEL: 01237 475605; home - same. SER: Restorations (re-upholstery, French polishing, cabinet work). VAT: Stan.

BOVEY TRACEY, Nr. Newton Abbot

Frank's Antiques

10 Town Hall Place. TQ13 9EH. (F.G. Tedd). Est. 1974. Open 10-5, prior telephone call advisable. SIZE: Small. *STOCK: Furniture, 17th-20th C; mechanical music including gramophones, 19th-20th C; clocks, 18th-20th C.* LOC: 5 minutes from A38. PARK: 100 yards. TEL: 01626 833325; home - same. SER: Valuations; restorations (gramophones, furniture including French polishing). FAIRS: National Vintage Communications (NEC).

BRAUNTON

Timothy Coward Fine Silver LAPADA

Marisco, Saunton. EX33 1LG. Open by appointment. *STOCK: Antique and early 20th C silver.* TEL: 01271 890466.

BRIXHAM

John Prestige Antiques

1 and 2 Greenswood Court. TQ5 9HN. Est. 1971. Open 8.45-6, appointment advisable. CL: Sat. and

Brixham continued

Sun. except by appointment. SIZE: Large + warehouse. *STOCK: Period and Victorian furniture; shipping goods.* TEL: 01803 856141; home - 01803 853739; fax - 01803 851649. VAT: Stan/Spec.

BUDLEIGH SALTERTON

Alison Gosling Antiques

46a High St. Est. 1983. Open 10-5, Tues. and Fri. 2-5, other times by appointment. CL: Thurs. and some Sats. SIZE: Medium. *STOCK: Furniture, 18th C to Edwardian, £200-£3,500; porcelain and decorative items, late 18th C to 1930's, £20-£600.* LOC: Next to Barclay's Bank. PARK: Easy. TEL: 01395 443737; home - 01395 271451. SER: Valuations.

David J. Thorn

2 High St. EX9 6LQ. Est. 1950. Open Tues. and Fri. 10-1 and 2.15-5.30, Sat. 10-1. SIZE: Small. *STOCK: English, Continental and Oriental pottery and porcelain, 1620-1850, £5-£5,000; English furniture, 1680-1870, £20-£5,000; paintings, silver, jewellery, £1-£1,000.* PARK: Easy. TEL: 01395 442448. SER: Valuations. VAT: Stan/Spec.

CHAGFORD

Mary Payton Antiques

The Old Market House. TQ13 8AB. (Mrs M. Essex). Est. 1968. Open 10-1 and 2.30-5. CL: Wed. and Mon. SIZE: Small. *STOCK: English pottery and porcelain especially Staffordshire, English glass, 18th-19th C; maps and prints (West Country), 17th-19th C.* Not Stocked: Jewellery, firearms, coins, silver, pewter. LOC: Coming from Whiddon Down (A30) by A382, turn right at Easton Court. Shop in the town square. PARK: Easy. TEL: 01647 432428; home - 01647 432388.

Rex Antiques

The Old Cinema. TQ13 8AB. (John Meredith). Est. 1979. Open by appointment. SIZE: Large. *STOCK: Country oak, 16th-19th C, £5-£2,000; Oriental brass and copper, weapons, large unusual items, granite, architectural items, old iron work.* PARK: Easy. TEL: 01647 433405. SER: Buys at auction. VAT: Stan/Spec. *Trade only.*

Whiddons Antiques and Tearooms

6 High St. TQ13 8AJ. (D. Meldrum). Est. 1979. Open 10.30-5.30. SIZE: Medium. *STOCK: General and country items - furniture including pine, clocks, prints, paintings, copper, brass, books and collectables.* LOC: Opposite church. PARK: Easy. TEL: 01647 433406; home - 01647 433303.

COLYTON

Colyton Antique Centre

Dolphin St. EX12 2UR. Open 10-5. SIZE: 30+ dealers. *STOCK: General antiques and collectables.* PARK: Easy. TEL: 01297 552339.

CULLOMPTON

Cobweb Antiques

The Old Tannery, Exeter Rd. EX15 1DT. (R. Holmes). Est. 1980. Open 10-5, Sun. 11-4. SIZE: Large. *STOCK: Pine and country furniture, painted, decorative and mahogany items, £5-£2,000.* LOC: Half a mile from junction 28, M5. PARK: Easy. TEL: 01884 855748. SER: Stripping; restorations; packing; courier. VAT: Stan/Spec.

Cullompton Antique Mirrors

The Old Tannery, Exeter Rd. EX15 1DT. (Peter Schicht). Est. 1996. Open 10-5.30, Sat. and Sun. 10-5. SIZE: Small. *STOCK: Overmantel mirrors, 19th C, £500-£2,000; wall mirrors, 18th-19th C, £50-£1,500.* LOC: M5 J28, left in Cullompton, shop on RHS before Esso garage. PARK: Easy. TEL: 01884 34856; home - 01823 672010. SER: Valuations; buys at auction.

Cullompton Old Tannery Antiques

Exeter Rd. EX15 1DT. (Cullompton Antiques Ltd). Est. 1989. Open 10-5.30, Sat. 10-5, Sun. 11-4. SIZE: Large. *STOCK: Pine, oak, mahogany and fruitwood country furniture; china, decorative items and mirrors.* LOC: Off M5, junction 28, through town centre, premises on right, approximately 1 mile. PARK: Easy. TEL: 01884 38476; fax - same; e-mail - mail@cullompton-antiques.ltd.uk.; internet - www.Cullompton-antiques.ltd.uk.VAT: Stan/Spec.

Mills Antiques

The Old Tannery, Exeter Rd. EX15 1DT. Est. 1979. Open 10-5.30, Sat. 10-5, Sun. 11-4. *STOCK: 17th C to Edwardian furniture; French bedroom suites, country furniture and decorative items.* PARK: Easy. TEL: 01392 860945.

Umborne Antiques

The Old Tannery, Exeter Rd. EX15 1DT. (Terence and Marilyn Warr). Est. 1987. Open 10-5.30, Sat., 10-5, Sun 11-4. SIZE: Small. *STOCK: Furniture, 1750-1920.* LOC: Off M5, junction 28 far end of High St. PARK: Easy. TEL: 01297 552596; fax - same; home - same.

DARTMOUTH

Chantry Bookshop and Gallery

11 Higher St. TQ6 9RB. (M.P. Merkel). Est. 1969. Open 10.30-5. CL: 15th Jan.-20th Mar. SIZE: Small. *STOCK: Antiquarian books and watercolours; decorative maps, town plans, prints, sea charts and battle plans.* LOC: Next to 'The Cherub' public house. PARK: Nearby. TEL: 01803 832796; home - 01803 834208.

EAST BUDLEIGH

Antiques at Budleigh House

Budleigh House. EX9 7ED. (W. Cook). Est. 1982. Open 10-5, Sat. 10-1. CL: Mon. and Wed. SIZE: Small. *STOCK: 18th-19th C small furniture and decorative objects, porcelain, glass, silver and metalware, £5-£1,000.* LOC: Opposite Sir Walter Raleigh public house. PARK: Easy. TEL: 01395 445368; home - same. SER: Valuations; buys at auction.

ERMINGTON, Nr. Ivybridge

Mill Gallery

Resident. (Christopher Trant). Est. 1984. CL: Sat. SIZE: Small. *STOCK: Oils and watercolours, 18th-20th C, £300-£1,000.* LOC: From A38 take Ivybridge exit, follows signs, 1st premises in village. PARK: Easy. TEL: 01548 830172. SER: Valuations; restorations (oils). VAT: Spec.

EXETER

The Antique Centre on the Quay

The Quay. EX2 4AP. Open 10-5 winter, 10-6 summer including Sun. SIZE: 20+ dealers. *STOCK: Antiques, collectables, books, records, tools and jewellery.* TEL: 01392 493501.

Exeter Rare Books

Guildhall Shopping Centre. EX4 3HG. ABA. (R.C. Parry). Est. 1975. Open 10-1 and 2-5. SIZE: Small. *STOCK: Books, antiquarian, secondhand, out-of-print, 17th-20th C, £5-£500.* LOC: City centre. PARK: Easy. TEL: 01392 436021. SER: Valuations; buys at auction. FAIRS: ABA Chelsea, Bath and Edinburgh.

Fagins Antiques

The Old Whiteways Cider Factory, Hele. EX5 4PW. (C.J. Strong). Open 9.15-5, Sat. 11-5. *STOCK: Furniture, decorative items, architectural and shipping items.* TEL: 01392 882062/01395 279660; fax - 01392 882194.

Gold and Silver Exchange

Eastgate House, Princesshay. EX4 3JT. *STOCK: Jewellery, watches including Rolex.* TEL: 01392 217478.

The House that Moved

24 West St. (L. Duriez). Open 10-5. *STOCK: Lace, shawls, babywear, linen, 1920's costume, Victorian and Edwardian bridal wedding dresses.* TEL: 01392 432643.

McBains of Exeter LAPADA

Exeter Airport, Clyst Honiton. EX5 2BA. SIZE: Large warehouse complex. *STOCK: Furniture.* LOC: A30, 2 miles from exit 30, M5. Below are listed the dealers who are trading from this address. TEL: 01392 366261; fax - 01392 365572. *Trade Only.*

Exeter continued

Ash Brothers Antiques

Art deco, unstripped pine, shipping goods. TEL: 01392 364483. VAT: Stan.

McBains of Exeter

(I.S., G., R. and M. McBain). Est. 1963. Open 9-6, weekends by appointment. *Furniture, period and Victorian; decorative and shipping goods.* TEL: 01392 366261; fax - 01392 365572.

Miscellany Antiques

Shipping goods. TEL: 01392 366261.

Leon Robertson Antiques

Furniture. TEL: 01392 366261.

Tredantiques

Georgian, Victorian and Edwardian furniture. TEL: 01392 366261.

The Meeting

38 South St. EX1 1ED. (L. Emanuel). Open 10-5.30. SIZE: Large - 30 dealers. *STOCK: Furniture and clocks, 18th-19th C, pianos, 20th C, £100-£5,000; porcelain, glass, silver, jewellery, rugs and textiles, fine art, books, boxes, treen, pens, instruments, 19th-20th C, £20-£1,500.* LOC: City centre, opposite White Hart. PARK: Opposite and 150 metres. TEL: 01392 412260. SER: Valuations.

Brian Mortimer

87 Queen St. EX4 3RP. *STOCK: General antiques, jewellery, silver, Victoriana.* TEL: 01392 79994. VAT: Stan/Spec.

John Nathan Antiques

153/154 Cowick St., St. Thomas. EX4 1AS. (I. Doble). Est. 1950. Open 9-5.30. SIZE: Small. *STOCK: Silver and jewellery, £5-£5,000; clocks, including Georgian and Victorian, £25-£3,000.* LOC: From Exeter inner by-pass over new Exe Bridge, take A30 Okehampton Rd. under railway arch, shop on right. PARK: Easy. TEL: 01392 278216. SER: Valuations; restorations (silver and jewellery); buys at auction. VAT: Stan.

Pennies

Pennies Furniture Centre, Unit 2, Wessex Estate, Station Rd., Exwick. EX4 4NZ. (Penelope and Michael Clark). Est. 1982. Open 9-6. SIZE: Medium. *STOCK: Furniture, from Victorian; china, glass and bric-a-brac, books.* LOC: Behind St. David's Station, over railway lines. PARK: Easy. TEL: 01392 271928/276532/216238. SER: Valuations. VAT: Stan/Spec.

Phantique

47 The Quay. EX2 4AN. Open daily - summer 10.30-5.30, winter 10.30-4.30. SIZE: 14 dealers. *STOCK: General antiques.* TEL: 01392 498995. SER: Restorations.

Exeter continued

The Quay Gallery Antiques Emporium

43 The Quay. EX2 4AP. (A. Nebbett). Est. 1984. Open 10-5 including Sun. SIZE: Large - 10 dealers. *STOCK: 18th-20th C oak and mahogany furniture, marine items, porcelain, silver, plate, glass and decorative items.* LOC: Next to Old Customs House. PARK: Easy. TEL: 01392 213283; fax - 01392 490585.

EXMOUTH

Boase Antiques

5 High St. EX8 1NN. Open 10-5. *STOCK: Jewellery, silver, Victorian collectables.* LOC: Town centre. PARK: Easy. TEL: 01395 271528.

Lilians

32 Exeter Rd. (L. Treasure). Open 9-5. *STOCK: General antiques.* TEL: 01395 279512.

HATHERLEIGH

Hatherleigh Antiques BADA

15 Bridge St. EX20 3HU. (S. and M. Dann). Open 9-1 and 2-5, anytime by appointment. CL: Wed. and Thurs. SIZE: Medium. *STOCK: Collectors' furniture and works of art, pre-1700.* PARK: Easy. TEL: 01837 810159/01837 810500. VAT: Spec.

HONITON

The Antique Centre Abingdon House

136 High St. EX14 8JP. (M.V. Melliar-Smith and J.J. Butler). Est. 1985. Open 10-5. SIZE: Large - 15 dealers. *STOCK: Arts and Crafts and general antiques including furniture, clocks and early metalwork, tools and country items.* LOC: Exeter end of High St. PARK: Nearby. TEL: 01404 42108.

Jane Barnes Antiques & Interiors

59 High St. EX14 8PW. Open 10-4. CL: Wed. SIZE: Medium. *STOCK: General antiques and country pine, glass, clocks.* LOC: Main St. PARK: Easy. TEL: 01404 41712. SER: Furniture copies made to order.

J. Barrymore and Co

73-75 High St. EX14 8PG. (J. and M. Ogden). Est. 1979. Open 10-5, Thurs. by appointment only. SIZE: Medium. *STOCK: Silver, 17th-20th C, £100-£15,000; Old Sheffield plate, Victorian electroplate, £100-£4,000; jewellery, £150-£5,000; all 19th C to early 20th C.* LOC: Main st. PARK: Easy. TEL: 01404 42244. VAT: Stan/Spec.

Roderick Butler BADA

Marwood House. EX14 8PY. Est. 1948. Open 9.30-5. SIZE: Large. *STOCK: 17th-18th C and Regency furniture, curiosities, unusual items, early metalwork.* LOC: Adjacent to roundabout at eastern end of High St. PARK: In courtyard. TEL: 01404 42169. VAT: Spec.

C & S Antiques

159 High St. EX14 8LJ. (I. Crackston and H. Sledge). Est. 1986. Open 10-5. SIZE: Medium. *STOCK: Period country antiques, copper, brass, ceramics, to 19th C.* PARK: Nearby. TEL: 01404 43436.

Fountain Antiques

132 High St. EX14 8JP. (J. Palmer and G. York). Open 9.30-5.30. *STOCK: General antiques including pictures, books and linen.* TEL: 01404 42074.

Honiton Antique Toys

38 High St. EX14 8PJ. (L. and S. Saunders). Est. 1986. Open 10.30-5. CL: Mon. and Thurs. *STOCK: Toys, dolls, teddies and children's books.* PARK: Easy. TEL: 01404 41194.

Honiton Clock Clinic

16 New St. EX14 8EY. (David Newton). Est. 1992. Open 10-5, Thurs. and Sat. 10-1. SIZE: Small. *STOCK: Clocks and barometers.* PARK: Nearby. TEL: 01404 47466.

Honiton Fine Art

189 High St. EX14 8LQ. (C.B. and P.R. Greenberg). Est. 1974. Open 11.30-5. SIZE: Medium. *STOCK: English watercolours and oil paintings, 18th-20th C, £300-£5,000; Old Master drawings, Dutch, Italian and French, 16th-18th C, £300-£1,500.* LOC: Town centre. PARK: Easy. TEL: 01404 45942. SER: Valuations; restorations (oil paintings and watercolours).

Honiton continued

The Honiton Lace Shop
44 High St. EX14 8PJ. Open 9.30-1 and 2-5. *STOCK: Lace including specialist and collectors; quilts, shawls and other textiles, bobbins and lace making equipment.* TEL: 01404 42416; fax - 01404 47797; e-mail - Honitonlace@compuserve.com.

Honiton Old Bookshop
Felix House, 51 High St. EX14 8PW. (R. Collicott). Est. 1991. Open 10-5.30. *STOCK: Books - travel, childrens' illustrated; plate books and bindings; all £5-£500.* LOC: Main street. PARK: Easy. TEL: 01404 47180. SER: Catalogues available (3 per annum). FAIRS: London PBFA. VAT: Stan.

House of Antiques
195 High St. EX14 8LQ. (Kevin Wheeler-Johns and Ian Baum). Est. 1992. Open 10-5. SIZE: Large. *STOCK: Edwardian and Victorian furniture, general antiques.* LOC: Exeter end of High St. PARK: Nearby. TEL: 01752 41648; home - 01752 224393.

L.J. Huggett and Son
Stamps Building, King St. EX14 8AG. Open 9.30-5, Sat 9.30-4. SIZE: Large. *STOCK: Furniture, 18th-19th C.* TEL: 01404 42043; home - 01404 47117.

Lombard Antiques
14 High St. EX14 8PU. Est. 1984. Open 10-5.30. SIZE: Small. *STOCK: 18th-19th C English furniture, porcelain and decorative items.* PARK: Easy. TEL: 01404 42140.

Merchant House Antiques
19 High St. EX14 8PR. (G. Giltsoff and R. Kirk). Open 10-5, Sun. by appointment. SIZE: Large. *STOCK: English and French fine and provincial furniture, 17th-19th C; period metalware, works of art, ironstone and later china, collectables and decorative items, upholstery and furnishings, £10-£8,000.* PARK: Easy. TEL: 01404 42694; fax - same; home - 01395 442979/01884 820944. SER: Valuations. FAIRS: NEC; Newark; Ardingly; Shepton Mallet. VAT: Stan/Spec.

The Old Dairy - Antiques & Bygones
Vine Passage, High St. EX14 8NN. (Miss N. J. Symes). Est. 1993. Open Tues.-Sat. 10-5 or by appointment. SIZE: Small. *STOCK: 19th-20th C country pine and oak furniture, £25-£1,000.* LOC: Off High St., opposite Vine Inn. PARK: Easy and at rear. TEL: 01404 44876. SER: Restorations (furniture including pine stripping).

Otter Antiques
69 High St. EX14 8PW. (G.F. Wilkin). Open 9-5, Thurs. by appointment only. *STOCK: Silver and plate including cutlery and flatware.* TEL: 01404 42627.

Honiton continued

Pilgrim Antiques LAPADA
145 High St. EX14 8LJ. (G. and J.E. Mills). Est. 1970. Open 9-5.30. SIZE: Large - trade warehouse. *STOCK: Period English and Continental furniture.* PARK: Easy. TEL: 01404 41219/45316; fax - 01404 45317. SER: Packing and shipping. VAT: Stan/Spec.

Upstairs, Downstairs
12 High St. EX14 8PU. Open 10-5.30. SIZE: Large. *STOCK: 18th-19th C furniture, porcelain, metalware, pictures and clocks.* PARK: Easy. TEL: 01404 44481/42140.

Wickham Antiques
191 High St. EX14 8LQ. (J. and E. Waymouth). Est. 1986. Open 9.30-5. SIZE: Medium. *STOCK: Mahogany and oak country furniture, decorative items.* PARK: Easy. TEL: 01404 44654.

Geoffrey M. Woodhead
53 High St. EX14 8PW. Est. 1950. Open 9.30-5. SIZE: Medium. *STOCK: Secondhand books and magazines.* LOC: A30 opposite largest tree in street. PARK: Limited. TEL: 01404 42969.

ILFRACOMBE

Relics
113 High St. Resident. (Nicola D. Bradshaw). Est. 1977. Open 10-1 and 2-5, Thurs. 10-1. SIZE: Small. *STOCK: General antiques and small collectables, Victorian and Edwardian.* LOC: Opposite The Bunch of Grapes. PARK: Nearby. TEL: 01271 865486; home - same. SER: Valuations. VAT: Stan.

KENTISBEARE, Nr. Cullompton

Sextons
Dulford Cottage. EX15 2DX. (B.A. and F.B. Ward-Smith). Est. 1979. Open 9-6, Sat. and Sun. by appointment. SIZE: Medium. *STOCK: English and French country furniture, 1720-1900, £100-£3,000.* LOC: Telephone for directions. PARK: Easy. TEL: 01884 266429; home - same. VAT: Stan. *Trade Only.*

KINGSBRIDGE

Avon House Antiques/Hayward's Antiques
13 Church St. TQ7 1BT. (D.H. and M.S. Hayward). Open 10-1 and 2-5. *STOCK: General antiques.* TEL: 01548 853718.

KINGSWEAR, Nr. Dartmouth

David L.H. Southwick Rare Art BADA
Beacon Lodge, Beacon Lane. TQ6 0BU. Open by appointment. *STOCK: Chinese and Japanese works of art.* TEL: 01803 752533; fax - 01803 752535.

LYDFORD, Nr. Okehampton

Skeaping Gallery

Townend House. EX20 4AR. Est. 1972. Open by appointment. *STOCK: Oils and watercolours.* TEL: 01822 820383; fax - same. VAT: Spec

LYNTON

Vendy Antiques

29A Lee Rd. EX35 6BS. (D.R. and T.W. Vendy). Est. 1964. Open 10-1 and 2-4, Sat. by appointment. *STOCK: General antiques including furniture and smalls, mainly Victorian, £10-£2,000.* PARK: Easy. TEL: 01598 752722; home - 01598 753227.

MAIDENCOMBE, Nr. Torquay

G.A. Whiteway-Wilkinson

Sunsea, Teignmouth Rd. TQ1 4TP. Est. 1943. Open by appointment only. *STOCK: General antiques, fine art and jewellery.* LOC: Approximately half-way on main Torquay/Teignmouth road. TEL: 01803 329692. VAT: Spec.

MERTON, Nr. Okehampton

Barometer World Ltd

Quicksilver Barn. EX20 3DS. Est. 1979. Open 8-5. SIZE: Medium. *STOCK: Mercurial wheel and*

Merton continued

stick barometers, 1780-1900, £650-£5,000; aneroid barometers, 1850-1930, £70-£1,200. LOC: Between Hatherleigh and Torrington on A386. PARK: Easy. TEL: 01805 603443; fax - 01805 603344. SER: Valuations; restorations (barometers). VAT: Stan/Spec.

MODBURY, Nr. Ivybridge

Fourteen A

14A Broad St. PL21 0PU. (Bridget Kirke). Est. 1986. Open 10-5. SIZE: Small. *STOCK: Lighting, door furniture, brass fire irons, copper, kitchenalia, 19th C boxes, new English blue and white china, tribal rugs.* LOC: Next to Post Office. PARK: Nearby. TEL: 01548 831136; home - 01548 560055; fax - same.

Quality Box Antiques

at Fourteen A, 14a Broad St. (Marjorie Ridsdill). Est. 1982. Open 10-5, Sun. by appointment. SIZE: Small. *STOCK: White linen and quilts, 19th to early 20th C, £5-£500; coloured embroidered linen, early 20th C, £2-£100; jewellery, silver and flatware, 19th-20th C, £5-£300; small furniture, 19th-20th C, £50-£500.* LOC: Shop next to Post Office. PARK: Nearby. TEL: 01548 831136; home - 01364 72376. FAIRS: Ardingly.

Wild Goose Antiques

34 Church St. PL21 0QR. (Mr and Mrs E. Christopher-Walsh). Open 10-5 and by appointment. CL: Mon. and Wed. *STOCK: General antiques, pictures, porcelain, chandeliers, silver, jewellery.* TEL: 01548 830715; home - 01548 830238. VAT: Stan.

Ye Little Shoppe

1B Broad St. PL21 0PS. (Eric W. Ridsdill). Est. 1990. Open 10-5. CL: Wed. SIZE: Small. *STOCK: Tea, writing and jewellery boxes, 19th C, £40-£350; woodworkers and saddlers tools, 19th C to early 20th C, £10-£150; small furniture and china, to £300; oil lamps, 19th-20th C, £18-£300.* LOC: Main street. PARK: Nearby. TEL: 01548 830732. SER: Restorations (writing boxes, including embossed and gilded leathers). FAIRS: Ardingly.

MONKTON, Nr. Honiton

Pugh's Farm Antiques

Pugh's Farm. EX14 9QH. (G. Garner and C. Cherry). Est. 1974. Open 9.30-5.30, Sun. am. by appointment. SIZE: Large. *STOCK: General antiques including Victorian and Edwardian furniture, beds and country farmhouse tables imported from France.* LOC: A30 2 miles from Honiton. PARK: Easy. TEL: 01404 42860; home - same; fax - 01404 47792. VAT: Stan.

MORCHARD BISHOP, Nr. Crediton

Morchard Bishop Antiques

Meadowbank. EX17 6PD. Resident. (J.C. and E.A. Child). Open by appointment. *STOCK: Mainly metalware boxes and pottery.* LOC: 8 miles west of Crediton, off A377 at Morchard Rd. PARK: Easy. TEL: 01363 877456.

MORETONHAMPSTEAD

The Old Brass Kettle

2-4 Ford St. TQ13 8LN. (H. Clark). Est. 1950. Open 9.30-1 and 2.15-5.30. CL: Sun. except by appointment, and Thurs. SIZE: Medium. *STOCK: Pottery, porcelain and furniture, 19th C.* LOC: A382 from Newton Abbot, B3212 from Exeter. TEL: 01647 440334. SER: Buys at auction. VAT: Spec.

NEWTON ABBOT

The Attic

9 Union St. TQ12 2JX. (G.W. Gillman). Est. 1976. CL: Mon. and Thurs., prior telephone call advisable. SIZE: Medium. *STOCK: General antiques, to £1,000.* LOC: Town centre. PARK: Easy. TEL: 01626 55124. SER: Valuations.

Newton Abbot Antiques Centre

55 East St. TQ12 2JP. (Paul Stockman). Est. 1973. Open every Tues. 9-3. SIZE: 50 stands. *STOCK: Furniture, silver, 18th-19th C pottery and porcelain, Victorian flatback, Staffordshire, jewellery, postcards.* LOC: 100yds. from clock tower. PARK: Through arch. TEL: 01626 215188. Below are listed some of the dealers at this centre. SER: Valuations.

Mrs Adams
China, glass, small furniture.

Sylvia Adams
Shipping goods and china.

Anne
Clocks, small furniture, jewellery and china, bottles, plate, Goss, badges.

Blockley
Decorative objects and furniture.

Bobs
Oak and mahogany furniture.

Caunter
Victoriana, 19th C china and pottery.

Mrs Churchill
Silver, jewellery, furniture, dolls.

Curio Corner
Plate, china, glass, jewellery.

Mrs Forster
Small furniture, plate, pottery and porcelain.

Vyvyan Goode
Furniture and silver, pictures, objets d'art, glass, plate.

Newton Abbot continued

Hendrika
General antiques and china.

Jo Hicks
Furniture, curios, pictures, silver, jewellery, Staffordshire.

H. Hill
Costume, china, glass, fabrics, lace.

B. Hunt
Silver and china, furniture, period tools.

Mrs Jones
China, glass, brass and copper, small furniture.

John Lawrence
Furniture and china, metal toys.

Mrs Lock
General antiques, china and pottery.

M. Morrell
Small china, collectables.

G. Mosdell
Antiquarian books and prints.

P. & D. Antiques
Victorian and shipping furniture; Staffordshire, 18th-19th C.

Prints Etc.
Prints, pictures.

P. Shearman
Furniture, china, brass and copper.

Paul and Dorothy Stockman
Pottery and porcelain, 18th-19th C, furniture, flat back Staffordshire.

Teignmouth Antiques
Cards, coins, paper money.

Village Antiques
Silver, china and furniture.

Liz Wheeleker
General antiques, decor, china, silver, jewellery.

Derick Wilson
Jewellery, shipping goods and furniture.

P. Winchester
Postcards, china.

P. Wright
General antiques, small items.

Mavis Young
Small general antiques, pictures.

NEWTON ST. CYRES, Nr. Exeter

Gordon Hepworth Fine Art

Hayne Farm, Sand Down Lane. EX5 5DE. (C.G. and I.M. Hepworth). Est. 1990. Open Wed.-Sat. during exhibitions or by appointment. SIZE: Large barn - 2 floors. *STOCK: Modern British paintings, post-war and contemporary especially West Country - West Cornwall and St. Ives School, £300-£5,000.* LOC: A377, 3 miles N.W. of Exeter turn left by village sign, into Sand Down Lane, farm entrance on left, after last white house. PARK: Easy. TEL: 01392 851351; home - same.

OKEHAMPTON

Alan Jones Antiques

Fatherford Farm. EX20 1QQ. Est. 1971. Open anytime by appointment. SIZE: Large - warehouse and showroom. *STOCK: Furniture, oak, walnut and mahogany, some pine; copper, brass, barometers, clocks.* LOC: On A30, one mile from Okehampton. PARK: Easy. TEL: 01837 52970; home - 01409 231428. SER: Valuations. VAT: Stan/Spec.

PLYMOUTH

Annterior Antiques

22 Molesworth Rd., Millbridge. PL1 5LZ. (A. Tregenza and R. Mascaro). Est. 1982. Open 9.30-5.30, Sat. 9.30-5, or by appointment. SIZE: Small. *STOCK: Stripped pine, 18th-19th C, £50-£3,000; some painted, mahogany and decorative furniture; brass and iron beds, 19th C, £250-£1,500; decorative small items.* LOC: Follow signs to Torpoint Ferry from North Cross roundabout, turn left at junction of Wilton St. and Molesworth Rd. PARK: Easy. TEL: 01752 558277; home - 01752 562774. SER: Buys at auction; finder. VAT: Stan/Spec.

Antique Fireplace Centre

30 Molesworth Rd., Stoke. PL1 5NA. (Brian Taylor). Est. 1988. Open 10-5 or by appointment. *STOCK: Fire surrounds - timber, marble, slate, cast iron, £100-£3,500; Georgian and Victorian fire grates, £100-£1,500; original accessories including scuttles, coal boxes, fire irons and overmantels, lamps and lanterns.* LOC: 50yds. from Victoria Park, map sent on request. PARK: Easy. TEL: 01752 559441; fax - 01752 605964. SER: Valuations. VAT: Stan/Spec.

Barbican Antiques Centre

82-84 Vauxhall St., Barbican. PL4 0EX. (T. Cremer-Price). Open 9.30-5 every day. SIZE: 60+ dealers. *STOCK: Silver and plate, art pottery, porcelain, glass, jewellery, coins, stamps, clocks, collectables.* PARK: Own. TEL: 01752 201752; fax - same.

Alan Jones Antiques

Applethorn Slade Farm, Near Plympton. PL7 5AS. Resident. Est. 1965. Open by appointment. SIZE: Small. *STOCK: Maritime and scientific*

Plymouth continued

items, navigational instruments, telescopes, optical toys and collectors items. LOC: Off A38, near Plymouth. TEL: 01752 338188.

M. and A. Antique Exporters

44 Breton Side. PL4 0AY. (M. Antonucci). Open 9-5. *STOCK: General antiques.* TEL: 01752 665419; fax - 01752 228058. SER: Imports; exports.

New Street Antique Centre

27 New St., The Barbican. (Turner Properties). Est. 1980. Open 10-5. SIZE: Medium. *STOCK: Clocks, silver, jewellery, weapons, general antiques.* PARK: Nearby. TEL: 01752 661165. VAT: Stan/Spec.

Anne-Marie Scott-Masson

Mount Stone House, Devil's Point. PL1 3RW. *STOCK: Small period pieces, prints, furnishing fabrics and wallpaper.* TEL: 01752 664413. SER: Interior design.

Brian Taylor Antiques

24 Molesworth Rd., Stoke. PL1 5LZ. Est. 1975. Open 10-5 Fri. and Sat., or by appointment. SIZE: Medium. *STOCK: Gramophones, phonographs, mechanical music, radios, 1840-1940, £50-£5,000+; Oriental items including buddhas and thankas, £50-£2,000; clocks, 18th-19th C, £50-£4,000.* LOC: 50yds. from Victoria Park, map sent on request. PARK: Easy. TEL: 01752 569061; home - same; fax - 01752 605964. SER: Valuations; restorations (clocks and gramophones).

Michael Wood Fine Art

Bedford Row, 54 North Hill. PL4 8EU. Est. 1971. Open 9.30-6, other times by appointment. SIZE: Medium. *STOCK: Oils, watercolours, original prints, bronzes, ceramics and art glass, Contemporary, Modern British, Newlyn, St Ives and Victorian, £35-£4,000.* LOC: 200 yds from City Museum & Art Gallery. PARK: Opposite. TEL: 01752 225533; mobile - 0468 960533. SER: Valuations; conservation/preservation advice.

SEATON

Etcetera Etc Antiques

12 Beer Rd. EX12 2PA. (B. Warren and M. Rymer). Est. 1969. Open 10-1 and 2-5. CL: Thurs. SIZE: Medium. *STOCK: General antique furniture, ceramics, glass, brass and decorative items.* PARK: Own. TEL: 01297 21965.

SHALDON, Nr. Teignmouth

Leigh C. Extence

49 Fore St. TQ14 0EA. Open 9.30-1 and 2.15-5. CL: Thurs. and Sat. pm. *STOCK: Clocks, 1730-1880; barometers, 1780-1880; collectables and pictures.* PARK: Outside shop. TEL: 01626 872636; fax - same; mobile - 0585 319226. SER: Buys at auction; clock finding service; horological research. VAT: Spec.

Shaldon continued

Tempus Fugit

16c Fore St. TQ14 0DE. (I. Gregory). Est. 1982. Open 9.30-5, Sat. and Sun. am. by appointment. CL: Thurs. pm. SIZE: Small. *STOCK: Clocks, watches, furniture, paintings, Chinese porcelain, cigarette cards, craftware.* LOC: From A379 take left turn over bridge to Shaldon. On bend turn left into Fore St., shop 75yds on right. PARK: Easy. TEL: 01626 872752. SER: Valuations; repairs/ restoration (clocks, watches, barometers).

W. J. Woodhams

28 Fore St. TQ14 0DE. Resident. Est. 1970. Open 10-5.30. SIZE: Small. *STOCK: Furniture, £5-£5,000; silver and porcelain, bric-a-brac, £5-£200; all 18th-19th C.* PARK: Easy. TEL: 01626 872630. SER: Valuations; restorations (furniture); buys at auction (furniture). VAT: Stan/Spec.

SIDMOUTH

Gainsborough House Antiques

Libra Court, Libra House, Fore St. EX10 8AJ. (K.S. Scratchley). Est. 1935. Open 9-5, Sat. 12.45. CL: Thurs. pm. except by appointment. SIZE: Small. *STOCK: Small general antiques, 1750-1950, £1-£1,000; medals and militaria, 1700 to date, £1-£1,500.* LOC: Down Fore St., 50 yds from seafront, left down York St., entrance to premises on left. PARK: 100 yds. TEL: 01395 514394; home - 01395 515112. SER: Valuations.

The Lantern Shop Gallery

5 New St. EX10 8AP. (Miss J.M. Creeke). Est. 1974. Open 10-4.45. SIZE: Medium. *STOCK: Lighting including table lamps, 1750-1960, £50-£2,000; shades, £50-£250; English porcelain, 1780-1970, £5-£1,500; watercolours and oils, 1800-1950, £15-£2,000; small furniture, decorative items and collectables, 1750-1970, £5-£1,000; topographical and decorative prints, especially East Devon, 1780-1930, maps, 1620-1880, £10-£700.* LOC: Town centre between Fore St. and Market Place. PARK: Nearby - disabled opposite. TEL: 01395 578462. SER: Valuations; restoration/cleaning (as stock); silk lampshade-making. VAT: Stan.

Sidmouth continued

Sidmouth Antiques and Collectors Centre

All Saints Rd. EX10 8ES. Open 10-5, Sun. 2-6. (Easter-Oct). SIZE: 10 dealers. *STOCK: Wide range of antiques and collectables, collectors' records, antiquarian and out of print books.* TEL: 01395 512588.

The Vintage Toy and Train Museum Shop

Sidmouth Antiques and Collectors Centre, All Saints Rd. EX10 8ES. (R.D.N., M.E. and J.W. Salisbury). Open 10-5. *STOCK: Hornby Gauge 0 and Dublo trains, Dinky toys, Meccano and other die-cast and tinplate toys, wooden jig-saw puzzles.* TEL: 01395 512588; home - 01395 513399.

SOUTH BRENT

Philip Andrade BADA LAPADA

White Oxen Manor, Rattery. TQ10 9JX. Usually open 9-5.30, Sat. 9-1, but prior 'phone call is advisable. *STOCK: English town furniture, 18th to early 19th C; interesting objects; all £100-£10,000.* TEL: 01364 72454; fax - 01364 73061.

P.M. Pollak

Moorview, Plymouth Rd. TQ10 9HT. ABA. (Dr. P.M. Pollak). Est. 1973. Open by appointment. SIZE: Small. *STOCK: Antiquarian books especially medicine and science; prints, some instruments, £50-£5,000.* LOC: On edge of village, near London Inn. PARK: Own. TEL: 01364 73457; fax - 01364 72918; e-mail - patrick.pollak@virgin.net. SER: Valuations; buys at auction; catalogues issued, computer searches.

L.G. Wootton Clocks and Watches

2 Church St. TQ10 9AB. Est. 1948. Open by appointment only. *STOCK: Clocks and watches, all periods; small antiques, unusual curios.* LOC: Just off A38. PARK: Easy. TEL: 01364 72553. SER: Valuations; repairs and restorations (clocks).

SOUTH MOLTON

Cobbs Curiosity Shop

24 East St. Est. 1984. Open 10-4. SIZE: Small. *STOCK: Small furniture, curios, jewellery and silver, interesting items, £5-£1,000.* PARK: Easy. TEL: 01769 574104.

The Furniture Market

14a Barnstaple St. EX36 3BQ. (R.M. and V.J. Golding). Est. 1971. Open 10-1 and 2-5, Wed 10-1. SIZE: Large - 20 dealers. *STOCK: Furniture, collectables, silver and glass, to early 20th C, £5-£2,000.* LOC: On old A361, 100 yards from town centre. PARK: Nearby. TEL: 01769 573401. SER: Valuations; buys at auction.

South Molton continued

The Lace Shop

Bay House, 33 East St. EX36 3DF. (Fenela Sadler). Est. 1985. *STOCK: Lace, 17th-20th C, £5-£1,000; linens, patchwork, bridal veils, head-dresses and dresses, 19th-20th C, £10-£4,000.* PARK: Easy. TEL: 01769 573184; home - same. SER: Valuations; restorations (handmade lace and embroidery); bridal gowns to order. VAT: Stan/Spec.

Memory Lane Antiques

100 East St. EX36 3DF. (D. Mason). Open 10-5. SIZE: 3 showrooms. *STOCK: General antiques including china, glass, silver, jewellery, plate, brass, copper and furniture.* TEL: 01769 574288.

Treasure Trove Antiques

101 East St. EX36 3DF. (D. Mason). Open 10-5. SIZE: 2 small showrooms. *STOCK: China, glass, clocks, kitchenalia and all small items.* TEL: 01769 574288.

J.R. Tredant

50/50a South St. EX36 4AG. Usually open. *STOCK: General antiques.* TEL: 01769 573006; home - 01769 572416. SER: Valuations.

STOCKLAND, Nr. Honiton

Colystock Antiques

Rising Sun Farm. EX14 9NH. (D.C. McCollum). Est. 1975. Open seven days. SIZE: Large. *STOCK: Pine and oak including English, Irish and Continental, 18th-19th C.* TEL: 01404 861271. SER: Container packing and documentation; courier.

TAVISTOCK

King Street Curios

5 King St. PL19 0DS. (T. and P. Bates). Est. 1979. Open 9-5. SIZE: Medium. *STOCK: Pine furniture, postcards, cigarette cards, china, glass, general collectables, jewellery, to £100.* LOC: Town centre.

TEIGNMOUTH

Charterhouse Antiques

1B Northumberland Place. TQ14 8DD. (A. and S. Webster). Est. 1974. Open 11-1 and 2.30-4, Sat. 11-1. CL: Mon. and Thurs. SIZE: Small. *STOCK: Pottery and porcelain, especially commemoratives, 18th C to 1930s, £1-£200; Victorian jewellery and small silver, 1800-1930, £5-£400; small furniture, paintings, 1780-1900, £10-£500.* LOC: If facing sea, turn right at Post Office, third left, shop round corner on left. PARK: Easy and nearby. TEL: 01626 54592.

Teignmouth continued

Extence Antiques
2 Wellington St. TQ14 8HH. (T.E. and L.E. Extence). Est. 1928. Open 9.30-1 and 2-5.30. SIZE: Medium. *STOCK: Furniture, 18th to early 19th C; jewellery, silver, objets d'art, clocks.* PARK: Limited. TEL: 01626 773353. VAT: Stan/Spec.

The Old Passage
13a Bank St. TQ14 8AW. (G. and R.H. Doel). Est. 1981. Open 11-1 and 2.30-4.30. CL: Mon. and Thurs. SIZE: Small. *STOCK: Porcelain, pottery, glass, treen and silver, mainly 19th-20th C, £5-£200.* LOC: Main street. PARK: Nearby. TEL: 01626 772634; home - 01626 776196. SER: Restorations (furniture, French polishing). FAIRS: Livestock Market, Exeter.

Timepiece
125 Bitton Park Rd. TQ14 9BZ. (Clive and Willow Pople). Est. 1988. Open 9.30-5.30, Sat. 9.30-6. CL: Mon. SIZE: Medium. *STOCK: Country furniture (including pine), clocks, 19th C, £25-£2,000; kitchenalia and collectables, 19th-20th C, £1-£100.* LOC: On main Newton Abbot road, next to Bitton Park. TEL: 01626 770275.

TIVERTON

Barrington Antiques
8-10 Barrington St. EX16 6PU. Est. 1967. Open 10-5. CL: Thurs. p.m. SIZE: Large. *STOCK:*

Tiverton continued

Period furniture. PARK: Easy. TEL: 01884 256141. SER: Oak furniture made to order; restoration (furniture and period property). VAT: Stan/Spec.

Bygone Days Antiques
40 Gold St. EX16 6PY. (N. Park). Open 10-1 and 2-5. CL: Thurs. *STOCK: Furniture, Victorian and Georgian; watercolours and oils.* TEL: 01884 252832; home - 01884 243615.

TOPSHAM, Nr. Exeter

The Ark Antiques & Design
76 Fore St. EX3 0HQ. Est. 1985. Open Tues.-Sat. SIZE: Large. *STOCK: Country and decorative furniture.* LOC: Centre of Fore St., next to Lloyds Bank. PARK: Easy. TEL: 01392 874301/873561; fax - 01392 873738. SER: Large breakfronted architectural furniture made to order; antiqued garden formal and country reconstituted stoneware; wholesale and export; shipping and packing. VAT: Spec. *Export and Trade.*

Mere Antiques
13 Fore St. EX3 0HF. Resident. (Marilyn Hawkins). Est. 1986. Open 9.30-5.30, Sat. 10-4.30, Sun. by appointment. SIZE: Small. *STOCK: English and Continental porcelain, 19th C, £50-£5,000; Japanese satsuma, 19th-20th C, £350-£5,000; furniture, 18th-19th C, £200-£5,000.*

Topsham continued

PARK: Easy and nearby. TEL: 01392 874224; fax - same. SER: Valuations. FAIRS: NEC; LAPADA; Earls Court; Guildford. VAT: Spec.

Mulberry House
6 & 7 Fore St. EX3 0HF. (M. J. Sellers). Est. 1989. Open 10-5.30. SIZE: Large (7 units). *STOCK: 19th C dining tables, £1,000-£10,000; desks, bookcases, £500-£5,000; occasional furniture, porcelain and smalls, £25-£400.* LOC: Off junction 30, M5. PARK: Public at rear. TEL: 01392 876321; fax - 01392 876297. SER: Valuations; restorations (furniture). FAIRS: NEC.

Pennies
40 Fore St. (Penelope and Michael Clark). Open 10-5. CL: Wed. pm. *STOCK: Antiques and collectables.* TEL: 01392 877020. VAT: Stan/-Spec.

TORQUAY

Birbeck Gallery
45 Abbey Rd. TQ2 5NQ. Est. 1952. Open by appointment. SIZE: Medium. *STOCK: Paintings and prints, 19th to early 20th C, to £10,000; general antiques.* LOC: 200yds. up Abbey Rd. from main street roundabout at Torquay G.P.O. PARK: Easy. TEL: 01803 291658/297144/324449. SER: Valuations; restorations; buys at auction.

Great Western Antiques
Torre Station, Newton Rd. TQ2 5DD. (J. Jefferies). Est. 1975. Open 10.30-5.30, including Sun. SIZE: Large. *STOCK: Victorian and Edwardian furniture, architectural and marine items, £1-£40,000.* LOC: Railway station on main road into town. PARK: Easy. TEL: 01803 200551.

Sheraton House Antiques
Sheraton House, 1 Laburnum Row, Torre. TQ2 5QX. (I.S. Hutton). Open 9.45-4.45, Wed. and Sat. 9.45-4. *STOCK: General antiques.* TEL: 01803 293334.

Spencers Antiques
187 Union St., Torre. TQ1 4BY. *STOCK: General antiques.* TEL: 01803 296598.

TOTNES

Collards Books
4 Castle St. TQ9 5NU. (B. Collard). Est. 1970. Open 10-5, restricted opening in winter. *STOCK: Antiquarian and secondhand books.* LOC: Opposite castle. PARK: Nearby. TEL: Home - 01548 550246.

Fine Pine Antiques
Woodland Rd., Harbertonford. TQ9 7SX. Est. 1973. Open 9.30-5. *STOCK: Stripped pine and country furniture.* TEL: 01803 732465; fax - 01803 732771. SER: Restorations; stripping.

Totnes continued

Past and Present
94 High St. TQ9 5SN. (James Sturges). CL: Lunch-times. SIZE: Large. *STOCK: Furniture, £100-£2,000; smalls, bygones, £5-£300; all 18th-20th C.* LOC: A38. PARK: 150 yards. TEL: 01803 866086. FAIRS: Sandown Park.

WHIMPLE, Nr. Exeter

Anthony James Antiques
Brook Cottage, The Square. EX5 2SL. Open by appointment. *STOCK: 17th-19th C furniture and works of art.* LOC: A30 between Exeter and Honiton. PARK: Easy. TEL: 01404 822146. SER: Valuations. VAT: Spec.

WOODBURY, Nr. Exeter

Woodbury Antiques
Church St. EX5 1HN. (H. Ballingull). Est. 1966. Open 10-5, Mon. and Sat. 10-1. CL: Wed. and Thurs. SIZE: Large. *STOCK: Victorian and Edwardian furniture and items.* PARK: Easy. TEL: 01395 232727. VAT: Stan/Spec.

YEALMPTON, Nr. Plymouth

Colin Rhodes Antiques LAPADA
15 Fore St. PL9 2JN. Est. 1969. *STOCK: 17th to early 19th C furniture, paintings and objets d'art.* TEL: 01752 881170/862232. SER: Valuations. VAT: Spec.

Dorset

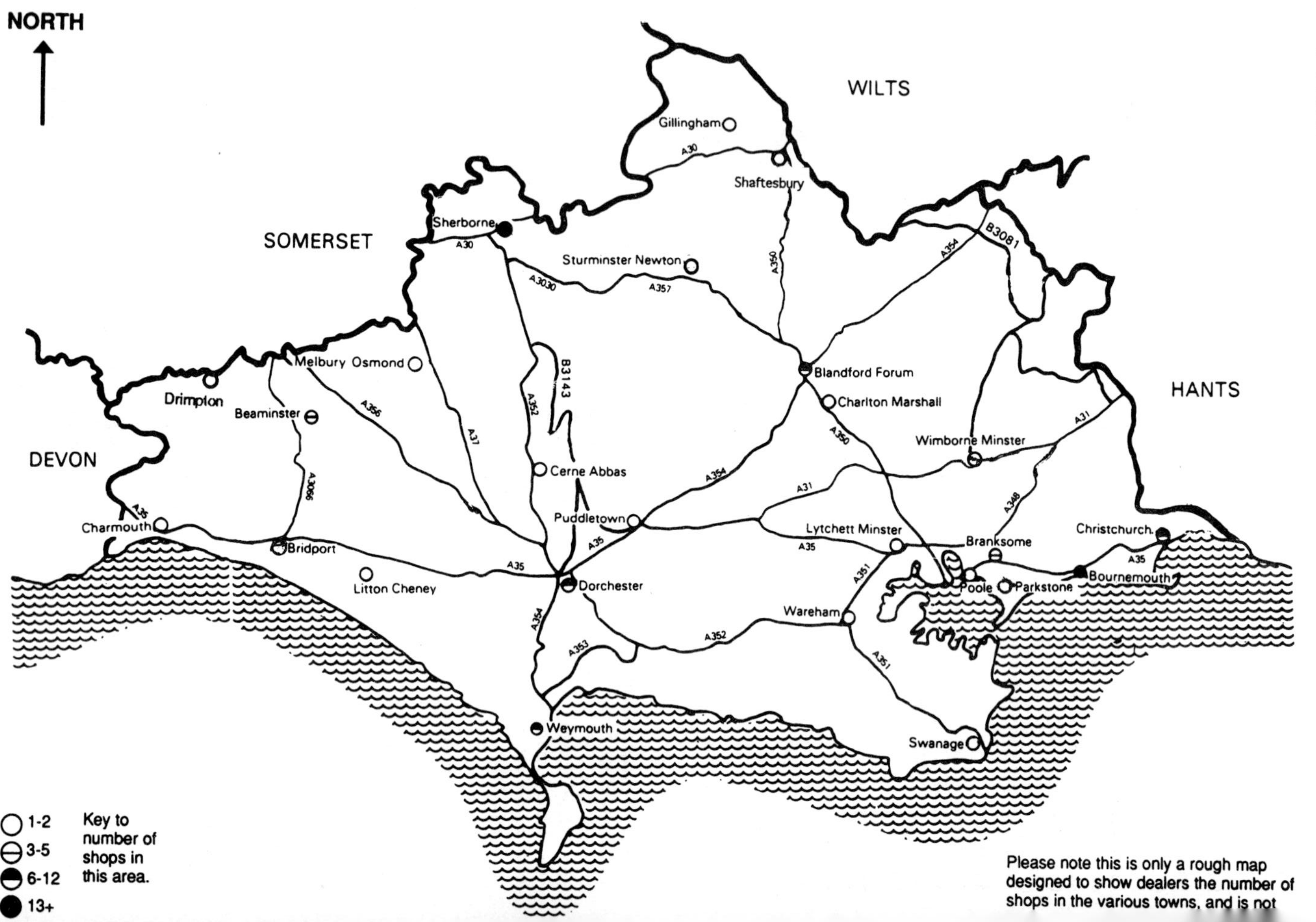

NORTH
WILTS
SOMERSET
DEVON
HANTS
Gillingham
Shaftesbury
Sherborne
Sturminster Newton
Melbury Osmond
Drimpton
Beaminster
Blandford Forum
Charlton Marshall
Wimborne Minster
Cerne Abbas
Puddletown
Charmouth
Bridport
Litton Cheney
Dorchester
Lytchett Minster
Branksome
Christchurch
Bournemouth
Poole
Parkstone
Wareham
Weymouth
Swanage
A30
A350
A354
B3081
A3030
A357
B3143
A352
A356
A37
A3066
A31
A348
A35
A351
A353
1-2
3-5
6-12
13+
Key to number of shops in this area.
Please note this is only a rough map designed to show dealers the number of shops in the various towns, and is not

BEAMINSTER

Beaminster Antiques

4 Church St. DT8 3JA. (Mrs T.P.F. Frampton). Est. 1982. Open 10-5. CL: Wed. SIZE: Small. *STOCK: Small furniture, £20-£1,400; silver, £10-£800; objets d'art, porcelain, boxes, 18th C to Art Deco, £5-£1,400; brass and pictures, 18th C to 1950s, £1-£1,000; thimbles and sewing objects, collectables.* Not Stocked: Coins and medals. LOC: Just off square. PARK: Easy. TEL: 01308 862591; home - 01935 891395.

Cottage Antiques

17 The Square. DT8 3AU. Open 10-5.30 or by appointment. CL: Wed. *STOCK: Furniture, paintings, clocks, prints, decorative items.* LOC: A3066. TEL: 01308 862136.

Good Hope Antiques

2 Hogshill St. DT8 3AE. (D. Beney). Est. 1980. Open 10-1 and 2-5. CL: Tues. and Wed. SIZE: Medium. *STOCK: Clocks especially longcase, bracket and wall, barometers, £500-£5,000; furniture, £200-£2,500; all 18th-19th C.* LOC: Town square. PARK: Easy. TEL: 01308 862119. SER: Valuations; restorations (clocks, including dials; barometers). VAT: Spec.

BLANDFORD FORUM

A & D Antiques

21 East St. DT11 7DU. (A. and D. Edgington). Est. 1981. Open 10-5, Sun. by appointment. CL: Mon. and Wed. pm. SIZE: Small. *STOCK: Silver, Georgian to Victorian, £50-£2,000; Lalique, £100-£5,000.* LOC: Town centre on main east-west route (one-way system). PARK: Easy. TEL: 01258 455643; home - same. VAT: Spec.

Ancient and Modern Bookshop (including Garret's Antiques)

84 Salisbury St. DT11 7QE. (Mrs P. Davey). Open 9.30-12.30 and 1.30-5. CL: Wed. *STOCK: Books and small antiques.* TEL: 01258 455276.

Antiques for All

Higher Shaftesbury Rd. Est. 1998. Open 9.30-5, Sun. 10.30-3.30. SIZE: Large. *STOCK: Furniture, 18th-20th C, £100-£10,000; ceramics and collectables, 18th-20th C, £5-£1,000; clocks and barometers, oil lamps, 18th-19th C, £100-£1,000.* LOC: A354 and A350 roundabout on by-pass; town exit, 3rd turning on right, 1st left. PARK: Easy. TEL: 01258 458011; fax - 01258 458022. SER: Buys at auction (furniture, oil lamps and ceramics).

Milton Antiques

Market Place. DT11 7HU. Open 9-5. CL: Wed. SIZE: Medium. *STOCK: Furniture, 18th-19th C, £50-£2,000; decorative items, 18th-20th C, £5-£200.* LOC: Opposite parish church, adjacent to town museum. PARK: Easy - Market Square. TEL: 01258 450100. SER: Valuations; restorations including polishing.

Blandford Forum continued

Stour Gallery

28 East St. DT11 7DR. (R. Butler). Est. 1966. Open 10-1 and 2-4, Sun. by appointment. CL: Mon. and Wed. pm. SIZE: Medium. *STOCK: Watercolours, oils and pastels, early 19th to 20th C, £50-£3,000.* LOC: On right-hand side of High St., on one way system. PARK: Opposite. TEL: 01258 456293; home - 01258 453174. SER: Restorations (oil, watercolours, wash line mounts); framing.

Strowger of Blandford

13 East St. DT11 7DU. Est. 1962. Open by appointment. SIZE: Medium. *STOCK: Period furniture and collectables.* LOC: A354. PARK: Easy. TEL: 01258 861138.

BOURNEMOUTH

Antiques and Furnishings

339 Charminster Rd. BH8 9QR. (P. Neath). Open 10-5.30. *STOCK: Furniture including Victorian stripped pine; brass, copper, china, textiles and decorative objects.* TEL: 01202 527976.

Bournemouth continued

Arcade Antiques

6 Westbourne Arcade, Westbourne. BH4 9AY. (Richard Samuel). Est. 1984. Open 10-4.30, Wed. 10-2, Fri. and Sat. 9.30-5. SIZE: Medium. *STOCK: General antiques, furniture, collectors' items, Poole pottery.* LOC: Just off A35 between Bournemouth and Poole. PARK: Easy. TEL: 01202 764800; fax - 01202 769537. SER: Valuations. VAT: Spec.

The Artist Gallery

1086 Christchurch Rd., Boscombe East. BH7 6BQ. Open 9.30-5. CL: Wed. *STOCK: Limited edition prints and original works of art - David Shepherd, Sir William Russell Flint, E.R. Sturgeon, Lowry, Gordon King and others.* PARK: Forecourt. TEL: 01202 417066.

Blade and Bayonet

884 Christchurch Rd., Boscombe. BH7 6DJ. Resident. (L.M. Martin). Est. 1982. Open 10-12 and 1-5. CL: Mon. SIZE: Medium. *STOCK: Militaria, mid 17th to 20th C, £75-£485.* LOC: Near Pokesdown station. PARK: Easy. TEL: 01202 429891. SER: Valuations; restorations (mainly cleaning weapons). FAIRS: Bournemouth, Southsea, Bovington Tank Museum, Midhurst, Dorking, Farnham.

Boscombe Militaria

86 Palmerston Rd., Boscombe. BH1 4HU. (E.A. Browne). Est. 1981. Open 10-1 and 2-5. CL: Wed. *STOCK: German militaria, £10-£500; British and American militaria, £5-£300, all 1914-1918 and 1939-1945.* LOC: Just off Christchurch Rd. PARK: Easy. TEL: 01202 304250; fax - 01202 733696. FAIRS: Farnham; Cheshunt; major South of England Arms.

Boscombe Models and Collectors Shop

802c Christchurch Rd., Boscombe. BH7 6DD. (Sylvia Hart). Open 10-1 and 2-4.30. CL: Wed. *STOCK: Collectors' toys, 19th-20th C, £1-£1,000.* LOC: On Somerset Rd. TEL: 01202 398884.

D & J Antiques

873 Christchurch Rd., Pokesdown. (J. Mortimer). Open 10-5, Wed. 10-1.30. SIZE: Medium. *STOCK: 18th C furniture, lighting, china, pictures.* PARK: Easy. TEL: 01202 417277; home - 01202 763935. SER: Valuations.

Peter Denver Antiques

36 Calvin Rd., Winton. BH9 1LN. (P. Denver-White). Est. 1961. Open 10-5. CL: Mon. SIZE: Small. *STOCK: Furniture, porcelain, pictures, glass, Georgian-Edwardian, £5-£800.* LOC: Off main Wimborne Rd. PARK: Easy. TEL: 01202 532536; home - 01202 513911.

Richard Dunton Antiques LAPADA

920 Christchurch Rd., Boscombe. BH7 6DL. Resident. (R.D. Dunton). Est. 1980. Open by appointment only. SIZE: Large. *STOCK: Antiques and decorative accessories - Staffordshire, majolica, glass, paintings, brass, oak and pine, sculpture and garden furniture, £20-£50,000.* PARK: Easy. TEL: 01202 425963; fax - 01202 418456. SER: Valuations. VAT: Stan/Spec. *Trade Only.*

Bournemouth continued

Lionel Geneen Ltd LAPADA

781 Christchurch Rd., Boscombe. BH7 6AW. BDADA. Est. 1902. Open 9-5, Sat. 9-12, other times by appointment. CL: Lunchtimes. SIZE: Large. *STOCK: English, Continental and Oriental furniture, china and works of art including bronzes, enamels, ivories, jades, Art Nouveau and Art Deco, all 17th C to early 20th C.* LOC: Main road through Boscombe. PARK: Easy. TEL: 01202 422961; home - 01202 520417. SER: Valuations. VAT: Stan/Spec.

H.L.B. Antiques

139 Barrack Rd. BH23 2AW. (H.L. Blechman). Est. 1969. SIZE: Large. *STOCK: Collectable items.* PARK: Easy. TEL: 01202 429252/482388.

Hampshire Gallery LAPADA

18 Lansdowne Rd. BH1 1SD. Est. 1971. *STOCK: Paintings and watercolours, 17th to early 20th C.* TEL: 01202 551211. SER: Valuations; restorations. VAT: Spec.

Hardy's Clobber

874 Christchurch Rd., Boscombe. BH7 6DQ. (J.W. Hardy). Open 10-5. *STOCK: Clothing and fabrics, from Victorian.* TEL: 01202 429794.

Hardy's Collectables

862 Christchurch Rd., Boscombe. BH7 6DQ. (J. Hardy). Open 10-5. SIZE: 20 dealers. *STOCK: Art Deco and Art Nouveau glass and 50's collectables especially Poole pottery.* TEL: 01202 422407/303030.

Libra Antiques

916 Christchurch Rd. Est. 1967. Open 10-5.30. CL: Wed. pm. SIZE: Medium. *STOCK: Furniture, Art Nouveau, silver and plate, copper, brass, shipping goods.* PARK: Opposite. TEL: 01202 427615. VAT: Stan.

G.B. Mussenden and Son Antiques, Jewellery and Silver

24 Seamoor Rd., Westbourne. BH4 9AR. Est. 1948. Open 9-5. CL: Wed. SIZE: Medium. *STOCK: Antiques, jewellery, silver.* LOC: Central Westbourne, corner of R.L. Stevenson Ave. PARK: Easy. TEL: 01202 764462. SER: Valuations. VAT: Stan/Global/Spec.

Geo. A. Payne and Son Ltd

742 Christchurch Rd., Boscombe. BH7 6BZ. FGA. (H.G. and N.G. Payne). Est. 1946. Open 9-5.30. SIZE: Small. *STOCK: Jewellery, 19th-20th C, £10-£3,000; silver, 18th-20th C, £30-£1,000; plate, £10-£200.* LOC: Opposite Browning Ave. and Chessel Ave. PARK: Browning Ave. TEL: 01202 394954. SER: Valuations; gemstone testing; restorations (silver, jewellery, clocks, watches). VAT: Stan/Spec.

Bournemouth continued

R.E. Porter

2-6 Post Office Rd. BH1 1BA. Est. 1934. Open 9.30-5. SIZE: Medium. *STOCK: Silver including early antique spoons, Georgian, £20-£5,000; jewellery, pot lids, Baxter and Le Blond prints, clocks including second-hand.* Not Stocked: Furniture, arms, armour, carpets. LOC: Walking from the Square, take the Old Christchurch Rd., then the first turning on the left. PARK: 300yds. at top of Richmond Hill. TEL: 01202 554289. SER: Valuations. VAT: Stan/Spec.

Portique

15/16/17 Criterion Arcade. BH1 1BU. Est. 1971. *STOCK: Silver, jewellery, Derby china, glass paperweights, cloisonné, clocks.* LOC: Coming from the square take the Old Christchurch Rd. from roundabout, arcade entrance is between first and second turnings on left. TEL: 01202 552979. SER: Repairs and restoration (silver and jewellery). VAT: Stan/Spec.

Sainsburys of Bournemouth Ltd LAPADA

23-25 Abbott Rd. BH9 1EU. Est. 1918. Open 8-1 and 2-6, appointment advisable. CL: Sat. *STOCK: Furniture especially bookcases and dining tables, 18th C, to £15,000.* PARK: Own. TEL: 01202 529271; home - 01202 763616; fax - 01202 510028. VAT: Stan/Spec.

Sandy's Antiques

790 Christchurch Rd., Boscombe. BH7 6DD. BDADA. SIZE: 2 shops + warehouse. *STOCK: Victorian, Edwardian and shipping goods.* TEL: 01202 301190; evenings - 01202 304955. VAT: Stan/Spec.

Peter Stebbing

7 Post Office Rd. BH1 1BB. (P.M. Stebbing). Est. 1960. Open 9.30-5. SIZE: Small. *STOCK: Furniture, £25-£1,000; glass, silver, £1-£100; metalware, jewellery; all 18th-19th C.* LOC: Next to Head Post Office. PARK: 200yds. TEL: 01202 552587. SER: Valuations.

Sterling Coins and Medals

2 Somerset Rd., Boscombe. BH7 6JH. (W.V. Henstridge). Est. 1969. Open 9.30-4. CL: Wed. pm. SIZE: Small. *STOCK: Coins, medals, militaria, World War II German items.* LOC: Next to 806 Christchurch Rd. TEL: 01202 423881. SER: Valuations. VAT: Stan.

D.C. Stuart Antiques

34-40 Poole Hill. BH2 5PS. Open 9-5.30. *STOCK: General antiques, hand-carved reproduction furniture.* TEL: 01202 555544.

M.C. Taylor

995 Christchurch Rd., Boscombe East. BH7 6BB. MAPH, CMBHI, BDADA. (Mark Taylor). Est. 1982. SIZE: Small. *STOCK: Clocks, barometers and music boxes, 19th C, £500-£5,000.* LOC:

Bournemouth continued

Opposite St. James' School and Kings Park entrance. PARK: Easy. TEL: 01202 429718. SER: Valuations; restorations. VAT: Stan/Spec.

Victorian Chairman

883 Christchurch Rd., Boscombe. BH7 6AU. (M. Leo). Open 9.30-5. *STOCK: Furniture especially chairs, sofas and tables.* TEL: 01202 420996. SER: Upholstery restoration.

Yesterday Tackle and Books

42 Clingan Rd., Boscombe East. BH6 5PZ. (David and Alba Dobbyn). Open by appointment. *STOCK: Fishing tackle and associated items including taxidermy; books.* TEL: 01202 476586. SER: Catalogues issued.

BRANKSOME

Allen's (Branksome) Ltd

447/449 Poole Rd. BH12 1DH. (D.L and P.J. D'Ardenne). Est. 1948. Open 9-5.30. SIZE: Large. *STOCK: Furniture.* TEL: 01202 763724; fax - 01202 763724. VAT: Stan/Spec.

Branksome Antiques

370 Poole Rd. BH12 1AW. (B.A. Neal). Est. 1973. Open 10-5. CL: Wed. and Sat. SIZE: Medium. *STOCK: Scientific and marine items, furniture and general small items.* PARK: Easy. TEL: 01202 763324; home - 01202 679932. SER: Buys at auction (as stock). VAT: Stan/Spec.

David Mack Antiques

434-436 Poole Rd. and 21 Crommer Rd. BH12 1DF. Est. 1963. Open 9-5.30 or by appointment. SIZE: Large. *STOCK: 18th-19th C tables, chairs, display cabinets, desks, bureaux, bookcases; later furniture and shipping goods.* LOC: 2 doors from Branksome rail station. PARK: Own. TEL: 01202 760005; fax - 01202 765100. SER: Restorations. VAT: Stan/Spec.

BRIDPORT

Batten's Jewellers

26 South St. DT6 3NQ. (R. Batten). Open 9.30-5. *STOCK: Jewellery and silver.* TEL: 01308 456910. SER: Valuations; repairs.

Bridport Antiques Centre

5 West Allington. DT6 5BJ. Open 9-5. SIZE: 10 dealers. *STOCK: Pine and country furniture, lace, linen, porcelain, glass, books, prints, watercolours, oils, postcards, jewellery, classical garden ornaments, taxidermy.* TEL: 01308 425885.

Hobby Horse Antiques

29 West Allington. DT6 5JB. Resident. (J. Rodber). Est. 1948. Open mornings and all day Fri. and Sat. SIZE: Medium. *STOCK: Mechanical antiques, toys, trains, porcelain, brass, copper, bygones, silver, jewellery.* LOC: West Bridport on south side of A35 between Dorchester and Exeter. PARK: Nearby. TEL: 01308 422801.

Bridport continued

PIC's Bookshop
11 South St. DT6 3NR. CL: Thurs. pm. *STOCK: Books, engravings and prints.* TEL: 01308 425689.

Tudor House Antiques LAPADA
88 East St. DT6 3LL. (P. Knight and D. Burton). Est. 1940. Open 9-1 and 2-5.30, Sun. by appointment. SIZE: Small. *STOCK: General antiques.* LOC: Left hand side of main street from Dorchester. PARK: Easy. TEL: 01308 427200; home - same. VAT: Stan/Spec.

CERNE ABBAS

Cerne Antiques
DT2 7LA. (I. Pulliblank). Est. 1972. Open 10-1 and 2-5, Sun. 2-5. CL: Mon. and Fri. SIZE: Medium. *STOCK: Silver, porcelain, furniture including unusual items, mainly 19th C, £1-£400.* LOC: A352. PARK: Easy. TEL: 01300 341490; home - same.

CHARLTON MARSHALL, Nr. Blandford

Zona Dawson Antiques
The Old Clubhouse. DT11 9PA. Est. 1958. Open 10-6. CL: Mon. *STOCK: Mainly furniture, clocks, 18th-19th C.* TEL: 01258 453146.

CHARMOUTH, Nr. Bridport

Charmouth Antique Centre
The Street. DT6 6QH. (S.R. Dodd). Open 10-5. CL: Sun. and Mon. SIZE: Medium - 10 dealers. *STOCK: General antiques; Shelley a speciality.* TEL: 01297 560122; mobile - 0378 107994.

CHRISTCHURCH

J.L. Arditti
88 Bargates. BH23 1QP. Est. 1964. Open 9-5.30. CL: Sun. except by appointment. SIZE: Medium. *STOCK: Oriental carpets and rugs, 18th to early 20th C, £500-£8,000.* LOC: From town centre take road towards Hurn airport, left side on corner of Bargates and Twynham Avenue. PARK: Twynham Avenue. TEL: 01202 485414. SER: Valuations; restorations; cleaning (Persian rugs). VAT: Stan/Spec.

Christchurch Carpets
55/57 Bargates. BH23 1QE. (J. Sheppard). Est. 1963. Open 9-5.30. SIZE: Large. *STOCK: Persian carpets and rugs, 19th-20th C, £100-£1,000.* LOC: Main road. PARK: Adjacent. TEL: 01202 482712. SER: Valuations. VAT: Stan/Spec.

Hamptons
12 Purewell. BH23 1EP. (G. Hampton). Open 10-6. CL: Sat. am. SIZE: Large. *STOCK: Furniture, 18th-19th C; general antiques, clocks, china, instruments, metalware, oil paintings, Chinese and Persian carpets and rugs.* PARK: Easy. TEL: 01202 484000.

Christchurch continued

M. & R. Lankshear Antiques
149 Barrack Rd. BH23 2AP. (M.I. Lankshear). Open 9.30-6. *STOCK: General antiques, especially militaria and swords; collectables, postcards, cigarette cards, medals and paintings.* PARK: Forecourt. TEL: 01202 473091. SER: Valuations.

The Old House Antiques & Collectors Centre
24 Bargates. BH23 4QL. (Ms M. Whitcher and Mr R. Wolstenholme). Open 10-5, Sat. 9.30-5. SIZE: Medium. *STOCK: General antiques and collectables - china, glass, metals, furniture, pictures, 19th-20th C, £10-£250.* PARK: Easy. TEL: 01202 475555.

The Old Stores
West Rd., Bransgore. BH23 8BQ. (W. and Mrs J. Collier). Open by appointment. *STOCK: General antiques.* TEL: 01425 672616; fax - same.

CRANBORNE, Nr.Wimborne

Tower Antiques
The Square. BH21 5PR. (P.W. Kear and P. White). Est. 1975. Open 8.30-5.30. CL: Sat. *STOCK: Georgian and Victorian furniture.* TEL: 01725 517552.

DORCHESTER

Box of Porcelain
51d Icen Way. DT1 1EW. (R.J. and Mrs. S.Y. Lunn). Est. 1984. Open 10-5. *STOCK: Porcelain including Worcester, Doulton, Belleek.* LOC: Close town centre, near Dinosaur Museum. TEL: 01305 250856; fax - same; e-mail - rlunn@compuserve.com. SER: Valuations; Beswick/Doulton collectors' finder service.

Colliton Antique Centre
Colliton St. DT1 1XH. Open daily, Sun. by appointment. SIZE: 14 dealers. *STOCK: 18th-20th C furniture, £25-£5,000; brass, bric-a-brac, pictures, china, pine, clocks, jewellery and silver, toys.* LOC: By town clock. PARK: Easy. TEL: 01305 269398/260115. SER: Restorations (cabinet work and metalware). VAT: Stan/Spec.

Michael Legg Antiques
8 Church St. DT1 1JN. (E.M.J. Legg). Open 9-5.30 or any time by appointment. SIZE: Medium. *STOCK: 17th-19th C furniture, porcelain, pictures, silver, glass.* TEL: 01305 264596. SER: Lectures on the Arts. VAT: Stan/Spec.

Legg of Dorchester
Regency House, 51 High East St. DT1 1HU. (W. and H. Legg). Est. 1930. *STOCK: General antiques, Regency and decorative furniture, stripped pine.* TEL: 01305 264964. VAT: Stan/Spec.

Dorchester continued

John Walker Antiques BADA

52 High West St. DT1 1UT. Open 9.30-5 or by appointment. SIZE: Small. ***STOCK: Early furniture, textiles, metalwork, ceramics, wood carvings, 16th-18th C; British folk art, 16th-19th C.*** **LOC: Main street. PARK: Easy. TEL: 01305 260324. SER: Valuations; buys at auction. VAT: Spec.**

Words Etcetera

2 Cornhill. DT1 1BA. PBFA, ABA. (Julian Nangle). Est. 1970. Open 9.30-5.30. SIZE: Medium. *STOCK: Antiquarian and quality second-hand books and prints; remainders on all subjects.* LOC: Close to museum. TEL: 01305 251919; fax - 01305 266898; home - 01258 820415. SER: Buys at auction (books). FAIRS: ABA London (June).

DRIMPTON, Nr. Crewkerne

Drimpton Antiques

The Old Barn, Netherhay. DT8 3RH. (Cliff Gibbs). Est. 1982. Open 10-6 including Sun. SIZE: 2 showrooms. *STOCK: Furniture, general antiques and smalls, £5-£2,000.* PARK: Easy. TEL: 01308 867597. SER: Valuations; restorations; French polishing; buys at auction.

GILLINGHAM

Talisman LAPADA

The Old Brewery, Wyke. SP8 4NW. Open 9-5, Sat. 10-4. SIZE: Large. ***STOCK: Unusual and decorative items, garden furniture, architectural fittings, 18th-19th C; English and Continental furniture.*** **TEL: 01747 824423/824222; fax - 01747 823544. VAT: Stan/Spec.**

LITTON CHENEY, Nr. Dorchester

F. Whillock

Court Farm. DT2 9AU. Open by appointment. *STOCK: Maps and prints.* TEL: 01308 482457. SER: Framing.

LYTCHETT MINSTER

Old Button Shop Antiques

BH16 6JF. (T. Johns). Est. 1970. Open Tues.-Fri. 2-5, Sat 11-1. *STOCK: Small antiques, brass, copper, curios, unusual items, and antique Dorset buttons.* TEL: 01202 622169.

MELBURY OSMOND, Nr. Dorchester

Hardy Country

Mearon View. DT2 0NA. Est. 1980. SIZE: Large. *STOCK: Edwardian and Victorian country furniture and antiques, £40-£800.* LOC: Off A37. PARK: Easy. TEL: 01935 83440.

PARKSTONE, Nr. Poole

D.J. Burgess

116-116a Ashley Rd. BH14 9BN. Open 9.30-5.30. CL: Wed. and Thurs. *STOCK: Clocks, watches, some furniture.* TEL: 01202 730542. SER: Restorations (clocks and watches).

Wiffen's Antiques

95/101 Bournemouth Rd. (C. A. Wiffen). Est. 1960. Open 9-5.30. SIZE: Large. *STOCK: Furniture including shipping; porcelain, pictures, silver and plate, clocks, brass and copper, jewellery, statuary and garden items.* TEL: 01202 736567; fax - 01202 717305. SER: Valuations; restorations.

Christopher Williams Antiquarian Bookseller

19 Morrison Ave. BH12 4AD. *STOCK: Books especially antiques, art, bibliography, cookery, wine, topography.* TEL: 01202 743157. FAIRS: Various book and craft. *Postal only.*

POOLE

G.D. and S.T. Antiques

(G.D. and S.T. Brown). Open by appointment. *STOCK: General antiques.* TEL: 01202 676340.

PUDDLETOWN, Nr. Dorchester

Antique Map and Bookshop

32 High St. DT2 8RU. (C.D. and H.M. Proctor). Open 9-5. *STOCK: Antiquarian and secondhand books, maps, prints and engravings.* TEL: 01305 848633; fax - 01305 848992. SER: Postal.

SHAFTESBURY

Mr. Punch's Antique Market

33 Bell St. SP7 8AE. Open 10-6. CL: Mon. SIZE: Large. *STOCK: Wide variety of general antiques, fine art and collectables. Also Punch and Judy collection.* LOC: On corner with Muston's Lane. PARK: Easy 100 yards. TEL: 01747 855775; fax - same. SER: Valuations; restorations; deliveries. *Trade Only.*

Shaston Antiques

16A Bell St. SP7 8AE. Resident. (J. D. Hine). Est. 1997. Open 9.30-1 and 2-5, Wed. 9.30-1. SIZE: Small. *STOCK: Furniture, 18th-19th C, £300-£5,000.* LOC: From town centre, turn right opposite Grosvenor Hotel into Bell St. TEL: 01747 850405; home - same. SER: Restorations (furniture).

SHERBORNE

Abbas Antiques

17 Newlands. DT9 3JG. Open 9-5. *STOCK: Small collectables and furniture.*

Sherborne continued

Antiques of Sherborne
1 The Green. DT9 3HZ. (C. and L. Greenslade). Open 10-5. *STOCK: Furniture, upholstery, decorative items, linen, rugs and collectables.* TEL: 01935 816549; home - 01963 210737. SER: Restorations (furniture); buys at auction; commission sales.

Jasper Burton Antiques
23 Cheap St. DT9 3PU. Est. 1964. Open 9-1 and 2-5. CL: Wed. SIZE: Medium. *STOCK: General antiques, especially furniture.* PARK: Easy. TEL: 01935 814434. VAT: Stan/Spec.

Dodge and Son LAPADA
28-33 Cheap St. DT9 3PU. (S. Dodge). Open 9-5.30. SIZE: Large. *STOCK: Furniture, all periods, mainly Georgian.* PARK: At rear. TEL: 01935 815151. VAT: Stan/Spec.

Greystoke Antiques
Swan Yard, Off Cheap St. DT9 3AX. (F.L. and N.E. Butcher). Est. 1970. Open 10-4.30. *STOCK: Silver, Georgian, Victorian and later; some 19th C pottery and porcelain.* LOC: Off main street. PARK: Adjacent to Swan Yard, or outside shop. TEL: 01935 812833. VAT: Stan/Margin/Global.

Heygate Browne Antiques
South St. DT9 3NG. (M. and W.Heygate Browne). Open 10-5. SIZE: Large. *STOCK: 18th-19th C furniture, pottery and porcelain.* LOC: Off Cheap St. towards station. PARK: Easy. TEL: 01935 815487. SER: Valuations; restorations. VAT: Stan/Spec.

The Nook
South St. DT9 3LX. (H.B. Bruton). *STOCK: General antiques - furniture, china, glass, brass and copper.* TEL: 01935 813987.

Pine on the Green
The Green. DT9 4EW. (S. Dodge). Open 9-5.30. SIZE: Medium. *STOCK: Restored antique pine furniture; period oak dressers and tables, elm furniture, walnut, fruitwood and chestnut pieces, antique and reconstituted, English and continental.* LOC: Off A30, 1st shop on left hand side at the top of the town. PARK: Easy. TEL: 01935 815216.

Piers Pisani Antiques
The Music House, The Green. DT9 3HX. Open 10-5. SIZE: Medium. *STOCK: 17th-19th C furniture and furnishings.* TEL: 01935 815209; fax - same. SER: Restorations; upholstery; chairs copied; cabinet-making. VAT: Spec.

Georgina Ryder LAPADA
The Music House, The Green. DT9 3HX. Resident. Est. 1977. Open 10-5. SIZE: Medium. *STOCK: 17th-18th C tapestries; 18th-19th C French furniture; decorative objects.* PARK: Easy. TEL: 01935 815209. SER: Valuations; restorations (upholstery). FAIRS: Olympia; LAPADA. VAT: Spec.

Sherborne continued

Sherborne Antique Centre
Mattar Arcade, 17 Newlands. DT9 3JG. Est. 1965. Open 9-5. SIZE: 5 shops. *STOCK: Fine arts, painting, furniture, rugs, objets d'art, jewellery, gold, silver.* LOC: From A30 via Greenhill. PARK: Easy. TEL: 01935 813464.

The Swan Gallery
51 Cheap St. DT9 3AX. (S. and Mrs K. Lamb). Est. 1977. Open 9.30-5, Wed. 9.30-1. SIZE: Large. *STOCK: Watercolours, 18th to early 20th C; prints, maps, antiquarian and secondhand books.* PARK: Easy, at rear. TEL: 01935 814465; fax - 01308 868195. SER: Valuations; restorations (paintings, watercolours and prints); framing. VAT: Stan/Spec.

Henry Willis (Antique Silver)
38 Cheap St. DT9 3PX. Est. 1973. Open 10-5. SIZE: Small. *STOCK: Silver, 17th-19th C, £15-£1,500.* LOC: Town centre, just off A30. PARK: Nearby. TEL: 01935 816828. SER: Valuations; restorations (silver); buys at auction (silver). FAIRS: Olympia (June). VAT: Stan/Spec.

STURMINSTER NEWTON

Quarterjack Antiques
Bridge St. DT10 1BZ. (Jon Neilson). Est. 1969. SIZE: Small. *STOCK: 18th-19th C glassware, furniture, pictures, walking sticks and horse brasses.* TEL: 01258 471344; home - 01258 472558; e-mail - 106012.1473@compuserve.com/; internet - http://ourworld.compuserve.com./homepages/jonneilson.

Tom Tribe and Son
Bridge St. DT10 1BZ. CMBHI. Resident. Open 9-5, Sat. 9-1 and by appointment. *STOCK: Longcase and mantle clocks, barometers.* PARK: At side of shop. TEL: 01258 472311. VAT: Stan/Spec.

SWANAGE

Georgian Gems Antique Jewellers
28 High St. BH19 2NU. NAG. (Brian Barker). Est. 1971. Open 9.30-1 and 2.30-5 or by appointment. SIZE: Small. *STOCK: Jewellery, £5-£2,000; silver, £5-£500; both from 1700.* LOC: Town centre. PARK: Nearby. TEL: 01929 424697. SER: Valuations; repairs; gem testing; special search.

Reference Works
12 Commercial Rd. BH19 1DF. (B. Lamb). Open by appointment. *STOCK: Reference books on ceramics, all subjects, new and out-of-print, £5-£600; some small British porcelain £10-£400.* TEL: 01929 424423; fax - 01929 422597; e-mail - RWrefworks@aol.com. SER: Mail order, catalogue available; six newsletters each year; ceramic research and consultancy. FAIRS: Details on request.

WAREHAM

Heirlooms Antique Jewellers and Silversmiths

21 South St. BH20 4LR. FGA, DGA, RJDip. (Mr. M. and Mrs G. Young). Est. 1986. Open 9.15-5. CL: Wed. SIZE: Medium. *STOCK: Jewellery, £30-£1,000; silver, £20-£500; both Georgian to Edwardian.* LOC: On main thoroughfare. PARK: At rear. TEL: 01929 554207. SER: Valuations; restorations; repairs; gem testing.

WEYMOUTH

Books Afloat

66 Park St. DT4 7DE. (J. Ritchie). Open 9.30-5.30. *STOCK: Rare and secondhand books especially nautical; maritime ephemera, liner memorabilia, ship models, paintings, prints.* LOC: Near railway station. PARK: Nearby. TEL: 01305 779774.

Books & Bygones

Great George St. DT4 7AR. (Mrs Denise Nash). Est. 1981. Open 11-5.30, Sun. 12-5. SIZE: Medium. *STOCK: Books including antiquarian, 50p to £1,000; antiques and collectables, from 18th C, £1-£750; ephemera, from 50p.* LOC: Near King's statue, on esplanade. PARK: Easy. TEL: 01305 777231; home - 01305 771529. SER: Valuations; buys at auction.

Finesse Fine Art

9 Coniston Crescent. DT3 5HA. (T. Wraight and W. Flint). Open by appointment only. *STOCK: Pre-war motoring accessories - metal mascots and Lalique glassware, including mascots, fine bronzes, picnic hampers, £500-£20,000.* TEL: 01305 854286; fax - 01305 852888; mobile - 0973 86937.

Nautical Antique Centre

3a Hope Square. DT4 8TR. (D.C. Warwick). Est. 1989. Open 10-1 and 2-5 - prior 'phone call advisable, Sat., Sun. and Mon. by appointment. SIZE: Medium. *STOCK: Exclusively nautical, including sextants, logs, clocks, flags, blocks, old sails, rope, bells, ship models, telescopes, ship badges, portholes and memorabilia, also restaurant/pub decorative items, 19th-20th C, £5-£2,000.* LOC: Off Brewers Quay, adjacent harbour. PARK: Nearby. TEL: 01305 777838; home - 01305 783180. SER: Buys at auction (nautical items).

North Quay Collector's Centre

26a Trinity Rd. DT4 8TJ. (R.A. Shorey). Open 10-5. SIZE: 11 dealers. *STOCK: General antiques and collectables.* TEL: 01305 779313.

Park Antiquities

37 Park St. DT4 7DF. (F. and Mrs. J.R. Ballard). *STOCK: General antiques, porcelain, small furniture, treen, advertising items.* LOC: Near railway station. PARK: Nearby. TEL: 01305 787666.

Weymouth continued

The Treasure Chest

29 East St. DT4 8BN. (P. Barrett). Open 10-5. CL: Wed. pm. *STOCK: Maps, prints, coins, medals; army, RN and RAF badges.* PARK: Next door. TEL: 01305 772757. SER: Lost medals replaced; medal mounting - full size or miniature, brooches and new ribbons.

WIMBORNE MINSTER

Bryan Chew

Quercus, 27 Leigh Rd. Est. 1985. Open 10.30-4.30, Sun. and Mon. by appointment. SIZE: Small. *STOCK: Oak and country furniture, clocks and paintings, £1,000-£10,000.* LOC: From A31 follow signs to town centre, left after cricket ground and pub, premises 100 yards on left, opposite car park. PARK: Easy and opposite. TEL: 01202 886275. SER: Valuations; restorations (oak and country furniture); buys at auction (oak and country furniture). FAIRS: Petworth, Harrogate, Snape, Arley Hall, Hoghton Tower, Chavenage. VAT: Spec.

Christina Doggrell Antiques

52 King St. BH21 1EB. Est. 1983. Open 10-5, Mon. and Sat. 10-4. CL: Wed. SIZE: Small. *STOCK: General antiques including porcelain and glass, silver and jewellery, paintings, boxes and furniture, mainly 19th C, £5-£500; some 20th C collectables - Poole, Doulton and commemorative.* LOC: Next to back entrance of Minster. PARK: Nearby. TEL: 01202 881988. SER: Restorations. FAIRS: Kempton Park; Sandown Park.

Four Seasons Gallery

24 West Borough. BH21 1NF. (Nigel and Maria Cox). Est. 1996. Open Wed.- Sat. 10-5.30. SIZE: Small. *STOCK: Small 18th-19th furniture, paintings, collectables; contemporary art gallery with regular exhibitions.* LOC: Near minster. PARK: Easy and nearby. TEL: 01202 882204; fax - 01202 881105.

J.B. Antiques

10A West Row. (J. Beckett). Est. 1978. Open 10-4, Fri. and Sat. 9.30-4. CL: Wed. SIZE: Small. *STOCK: Copper, £5-£360; brass, £1-£350; furniture, £30-£1,200; all 18th-20th C.* LOC: 2 mins. from Sq. PARK: Nearby. TEL: Home - 01202 882522. SER: Valuations; restorations (metalware); buys at auction (copper).

Wimborne Antiques and Collectables Centre

21 Newborough, Off Poole Rd. BH21 1RB. (J. Spendier). Est. 1990. Open Thurs.-Sun. 9-5 and Bank Holidays. SIZE: Large. *STOCK: Victorian furniture, collectables and bric-a-brac.* LOC: Corner of Grove Rd and Newborough. PARK: Nearby. TEL: 01202 841251.

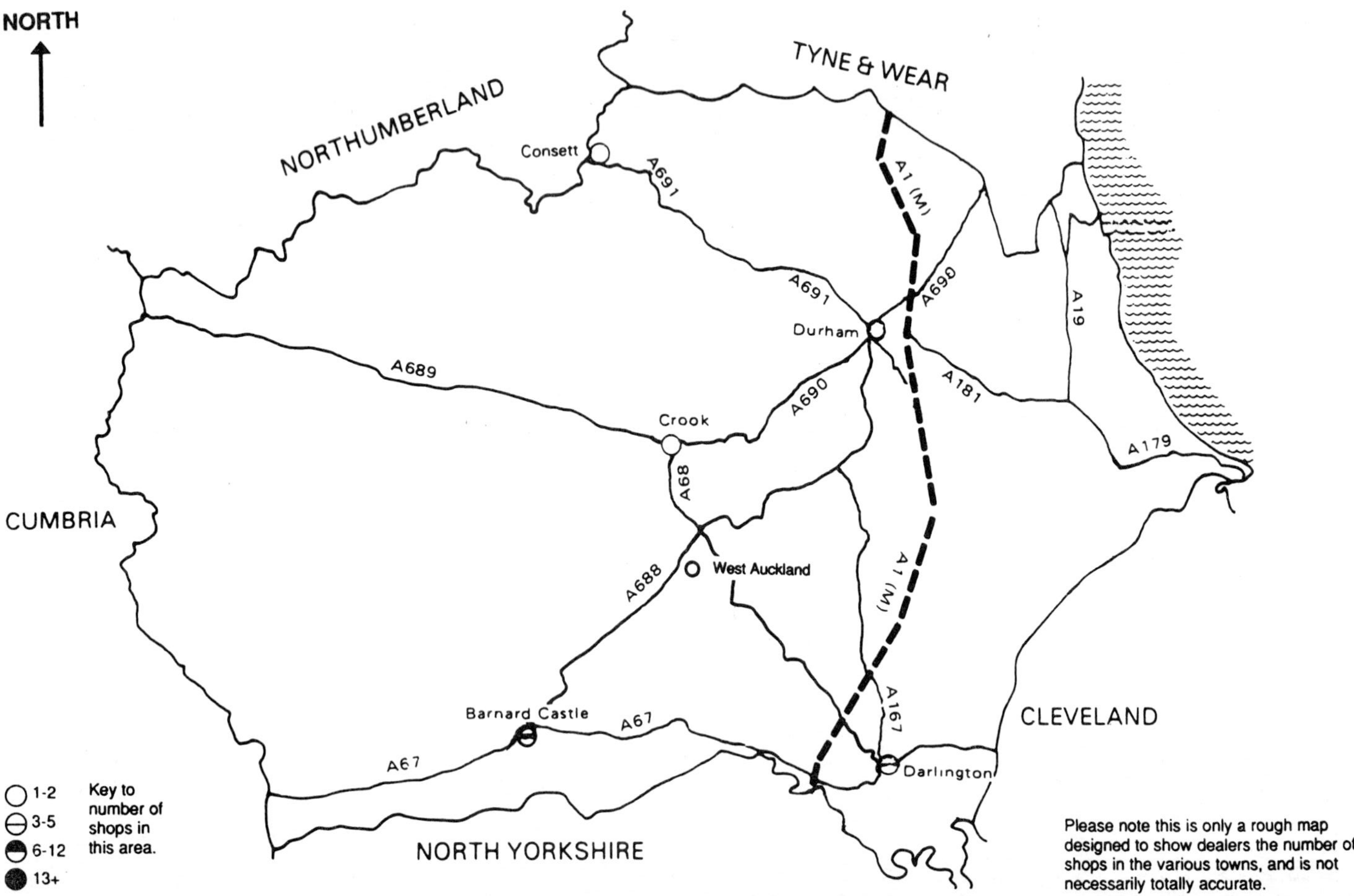
NORTH
NORTHUMBERLAND
TYNE & WEAR
CUMBRIA
CLEVELAND
NORTH YORKSHIRE
Consett
Durham
Crook
West Auckland
Barnard Castle
Darlington
A691
A691
A1 (M)
A1 (M)
A690
A690
A19
A689
A181
A179
A68
A688
A167
A67
A67
1-2
3-5
6-12
13+
Key to number of shops in this area.
Please note this is only a rough map designed to show dealers the number of shops in the various towns, and is not necessarily totally accurate.

BARNARD CASTLE

Brown's Antiques LAPADA

34 The Bank. DL12 8PN. Resident. (Philip and Judy Brown). Est. 1978. Open 10-5, Sun., Mon. and Tues. by appointment only. SIZE: Medium. *STOCK: Georgian mahogany, 18th-19th C oak, £500-£1,000+; pottery and paintings, 19th C, £100-£1,000.* LOC: A66 off A1M at Scotch Corner heading west. PARK: Easy. TEL: 01833 637891. SER: Valuations; restorations (furniture, pictures, pottery and porcelain, carpets and tapestries). VAT: Spec.

The Collector

Douglas House, The Bank. DL12 8PH. (Robert A. Jordan). Est. 1970. Open Sat. 10-5 or by appointment. SIZE: Medium. *STOCK: Early furniture and objects, decorative interior fittings and Eastern rugs.* TEL: 01833 637783; fax - same. SER: Restorations (especially metal work, early furniture and interiors).

Grant's Antiques

The Ancient Manor House, The Bank. DL12 8PN. Resident. (Carl and Stephanie Grant). Est. 1976. Open 10-5. SIZE: Small. *STOCK: Oak furniture, £100-£5,000; pottery, £20-£500; rugs, £50-£1,000; all 17th C; interesting items.* LOC: Main road. PARK: Nearby. TEL: 01833 637437. SER: Valuations; restorations; buys at auction. VAT: Stan.

Joan and David White Antiques

Neville House, 10 The Bank. Est. 1975. Open Thurs.-Sat. 11-5. *STOCK: Georgian, Victorian and export furniture and decorative items.* LOC: 100yds. from Market Cross. TEL: 01833 638329; home - 01325 374303. VAT: Stan/Spec.

CONSETT

Harry Raine Antiques

Kelvinside House, Villa Real Rd. DH8 6BL. Appointment advisable. SIZE: Large. *STOCK: General antiques.* TEL: 01207 503935.

CROOK

Jo Patterson Antiques

DL15 0LZ. Est. 1968. Open by appointment only. SIZE: Small. *STOCK: Furniture and smalls, 19th-20th C.* LOC: 6 miles from A68. TEL: 01388 746586.

DARLINGTON

S. Brown and Sons 'The Popular Mart'

26 Hollyhurst Rd. DL3 6HT. Est. 1976. Open 9.30-5. CL: Wed. pm. and Sat. pm., except by appointment. SIZE: Large. *STOCK: General antiques, from late 19th C, £5-£500.* LOC: From town centre, along Woodlands Rd. to Hollyhurst Rd., shop adjacent to Memorial Hospital. PARK: Easy. TEL: 01325 354769; home - 01325 355490. SER: Valuations; buys at auction.

Darlington continued

Robin Finnegan (Jeweller)

83 Skinnergate. DL3 7LX. Est. 1974. Open 10-5.30. SIZE: Medium. *STOCK: Jewellery, general antiques, coins and medals, £1-£2,000.* TEL: 01325 489820. SER: Valuations. VAT: Stan.

Alan Ramsey Antiques LAPADA

Unit 10-11 Dudley Rd, Yarm Road Industrial Estate. DL1 4GG. Est. 1973. Open Mon., Tues., Thurs. and Fri. 9.30-4, or by appointment. SIZE: Warehouse. *STOCK: Victorian, Edwardian and Georgian furniture; interesting pine.* PARK: Easy. TEL: 01325 361679; home - 01642 711311; mobile - 0402 523246. VAT: Stan/Spec. *Trade Only.*

DURHAM

J. Shotton Antiquarian Books, Prints and Coins

89 Elvet Bridge. DH1 3AG. Est. 1967. Open 9.30-5. CL: Mon. *STOCK: Antiquarian books, prints, maps and coins.* TEL: 0191 386 4597.

WEST AUCKLAND

Eden House Antiques

10 Staindrop Rd. DL14 9JX. (Chris and Margaret Metcalfe). Est. 1978. Open daily including Sun. SIZE: Small. *STOCK: Clocks, 18th-19th C, £50-£1,500; furniture, 18th-20th C, £250-£750; bric-a-brac, 19th-20th C, £25-£75; good quality oak, walnut, pine and mahogany reproduction furniture.* LOC: A68, approximately 7 miles west of A1M. PARK: Easy. TEL: 01388 833013; home - same. SER: Valuations; restorations (clocks and furniture); buys at auction (clocks and furniture).

Lawrence Stephen Lowry, Canal Scene with figures, signed, 1937, 10½in. x 13¼in., £2,700. Andrew Hartley Fine Arts.

From a feature on Saleroom Prices which appeared in the April 1998 issue of **Antique Collecting**

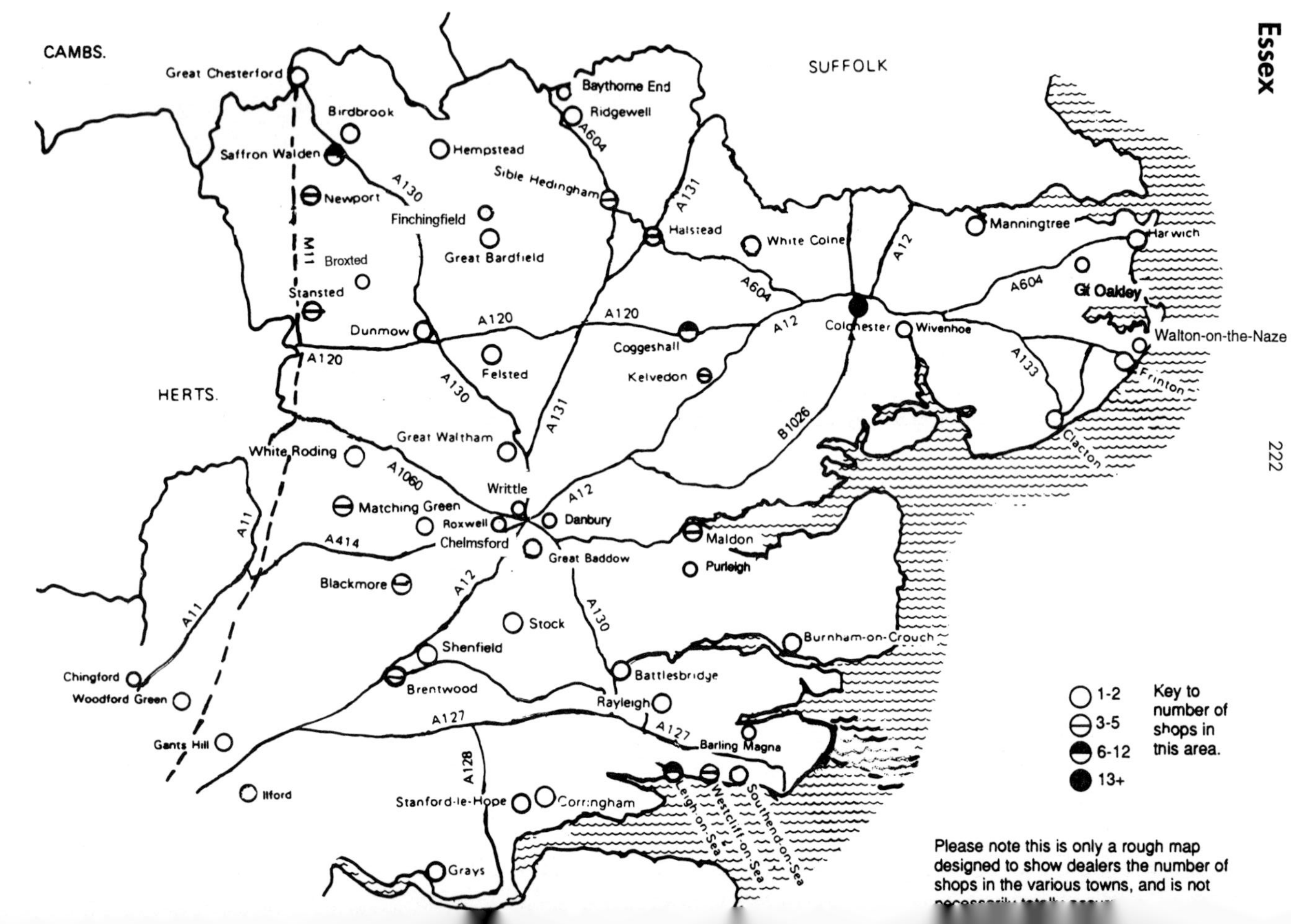
NORTH
CAMBS.
SUFFOLK
HERTS.
Great Chesterford
Birdbrook
Saffron Walden
Newport
Broxted
M11
Stansted
Hempstead
A130
Sible Hedingham
Baythorne End
Ridgewell
A604
Finchingfield
Great Bardfield
Halstead
A131
White Coine
A604
Colchester
A12
Manningtree
Harwich
A604
Gt Oakley
Walton-on-the-Naze
Frinton
Wivenhoe
A133
Clacton
Dunmow
A120
A120
Coggeshall
Kelvedon
A12
B1026
A120
Felsted
A130
A131
Great Waltham
White Roding
A1060
Writtle
A12
Danbury
Matching Green
Roxwell
Chelmsford
Great Baddow
Maldon
Purleigh
A11
A414
Blackmore
A12
A11
Stock
A130
Burnham-on-Crouch
Shenfield
Battlesbridge
Brentwood
Rayleigh
A127
A127
Barling Magna
Chingford
Woodford Green
Gants Hill
Ilford
A128
Stanford-le-Hope
Corringham
Leigh-on-Sea
Westcliff-on-Sea
Southend-on-Sea
Grays
1-2
3-5
6-12
13+
Key to number of shops in this area.
Please note this is only a rough map designed to show dealers the number of shops in the various towns, and is not

ABRIDGE

Revival

Coach House, Market Place. RM4 1UA. (R. Y. Jefferson). Est. 1988. Open 11-5.30 including Sun. CL: Fri. SIZE: Large. *STOCK: Furniture, Georgian to Deco, £20-£3,000; china and glass, silver, 1800-1960, £5-£500.* LOC: From London - off M11, junction 5, turn right then left on to A113. From M25, junction 26 follow A121, then B172. PARK: Opposite. TEL: 01992 814000; fax - 01992 814300. SER: Valuations; restorations (furniture and upholstery).

BARLING MAGNA

Domino Antiques

Potash Cottage, Barling Rd. SS3 0LY. Resident. (S. Parish). By appointment only. *STOCK: English porcelain including Royal Worcester, £100-£4,000; watercolours, £300-£2,500.* TEL: 01702 218691; fax - same. FAIRS: Wakefield Ceramic.

BATTLESBRIDGE

Battlesbridge Antique Centre

SS11 7RF. SIZE: Over 80 units within adjacent premises (see below). *STOCK: Wide range from large furniture to jewellery, all periods with specialist dealers for most items.* LOC: A130, mid-way between Chelmsford and Southend. Junction 29, M25, east on A127 to A130, then north for 3 miles. By rail: Liverpool St.-Southend-on-Sea, change at Wickford for Battlesbridge. PARK: Own. SER: Restorations (furniture); container facilities; nationwide and overseas delivery service.

Battlesbridge continued

Cromwell House Antique Centre

TEL: Management : Jim Gallie - 01268 575000; ground floor dealers - 01268 762612; first floor dealers - 01268 734030.

Haybarn and Bridgebarn Antique Centres

(J. P. Pettitt). TEL: 01268 763500/735884.

Muggeridge Farm Buildings

(Jim Gallie). TEL: 01268 575000.

The Old Granary Antique and Craft Centre

(Jim Gallie). TEL: Office - 01268 575000; showrooms - 01268 764197.

Farmhouse Antiques

Maltings Rd. SS11 7RF. EADA. (Ian F. Vince). Open Wed.-Sun. 10-5. *STOCK: Furniture and smalls.* LOC: Battlesbridge Antique Centre A130. TEL: 01268 561586 or 01245 400046.

BAYTHORNE END

Swan Antiques

The Swan. CO9 4AF. (Mr and Mrs K. Mercado). Est. 1983. Open 9.30-6 including Sun. SIZE: Medium. *STOCK: Furniture, 18th-19th C and some Edwardian, £50-£2,000; porcelain, 19th C, £5-£1,000; small silver and collectables, 19th-20th C, £5-£500.* LOC: A1017 (formerly A604) junction with A1092 to Clare and Long Melford. PARK: Easy. TEL: 01440 785306; home - same. SER: Valuations; restorations. FAIRS: Newark and Ardingly.

BIRDBROOK, Nr. Halstead

I. Westrope

The Elms. CO9 4AB. Est. 1958. Open 9-5, Sat. 10-1, or by appointment. *STOCK: Furniture, china, dolls house furniture, garden ornaments including birdbaths, fountains, statues, animals, etc.* LOC: A604. TEL: 01440 785365; evenings - 01440 785426.

BLACKMORE, Nr Ingatestone

Blackmore Antiques & Craft Centre

Horsefayre Green, Fingrith Hall Rd. CM4 0RL. (David Lee). Est. 1988. Open 10-5 including Sun. SIZE: Large. *STOCK: Period furniture, clocks, books and collectables.* LOC: Just off A144. PARK: Easy. TEL: 01277 821475; fax - 01277 823661; home - same. SER: Valuations; restorations.

Hay Green Antiques

Hay Green Farmhouse. CM4 0QE. (T. Harding). Open 9.30-5.30. CL: Mon. *STOCK: Pine, some mahogany and Victorian furniture.* TEL: 01277 821275.

Megarry's and Forever Summer

Jericho Cottage, The Duckpond Green. CM4 0RR. EADA. (Peter and Judi Wood). Est. 1986. Open 10-6 including Sun.; winter - open 11-5 including Sun. CL: Wed. SIZE: Medium. *STOCK: Furniture, mainly 18th-19th C, some 20th C, £60-£3,500; ceramics, glass, treen and metalware, 19th-20th C, £5-£200; small silver and plate, jewellery and collectables, 19th-20th C, £5-£100; pine, 19th to early 20th C, £75-£1,000.* LOC: From A12, turn left at war memorial, premises behind Bull garden. PARK: Own. TEL: 01277 821031; home - 01277 822170. SER: Valuations; restorations (furniture including French polishing, clocks and jewellery).

BRENTWOOD

Brandler Galleries

1 Coptfold Rd. CM14 4BM. (J. Brandler). Est. 1973. Open 10-5.30, Sun. by appointment. CL: Mon. SIZE: Medium. *STOCK: British pictures, 20th C, £100-£30,000.* LOC: Near Post Office. PARK: Own at rear. TEL: 01277 222269 (24 hrs); fax - 01277 222786. SER: Valuations (photographs); restorations (picture cleaning, relining, framing); buys at auction (pictures); 2-3 free catalogues annually.

Brentwood continued

Neil Graham Gallery

11 Ingrave Rd. CM15 8AP. EADA. FATG. Est. 1977. CL: Mon. SIZE: Large. *STOCK: 19th to early 20th C watercolours, oils and prints, £50-£1,000; Victorian and Edwardian occasional furniture, £100-£1,500; silver, pottery and porcelain, 19th-20th C, £25-£500.* LOC: Near junction of Wilson's Corner, town centre. PARK: Easy and High St. TEL: 01277 215383; fax - same. SER: Valuations; restorations (paintings); buys at auction. FAIRS: NEC Spring and Summer. VAT: Stan/Spec.

Simpsons - Bespoke Carvings

449 Ongar Rd. CM15 9JG. (S. Yardy). Open by appointment. *STOCK: Mirrors - antique including pine and new hand-carved; decorative pieces.* TEL: 01277 374541.

BROXTED

Church Hall Farm Antique & Craft Centre

Church Hall Farm. CM6 2BZ. (Jan and Tony Wildman). Est. 1996. Open 10-6 including Sun. SIZE: Large - 60+ dealers. *STOCK: Wide range of general antiques, from smalls to large furniture, £1-£1,500+.* LOC: B1051 next to Whitehall conference centre. PARK: Easy. TEL: 01279 850858; home and fax - same.

BURNHAM ON CROUCH

Quay Antiques

28 High St. CM0 8AA. (C. McMullan). Est. 1961. Open 10-5 or by prior appointment. CL: Mon., Tues., Wed. *STOCK: Paintings, prints, china, glass, Victoriana, jewellery, small furniture.* TEL: Home - 01621 782468.

CHELMSFORD

Hutchison Antiques

163 Main Rd., Broomfield. EADA. (G. Hutchison). Est. 1980. Open 11-5.30, Sun. by appointment. CL: Mon. SIZE: Medium. *STOCK: Furniture, 18th-19th C, £300-£1,000+; china, mainly 19th C, from £50; paintings, from 19th C, from £100.* LOC: On main road, near Broomfield hospital. PARK: Easy.TEL: 01245 441184. SER: Valuations; restorations (as stock).

CHINGFORD

Nicholas Salter Antiques

8 Station Approach, Station Rd. E4 7AZ. Est. 1971. Open 9.30-5, Fri. and Sat. 9.30-6. CL: Thurs. SIZE: Large. *STOCK: Furniture, 1850-1930, £150-£1,500; china and linen, 1870-1950, £30-£150.* LOC: Next door to North Chingford station. PARK: Easy. TEL: 0181 529 2938.

CLACTON-ON-SEA

L.R. Sharman

80B Rosemary Rd. CO15 1TG. Est. 1973. Open 9.30-5.15. CL: Wed. SIZE: Small. *STOCK: Furniture, 19th C decorative arts, £100-£5,000; jewellery, bronzes, clocks, music boxes, militaria.* LOC: Town centre. PARK: Own. TEL: 01255 424620. SER: Valuations; jewellery repairs.

COGGESHALL

Antique Metals

9A East St. CO6 1SH. (M.C. Chaplin). Est. 1959. Open 9-5, Sun. 12-5. *STOCK: Brass, copper and polished steel, especially fenders and fireside equipment; lighting including oil lamps.* TEL: 01376 562252; fax - same.

Argentum Antiques

1 Church St. CO6 1TU. EADA. (Mrs. Dianne M. Carr). Open 10-5. CL: Tues. and Wed. SIZE: Medium. *STOCK: Silver and Old Sheffield plate, 19th-20th C, £100-£1,000; furniture, mainly oak, 17th-19th C, £200-£2,000; decorative items, object d'art, garden ornaments, 19th C.* LOC: Between A120 and A12, village centre. PARK: Nearby. TEL: 01376 561365. VAT: Spec.

Coggeshall Antiques

Doubleday Corner. CO6 1NJ. Open 10-5, Sun. 2-5. SIZE: Large. *STOCK: Furniture, paintings and decorative items, 18th-19th C.* LOC: A120 opposite White Hart Hotel. PARK: At rear. TEL: 01376 562646; home - 01245 256027.

Elkin Mathews

16 Stoneham St. CO6 1TT. (D.C. Muir). Est. 1887. Open 9.30-1 and 2-4.30, Sat. 10-1 and 2-5. CL: Wed. SIZE: Medium. *STOCK: Antiquarian and secondhand books, 50p-£1,000.* LOC: Just off A120 between Colchester and Braintree. PARK: Own, at rear. TEL: 01376 561730. SER: Valuations; restorations; buys at auction. FAIRS: Major London. VAT: Stan.

English Rose Antiques

7 Church St. CO6 1TU. (Mark J. Barrett). Est. 1983. Open 10-1 and 2-5.30 including Sun., Wed. by appointment. SIZE: Medium. *STOCK: English and Continental pine including dressers, chests, tables and wardrobes, 19th C, £50-£500; fruitwood, ash and elm country furniture and kitchenalia.* LOC: In village centre. PARK: Loading or 50 yds. TEL: 01376 562683; home - same. SER: Valuations; restorations (cabinet work, small repairs, stripping and finishing).

Lindsell Chairs

11 Market Hill. CO6 1TS. (T.J.L. and A.M. Martin). Est. 1982. Open 10.30-6. SIZE: Large. *STOCK: Chairs and other seating, some tables, mid-18th C to 1914, £100-£4,000+.* Not Stocked: Windsor, caned, rush seated or commode chairs. LOC: Town centre. PARK: Nearby. TEL: 01376 562766; home - 01371 870222. SER: Restorations. VAT: Stan/Spec.

Coggeshall continued

Mark Marchant (Antiques)

3 Market Sq. CO6 1TS. Resident. Est. 1960. Open 11-5, Sun. 2.30-5.30. SIZE: Small. *STOCK: Clocks, barometers and music boxes only.* LOC: A120. PARK: Easy. TEL: 01376 561188. SER: Valuations; restorations; buys at auction. VAT: Spec.

Partners in Pine

63/65 West St. CO6 1NS. Resident. (W.T. Newton). Open 7 days 10-6. *STOCK: Victorian stripped pine.* TEL: 01376 561972.

Times Past

5A Church St. CO6 1TU. (Victoria Waine). Est. 1981. Open 10-5. CL: Mon. and Wed. SIZE: Medium. *STOCK: Art Deco and Art Nouveau, glass, china, metalware, lighting and small furniture, £5-£1,000; Clarice Cliff, Cooper, Shelley, figurines, Lalique, Sabino, Vasart, Monart.* TEL: 01376 563600.

COLCHESTER

101 Antiques

101 Crouch St. CO3 3HA. (Mrs S.P. Edwards). Est. 1969. Open 9.30-4. CL: Thurs. SIZE: Small. *STOCK: Glass, china, metalware and furniture, 19th-20th C, £1-£500.* LOC: Almost opposite the old Essex County Hospital on Lexden Rd. PARK: Easy. TEL: 01206 549150.

Badger Antiques

The Old House, The Street, Elmstead Market. CO7 7AA. Resident. (A. Johnson). Est. 1977. Open 9.30-5.30, Sun. by appointment. SIZE: Medium. *STOCK: Furniture, pine, ceramics, glass, lace, linen and unusual bygones.* LOC: 4 miles from Colchester on old A133 Clacton road. PARK: Easy. TEL: 01206 822044. SER: Valuations; restorations (furniture and clocks).

Barntiques

Lampitts Farm, Turkeycock Lane, Stanway. CO3 5ND. Resident. (A. Jones and S. Doubleday). Est. 1978. Open weekends. SIZE: Medium. *STOCK: General antiques and pine.* LOC: Turn left at Eight Ash Green from A604. PARK: Easy. TEL: 01206 210486; home - 01206 212421.

S. Bond and Son

14/15 North Hill. CO1 1DZ. (R. Bond). Open 9-5.30. SIZE: Large. *STOCK: Furniture and pictures.* TEL: 01206 572925. SER: Restorations. VAT: Stan/Spec.

Elizabeth Cannon Antiques

85 Crouch St. CO3 3EZ. Open 9-5.30. *STOCK: General antiques including jewellery, silver, glass, porcelain, engravings and furniture.* PARK: Easy. TEL: 01206 575817.

Colchester continued

Castle Bookshop
37 North Hill. CO1 1QR. (R.J. Green). *STOCK: Antiquarian and secondhand books, maps & prints.* TEL: 01206 577520.

Dean Antiques
Mill Farm, Harwich Rd., Gt. Bromley. CO7 7JQ. Est. 1947. Open 9-5, including Sun. SIZE: Medium. *STOCK: Mahogany, country and pine furniture, 18th-19th C.* Not Stocked: Reproductions. LOC: 6 miles from Colchester. 1 1/2 miles off A120 Harwich road, follow signs for Mill Farm camping. PARK: Own. TEL: 01206 250485; home - same; fax - 01206 252040. SER: Valuations.

Grahams of Colchester
19 Short Wyre St. CO1 1LN. Open 9-5.30. *STOCK: Jewellery and silver.* TEL: 01206 576808. SER: Valuations; restorations.

Richard Iles Gallery
10a, 10 and 12 Northgate St. CO1 1HA. (R. and C. Iles). Est. 1970. Open 9.30-4.30. SIZE: Small. *STOCK: Watercolours, 19th to early 20th C, £75-£700.* LOC: Off North Hill. PARK: NCP nearby. TEL: 01206 577877.

E.J. Markham & Son Ltd
122/3 Priory St. CO1 2PX. (Mrs S. Campbell). NAG, NPA. Open 9.30-5.30. SIZE: Medium. *STOCK: Jewellery, 19th-20th C, £25-£8,000; porcelain, 18th-20th C, £25-£2,000; furniture, 19th-20th C, £100-£1,500.* LOC: Opposite St. Botolph's priory ruins. PARK: NCP Priory St. TEL: 01206 572646. SER: Valuations; restorations (porcelain). VAT: Stan.

Mayflower Antiques
14/15 North Hill. CO1 1DZ. Est. 1970. Open 9-5.30. *STOCK: 19th C furniture, clocks, decorative antiques, paintings.* PARK: Easy. TEL: 01206 572925; mobile - 0860 315101; e-mail - mayflower@anglianet.co.uk. VAT: Stan/Spec.

Anthony Rush - Colne Valley Antiques
85 High St., Earls Colne. CO6 2QX. *STOCK: Furniture, china, glass, jewellery, pictures, prints and bric-a-brac.* TEL: 01787 223348.

Stock Exchange
The Old Saleroom, 4 North Station Rd. CO1 1RD. (J. Mellish and G. Dean). Open 10-5. *STOCK: General antiques and continental furniture.* TEL: 01206 561997.

Trinity Antiques Centre
7 Trinity St. CO1 1JN. Est. 1976. Open 9.30-5. SIZE: 7 dealers + cabinets. *STOCK: General antiques - small furniture, copper, clocks, brass, porcelain, silver, jewellery, collectors' items, Victoriana, maps and prints, linen, pine furniture.* TEL: 01206 577775.

CORRINGHAM, Nr. Stanford-le-Hope

Bush House
Church Rd. SS17 9AP. (F. Stephens). Est. 1976. Open by appointment. *STOCK: Staffordshire animals, portrait figures, 1770-1901, £50-£5,000.* LOC: Opposite the church. PARK: Own. TEL: 01375 673463; home - same; fax - same. FAIRS: Park Lane Hotel; NEC, Birmingham; K.M. Ceramic.

DANBURY

Danbury Antiques
Eves Corner (by the Village Green). CM3 4QF. (Mrs Pam Southgate). Est. 1983. Open 10-5, Wed. 10-1, Sun. 10.30-1. SIZE: Medium. *STOCK: Jewellery and silver, ceramics, metalware, furniture, 18th to early 20th C, £5-£1,800.* LOC: Off M25, take A12, then A414. PARK: Easy. TEL: 01245 223035. SER: Valuations; restorations (jewellery, upholstery, furniture). FAIRS: Furzehill, Margaretting, Billericay. VAT: Stan/Spec.

DUNMOW

Julia Bennet (Antiques) LAPADA
Flemings Hill Farm, Gt. Easton. CM6 2ER. Open by appointment. *STOCK: 18th C mahogany, 17th-19th C oak and country furniture, decorative and garden pieces.* TEL: 01279 850279.

Simon Hilton
Flemings Hill Farm, Gt. Easton. CM6 2ER. Resident. Est. 1937. Open by appointment. *STOCK: Oil paintings, watercolours and drawings, £100-£10,000; fine prints and sculpture, £50-£5,000; all 17th-20th C.* TEL: 01279 850107/850279. SER: Valuations; restorations (oil paintings, watercolours and drawings); buys at auction. VAT: Spec.

FELSTED, Nr. Great Dunmow

Argyll House Antiques
Argyll House, Station Rd. CM6 3DG. EADA. (J. Howard and C. Downing). Est. 1978. CL: Wed. SIZE: Medium. *STOCK: Furniture, Victorian and Edwardian, £25-£1,000; porcelain, 19th C to mid-20th C, £5-£500; collectors' items and ephemera, £1-£250.* LOC: Village centre. PARK: Easy. TEL: 01371 820682; home - same.

FINCHINGFIELD

Finchingfield Antiques Centre
The Green. CM7 4JX. (Peter Curry). Est. 1992. Open 10-6, including Sun. SIZE: Large - 40 dealers. *STOCK: Wide range of general antiques and collectables.* LOC: From M11, A120 to Gt. Dunmow, then B1057. PARK: Easy. TEL: 01371 810258; fax - same.

FRINTON-ON-SEA

Dickens Curios

151 Connaught Ave. CO13 9AH. (Miss M. Wilsher). Est. 1970. Open 9.45-1 and 2-5.30, Sat. 9.45-1 and 2-5. CL: Wed. pm. SIZE: Small. *STOCK: Postcards and ephemera, Victorian and later items, £5-£200.* Not Stocked: Firearms, watches and clocks. LOC: From Frinton Station quarter of mile down Connaught Ave. PARK: Easy. TEL: 01255 674134.

Frinton Antiques

CO13 9BT. (Mrs. G.M. Pethick). Est. 1952. Open by appointment. *STOCK: Small decorative furniture; fine porcelain, silver, glass and pottery.* TEL: 01255 671894. VAT: Stan/Spec.

GANTS HILL

Antique Clock Repair Shoppe

26 Woodford Ave. IG2 6XG. (K. Ashton). Est. 1971. Open 10-5. *STOCK: Clocks, pictures, bric-a-brac.* TEL: 0181 550 9540.

GRAYS

Kendons and Atticus Books

10 London Rd. RM17 5XY. Open Mon., Thurs., Fri. and Sat. 9.30-5. *STOCK: Collectables - jewellery, clocks, watches, children's books and comics, toys, silver, Goss/crested china, military items, furniture, pictures, antiquarian and Essex books.* LOC: Town centre, 5 mins from station, 10 mins from M25. TEL: 01375 371200. SER: Framing; jewellery repairs; medal mounting.

GREAT BADDOW

Baddow Antique Centre

The Bringy, Church St. CM2 7JW. Est. 1969. Open 10-5, Sun. 11-5. SIZE: 22 dealers. *STOCK: Furniture, general antiques, Victorian brass bedsteads, bric-a-brac and shipping goods.* PARK: Easy. TEL: 01245 476159. SER: Restorations; upholstery.

GREAT BARDFIELD

Golden Sovereign

The Old Police House, High St. CM7 4SP. EADA. (C. and W. Leitch). Est. 1969. Open Mon., Tues. and Thurs. 10-6 and Wed., Fri. and Sat. afternoons. SIZE: Small. *STOCK: Glass, silver, small furniture, small items, 18th-19th C, from £5.* LOC: B1057. From Dunmow, 100yds. beyond Thaxted turning, 2nd shop on left. PARK: Easy. TEL: 01371 810507; home - same.

GREAT CHESTERFORD, Nr. Saffron Walden

C. and J. Mortimer and Son

School St. CB10 1NN. Est. 1962. Open Thurs., Sat. and Sun. 2.30-5 or by appointment. SIZE: Medium. *STOCK: Oak furniture, 16th-17th C, from £400; portrait paintings, 16th-17th C, from £1,500.* LOC: From London on B1383. PARK: Easy. TEL: 01799 530261.

Great Chesterford continued

GREAT OAKLEY, Nr. Harwich

John Burls

1 The Plains. CO12 5AS. (John and Jonathan Burls). Est. 1960. Open in summer 10-1 and 2-4, Sun. 11-1 and 2-4; prior telephone call advisable in winter. SIZE: Small. *STOCK: Pottery and porcelain, 18th-20th C, £2-£300; furniture, £40-£500; paintings, £20-£350; both 19th-20th C. Clocks, silver, brass and copper, jewellery and prints.* LOC: 3 miles from A120 Colchester to Harwich road. PARK: Easy. TEL: 01255 880141; home - same. SER: Valuations; restorations (furniture); buys at auction.

GREAT WALTHAM, Nr. Chelmsford

The Stores

CM3 1DE. (M. Webster). Est. 1974. Open 10-5. CL: Sun. and Tues. SIZE: Large. *STOCK: Pine furniture.* LOC: On A130. PARK: At rear. TEL: 01245 360277; home - 01376 26997. VAT: Stan.

HALSTEAD

Antique Bed Shop

Napier House, Head St. CO9 2BT. EADA. (Veronica McGregor). Est. 1977. Open Wed.-Sat., Sun., Mon. and Tues. by appointment. SIZE: Large. *STOCK: Antique wooden beds in mahogany, rosewood, walnut, chestnut, oak, bergere, 19th-20th C, £1,295-£2,795 including new base, mattress and UK delivery.* Not Stocked: Brass, iron or pine beds. LOC: On A131 to Sudbury, 200 yds from Halstead High Street. PARK: Own. TEL: 01787 477346; fax - 01787 478757. SER: Worldwide delivery. VAT: Spec.

Causeway Antiques

The Forecourt, Townsford Mill Antiques Centre, The Causeway. CO9 1ET. (Mr and Mrs L.W. Stevens-Wilson). Est. 1966. Open Sat. 10-5, Sun. 11-5, other times by appointment. SIZE: Small. *STOCK: Furniture, £50-£1,500; porcelain and glass, £10-£500; general antiques and metalware, £10-£1,000.* LOC: Off A604 in town centre. PARK: Easy. TEL: 01787 478931; home - same. SER: Valuations; lectures.

Halstead Antiques

71 Head St. CO9 2AU. (P. Earl). Est. 1973. *STOCK: Small general antiques, glass, bric-a-brac.* TEL: 01787 473265.

Townsford Mill Antiques Centre

The Causeway. CO9 1ET. (M.T. Stuckey). Open 10-5, Sun. and Bank Holidays 11-5. SIZE: 70 dealers. *STOCK: General antiques and collectables.* LOC: On A131 Braintree/Sudbury road. TEL: 01787 474451.

HARWICH

Harwich Antiques Centre

19 Kings Quay St. CO12 3ER. (David Edwards and John Tanner). Open 10-5, Sun. 1-5. CL: Mon. SIZE: Medium. *STOCK: Furniture, porcelain, china, glass, 19th C, £40-£800; collectables, 19th-20th C.* PARK: Nearby. TEL: 01255 554719. VAT: Stan.

Mayflower Antiques

105 High St., Dovercourt. CO12 3AP. (J.W. Odgers). Est. 1970. Open 10-6. CL: Sat. SIZE: Medium. *STOCK: Clocks, mechanical music, scientific and marine instruments, collectors' items.* LOC: Main road. PARK: Easy. TEL: 01255 504079; mobile - 0860 843569; e-mail - mayflower@anglianet.co.uk. VAT: Stan/Spec.

HEMPSTEAD, Nr. Saffron Walden

Michael Beaumont Antiques

Hempstead Hall. CB10 2PR. Open Sat., Sun., Mon. and Wed. 10.30-5. SIZE: Large. *STOCK: Furniture - oak, mahogany, walnut, rosewood, 17th-20th C, £50-£4,000.* LOC: On B1054 between Hempstead and Steeple Bumpstead. PARK: Easy. TEL: 01440 730239. SER: Restorations (furniture). VAT: Stan/Spec.

ILFORD

Belgrave Antiques and Bric-a-Brac

89b Belgrave Rd. IG1 3AL. (Mrs M.M. Germain). Est. 1969. Open 10.30-2 and 3.30-6.30. *STOCK: Furniture, paintings, bric-a-brac, books and collectables.* TEL: 0181 554 8032.

Flowers Antiques

733 High Rd., Seven Kings. IG3 8RL. (J.C. and A.D. Meeson). Est. 1988. Open 9.30-5.30. *STOCK: Furniture, Edwardian, Victorian; glass, china.* PARK: Easy. TEL: 0181 599 9959.

KELVEDON, Nr. Colchester

Colton Antiques

Station Rd. CO5 9NP. (Gary Colton). Est. 1993. Open 8-5, Sun. by appointment. SIZE: Medium. *STOCK: Furniture, 18th-19th C, £300-£10,000.* PARK: Own. TEL: 01376 571504. SER: Restorations. VAT: Stan/Spec.

Kelvedon Antiques

2 High St. CO5 9AG. (Sarah Mabey). Open 10-5. SIZE: Large. *STOCK: Furniture, paintings and decorative items, 18th-19th C.* PARK: Easy - own. TEL: 01376 573065; home - 01245 256027.

Millers Antiques Kelvedon

46 High St. CO5 9AG. Est. 1920. Open Tues.-Fri. 9-5, Sat. 10-4, or by appointment. SIZE: Large. *STOCK: 17th-19th C mahogany, walnut, fruitwood, oak, English and French furniture.* PARK: Own. TEL: 01376 570098; fax - 01376 572186. VAT: Stan/Spec.

Kelvedon continued

G.T. Ratcliff Ltd

Greys Mill. (W.D. Boyd Ratcliff and F.D. Campbell). Est. 1935. Open 9-5, Sat. and Sun. by appointment. SIZE: Large. *STOCK: Furniture and smalls, mainly 18th-19th C.* LOC: A12. PARK: Easy. TEL: 01376 570234; fax - 01376 571764. VAT: Stan. *Trade Only.*

Thomas Sykes Antiques LAPADA

16 High St. CO5 9AG. (T.W. Sykes and O.P. Folkard). Est. 1983. Open 10-5, Sun. by appointment. SIZE: Large. *STOCK: 18th-19th C furniture and Victorian pictures, £500-£35,000.* LOC: Off A12. PARK: Own. TEL: 01376 571969; fax - 01376 571063. SER: Buys at auction. VAT: Spec.

LEIGH-ON-SEA

K.S. Buchan

135 The Broadway. SS9 1PJ. Open 10-5. *STOCK: Furniture and general antiques.* TEL: 01702 79440.

Castle Antiques

PO Box 1911, 72 Broadway. SS9 1JG. (B.L. and J.A. Gair). Open strictly by appointment only. *STOCK: 18th-19th C English pottery including Mason's Ironstone; Staffordshire figures, tribal edged weapons, ethnic weapons, cased birds and fish.* TEL: 01702 711390; fax - 01702 75732; mobile - 0973 674355.

Collectors' Paradise

993 London Rd. SS9 3LB. (H.W. and P.E. Smith). Est. 1967. Open 10-5.30. CL: Fri. SIZE: Small. *STOCK: Clocks, 1830-1930, from £85; bric-a-brac; postcards, 1900-1930s; cigarette cards, 1889-1939.* LOC: On A13. PARK: Easy. TEL: 01702 73077.

Pall Mall Antiques

104c/104d Elm Rd. SS9 1SQ. EADA. (M. Sherman). Open 10-5. *STOCK: Porcelain, glass, metalware and collectables.*TEL: 01702 77235.

Penny Farthing

104 Elm Rd. SS9 1SQ. (R. and N. Cameron). Open 10-5. CL: Mon. and Wed. *STOCK: Furniture, clocks and jewellery.* TEL: 01702 79796

John Stacey and Sons

86-90 Pall Mall. SS9 1RG. Est. 1946. Open 9-5.30. CL: Sat. pm. *STOCK: General antiques.* TEL: 01702 77051. SER: Valuations; exporters; auctioneers. VAT: Stan.

J. Streamer Antiques

86 Broadway and 212 Leigh Rd. SS9 1AE. Est. 1965. Open 9.30-5.30. CL: Wed. *STOCK: Jewellery, silver, bric-a-brac, small furniture.* TEL: 01702 72895/711633.

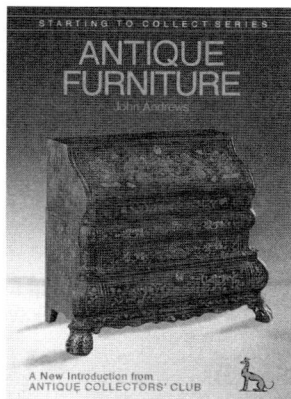

Leigh-on-Sea continued

Tilly's Antiques

1801 London Rd. SS9 2ST. (S.T. and R.J. Austen). Est. 1972. Open 10-5. CL: Wed. SIZE: Medium. *STOCK: Furniture, 19th C, £100-£500+; Victorian and Edwardian dolls, £100-£500; general antiques, 19th-20th C, £5-£200.* LOC: A13. PARK: Easy. TEL: 01702 557170. SER: Valuations; restorations (furniture and dolls).

Richard Wrenn Antiques

113/115 Broadway West. SS9 2BU. Est. 1950. Open 10.30-5.30. CL: Mon., Wed. and Sat. SIZE: Large. *STOCK: Furniture, £250-£5,000; porcelain, glass, £30-£1,000; jewellery, silver, objets d'art, £40-£2,000; metalware, brass, copper, £20-£500.* LOC: 250yds. west of Leigh church. TEL: 01702 710747; fax - same. VAT: Stan/Spec.

MALDON

Abacus Antiques

105 High St. CM9 7EP. (Mrs J. Davidson). Open Thurs., Fri. and Sat. 10-4.30. SIZE: Medium. *STOCK: Jewellery, 19th to early 20th C, £10-£500; porcelain, pottery, glass, small silver and collectors' items, 1800-1930, £5-£500; furniture,*

Maldon continued

19th C and Edwardian, £20-£2,000. Not Stocked: Firearms, coins, stamps, books. LOC: Town centre. PARK: Easy. TEL: 01621 850528; home - same. SER: Valuations.

The Antique Rooms

63D High St. CM9 7EB. (Mrs E. Hedley). Est. 1966. Open 10-4. CL: Wed. SIZE: Medium. *STOCK: Furniture, pottery, porcelain, glass and silver, costume, linen and lace, jewellery, lace-making equipment, collectors' items.* LOC: Just off High St. PARK: Nearby. TEL: 01621 856985.

Clive Beardall Antiques

104B High St. CM9 5ET. BAFRA, EADA. Est. 1982. Open 8-5.30, Sat 8-4.30. SIZE: Medium. *STOCK: Furniture, 18th-19th C, £100-£5,000.* LOC: Off High St. up alleyway between Just Fabrics and Peter Foulkes. PARK: Easy. TEL: 01621 857890. SER: Restorations (furniture). VAT: Stan/Spec.

Maldon Antiques and Collectors Market

All Saints Church Hall, London Rd. Est. 1975. Open first Sat. every month 9-4. LOC: Top of High St., opposite Police Station. PARK: Own. TEL: 01702 230746.

MANNINGTREE

Forty Nine
High St. CO11 1AH. (A. Patterson). Open 10-1 and 2-5. *STOCK: General and country antiques.* PARK: Easy. TEL: 01206 396170.

F. Freestone
Kiln Tops, 29 Colchester Rd. Open 9-6, appointment advisable. *STOCK: General antiques, furniture, clocks.* TEL: 01206 392998.

MATCHING GREEN, Nr. Harlow

Old Barn Antiques
Downhall Rd. CM17 0RA. Est. 1971. Open 9-5.30, Sat. and Sun. by appointment. SIZE: Warehouse. *STOCK: French, English and Continental furniture and smalls, 17th-19th C, £20-£5,000.* LOC: Turning off A1060 at Hatfield Heath. PARK: Own. TEL: 01279 731440. VAT: Stan.

Stone Hall Antiques
Downhall Rd. CM17 ORA. Est. 1971. Open 9-5.30, Sat. and Sun. by appointment. SIZE: Warehouse. *STOCK: Furniture, 17th-19th C, £50-£10,000.* LOC: Turning off A1060 at Hatfield Heath. PARK: Own. TEL: 01279 731440; home - same. VAT: Stan.

West Essex Antiques
Downhall Rd. CM17 0RA. Est. 1982. Open 9-5.30, Sat and Sun. by appointment. SIZE: Large warehouse. *STOCK: English furniture, 17th-19th C, £50-£5,000.* LOC: Turning off A1060 at Hatfield Heath. PARK: Own. TEL: 01279 730607. SER: Restorations. VAT: Stan.

NEWPORT, Nr. Saffron Walden

Brown House Antiques
High St. CO11 3QY. (B.E. and J. Hodgkinson). Est. 1978. Open 10-5. SIZE: Medium. *STOCK: Furniture, from 18th C, £50-£2,500.* LOC: B1383, off M11 at Stansted interchange. PARK: Easy. TEL: 01799 540238; home - same. SER: Valuations; restorations; buys at auction (furniture). VAT: Stan/Spec.

Gostick Hall Antiques
CB11 3PP. Est. 1979. Open by appointment. *STOCK: Victorian and Edwardian jewellery, silver, porcelain, glass.* TEL: 01799 540633.

Newport Gallery
High St. CB11 3QZ. (W. Kemp and E.C. Hitchcock). Open 9.30-5. CL: Mon. *STOCK: Watercolours, prints and oils.* LOC: On B1383, two miles from Saffron Walden. PARK: At rear. TEL: 01799 540623.

PURLEIGH, Nr. Chelmsford

David Lloyd Gallery
The Studio, Turnstone, The Street. CM3 6QL. Open by appointment. *STOCK: 19th-20th C watercolours and oils.* TEL: 01621 828093.

RAYLEIGH

F.G. Bruschweiler (Antiques) Ltd LAPADA
41-67 Lower Lambricks. SS6 7EN. Est. 1963. Open 9-5, Sat. by appointment. SIZE: Warehouses. *STOCK: Furniture, 18th-19th C.* LOC: A127 to Weir roundabout through Rayleigh High St. and Hockley Rd., first left past cemetery, then second left, warehouse round corner on left. PARK: Easy. TEL: 01268 773761/773932; home - 0162 182 8152; fax - 01268 773318. VAT: Stan.

RIDGEWELL, Nr. Halstead

Ridgewell Crafts and Antiques
CO9 4SG. (C.M.J. Godsell). Est. 1952. Open 10-6.30 including Sun. CL: Wed. SIZE: Medium. *STOCK: Clocks and watches, 19th C, £5-£500; china, brass, copper, some furniture.* LOC: On A604, 6 miles from Haverhill towards Colchester. PARK: Easy. TEL: 01440 785272.

ROXWELL, Nr. Chelmsford

Freemans Antiques
CM1 4NJ. By appointment only. *STOCK: 17th-18th C oak, especially coffers.* TEL: 01245 231286.

SAFFRON WALDEN

Bush Antiques
26-28 Church St. CB10 1JQ. EADA. (Mrs. B.E. Bush and Mrs. J.M. Hosford). Est. 1962. Open 10.30-4.30. CL: Thurs. SIZE: Medium. *STOCK: English ceramics including blue and white transfer printed pottery, copper lustre and pink lustre, £25-£250; mahogany and country furnitutre, to £1,000; copper and brass, to £250; all 1800-1860.* LOC: 300 yards north of Market Sq., on crossroads with Museum St. PARK: Nearby. TEL: 01799 523277. FAIRS: Bury St. Edmunds (Spring and Autumn).

The Interior Design Shop
4 & 5 Rose & Crown Walk. CB10 1JH. (Peter Mileham). Est. 1981. Open 9-5. *STOCK: Victorian mahogany, £200-£3,000; upholstered items, Georgian to 1930's, £300-£2,000; oak and early mahogany, 1790-1900, £300-£2,000.* TEL: 01799 516456; fax - 01799 516699. SER: Valuations; restorations; interior design. VAT: Stan/ Spec.

Lankester Antiques and Books
Old Sun Inn, Church St., and Market Hill. CB10 1HQ. (P. Lankester). Est. 1965. Open 9.30-5.30. SIZE: Large. *STOCK: Furniture, porcelain, pottery, metalwork, general antiques, books, prints and maps.* TEL: 01799 522685. VAT: Stan

Saffron Walden continued

Littlebury Antiques - Littlebury Restorations Ltd

58/60 Fairycroft Rd. CB10 1LZ. (N.H. D'Oyly). Est. 1962. Open 9-5. CL: Sat. and Sun. except by appointment. SIZE: Medium. *STOCK: Barometers, marine antiques, chess sets, walking sticks and curios.* PARK: Easy. TEL: 01799 527961; fax - same; home - 01279 771530. SER: Valuations; restorations; buys at auction. VAT: Stan/Spec.

Maureen Morris BADA LAPADA

CB11 4TA. Open by appointment. *STOCK: Samplers, needleworks, textiles and small country furniture.* TEL: 01799 521338; fax - 01799 522802.

Saffron Walden Antiques Centre

1 Market Row. CB10 1HA. Open 9-5.30, Sun. 10-4. CL: Mon. SIZE: Medium - 40+ dealers*STOCK: Wide range of general antiques.* LOC: Town centre. PARK: Easy. TEL: 01799 524534.

SHENFIELD

The Chart House

33 Spurgate, Hutton Mount. CM13 2JS. (C.C. Crouchman). Est. 1974. Open by appointment only. SIZE: Small. *STOCK: Nautical items.* PARK: Easy. TEL: 01277 225012; home - same. SER: Hire of nautical items and equipment; buys at auction.

SIBLE HEDINGHAM, Nr. Halstead

Churchgate Antiques

Prayors Farm, Prayors Hill. CO9 3LE. (B. Wilkinson). Est. 1979. Open 10-5, Sun. by appointment. CL: Mon. SIZE: Large. *STOCK: English and Irish period pine, £75-£1,800; architectural antiques - fireplaces, doors, baths, sinks, tiles, garden statuary.* PARK: Easy. TEL: 01787 462269; home - 01787 461311. SER: Valuations; restorations (stripping). VAT: Stan.

Hedingham Antiques

100 Swan St. CO9 3HP. EADA. (P. Patterson). Open 10-12.30 and 1.30-5 or by appointment. SIZE: Medium and warehouse. *STOCK: Shop - furniture, 1790-1910; china, glass, silver plate, Victorian to Art Deco, bric-a-brac. Warehouse - old and modern furniture and effects.* LOC: On A1017, village centre. PARK: Easy. TEL: 01787 460360; home - same. SER: Restorations.

Sible Hedingham continued

Lennard Antiques LAPADA

c/o W.A. Pinn & Sons, 124 Swan St. CO9 3HP. Est. 1978. *STOCK: Oak and country furniture, English Delftware, 18th to early 19th C.* LOC: On A604 opposite Shell garage in middle of village. TEL: 01787 461127. FAIRS: Chelsea; West London; Olympia (June); Harrogate (Feb.); Chester.

W.A. Pinn and Sons BADA LAPADA

124 Swan St. CO9 3HP. (K.H. and W.J. Pinn). Est. 1943. CL: Sun. except by appointment. SIZE: Medium. *STOCK: Furniture, 17th to early 19th C, £100-£5,000; clocks, 18th to early 19th C, £500-£6,000; Chinese export porcelain, £25-£1,000; interesting items, prior to 1830, £10-£1,500.* LOC: On A604 opposite Shell Garage. PARK: On premises. TEL: 01787 461127. FAIRS: Chelsea Spring and Autumn. VAT: Stan/Spec.

SOUTHEND-ON-SEA

Lonsdale Antiques

86 Lonsdale Rd, Southchurch. SS2 4LR. (H.M. Clark). Open 9-5.30. CL: Wed. *STOCK: Jewellery, pictures, porcelain, general small antiques.* TEL: 01702 462643.

Reddings Art and Antiques

98 London Rd. SS1 1PG. Resident. (F.H. Redding). *STOCK: Oils and watercolours, general antiques.* TEL: 01702 354647.

STANFORD-LE-HOPE

Barton House Antiques

Wharf Rd. SS17 0DY. (L. and J. Pigney). Est. 1973. Open all times but appointment advisable. SIZE: Medium. *STOCK: 17th-19th C furniture; 18th-19th C English porcelain, including English 18th C blue and white, copper, brass and glass.* LOC: Turn off A13 to centre of town, 200yds. on

Stanford-le-Hope continued

right hand side. PARK: Easy. TEL: 01375 672494. SER: Valuations; buys at auction. VAT: Spec. *Mainly Trade.*

STANSTED

Harris Antiques (Stansted)

40 Lower St. CM24 8LR. Resident. EADA. (F.A.D. and B.D.A. Harris, and E.V. Bradshaw). Est. 1956. Open 9-5, Sun. by appointment only. SIZE: Medium. *STOCK: Quality period furniture, ceramics and clocks, 16th-19th C, £200-£20,000+.* LOC: Near M11 and Stansted Airport. PARK: Easy. TEL: 01279 812233; home - same. SER: Valuations; restorations (furniture and ceramics). VAT: Spec.

Linden House Antiques

3 Silver St. CM24 8HA. (A.W. and K.M. Sargeant). Est. 1961. Open 9-5.30. CL: Sun. except by appointment. SIZE: Large. *STOCK: English furniture, 18th-19th C, £100-£10,000; small decorative items, including library and dining room furniture.* LOC: A11. TEL: 01279 812372. VAT: Spec.

Valmar Antiques LAPADA

Croft House, High Lane. CM24 8LQ. Resident. (John and Marina Orpin). Est. 1960. Open by appointment. SIZE: Large. *STOCK: Furniture and decorative items, £50-£10,000.* TEL: 01279 813201; fax - 01279 816962; mobile - 0831 093701. FAIRS: Major British.

STOCK

Sabine Antiques

38 High St. CM4 9BW. EADA. (C.E. Sabine). Est. 1974. Open 10-5 or by appointment. CL: Mon. *STOCK: Furniture, from £50; china and glass, from £5.* LOC: Village centre on B1007. PARK: Easy. TEL: 01277 840553. SER: Valuations; restorations (furniture); silver plating; framing.

WALTON-ON-THE-NAZE

Walton Antique Centre

27-31 High St. CB13 8BW. (B. Gore). Est. 1995. Open 10-4, Sat. 10-5 and Sun. June to Sept. CL: Wed. SIZE: Medium. *STOCK: Victorian and Edwardian items, £5-£1,000.* PARK: Easy. TEL: 01255 674385.

WESTCLIFF-ON-SEA

David, Jean and John Antiques

Lincoln House Gallery, 587 London Rd. SS0 9PQ. Est. 1963. Open 10-5. CL: Wed. SIZE: Large. *STOCK: Clocks, furniture, £25-£3,000; porcelain, bronzes, weapons, objets d'art, some shipping goods.* LOC: Opposite Jewsons. TEL: 01702 339106; home - 01268 733330; fax - same; evenings - 01268 785815. SER: Valuations; restorations (clocks, barometers and small furniture). VAT: Stan/Spec.

Westcliff-on-Sea continued

It's About Time

863 London Rd. SS0 9SZ. EADA. (R. and V. Alps). Est. 1980. Open 9-5.30. SIZE: Large. *STOCK: Clocks, 18th-19th C, £200-£4,000; barometers, Victorian and Edwardian furniture.* LOC: A13. PARK: Easy. TEL: 01702 72574; fax - same; home - 01702 205204.

Ridgeway Antiques

66 The Ridgeway. SS0 8NU. EADA. (Trevor Cornforth and Charles Jackson). Est. 1987. Open 10.30-5. SIZE: Small. *STOCK: General antiques, £5-£1,000.* LOC: A13 London road, right at Chalkwell Ave., right to The Ridgway. PARK: Easy. TEL: 01702 710383. SER: Valuations. FAIRS: Ridgeway and Hallmark.

WHITE COLNE, Nr. Colchester

Fox and Pheasant Antique Pine

CO6 2PS. (J. and J. Kearin). Est. 1978. Open 8-6. SIZE: Large. *STOCK: Stripped pine.* LOC: A604. PARK: Easy. TEL: 01787 223297. SER: Pine stripping; restorations; kitchens; joinery.

WHITE RODING

White Roding Antiques

'Ivydene', Chelmsford Rd. CM6 1RG. (F. and J. Neill). Est. 1971. Open by appointment. SIZE: Medium. *STOCK: Furniture and shipping goods, 18th-19th C, £10-£1,500.* LOC: A1060 between Bishops Stortford and Chelmsford. PARK: Easy. TEL: 01279 876376; home - same. VAT: Stan/Spec.

WOODFORD GREEN

P. Blake - Lanehurst Antiques LAPADA

403 High Rd. IG8 0XG. Est. 1952. Open by appointment only. SIZE: Medium. *STOCK: Furniture, general antiques.* LOC: A11, close to Castle public house. TEL: 0181 504 9264; fax - same; mobile - 04100 31079. SER: Valuations; buys at auction. VAT: Stan/Spec.

Galerie Lev

1 The Broadway. Open 10-5. *STOCK: Oils, watercolours, collectors' items, silver plate, porcelain.* LOC: Near Woodford underground station. TEL: 0181 505 2226. SER: Framing (Trade only).

WRITTLE, Nr. Chelmsford

Whichcraft Jewellery

54-56 The Green. CM1 3DU. EADA. (A. Turner). Est. 1978. Open 9.30-5.30. CL: Mon. SIZE: Small. *STOCK: Jewellery, silver and watches, 19th C, £30-£100.* PARK: Easy. TEL: 01245 420183. SER: Valuations; restorations (jewellery). VAT: Stan/Spec.

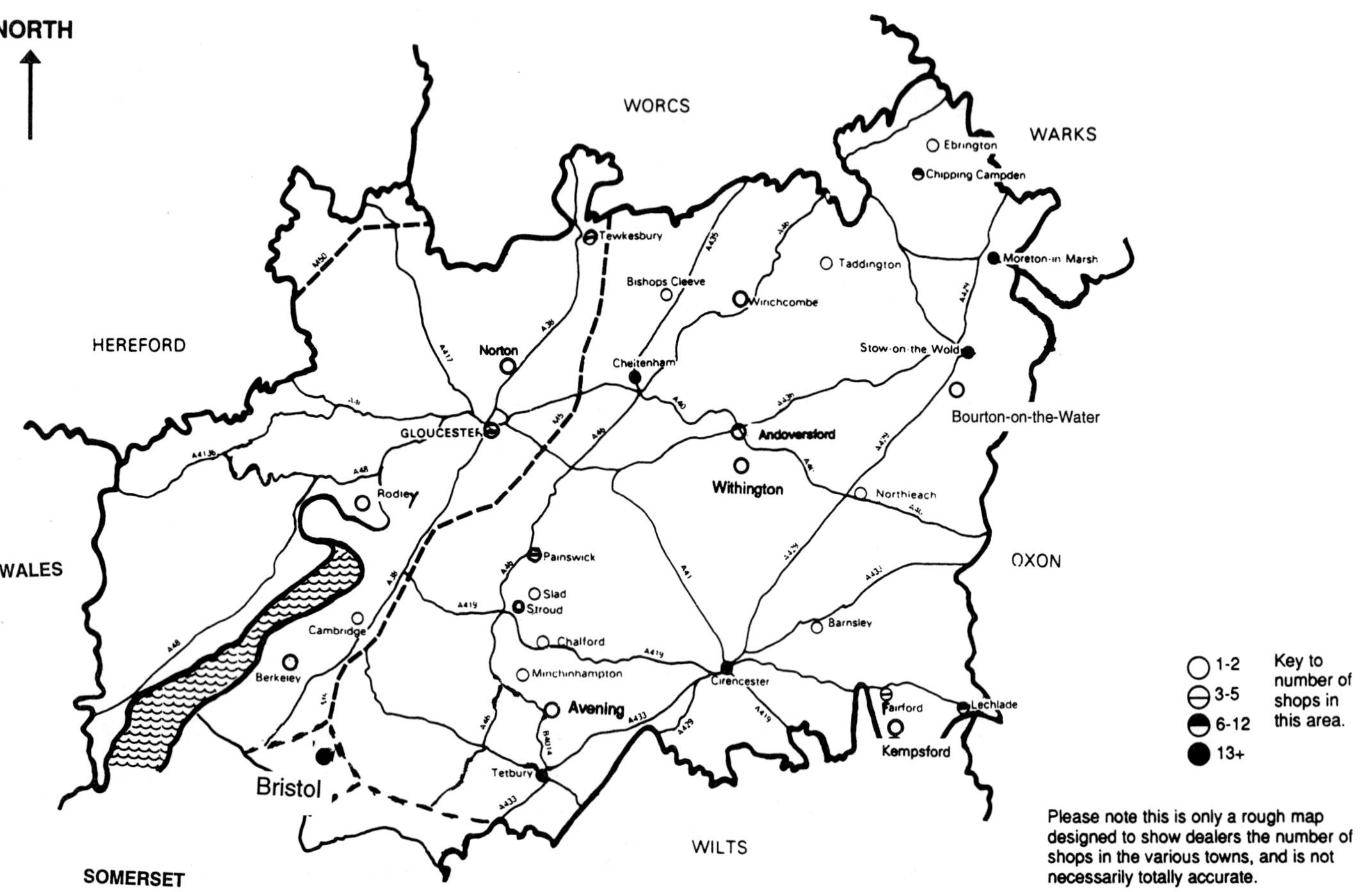
NORTH
WORCS
WARKS
HEREFORD
WALES
OXON
WILTS
SOMERSET
Ebrington
Chipping Campden
Tewkesbury
Taddington
Moreton-in Marsh
Bishops Cleeve
Winchcombe
Norton
Cheltenham
Stow-on-the Wold
Bourton-on-the-Water
GLOUCESTER
Andoversford
Withington
Rodley
Northleach
Painswick
Slad
Stroud
Chalford
Cambridge
Barnsley
Berkeley
Minchinhampton
Cirencester
Avening
Fairford
Lechlade
Kempsford
Tetbury
Bristol
1-2
3-5
6-12
13+
Key to number of shops in this area.
Please note this is only a rough map designed to show dealers the number of shops in the various towns, and is not necessarily totally accurate.

ANDOVERSFORD, Nr. Cheltenham

Julian Tatham-Losh

Brereton House, Stow Rd. GL54 4JN. Resident. (Julian and Patience Tatham-Losh). Est. 1980. Open Mon.-Fri. 9-6, at any other time by appointment. SIZE: Large. *STOCK: 19th C decorative smalls, bamboo and interesting furniture, majolica, flow blue, Staffordshire figures and animals, boxes and caddies, candlesticks, decorative glass, primitive and folk art items, kitchenalia, mirrors, £2-£5,000.* Not Stocked: Reproductions and jewellery. LOC: From A40 Oxford to Cheltenham road take A436 to Stow-on-the-Wold, premises first house on left. PARK: Own large. TEL: 01242 820646; mobile - 0850 574924. SER: Antique and decorative items supplied to order, especially repeat bulk shipping items; courier (air-conditioned transport); free storage. FAIRS: Newark; NEC; Earls Court. VAT: Stan/Spec. *Trade Only.*

AVENING, Nr. Tetbury

Andrew Lelliott

Avening Park Workshop, West End. GL8 8LT. BAFRA. Open Mon.-Fri. 8.30-1 and 2-5 (appointment advisable), other times by appointment. SIZE: Small. *STOCK: 17th-19th C chests of drawers, bureaux and occasional tables, mainly English oak and mahogany.* LOC: Map available. TEL: 01453 835783; home - 01453 832652. SER: Restorations (furniture).

Avening continued

BARNSLEY, Nr. Cirencester

Denzil Verey

Barnsley House. GL7 5EE. CADA. Resident. Est. 1980. Open 9.30-5.30, Sat. 10-5.30, other times by appointment. SIZE: Large. *STOCK: Country furniture, including pine, 18th-19th C; brass, country and kitchen bygones, unusual and decorative items.* LOC: 4 miles from Cirencester on B4425 to Burford, 1st large house in village, set back off road on the right. PARK: Easy. TEL: 01285 740402; fax - 01285 740628. VAT: Stan/Spec.

BERKELEY

Berkeley Antiques Market

GL13 9BP. Open 9.30-1 and 2-5. CL: Mon. SIZE: Large - 10 dealers. *STOCK: General antiques, oak, mahogany, pine, linen and smalls, £1-£1,000.* LOC: Village centre, 1 mile from A38. PARK: Easy. TEL: 01453 511032.

Berkeley continued

The Stuffed Dog Antiques

The Old Forge, Canonbury St. (Mrs S.L. Giddens). Est. 1995. Open by appointment or chance (prior telephone call advisable). SIZE: Small. *STOCK: Samplers, folk art, pottery, textiles, miniatures, naive paintings, decorative country items and small furniture, 18th-19th C, £20-£2,000.* LOC: From A38 on main steet through Berkeley on left-hand side, 100 yards up from castle entrance. PARK: Easy. TEL: 01453 810024. FAIRS: NEC; Shepton; Westpoint; Newark.

BISHOPS CLEEVE, Nr. Cheltenham

Cleeve Picture Framing

Church Rd. GL52 4LR. (J. Gardner). Open 9-1 and 2-5.30, Sat. 9-1. *STOCK: Prints and pictures.* TEL: 01242 672785. SER: Framing, cleaning, restoring (oils, watercolours and prints).

The Priory Gallery

The Priory, Station Rd. GL52 4HH. (R.M. and E. James). Est. 1977. SIZE: Large. *STOCK: British and European watercolours and oils, late 19th-20th C, £500-£50,000.* LOC: A435. PARK: Easy. TEL: 01242 673226. SER: Buys at auction (as stock). VAT: Stan/Spec.

BOURTON-ON-THE-WATER

Bell Antiques LAPADA

Moore Rd. GL54 2AZ. (Nick Ball). Open Thurs.-Sat 10-5, Sun. 12-5, other days by appointment. SIZE: Small. *STOCK: Glass, £100-£3,000; wine related antiques, £100-£1,000; small furniture, £100-£2,500; all 18th-19th C.* LOC: Just off the High Street. PARK: Easy. TEL: 01421 822498; fax - 0121 745 9034; home - same. SER: Valuations. FAIRS: NEC (April, Aug.); Glass Collectors (May, Nov.). VAT: Stan/Spec.

BRISTOL

Alexander Gallery

122 Whiteladies Rd. BS8 2RP. (P.J. Slade and H.S. Evans). Open 9-5.30, Wed. 9-1. *STOCK: 19th-20th C paintings, watercolours and prints.* TEL: 0117 9734692; fax - 0117 9466991.

Antique Corner with A & C Antique Clocks

86 Bryants Hill, Hanham. BS5 8QT. (D.A. and J.P. Andrews). Est. 1985. Open 10-5. CL: Mon. and Wed. SIZE: Large - 2 floors. *STOCK: Clocks including longcase, wall and mantle; furniture and ceramics, £5-£5,000.* LOC: Next to The Trooper public house, A431 Bristol to Bath road. PARK: Easy. TEL: 0117 9476141. SER: Clock and watch repairs.

Antique Four-Poster Beds

18 Richmond Hill. BS8. (Val Dewdney). Est. 1973. Open at all times but appointment advisable. SIZE: Large. *STOCK: Four-poster beds and bedposts, 18th-19th C, £950-£6,500.* LOC: Near suspension bridge. PARK: Easy. TEL: 0117 9744450; home - same; fax - same.

Bristol continued

Au Temps Perdu

5 Stapleton Rd., Easton. BS5 0QR. (Peter C. Chapman). Open 10-6. SIZE: Large + yard. *STOCK: Period fireplaces, bathroom ware and doors; traditional building materials.* LOC: On edge of Old Market. PARK: Easy. TEL: 0117 9555223.

Bizarre Antiques

210 Gloucester Rd., Bishopston. BS7 8NZ. (E.J. Parkin). Open 8.15-5. *STOCK: General antiques.* TEL: 0117 9427888; home - 0117 9503498.

The Bristol Antiques Centre

Broad Plain. BS20 9HR. Open 10-4.30, Sun. 12-4. *STOCK: General antiques including furniture, decorative and collectors' items, jewellery.* TEL: 0117 9297739.

Bristol Guild of Applied Art Ltd

68/70 Park St. BS1 5JY. Est. 1908. Open 9-5.30, Mon. and Sat. 9.30-5.30. *STOCK: Furniture, late 19th-20th C.* TEL: 0117 9265548.

Bristol Trade Antiques

192 Cheltenham Rd. BS6 5RB. (L. Dike). Est. 1970. SIZE: Large and warehouse. *STOCK: General antiques.* TEL: 0117 9422790.

Robin Butler BADA

20 Clifton Rd. BS8 1AQ. Est. 1978. Open 9.30-5.30, Sat. 10-3. SIZE: Medium. *STOCK: Fine furniture, silver, wine antiques, glass and works of art, 1600-1850, from £50.* Not Stocked: Victoriana, weapons, carpets, shipping goods. LOC: Map showing location sent on request. PARK: Easy, in drive to left of shop. TEL: 0117 9733017. SER: Valuations. VAT: Spec.

Cleeve Antiques

282 Lodge Causeway, Fishponds. BS16 3RD. (T. and S.E. Scull). Est. 1978. Open 9.30-5.30. CL: Wed. *STOCK: Furniture and bric-a-brac.* TEL: 0117 9658366; home - 0117 9567008.

Cotham Galleries

22 Cotham Hill, Cotham. BS6 6LF. (D. Jury). Est. 1960. Open 9-5.30. SIZE: Small. *STOCK: Furniture, glass, metal.* LOC: From city centre up Park St. into Whiteladies Rd. Turn right at Clifton Down station. PARK: Easy. TEL: 0117 9736026. SER: Valuations.

Cotham Hill Bookshop

39A Cotham Hill, Cotham. BS6 6JY. (R. Plant) Open 9.30-5.30. *STOCK: Antiquarian and secondhand books especially fine art; antiquarian prints.* TEL: 0117 9732344.

Richard Essex Antiques

BS40 5BP. Est. 1969. *STOCK: General antiques from mid-18th C.* TEL: 01934 863302.

Flame and Grate
159 Hotwells Rd., Hotwells. BS8 4RU. Open 9-5. *STOCK: Original cast-iron fireplaces, marble surrounds and fireplace accessories.* PARK: Easy. TEL: 0117 9252560/9292930.

Grey-Harris and Co
12 Princess Victoria St., Clifton. BS8 4BP. Est. 1963. Open 9.30-5.30. *STOCK: Jewellery, Victorian; silver, old Sheffield plate.* TEL: 0117 9737365. SER: Valuations. VAT: Stan/Spec.

Chris Grimes Militaria
13 Lower Park Row. BS1 5BN. Open 11-5.30. *STOCK: Militaria, scientific instruments, nautical items.* TEL: 0117 9298205.

A.R. Heath
62 Pembroke Rd., Clifton. BS8 3DX. Open by appointment only. *STOCK: Rare books, pamphlets, broadsides, pre-1850.* TEL: 0117 9741183; fax - 0117 9732901.

Kemps
9 Carlton Court, Westbury-on-Trym. BS9 3DF. (P.M. Kemp). Open 9-5.30. *STOCK: Jewellery.* TEL: 0117 9505090.

Michael's Antiques
150 Wells Rd. Resident. (M. Beese). TEL: 0117 9713943.

Robert Mills Architectural Antiques Ltd
Narroways Rd., Eastville. BS2 9XB. Est. 1969. Open 9.30-5. CL: Sat. SIZE: Large. *STOCK: Architectural items, panelled rooms, shop interiors, Gothic Revival, stained glass, church woodwork, bar and restaurant fittings, 1750-1920, £50-£30,000.* LOC: Half mile from Junction 2, M32. PARK: Easy. TEL: 0117 9556542; fax - 0117 9558146. VAT: Stan.

Oldwoods
4 Colston Yard. BS1 5BD. (S. Duck). Open 11-5.30, Sat. 11-4. *STOCK: Victorian and Edwardian furniture, pine and other woods.* TEL: 0117 9299023. SER: Restorations.

Period Fireplaces
The Old Station, Station Rd., Montpelier. BS6 5EE. (John Ashton and Martyn Roberts). Est. 1987. Open daily. SIZE: Small. *STOCK: Fireplaces, originals and reproduction, £100-£500.* LOC: Just off Gloucester Rd. PARK: Easy. TEL: 0117 9444449. SER: Valuations; restorations; fitting. VAT: Stan.

Potter's Antiques and Coins
60 Colston St. BS1 5AZ. (B.C. Potter). Est. 1965. Open 10.30-5.30. SIZE: Small. *STOCK: Antiquities, 500 B.C. to 1600 A.D., £5-£500; commemoratives, 1770-1953, £4-£300; coins, 500 B.C. to 1967, £1-£100; drinking glasses, 1770-1953, £3-£200; small furniture, from 1837, £10-£200.* LOC: Near top of Christmas Steps, close to city centre. PARK: N.C.P. Park Row. TEL: 0117 9262551. SER: Valuations; buys at auction. VAT: Stan/Spec.

Bristol continued

Relics - Pine Furniture
109 St. George's Rd., College Green. BS1 5UW. (R. Seville and S. Basey). Est. 1972. Open 10-6. SIZE: Large. *STOCK: Victorian style pine furniture, £25-£700.* LOC: Near cathedral, 1/2 mile from city centre. PARK: Easy. TEL: 0117 9268453; fax - same. VAT: Stan.

Something Old, Something New
115 Coldharbour Rd., Redland. BS6 7SD. (Z. Bouyamourn). Open 10-5.30. *STOCK: General antiques and French furniture.* TEL: 0117 9247479.

St. Nicholas Markets
The Exchange Hall, Corn St. BS1 1JQ. (Steve Morris). Est. 1975. Open 9.30-5. *STOCK: Wide range of general antiques and collectors' items.* TEL: 0117 9224014.

John and Sheila Symes
93 Charlton Mead Drive, Westbury-on-Trym. BS10 6LW. Open by appointment. *STOCK: Postcards, ephemera and autographs.* TEL: 0117 9501074.

Triangle Books (inc. John Roberts Bookshop Est. 1955)
43 Triangle West, Clifton. BS8 1ES. Open 10-5.30. SIZE: Large. *STOCK: Secondhand and antiquarian books and prints.* LOC: Just off Queens Rd. PARK: Meters or nearby multi-storey. TEL: 0117 9268568; fax - 0117 9226653. VAT: Spec.

The Wise Owl Bookshop
26 Upper Maudlin St. BS2 8DJ. Open 10.30-5.30. *STOCK: Antiquarian and secondhand books, all subjects including music and the performing arts; sheet music, records, tapes and CDs.* TEL: 0117 9262738; evenings - 0117 9246936.

CAMBRIDGE, Nr. Gloucester

Bell House Antiques
Bell House. GL2 7BD. Resident. (G. and J. Hawkins). Open 10-1 and 2-5. SIZE: Medium. *STOCK: Furniture, shipping goods, stripped pine, small items, bygones, £5-£500.* LOC: Near Slimbridge, on main A38. PARK: Easy. TEL: 01453 890463. SER: Valuations.

CHALFORD

J. and R. Bateman Antiques
Green Court, High St. Est. 1975. Open 9-6 or by appointment. *STOCK: Furniture, oak and country, 17th-19th C; decorative items.* PARK: Easy. TEL: 01453 883234. SER: Restorations; cabinet making, rushing and caning. VAT: Stan/Spec.

CHELTENHAM

Art and Antiques LAPADA
16/17 Montpellier Walk. GL50 1SD. (Joy Turner). Est. 1950. Open 10-4.30. CL: Wed. *STOCK: General antiques.* TEL: 01242 522939. VAT: Stan/Spec.

Cheltenham continued

David Bannister FRGS

26 Kings Rd. GL52 6BG. PBFA. Est. 1963. Open by appointment only. SIZE: Medium. *STOCK: Early maps and prints, 1480-1850, from £25; decorative and topographical prints; atlases and colour plate books.* TEL: 01242 514287; fax - 01242 513890; e-mail - db@antiquemaps.co.uk. SER: Valuations; restorations; lectures; buys at auction. FAIRS: Organiser - Antique Map and Print (Bonnington Hotel). VAT: Stan.

Bed of Roses

12 Prestbury Rd. GL52 2PW. (Martin Losh). Est. 1978. Open Tues.-Fri. 10-1 and 2-5, Sat. 9.30-5.30. SIZE: Large. *STOCK: Fine stripped pine.* LOC: 200 metres on town side of roundabout, B4632, close to Pittville Circus. PARK: Easy. TEL: 01242 231918. VAT: Stan/Spec.

Edward Bradbury and Son

32 High St. GL50 1DZ. Resident. (O. Bradbury). Est. 1986. Open by appointment. SIZE: Small. *STOCK: Works of art, tribal art, furniture, 18th-19th C; books on art reference, monographs on artists and photographers, manuscripts.* PARK: Nearby. TEL: 01242 254952. SER: Valuations. VAT: Spec.

Butler and Co

111 Promenade. GL50 1NW. (D.J. Butler). Est. 1968. Open Sat. only. SIZE: Small. *STOCK: English coins, 1st to 20th C; world coins, 19th C; both £5-£25; British campaign medals, 19th-20th C, £50-£100.* PARK: Easy. TEL: 01242 522272; home - 01242 234439. SER: Valuations. FAIRS: Cheltenham.

Charlton Kings Antiques Centre

199 London Rd., Charlton Kings. GL52 6HU. Est. 1984. Open 9.30-5.30. SIZE: Large - 11 dealers. *STOCK: General antiques, pine, painted furniture, china, glass, prints, silver, plate, linen, flatware and collectibles, £5-£1,000.* LOC: On A40. PARK: Easy. TEL: 01242 510672.

Cheltenham Antique Market

54 Suffolk Rd. GL50 2AQ. (K.J. Shave). Est. 1970. Open 9.30-5.30. SIZE: 14 dealers. *STOCK: General antiques.* TEL: 01242 529812.

Cocoa

9 Clarence Parade. GL50 3NY. (Cara Wagstaff). Est. 1973. Open 10-5. SIZE: Small. *STOCK: Lace, antique wedding dresses and accessories, 19th-20th C, £1-£2,000.* TEL: 01242 233588. SER: Recreations; restorations (period textiles). VAT: Stan.

Government House

Suffolk Rd. GL50 2AQ. Open Sat. 10.30-6, other times by appointment. *STOCK: Antique and pre-war lighting and accessories.* LOC: In antique area. PARK: Private. TEL: 01242 255897. SER: Spare parts stocked.

Greens of Cheltenham Ltd

15 Montpellier Walk. GL50 1SD. Est. 1946. Open 9-5. CL: Wed. pm. SIZE: Large. *STOCK: Victorian and diamond set jewellery, porcelain, silver, glass and some furniture.* LOC: Conjunction of Promenade and main shopping centre. PARK: Easy. TEL: 01242 512088. SER: Buys at auction. VAT: Stan/Spec.

Cheltenham continued

Heydens Militaria

420 High St. GL50 3JA. (R.E.J. Heyden). Open 10-5.30. *STOCK: Bric-a-brac and militaria.* TEL: 01242 690909.

David Howard

42 Moorend Crescent. GL53 0EL. Est. 1983. Open by appointment. *STOCK: Fine oil paintings, watercolours and drawings, 19th-20th C, £500-£5,000.* PARK: Easy. TEL: 01242 243379; home - same. SER: Valuations; buys at auction; research (pictures). VAT: Spec.

H.W. Keil (Cheltenham) Ltd — BADA

129-131 Promenade. GL50 1NW. Est. 1953. SIZE: Large. *STOCK: Furniture, paintings, 17th-18th C; metalwork, chandeliers.* LOC: Opposite Queens Hotel, at top of Promenade. PARK: Easy. TEL: 01242 522509. SER: Upholstery. VAT: Spec.

Latchford Antiques

215 London Rd., Charlton Kings. GL52 6HY. (K. and R. Latchford). Est. 1985. Open 10-5. SIZE: Small. *STOCK: Furniture, china, glass and objets d'art, 18th-19th C, £5-£1,000.* LOC: 2 miles from Cheltenham, on A40 towards London at Sixways Shopping Centre, on right. PARK: Easy. TEL: 01242 226263. VAT: Stan/Spec.

The Loquens Gallery

3 Montpellier Avenue. GL50 1SA. Est. 1975. Open 10.15-5. SIZE: Small. *STOCK: 18th-20th C watercolours and some oils.* LOC: Adjacent to The Queens Hotel. TEL: 01242 254313. SER: Valuations: framing; restorations.

Manor House Antiques — LAPADA

42 Suffolk Rd. GL50 2AQ. (J.G. Benton). Est. 1972. Open Fri. and Sat. 10-5.30, other times by appointment only. SIZE: Large. *STOCK: Furniture, 18th-19th C; general antiques, 19th C and Victorian, all £50-£5,000; paintings and ceramics.* Not Stocked: Small items, china and jewellery. LOC: A40. PARK: Nearby. TEL: 01242 232780 and 01278 760159.

Manor House Gallery

16 Royal Parade, Bayshill Rd. GL50 3AY. Resident. (Geoff Hassell). Open anytime by appointment. *STOCK: Oils and watercolours, £200-£2,000; prints, under £100; all 20th C.* LOC: Central. PARK: Easy. TEL: 01242 228330; home - same; fax - 01242 228328; e-mail - geoffatmhg@mcmail.com. SER: Valuations; restorations (oils). VAT: Stan/spec.

Martin and Co. Ltd

19 The Promenade. GL50 1LP. (I.M. and N.C.S. Dimmer). Est. 1890. *STOCK: Silver, Sheffield plate, jewellery, objets d'art.* TEL: 01242 522821; fax - 01242 570430. VAT: Stan/Spec.

Cheltenham continued

Montpellier Clocks BADA

13 Rotunda Terrace, Montpellier. GL50 1SW. (B. Bass and T. Birch). Open 9-5.30. *STOCK: Clocks, 17th-19th C; barometers.* LOC: Close to Queens Hotel. PARK: Easy. TEL: 01242 242178; fax - same. SER: Repairs and restorations by West Dean/BADA Dip. conservator.

Patrick Oliver LAPADA

4 Tivoli St. GL50 2UW. Est. 1896. SIZE: Large. *STOCK: Furniture and shipping goods.* PARK: Easy. TEL: 01242 519538. VAT: Stan/Spec.

Past & Present

31 Suffolk Parade. (Melanie Trundle). Est. 1997. Open daily. SIZE: Small. *STOCK: 19th C mahogany and oak furniture, mirrors and decoratives.* PARK: Easy. TEL: 01242 511100. SER: Repairs. VAT: Spec.

Eric Pride Oriental Rugs

44 Suffolk Rd. GL50 2AQ. Est. 1980. Open by appointment only. SIZE: Medium. *STOCK: Rugs and carpets, £100-£4,000; kilims, £300-£2,000; saddle-bags and horse covers, £150-£800; all 19th to early 20th C.* LOC: A40 near Cheltenham College. PARK: Nearby. TEL: 01242 580822 (answerphone); fax - 01242 700549. SER: Valuations; restorations (cleaning and repairs).

Michael Rayner

11 St. Luke's Rd. GL53 7JQ. Open 10-6, other times by appointment. CL: Mon. and Tues. *STOCK: Books, antiquarian and secondhand.* TEL: 01242 512806.

Robson Antiques

New Barn Farm, Farmington. Est. 1982. Open daily by appointment. *STOCK: Furniture, from 18th C, £50-£5,000.* PARK: Easy. TEL: 01451 861006/861071.

Scott-Cooper Ltd BADA

52 The Promenade. GL50 1LY. Est. 1912. *STOCK: Silver, plate, jewellery, clocks, ivory, enamel, objets de vertu.* TEL: 01242 522580. SER: Restorations and repairs (silver and jewellery). VAT: Stan/Spec.

Tapestry

33 Suffolk Parade. GL50 2AE. Open 10-5.30. SIZE: Medium. *STOCK: Antique and decorative furniture and objects, including brass and iron beds, soft furnishings and garden items.* LOC: 10 mins. walk from The Promenade. PARK: Easy. TEL: 01242 512191.

John P. Townsend

Ullenwood Park Farm, Ullenwood. GL53 9QX. Est. 1969. Open 9-5. CL: Sat. SIZE: Medium. *STOCK: Furniture - stripped pine, country and shipping, to 1940's; books.* TEL: 01242 870223.

Triton Gallery

27 Suffolk Parade. GL50 2AE. Resident. (L. Bianco). Open 9-5.30, other times by appointment. *STOCK: Period furniture, 18th C paintings, mirrors and lighting.* TEL: 01242 510477.

CHIPPING CAMPDEN

Antique Heritage

High St. GL55 6AT. (D.B. Smith). Est. 1981. Open 10-5, Sun. 11-4. SIZE: Small. *STOCK: Small items, china, porcelain, tables, boxes, Georgian and Victorian, £15-£400.* LOC: Village centre. PARK: Easy. TEL: 01386 840727.

Campden Country Pine Antiques

High St. GL55 6HN. (Jane and Frank Kennedy). Est. 1988. Open 10-12 and 2-5 including Sun. SIZE: Large. *STOCK: 17th-19th C English pine.* LOC: On village green at Leasebourne end of High St. PARK: Easy. TEL: 01386 840315; home - same; fax - 01386 841740; e-mail - TheKettle@aol.com. SER: National and international delivery.

Pedlars

Lower High St. GL55 6AL. (A. Yates). Open 10-5. *STOCK: General antiques.* TEL: 01386 840680.

Saxton House Gallery LAPADA

High St. GL55 6HQ. (S.D. and J. Coy). Open 9-5.30. CL: Thurs. SIZE: Medium. *STOCK: Fine English clocks and barometers, unusual carriage clocks, jewellery, Georgian furniture, paintings and watercolours.* LOC: Village centre. PARK: Easy. TEL: 01386 840278. VAT: Stan/Spec.

School House Antiques LAPADA

School House, High St. GL55 6HB. (G. Hammond). Open 9.30-5 including Sun.(June-Sept.). CL: Thurs. (Oct.-May). *STOCK: Clocks, 18th-19th C; furniture including oak and shipping, 17th-19th C; works of art, oils and watercolours.* TEL: 01386 841474; fax - 01386 841367. SER: Restorations.

Stuart House Antiques

High St. GL55 6HB. (J. Collett). Est. 1985. Open 10-1 and 2-5.30 including Sun. SIZE: Large. *STOCK: China, 19th C; general antiques, from 18th C; all £1-£1,000.* LOC: Opposite market hall. PARK: Easy. TEL: 01386 840995. SER: Valuations; china search; restorations (ceramics).

Swan Antiques

High St. GL55 6HB. (J. Stocker). Est. 1960. Open 10-1 and 2-4.45, Thurs. and Sun. by appointment. SIZE: Medium. *STOCK: Silver, George II to 1920; jewellery including Victorian; porcelain; furniture, 17th C oak to 1860 mahogany; decorative items.* LOC: Village centre. PARK: Easy. TEL: 01386 840759. SER: Gemmologist.

CHIPPING SODBURY, Nr. Bristol

Sodbury Antiques

70 Broad St. (Millicent Brown). Est. 1986. CL: Wed. SIZE: Small. *STOCK: Porcelain and china, mainly 18th-19th C; antique and secondhand jewellery, £5-£1,000.* PARK: Easy. TEL: 01454 273369.

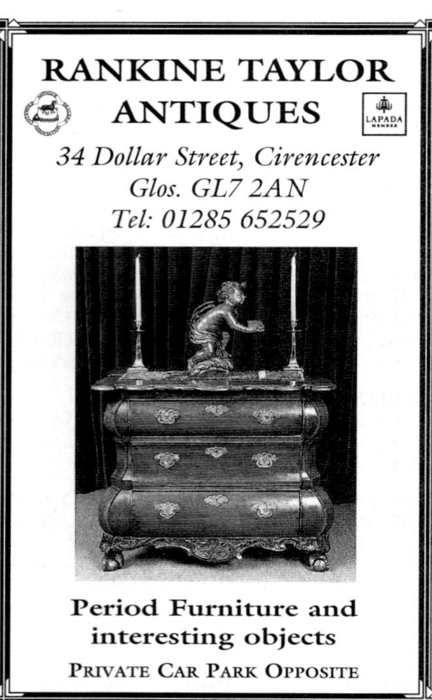

RANKINE TAYLOR
ANTIQUES
LAPADA
34 Dollar Street, Cirencester
Glos. GL7 2AN
Tel: 01285 652529
Period Furniture and
interesting objects
PRIVATE CAR PARK OPPOSITE

CIRENCESTER

Walter Bull and Son (Cirencester) Ltd

10 Dyer St. GL7 2PF. Est. 1815. Open 9-5. SIZE: Small. *STOCK: Silver, from 1700, £50-£3,000; objets d'art.* LOC: Lower end of Market Place. PARK: At rear. TEL: 01285 653875; fax - 01285 641751. VAT: Stan/Spec.

Cirencester Antique Market

Market Place. GL7 2PP. (Antique Forum Ltd). Open Fri. SIZE: 60 dealers. *STOCK: General antiques.* TEL: 01225 765586.

Corner Cupboard Curios

2 Church St. GL7 1LE. (P. Larner). *STOCK: General antiques and gramophonalia.* TEL: 01285 655476.

Forum Antiques

Springfield Farm, Perrotts Brook. (W. Mitchell). Est. 1986. Open Mon.-Fri. 8.30-5.30 by appointment only. SIZE: Small. *STOCK: Period furniture, pre-1850.* TEL: 01285 831821. SER: Valuations; restorations. VAT: Spec.

Hares

4 Black Jack St. Est. 1972. Open 10-5.30, Sun. by appointment. SIZE: Large. *STOCK: Furniture, especially dining tables and long sets of chairs, 18th to early 19th C, £100-£50,000; upholstery and decorative objects.* LOC: Near Market Sq.

Cirencester continued

PARK: Own. TEL: 01285 640077; mobile - 0860 350097; e-mail - hares@star.co.uk. SER: Restorations; traditional upholstery. VAT: Spec.

Thomas and Pamela Hudson

At the Sign of the Herald Angel, 17 Park St. GL7 2BX. Resident. Est. 1959. Open by appointment only. *STOCK: Work boxes, needlework tools and needleworks.* TEL: 01285 652972. SER: Mail order.

Silver Street Antiques and Things

9 Silver St. GL7 2BJ. Resident. (S.A. Tarrant). Est. 1992. Open 10-5.30. SIZE: Medium. *STOCK: General antiques including small furniture, £5-£800.* LOC: Between Corn Hall and museum. PARK: Nearby. TEL: 01285 641600.

William H. Stokes BADA

The Cloisters, 6/8 Dollar St. GL7 2AJ. CADA. (W.H. Stokes and P.W. Bontoft). Est. 1968. Open 9.30-5.30, Sat. 9.30-4.30. *STOCK: Early oak furniture, £1,000-£30,000; brassware, £150-£5,000; all 16th-17th C.* TEL: 01285 653907; fax - same. VAT: Spec.

Rankine Taylor Antiques LAPADA

34 Dollar St. GL7 2AN. CADA. Est. 1969. Open 9-5.30, Sun. by appointment. SIZE: Large. *STOCK: Furniture, 17th to early 19th C, £300-£35,000; glass, 18th-20th C, £8-£350; silver, rare interesting objects and decorative items, 17th-20th C, £20-£4,000.* Not Stocked: Victoriana. LOC: From church, turn right into West Market Place, via Gosditch St. into Dollar St. PARK: Own - private opposite. TEL: 01285 652529. VAT: Spec.

Patrick Waldron Antiques

18 Dollar St. GL7 2AN. Resident. Est. 1965. Open 9.30-1 and 2-6, Sun. by appointment. SIZE: Medium. *STOCK: Furniture, 18th-19th C.* LOC: In street behind church. PARK: Easy and public behind shop. TEL: 01285 652880; home - same; workshop - 01285 643479. SER: Restorations (furniture); buys at auction. VAT: Stan./Spec.

P.J. Ward Fine Paintings

11 Gosditch St. GL7 2AG. Open 9-5. *STOCK: 17th-19th C paintings.* TEL: 01285 658499. SER: Valuations; restorations; framing. VAT: Spec.

Waterloo Antiques

20 The Waterloo. GL7 2PZ. (Philip A. Ruttleigh). Est. 1990. Open 9.30-5.30 including Sun. SIZE: Medium. *STOCK: Furniture - 18th-19th C mahogany, 17th-18th C oak, elm and country, 19th C English and Continental pine, all £50-£3,000; ceramics, from 1700, £10-£2,000.* LOC: Left at traffic lights after Market Place or right from London Rd. PARK: Opposite. TEL: 01285 644887; home - same. SER: Restorations (furniture including paint stripping); upholstery.

Cirencester continued

Bernard Weaver Antiques

28 Gloucester St. GL7 2DH. CADA. Open 9.30-6, Sat. 9.30-1. SIZE: Medium. *STOCK: Furniture, mahogany and oak, 18th-19th C; Art Nouveau and Arts and Crafts.* LOC: Continuation of Dollar St. PARK: Easy. TEL: 01285 652055; home - same. SER: Valuations.

Woodminster Antiques

14 Dollar St. GL7 2AJ. Resident. (M. Sharpe). Est. 1988. Open 10-6. SIZE: Medium. *STOCK: Town and country furniture, 17th-19th C, £100-£10,000; Staffordshire and faience pottery, 18th-19th C, £25-£500.* LOC: From church, turn right up West Market Place via Gosditch St. PARK: Easy. TEL: 01285 644485; mobile - 0836 718982. SER: Valuations; restorations (pottery); buys at auction. VAT: Spec.

EBRINGTON, Nr. Chipping Campden

John Burton Natural Craft Taxidermy

21 Main St. GL55 6NL. Est. 1973. Open by appointment. SIZE: Medium. *STOCK: Taxidermy - Victorian and Edwardian cased fish, birds and mammals, from £40-£2,500; glass domes, sporting trophies.* LOC: Village centre. PARK: Easy. TEL: 01386 593231; home - same. SER: Valuations; restorations (taxidermy); buys at auction (taxidermy). VAT: Stan.

FAIRFORD

Blenheim Antiques

Market Place. GL7 4AB. CADA. Resident. (N. Hurdle). Est. 1972. Open 9.30-6.30. *STOCK: 18th-19th C furniture.* TEL: 01285 712094. VAT: Stan/Spec.

Mark Carter Antiques

5 Macaroni Wood, Eastleach. GL7 3NF. Est. 1979. SIZE: Large - warehouse. *STOCK: English mahogany, oak and fruitwood furniture, 17th-19th C, £300-£5,000.* LOC: Telephone for directions. PARK: Own. TEL: 01367 850483; mobile - 0836 260567. SER: Valuations. VAT: Spec.

Gloucester House Antiques Ltd

Market Place. GL7 4AB. CADA. (Mrs Scilla Chester-Master). Est. 1972. Open 9-5.30. SIZE: Large. *STOCK: English and French country furniture in oak, elm, fruitwood, pine; pottery, faïence and decorative items.* PARK: Easy. TEL: 01285 712790; home - 01285 653066; fax - 01285 713324. VAT: Spec.

Anthony Hazledine

Antique Oriental Carpets, High St. GL7 4AD. Est. 1976. Mon., Fri. and Sat. 9-5, other days by appointment. SIZE: Small. *STOCK: Oriental carpets and textiles, 18th-19th C, £150-£4,000.* PARK: Easy. TEL: 01285 713400; home and fax - same. SER: Sales; purchases; restoration and cleaning. VAT: Stan/Spec.

GLOUCESTER

Steven D. Bartrick

The Antique Centre, Severn Rd. GL1 2LE. Est. 1985. Open 9-5, Sat. 9-4.30, Sun. 1-4.30. *STOCK: Topographical prints and some maps.* LOC: Gloucester dock area. PARK: At side of building. TEL: 01452 529716; home - 01242 231691.

Gloucester Antique Centre

1 Severn Rd. GL1 2LE. Est. 1949. Open 10-5, Sun. 1-5. SIZE: 110 dealers. 50p admission charge - Trade free. *STOCK: General antiques - furniture, jewellery, silver, clocks, ceramics, collectables.* LOC: Within the Dock area. PARK: Easy. TEL: 01452 529716; fax - 01452 307161.

Arthur S. Lewis LAPADA

Est. 1969. By appointment. *STOCK: Antique clocks and mechanical music.* TEL: 01452 780258.

Military Curios, HQ84

(The Curiosity Shop), Southgate. GL1 2DX. (B. Williams). Est. 1964. Open 10-6, including Sun. *STOCK: Medals, badges, (3rd Reich specialities), militaria, blazer badges, Govt. surplus, edged weapons, replicas, air weapons; Jaguar - spares, mascots.* LOC: A38, city centre. PARK: 100 yds (Docks). TEL: 01452 527716; fax - 01452 554056. SER: Valuations; medal find, mounting and framing; costume hire; badge-making; mail order;

A.J. Ponsford Antiques

Decora, Northbrook Rd., off Eastern Avenue, Barnwood. GL4 3DP. (A.J. and R.L. Ponsford). Est. 1962. Open 8-5.30. CL: Sat. SIZE: Large. *STOCK: Furniture, 1800-1880, £25-£4,000; furniture, 1650-1800, £200-£15,000; copper, brass.* LOC: 1 mile from M5, Wall's roundabout, south into Eastern Ave. ring road, past Royal Mail on right, 100 yds. turn right into Northbrook Rd. 150 yds. on left. PARK: Own. TEL: 01452 307700. SER: Valuations; restorations (furniture and oil paintings); rushing, caning, upholstery, picture framing; manufacturers of false books and decorative accessories. VAT: Stan/Spec.

KEMPSFORD, Nr. Fairford

Outhouse Antiques

Cross Tree Cottage. GL7 2EU. Resident. (R. W. King). Est. 1981. Open 8.30-5.30 including Sun. SIZE: Small. *STOCK: Country furniture, 18th-19th C; decorative items, kitchenalia, china and glass.* LOC: A417 to Fairford, Kempsford 4 miles south past air base. PARK: Easy. TEL: 01285 810318. FAIRS: Stoneleigh, Cheltenham.

LECHLADE

Apsley House Antiques Centre

Market Place. GL7 3AD. (Ian Smith). Est. 1979. Open 10-5.30, Sun. 11.30-4.30. SIZE: Large. *STOCK: Town and country furniture, silver, brass, copper, glass, porcelain, tools and kitchenalia, Oriental rugs.* LOC: A361 midway between Cirencester and Burford. PARK: Easy. TEL: 01367 253697. SER: Valuations; restorations.

Gerard Campbell BADA

Maple House, Market Pl. GL7 3AB. (J. and G. Campbell). Est. 1980. Open by appointment. SIZE: Large. *STOCK: Clocks especially Biedermeier Vienna regulators, 18th-19th C, £1,500-£15,000; oils, 20th C, £200-£5,000.* PARK: Easy. TEL: 01367 252267; home - same. SER: Valuations; buys at auction. VAT: Spec.

D'Arcy Antiques

High St. GL7 3AE. (J.W. and Mrs. M.A. Corbey). Est. 1986. Open 10-5. SIZE: Medium. *STOCK: Furniture, 1800-1960, £50-£1,800; china, 1800-1960, £1-£100; brass, 1780-1960, £2-£100.* LOC: A361, town centre. PARK: Easy. TEL: 01367 252471; home - 01793 852792.

Greystones Antiques and Interiors

High St. GL7 3AE. Resident. (S.J. and M.E. Sheppard). Open 9-6, including Sun. SIZE: Large - 4 showrooms. *STOCK: Arts & Crafts furniture and accessories; general antiques.* PARK: Easy, next to shop. TEL: 01367 253140 (24 hours).

Jubilee Hall Antiques Centre

Oak St. GL7 3AY. Open 10-5, Sun. 11-5. SIZE: Large. LOC: On left 350 yds from town centre going north towards Burford. PARK: Own. TEL: 01367 253777. SER: Shipping. Listed below are the dealers at this centre.

Lechlade continued

Nick Allen
Watercolours, oil paintings and engravings.

Mandy Barnes
Georgian and Victorian furniture and decorative objects.

John Calgie
Period furniture, mirrors, copper, brass and interesting objects.

Collingridge & Allen
18th-19th C furniture and mirrors, architectural items and prints.

Bryan Collyer
Corkscrews and wine related items.

Cooke & Dunn
Porcelain, glass, silver and objects of art.

Paul Eisler
18th-19th C ceramics, metalware and treen.

Peter Gibbons
Period pewter, treen, brass, arms and armour, country furniture.

John and Sally Gormley
18th-19th C furniture and decorative objects.

Caroline Haillay
Furniture, pottery, glass, small silver and objects of art.

Sue Herrington
Art objects, ceramics and small silver.

Colin and Mary Lee
Glass, porcelain, silver and objects.

Colin Morris
Country furniture, Staffordshire, brass, copper and period objects.

Cathy Nix
Moorcroft and other Art Deco ceramics, and early British telephones.

Oak Antiques
(David and Vicky Wilson) *Period country oak furniture and metalware.*

Mary Pennel
Porcelain, small silver and jewellery.

Red Lane Antiques
(Terry Sparks) *17th-19th C ironwork, treen, copper and brass.*

Keith Robinson
18th-19th C English furniture, engravings, ceramics, lighting and Japanese and English objects of art.

Lechlade continued

Betty Schwager
Georgian furniture and period decorative furnishings.

Fiona Taylor
Sporting antiques including golf, cricket and rowing; antique luggage.

Fred and Margaret Taylor
Small period silver, period glass and porcelain and objects of art.

Unicorn Antiques
(John Ward) *18th-19th C furniture, period metalware and country objects.*

Winniwood Antiques
(Tony Alock) *19th C furniture and furnishings.*

Lechlade Antiques Arcade
5, 6 and 7 High St. GL7 3AD. (J. Dickson). Open 10-6 including Sun. SIZE: 40+ dealers. *STOCK: General antiques, collectables, books, bric-a-brac.* TEL: 01367 252832.

Riverside Marina Arcade
Park End Wharf. GL7 3AQ. Est. 1995. Open 7 days from 8 am. SIZE: Medium. *STOCK: Art gallery, general antiques and collectables, gifts and crafts, £5-£500.* PARK: Easy. TEL: 01367 252366.

Mark A. Serle (Antiques and Restoration)
6 Burford St. GL7 3AP. Est. 1978. Open 9.30-5.30. SIZE: Small. *STOCK: Collectables, £5-£100; woodworking tools, £5-£50; furniture, £50-£1,000; all 19th C; militaria, £5-£150.* LOC: A361. PARK: Easy. TEL: 01367 253145; home - 01993 851664. SER: Restorations (furniture).

The Swan Antiques and Crafts Centre
Burford St. (Cilla and Ivor Littleton). Est. 1986. Open 10.30-4.30 including Sun. SIZE: 50 dealers. *STOCK: General antiques including furniture, collectables, books and pictures, jewellery and ceramics, 19th to early 20th C, £5-£1,500.* PARK: Own. TEL: 01367 252944; home - 01367 252129.

MINCHINHAMPTON, Nr. Stroud

Mick and Fanny Wright
'The Trumpet', West End. GL6 9JA. Open 10.30-5.30. CL: Mon. and Tues. SIZE: Medium. *STOCK: General antiques - watches, clocks, furniture, china, silver and plate, 50p-£1,500.* LOC: 200 yards from crossroads at bottom of High St. PARK: Nearby. TEL: 01453 883027.

MORETON-IN-MARSH

Antique Centre

London House, High St. GL56 OAH. Est. 1979. Open 10-5 including Sun. SIZE: Large. *STOCK: Furniture, paintings, watercolours, prints, pottery, porcelain, domestic artifacts, clocks, silver, jewellery and plate, mainly 17th-19th C, £5-£3,000.* LOC: Centre of High St. (A429). PARK: Easy. TEL: 01608 651084. VAT: Stan/Spec.

Astley House - Fine Art LAPADA

Astley House, High St. GL56 0LL. CADA. (D. and N. Glaisyer). Est. 1974. Open 9-5.30. CL: Wed. SIZE: Medium. *STOCK: Oil paintings and botanical watercolours, 19th-20th C, £200-£10,000.* LOC: Main street. PARK: Easy. TEL: 01608 650601; fax - 01608 651777. SER: Restorations (oils and watercolours); framing. VAT: Spec.

Astley House - Fine Art LAPADA

Astley House, London Rd. GL56 0LE. CADA. (D. and N. Glaisyer). Est. 1974. Open 10-1 and 2-5. CL: Wed. SIZE: Large. *STOCK: Oil paintings, 19th-20th C; large decorative paintings and portraits.* LOC: Town centre. PARK: Easy. TEL: 01608 650601; fax - 01608 651777. SER: Restorations (oils and watercolours); porcelain framing. VAT: Spec.

Moreton-in-Marsh continued

Berry Antiques LAPADA

3 High St. GL56 0AH. (Chris Berry). Est. 1989. Open 10-5.30, Sun. 11-5.30. CL: Tues. SIZE: Medium. *STOCK: Furniture, late 18th to 19th C, £1,000-£10,000; porcelain, £50-£500; paintings, £200-£5,000; both 19th C.* LOC: Near junction with Broadway road. PARK: Easy. TEL: 01608 652929; home - same. SER: Valuations. FAIRS: NEC, LAPADA (NEC). VAT: Spec.

Simon Brett BADA

Creswyke House, High St. GL56 0LH. Est. 1972. Open by appointment only. *STOCK: Antique and collectors' fishing tackle and carved wood fish models; portrait miniatures.* TEL: 01608 650751; fax - 01608 651791. VAT: Spec.

Chandlers Antiques

High St. GL56 0AD. (I. Kellam and P. Grout). Prior telephone call advisable. *STOCK: Pottery, porcelain, glass, silver, jewellery, small furniture and general antiques.* TEL: 01608 651347.

Cox's Architectural Reclamation Yard

Unit 10, Fosseway Industrial Estate. GL55 6AZ. (P. Watson). Est. 1991. Open 8.30-6, Sat. 9.30-5, Sun. by appointment. SIZE: Large. *STOCK: Architectural antiques, fire surrounds and places, £250-£500; doors, £50-£100, all 19th C.* LOC: Just off Fosseway on northern end of Moreton in

Moreton-in-Marsh continued

Marsh. PARK: Easy. TEL: 01608 652505; fax - 01608 632881. SER: Valuations. FAIRS: Newark. VAT: Stan.

Dale House Antiques

High St. GL56 0AD. (Anthony Sampson). Open 9.30-5.30. SIZE: Large - 12 dealers. *STOCK: 17th-19th C town and country furniture, English and Continental porcelain and pottery; glass, silver, Oriental paintings, metalwork, objets, arms and armour, militaria, occasional garden ornaments and architectural items, decorative objects.* LOC: Main street. PARK: Easy. TEL: 01608 650763; fax - 01608 652424; e-mail - dalehouseantiques@antiques-uk.co.uk. VAT: Spec.

Europa Antiques

The Old Dairy, Fosse Way Industrial Estate. GL55 6AZ. (Graham Gadsby). Est. 1994. Open 9-5. SIZE: Large. *STOCK: Pine, 19th C, £50-£500; English mahogany and oak, 18th-19th C.* LOC: A429 Fosse Way. PARK: Easy. TEL: 01608 652241; fax - 01608 652250; home - 01386 841504. SER: Restorations and stripping; buys at auction. FAIRS: Newark; Archenliesh. VAT: Stan.

Jeffrey Formby Antiques LAPADA

Orchard Cottage, East St. GL56 0LQ. Resident. Est. 1994. Open by appointment. SIZE: Small. *STOCK: Fine English clocks, pre 1850, £2,000-£10,000; horological books, old and new, £5-£500.* LOC: 100 yards from High St. PARK: Easy. TEL: 01608 650558. SER: Restorations (clock movements and cases); buys at auction. FAIRS: Chelsea; NEC; Chester; Solihull; Guildford. VAT: Spec.

Grimes House Antiques & Fine Art

High St. GL56 0AT. (S. and V. Farnsworth). Est. 1978. Open 9.30-1 and 2-5, other times by appointment. *STOCK: Old cranberry glass, furniture, boxes and fine paintings.* TEL: 01608 651029.

Lemington House Antiques LAPADA

Oxford St. GL56 0LA. (K.W. and Y. Heath). Open 10.30-5.30. *STOCK: Early walnut, satinwood, mahogany and oak furniture, 17th-19th C.* LOC: Close to junction with High St. PARK: Own. TEL: 01608 651443.

Mrs M.K. Nielsen

Seaford House, High St. GL56 0AD. Est. 1965. Open Thurs., Fri. and Sat. 9.30-1 and 2-5 or by appointment. SIZE: Medium. *STOCK: Derby porcelain, £45-£5,000; Worcester, £65-£5,000; furniture, £150-£4,500.* LOC: A429 Fosseway. PARK: Easy. TEL: 01608 650448. VAT: Stan/Spec.

Oriental Gallery

High Barn, Longborough. (Patricia Cater). Open by appointment only. *STOCK: Oriental ceramics and works of art.* TEL: 01451 830944; fax - 01451 870126.

Moreton-in-Marsh continued

Elizabeth Parker

High St. GL56 0LL. (P.J. and T.M. King-Smith). Est. 1975. Open 9-6. *STOCK: 18th-19th C furniture, £500-£10,000; clocks, silver, boxes, porcelain, brass and copper.* LOC: Opposite Manor House Hotel, on Fosseway junction of A44 from Broadway. TEL: 01608 650917. SER: Buys at auction. VAT: Stan/Spec.

Southgate Gallery

Fosse Manor Farm. GL56 9NQ. (J. Constable and N. Collins). Est. 1968. Open by appointment only. *STOCK: Modern British paintings.* TEL: 01608 650051. SER: Restorations (oils).

Windsor House Antiques Centre

High St. GL56 0AD. Open 10-5.30, Sun. 12-5.30. SIZE: 40 dealers. *STOCK: General antiques.* TEL: 01608 650993.

Gary Wright Antiques

Unit 5, Fosseway Business Park, Stratford Rd. Est. 1983. Open 9.30-5.30, Sun. by appointment. SIZE: Large. *STOCK: English and Continental furniture, 18th-19th C, £500-£30,000; unusual and decorative objects, 17th-20th C, £200-£4,000.* LOC: Entrance adjacent to railway bridge on north side of Moreton, on Fosseway (A429). PARK: Easy, TEL: 01608 652007; fax - same; home - 01608 674297. SER: Valuations; restorations; buys at auction (furniture). VAT: Stan/Spec.

NORTHLEACH, Nr. Cheltenham

The Doll's House

Market Place. GL54 3EJ. (Miss Michal Morse). Est. 1971. Open Thurs. Fri. and Sat. 10-5 and some Sun. 11-4, other times prior telephone call advisable. SIZE: Small. *STOCK: Handmade doll's houses and miniature furniture in one twelfth scale.* LOC: A40. PARK: Easy. TEL: 01451 860431; home and fax - same. SER: Restorations (as stock). VAT: Stan.

Keith Harding's World of Mechanical Music

The Oak House, High St. GL54 3ET. (K. Harding, FBHI and C.A. Burnett, CMBHI). Est. 1961. Articles on clocks, musical boxes. Open 10-6 including Sun. *STOCK: Clocks, musical boxes and automata.* TEL: 01451 860181; fax - 01451 861133. SER: Guided tours and demonstrations; valuations; restorations (musical boxes, clocks); buys at auction. VAT: Stan/Spec.

A farmer and his wife (both looking very depressed) stand on a green mound with grasses modelled in relief. The well known 'Umbrella Courtship' is also mounted on the same kind of base. The figures also appear on clock or watch stand groups, and attending large sheep or cows. c.1810. 5½in. high.

From an article entitled "Pratt Ware" by Griselda Lewis which appeared in the October 1997 issue of **Antique Collecting**

Northleach continued

Lion, Witch and Lampshade

Broxborn Barn, High St. GL54 3ES. (Mr. and Mrs. I. Dixon). Open by appointment. *STOCK: Unusual decorative objects, 18th-early 20th C, £5-£150; lamps, wall brackets, chandeliers and candlesticks, £50-£1,000; rocking horses.* TEL: 01451 860855.

NORTON, Nr. Gloucester

Ronson's Architectural Effects

Norton Barn, Wainlodes Lane. GL2 9LN. (A.P. Jones). Est. 1988. Open 8-5, Sat. 8-1. SIZE: Large. *STOCK: Architectural items including garden ornaments and architectural effects, £25-£1,000; antique pine, £50-£1,000.* LOC: A38 between Gloucester and Tewkesbury. PARK: Easy. TEL: 01452 731236. SER: Buys at auction (garden ornaments and statues). FAIRS: Restorex Period Living, Olympia. VAT: Stan.

PAINSWICK

Craig Carrington Antiques

Pincot House, Pincot Lane. GL6 7QP. Est. 1970. Open by appointment. *STOCK: English and Continental furniture and works of art.* TEL: 01452 813248. SER: Buys at auction. VAT: Spec.

Painswick Antique Centre

New St. GL6 6XH. (R.J.B. Short). Open 10-5, Sat. 10-5.30, Sun. 10.30-5.30. *STOCK: General antiques from jewellery to period furniture.* LOC: A46, near Painswick church. PARK: Easy. TEL: 01452 812431.

Nina Zborowska BADA

Damsels Mill, Paradise. GL6 6UD. Est. 1980. By appointment, except during exhibitions (May-June and Oct.-Nov) 11-5 including Sun. SIZE: Medium. *STOCK: Modern British paintings and drawings, St Ives, Newlyn, NEAC and Bloomsbury schools, 1900-1970, £500-£20,000.* LOC: From Cheltenham towards Stroud on A46, take first turning on left to Sheepscombe. PARK: Easy. TEL: 01452 812460; fax - 01452 812912. SER: Valuations; restorations. FAIRS: Olympia (Feb); 20th C British Art.

RODLEY, Nr. Westbury on Severn

Kelly Antiques

Landeck, Upper Rodley Rd. GL14 1QZ. Resident. (G. Kelly). Always open. *STOCK: Antique pine.* TEL: 01452 760315.

SLAD, Nr. Stroud

Ian Hodgkins and Co. Ltd

Upper Vatch Mill, The Vatch. GL6 7JY. Open by appointment only. *STOCK: Antiquarian books*

Slad continued

including pre-Raphaelites and associates, the Brontës, Jane Austen; 19th C illustrated, children's art and literature books, European royalty. TEL: 01453 764270; fax - 01453 755233.

STOW-ON-THE-WOLD

Acorn Antiques
Sheep St. GL54 1AA. (Maggie Masters). Est. 1987. Open 9.30-1 and 2.15-5, Sat. 9.30-1 and 2.30-5. CL: Wed. pm. SIZE: Medium. *STOCK: 19th C Staffordshire figures and animals; small furniture, Georgian, Victorian and Edwardian; collectables.* PARK: Easy. TEL: 01451 831519.

Ashton Antiques
7a Talbot Court. GL54 1BQ. Est. 1966. Open 11-5. SIZE: Large - 2 floors. *STOCK: Fine English furniture including furniture, china and pictures.* PARK: Easy. TEL: 01451 870067. VAT: Spec.

Duncan J. Baggott LAPADA
Woolcomber House, Sheep St. GL54 1AA. CADA. Est. 1967. Open 9-5.30 or by appointment. SIZE: Large. *STOCK: 17th-20th C English furniture, paintings, domestic metalwork and decorative items; garden statuary and ornaments.* PARK: Sheep St. or Market Sq. TEL: 01451 830662; fax - 01451 832174.

Baggott Church Street Ltd BADA
Church St. GL54 1BB. CADA. (D.J. and C.M. Baggott). Est. 1978. Open 9.30-5.30 or by appointment. SIZE: Large. *STOCK: English furniture, 17th-19th C; portrait paintings, metalwork, pottery, treen and decorative items.* LOC: South-west corner of market square. PARK: In market square. TEL: 01451 830370; fax - 01451 832174.

Colin Brand Antiques
Tudor House, Sheep St. GL54 1AA. Est. 1985. Open 10-1 and 2-5, Sun. by appointment. CL: Wed. SIZE: Medium. *STOCK: Clocks, small furniture, £200-£4,000; porcelain, £30-£600, all pre-1900.* LOC: Opposite Post Office. PARK: Main square. TEL: 01451 831760; fax and home - same. VAT: Spec.

Stow-on-the-Wold continued

J. and J. Caspall Antiques
Sheep St. GL54 1AA. Author of "Fire and Light in the Home pre-1820". Est. 1971. Open 10-5.30 or by appointment. *STOCK: Period oak, 16th C to 1760; early metalwork, especially lighting and hearth, early woodcarvings, period domestic and decorative items.* PARK: Nearby. TEL: 01451 831160. VAT: Spec.

Annarella Clark Antiques
11 Park St. GL54 1AQ. Est. 1968. Open by appointment any time. SIZE: Medium. *STOCK: Wicker and garden, English and French country and painted furniture, needlework, pottery, quilts and decorative objects.* LOC: Park St. leads from Sheep St., 1st right at lights leading into town. PARK: Easy. TEL: 01451 830535; home - same.

Christopher Clarke Antiques Ltd
The Fosseway. GL54 1JS. CADA. (C.J. and I.D. Clarke). Est. 1961. Open 9.30-5.30 or by appointment. SIZE: Large. *STOCK: Furniture, 17th-19th C; works of art, metalware, treen, pictures and decorative items.* LOC: Corner of The Fosseway and Sheep St. PARK: Easy. TEL: 01451 830476; fax - 01451 830300.

Cotswold Galleries
GL54 1AB. CADA. (Richard and Cherry Glaisyer). Est. 1961. Open 9-5.30 or by appointment. SIZE: Large. *STOCK: Oil paintings, especially 19th-20th C landscape.* TEL: 01451 870567; fax - 01451 870678. SER: Restorations; framing.

Country Life Antiques
Grey House, The Square. GL54 1AF. Open 10-5. *STOCK: Scientific instruments, decorative accessories, pewter, brass, copper, furniture.* PARK: Easy. TEL: 01451 831564; fax - same.

The John Davies Gallery
Church St. GL54 1BB. CADA. Est. 1977. Open 9.30-1.30 and 2.30-5.30. SIZE: Large. *STOCK: Contemporary and late period paintings; limited edition bronzes.* PARK: In square. TEL: 01451 831698; fax - 01451 832477. SER: Restoration and conservation to museum standard.

Stow-on-the-Wold continued

Durham House Antiques Centre
Sheep St. GL54 1AA. Open 10-5, Sun. 11-5. SIZE: 30+ dealers. PARK: Easy. TEL: 01451 870404; fax - same; e-mail - DurhamHouse@ Compuserve.com. SER: Buys at auction. FAIRS: NEC (Aug); Newark; Ardingly. Below are listed the dealers at this market.

Ancient and Oriental Ltd
Ancient art and items of archeological interest, all periods, from around the world.

Aston Antiques
Arts and Crafts, Victorian and decorative objects, fabrics, pillows, crystal and porcelain.

John Benson-Wilson
Continental porcelain and cabinet pieces, Meissen, Samson.

Judi Bland Antiques
Toby jugs, Staffordshire, oak furniture, metalware and decorative items.

Bread and Roses
19th and 20th C kitchen, dairy, laundry, garden and outdoor objects.

Castle Antiques
Art, small furniture, brass, copper and period metalware, pottery and treen.

Victoria Charles Antiques
Furniture, clocks, silverware, ceramics, glass and metalware.

Brian Collyer
English pottery and Staffordshire figures; corkscrews and wine related items.

Crockwell Antiques
(Philip Dawes) *Longcase clocks, 18th C oak and country furniture, brass, copper and Ironstone china.*

Jane Fairfield
Elegant silver and plate, Continental porcelain and objet d'art.

Stow-on-the-Wold continued

Tony and Jane Finnegan
Traditional furniture, interesting home accessories and comforts.

John and Sally Gormley
General antique furniture and decorative objects, 18th and 19th C.

Beryl and Brian Harrison
Linen, lace, tableware and fabrics.

Erna Hiscock
Samplers, country furniture and interesting objects.

Harry Horner
Silver and silver plated flatware and cutlery including classical designs.

Dorothy and Christopher Hyatt
Glass, 18th-20th C., early English porcelain and pottery.

Lineage Antiques
Small silverware, jewellery, Mauchline ware, portrait miniatures and interesting small objects.

Little Nells
(Helen Middleton) *Antiques and collectables, 18th-20th C; cabinet pieces and collectables.*

Audrey McConnell
Silver, picture frames, jewellery, china and pottery.

Colin Morris
Treen, early metalware, glass and pewter.

Peggy Nichols
Silver and plate, jewellery, glass and ceramics.

Outram Antiques
(Philip and Dorothy Lipman) *Oak and country furniture and collectables.*

Paper Moon Books
Fine leather bindings, 19th and early 20th C, English poetry, prose,history, etc.

Pauline Parkes
Sewing ephemera, Mauchline ware, treen and interesting objects.

Stow-on-the-Wold continued

Edith Prosser Antiques
English furniture, 18th-20th C; mirrors and period accesories.

Quartz & Clay
Deco, Arts & Crafts, pottery, ceramics and glass - Clarice Cliff, Whitefriar (Powell), Denby.

Betty Thornley Antiques
Tôle, glassware, decorative prints, late 18th-early 19th C, objects of merit.

Margaretha and David Walter-Ellis
Small furniture and decorative objects, 18th-20th C.

Paul Wright Antiques
Georgian and Victorian furniture, fine jewellery and silver. SER: Restorations; stones supplied and matched.

Yorca Antiques
(P. and P. Hughes) *18th-20th C porcelain and objets d'art.*

The Fosse Gallery

The Square. Est. 1979. Open 10-5.30. SIZE: Large. *STOCK: English and Scottish painters, many RA, RSA and Royal Glasgow Institute members, including Gore, Howard, Ward, Dunstan, Spear, Weight, Morrocco, Donaldson, McClure, Haig, Devlin and Boyd.* LOC: Off Fosseway, A429. PARK: Easy. TEL: 01451 831319. SER: Valuations; buys at auction. VAT: Spec.

Fosse Way Antiques

Ross House, The Square. GL54 1AF. CADA. (M. Beeston). Est. 1969. Open 10-5. SIZE: Large. *STOCK: Furniture and oil paintings, £300-£8,000; bronzes, Sheffield plate, caddies, boxes and decorative objects, £50-£1,000; all 18th-19th C.* LOC: East side of the Square, behind the Town Hall. PARK: Easy. TEL: 01451 830776. SER: Valuations; buys at auction. VAT: Spec.

Fox Cottage Antiques

Digbeth St. GL54 1BN. (Sue London). Est. 1995. Open 10-5. SIZE: 7 dealers. *STOCK: Wide variety of general antiques including pottery and porcelain, silver and plate, metalware, prints, small furniture, country and decorative items, mainly pre 1900, £5-£500.* LOC: Left hand side at bottom of narrow street, running down from The Square. PARK: Nearby. TEL: 01451 870307.

Keith Hockin (Antiques) Ltd BADA

The Square. GL54 1AF. CADA. Est. 1968. Open Thurs., Fri., Sat., 9-6, other times by appointment. SIZE: Medium. *STOCK: Oak furniture, 1600-1750; country furniture in oak, fruitwoods, yew, 1700-1850; pewter, copper, brass, ironwork, all periods.* Not Stocked: Mahogany. PARK: Easy. TEL: 01451 831058. SER: Buys at auction (oak, pewter, metalwork). VAT: Stan/Spec.

Stow-on-the-Wold continued

Huntington Antiques Ltd LAPADA

The Old Forge, Church St. GL54 1BE. CADA. CINOA. TEFAF. Resident. (M.F. and S.P. Golding). Est. 1974. Open 9.30-5.30 or by appointment. *STOCK: Early period and fine country furniture, metalware, treen and textiles, tapestries and works of art.* TEL: 01451 830842; fax - 01451 832211. SER: Valuations; buys at auction. FAIRS: Maastricht; Madrid. VAT: Spec.

Kenulf Fine Arts LAPADA

Digbeth St. GL54 1BN. (E. and J. Ford). Est. 1978. Open 9.30-1 and 2-5.30. *STOCK: 19th to early 20th C oils, watercolours and prints; decorative items and 20th C ceramics; small furniture.* TEL: 01451 870878 or 01242 603204. SER: Valuations; restorations (oils and watercolours, period framing).

Roger Lamb Antiques & Works of Art

LAPADA

The Square. GL54 1AB. CADA. Open 10-5. *STOCK: 18th to early 19th C furniture especially small items, lighting, decorative accessories, oils and watercolours.* TEL: 01451 831371. SER: Search.

Park House Antiques

Park St. GL54 1AQ. (G. and B. Sutton). Est. 1986. Open 10-5, winter - 11-4.30. CL: Tues. and all of May. SIZE: Large. *STOCK: Early dolls, teddy bears, toys, Victorian linen and lace, porcelain, collectables, small furniture and pictures.* PARK: Easy. TEL: 01451 830159; home - same. SER: Museum of dolls, teddies, toys, textiles and collectables. VAT: Stan/Spec.

Antony Preston Antiques Ltd BADA

The Square. GL54 1AB. CADA. Est. 1965. Open 9.30-5.30 or by appointment. *STOCK: 18th-19th C English and Continental furniture and objects; barometers and period lighting.* TEL: 01451 831586; fax - 0171 581 5076. VAT: Stan/Spec.

Priests Antiques

The Malt House, Digbeth St. GL54 1BN. (A.C. Priest). Est. 1986. Open 10-5. SIZE: Large. *STOCK: English furniture, oak, walnut, fruitwood and mahogany, 17th-19th C.* PARK: Easy. TEL: 01451 830592; fax - 01451 830592. SER: Valuations. VAT: Spec.

Queens Parade Antiques Ltd BADA

The Square. GL54 1AB. CADA. (Antony Preston Antiques Ltd). Est. 1965. Open 9.30-5.30. SIZE: Large. *STOCK: 18th-19th C furniture, papier mâché, tôle peinte, needlework and period lighting.* LOC: Off Fosse Way. PARK: Easy. TEL: 01451 831586. VAT: Stan/Spec.

Stow-on-the-Wold continued

Michael Rowland Antiques
Little Elms, The Square. GL54 1AF. (Michael Rowland). Open 10.30-5. SIZE: Medium. *STOCK: Furniture, including Welsh dressers, farmhouse tables, gate legs, side tables and bureaux, 17th-18th C, £500-£8,000.* PARK: Easy. TEL: 01451 870089; home - same. VAT: Spec.

Ruskin Antiques
5 Talbot Court. GL54 1DP. CADA. (Anne and William Morris). Est. 1990. Open 9.30-1 and 2-5.30. SIZE: Small. *STOCK: Interesting and unusual decorative objects - Arts & Crafts movement and Art Deco glass and pottery, 1860-1940.* LOC: Between The Square and Sheep Street. PARK: Nearby. TEL: 01451 832254; home - 01993 831880. SER: Valuations.

Samarkand Galleries LAPADA
8 Brewery Yard, Sheep St. GL54 1AA. CADA. CINOA. (Brian MacDonald). Est. 1980. Open 10-5.30, Sun. by appointment. SIZE: Medium. *STOCK: Tribal and village rugs and artefacts, 19th C, £100-£10,000; fine decorative carpets, 19th-20th C, £1,000-£10,000+; kelims, 19th-20th C, £200-£2,000.* LOC: Street adjacent to Market Sq. PARK: Easy. TEL: 01451 832322; fax - same. SER: Exhibitions; valuations; restorations; cleaning. VAT: Stan/Spec.

Arthur Seager Antiques
50 Sheep St. Open 10-5.30. SIZE: Medium. *STOCK: Fine 16th-18th C oak furniture, carvings, metalware, paintings, pewter and period accessories, £200-10,000.* PARK: Easy. TEL: 01451 831605. SER: Valuations (furniture). VAT: Spec.

Geoffrey Stead BADA
1 Waddington Warehouses, Bourton Industrial Park, Bourton-on-the Water. GL54 2HQ. Est. 1963. Open by appointment only. *STOCK: English and Continental furniture, decorative objects and paintings.* LOC: 3 miles from Stow-on-the-Wold, on A429. TEL: 01608 674364; fax - 01608 674533; mobile - 0468 460450.

Stow Antiques LAPADA
The Square. GL54 1AF. CADA. Resident. (Mr and Mrs J. Hutton-Clarke). Est. 1969. Open Mon.-Thurs. 2-5.30, Sat. 11-1 and 2-5.30, other times by appointment. SIZE: Large. *STOCK: Furniture, mainly Georgian, £500-£30,000; decorative items, gilded mirrors, £50-£10,000.* PARK: Easy. TEL: 01451 830377; fax - 01451 870018. SER: Shipping worldwide.

Styles of Stow
The Little House, Sheep St. GL54 1AA. (Mr and Mrs W.J. Styles). Est. 1981. Open 10-5.30. SIZE: Medium. *STOCK: Longcase (50+) and bracket clocks, barometers, 18th-19th C, £400-£30,000; fine furniture, 18th-19th C, £250-£15,000; paintings and collectables, 19th-20th C, £25-£10,000.* LOC: Opposite post office. PARK: Easy. TEL: 01451 830455; home and fax - same. SER: Valuations; restorations; buys at auction (longcase and bracket clocks). VAT: Margin.

Stow-on-the-Wold continued

Talbot Court Galleries
Talbot Court. GL54 1BQ. (J.P. Trevers). Est. 1988. Open 9.30-1 and 1.30-5.30, Sun. by appointment. SIZE: Medium. *STOCK: Prints and maps, 1580-1880, £10-£5,000.* LOC: Behind Talbot Hotel in precinct between the Square and Sheep St. PARK: Nearby. TEL: 01451 832169; fax - 01451 832167. SER: Valuations; restorations (cleaning, colouring); framing; buys at auction (engravings). VAT: Stan.

Vanbrugh House Antiques
Park St. GL54 1AQ. Resident. (J. and M.M. Sands). Est. 1972. Open 10-6 or by appointment. *STOCK: Furniture and decorative items, 17th to early 19th C; early maps, music boxes, square pianos, clocks and barometers.* LOC: Opposite the Bell Inn. PARK: Easy. TEL: 01451 830797; fax - same. SER: Valuations. VAT: Stan/Spec.

STROUD

Gnome Cottage Antiques
55 Middle St. GL5 1DZ. (G.I. Fry). Est. 1961. Open Sat.10.30-5.30, or by appointment. SIZE: Bookshop attached. *STOCK: Antique and modern furniture, collectables, curios and militaria.* TEL: 01453 755788.

Shabby Tiger Antiques
18 Nelson St. GL5 2HN. (S. Krucker). Est. 1975. Open 11-6. *STOCK: 19th C furniture, pictures, jewellery, silver and plate, china, glass, metalware, decorative items.* LOC: Nelson St. is adjacent to Parliament St. car park. PARK: Opposite. TEL: 01453 759175.

TADDINGTON, Nr. Cutsdean

Architectural Heritage
Taddington Manor. GL54 5RY. CADA. Est. 1978. Open 9.30-5.30, Sat. 10.30-4.30. SIZE: Large. *STOCK: Period panelling, oak, mahogany and pine; chimney pieces in marble, stone, oak and mahogany; garden statuary, fountains, seats and urns.* PARK: Easy. TEL: 01386 584414; fax - 01386 584236. VAT: Stan.

TETBURY

Philip Adler Antiques
32 Long St. GL8 8AQ. TADA. Open 10-5 or by appointment. *STOCK: Eclectic and general decorative and period antiques.* TEL: 01666 505759.

The Antique and Interior Centre
51A Long St. TADA. Open 10-5, Sun. 11-5 and most Bank Holidays. SIZE: 8 dealers. *STOCK: Furniture, porcelain, silver and pictures; interior design items.* TEL: 01666 505083.

The Antiques Emporium
The Old Chapel, Long St. GL8 8AA. TADA. (C. and D. Sayers). Est. 1993. Open 10-5, Sun. 1-5. SIZE: Large - 38 dealers. *STOCK: Fruitwood and country furniture, fine oak and mahogany, china, porcelain, treen, copper and brass, jewellery, silver, kitchenalia, militaria, £1-£15,000.* Not Stocked: Reproductions. PARK: Nearby. TEL: 01666 505281. SER: Export. VAT: Stan/Spec.

Tetbury continued

Artique
18 Long St. GL8 8AQ. TADA. (George Bristow). Open 9-5. *STOCK: Interiors, textiles, carpets and kelims and objets d'art from the Orient.* TEL: 01666 503597.

Ball and Claw Antiques
45 Long St. GL8 8AA. TADA. (Chris and Nick Kirkland). Est. 1995. Open 10-1 and 2-5. SIZE: Medium. *STOCK: Furniture, 18th-19th C, £50-£5,000; decorative items, objects and prints, some country items.* PARK: Easy. TEL: 01666 502440; internet - http://www.all-about-antiques.co.uk/ballc.html. SER: Valuations; buys at auction. VAT: Stan/Spec.

Balmuir House Antiques LAPADA
14 Long St. GL8 8AQ. TADA. (P. Whittam). Est. 1946. Open 9.30-5.30, Sun. by appointment. SIZE: Large. *STOCK: Furniture, paintings, mirrors, 19th C, £500-£5,000.* LOC: Town centre. PARK: Easy. TEL: 01666 503822; home - same. SER: Valuations; restorations (furniture, upholstery, paintings). VAT: Spec.

Breakspeare Antiques LAPADA
36 and 57 Long St. GL8 8AQ. CADA. Resident. (M. and S. Breakspeare). Est. 1962. Open 10-5 or by appointment. CL: Thurs. SIZE: Medium. *STOCK: English period furniture - early walnut, 1690-1740, mahogany, 1750-1835.* PARK: Own. TEL: 01666 503122; fax - same. VAT: Stan/Spec.

The Chest of Drawers
24 Long St. GL8 8AQ. TADA. Resident. (A. and P. Bristow). Est. 1969. Open 9.30-6 or by appointment. CL: Thurs. am. SIZE: Medium + trade store. *STOCK: Late Georgian, Regency and Victorian furniture; country pieces, 17th-18th C; china and brass.* LOC: On A433. PARK: Easy. TEL: 01666 502105; home - same. VAT: Spec.

The Coach House Bookshop
4 The Chipping. TADA. (Philip Gibbons). Open 10-6, Sun. 11-5. *STOCK: Secondhand and antiquarian titles including A & C Black colour plate books; prints, antique furniture and small items.* TEL: 01666 504330; e-mail - bookshop@tetbury.co.uk SER: Booksearch.

Country Homes
30 Long St. GL8 8AQ. Est. 1984. Open 9-5.30, Sun. 1-5.30. SIZE: Large. *STOCK: Pine, fruitwood and painted country furniture, £50-£4,000.* PARK: Easy. TEL: 01666 502342.

Day Antiques
5 New Church St. GL8 8DS. CADA. TADA. Est. 1975. Open 9-6. SIZE: Medium. *STOCK: Oak and country furniture, early pottery, metalware, treen, some period mahogany.* TEL: 01666 502413. VAT: Stan/Spec.

Tetbury continued

The Decorator Source
39a Long St. GL8 8AA. TADA. (Colin Gee). Open 10-5 or by appointment. SIZE: Large. *STOCK: French provincial furniture - armoires, farm tables, buffets; decorative items and accessories of interest to interior decorators.* PARK: Easy. TEL: 01666 505358. VAT: Stan/Spec.

Dolphin Antiques
48 Long St. GL8 8AQ. TADA. (P. and L. Davis). Est. 1986. Open 10-5.30. CL: Thurs. SIZE: Small. *STOCK: Mainly 19th C decorative porcelain including Meissen, Dresden, Royal Worcester, Samson, Coalport and Sitzendorf; some general antiques; all 1750-1930, £20-£2,000.* Not Stocked: Furniture. PARK: Nearby. TEL: 01666 504242; home - same.

Fifty-One Antiques Et Cetera
51 Long St. TADA. (Sylvia Powell). Est. 1977. Open 10-5, Sun. by appointment. SIZE: Small. *STOCK: English and French country furniture, £50-£5,000; decorative items.* PARK: Easy. TEL: 01666 505026.

Anne Fowler
35 Long St. GL8 8AA. TADA. Est. 1971. Open 10-5.30, Sun. by appointment. SIZE: Medium. *STOCK: Mainly French painted and decorative items including garden furniture and accessories, mirrors, faience and pots, wirework, lighting and prints, £20-£2,000.* PARK: Easy. TEL: 01666 504043; home - same; fax - 01666 504900. VAT: Stan/Spec.

Gales Antiques
52 Long St. GL8 8AQ. TADA. (M.R. Mathews). Est. 1979. Open 10-5.30. SIZE: Medium. *STOCK: English and French country furniture and decorative items, 17th-19th C, £5-£5,000.* PARK: Easy. TEL: 01666 502686. VAT: Stan/Spec.

Hampton Gallery
8 Tetbury Upton. GL8 8LP. Resident. (P. Downey). Est. 1969. Open by appointment. SIZE: Large. *STOCK: Weapons, arms and armour, 1700-1880, £50-£5,000.* LOC: Off junction 17, M4. PARK: Easy. TEL: 01666 502971. SER: Valuations; buys at auction (arms). FAIRS: All major. VAT: Spec.

Jester Antiques
10 Church St. TADA. (Lorna Coles and Peter Bairstow). Open every day 10-5.30. *STOCK: Furniture, decorative items, lamps, lanterns, mirrors, clocks, memorabilia, curios, pictures, copper and brass, Oriental items.* TEL: 01666 505125.

Lyon Oliver Antiques
TADA. By appointment. *STOCK: English and Irish country house furniture, large mirrors, upholstery and decorative sculpture.* TEL: 01666 577603; e-mail - kate.oliver@virgin.net

Tetbury continued

Bobbie Middleton

58 Long St. TADA. Open 10-1 and 2-5, Sun. by appointment. *STOCK: 18th-19th C mahogany, oak, fruitwood and painted furniture, mirrors, upholstery and decorative items.* LOC: Corner of Long St. and New Church St. TEL: 01666 502761; mobile - 0374 192660. VAT: Spec.

Morpheus - Elgin House

1 New Church St. GL8 8DT. TADA. (B. Symes). Open every day 9-5.30. *STOCK: 18th-19th C oak, mahogany and pine furniture; restored wood, brass and upholstered beds, 4-posters, half-testers and lit bateau styles.* TEL: 01666 504068; fax - 01666 503352.

Peter Norden Antiques

61 Long St. GL8 8AA. TADA. Open 10-5.30, Sun. by appointment. SIZE: Medium. *STOCK: Early oak furniture, 16th-18th C, £250-£10,000; country furniture, 15th-19th C, £75-£10,000; early carvings, metalware, pewter, pottery, 14th-19th C, £10-£2,000.* PARK: Nearby. TEL: 01666 503854; home - 01993 831607. SER: Valuations; buys at auction. FAIRS: NEC. VAT: Spec.

Old Mill Market Shop

12 Church St. GL8 8JG. TADA. (Mr and Mrs M. Green). Open 10-5.30, Thurs. 10-1. *STOCK: General antiques, collectables and bric-a-brac.* TEL: 01666 503127.

Porch House Antiques

40/42 Long St. GL8 8AQ. TADA. Open 10-5. *STOCK: 17th-20th C furniture and decorative items.* TEL: 01666 502687.

Simon Seiff Antiques

30 Long St. GL8 8AQ. TADA. Est. 1994. Open 9-5.30, Sun. by appointment. SIZE: Large. *STOCK: French and English provincial country furniture, 1780-1900, £50-£8,000.* PARK: Easy. TEL: 01666 502342. SER: Valuations; buys at auction. FAIRS: Hervey Decorative Antique & Textile. VAT: Stan/Spec.

Tetbury Gallery

18 Market Place. FATG. TADA. (Jane Maile). Open every day. *STOCK: Original and limited edition prints, from Victorian watercolours and oils to contemporary artists including Russell Flint, David Shepherd and Ben Maile.* TEL: 0166 503412.

Westwood House Antiques

29 Long St. TADA. Resident. (Richard Griffiths and Lynne Petersen). Open 10-5.30 or by appointment. *STOCK: Oak, elm and ash country furniture especially dressers, dresser bases and tables, 17th-19th C; occasional French pieces; decorative pottery, pewter and treen.* TEL: 01666 502328; fax - same.

TEWKESBURY

Abbey Antiques

62 Church St. GL20 5RZ. Est. 1945. CL: Thurs. pm. *STOCK: General antiques, Victoriana, trade and shipping goods.* TEL: 01684 292378.

Berkeley Antiques

132 High St. GL20 5JR. (P. & S. Dennis). Open 9.30-5.30. CL: Thurs. pm. SIZE: Large. *STOCK: Mahogany, oak, walnut and pine, 17th-19th C, £50-£2,000; brass, copper, silver, china and glass.* TEL: 01684 292034. SER: Restorations. VAT: Stan/Spec.

Gainsborough House Antiques

81 Church St. GL20 5RX. (A. and B. Hilson). Open 9.30-5. *STOCK: Furniture, 18th to early 19th C; glass, porcelain.* TEL: 01684 293072. SER: Restorations; conservation.

Tewkesbury Antique & Curio Centre

Tolsey Hall, Tolsey Lane. Open 10-5, including Sun. SIZE: 10+ units. *STOCK: General antiques, toys, books, collectables.* LOC: Town centre. TEL: 01684 294091. SER: Restorations.

WICKWAR

Bell Passage Antiques LAPADA

38 High St. GL12 8NP. (Mrs D.V. Brand). Est. 1966. Open 9-5. CL: Mon. and Thurs. SIZE: Large. *STOCK: Furniture, glass, porcelain, some pictures.* LOC: On B4060. PARK: Easy. TEL: 01454 294251; fax - same. SER: Valuations; restorations; upholstery.

WINCHCOMBE, Nr. Cheltenham

Muriel Lindsay

Queen Anne House. GL54 5LJ. Resident. Est. 1965. Open Thurs.-Sat. 9.30-5.30. *STOCK: Metalwork, Staffordshire, glass, some furniture, silver.* TEL: 01242 602319. VAT: Spec.

Prichard Antiques

16 High St. GL54 5LJ. CADA. (K.H. and D.Y. Prichard). Est. 1979. Open 9-5.30, Sun. by appointment. SIZE: Large. *STOCK: Period and decorative furniture, £10-£10,000; treen and metalwork, £5-£500; interesting and decorative accessories.* LOC: On B4632 Broadway to Cheltenham road. PARK: Easy. TEL: 01242 603566. VAT: Spec.

WITHINGTON, Nr. Cheltenham

Brian Sinfield - Compton Cassey Gallery

GL54 4DE. Open Sat. 10-5, other times by appointment. *STOCK: Mainly contemporary, but some Victorian and Edwardian paintings and sculptures.* TEL: 01242 890500; fax - 01242 890599. SER: Commission sales.

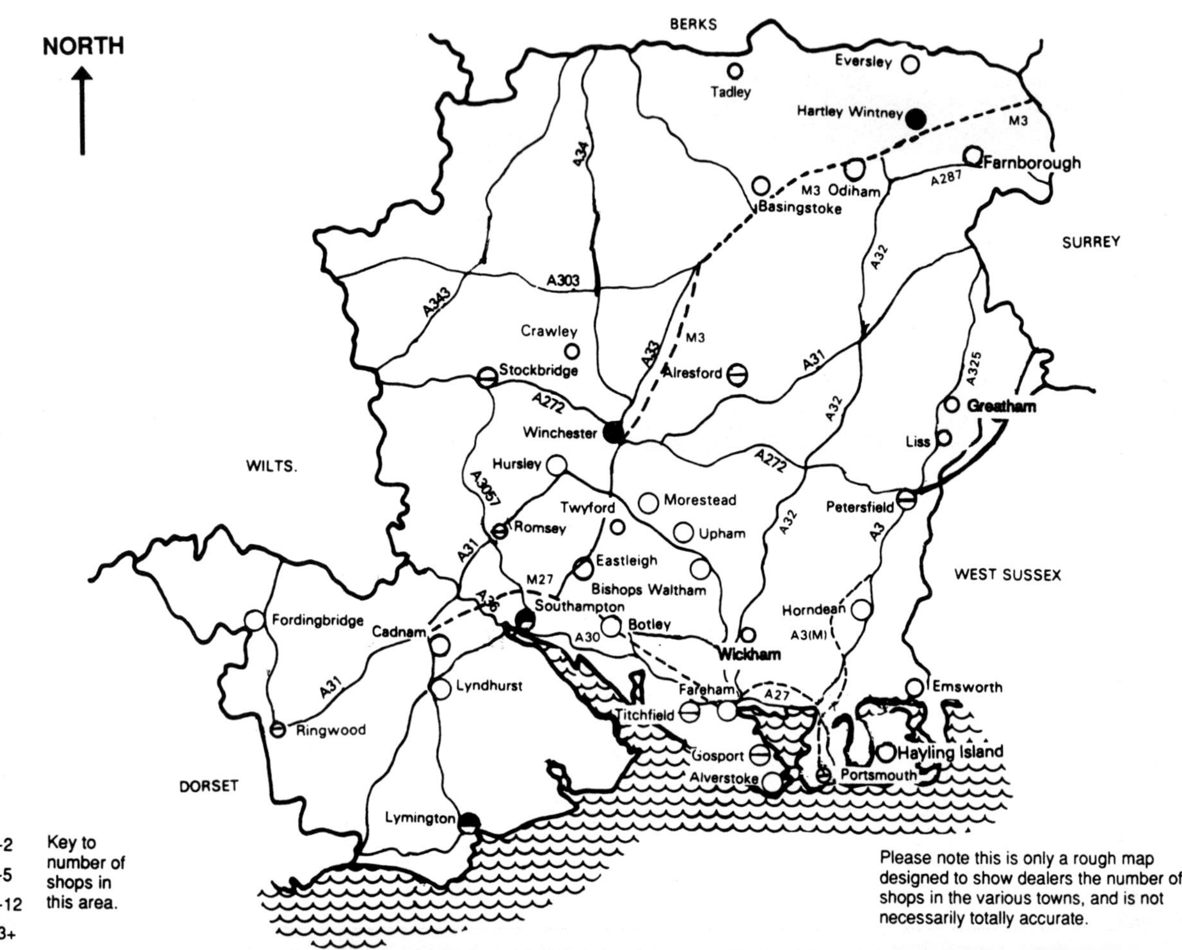
NORTH
BERKS
SURREY
WEST SUSSEX
WILTS.
DORSET
Eversley
Tadley
Hartley Wintney
M3
Farnborough
A287
M3 Odiham
Basingstoke
A34
A303
A343
A32
Crawley
M3
A33
Alresford
A31
A325
Stockbridge
A272
Greatham
Liss
Winchester
A272
Hursley
A3057
Morestead
Petersfield
Twyford
Romsey
Upham
A32
A3
A31
Eastleigh
M27
Bishops Waltham
A36
Southampton
Horndean
Fordingbridge
Cadnam
Botley
A30
A3(M)
Wickham
A31
Lyndhurst
Fareham
A27
Emsworth
Titchfield
Ringwood
Gosport
Hayling Island
Alverstoke
Portsmouth
Lymington
1-2
3-5
6-12
13+
Key to number of shops in this area.
Please note this is only a rough map designed to show dealers the number of shops in the various towns, and is not necessarily totally accurate.

ALRESFORD

Alresford Antiques

at Artemesia, 16 West St. SO24 9AT. (Mr and Mrs C. Carpenter). Est. 1992. Open 10.30-5. SIZE: Small. *STOCK: Small curios, china and glass, 18th-20th C, £5-£200; Oriental items, 18th-19th C, £25-£300.* TEL: 01962 733160. FAIRS: Sandown Park; Alexandra Palace.

Artemesia LAPADA

16 West St. SO24 9AT. (D.T.L. Wright). Est. 1972. Open 9.30-5. SIZE: Medium. *STOCK: English and Continental furniture, English, Continental and Oriental porcelain and works of art, £20-£6,000.* LOC: A31. PARK: Nearby. TEL: 01962 732277. SER: Valuations. VAT: Spec.

Evans and Evans LAPADA

40 West St. SO24 9AU. (D. and N. Evans). Est. 1953. Open Fri. and Sat. or by appointment. SIZE: Medium. *STOCK: Clocks, watches, 1680-1900, £250-£50,000; musical boxes, 19th C, £500-£12,000; Regency and Victorian barometers, £200-£2,000. Stock only as listed.* LOC: A31. Shop on left going east. PARK: Easy. TEL: 01962 732170. SER: Valuations; buys at auction. VAT: Stan/Spec.

Laurence Oxley

Studio Bookshop and Gallery, 17 Broad St. SO24 9AW. ABA. Est. 1951. Open 9-5. SIZE: Large. *STOCK: Antiquarian books, £5-£2,500; topographical prints, £2-£250; maps, £5-£800; watercolours, £75-£9,000.* LOC: B3046. PARK: Easy. TEL: 01962 732188. SER: Valuations; restorations (oil paintings/watercolours, prints, books); framing; book-binding. FAIRS: London ABA. VAT: Stan.

ALVERSTOKE, Nr. Gosport

Alverstoke Antiques

47 Village Rd. (Dyer and Follett Ltd). Est. 1960. Open 9-12.45 and 2.15-5.30. SIZE: Small. *STOCK: Furniture.* PARK: Easy. TEL: 01705 582204; fax - 01705 588499. SER: Restorations. VAT: Stan/Spec.

Olive Antiques

2A Church Rd. PO12 2LB. Est. 1976. Open 8.15-5. SIZE: Medium. *STOCK: Gold, silver, diamonds, jewellery, clocks, barometers, mirrors and porcelain, £10-£1,000.* LOC: Main road from Fareham to Gosport and then to Alverstoke. PARK: Easy. TEL: 01705 522812. SER: Valuations; gem stone testing.

BASINGSTOKE

Squirrel Collectors Centre

9 New St. RG21 1DF. (A.H. Stone). Est. 1981. Open 10-5.30. SIZE: Small. *STOCK: Jewellery and silver, Victorian and Edwardian, £5-£1,500; books,*

Basingstoke continued

cigarette and post cards, watches, collectors' and small items, toys and records. LOC: Near traffic lights at junction with Winchester St. PARK: Nearby. TEL: 01256 464885. SER: Valuations. FAIRS: Farnham Maltings monthly. VAT: Stan.

BISHOPS WALTHAM, Nr. Southampton

Pinecrafts

4 Brook St. (A. Robinson). Open 10-5. SIZE: Large. *STOCK: Pine furniture.* TEL: 01489 892878. SER: Restorations; stripping. VAT: Stan.

BOTLEY, Nr. Southampton

Butterfly Pine

Furniture Trading Co., Old Flour Mills. S03 2GB. (L. Davies). Est. 1986. Open 10-5.30, Sun. 12-5. SIZE: Medium. *STOCK: Pine, £500-£1,000; darkwood furniture, £250-£1,500; associated items, porcelain and prints, £50-£500; all 18th-19th C.* LOC: Off M27, exit 7. PARK: Easy. TEL: 01489 788194; fax - 01489 784629. SER: Valuations; restorations (clocks, furniture including upholstery, caning and French polishing); buys at auction; finder; furniture made to order from old and new pine. VAT: Stan.

CADNAM

C.W. Buckingham

Twin Firs, Southampton Rd. SO40 2NQ. Resident. Open 9-6 or by appointment. CL: Thurs. *STOCK: Mainly pine, some period and Victorian furniture.* TEL: 01703 812122.

CRAWLEY, Nr. Winchester

Folly Farm Antiques

Folly Farm. (S. Baker). Open 9-5, including Sun. *STOCK: Pine and country furniture.* TEL: 01962 776687.

EASTLEIGH

Tappers Antiques

186 Southampton Rd. SO5 5QW. (P.A. Passell). Open 10-5. *STOCK: General collectables and curios.* LOC: 1 mile off M27. TEL: 01703 643105.

EMSWORTH

Clockwise

10 South St. PO10 7EH. AHS. GMC. (D. Judge). Est. 1976. Open daily. SIZE: Small. *STOCK: Longcase, wall, mantle, bracket and carriage clocks, 18th-19th C, £300-£12,000; barometers, books and tools.* LOC: A259 off A27, head for harbour. PARK: Easy. TEL: 01243 377558. SER: Valuations; restorations (clocks and barometers). VAT: Margin.

Emsworth continued

Dolphin Quay Antique Centre

Queen St. PO10 7BU. (M. and N. Farmer). Est. 1996. Open 10-5, Sun. and Bank Holidays 10-4. SIZE: Large - 30+ dealers. *STOCK: English, French and country furniture, 18th C to 1939, £50-£3,000; marine antiques, including instruments; paintings, watercolours, clocks, jewellery, silver, glass, period lighting, decorative arts, brocante, commemorative and crested china, sporting, garden and conservatory antiques, £25-£1,500.* PARK: Easy, in square. TEL: 01243 379994. SER: Valuations; restorations.

Tiffins Antiques

12 Queen St. PO10 7BL. (Mrs P. Hudson). Est. 1987. Open 10-5. SIZE: Small. *STOCK: General antiques, oil lamps and clocks.* TEL: 01243 372497; home - same. SER: Restorations (clocks).

EVERSLEY, Nr. Wokingham

Kingsley Barn Antique Centre

Church Lane. RG27 0PX. (G. Bazely). Est. 1988. Open 10.30-5. CL: Mon. SIZE: Large. *STOCK: Furniture, china and bric-a-brac.* LOC: 1.5 miles from Blackbush airport. PARK: Easy. TEL: 0118 9328518.

FAREHAM

Elizabethans

58 High St. PO16 7BG. (E.J. Keeble). Est. 1961. Open Mon., Thurs. and Sat. 10-4. *STOCK: Small general antiques including furniture.* TEL: 01329 234964 (answerphone).

FARNBOROUGH

Martin and Parke — LAPADA

97 Lynchford Rd. (J. Martin and J. Warde). Est. 1971. Open 9-5. SIZE: Large. *STOCK: Furniture, shipping goods and books.* TEL: 01252 515311. VAT: Stan.

FORDINGBRIDGE

Mark Collier — BADA

24 High St. SP6 1AX. *STOCK: Period and decorative antiques.* Not Stocked: Coins, medals and stamps. TEL: 01425 652555; fax - 01425 656886.

Quatrefoil

Burgate. SP6 1LX. Resident. (C.D. and Mrs I. Aston). Est. 1972. Always open. SIZE: Large. *STOCK: Early oak furniture, 16th-18th C, £50-£15,000; carvings and sculpture, 13th-17th C, £20-£20,000; antiquities and coins, £50-£10,000.* LOC: On A338, adjacent Tudor Rose Inn. PARK: Easy. TEL: 01425 653309. VAT: Stan/Spec.

GOSPORT

E.T. Cooper

20 Stoke Rd. PO12 1JB. Est. 1972. Open 9.30-12.30 and 1.30-5. CL: Wed. pm. SIZE: Medium. *STOCK: Silver, china, glass, furniture, mechanical music, fairground equipment.* LOC: Main road from Lee-on-Solent through Gosport. PARK: In side road. TEL: 01705 585032. SER: Valuations; buys at auction.

Peter Pan's Bazaar

87 Forton Rd. PO12 4TG. (S.V. Panormo). Est. 1960. CL: Mon., Tues. and Wed. *STOCK: Vintage cameras, early photographica, images, 1850-1950, £5-£1,500.* LOC: Main road into town. PARK: Easy. TEL: 01705 524254. FAIRS: Main south of England.

Peter Pan's of Gosport

87 Forton Rd. PO12 4TG. (J. McClaren). Est. 1965. CL: Mon., Tues. and Wed. *STOCK: Jewellery, dolls, toys and miniatures.* LOC: Main road into town. PARK: Easy. TEL: 01705 524254. FAIRS: Main south of England.

GREATHAM, Nr. Liss

Jardinique

Kemps Place, Selborne Rd. GU33 6HG. (Edward and Sarah Neish). Est. 1994. Open 10-5. CL:

Greatham continued

Mon. SIZE: Very large. *STOCK: Garden ornaments, urns, statuary and furniture, £100-£3,000.* LOC: West of A3 roundabout at Liss, turn left after 750 yards onto B3006, premises 200 yards on left. PARK: Easy. TEL: 01420 538000; fax - 01420 538700. SER: Valuations; buys at auction (as stock). VAT: Stan/Spec.

HARTLEY WINTNEY

Nicholas Abbott LAPADA

High St. RG27 8NY. (C.N. Abbott). Est. 1962. Open 9.30-5.30. *STOCK: English furniture, 18th to early 19th C.* LOC: A30. PARK: Easy. TEL: 01252 842365.

Airdale Antiques

at Deva, High St. RG27 8NY. (E.J. Andreae). Est. 1972. *STOCK: Country furniture, 17th-19th C; polished pine.* TEL: 01252 843538.

Andwells LAPADA

High St. RG27 8NY. Est. 1967. Open 9-5.30, Sat. 9.30-5.30. SIZE: Large. *STOCK: Georgian and Regency furniture, mainly mahogany.* LOC: Main street. PARK: Easy. TEL: 01252 842305; fax - 01252 845149. VAT: Stan/Spec.

Hartley Wintney continued

Antique House
22 High St. RG27 8NY. (R.M. Campbell and P. Weaver). Open 9.30-5.30, Sun. by appointment. *STOCK: Furniture in walnut, mahogany, rosewood, oak and fruitwoods, 1710-1910; inlaid Edwardian furniture, mirrors, oils, watercolours and prints, £50-£5,000.* PARK: Easy. TEL: 01252 844499; fax - 01252 845270. SER: Restorations (furniture and porcelain).

The Antiques Centre
Primrose House, London Rd. (Mrs. Shelagh Lister). Open 10-5, Sun. 11-4. SIZE: Large - 15+ dealers. *STOCK: Pine, Georgian and Victorian furniture, £50-£5,000; prints, brass, copper, silver, 19th-20th C china including Art Deco; general decorative items, all £5-£500.* PARK: Easy. TEL: 01252 843393; mobile - 0836 734838.

Cedar Antiques Centre Ltd.
High St. RG27 8NY. (Derek and Sally Green). Open 10-5.30, Sun. 10-4. SIZE: Large - 40+ dealers. *STOCK: Quality furniture, glass, porcelain and pottery, paintings, silver, collectibles from teddy bears to treen.* LOC: A30 village centre. PARK: Opposite. TEL: 01252 843222; fax - 01252 842111. VAT: Stan/Spec.

Hartley Wintney continued

Cedar Antiques Limited
High St. RG27 8NY. (Derek and Sally Green). Est. 1964. Open 9-5.30. SIZE: Large. *STOCK: Fine English oak, walnut and country furniture, 17th-18th C, £50-£10,000; French provincial furniture, 1680-1780, £800-£5,000; steel and brasswork, £30-£1,000.* Not Stocked: China, glass, silver. LOC: A30. PARK: Opposite. TEL: 01252 843252; fax - 01252 842111. SER: Valuations; restorations (period furniture); interior design and furnishing. VAT: Stan/Spec.

Bryan Clisby Antique Clocks
at Andwells Antiques, High St. RG27 8NY. Est. 1976. Open 9.30-5.30. SIZE: Large. *STOCK: Longcase clocks, 1700-1830, £1,500-£15,000; barometers, 1770-1850, £350-£3,000; bracket, wall and mantel clocks.* LOC: A30 village centre. PARK: Easy. TEL: 01252 716436. SER: Valuations; restorations (clocks and barometers). VAT: Spec.

Deva Antiques
High St. RG27 8NY. (A. Gratwick). Open 9-5.30. SIZE: Large. *STOCK: 18th-19th C English mahogany and walnut furniture.* PARK: Easy. TEL: 01252 843538/843656; fax - 01252 842946. VAT: Stan/Spec.

Colin Harris Antiques
at Deva, High St. Est. 1966. Open 9-5.30. *STOCK: General antiques, mainly furniture and small decorative items, 18th-19th C, £20-£3,000.* LOC: A30. PARK: Easy. TEL: 01252 843538; home - 01734 732580. VAT: Spec.

David Lazarus Antiques BADA
High St. RG27 8NS. Resident. Est. 1973. Open 9.30-5.30; some Sundays, other times by appointment. SIZE: Medium. *STOCK: 17th to early 19th C English and Continental furniture; objets d'art.* LOC: Main street. PARK: Own. TEL: 01252 842272. VAT: Stan/Spec.

Millon Antiques
Antique House, 22 High St. RG27 8NY. (J.D. Millon-Milovanovich). Open 9.30-5. SIZE: Medium. *STOCK: English furniture, 1700-1850.* TEL: 01252 844499. VAT: Spec.

Old Forge Cottage Antiques
The Green. RG27 8PG. (Sue Carpenter). Open Tues., Thurs., Fri. and Sat. 10-4, other days by appointment. SIZE: Medium. *STOCK: Country and general antiques.* LOC: A30. PARK: Easy. TEL: 01252 842916.

Phoenix Green Antiques
London Rd. RG27 8RT. (J. Biles). Open 9.30-5.30, Sat. 10-5 or by appointment. SIZE: Large. *STOCK: English and Continental country furniture, Georgian mahogany, 18th-19th C.* TEL: 01252 844430.

Hartley Wintney continued

A.W. Porter and Son

High St. RG27 8NY. (M.A. Porter). Est. 1844. Open 9.30-5, Sat. 9.30-4.45. *STOCK: Clocks, silver, jewellery, glass.* LOC: Opposite Lloyds Bank. TEL: 01252 842676. SER: Restorations (clocks). VAT: Stan/Spec.

Sheila Revell Antiques

at Deva, High St. RG27 8NY. Open 9-5.30. *STOCK: 18th-19th C decorative objects, small furniture and collectors' items especially tea caddies and boxes.* TEL: 01252 843538.

HAYLING ISLAND

J. Morton Lee BADA

Cedar House, Bacon Lane. PO11 0DN. Est. 1984. Open by appointment. *STOCK: Watercolours, 18th-20th C, £50-£10,000.* PARK: Easy. TEL: 01705 464444. SER: Valuations; buys at auction; exhibitions in July and Dec. FAIRS: World of Watercolours, Chester, BADA, Harrogate, Buxton, Olympia (June), NEC (Aug), Northern. VAT: Stan/Spec.

HORNDEAN

Goss and Crested China Centre and Goss Museum

62 Murray Rd. PO8 9JL. (L.J. Pine). Est. 1968.

Horndean continued

SIZE: Medium. *STOCK: Goss, 1860-1930, £2-£1,000; other heraldic china, Art Deco pottery including Carlton ware, Charlotte Rhead, Chamelion, 1890-1930, £1-£1,000.* PARK: Easy. TEL: 01705 597440. SER: Valuations. VAT: Stan.

HURSLEY, Nr. Winchester

Hursley Antiques

SO21 2JY. Coppersmith. (S. Thorne). Est. 1980. Open 10-6. *STOCK: Pine.* LOC: 4 miles from Winchester on Romsey Rd. PARK: Easy. TEL: 01962 775488. SER: Restorations and repairs (metalware).

LISS

Plestor Barn Antiques

Farnham Rd. GU33 6JQ. Open 9-5. SIZE: Large. *STOCK: Furniture, including upholstered, Victorian and Edwardian, shipping goods, pine; china and glass, copper and brass.* LOC: A325, 2 mins from A3 roundabout. TEL: 01730 893922.

LYMINGTON

Corfields Ltd

120 High St. SO41 9AQ. Open 9.15-5.30. SIZE: Large. *STOCK: English furniture, porcelain, English School watercolours and oil paintings.* TEL: 01590 673532; fax - 01590 678855. SER: Restorations. VAT: Stan/Spec.

Hughes and Smeeth Ltd

1 Gosport St. SO41 9BG. ABA. (P. Hughes and S. Smeeth). Est. 1976. Open 9.30-5. SIZE: Small. *STOCK: Antiquarian and secondhand books, maps and prints.* LOC: At bottom of High St. PARK: Nearby. TEL: 01590 676324. SER: Valuations; binding; framing. VAT: Stan.

Lymington Antiques Centre

76 High St. SO41 9AL. Open 10-5, Sat. 9-5. SIZE: 30 dealers. *STOCK: General antiques and books.* TEL: 01590 670934.

Barry Papworth

28 St. Thomas St. SO41 9NE. Est. 1960. Open 9-5. SIZE: Small. *STOCK: Diamond jewellery, £50-£4,000; silver, £25-£1,500; both 18th-19th C. Watches, 19th C, £50-£1,000.* LOC: A337 into town, bay window on left. TEL: 01590 676422. SER: Valuations; restorations. VAT: Stan/Spec.

Robert Perera Fine Art

19 St. Thomas St. SO41 9NB. (R.J.D. Perera). Open 10-1 and 2-5, lunch-times and Sun. by appointment. SIZE: Small. *STOCK: British paintings, 19th-20th C, £100-£5,000; occasional ceramics and sculpture, 19th-20th C, £50-£1,500.* LOC: Top (west) end of main shopping area. PARK: Easy. TEL: 01590 678230; home - 01590 673190; internet - http://www./ART-GALLERY.co.uk.

Lymington continued

Charles Wallrock - Wick Antiques

(Mr and Mrs C. Wallrock). Est. 1985. Open by appointment only. SIZE: Medium. *STOCK: French and English furniture, 19th C, £1,000-£5,000; small 19th C, £300-£800; late 19th to early 20th C items, £70-£150.* TEL: 01590 677558; evenings - 01590 672515. SER: Valuations; restorations (furniture polishing, repairs, upholstery and re-gilding); buys at auction. FAIRS: Olympia. VAT: Spec.

LYNDHURST

Lita Kaye of Lyndhurst

13 High St. SO43 7BB. (S. and S. Ferder). Est. 1947. Open 9.30-1 and 2.15-5. SIZE: Large. *STOCK: Furniture, clocks, 1690-1820; decorative porcelain, 19th C.* LOC: A35. PARK: 100yds. in High St. TEL: 01703 282337. VAT: Stan/Spec.

MORESTEAD, Nr. Winchester

Burgess Farm Antiques

SO21 1LZ. (N. Spencer-Brayn). Est. 1970. Open 9-5. SIZE: Large. *STOCK: Furniture, especially pine and country, 18th-19th C, £25-£5,000; architectural items - doors, panelling, fire-places.* LOC: 2 miles south of Winchester, off Corehampton road at Jackmans Hill corner. PARK: Easy. TEL: 01962 777546. SER: Stripping; export. VAT: Stan/Spec.

ODIHAM

The Odiham Gallery LAPADA

78 High St. (I. Walker). Open 10-5, Sat. 10-1. *STOCK: Decorative and Oriental rugs and carpets.* TEL: 01256 703415.

PETERSFIELD

The Barn

North Rd. GU31 4AH. (P. Gadsden). Est. 1956. Open 9-5. *STOCK: Victoriana, bric-a-brac; also large store of trade and shipping goods.* TEL: 01730 262958. VAT: Stan.

Cull Antiques LAPADA

62 Station Rd. GU32 3ES. (J. Cull). Est. 1978. Open by appointment. *STOCK: 18th C English furniture and metalwork.* TEL: 01730 263670.

The Folly Antiques Centre

Folly Market, College St. GU31 4AD. (Red Goblet Ltd). Est. 1980. Open 9.30-5.30. SIZE: Medium. *STOCK: Furniture, 19th-20th C, £20-£1,000; ceramics and silver, 18th-20th C, £5-£100; clocks, 19th-20th C, £10-£250; pictures, general.* LOC: Town centre. PARK: Nearby. TEL: 01730 265937/269888.

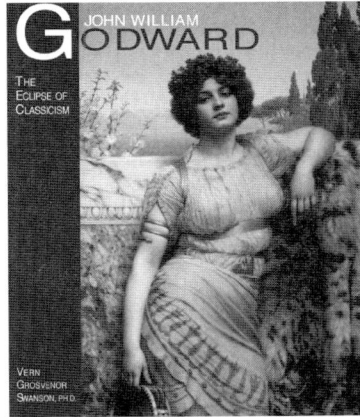

Petersfield continued

The Petersfield Bookshop BADA

16a Chapel St. GU32 3DS. ABA. (F. Westwood). Est. 1918. Open 9-5.30. SIZE: Large. *STOCK: Books, old and modern, £500; maps and prints, 1600-1859, £1-£200; oils and watercolours, 19th C, £20-£1,000.* LOC: Chapel St. runs from the Square to Station Rd. PARK: Opposite. TEL: 01730 263438. SER: Restorations and rebinding of old leather books; picture-framing and mount-cutting. FAIRS: Buxton and London ABA. VAT: Stan.

PORTSMOUTH

Affordable Antiques

89 Albert Rd., Southsea. PO5 2SG. (Max Gosling). Est. 1987. Open 10.30-3, Sat. 9.30-5. SIZE: Medium. *STOCK: Furniture, Victorian, Edwardian and 1930's, £2-£5,000.* LOC: Near Kings Theatre. PARK: Easy. TEL: 01705 293344/421993; fax - 01705 293344. SER: Valuations.

Affordable Pine

89 Albert Rd., Southsea. PO5 2SJ. (Una Gosling). Est. 1995. Open 10.30-3, Sat. 9.30-5. SIZE: Small/medium. *STOCK: Victorian pine and satinwoods, teapots, £5-£1,000.* Not Stocked: Reproduction. LOC: Nr. King's Theatre. PARK: Easy. TEL: 01705 293344/421993.

A. Fleming (Southsea) Ltd

The Clock Tower, Castle Rd., Southsea. PO5 3DE. Est. 1905. Open 9.30-5.30, Sat. 9.30-1, or by appointment. *STOCK: Furniture, silver and general antiques.* TEL: 01705 822934; fax - 01705 293501. SER: Restorations. VAT: Stan/Spec.

The Gallery

11 and 19 Marmion Rd., Southsea. PO5 2AT. (I. Murphy). Open 10-5. *STOCK: At No.19 - Victorian chairs and chesterfields; at No.11 - furniture, mainly Victorian and Edwardian.* PARK: Nearby. TEL: 01705 822016.

Oldfield Gallery

76 Elm Grove, Southsea. PO5 1LN. Est. 1970. Open 10-5. CL: Mon. SIZE: Large. *STOCK: Maps and engravings, 16th-19th C, £5-£1,000; decorative prints and some paintings, 19th-20th C, £5-£1,000.* PARK: Easy. TEL: 01705 838042; fax - 01705 838042. SER: Valuations; restorations (maps and prints); framing. FAIRS: Bonnington Hotel Map (monthly). VAT: Stan.

RINGWOOD

Millers of Chelsea Antiques Ltd LAPADA

Netherbrook House, 86 Christchurch Rd. BH24 1DR. Est. 1897. Open 9-5, Sat. 10-4, other times by appointment. SIZE: Large. *STOCK: Furniture - English and Continental country, mahogany and gilt, military, decorative items, treen, majolica and fäience, 18th-19th C, £25-£5,000.* LOC: On B3347 towards Christchurch. PARK: Own. TEL: 01425 472062; fax - 01425 472727. FAIRS: Decorative Antiques; Kensington Antique Fairs; Goodwood; Wilton; Earls Court. VAT: Stan/Spec.

Ringwood continued

R. Morgan Antiques

9 Christchurch Rd. BH24 1DR. Est. 1984. Open Wed. and Sat. 9.30-5.30, other days (including Sun.) by appointment. SIZE: Small. *STOCK: Oriental, 19th C, £50-£200; glass, 19th-20th C, £50-£100; unusual items, £50-£500.* LOC: Off A31 into Ringwood, straight over 1st roundabout, left at next roundabout, shop 150yds. on left. PARK: Easy, and at rear. TEL: 01425 479400; fax - same; mobile - 0467 416106. SER: Valuations; restorations; buys at auction. FAIRS: Park Lane; Cumberland Hotel. VAT: Stan/Spec.

The Old Toy Shop

7 Monmouth Court. (David and Patricia Wells). Est. 1973. Open 10-4, Mon. and Tues. by appointment. SIZE: Small. *STOCK: Toy soldiers, board games, diecast models, 19th-20th C, £1-£1,000.* LOC: 50yds. from A31, opposite Phillips Auction Rooms. PARK: Easy, and at rear. TEL: Mobile - 0802 924775; home - 01425 476899. SER: Valuations; buys at auction.

Smith & Sons

104 Christchurch Rd. BH24 1DR. (D.R., M. and T. Smith). Est. 1978. Open 9.30-5.30. SIZE: Large. *STOCK: Pine and other woods, 18th-19th C, £30-£1,000.* Not Stocked: Silver, fine china, bric-a-brac. LOC: Almost opposite fire station. PARK: Own. TEL: 01425 476705; home - same. SER: Makers of cherry and oak replica items; restorations. VAT: Stan.

ROMSEY

Bell Antiques

8 Bell St. SO51 8GA. FGA. (M. and B.M. Gay). Est. 1979. Open 9.30-5.30. CL: Wed. pm. (winter). SIZE: Large. *STOCK: Jewellery and silver, glass, pottery, porcelain, small furniture, prints and maps, mainly 19th and 20th C.* LOC: Near market place. PARK: Town centre. TEL: 01794 514719. VAT: Global/Stan/Spec.

Cambridge Antiques LAPADA

5 Bell St. SO51 8GY. Open 9-5. SIZE: Large. *STOCK: Furniture, small china, jewellery, paintings.* LOC: From the West, Romsey bypass, left into Palmerston St., first left then first right, 100yds. on left. PARK: Nearby. TEL: 01794 512885/523089/512069. VAT: Stan/Spec.

Lacewing Fine Art Gallery

4 Tee Court, Bell St. SO51 8GY. (N. James). Open 10-5. CL: Wed. *STOCK: Paintings, watercolours and sculpture, 16th-20th C, £200-£10,000.* TEL: 01794 523443; fax - same.

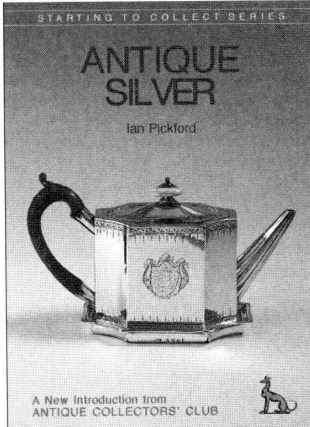

Romsey continued

"Old Cottage Things"

Broxmore Park, Sherfield English. SO5 6FU. (R. Comport). Est. 1970. *STOCK: Original building, architectural and garden materials; old pine country kitchens and furniture.* LOC: A27. TEL: 01794 884538.

Romsey Medal and Collectors Centre

5 Bell St. SO51 8GY. (T. Cambridge, OMRS). Est. 1980. Open 9-5.30. *STOCK: Medals, badges, militaria, and commemorative china.* LOC: From the west, Romsey by-pass, left into Palmerston St., first left then first right, 100yds. on left. PARK: Nearby. TEL: 01794 512069/512885; fax - 01794 830332.

SOUTHAMPTON

Mr. Alfred's "Old Curiosity Shop" and The Morris Gallery

280 Shirley Rd., Shirley. SO15 3HL. Est. 1952. Open 9-6, including Sun. *STOCK: Furniture, 18th-20th C; paintings, porcelain, bronzes, brass, glass, books, silver, jewellery and general antiques.* LOC: On left of main Shirley road, 3/4 mile from Southampton central station. PARK: Easy. TEL: 01703 774772. SER: Fine art dealer; valuer; auctioneer; curator; restorer.

Meg Campbell

10 Church Lane, Highfield. SO17 1SZ. Est. 1967. Open by appointment only. *STOCK: English, Scottish and Irish silver, collectors' pieces, Old Sheffield plate, portrait miniatures.* TEL: 01703 557636. SER: Mail order; catalogues available. VAT: Spec.

Cobwebs

78 Northam Rd. SO14 0PB. (P.R. and J.M. Boyd-Smith). Open 10.30-4. CL: Wed. SIZE: Medium. *STOCK: Ocean liner memorabilia, china, silver-plate, ephemera, paintings, furniture, shop fittings, 1840-1990, £5-£5,000.* LOC: Main road into city centre from the east. PARK: 20yds. TEL: 01703 227458; fax - same. SER: Valuations. FAIRS: Beaulieu Boat & Auto; Ship Show, Westminster.

H.M. Gilbert and Son

2 1/2 Portland St. SO14 7EB. ABA. (R.C. and A.M. Gilbert). Est. 1859. Open 9-5. *STOCK: Antiquarian and secondhand books, £1-£500.* PARK: Easy. TEL: 01703 226420. SER: Valuations; bookbinding; repairs.

L. Moody

70 Bedford Place. SO15 2DS. (J. and A.H. Gubb). Est. 1905. Open 9-5. CL: Wed. pm. SIZE: Large. *STOCK: Furniture, 1650-1910; silver, porcelain, to 1900.* LOC: Half mile north of Civic Centre. PARK: 50yds. in next block. TEL: 01703 333720. SER: Valuations. VAT: Stan/Spec.

Southampton continued

Parkhouse and Wyatt Ltd

96 Above Bar. SO9 4FF. Est. 1794. SIZE: Small. *STOCK: Silver, jewellery.* LOC: City centre. PARK: Pay & display and multi-storey. TEL: 01703 226653 ext. 25. SER: Valuations; repairs.

STOCKBRIDGE

George Hofman & Ian Lemon at the Sign of the Black Cat

High St. SO20 6EY. Est. 1973. Open Tues., Thurs., Fri., Sat. 10-5.30, or by appointment. SIZE: Medium. *STOCK: General antiques and decorative items.* LOC: A30. PARK: Easy. TEL: 01264 810570/323657.

Lane Antiques

High St. SO20 6EU. (E.K. Lane). Est. 1981. Open 10-5. CL: Wed. SIZE: Small. *STOCK: English and Continental porcelain, 18th-19th C; silver and plate, decorative items, glass, small furniture.* PARK: Easy. TEL: 01264 810435.

Stockbridge Antique Centre

Old London Rd. SO20 6EJ. (Peter Rogers). Est. 1962. Open 10-5.30. SIZE: Large. *STOCK: Furniture - oak and pine, 18th-20th C, £50-£2,000; decorative items, silver and plate.* LOC: On White Hart public house roundabout. PARK: Easy. TEL: 01264 811008; fax - same. SER: Restorations (silver and jewellery). VAT: Stan/Spec.

Elizabeth Viney BADA

Jacob's House, High St. SO20 6HF. (Miss E.A. Viney MBE). Est. 1967. Open 9-5, appointment advisable Mon. and Wed. CL: Sun except by appointment. SIZE: Small. *STOCK: Period furniture - mahogany, walnut, oak and country; treen, brass and copper, especially candlesticks.* Not Stocked: Victoriana. LOC: A30. Opposite old Post Office. PARK: Easy. TEL: 01264 810761. VAT: Stan/Spec.

TADLEY

Gasson Antiques and Interiors LAPADA

P O Box 7225. RG26 5IY. Open by appointment. *STOCK: Georgian, Victorian and Edwardian furniture, clocks, porcelain and decorative items.* TEL: 01189 813636; mobile - 0860 827651.

TITCHFIELD, Nr. Fareham

Alexanders

13 South St. PO14 4DL. Open Thurs.-Sat. 10-5. *STOCK: General antiques including Art Nouveau and Art Deco.* PARK: Easy. TEL: 01329 315962. SER: Restorations (furniture); silver and chrome plating.

J.W. BLANCHARD LTD
Trade suppliers of Antique Furniture
Exports throughout the World
Described in Antiques of Britain as having
one of the largest & most comprehensive
stocks of Antiques in the South of Britain
A short journey by train from London
Incorporating: Blanchard (London) Ltd.,
86-88 Pimlico Road, London SW1
12 Jewry St., Winchester, Hampshire,
England. Phone 854547 & 852041

Titchfield continued

Gaylords

75 West St. PO14 4DG. (I. Hebbard). Est. 1970. Open 9.30-5.30. SIZE: Large. *STOCK: Furniture, from 18th C; clocks, £50-£10,000.* LOC: Junc. 9 off M27. PARK: Easy. TEL: 01329 843402; home - 01329 847134. SER: Valuations. VAT: Stan/Spec.

Robin Howard Antiques

6 & 8 South St. PO14 4DJ. Open Tues.-Sat. SIZE: Small. *STOCK: Antique and modern jewellery, silver and plate, boxes and small collectables, £10-£500.* LOC: 1/4 mile from A27. PARK: Easy. TEL: 01329 842794. SER: Valuations.

TWYFORD, Nr. Winchester

Twyford Antiques

High St. SO21 1NH. Open 9.30-5.30. SIZE: Large. *STOCK: Clocks, furniture.* TEL: 01962 713484. SER: Valuations; restorations (clocks).

UPHAM, Nr. Southampton

Susanna Fisher

Spencer. SO32 1JD. Est. 1971. Open by appointment only. *STOCK: Navigational charts and sailing directions, 16th-19th C.* TEL: 01489 860291; fax - 01489 860638. SER: Buys at auction; catalogues available. *Mainly Postal.*

WICKHAM, Nr. Fareham

Bridge House Antique Centre

Bridge St. PO17 5JH. (Barry and Jan Mapson). Est. 1995. Open 10-5 including Sun. CL: Mon. SIZE: Large - several dealers. *STOCK: Wide variety of general antiques including furniture, clocks, paintings, porcelain, silver and jewellery, Art Deco, kitchenalia, collectables, from Georgian to Edwardian and later.* LOC: Into Bridge St. from A32, premises 50 yards, adjacent to river. PARK: Wickham Sq. TEL: 01329 833079; fax - same. VAT: Stan/Spec.

WINCHESTER

Bell Fine Art

67b Parchment St. SO23 8AT. (L.E. Bell). Open 9.30-5.30. *STOCK: Watercolours, oils and prints, 1750-1950, £5-£5,000.* TEL: 01962 860439; fax - same; home - 01962 733556. SER: Valuations; restorations (oils and watercolours); buys at auction. VAT: Spec.

J.W. Blanchard Ltd LAPADA

12 Jewry St. SO23 8RZ. Est. 1940. Open 9-5. SIZE: Large. *STOCK: 18th-19th C bookcases and dining room furniture.* PARK: Own. TEL: 01962 854547/852041; fax - 01962 842572. VAT: Stan/Spec.

Winchester continued

Burns and Graham
27 St. Thomas St. SO23 9HJ. (M. and G. Rollitt). Est. 1971. Open 9.30-5.30, or by appointment. *STOCK: English furniture, mirrors, period decorative items, 1680-1840.* LOC: Town centre. PARK: At rear. TEL: 01962 853779. SER: Valuations. VAT: Stan/Spec.

Cabbages & Kings
20a Jewry St. SO23 8RZ. Open 9.30-5. SIZE: Large. *STOCK: Mainly 18th-19th C furniture, pine, pictures, old woodworking tools, architectural artefacts, unusual and decorative items, porcelain, weapons, collectors items, smalls, shipping goods.* TEL: 01962 852363; fax - 01962 855763.

The Clock-Work Shop
6a Parchment St. SO23 8AT. (P. Ponsford-Jones). Est. 1997. Open daily. SIZE: Medium. *STOCK: Longcase, wall, mantle, bracket and carriage clocks, 18th-19th C, £300-£7,000; barometers, books and tools.* LOC: Central, off main pedestrian precinct, near Smiths. PARK: Easy. TEL: 01962 842331. SER: Valuations; restorations (clocks and barometers).

Peter M. Daly
Rear of Cabbages and Kings, 20a Jewry St. SO23 8RZ. PBFA. Open Wed., Fri. and Sat. 10-5. *STOCK: Rare and secondhand books; some pictures and prints, maps.* TEL: Home - 01962 867732.

H.M. Gilbert
19 The Square. SO23 9EY. ABA. (R.C. and A.M. Gilbert). Open 9-5.30. *STOCK: Antiquarian and secondhand books, £1-£1,000.* TEL: 01962 852832. SER: Valuations; repairs; rebinding.

G.E. Marsh Antique Clocks Ltd BADA
32a The Square. SO23 9EX. Est. 1947. Open 9.30-5, Sat. 9.30-1 and 2-5. *STOCK: English clocks, watches and barometers c1680-1880, including longcase, bracket, French and Continental.* LOC: Near Cathedral. PARK: Easy. TEL: 01962 844443; fax - same. SER: Saleroom valuations; restorations; commissions.

The Pine Cellars
39 Jewry St. and 7 Upper Brook St. SO23 8RY. (N. Spencer-Brayn). Est. 1970. Open 10-5. SIZE: Large and warehouses. *STOCK: Pine and country furniture, 18th-19th C, £10-£5,000; painted furniture, architectural items, panelled rooms.* LOC: One way street, a right turn from top of High St. or St. Georges St., shop 100yds. on right. Brook St. premises - opposite Brooks Shopping Centre. PARK: Nearby. TEL: 01962 867014/ 777546/870102. SER: Stripping and export. VAT: Stan/Spec.

Winchester continued

Printed Page
2/3 Bridge St. SO23 9BH. CL: Mon. SIZE: Small. *STOCK: Maps and prints, 17th-19th C, £5-£500.* LOC: Bottom of High St., cross over river and shop is on left. PARK: Chesil St. car park close to shop. TEL: 01962 854072; fax - 01962 862995; e-mail - richard@printed-page.co.uk; internet - www.printed-page.co.uk. SER: Framing (pictures, tapestries, medals, etc). VAT: Stan.

Mary Roofe Antiques
1 Stonemason's Court, 67 Parchment St. SO23 8AT. (R. and M. Roofe). Est. 1983. Open 10-5, Mon. by appointment. SIZE: Small. *STOCK: 18th-19th C furniture, boxes, Tunbridgeware, treen, small collectors' items, £5-£2,500.* LOC: 200yds. from High St. and Buttercross. TEL: 01962 840613; home - 01962 862619.

Samuels Spencers Antiques and Decorative Arts Emporium
39 Jewry St. SO23 8RY. (N. Spencer-Brayn). Open 10-5. SIZE: 31 dealers. *STOCK: General antiques.* LOC: One way street, right turn from top of High St. or St. George St., shop 100yds. on right. PARK: Nearby. TEL: 01962 867014/ 777546.

SPCK Bookshops
24 The Square. SO23 9EX. Open 9-5.30. *STOCK: Secondhand theological books.* TEL: 01962 866617.

Todd and Austin Antiques of Winchester
2 Andover Rd. SO23 7BS. (G. Austin). Est. 1964. Open by appointment only. SIZE: Medium. *STOCK: 19th C paperweights, silver tea caddies, boxes, objets d'art and decorative items.* LOC: 1 minute from Winchester Station. PARK: Easy. TEL: 01962 869824. SER: Selected range on view at Lainston House Hotel, Sparsholt, Nr Winchester; finder service.

Webb Fine Arts
38 Jewry St. SO23 8RY. (D.H. Webb). Est. 1955. Open 9-5, Sat. 9-1. SIZE: Large - 4 floors. *STOCK: Oil paintings and furniture.* PARK: Own. TEL: 01962 842273. SER: Valuations; restorations (oil paintings); lining and framing; buys at auction (paintings). VAT: Stan/Spec.

Herefordshire

Key to number of shops in this area.

- ○ 1–2
- ⊖ 3–5
- ◓ 6–12
- ● 13+

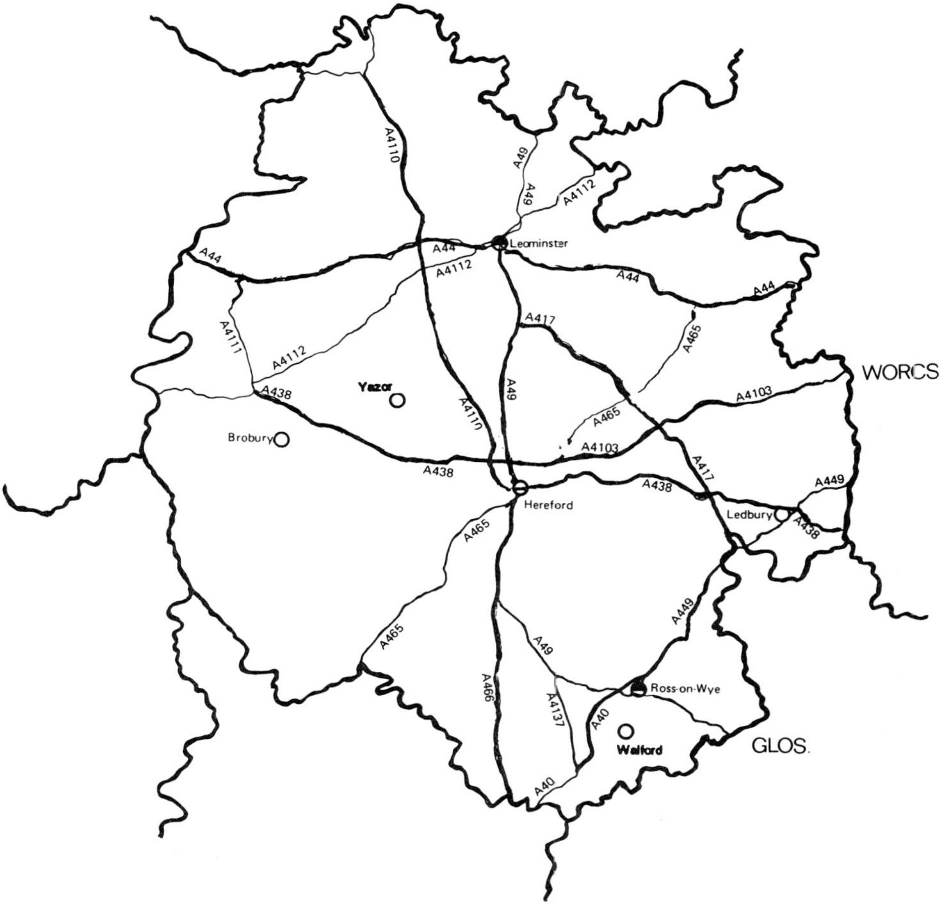

Leominster

Yazor

Brobury

Hereford

Ledbury

Ross-on-Wye

Walford

WORCS

GLOS.

Please note this is only a rough map designed to show dealers the number of shops in the various towns, and is not necessarily totally accurate.

BROBURY, Nr. Hay-on-Wye

Brobury House Gallery

HR3 6BS. Resident. (L. Weaver). Est. 1972. Open 9-4.30, 9-4 in winter. *STOCK: Old prints, 17th-20th C; watercolours, 19th-20th C.* PARK: Easy. TEL: 01981 500229. SER: Restorations (framing). VAT: Stan.

HEREFORD

I. and J.L. Brown Ltd

58-59 Commercial Rd. HR1 2BP. Open 8-5.30. SIZE: Large. *STOCK: Matched sets of period country chairs, £500-£4,000; English country and French provincial furniture, decorative items.* LOC: A465, 300 metres from railway station, 100 metres from city ring road. PARK: 2 minutes walk from shop. TEL: 01432 358895; fax - 01432 275338; home - 01432 840674. SER: Restorations; re-rushing chairs. VAT: Stan/Spec.

Chatelain Antiques and Interior Decoration

4 St. Nicholas St. HR4 0BG. Est. 1970. Open Wed.-Sat. 10-5 or by appointment. SIZE: Medium. *STOCK: General antiques including beds and mirrors, 17th-20th C.* PARK: Easy. TEL: 01432 350389; fax - same. SER: Valuations; restorations. VAT: Stan/Spec.

Great Brampton House Antiques Ltd

LAPADA

Great Brampton House, Madley. HR2 9NA. (Lady Pidgeon). Est. 1969. Open 9-5 or by appointment. SIZE: Large. *STOCK: English and French furniture and fine art.* TEL: 01981 250244; fax - 01981 251333.

Hereford Antique Centre

128 Widemarsh St. HR4 9HN. (L. F. Mitchell). Est. 1991. Open 9-5, Sun. 1-5. SIZE: 30 dealers. *STOCK: General antiques and collectables.* PARK: Easy. TEL: 01432 266242. SER: Restorations; shipping.

Warings of Hereford

45-47 St. Owen St. HR1 2JB. Open 9-6 including Sun. *STOCK: Fine 19th C furniture, farmhouse pine; gold and silver.* TEL: 01432 276241.

LEDBURY

John Nash Antiques and Interiors

LAPADA

Tudor House, 17c High St. HR8 1DS. (J. Nash and L. Calleja). Est. 1972. Open 10-5.30, Sun. by appointment. SIZE: Medium. *STOCK: Mahogany, oak and walnut furniture, 18th-20th C, £300-£10,000; decorative items, fabrics and wallpapers.* TEL: 01531 635714; fax - 01531 635050; home - 01684 540432. SER: Valuations; restorations; buys at auction (furniture, silver). VAT: Stan/Spec.

Ledbury continued

Serendipity

The Tythings, Preston Court. HR8 2LL. (Mrs R. Ford). Open 9-5 or by appointment. SIZE: Large. *STOCK: 17th-20th C furniture and general antiques.* LOC: Take A449 for 3 miles from Ledbury, at roundabout turn left on B4215, premises 500yds. on left behind half-timbered house. TEL: 01531 660245/660380. SER: Restorations (furniture); buys at auction. FAIRS: Kensington; Olympia. VAT: Stan/Spec.

LEOMINSTER

Barometer Shop

New St. HR6 8BT. (R. Cookson). Est. 1965. Open 9-5 or by appointment. *STOCK: Barometers, barographs, clocks, scientific instruments, period furniture.* LOC: Corner of A49 and Broad St. PARK: Easy. TEL: 01568 613652/610200. SER: Valuations; restorations (workshop on the Register of the Conservation Unit of the Museums and Galleries Commission); barometers and clock spares.

Coltsfoot Gallery

Hatfield. HR6 0SF. (Edwin Collins). Est. 1971. SIZE: Medium. *STOCK: Sporting and wildlife watercolours and prints, £20-£2,000.* PARK: Easy. TEL: 01568 760277; home - same. SER: Restoration and conservation of works of art on paper; mounting; framing.

Courts Miscellany

48A Bridge St. Open 10.30-5. *STOCK: General curios including corkscrews, social and political history, police, fire brigade and sporting items; tools, horse brasses, enamel signs - advertising, military, brewery; studio pottery and commemoratives.* TEL: 01565 612995.

P. and S.N. Eddy

22 Etnam St. HR6 8AQ. Resident. Est. 1951. Open 9-6. CL: Sun. except by appointment. SIZE: Small. *STOCK: Oak and mahogany furniture; saltglaze stoneware, 18th C brass and copper, early metalware, treen and bygones.* Not Stocked: Arms, armour, coins, medals, jewellery. LOC: A44. PARK: Easy. TEL: 01568 612813; home - same.

Farmers Gallery

1 High St. SIZE: 6 galleries. *STOCK: 18th-19th C furniture, paintings, prints, maps, frames, needlework, porcelain and decorative items.* LOC: Town centre. PARK: Easy. TEL: 01568 611413; fax - 01568 611141. SER: Exhibition gallery available.

Leominster continued

Jeffery Hammond Antiques LAPADA

'Shaftesbury House', 38 Broad St. HR6 8BS. Resident. (J. and E. Hammond). Est. 1970. Open 9-6, Sun. by appointment. SIZE: Medium. *STOCK: Furniture and works of art, 18th to early 19th C.* LOC: Town centre. PARK: Own. TEL: 01568 614876; fax - same; internet - www.gen.com/creative-eye/jhshop.htm. SER: Valuations; buys at auction (furniture). VAT: Stan/Spec.

Hubbard Antiques LAPADA

The Golden Lion, Bridge St. HR6 8DU. Resident. (D. T. and P. Saunders). Open by appointment. *STOCK: 16th-18th C oak furniture, especially dressers and coffers; copper, 18th-19th C; patchwork quilts.* LOC: North side of town, just off by-pass. PARK: Own. TEL: 01568 614362; mobile - 0410 639935.

Leominster Antiques Market

14 Broad St. Open 10-5. SIZE: 15 traders - 3 floors. *STOCK: General antiques, country and painted furniture, mahogany, oak, pine, treen, kitchenalia, pottery, porcelain, collectables, textiles, pictures, tools, metalware, silver, jewellery, clocks and architectural antiques, etc.* TEL: 01568 612189.

Moreden Prints

at The Old Shoe Box, Church St. (B. Croxton). Open by appointment. *STOCK: Antiquarian and collectable prints and maps, furniture and smalls.* TEL: 01568 611414. SER: Book and print search; mount cutting; framing.

ROSS-ON-WYE

Baileys Architectural Antiques

The Engine Shed, Ashburton Industrial Estate. HR9 7BW. (M. and S. Bailey). Est. 1978. Open 9-5. SIZE: Medium. *STOCK: Garden tools and furniture, French and English lighting, pews, chapel chairs, ironwork, dressers, tables, cast iron fireplaces, marble and wood surrounds, mirrors, tiles, bathroom taps, baths and basins, kitchen sinks, buckets, apple boxes, flower pots, trugs, pictures and planters.* LOC: Gloucester side of Ross, just off A40. TEL: 01989 563015; fax - 01989 768172.

The Elizabethan Shop

23/24 Brookend St. HR9 7EE. Est. 1970. Open 9.30-5.30. SIZE: Large - 5 showrooms. *STOCK: Country oak, 17th-19th C, especially dressers, gatelegs, Windsors; French country furniture, fruitwood, bookcases, farmhouse tables, longcase clocks, candlesticks, metalware.* LOC: 100yds. downhill from Market Hall. PARK: Nearby. TEL: 01989 562123; fax - same. SER: Restorations (furniture, oil paintings, metalware and long case clocks). VAT: Global/Spec.

Ross-on-Wye continued

Fritz Fryer Antique Lighting

12 Brookend St. HR9 7EG. (F. Fryer and J. Graham). Est. 1981. Open 10-5.30, Sun. by appointment. SIZE: Large. *STOCK: Decorative lighting, original shades, Georgian to Art Deco.* TEL: 01989 567416; fax - 01989 566742. SER: Restorations; lighting scheme design.

Relics

31 High St. HR9 5HD. (Mr and Mrs I. Power). Open 10-5. CL: Wed. *STOCK: Jewellery, linen, silver, clocks, smalls and furniture.* TEL: 01989 564539. SER: Restorations and repairs (clocks and jewellery).

Ross Old Book and Print Shop

51 and 52 High St. HR9 5HH. Open 10-5. *STOCK: Antiquarian and secondhand books, prints and maps.* TEL: 01989 567458.

Singleton Antiques

29-30 Brookend St. HR9 7EF. (J.W. & A.A Chapman). Est. 1994. Open 9.30-5.30. SIZE Medium. *STOCK: Oak, 17th-19th C, £500-£5,000; country furniture, 18th-19th C, £100-£2,000; decorative items and pictures, 19th-20th C, £10-£2,000.* LOC: Main shopping street. PARK: Easy. TEL: 01989 763400; fax - 01989 763200. SER: Valuations. VAT: Stan/Spec.

Ross-on-Wye continued

Trecilla Antiques

36 High St. HR9 5HD. (Lt. Col. and Mrs I.G. Mathews). Est. 1969. Open 9.30-5. CL: Sun. and Wed pm., except by appointment. SIZE: Large. *STOCK: Furniture, longcase clocks, all periods; arms and armour, £50-£7,500; silver, china, glass, metalware, £10-£3,000; prints, maps, militaria and bygones, £1-£500.* LOC: A40. PARK: Private. TEL: 01989 563010; home - 01981 540274. SER: Valuations; restorations; buys at auction. VAT: Stan/Spec.

WALFORD, Nr. Ross-on-Wye

Old Pine Shop

Warryfield Barn. HR9 5QW. Open 10-5 or by appointment. SIZE: Large. *STOCK: Pine furniture, especially dressers, chests, tables, desks, blanket boxes, wardrobes, linen presses; Victorian brass and iron bedsteads.* LOC: Approx. 3 miles from Ross town. TEL: 01989 566331; workshop - 01989 768278. SER: Restorations.

YAZOR

M. and J. Russell

The Old Vicarage. HR4 7BA. Est. 1969. Usually open Fri. to Mon. and evenings, other times appointment advisable. *STOCK: English period oak and country furniture, some garden antiques.* LOC: 7 miles west of Hereford on A480. TEL: 01981 590674. *Mainly Trade.*

Quite topical. 1953 'Titanic' poster offered at Christie's South Kensington on 9th March 1998 in their Vintage Film Poster sale – estimate £300-£500.

From an Auction Preview which appeared in the March 1998 issue of **Antique Collecting**

Hertfordshire

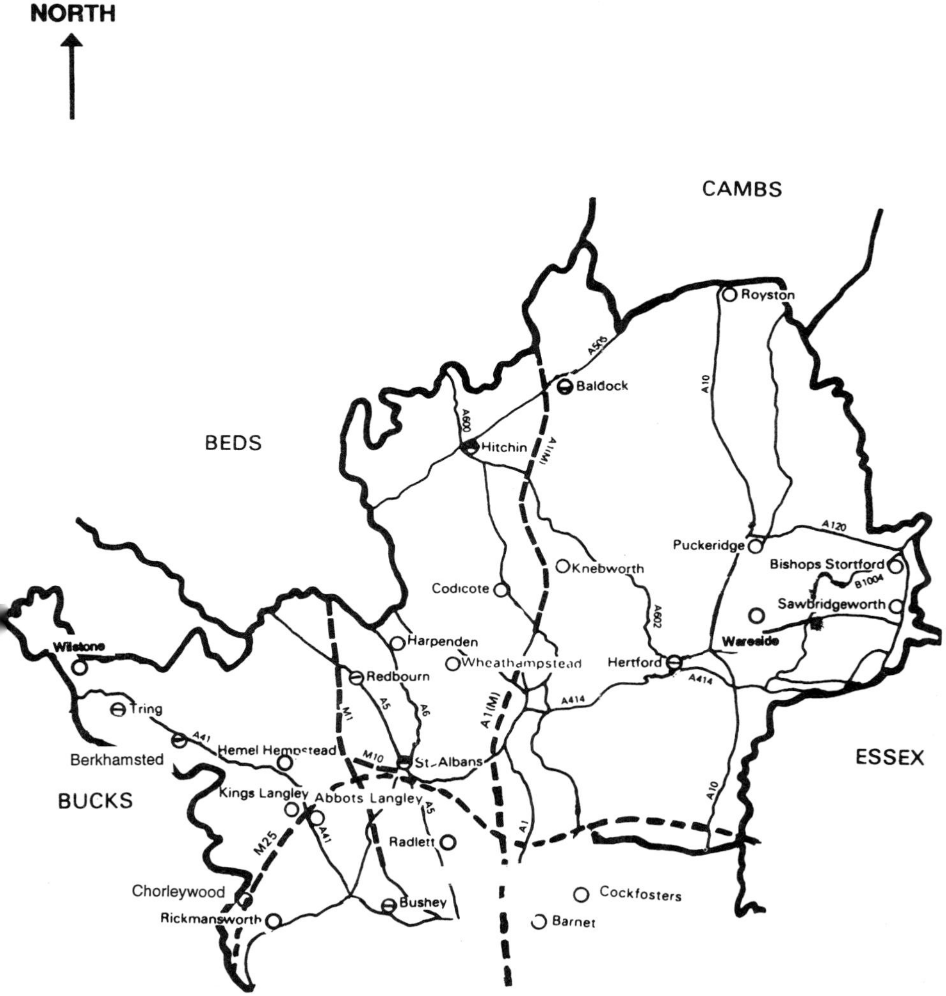

CAMBS
BEDS
BUCKS
ESSEX
Royston
A505
Baldock
A10
A600
Hitchin
A1(M)
A120
Puckeridge
Bishops Stortford
B1004
Knebworth
Codicote
Sawbridgeworth
A602
Harpenden
Wareside
Wilstone
Wheathampstead
Hertford
Redbourn
A414
A414
A5
A6
A1(M)
Tring
M1
A41
Hemel Hempstead
M10
St. Albans
Berkhamsted
Kings Langley
Abbots Langley
A5
A10
A1
A41
M25
Radlett
Chorleywood
Bushey
Cockfosters
Rickmansworth
Barnet

○ 1-2	Key to number of shops in this area.
⊖ 3-5	
◒ 6-12	
● 13+	

Please note this is only a rough map designed to show dealers the number of shops in the various towns, and is not necessarily totally accurate.

ABBOTS LANGLEY, Nr. Watford

Dobson's Antiques

53 High St. WD5 0AA. Est. 1926. Open 8.30-5.30. CL: Tues. pm. *STOCK: Carved oak, stripped pine, shipping goods, bric-a-brac, £5-£2,000.* LOC: 4 miles north of Watford. TEL: 01923 263186. VAT: Stan/Spec.

BALDOCK

The Attic

20 Whitehorse St. SG7 6QN. (P. Sheppard). Est. 1977. CL: Thurs. SIZE: Small. *STOCK: Small furniture, china, brass and copper, dolls and teddy bears, £5-£100.* LOC: 3 minutes from A1(M). PARK: Easy. TEL: 01462 893880.

Anthony Butt Antiques

7/9 Church St. SG7 5AE. Resident. Usually open. *STOCK: English furniture, 17th-19th C, £500-£5,000; works of art and objects of interest.* Not Stocked: Bric-a-brac, shipping goods. PARK: Easy. TEL: 01462 895272. SER: Valuations. VAT: Spec.

Howards

33 Whitehorse St. SG7 6QF. (D.N. Howard). Est. 1970. Open 9.30-5.00. CL: Mon. *STOCK: Clocks, 18th-19th C, £200-£5,000.* PARK: Easy. TEL: 01462 892385. SER: Valuations; restorations and repairs (clocks). VAT: Spec.

Ralph and Bruce Moss

26 Whitehorse St. SG7 6QQ. (R.A. and B.A. Moss). Est. 1973. Open 9-6. SIZE: Large. *STOCK: Furniture, £100-£10,000; general antiques, £5-£5,000.* LOC: A505, in town centre. PARK: Own. TEL: 01462 892751; fax - same. VAT: Stan/Spec.

The Wheelwright

1 Mansfield Rd. SG7 6EB. Resident. (E. and L. Hurst). Est. 1976. Open 9.30-5.30. CL: Thurs. SIZE: Medium. *STOCK: Small porcelain and china, jewellery, small furniture, bric-a-brac, 19th C, £5-£500.* LOC: Off A1. PARK: Easy. TEL: 01462 893876.

BARNET

C. Bellinger Antiques

91 Wood St. EN5 4BX. Est. 1974. Open Thurs., Fri. and Sat. 10-4 or by appointment. SIZE: Medium. *STOCK: Furniture, silver and plate, smalls.* LOC: Opposite Ravenscroft Park. PARK: Within 100yds. TEL: 0181 449 3467. VAT: Stan/Spec.

Scrummager's Haunt

188 High St. EN5 5SZ. Est. 1995. Open 10-5, Sat. 10-5.30, Sun. 12-5. SIZE: Medium. *STOCK: Collectibles, £5-£100; pine furniture, £100-£900; jewellery, £10-£100; all 19th-20th C.* PARK: At Hadley Green. TEL: 0181 441 6050; fax - 0181 441 4642.

BERKHAMSTED

Gossoms End Antiques

Entreat, Gossoms End. (David White). Est. 1970. Open 10-6 including Sun. SIZE: Small. *STOCK: Furniture and decorative items, £50-£2,000; mirrors, books, pine, china, glass, toys, sporting relics, collectibles, £5-£2,000; oil paintings, watercolours and prints, £25-£2,000; all 18th-20th C.* LOC: From junction 20, M25 onto A41 or junction 8, M1 onto A414, through Berkhamsted to Gossoms End. PARK: Easy. TEL: 01442 878786; home - same. SER: Valuations; restorations; buys at auction. FAIRS: Kensington Brocante; Sandown Park. VAT: Stan/Spec.

Home and Colonial

134 High St. HP4 3AT. (Alison and Graeme Reid-Davies and Liz and Tony Stanton-Kipping). Open 10-5.30, Sun. 11-4.30. CL: Wed. SIZE: Large. *STOCK: Furniture, country antiques and collectables, clocks and barometers, art, pictures, china and jewellery, 18th-19th C, £100-£1,500.* PARK: Easy. TEL: 01442 877007. SER: Valuations.

BISHOP'S STORTFORD

The Windhill Antiquary

4 High St. CM23 2LT. (G.R. Crozier). Est. 1951. Open 10-1 and 2-4, appointment advisable. CL: Wed. pm. SIZE: Medium. *STOCK: English furniture, 18th C; carved and gilded wall mirrors, 17th-19th C.* Not Stocked: Shipping goods. LOC: Next to George Hotel. PARK: Up hill - first right. TEL: 01279 651587; home - 01920 821316.

BUSHEY, Nr. Watford

Bushey Antique Centre

39 High St. WD2 1NB. (Graham Lindsay). Est. 1983. Open 9.30-5.30, Sun. 10-4.30. SIZE: 30 dealers. *STOCK: Furniture, 18th-20th C, £50-£500; smalls, collectables, clocks, dolls and jewellery, £5-£250; fireplaces and chimney pieces, 18th-19th C, £160-£800.* LOC: Between Harrow and Watford. PARK: At rear. TEL: 0181 950 5040; home - same. SER: Valuations; restorations (woodwork and furniture); buys at auction (furniture and fires). VAT: Spec.

Circa Antiques

43 High St., Bushey Village. (K. Wildman). Est. 1978. Open 9.30-5.30 or by appointment. SIZE: Medium. *STOCK: General antiques, furniture, porcelain, silver and clocks.* TEL: 0181 950 9233.

Country Life Antiques

33a High St. WD2 1BDA. (Peter Myers). Est. 1981. Open 9-5. SIZE: Large. *STOCK: Victorian and Edwardian, European and Scandinavian original pine, French country oak; kitchenalia, watercolours, china and Art Deco.* PARK: Easy. TEL: 0181 950 8576. VAT: Stan.

Bushey continued

Thwaites and Co
33 Chalk Hill, Oxhey. WD1 4BL. Est. 1971. Open 9-5, Sat. 9.30-12.30. *STOCK: Stringed instruments, from violins to double basses.* TEL: 01923 232412. SER: Restorations.

CHORLEYWOOD

The Architectural Salvage Store
Unit 6, Darvells Works, Common Rd. WD3 5LP. (Tony Pattison). Open 9.30-6, Sun. 11-2. CL: Mon. SIZE: Large *STOCK: Doors, glass, 18th `C to 1930, £5-£1,000; fireplaces, marble and stone, 18th C to 1920, £500-£3,000; garden ornaments, 19th C to 1950, £1,000-£2,000.* LOC: A404 from M25, junction 18. After .75 mile, turn left at lights to town centre, premises 500yds. on right. PARK: Easy. TEL: 01923 284196; fax - 01923 284146. SER: Restorations (glass, marble, stone). VAT: Stan/Spec.

COCKFOSTERS

H. Pordes Ltd
383 Cockfosters Rd. EN4 0JS. *STOCK: Antiquarian books including scientific and learned; periodicals, overstocks and remainders.* TEL: 0181 449 2524; fax - 0181 441 9595. *Postal Only.*

CODICOTE

Wheldon and Wesley Ltd
Lytton Lodge. SG4 8TE. Est. 1921. Open by appointment only. *STOCK: Antiquarian books on Natural History.* TEL: 01438 820370; fax - 01438 821478. SER: Buys at auction. *Mail Order Only.*

HARPENDEN

Meg Andrews
23 Cowper Rd. AL5 5NF. Est. 1982. Open by appointment. *STOCK: Worldwide collectable, hangable and wearable antique costume and textiles including Chinese embroideries and woven fabrics, robes, shoes, hats, large hangings, Morris and Arts and Crafts embroideries and woven cloths, Paisley shawls, samplers, silkwork pictures; European costumes and textiles.* TEL: 01582 460107; home - same; fax - same. SER: Valuations; advice; buys at auction.

HEMEL HEMPSTEAD

Abbey Antiques - Fine Jewellery & Silver
97 High St., Old Town. HP1 3AH. (L., E., S. and C. Eames). Est. 1962. Open 9.30-5.30. SIZE: Medium. *STOCK: Silver, plate, jewellery, £5-£5,000.* LOC: M1, junction 8, M25, junction 20, bypass main shopping centre to old town. PARK: Easy. TEL: 01442 264667. SER: Valuations; jewellery design and repair. VAT: Stan/Global.

Hemel Hempstead continued

Cherry Antiques
101-103 High St. HP1 3AH. (A. and R.S. Cullen). Open 9.30-4.30. CL: Wed. pm. SIZE: Medium. *STOCK: Victorian, Edwardian, and some period furniture, pine, general antiques, collectors' and decorative items, bric-a-brac, needlework tools, dolls, linens, some silver, plate, jewellery, glass, pottery, porcelain, brass, copper, some shipping items.* PARK: Easy. TEL: 01442 64358. VAT: Stan/Spec.

HERTFORD

Beckwith and Son
St. Nicholas Hall, St. Andrew St. SG14 1HZ. (G.C.M. Gray). Est. 1904. Open 9-1 and 2-5.30. SIZE: Large. *STOCK: General antiques, furniture, silver, pottery, porcelain, prints, weapons, clocks, watches, glass.* Not Stocked: Fabrics. LOC: A414/B158. PARK: Adjacent. TEL: 01992 582079. SER: Valuations; restorations (fine porcelain, furniture, upholstery, silver, clocks). VAT: Spec.

Hertford Antiques
51 St Andrew St. SG14 1HZ. (S.D. Garratt and R.F. Norris). Est. 1994. Open 10-5.30 including Sun. SIZE: Large - 50+ dealers. *STOCK: Furniture, jewellery, porcelain, silver, glass, books, £5-£4,000.* LOC: Next to St Andrew's Church. PARK: Easy. TEL: 01992 504504.

Robert Horton Antiques
13 Castle St. SG14 1ER. Est. 1972. Open 9-5. *STOCK: Clocks, barometers, furniture.* TEL: 01992 587546. VAT: Stan/Spec.

HITCHIN

Bexfield Antiques
13 and 14 Sun St. SG5 1AH. (A.B. Bexfield). Est. 1962. Open 9.30-5. CL: Mon. and Wed. *STOCK: Jewellery, silver, porcelain, copper, pewter and furniture.* PARK: Nearby. TEL: 01462 432641; fax - 01462 631555; e-mail - arthur@bexfield.demon.co.uk. SER: Valuations (probate and insurance).

Countrylife Gallery
41-43 Portmill Lane. SG4 7SH. (David and Monica Moore). Open by appointment only. SIZE: Small. *STOCK: Watercolours - botanical, flower and natural history, 1780-1930, £50-£500; oils - flowers and natural history, 1850-1930, £500-£5,000.* LOC: Town square. PARK: 50yds. TEL: 01462 433267; home - same. SER: Valuations; restorations; buys at auction (English watercolours and pictures). FAIRS: Royal Horticultural Socy. VAT: Spec.

Michael Gander
10-11 Bridge St. SG5 2DE. Est. 1973. Open 9-6. *STOCK: Period furniture, metalware.* TEL: 01462 432678.

Hitchin continued

Hanbury Antiques

86 Tilehouse St. SG5 2DU. (Mrs M.D. Hanbury). Est. 1988. CL: Wed afternoons. SIZE: Small. *STOCK: Period furniture, porcelain, silver, jewellery.* LOC: Continuation of Bridge St. PARK: 100 yards. TEL: 01462 420487; home - same. SER: Valuations.

Eric T. Moore

24 Bridge St. SG5 2DF. Open 9.30-1 and 2.15-5.30, Wed. 9-12.30, Sat. 9.30-5.30. *STOCK: Antiquarian books, maps and prints.* TEL: 01462 450497. SER: Picture framing, mount cutting.

Phillips of Hitchin (Antiques) Ltd BADA

The Manor House. SG5 1JW. (M. and J. Phillips). Est. 1884. Open 9-5.30. SIZE: Large. *STOCK: Furniture, walnut and mahogany, 18th to early 19th C, £500-£20,000.* LOC: In Bancroft, main street of Hitchin. PARK: Easy. TEL: 01462 432067; fax - 01462 441368. SER: Restorations (furniture); books on collecting. FAIRS: Specialist antique exhibitions at the Manor House. VAT: Spec.

Tom Salusbury Antiques

9A Bridge St. Est. 1963. SIZE: Small. *STOCK: Furniture, 18th-19th C, £100-£3,000; accessories, 18th-20th C, £10-£500.* LOC: 3 miles from A1, junction 8. PARK: At rear. TEL: 01462 454274; fax - same. SER: Valuations; restorations; buys at auction. FAIRS: Luton. VAT: Stan/Spec.

Carole Thomas (Fine Arts)

28 Bridge St. SG5 1DF. Est. 1976. Open 11-5.30, appointment advisable on Wed. *STOCK: English watercolours, 1800-1950, £100-£4,000; oil paintings, drawings, etchings from £60.* LOC: Near town centre. PARK: Own. TEL: 01462 436077. SER: Valuations; cleaning; restoring; framing. VAT: Stan.

KING'S LANGLEY

Frenches Farm Antiques

Tower Hill, Chipperfield. WD4 9LN. (I. Cross). Est. 1972. Open 2-6 or by appointment. SIZE: Large. *STOCK: Furniture including pine, £15-£700; porcelain, Victoriana, copper, brass, £3-£100; mainly 18th-19th C.* Not Stocked: Silver, jewellery, firearms, paintings. LOC: From Chipperfield take Bovingdon Rd. On right 500yds. from Royal Oak public house. PARK: Easy. TEL: 01923 265843.

KNEBWORTH

Hamilton Billiards & Games Co.

Park Lane. SG3 6PJ. (H. Hamilton). Est. 1980. Open 9-5, weekends and evenings by appointment. SIZE: Large. *STOCK: Victorian and Edwardian billiard tables, £3,000-£18,000; 19th C convertible billiard/dining tables and accessories, £30-£5,000; indoor and outdoor games.*

Knebworth continued

LOC: Near railway station. PARK: Easy. TEL: 01438 811995. SER: Valuations; restorations (billiard tables and furniture); buys at auction (as stock). VAT: Stan.

PUCKERIDGE

St. Ouen Antiques

Vintage Corner, Old Cambridge Rd. SG11 1SA. (J., J. and S.T. Blake and Mrs P.B. Francis). Est. 1918. Open 10.30-5. SIZE: Large. *STOCK: English and Continental furniture, decorative items, silver, porcelain, pottery, glass, clocks, barometers, paintings.* TEL: 01920 821336. SER: Valuations; restorations.

RADLETT

Hasel-Britt Ltd

157 Watling St. WD7 7NQ. (Mrs Britton). Est. 1962. Open 10-5.30. CL: Wed. pm. *STOCK: General antiques, 19th C; pottery and porcelain.* TEL: 01923 854477.

REDBOURN, Nr St. Albans

Bushwood Antiques LAPADA

Stags End Equestrian Centre, Gaddesden Lane. HP2 6HN. Est. 1967. Open Mon.-Fri. 8.30-4, or by appointment. SIZE: Medium. *STOCK: 18th-19th C furniture, decorative items, works of art and clocks.* TEL: 01582 794700; fax - 01582 792299. VAT: Spec.

J.N. Antiques

86 High St. AL3 7BD. (M. and J. Brunning). Est. 1975. Open 9-6. SIZE: Medium. *STOCK: Furniture, 18th-20th C, £5-£3,000; brass and copper, porcelain, 19th C, £5-£100; pictures, 19th-20th C.* PARK: 50 yds. TEL: 01582 793603; fax - same. SER: Valuations. VAT: Spec.

Tim Wharton Antiques LAPADA

24 High St. AL3 7LL. Est. 1970. Open 10-5.30, Sat. 10-4. CL: Mon. and usually Thurs. *STOCK: Oak and country furniture, 17th-19th C; some mahogany, 18th to early 19th C; copper, brass, ironware and general small antiques.* LOC: On left entering village from St. Albans on A5183. PARK: Easy. TEL: 01582 794371. VAT: Stan/Spec.

RICKMANSWORTH

Clive A. Burden

Elmcote House, The Green, Croxley Green. WD3 3HN. Est. 1966. Open by appointment only. SIZE: Medium. *STOCK: Maps, 1500-1860, £5-£1,500; natural history, botanical and Vanity Fair prints, 1720-1870, £1-£1,000; antiquarian books, pre-1870, £10-£5,000.* TEL: 01923 778097; fax - 01923 896520; home - 01923 772387. SER: Valuations; buys at auction (as stock). VAT: Stan.

For 100 years and over three generations discerning collectors from all over the world have come to find carefully chosen English period furniture displayed in the period rooms of this Georgian manor house only 30 miles (1 hour by car) from London.

PHILLIPS of HITCHIN

(ANTIQUES) LTD

The Manor House
Hitchin, Herts.

SG5 1JW

Members of the British Antique Dealers Association

Telephone: Hitchin 432067
STD 01462

Facsimile: Hitchin 441368
STD 01462

Rickmansworth continued

Galliard Antiques
2 Station Rd. WD3 1QZ. (Ellen Harriman). Open 10-5.30. CL: Mon. *STOCK: Clocks, furniture, china, silver, militaria, pictures, bronzes, coins, Art Nouveau, Art Deco.* TEL: 01923 778087; fax - 01923 773995.

ROYSTON

Royston Antiques
29 Kneesworth St. SG8 5AB. (J. and M. Newnham). Est. 1965. Open 10-5, Sat. 9.30-5. CL: Thurs. SIZE: Medium. *STOCK: Furniture, 1750-1930, £50-£2,500; porcelain, books, £5-£500; collectors' items, pine, metalware, bygones.* TEL: 01763 243876.

SAWBRIDGEWORTH

The Herts and Essex Antiques Centre
The Maltings, Station Rd. CM21 9JX. Est. 1982. Open 10-5, Sat. and Sun. 10.30-6. CL: Mon. SIZE: Large - over 100 dealers. *STOCK: General antiques and collectables, £1-£2,000.* LOC: Opposite B.R. station. PARK: Easy. TEL: 01279 722044. SER: Restorations.

ST. ALBANS

By George! Antiques Centre
23 George St. Open 10-5, Sun. 1-5. SIZE: 20 dealers. *STOCK: A wide range of general antiques, jewellery and collectables.* LOC: 100yds. from Clock Tower. PARK: Internal courtyard (loading) and Christopher Place (NCP) nearby. TEL: 01727 853032. SER: Restorations.

The Clock Shop - Philip Setterfield of St. Albans
161 Victoria St. AL1 3TA.. Est. 1974. Open 11-5, Sat. 11-4. CL: Thurs. *STOCK: Clocks and watches.* LOC: City station bridge. TEL: 01727 856633; fax - same. SER: Restorations; repairs (clocks, watches, barometers). VAT: Stan/Spec.

Forget-me-Knot Antiques
at Over the Moon, 27 High St. AL3 4EH. (Heather Sharp). Est. 1987. Open 9.30-5.30, Sun. by appointment. *STOCK: Mainly Victorian jewellery and collectables, specializing in silver name brooches.* TEL: 01727 848907. SER: Valuations. VAT: Stan.

St. Albans continued

James of St Albans

11 George St. AL3 4ER. (S.N. and W. James). Est. 1957. Open 10-5, Thurs. 10-1. *STOCK: Furniture including reproduction; smalls, brass and copper; topographical maps and prints of Hertfordshire.* TEL: 01727 856996. VAT: Stan/Spec.

Magic Lanterns

at By George! Antiques Centre, 23 George St. AL3 4ES. (Josie A. Marsden). Est. 1987. Open 10-5, Thurs. 11-5, Sat. 10-5.30, Sun. 1-5. SIZE: Medium. *STOCK: Lighting - candle, gas and early electric, 1800-1950's, £35-£1,000; small furniture, prints, mirrors, china, metalware, fire accessories, 1850-1950, £25-£500.* LOC: Near the abbey. PARK: Multi-storey nearby. TEL: 01727 853032/865680.

Oriental Rug Gallery Ltd

42 Verulam Rd. AL3 4DQ. (R. Mathias and J. Blair). Open 9-6, Sun. 10.30-4. *STOCK: Russian, Afghan, Turkish and Persian carpets, rugs and kelims; Oriental objets d'art.* TEL: 01727 841046.

St. Albans Antique Market

Town Hall, Chequer St. AL4 0XS. Est. 1978. Open Mon. 9.30 (8.30 trade)-4, some Bank Holidays. SIZE: 30 stands. *STOCK: A wide variety of antiques.* TEL: 01727 844957.

Stuart Wharton

1 George St. AL3 4ER. FGA DGA. Est. 1967. Open 9-5.30. SIZE: Medium. *STOCK: Silver, 18th-20th C, £20-£2,000; jewellery, mainly modern, £20-£5,000.* LOC: Near clock tower. PARK: Multi-storey, city centre. TEL: 01727 859489; fax - 01727 855474. SER: Registered valuer (jewellery and silver); goldsmithing, gem testing; buys at auction (silver). VAT: Stan.

TRING

John Bly BADA

The Old Billiards Room, Church Yard. HP23 5AG. Est. 1891. Open Wed., Thurs., and Sat. 9.30-4.30. SIZE: Large. *STOCK: English furniture.* TEL: 01442 890802.

Country Clocks

3 Pendley Bridge Cottages, Tring Station. HP23 5QU. Resident. (T. Cartmell). Est. 1976. Open daily, prior 'phone call advisable. SIZE: Small. *STOCK: Clocks, 18th-19th C.* LOC: One mile from A41 in village, cottage nearest canal bridge. PARK: Easy. TEL: 01442 825090. SER: Restorations (clocks).

Farrelly Antiques

The Long Barn, 50 High St. (P. Farrelly). Open 9-4. *STOCK: Furniture.* TEL: 01442 891905. SER: Restorations. VAT: Spec.

Tring continued

New England House Antiques

50 High St. HP23 5AG. (Jennifer and Suj Munjee). Est. 1990. Open 10-5. SIZE: Large - 6 showrooms on 3 floors. *STOCK: Fine Georgian and Victorian furniture, £100-£10,000; paintings, glass, silver, decorative furnishings.* LOC: A41 towards Aylesbury. PARK: Next to shop. TEL: 01442 827262; home - 01462 431914. SER: Valuations; restorations (paintings, metalwork and furniture); searches undertaken. FAIRS: Luton. VAT: Stan/Spec.

Tring Triangle Antiques Centre

15 Western Rd. HP23 4BQ. (M. Chase). Est. 1994. Open Wed.-Sun. 11-5. SIZE: Large - 20 dealers. *STOCK: General antiques, 19th C, £5-£800; Susie Cooper, Art Deco, clocks, cigarette cards, Victorian and Edwardian furniture, porcelain and collectors' items.* LOC: Continuation of the High St. PARK: Side street.TEL: 01442 825060.

WARESIDE

Wareside Antiques

SG12 7QY. (David Broxup). Est. 1983. Open by appointment only. SIZE: Medium. *STOCK: Furniture, dining tables, sets of chairs.* LOC: On Ware to Much Hadham road. PARK: Easy. TEL: 01763 281234.

WHEATHAMPSTEAD

Collins Antiques (F.G. and C. Collins Ltd.)

Corner House. AL4 8AP. (S.J. and M.C. Collins). Est. 1907. Open 9-1 and 2-5. SIZE: Large. *STOCK: Furniture, mahogany, 1730-1920, £100-£8,000; oak, 1600-1800, £50-£5,000; walnut, 1700-1740, £75-£3,000.* Not Stocked: Silver. LOC: London, A1(M) junction 4 to B653. PARK: Easy. TEL: 01582 833111. VAT: Stan/Spec.

The Old Bakery Antiques

3 Station Rd. (Maurice Shifrin). Open 10-6, Sun. 11-4. CL: Wed. SIZE: Large. *STOCK: 19th C furniture, £500-£1,000.* PARK: Easy, own. TEL: 01582 831999; fax - 01582 831555. VAT: Stan/Spec.

WILSTONE, Nr. Tring

Michael Armson (Antiques) Ltd

The Old Post Office, 34 Tring Rd. HP23 4PB. Open 8.30-5.30. SIZE: Large. *STOCK: Furniture, 17th-19th C.* TEL: 01442 890990; fax - 01442 891167; mobile - 0860 910034.

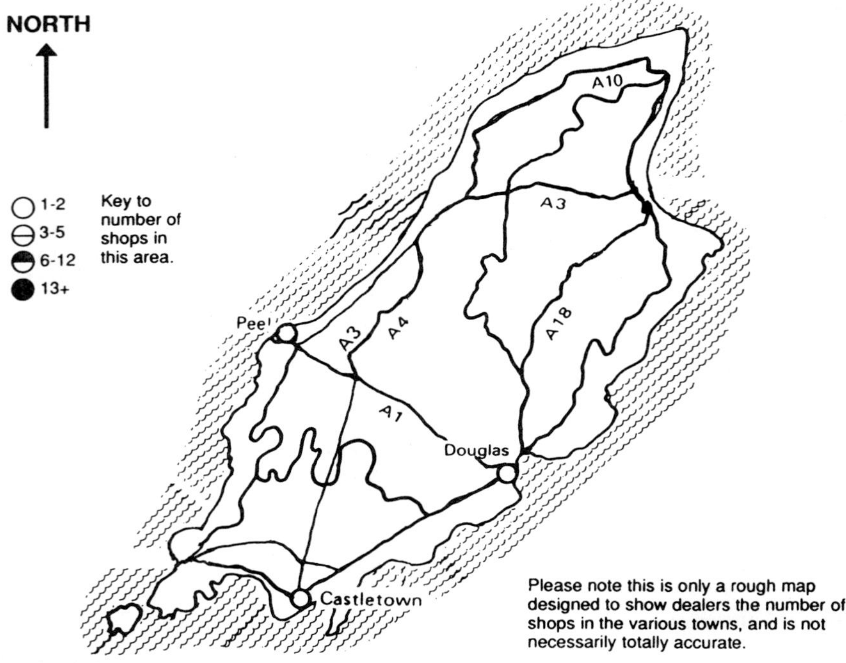

CASTLETOWN

J. and H. Bell Antiques

22 Arbory St. IM9 1LJ. Est. 1965. Open Wed., Fri. and Sat. 10-5. SIZE: Medium. *STOCK: Jewellery, silver, china, early metalware, furniture, 18th-20th C, £5-£5,000.* TEL: 01624 823132 or 01624 822414. VAT: Stan/Spec.

DOUGLAS

John Corrin Antiques

73 Circular Rd. IM1 1AZ. Est. 1972. Open Sat. 9-5.30 otherwise by appointment. SIZE: Medium. *STOCK: Furniture, 18th-19th C, £100-£6,000; clocks, barometers, 19th C.* LOC: From the promenade, travel up Victoria St., this becomes Prospect Hill and Circular Rd. is on left. PARK: Easy. TEL: 01624 629655; home - 01624 621382.

PEEL

Dorothea Horn At The Golden Past

18A Michael St. Est. 1982. Open 1-4.30, Sat. 10.30-4.30. CL: Thurs. Oct.-Mar. SIZE: Medium. *STOCK: Jewellery, porcelain, silver, glass, books and paintings, 1840-1940, £5-£100.* LOC: Main shopping street. PARK: Easy. TEL: 01624 842170; home - 01624 843839.

Isle of Wight

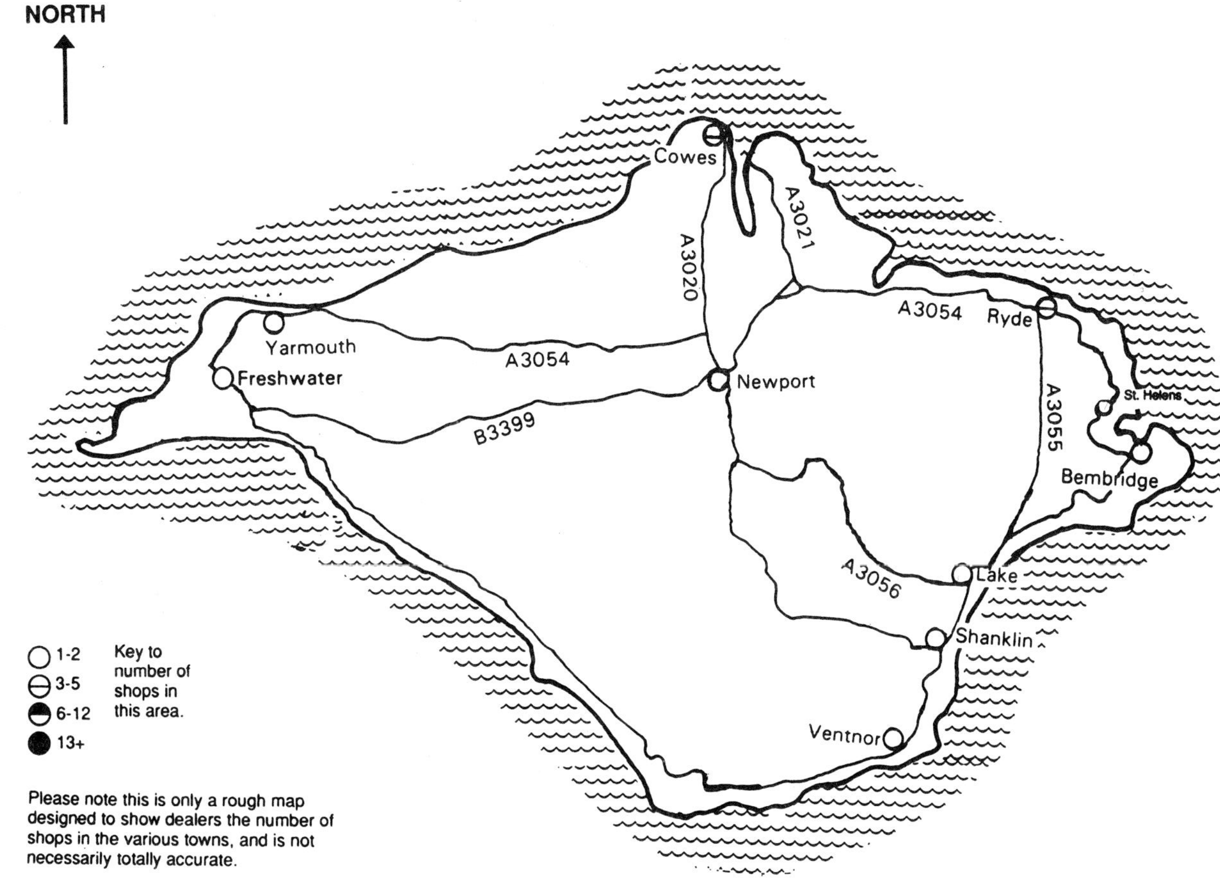
NORTH
Cowes
A3021
A3020
A3054
Ryde
Yarmouth
Freshwater
A3054
Newport
St. Helens
A3055
B3399
Bembridge
A3056
Lake
Shanklin
Ventnor
1-2
3-5
6-12
13+
Key to number of shops in this area.
Please note this is only a rough map designed to show dealers the number of shops in the various towns, and is not necessarily totally accurate.

BEMBRIDGE

Windmill Antiques LAPADA

1 Foreland Rd. PO35 5XN. (E.J. de Kort). Est. 1970. CL: Thurs. pm. SIZE: Medium. *STOCK: Furniture, silver, porcelain, jewellery.* TEL: 01983 873666. SER: Valuations; buys at auction. VAT: Stan/Spec.

COWES

Julia Margaret Cameron Gallery

90B High St. PO31 7AW. (J. Flynn). *STOCK: Antiquarian books, maps and prints especially local, postcards.* TEL: 01983 290404.

Charles Dickens Bookshop

65 High St. PO31 7RL. *STOCK: Antiquarian and secondhand books, especially 19th C English literature, nautical and children's.* TEL: 01983 293598/280586.

Galerias Segui

75 High St. PO31 7AJ. Est. 1976. Open 10-5. SIZE: Medium. *STOCK: Pine furniture, £60-£600; prints and watercolours, £15-£200; bric-a-brac.* LOC: Between Midland and Lloyds Bank, near Red Funnel Pier. PARK: 200yds. TEL: 01983 292148.

Royal Standard Antiques

70-72 Park Rd. PO31 7LY. Resident. (Dennis and Caroline Bradbury). Est. 1992. Open 10.30-5.30, or any time by appointment. SIZE: Medium. *STOCK: Victorian, Edwardian and French provincial furniture, £100-£1,000; architectural items, £50-£800; pictures, commemoratives, breweriana, £5-£500.* LOC: 5 mins. walk from hydrofoil terminus; corner of Victoria Rd. PARK: Own, behind premises. TEL: 01983 281672; home - same.

FRESHWATER

Aladdin's Cave

147/149 School Green Rd. PO40 9BB. (Mrs J. Dunn). Est. 1984. Open 9.30-4.30, including Sun. SIZE: Medium. *STOCK: China, collectors' items,*

Freshwater continued

glass, linen, old pine, furniture, memorabilia, books, 19th-20th C, £5-£500. PARK: Easy. TEL: 01983 752934; home - 01983 753846.

LAKE

Lake Antiques

Sandown Rd. PO36 9JP. (P. Burfield). Est. 1982. Open 10-4. CL: Wed. *STOCK: General antiques, Victorian and Edwardian furniture, clocks.* LOC: On the main Sandown-Shanklin Rd. PARK: On forecourt. TEL: 01983 406888/865005; mobile - 04100 67678.

NEWPORT

Mike Heath Antiques

3-4 Holyrood St. PO30 5AU. (M. and B. Heath). Est. 1974. Open 9.30-5. CL: Thurs. SIZE: Medium. *STOCK: General antiques and bric-a-brac, 19th-20th C, £5-£500.* LOC: Off High St. PARK: Nearby. TEL: 01983 525748; home - same. SER: Restorations (copper and brass).

RYDE

Hayter's

19-20 Cross St. PO33 2AD. (R.W. and F.L. Hayter). Est. 1956. Open 9-1 and 2-5.30. CL: Thurs. SIZE: Large. *STOCK: Furniture including Victorian.* LOC: Through main traffic flow from sea front to town centre. TEL: 01983 563795. VAT: Stan/Spec/Global.

Royal Victoria Arcade

Union St. Open 9-5.30; basement market open Thurs., Fri. and Sat. in summer. TEL: 01983 564661. Below are listed some of the dealers in this Arcade.

Crocus

Collectables, art deco to 1950's.

Echoes

Costume jewellery, militaria and general antiques.

Uriah's Heap

Jewellery, writing equipment, instruments, china, glass and collectables.

Ryde continued

Uriah's Heap

9 Royal Victoria Arcade, Union St. PO33 2LQ. (F. Cross). Open Wed., Fri. and Sat. 10-5. *STOCK: Small antiques, china, silver, collectables, linen, lace, fountain pens, jewellery.* TEL: 01983 564661.

SHANKLIN

The Shanklin Gallery

67 Regent St. PO37 7AE. Open 9-5. SIZE: Medium. *STOCK: Oils, watercolours, engravings, prints, maps, 17th-20th C, £10-£2,000.* LOC: Town centre near railway station. PARK: Easy. TEL: 01983 863113. SER: Valuations; restorations (oils, watercolours and prints); framing.

ST. HELENS, Nr. Bembridge

St. Helens Antiques

19 Lower Green Rd. PO33 1UB. Open daily in summer 10-1 and 2.30-5.30; winter - Mon., Wed., Fri. and Sat. 10-1 and 2.30-5. *STOCK: General antiques, ceramics, furniture, textiles, glass, Victorian jewellery, prints and violins.* TEL: 01983 874896.

VENTNOR

Peter Goodall

29 Pier St. PO38 1SX. Est. 1965. Open by appointment only. SIZE: Medium. *STOCK: Engravings, etchings, lithographs and aquatints, 17th-20th C, £5-£1,000.* TEL: 01983 856116. SER: Valuations.

Ventnor Rare Books

19 Pier St. PO38 1ST. ABA. (N.C.R. and T.A. Traylen). *STOCK: Antiquarian and secondhand books, prints.* TEL: 01983 853706; fax - 01983 853357.

YARMOUTH

Marlborough House Antiques

St. James Sq. PO41 0NS. (P.A. Webb). Est. 1972. *STOCK: Local prints and maps, silver, jewellery, pottery, glass and furniture.* TEL: 01983 760498.

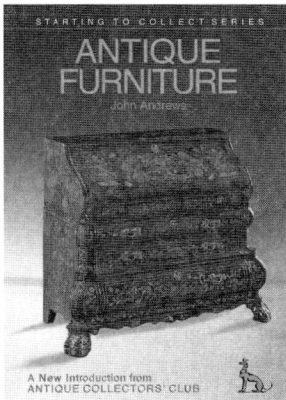

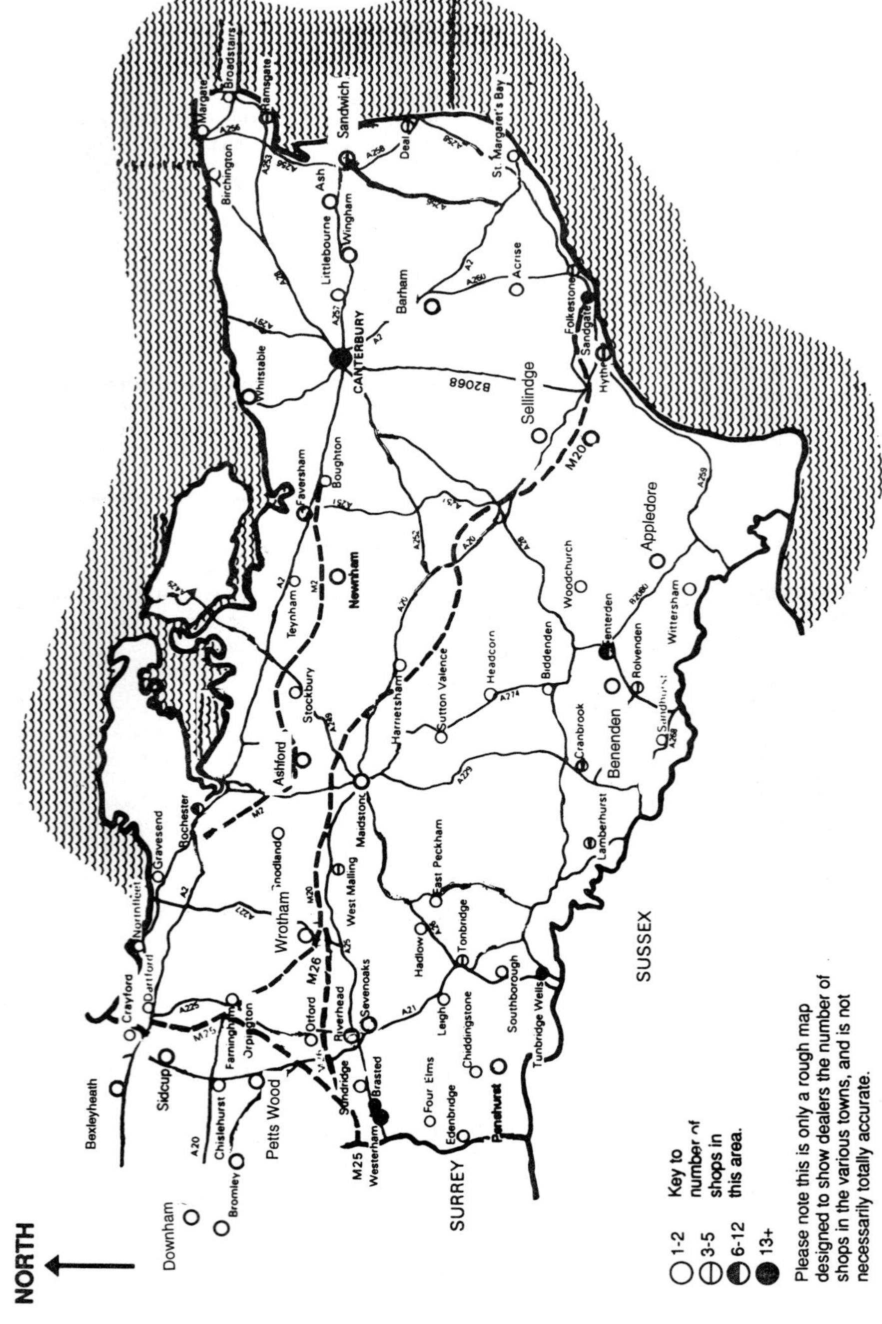
NORTH
Downham
Bromley
Chislehurst
Bexleyheath
Sidcup
Petts Wood
Crayford
Dartford
Farningham
Orpington
Northfleet
Gravesend
Rochester
Wrotham
Snodland
Ashford
Stockbury
Maidstone
West Malling
Otford
Riverhead
Sevenoaks
Sundridge
Brasted
Westerham
Four Elms
Edenbridge
Chiddingstone
Penshurst
Leigh
Hadlow
Tonbridge
Southborough
Tunbridge Wells
East Peckham
Lamberhurst
Cranbrook
Benenden
Harrietsham
Sutton Valence
Headcorn
Biddenden
Tenterden
Rolvenden
Wittersham
Woodchurch
Appledore
Teynham
Newnham
Faversham
Boughton
Whitstable
CANTERBURY
Sellindge
Hythe
Sandgate
Folkestone
Acrise
Barham
Littlebourne
Wingham
Ash
Sandwich
Deal
St. Margaret's Bay
Birchington
Margate
Broadstairs
Ramsgate
M25
M26
M20
M2
SURREY
SUSSEX
Key to number of shops in this area.
1-2
3-5
6-12
13+
Please note this is only a rough map designed to show dealers the number of shops in the various towns, and is not necessarily totally accurate.

ACRISE, Nr. Folkestone

R. Kirby Antiques

Caroline Cottage, Ridge Row. Open by appointment only. CL: Mon. *STOCK: Early period oak.* TEL: 01303 893230.

APPLEDORE, Nr. Ashford

Richard Moate Antiques and Back 2 Wood Pine Stripping

The Old Goods Shed, Station Rd. Est. 1987. Open 8.30-5, Sat. 10-12. *STOCK: Unstripped and finished pine furniture.* LOC: Adjacent to Appledore station. PARK: Easy. TEL: 01233 758109; mobile - 0831 655414; home - 01233 860400. VAT: Stan/Margin. *Trade Only.*

ASH, Nr. Canterbury

Henry's of Ash

51 The Street. CT3 2EN. (P.H. Robinson). Est. 1988. Open 10-12 and 2-5. CL: Tues. pm and Wed. SIZE: Small. *STOCK: General antiques, Victorian and Art Deco, £5-100; small furniture, £50-£500.* LOC: Main street. PARK: Outside. TEL: 01304 812600. SER: Buys at auction (small items). FAIRS: Copthorne; Ashford; Great Danes.

ASHFORD

County Antiques

Old Mill Cottage, Kennett Lane, Stanford North. TN25 6DG. (B. Nilson). Open by appointment. *STOCK: General antiques.* TEL: 01303 813039.

BARHAM

Stablegate Antiques

(Mrs. G. Giuntini). Open nearly every day, but prior 'phone call advisable. SIZE: Large. *STOCK: Georgian and Victorian dining tables, chairs, sideboards.* LOC: Village just off the A2 to Dover. PARK: Easy. TEL: 01227 831639.

BECKENHAM

Beckenham Antique Market

Old Council Hall, Bromley Rd. Est. 1979. Open Wed. only 9.30-2. SIZE: 20 stalls. *STOCK: General antiques.* TEL: 0181 777 6300.

Pepys Antiques

9 Kelsey Park Rd. BR3 2LH. (S.P. Elton). Est. 1969. Open 10-2. CL: Wed. *STOCK: Furniture, paintings, clocks, silver, porcelain, copper, brass.* LOC: Central Beckenham. TEL: 0181 650 0994.

BENENDEN

Harriet Ann Sleigh Beds

(Mrs R. Churchod). Est. 1987. Open by appointment only. SIZE: Medium. *STOCK: Eastern European and Scandinavian sleigh beds; French fruitwood doubles or singles; European pine armoires, chests and cabinets; bedside lights, bedroom decorative accessories especially*

Benenden continued

childrens. PARK: Easy. TEL: 01580 243005. SER: Mattresses available to order; reproduction beds in certain styles.

BEXLEYHEATH

Bexleyheath Antiques Centre

241 Broadway. DA6 8DB. (Jackie Marriott-Smith). Est. 1977. Open 10-5, Sat. 9.30-5.30, Sun. 11-4. SIZE: Large. *STOCK: Furniture, £20-£1,000+; jewellery, china and glass, collectables, £2-£1,000–.* LOC: Main road. PARK: Loading and nearby. TEL: 0181 303 5147; fax - same. SER: Valuations; monthly auctions held. FAIRS: Ardingly; Newark.

BIDDENDEN, Nr. Ashford

Two Maids Antiques

6 High St. TN27 8AH. (J. Thornley). Est. 1979. Open 10-5 and by appointment. CL: Mon. and Wed. SIZE: Medium. *STOCK: 17th-18th C metalwork, lace bobbins, Victorian picture frames, wood carvings, treen, miniatures and small furniture.* LOC: A262. PARK: Opposite. TEL: 01580 291807; home - same.

BIRCHINGTON, Nr. Margate

John Chawner

36 Station Approach. CT7 9RD. Open 10.30-12.30 and 2-5. CL: Tues. *STOCK: Clocks, barometers, smalls and bureaux.* PARK: Easy. TEL: 01843 843309. SER: Repairs (clocks and barometers).

BOUGHTON, Nr. Faversham

Clockshop

187 The Street. ME13 9BH. LBHI. Resident. (S.G. Fowler). Est. 1968. Open 10-6. SIZE: Small. *STOCK: Clocks.* PARK: Easy. TEL: 01227 751258. SER: Repairs (clocks).

Jean Collyer Antiques

194 The Street. ME13 9AL. (Mrs J.B. Collyer). Est. 1977. Open Tues. and Fri. 2-5, Sat. 10-5. SIZE: Small. *STOCK: Porcelain, glass, furniture, general antiques, 18th to mid-19th C.* PARK: Easy. TEL: 01227 751454; home - same. SER: Valuations. VAT: Stan/Spec.

BRASTED, Nr. Westerham

David Barrington

The Antique Shop. TN16 1JA. Est. 1947. Open 9-6. SIZE: Medium. *STOCK: Furniture, 18th C.* LOC: A25. PARK: Easy. TEL: 01959 562537. VAT: Stan/Spec.

Cooper Fine Arts Ltd

Swan House, High Street. TN16 1JJ. (J. Hill-Reid). Est. 1976. Open 10-6. SIZE: Medium. *STOCK: Furniture, sculpture, oils and watercolours, 1750-1950, £100-£10,000.* PARK: Easy. TEL: 01959 565818. VAT: Stan/Spec.

Brasted continued

Courtyard Antiques

High St. TN16 1JE. (H. La Trobe). Open 10-5.30. *STOCK: General antiques including silver, jewellery, furniture especially extending Victorian dining tables and sets of chairs.* PARK: Easy. TEL: 01959 564483. SER: Valuations; restorations (furniture); French polishing and re-leathering.

Peter Dyke

Kentish House, High St. Est. 1977. Open 10-5, Sat. 1-5. SIZE: Small. *STOCK: Furniture, 18th-19th C, £500-£10,000; paintings, 19th-20th C, £500-£1,000+; decorative objects, 19th C, £150-£1,000.* LOC: A25. PARK: Easy. TEL: 01959 565020. SER: Valuations; buys at auction. VAT: Spec.

Kashan Carpets Ltd.

High St. TN16 1JA. (J. Caslake). Open 10-6, Sun. by appointment. *STOCK: Oriental carpets and rugs, £250-£10,000; kilim stools, £85-£550; kilim and carpet cushions, £20-£75.* TEL: 01959 565866; fax - same. SER: Valuations; restorations; hand-cleaning; kilim stools and cushions made to order. FAIRS: Olympia (June).

Keymer Son & Co. Ltd

Swaylands Place, The Green. TN16 1JY. Est. 1977. Open 10-1 and 2.30-5. CL: Sat. SIZE: Small. *STOCK: 18th-19th C furniture, £100-£3,000.* LOC: A25. PARK: Easy. TEL: 01959 564203; fax - 01959 561138.

Roy Massingham Antiques LAPADA

The Coach House. TN16 1JJ. Open 9-5 or by appointment. *STOCK: 18th-19th C furniture, pictures and decorative items.* TEL: 01959 562408; mobile - 0860 326825.

Old Manor House Antiques

The Green. TN16 1JL. Open daily. *STOCK: Clocks, barometers, lighting, copper and brass, mirrors, furniture and general antiques.* TEL: 01959 562536.

Southdown House Antique Galleries

High St. TN16 1JE. (R. and D. Thomas). Est. 1978. Open 9.30-5.30. *STOCK: Furniture, porcelain, glass, metalware, tapestries, 18th-19th C; paintings, books.* TEL: 01959 563522.

Graham Stead Antiques

Southdown House, High St. Open 9.30-5.30. *STOCK: Furniture, mainly 19th C mahogany and walnut, decorative items and porcelain, £50-£3,000.* PARK: Own. TEL: 01959 563522. VAT: Spec.

Dinah Stoodley & Celia Jennings

High St. TN16 1JE. Est. 1965. Open 9.30-5.30. SIZE: Medium. *STOCK: Period oak and country furniture, 1600-1800; ceramics, early European woodcarving and sculpture.* Not Stocked: Victoriana, jewellery, silver. LOC: A25. PARK: Easy. TEL: 01959 563616. VAT: Spec.

Brasted continued

Tilings Antiques

High St. TN16 1JA. (H. Loveland and P. Fawcett). Est. 1974. Open 10-5.30 or by appointment. SIZE: Medium. *STOCK: Furniture, ceramics, decorative items, 18th-19th C, £20-£2,000.* LOC: Village centre on A25. PARK: Easy. TEL: 01959 564735. VAT: Stan/Spec.

The Village Antique Centre

4 High St. (Ms K. Phillips). Est. 1983. Open 10-5, including Sun. SIZE: Large. *STOCK: Furniture, ceramics, silver, jewellery, glass, decorative and collectibles, 15th-20th C, £5-£10,000.* LOC: A25 between Sevenoaks and Westerham. PARK: Own. TEL: 01959 564545; home - 01293 824173. SER: Valuations; restorations (furniture).

W.W. Warner (Antiques) Ltd BADA

The Green. TN16 1JL. (Mrs C.U. Warner). Est. 1957. Open 10-1 and 2-5. SIZE: Medium. *STOCK: English pottery, porcelain, glass and mahogany furniture, 18th-19th C, £100-£1,000.* Not Stocked: Silver, Victoriana. LOC: A25. PARK: Easy. TEL: 01959 563698. SER: Buys at London auctions. VAT: Spec.

BROADSTAIRS

Broadstairs Antiques and Collectables

49 Belvedere Rd. CT10 1PF. (P. Edwards). Est. 1980. Open winter 10-4.30 (closed Wed), April-end Sept. 10-5, including Wed. *STOCK: General antiques, linen, lace, china and small furniture.* LOC: Road opposite Lloyds Bank. TEL: 01843 861965.

BROMLEY

Antica

Rear of 35-41 High St. BR1 1LE. (L. and P. Muccio). Open 10-5.30. *STOCK: General antiques.* LOC: Opposite Habitat. TEL: 0181 464 7661. VAT: Stan.

Bromley Antique Market

Widmore Rd. Est. 1968. Open Thursday 7.30-3. SIZE: 70 stalls. *STOCK: General antiques, jewellery, books, bric-a-brac, copper, brass and clocks, collectors' items, coins, furs, stamps, postcards.* VAT: Stan.

CANTERBURY

Antique and Design

The Old Oast, Hollow Lane. (Steve Couchman). Est. 1988. Open 9-6, Sun. 10-4. SIZE: Large. *STOCK: Pine furniture, decorative items, 1800-1950, £5-£1,500.* LOC: M2 from London, Canterbury exit, straight at first roundabout, right at second and third roundabouts, left at second pedestrian lights, shop 500 yds. TEL: 01227 762871. SER: Restorations; buys at auction; import and export. VAT: Stan/Spec.

Canterbury continued

R. J. Baker

16 Palace St. CT1 2DZ. Est. 1971. Open 9.30-5.30. CL: Thurs. SIZE: Small. *STOCK: Silver and jewellery, 18th-19th C, £500-£2,000; handmade modern silverware, modern jewellery.* LOC: 5 minutes from cathedral, opposite The King's School. PARK: Easy. TEL: 01227 463224. SER: Valuations; restorations; gold and silversmiths; manufacturers. VAT: Stan/Spec.

Brass Bed Shop

37a Broad St. CT1 2LR. Open 9-6. *STOCK: Victorian brass beds.* TEL: 01227 769055. VAT: Stan/Spec.

Burgate Antique Centre

10c Burgate. CT1 2HG. (Mr and Mrs Winterflood). Est. 1986. Open 10-5. SIZE: 12 dealers. *STOCK: Furniture, silver, porcelain, Art Deco, paintings, prints, books, militaria, lead soldiers and toys, 19th-20th C.* LOC: City Wall overlooking Cathedral Gardens. TEL: 01227 456500. SER: Valuations.

The Canterbury Bookshop

23a Palace St. CT1 2DZ. (David Miles). Open 10-5. *STOCK: Antiquarian and children's books, pictures and prints.* TEL: 01227 464773; fax - 01227 780073.

Chaucer Bookshop

6-7 Beer Cart Lane. CT1 2NY. ABA, PBFA. (Sir Robert Sherston-Baker, Bt.). Est. 1977. Open 10-5. *STOCK: Books and prints, 18th-20th C, £5-£150; maps, 18th-19th C, £50-£250.* LOC: 5 minutes walk from cathedral, via Mercery Lane and St. Margaret's St. PARK: Castle St. TEL: 01227 453912; fax - 01227 451893. SER: Valuations; restorations (book binding); buys at auction (books, maps and prints). VAT: Stan.

Coach House Antiques

2A Duck Lane, St. Radigunds. CT1 2AE. Est. 1975. Open daily. SIZE: Large. *STOCK: General antiques, small furniture, ceramics, glass, linen, books, collectors' items and bygones.* Not Stocked: Jewellery. TEL: 01227 463117.

Conquest House Antiques

17 Palace St. CT1 2DZ. (C.C. Hill and D.A. Magee). Open 10-5. *STOCK: 18th-19th C furniture and decorative items.* TEL: 01227 464587; fax - 01227 451375.

H.S. Greenfield and Son, Gunmakers (Est. 1805)

4/5 Upper Bridge St. CT1 2NB. (T.S. Greenfield). *STOCK: English sporting guns, in pairs and singles; Continental sporting guns, firearms.* TEL: 01227 456959. SER: Valuations; restorations (antique firearms). VAT: Stan.

Leadenhall Gallery

12 Palace St. CT1 2DZ. (D.L. Greenaway). Open 10-5.30. *STOCK: Prints and maps.* TEL: 01227 457339.

Canterbury continued

Nan Leith's Brocanterbury

Errol House, 68 Stour St. CT1 2NZ. Resident. Open Mon., Wed., Fri. and Sat. 12-6. *STOCK: Art Deco, Victoriana, pressed glass, costume jewellery.* LOC: Close to Heritage Museum. TEL: 01227 454519.

Michael Pearson Antiques

2 The Borough, Northgate. CT1 2DR. Open 10-6. *STOCK: 17th and 18th C furniture, including early oak, clocks and country furniture; wood carvings.* TEL: 01227 459939. SER: Valuations; restorations (clocks and furniture).

Pine and Things

Oast Interiors, Wincheap Rd. CT1 3TY. Est. 1977. Open 9-5.30. SIZE: Large. *STOCK: Pine furniture, 19th C and reproduction, £100-£500; ornaments and collectors' items.* LOC: A28 towards Ashford, 1 mile from city centre. PARK: Easy. TEL: 01227 470283. VAT: Stan.

Rastro Antiques

44a High St. CT1 2SA. (J. Coppage). Est. 1981. Open 10-5. SIZE: 8 dealers. *STOCK: Bric-a-brac, vintage clothing, books, stamps, ephemera.* LOC: Up narrow lane off High St. PARK: Nearby. TEL: 01227 463537.

The Saracen's Lantern

8-9 The Borough. CT1 2DR. (W.J. Christophers). Est. 1970. *STOCK: General antiques, silver, jewellery, clocks, watches, Victorian bottles and pot-lids, Georgian, Victorian and Edwardian furniture.* LOC: Near Cathedral opposite King's School. PARK: At rear, by way of Northgate and St. Radigun's St. TEL: 01227 451968.

Stablegate Antiques

19 The Borough, Palace St. CT1 2DR. (Mrs G. Giuntini). Est. 1989. Open 10-5.30. SIZE: Small. *STOCK: General antiques, furniture and porcelain, Georgian, Victorian and Edwardian, £5-£4,000; jewellery, glass, objets d'art, collectables.* LOC: Between Mint Yard Gate and King's School. PARK: Nearby. TEL: 01227 764086; home - 01227 831639.

Town and Country Furniture

141 Wincheap. CT1 3SE. (V. Keen). Est. 1986. Open 9-5. SIZE: Medium. *STOCK: Furniture, country collectables, 50p-£1,000.* LOC: A28 Wincheap road. PARK: Nearby. TEL: 01227 762340. SER: Paint and metal stripping; restorations (furniture); French polishing; lead light repairs; reclaimed pine furniture made to order.

Victorian Fireplace

Thanet House, 92 Broad St. CT1 2LU. (J.J. Griffith). Est. 1980. Open 10-5.30. CL: Mon. SIZE: Medium. *STOCK: Georgian to Victorian fireplaces.* LOC: Town centre. PARK: Nearby. TEL: 01227 767723. SER: Restorations; fitting. VAT: Stan/Spec.

CHIDDINGSTONE, Nr. Edenbridge

Barbara Lane Antiques

Tudor Cottage. TN8 7AH. (Mrs E.B. Avery). Est. 1967. Open 10-5. *STOCK: General antiques, furniture, silver and plate, porcelain and 20th C collectables.* LOC: Behind Castle Inn. PARK: Easy. TEL: 01892 870577.

CHISLEHURST

Chislehurst Antiques LAPADA

7 Royal Parade. BR7 6NR. (Mrs M. Crawley). Est. 1976. Open 10-5. SIZE: Large. *STOCK: Furniture, 1760-1910; lighting - oil, gas, electric, 1850-1910; decorative antiques.* LOC: Half mile from A20, 3 miles from M25. PARK: Easy. TEL: 0181 467 1530; mobile - 0468 081577. VAT: Spec.

Michael Sim

1 Royal Parade. BR7 5PG. Open 9-6 including Sun. SIZE: Medium. *STOCK: English furniture, Georgian and Regency, £500-£50,000; clocks, barometers, globes and scientific instruments, £500-£50,000; Oriental works of art, £50-£5,000; pictures, Victorian, £100-£10,000; portrait miniatures, £300-£5,000; animalier bronzes, £1,000-£10,000.* LOC: 50yds. from War Memorial at junction of Bromley Rd. and Centre Common Rd. PARK: Easy. TEL: 0181 467 7040; home - same; fax - 0181 467 4352. SER: Valuations; restorations; buys at auction. VAT: Spec.

CRANBROOK

Douglas Bryan BADA LAPADA

The Old Bakery, St. David's Bridge. TN17 3HN. (Douglas and Catherine Bryan). Est. 1971. Open 9.30-5, Wed. 9.30-1 and by appointment. SIZE: Medium. *STOCK: Mainly English oak furniture, 17th-18th C; woodcarvings, some metalware.* LOC: Adjacent Tanyard car park - off road towards Windmill. PARK: Adjacent. TEL: 01580 713103; fax - 01580 712407.

Cranbrook Antique Centre

15 High St. (Mr. and Mrs R. Bisram). Open 10-5. SIZE: 7 dealers - 2 floors. *STOCK: 19th C furniture, collectables and silver.* TEL: 01580 712173.

Cranbrook Gallery

21B Stone St. TN17 3HE. (P.A. Donovan). Open 9.15-5, Sat. 9.15-4. CL: Mon. *STOCK: Watercolours, prints and maps, 18th-19th C.* TEL: 01580 713021.

Swan Antiques

Stone St. (R. White). Est. 1982. Open 10-5, Wed. 10-1. SIZE: Medium. *STOCK: Country furniture, 17th-19th C, from £500+; folk art and nâive paintings.* LOC: Town centre. PARK: Easy. TEL: 01580 712720; home - 01580 291864. SER: Valuations; buys at auction. FAIRS: Olympia; Battersea Decorative and Fine Art. VAT: Spec.

CRAYFORD

Watling Antiques

139 Crayford Rd. DA1 4AS. Open 10-6.30. *STOCK: General antiques and shipping goods.* TEL: 01322 523620.

DARTFORD

Copperfields Antique & Craft Centre

3c/4 Copperfields, Spital Street. (R.J. Overton). Open 10-5. SIZE: Medium - 20 dealers. *STOCK: China, glass, clocks, general antiques, 18th-20th C, £5-£1,000.* PARK: Orchard Street multi-storey. TEL: 01322 281445. SER: Valuations; restorations; buys at auction.

Dartford Antiques

27 East Hill. (M. Skudder). Est. 1976. Open 10-4. SIZE: Medium. *STOCK: Furniture, 19th-20th C, £25-£100; collectors' items.* LOC: On hill into town from tunnel. PARK: Easy. TEL: 01322 291350. SER: Valuations.

DEAL

Decors

67 Beach St. CT14 6HY. (N. Loftus-Potter). Est. 1973. Open 9.30-7 including Sun; open in winter Fri.-Mon. or by appointment. *STOCK: Decorative items, general antiques and fabrics (including modern).* PARK: Easy. TEL: 01304 368030; home - same.

Pretty Bizarre

170 High St. CT14 6BQ. (Philip Hartley). Open Mon. 9-1, Fri. and Sat. 9-5 or by appointment. SIZE: Medium. *STOCK: Art Deco, ceramics, furniture.* TEL: 01304 367480.

Quill Antiques

12 Alfred Sq. CT14 6LR. (A.J. and A.R. Young). Open 9-5.30. *STOCK: General antiques, porcelain, postcards.* TEL: 01304 375958.

Serendipity

168 High St. CT14 6BQ. (M. and K. Short). Est. 1976. Open 10-12.30 and 2-4.30, Sat. 9.30-5, or by appointment. CL: Thurs. SIZE: Medium. *STOCK: Staffordshire figures, ceramics, pictures, furniture.* PARK: Easy. TEL: 01304 369165; home - 01304 366536. SER: Valuations; restorations (ceramics, oil paintings).

DOWNHAM, Nr. Bromley

The Gallery

427 Bromley Rd. BR1 4PJ. (P. Cockton). Est. 1991. Open 11-5. SIZE: Medium. *STOCK: Victorian pine, £50-£750; mahogany, 19th C, £100-£400; oak, 1930's, £50-£100.* LOC: On main road between Catford and Bromley. PARK: Easy. TEL: 0181 698 8578.

EAST PECKHAM, Nr.Tonbridge

Desmond and Amanda North

The Orchard, Hale St. TN12 5JB. Est. 1971. Open daily, appointment advisable. SIZE: Medium. *STOCK: Oriental rugs, runners, carpets and cushions, 1800-1939, £60-£3,500.* LOC: On A228 (was B2015), 150yds. south of junction with B2016. PARK: Easy. TEL: 01622 871353; home - same. SER: Valuations; restorations (reweaving, re-edging, patching, cleaning).

EDENBRIDGE

Lennox Cato BADA LAPADA

1 The Square. TN8 5BD. (Mr and Mrs Cato). Est. 1975. Open 9.30-5.30, Sat. 10-5. SIZE: Medium. *STOCK: 18th C English and Continental furniture and related items, garden furniture.* TEL: 01732 865988; mobile - 0836 233473. SER: Valuations; restorations. FAIRS: Major London. VAT: Stan/Spec.

Chevertons of Edenbridge Ltd LAPADA

Taylour House, 67-73 High St. TN8 5AL. (D. and A. Adam). Open 9-5.30. SIZE: Large. *STOCK: Furniture and accessories, £250-£25,000.* LOC: From Westerham, on B2026 to Edenbridge. PARK: Own. TEL: 01732 863196/ 863358; fax - 01732 864298. VAT: Stan/Spec.

FARNINGHAM

Antiques & Pine and Farningham Pine

High St. DA4. (P. and Mrs. T.A. Dzierzek). Est. 1952. Open 10-5. CL: Wed. *STOCK: Pine furniture, from 1830, £25-£5,000.* LOC: 1 mile from M25, J3, on A20, first turn off (A225), before Brands Hatch if heading south. PARK: Easy. TEL: 01322 863168/863230; fax - 01322 863168. VAT: Stan/Spec.

P.T. Beasley

Forge Yard, High St. DA4 0DB. (P.T. and R. Beasley). Est. 1964. CL: Tues. *STOCK: English furniture, some pewter, brass, Delft, woodcarvings.* LOC: Opposite Social Club. TEL: 01322 862453.

FAVERSHAM

Collectors' Corner

East St/Crescent Rd. ME13 8AD. Est. 1952. Open Mon., Tues., Fri. 10-5, Sat. 10-4. SIZE: Small. *STOCK: Collectors' items - coins and medals, stamps, cigarette and post cards, badges, ceramics and silver, jewellery, prints, oils and watercolours, antique and secondhand woodworking and engineering tools, £1-£20,000.* LOC: Opposite P.O., at only set of traffic lights. PARK: Easy and at rear by arrangement. TEL: 01795 539721; home - 01795 536642. SER: Valuations.

Faversham continued

Squires Antiques (Faversham)
3 Jacob Yard, Preston St. ME13 8NY. (A. Squires). Est. 1985. Open 10-5. CL: Wed. and Thurs. *STOCK: General antiques.* TEL: 01795 531503.

FOLKESTONE

Richard Amos
37 Cheriton High St. CT19 4EY. Open 9.30-12 and 2-5. CL: Wed. pm. *STOCK: General antiques.* TEL: 01303 275449.

Alan Lord Antiques
71 Tontine St. CT20 1JR. (A.G., J.A. and R.G. Lord). Est. 1956. Open 9-1 and 2-5. CL: Sat. pm. SIZE: Large. *STOCK: Period and Victorian furniture, china, silver. Rear warehouse - trade and shipping goods.* LOC: Road up from harbour. PARK: Easy. TEL: 01303 253674 anytime. VAT: Stan/Spec.

G. and D.I. Marrin and Sons
149 Sandgate Rd. CT20 2DA. ABA. Est. 1949. Open 9.30-1 and 2.30-5.30. SIZE: Large. *STOCK: Maps, early engravings, topographical and sporting prints, paintings, drawings, books, engravings.* TEL: 01303 253016; fax - 01303 850956. SER: Restorations; framing. VAT: Stan.

FOUR ELMS, Nr. Edenbridge

Treasures
The Cross Roads. (B. Ward-Lee). Open 10-5. *STOCK: Copper, brass, glass, porcelain, silver, jewellery, linen, books, toys, pine, small furniture and collectables.* TEL: 01732 700363.

Yew Tree Antiques
The Cross Roads. TN8 7NH. (G. Nixon). Est. 1984. Open 10-5. SIZE: Medium. *STOCK: Porcelain and copper, 19th-20th C, £5-£500; glass, jewellery, linen, small furniture and collectables.* LOC: Off A25 - B269. PARK: Easy. TEL: 01732 700215.

GRAVESEND

Alan Wood
Open by appointment. *STOCK: Specialist in Staffordshire portrait figures.* TEL: 01474 533722.

HADLOW, Nr. Tonbridge

The Pedlar's Pack
The Square. TN11 0DA. (Mrs Nina Joy). Est. 1976. Open 10-5.30, Wed. 10-1. CL: Mon. SIZE: Medium. *STOCK: Country furniture, £50-£600; brass, copper, glass and china, £25-£300; all 18th-19th C; small interesting items, 19th-20th C; jewellery, £40-£600.* LOC: On Tonbridge to Maidstone Rd. PARK: Easy. TEL: 01732 851296; home - same.

Hadlow continued

Rosewood Gallery
High St. (R. and G. King). Est. 1969. *STOCK: Oriental carpets, general antiques and curios.* LOC: A26. PARK: Easy. TEL: 01732 852359; for enquiries re. carpets - 01732 850228. SER: Repairs and hand cleaning (carpets). VAT: Stan.

HARRIETSHAM, Nr. Maidstone

Judith Peppitt
Chegworth Manor Farm, Chegworth. ME17 1DD. Open by appointment. *STOCK: English water-colours, 19th-20th C.* LOC: 1 mile from Leeds Castle. PARK: Easy. TEL: 01622 859313.

HEADCORN, Nr. Ashford

Penny Lampard
31-33 High St. TN27 9NE. (Mrs P. Lampard). Est. 1981. Open 9.30-5.30. SIZE: Large. *STOCK: Stripped pine and dark wood furniture.* PARK: Easy. TEL: 01622 890682. FAIRS: Sutton Valence. VAT: Stan.

HYTHE

Malthouse Arcade
High St. CT21 5BW. (Mr and Mrs R.M. Maxtone Grahame). Est. 1974. Open Fri., Sat. and Bank Holiday Mon. 9.30-5.30. SIZE: Large - 37 stalls. *STOCK: Furniture, jewellery and collectors' items.* LOC: West end of High St. PARK: 50yds. TEL: 01303 260103; home - 01304 613270.

Owlets
99 High St. CT21 5JH. Open 9-5. *STOCK: Antique and estate jewellery and silver.* TEL: 01303 230333.

Samovar Antiques
158 High St. CT21 5JR. (Mrs F. Rignault). Open 9.30-5, Wed. 9.30-1. *STOCK: 19th C furniture, French provincial furniture, Oriental carpets and rugs and general antiques.* PARK: Own. TEL: 01303 264239.

Traditional Pine Furniture
248 Seabrook Rd., Seabrook. CT21 5RQ. (M. Hannant). Est. 1977. Open daily. SIZE: Large. *STOCK: Pine, 19th C, £50-£500.* LOC: 1.5 miles from end of M20 on A259. PARK: Easy. TEL: 01303 239931. VAT: Stan.

LAMBERHURST

The China Locker
TN3 8HN. (G. Wilson). Open by appointment only. SIZE: Small. *STOCK: Prints, 18th-19th C, £5-£40.* TEL: 01892 890555. FAIRS: Penshurst Village Hall; Sutton Valence School.

LEIGH, Nr. Tonbridge

Clive Marsden
TN11 8RL. Open by appointment only. *STOCK: Furniture and clocks.* TEL: 01732 833794. SER: Restorations (furniture and clocks); furniture and clock cases made to order.

Leigh continued

Anthony Woodburn BADA LAPADA
Orchard House, High St. TN11 8RH. Est. 1975. Open daily, Sun. by appointment. SIZE: Medium. *STOCK: Clocks and barometers, 17th to early 19th C.* LOC: Off A21. PARK: Easy. TEL: 01732 832258; fax - 01732 838023. SER: Valuations; buys at auction (clocks). VAT: Spec.

LITTLEBOURNE, Nr. Canterbury

Jimmy Warren Antiques
Cedar Lodge, 28 The Hill. CT3 1TA. Est. 1969. Open 9-6 including Sun. *STOCK: Decorative antiques, 18th-19th C; garden ornaments.* LOC: A257. PARK: Own. TEL: 01227 721510; fax - 01227 722431. SER: Valuations; restorations. VAT: Stan/Spec.

MAIDSTONE

Newnham Court Antiques
Newnham Court Shopping Village, Bearsted Rd. (Mr and Mrs Draper). Est. 1991. Open 9-5.45, Sun. 10.30-4.30. SIZE: Medium. *STOCK: Dining furniture including sideboards and cabinets, late Victorian to 1930's, £300-£2,500; collectables, £1-£250.* PARK: Easy. TEL: 01622 631526. SER: Restorations (dining tables and chairs). VAT: Stan/Spec.

Sutton Valence Antiques LAPADA
Unit 4 Haslemere Parkwood Estate, Sutton Rd. ME15 9NL. (T. and N. Mullarkey). Est. 1971. Open 9-5.30, Sun. 11-4. SIZE: Large warehouse. *STOCK: Antique and shipping furniture.* LOC: Approx. 3 miles south of Maidstone town centre, just off A274. PARK: Easy. TEL: 01622 675332; fax - 01622 692593. SER: Container packing and shipping; courier; buys at auction.

MARGATE

Furniture Mart
Grotto Hill. CT9 2BU. (R.G. Scott). Est. 1971. CL: Wed. SIZE: Large. *STOCK: General antiques £1-£1,500; shipping goods.* LOC: Corner of Bath Place. TEL: 01843 220653. SER: Restorations; stripping; restoration materials supplied. VAT: Global/Stan.

NEWNHAM, Nr. Sittingbourne

Periwinkle Press
47 The Street. ME9 0LN. (A.L. and C. Swain). Est. 1967. Open 9-6, Sun. 12-6. *STOCK: Antiquarian books and prints, maps, watercolours.* LOC: Village centre. PARK: Easy. TEL: 01795 890388. SER: Restorations (prints and oils); framing.

NORTHFLEET

Northfleet Hill Antiques
36 The Hill. DA11 9EX. (Mrs M. Kilby). Est. 1986. Open Tues., Fri. and Sat. 9.30-5. SIZE: Small. *STOCK: Furniture, 19th to early 20th C, £50-£800; bygones and collectables, £1-£100.* LOC: A226 near junction with B261 and B2175. PARK: Easy (behind Ye Olde Coach and Horses Inn). TEL: 01474 321521.

ORPINGTON

Antica
48 High St., Green Street Green. Open 10-5.30. *STOCK: General antiques.* TEL: 01689 851181.

OTFORD

Ellenor Antiques and Tea Shop
11a High St. (Ellenor Hospice Care). Open 10-5. SIZE: Medium. *STOCK: Furniture, ceramics, glass, 18th to early 20th C, £5-£1,500.* LOC: Towards Sevenoaks, 3 miles south of junction 4, M25. PARK: Nearby. TEL: 01959 524322. SER: Items sold on donation or commission basis for hospice charity.

Mandarin Gallery - Oriental Art
The Mill Pond, 16 High Street. TN14 5PQ. (J. and M.C. Liu). Est. 1984. Open 10-5. CL: Wed. and Thurs. SIZE: Medium. *STOCK: Chinese rosewood and lacquer furniture, 18th-19th C; jade and soap stone, ivory and wood carvings.* Not Stocked: Non-Oriental items. LOC: A225. PARK: Easy. TEL: 01959 522778; home - 01732 457399; fax - same. SER: Restorations (Chinese rosewood furniture).

PENSHURST, Nr. Tonbridge

Buxton House Stores
TN11 8BT. (Sali Morant and Jonny Farringdon). Est. 1995. Open Thurs., Fri., Sat. 12-5, Sun. 2-5. *STOCK: Furniture, textiles, linens and decorative items, £2-£250.* LOC: Main road. PARK: Easy. TEL: 01892 870220; home - same; internet - http://www.wizzo.demon.co.uk/.

PETTS WOOD

Beehive
22 Station Sq. BR5 1NA. (Mrs R. Miller). Est. 1994. Open 9.30-5, Sat. 9.30-4.30. SIZE: Medium. *STOCK: Collectables, china, glass and furniture, 19th-20th C, £1-£1,000.* PARK: Easy. TEL: 01689 890675.

RAMSGATE

De Tavener Antiques
24 Addington St. CT11 9JJ. (Mr and Mrs I.E. Gregg). Est. 1983. Open 9.30-5.30, Wed. 9.30-12.30. SIZE: Small. *STOCK: Clocks and barometers, bric-a-brac.* LOC: End of A299, above Sally Line berth. PARK: Easy. TEL: 01843 582213; home - same. SER: Valuations; restorations (clocks and barometers). FAIRS: Great Danes Hotel, Maidstone; Inn on the Lake Hotel, Gravesend.

Ramsgate continued

Granny's Attic
2 Addington St. CT11 9JL. (Penelope J. Warn). Est. 1987. Open 10-5. CL: Thurs. pm. SIZE: Medium. *STOCK: Pre-1940's items, £2-£500.* LOC: Left off harbour approach road or right off Westcliffe Rd. PARK: Easy. TEL: 01843 588955; home - 01843 596288.

Thanet Antiques Trading Centre
45 Albert St. CT11 9EX. (Mr and Mrs R. Fomison). Est. 1971. Open 9-5, Sun. by appointment. SIZE: Large. *STOCK: Furniture and bric-a-brac, 18th-20th C, £1-£5,000.* LOC: From London Rd. right to seafront. With harbour on right turn first left down Addington St., then last right. PARK: Own. TEL: 01843 597336; home - 01843 597540.

RIVERHEAD

Amherst Antiques LAPADA
23 London Rd. TN13 2BU. (D. Brick). Est. 1985. Open 9.30-5. CL: Wed. SIZE: Small. *STOCK: Furniture, £500-£3,000; porcelain, silver and Tunbridge ware £50-£3,000.* LOC: A25. PARK: Nearby. TEL: 01732 455047. FAIRS: Olympia; NEC; Buxton; Guildford; West London; Chester; Harrogate. VAT: Stan/Spec.

Roundabout Antiques
28a London Rd. TN13 2DE. (Mrs C. Ledamun and Mrs L. López Fonseca). Est. 1991. Open 9.30-5. CL: Wed. SIZE: Small. *STOCK: Collectables, china, glass, smalls, including Victorian and Art Deco, £5-£100; furniture, to £1,000; lace, linen and embroideries, Victorian to 1930's, £1-£200.* LOC: A25, then take London Rd. towards Dunton Green, shop 50 yards from mini roundabout. PARK: Easy. TEL: 01732 741873.

ROCHESTER

Authentiques
39 High St. ME1 1LN. (P. Farmer). Open 10-5. *STOCK: Furniture, objets d'art, collectables, bronzes.* TEL: 01634 830575.

Baggins Book Bazaar - The Largest Secondhand Bookshop in England
19 High St. ME1 1PY. Open 10-6 including Sun. *STOCK: Secondhand and antiquarian books.* TEL: 01634 811651; fax - 01634 840591.

Cottage Style Antiques
24 Bill Street Rd. ME2 4RB. (W. Miskimmin). Open 9.30-5.30. *STOCK: General and architectural antiques.* TEL: 01634 717623.

Deo Juvante Antiques
43 High St. ME1 1LN. (Lorraine and Margaret Petrie). Est. 1969. SIZE: Medium. *STOCK: Furniture, 1650-1930's, £100-£500; smalls, 1800-1950's, £5-£100; gold and silver, 1750-1950's, £20-£100.* LOC: A2 into town, turn right into High St, then first right again. PARK: Limited and nearby. TEL: 01634 843750. SER: Valuations; restorations. VAT: Stan/Spec.

Rochester continued

Droods
62 High St. (A.J. Stewart and C. Morgan). Open 10-5.30. *STOCK: General antiques.* TEL: 01634 829000.

Francis Iles
Rutland House, La Providence, High St. ME1 1LX. (The Family Iles). Est. 1960. Open 9.30-5.30. SIZE: Large. *STOCK: Watercolours and oils, mainly 20th C, £50-£10,000.* LOC: Off central High St. PARK: 40yds. TEL: 01634 843081; fax - 01634 846681. SER: Restorations (cleaning and relining); framing. VAT: Stan/Spec.

Kaizen International
88 High St. ME1 1JT. (Jason Hunt). Est. 1980. Open 9-5.30, Sun. 12-6. SIZE: Medium. *STOCK: General antiques including antique and second-hand jewellery.* LOC: A20, centre of High St. PARK: Nearby. TEL: 01634 814132; home - 01634 850727. SER: Valuations; restorations (jewellery). FAIRS: Barbican, Olympia, Kenilworth, Goodwood, NEC (Aug), Café Royal. VAT: Stan/Spec.

Langley Galleries
143 High St. ME1 1EL. (K.J. Cook). Est. 1978. Open 9-5.30. *STOCK: Prints, watercolours, oils, 19th-20th C.* TEL: 01634 811802. SER: Restorations and cleaning (watercolours and oils); framing.

Memories
128 High St. ME1 1JT. (Mrs V.A. Lhermette). Est. 1985. Open 9-5, Sun. 11-5. SIZE: Medium. *STOCK: Small furniture, £50-£500; china, £5-£75; both 1900-1950; pictures, late Victorian to Edwardian, £20-£70; collectables, bric-a-brac, linen, corkscrews and books.* PARK: Opposite. TEL: 01634 811044.

Rochester Antiques Centre
93 High St. ME1 1LX. (Jane Staff and Jim Field). Open 10-5. SIZE: Large - 4 showrooms. *STOCK: General antiques and collectables.* LOC: Centre of High St. TEL: 01634 846144.

ROLVENDEN, Nr. Cranbrook

Falstaff Antiques
63-67 High St. TN17 4LP. (C.M. Booth). Est. 1964. Open 9-6, Sun. by appointment. SIZE: Medium. *STOCK: English furniture, £5-£700; china, metal, glass, silver, £1-£200.* Not Stocked: Paintings. LOC: On A28, 3 miles from Tenterden, 1st shop on left in village. PARK: Easy. TEL: 01580 241234. SER: Valuations. VAT: Stan/Spec.

Kent Cottage
39 High St. TN17 4LP. (Mrs R. Amos). Open by appointment. *STOCK: Porcelain - Continental including Meissen, and English; English scent bottles, silver and small furniture.* LOC: A28, 3 miles S.E of Tenterden. PARK: Easy. TEL: 01580 241719.

Rolvenden continued

J.D. and R.M. Walters

10 Regent St. TN17 4PE. Est. 1977. Open 8-6. SIZE: Small. *STOCK: Mahogany furniture, 18th-19th C.* LOC: A28 turn left in village centre onto B2086, shop on left. PARK: Easy. TEL: 01580 241563; home - same. SER: Handmade copies of period furniture including chairs; restorations (GMC). VAT: Stan/Spec.

SANDGATE, Nr. Folkestone

Christopher Buck Antiques BADA

56-60 High St. CT20 3AP. Est. 1983. Open 10-5. CL: Wed. SIZE: Medium. ***STOCK: English furniture, 18th C, £500-£30,000; decorative items, 18th-19th C, £100-£2,000.*** **LOC: 5 mins. from M20 and Channel Tunnel. PARK: Easy. TEL: 01303 221229. SER: Valuations; restorations (furniture); buys at auction. FAIRS: Olympia, Chelsea. VAT: Stan/Spec.**

Dench Antiques

Cromwell House, 32 High St. CT20 3AP. (Mr and Mrs J.W.G. Elcombe). Est. 1980. Open by appointment only. SIZE: Medium + warehouse. *STOCK: 18th-19th C Continental and English furniture, decorators' items and statuary.* PARK: Easy. TEL: 01303 240824; fax - 01303 257346. VAT: Stan/Spec.

Michael File Antiques

13 Sandgate High St. CT20 3BA. Est. 1972. Open

Sandgate continued

9.30-5.30. *STOCK: Furniture, silver plate, Victoriana, decorator's items and collectables.* TEL: 01303 249574.

Finch Antiques

40 High St. CT20 3AP. (Robert and Sylvia Finch). Est. 1978. Open 9.30-6, Sun. 11-5. SIZE: Medium. *STOCK: Furniture, 1800-1920, £150-£3,000; silver plate and writing items, £5-£400.* PARK: Easy. TEL: 01303 240725. SER: Restorations (furniture, French polishing).

Michael Fitch Antiques LAPADA

99 High St. CT20 3BY. Open 10-5.30, Sun. by appointment. ***STOCK: Georgian, Victorian and Edwardian furniture and clocks.*** **TEL: 01303 249600; fax - same; evenings - 01303 230839.**

Freeman and Lloyd Antiques BADA LAPADA

44 High St. CT20 3AP. (K. Freeman and M.R. Lloyd). Est. 1968. Open 10-5.30, Mon. and Wed. by appointment only. SIZE: Medium. ***STOCK: Fine Georgian and Regency English furniture; clocks, paintings and other period items.*** **LOC: On main coast road between Hythe and Folkestone (A259). PARK: Easy. TEL: 01303 248986; fax - same; mobile - 0860 100073. SER: Valuations. FAIRS: Chelsea (Sept); BADA (March); Olympia (Gold Section-June, BADA Pavilion-Nov). VAT: Spec.**

Sandgate continued

David Gilbert Antiques
30 High St. CT20 3AP. Est. 1975. Open 9-5. SIZE: Medium. *STOCK: Furniture, smalls, glass, 1790-1930, £5-£1,000.* LOC: A259. PARK: Easy. TEL: 01303 850491; home - 01304 812237. SER: Valuations.

Robin Homewood Antiques
59a Sandgate High St. CT20 3AH. (R.A. Homewood). Est. 1984. Open 9.30-5.30, Sun. by appointment. *STOCK: General antiques.* TEL: 01303 249466.

Nordens
43/43a High St. CT20 3AH. Est. 1946. Open 10-1 and 2.30-5.30 or by appointment. *STOCK: General antiques, Victoriana, bric-a-brac.* LOC: Main Folkestone to Hythe Rd. TEL: 01303 248443.

Old English Oak
102 High St. CT20 3BY. (A. Martin). *STOCK: Oak furniture and interesting items.* TEL: 01303 248560.

Old English Pine
100 High St. CT20 3BY. (A. Martin). Open 10-6. *STOCK: Pine furniture and interesting items.* TEL: 01303 248560.

J.T. Rutherford and Son
55 High St. CT20 3AH. Est. 1963. Open 9-6, Sun. 9-2 or by appointment. SIZE: Medium. *STOCK: Furniture and longcase clocks; weapons - flintlock percussion pistols, muskets, edged weapons, swords including dress.* LOC: A295. PARK: Easy. TEL: 01303 249515; home - 01303 260822. SER: Restorations (furniture); buys at auction. VAT: Stan/Spec.

Sandgate Antiques Centre LAPADA
61-63 High St. CT20 3AH. (Jonathan Greenwall Antiques). Est. 1964. Open 9.30-5.30. SIZE: Large. LOC: Folkestone-Brighton road. PARK: Easy. TEL: 01303 248987. SER: Valuations.

SANDHURST

Forge Antiques and Restorations
Rye Rd. TN18 5JG. (J. Nesfield). Open 9-6. *STOCK: Victoriana, ceramics, glass, furniture including pine, £1-£5,000.* LOC: A268. PARK: Own. TEL: 01580 850308/850665. SER: Restorations (furniture). VAT: Spec.

SANDWICH

Delf Stream Gallery
14 New St. CT13 9AB. (N. Rocke). Est. 1985. Open 10-5. CL: Wed. SIZE: Small. *STOCK: European and American art pottery, 19th-20th C, £25-£4,000.* LOC: Main one-way road in town centre, around corner from Guildhall. PARK: Easy. TEL: 01304 617684; home - same; fax - 01304 615479. SER: Valuations; restorations (as stock); buys at auction. FAIRS: Ardingly; Newark; Kensington Decorative Arts, etc.

Noah's Ark Antique Centre
King St. CT13 9BT. (Mr and Mrs R.M. Maxtone Grahame). Est. 1978. Open 10-4. CL: Wed. SIZE: Medium. *STOCK: Staffordshire figures, china, porcelain, antiquarian books, watercolours, oil paintings, prints, small furniture, silver, jewellery, copper and brass.* PARK: Guildhall. TEL: 01304 611144; home - 01304 613270.

James Porter Antiques
5 Potter St. CT13 9DR. Est. 1948. Open 9.30-5.30. CL: Wed. *STOCK: Period furniture, brass and copper.* TEL: 01304 612218.

Nancy Wilson
Monken Quay, Strand St. CT13 9HP. Open 11-5, other times by appointment. SIZE: Large. *STOCK: Period furniture, longcase clocks, £100-£5,000.* LOC: 100yds. from King's Arms public house. PARK: Easy. TEL: 01304 612345; home - same.

SELLINDGE

Cobwebs
Cobden House, Main Rd. TN25 6EQ. (Mrs K.S. Staines). Est. 1978. Open 10-4.30, Thurs. and Fri. 1-4.30. SIZE: Small. *STOCK: Collectables, late 19th C to 1970's, £5-£100.* LOC: A20. PARK: Easy. TEL: 01303 812003; home - same. FAIRS: Ardingly.

SEVENOAKS

The Antiques Centre
120 London Rd., Tubs Hill. TN13 1BA. (Ruth Harrison). Est. 1964. Open 10-1 and 2-4.30, Wed. and Sat. 10-1, other times by appointment. SIZE: Large. *STOCK: Furniture, 17th-19th C; interesting and decorative items.* LOC: Near station, on left side of hill. PARK: Opposite or in driveway. TEL: 01732 452104. VAT: Stan/Spec.

Sevenoaks continued

Bradbourne Gallery
4 St. John's Hill. TN13 3NP. Open 9.30-5, Sat. 9-1. SIZE: Several dealers. *STOCK: Silver, furniture, ceramics, jewellery, glass, prints and paintings, treen, upholstery and fabrics, 18th C to Edwardian.* LOC: 1 mile from town centre, continuation of High St./Dartford Rd. PARK: Easy. TEL: 01732 460756; fax - same.

Time to Remember
18 London Rd., Dunton Green. TN13 2UE. (A Lyons). Est. 1982. Open 10-6, Mon. and Tues. 10-5, Sun. 2-6. SIZE: Large. *STOCK: Clocks and watches, period furniture, porcelain, glass, toys, bric-a-brac.* LOC: London road into town, opposite Whitmore's Vauxhall showroom. PARK: Easy. TEL: 01732 454549; home - 01689 855295. SER: Valuations; restorations (clocks and watches, furniture); buys at auction (clocks and furniture).

SIDCUP

Sidcup Antique and Craft Centre
Elm Parade, Main Rd. DA14 6NF. (M.H. and G.M. Tripp). Est. 1993. Open 10-5 including Sun. SIZE: 90+ dealers. *STOCK: Wide range of antiques and craft items.* LOC: M25, junction 3 then A20 to Sidcup (Queen Mary's Hospital). Premises near traffic lights, opposite police station. PARK: Easy. TEL: 0181 300 7387.

SNODLAND

Aaron Antiques
90 High St. ME6 5AL. (R.J. Goodman). Open 10-5 or by appointment. *STOCK: Clocks and pocket watches, paintings and prints, period and shipping furniture, English, Continental and Oriental porcelain; antiquarian books, postcards, coins and medals.* TEL: 01634 241748. VAT: Stan.

SOUTHBOROUGH Nr. Tunbridge Wells

Henry Baines LAPADA
14 Church Rd. TN4 0RX. Est. 1968. Open Tues.-Fri. 10-5, Sat. 10-4.30, prior telephone call advisable. *STOCK: Early oak and country furniture especially tables and sets of chairs; French provincial furniture and decorative items.* PARK: Easy. TEL: 01892 532099. VAT: Stan/Spec.

ST. MARGARET'S BAY, Nr. Dover

Alexandra's Antiques
1-2 The Droveway. CT15 6DY. (J. Cox-Freeman). Est. 1979. Open 10-1 and 2.15-4.30, Wed. and Sat. pm. by appointment only. SIZE: Small. *STOCK: Paintings by Victorian and local artists; furniture, porcelain and jewellery.* LOC: Between Dover and Deal at top of hill. PARK: Easy. TEL: 01304 853102; fax - 01304 853306; home - 01304 852682.

STOCKBURY

Steppes Hill Farm Antiques BADA
The Hill Farm, South St. ME9 7RB. (W.F.A. Buck). Est. 1965. Always open, appointment advisable. SIZE: Medium. *STOCK: English porcelain, pottery, pot-lids, 18th-20th C, £5-£5,000; small silver; caddy spoons, wine labels, silver boxes, 18th-19th C, to £1,000; furniture, 18th-19th C, £10-£5,000.* LOC: 5 mins. from M2 on A249. Enquire in village for Steppes Hill Antiques. PARK: Easy. TEL: 01795 842205. SER: Valuations; buys at auction. FAIRS: BADA; Chelsea; International Ceramics. VAT: Spec.

SUNDRIDGE, Nr. Sevenoaks

Sundridge Gallery
9 Church Rd. TN14 6DT. (T. and M. Tyrer). Open 10-5.30. *STOCK: Watercolours and oils, 19th-20th C; some Oriental rugs.* TEL: 01959 564104.

Colin Wilson Antiques
99-103 Main Rd. TN14 6EQ. Open 10-6. *STOCK: Victorian mahogany and inlaid Edwardian furniture.* TEL: 01959 562043. SER: Repairs; restorations. VAT: Stan/Spec.

SUTTON VALENCE, Nr. Maidstone

Sutton Valence Antiques LAPADA
North St. ME17 3AP. (T. and N. Mullarkey). Est. 1971. Open 9.30-5, Sun. 11-4. SIZE: Large. *STOCK: Furniture, porcelain, clocks, silver, metalware, shipping items, 18th-19th C.* LOC: On A274 Maidstone/Tenterden Rd. PARK: Side of shop. TEL: 01622 843333; fax - 01622 843499. SER: Valuations.

TENTERDEN

Flower House Antiques
90 High St. TN30 6JB. (Barry Rayner and Quentin Johnson). Est. 1965. Open 9.30-5.30, Sun. by appointment. SIZE: Medium. *STOCK: English and Continental furniture, 16th to early 19th C; Oriental works of art, 16th-19th C; pictures, lighting, mirrors, objets d'art.* LOC: A28. PARK: Easy and private. TEL: 01580 763764. SER: Valuations; restorations. VAT: Spec.

Garden House Antiques
116-118 High St. TN30 6HT. Resident. (H. Kirkham). Always open. *STOCK: Mainly 18th-19th C furniture, paintings and porcelain; old fishing reels and rods.* PARK: Easy. TEL: 01580 763664. SER: Valuations; interior design.

The Lace Basket
at Garden House, 116 High St. TN30 6HD. (C. Walls). Open 10.30-5. *STOCK: Textiles, Victorian linen and lace, samplers and quilts.* PARK: Opposite. TEL: 01580 763664. SER: Valuations.

Tenterden continued

Sparks Antiques

Rear of 4 Manor Row, High St. TN30 6HP. (Patrick Robbins and Philip Ingham). Est. 1967. Open 9.30-5.30, Sun. by appointment. SIZE: Medium + warehouse. *STOCK: English and Continental furniture, 17th-19th C, £200-£8,000; paintings and prints, 18th-19th C, £200-£5,000; pottery and metalwork, 18th-19th C, £50-£1,000.* LOC: A28. PARK: Easy. TEL: 01580 766696; home - 01424 431233 or 01797 344566. SER: Valuations; restorations (furniture). VAT: Spec.

Sparks Antiques Centre

4 Manor Row, High St. TN30 6HP. Open 9.30-5.30, Sun. 11-4.30. SIZE: 12 dealers. *STOCK: Wide range of furniture and paintings, £100-£5,000; pottery, metalwork and collectors items, £50-£1,000.* LOC: A28. PARK: Easy. TEL: 01580 766211.

Tenterden Antiques Centre

66 High St. TN30 6AU. (B.M. Jackson). Open 10-5 including Sun. SIZE: 20 dealers. *STOCK: Wide range of general antiques.* TEL: 01580 765885/765655.

TEYNHAM, Nr. Sittingbourne

Jackson-Grant Antiques

The Old Chapel, 133 London Rd. ME9 9QJ. (D.M. Jackson-Grant). Est. 1966. Open 10-5, Sun. 1-5. SIZE: Large. *STOCK: Country furniture, oak, 17th-19th C, £50-£2,000; period walnut, £450-£1,500; mahogany, £100-£1,000; some pine; smalls, 18th C to Art Deco, £5-£500.* LOC: A2 between Faversham and Sittingbourne. PARK: Easy. TEL: 01795 522027; home - same; mobile - 0831 591881. VAT: Stan/Spec.

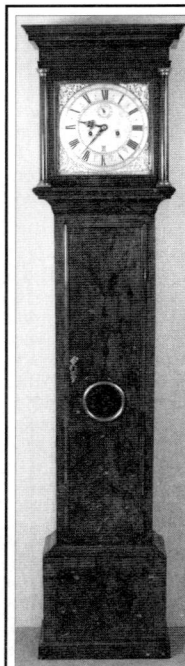

Teynham continued

TONBRIDGE

Barden House Antiques

1-3 Priory St. TN9 2AP. (Mrs B.D. Parsons). Open 10-5. SIZE: 5 dealers. *STOCK: General antiques and collectables.* TEL: 01732 350142; evenings - 01732 355718.

Lawson Antiques Limited

165 High St. TN9 1BX. (M.P. Baldwin). Est. 1735. Open 10-5.30. SIZE: Large. *STOCK: Furniture, pictures, collectables, £5-£5,000.* LOC: North end of High St. PARK: Public at rear. TEL: 01732 367606.

Derek Roberts Fine Antique Clocks, Music Boxes, Barometers BADA

25 Shipbourne Rd. TN10 3DN. Author of several books on clocks. Est. 1968. Open 9.30-5.30 or by appointment. SIZE: Large. *STOCK: Fine restored clocks, mostly £1,000-£80,000; music boxes.* LOC: A227. From London A21 Tonbridge North turnoff, left 20 yds before first lights, left again and 50 yds up on right. PARK: Easy. TEL: 01732 358986; fax - 01732 771842. SER: Cabinet making. VAT: Spec.

Tonbridge continued

B. Somerset

Stags Head, 9 Stafford Rd. TN9 1HT. Est. 1948. Open 11-6.30. *STOCK: Clocks, £500-£5,000.* LOC: Off High Street beside castle. TEL: 01732 352017. SER: Valuations; restorations (cabinets, gilt and French polishing); buys at auction (longcase and bracket clocks). VAT: Stan.

TUNBRIDGE WELLS

Aaron Antiques

77 St. Johns Rd. TN4 9TT. (R.J. Goodman). Open 9-5. *STOCK: Clocks and pocket watches, paintings and prints; period and shipping furniture; English, Continental and Oriental porcelain; antiquarian books, postcards, coins and medals.* TEL: 01892 517644. VAT: Stan/Spec.

Amadeus Antiques

32 Mount Ephraim. TN3. (P.A. Davies). Open 10-5, Sun. by appointment. SIZE: Medium. *STOCK: Unusual furniture, to Art Deco, £50-£5,000; china and bric-a-brac, £25-£500; chandeliers, £100-£1,000.* LOC: Near hospital. PARK: Easy. TEL: 01892 544406; 01892 864884. SER: Valuations.

Baskerville Books

13 Nevill St. TN2 5RU. (Mike Banwell). Est. 1982. Open 10-5. CL: Wed. SIZE: Small. *STOCK: Antiquarian and secondhand books; small collectible antiques and occasional period and shipping furniture.* LOC: 50 yards from entrance to Pantiles. PARK: Nearby. TEL: 01892 526776. SER: Valuations.

Nicholas Bowlby

9 Castle St. TN1 1XJ. Est. 1981. Open 10-5.30. CL: Mon. and Wed. SIZE: Large. *STOCK: 19th-20th C watercolours, contemporary paintings and sculpture, £200-£20,000.* LOC: Near The Pantiles. TEL: 01892 510880. SER: Valuations; restorations; buys at auction (watercolours and drawings). VAT: Spec.

Chapel Place Antiques

9 Chapel Place. TN1 1YQ. (J. and A. Clare). Open 9-6. *STOCK: Antique and modern silver, old watches, jewellery, carriage clocks; some porcelain and dolls.* TEL: 01892 546561.

Claremont Antiques

6 Chapel Place. TN1 1YQ. (Anthony Broad). Open 10-5.30, other times by appointment. SIZE: Medium + warehouse. *STOCK: Irish, Eastern European, French pine, hardwood and painted country furniture, 18th-19th C; decorative items, all £10-£3,000.* LOC: Pedestrian precinct, lower end of High St. PARK: Nearby. TEL: 01892 511651; fax - 01892 517360. SER: Restorations (furniture). VAT: Stan/Spec.

Tunbridge Wells continued

Corn Exchange Antiques Centre

64 The Pantiles. TN2 5TN. (B. Henderson). Open 9.30-5. *STOCK: Furniture, clocks, books, prints, ceramics and silver.* TEL: 01892 539652.

County Antiques

94 High St. TN1 1YF. (Mrs. I. Hale). Open 10-5, Wed. 10-1. *STOCK: Small antiques and decorative items.* TEL: 01892 530767.

Cowden Antiques

24 Mount Ephraim Rd. TN1 1ED. (A. Linstead). Est. 1970. Open 10-5. CL: Wed. SIZE: Medium. *STOCK: Mahogany, decorative items and curtains.* PARK: Reasonable. TEL: 01892 520752. SER: Interiors. VAT: Stan/Spec.

Devron Green Antiques

39-41 The Pantiles. TN2 5TE. Est. 1992. Open 9.30-5, Sun. by appointment. SIZE: Large. *STOCK: Furniture, 18th-19th C, £500-£5,000; barometers, 19th C, £1,000-£2,500; pictures, prints and maps, 17th-20th C, £1,000-£4,000.* PARK: 100 yds. TEL: 01892 510688. SER: Valuations.

Glassdrumman Antiques

at Pantiles Spa Antiques, 4/6 Union Sq., The Pantiles. TN4 8LX. (G. and A. Dyson Rooke). Open 9.30-5, Sat. 9.30-5.30. SIZE: Large. *STOCK: Jewellery, silver, furniture, glass, china and collectables, 18th-19th C.* PARK: Nearby. TEL: 01892 541377.

Graham Gallery

1 Castle St. TN1 1XJ. (Joyce Graham). Est. 1987. Open 10.30-5, Sat. 10-5.30. CL: Mon. and Wed. *STOCK: 19th-20th C watercolours and Modern British paintings, £200-£5,000.* LOC: Off High St. PARK: Nearby. TEL: 01892 526695. VAT: Spec.

Hadlow Antiques

P.O Box 134. TN2 5YA. (M. and L. Adler). Est. 1966. Open by appointment only. SIZE: Small. *STOCK: Clocks, watches, 17th-20th C; dolls and accessories, automata, 18th-20th C; scientific and medical instruments, music boxes, singing birds, gramophones and collectors' items.* TEL: 01825 830368; fax - same. SER: Valuations; restorations; buys at auction. VAT: Stan/Spec.

Hall's Bookshop

20 Chapel Place. TN1 1YQ. Est. 1898. Open 9.30-5. *STOCK: Antiquarian and secondhand books.* TEL: 01892 527842.

Kentdale Antiques

Forge Rd., Eridge Green. TN3 9LJ. (C. Bigwood and T. Rayfield). Open 8.30-5.00. CL: Sat. *STOCK: Victorian furniture including extending tables.* TEL: 01892 863840. SER: Restorations (furniture); upholstery.

Tunbridge Wells continued

Linden Park Antiques

7 Union Sq., The Pantiles. TN4 8HE. (H.A. La Trobe and C. Bigwood). Est. 1993. Open 10-5.30, Sun. by appointment. SIZE: Medium. *STOCK: Victorian dining room furniture, £300-£5,000; other occasional furniture, £100-£2,000; prints, watercolours, copper and brass, pottery and porcelain, £10-£500.* PARK: Easy. TEL: 01892 538615. SER: Restorations; French polishing and re-leathering.

Howard Neville Antiques

21 The Pantiles. (H.C.C. Neville). Est. 1967. Open by appointment. SIZE: Medium. *STOCK: General antiques, furniture, sculpture and works of art, 16th-18th C.* PARK: Easy. TEL: 01892 511461; home - 01435 882409. SER: Valuations; restorations. VAT: Spec.

The Pantiles Antiques

31 The Pantiles. (Mrs E.M. Blackburn). Est. 1979. Open 10-5. SIZE: Medium. *STOCK: Georgian, Victorian and Edwardian furniture; 19th C porcelain, barometers, Jobling glass, silver.* PARK: Easy. TEL: 01892 531291.

Pantiles Spa Antiques

4/5/6 Union House, The Pantiles. TN4 8HE. (J.A. Cowpland). Est. 1985. Open 9.30-5, Sat. 9.30-5.30. SIZE: Large. *STOCK: Furniture especially

Tunbridge Wells continued

dining tables and chairs, £200-£10,000; pictures, £50-£3,000; clocks, £100-£5,000; porcelain, £50-£2,000; jewellery, £50-£200; silver, £50-£1,000; all 17th-19th C; dolls, bears and toys.* PARK: Nearby. TEL: 01892 541377; fax - 01435 865660. SER: Restorations (furniture). VAT: Spec.

Phoenix Antiques

48 and 51 St. John's Rd. TN4 9TP. (P. Janes, Miss J. Stott and R. Pilbeam). Est. 1982. Open 10-5.30 or by appointment. SIZE: Medium. *STOCK: Country and mahogany furniture, 18th-19th C, £50-£1,000; decorative furnishings, 18th-19th C, £5-£500.* LOC: On A26 from A21 into town, by St. John's church. PARK: Easy. TEL: 01892 549099.

Ian Relf Antiques

132/134 Camden Rd. Open 9.30-1.30 and 2.30-5.30. *STOCK: Mainly furniture.* TEL: 01892 538362.

John Thompson

27 The Pantiles. TN2 5TD. Est. 1982. Open 9.30-1 and 2-5. SIZE: Medium. *STOCK: Furniture, late 17th to early 19th C; paintings 17th-20th C; decorative items.* Not Stocked: Jewellery, silver and militaria. PARK: Linden Road or Warwick Park. TEL: 01892 547215. VAT: Spec.

Tunbridge Wells Antique Centre

12 Union Sq., The Pantiles. TN4 8HE. (N.J. Harding). Est. 1980. Open 9.30-5. SIZE: Large. *STOCK: Antiques and collectables including silver, jewellery, Georgian and Victorian furniture, soft furnishings, Victorian Staffordshire figures, clocks and watches, Tunbridgeware, antique-related books, fountain pens, Oriental rugs.* PARK: Nearby. TEL: 01892 533708. SER: Valuations; shipping. VAT: Stan/Spec.

Up Country

The Corn Stores, 68 St. Johns Rd. TN4 9PE. (G.J. Price and C.M. Springett). Est. 1988. Open 9-5.30. SIZE: Large. *STOCK: British and European country furniture, £50-£5,000; associated decorative and interesting items, £5-£500; all 18th-19th C.* LOC: On main London Rd. to Southborough and A21 trunk road which joins M25 and M26 at Sevenoaks intersection. PARK: Own at rear. TEL: 01892 523341. VAT: Stan.

WEST MALLING

The Old Clock Shop

63 High St. ME19 6NA. (S.L. Luck). Est. 1970. Open 9-5. SIZE: Large. *STOCK: Grandfather clocks, 17th-19th C; carriage, bracket and wall clocks.* LOC: Half a mile from M20. PARK: Easy. TEL: 01732 843246. VAT: Spec.

West Malling continued

Rose and Crown Antiques
40 High St. (Candy and Julian Lovegrove). Est. 1995. Open 9.30-5.30. SIZE: Small. *STOCK: General antiques including furniture, 18th to early 20th C.* PARK: Limited and nearby. TEL: 01732 872707; home/fax - same. SER: Restorations (furniture including French polishing and upholstery)

Andrew Smith Antiques
89 High St. ME19 6NA. Est. 1978. Open 9.30-5.30, Sun. by appointment. SIZE: Medium. *STOCK: Jewellery, silver, porcelain and clocks; £50-£2,000.* LOC: Off M20, junction 4, A228. PARK: Easy. TEL: 01732 843087; home - same. VAT: Stan/Spec.

WESTERHAM

Apollo Antique Galleries LAPADA
19 -21 Market Sq. TN16 1AN. Open 9.30-5.30. SIZE: Large. *STOCK: Georgian, Victorian and Edwardian furniture; 19th C oils and watercolours; bronze and marble statuary; clocks, silver.* TEL: 01959 562200. VAT: Spec.

Aquarius Antiques
Market Square. TN16 1AY. (G.W. Barr). Open 9.30-5.30. *STOCK: Mainly pictures, bronzes and small furniture.* TEL: 01959 561792; mobile - 0802 689253/0585 883441.

Brazil Antiques LAPADA
2 The Green. TN16 1AS. *STOCK: Furniture, 18th-20th C.* TEL: 01959 563048; fax - 01959 563020. VAT: Stan/Spec.

Castle Antiques Centre
1 London Rd. TN16 1BB. (Stewart Ward Properties). Est. 1974. Open 10-5. SIZE: Small - 8 dealers. *STOCK: General antiques including tools, lace and linen, £5-£500.* LOC: Just off town centre. PARK: Easy - nearby. TEL: 01959 562492. SER: Valuations; clock repair; props for stage productions.

Westerham continued

Anthony J. Hook
3 The Green. TN16 1AT. Est. 1948. Open 9-5.30, Sat. 10.30-4.30. SIZE: Medium. *STOCK: English furniture, 18th-19th C.* LOC: A25. TEL: 01959 562161. VAT: Stan/Spec.

London House Antiques
4 Market Sq. TN16 1AW. Est. 1977. Open 10-5, Sun. 12-4. SIZE: Medium. *STOCK: Furniture, 18th-19th C, £500-£10,000; paintings, prints and engravings, 19th-20th C, £100-£2,000; English and German teddy bears and dolls, 19th-20th C, £100-£3,000; clocks and bronzes, 19th C, £300-£5,000; silver and porcelain, 19th-20th C, £50-£1,500.* LOC: Off M25, junction 6 on A25 to Westerham. PARK: Easy. TEL: 01959 564479.

Marks Antiques
5 The Green. TN16 1AS. (Alan and Michael Marks). Est. 1954. Open 9.30-5. SIZE: Medium. *STOCK: Furniture, £500-£30,000; clocks, barometers, porcelain, bronzes and pictures, £200-£3,000: all 18th-19th C.* LOC: A25. PARK: Easy. TEL: 01959 562017; home - 01268 542621. SER: Valuations; restorations (furniture, including upholstery); buys at auction (furniture). VAT: Stan/Spec.

Modern Design Classics
4 London Rd. TN16 1BD. (Joseph and Eva M. Myler). Est. 1967. Open Wed.-Sat. 12-5.30, Mon. and Tues. by appointment. SIZE: Small. *STOCK: Art Deco furniture, £500-£7,000; bronzes, 1870-1930, £800-£5,000; small decorative items, £50-£500.* PARK: The Green. TEL: 01959 564406; home - 0181 658 0803; fax - same. VAT: Stan.

Regal Antiques
2 Market Square. TN16 1AW. (E. Lawrence). Open 10-5. CL: Mon. and Tues. *STOCK: Vintage watches, portrait miniatures, porcelain and jewellery.* TEL: 01959 561778.

Westerham continued

Denys Sargeant

21 The Green. TN16 1AX. Est. 1949. Open 9.30-5.30. *STOCK: Glass, especially chandeliers and candelabras, decanters and lustres.* TEL: 01959 562130. SER: Restoration and cleaning (chandeliers, candelabras, lustres); electrification. VAT: Stan/Spec.

Taylor-Smith LAPADA

4 The Grange, High St. TN16 1AH. Open 10-5. CL: Wed. *STOCK: Fine 18th and 19th C furniture; paintings, porcelain, glass and decorative items.* TEL: 01959 563100; fax - 01959 561561.

Taylor-Smith LAPADA

2 High St. TN16 1RF. Open 10-5, Sun. 2.30-5. CL: Mon. and Tues. *STOCK: Books and Sir Winston Churchill items.* TEL: 01959 561561; fax - 01959 561561.

Westerham House Antiques

The Green. TN16 1AY. (R.W. Barr). Open 9.30-5.30. *STOCK: Victorian and period furniture, pictures and bronzes.* TEL: 01959 561622; mobile - 0802 689253/0585 883441.

WHITSTABLE

Laurens Antiques

2 Harbour St. CT5 1AG. (G. A. Laurens). Est. 1965. Open 9.30-5.30. SIZE: Medium. *STOCK: Furniture, 18th-19th C, £300-£500+.* LOC: Turn off Thanet Way at Longreach roundabout, straight down to one-way system in High St. PARK: Easy. TEL: 01227 261940; home - same. SER: Valuations; restorations (cabinet work); buys at auction.

Whitstable continued

Tankerton Antiques

136 Tankerton Rd. CT5 2AN. (Mrs. F. Holland). Est. 1985. Open 10-5, Tues. 10-4, Wed. 10-1. CL: Mon. SIZE: Medium. *STOCK: Furniture, Regency to 1930's, £50-£1,500; china, from 18th C, to £1,500; glass, Regency to 1930's, to £400; clocks and barometers, from 1800, £30-£2,500; French, English and German costume jewellery, £30-£300.* LOC: From A299 Thanet Way take A290/B2205 turn off to Whitstable. Through town and into Tankerton. Shop on right just past roundabout. TEL: 01227 266490. SER: Valuations.

WINGHAM, Nr. Canterbury

Bridge Antiques

97 High St. CT3 1DE. Resident. (A. and C. Cripps). Est. 1968. Open Thurs., Fri. and Sat. 9-5, or by appointment any time. SIZE: Large. *STOCK: English and Continental furniture, clocks, dolls and toys, books, shipping goods, bric-a-brac.* TEL: 01227 720445.

Silvesters LAPADA

33 High St. CT3 1AB. (S.N. Hartley and G.M.A. Wallis). Est. 1953. Open 9.30-5 by appointment. *STOCK: Furniture, Georgian and Victorian; decorative items, silver, porcelain, glass.* LOC: At main junction in town. TEL: 01227 720278 and 01843 841524.

WITTERSHAM

Old Corner House Antiques

6 Poplar Rd. TN30 7PG. (G. and F. Shepherd). Open 10-5. CL: Fri. *STOCK: General antiques, country furniture, samplers; 18th-19th C English pottery including blue and white and creamware; watercolours, 19th to early 20th C.* PARK: Easy. TEL: 01797 270236.

WOODCHURCH, Nr. Ashford

Treasures of Woodchurch

1-3 The Green. TN26 3PE. (Mrs S. Cottrell). Open 10-5.30. CL: Thurs. SIZE: Medium. *STOCK: Continental and English pine, some dark wood; china, linen, domestic collectables, £1-£800.* LOC: At top of green close to church. TEL: 01233 860249.

WROTHAM

Charles International Antiques LAPADA

The Poplars, London Rd. TN15 7RR. (Mr and Mrs C. Bremner). Est. 1968. Open 9-4.30. *STOCK: Victorian, Edwardian and shipping goods.* LOC: A20. TEL: 01622 682882. SER: Valuations; full container and documentation facilities.

Lancashire

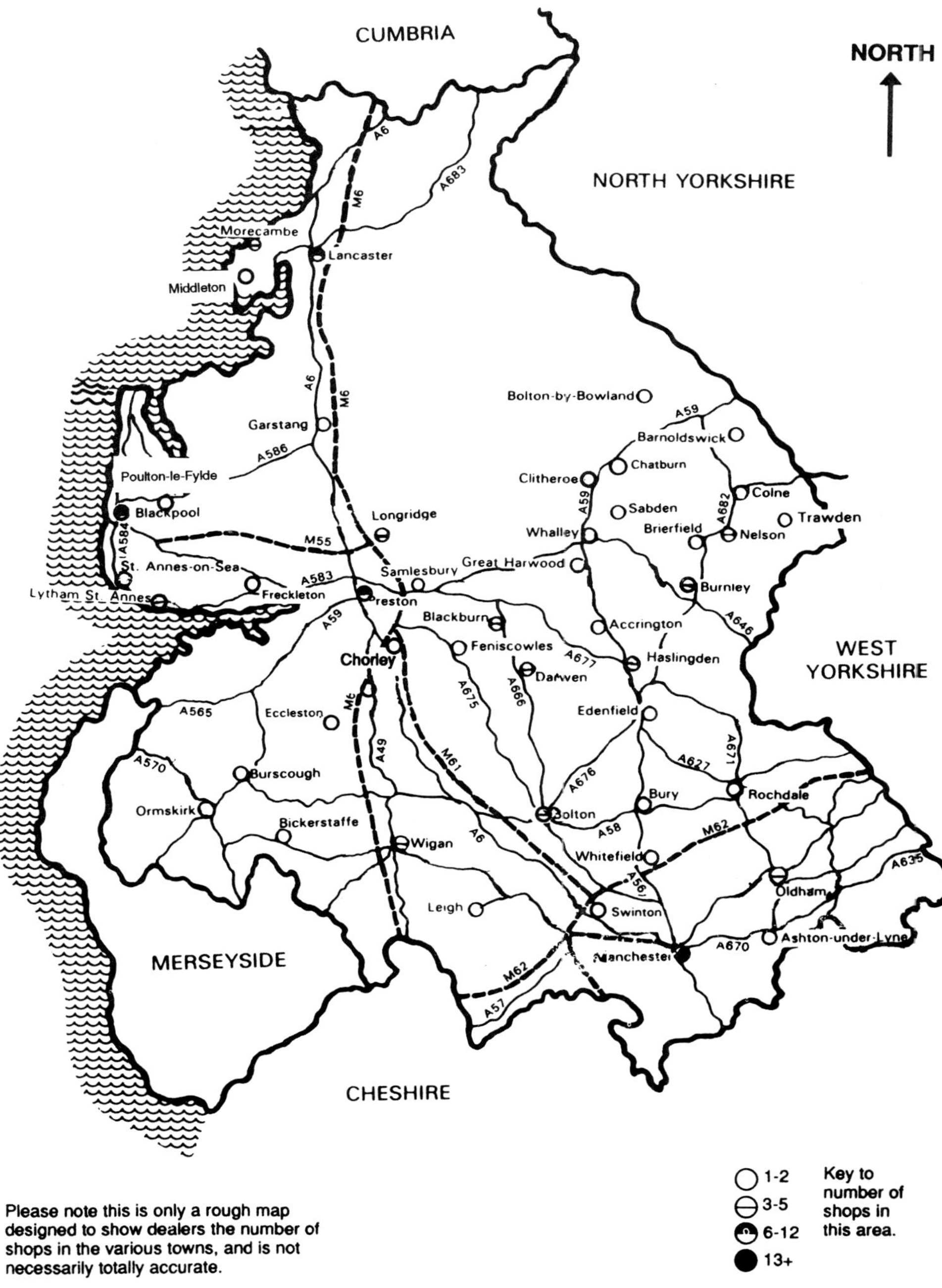

Please note this is only a rough map designed to show dealers the number of shops in the various towns, and is not necessarily totally accurate.

ACCRINGTON

The Coin and Jewellery Shop

129a Blackburn Rd. BB5 0AA. Est. 1977. Open 9.30-5. CL: Wed. *STOCK: Coins, jewellery and small antiques.* TEL: 01254 384757.

ASHTON-UNDER-LYNE

Kenworthys Ltd BADA

226 Stamford St. OL6 7LW. (C.J. and M. Collings). Est. 1880. Open by appointment only. *STOCK: Silver and jewellery, all periods, £1-£5,000.* PARK: 50yds. away behind shop. TEL: 0161 330 3043 (2 lines). SER: Valuations; restorations; buys at auction. FAIRS: Harrogate (NADF); Chester; Buxton; Olympia (June and Autumn). VAT: Stan/Spec.

BARNOLDSWICK, Nr. Colne

Roy W. Bunn LAPADA

34/36 Church St. BB8 5UT. Est. 1986. Open by appointment only. *STOCK: Staffordshire figures, 18th-19th C, £45-£2,000.* LOC: Main road. PARK: Easy. TEL: 01282 813703; fax - same; home - same. SER: Valuations; restorations (ceramics); buys at auction. VAT: Spec.

BICKERSTAFFE, Nr. Ormskirk

E.W. Webster

Wash Farm, Rainford Rd. L39 0HG. Est. 1975. Open anytime by appointment. SIZE: Medium. *STOCK: Furniture, early metal, needlework, treen, decorative items, 1650-1850.* Not Stocked: Bric-a-brac. LOC: Exit 3, M58 on to A570, turn left 100yds. PARK: Easy. TEL: 01695 580530. VAT: Spec.

BLACKBURN

Ancient and Modern

17 New Market St. BB1 7DR. Est. 1943. Open 9-5.30. *STOCK: Jewellery, Victorian to date, up to £25,000; clocks, watches, paintings, militaria, antique and modern silver, objets de vertu.* LOC: Town centre, opposite side entrance of Marks & Spencer. PARK: Easy. TEL: 01254 677866. SER: Valuations; repairs; restorations.

Mitchell's (Lock Antiques)

76 Bolton Rd. BB2 3PZ. (S. Mitchell). Open 9-5. *STOCK: General antiques, gold and silver jewellery, wrist watches.* TEL: 01254 664663.

BLACKPOOL

Chard Coins

521 Lytham Rd. FY4 1RJ. Est. 1965. Open 9-5. CL: Sat. SIZE: Large. *STOCK: Paintings and furniture, English and ancient coins, gold bullion coins, jewellery and silver, £50-£20,000+.* LOC: Lytham Rd. runs from Central Promenade south to Blackpool Airport main gates. Shop is 1/4 mile from airport. PARK: Easy. TEL: 01253 343081. SER: Valuations. VAT: Stan/Spec.

Blackpool continued

Ann and Peter Christian

400/402 Waterloo Rd., Marton. FY4 4BL. Open 10-5.30. *STOCK: Decorative arts and pine furniture.* TEL: 01253 763268.

R.H. Latham Antiques

45 Whitegate Drive. FY3 9DG. Resident. Est. 1958. Open 10-5.30. SIZE: Large. *STOCK: Stripped pine, brass, copper and porcelain.* TEL: 01253 393950; home - same. SER: Shipping and courier.

Nostalgia

95 Coronation St. FY1 4QE. (P. Jackson). Est. 1978. Open 10-4, including Sun. in summer. SIZE: Small. *STOCK: Royal commemoratives, 19th-20th C, £3-£500; also antiquarian and modern prints.* LOC: Town centre, near Winter Gardens. PARK: Easy. TEL: 01253 293251.

BOLTON

Bolton Antique Centre

Central St. Open 10-4.30. *STOCK: General antiques and collectables.* LOC: Town centre behind McDonalds. PARK: Opposite. TEL: 01204 362694.

Drop Dial Antiques

Last Drop Village, Hospital Rd., Bromley Cross. BL7 9PZ. (I.W. and I.E. Roberts). Est. 1975. Open every afternoon except Mon. and Fri. SIZE: Small. *STOCK: Clocks, mainly English and French, 18th-20th C, £100-£4,000; mercury barometers, 19th-20th C, £100-£500; paintings, silver and general antiques, £20-£500.* Not Stocked: Stamps and armour. PARK: Easy. TEL: 01204 307186; home - 01257 480995. SER: Valuations; restorations (clocks and barometers). VAT: Stan/Spec.

Ironchurch Antiques Centre

Blackburn Rd. BL1 8DR. (P.J. Wilkinson). Est. 1975. Open 10-5 including Sun. SIZE: Large. *STOCK: Furniture, china, glass, clocks, books, jewellery, 17th C to date, £1-£10,000.* PARK: Free nearby. TEL: 01204 383616. SER: Valuations; restorations.

G. Oakes and Son

160-162 Blackburn Rd. BL1 8DR. Est. 1958. Open 9-5. *STOCK: Furniture and bric-a-brac.* TEL: 01204 526587; e-mail - 100410.3406@compuserve.com. SER: Shipping and packing; buys at auction. VAT: Stan.

Park Galleries Antiques, Fine Art and Decor

167 Mayor St. BL1 4SJ. (Mrs S. Hunt). Est. 1964. Open Thurs., Fri. and Sat. 11-4 or by appointment. SIZE: Medium. *STOCK: English and Continental furniture, 17th to early 20th C; English and Continental pottery and porcelain,*

Blackpool continued

miniatures, glass, brass, silver, copper; paintings, 19th C; decorative and collectable items. Not Stocked: Weapons, coins, medals, stamps. LOC: On B6202. PARK: Side and rear. TEL: 01204 529827; home - 0161 764 5853. SER: Valuations; restorations (furniture; metalwork replating, pottery and porcelain, paintings; frames regilded; clock movements).

BOLTON-BY-BOWLAND, Nr. Clitheroe

Farmhouse Antiques

23 Main St. BB7 4NY. (M. Howard). Est. 1980. Open Sat., Sun. and Bank Holidays 12-4.30, or by appointment. SIZE: Small. *STOCK: Textiles, linen and quilts, from 1830; beads and jewellery, Victoriana, china, kitchenalia and brasses.* LOC: Off A59, past Clitheroe, through Sawley to village. PARK: Easy. TEL: 01200 441457/ 447294.

Harrop Fold Clocks (F. Robinson)

Harrop Fold, Lane Ends. BB7 4PJ. Est. 1974. Open by appointment. SIZE: Medium. *STOCK: British clocks, barometers, 18th-19th C, £1,000-£10,000.* LOC: Through Clitheroe to Chatburn and Grindleton. Take Slaidburn road, turn left after 3 miles. PARK: Own. TEL: 01200 447665; home - same. SER: Valuations; restorations (clocks).

BRIERFIELD, Nr. Nelson

J.H. Blakey and Sons Ltd (Est. 1905)

Burnley Rd. BB9 5AD. *STOCK: Furniture, brass, copper, pewter, clocks, curios.* TEL: 01282 613593. SER: Restorations. VAT: Stan.

BURNLEY

Brun Lea Antiques

3/5 Standish St. BB11 1AP. Open 9.30-5.30. *STOCK: General antiques and shipping goods.* TEL: 01282 413513.

Brun Lea Antiques (J. Waite Ltd)

Unit 1, Rear Elm Street Mill, Travis St. BB10 1NZ. Open 8.30-5.30, Fri. and Sat. 9-4, Sun. 12-4. SIZE: Warehouse. *STOCK: Georgian furniture to 1930's shipping goods.* TEL: 01282 413513.

King's Mill Antique Centre

Unit 2 King's Mill, Queen St., Harle Syke. (Michael and Linda Helier). Open 10-5, Thurs. 10-8, Sun. 11-4. SIZE: Large. *STOCK: Furniture and bric-a-brac, Edwardian and Victorian, £5-£1,000.* LOC: From General Hospital, follow brown tourist signs for Queen's Mill. PARK: Easy. TEL: 01282 431953; mobile - 0421 023634. SER: Restorations (furniture).

BURSCOUGH, Nr. Ormskirk

West Lancs. Antique Exports LAPADA

Victoria Mill, Victoria St. L40 0SN. (W. and B. Griffiths). Est. 1959. Open 9-5.30, Sat. and Sun.10-5. SIZE: Large. *STOCK: Shipping furniture.* TEL: 01704 894634/896036; fax - 01704 894486. SER: Courier; packing and shipping. VAT: Stan.

BURY

Newtons

151 The Rock. BL9 0ND. (Newtons of Bury). Est. 1931. Open 9-5. SIZE: Small. *STOCK: General antiques, 18th-19th C, £5-£500.* Not Stocked: Continental furniture. LOC: From Manchester through Bury town centre, shop is on left 200yds. before Fire Station. PARK: 50yds. behind shop. TEL: 0161 764 1863. SER: Valuations; restorations (furniture). VAT: Stan.

CHATBURN, Nr. Clitheroe

T. Brindle Antiques LAPADA

6 and 8 Sawley Rd. BB7 4AS. Open 9.30-5.00, Sat. and other times by appointment. *STOCK: Antique and decorative items.* TEL: 01200 440025; fax - 01200 440090.

CHORLEY

Antiques and Crafts Centre

Botany Bay Villages Ltd., Canal Mill, Botany Brow. PR6 8AX. Open daily including Sun. SIZE: Large - 5 floors. *STOCK: Porcelain, china and jewellery; furniture, memorabilia and curios andcrafts.* LOC: Opposite J8, M61. PARK: Easy. TEL: 01257 261220. VAT: Stan.

CLITHEROE

Folly Antiques

22 Moor Lane. BB7 1BE. (N.P. Medd). Est. 1967. Open 9-6, Wed. and Sun. by appointment. SIZE: Medium. *STOCK: Decorative and upholstered items, furniture, £100-£2,000; pictures, brass and objects, £5-£2,000; all 19th-20th C; garden furniture, small architectural items, 18th-20th C, £20-£2,000.* LOC: 15 miles from junction 31, M6, via A59. PARK: Opposite. TEL: 01200 429461. VAT: Stan/Spec.

Lee's Antiques

59 Whalley Rd. BB7 1EE. (P.A. Lee). *STOCK: General antiques.* TEL: 01200 424921; home - 01200 425441.

COLNE

Enloc Antiques

96 Keighley Rd. BB8 0PH. Est. 1978. Open 9-5, Sun. 12-4. SIZE: Large. *STOCK: Pine - antique, reclaimed timber, reproduction.* TEL: 01282 867101; fax - 01282 867601. SER: Restorations (hot stripping, polishing and joinery). VAT: Stan.

DARWEN

Cottage Antiques

135 Blackburn Rd. SIZE: Small. *STOCK: Fine porcelain including Crown Derby, Worcester and Doulton, £100-£2,000; 19th C furniture, £100-£5,000.* LOC: A666 towards Blackburn, opposite St Cuthbert's Church. PARK: Opposite. TEL: 01254 775891 or 01254 676840 (24 hour).

Darwen Antiques

Percival St. BB3 1HG. Est. 1971. Open 9.30-5, Sun 11-5. *STOCK: Pottery, glass, pictures and furniture, £1-£5,000.* PARK: Easy. TEL: 01254 760565; home - 01254 776644/776551. SER: Valuations; buys at auction. VAT: Stan/Spec.

K.C. Antiques

538 Bolton Rd. BB3 2JR. Resident. (K. and J. Anderton). Open 9-6, Sun. 12-5. *STOCK: Georgian, Victorian and Edwardian furniture and decorative items.* LOC: A666. PARK: Easy. TEL: 01254 772252. SER: Buys at auction. VAT: Stan/Spec.

ECCLESTON

3 L's Antiques

Units 3 & 4, Grove Development Centre. PR7 5PD. (L. and L.C. Frost). Est. 1989. Open 12-3.30, Sun. 11-5. SIZE: Small. *STOCK: Furniture, 1850-1940, £50-£700; gramophones, £50-£500; pottery, porcelain and brassware.* LOC: Junction 27, M6, village is 4 miles north via Mossy Lea Rd. Shop situated at Bygone Times Centre. PARK: Easy. TEL: 01257 450290.

Bygone Times International Plc

Grove Mill, The Green. PR7 5PD. (S. Higham). Open 9-5 including Sun. SIZE: 2 warehouses. *STOCK: Architectural and general antiques; Americana.* TEL: 01257 453780.

EDENFIELD, Nr. Bury

The Antique Shop

17 Market St. BL0 0JA. (J. and J.C. Salisbury). Est. 1964. Open 10-4. SIZE: Large. *STOCK: General antiques, shipping goods, £1-£10,000.* LOC: On A56. PARK: Easy. TEL: 0170 682 3107/2351. SER: Valuations. VAT: Stan/Spec.

FENISCOWLES, Nr. Blackburn

Old Smithy

726 Preston Old Rd. BB2 5EP. (R.C. Lynch). Est. 1967. Open 9.30-5. SIZE: Large. *STOCK: Period and Victorian fireplaces, pub and architectural items, violins and musical instruments, pictures and prints, furniture, shipping items, jewellery, brass, copper, Victorian lace and linen.* LOC: Opposite Fieldens Arms. PARK: Own or nearby. TEL: 01254 209943/580874. SER: Valuations; restorations (wooden items); buys at auction. FAIRS: Park Hall, Charnock Richard, Newark, Lincs.

FRECKLETON, Nr. Preston

L. Booth Antiques and Reproductions

Freckleton Boat Yard, Poolside. PR4 1HB. Open 10-5 including Sun. *STOCK: Victorian and Edwardian furniture.* TEL: 01772 632439. SER: Restorations.

GARSTANG

Clare's Antiques and Auction Galleries

Wheatsheaf Buildings, Park Hill. PR3 1EL. (Mrs C.A.L. Campbell-Cameron and Mrs C.L. Allen). Est. 1960. Open Thurs., Fri. and Sat. 10-4. SIZE: Large. *STOCK: Royal Worcester porcelain, early 20th C, £150-£4,000; Rudelstadt, Meissen, Dresden figures, 19th C, £500-£2,000; silver, jewellery, small furniture.* LOC: Off A6. PARK: Easy. TEL: 01995 605702; home - same. SER: Valuations; restorations (porcelain, jewellery); buys at auction.

GREAT HARWOOD, Nr. Blackburn

Benny Charlesworth's Snuff Box

51 Blackburn Rd. BB6 7DF. (N. Walsh). Est. 1984. Open 10-5. SIZE: Small. *STOCK: Furniture, china, linen, costume jewellery, teddies.* LOC: 200yds. from town centre, off A680. PARK: Next to shop. TEL: 01254 888550. FAIRS: Local.

HASLINGDEN

P.J. Brown Antiques

8 Church St. BB4 5QU. Open 10-5, Sat. and Sun. by appointment. SIZE: Large and warehouse. *STOCK: Georgian, Victorian and Edwardian furniture, shipping goods, old advertising items, bottles and related items.* LOC: Town centre, off Bury Road and Regent St. PARK: Easy. TEL: 01706 224888. VAT: Stan/Spec.

Fieldings Antiques

176, 178 and 180 Blackburn Rd. BB1 2LG. Est. 1956. Open 9-4.30, Fri. 9-4. CL: Thurs. SIZE: Large. *STOCK: Longcase clocks, £30-£2,000; wall clocks, sets of chairs, pine, period oak, French furniture, glass, shipping goods, toys, steam engines, veteran cars, vintage and veteran motor cycles.* PARK: Easy. TEL: 01706 214254; mobile - 0973 698961; home - 01254 263358.

P.W. Norgrove - Antique Clocks

38 Bury Rd. BB4 5LR. Normally open 9-5.30, Sat. 10-5, but prior 'phone call advisable. *STOCK: Longcase, wall, bracket and mantel clocks.* TEL: 01706 211995.

LANCASTER

The Assembly Rooms Market

King St. Open Thurs., Fri. and Sat. 10-4.30. SIZE: Several dealers. *STOCK: General antiques, jewellery, collectables, model railways, period costume/clothing, books, records and collectors' comics.* TEL: Market Superintendent - 01524 66627.

Lancaster continued

G.B. Antiques Ltd

Lancaster Leisure Park, Wyresdale Rd. LA1 3LA. (Mrs G. Blackburn). Open 10-5 including Sun. SIZE: Large. 100+ dealers. *STOCK: Porcelain, glass and silver, late 19th to early 20th C; small furniture, Victorian to early 20th C.* LOC: Off M6, junction 33 or 34. PARK: Easy. TEL: 01524 844734; fax - 01524 844735; home - 01772 861593. SER: Valuations; buys at auction. VAT: Stan/Spec.

Lancaster Leisure Park Antiques Centre

Wyresdale Rd. (on site of former Hornsea Pottery Plant). LA1 5LA. Open every day 10-5. SIZE: 140 dealers. *STOCK: Wide range of general antiques.* LOC: Off M6, junction 33. TEL: 01524 844734.

Lancastrian Antiques & Co

70/72 Penny St. LA1 1XN. (S.P. and H.S. Wilkinson). Open 10-4. CL: Wed. *STOCK: Furniture, lighting, period beds, bric-a-brac.* TEL: 01524 847004.

W.B. McCormack

6 and 6a Rosemary Lane. LA1 1NR. Open 10-5. CL: Wed. *STOCK: Rare and secondhand books; maps and prints.* TEL: 01524 36405.

Vicary Antiques

18a Brock St. LA1 1VV. Est. 1974. Open 10-5. CL: Wed. SIZE: Small. *STOCK: Paintings, prints, art pottery, works of art, 1850-1950; arts and crafts, furniture, quilts.* TEL: 01524 843322.

LEIGH

Leigh Jewellery

3 Queens St. (R. Bibby). Open 9.30-5.30, Wed. 9.30-12.30. *STOCK: Jewellery.* TEL: 01942 607947.

LONGRIDGE, Nr. Preston

The Attic Centre

29-33 Berry Lane. (Mrs T. Harber). Est. 1986. Open 10.30-4.30, Sat. and Sun. 10-4, prior telephone call advisable. CL: Mon. SIZE: Large - 20 units. *STOCK: Wide variety of general antiques, Victorian to 1950's, £5-£1,000.* LOC: Main road, top floor of old Co-op Building. PARK: Easy and nearby. TEL: 01772 786366; home - 01254 813868. SER: Valuations; restorations; buys at auction. FAIRS: Newark, Ardingly, Kempton, Parkhall (Lancs).

Charnley Fine Arts

Charnley House, Preston Rd. PR3 3BD. (R. and J. Crosbie). Est. 1989. Open by appointment. SIZE: Medium. *STOCK: Paintings, 19th-20th C, £100-£10,000.* LOC: Off M55/M6, north of Preston on B6243. PARK: Easy. TEL: 01772 782800; home - same. SER: Restorations; cleaning.

Longridge continued

Joys

83 Berry Lane. PR3 3WH. (Mrs J. Roberts). Est. 1986. Open 9-5. CL: Wed. SIZE: Small. *STOCK: Pine and oak furniture, Art Deco china, jewellery, mirrors, lamps, rugs.* LOC: 6 miles from exit 31, M6. PARK: Easy. TEL: 01772 782083.

Kitchenalia

'The Old Bakery', 36 Inglewhite Rd. PR3 3JS. (J. Chilton). *STOCK: Kitchenalia, brass, copper ware, pottery, pine and oak country furniture, butchers' blocks, Victorian church pews.* TEL: 01772 785411. VAT: Stan/Spec.

LYTHAM ST. ANNES

All Our Yesterdays of Lytham

3 Station Rd. FY8 5DH. (S. Brickwood and P. Harrison). Open 11-5. CL: Mon. and Wed. *STOCK: General antiques.* TEL: 01253 734748.

Snuff Box

5 Market Buildings, Hastings Pl. FY8 5LW. (Mrs J.C. Rimmer). Open 10-5. CL: Wed. *STOCK: Silver and plate, jewellery, watches and linen.* TEL: 01253 738656.

John Treasure Antiques & Restorations

Warton Close, Lodge Lane. FY8 5RP. Open by appointment. *STOCK: Furniture, 1650-1900.* TEL: 01253 736801.

MANCHESTER

A.S. Antique Galleries

26 Broad St, Salford. M6 5BY. (A. Sternshine). Est. 1975. Open 10-5.30. CL: Tues. SIZE: Large. *STOCK: Art Nouveau and Art Deco bronzes, bronze and ivory figures, silver, glass, furniture, jewellery, lighting and general antiques.* Not Stocked: Weapons. LOC: On A6, one mile north of Manchester city centre, next to Salford University College. PARK: Easy. TEL: 0161 737 5938; mobile - 0836 368230; fax - 0161 737 6626. SER: Valuations; restorations; commission purchasing.

Antique Fireplaces

1090 Stockport Rd, Levenshulme. M19 2SU. (J. McMullan & Son). Open 9-6, Sun. 11-5. *STOCK: Fireplaces and architectural items.* TEL: 0161 431 8075.

Antiques Village

The Old Town Hall, 965 Stockport Rd., Levenshulme. M19 3NP. Est. 1978. Open 10.15-5, Sun. 12-4.45. SIZE: 40+ dealers. *STOCK: Furniture, fireplaces, collectables.* LOC: A6 between Manchester and Stockport. PARK: Own. TEL: 0161 256 4644. SER: Valuations; pine stripping; picture framing. FAIRS: Newark; G MEX. VAT: Stan/Spec.

Authentiques

(S.G. Rubenstein). Est. 1978. Open by appointment only. *STOCK: Decorative items - silver, plate, porcelain, glass, boxes, Staffordshire, watercolours and prints, small furniture, miniatures, brass, curios, early 19th C to 1920s, £50-£500.* LOC: 1/2 mile from junction 17, M62 on A56. PARK: Easy. TEL: 0161 773 9601; fax - same. SER: Valuations; restorations (silver); buys at auction (pictures, silver, furniture). FAIRS: British International, Birmingham.

The Baron Antiques

1-11 Church Lane, Prestwich. M25 5AN. (S. Brunsveld). Open 9.30-6. SIZE: Large. *STOCK: 18th C mahogany and early oak furniture, Victorian walnut, clocks, porcelain, objets d'art, shipping goods.* TEL: 0161 773 9929; fax - 01925 758101. SER: Valuations; restorations.

Boodle and Dunthorne Ltd

1 King St. M2 6AW. Est. 1798. Open 9-5.30. SIZE: Large. *STOCK: 18th-19th C silver, Victorian jewellery, £100-£30,000; clocks and clock sets, mid-19th C, £100-£1,000.* Not Stocked: Furniture. TEL: 0161 833 9000. VAT: Stan/Spec.

Bulldog Antiques

393 Bury New Rd., Prestwich. M25 1AW. (P. Wordsworth). Est. 1971. Open 10.30-6. CL: Sun. except by appointment. SIZE: Large. *STOCK: Georgian, Victorian and Edwardian furniture; clocks especially longcase and wall clock sets, 18th-19th C; militaria, swords, guns, pistols,*

Manchester continued

shotguns, war medals, pottery, prints, pictures, general antiques and shipping goods. LOC: Exit 17, M62. PARK: At rear. TEL: 0161 798 9277; home - 0161 790 7153. SER: Restorations (furniture); French polishing, watch and clock repairs.

Bus Stop Curios

1 Beech Rd., Chorlton-cum-Hardy. M21 8BX. Resident. (John and Jean Higginbotham). Est. 1989. Open Thurs. 11-5.30, Fri. 11.15-5.45, Sat. 10.30-4.30. SIZE: Medium. *STOCK: Militaria, WW1 & WW2, £1-£100; Victorian and Art Deco pottery and glass and smalls, £1-£100.* PARK: Easy. TEL: 0161 860 6232.

Cathedral Jewellers

4 Todd St. M3 1WU. Open 9.30-5. *STOCK: Jewellery.* TEL: 0161 832 3042.

Family Antiques

405/407 Bury New Rd., Prestwich. (J. and J. Ditondo). Open daily. *STOCK: General antiques.* TEL: 0161 798 0036.

Fernlea Antiques

Failsworth Antique Centre, Failsworth Mill, Ashton Rd West, Failsworth. (A.J. and Mrs B. McLaughlin). Open 10-5. *STOCK: General antiques and shipping goods.* TEL: 0161 682 0589.

Forest Books of Cheshire

in The Ginnel, 18-22 Lloyd St. M2 5WA. (Mrs E. Mann). Open 9.30-5.30. *STOCK: Antiquarian, art, collecting, drama and humanities books and prints.* TEL: 0161 834 0747; 0161 833 9037 (The Ginnel).

Fulda Gallery Ltd

19 Vine St., Salford. M7 3PG. (M.J. Fulda). Est. 1969. Open by appointment only. *STOCK: Oil paintings, 1500-1950, £500-£30,000; watercolours, 1800-1930, £350-£10,000.* LOC: Near Salford Police Station off Bury New Rd. TEL: 0161 792 1962; mobile - 0836 518313. SER: Valuations; restorations; buys at auction.

Gibb's Bookshop Ltd

10 Charlotte St. M1 4FL. Est. 1926. *STOCK: Books.* TEL: 0161 236 7179.

The Ginnell Gallery Antique Centre

18-22 Lloyd St. M2 5WA. (Mr and Mrs J.K. Mottershead). Est. 1973. Open 9.30-5.30. *STOCK: Art Deco and Art Nouveau, 1950's pottery, furniture, glass, fishing tackle, antiquarian and other books.* LOC: Opposite Town Hall. TEL: 0161 833 9037.

In-Situ Architectural Antiques

Worsley St. M15 4LD. (Laurence Green and Stan Newsham). Est. 1983. Open 9-5.30, Sun. 10-4. SIZE: Large. *STOCK: Architectural items including fireplaces, doors, panelling, sanitary*

Manchester continued

ware, radiators, flooring, glass, gardenware, staircasing. PARK: Easy. TEL: 0161 839 2010. SER: Valuations; restorations (architectural items). VAT: Stan.

Irving Antique Toys

c/o Ginnel Gallery, 18-22 Lloyd St. M2 5WA. SIZE: Large. *STOCK: Dinkies, teddies and dolls.* LOC: Off Albert Square. TEL: 0161 833 9037.

Manchester Antique Company

Ballbrook Ave., West Didsbury. M20 0UT. (J. Long). Est. 1964. Open 9.30-5.30. SIZE: Large. *STOCK: Mainly marquetry walnut and mahogany, some period furniture, silver, and pianos.* LOC: 3 miles from airport on M56 towards city. PARK: Easy. TEL: 0161 434 7752. SER: Valuations; buys at auction (clocks). VAT: Stan.

Eric J. Morten

Warburton St., Didsbury. M20 6WA. Est. 1959. Open 10-6. SIZE: Medium. *STOCK: Antiquarian books, 16th-20th C, £5-£5,000.* LOC: Off Wilmslow Rd., near traffic lights in Didsbury village. A34. PARK: Easy. TEL: 0161 445 7629 and 01265 277959. SER: Valuations; buys at auction (antiquarian books).

R.J. O'Brien and Son Antiques Ltd

Failsworth Mill, Ashton Rd. West, Failsworth. M35 0FD. Est. 1970. Open 9-5. CL: Sat. SIZE: Large. *STOCK: Furniture, Victorian, Edwardian and 1930's; shipping goods, general antiques and pianos.* PARK: Own. TEL: 0161 688 4414; mobile - 0850 485201. SER: Container and courier service.

Premiere Antiques

373 Bury New Rd., Prestwich. M25 5AW. GADAR. (S. Harris). *STOCK: Furniture, mainly Victorian and Edwardian inlaid.* TEL: 0161 773 0500; fax - 0161 792 0232. SER: Restorations (furniture).

Prestwich Antiques Ltd

371-373 Bury New Rd., Prestwich. (T. Finn and Y. Gray). Est. 1973. Open 10.30-6, Sun. 11.30-5. SIZE: Large. *STOCK: Victorian furniture, decorative lighting, to £1,000.* LOC: Off junction 17,

Manchester continued

M62. PARK: Own at rear. TEL: 0161 798 0911; home - 01282 618270. SER: Valuations; restorations (upholstery, polishing and repairs). VAT: Stan/Spec.

Paul Quentin

626 Manchester Rd., Bury. BL9 9SU. (D. and P. Eccleston). Est. 1965. Open 10-6. SIZE: Large. *STOCK: General antiques, weapons, copper, brass, pewter, 1650-1920.* Not Stocked: Fine porcelain. LOC: On A56, 2 miles north of junction 17, M62; 1 mile west of junction 3, M66. PARK: Easy. TEL: 0161 766 6673.

Secondhand and Rare Books

Corner Church St/High St. M4 1PN. Open 12-4. *STOCK: Books.* TEL: 0161 834 5964 or 01625 861608.

St. James Antiques

41 South King St. M2 6DE. *STOCK: Jewellery, silver and paintings.* LOC: Off Deansgate, in town centre. TEL: 0161 834 9632.

Village Antiques

416 Bury New Rd., Prestwich. M25 1BD. (R. Weidenbaum). Est. 1981. Open 10-5, Wed. 10-1. SIZE: Medium. *STOCK: 19th C pottery and porcelain, £5-£300; 18th C glass; small furniture; Art Deco clocks, figurines and lamps; Art Nouveau figurines.* LOC: Village centre, 2 mins. from M62. PARK: Easy - side and opposite. TEL: 0161 773 3612.

MIDDLETON VILLAGE, Nr. Morecambe

G.G. Exports

Newfield House, Middleton Rd. LA3 3JS. (G. Goulding). Est. 1970. Always available but prior telephone call essential. SIZE: Large. *STOCK: Shipping goods, £30-£500; Victoriana, £50-£3,000; general antiques and pine.* LOC: On main road between Morecambe promenade and Middleton village. PARK: Easy. TEL: 01524 850757; fax - 01524 851565. SER: Courier; packing; 40ft containers weekly worldwide. VAT: Stan. *Trade Only.*

MORECAMBE

The Magpies Nest

Unit 1 Plaza Arcade and 48 Pedder St. LA4 5YJ. (B. Byrne). Open 10-5. CL: Wed. *STOCK: Bric-a-brac, cutlery, china, glass, militaria.* TEL: 01524 423328.

Tyson's Antiques

Clark St. (George, Andrew and Shirley Tyson). Est. 1952. Open Sat. 9-12, other times by appointment. SIZE: Large. *STOCK: Georgian, Victorian and Edwardian furniture.* LOC: Opposite fire station. PARK: Easy. TEL: 01524 416763/ 425235/420098; home - 01524 416763. VAT: Stan/Spec. *Trade Only.*

Luigino Vescovi

1 and 3 Back Avondale Rd. East. LA3 1JX. Est. 1970. Open by appointment every day. SIZE: Warehouse. *STOCK: Georgian, Victorian and Edwardian items, £50-£5,000.* PARK: Easy. TEL: 01524 416732; mobile - 0860 784856. VAT: Stan/Spec.

NELSON

Colin Blakey Fireplaces

115 Manchester Rd. BB10 2LS. Est. 1906. Open 9.30-5.30, Sat. 9.30-5, Sun. 12-4. *STOCK: Fireplaces and hearth furniture, paintings and prints.* LOC: Exit 12, M65. PARK: Opposite. TEL: 01282 614941. SER: Manufacturers and suppliers of hand-carved marble fireplaces and hardwood mantels. VAT: Stan.

Brittons Jewellers and Antiques

34 Scotland Rd. BB9 7UU. Est. 1970. CL: Tues. *STOCK: Jewellery, collectors' watches and general small antiques.* PARK: Opposite. TEL: 01282 697659; fax - 01282 618867.

Brooks Antiques

7 Russell St. BB9 7NL. (D. and S.A. Brooks). Est. 1987. Open 9-5, Sun. and Tues. by appointment. SIZE: Medium. *STOCK: Furniture, £50-£2,000; smalls, £5-£500; both 1750-1930; postcards, ephemera, early 20th C, to £20.* LOC: Town centre, 2 mins. from junction 13, M65. PARK: Easy. TEL: 01282 698148; home - 01282 866234. SER: Valuations.

Nelson continued

Margaret's Antique Shop
79a Scotland Rd. BB9 7UY. (S. Rhodes). Est. 1948. Open 10-6. CL: Tues. SIZE: Small. LOC: Town centre. PARK: Easy.

OLDHAM

Charles Howell Jeweller
2 Lord St. OL1 3EY. NAG. (N.G. Howell). Est. 1870. Open 9.15-5.15. SIZE: Small. *STOCK: Edwardian and Victorian jewellery, £25-£2,000; silver, early to mid 20th C, £40-£1,500; watches, Victorian to mid 20th C, £50-£800.* LOC: Town centre, off High St. PARK: Limited or by arrangement. TEL: 0161 624 1479. SER: Valuations; restorations (jewellery and watches); buys at auction (jewellery and watches). VAT: Stan/Spec.

H.C. Simpson and Sons Jewellers (Oldham)Ltd
37 High St. OL3 5AW. Open 9-5.30. *STOCK: Clocks, jewellery, watches.* TEL: 0161 624 7187. SER: Restorations (clocks).

Valley Antiques
Soho St. OL4 2AD. (J. Chadwick). Est. 1973. Open 10-6. SIZE: Warehouse. *STOCK: General antiques including stripped pine, oak furniture, 19th C, £25-£600.* PARK: Easy. TEL: 0161 624 5030. SER: Valuations; restorations (pine stripping, upholstery, clocks).

Waterloo Antiques
16 Waterloo St. OL1 1SG. (B.J. and S. Marks). Est. 1969. Open 9.30-5. SIZE: Medium. *STOCK: General antiques, furniture, jewellery.* LOC: Town centre. TEL: 0161 624 5975; fax - same. SER: Valuations; gemmologist.

ORMSKIRK

Alan Grice Antiques
106 Aughton St. L39 3BS. Open 10-6. *STOCK: Period furniture.* PARK: Easy. TEL: 01695 572007.

POULTON-LE-FYLDE

Ray Wade Antiques
PO Box 39. FY6 9GA. Est. 1978. By appointment. *STOCK: Decorative items, sculpture, European and Oriental works of art, paintings.* TEL: 01253 700715; fax - 01253 702342; mobile - 0836 291336. SER: Finder; valuations; buys for export. VAT: Stan/Spec.

PRESTON

The Antique Centre
56 Garstang Rd. PR1 1NA. (Paul Allison). Open 9-5.30, Sat. 9.30-5.30, Sun. 10.30-5.30. SIZE: 35

Preston continued

dealers. *STOCK: Furniture, including pine, Georgian-Edwardian; porcelain, bric-a-brac and pictures.* TEL: 01772 882078; fax - 01772 252842. SER: Worldwide shipping; containers.

Duckworth's
45 New Hall Lane. PR1 5NX. (V.K. and M. Duckworth). Est. 1960. Open 9.30-4. SIZE: Small. *STOCK: Shipping goods, kitchenalia.* LOC: Main road leading from M6 motorway. PARK: Easy. TEL: 01772 794336; home - 01772 742720.

Hackler's Jewellers
6b Lune St. FBHI. (N.E. Oldfield). *STOCK: Antique clocks.* TEL: 01772 258465. VAT: Stan.

Halewood and Sons
37 Friargate. PR1 2AT. Est. 1867. CL: Thurs. pm. *STOCK: Antiquarian books and maps.* TEL: 01772 252603.

Nelson's Antiques
113 New Hall Lane. PR1 5PB. (W. and L. Nelson). Open 9.30-5.30 or by appointment. *STOCK: General antiques and collectors' items, dolls.* LOC: Half mile from J31, M6. PARK: Easy. TEL: 01772 794896/862066. SER: Valuations.

The Odd Chair Company
70-72 Blackbull Lane, Fulwood. PR2 3JX. (Sue and James Cook). Est. 1969. Open daily by appointment, evenings and weekends by arrangement. SIZE: Large. *STOCK: Upholstered 19th chairs and sofas, including Knole.* LOC: 1.3 miles from M6, junction 32. Follow signs towards Preston until 2nd set of traffic lights, then turn right into Blackbull Lane, premises 800 yards on left. PARK: Own. TEL: 01772 787990; fax - 01772 787950. SER: Valuations; restoration and re-upholstery using traditional methods and materials (horsehair, coarfibre, wool wadding and feathers); complementary curtains and loose covers made; buys at auction.

Preston Antique Centre
The Mill, New Hall Lane. PR1 5UH. Open 8.30-5.30, Sat.10-4, Sun. 9-4. SIZE: Large - 40+ dealers. *STOCK: General antiques, Georgian, Victorian and Edwardian; shipping furniture.* TEL: 01772 794498/654531/651548; fax - 01772 651694.

Preston Book Co
68 Friargate. PR1 2ED. Est. 1950. Open 9.30-5.30. *STOCK: Antiquarian books.* TEL: 01772 252613. SER: Buys at auction.

Preston continued

Swag
24 Leyland Rd., Penwortham. PR1 9XS. (M. Fletcher). Est. 1967. Open 9-6. CL: Thurs. pm. SIZE: Small. *STOCK: Dolls, especially 1830-1920, £5-£250; pottery, porcelain, furniture.* LOC: 3 miles from exit 29, M6, following St. Anne's signs. PARK: Easy. TEL: 01772 744970. SER: Restorations (dolls).

ROCHDALE

S.C. Falk LAPADA
OL12 6LE. Open by appointment only. *STOCK: Fine English period furniture.* TEL: 01706 644946. VAT: Stan/Spec.

Owen Antiques
191 Oldham Rd. OL16 5QZ. (J.G.T. Owen). Est. 1891. Open 11.30-7, Sun. 2-6. *STOCK: Clocks and paintings, 17th-19th C, £100-£5,000; early oak and walnut, spinning wheels, silver, pewter, pistols, phonographs, wireless sets, coins, model ships, orreries and gothic clocks, nautical items, violins, antiquarian books, early ciné equipment.* LOC: A627 from town centre up hill (Oldham road) for 1/2 mile. Next block to high level pavement on left hand side past railway bridge. PARK: Nearby. TEL: 01706 48138; home - 01706 353270. SER: Valuations; restorations (clocks and furniture).

SABDEN, Nr. Blackburn

Walter Aspinall Antiques
Pendle Antiques Centre, Union Mill, Watt St. BB7 9ED. Est. 1964. Open 9-5, Sat. and Sun. 11-4, or by appointment. SIZE: Large. *STOCK: Furniture and bric-a-brac.* LOC: On Pendle Hill between Clitheroe and Padiham. TEL: 01282 778642; fax - 01282 778643. SER: Export; packing; courier; containers.

Pendle Antiques Centre Ltd
Union Mill, Watt St. BB7 9ED. Est. 1993. Open 9-5, Sat. and Sun. 11-5. *STOCK: Large furniture, bric-a-brac.* LOC: On Pendle Hill, between Clitheroe and Padiham. TEL: 01282 776311; fax - 01282 778643.

SAMLESBURY, Nr. Preston

Samlesbury Hall
(Dating from 1325). Preston New Rd. PR5 0UP. (Samlesbury Hall Trust). Est. 1969. Open 11-4.30. Admission - adults £2.50, children £1. CL: Mon. SIZE: Large. *STOCK: General collectable antiques.* LOC: Exit 31, M6 on A677 between Preston and Blackburn. PARK: Easy. TEL: 01254 812010/2229.

ST. ANNES-ON-SEA

The Victorian Shop
19 Alexandria Drive. FY8 1JF. (G.O. Freeman). Open 10-5. *STOCK: General antiques.* TEL: 01253 725700.

SWINTON

Ambassador House
273 Chorley Rd. M27 2AZ. (G. White). Open 2-6, prior telephone call advisable. *STOCK: General antiques including clocks, silver, paintings, furniture, pottery and porcelain, 17th-18th C.* TEL: 0161 794 3806. SER: Valuations.

TRAWDEN, Nr. Colne

Jack Moore Antiques and Stained Glass
The Old Rock, Keighley Rd. BB8 8RW. Open Mon.-Fri. 9-5, or by appointment. SIZE: Large. *STOCK: Furniture and stained glass.* PARK: Easy. TEL: 01282 869478; home - same; fax - 01282 865193; mobile - 0831 145325. SER: Restoration and manufacture of stained glass; container packing; courier. VAT: Stan.

WHALLEY, Nr. Blackburn

Davies Antiques
32 King St. BB7 9SL. (G.E. and P. Davies). Est. 1960. Open 10-5. SIZE: Medium + trade warehouse. *STOCK: Oak and country furniture, longcase clocks, to £10,000; jewellery, to £500.* Not Stocked: Reproductions. LOC: A59 (11 miles from M6). PARK: Easy. TEL: 01254 823764. VAT: Stan/Spec.

WHITEFIELD, Nr. Manchester

Henry Donn Gallery
138/142 Bury New Rd. M45 6AD. Est. 1954. Open 9.30-5.30. *STOCK: Paintings, 19th-20th C, £20-£20,000.* LOC: Off M62, junction 17 towards Bury. TEL: 0161 766 8819. SER: Valuations; framing; restorations (pictures). VAT: Stan/Spec.

WIGAN

Colin de Rouffignac
57 Wigan Lane. WN1 2LF. Open 10-5. CL: Wed. *STOCK: Furniture, jewellery, oils and watercolours.* TEL: 01942 237927.

Frank Nunan Antiques
12 Lord St. WN1 2BN. Open 10-5. CL: Sat. and Wed. *STOCK: Oak furniture, to 1940; pottery, paintings, jewellery.* TEL: 01942 243600. Exports.

John Robinson Antiques
172-176 Manchester Rd., Higher Ince. WN2 2EA. Est. 1965. Open any time. SIZE: Large. *STOCK: General antiques.* LOC: A577 near Ince Bar. PARK: Easy. TEL: 01942 247773/241671. SER: Export packing. VAT: Stan. *Export and Trade Only.*

John Roby Antiques
12 Lord St. WN1 2BN. Open 10-5. CL: Sat. and Wed. *STOCK: Furniture, to 1940; bric-a-brac.* TEL: 01942 230887.

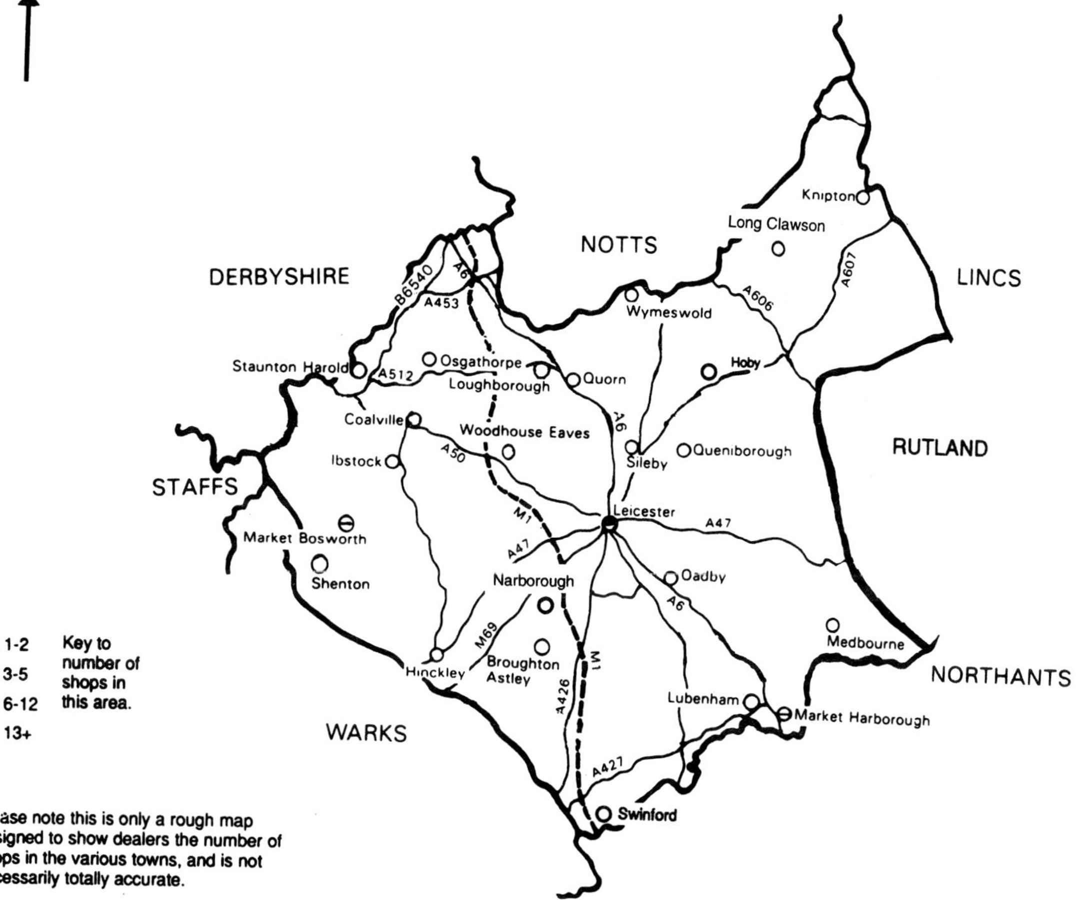
NORTH
DERBYSHIRE
NOTTS
LINCS
RUTLAND
STAFFS
WARKS
NORTHANTS
Knipton
Long Clawson
A607
A606
Wymeswold
Hoby
B6540
A6
A453
Staunton Harold
A512
Osgathorpe
Loughborough
Quorn
Coalville
Woodhouse Eaves
A6
Sileby
Queniborough
Ibstock
A50
Leicester
A47
M1
Market Bosworth
A47
Shenton
Narborough
Oadby
A6
Medbourne
M69
Broughton Astley
Hinckley
M1
A426
Lubenham
Market Harborough
A427
Swinford
1-2
3-5
6-12
13+
Key to number of shops in this area.
Please note this is only a rough map designed to show dealers the number of shops in the various towns, and is not necessarily totally accurate.

BROUGHTON ASTLEY

Nr. Leicester

Old Bakehouse Antiques and Gallery

10 Green Rd. LE9 6RA. (S.R. Needham). Open Thurs.-Sat. 10-6, Sun. 2-5. *STOCK: Period furniture.* PARK: Easy. TEL: 01455 282276.

COALVILLE

Keystone Antiques LAPADA

9 Ashby Rd. LE67 3LF. FGA. (I. and H. McPherson). Est. 1979. Open 10-5, Sat. 10-4. CL: Wed. SIZE: Medium. *STOCK: Jewellery, Victorian and Georgian, £25-£1,500; silver, 1700-1920, £20-£500; small collectable items, 18th-19th C, £15-£300; furniture, cranberry, needlework tools, Victorian and Georgian table glass.* LOC: A50, town centre. PARK: At rear. TEL: 01530 835966. SER: NAG registered valuer; gem testing. VAT: Stan/Spec.

Massey's Antiques

26 Hotel St. LE67 2EP. (Mr and Mrs C.A. Irons). Est. 1969. Open 9-5. CL: Wed. SIZE: Small. *STOCK: Bric-a-brac and bygones, small furniture, 1890-1960.* PARK: Rear. TEL: 01530 832374; home - 01530 832448.

HINCKLEY

House Things Antiques

Trinity Lane, 44 Mansion St. LE10 0AU. (P.W. Robertson). Est. 1976. Open 10-6. SIZE: Small. *STOCK: Stripped pine, satinwood, oak and walnut, mainly Victorian and Edwardian, £50-£600; small collectors' items, 1860-1930s, £5-£100; cast iron fireplaces, brass and iron beds, 1890-1920's, £50-£1,000.* LOC: On inner ring road 200yds. from Leisure Centre. PARK: Easy. TEL: 01455 618518; home - 01455 212797.

HOBY, Nr. Melton Mowbray

Withers of Leicester

The Old Rutland, Church Lane. LE14 3DU. (S. Frings). Est. 1860. Open 9-5.30. CL: Thurs. pm. and Sat. SIZE: Medium. *STOCK: Furniture, 17th-19th C, £50-£3,000; china, 18th-19th C, £10-£300; oil paintings, 19th C, £5-£500.* Not Stocked: Jewellery and coins. PARK: Easy. TEL: 01664 434803. SER: Valuations; restorations (furniture). VAT: Stan/Spec.

IBSTOCK, Nr. Leicester

Mandrake Stevenson Antiques

99 and 101 High St. LE67 6LJ. Est. 1979. Open 10-5, Sat. 10-2.30. SIZE: Small. *STOCK: Furniture, pre 1930's.* PARK: Easy. TEL: 01530 260898. SER: Valuations; restorations (furniture).

KNIPTON, Nr. Grantham

Anthony W. Laywood

NG32 1RF. ABA. Est. 1967. Open by appointment. SIZE: Medium. *STOCK: Antiquarian books, pre-1850, £20-£2,000.* LOC: 1.5 miles off the Grantham-Melton Mowbray road. PARK: Easy. TEL: 01476 870224; fax - 01476 870198. SER: Valuations; buys at auction.

Knipton continued

LEICESTER

Betty's

9 Knighton Fields Rd. West. LE2 6LH. (A. Smith). Est. 1968. Open 9.30-5. SIZE: Small. *STOCK: Satinwood and pine items, brass and copper, pictures.* LOC: Off Saffron Lane. PARK: Easy. TEL: 0116 2839048. SER: Valuations; buys at auction.

Boulevard Antique and Shipping Centre

Bow Bridge Centre, Richard III Rd. LE3 5PT. Open Mon.-Fri. 9-6 or anytime by appointment. SIZE: Large. *STOCK: Furniture including oak, mahogany, pine and shipping; general antiques, some smalls.* LOC: A46 from junction 21, M1. PARK: Own. TEL: 0116 233 8802/287 8500; fax - 0116 233 8829. VAT: Stan.

Britain's Heritage

Shaftesbury Hall, 3 Holy Bones. (Mr and Mrs J. Dennis). Est. 1980. Open daily, Sun. 2-5. SIZE: Large. *STOCK: Fireplaces, 18th-20th C, £100-£12,000.* LOC: Off Vaughan Way, 70 yards from Holiday Inn. PARK: Easy. TEL: 0116 2519592. SER: Valuations; restorations (antique fireplaces). VAT: Stan/Spec.

Corry's LAPADA

24 Francis St., Stoneygate. LE2 2BD. (Mrs E.I. Corry). Est. 1962. Open 10-5. CL: Wed. SIZE: Medium. *STOCK: Furniture, 18th-19th C, £500-£10,000; paintings, 19th C, £100-£8,000; silver, porcelain and jewellery, 19th-20th C, £5-£5,000.* TEL: 0116 270 3794; mobile - 0860 195376. SER: Restorations. FAIRS: NEC (Jan., April, Aug.); LAPADA London; Robert Baileys'; Dorchester; Claridges; Park Lane. VAT: Spec.

Letty's Antiques

6 Rutland St. LE1 1RA. Est. 1952. *STOCK: Silver, jewellery, china and brass.* TEL: 0116 2626435.

Walter Moores and Son LAPADA

89 Wellington St. LE1 6HJ. (P. Moores). Est. 1925. Open 8.30-5.30, Sat. 8.30-12.30. CL: Mon. except by appointment. *STOCK: Mainly furniture, 1680-1880, £10-£10,000.* LOC: From London Rd. railway station go up Waterloo Way, first right into South Albion St., left at T-junction. PARK: Easy. TEL: 0116 2551402; mobile - 04100 19045. VAT: Spec.

Oxford Street Antique Centre

16-26 Oxford St. LE1 5XU. Open 10-5.30, Sun. 2-5, or by appointment. SIZE: Large trade warehouse. *STOCK: Period furniture, shipping goods,*

Leicester continued

pine, bric-a-brac and general antiques, 18th to mid-20th C, 50p-£5,000. LOC: Main ring road. PARK: Own. TEL: 0116 2553006; fax - 0116 2555863. SER: Container loading facilities. VAT: Stan/Spec.

The Rug Gallery

50 Montague Rd., Clarendon Park. LE2 1TH. (Dr. Roy Short). Est. 1987. Open Fri. and Sat. 10-4 or by appointment. SIZE: Medium. *STOCK: Oriental rugs and kilims, early 19th to 20th C, £100-£2,000; Swat, Afghan, Indian and Chinese furniture, 18th-19th C, £50-£1,000; tribal embroidery and jewellery, 19th-20th C, £10-£1,000.* LOC: From London Rd. A6, take Victoria Park Rd., to Queen's Rd., then Montague Rd. PARK: Easy. TEL: 0116 2700085; home - 0116 2700113.

Hammond Smith (Fine Art)

31 Dukes Drive. LE2 1TP. Est. 1981. Open by appointment. Also available by appt. in London W1. SIZE: Small. *STOCK: British watercolours, 1750-1950, £300-£10,000; British etchings, 19th-20th C, £100-£500.* TEL: 0116 270 9020; fax - same; mobile - 0973 483231. SER: Valuations; restorations (watercolours and prints cleaned, mounted and framed); buys at auction (watercolours). VAT: Spec.

LONG CLAWSON, Nr. Melton Mowbray

Victoriana Architectural

Old Hall Farm, Hose Lane. LE14 4NG. Open 8.30-5.30. *STOCK: Pine, French antiques, gas (electric) wall lights and shades, architectural items.* TEL: 01949 860274; fax - 01949 861231. SER: Restorations (oak, mahogany, architectural items, pine stripping); furniture, windows and doors made from reclaimed pine.

LOUGHBOROUGH

Lowe of Loughborough

37-40 Church Gate. LE11 1UE. Est. 1846. CL: Sat. SIZE: Large and warehouse. *STOCK: Furniture and period upholstery from early oak, 1600 to Edwardian; mahogany, walnut, oak, £20-£8,000; clocks, bracket and longcase, £95-£2,500; porcelain, maps, copper and brass.* Not Stocked: Jewellery. LOC: Opposite parish church. PARK: Own. TEL: 01509 212554/217876. SER: Upholstery; restorations; interior design. VAT: Stan/Spec.

LUBENHAM, Nr. Market Harborough

Leicestershire Sporting Gallery and Brown Jack Bookshop

The Old Granary, 62 Main St. LE1 9DG. (Reg Leete). Est. 1958. Prior 'phone call advisable. SIZE: Large. *STOCK: Oil paintings, prints*

Lubenham continued

including Vanity Fair and sporting; engravings, maps, furniture (including pine, mahogany and oak); antiquarian books, horse brasses, martingales, swingers. LOC: Centre of village. PARK: Rear of village green opposite. TEL: 01858 465787.

Stevens and Son

61 Main St. LE16 9TF. Resident. (M.J. Stevens). Est. 1977. Open 10-5. *STOCK: General antiques, mainly furniture.* LOC: A427 via junction 20 M1. TEL: 01858 463521. SER: Restorations (furniture).

MARKET BOSWORTH

Corner Cottage Antiques

7 Market Place, The Square. CV13 0LF. (J. and B. Roberts). Est. 1969. Open 10-5 or by appointment. *STOCK: 18th-20th C furniture, silver, paintings; clocks, porcelain, glass, brass and copper, general antiques.* PARK: Easy. TEL: 01455 290344; home - 01455 282583. VAT: Global/Stan/Spec.

Country Pine Antiques

4 Main St. CV13 0JW. (M. and A. Boylan). Est. 1980. Open 10-5.30, Thurs. 10-3. CL: Mon. SIZE: Medium. *STOCK: Stripped pine and interesting and unusual decorative items.* LOC: Off A447 in Market Place. PARK: Easy. TEL: 01455 291303.

P. Stanworth (Fine Arts)

The Grange, 2 Barton Rd. CV13 0LQ. Resident. (Mr and Mrs G. and Mr James Stanworth). Est. 1965. Open by appointment. SIZE: Medium. *STOCK: Oil paintings and watercolours, 18th to early 20th C.* LOC: Road just off town square. PARK: Easy. TEL: 01455 291023. VAT: Spec.

MARKET HARBOROUGH

Abbey Antiques

17 Abbey St. LE16 9AA. (M. and M.A. Muckle). Est. 1977. Open 10.30-5. SIZE: Medium. *STOCK: Furniture, 18th-19th C, £50-£2,000; decorative items, bric-a-brac, £1-£250; pine.* LOC: 100yds. off town centre. PARK: Easy. TEL: 01858 462282; home - 01858 464085. SER: Valuations. VAT: Global/Stan/Spec.

Graftons of Market Harborough

92 St Mary's Rd. LE16 7DX. (F. Ingall). Est. 1967. Open Mon., Tues., Fri. and Sat. 10-5.30, other times by appointment. *STOCK: Oils, watercolours, etchings and engravings, 18th-19th C.* TEL: 01858 433557.

Richard Kimbell Ltd

Rockingham Rd. and warehouse - Riverside. Est. 1966. Open 9-6, Sun. 10.30-4.30; warehouse - trade only by appointment. SIZE: Large. *STOCK: Antique pine and country furniture.* TEL: 01858 433444; warehouse - 01858 461800.

Market Harborough continued

J. Stamp and Sons

The Chestnuts, 15 Kettering Rd. LE16 8AN. Resident. (M. Stamp). Est. 1947. Open 8-5.30, Sat. 9-12.30 or by appointment. SIZE: Medium. *STOCK: Mahogany and oak furniture, 18th-19th C, £500-£5,000; Victorian furniture, £250-£2,500; Edwardian furniture, £100-£1,000.* LOC: On A6. PARK: Easy. TEL: 01858 462524; fax - 01858 465643. SER: Valuations (furniture); restorations (furniture). VAT: Stan/Spec.

MEDBOURNE

E. and C. Royall Antiques

10 Waterfall Way. LE16 8EE. Open 9-5. *STOCK: Furniture, pictures, silver, porcelain, glassware, ivories and Oriental bronzes.* TEL: 01858 565744; home - same. SER: Restorations (bronzes, ivories, brass including inlay work, metalware, wood-carving, upholstery, French polishing).

NARBOROUGH

Ken Smith Antiques Ltd LAPADA

215-217 Leicester Rd. (K.W. Sansom). Est. 1888. Open 9.30-5, Sun. 11-5. SIZE: Large. *STOCK: Furniture, mainly 1880-1930, £100-£5,000; clocks, smalls and paintings.* TEL: 0116 286 2341; fax - 0116 275 3151. VAT: Stan/Spec.

OADBY

John Hardy Antiques

91 London Rd. LE2 5DP. Open every day. *STOCK: General antiques.* TEL: 0116 2712862. VAT: Stan/Spec.

OSGATHORPE, Nr. Loughborough

David E. Burrows LAPADA

Manor House Farm. LE12 9SY. Est. 1973. *STOCK: Pine, oak, mahogany and walnut furniture, clocks, smalls, £50-£20,000.* LOC: Exit 23, M1, turn right off Ashby road, farm next to church. TEL: 01530 222218; mobile - 0836 598664; fax - 01530 223139. VAT: Stan/Spec.

QUENIBOROUGH, Nr. Leicester

J. Green and Son

1 Coppice Lane. LE7-3DR. Resident. (R. Green). Est. 1932. Appointment advisable. SIZE: Medium. *STOCK: 18th-19th C English and Continental furniture.* LOC: Off A607 Leicester-Melton Mowbray Rd. PARK: Easy. TEL: 0116 2606682. SER: Valuations; buys at auction. VAT: Stan/Spec.

QUORN

Mill on the Soar Antiques Ltd

1/3 High St. LE12 8DS. (T.O. and J. York). CL: Sun. and Mon. except by appointment. *STOCK: 17th-19th C furniture and associated articles.* LOC: In centre of village, on old A6. PARK: Easy. TEL: 01509 414218.

Quorn continued

Quorn Pine and Decoratives

The New Mills, Leicester Rd. LE12 8ES. (S. Yates and S. Parker). Open 9-6, Sat. 9.30-5.30. *STOCK: Pine and country furniture.* TEL: 01509 416031. SER: Stripping and restorations (pine). VAT: Stan/Spec.

SHENTON, Nr. Market Bosworth

Whitemoors Antiques and Fine Art

CV13 6BZ. Est. 1987. Open 11-5, Sun. and Bank Holidays (except Christmas) 10-6. SIZE: Large - 20+ unitholders. *STOCK: Furniture, £25-£2,000; smalls, £5-£200; prints and pictures, Victorian to early 20th C, £40-£400.* LOC: A5 onto A444 towards Burton-on-Trent, first right then second left. PARK: Easy. TEL: 01455 212250; home - 01455 212981.

SILEBY, Nr. Loughborough

R. A. James Antiques

Ammonite Gallery, 15a High St. LE12 7RX. *STOCK: Mainly stripped pine, general antiques.* TEL: 01509 812169.

STAUNTON HAROLD

Ropers Hill Antiques

Ropers Hill Farm. LE65 1SE. (S. and R. Southworth). Est. 1974. Open by appointment. SIZE: Small. *STOCK: General antiques, silver and metalware.* LOC: On old A453. PARK: Easy. TEL: 01530 413919. SER: Valuations.

SWINFORD, Nr. Lutterworth

Old Timers

Holmwood, High St. LE17 6BL. (M. S. Harris). Est. 1993. Open every day but appointment preferred. SIZE: Small. *STOCK: 18th-19th C clocks - longcase, £1,000-£5,000; wall, £150-£1,500; bracket and mantle, £150-£3,000; some brass and copper.* LOC: Village centre, half a mile from M1, junction 19. PARK: Nearby. TEL: 01788 860311; home - same. SER: Valuations; restorations (clocks).

WOODHOUSE EAVES, Nr. Leicester

Paddock Antiques

The Old Smithy, Brand Hill. LE12 8SS. (M., C.A. and T.M. Bray). Open Thurs. - Sat. 10-5.30, other times by appointment. *STOCK: Furniture, 1750-1910, to £5,000; porcelain, 1750-1940's, to £3,500; prints and glass.* PARK: Easy.

WYMESWOLD, Nr. Loughborough

N. Bryan-Peach Antiques

28 Far St. LE12 6TZ. Resident. Open 10-6, Sun. by appointment. SIZE: Medium. *STOCK: Clocks, barometers, watches; 18th-19th C furniture, £50-£5,000.* PARK: Easy. TEL: 01509 880425. SER: Valuations; restorations; buys at auction. VAT: Spec.

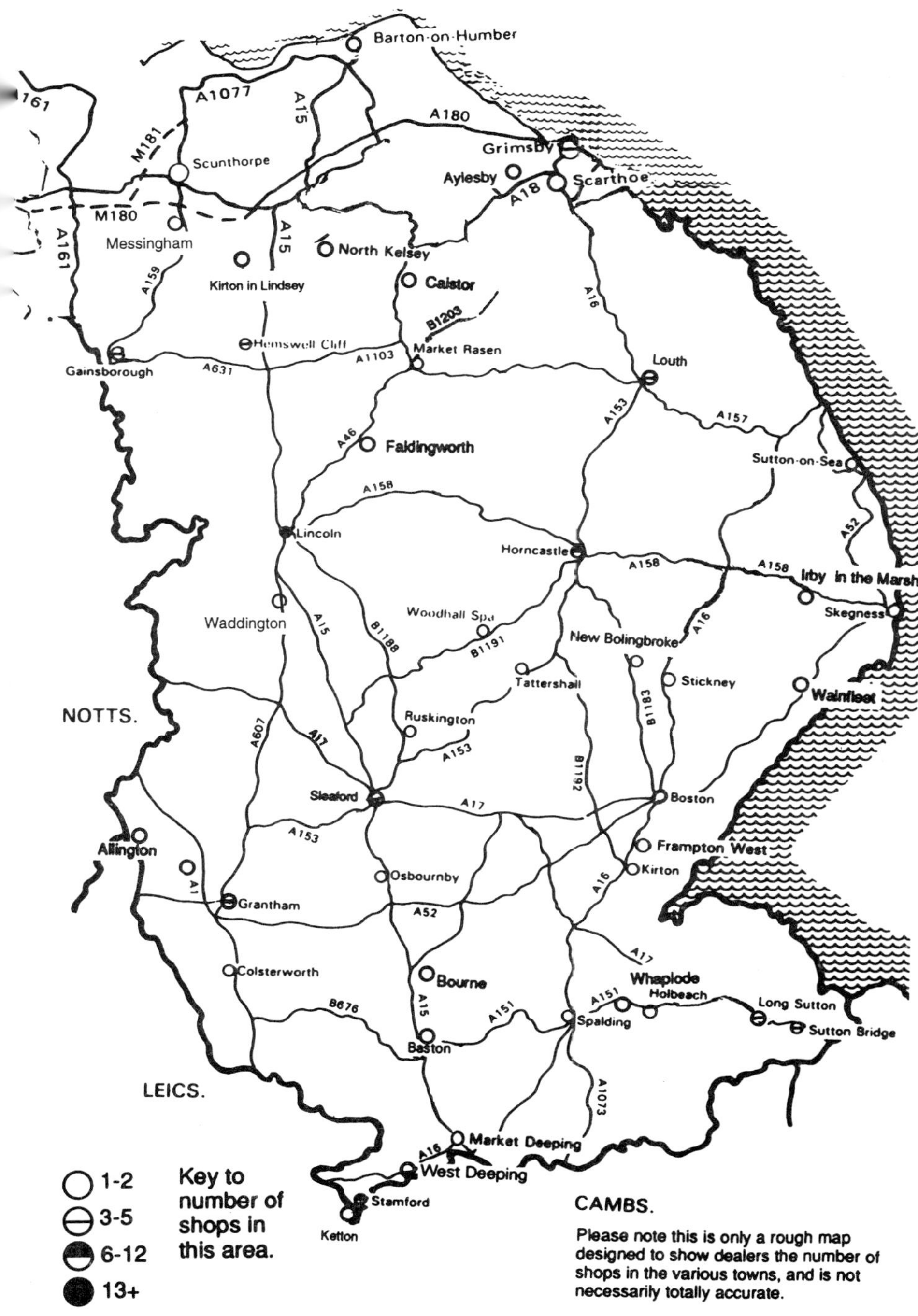

Please note this is only a rough map designed to show dealers the number of shops in the various towns, and is not necessarily totally accurate.

ALLINGTON, Nr. Grantham

Garth Vincent Antique Arms and Armour LAPADA

The Old Manor House. NG32 2DH. Est. 1979. Open by appointment. SIZE: Medium. *STOCK: Militaria including firearms, swords, rapiers and daggers; armour, 16th-19th C, £50-£15,000.* LOC: Opposite church. PARK: Easy. TEL: 01400 281358; home - same; fax - 01400 282658. SER: Valuations; restorations; buys at auction. FAIRS: London and major city Arms; Period Homes and Gardens, NEC Aug. VAT: Spec.

AYLESBY
Nr. Grimsby

Robin Fowler (Period Clocks) LAPADA

Washing Dales, Washing Dales Lane. DN37 7LH. Open by appointment. SIZE: Large. *STOCK: Clocks and barometers, 17th-18th C.* TEL: 01472 751335. SER: Restorations (clocks, barometers).

BARTON-ON-HUMBER

Streetwalker Antiques Warehouse

The Old Leisure Centre, Brigg Rd. DN18 5DH. (J.N. Chapman). Open 9-5.30. SIZE: Large. *STOCK: General antiques and shipping furniture, oak and mahogany.* TEL: 01652 660050; fax - 01652 633472. *Trade Only.*

BASTON, Nr. Peterborough

The Complete Automobilist

Dept. GD, 35 Main St. PE6 9NX. Est. 1967. Open 9-5. CL: Sat. *STOCK: Hard-to-get parts for older vehicles.* LOC: On A15, east of Stamford. PARK: Easy. TEL: 01778 560312; fax - 01778 560738. SER: Catalogue available £1.

BOSTON

Tony Coda Antiques

121 High St. PE21 8TS. Est. 1967. Open 9.30-12.30 and 1.30-5.30. SIZE: Medium. *STOCK: Furniture, 17th-19th C, from £100; paintings, 19th C, to £500; china, silver and clocks, to £200.* LOC: From A16 turn right at roundabout in to London Rd. and then to High St. PARK: Easy. TEL: 01205 352754; home - 01205 722104. SER: Valuations. FAIRS: International Antique and Collectors.

Portobello Row Antique & Collectors' Centre

93-95 High St. Open 10-4. SIZE: 9 dealers. *STOCK: Shipping furniture, kitchenalia, blue and white china, 1940's-60's clothing, bric-a-brac.* TEL: 01205 368692.

Antique and Secondhand Traders

39 West St. (C.A. and A.L. Thompson). Est. 1962. Open 9-5, Tues and Wed. by appointment.

Boston continued

SIZE: Warehouse. *STOCK: Furniture, antique shipping oak, pine, modern and smalls, £5-£5,000.* LOC: On A15, 8 miles from Stamford A1. PARK: Own. TEL: 01778 394700; mobiles - Alan - 0585 694299, Clyde - 0860 734742. SER: Valuations. FAIRS: Newark; Ardingly. VAT: Spec/Global.

CAISTOR

Caistor Antiques

12 High St. (Susan Rutter). Est. 1982. Open by appointment day or night. *STOCK: Pottery, furniture, jewellery, dolls, linen, 18th-20th C.* LOC: Off A46 between Grimsby and Market Rasen. PARK: Own. TEL: 01472 851975; home - same. SER: Valuations.

COLSTERWORTH

Clive Underwood Antiques

46 High St. NG33 5NF. Est. 1970. Open 9.30-5.30. *STOCK: Furniture, oak, mahogany, 17th-19th C, £45-£10,000; some pictures, glass, porcelain.* LOC: 1/2 mile off A1 between Stamford and Grantham. TEL: 01476 860689. SER: Valuations; restorations; rushing; caning. VAT: Stan/Spec.

FALDINGWORTH, Nr. Market Rasen

Brownlow Antiques Centre

Lincoln Rd. LN8 3SF. (Sylvia and Alex Stephens). Est. 1994. Open 10-6 including Sun. and by appointment. CL: Mon. SIZE: Large. *STOCK: Furniture, 18th C to pre-1940, £50-£3,000; bric-a-brac, collectables, from £2.* LOC: A46 towards Grimsby, 10 miles north of Lincoln. PARK: Own. TEL: 01673 885367; home - same. FAIRS: Local.

FRAMPTON WEST, Nr. Boston

Robert J. Kent Antiques

Pinewood, Ralphs Lane. PE20 1QZ. *STOCK: Pine furniture.* LOC: B1391. TEL: 01205 723739. VAT: Stan.

GAINSBOROUGH

S. Carrick's Antiques and Shipping

130 Trinity St. DN21 5PD. Open 8.30-5. *STOCK: General antiques and shipping furniture.* TEL: 01427 611393/810409.

Stanley Hunt Jewellers

22 Church St. (S. and R.S. Hunt). Est. 1952. Open 9-5. CL: Wed. SIZE: Medium. *STOCK: Jewellery, 19th C, £50-£500+.* LOC: Main street from Market Place. PARK: Easy. TEL: 01427 613051; home - same. SER: Valuations; restorations (gold, silver, clocks).

Gainsborough continued

Pilgrims Antiques Centre
66 Church St. DN21 2JR. Est. 1986. CL: Mon. and Wed. SIZE: Large. *STOCK: Jewellery and silver, £5-£1,000; pictures, ceramics and textiles, £5-£1,000; pine and furniture, £50-£1,000.* LOC: Near Old Hall. PARK: Easy. TEL: 01427 810897. SER: Valuations. FAIRS: Newark; Birmingham.

GRANTHAM

Grantham Clocks
30 Lodge Way. NG31 8DD. Resident. (R. Conder). Open by appointment. *STOCK: Clocks.* PARK: Easy. TEL: 01476 561784. SER: Restorations.

Grantham Furniture Emporium
4-6 Wharf Rd. NG31 6BA. (K. and J.E. Hamilton). Est. 1970. Open 10-4.30, Sun. 11-4. CL: Mon. and Wed. SIZE: Large. *STOCK: Victorian, Edwardian and shipping furniture, £5-£3,000.* LOC: Town centre, near Post Office. PARK: Own at rear. TEL: 01476 562967.

Notions
2a Market Place. NG31 6LQ. (Mrs S. Checkley). Est. 1982. Open 10-5, Sat. 9.30-5, Sun. 1-4. SIZE: Medium. *STOCK: China, collectables and decorative accessories, £1-£500; furniture, £30-£800, 19th-20th C.* LOC: Down from Angel and Royal Hotel. PARK: Easy. TEL: 01476 563603. SER: Repairs; re-upholstery; French polishing. FAIRS: Newark; Ardingly; Stoneleigh; Peterborough.

William Redmile Antiques
15 Elmer St. North. NG31 6RE. (J.W. Redmile). Est. 1936. Open 9-6. *STOCK: General antiques.* LOC: From London turn right at Angel Hotel. TEL: 01476 564074.

Wilkinson's
The Tyme House, 1 Blue Court. NG31 6NJ. (M. and P. Wilkinson). Est. 1935. Open 10-1 and 2-4. CL: Wed. SIZE: Small. *STOCK: Jewellery, watches and silver, 19th C, £50-£1,000.* PARK: Nearby. TEL: 01476 560400 and 01529 413149. SER: Valuations; restorations (including clock and watch movements); buys at auction (rings and watches). VAT: Spec.

GRIMSBY

Abbeygate Antique & Craft Centre
14 Abbeygate. DN31 1JY. (Sue Patterson). Est. 1987. Open Tues.-Fri. 9.30-4.30, Sat. 9.30-5. SIZE: Medium. *STOCK: Pottery and glass, militaria, coins and medals, £5-£100; small furniture, £25-£500; all 19th-20th C.* LOC: Near railway station, precinct entrance on Bethlehem St. PARK: Rear of precinct. TEL: 01472 361129; home - 01472 354312. SER: Valuations. FAIRS: Donnington Park; RAF Swinderby.

Grimsby continued

Bell Antiques

68 Harold St. DN32 7NQ. (V. Hawkey). Est. 1964. Open by appointment, telephone previous evening. SIZE: Large. *STOCK: Antique pine and grandfather clocks.* Not Stocked: Reproduction. PARK: Easy. TEL: 01472 695110; home - same.

HEMSWELL CLIFF, Nr. Gainsborough

Astra House Antiques Centre

RAF Hemswell. DN21 5TL. (M. Frith). Open daily including Sun. 10-5. SIZE: 50 dealers. *STOCK: Wide variety of general antiques and shipping goods, including Victorian, Edwardian and Continental furniture and smalls.* LOC: Near Caenby Corner Roundabout A15/A631. TEL: 01427 668312.

Hemswell Antiques Centre

Caenby Corner Estate. DN21 5TJ. (P.J. and A.R. Miller). Est. 1986. Open 10-5 including Sun. SIZE: 270+ dealers. *STOCK: Period furniture, 17th-19th C; watercolours and oils, 19th C; silver and plate, clocks, porcelain, china, jewellery, dolls, toys, books, prints, clothes.* LOC: A15 from Lincoln then A631 towards Gainsborough, 1 mile from roundabout, follow signs. PARK: Easy. TEL: 01427 668389; fax - 01427 668935. SER: Valuations; restorations (oak, mahogany and pine; upholstery); container packing.

Kate

Kate House, Caenby Corner Estate. DN21 5TJ. (Mr Shamsa). Open 9-4.30, Sat. 10-1. *STOCK: Pine including reproduction.* TEL: 01427 668724/668904; fax - 01427 668905.

Second Time Around

Hemswell Antique Centre, Caenby Corner Estate. DN21 5TJ. (G.L. Powis). Open 10-5 including Sun. *STOCK: Longcase and bracket clocks, pre 1830, £1,450-£25,000.* LOC: A15 from Lincoln to Caenby Corner roundabout, left towards Gainsborough for 1 mile. (A631). PARK: Easy. TEL: 01427 668389; home - 01522 543167; mobile - 0860 679495. SER: Restorations (clocks).

HOLBEACH, Nr. Spalding

P.J. Cassidy (Books)

1 Boston Rd. PE12 7LR. Est. 1974. Open 10-6. SIZE: Medium. *STOCK: Books, 19th-20th C, £2-£300; maps, prints and engravings, 17th-19th C, £10-£500.* LOC: 1/4 mile from A17. PARK: Nearby. TEL: 01406 426322; fax - same; e-mail - bookscass@aol.com. SER: Valuations; framing and mount cutting. VAT: Stan.

HORNCASTLE

Clare Boam

22-38 North St. LN9 5DX. Est. 1977. Open 9-5, Sun 2-4.30. SIZE: Large. *STOCK: Furniture and bric-a-brac, 19th-20th C, to £1,000.* LOC: Louth/Grimsby road out of town. PARK: Easy. TEL: 01507 522381; home - same. VAT: Stan.

Great Expectations

39-41 East St. (Clare Boam). Est. 1977. Open 9-5, Sun. and Bank Holidays 1-4.30. SIZE: Large. *STOCK: Wide variety of general antiques including pine, oak, mahogany, kitchenalia, luggage, books, china, glass, collectables, 50p to £1,000.* LOC: A158, 100 yards from traffic lights. PARK: At rear or in street opposite. TEL: 01507 524202; home - 01507 522381. SER: Restorations (china, glass and furniture).

Robert Kitching

9-11 West St. LN9 5JE. Open 9.30-5. *STOCK: Clocks and general antiques.* TEL: 01507 522120.

Lindsey Court Antiques

The Lincolnshire Antiques Centre, Lindsey Court. LN9 5DH. (Lindsay and Karen White). Open 10-4 or by appointment. SIZE: Medium. *STOCK: Period furniture and general antiques, £5-£10,000.* LOC: Behind the Library. PARK: Own. TEL: 01507 527794; fax - 01507 526670. SER: Weekly auction. VAT: Stan/Spec.

Alan Read Period Furniture

60 & 62 West St. LN9 5AD. Open 10-4.30. CL: Mon. and Wed. *STOCK: 17th-18th C furniture; decorative items, Eastern rugs.* TEL: 01507 524324/525548. SER: Bespoke copies.

Seaview Antiques

Stanhope Rd. LN9 5DG. (M. Chalk and Tracey Collins). Open 9-5. SIZE: Large + warehouse. *STOCK: Victorian, Edwardian and decorative furniture; smalls, brassware, silver, silver plate, lamps, boxes.* LOC: A158. PARK: Easy. TEL: 01507 524524.

Laurence Shaw Antiques

77 East St. LN9 6AA. Open 8.30-5. SIZE: Medium. *STOCK: Furniture, china, glass, metalware, books, collectables, general antiques, 17th-20th C.* LOC: Opposite Tourist Information Centre. TEL: 01507 527638. SER: Consultant; valuations. VAT: Stan/Spec.

Staines Antiques

25 Bridge St. LN9 5HZ. (Mrs M. Staines). Est. 1991. Open 10-5. CL: Mon. SIZE: Large. *STOCK: Furniture, pictures and clocks, £50-£5,000; ceramics, £20-£500; all 18th-20th C.* LOC: A158 Lincoln to Skegness road, turn off by-pass towards town centre. Shop 200 yards on right, opposite Antiques Centre. PARK: Easy and nearby. TEL: 01507 527976; home - same. SER: Valuations.

IRBY-IN-THE-MARSH, Nr. Skegness

Irby Antiques Centre

Pinfold Lane. Resident. (P. and K. Hines). Est. 1975. Open 10.30-5 including Sun. CL: Wed. SIZE: Medium. *STOCK: Porcelain, brass, pictures and collectables, 19th and 20th C, £5-£500.* LOC: B1195 Wainfleet to Spilsby road. PARK: Own. TEL: 01754 810943. FAIRS: Local.

KETTON, Nr. Stamford

Robin Cox Antiques

Manor Farmhouse, High St. PE9 3TA. Est. 1965. Open strictly by appointment. *STOCK: English and Continental furniture, and works of art, including early oak, mahogany and decorated, wood carvings and sculpture, architectural fittings, garden items, £50-£10,000.* TEL: 01780 720240. VAT: Stan/Spec.

KIRTON

Kirton Antiques LAPADA

3 High St. PE20 1DR. (A.R. Marshall). Est. 1973. Open 8.30-5, Sat. 8.30-12, or by appointment. SIZE: Large - warehouse. *STOCK: Furniture, all periods; painted pine, chairs, decorative items, glass, metal, pottery, china, picture frames.* TEL: 01205 722595; evenings - 01205 722134; fax - 01205 722895. VAT: Stan.

KIRTON IN LINDSEY

Mr Van Hefflin

12 High St. DN21 4LU. Est. 1820. Open 10-5. *STOCK: Jewellery, curios, silver, paintings.* PARK: Easy. TEL: 01652 648044. SER: Guide.

LINCOLN

20th Century Frocks

65 Steep Hill. LN1 1YN. (Patricia Rowberry). Est. 1986. Open 11-5. SIZE: Small. *STOCK: Ladies clothes, hats and accessories, jewellery including costume, mainly '20's and '30's, to 1970, £5-£150; textiles including Canton and paisley shawls, curtains and chenille cloths, £5-£300.* LOC: Opposite the Jews House, bottom of Steep Hill. PARK: Danes Terrace. TEL: 01522 545916; home - 01507 533638. SER: Valuations. FAIRS: Newark.

Annette Antiques

77 Bailgate. LN1 3AR. (Mrs A. Bhalla). Est. 1972. Open Mon. 11-5, Tues.-Sat. 12-6. SIZE: Small. *STOCK: Porcelain, glass and small silver, 19th-20th C; clocks, silver flatware, watercolours, prints and drawings, 18th-20th C; all £10-£500.* LOC: 2 minutes from castle and cathedral. PARK: Nearby. TEL: 01522 546838; home - 01205 260219. SER: Restorations (furniture, clocks). FAIRS: Alexandra Palace.

Lincoln continued

Michael Brewer

Northgate Lodge, Northgate. LN2 1QS. (M.N. Brewer). Est. 1954. Open by appointment. SIZE: Medium. *STOCK: Furniture, oil paintings, silver, porcelain, bronzes, works of art.* Not Stocked: Coins. LOC: Close to Cathedral. PARK: 20yds. TEL: 01522 545854. SER: Valuations; buys at auction. VAT: Stan/Spec. *Trade Only.*

C. and K.E. Dring

111 High St. LN5 7PY. Open 10-5.30. CL: Wed. *STOCK: Victorian and Edwardian inlaid furniture; shipping goods, porcelain, clocks, musical boxes, tin-plated toys, trains and Dinkys.* TEL: 01522 540733/792794.

Golden Goose Books

20 and 21 Steep Hill. LN2 1LT. (R. West-Skinn and Mrs A. Cockram). Est. 1983. Open 10-5.30. *STOCK: Antiquarian and secondhand books, maps and prints.* TEL: 01522 522589; home - 01673 878622.

Harlequin Gallery

22 Steep Hill. LN2 1LT. (R. West-Skinn). Est. 1962. Open 10-5.30. *STOCK: Antiquarian and secondhand books, maps and prints.* TEL: 01522 522589; home - 01673 858294.

Dorrian Lambert Antiques

64 Steep Hill. LN1 1YN. (R. Lambert). Est. 1981. Open 10-5, Wed. and Sun. by appointment. SIZE: Medium. *STOCK: Small furniture, clocks, chairs, pottery, porcelain, jewellery, books, sporting antiques, books and collectables, 18th to early 20th C.* PARK: Loading only or nearby. TEL: 01522 545916; home - 01427 848686. SER: Valuations; restorations (clocks). FAIRS: Newark Showground.

Lincoln Fine Art

Dernstall House, 33 The Strait. LN2 1JD. (Mrs D. Glen-Doepel). Est. 1973. Open 10-1 and 2-5.30. *STOCK: Oil paintings including decorative portraits, landscapes, marine, watercolours, abstracts (Dorothy Lee Roberts), miniatures, Old Master paintings, drawings, porcelain and objets d'art, 17th-20th C, £80-£10,000.* LOC: Top of High St., opposite O'Neills bar. PARK: Nearby. TEL: 01522 533029. SER: Valuations.

Mansions

5a Eastgate. LN2 1QA. Open 10-5. *STOCK: General antiques, decorative items, period lighting.* TEL: 01522 513631/560271.

Rowletts of Lincoln

338 High St. LN5 7DQ. (A.H. Rowlett). Open 9-5. *STOCK: Antique and secondhand jewellery.* TEL: 01522 524139.

James Usher and Son Ltd

6 Silver St. LN2 1DY. Open 9-5.30. *STOCK: Silver, jewellery.* TEL: 01522 527547.

LONG SUTTON

The Chapel Emporium Antique Centre

London Rd. (J.A. Beck and B. Hill). Est. 1984. Open 10-5, including Sun. SIZE: Large. *STOCK: Furniture, 18th-19th C, £100-£2,000; collectables, 19th-20th C, 50p-£300; ephemera, 19th C, 50p-£25.* LOC: Opposite playing fields. PARK: Easy. TEL: 01406 364808. VAT: Stan/Spec.

J.W. Talton

15-19 Market St. PE12 9DD. Resident. (J., W. and J.J. Talton). Est. 1952. Open 9-5, Wed. 9-12. SIZE: Small. *STOCK: General antiques.* LOC: On old A17. PARK: Easy. TEL: 01406 362147; home - same. SER: Restorations (furniture and cabinet making).

Trade Antiques

7 Market St. PE12 9EF. (P.E. Poole). Est. 1961. CL: Sat. SIZE: Medium. *STOCK: General shipping goods, clocks and watches.* LOC: Old A17. PARK: Easy. TEL: 01406 363758. *Trade Only.*

LOUTH

A Barn Full of Brass Beds

Abbey House, Eastfield Rd. LN11 7HJ. (J.J. Tebbs). Est. 1985. Open by appointment. SIZE: Large. *STOCK: Brass and iron beds, 1860-1910, £250-£1,000.* LOC: 1/4 mile from Louth on right, off Eastfield Rd. PARK: Easy. TEL: 01507 603173; home - same. SER: Valuations; restorations. FAIRS: Lincolnshire Show. VAT: Stan.

Jocelyn Chatterton

82 Westgate. LN11 9YD. Open by appointment. SIZE: Small. *STOCK: Formal Chinese court costume, Qing dynasty, £200-£5,000; informal Chinese costume, 19th to early 20th C, £50-£3,000; Chinese dress accessories and embroidery, 19th to early 20th C, £20-£500.* LOC: Adjacent St James' church (large spire) in town centre. PARK: Available by appointment. TEL: 01507 608239; fax - same; home - 01507 602251; internet - www.mernet.co.uk/~tofh/SER: Buys at auction (Chinese costume). FAIRS: Newark.

Louth continued

Haydn Earl Antiques and Period Interiors

119a Eastgate. LN11 9QE. Est. 1990. Open Tues.-Sat. 10-5. *STOCK: Furniture, Georgian, Regency and country; decorative items.* TEL: 01507 609906. SER: Valuations; restorations (polishing, re-upholstery, re-leathering, metal). FAIRS: Newark, Ardingly and NEC. VAT: Stan/Margin/EC.

Old Maltings Antique Centre

Aswell St. Est. 1982. Open 10-4. SIZE: Large. *STOCK: Victorian, Edwardian and secondhand furniture.* LOC: 2 minutes walk from town centre. PARK: Easy. TEL: 01507 600366. SER: Valuations; restorations; pine stripping.

MARKET DEEPING

Portland House Antiques

23 Church St. PE6 8AN. (G.W. Cree and V.E. Bass). Est. 1987. Open Mon.-Sat. or by appointment. SIZE: Medium. *STOCK: Porcelain, glass, furniture, 18th-19th C, £100-£10,000.* PARK: Easy. TEL: 01778 347129; home - same. SER: Buys at auction. FAIRS: Kings College. VAT: Stan/Spec.

MARKET RASEN

Harwood Tate

Church Mill, Caistor Rd. LN8 3HX. (J. Harwood Tate). Open 9.30-5.30, Sat. 10-1. SIZE: Large. *STOCK: Furniture, mahogany, rosewood, oak; clocks, 18th to early 19th C; ornamental items including pictures and prints, 18th-19th C.* Not Stocked: Shipping goods. LOC: Take A46 from Lincoln, Church Mill is off town centre, north of church. PARK: Easy. TEL: 01673 843579. VAT: Stan/Spec.

MESSINGHAM, Nr Scunthorpe

Beckside Antiques

38 High St. DN17 3RS. Resident. (S.S. Bowden). Open Fri. and Sun. 10-4, other days by appointment. SIZE: Medium. *STOCK: Furniture and*

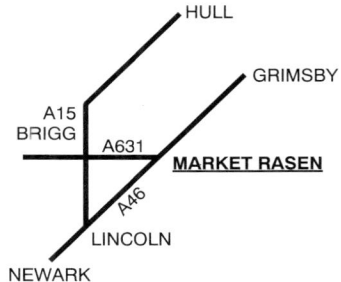

Messingham continued

clocks, Victorian and Edwardian, £5-£2,000. LOC: On the A159 Gainsborough/Scunthorpe road. PARK: Easy. TEL: 01724 765445; mobile - 0410 016018; home - 01724 762842. SER: Valuations; restorations (furniture). FAIRS: Newark. VAT: Spec.

NEW BOLINGBROKE, Nr. Boston

Junktion

The Old Railway Station. (J. Rundle). Est. 1981. Open Wed., Thurs. and Sat. SIZE: Large. *STOCK: Early advertising, decorative and architectural items; toys, automobilia, mechanical antiques and bygones; early slot machines, wireless, telephones, 20th C collectables.* Not Stocked: Porcelain and jewellery. LOC: B1183 Boston to Horncastle. PARK: Easy. TEL: 01205 480087/480068.

NORTH KELSEY MOOR, Nr. Caistor

Moor Pine

New Warehouse, Station Yard. LN7 6HD. SIZE: Large. *STOCK: English and Continental pine and French furniture; old pine reproduction furniture.* PARK: Own. TEL: 01652 678036. SER: Containers. VAT: Stan.

OSBOURNBY, Nr. Sleaford

Audley House LAPADA

35 High St. NG34 0DN. (R. and S. Galloway). Est. 1948. Open by appointment only. *STOCK: 17th-18th C oak and country furniture, textiles and treen.* PARK: Easy. TEL: 01529 455473; mobile - 0850 876752.

RUSKINGTON

Pinfold Antiques LAPADA

3 Pinfold Lane. NG34 9EU. (J. and G.D. Ballinger). Est. 1981. Open by appointment. SIZE: Medium. *STOCK: Longcase clocks, £1,500-£15,000; period English furniture, £200-£10,000; also wall, bracket and mantel clocks.* PARK: Easy. TEL: 01526 832057; fax - 01526 834550. SER: Valuations; restorations (longcase and bracket clocks, period furniture); buys at auction. FAIRS: Olympia, Robert Bailey, NEC.

SCARTHOE, Nr. Grimsby

Scarthoe Gifts and Antiques

38 Louth Rd. DN33 2EP. (P. Bridges). Est. 1975. Open 10-5. CL: Mon. and Thurs. SIZE: Medium. *STOCK: Jewellery, silver, porcelain, collectors' items, maps, prints, linen.* LOC: A16. PARK: Easy. TEL: 01472 877394.

SCUNTHORPE

Antiques & Collectables

251 Ashby High St. DN16 2SQ. (J.A. Bowden). Open 9-5. *STOCK: Clocks, furniture, arms and collectables.* TEL: 01724 865445/720606. SER: Restorations and repairs (clocks and guns).

SKEGNESS

G & J Crowson

50 High St. PE25 3NW. Open daily 10-6. *STOCK: General antiques and reproductions.* TEL: 01754 764360. *Mainly Trade.*

SLEAFORD

Mill Antiques

19A Northgate. NG34 7BH. (John Noble and A. Crabtree). Est. 1988. Open 9-5. SIZE: Medium. *STOCK: General antiques including furniture, porcelain and pictures, 18th-20th C, £5-£1,500.* LOC: 100 yds. from Market Square. PARK: Loading only. TEL: 01529 413342; home - 01529 415101. SER: Valuations; restorations (furniture and porcelain).

Victoriana

1 Jermyn St. (Mrs P.C. Pywell). Est. 1970. Open Mon. and Fri. 10.30-5 and usually Sat. 11-5. SIZE: Small. *STOCK: General small antiques, 1820's to 1940's, £5-£250.* LOC: A17. PARK: Nearby. TEL: Home - 01205 722785.

Wilkinson's

The Little Tyme House, 13 Southgate. NG34 7SU. (M. and P. Wilkinson). Est. 1935. Open 10-1 and 2-4. CL: Thurs. SIZE: Small. *STOCK: Jewellery, watches and silver, £50-£1,000.* PARK: Nearby. TEL: 01529 413149 and 01476 60400. SER: Valuations; restorations (including clock and watch movements); buys at auction (rings and watches). VAT: Stan.

SPALDING

Dean's Antiques

"The Walnuts", Weston St. Mary's. PE12 6JB. (Mrs B. Dean). Est. 1969. Open daily. SIZE: Medium. *STOCK: General antiques, farm and country bygones, £2-£200.* LOC: On Spalding to Holbeach main road A151. PARK: Easy. TEL: 01406 370429.

STAMFORD

Dawson of Stamford Ltd

6 Red Lion Sq. PE9 2AJ. (J Dawson). Open 9-5.30. *STOCK: Fine antique furniture, jewellery and silver.* LOC: Town centre between St. John's church and All Saint's church. TEL: 01780 754166. VAT: Stan/Spec.

Claire Langley Antiques

9a St. Mary's Hill. PE9 2DP. Open 9.30-5.30. CL: Thurs. SIZE: Medium. *STOCK: Period mahogany and oak furniture, clocks, barometers and unusual*

Stamford continued

decorative items. LOC: Just over town bridge, on the left. PARK: George Hotel. TEL: 01780 480544. SER: Restorations (furniture, clocks and barometers). VAT: Stan/Spec.

Graham Pickett Antiques

7 High St., St Martins. PE9 2LF. (G.R. Pickett). Est. 1990. Open 10-5, Sun. and Thurs. by appointment. SIZE: Medium. *STOCK: Furniture - country, 1650-1900, French provincial, 1700-1900, both £50-£2,000; French and English beds, 1750-1900, £350-£2,000.* LOC: From A1 north into town, on right by 1st lights opposite George Hotel. PARK: Easy. TEL: 01780 481064; home - 01780 764502. SER: Valuations; buys at auction. FAIRS: Newark IACF. VAT: Stan/Spec.

Sinclair's

11/12 St. Mary's St. (J.S. Sinclair). Est. 1970. Open 9-5.30. SIZE: Large. *STOCK: Oak country furniture, 18th C, £200-£3,000; Victorian mahogany furniture, £100-£1,000; Edwardian furniture.* LOC: Near A1. PARK: George Hotel. TEL: 01780 765421. VAT: Stan/Spec.

St. George's Antiques

1 St. George's Sq. PE9 2BN. (G.H. Burns). Est. 1974. Open 9-1 and 2-4.30. CL: Sat. SIZE: Shop + trade only warehouse. *STOCK: Period and Victorian furniture, some small items.* TEL: 01780 754117; home - 01780 460456. VAT: Stan/Spec.

St. Martins Antiques Centre

23a High St., St. Martin's. PE9 2LF. (P. B. Light). Open 10-5, Sat., Sun. 10.30-5. SIZE: 40 dealers. *STOCK: Period, Art Nouveau and Art Deco furniture, porcelain, ceramics, pictures, prints, clocks, watches, silver, jewellery, books, toys, military books, textiles, clothes, glass and all sorts of collectables.* TEL: 01780 481158; fax - 01780 766598. SER: Restoration; shipping arranged.

St. Mary's Galleries

5 St. Mary's Hill. PE9 2DP. (David E. Clark and Mrs O.M. and R.D. Cox). Est. 1955. Open 9-5. SIZE: Medium. *STOCK: Furniture, 18th-19th C, £50-£10,000; Victorian and Georgian jewellery, £5-£1,000; unusual items, textiles, oil paintings.* LOC: Nr. Stamford river bridge. PARK: At rear of shop. TEL: 01780 764159; mobile - 0860 340358.

Stamford Antiques Centre

The Exchange Hall, Broad St. PE1 9PX. Open 10-5, Sun. 11.30-5.30. SIZE: 35 dealers. *STOCK: General antiques (with dateline); collectables; specialist in Art Nouveau.* LOC: Town centre. PARK: Easy. TEL: 01780 762605.

Staniland (Booksellers)

4/5 St. George's St. PE9 2BJ. (M.G. Staniland and B.J. Valentine-Ketchum). Est. 1973. Open 10-5. CL: Thurs. SIZE: Large. *STOCK: Books, mainly 19th-20th C, 50p-£500.* LOC: High St. PARK: St. Leonard's St. TEL: 01780 755800.

Stamford continued

Andrew Thomas

Old Granary, 10 North St. PE9 2YN. Est. 1970. Open 9-6. SIZE: Large. *STOCK: Pine and country furniture in original paint; ironware.* LOC: From south take old A1 through Stamford. Turn right at second set of traffic lights, warehouse on right. PARK: Opposite. TEL: 01780 762236; home - 01780 410627. VAT: Stan.

STICKNEY

B and B Antiques

Main Rd. PE22 8AD. (B.J. Whittaker and J. Shooter). Open by appointment. *STOCK: General antiques.* PARK: Easy. TEL: 01205 480204.

SUTTON BRIDGE

The Antique Shop

100 Bridge Rd. PE12 9SA. (G. and R. Gittins). Est. 1973. Open 9-5.30, Sun. 1-5. SIZE: Large - 10 showrooms + Trade warehouse. *STOCK: Victorian furniture, glass, china, oil lamps and clocks.* Not Stocked: Pine. LOC: On old A17 opposite church. PARK: Easy. TEL: 01406 350535. VAT: Spec.

Bridge Antiques

30-32 Bridge Rd. PE12 9UA. Open 8-5. CL: Sat. SIZE: Large. *STOCK: Shipping furniture - barleytwist, linenfold, pineapple, Jacobean styles.* LOC: Old A17. PARK: Easy. TEL: 01406 350704/351669.

Old Barn Antiques Warehouse

220 New Rd. PE12 9QE. (S. and Mrs T.J. Jackson). Open 9-5.30, or by appointment. SIZE: Large. *STOCK: 19th -20th C furniture - shipping oak, carved, pineapple, Jacobean, barley twist; mahogany, walnut and pine original and reclaimed timber copies.* LOC: 1 mile out of village, turn by Barclays Bank. PARK: Own. TEL: 01406 350435; fax - same; mobile - 0468 744050. SER: Container facilities. *Trade & Export Only.*

SUTTON-ON-SEA

Knicks Knacks Emporium

41 High St. LN12 2EY. (Mr and Mrs R.A Nicholson). Est. 1983. Open 10-1 and 2-5, including Sun. CL: Mon. SIZE: Medium + small warehouse. *STOCK: Victorian gas lights, brass and iron beds, cast-iron fireplaces, bygones, curios, tools, collectables, pottery, porcelain, Art Deco, Art Nouveau, advertising items, furniture and shipping goods, £1-£1,000.* LOC: A52. PARK: Easy. TEL: 01507 441916; home - 01507 441657.

TATTERSHALL

Wayside Antiques

Market Place. LN4 4LQ. (G. Ball). Est. 1969. Open 10-5.30. *STOCK: General antiques.* LOC: A158. PARK: Easy. TEL: 01526 342436.

WADDINGTON, Nr Lincoln

J. and R. Ratcliffe

The Manor, Manor Lane. LN5 9QD. Est. 1954. Appointment advisable. *STOCK: English and Continental furniture, 1600-1830.* LOC: 4 miles from Lincoln on Grantham road. PARK: Opposite. TEL: 01522 720996.

WAINFLEET, Nr. Skegness

Haven Antiques

Bank House, 36 High St. PE24 4BJ. (Colin and Julie Crowson). Est. 1980. Open daily except Thurs., Sun. by appointment. SIZE: Small. *STOCK: General antiques, mainly jewellery, porcelain and small furniture.* LOC: A52. PARK: Easy and opposite. TEL: 01754 880661; home - same. SER: Valuations; restorations (pottery).

WEST DEEPING

Quality Antiques

The Barn, 43a King St. PE6 9HP. (Barry and Lindy Vaughan). Est. 1993. Open seven days. SIZE: Large. *STOCK: Furniture and smalls.* TEL: 01778 342053.

WHAPLODE, Nr. Spalding

Francis Bowers Chess Suppliers

34 Middle Rd. PE12 6TW. Resident. Est. 1991. Open 9-9, Fri. 9-6, Sat. and Sun. by appointment. SIZE: Small. *STOCK: Chess sets, boards, clocks and tables, 18th-20th C, £20-£1,000; books on chess and others, 18th-20th C, £1-£1,000; garden chess sets, computers, 19th-20th C, £50-£1,500.* LOC: From north - A1, A17, A151, 4th turning on left, near Texaco garage. From south - A1, A15, A1073, A151, 5th turning on right. PARK: Easy. TEL: 01406 370166; fax - same; mobile - 0860 408992. SER: Valuations; restorations (minor repairs, book binding); buys at auction (chess related items). FAIRS: Spalding, King's Lynn, Peterborough, Skegness, Grantham Chess Congress.

WOODHALL SPA

Underwoodhall Antiques

The Broadway. LN10 6ST. Open 10-5. CL: Wed. SIZE: Medium. *STOCK: Furniture, £10-£1,000; porcelain and china, £5-£500; general antiques, £1-£500; pictures, £5-£500, all 1750 to date.* LOC: B1191. PARK: Easy. TEL: 01526 353815.

V.O.C. Antiques LAPADA

27 Witham Rd. LN10 6RW. Resident. (D.J. and C.J Leyland). Est. 1970. Open 9.30-5.30, Sun. 2-5. SIZE: Medium. *STOCK: 17th-19th C furniture, to £5,000; period brass and copper, pottery, porcelain and pictures.* LOC: B1191. PARK: Easy. TEL: 01526 352753; fax - same; home - same. SER: Valuations.

Please note this is only a rough map designed to show dealers the number of shops in the various towns, and is not necessarily totally accurate.

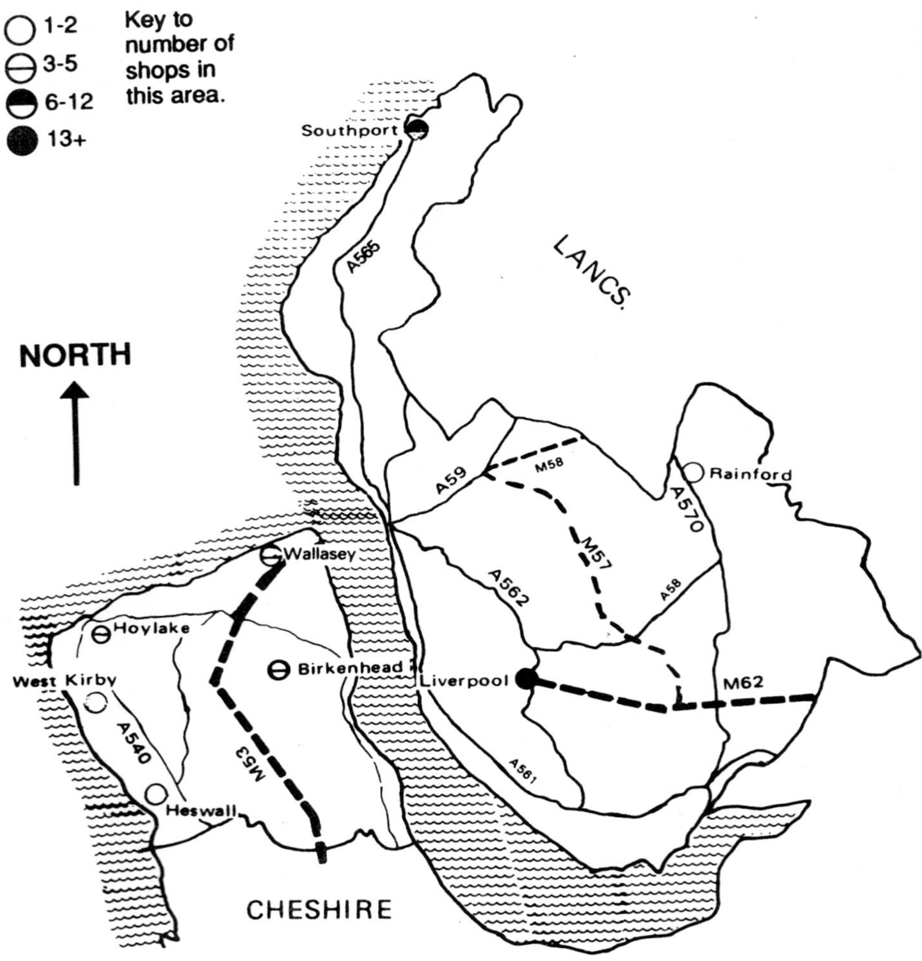

BIRKENHEAD

David Allan Antiques

281 Woodchurch Rd., Prenton. L42 9LE. Est. 1975. Open 10-6. SIZE: Medium. *STOCK: 19th C fireplaces, paintings, flintlock pistols.* LOC: Main road. PARK: Easy. TEL: 0151 608 7118; home - same. SER: Valuations; restorations (fireplaces).

Bodhouse Antiques

379 New Chester Rd., Rock Ferry. (G. and F.M. Antonini). Open 9-5, Sat. and Sun. by appointment. SIZE: Large. *STOCK: Furniture, 19th C; ceramics, from 19th C; silver plate, 18th-20th C; all £5-£1,000+; prints and pictures, 19th C, £25-£1,000+.* LOC: 1/2 mile from Birkenhead Tunnel, A41 towards Chester. PARK: Easy. TEL: 0151 644 9494; home - 0151 327 6233. SER: Packing; courier; regular containers to Italy and Spain. VAT: Stan/Spec.

Rose Mount

2 Rose Mount. (A.J. Bampton). Open 10-5. *STOCK: General antiques.* TEL: 0151 653 9060.

HESWALL

C. Rosenberg

The Antique Shop, 120-122 Telegraph Rd. L60 0AQ. Est. 1960. Open 10-5. CL: Wed. pm. *STOCK: Jewellery, silver, porcelain, objets d'art.* TEL: 0151 342 1053. VAT: Stan.

HOYLAKE

M. Fearn Antiques

124A Market St. L47 3BH. (Marion Fearn). Est. 1994. Open 10-5, Wed. 10-1, Sat. 10-2. SIZE: Small. *STOCK: Furniture, china, glass and silver, from £10.* PARK: At rear. TEL: 0151 632 0892.

Hoylake Antique Centre

128-130 Market St. L47 3BH. Open 9.15-5.30. CL: Wed. *STOCK: Furniture, pine, silver, pictures, porcelain, glass and decorative arts.* LOC: A540, in town centre. PARK: At rear. TEL: 0151 632 4231.

Market Antiques

80 Market St. L47 3BB. (W. Bateman). Est. 1969. Open Thurs. and Fri. 10-1 and 2.15-5, Sat. 10-5, other times by appointment. SIZE: Medium. *STOCK: Furniture, £10-£1,000; trade and shipping goods, silver, glass, china, £2-£250; paintings, prints, £5-£500.* Not Stocked: Weapons, medals, coins. LOC: On main street in town centre A563 or A540. PARK: From Ship Inn forecourt, cars drive in, vans at rear. TEL: 0151 632 4059 (24 hr).

Kevin Whay's Clock Shop and Antiques

The Quadrant. L47 2EE. Est. 1969. Open Thurs. and Fri. 10-4.30, Sat. 10-2 and by appointment. *STOCK: Clocks, barometers, furniture and jewellery.* PARK: Easy. TEL: 0151 631 1888; fax - 0151 236 1070; e-mail - 110213.544@compuserve.com. SER: Restorations (clocks, barometers, dials and cases).

LIVERPOOL

Antique Fireplaces

43a Crosby Rd. North, Waterloo. (J. Toole). Est. 1978. Open 10-5, Sat. 10-5.30. SIZE: Medium. *STOCK: Fireplaces, 18th-19th C, £100-£1,000+; doors, 19th C, from £35.* PARK: Easy. TEL: 0151 949 0819. SER: Valuations; restorations. VAT: Stan.

Boodle and Dunthorne Ltd

Boodles House, Lord St. L2 9SQ. Est. 1798. Open 9-5.30. SIZE: Large. *STOCK: Silver, 18th-19th C, £100-£5,000; clocks and clock-sets, mid-19th C, £200-£4,000; jewellery, Victorian and Georgian, £100-£30,000.* Not Stocked: Furniture. PARK: Paradise St. TEL: 0151 227 2525. VAT: Stan/Spec.

Edward's Jewellers

45a Whitechapel. FGA. (R.A. Lewis). Est. 1967. Open by appointment. CL: Sat. SIZE: Small. *STOCK: Jewellery, silver and plate, 19th-20th C, £50-£600.* LOC: City centre. TEL: 0151 236 2909. SER: Valuations. VAT: Stan/Spec.

Kensington Tower Antiques Ltd

Christ Church, 170 Kensington. L7 2RJ. (R. Swainbank). Est. 1960. Open 9-5, Sat. and Sun. by appointment. CL: Mon. SIZE: Large. *STOCK: Shipping goods, general antiques.* LOC: A57. PARK: Easy. TEL: 0151 260 9466; fax - 0151 260 9130; home - 0151 924 6538. VAT: Stan. *Trade Only.*

Lyver & Boydell Galleries LAPADA

15 Castle St. L2 4SX. Est. 1861. Open 10.30-5.30. CL: Sat. SIZE: Medium. *STOCK: Paintings and watercolours, 18th-20th C, £50-£10,000; maps and prints, 16th-19th C, £1-£1,500.* LOC: City centre, opposite Town Hall. PARK: Pay & Display. TEL: 0151 236 3256; fax - 0151 227 3293. SER: Valuations; cleaning; framing; restorations; buys at auction. FAIRS: National. VAT: Stan/Spec.

Maggs Antiques Ltd

26-28 Fleet St. L1 4AR. (G. Webster). Est. 1965. Open daily. *STOCK: General antiques, period and shipping smalls, £1-£1,000.* LOC: In town centre by Central station. PARK: Meters. TEL: 0151 708 0221; evenings - 01928 564958. SER: Restorations; container packing, courier.

The Original British American Antiques

Halsall Hall, 2 Carrmoss Lane, Halsall. L39 8RS. (John Nolan). Est. 1970. Open by appointment including Sun. and evenings. SIZE: Large. *STOCK: Export items, especially for US decorator market.* LOC: On A5147. TEL: 01704 841065; mobile - 0802 604007. SER: Courier; packing and shipping. VAT: Stan/Spec. *Trade Only*

Liverpool continued

E. Pryor and Son

110 London Rd. L3 5NL. (Mr Wilding). Est. 1876. Open 8-4. CL: Wed. *STOCK: General antiques, jewellery, Georgian and Victorian silver, pottery, porcelain, coins and medals, clocks, paintings, ivory and carvings.* TEL: 0151 709 1361. VAT: Stan.

Ryan-Wood Antiques

102 Seel St. L1 4BL. Est. 1972. Open 9.30-5. *STOCK: Furniture, paintings, china, silver, curios, bric-a-brac, Victoriana, Edwardiana, Art Deco.* TEL: 0151 709 7776; home/fax - 0151 709 3203. SER: Restorations; valuations. VAT: Stan/Spec.

Stefani Antiques

497 Smithdown Rd. L15 5AE. (T. Stefani). Est. 1969. Open 10-5. SIZE: Medium. *STOCK: Furniture, to 1910, £200-£2,000; jewellery, £25-£2,000; pottery, silver, old Sheffield plate, porcelain, bronzes.* LOC: On main road, near Penny Lane. PARK: Easy. TEL: 0151 734 1933; home - 0151 737 1360. SER: Valuations; restorations.

Swainbanks Ltd

Christchurch, 170 Kensington. L7 2RJ. Open 9-5 or by appointment. CL: Sat. SIZE: Large. *STOCK: Shipping goods and general antiques.* TEL: 0151 260 9466/924 6538; fax - 0151 260 9130. SER: Containers. VAT: Stan.

Theta Gallery

29-33 Parliament St. (J. Matson). Open by appointment. SIZE: Warehouse. *STOCK: General antiques, especially furniture and clocks.* TEL: 0151 709 1217. *Trade Only.*

RAINFORD, Nr. St. Helens

Colin Stock BADA

8 Mossborough Rd. WA11 8QN. Est. 1895. Open by appointment. *STOCK: Furniture, 18th-19th C.* TEL: 0174 488 2246.

SOUTHPORT

C.K. Broadhurst and Co Ltd

5-7 Market St. PR8 1HD. Est. 1926. Open 9-5.30. *STOCK: Rare books, first editions, art and architecture, collecting.* TEL: 01704 532064/534110; fax - 01704 542009.

Decor Galleries

52 Lord St. PR8 1QB. (F.D. Glover). CL: Tues. *STOCK: Decorative items, furniture, 18th-19th C.* TEL: 01704 535134. VAT: Stan/Spec.

King Street Antiques

27 King St. PR8 1LH. (John Nolan). Open 10-5. *STOCK: General antiques.* TEL: 01704 540808; home - 01704 841065; mobile - 0802 438688.

Southport continued

Molloy's Furnishers Ltd

6-8 St. James St. PR8 5AE. (P. Molloy). Est. 1955. Open daily. SIZE: Large. *STOCK: Mahogany and oak, shipping and Edwardian furniture.* LOC: On A570, Scarisbrick new road. PARK: Easy. TEL: 01704 535204; fax - 01704 548101. VAT: Stan.

John Nolan Antiques Ltd

29 King St. PR8 1LH. Open Mon.-Sat. *STOCK: Furniture and decorative items.* TEL: 01704 540808; mobile - 0802 438688; home - 01704 841065. SER: Courier; packing and shipping.

Osiris Antiques

104 Shakespeare St. (C. and P. Wood). Est. 1983. Open 10.45-4.45, Sat. 11-5.15, Sun. by appointment. CL: Tues. SIZE: Small. *STOCK: Art Nouveau and Art Deco, £10-£1,000; period clothing and accessories, 1850-1950, £5-£200; jewellery, 1880-1960, to £150.* LOC: Just out of town, off main road leading to motorway. PARK: Easy. TEL: 01704 500991; mobile - 0802 818500; home - 01704 560418. SER: Valuations; buys at auction (Art Nouveau, Art Deco); lectures given on Decorative Arts 1895-1930.

The Southport Antiques Centre

27/29 King St. PR8 1LH. (J. Nolan). Open 10-5. TEL: 01704 540808; mobile - 0802 438688. Below are listed the dealers at this centre.

British-American Antiques
Shipping goods.

Halsall Hall Antiques
Country furniture.

King St. Antiques
General antiques.

John Nolan
Period furniture.

Pine Antiques
Country pine furniture.

S.M.
Collectors items.

The Spinning Wheel

1 Liverpool Rd., Birkdale. PR8 4AR. (R. Bell). Est. 1966. Open 10-5. CL: Tues. SIZE: Small. *STOCK: General antiques, old golf items, £5-£1,000+.* TEL: 01704 568245; home - 01704 567613.

Tony and Anne Sutcliffe Antiques

130 Cemetery Rd. and warehouse - 37A Linaker St. Est. 1969. Open 8.30-5 including Sun. or by appointment. SIZE: Large. *STOCK: Shipping goods, Victorian and period furniture.* LOC: Town centre. TEL: 01704 537068; home - 01704 533465. SER: Containers; courier. VAT: Stan/Spec.

Southport continued

H.S. Walne

183 Lord St. PR8 1PF. Open 9-4.45. *STOCK: Diamonds, gold, silver, jewellery.* TEL: 01704 532469.

Weldons Jewellery and Antiques

567 Lord St. PR9 0BB. (H.W. and N.C. Weldon). Est. 1914. Open 9.30-5.30. SIZE: Medium. *STOCK: Furniture, clocks, watches, jewellery, silver, coins.* Not Stocked: Militaria. PARK: Easy. TEL: 01704 532191; fax - 01704 500091. SER: Valuations; restorations. VAT: Stan.

WALLASEY

Arbiter

10 Atherton St., New Brighton. L45 2NY. Resident. (W.D.L. Scobie and P.D. Ferrett). Est. 1983. Open Tues.-Sat. 1-5, or by appointment. *STOCK: Decorative arts, 1850-1980; base metal and treen, £20-£2,000; Oriental, ethnographic and antiquities, £40-£1,500; original prints and drawings, £80-£500.* LOC: Opposite New Brighton station. PARK: Easy. TEL: 0151 639 1159. SER: Valuations; buys at auction; consultant.

Decade Antiques

62 Grove Rd. L45 3HW. (A.M. Duffy). Open 10-5. SIZE: Large. *STOCK: General antiques, textiles, decorative items, Continental furniture.* LOC: J1 M53, take A554 to Wallasey/New Brighton, turn right along Harrison Drive into Grove Rd. TEL: 0151 638 0433; 0151 639 6905/8728.

Victoria Antiques/City Strippers

155-157 Brighton St. L44 8DU. (J.M. Colyer). Open 9.30-5.30. *STOCK: Pre-1930 furniture.* TEL: 0151 639 0080.

Yarnall Antiques

244A Wallasey Village. L45 0JT. (Richard and Joy Yarnall). Est. 1970. Open 10.30-1 and 2-5, Wed. by appointment, Sat. 11-5. SIZE: Large. *STOCK: Furniture, 18th-19th C, £100-£3,000; collectables, 18th-20th C, £5-£500; curios, £5-£1,000.* LOC: Main road, 5 minutes from end of M53. PARK: Easy. TEL: 0151 638 2286; home - 0151 639 5204. SER: Valuations. FAIRS: Newark, Stafford, Ardingly, Bluith Wells, G-Mex. VAT: Stan/Spec.

WEST KIRBY

Helen Horswill Antiques and Decorative Arts

62 Grange Rd. L48 4EG. Open 10-5 or by appointment. SIZE: Medium. *STOCK: Furniture, 17th-19th C; decorative items.* LOC: A540. PARK: Easy. TEL: 0151 625 2803/8660.

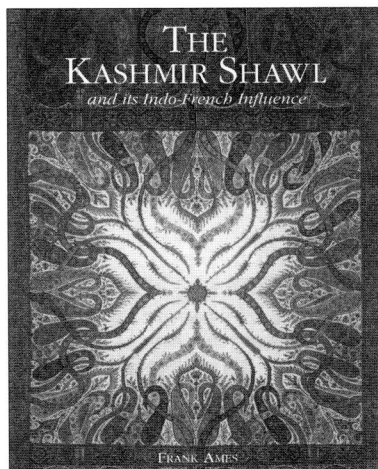

Middlesex

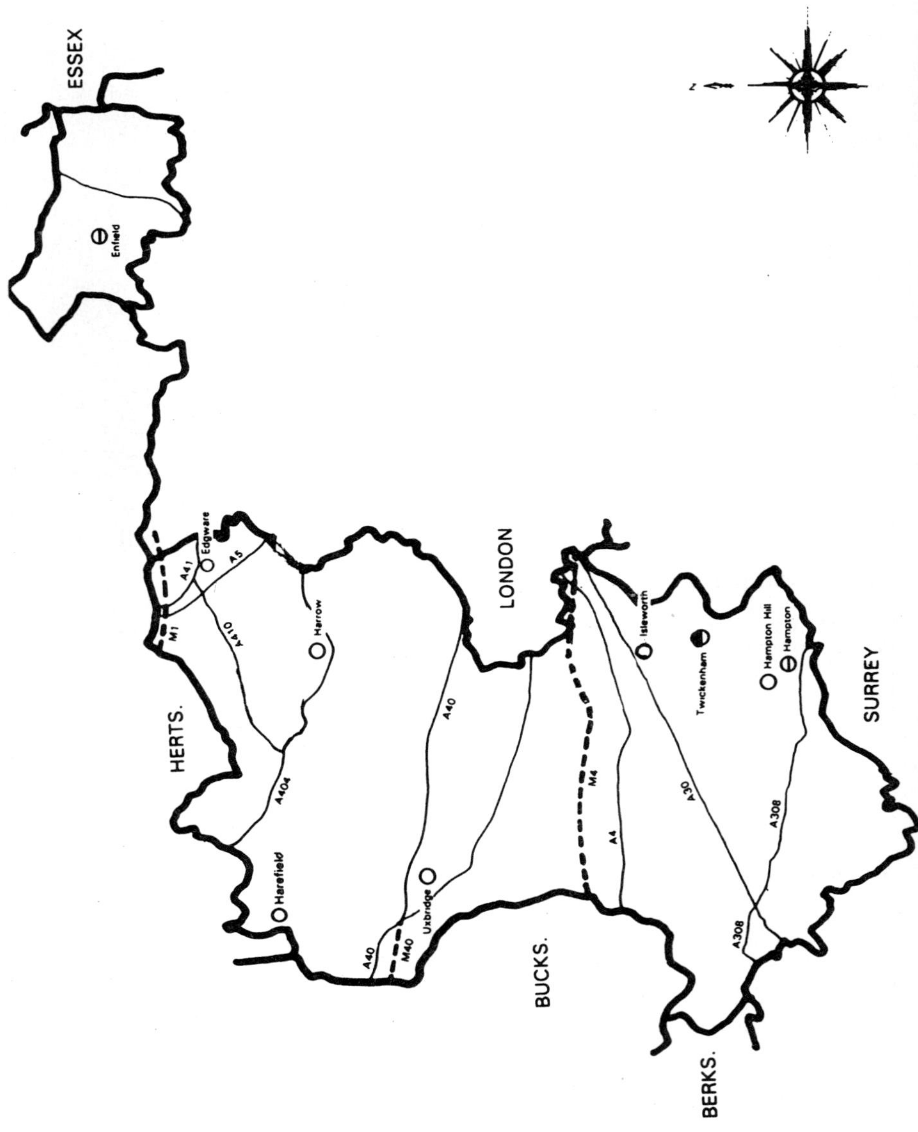

○ 1–2
⊖ 3–5
◓ 6–12
● 13+

Key to number of shops in this area.

Please note this is only a rough map designed to show dealers the number of shops in the various towns, and is not necessarily totally accurate.

EDGWARE

Edgware Antiques

19 Whitchurch Lane. HA8 7JZ. (E. Schloss). Est. 1972. Open Thurs.- Sat. 10-5 or by appointment. SIZE: Medium. *STOCK: Furniture, pictures, silver and plate, brass and copper, clocks, bric-a-brac, porcelain and shipping goods.* PARK: Easy. TEL: 0181 952 1606; home - 0181 952 5924.

ENFIELD

Richard Kimbell

Country World, Cattlegate Rd., Crews Hill. Est. 1966. Open 9-6 including Sun. SIZE: Large. *STOCK: Pine, 19th C, £50-£1,000.* LOC: Off junction 24, M25 via A1005 to Enfield, then left into East Lodge Lane. PARK: Easy. TEL: 0181 364 6661. VAT: Stan.

La Trouvaille

1A Windmill Hill. EN2 6SE. (Mrs C.M. Waring). Est. 1982. Open 10-5. CL: Mon. and Wed. SIZE: Medium. *STOCK: Small general antiques, collectors' items, furniture and prints, 1800-1930.* Not Stocked: Weapons. LOC: West of town. PARK: Easy. TEL: 0181 367 1080.

Cynthia Morgan Interiors

Unit 41, 26-28 The Queensway, Ponders End. EN3 4SA. Open by appointment. SIZE: Medium. *STOCK: 18th-19th C furniture.* LOC: Off Hertford road, off A10. PARK: At rear. TEL: 0181 805 0353; fax - 0181 372 9946.

HAMPTON

Peco

72 Station Rd. TW12 2BT. (C.D. and E.S. Taylor). Est. 1969. Open 9-5.15. SIZE: Large. *STOCK: Doors, 18th-20th C, £75-£250; fireplaces including French and marble, 18th-19th C, £350-£3,500; stoves; French beds.* LOC: 1.5 miles from Hampton Court. Turning off Hampton Court/Sunbury Rd. PARK: Own. TEL: 0181 979 8310. SER: Restorations (stained glass, cast iron fireplaces, doors); stained glass made to order. VAT: Stan.

Ian Sheridan's Bookshop Hampton

Thames Villa, 34 Thames St. TW12 2DX. Est. 1960. Open 10.30-6 including Sun. SIZE: Large. *STOCK: Antiquarian and secondhand books.* LOC: 1 mile from Hampton Court Palace. TEL: 0181 979 1704.

Valtone Pine

78-80 Station Rd. TW12 2RX. (A.P. Frost). Open 9-6. *STOCK: Painted furniture.* TEL: 0181 255 6224.

HAMPTON HILL

The Hampton Hill Gallery

203 and 205 High St. TW12 1NP. *STOCK: Watercolours, drawings, prints, 18th-20th C.* TEL: 0181 977 1379; fax - 0181 977 3876. SER: Restorations and cleaning (watercolours, prints and paintings); mounting; framing. VAT: Stan/Spec.

HAREFIELD

The Jay's Middlesex Antique Centre

27/29 High St. Open 10-6, Sun. 11-5. SIZE: 15 dealers. *STOCK: General antiques, bric-a-brac, gold and silver.* TEL: 01895 824738.

Riverside Antiques

Unit 7, Summerhouse Lane. UB9 6HU. (Alan Rooke and Phil Burroughs). Est. 1980. Open 10-5 including Sun. SIZE: Large - 15 dealers. *STOCK: Primarily a picture gallery, with antique clocks, barometers, Victorian and Edwardian furniture, books, smalls, £5-£1,000.* LOC: By Fisheries public house.PARK: OwnTEL: 01895 824394; fax - 01895 823729. SER: Restorations (furniture and pictures); buys at auction (furniture and pictures). VAT: Stan.

HARROW

Kathleen Mann - The Other Shop

49 High St. HA1 3HT. Est. 1973. Open Thurs., Fri. and Sat. 9.30-5. SIZE: Medium. *STOCK: Furniture, 19th-20th C, £25-£4,000; decorative items, £5-£1,000.* LOC: Follow Harrow road, or take A40 turning at Greenford roundabout. PARK: Easy. TEL: 0181 422 1892. SER: Buys at auction; cat museum.

ISLEWORTH

Crowther of Syon Lodge Ltd

Busch Corner, London Rd. TW7 5BH. Open 9-5, Sat. and Sun. 11-4.30. SIZE: Large. *STOCK: Period panelled rooms, in pine and oak; chimneypieces in marble, stone and wood; life-sized classical bronze and marble statues; wrought iron entrance gates, garden temples, vases, wellheads, tanks, animal figures, seats, fountains and other statues.* LOC: Just off the A4, half-way between the West End and London Airport. TEL: 0181 560 7978. SER: Bespoke summerhouses; quality reproduction ornaments. VAT: Stan/Spec.

TWICKENHAM

Ailsa Gallery

32 Crown Rd. (C.A. Wiltshire). Open Thurs., Fri. and Sat. 10-5, other times by appointment. SIZE: Small. *STOCK: Paintings, 19th-20th C, £200-£3,000; bronze, decorative arts, small furniture, silver and glass.* LOC: Off St. Margarets Rd., near station. PARK: Easy. TEL: 0181 891 2345; home - 0181 892 0188.

PHELPS
Antiques
Established 1870
12,000 SQ FT
SHOWROOMS
ONE OF THE FINEST AND
LARGEST SELECTIONS
OF 19TH & EARLY 20TH CENTURY
FURNITURE WITHIN THE M25
*****
WE ARE 9 MILES FROM CENTRAL LONDON
(BR station 2 mins., Richmond underground
station 10 mins.)
10 mins. drive from M3 and 15mins. from M25
*****
Open: Monday-Friday 9-5.30
Saturday 9.30-5.30, Sunday 12.00-4.00
Phelps Antiques
133-135 St. Margarets Road,
East Twickenham TW1 1RG
Tel: 0181 892 1778
Fax: 0181 892 3661
Please apply for leaflet & directions

Twickenham continued

Alberts Cigarette Card Specialists

308 Nelson Rd.,Whitton. TW2 7AJ. (J.A. Wooster). Open 10-6, Sat. 10-4. CL: Mon. *STOCK: Original cigarette cards; accessories.* TEL: 0181 891 3067; fax - 0181 744 3133. SER: Mail order; shipping; framing; catalogue; Guide to Cigarette Card Collecting; postal auctions - worldwide service.

Golden Oldies

113 London Rd. TW1 1EE. (Janet S. Wooster). Open 10-6, Sat. 10-4. CL: Mon. *STOCK: Film memorabilia - stills, photos, posters, postcards, prints, statues, models, film magazines, books.* TEL: 0181 891 3067; fax - 0181 744 3133. SER: Regular catalogues/stock lists available; world-wide mailing.

Anthony C. Hall

30 Staines Rd. TW2 5AH. Est. 1966. Open 9-5.30. CL: Wed. pm. and Sat. SIZE: Medium. *STOCK: Antiquarian books.* PARK: Easy. TEL: 0181 898 2638; fax - same.

John Ives Bookseller

5 Normanhurst Drive, St. Margarets. TW1 1NA. Resident. Est. 1977. Open by appointment at any time. SIZE: Medium. *STOCK: Scarce and out of print books on antiques and collecting, £1-£500.* LOC: Off St. Margarets Rd. near its junction with Chertsey Rd. PARK: Easy. TEL: 0181 892 6265; fax - 0181 744 3944. SER: Valuations (as stock).

Twickenham continued

Tobias Jellinek Antiques — BADA

29 Broadway Avenue, St Margarets. TW1 1HR. (Mrs D.L. and T.P. Jellinek). Est. 1963. By appointment only. SIZE: Small. *STOCK: Fine early furniture and objects, 16th-17th C or earlier, £500-£5,000+.* LOC: Near Richmond Bridge. PARK: Easy. TEL: 0181 892 6892; home - same; fax - 0181 744 9298. SER: Valuations; buys at auction (as stock). VAT: Stan/Spec.

Marble Hill Gallery

70/72 Richmond Rd. TW1 3BE. (D. and L. Newson). Est. 1974. Open 10-5.30. *STOCK: Victorian watercolours and fireside furniture, French marble, pine and white Adam style mantels.* PARK: Easy. TEL: 0181 892 1488. VAT: Stan/Spec.

David Morley Antiques

371 Richmond Rd. TW1 2EF. Est. 1968. Open 10-1 and 2-5. CL: Wed. SIZE: Medium. *STOCK: General antiques, collectors' items, old toys.* Not Stocked: Large furniture. LOC: Approx. 200yds. from Richmond Bridge. PARK: In side road (adjacent to shop). TEL: 0181 892 2986.

Phelps Antiques — LAPADA

133-135 St. Margarets Rd. TW1 1RG. (R.C. Phelps). Est. 1870. Open 9-5.30, Sat. 9.30-5.30, Sun. 12-4. SIZE: Large - several dealers. *STOCK: Furniture, 1800-1920's.* LOC: Adjacent St. Margaret's station. PARK: Easy, at rear of shop. TEL: 0181 892 1778/7129; fax - 0181 892 3661. SER: Restorations. VAT: Stan/Spec.

Rita Shenton

142 Percy Rd. TW2 6JG. Est. 1973. Open by appointment only. SIZE: Medium. *STOCK: Clocks, watches, barometers, sundials, scientific instruments, automata and ornamental turning books, £1-£1,000.* LOC: Continuation of Whitton High St. PARK: Easy. TEL: 0181 894 6888; fax - 0181 893 8766; e-mail - rita@shentonbooks.demon.co.uk SER: Valuations; buys at auction (horological books, clocks); catalogues available. *International postal service.*

Neil Willcox

113 Strawberry Vale. TW1 4SJ. Open by appointment. *STOCK: Wine, apothecary, medical and other bottles, British and Continental, 17th to mid 19th C.* TEL: 0181 892 5858 (24 hrs). SER: Valuations; mail order, photos supplied; prop hire.

UXBRIDGE

Antiques Warehouse (Uxbridge)

34-36 Rockingham Rd. UB8 2TZ. Est. 1966. Open 10-6. SIZE: Large. *STOCK: General antiques, shipping items, £1-£4,000.* PARK: Easy. TEL: 01895 256963/271012. VAT: Stan.

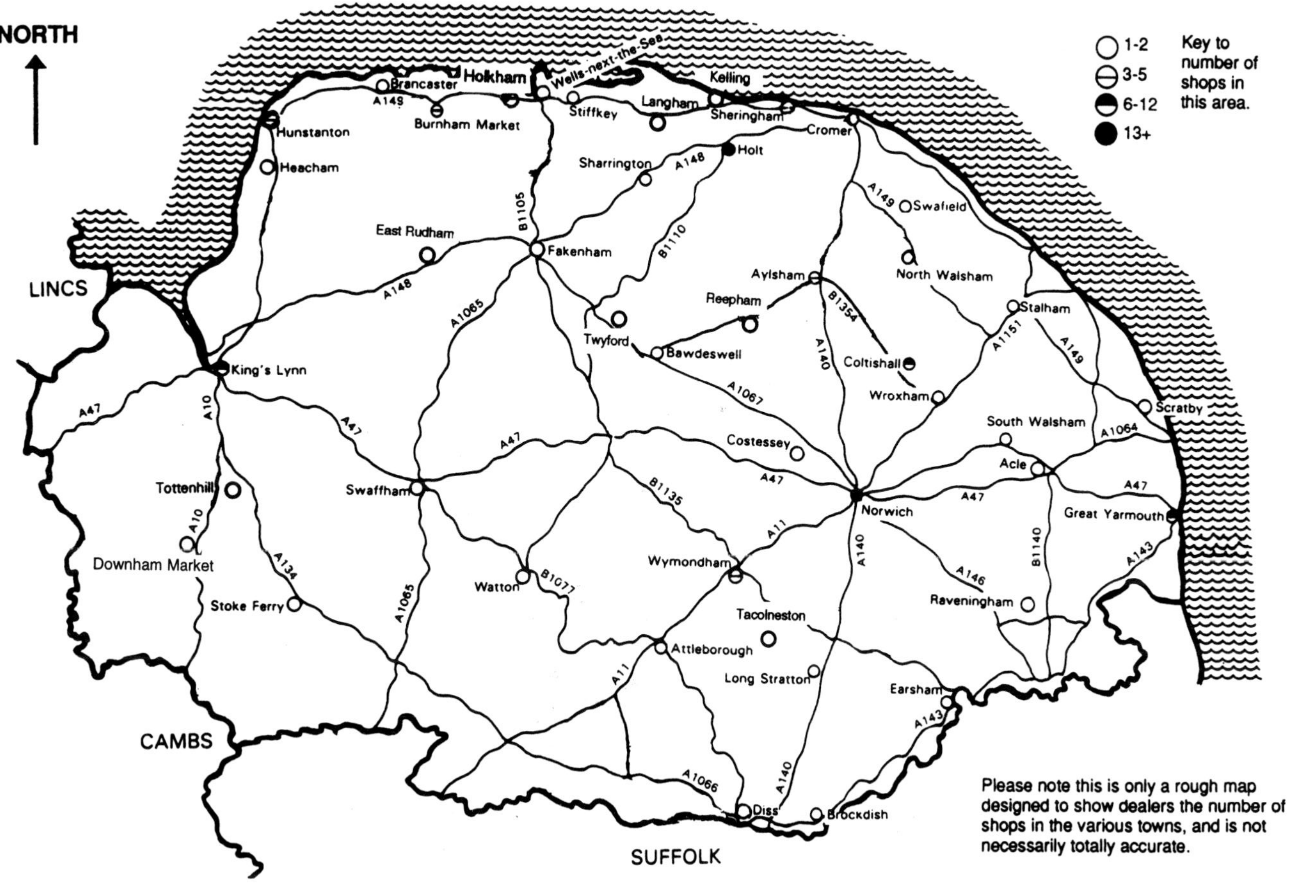
NORTH
Key to number of shops in this area.
1-2
3-5
6-12
13+
LINCS
CAMBS
SUFFOLK
Hunstanton
Heacham
Brancaster
Burnham Market
Holkham
Wells-next-the-Sea
Stiffkey
Langham
Kelling
Sheringham
Cromer
Holt
Sharrington
Fakenham
East Rudham
King's Lynn
Tottenhill
Downham Market
Stoke Ferry
Swaffham
Watton
Twyford
Bawdeswell
Reepham
Aylsham
Costessey
Swafield
North Walsham
Coltishall
Wroxham
Stalham
Scratby
South Walsham
Acle
Great Yarmouth
Norwich
Raveningham
Earsham
Brockdish
Long Stratton
Tacolneston
Wymondham
Attleborough
Diss
A149
A148
B1105
A1065
A47
A10
A134
B1110
B1135
B1077
A1067
A140
B1354
A1151
A1064
A143
B1140
A146
A11
A1066
Please note this is only a rough map designed to show dealers the number of shops in the various towns, and is not necessarily totally accurate.

ACLE, Nr. Norwich

Ivy House Antiques

Ivy House, The Street. NR13 3BH. (N. Pratt). Est. 1970. Open 9-5. SIZE: Small. *STOCK: Furniture, porcelain, pottery, glass, metalware, 18th-20th C, £25-£2,000; pictures, 19th C; garden furniture, 19th-20th C, both £50-£500.* LOC: Village centre. PARK: Easy. TEL: 01493 750682; home - same. SER: Valuations. FAIRS: Norwich. VAT: Stan/Spec.

ATTLEBOROUGH

A.E. Bush and Partners

Vineyards Antiques Gallery, Leys Lane. NR17 1NE. (A.G., M.S. and J.A. Becker). Est. 1940. Open 9-1 and 2-5.30. SIZE: Large. *STOCK: Walnut and mahogany, 18th-19th C.* LOC: Town outskirts. PARK: Easy. TEL: 01953 454239/ 452175. SER: Restorations; wholesale antiques and export; storage; buys at auction. VAT: Stan/Spec.

AYLSHAM

As Time Goes By - Antique and Exterior Clocks

Blofields Loke, Off Red Lion St. NR11 6ES. MBHI. (S. Phillips). Est. 1981. Open 9.30-5, Sat. 9.30-1. CL: Wed. SIZE: Small. *STOCK: Clocks, £150-£8,000.* LOC: Off A140 between Cromer and Norwich. PARK: Easy. TEL: 01263 731069; home - 01603 278080; fax - same; mobile - 0836 753869. SER: Valuations; restorations (clocks). VAT: Stan/Spec.

Sheila Hart and John Giles LAPADA

NR11 7QQ. Open by appointment. *STOCK: Furniture, 18th-19th C, £200-£5,000; objects, £50-£1,000.* PARK: Easy. TEL: 01263 768216; fax - same. SER: Courier. *Trade Only.*

Pearse Lukies

The Old Vicarage. Open preferably by appointment. *STOCK: Period oak, sculpture, objects, 18th C furniture.* TEL: 01263 734137. *Trade Only.*

BAWDESWELL, Nr. East Dereham

Norfolk Polyphon Centre

Wood Farm. NR20 4RX. (N.B. Vince). Open weekends, week days preferably by appointment. *STOCK: Mechanical music - polyphons, cylinder musical boxes, organs, orchestrions, automata.* LOC: On B1145, 1 mile east of Bawdeswell village and junction with A1067. TEL: 01362 688230. VAT: Stan/Spec.

BRANCASTER STAITHE, Nr. King's Lynn

Brancaster Staithe Antiques

Coast Rd. PE31 8BJ. (M.J. Wilson). Open every day including Sun. *STOCK: Victorian tables, chairs; oak, unusual pine, bookpresses, Art Deco.* TEL: 01485 210600.

BROCKDISH, Nr. Diss

Brockdish Antiques

Commerce House. IP21 4JL. (M. and L.E. Palfrey). Est. 1975. Open 9-5.30. CL: Wed. *STOCK: Mainly 19th C furniture and upholstery.* LOC: A143. TEL: 01379 668498. SER: Restorations; re-upholstery.

BURNHAM MARKET

M. and A. Cringle

The Old Black Horse. PE31 8HD. Est. 1965. Open 10-1 and 2-5. CL: Wed. SIZE: Medium. *STOCK: 18th to early 19th C furniture, £50-£2,000; china, glass, pottery, prints, maps, £10-£500.* Not Stocked: Large furniture. LOC: In village centre. PARK: Easy. TEL: 01328 738456. VAT: Spec.

Anne Hamilton Antiques

North St. PE31 8HG. (A. Hudson). Open 10-1 and 2-5. SIZE: Medium. *STOCK: Georgian furniture; porcelain, decorative items.* LOC: 20yds. from village green towards coast. PARK: Easy. TEL: 01328 738187; fax - same. VAT: Stan/Spec.

Market House BADA

PE31 8HF. Resident. (D.H. and J. Maufe). Est. 1978. Open 10-6 or by appointment. SIZE: Medium. *STOCK: English furniture - walnut, mahogany, rosewood, late 17th to mid-19th C,*

Burnham Market continued

***£25-£20,000; works of art, mirrors, small decorative items.* Not Stocked: Silver, jewellery. LOC: B1355, large Queen Anne house on green in village centre. PARK: Easy. TEL: 01328 738475; fax - 01328 730750. SER: Valuations; buys at auction. FAIRS: Olympia. VAT: Spec.**

COLTISHALL

Liz Allport-Lomax

NR12 7EF. Open by appointment only. *STOCK: Objets de vertu, collectors' items, porcelain, pottery and silver, 18th-19th C; glass, watercolours and oils, all £5-£1,000; copper, brass and furniture, 19th C, £5-£2,000.* TEL: 01603 737631. FAIRS: Langley Park Spring, East Anglian Antique Dealers, Woolverstone Fine Art & Antiques, Norwich Fine Art & Antiques (organiser).

Roger Bradbury Antiques

Church St. NR12 7DJ. Est. 1967. Open by appointment. *STOCK: Nanking cargo, Diana cargo, period furniture and objets d'art.* PARK: Easy. TEL: 01603 737444. VAT: Stan.

Coltishall Antiques Centre

High St. NR3 7AA. (I. Ford). Est. 1980. Open 10-5. SIZE: Several specialists. *STOCK: A wide variety of items including porcelain and pottery, silver and plate, copper, brass, dolls, lamps, furniture, jewellery, collectors' items, militaria, glass, Oriental porcelain, clocks.* LOC: B1150 on corner of main street. PARK: Easy. TEL: 01603 738306. SER: Valuations.

Gwendoline Golder

Point House, 5 High St. NR12 7AA. Est. 1974. Open 11-5. CL: Sun. except by appointment. *STOCK: General antiques and collectors' items.* PARK: Easy. TEL: 01603 738099.

Isabel Neal Cabinet Antiques

Bank House, 20 High St. NR12 7DH. Est. 1968. Open 10-5. SIZE: Small. *STOCK: Porcelain, pottery, including Delft, 17th-20th C; small furniture, pictures, collectors' items.* LOC: B1150 towards North Walsham, shop - blue door on right. PARK: Easy. TEL: 01603 737379.

Village Clocks

9 High St. Open Tues.-Sat. *STOCK: Clocks - 18th-19th C longcase and bracket, 19th C regulators, wood and marble mantel clocks.* LOC: Main North Walsham road. PARK: Easy. TEL: 01603 736047. SER: Valuations; restorations (cases and movements).

COSTESSEY, Nr. Norwich

The Coach House

Townhouse Rd., Old Costessey. NR8 5BX. Resident. (J. Hines). Open by appointment. *STOCK: Modern British paintings; drawings, Victorian watercolours and post-war artists; original prints, etchings, engravings; Baxter and Le Blond.* TEL: 01603 742977. SER: Cleaning prints and watercolours; framing.

CROMER

Bond Street Antiques (inc. Jas. J. Briggs Est. 1820)

6 Bond St. and 38 Church St. NR27 9DA. NAG, FGA. (M.R.T. and J.A. Jones). Est. 1958. Open 9-1 and 2.15-5.30, Sat. 9-6, Sun. by appointment. SIZE: Medium. *STOCK: Jewellery, silver, porcelain, china, glass, small furniture, 18th-20th C, £50-£5,000.* LOC: From Church St. bear right to Post Office, shop on opposite side on street further along. PARK: Easy. TEL: 01263 513134; home - same. SER: Valuations; restorations (watches and jewellery); gem testing and analysis. VAT: Stan.

A.E. Seago

15 Church St. NR27 9ES. (D.C. Seago). Est. 1937. Open 9-1 and 2-5.15. CL: Sun. and Wed. October to April. SIZE: Small. *STOCK: Furniture, 1790-1910, £25-£2,500.* Not Stocked: Silver, garden furniture, oil paintings. LOC: From Sheringham take main coast road, then New St. into High St. PARK: Easy. 50 yds away around church. TEL: 01263 512733. SER: Valuations.

DISS

Diss Antiques LAPADA

2 & 3 Market Place. Open 9-1 and 2-5, or by appointment. SIZE: Large. *STOCK: Furniture, barometers, clocks, porcelain, copper, brass.* PARK: Nearby. TEL: 01379 642213; home - 01379 651369. SER: Restorations; restoration materials; export facilities. VAT: Stan/Spec.

DOWNHAM MARKET

B & T Addrison

47 Bridge St. PE38 9DW. Est. 1980. Usually open 11-5. SIZE: Medium. *STOCK: Furniture - pine, oak, mahogany; brass and iron beds, Victorian to 1930, £1-£900.* PARK: Free opposite.

EARSHAM, Nr. Bungay

Earsham Hall Pine

Earsham Hall. NR35 2AN. (R. Derham). Est. 1976. Open 8-5, Sat. 10-5, Sun. 11-5. SIZE: Large. *STOCK: Pine furniture.* LOC: On Earsham to Hedenham Rd. PARK: Easy. TEL: 01986 893423; fax - 01986 895656. SER: Containers.

EAST RUDHAM

Anne Hamilton Antiques

Mulberry Tree House, The Green. PE31 8RD. (A. Hudson). Open by appointment. SIZE: Medium. *STOCK: Georgian furniture; longcase clocks, porcelain, decorative items.* LOC: On A148. PARK: Easy, on village green. TEL: 01485 528387. VAT: Stan/Spec.

FAKENHAM

Fakenham Antique Centre

Old Congregational Chapel, 14 Norwich Rd. NR21 8AZ. (Mrs Quainton Allen). Est. 1972. Open 10-4.30, until 5 in summer (Easter onwards), Thurs. 9-4.30. SIZE: 15 dealers. LOC: Turn off A148 at roundabout to town, turn right at traffic lights, to town centre, turn left, centre 50yds. on right. PARK: Easy. TEL: 01328 862941; home - 01328 738131. SER: Restorations (furniture and china); polishing; replacement handles.

Sue Rivett Antiques and Bygones

6 Norwich Rd. (Mrs S. Rivett). Est. 1969. Open 10-1. *STOCK: General antiques and bygones.* LOC: On Norwich Rd. into Fakenham. TEL: 01328 862924; home - 01263 860462.

GT. YARMOUTH

Barry's Antiques

35 King St. NR30 2PN. Open 9.30-5. SIZE: Large. *STOCK: Jewellery, porcelain, clocks, glass, pictures.* LOC: In main shopping street. PARK: Opposite. TEL: 01493 842713. VAT: Stan/Spec.

David Ferrow

77 Howard St. South. NR30 1LN. ABA, PBFA. Est. 1940. Open 9.30-5.30. CL: Thurs. SIZE: Large. *STOCK: Books, some antiquarian maps, local prints, manuscripts.* LOC: From London, sign before river bridge to The Docks, keep to nearside, turn left and then right to car park. PARK: Easy. TEL: 01493 843800; home - 01493 662247. SER: Valuations; restorations (books and prints). VAT: Stan.

The Ferrow Family Antiques LAPADA

6 and 7 Hall Quay and 1 George St. NR30 1HX. Est. 1957. Open 9-5. CL: Thurs. pm. *STOCK: General antiques, £50-£5,000.* Not Stocked: Guns, medals, coins, jewellery. LOC: Near Haven Bridge, off A12. TEL: 01493 855391; home - 01493 663605. SER: Valuations; restorations; buys at auction; hire. VAT: Stan/Spec.

Folkes Antiques and Jewellers

74 Victoria Arcade. NR30 2NU. (Mrs J. Baldry). Est. 1946. Open 10-4. *STOCK: General antiques especially jewellery and collectables.* LOC: From A47 into town centre, shop on right. PARK: Easy. TEL: 01493 851354. SER: Valuations. FAIRS: Local collectors.

Gold and Silver Exchange

Theatre Plain. NR30 2BE. (C. Birch). Open 9.30-5.15. *STOCK: Coins, medals and secondhand jewellery.* TEL: 01493 859430.

The Haven Gallery LAPADA

6/7 Hall Quay. NR30 1HX. (M. and J. Ferrow). Open 9-5. CL: Thurs. pm. *STOCK: Watercolours, drawings, prints, oil paintings, 19th C, £10-£6,000.* LOC: Near Haven Bridge, off A12.

Gt. Yarmouth continued

TEL: 01493 855391; home - 01493 663605. SER: Valuations; restorations (framing, collections). VAT: Stan/Spec.

Peter Howkins

39, 40, 132 and 135 King St. NR30 2PQ. Est. 1946. Open 9-5. SIZE: Large. *STOCK: At 135 King St. - jewellery, Victorian to present day, £5-£5,000; silver, George III to present day, £1-£2,000; at 39 and 40 King St. - furniture, upholstery, Georgian to Victorian, £5-£5,000; at 132 King St. - investment antiques.* LOC: From Norwich through town one-way system to road signposted Lowestoft which intersects King St. PARK: Easy. TEL: 01493 844639/851180. SER: Valuations; restorations (jewellery, silver, gold, furniture).

Wheatleys

16 Northgate St., White Horse Plain and Fullers Hill. NR30 1BA. Est. 1971. Open 9.30-5, Thurs. 9.30-1. SIZE: Large. *STOCK: Jewellery and general antiques.* LOC: 2 minutes walk from Market Place. PARK: Easy. TEL: 01493 857219. VAT: Stan.

HEACHAM, Nr. King's Lynn

Peter Robinson

Pear Tree House, 7 Lynn Rd. PE31 7HU. Est. 1880. Open 9-5. Appointment advisable Mon. and Sat. SIZE: Small. *STOCK: Furniture, 1600-1900, £10-£5,000; china, 1750-1900, metalwork, 1700-1870; both £2-£1,000.* LOC: Shop on left on entry to village. PARK: Easy. TEL: 01485 570228. SER: Valuations; buys at auction. VAT: Stan/Spec.

HOLKHAM, Nr. Wells-next-the-Sea

The Potting Shed

Main Rd. (Bill Jellings). Est. 1993. Open Sun. afternoons only, trade mid-week by appointment. SIZE: Medium. *STOCK: Antique flowerpots.* LOC: On north Norfolk coast road (A149) by entrance to Holkam Hall. PARK: Easy. TEL: 01692 402424; home - same.

HOLT

Baron Art

9 Chapel Yard, Albert St. NR25 6HG. (Anthony R. Baron and Michael J. Bellis). Est. 1992. Open 9.30-5.30, Sun. by appointment. SIZE: Medium. *STOCK: Paintings, 19th-20th C, £50-£5,000; prints and lithographs, 19th-20th C, £5-£500; collectables, 1830-1940, £5-£500.* PARK: Easy. TEL: 01263 713906; home - 01263 588227. SER: Valuations; buys at auction (paintings). VAT: Stan/Spec.

Collectors Cabin

7 Cromer Rd. NR25 6HA. (J.M.E. Codling). Est. 1983. Open 10-1 and 2-4.30. CL: Thurs. pm. SIZE: Small. *STOCK: Bric-a-brac, bygones, toys, 19th C, £5-£25.* LOC: Near Post Office. PARK: Bull St. TEL: 01263 712241.

Holt continued

Simon Gough Books
5 Fish Hill. NR25 6BD. Est. 1976. Open 10-5. *STOCK: Antiquarian and secondhand books; bindings.* TEL: 01263 712650.

Heathfield Antiques
15 Chapel Yard, Albert St. NR25 6HQ. (J.E., H.B. and S.M. Heathfield). Est. 1990. Open 11-5. CL: Thurs. SIZE: Medium. *STOCK: Stripped pine, 19th-20th C, £20-£800; bric-a-brac, £1-£100.* PARK: Easy. TEL: 01263 711122; home - 01263 711531. VAT: Stan/Global.

Heathfield Country Pine
The Warehouse, 39 Hempstead Rd. (J.E., H.B. and S.M. Heathfield). Est. 1994. Open 9-5. SIZE: Large. *STOCK: Pine furniture, £50-£1,000.* LOC: Follow signs to Hempstead. PARK: Own. TEL: 01263 711609; home - 01263 711531. VAT: Stan/Global.

Maura Henry Antiques and Interiors
17 Chapel Yard, Albert St. NR25 6HG. (Mrs M.E. Henry). Est. 1974. CL: Thurs. SIZE: Medium. *STOCK: Furniture, 18th-19th C; mirrors, objects, £10-£3,000.* PARK: Easy. TEL: 01263 711240; home - 01362 668796. SER: Valuations.

Judy Hines of Holt - The Gallery
3 Fish Hill. NR25 6BD. *STOCK: 20th C prints and paintings.* TEL: 01263 713000; fax - same. SER: Framing.

Holt Antique Centre
Albert Hall, Albert St. (David Attfield). Est. 1980. Open 10-5, Sat. 10-5.30 (Sun. Easter-October) SIZE: Large. *STOCK: Pine and country furniture, china, glass, lighting, silver plate and kitchenalia, jewellery, clothes, soft furnishings, 18th-20th C, £1-£1,500.* LOC: Turn right from Chapel Yard car park, 100 yards. PARK: Easy. TEL: 01263 712097; home - 01263 860347.

In the Picture (The Golf Collection)
16 Chapel Yard. NR25 6HG. (T.R. Groves). Open 10-4. SIZE: Medium. *STOCK: Decorative prints, limited editions, maps, sporting (especially golf), £5-£500.* PARK: Easy. TEL: 01263 713720/ 822265/824728; fax - 01263 822097. SER: Framing. VAT: Stan.

Past Caring
6 Chapel Yard. NR25 6HG. (L. Mossman). Est. 1988. Open 11-5. CL: Thurs. SIZE: Medium. *STOCK: Period clothes, linen and textiles, Victorian to 1950, £5-£100; jewellery and accessories, Victorian to 1960, £2-£75.* PARK: Easy. TEL: 01263 713771; home - 01362 683363. SER: Valuations; restorations (christening gowns and some beadwork). FAIRS: Alexandra Palace, Stand W60.

Richard Scott Antiques
30 High St. NR25 6BH. Est. 1967. Open 11-5. CL: Thurs. SIZE: Large. *STOCK: Pottery, porcelain, period furniture, oil lamps and spares, general antiques.* LOC: On A148. PARK: Easy. TEL: 01263 712479. SER: Valuations; conservation advice. VAT: Stan.

HUNSTANTON

Delawood Antiques
10 Westgate. PE36 5AL. Resident. (R.C. Woodhouse). Est. 1975. Open 10-5 Wed., Fri., Sat. and most Sun., other times by chance or appointment. SIZE: Small. *STOCK: General antiques, furniture, jewellery, collectors' items, books, £1-£1,000.* LOC: Near town centre and bus station. PARK: Easy. TEL: 01485 532903; home - same. SER: Valuations: restorations (porcelain and china); items sold on commission.

Le Strange Old Barns Antiques, Arts & Craft Centre
Golf Course Rd., Old Hunstanton. PE36 6JG. (R.M. Weller). TEL: 01485 533402.

R.C. Woodhouse (Antiquarian Horologist)
10 Westgate. PE36 5AL. MBHI and BWCG. Resident. Est. 1975. Open Wed., Fri, Sat., usually Sun. Other days or eves. by chance or appointment. SIZE: Small. *STOCK: Georgian, Victorian and Edwardian longcase, dial, wall and mantle clocks; some watches and barometers.* LOC: Near town centre and bus station. PARK: Easy. TEL: 01485 532903; home - same. SER: Valuations; restorations (longcase, bracket, chiming, carriage, French, wall clocks, dials, barometers); small locks repaired and lost keys made - postal service if required.

KELLING, Nr. Holt

Baron Art
The Old Reading Room. NR25 7EL. (Anthony R. Baron and Michael J. Bellis). Est. 1994. Open 10-5.30 including Sun. Easter to Oct. SIZE: Large. *STOCK: Paintings and prints, 19th-20th C, £5-£5,000; modern, first editions, poetry, art and children's books, £1-£500; furniture and collectables, 1830-1940, £5-£2,000.* LOC: A149 coast road between Weybourne and Cley, at war memorial in village. PARK: Easy. TEL: 01263 588227; home - 01263 588435. SER: Valuations; buys at auction (paintings and books). VAT: Stan/Spec.

KING'S LYNN

Tim Clayton Jewellery
21-23 Chapel St. PE30 1EG. Open 9-5. *STOCK: Jewellery, clocks, watches, furniture and pictures.* TEL: 01553 772329; fax - 01553 776583. SER: Restorations (silver); bespoke jewellery made to order.

Norfolk Galleries
Railway Rd. PE30 1PF. (B. Houchen and G.R. Cumbley). Open 8.30-5.30, Sat. 8.30-12.30. *STOCK: Victorian and Edwardian furniture.* PARK: Nearby. TEL: 01553 765060.

King's Lynn continued

Old Curiosity Shop

25 St. James St. PE30 5DA. (Mrs R.S. Wright). Est. 1980. Open 10.30-5, Sat. 9.30-6. SIZE: Small. *STOCK: General collectable smalls, glass, clothing, linen, jewellery, lighting, Art Deco and Art Nouveau, furniture, prints, stripped pine and paintings, pre 1930, £1-£500.* LOC: Off Saturday market place towards London Rd. PARK: At rear or nearby. TEL: 01553 766591. FAIRS: Alexandra Palace, Newark and local.

The Old Granary Antiques and Collectors Centre

King Staithe Lane, Off Queens St. PE30 1LZ. Open 10-5. *STOCK: China, glass, books, silver, jewellery, brass, copper, postcards, linen, some furniture, and general antiques.* PARK: Easy. TEL: 01553 775509.

Pine and Things

28 Tower St. Open 9-5.30. CL: Wed. SIZE: 8 dealers. *STOCK: General antiques including small items, pine, mahogany and oak furniture, bygones, ornate plasterwork, ceiling roses and Adam style fireplaces.* TEL: 01553 766532.

Silverton Antiques

21-23 Chapel St. PE30 1EG. (Mrs S. Clayton). Open 9-5. *STOCK: Glass, porcelain, clocks, barometers, furniture and paintings, pre-1900.* TEL: 01553 772329; fax - 01553 776583. SER: Restorations (clocks, barometers and jewellery).

LANGHAM, Nr. Holt

Sue Miller Antiques and Collectables

The Courtyard, Langham Glass. Est. 1993. Open 10-1.30 and 2-5 including Sun. SIZE: Small. *STOCK: Glass - table, decorative and unusual, 18th-20th C, £1-£1,000; porcelain and pottery, mainly 19th to early 20th C, £10-£500; furniture, including early country oak, walnut and mahogany, 17th-19th C, £500-£2,500.* LOC: Turn off A148 Cromer/Fakenham road at Bale and follow Langham signs. PARK: Own. TEL: 01328 830511. SER: Valuations.

LONG STRATTON

Old Coach House

Ipswich Rd. NR15 2TA. Est. 1976. Open 10-1 and 2-5. CL: Mon. *STOCK: General antiques, pine, Victorian and Edwardian export furniture, paintings, copper, brass, china.* TEL: 01508 530942.

NORTH WALSHAM

Eric Bates and Sons

Melbourne House, Bacton Rd. NR28 0RA. Est. 1973. Open 8-5. SIZE: Large. *STOCK: Victorian and Edwardian furniture.* TEL: 01692 403221; fax - 01692 404388. SER: Restorations (furniture); manufacturer of period-style furniture; upholstery; shipping and container packing. VAT: Stan/Spec.

NORWICH

Albrow and Sons Family Jewellers

10 All Saints Green. NR1 3NA. NAG Registered Valuer. (R. Albrow). Open 9.30-4.30. *STOCK: Jewellery, silver, plate, china, glass, furniture.* LOC: Opposite Bond's store. PARK: Behind Bond's store. TEL: 01603 622569. SER: Valuations; repairs.

The Bank House Gallery LAPADA

71 Newmarket Rd. NR2 2HW. Resident. (R.S. Mitchell). Est. 1979. Open by appointment. *STOCK: English oil paintings especially Norwich and Suffolk schools, 19th C, £1,000-£50,000.* LOC: On A11 between city centre and ring road. PARK: Own. TEL: 01603 633380; fax - 01603 633387. SER: Valuations; restorations. VAT: Stan/Spec.

Arthur Brett and Sons Ltd BADA

42 St. Giles St. NR2 1LW. Est. 1870. Open 9.30-1 and 2-5. CL: Sat. except by appointment. SIZE: Large. *STOCK: Antique furniture, mahogany, walnut and oak; sculpture and metalwork.* LOC: Near City Hall. PARK: Easy. TEL: 01603 628171; fax - 01603 630245. FAIRS: Olympia. VAT: Stan/Spec.

J & D Clarke Book and Print Dealers

St Michael at Plea Church, Redwell St. NR2 4SN. Est. 1988. Open 9.30-5. SIZE: Medium. *STOCK: Books and prints, £1-£1,000.* LOC: Twixt Elm Hill and city centre. PARK: Limited. TEL: 01603 617700/619226. SER: Book repairs; print colouring and mounting.

Norwich continued

Cloisters Antiques Fair
St. Andrew's and Blackfriars Hall, St. Andrew's Plain. NR3 1AU. (Norwich City Council). Est. 1976. Open Wed. only 9.30-3.30. SIZE: 23 dealers. *STOCK: Wide variety of general antiques.* PARK: Easy. TEL: 01603 628477; fax - 01603 762182; bookings - 01603 425158.

Country and Eastern
8 Redwell St. (J. Millward). Est. 1978. Open daily. *STOCK: Oriental rugs, kelims and textiles, late 19th C to early 20th C, £50-£500; primitive and country furniture, 18th-19th C, £25-£500; woolwork pictures, 17th-19th C, £10-£200; bygones, 18th-19th C, £2-£75.* LOC: Top of Elm Hill. PARK: Nearby. TEL: 01603 623107. VAT: Stan/Spec.

Crome Gallery and Frame Shop
34 Elm Hill. NR3 1HG. (J. Willis). Est. 1971. Open 9.30-5. SIZE: Medium. *STOCK: Mainly 20th C watercolours, oils and prints; some 19th C.* LOC: Near cathedral. PARK: Free. TEL: 01603 622827. SER: Crome Gallery Conservation (oils, watercolours, prints, frames, furniture, porcelain).

Peter Crowe, Antiquarian Book Seller
75-77 Upper St. Giles St. NR1 2AB. Open 9.30-5.30. *STOCK: Antiquarian books, 17th-18th C, calf, 19th C, cloth and fine bindings, travel, topography and Norfolk; maps and prints.* TEL: 01603 624800.

Clive Dennett Coins
66 St. Benedicts St. NR2 4AR. BNTA. Est. 1970. CL: Thurs. and lunchtime. SIZE: Small. *STOCK: Coins and medals, ancient Greek to date, £5-£5,000; jewellery, 19th-20th C; banknotes, 20th C; both £5-£1,000.* PARK: Easy. TEL: 01603 624315. SER: Valuations; buys at auction (as stock). FAIRS: All Simmons; Cumberland Hotel, London; Coinex; Marriott Hotel, London; Tienan, Belgium.

The Fairhurst Gallery
Bedford St. NR2 1AR. Est. 1951. Open 9-5. CL: Sat. pm. SIZE: Medium. *STOCK: Oil paintings, £5-£5,000; watercolours, £5-£2,000, both 19th-20th C; frames, 18th-20th C; furniture, £500-£10,000.* LOC: Behind Travel Centre. TEL: 01603 614214. SER: Valuations; restorations; cleaning; framemakers. VAT: Spec.

Nicholas Fowle Antiques BADA
Websdale Court, Bedford St. NR2 1AR. Est. 1965. Open 9-5, Sat. 9-1. SIZE: Medium. *STOCK: Furniture, £500-£10,000; works of art, £5-£1,000; both 17th-19th C.* LOC: City centre pedestrian area (limited access for loading and unloading). PARK: St Andrews multi-storey. TEL: 01603 219964; fax - same. SER: Valuations; restorations (furniture). VAT: Stan/Spec.

Norwich continued

Michael Hallam Antiques

Black Horse Gallery, Wensum St. (M.J. Hallam). Est. 1969. Open 9.30-5. SIZE: Small. *STOCK: Furniture, porcelain, pictures and small items, mainly 19th C, £10-£2,000.* LOC: Near Cathedral. TEL: 01603 413692. SER: Valuations.

John Howkins Antiques

1 Dereham Rd. NR2 4HX. (J.G. Howkins). Est. 1973. Open 10-5, prior telephone call advisable. SIZE: Large. *STOCK: Furniture and smalls, 18th to early 20th C, £25-£15,000.* LOC: Inner ring road, junction of Dereham Road and Grapes Hill. PARK: Own at rear. TEL: 01603 627832; fax - 01603 666626. SER: Valuations; restorations (furniture, clocks, upholstery); buys at auction. VAT: Stan/Spec.

Leona Levine Silver Specialist BADA

35 St. Giles St. NR2 1JN. Est. 1865. Open 9.30-5. CL: Thurs. *STOCK: Silver and Sheffield plate.* TEL: 01603 628709; fax - same. SER: Valuations; engraving; restorations. VAT: Stan/Spec.

Maddermarket Antiques

18c Lower Goat Lane. NR2 1EL. Est. 1955. Open 9.30-4.30. *STOCK: Jewellery, silverware.* TEL: 01603 620610. SER: Part exchange.

Norwich continued

Mandell's Gallery BADA

Elm Hill. NR3 1HN. Est. 1964. Open 9-5.30. SIZE: Large. *STOCK: Oils and watercolours, especially English and Continental works and Norwich and Suffolk painters, 19th-20th C.* LOC: Near shopping centre, close to cathedral. PARK: Easy. TEL: 01603 626892/629180; fax - 01603 767471. SER: Conservation; framing. VAT: Spec.

The Movie Shop

Antiquarian and Nostalgia Centre, 11 St. Gregory's Alley. NR2 1ER. Open 10-5. SIZE: Large. *STOCK: Books, magazines and movie ephemera; telephones, pre-1940 clothes and textiles, collectables and general antiques.* TEL: 01603 615239.

Norwich Antique, Collectors & Interiors Centre

St Mary's Church, St Mary's Plain, Duke St. NR3 3AF. (I. Ford). Est. 1982. Open 10-4.30. SIZE: Large - 30 dealers. *STOCK: Wide range of general antiques including furniture, porcelain, toys and teddies, trains and dolls, jewellery, militaria, paintings and prints, plated ware, art, period clothes, watches, clocks and collectables.* LOC: Near HMSO. PARK: 200 yds. TEL: 01603 612582. SER: Valuations.

Alfred Daniels, RWS, RBA (born London, 1924), 'The Pavilion, the Garden and School Brass Band, Brighton', oil on canvas, 24in. x 40in., signed and dated 1980. Exhibited at the 1980 Royal Summer Exhibition, number 869. Price guide: watercolours, £500-£700; oil paintings (the artist is currently using the oil-modified alkyd resin, Griffin Alkyd, which is manufactured by Winsor & Newton. 'The quick-drying time of this paint means that subsequent coats do not pick up, so that I can make very fine details and overpaint in multiple layers.'), £1,500-£3,300. (Manya Igel Fine Art)

From an article entitled "Contemporary British Artists: A Personal Choice" by Anthony J. Lester which appeared in the September 1997 issue of **Antique Collecting**

Norwich continued

Norwich Antiques Centre

Augustine Steward House, 14 Tombland. NR3 1HF. (Mrs Betty Godsafe). Est. 1974. Open 10-5. SIZE: Large. *STOCK: Furniture, 19th to early 20th C, £50-£1,000; china and porcelain, 1850-1950, £20-£200; collectables, 1850-1950, £5-£50.* LOC: City centre, opposite cathedral. PARK: Elm Hill. TEL: 01603 619129. SER: Valuations; restorations (furniture, caning).

The Scientific Anglian (Bookshop)

30-30a St. Benedict St. NR2 4AQ. (N.B. Peake). Est. 1965. Open 12-6. SIZE: Large. *STOCK: Secondhand books, old and modern, 30p-£200; antiquarian items, 1500-1900, from £1.* Not Stocked: Maps or prints. LOC: 3 minutes walk from City Hall straight down Upper Goat Lane, turn left into St. Benedict's. PARK: Limited nearby or multi-storey St. Andrew's St. TEL: 01603 624079. SER: Valuations; buys at auction. VAT: Stan.

Oswald Sebley

20 Lower Goat Lane. NR2 1EL. (P.H. Knights). Est. 1895. Open 9-5.15. CL: Thurs. SIZE: Small. *STOCK: Silver, 18th-20th C, £15-£2,000; jewellery, Victorian, £10-£4,000.* LOC: 150yds. to right of City Hall, down paved street. PARK: Nearby. TEL: 01603 626504. SER: Valuations; restorations (silver and gold jewellery). VAT: Stan/Spec.

St. Michael at Plea Antiques Centre

Bank Plain. NR2 4SN. (Manager - K.J. Burton). Est. 1984. Open 9.30-5. SIZE: Medium - 30 dealers. *STOCK: General antiques, pre-1940, £1-£2,500.* LOC: Near top of Elm Hill. PARK: 30 minutes roadside, multi-storey nearby. TEL: 01603 618989. SER: Restorations and repair (clocks, china); French polishing; re-caning.

James and Ann Tillett LAPADA

12 and 13 Tombland. NR3 1HF. Est. 1972. Open 9-6, Sat. 9-1.30. *STOCK: English domestic silver, flatware and jewellery, from 17th C; mustard pots, collectors' items, barometers, barographs, from 18th C.* LOC: Opposite Erpingham Gate, Norwich Cathedral and Maid's Head Hotel. TEL: 01603 624914; fax - 01603 764310. SER: Valuations; restorations (silver); export facilities. VAT: Stan/Spec.

Thomas Tillett & Co

17 St. Giles St. NR2 1JL. Open daily. SIZE: Medium. *STOCK: Diamond jewellery, 19th-20th C, £50-£2,000; silver, 18th-19th C, £20-£1,000.* PARK: Easy. TEL: 01603 625922. SER: Valuations; restorations (jewellery, silver). VAT: Stan/Spec.

The Tombland Bookshop

8 Tombland. NR3 1HF. (J.G. and A.H. Freeman). Open 9.30-5. *STOCK: Antiquarian and secondhand books.* TEL: 01603 490000; fax - 01603 611631.

Norwich continued

Malcolm Turner

15 St. Giles St. NR2 1JL. Open 9-5. CL: Thurs. SIZE: Small. *STOCK: Bronzeware, Oriental ceramics, silver, Staffordshire, Imari, mostly 19th C, £50-£1,000.* PARK: Nearby. TEL: 01603 627007. SER: Valuations. VAT: Stan/Spec.

RAVENINGHAM

M.D. Cannell Antiques

Castell Farm, Beccles Rd. NR14 6NU. Resident. Open 10-6 including Sun. SIZE: Large. *STOCK: Oriental rugs and carpets, Eastern furniture, pine, metalwork.* LOC: On B1140. PARK: Easy. TEL: 01508 548441. VAT: Stan/Spec.

REEPHAM

Echo Antiques

Church Hill. NR10 4JL. (Ms M. Stiefel and N. Bundock). Est. 1986. Open 10-5. CL: Thurs. SIZE: Medium. *STOCK: Furniture, 1650-1900, £10-£2,000; pine, 1800-1900, £50-£1,000; small items, 1650-1900, £10-£1,000.* Not Stocked: Jewellery. PARK: Market Sq. TEL: 01603 873291; home - 01603 872068. SER: Valuations; restorations (furniture); buys at auction.

SCRATBY, Nr. Gt. Yarmouth

Keith Lawson Antique Clocks

Scratby Garden Centre, Beach Rd. NR29 3AJ. LBHI. Est. 1979. Open seven days 9-6. SIZE: Large. *STOCK: Clocks and barometers.* LOC: B1159. PARK: Easy. TEL: 01493 730950. SER: Valuations; restorations. VAT: Stan/Spec.

SHARRINGTON, Nr. Holt

Sharrington Antiques

NR24 2PQ. (P. Coke). Est. 1944. Open by chance 9.30-5.00, or by appointment. CL: Jan.-Mar. SIZE: Medium. *STOCK: Small and interesting items, £5-£1,500; china, pictures, embroideries, treen, papier mâché.* LOC: 3 miles west of Holt. PARK: Easy. TEL: 01263 861411; home - 01263 860719.

SHERINGHAM

R.L. Cook

12 Sycamore Grove. NR26 8PG. Est. 1950. Open by appointment. *STOCK: Antiquarian books.* TEL: 01263 822050.

Dorothy's Antiques

23 Waterbank Rd. NR26 8RB. (Mrs D.E. Collier). Est. 1975. *STOCK: Cranberry glass, Royal Worcester, Royal Dux commemorative and other china; small furniture.* TEL: 01263 822319; home - 01263 823018.

Parriss

20 Station Rd. NR26 8RE. (J.H. Parriss). Est. 1947. Open 9-5.30. CL: Wed. SIZE: Medium. *STOCK: Jewellery, £30-£2,500; silver, £40-£2,000; clocks, £100-£3,000.* LOC: A1082, in main street. PARK: Within 150yds. TEL: 01263 822661. SER: Valuations; restorations (jewellery, silver, clocks). VAT: Stan.

Sheringham continued

The Westcliffe Gallery

2-8 Augusta St. NR26 8LA. Resident. (Richard and Sheila Parks). Est. 1979. Open 9.30-1 and 2-5.30, Sat. 9.30-5.30, Sun. 10-4. SIZE: Medium. *STOCK: Oils, watercolours and drawings, 19th-20th C, £100-£15,000; furniture.* LOC: Town centre. PARK: Easy. TEL: 01263 824320. SER: Valuations; restorations (oils, watercolours, prints); gilding. VAT: Stan/Spec.

SOUTH WALSHAM

Leo Pratt and Son LAPADA

Old Curiosity Shop. NR13 6EA. (R. and E.D. Pratt). Est. 1890. Open 9-1 and 2-5.30. SIZE: Large. *STOCK: Furniture, from 1700; porcelain, glass, pottery, 1830; shipping furniture, metalware.* PARK: Easy. TEL: 01603 270204. SER: Restorations (furniture); buys at auction. FAIRS: Norwich; Snape; Bury St Edmunds. VAT: Stan/Spec.

STALHAM

Stalham Antique Gallery LAPADA

High St. NR12 9AH. (M.B. Hicks). Est. 1970. Open 9-1 and 2-5. CL: Sat pm. SIZE: Medium. *STOCK: Furniture, 17th C to 19th C; pictures,*

Stalham continued

***china, glass, brass.* Not Stocked: Reproductions. PARK: Easy. TEL: 01692 580636. SER: Valuations; restorations. VAT: Spec.**

STIFFKEY

Stiffkey Antiques

The Old Methodist Chapel. NR23 1AJ. Open by arrangement with Stiffkey Lamp Shop. *STOCK: Victorian and Edwardian bathroom fittings; fire irons, door furniture, bric-a-brac, Japanese and other tinplate toys (many boxed and mint).* PARK: Easy. TEL: 01328 830460; fax - 01328 830005.

The Stiffkey Lamp Shop

Townshend Arms. NR23 1AJ. (R. Belsten and D. Mann). Est. 1976. Open 10-5 including Sun. SIZE: Medium. *STOCK: Lamps, gas, electric and oil, 1800-1920, £25-£2,000; rare lamp fittings.* LOC: Coast road near Wells-on-Sea. PARK: Easy. TEL: 01328 830460; fax - 01328 830005. VAT: Stan.

STOKE FERRY, Nr. King's Lynn

Farmhouse Antiques

White's Farmhouse, Barker's Drove. PE33 9TA. Resident. (P. Philpot). Est. 1969. Open by appointment. *STOCK: General antiques.* TEL: 01366 500588. SER: Restorations; furniture made to order in old timber.

SWAFFHAM

Cranglegate Antiques

Market Place. PE37 7LE. Resident. (Mrs R.D. Buckie). Est. 1965. Open Tues., Thurs. and Sat. 10-1 and 2-5.30. SIZE: Small. *STOCK: Small furniture, general antiques and collectors items, 17th-20th C.* LOC: A47. PARK: In square opposite or in passage at rear. TEL: Home - 01760 721052.

Swaffham Antiques Supplies

The Old Cold Store Buildings, 7 Cley Rd. PE37. (M. and R. Cross). Est. 1959. Open by appointment only. SIZE: Large. *STOCK: General antiques, 18th-19th C; shipping furniture, £100-£5,000.* LOC: Off Market Place. PARK: Easy. TEL: 01760 721697/725418; home - 01760 721697.

SWAFIELD, Nr. North Walsham

Staithe Lodge Gallery

Staithe Lodge. NR28 0RQ. Resident. (M.C.A. Foster). Est. 1976. Open 9-5, Sun. by appointment. CL: Wed. pm. SIZE: Medium. *STOCK: Watercolours, paintings and prints, 1800-1950, £50-£500.* LOC: On B1145 at the Mundesley end of the North Walsham by-pass. PARK: Easy. TEL: 01692 402669. SER: Restorations; framing; buys at auction (mainly watercolours).

TACOLNESTON, Nr. Norwich

Freya Antiques

St. Mary's Farm, Cheneys Lane. NR16 1DB. Usually open but appointment advisable; evenings by appointment. SIZE: Large. *STOCK: General antiques, especially pine and country furniture; upholstery.* TEL: 01508 489252; mobile - 0370 757259. SER: Valuations; restorations; re-upholstery.

TOTTENHILL, Nr. King's Lynn

Jubilee Antiques

Coach House, Whin Common Rd. PE33 0RS. (Mr and Mrs A.J. Lee). Est. 1953. Open daily including Sun. SIZE: Medium. *STOCK: Furniture especially Victorian chairs, £50-£4,000; post boxes, interesting items.* LOC: Between King's Lynn and Downham Market, adjacent to A10. PARK: Easy. TEL: 01553 810681; home - same. SER: Valuations; restorations (furniture); buys at auction (furniture).

TWYFORD, Nr. Fakenham

Norton Antiques

(T. and N. Hepburn). Est. 1966. Open by appointment only. *STOCK: Furniture 1680-1900, £25-£3,500; oils and watercolours, 19th to early 20th C, £25-£2,500; clocks, 18th-19th C, £40-£3,500; woodworking and craftsman's hand tools.* TEL: 01362 683331. SER: Valuations.

WATTON

Clermont Antiques

Clermont Hall. IP25 6LY. Resident. (P. Jones). Est. 1983. Open daily. SIZE: Large. *STOCK: Furniture, decorative items, 18th to early 19th C.* LOC: Down farm track, off B1108. PARK: Easy. TEL: 01953 882189. VAT: Spec.

WELLS-NEXT-THE-SEA

Church Street Antiques

2 Church St. NR23 1JA. (Paula Ford and Lesley Ann Irons). Open 10-4 including Sun., Mon. by appointment. SIZE: Small. *STOCK: Textiles, lace, costume jewellery, hat pins, kitchenalia, ephemera, collectables, £1-£500.* LOC: A149 main coast road, opposite church. PARK: Easy. TEL: 01328 711698.

Wells Antique Centre

The Old Mill, Maryland. NR23 1LX. Open 10-5 including Sun. SIZE: 12 dealers. *STOCK: General antiques and collectables.* PARK: Easy. TEL: 01328 711433.

WROXHAM

T.C.S. Brooke BADA

The Grange. NR12 8RX. (S.T. Brooke). Est. 1952. Open 9.30-1 and 2.15-5.30. CL: Mon. ***STOCK: English porcelain, 18th C; furniture, mainly Georgian; silver, glass, works of art, Oriental rugs.*** **PARK: Easy. TEL: 01603 782644. SER: Valuations. VAT: Spec.**

WYMONDHAM

King

Market Place. NR18 0AX. (M. King). Est. 1969. Open 9-4. CL: Mon. and Wed., except by appointment. *STOCK: General antiques, furniture, copper, brass, silver, jewellery, porcelain.* PARK: Easy. TEL: 01953 604758; evenings - 01953 602427.

M.E. and J.E. Standley

"Acorns", 23 Norwich Rd. and warehouses at Chandlers Hill. NR18 0NT. Open Sat. or by appointment. *STOCK: Furniture, 17th-19th C and Victorian.* TEL: 01953 602566.

Turret House

27 Middleton St. NR18 0AB. PBFA. Resident. (Dr and Mrs D.H. Morgan). Est. 1972. SIZE: Small. *STOCK: Antiquarian books, especially science and medical; scientific instruments.* LOC: Corner of Vicar St., adjacent to War Memorial. TEL: 01953 603462. SER: Buys at auction. FAIRS: London and major provincial PBFA. VAT: Stan/Spec.

Northamptonshire

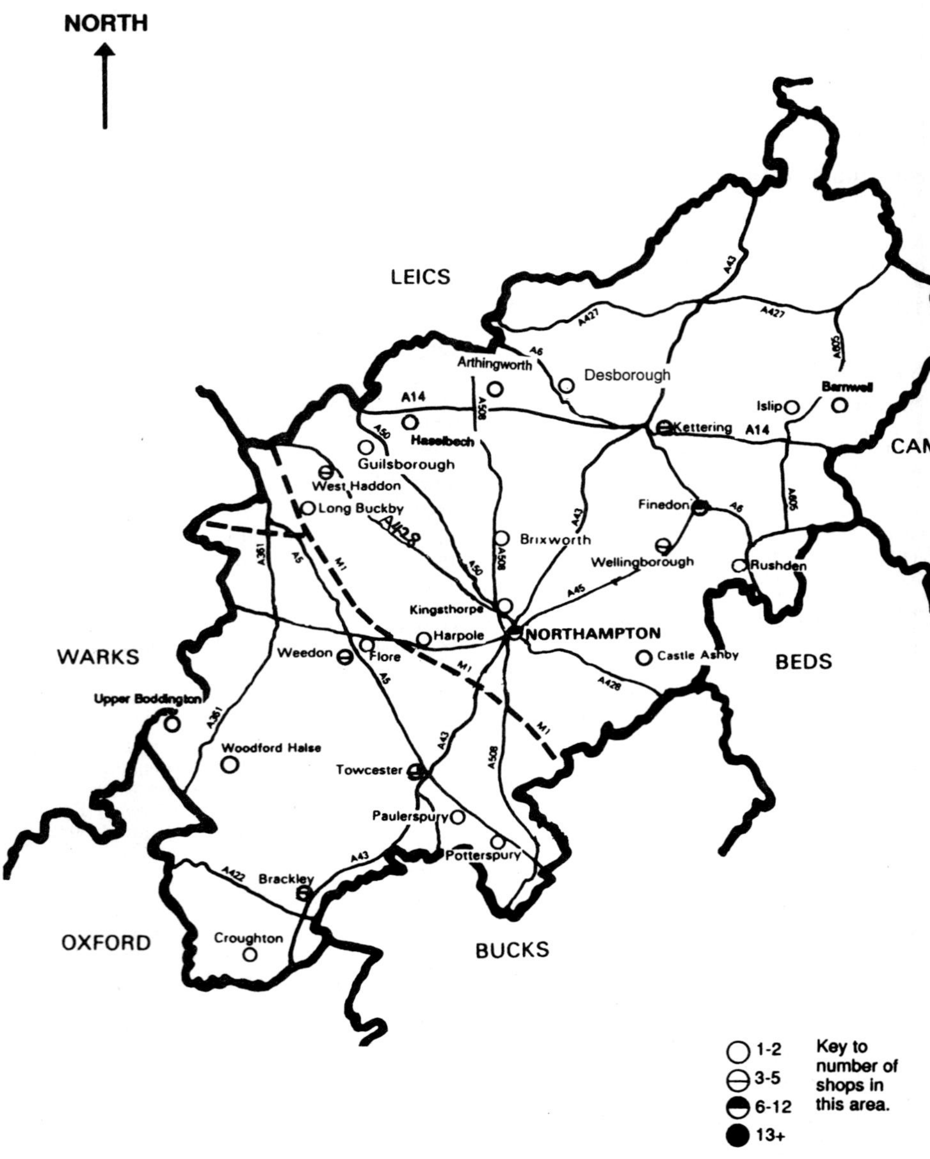

○ 1-2
⊖ 3-5
◓ 6-12
● 13+

Key to number of shops in this area.

Please note this is only a rough map designed to show dealers the number of shops in the various towns, and is not necessarily totally accurate.

ARTHINGWORTH
Nr. Market Harborough (Leics)

Coughton Galleries Ltd
The Old Manor. LE16 8JT. (Lady Isabel Throckmorton). Est. 1968. Open Wed., Thurs., Sat. and Sun. 10.30-5, or by appointment. SIZE: Medium. *STOCK: Modern British and Irish oil paintings and watercolours.* TEL: 01858 525436. VAT: Spec.

BARNWELL, Nr. Oundle

Berengar Antiques LAPADA
Barnwell Manor. PE8 5JP. (Paul R.M. Howell). Est. 1995. Open 10-5, Sun. by appointment. SIZE: Large. *STOCK: Furniture, 17th-19th C, £500-£50,000; paintings, 17th-20th C, £100-£20,000.* LOC: 5 miles north of A14 (Junc.13) on the A605. PARK: Own. TEL: 01832 274070; home - same; fax - 01832 272726. VAT: Spec.

BRACKLEY

Brackley Antiques
69 High St. NN13 7BW. (Mrs B.H. Nutting). Est. 1977. Open 10-6, Wed. 10-12, Sun. by appointment. SIZE: Medium. *STOCK: Furniture, especially traditionally upholstered, 19th C, £50-£2,000; ceramics, 18th-20th C, £2-£400; interesting and unusual items.* LOC: A43. PARK: Easy. TEL: 01280 703362; home - same. SER: Restorations (furniture and upholstery).

Peter Jackson Antiques
3 Market Place. NN13 7AB. Open 10.30-1 and 2-5. *STOCK: English and Continental porcelain and pottery, 18th-19th C; furniture, paintings, silver, jewellery, glass, watercolours and prints.* TEL: 01280 703259; mobile - 04022 30074. SER: Valuations; restorations.

Juno Antiques
4 Bridge St. NN13 7EP. Open 10-1 and 2-5. CL: Wed. *STOCK: General antiques.* LOC: Northampton/Oxford road. TEL: 01280 700639.

The Old Hall Bookshop
32 Market Place. NN13 7DP. (J. and Lady Juliet Townsend). Est. 1977. Open 9.30-1 and 2-5.30. SIZE: Large. *STOCK: Antiquarian, secondhand and new books and maps.* LOC: Town centre on east side of Market Place. PARK: Easy. TEL: 01280 704146; fax - 01280 705131. VAT: Stan.

Right Angle
24 Manor Rd. NN13 6AJ. Open 9.30-5.30, Wed. 9.30-1. *STOCK: Watercolours, oils, prints and maps.* TEL: 01280 702462. SER: Restorations (frames); gilding and framing.

BRIXWORTH, Nr. Northampton

B.R. & J.B. Gunnett
128 Northampton Rd. NN6 9BU. Open by appointment. *STOCK: Pine and country furniture.* TEL: 01604 880057. SER: Picture framing.

CASTLE ASHBY

Castle Ashby Gallery
The Old Farmyard. NN7 1LF. (G.S. Wright - Fine Paintings). Open 10-5. CL: Mon. *STOCK: Oil paintings - British, 1850-1950, £200-£20,000; significant Contemporary artists.* LOC: Adjacent to Castle Ashby House. PARK: Easy. TEL: 01604 696787; fax - 01604 415055. SER: Valuations; restorations (oils). VAT: Spec.

CROUGHTON, Nr. Brackley

Croughton Antiques
29 High St. NN13 5LT. (L.T. and N. Cross). Est. 1971. Open Wed.-Sun. 10-6 or by appointment. SIZE: Medium. *STOCK: General antiques, decorators' items and shipping goods.* LOC: B4031. PARK: Easy. TEL: 01869 810203.

DESBOROUGH, Nr Kettering

Richard Kimbell Ltd
The Old Bus Station, Harborough Rd. SIZE: Warehouse. *STOCK: Antique pine and country furniture.* TEL: 01536 762093. SER: Shipping and packing; stripping. *Trade only.*

FINEDON

Aspidistra Antiques
51 High St. NN9 5JN. Resident. (Pat and Geoff Moss). Est. 1993. Open Thurs.-Sat. 9-5.30, Sun. 11-5. SIZE: Large. *STOCK: Art Nouveau and Art Deco metal, ceramics, plaster and furniture, £25-£1,000; general antiques, £1-£500.* LOC: Off A14 junction 10 - turn right just before roundabout in village centre. From junction 11, turn right at roundabout and immediate left. PARK: Easy. TEL: 01933 680196; mobile - 0468 071948. SER: Valuations; restorations (furniture); buys at auction. FAIRS: IACF; Alexander Palace, Sandown, NEC.

Simon Banks Antiques
28 Church St. NN9 5NA. (S. Banks). Est. 1984. SIZE: Medium. *STOCK: 17th-20th C furniture, £30-£3,000; glass, silver, ceramics, prints, copper, decorative and collectable items.* TEL: 01933 680371; mobile - 0976 787539. VAT: Stan/Spec.

M.C. Chapman LAPADA
11-25 Bell Hill. NN9 5ND. Est. 1967. Open 9-5.30, Sun. 11-5. SIZE: Large. *STOCK: Furniture, 18th-19th C; clocks, 18th-20th C; both £100-£3,000; decorative items, 19th-20th C.* LOC: 400 yds. off A510. PARK: Easy. TEL: 01933 681260. SER: Container facilities. FAIRS: Newark. VAT: Stan/Spec.

Robert Cheney Antiques
11-13 High St. NN9 5JN. Est. 1991. Open 9-5.30, Sun. 11-5. SIZE: Medium. *STOCK: 18th C furniture, £500-£1,000; 19th C china, £50-£100; 20th C collectables, £5-£25.* LOC: A6. PARK: Easy. TEL: 01933 681048; home - 01933 680085. SER: Valuations.

Finedon continued

E.K. Antiques
37 High St. NN9 5NB. Est. 1967. Open 9.30-5.30, Sun. 11-5. SIZE: Medium- several dealers. *STOCK: Furniture, china, silver, glass, pictures, needlework and decorative items, 1780-1950, £5-£3,500.* PARK: Easy. TEL: 01933 681882; home - 01933 410245. SER: Restorations (furniture); French polishing; period interiors; valuations.

Finedon Antiques (Antiques Centre)
11-25 Bell Hill. NN9 5ND. (M.C. Chapman). Est. 1973. Open 9-5.30, Sun. 11-5. SIZE: Large - 30 dealers. *STOCK: Furniture, ceramics, glass, paintings, prints and clocks, silver and plate, mainly 18th to early 20th C.* LOC: From roundabout at junction of A6 and A510 take A510 towards Wellingborough, turn right after half a mile, premises 400yds. on right. PARK: Easy. TEL: 01933 681260. SER: Export facilities. VAT: Stan/Spec.

FLORE, Nr. Weedon

Huntershield Antiques
The Huntershields. NN7 4LZ. (Mrs. C. Madeira). Est. 1968. Open 9-7, Sun. by appointment. SIZE: Large. *STOCK: Furniture, 17th-19th C, £50-£5,000; decorative items, 19th C, £50-£2,000; metalware, 18th-19th C, £10-£1,000.* LOC: Off M1, junction 16, into Flore, last turning on left, premises on right. PARK: Easy. TEL: 01327 340718; home - same; fax - 01327 349263. VAT: Stan/Spec.

Christopher Jones at Flore House
Flore House, The Avenue. NN2 4LZ. Est. 1977. Open 10-5, Sat. 11-4.30, Sun. by appointment. SIZE: Large. *STOCK: Period and decorative furniture, lighting, porcelain, glass and objects, 18th-20th C.* PARK: Easy. TEL: 01327 342165. SER: Interior decor advice. FAIRS: Olympia. VAT: Spec.

GUILSBOROUGH

Nick Goodwin Exports
The Firs, Nortoft Rd. NN6 8QB. Open every day by appointment. SIZE: Warehouse. *STOCK: Oak, mahogany, walnut, stripped and painted pine, smalls.* TEL: 01280 813115; 01604 740234; fax - same. SER: Restorations; pine stripping, export, shipping and packing; courier.

HARPOLE

Inglenook Antiques
23 High St. NN7 4DH. (T. and P. Havard). Est. 1971. Open 9-7. CL: Wed. SIZE: Small. *STOCK: General antiques, £1-£500.* LOC: In main street. PARK: Easy. TEL: 01604 830007.

HASELBECH, Nr. Northampton

Savage Fine Art — LAPADA
R.S.J. Savage & Son, The Gate House. NN6 9LQ. (Michael Savage). Est. 1905. Open by appointment only. *STOCK: Oils and watercolours, 19th and 20th C; local antiquarian maps and prints, mirrors, work by local artists past and present.* TEL: 01604 686232; fax - 01604 686378. SER: Valuations; restorations (paintings and frames); framing. FAIRS: LAPADA; World of Drawings & Watercolours, Park Lane; Buxton; Snape.

ISLIP, Nr. Thrapston

John Roe Antiques
The Furnace Site, Kettering Rd. NN14 3JW. Est. 1968. Open 9-5.30, Sat. 10-4. *STOCK: General antiques; Continental and American shipping goods.* TEL: 01832 732937. VAT: Stan.

KETTERING

Alexis Brook
74 Lower St. NN16 8DL. (Mrs A. Brook). Est. 1959. Open from 11.30, appointment advisable. CL: Sun. am. SIZE: Medium. *STOCK: General small antiques, £1-£1,500.* LOC: On A6 from Market Harborough. House halfway up hill on left before main shopping centre. PARK: At Collingwood Motors, adjacent. TEL: 01536 513854.

Dragon Antiques
85 Rockingham Rd. NN16 8LA. Open 10-4. CL: Thurs. *STOCK: Watercolours and oils; Oriental items and general antiques.* TEL: 01536 517017. SER: Framing.

C.W. Ward Antiques
Deene House, 40 Lower St. NN16 8DJ. (Mrs J. Wilson). Est. 1912. Open by appointment only. SIZE: Medium. *STOCK: General antiques, furniture, pottery, porcelain, pewter, glass and pictures.* LOC: 25yds. from GPO on A6. PARK: Opposite. TEL: 01536 513537. SER: Valuations; upholstery and curtain making. VAT: Stan.

KINGSTHORPE, Nr. Northampton

Laila Gray Antiques
25 Welford Rd. NN2 8AQ. Open 9-5.30. *STOCK: Pine.* TEL: 01604 715277. SER: Waxing; stripping.

The Old Brigade
10a Harborough Rd. NN2 7AZ. (S.C. Wilson). Est. 1978. Open by appointment. SIZE: Small. *STOCK: Military items, 1850's to 1945, £5-£5,000.* LOC: Junction 15, M1. PARK: Easy. TEL: 01604 719389; fax - 01604 712489. SER: Valuations; illus. catalogue (£4 + SAE). VAT: Stan/Spec.

LONG BUCKBY

Antique Coffee Pot

15 High St. NN6 7RE. Open 8-5, Sun. 11-2. *STOCK: Furniture and bric-a-brac.* TEL: 01327 843849.

R.E. Thompson

17 Church St. NN6 7QH. Est. 1968. Open 8-5. SIZE: Large. *STOCK: Shipping goods, furniture, 19th-20th C; stripped pine, clocks, £1-£1,000.* PARK: Easy. TEL: 01327 842242/843487. VAT: Stan.

NORTHAMPTON

The Bookstore

26 St Michael's Rd. NN1 5NA. (E.J. Whitehouse). Est. 1994. Open 10-6, Sat. 9-6. SIZE: Small. *STOCK: Secondhand, rare and antiquarian books, prints and maps, 1650-1997, 50p-£100.* PARK: Next to shop. TEL: 01604 620800; home - 01604 621064. SER: Valuations.

F. and C.H. Cave

111 Kettering Rd. NN1 4BA. Est. 1879. Open 9-5.30. CL: Thurs. SIZE: Large. *STOCK: Furniture - Georgian, Victorian and decorative; general antiques.* LOC: Near town centre, quarter mile outside pedestrianised area. PARK: Adjoining side streets. TEL: 01604 638278. VAT: Spec.

Hickey Books

Market Hall. (Karl J. Hickey). Est. 1997. Wed.and Fri. 9-4, Sat. 9-5. SIZE: Small. *STOCK: Books, 1800 to modern, 50p to £100; comics, 1950's to date, 50p to £75; prints, 1800 to date, £3-£20.* LOC: Top of The Drapery, opposite Market Sq. PARK: Nearby.

Michael Jones Jeweller

1 Gold St. NN1 1SA. Est. 1919. *STOCK: Silver, gold and gem jewellery, French and carriage clocks.* TEL: 01604 32548. VAT: Stan/Spec.

Occultique

73 Kettering Rd. NN1 4AW. (M.J. Lovett). Est. 1973. Open 10-5. SIZE: Small. *STOCK: Books, 50p-£500.* PARK: Nearby. TEL: 01604 27727; fax - 01604 603860. VAT: Stan.

Penny's Antiques

83 Kettering Rd. NN1 4AW. (Mrs P. Mawby). Est. 1976. Open 11-4, Sat. 10-5. CL: Thurs. SIZE: Small. *STOCK: Shipping goods, kitchen chairs, pictures, army badges, furniture, china, smalls, glass and brass, Victorian to 1940, £5-£100.* LOC: On A43 near town centre. PARK: Easy. TEL: 01604 32429.

PAULERSPURY, Nr. Towcester

The Antique Galleries BADA

Watling St. NN12 6LQ. (M. Cameron). Est.

Paulerspury continued

1948. Open 10-5.30. SIZE: Large. *STOCK: English furniture, 1650-1830; barometers, 1780-1830.* LOC: 3 miles south of Towcester on A5. PARK: Own. TEL: 01327 811238. VAT: Spec.

POTTERSPURY, Nr. Towcester

Reindeer Antiques Ltd BADA LAPADA

43 Watling St. NN12 7QD. (J.W. Butterworth). Est. 1959. Open 9-6. SIZE: Large. *STOCK: Period English furniture, paintings, metal, clocks, garden furniture and statuary.* LOC: A5. TEL: 01908 542407/542200; fax - 01908 542121. VAT: Stan/Spec.

RUSHDEN

Magpies

1 East Grove. NN10 0AP. (Jim and Janet Ward). 1993. Open 10-5, Sun. 12-4. SIZE: Large. *STOCK: Furniture, £20-£1,000; china, glass, kitchenalia and bric-a-brac, £1-£25; all 19th-20th C.* LOC: A6 south on one-way system, first left after passing old station. PARK: Easy. TEL: 01933 411404.

D.W. Sherwood Antiques Ltd

59 Little St. NN10 0LS. Est. 1960. *STOCK: General antiques.* TEL: 01933 353265.

TOWCESTER

Clark Galleries

215 Watling St. NN12 6BX. FABPR. (A. Clark). Est. 1964. Open 8.30-5.30, Sat. 9.30-4. SIZE: Medium. *STOCK: Landscape paintings, 18th C, £500-£15,000; portraits, 17th-18th C, £500-£5,000.* LOC: M1, junction 15, on A5. PARK: Easy and at rear. TEL: 01327 352957. SER: Valuations; restorations and re-lining (oil paintings). VAT: Stan/Spec.

Ron Green

227-239 Watling St. West. NN12 7BX. Est. 1952. Open 9-6 or by appointment. SIZE: Large. *STOCK: English and Continental furniture, £30-£30,000; oil paintings, £100-£10,000; decorative items.* TEL: 01327 350387/350615.

R. and M. Nicholas

161 Watling St. NN12 6BX. Open 9.30-5. SIZE: Small. *STOCK: 18th-19th C porcelain, silver and glass.* TEL: 01327 350639.

Towcester continued

Shelron Collectors Shop

9 1/2 Brackley Rd. NN12 6DH. PTA. Resident. (R. Grosvenor). Est. 1973. Open Tues.-Fri. 10-4, Sat. 10-1. SIZE: Medium. *STOCK: Postcards, from 1890; cigarette and trade cards, from 1880; ephemera, bric-a-brac, books, prints, models, £1-£100.* LOC: Leave M1, junction 15A, 100yds. from A5 traffic lights going west. PARK: Easy. TEL: 01327 350242. SER: Valuations (postcards and cigarette cards).

UPPER BODDINGTON

Doric Antiques LAPADA

Cherry Tree House, Warwick Rd. NN11 6DH. (Keith and Jane Riley). Est. 1975. SIZE: Medium. *STOCK: English oak, 17th-19th C, £50-£5,000; associated items and pottery.* LOC: Midway between Banbury and Daventry. PARK: Easy. TEL: 01327 263125; home - same. SER: Buys at auction (country furniture). FAIRS: NEC; ICAF. VAT: Stan/Spec.

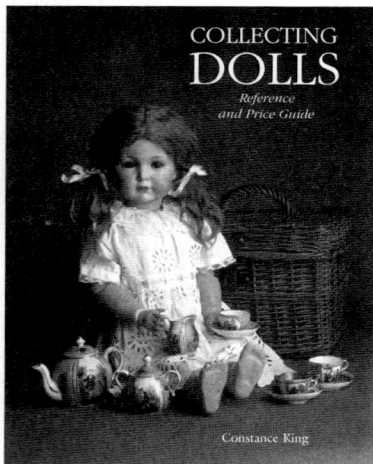

WEEDON

Architectural Heritage of Northants

The Woodyard. NN7 4LB. Open Tues.-Sat. 10-5, Sun. 11-5. *STOCK: Architectural antiques.* LOC: A5, 2 miles north of Weedon. TEL: 01327 349249; fax - 01327 349397.

Helios & Co (Antiques)

25/27 High St. NN7 4QD. (J. Skiba and B. Walters). Open 9-6 including Sun. SIZE: Large. *STOCK: English and Continental furniture especially dining tables; decorative accessories.* PARK: Easy. TEL: 01327 340264; fax - 01327 342235. SER: Suppliers and restorers to H. M. Govt. VAT: Spec.

Rococo Antiques and Interiors

5 New St., Lower Weedon. NN7 4QS. Resident. (N.K. Griffiths). Usually available. *STOCK: Ironwork, brass and iron beds, fireplaces, pine furniture, sanitary ware - toilets, sinks, taps.* LOC: 3 miles junction 16, M1, quarter mile off A5. PARK: Easy. TEL: 01327 341288. VAT: Stan/Spec.

The Village Antique Market

62 High St. NN7 4QD. (E.A. and J.M. Saunders). Est. 1967. Open 9.30-5.30, Sun. 10.30-5.30. SIZE: Large - 40 dealers. *STOCK: General antiques and interesting items.* LOC: On A45, just off A5. PARK: At side of market. TEL: 01327 342015.

WELLINGBOROUGH

Antiques and Bric-a-Brac Market

Market Sq. NN8 1BN. Open Tues. 9-4. SIZE: 135 stalls. *STOCK: General antiques and collectables.* LOC: Town Centre.

Park Gallery & Bookshop

16 Cannon St. NN8 5DJ. (Mrs J.A. Foster). Est. 1979. Open 10-5.30. SIZE: Medium. *STOCK: Books, maps and prints, 18th-19th C, £2-£300.* LOC: Continuation of A510 into town. PARK: Easy. TEL: 01933 222592.

Bryan Perkins Antiques

Finedon Rd. NN8 4DJ. (J., B.H. and S.C. Perkins). Est. 1971. Open 9-5. CL: Sat. pm. SIZE: Large. *STOCK: Furniture and paintings, 19th C, £200-£2,000; small items.* PARK: Easy. TEL: 01933 228812; home - 01536 790259. SER: Valuations; restorations (furniture). VAT: Spec. *Trade Only.*

WEST HADDON

The Country Pine Shop

The Romney Building, Northampton Rd. NN6 7AS. (Ryan and Dodd). Est. 1985. Open 8-5. SIZE: Large. *STOCK: English and Continental stripped pine, £30-£1,200.* LOC: A428. TEL: 01788 510430.

West Haddon continued

Paul Hopwell Antiques BADA LAPADA

30 High St. NN6 7AP. Est. 1974. Open 9-6. CL: Sun. except by appointment. SIZE: Large. *STOCK: 17th-18th C oak and walnut country furniture, longcase clocks, metalware: oil paintings and prints mainly sporting and country pursuits.* LOC: A428. PARK: Easy. TEL: 01788 510636; fax - 01788 510044. SER: Valuations; restorations (furniture and metalware); buys at auction. VAT: Spec.

Mark Seabrook Antiques

9 West End. NN6 7AY. Open 10-5.30. SIZE: Medium. *STOCK: Country furniture, period metalware, brass and copper, treen and other domestic items.* LOC: A428. PARK: Easy. TEL: 01788 510772; home - 01480 861339.

WOODFORD HALSE, Nr. Daventry

The Corner Cupboard

18 & 28 Station Rd. NN11 6RB. (Mr and Mrs J.R. Bacon). Est. 1980. Open 9-7 six days a week. CL: Tues. SIZE: Medium. *STOCK: English and Continental stripped pine, Victorian and Edwardian, £50-£1,000; iron and brass beds, Victorian, £175-£650; sofas, chairs, chesterfields, Victorian, £50-£450.* LOC: Off A361 towards village. After 1 mile turn right up Phipps Rd. to village centre, shops in parade at top of hill. PARK: Easy. TEL: 01327 260725; home - same.

Northumberland

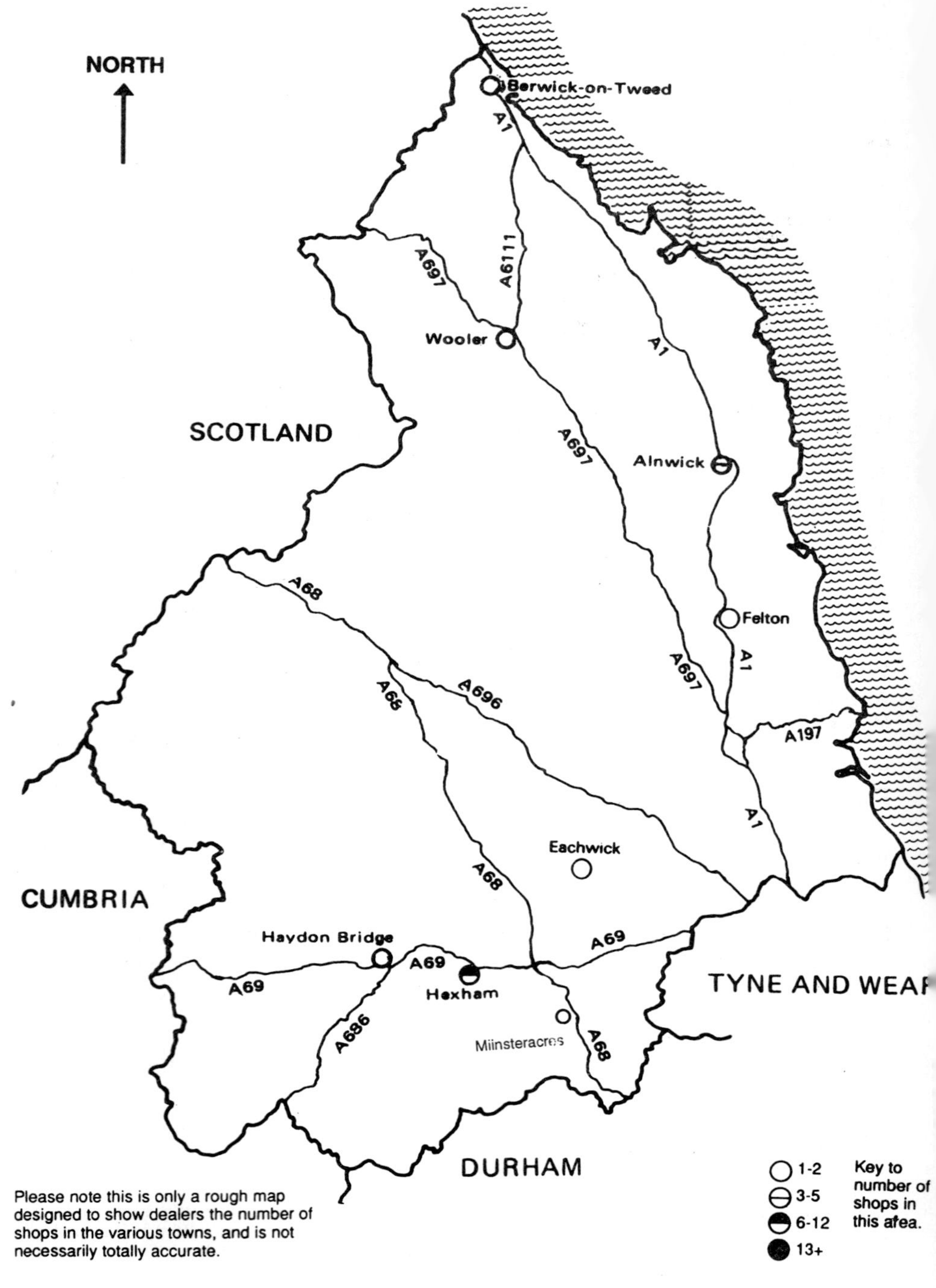

Please note this is only a rough map designed to show dealers the number of shops in the various towns, and is not necessarily totally accurate.

ALNWICK

G.M. Athey
Castle Corner, Narrowgate. NE66 0NP. *STOCK: English oak, mahogany furniture, glass, china and brass, 18th-19th C.* TEL: 01665 604229.

Bailiffgate Antique Pine
22 Bailiffgate. NE66 1LX. (S. Aston). Est. 1994. Open Thurs.-Sat. 10-4.30. SIZE: Large. *STOCK: Country pine furniture.* LOC: Opposite the castle. PARK: Easy. TEL: 01665 603616. SER: Valuations; restorations; buys at auction.

Tamblyn
12 Bondgate Without. NE66 1PP. (Mrs S.M. Hirst). Est. 1981. Open 10-4.30. SIZE: Medium. *STOCK: General antiques including country furniture, pottery, pictures; antiquities, glass, to 20th C, £5-£1,500.* LOC: Diagonally opposite war memorial at southern entrance to town. PARK: Easy. TEL: 01665 603024; home - same. SER: Valuations.

BERWICK-ON-TWEED

Treasure Chest
43 Bridge St. TD15 2DX. (Y. Scott). Est. 1988. Open 10.30-4. SIZE: Medium. *STOCK: China, jewellery, glass, silver plate and small furniture, from 1860, £5-£150.* LOC: Approximately 1 mile from A1. PARK: Easy. TEL: Home - 01289 307736. SER: Restorations (china). FAIRS: Local.

EACHWICK

Hazel Cottage Clocks
Hazel Cottage. NE18 0BE. (E. and M. Charlton). Open 9.30-5.30. SIZE: Medium. *STOCK: Clocks, £300-£8,000.* LOC: Just off Darras Hall to Stamfordham road, opposite Wylam turn-off. PARK: Easy. TEL: 01661 852415. SER: Restorations and repairs (clocks). VAT: Spec.

FELTON, Nr. Morpeth

Felton Park Antiques
Felton Park. NE65 9HN. Resident. (D. and A. Burton). Est. 1973. By appointment only. *STOCK: Pottery and porcelain, 1795-1935.* PARK: Easy. TEL: 01670 787319. SER: Valuations; restorations; polishing.

HAYDON BRIDGE, Nr. Hexham

Haydon Bridge Antiques
3 Shaftoe St. NE47 6BQ. (J. and J. Smith). Est. 1974. Open 10.30-5 and by appointment. CL: Mon. and Thurs. SIZE: Large. *STOCK: Stripped pine, £5-£500; Victorian and Edwardian oak and mahogany, shipping goods, Victorian oils and watercolours.* PARK: Easy. TEL: 01434 684200; home - 01434 684461. VAT: Stan.

Haydon Bridge continued

Haydon Gallery
3 Shaftoe St. NE47 6BQ. (J. Smith). Est. 1975. Open 10.30-5.30, Sun., Mon. and Thurs. by appointment. SIZE: Small. *STOCK: Oils and watercolours by North Eastern artists and others, mainly 19th C; some bronzes.* TEL: 01434 684200; home - 01434 684461. SER: Valuations; restorations (oil paintings).

HEXHAM

Boadens Antiques LAPADA
29 and 30 Market Place. NE46 3PB. (R.J. Boaden). Est. 1948. Open 9-5. SIZE: Large. *STOCK: Small furniture, antique and Victorian, £100-£3,000; Victorian bric-a-brac, £10-£500; paintings, 19th-20th C, £50-£1,000; Victorian jewellery, from £30.* LOC: Opposite Hexham Abbey, off A69. PARK: Nearby. TEL: 01434 603187. SER: Valuations; jewellery repairs. VAT: Stan/Spec.

Gordon Caris
16 Market Place. NE46 1XQ. Est. 1972. Open 9-5. CL: Thurs. *STOCK: Clocks and watches.* TEL: 01434 602106. SER: Restorations (clocks and watches).

Victorian occasional table, painted with flowers, heightened in gilt and mother-of-pearl, £748, May 1997.

From an article entitled "English Papier Mâché" by Paul Davidson which appeared in the July/August 1997 issue of **Antique Collecting**

Hexham continued

Hallstile Antiques

17 Hallstile Bank. NE46 3PG. (Mrs P. Neumann). Est. 1982. Open 10-5. CL: Thurs. SIZE: Large. *STOCK: Furniture, 18th to early 20th C, 50-£5,000; paintings and prints, £15-£400; clocks, silver plate, china, porcelain and glass.* LOC: Town centre, just off Market Place. PARK: Nearby. TEL: 01434 602239. SER: Buys at auction.

Hedley's of Hexham

3 St. Mary's Chare. NE46 1NQ. (P. Torday). Est. 1819. Open 9-5. SIZE: Medium. *STOCK: Furniture, 17th C to Edwardian; porcelain, silver and glass, 18th-20th C.* LOC: Off Market Place. PARK: 200 yds. TEL: 01434 602317. SER: Valuations; restorations. VAT: Stan/Spec.

Hexham Antiques (Inc. Hotspur Antiques)

6 Rear Battle Hill. NE46 1BB. (J. and D. Latham). Est. 1977. Open 10.30-4, Sat. 9.30-4. CL: Wed. and Thurs. SIZE: Large. *STOCK: Furniture, clocks, pictures, glass, china, boxes and collectors' items, to Art Deco.* LOC: Main shopping street, opposite NatWest Bank. PARK: 400 metres. TEL: 01434 603851; home - 01434 604813. SER: Valuations; buys at auction.

The Violin Shop

27 Hencotes. NE46 2EQ. (N. Cain and D. Mann). Est. 1970. Open 10-5 or by appointment. *STOCK: Violins, violas, cellos, basses and bows.* TEL: 01434 607897.

MINSTERACRES

Minsteracres Pine & Oak

Ivy Cottage. DH8 9RR. Est. 1984. Open by appointment. SIZE: Medium. *STOCK: Stripped pine including wardrobes, dressers; also pine furniture made to order in reclaimed wood, oak furniture to order.* LOC: Turn into Minsteracres monastry off A68. PARK: Easy. TEL: 01434 682601; home - same; workshop - 01434 673075.

WOOLER

Hamish Dunn Antiques

17 High St. NE71 6BU. Est. 1986. Open 9.30-12 and 1-4.30, Thurs. 9.30-12. SIZE: Medium. *STOCK: Curios and collectables, 19th-20th C, £5-£500; antiquarian and secondhand books, 18th-20th C, £1-£200; small furniture, 19th-20th C, £15-£1,000.* LOC: Off A697. PARK: Easy. TEL: 01668 281341; home - 01668 282013. VAT: Stan/Spec.

James Miller Antiques LAPADA

1-5 Church St. NE71 6BZ. Est. 1947. Open Mon.-Fri. 9.30-5. SIZE: Large, and warehouses. *STOCK: Georgian, Regency and Victorian furniture.* LOC: A697. PARK: Nearby. TEL: 01668 281500; fax - 01668 282383; home - 01668 217281. VAT: Stan/Spec.

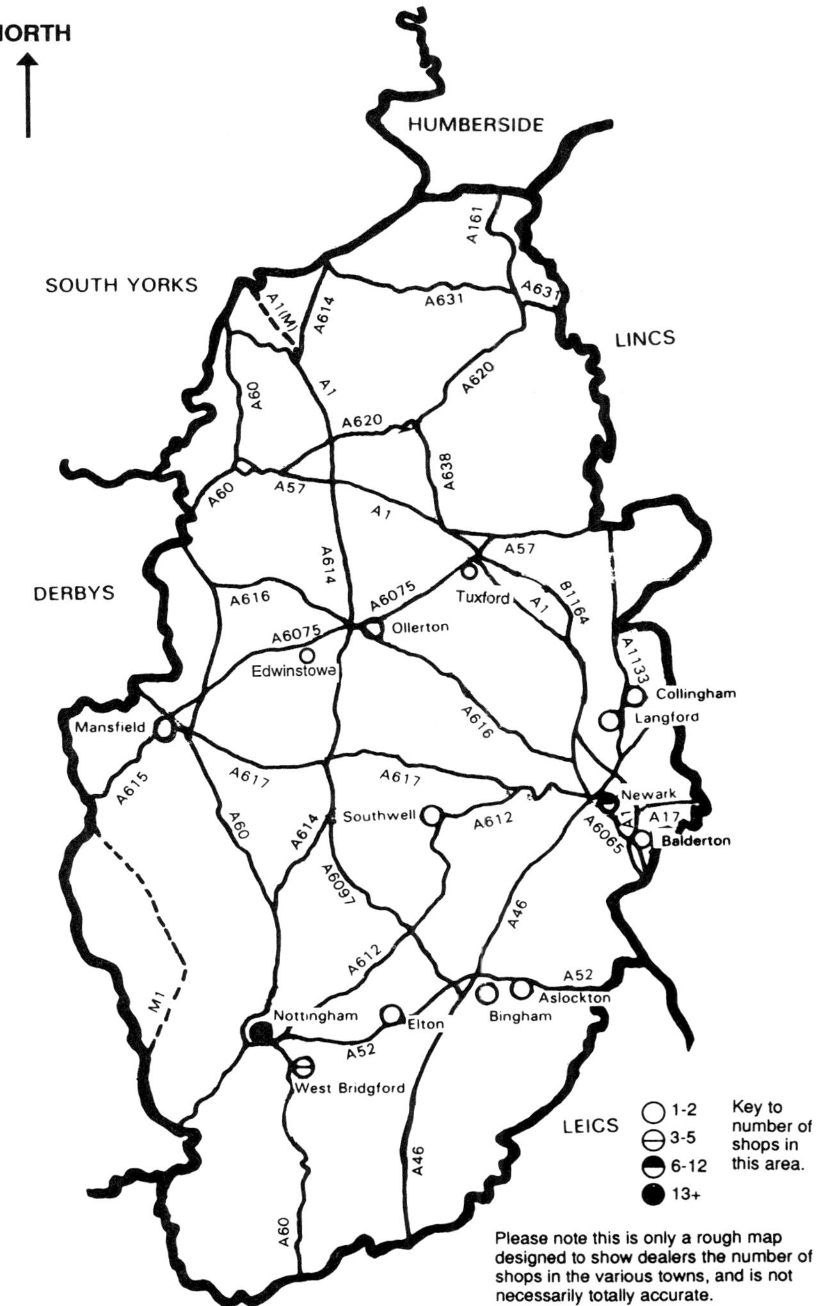

Please note this is only a rough map designed to show dealers the number of shops in the various towns, and is not necessarily totally accurate.

ASLOCKTON, Nr. Nottingham

Jane Neville Gallery

Elm House, Abbey Lane. NG13 9AE. Resident. (R. Repetto-Wright and J. Neville). Est. 1979. Open 10-4. SIZE: Medium. *STOCK: Paintings and prints including sporting, 19th-20th C, £50-£5,000.* LOC: A52. PARK: Easy. TEL: 01949 850220. SER: Valuations; restorations; framing; research; print publishers; buys at auction (sporting paintings). VAT: Stan/Spec.

BALDERTON

Blacksmiths Forge

74 Main St. NG24 3NP. (K. and J. Sheppard). Est. 1982. Open 9-6, Sun. by appointment. SIZE: Small. *STOCK: Original pine furniture, kitchenalia, architectural items - doors, fireplaces, cast iron and pine surrounds, Georgian to 1920, £20-£450; original beds, mainly Victorian, £100-£650.* LOC: Off A1, follow signs to village, turn right at traffic lights, shop on right next to church. PARK: Easy. TEL: 01636 700008; home - same. SER: Valuations; restorations; stripping; polishing; buys at auction (furniture).

BINGHAM

E.M. Cheshire — BADA LAPADA

Banks House, The Banks. NG13 8BT. By appointment only. *STOCK: Furniture, 17th C oak; 18th-19th C mahogany, early metalware.* TEL: 01949 838861/838455. FAIRS: All premier. VAT: Stan/Spec.

COLLINGHAM, Nr. Newark

The Barn

NG23 7NL. (J. Richardson). Open by appointment. *STOCK: 18th-19th C furniture and furnishings, treen, textiles, linen and lace, Baxter prints and licencees, Stevengraphs.* TEL: 01636 892884.

EDWINSTOWE, Nr Mansfield

Occleshaw Antiques Centre

The Old Major Cinema, 11 Mansfield Rd. NG21 9NL. (G. Occleshaw). Est. 1995. Open 10-5, including Sun. SIZE: Large. *STOCK: Furniture, Georgian, Victorian, £50-£1,000; brass, metalware, pottery, porcelain, glass, books, fireplaces, Georgian to 1950s; jewellery, pictures, cameras, clocks, militaria, Georgianto date, £5-£1,000.* LOC: A614 Nottingham road, village centre. PARK: Easy, own. TEL: 01623 825370; fax - 0115 953 0409; mobile - 0498 864104. SER: Valuations; restorations (furniture, book-binding); French polishing; upholstery.

ELTON, Nr. Bingham

Rectory Bungalow Workshop

Main Rd. NG13 9LF. (E.M. and Mrs M.G. Mackie). Est. 1981. Open Sat. 9.30-4.30 in summer, 10-12 and 2-3 in winter, other times by

Elton continued

appointment. SIZE: Small. *STOCK: Furniture, 18th-20th C; hand-painted, decorative items.* LOC: A52 between Nottingham and Grantham, near Granby/Orston crossroads. PARK: Easy. TEL: 01949 850330/850878; home - same. SER: Restorations (cane and rush seating).

LANGFORD, Nr. Newark

T. Baker

Langford House Farm. NG23 7RR. Est. 1966. CL: Sun. except by appointment and Sat. SIZE: Medium. *STOCK: Victoriana, period furniture and oak.* LOC: A1133. PARK: Own. TEL: 01636 704026. *Trade Only.*

MANSFIELD

The Book Shelf

7A Albert St. NG18 1EA. (S. Payton). Open 9.30-5. CL: Wed. SIZE: Medium. *STOCK: Antiquarian and secondhand books.* LOC: Town centre. TEL: 01623 648231; home - 01623 640601. SER: Book search.

Fair Deal Antiques

138 Chesterfield Rd. North. NG19 7JD. (D. Lowe). Est. 1972. Open 9.30-5.30. CL: Sat. pm. and Sun. except by appointment. SIZE: Large. *STOCK: Shipping goods, £50-£100; furniture, mainly mahogany, Victorian, £100-£1,000; period furniture, metalware and small items.* PARK: Easy. TEL: 01623 653768/512419. VAT: Stan. *Trade Only.*

NEWARK

Castle Gate Antiques Centre

55 Castle Gate. NG24 1BE. Est. 1985. Open 9.30-5. SIZE: Large. LOC: A46 through town, 250yds. from castle. PARK: Easy. TEL: 01636 700076. SER: Restorations. Below are listed the dealers at this centre.

& Barrington

Fine antique and modern silver. TEL: 0850 577724.

N. Bryan-Peach Antiques

18th-19th C furniture, clocks and barometers, metalware, £50-£3,000. TEL: Home - 01509 880425. VAT: Stan/Spec.

Evelyn Buckle Antiques

Oak and mahogany furniture, 18th-19th C; decorative items. TEL: Home - 01476 870796. VAT: Stan/Spec.

Mrs E.M. Cheshire BADA LAPADA

***18th and 19th C furniture and related items.* TEL: 01949 838455.**

Sylvia Cozens

Victorian and Edwardian mahogany furniture.

Newark continued

Leasingham Antiques

18th-19th C mahogany and porcelain.

Parkside Antiques

Georgian and Victorian furniture, £100-£3,500. TEL: Home - 0115 920 9734. VAT: Stan/Spec.

Margaret M. Thompson Antiques LAPADA

***19th C oak and mahogany furniture, pictures and decorative items.* TEL: Home - 01949 850204. SER: Valuations. VAT: Stan/Spec.**

John Winterbotham

Oak and country furniture, 17th and 18th C.

R.R. Limb Antiques

31-35 Northgate. NG24 1HD. Open 9-6. *STOCK: General antiques and pianos.* TEL: 01636 674546.

Newark Antiques Centre

Regent House, Lombard St. NG24 1XP. (Marks Tinsley). Open 9.30-5, Sun. 11-4. SIZE: 55 units and 30 cabinets. *STOCK: Georgian, Victorian and period furniture, pottery, porcelain, glass, textiles, militaria, clocks, pictures, books, silver, antiquities, jewellery, paintings, coins, Oriental, pine, oil lamps.* TEL: 01636 605504.

Newark Antiques Warehouse

Old Kelham Rd. NG24 1BX. Open 8.30-5.30, Sat. 10-4. LOC: Just off A1. PARK: Easy. TEL: 01636 674869; fax - 01636 612933. Below are listed the dealers at this warehouse. *Trade Only.*

A. M. Antiques

17th-19th C furniture. VAT: Stan/Spec.

Atkinson Antiques

17th-19th C furniture and architectural items. VAT: Stan/Spec.

Chris Baylis

Windsor chairs and country furniture.

B. Benson

Furniture, clocks and decorative items.

G. Brodie

Period furniture.

M. Chapman

18th-19th C furniture.

Clare Cottage Antiques

19th C furniture.

John Dench Antiques

17th-19th C furniture, English pottery, decorative items, longcase clocks. VAT: Stan/Spec.

Dukeries Antiques

(J. and J. Coupe). *17th-19th C furniture; vintage and classic cars.* VAT: Stan/Spec.

Hexham continued

D.J. Green Antiques
Furniture and decorative items. VAT: Stan/Spec.

R. Harrison
17th-19th C furniture.

John Hetherington
17th-18th C oak furniture.

Highfields Antiques
19th C mahogany, walnut and shipping furniture. VAT: Stan/Spec.

R. Leverton
19th C and shipping furniture.

Mansfield Antiques
18th-19th C furniture and decorative items. VAT: Stan/Spec.

St. Georges Antiques
17th-19th C furniture. VAT: Stan/Spec.

Charles Walmsley Restorations

Wickersley Antiques
Mainly Victorian and Edwardian furniture. VAT: Stan/Spec.

Portland Antiques
20 Portland St. NG24 4XG. Est. 1968. Open 9.30-5. CL: Mon.-Thurs. SIZE: Medium. *STOCK: General antiques and smalls, shipping items, £5-£1,000.* LOC: A46, 2 mins. from town centre. PARK: At rear. TEL: 01636 701478. SER: Valuations.

Portland Street Antiques Centre
Portland St. NG24 4XF. (Barbara Conlon). Est. 1972. Open 10-5. SIZE: 100 dealers. *STOCK: Furniture, Art Deco, clocks including longcase, silver, glass, ceramics, militaria, toys, dolls and taxidermy, mainly 18th-19th C, £1-£5,000.* LOC: A46 200 yards from traffic lights in town centre. PARK: Own at rear. TEL: 01636 674397; home - 01636 702836.

Jack Spratt Antiques
Unit 5, George St. NG24 1LU. Open 8-5.30, Sat. 8-4, Sun. 10.30-3.30. SIZE: Warehouse. *STOCK: Pine and oak.* PARK: Easy. TEL: 01636 681666/7; fax - 01636 681700. VAT: Stan.

Tudor Rose Antiques Centre
12-13 Market Place. NG24 1DU. Open 10-5. SIZE: 25 cabinets + 10 stands. *STOCK: Furniture including oak and country, pine, mahogany and fine; metalware, copper, brass and silver, militaria, clocks, English, Continental and Oriental porcelain, pottery, glass, decorative items and soft furnishings, treen, toys, pictures and linen, dateline 1940.* PARK: Nearby. TEL: 01636 610311. VAT: Stan/Spec.

NOTTINGHAM

N.J. Doris - 'Dorisbooks'
Cathedral Antiques, 66-68 Derby Rd. NG1 5FD. Open 9.30-5. *STOCK: Books, antiquarian and secondhand; music, maps and prints.* TEL: 0115 947 3913; fax - same; e-mail - treasure@btinternet.com; internet - http://www.btinternet.com/treasure.

The Golden Cage
99 Derby Rd., Canning Circus. NG5 4FE. (J. Pearson and D. Walker). Open 10-5. *STOCK: Formal wear to buy or hire.* TEL: 0115 9411600/9476478. SER: Hire (including 20's-40's and period costume); clothes copied to order.

Granny's Attic
308 Carlton Hill, Carlton. NG4 1GD. (Mrs A. Pembleton). Open Tues., Thurs., Fri. and Sat. 9-5. *STOCK: Dolls, miniatures, general antiques and furniture.* TEL: 0115 9265204.

Harlequin Antiques
79 Mansfield Rd., Daybrook. (P.R. Hinchley and J.W. Attenborough). Est. 1992. Open daily, Sun. by appointment. SIZE: Medium. *STOCK: 18th-19th C pine furniture, £300-£1,200; oak and mahogany, 18th to early 19th C, £300-£1,000.* LOC: A60 Mansfield road, north from Nottingham. PARK: Easy. TEL: 01159 674590; home - 01159 654197/569117. SER: Valuations; restorations (oak and mahogany). FAIRS: Newark. VAT: Stan/Spec.

Hockley Coins
170 Derby Rd. NG7 1LR. (D.T. Peake). Open 10-4. CL: Thurs. *STOCK: Coins, medals, badges, postcards, cigarette cards, toys, silver, collectables.* TEL: 0115 9790667.

Melville Kemp Ltd LAPADA
79-81 Derby Rd. NG1 5BA. Est. 1900. Open 9-5.30. CL: Thurs. SIZE: Small. *STOCK: Jewellery, Victorian; silver, Georgian and Victorian, both £5-£10,000; ornate English and Continental porcelain, Sheffield plate.* LOC: From Nottingham on main Derby Rd. PARK: Easy. TEL: 0115 9417055; fax - 0115 9417055. SER: Valuations; restorations (silver, china, jewellery); buys at auction. VAT: Stan/Spec.

Michael D. Long - Trident Arms
96-98 Derby Rd. NG1 5FB. Est. 1970. Open 9.30-5, Sat. 10-4. SIZE: Large. *STOCK: Arms and armour of all ages and nations.* LOC: From city centre take main Derby Rd., shop on right. PARK: Easy. TEL: 0115 9474137; fax - 0115 9414199. SER: Valuations. VAT: Stan/Spec.

Nottingham continued

Meadow Lane Antiques

Meadow Lane. NG2 3HG. (Dave Buckley). Open 8-6, Sat. 7.30-2.30 and Sun. prior to Newark Antiques Fair. SIZE: Large warehouse. *STOCK: Period, Victorian and Edwardian furniture and shipping goods, smalls and bric-a-brac for US, European and Japanese markets.* LOC: Opposite Arthur Johnson's Auction Rooms, near Trent bridge. 30 minutes from Newark Showground. TEL: 0115 9867374; fax - 0115 9867375; e-mail - antiques@mcmail.com. SER: Container packing; export facilities.

Anthony Mitchell Fine Paintings

Sunnymede House, 11 Albemarle Rd., Woodthorpe. NG5 4FE. (M. Mitchell). Est. 1965. Open by appointment. *STOCK: Oil paintings, £2,000-£100,000; watercolours, £500-£30,000.* LOC: North on Nottingham ring road to junction with Mansfield road, turn right, then 3rd left. PARK: Easy. TEL: 0115 9623865; fax - same. SER: Valuations; restorations. VAT: Spec.

Pegasus Antiques

62 Derby Rd. NG1 5FD. (P. and J. Clewer). Est. 1985. Open 9.30-5. *STOCK: English furniture and decorative antiques, mainly Georgian and Victorian; brass, copper, silver, jewellery and Staffordshire figures, 19th C.* TEL: 0115 9474220. SER: Stockist of Liberon Restoration products.

S. Pembleton

306 Carlton Hill, Carlton. Open Tues., Thurs. and Fri. 9-5, Sat. 10-5. *STOCK: General antiques.* TEL: 0115 9265204.

David and Carole Potter Antiques

LAPADA

76 Derby Rd. NG1 5FD. Est. 1966. Open by appointment only. SIZE: Medium. *STOCK: Clocks, 18th-19th C, £50-£5,000; period furniture, 17th-19th C; pottery, porcelain and glass, 18th-19th C, £20-£7,000; trade and shipping goods.* LOC: From Nottingham centre, take main Derby Rd., shop on right. PARK: Easy. TEL: 0115 9417911; mobile - 0973 689962. VAT: Stan/Spec.

Val Smith Coins and Antiques

170 Derby Rd. NG7 1LR. Open 10-4.30. CL: Thurs. *STOCK: Coins, medals, badges, postcards, cigarette cards, toys, jewellery, small collectables.* TEL: 0115 9781194.

Top Hat Antiques Centre

70-72 Derby Rd. NG1 3EN. (Top Hat Exhibitions). Est. 1978. Open 9.30-5. SIZE: Large. *STOCK: Furniture, Georgian to Edwardian; small porcelain and metal items, to Art Deco; oils, watercolours and prints, 19th-20th C, £30-£1,000.* LOC: A52 town centre. PARK: Easy. TEL: 0115 9419143; home - 0115 9258769. VAT: Stan/Spec.

Nottingham continued

Vintage Wireless Shop

The Hewarths, Sandiacre. NG10 5NQ. (Mr Yates). *STOCK: Early wireless and pre-war televisions, crystal sets, horn speakers, valves, books and magazines.* TEL: 0115 9393139; fax - 0115 9490180; mobile - 0860 362655.

OLLERTON

Hamlyn Lodge

Station Rd. NG22 9BN. (N., J.S. and M.J. Barrows). Open 10-5, Sat. and Sun. by appointment. SIZE: Small. *STOCK: General antiques, 18th-19th C, £100-£3,000.* LOC: Off A614. PARK: Easy. TEL: 01623 823600. SER: Restorations (furniture).

SOUTHWELL

Strouds (of Southwell Antiques)

3-7 Church St. NG25 0HQ. (V.N. and J. Stroud). Est. 1972. Open 9.30-5, or by appointment. SIZE: Large. *STOCK: Furniture, clocks, metalware and decorative items, 17th-19th C, £10-£50,000.* LOC: Town centre. PARK: Easy. TEL: 01636 815001. VAT: Stan/Spec.

TUXFORD

Sally Mitchell's Gallery

9 Eldon St. NG22 0LB. FATG. Est. 1966. Open 10-5, Sun. by appointment. SIZE: Medium. *STOCK: Contemporary sporting and animal paintings, £200-£5,000; limited edition sporting and animal prints, 20th C, £20-£350; sporting paintings.* LOC: 1 minute from A1, 14 miles north of Newark. PARK: Easy. TEL: 01777 838 234/655. FAIRS: CLA Game and Burghley Horse Trials. VAT: Stan/Spec.

WEST BRIDGFORD

Bridgford Antiques

2A Rushworth Ave. NG2 7LF. Open 10-5, Sat. 10-1. SIZE: Small. *STOCK: Furniture and general antiques, pictures, books and postcards.* LOC: Opposite County Hall. TEL: 0115 9821835; home - 0115 9817161.

Joan Cotton (Antiques)

5 Davies Rd. NG2 5JE. Est. 1969. Open 9-4.30. CL: Wed. *STOCK: General antiques, Victoriana, jewellery, silver, china, glass and bygones.* LOC: 1/2 mile along Bridgford Rd. from Trent Bridge, in town centre. PARK: On forecourt. TEL: 0115 9813043.

Moulton's Antiques

5 Portland Rd. NG2 6DN. (J. Moulton). Open 10-5. CL: Mon. *STOCK: General antiques; fabrics.* TEL: 0115 9814354. SER: Restorations (furniture); stripping (pine); pine furniture made to order.

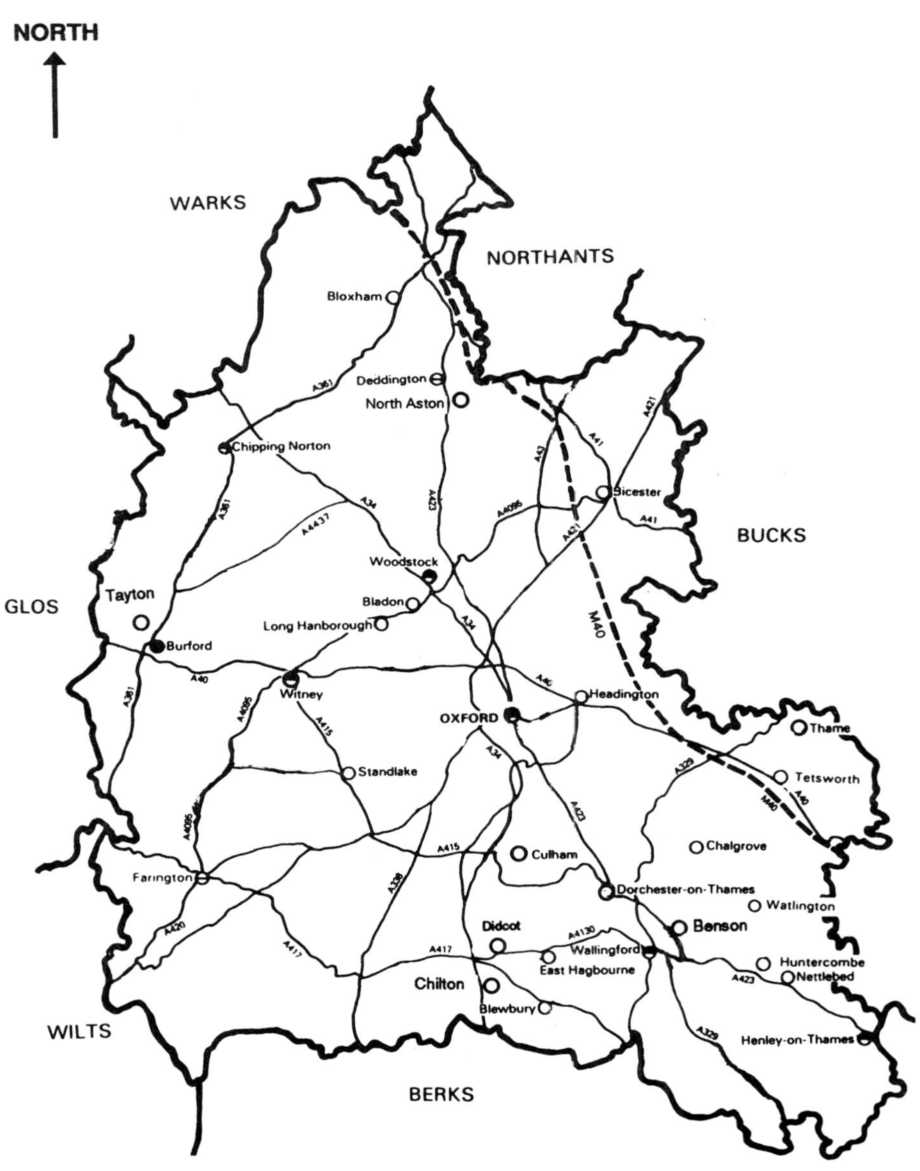

○ 1-2
⊖ 3-5
◓ 6-12
● 13+

Key to number of shops in this area.

Please note this is only a rough map designed to show dealers the number of shops in the various towns, and is not necessarily totally accurate.

ASTON TIRROLD, Nr. Didcot

John Harrison Fine Art

Skirmers, Aston St. OX11 9DQ. TVADA. (J.M.C. Harrison). Strictly by appointment. *STOCK: Drawings and watercolours, 18th-19th C.* TEL: 01235 850260. SER: Commissions undertaken.

BENSON, Nr. Wallingford

Benson Antiques Centre & Gallery

The Old Bakehouse, Castle Sq. OX10 6SD. TVADA. (Dane Clouston). Est. 1978. Open 10-5, Sun. 2-5. CL: Mon. SIZE: Medium. *STOCK: Furniture, 17th to early 20th C, £100-£5,000; ceramics, glass, silver, 18th to early 20th C, £5-£1,000; bronze, pewter, oils and watercolours, 19th-20th C, £25-£5,000.* LOC: Village centre. PARK: Easy. TEL: 01491 832525. SER: Valuations. FAIRS: TVADA.

BICESTER

Lisseter of Bicester

3 Kings End. OX6 7DR. (D. Lisseter). Est. 1945. Open 9-5. *STOCK: Furniture, all periods; Victoriana.* PARK: Easy, opposite. TEL: 01869 252402. VAT: Stan/Spec.

BLADON, Nr. Woodstock

Park House Tearoom & Antiques

26 Park St. OX7 0BY. Resident. (H.R. and T. Thomas). Open daily. *STOCK: Small furniture and decorative smalls.* PARK: Own. TEL: 01993 812817; fax - 01993 812912. SER: Valuations; restorations; courier; shipping; consultant.

BLEWBURY

Blewbury Antiques

London Rd. OX11 9NX. (S. and E. Richardson). Est. 1973. Open 10-6 including weekends. CL: Tues. *STOCK: General antiques, books, bric-a-brac, country and garden items, oil lamps and oil lamp parts.* PARK: Easy. TEL: 01235 850366.

BLOXHAM, Nr. Banbury

H.C. Dickins

High St. OX15 4LT. (P. and H.R. Dickins). Open 10-5.30, Sat. 10-1. *STOCK: 19th-20th C British sporting and landscape paintings, watercolours, drawings and prints.* TEL: 01295 721949.

BURFORD

Ashton Gower Antiques LAPADA

Cheltenham Rd., Burford Roundabout. OX18 4JA. (C. Gower and B. Ashton). Est. 1987. Open 10-5.30 and Sun. pm. *STOCK: English and Continental furniture, mirrors and decorative accessories, 18th-20th C, £25-£5,000.* LOC: On roundabout (A40) Oxford/ Cheltenham road. PARK: Easy. TEL: 01993 822450; fax - same. SER: Valuations; restorations; buys at auction. VAT: Stan/Spec.

Burford continued

Burford Antique Centre

Cheltenham Rd., At the Roundabout. (G. Viventi). Est. 1979. Open 10-6 including Sun. SIZE: Large. *STOCK: Furniture, 18th-19th C, £100-£5,000; china and pictures.* LOC: A40. PARK: Easy. TEL: 01993 823227. SER: Restorations (furniture including re-leathering).

The Burford Gallery

Classica House, High St. OX18 4QA. (B. Etheridge). Est. 1976. Open 9.30-5.30. SIZE: Medium. *STOCK: British and Continental watercolours, 18th-20th C, £40-£6,000.* LOC: 400yds. from A40 roundabout. PARK: Easy. TEL: 01993 822305; home - same. SER: Valuations; framing and mounting; buys at auction (watercolours). VAT: Spec.

Denver House Antiques and Collectables

Denver House, Witney St. OX18 4RU. Resident. (T. and B. Radman). Est. 1976. Open 10-5.30, Sun. by appointment. SIZE: Medium. *STOCK: Coins and medals, B.C. to date; orders, medals, badges, decorations, specialist in miniature orders, medals and decorations of the world; military books, police and fire brigade memorabilia, stamps and paper money, 1560 to date; maps, books.* PARK: Easy and nearby. TEL: 01993 822040; fax - 01993 822769. SER: Valuations; buys at auction (coins, stamps, medals, sovereign and stamp cases, maps, covers and tokens). VAT: Stan.

Jonathan Fyson Antiques

50 High St. OX18 4QF. CADA. (J.R. Fyson). Est. 1970. Open 9.30-1 and 2-5.30. SIZE: Medium. *STOCK: English and Continental furniture, decorative brass and steel including lighting and fireplace accessories; papier mâché, tôle, treen, porcelain, glass, jewellery.* LOC: At junction of A40/A361 between Oxford and Cheltenham. PARK: Easy. TEL: 01993 823204; fax - same; home - 01367 860223. SER: Valuations. VAT: Spec.

Gateway Antiques

Cheltenham Rd., Burford Roundabout. OX8 4JA. CADA. (M.C. Ford and P. Brown). Est. 1986. Open 10-5.30 and Sun. pm. SIZE: Large. *STOCK: English and Continental furniture, 18th-19th C; decorative accessories.* LOC: On roundabout (A40) Oxford/Cheltenham road. PARK: Easy. TEL: 01993 823678. SER: Valuations. VAT: Stan/Spec.

Horseshoe Antiques and Gallery

97 High St. OX18 4QA. (B. Evans). Open 9-5.30, Sun. by appointment only. SIZE: Medium. *STOCK: Clocks including longcase (all fully restored); early oak and country furniture; oil paintings and watercolours; copper and brass, horse brasses.* LOC: East side of High St. PARK: Easy. TEL: 01993 823244; home - 01993 822429. VAT: Spec.

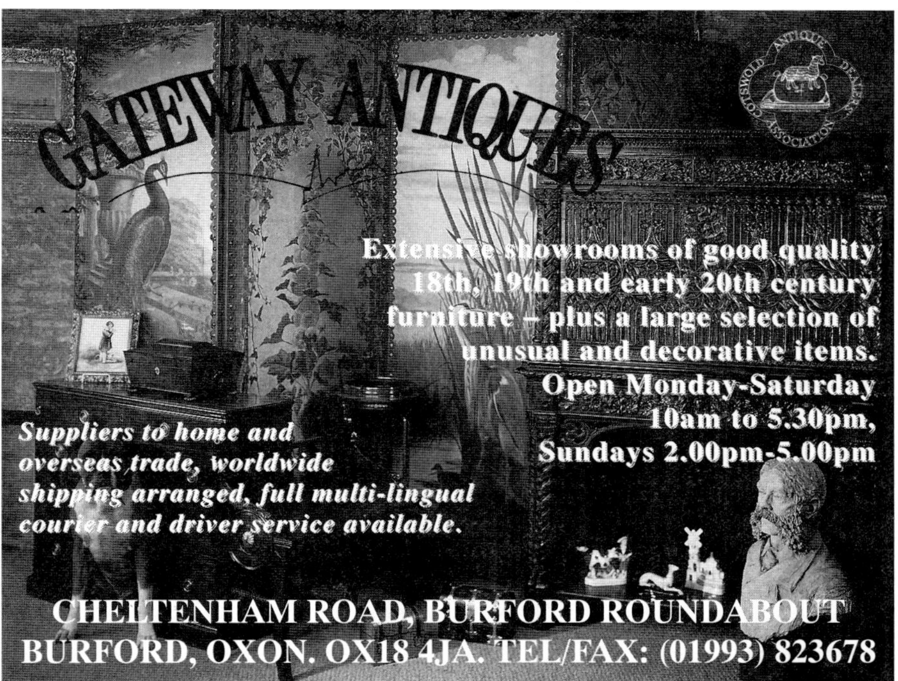

GATEWAY ANTIQUES
COTSWOLD ANTIQUE DEALERS ASSOCIATION
Extensive showrooms of good quality 18th, 19th and early 20th century furniture – plus a large selection of unusual and decorative items.
Open Monday-Saturday 10am to 5.30pm, Sundays 2.00pm-5.00pm
Suppliers to home and overseas trade, worldwide shipping arranged, full multi-lingual courier and driver service available.
CHELTENHAM ROAD, BURFORD ROUNDABOUT
BURFORD, OXON. OX18 4JA. TEL/FAX: (01993) 823678

Burford continued

Hubert's Antiques LAPADA

Burford Roundabout, Cheltenham Rd. OX18 4JA. (Michael R. Hinds). Est. 1987. Open 10-5.30. SIZE: Large. *STOCK: Furniture, £150-£10,000; oils, £50-£5,000; clocks, £250-£5,000; all 17th-19th C.* LOC: A40 half way between Oxford and Cheltenham. TEL: 01993 822151; fax - same.

Anthony Nielsen Antiques

80 High St. OX18 4QF. Est. 1977. Open 9.30-1 and 2-5.30. SIZE: Large. *STOCK: Furniture, mahogany, walnut, rosewood, oak, William and Mary to Edwardian, £200-£20,000; copper, brass, £20-£500.* PARK: Easy. TEL: 01993 822014; fax - same; after hours - 01451 821710.

Old George Inn Antique Galleries

104 High St. (E. Lyle-Cameron). Est. 1992. Open 10-5, Sun. 12-5. SIZE: Large. *STOCK: General antiques including oak, mahogany, china and treen, early 18th C to 1930's.* LOC: Main road. PARK: Around corner. TEL: 01993 823319.

David Pickup BADA

115 High St. OX18 4RG. CADA. Est. 1977. Open 9.30-1 and 2-5.30, Sat. 10-1 and 2-4. SIZE: Medium. *STOCK: Fine furniture, works of art, from £500+; decorative objects, from £100+; all late 17th to mid 20th C, specialising in Arts & Crafts.* PARK: Easy. TEL: 01993 822555. FAIRS: BADA; Olympia. VAT: Spec.

Burford continued

Richard Purdon BADA

158 High St. OX18 4QY. CADA. Open 9.30-5.30. SIZE: Medium. *STOCK: Antique Eastern and European carpets, village and tribal rugs, needlework, textiles and related items.* TEL: 01993 823777; fax - 01993 823719. SER: Valuations; restorations. VAT: Stan/Spec.

Manfred Schotten Antiques

109 High St. OX18 4RH. CADA. Est. 1974. Open 9.30-5.30 or by appointment. *STOCK: Sporting antiques and library furniture.* TEL: 01993 822302; fax - 01993 822055; internet - http:/ www.schotten.com. SER: Restorations.

The Stone Gallery

93 High St. OX18 4QA. (Mrs Phyllis M. and Simon Marshall). Est. 1918. Open 9.15-6. SIZE: Medium. *STOCK: Pre-Raphaelite and modern British pictures, 1840-1980, £120-£30,000; paperweights, from 1845, £50-£15,000; enamel boxes, from 1760, £50-£1,000.* LOC: Halfway down High St. PARK: Easy. TEL: 01993 823302; fax/home - same. SER: Valuations (paperweights); buys at auction (pictures and paperweights). VAT: Stan/Spec.

Burford continued

Swan Gallery LAPADA
High St. OX18 4RE. CADA. (D. Pratt). Est. 1966. Open 9.30-5.30. SIZE: Large. *STOCK: Country furniture in oak, yew, walnut and fruitwood, 17th-19th C, £300-£9,000; oil paintings; Staffordshire figures and small decorative items, 18th-20th C, £50-£800.* PARK: Easy. TEL: 01993 822244. VAT: Mainly Spec.

Walkers
101 High St. OX8 3RG. (A.E. Walker). Est. 1954. Open 9-5. SIZE: Large. *STOCK: 18th-19th C English furniture.* TEL: 01993 823284. VAT: Stan/Spec.

Wren Gallery
4 Bear Court, High St. OX18 4RR. (S. Hall and G. Mitchell). Est. 1986. Open 10-5.30. SIZE: Medium. *STOCK: 19th-20th C watercolours and drawings.* TEL: 01993 823495. SER: Valuations; restorations (watercolours); buys at auction (watercolours). VAT: Spec.

CHALGROVE, Nr. Oxford

Rupert Hitchcox Antiques
Warpsgrove Lane. OX44 7RW. (P. and R. Hitchcox). Est. 1957. Open 9-5, Sun. 2-5 or by appointment. SIZE: Large - 6 barns. *STOCK: Georgian, Victorian, Edwardian and 1920's furniture.* LOC: Halfway between Oxford and Henley, just off the B480, 6 miles from junction 6 M40. TEL: 01865 890241; fax - same. VAT: Stan/Spec.

CHILTON, Nr. Oxford

Country Markets Antiques and Collectables
at Country Gardens Garden Centre, Newbury Rd. OX11 0QN. Est. 1991. Open 10-5.30, Mon. 10.30-5.30, Sun. 10.30-4.30. SIZE: Large - 30 dealers. *STOCK: Wide variety of general antiques including furniture, books, jewellery and porcelain, £5-£5,000.* LOC: Off A34 near Harwell, 10 mins. from junction 13, M4, 20 mins. from Oxford. PARK: Easy. TEL: 01235 835125; fax - 01235 831266. SER: Restorations (furniture and ceramics).

CHIPPING NORTON

Bugle Antiques LAPADA
9 Horsefair. OX7 5AL. CADA. (M. and D. Harding-Hill). Est. 1971. Open 9.30-6. *STOCK: Windsor chairs including sets; English country furniture.* TEL: 01608 643322; fax - same; e-mail - bugle-windsor-chairs@dial.pipex.com. VAT: Stan/Spec.

Chipping Norton Antique Centre
Ivy House, 1 Middle Row and 21/44 West St. OX7 5NH. (G. Wissinger). Open 10-5.30 including Sun. SIZE: 20 dealers. *STOCK: A wide variety of smalls and furniture.* PARK: Own. TEL: 01608 644212.

Chipping Norton continued

The Emporium
26 High St. OX7 5AD. Open 10-1 and 2-5.30. Collectors Room open 2-5, Sat. 10-1 and 2-5. CL: Mon. *STOCK: Bric-a-brac, china, glass, postcards and prints.* TEL: 01608 643103.

Georgian House Antiques LAPADA
21 West St. OX7 5EU. Open 9-6. *STOCK: 17th-19th C furniture and paintings.* TEL: 01608 641369.

Jonathan Howard
21 Market Place. OX7 5NA. (J.G. Howard). Est. 1979. Open by appointment or ring bell. SIZE: Small. *STOCK: Clocks - longcase, wall and carriage, 18th-19th C.* PARK: Easy. TEL: 01608 643065. SER: Valuations; restorations (movement, dials and cases).

Key Antiques BADA
11 Horse Fair. OX7 5AL. CADA. Resident. (D. and M. Robinson). Open 9.30-5.30 or by appointment. SIZE: Medium. *STOCK: Period oak and country furniture, domestic metalware including lighting and downhearth equipment, early carvings, firemarks, keys.* LOC: On main road. PARK: Easy. TEL: 01608 643777. VAT: Spec.

Station Mill Antiques
Station Mill, Station Rd. OX7. (R. Stewart). Est. 1994. Open 10-5 including Sun. SIZE: Large. *STOCK: Furniture, fine art, bric-a-brac and collectables, 17th-20th C, £2-£2,000.* LOC: Just out of town off A44 towards Moreton in Marsh. PARK: Easy. TEL: 01608 644563; fax - same. SER: Valuations; restorations.

TRADA
21 High St. OX7 5AD. Open 9-5.30. CL: Thurs. *STOCK: Antiquarian prints, maps and engravings, 1600-1900.* TEL: 01608 644325. SER: Print renovation and colouring; picture frame making.

Peter Wiggins
Raffles Farm, Southcombe. OX7 5QH. Est. 1969. Usually available. *STOCK: Barometers.* LOC: 1 mile from Chipping Norton on A34. TEL: 01608 642652; home - same. SER: Valuations; restorations (barometers, clocks, automata); clock repairs; buys at auction.

CULHAM, Nr. Abingdon

Rob Dixon Fine Engravings
Warren Farmhouse, Thame Lane. OX14 3DT. By appointment only. *STOCK: Fine and decorative English and French prints, to 18th C; portraits including fine mezzotints, 16th-19th C; period frames.* LOC: Behind European School. TEL: 01235 524676.

DEDDINGTON

Castle Antiques Ltd LAPADA

Manor Farm, Clifton. OX15 0PA. (J. and J. Vaughan). Est. 1968. Open 10-5, Sun. 10-4. SIZE: Large. *STOCK: Furniture, £25-£3,000; silver, metalware, £10-£1,000; pottery, porcelain, £10-£200; kitchenalia.* LOC: B4031 (Aynho Road), 6 miles from junction 10, M40. PARK: Easy. TEL: 01869 338688; evenings - 01869 338294. VAT: Stan/Spec.

The Country Store and Linen Cupboard

Market Place. OX15 0SA. (R. Gregory). Open daily and Sun. SIZE: Medium. *STOCK: Country furniture, collectors items, 18th-19th C, paintings and prints, £50-£500; Victorian and later linen, lace and costume.* PARK: Outside. TEL: 01869 338215; home - 01295 812266. SER: Valuations; restorations; cleaning (oil paintings). VAT: Stan./ Spec.

Deddington Antiques Centre

Laurel House, Bull Ring, Market Sq. OX15 0TT. TVADA. (Mrs B. J. Haller). Est. 1972. Open 10-5, including Sun. SIZE: 27 dealers. *STOCK: Furniture, Georgian to 1930's, £40-£4,000; porcelain, silver, pictures, jewellery, 1700-1930, £5-£500; collectables, £10-£200.* LOC: Off A4260 Oxford-Banbury road at Deddington traffic lights. PARK: Easy, free. TEL: 01869 338968; fax - 01869 338916. SER: Valuations. FAIRS: NEC; Oxford; Eton; Goodwood House.

DIDCOT

Didcot Antiques Centre

220 The Broadway. OX11 8RS. TVADA. (Dr. A. Vetta). Est. 1995. Open 10-5, Sun. 11-4. CL: Mon. SIZE: Large. *STOCK: Furniture, £50-£1,000; silver and plate, books and ephemera, all 19th-20th C.* PARK: Own. TEL: 01235 510819; fax - 01235 512178. SER: Valuations.

DORCHESTER-ON-THAMES

Dorchester Antiques LAPADA

(formerly The Shambles), The Barn, 3 High St. OX10 7HH. TVADA. (J. and S. Hearnden). Est. 1992. Open Tues.-Sat. 10-5. SIZE: Medium. *STOCK: Furniture including chairs and decorative country pieces, 18th-19th C.* LOC: Opposite Abbey. PARK: Easy. TEL: 01865 341373. SER: Restorations; upholstery; finder.

Hallidays (Fine Antiques) Ltd LAPADA

The Old College, High St. OX10 7HL. TVADA. Est. 1950. Open 9-5, Sat. 10-1 and 2-4. SIZE: Large. *STOCK: Furniture, 17th-19th C, £100-£40,000; paintings, 18th-19th C, £100-£20,000; decorative and small items, pine and marble mantelpieces, firegrates, fenders, 18th-20th C; room panelling.* PARK: At rear. TEL: 01865 340028; fax - 01865 341149. FAIRS: Olympia. VAT: Stan/Spec.

EAST HAGBOURNE

Craig Barfoot

Tudor House. OX11 9LR. (I.C. Barfoot). Est. 1993. Open any time by appointment. SIZE: Medium. *STOCK: Longcase clocks, £1,500-£8,500; wall clocks, £250-£1,000; all 1680-1900; lantern clocks.* LOC: Just off A34 halfway between Oxford and Newbury. PARK: Easy. TEL: 01235 818968; home - same; mobile - 0410 858158. SER: Restorations (clocks); buys at auction (clocks, English oak furniture). VAT: Spec.

E.M. Lawson and Co

Kingsholm. OX11 9LN. (W.J. and K.M. Lawson). Est. 1921. Usually open 10-5 but appointment preferred. CL: Sat. *STOCK: Antiquarian and rare books, 1500-1900.* PARK: Easy. TEL: 01235 812033. VAT: Stan.

FARINGDON

Aston Pine Antiques

16-18 London St. SN7 7AA. (P. O'Gara). Est. 1982. Open Tues.-Sat. 9-5. *STOCK: Victorian and Continental pine; Victorian fireplaces, doors and bathrooms.* TEL: 01367 243840.

The Faringdon Antique Centre

35 Marlborough St. SN7 7JL. Open 10-5 including Sun. CL: Mon. except Bank Holidays. SIZE: Large. *STOCK: Mahogany, oak, walnut and pine furniture, Georgian to Edwardian, £500-£1,000+.* LOC: Off A420 at Faringdon roundabout, signposted A417 Lechlade, opposite Peugeot garage. PARK: Easy. TEL: 01367 243650. SER: Valuations; restorations (furniture, clocks, porcelain and china).

La Chaise Antique LAPADA

30 London St. SN7 7AA. (Roger Clark). Est. 1968. Open 10-6. CL: Sun. except by appointment. SIZE: Large. *STOCK: Chairs, pre-1860; furniture, 18th-19th C; general antiques, decorators' items.* Not Stocked: Silver, porcelain and glass. LOC: A420. PARK: At rear. TEL: 01367 240427; mobile - 0831 205002; fax - 01367 241001. SER: Valuations; restorations; upholstery (leather and fabrics); table top liners. FAIRS: NEC (April and Aug); LAPADA NEC (Jan.). VAT: Spec.

Faringdon continued

Oxford Architectural Antiques

16-18 London St. SN7 7AA. (M. O'Gara). Open Tues.-Sat. 9-5. *STOCK: Fireplaces, fixtures and fittings, doors.* TEL: 01367 242268; mobile - 0973 922393.

HEADINGTON, Nr. Oxford

Barclay Antiques

107 Windmill Rd. OX3 7BT. (C. Barclay). Est. 1979. Open 10-5.30. CL: Wed. SIZE: Small. *STOCK: Porcelain, silver and jewellery, 18th-19th C, £50-£100; period lamps, 20th C, £50-£500.* PARK: Easy. TEL: 01865 69551. SER: Valuations. FAIRS: Oxford.

HENLEY-ON-THAMES

Friday Street Antique Centre

4 Friday St. RG9 4QL. Open 9.30-5.30, Sun. 12-5. SIZE: 10 dealers. *STOCK: Furniture, china, silver, engravings and prints.* LOC: First left after Henley bridge, then first right, business on left. PARK: Nearby. TEL: 01491 574104. SER: Valuations; buys at auction.

Henley Antique Centre

Rotherfield Arcade, 2-4 Reading Rd. RG9 1AG. Open 9.30-5.30, Sun. 12-5.30, including Bank Holidays. SIZE: Large. *STOCK: General antiques, furniture, curios and fine arts.* TEL: 01491 411468.

The Barry M. Keene Gallery

12 Thameside. RG9 1BH. TVADA, FATG. (B.M. and J.S. Keene). Est. 1971. Open 9.30-5.30, Sun. 11-5.30, and by appointment. *STOCK: Paintings, watercolours, drawings, etchings, prints, 18th C to 1998; modern sculpture.* LOC: Junction 8/9 M4, over bridge, immediate left, 5th building on right. TEL: 01491 577119. SER: Restorations; framing, cleaning, relining, gilding, export. VAT: Stan/Spec.

Henley-on-Thames continued

Richard J. Kingston BADA

95 Bell St. RG9 2BD. TVADA. Open 9.30-5 or by appointment. SIZE: Medium. *STOCK: Furniture, 17th to early 19th C; silver, porcelain, glass, paintings, antiquarian and secondhand books.* PARK: Easy. TEL: 01491 574535; home - 01491 573133. SER: Restorations. FAIRS: Surrey, Buxton, Snape. VAT: Stan/Spec.

Thames Gallery

Thameside. RG9 2LJ. TVADA. (S. Came). Open 10-5. *STOCK: Georgian and Victorian silver; paintings, 19th C.* TEL: 01491 572449; fax - 01491 410273.

Thames Oriental Rug Co

Thames Carpet Cleaners Ltd, 48/56 Reading Rd. RG9 1AG. Resident. (D. Benardout and C. Aigin). Est. 1955. Open 9-12.30 and 1.30-5, Sat. 9-12.30. SIZE: Medium. *STOCK: Oriental rugs, mid-19th C to modern.* PARK: Easy. TEL: 01491 574676. SER: Valuations; restorations and cleaning (carpets). VAT: Stan.

A fine cut velvet and fur-trimmed evening cape, late 1930s, which made £420.

From an article entitled "Auction Report: Costume and Textiles at Sotheby's, 13th March" by Tom Flynn which appeared in the June 1997 issue of **Antique Collecting**

HUNTERCOMBE

The Country Seat LAPADA

Huntercombe Manor Barn. RG9 5RY. TVADA. (Harvey Ferry and William Clegg). Est. 1965. Open 9-5.30, Sun. by appointment. SIZE: Large. *STOCK: Furniture - signed and designed, 1700-1910, Chinese, 19th C; garden statuary, panelled rooms, metalwork and art pottery, upholstered furniture and ancient artefacts.* LOC: 200 yds down right-hand turn off A4130 Nettlebed-Wallingford. PARK: Easy. TEL: 01491 641349; fax - 01491 641533. SER: Restorations. VAT: Spec.

LONG HANBOROUGH

Hanborough Antiques

125-127 Main Rd. OX8 8JX. Open 10.30-5.30 (Sun. 11-4 from Easter through summer). CL: Mon. SIZE: Medium. *STOCK: Furniture, country and period; pottery, porcelain, Victoriana, rural and domestic bygones, brass and copper, collectors' items.* LOC: Going north from Oxford on A34 turn left before Woodstock on to A4095 near Witney. PARK: Easy. TEL: 01993 882767.

NETTLEBED, Nr. Henley-on-Thames

Willow Antiques and the Nettlebed Antique Merchants

The Barns, 1 High St. RG9 5DA. TVADA. (Willow Bicknell, Michael Plummer, Gregory Cupitt-Jones and Robert Wookey). Open Tues.-Sat 10-5.30, Sun. 11-4, other times by appointment. SIZE: Large. *STOCK: Decorative, fine and unusual furniture, objects and decorations, including architectural items, original painted or stripped and wax finished pine.* LOC: Between Wallingford and Henley on A4031. PARK: Easy. TEL: 01491 642062; fax - same; mobile - 0370 554559. SER: Cottage Upholstery - fabrics; upholstery.

NORTH ASTON

Elizabeth Harvey-Lee

1 West Cottages, Middle Aston Lane. OX6 3QB. TVADA. Est. 1986. Open by appointment. *STOCK: Original prints, 15th-20th C; artists' etchings, engravings, lithographs, £100-£6,000.* LOC: 6 miles from junction 10, M40, 15 miles north of Oxford. TEL: 01869 347164. SER: Illustrated catalogue available twice yearly (£12 p.a.). FAIRS: London Original Print, Royal Academy; Olympia (June and Nov).VAT: Spec.

Gerald E. Marsh (Antique Clocks) BADA

Jericho House. OX6 4HX. Open by appointment only. *STOCK: Clocks, watches, barometers; some furniture, mid-18th C and Regency.* TEL: 01869 340087; fax - same.

OXFORD

Blackwell's Rare Books

38 Holywell St. OX1 3SW. Est. 1879. Open 9-6, Tues. 9.30-6. *STOCK: Antiquarian and rare modern books.* TEL: 01865 792792; fax - 01865 248833; internet - http://www.blackwell.co.uk/bookshops/rarebooks/; e-mail - rarebooks@blackwell.co.uk. SER: Buys at auction. VAT: Stan/Spec.

The Corner Shop

Walton St. (P. Hitchcox and D. Florey). Est. 1978. Open 10-5. *STOCK: Pictures, china, glass, silver, small furniture and general items.* LOC: Central north Oxford. TEL: 01865 553364.

Reginald Davis Ltd BADA

34 High St. OX1 4AN. Est. 1941. Open 9-5. CL: Thurs. *STOCK: Silver, English and Continental, 17th to early 19th C; jewellery, Sheffield plate, Georgian and Victorian.* Not Stocked: Glass, china, pewter. LOC: On A40. PARK: Easy. TEL: 01865 248347. SER: Valuations; restorations (silver, jewellery). VAT: Stan/Spec.

Jeremy's (Oxford Stamp Centre)

98 Cowley Rd. OX4 1JE. Open 10-12.30 and 2-5. *STOCK: Stamps, postcards and cigarette cards.* TEL: 01865 241011.

Christopher Legge Oriental Carpets

25 Oakthorpe Rd., Summertown. OX2 7BD. (C.T. Legge). Est. 1970. SIZE: Medium. *STOCK: Rugs, various sizes, 19th-early 20th C, £100-£6,000.* LOC: Near shopping parade. PARK: Easy. TEL: 01865 557572; fax - 01865 554877. SER: Valuations; restorations; re-weaving; hand-cleaning. VAT: Stan.

Laurie Leigh Antiques LAPADA

36 High St. OX1 4AN. (L. and D. Leigh). Est. 1963. Open 10.30-5.30. CL: Thurs. *STOCK: Glass, keyboard musical instruments, clocks.* TEL: 01865 244197. VAT: Stan/Spec.

Magna Gallery

41 High St. OX1 4AP. TVADA. (Martin J. Blant). Est. 1969. Open 10-5.30. SIZE: Medium. *STOCK: Maps especially Oxfordshire, general topography, prints including botanical, caricatures, 1550-1895.* TEL: 01865 245805. SER: Valuations; framing. VAT: Stan.

The Oxford Antique Trading Co

40/41 Park End St. OX1 1JD. (D.A. Jones and R.S.J. Howse). Open 10-6. SIZE: Large. *STOCK: General antiques, from 18th C to 1930s, £50-£5,000.* LOC: 150yds. from railway station. PARK: Easy. TEL: 01865 793927. SER: Valuations; restorations (furniture, upholstery). VAT: Stan/Spec.

Payne and Son (Goldsmiths) Ltd BADA

131 High St. OX1 4DH. (E.P., G.N. and J.D. Payne, P.J. Coppock, A. Salmon and D.

Oxford continued

Thornton). Est. 1790. Open weekdays 9-5. SIZE: Medium. *STOCK: British silver, antique, modern and secondhand; jewellery, all £50-£10,000+.* LOC: Town centre near Carfax traffic lights. PARK: 800yds. TEL: 01865 243787; fax - 01865 793241. SER: Restorations (English silver). VAT: Stan/Spec.

Sanders of Oxford Ltd

Salutation House, 104 High St. OX1 4BW. Open 10-6, Sun. 11-4. SIZE: Large. *STOCK: Prints, especially Oxford; maps and Japanese woodcuts.* TEL: 01865 242590; fax - 01865 721748; e-mail - info@sanders-oxford.co.uk; internet - www.oxlink.co.uk/antiques/sanders.html. VAT: Stan/Spec.

A.J. Saywell Ltd. (The Oxford Stamp Shop)

15 Hollybush Row. OX1 1JH. (I.H. and H.J. Saywell). Est. 1943. Open 10-5.30, Thurs. 10-1. SIZE: Small. *STOCK: Stamps, accessories, coins and some medals.* LOC: Off Park End St. near railway station. PARK: Easy. TEL: 01865 248889. SER: Valuations. VAT: Stan.

Thorntons of Oxford Ltd

11 Broad St. OX1 3AR. Open 9-6. SIZE: Large. *STOCK: Antiquarian books.* TEL: 01865 242939; fax - 01865 204021; e-mail - Thorntons@booknews.demon.co.uk

Titles - Old and Rare Books

15 Turl St. OX1 3DQ. Est. 1972. Open 9.30-5.30. *STOCK: Antiquarian and secondhand books, general subjects, especially literature, natural history, travel, history of science, bindings, illustrated.* TEL: 01865 727928; fax - same.

Waterfield's

36 Park End St. OX1 1HJ. Open 9.30-5.30, Sat. 9.30-6. *STOCK: Antiquarian and secondhand books, all subjects, especially academic in the humanities; literature, history, philosophy, 17th-18th C English books.* TEL: 01865 721809.

STANDLAKE, Nr. Witney

Manor Farm Antiques

Manor Farm. OX8 7RL. (C.W. Leveson-Gower). Est. 1964. Open daily, Sun. by appointment. SIZE: Large. *STOCK: Victorian brass and iron beds.* PARK: Easy, in farmyard. TEL: 01865 300303.

TAYNTON, Nr. Burford

Wychwood Antiques

Upper Farm Cottage. Open by appointment only. *STOCK: English country furniture and decorative items.* TEL: 01993 822860.

TETSWORTH, Nr. Thame

The Swan at Tetsworth

High St. OX9 7AB. TVADA. Est. 1995. Open every day including Sun. LOC: A40, 5 minutes from junctions 6 and 8, M40. PARK: Own large. TEL: 01844 281777; fax - 01844 281770. SER: Valuations; restorations (clocks, cabinet work and gilding). Below are listed the dealers at this centre.

Deborah Abbot
Jewellery and objet d'art.

Jason Abbot
Antique sporting guns.

Acanthus Antiques
Arts & Crafts and Art Nouveau furniture and accessories.

S.J. Allison
Decorative ceramics, small furniture and silver.

Antiquus
Victorian furniture, frames, ceramics and objet d'art.

Denis Ashworth
Jewellery and ceramics.

Beagle Antiques
Fine porcelain and paintings.

David Binns
Books and paperweights.

Peter Bond
Prints, watercolours. SER: Gilding.

G. Buckle
Clocks and Oriental antiques.

C and C Architectural
Brass door and window furniture and architectural items.

John Chaffer
Framed antiquarian prints and maps.

Lakis Charambides
Antiques and collectable silver.

Clavic Lee Antiques
Silverware.

Audrey Cooper
Kitchenalia and country items.

Jenny Corkhill-Callin
Antique textiles including cushions, curtains, braids and quilts.

S and K Cullup
Antique linens and textiles.

Bridget Farwagi
Ceramics, furniture and objet d'art.

Mavis Foster-Abbott
20th C glass, specialising in Latticinio.

Framed Antiques
Collectable framed cigarette cards.

Tetsworth continued

Uta Gosling
Ceramics and collectables.

Gillian Gould
Maritime antiques.

Grate Expectations
Fireplaces, Cornish ranges, tiles, garden items and architectural salvage.

Grove Antiques Limited
Decorative and Continental furniture and lighting.

V. Gwilliam and K. Martin
Dolls, teds and ceramics.

Hampden Trading Company
Decorative antiques for house and garden.

Gill Hedge
Silver, glassware, ceramics and paintings.

Martin Isenberg
Period/decorative furniture, treen and ceramics.

Nigel Johnston Antiques
Useful antique household furniture.

Wendy Lancaster
Fine antiques, chandeliers, sidelights and lamps.

Russell Lane Antiques
Fine jewellery.

Sandra Lawless
Antique needle and sewing related items.

Gerald and Elisabeth Ledger
18th and 19th C furniture and ceramics.

Loryman Antiques
Period English and French furniture and smalls.

J. MacNaughton-Smith
TVADA. *Mainly 18th-19th C English furniture including desks, writing tables, chiffoniers, chests of drawers; small decorative items, 19th C watercolours*

Manzaroli
Fine antique paintings.

Marquetry Antiques
Chinese antiques and object d'art.

Millroyal Antiques
Fine furniture and smalls.

Nicholas Mitchell
Unusual period furniture and smalls.

Patsy Morgan
Victorian furniture - desks and bookcases.

George Morris
Jewellery.

Old Cottage Antiques
Period to Victorian furniture and metalware.

Tetsworth continued

Otter Antiques
Victorian and Regency furniture and writing slopes.

Penningtons
Pine and kitchenalia.

Quail Collectables
Fine antique glass, Georgian to Lalique.

Janet Raisey
Silverware.

T.H.A. & F.M. Sharland
Frames, prints and watercolours.

Carole Solway
China, prints and smalls.

Sovereign Art
Collectors' silver items.

Steeple Antiques LAPADA
Large period furniture and chandeliers.

Brian Stepney
Silver and flatware.

Peter Stevens
Ceramics, particularly blue and white transferware.

Jackie Stewart-Jones
Desk and writing accessories.

Tartan Antiques
Object d'art, pictures and toys.

Geoff and Coral Taylor-Robinson
French provincial furniture and decorative accessories.

Tudor House Antiques
Georgian to Victorian furniture.

J.D. Tye
Furniture, porcelain and oil paintings.

Allan Wardle
Period clocks and watches.

Carol Wardle
Furniture, clocks and watches.

John Weal
Decorative country antiques.

Wells Farm Designs
Upholstered furniture and upholstery.

Tim and Julia Williamson
Gardenalia and antiques restoration products.

Susan Wilson
Pine, kitchenalia and sporting antiques.

Wright Associates
Jewellery, glass and boxes.

Angela Yannaghas
Victorian and Georgian silver and glass.

Tetsworth continued

Tetsworth Antiques

High St. OX9 7DU. (M. and D. Vine). Open 11-5 including Sun., Sat. 10-5. CL: Mon. and Wed. SIZE: Medium. *STOCK: Furniture, china, glass, pine, clocks, £1-£4,000.* LOC: A40 between exits 6 and 7, M40. PARK: Easy. TEL: 01844 281636. SER: Valuations; restorations. VAT: Stan/Spec.

THAME

Rosemary and Time

42 Park St. OX9 3HR. Open 9-6. *STOCK: Clocks, watches, barometers.* TEL: 01844 216923. SER: Valuations; restorations; old spare parts. VAT: Stan/Spec.

WALLINGFORD

de Albuquerque Antiques

12 High St. OX10 0BP. Est. 1982. Open 10-5. SIZE: Medium. *STOCK: Furniture and objects, 18th-19th C.* PARK: At rear. TEL: 01491 832322; fax - same. SER: Framing; gilding.

The Lamb Arcade

83 High St. OX10 0BX. TVADA. Open 10-5, Sat. 10-5.30. TEL: 01491 835166. SER: Restorations (furniture). Below are listed some of the dealers at this centre.

Alicia Antiques

(A. Collins). *China, silver and collectors' items.* TEL: 01491 33737.

Anne Brewer Antiques

TVADA. *Furniture, china, jewellery and objets d'art.* TEL: 01491 38486.

Great Expectations

(N. McKie). *Victorian brass bedsteads, linens and bedroom furnishings.* TEL: 01491 39909.

Griffin Antiques

(Margaret and John Riordan). *18th-19th C furniture and decorative items including stamped, signed and attributed pieces.*

Pat Hayward

Antiques and decorative furnishings.

Wallingford continued

John Hedge

Secondhand and antiquarian books.

Phoenix Antiques

Victorian furniture, Continental and English pine, lighting.

Margaret Richmond

Small 17th-19th C oak country furniture, accessories, decorative items and kitchenalia. TEL: 01491 35166.

Simply Antiques

General antiques and collectables. TEL: 01491 824854.

Gretel Stone

Small furniture, porcelain, silver, pictures and objets d'art.

Julie Strachey

Pine. TEL: 01491 35166.

Tags

(T.and A. Green). *Collectors' items, curios, dolls' house furniture, jewellery, militaria, scientific instruments and furniture.* TEL: 01491 35048; home - 01491 872962.

Waters Violins

Old violins, violas and cellos. TEL: 01491 25616. SER: Valuations; restorations.

MGJ Jewellers Ltd.

1A St. Martins St. OX10 0AQ. (Mrs M. Jane). Est. 1971. Open 10-4.30, Sat. 10-5. SIZE: Small. *STOCK: Jewellery, Victorian and secondhand, £100-£2,500.* LOC: Town centre. PARK: Nearby. TEL: 01491 834336. VAT: Stan/Spec.

Chris and Lin O'Donnell Antiques

26-27 High St. OX10 0BU. Open 9.30-1 and 2-5. SIZE: Large. *STOCK: Furniture, 18th C to Edwardian, to £3,000; rugs, to £500; small collectables, especially Oriental items; maps.* LOC: Into town over Wallingford Bridge, 150yds. along High St. on left-hand side. PARK: Thames St. TEL: 01491 839332. VAT: Spec.

Wallingford continued

Otter Antiques

20 High St. (P.B. Otter). Open 9.30-5.30, Sun. 10.30-5. SIZE: Medium. *STOCK: Furniture, £300-£3,000; writing boxes, caddies, jewellery and sewing boxes, £100-£1,500; all 18th-19th C.* PARK: Easy, rear of shop. TEL: 01491 825544; internet - www.otterantiques.co.uk. SER: Restorations (boxes). VAT: Stan/Spec.

Mike Ottrey Antiques

16 High St. (M.J. Ottrey). Est. 1955. Open 9-5.30. CL: Sat. SIZE: Large. *STOCK: Furniture, 17th-19th C; oil paintings, copper and brass, decorative and unusual items.* LOC: A429. PARK: At rear. TEL: 01491 836429. VAT: Stan/Spec.

Summers Davis Antiques Ltd LAPADA

Calleva House, 6 High St. OX10 0BP. CINOA, TVADA. (Graham Wells). Est. 1917. Open 8.30-5.30, Sat. 9-5, Sun. 11-5. SIZE: Large. *STOCK: English and Continental furniture, decorative items and objects.* Not Stocked: Silver, shipping goods. LOC: From London, shop is on left, 50yds. from Thames Bridge. PARK: Opposite, behind castellated gates. TEL: 01491 836284; fax - 01491 833443; e-mail - summersdavisantiques@msn.com VAT: Spec.

WATLINGTON, Nr. Oxford

F.E.A. Briggs Ltd

The Antiques Warehouse, Shirburn Rd. OX9 5BZ. *STOCK: Furiture and textiles, Victorian, Edwardian and Georgian.* TEL: 0171 727 0909/221 4950. SER: Valuations. VAT: Stan/Spec.

Cross Antiques

37 High St. OX9 5PZ. TVADA. (R.A. and I.D. Crawley). Est. 1986. Open 10-6, Sun. and Wed. by appointment. SIZE: Small. *STOCK: Furniture, £100-£5,000; decorative smalls, clocks and garden items, £50-£2,000; all 1600-1900.* LOC: Off B4009 in village centre. PARK: Easy and at rear. TEL: 01491 612324; home - same.

Stephen Orton Antiques

The Antiques Warehouse, Shirburn Rd. OX9 5BZ. TVADA. Open Mon.-Fri. 9-5, other times by appointment. SIZE: Warehouse. *STOCK: 18th-19th C furniture, some decorative items.* LOC: 2 mins. from exit 6, M40. TEL: 01491 613752; fax - 01491 613875. SER: Valuations; restorations; buying agent. VAT: Stan/Spec.

Watlington continued

Mark Shanks BADA

The Royal Oak, High St. OX9 5QB. TVADA. Est. 1960. Open Tues.-Sat. 10-5, or by appointment. *STOCK: Furniture, £100-£20,000; barometers, £100-£10,000; both mainly 18th-19th C. Decorative items, £50-£5,000.* Not Stocked: Silver, jewellery, coins. LOC: 3 miles from junction 6, M40. Turn right into High St. (one-way). PARK: Own. TEL: 01491 613317; fax - 01491 613318.

WITNEY

The Clock Work Shop

79 Corn St. OX8 7DH. (Steve Fletcher). Est. 1973. Open Tues.-Fri. 9-12 and 2-5, Sat. 9-5. CL: Mon. SIZE: Small. *STOCK: Clocks, furniture, £30-£4,000; treen, £30-£150; all 18th-19th C.* PARK: Easy. TEL: 01993 772123. SER: Valuations; restorations (clock movements, furniture); buys at auction. VAT: Stan/Spec.

Louis Rayner, 'The Bell Inn', watercolour and bodycolour, 7in. x 11½in. (Russell-Cotes Art Gallery and Museum).

Louise Rayner was born into a family where sketching and painting were second nature and where artistic ambitions were encouraged. Life as an artist could be difficult enough, particularly as a woman. It was being part of an artistic family who supported her artistic endeavours that gave her an invaluable grounding.

From an article entitled "Louise Rayner: Picturesque Scenes of Living Architecture" by Mark Bills which appeared in the February 1998 issue of **Antique Collecting**

Witney continued

Colin Greenway Antiques

90 Corn St. OX8 7BU. Resident. Est. 1975. Open 9.30-6 or by appointment. SIZE: Large. *STOCK: Furniture, 17th-20th C; metalware, decorative and unusual items.* LOC: Along High St. to town centre, turn right, shop 400yds. on right. PARK: Easy. TEL: 01993 705026. VAT: Stan/Spec.

W.R. Harvey & Co (Antiques) Ltd BADA

86 Corn St. OX8 7BU. CADA. GMC. Open 9.30-5.30, and by appointment. SIZE: Large. *STOCK: Fine English furniture, £500-£50,000; clocks, mirrors, objets d'art, £250-£20,000; all 1680-1830.* LOC: 100 yds. from Market Place. TEL: 01993 706501; fax - 01993 706601. SER: Valuations; restorations; consultancy. FAIRS: BADA; Chelsea (March & Sept.) VAT: Stan/Spec.

Joan Wilkins Antiques

158 Corn St. OX8 7BY. (Mrs J. Wilkins). Est. 1973. Open 10-5. CL: Tues. *STOCK: Furniture, 18th-19th C, £150-£3,500; 19th C glass, metalware, £10-£1,500.* LOC: Town centre. PARK: Easy. TEL: 01993 704749. VAT: Spec.

W. R. Harvey & Co (Antiques) Ltd.

FINE ANTIQUE FURNITURE
& WORKS OF ART,
CONSERVATION & CONSULTANCY

86 Corn Street, Witney,
Oxfordshire OX8 7BU.
Tel: 01993 706501
Fax: 01993 706601

Web Site: www.wrharvey.co.uk
Email: antiques@wrharvey.co.uk

An excellent George I Walnut Bureau. Ca. 1720

Witney continued

Windrush Antiques

107 High St. OX8 6HG. Resident. (B. Tollett). Est. 1978. Open 10-5. SIZE: Large. *STOCK: Furniture, especially 17th-18th C oak and country chairs; Georgian mahogany, some metalware and porcelain.* LOC: A40, corner of Mill St. and High St. PARK: Private at rear. TEL: 01993 772536.

Witney Antiques BADA LAPADA

96/100 Corn St. OX8 7BU. CADA. (L.S.A. and C.J. Jarrett and R.R. Jarrett-Scott). Est. 1962. Open 10-5. SIZE: Large. *STOCK: English furniture, 17th-18th C; bracket and longcase clocks, mahogany, oak and walnut, metalware, needleworks and works of art.* LOC: From Oxford on old A40 through Witney via High St., turn right at T-junction, 400yds. on right. PARK: Easy. TEL: 01993 703902/703887; fax - 01993 779852. SER: Restorations. FAIRS: BADA; Grosvenor House. VAT: Spec.

WOODSTOCK

Chris Baylis Country Chairs

Minstrel House, 60 Oxford St. OX20 1TT. TVADA. Open 10.30-5.30 including Sun. *STOCK: English country chairs, from 1780; Windsors, ladder and spindlebacks, kitchen chairs; also good country furniture and reproductions including farm tables and chairs.* TEL: 01993 813887; fax - 01993 812379.

Bees Antiques

30 High St. OX20 1TG. TVADA. (Jo and Jim Bateman). Est. 1991. Open 10-1 and 1.30-5, Sun. 11-5. CL: Tues. SIZE: Small. *STOCK: Pottery, porcelain and glass, 18th-20th C, £30-£1,500; small furniture, 19th to early 20th C, £50-£2,000; metalware, 19th C, £30-£200; jewellery, 19th-*

Woodstock continued

20th C, £30-£1,000. LOC: Just off A3440 Oxford/Stratford-on-Avon road, in town centre. PARK: Opposite. TEL: 01993 811062; home - 01993 771593. SER: Valuations; buys at auction (as stock). FAIRS: TVADA.

Le Print Antique Centre

16 High St. OX20 1TF. Est. 1973. Open 10-5, Sun. 11-5. SIZE: 20+ dealers. *STOCK: General antiques and collectables including porcelain, pottery, glass, brass, copper, silver and plate, books, woodworking tools, furniture.* PARK: Easy. TEL: 01993 813900; home (Manager) - 01865 766181. SER: Valuations; restorations (ceramics and furniture repairs including re-covering); picture framing. FAIRS: Various specialist.

Robin Sanders and Sons LAPADA

11 Market St. OX20 1SU. CINOA. *STOCK: English and some French furniture, 17th-19th C; Staffordshire and Masons ironstone pottery, brass, treen and English glass pictures.* TEL: 01993 813930.

Span Antiques

6 Market Place. OX20 1TA. TVADA. Est. 1978. Open 10-1 and 2-5, Sun 1-5. SIZE: Medium. LOC: Near Town Hall. PARK: Easy. Below are listed some of the dealers selling from these premises. TEL: 01993 811332.

Woodstock continued

Doreen Caudwell
Table linen and textiles.

Diana Clark
Old and interesting books.

Mike and Kate Cowdy
Silver.

Andrew Crawforth
Iron, copper, brass, kitchen bygones, corkscrews.

Liz Hall-Bakker
Art Nouveau and Deco.

Jasper Antiques
Silver and decorative items.

Ilona Johnson Gibbs
Oil paintings and watercolours.

Rebecca Stuart-Mobey
Furniture and glass.

Thistle House Antiques

14 Market Place. OX7 1TA. Open 10-6. *STOCK: 18th-19th C furniture, porcelain, pictures.* TEL: 01993 811736. SER: Restorations.

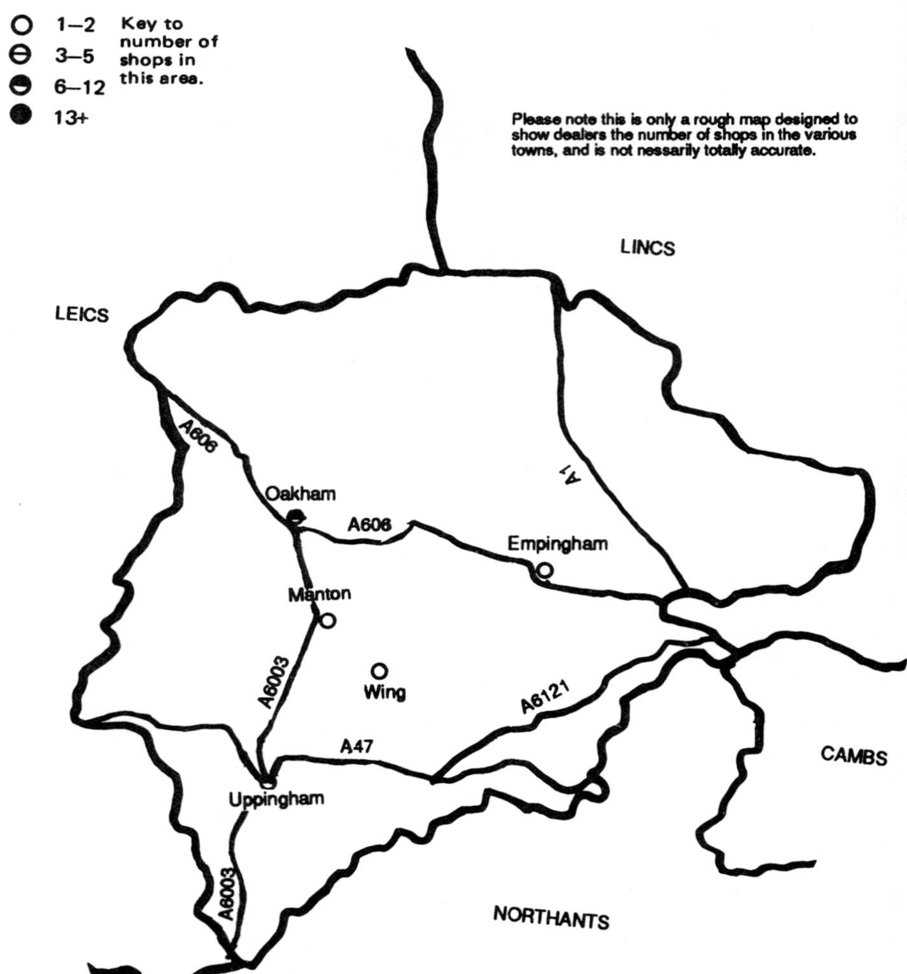
NORTH
1–2
3–5
6–12
13+
Key to number of shops in this area.
Please note this is only a rough map designed to show dealers the number of shops in the various towns, and is not nessarily totally accurate.
LINCS
LEICS
A606
A1
Oakham
A606
Empingham
Manton
A6003
Wing
A6121
A47
CAMBS
Uppingham
A6003
NORTHANTS

EMPINGHAM, Nr. Oakham

Churchgate Antiques

13 Church St. LE15 8PN. (R. Wheatley). Open Wed., Fri., Sat. and Sun. 12-6, other times by appointment. SIZE: Medium. *STOCK: Furniture, mainly 18th-19th C, £50-£4,000; paintings and prints, £25-£1,000; silver and plate, 19th-20th C, £5-£1,000.* LOC: Opposite church, off A606. PARK: Easy. TEL: 01780 460528.

MANTON

David Smith Antiques

Old Cottage, 20 St. Mary's Rd. LE15 8SU. Est. 1953. Open 9-5. CL: Sun., except by appointment. *STOCK: Furniture, glass, silver.* PARK: Easy. TEL: 01572 737244/737607.

OAKHAM

Fine Art of Oakham BADA LAPADA

4 High St. LE15 6AL. (Dr A.J. Smith). Open 10-5. CL: Mon. *STOCK: Continental oils and watercolours, Victorian and 19th C.* TEL: 01572 755221; fax - 01572 770047.

The Old House Gallery

13-15 Market Place. LE15 6DT. (R.A. Clarke). Est. 1979. Open 9.30-5, Sat. 9.30-4. CL: Thurs. SIZE: Medium. *STOCK: Oil paintings, £50-£3,500; art studio pottery, 1850-1990, £5-£500; watercolours, £25-£2,000; prints and objets d'art, £5-£500; antiquarian county maps, £15-£250.* PARK: Easy. TEL: 01572 755538. SER: Valuations; restorations (oils, watercolours, prints, frames); framing.

C. Reynolds Antiques

The East Lodge, Burley Mansion House, Burley-on-the-Hill. LE15 7TE. Est. 1972. Resident. Usually available but telephone call advisable. SIZE: Large. *STOCK: Early verge watches, repeater and other unusual clocks and watches.* TEL: 01572 771551.

Rutland Antique Clock Gallery

37 Trent Rd. LE15 6HE. (K.G. Neale). Est. 1986. Open by appointment only. SIZE: Small. *STOCK: 17th C clocks, £45-£2,000.* LOC: A606, Oakham High St., Mill St., Brooke Rd., corner plot between Trent Rd. and Spey Rd. PARK: Easy. TEL: 01572 723375; home - same. SER: Valuations; restorations.

Rutland Antiques

16 Melton Rd. (Mrs J. Freeman). Open 10-3 or by appointment. CL: Tues. and Thurs. *STOCK: Brass, glass, small furniture, postcards, lamps, pictures, prints, silver.* TEL: 01664 474571.

Oakham continued

Swans LAPADA

27 Mill St. LE15 6EA. (P.W. Jones). Est. 1988. Open 9.30-5.30, Sun. 2-5.30. SIZE: Large. *STOCK: French and English beds and associated furniture; 18th-19th C antiques, mainly decorative and upholstered.* LOC: 150yds. from High St. PARK: Easy. TEL: 01572 724364; home - 01572 757252. SER: Manufactures new bases and mattresses; valuations; restorations. VAT: Stan/Spec.

UPPINGHAM

Clutter

14 Orange St. LE15 9SQ. (M.C. Sumner). Est. 1982. Open 10-5. *STOCK: Victorian linen and lace; textiles including Durham quilts, chenilles; interesting silver, porcelain, glass, small furniture, kitchenalia, 10p-£1,000.* LOC: Take old A47 from by-pass, shop 25yds. from traffic lights. PARK: Nearby. TEL: 01572 823745; home - 01572 717243. SER: Valuations; restorations (furniture, brass, copper, silver, bronze, ivory, lacquer, shibayama and associated materials, ceramics); hire (christening gowns and Victorian wedding dress and accessories).

John Garner

51-53 High St. East. LE15 9PY. Est. 1966. Open 9-5.30, Sun. 2-5, prior telephone call advisable. SIZE: Large + warehouse. *STOCK: Furniture, 18th-19th C; clocks, bronzes, chandeliers, decorative pieces, period frames, mirrors, garden statuary. Warehouse - old wood, pine and 20th C furniture.* LOC: Just off A47, close to market place. PARK: Easy. TEL: 01572 823607; fax - 01572 821654. SER: Valuations; restorations (furniture, paintings, prints); framing (trade); courier; export. VAT: Stan/Spec.

Gilberts of Uppingham

Ayston Rd. (M. Gilbert). Open Wed., Fri. and Sat. 9.30-5, Mon. and Tues. 9.30-1 and 2-5. *STOCK: General antiques.* TEL: 01572 823486.

Goldmark Books

14 Orange St. LE15 9SQ. (M.M. Goldmark). Open 9.30-5.30 and Sunday afternoons. *STOCK: Antiquarian and secondhand books.* LOC: Between Market Sq. and traffic lights. PARK: Nearby. TEL: 01572 822694.

Marc Oxley Fine Art

10 Orange St. LE15 9SQ. Resident. Est. 1981. Open 9.30-5.30, Sat. 10-6, Sun. 2.30-5.30. *STOCK: Original watercolours and drawings, 1700-1950, £5-£850; oils, 19th-20th C, £100-£1,500; prints, mainly 19th C, £5-£50; maps, 17th-19th C, £10-£375.* LOC: From A47 on main road into town, just before Market Sq. PARK: Market Sq. TEL: 01572 822334; home - same. SER: Valuations; restorations (watercolours, drawings and prints); buys at auction (watercolours and drawings).

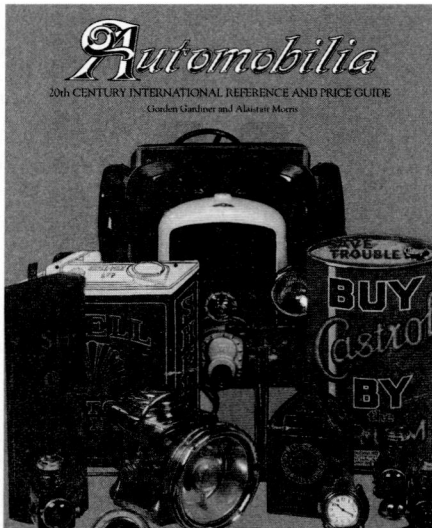

Uppingham continued

T.J. Roberts

39/41 High St. East. LE15 9PY. Resident. Open 9.30-5.30. *STOCK: Furniture, 18th-19th C; porcelain, pottery, English, Chinese, European, 18th-19th C; Staffordshire figures, paintings.* PARK: Easy. TEL: 01572 821493.

E. and C. Royall Antiques

Printers Yard, High St. East. LE15 1XX. Open 10-4.30. CL: Thurs. *STOCK: Furniture, pictures, silver, porcelain, glassware, ivories and Oriental bronzes.* TEL: 01858 565744.

Tattersall's

14b Orange St. LE15 9SQ. (J. Tattersall). Est. 1985. Open 9.30-5. CL: Thurs. SIZE: Small. *STOCK: Persian rugs, mirrors, sofas, 19th-20th C.* PARK: Easy, 200yds. TEL: 01572 821171. SER: Restorations (rugs, carpets).

Uppingham continued

Woodman's House Antiques

35 High Street East. (Mr. and Mrs. James Collie). 1991. SIZE: Small. *STOCK: Furniture, 18th-19th C.* PARK: Easy. TEL: 01572 821799; fax - same. SER: Valuations; restorations; buys at auction. FAIRS: Newark.

WING, Nr. Oakham

Robert Bingley Antiques

Home Farm, Church St. LE15 8RS. Open 9-5, Sun. 11-4. SIZE: Large. *STOCK: Furniture, 17th-19th C, £50-£5,000; glass, clocks, silver and plate, pictures and porcelain.* LOC: Next to church. PARK: Own. TEL: 01572 737725; home - 01572 737314. SER: Valuations; restorations. VAT: Spec.

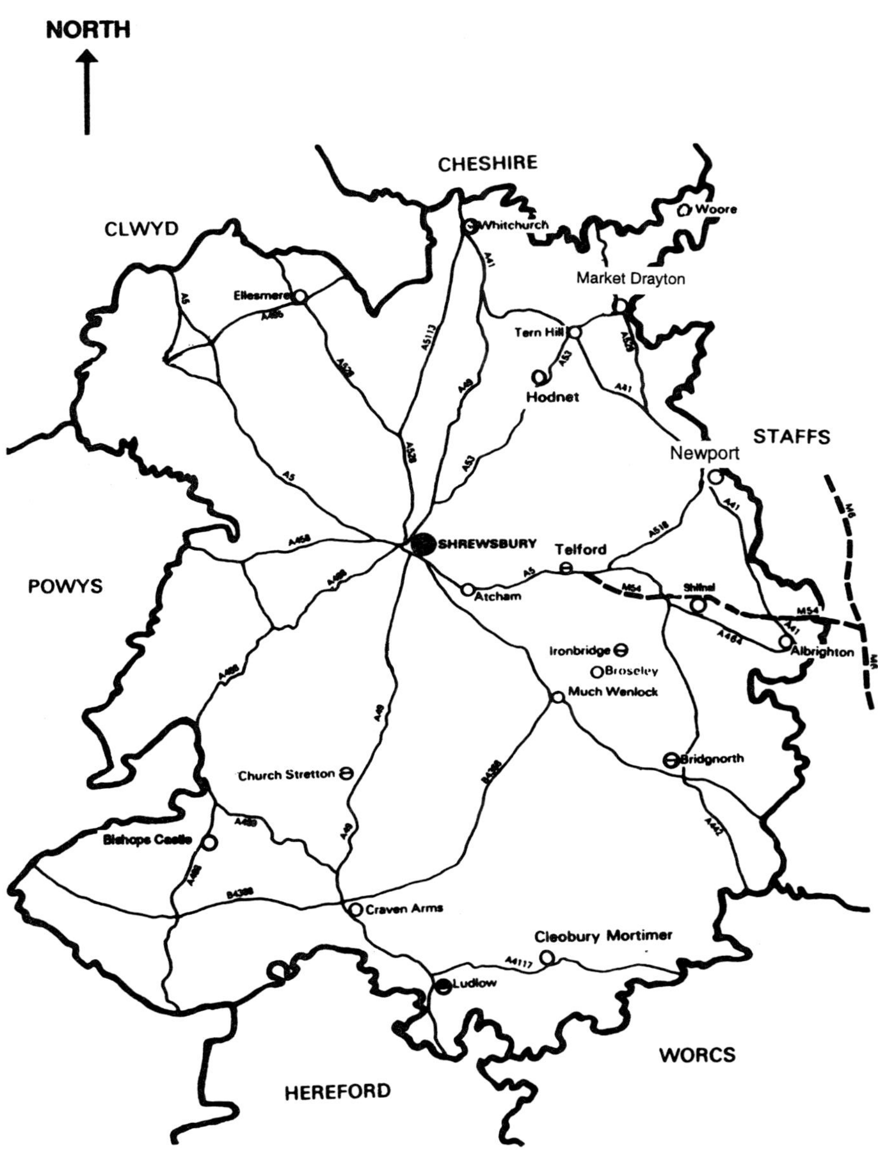

1-2
3-5
6-12
13+

Key to number of shops in this area.

Please note this is only a rough map designed to show dealers the number of shops in the various towns, and is not necessarily totally accurate.

ALBRIGHTON (NEACHLEY)

Doveridge House of Neachley BADA LAPADA

Long Lane (alongside RAF Cosford). TF11 8PJ. CINOA. (Cdr and Mrs H.E.R. Bain). Est. 1967. Open 9-5 seven days a week and/or by appointment. SIZE: Large. *STOCK: 17th-19th C English and Continental furniture, fine art, clocks, decorative artifacts.* LOC: From London M1 or M40 to M6. Junction 10A via M54 for North and Mid Wales. Leave at Junction 3 (A41) in Wolverhampton/Cosford direction. 40mph symbol after quarter mile, RH lane, turn right at Neachley sign into Long Lane, 6th entrance (lodge gates). From the North, M6 Junction 11, A460 towards Wolverhampton. Join M54 at Junction 1 then as Junction 3 above. PARK: Easy. TEL: 01902 373131. SER: Valuations; restorations (furniture and oils); interior design; export.

ATCHAM, Nr. Shrewsbury

Mytton Antiques

Norton Cross Roads. SY4 4UM. (M.A., E.A. and J.M. Nares and Manager - Hugh Norton). Est. 1972. Open 9.30-5.30 or by appointment. SIZE: Medium. *STOCK: General antiques, furniture, 1700-1900, £50-£3,000; clocks, all types, £35-£2,000; smalls, £15-£1,000.* LOC: On B5061 (the old A5) between Shrewsbury and Wellington. PARK: Own. TEL: 01952 740229(24hrs.); fax - 01952 461154; internet - http://www.enta. net/mytton. SER: Buys at auction; suppliers of reference books and restoration materials. VAT: Stan/Spec.

BISHOP'S CASTLE

Ark Antiques

9 Market Square. (Jill Thomas). Est. 1974. Open 10.30-4.30 and Bank Holidays. CL: Mon. and Wed. SIZE: Small. *STOCK: Oak and pine country furniture, 18th-19th C; country and rural tools, brass and iron beds.* PARK: Easy. TEL: Home - 01588 638608. SER: Valuations; restorations (metal and wood); buys at auction (cottage furniture and artifacts).

BRIDGNORTH

Bridgnorth Antiques Centre

Whiteburn St. WV16 4QT. (R.C. Lewis). 1992. Open 9.30-5.30, Sun. 10.30-4.30. SIZE: Large. *STOCK: 19th-20th C furniture, £25-£1,000, pianos, £250-£5,000, ceramics, £1-£300; 18th-20th C clocks, £25-£3,000.* PARK: Nearby. TEL: 01746 768055. SER: Restorations (clocks, pianos).

English Heritage

2 Whitburn St., High Town. WV16 4QN. (P.J. Wainwright). Open 10-5. CL: Thurs. SIZE: Medium. *STOCK: Jewellery, silverware and general antiques, militaria.* LOC: Just off High St. PARK: High St. TEL: 01746 762097. SER: Framing. VAT: Stan/Spec.

Bridgnorth continued

Micawber Antiques

64 St. Mary's St. WV16 4DR. (M. and N. Berthoud). Open 10-5, other days by appointment. CL: Mon. and Thurs. SIZE: Medium. *STOCK: English porcelain and pottery, decorative items, £5-£500; small furniture, £100-£1,000.* LOC: 100yds. west of town hall in High St. PARK: Easy. TEL: 01746 763254; home - same. SER: Buys at auction (English porcelain).

Old Mill Antique Centre

Mill St. WV15 5AG. (D.A. and J.R. Ridgeway). Est. 1996. Open 10-6 including Sun. SIZE: Large - 70 dealers. *STOCK: Wide range of general antiques including period furniture, porcelain and silver, jewellery, prints and watercolours, collectables.* LOC: Main road. PARK: Own. TEL: 01746 768778; fax - 01746 762248. SER: Valuations; restorations. VAT: Stan.

BROSELEY

John Boulton Fine Art

6 Church St. TF12 5DG. Resident. Est. 1983. Open 9-5, Sun. 2-5. SIZE: Medium. *STOCK: Oils, watercolours and prints, late 19th C to contemporary, £100-£2,500.* LOC: Junction 4, M54, take A442. PARK: Easy. TEL: 01952 882860. FAIRS: Buxton; NEC Birmingham; Shrewsbury; Edinburgh.

CHURCH STRETTON

Antiques on the Square

2 Sandford Court, Sandford Ave. SY6 6DA. (Chris Radford). Est. 1985. Open 9.30-5, Sun. by appointment. SIZE: Medium. *STOCK: Art Deco ceramics, Clarice Cliff, furniture, glass, 1920-1930, £5-£3,000; collectors items, TV's, radios, £5-£500; decorative items, £5-£1,000; both pre-1939.* Not Stocked: Armour, stamps, period furniture. LOC: Off A49. PARK: Easy. TEL: 01694 724111; home - 01694 723072; mobile - 0831 336052. SER: Valuations; restorations (furniture, glass, tapestry, metalware, paintings and ceramics); buys at auction (English furniture pre-1830); research; Clarice Cliff exhibition annually. FAIRS: Battersea (Art Deco); Loughborough; Warwick (Art Deco). VAT: Stan/Spec.

Cardingmill Antiques

1 Burway Rd. SY6 6DL. (Mrs P. A. Benton). Est. 1976. Open Thurs., Fri. and Sat. 10.30-5, Mon., Tues. and Wed. by appointment. *STOCK: Wall clocks and furniture, 18th-19th C, £250-£1,250; Measham teapots, 19th-20th C, £100-£450; ribbon and lace plates, 19th-20th C, £10-£40; horse brasses (NHBS), 19th-20th C, £10-£250.* LOC: A49. PARK: Valuations; restorations (longcase and wall clocks). TEL: 01694 724555; home - 01584 877880.

Church Stretton continued

Longmynd Antiques

Crossways. SY6 6PG. (David Coomber). Est. 1994. Open 10.30-5, Sun. 11-5. CL: Wed. SIZE: Large. *STOCK: Furniture, 17th C to Edwardian, £100-£10,000; collectables, 19th-20th C, £5-£500.* LOC: A49. Premises immediately south of traffic lights. PARK: Own. TEL: 01694 724474; fax - same. SER: Buys at auction. VAT: Spec.

Stretton Antiques Market

36 Sandford Ave. SY6 6BH. (T. and L. Elvins). Est. 1986. Open 9.30-5.30, Sun. and Bank Holidays 10.30-4.30. SIZE: Large - 55 dealers. *STOCK: General antiques, shipping items and collectables.* LOC: Town centre. PARK: Easy. TEL: 01694 723718. SER: Valuations; buys at auction.

CLEOBURY MORTIMER, Nr. Kidderminster

Cleobury Mortimer Antique Centre

Childe Rd. DY14 8PA. Open 10-5 including Sun. SIZE: Large. *STOCK: Georgian, Victorian, Edwardian and old pine furniture, period beds, bric-a-brac and architectural items.* PARK: Own. TEL: 01299 270513.

CRAVEN ARMS

I. and S. Antiques

Stokesay, Ludlow Rd. SY7 9QL. (J. Briscoe). Open 9-5, Sun. 10.30-4.30 in summer. *STOCK: Unstripped pine, shipping goods, treen, country items, bric-a-brac, books, 19th to early 20th C.* TEL: 01588 672263; home - 01588 640374.

ELLESMERE

White Lion Antiques

Market St. SY12 0AP. (Lynne Davies). Open 9.30-5.30. SIZE: Medium. *STOCK: Furniture, glass, china, silver, jewellery.* TEL: 01691 623835.

HODNET, Nr. Market Drayton

Hodnet Antiques

13a and 19a Shrewsbury St. TF9 3NP. (Mrs J. Scott). Est. 1976. Open Tues. and Thurs. 2-5, other times by appointment. SIZE: Small. *STOCK: General antiques - china, glass, silver, jewellery, pictures, brass and copper, collectables and unusual decorative items, £5-£1,000; 18th-20th C furniture, £100-£5,000.* LOC: A53. PARK: Outside shop. TEL: Home - 01630 638591. SER: Valuations; buys at auction.

IRONBRIDGE

Ironbridge Antique & Reproduction Centre

Dale End. TF8 7DS. (F.G. Cooke). Est. 1968. Open 10-5, Sun. 2-5. SIZE: Large. *STOCK:*

Ironbridge continued

Porcelain, pictures, jewellery, bric-a-brac, furniture and reproductions. PARK: Easy. TEL: 01952 433784.

Tudor House Antiques (Bill Dickenson)

11 Tontine Hill. TF8 7AL. Open 10-5, Sun. 2-5. CL: Mon. *STOCK: General antiques, especially porcelain including Caughley and Coalport.* LOC: Opposite bridge. TEL: 01952 433783.

A group of French weights, c.1850. (Top to bottom, left to right). A Baccarat blue camomile with red bud, a Baccarat yellow wheatflower, a St. Louis blue jasper with yellow dablia, a St. Louis faceted upright bouquet, a Baccarat butterfly and white clematis weight, a Baccarat strawberry weight. Average diameter 2¾in.

Since the start of their production, glass paperweights have been popular with collectors. Although some of the classic, early French weights are out of reach of all but the wealthiest, many later pieces, every bit as skilful and as creative as their predecessors, are available to new collectors.

From an article entitled "Weight-Watching: Collecting Glass Paper-weights" by Simon Cottle which appeared in the March 1998 issue of **Antique Collecting**

LUDLOW

Architectural Antiques and Interiors

140 Corve St. SY8 2PG. (R.G. and J. Dickinson). Open 10-5. *STOCK: Bathrooms, fireplaces, lighting, doors and other architectural antiques.* TEL: 01584 876207.

Bayliss Antiques

22 Old St. SY8 1NP. Resident. *STOCK: Furniture, silver, paintings, decorative items.* TEL: 01584 873634.

R.G. Cave and Sons Ltd BADA LAPADA

17 Broad St. SY8 1NG. Resident. Est. 1962. Open 9.30-5.30. *STOCK: Furniture, 1630-1830; clocks, barometers, metalwork, fine art and collectors' items.* PARK: Easy. TEL: 01584 873568; fax - 01584 875050. SER: Valuations. VAT: Spec.

John Clegg

12 Old St. SY8 1NP. Resident. Est. 1960. Open 8.30-5. *STOCK: Country and other period furniture, metalware and decorative items.* TEL: 01584 873176.

The Curiosity Shop

127 Old St. SY8 1NU. Resident. (J. Luffman). Open 9.30-5 or by appointment. *STOCK: Longcase, bracket and mantel clocks, music boxes, country furniture, paintings and militaria, £5-£20,000.* TEL: 01584 875927; mobile - 0836 592898. SER: Valuations; buys at auction (militaria, paintings). VAT: Spec.

Ludlow continued

G. & D. Ginger Antiques

5 Corve St. SY8 1DA. Resident. Open 9-5. SIZE: Large. *STOCK: Oak dressers and farmhouse tables, Welsh cupboards and presses, country and mahogany furniture; decorative and associated items.* TEL: 01584 876939; mobile - 07970 666437.

Mitre House Antiques

Corve Bridge. SY8 1DY. (L. Jones). Open 9-5.30. SIZE: Shop + trade warehouse. *STOCK: Clocks, pine and general antiques. Warehouse - unstripped pine and shipping goods.* TEL: 01584 872138.

Pepper Lane Antiques

Pepper Lane. SY8 1PX. (D. Nicholas and C. Reid). Est. 1985. Open 10-5. SIZE: Large. *STOCK: Furniture, porcelain, silver and plate.* LOC: Just off King St. PARK: Easy. TEL: 01584 876494. SER: Re-upholstery.

M. and R. Taylor (Antiques)

53 Broad St. SY8 1NH. (M. Taylor). Est. 1977. Open from 9 am. including evenings. SIZE: Medium. *STOCK: Furniture, mahogany, oak and walnut, Persian rugs, brass and copper, 17th-19th C.* PARK: Nearby. TEL: 01584 874169; home - same. VAT: Stan/Spec.

Ludlow continued

Teme Valley Antiques

1 The Bull Ring. SY8 1AD. (C.S. Harvey). Est. 1979. Usually open 10-5.30, Sun. by appointment. SIZE: Medium. *STOCK: English and Continental porcelain, 18th to early 20th C, £25-£2,500; furniture, oil and watercolour paintings, £50-£2,500; jewellery, silver, plate, metalware and glass, £10-£3,500; both 17th to early 20th C.* Not Stocked: Militaria, coins and carpets. LOC: Town centre opposite Lunn Poly. PARK: Easy. TEL: 01584 874686. SER: Valuations; buys at auction (porcelain). VAT: Stan/Spec.

Valentyne Dawes Gallery

Dawes Mansion, Church St. SY8 1AP. (B.S. McCreddie). Open 10-5.30, Sun. in summer and Bank Holidays. SIZE: Medium. *STOCK: Paintings, 19th to early 20th C, £200-£40,000; furniture, 17th-19th C, £50-£4,000; porcelain, 19th C, £5-£500.* LOC: Town centre near Buttercross. PARK: Nearby. TEL: 01584 874160. SER: Valuations; restorations (oil paintings, watercolours, furniture). VAT: Spec.

MARKET DRAYTON

Peter Wain BADA

Glynde Cottage, Longford. TF9 3PW. Open by appointment only. SIZE: Medium. *STOCK: Oriental ceramics and works of art, £100-£10,000.* TEL: 01630 647118; fax - same. SER: Valuations; buys at auction.

MUCH WENLOCK

Cruck House Antiques

23 Barrow St. TF13 6EN. (B. Roderick Smith). Est. 1985. Open 9.30-5.30. CL: Wed. SIZE: Small. *STOCK: Silver and watercolours, 19th-20th C, £25-£300; furniture, 19th C, £50-£500; general antiques.* Not Stocked: Weapons and gold. LOC: Near Square. PARK: Easy. TEL: 01952 727165.

Wenlock Fine Art

3 The Square. TF13 6LX. (P. Cotterill). Est. 1990. Open Wed.-Sat. 10-5. SIZE: Medium. *STOCK: Modern British paintings, mainly 20th C, some late 19th C, £100-£6,000.* PARK: Nearby. TEL: 01952 728232; home - 01952 252376. SER: Valuations; restorations (cleaning); mounting; framing; buys at auction (as stock). VAT: Spec.

NEWPORT

Amanda's Antique Centre/Flea Market

The Old Town Hall, Stafford St. TF10 7AG. (Amanda Sutton). 1992. Open 10-5. SIZE: Large. *STOCK: General antiques.* LOC: Off A41 Wolverhampton-Whitchurch. PARK: 50 yds. TEL: 01952 820364; home - 01952 606385.

SHIFNAL

Antiques of Shifnal

2 Church St. TF11 9AA. (C. Weaver). Open 10-5.30. CL: Mon. and Thurs. SIZE: Medium. *STOCK: Furniture, 18th-19th C, £200-£1,000; ceramics, silver and prints, 19th C, £25-£500; works of art, £25-£100.* LOC: Town centre, under railway bridge, follow road round then 1st right into one-way street (Church St). PARK: 100 yards to right of shop on left. TEL: 01952 462986. SER: Cane and rush seating; picture framing.

SHREWSBURY

Candle Lane Books

28-29 Princess St. SY1 1LW. (J. Thornhill). Open 9.30-5. *STOCK: Antiquarian and secondhand books.* TEL: 01743 365301.

Juliet Chilton Antiques and Interiors

69 Wyle Cop. SY1 1UX. Open 9.30-6. SIZE: Large. *STOCK: Furniture and smalls, mainly 1700's-1920's and some reproduction.* TEL: 01743 358699/366553; fax - 01743 366563. SER: Shipping and packing.

Shrewsbury continued

Collectors' Gallery

7 Castle Gates. SY1 2AE. Open 9-5.30. SIZE: Large. *STOCK: Coins and medals; stamps and postcards; related books and accessories.* TEL: 01743 272140; fax - 01743 366041.

Collectors' Place

29a Princess St., The Square. SY1 1LW. (Keith Jones). Open Wed.-Sat. 9.30-5. *STOCK: Collectables especially Prattware, potlids and bottles, 1700-1900.* TEL: 01743 246150.

Sue Dyer Antiques

9 St John's Hill. SY1 1JD. Est. 1971. Open 9.30-5.30, Mon. and Wed. 9.30-5, Sun. pm and other times by appointment. SIZE: Small. *STOCK: Small silver collectables and cutlery, 1850-1930's; china, objet d'art, coloured glass, 1800-1940; both £5-£200; small furniture, 1800-1940, £5-£1,000.* LOC: Straight on at bottom of Pride Hill, shop 200yds on left. PARK: Loading only or Barker St.TEL: 01743 350358; home - 01743 873354. VAT: Spec.

Expressions

17 Princess St. SY1 1LP. Open 10.30-4.30. CL: Thurs. *STOCK: Art Deco originals, ceramics, furniture, jewellery, lighting, mirrors, prints.* TEL: 01743 351731.

Hutton Antiques

18 Princess St. SY1 1LP. (Mrs C. Brookfield). Est. 1978. Open 9-12.30 and 1.30-4. CL: Mon. SIZE: Medium. *STOCK: Silver, porcelain and glass, 18th-19th C, £25-£500; small furniture, £100-£2,000; Victorian jewellery.* LOC: Off square, near Music Hall. PARK: Easy. TEL: 01743 245810. SER: Valuations.

The Little Gem

18 St. Mary's St. SY1 1ED. (M.A. Bowdler). Est. 1969. Open 9-5.30. CL: Thurs. (except Dec.). SIZE: Medium. *STOCK: Georgian and Victorian jewellery; unusual gem stones, watches; handmade jewellery.* Not Stocked: Weapons, coins, medals, furniture. LOC: Opposite St. Mary's Church along from G.P.O. PARK: In side road (St. Mary's Place) opposite shop. TEL: 01743 352085. SER: Repairs.

F.C. Manser and Son Ltd LAPADA

53/54 Wyle Cop. SY1 1XJ. Est. 1944. Open 9-5.30. CL: Thurs. pm. SIZE: Large. *STOCK: Furniture, 17th-20th C, £150-£12,000; Oriental items, 15th-20th C, £5-£3,000; silver, plate, copper, 18th-20th C, £5-£6,000; oils and watercolours, £100-£20,000; jewellery, 19th-20th C, £50-£6,000.* Not Stocked: Coins, books. LOC: 150yds. town side of English bridge. PARK: Own. TEL: 01743 351120/245730; fax - 01743 271047. SER: Valuations; restorations. VAT: Stan/Spec.

Shrewsbury continued

Princess Antique Centre
14a The Square. (J. Langford). Open 9.30-5.30. SIZE: 35 dealers. *STOCK: General antiques and collectables.* TEL: 01743 343701.

Quayside Antiques
9 Frankwell. (Jean and Chris Winter). Open Tues. and Wed. 10-4, Fri. and Sat. 9.30-5. SIZE: Large. *STOCK: Victorian and Edwardian furniture, especially dining tables and sets of chairs, desks, bookcases, beds, wardrobes.* LOC: Near Halls Saleroom. PARK: Own. TEL: 01743 360490; workshop - 01948 665838; home - 01948 830363. SER: Restorations (furniture).

Raleigh Antiques
23 Belle Vue Rd. SY3 7LN. (R. and E. Handbury-Madin). Est. 1968. Open 9-5. *STOCK: Furniture, pottery, porcelain, glass, jewellery, silver.* PARK: Easy. TEL: 01743 359552. SER: Valuations; restorations (furniture, clocks).

Shrewsbury Antique Centre
15 Princess House, The Square. SY1 1JZ. (J. Langford). Est. 1978. Open 9.30-5.30. SIZE: Large - 50 dealers. *STOCK: General antiques and collectables.* LOC: Town centre just off the Square. PARK: Nearby. TEL: 01743 247704.

Shrewsbury Antique Market
Frankwell Quay Warehouse. SY3 8LG. (J. Langford). Open 9.30-5. SIZE: Large - 45 units. *STOCK: General antiques and collectors' items, £1-£2,000.* LOC: Alongside Frankwell Quay car park. PARK: Easy. TEL: 01743 350916.

Tiffany Antiques
Shrewsbury Antique Centre, 15 Princess House, The Square. SY1 1JZ. (A. Wilcox). Est. 1988. Open 9.30-5.30. *STOCK: Metalware, collectables, curios, china and glass.* LOC: Town centre. PARK: Multi-storey. TEL: Home - 01270 257425; mobile - 0370 380261. SER: Buys at auction.

STANTON, Nr. Shrewsbury

Marcus Moore Antiques
Booley House, Booley. SY4 4LY. (M.G.J. and M.P. Moore). Est. 1980. Usually open but prior telephone call advisable. SIZE: Medium. *STOCK: Oak and country furniture, late 17th to 18th C; Georgian mahogany furniture, 18th to early 19th C; all £50-£7,000; some Victorian furniture; associated items.* LOC: Half a mile north of Stanton on right. PARK: Easy. TEL: 01939 200333. SER: Restorations (furniture); polishing; search; shipping. VAT: Stan/Spec.

TELFORD

Haygate Gallery
40 Haygate Rd., Wellington. TF1 1QT. (Mrs M. Kuznierz). Open 9-5, Sat. 9-1. CL: Wed. *STOCK:*

Telford continued

Watercolours, oils and general antiques. LOC: One mile from junction 7, M54. PARK: Easy. TEL: 01952 248553. SER: Framing.

Brian James Antiques
Old Maltings, The Lawns, Wellington. TF1 3AF. Est. 1985. Open 9-6, Sat. 9.30-12.30, Sun. by appointment. SIZE: Large. *STOCK: Chests of drawers, Georgian to Victorian, £50-£1,500.* LOC: Off M54, junction 6. Follow signs for Telford Hospital then Wellington Centre, turn right at Red Lion. PARK: Easy. TEL: 01952 256592/243906. SER: Restorations and conversions; linen presses and chests made to order. VAT: Stan. *Trade Only.*

Oddfellows Antiques
120 High St., Wellington. TF1 1JU. Resident. (Bernie Pugh). Open by appointment only. *STOCK: Furniture.* TEL: 01952 256184.

St. George's Antiques
The Chapel, Church St., St George's. (McNulty Wholesalers). Est. 1983. Open 11-5. CL: Mon. SIZE: Large. *STOCK: Painted pine, mahogany; small interesting items.* LOC: 5 minutes from town centre. PARK: Easy. TEL: 01952 616613. FAIRS: Newark. VAT: Stan.

TERN HILL, Nr. Market Drayton

L. Onions - White Cottage Antiques
White Cottage, 8 Tern Hill. TF9 3PR. Est. 1965. Open 9.30-5.30. SIZE: Medium. *STOCK: Furniture, oak and some walnut, brass, 16th-18th C.* LOC: On A41, 200yds. from roundabout at Tern Hill cross roads. PARK: Easy. TEL: 01630 638222. VAT: Stan/Spec.

WHITCHURCH

Dodington Antiques
15 Dodington and The Old Music Hall. SY13 1EA. Resident. (G. MacGillivray). Est. 1978. By appointment. SIZE: Large. *STOCK: Oak, fruitwood, walnut country and 18th to early 19th C mahogany furniture, longcase clocks, barometers, £10-£6,000.* LOC: On fringe of town centre. PARK: Easy. TEL: 01948 663399. SER: Buys at auction. VAT: Stan/Spec.

WOORE, Nr. Crewe

The Mount
12 Nantwich Rd. CW3 9SA. Est. 1978. Open most afternoons and weekends (prior telephone call advisable). *STOCK: Watercolours, oils and drawings, Victorian to early 20th C; county maps, prints, engravings and topographical items, from 17th C; all £2-£500.* LOC: Junction of A51 and A525. PARK: Easy. TEL: 01630 647274; home - same. SER: Framing; finder (maps and topography).

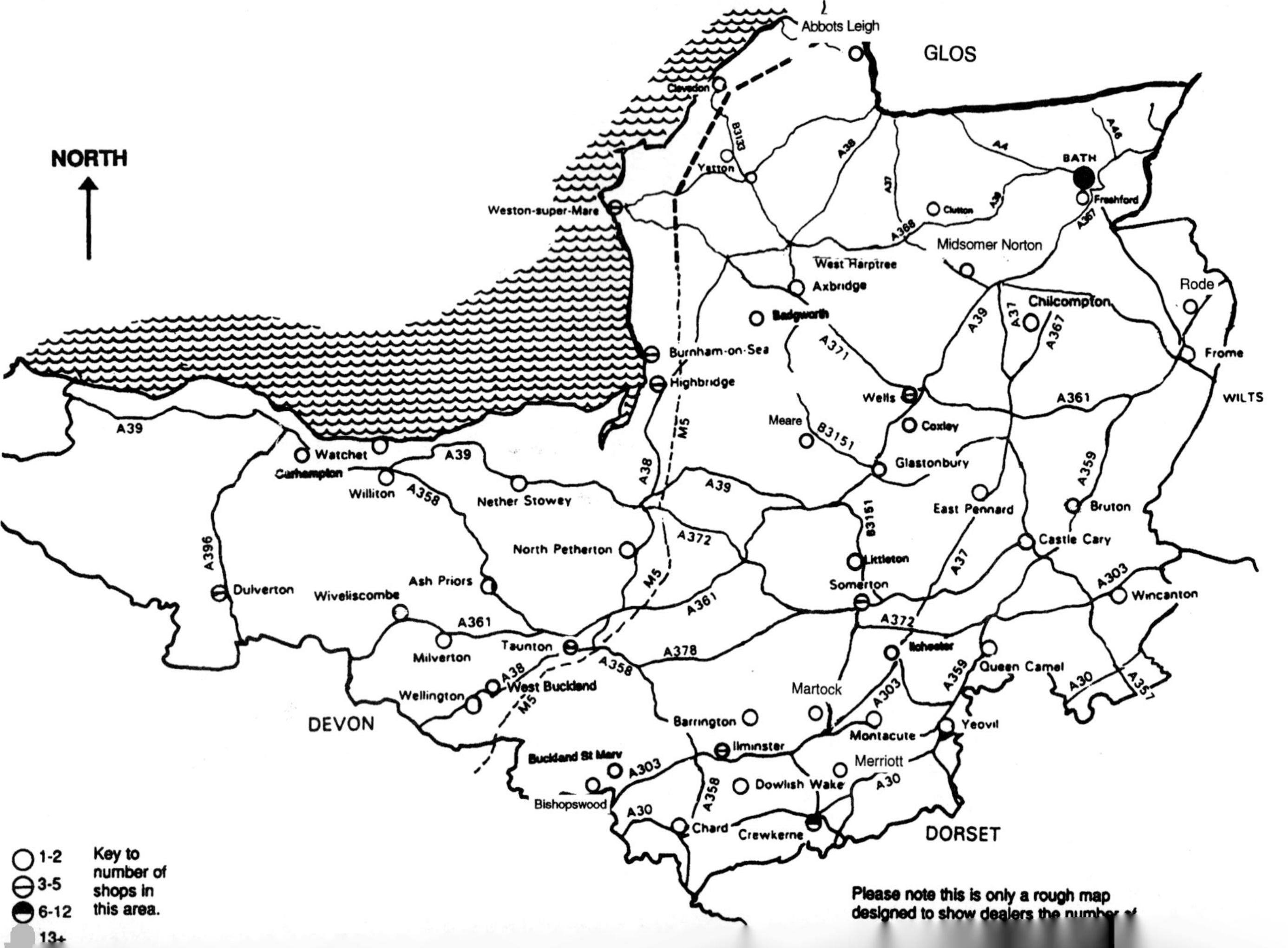

NORTH
GLOS
WILTS
DORSET
DEVON
Abbots Leigh
Clevedon
Yatton
Weston-super-Mare
BATH
Freshford
Clutton
Midsomer Norton
West Harptree
Axbridge
Badgworth
Chilcompton
Rode
Frome
Burnham-on-Sea
Highbridge
Wells
Coxley
Meare
Glastonbury
East Pennard
Bruton
Castle Cary
Wincanton
Littleton
Somerton
Ilchester
Queen Camel
Yeovil
Martock
Montacute
Merriott
Barrington
Ilminster
Dowlish Wake
Crewkerne
Chard
Buckland St Mary
Bishopswood
Taunton
West Buckland
Wellington
Milverton
Wiveliscombe
Ash Priors
North Petherton
Nether Stowey
Williton
Watchet
Carhampton
Dulverton
A4
A46
A38
A37
A39
A368
A367
B3133
A371
A361
B3151
A359
A372
A303
A30
A357
A378
A358
A396
M5
1-2
3-5
6-12
13+
Key to number of shops in this area.
Please note this is only a rough map designed to show dealers the number of

ABBOTS LEIGH, Nr. Bristol

David and Sally March Antiques LAPADA

Oak Wood Lodge, Stoke Leigh Woods. BS8 3QB. (D. and S. March). Est. 1981. Open by appointment. *STOCK: 18th to early 19th C English porcelain especially figures and Bristol.* PARK: Easy. TEL: 01275 372422; mobile - 0374 838376; fax - 01275 371032. SER: Valuations; buys at auction (as stock). FAIRS: LAPADA; Chelsea; NEC; Cumberland Ceramic. VAT: Spec.

ASH PRIORS, Nr. Taunton

The Granary Galleries

Court House. TA4 3NQ. (R. Hall). Est. 1969. Open 8.30-5.30. SIZE: Large. *STOCK: Period items, general antiques, 18th-19th C furniture, some shipping goods.* PARK: Easy. TEL: 01823 432402; home - (after 6.30) 01823 432816. VAT: Stan/Spec.

Hall's Antiques

Court House. TA4 3NQ. (A.R. and J.M. Hall). Est. 1945. Open 8.30-5.30. CL: Sun. except by appointment. SIZE: Large. *STOCK: English and Continental furniture, 18th-19th C; oil paintings, watercolours, 17th-19th C; all £25-£10,000; shipping goods.* LOC: On A358. PARK: Easy. TEL: 01823 432402; home - same. SER: Valuations; buys at auction. VAT: Stan/Spec.

AXBRIDGE

The Old Post House

Weare, Bridgewater Rd. BS26 2JF. (Ray and Mollie Seaman). *STOCK: General antiques and country furniture.* TEL: 01934 732372.

BADGWORTH, Nr. Axbridge

John Hawley (MBHI) Antique Clocks

Court Barn, Church Lane. BS26 2QP. Est. 1972. Open by appointment. *STOCK: Clocks especially longcase, bracket, wall and carriage.* TEL: 01934 733444. SER: Valuations; restorations; repairs.

BARRINGTON, Nr. Ilminster

Stuart Interiors (Antiques)Ltd LAPADA

Barrington Court. TA19 0NG. Open 9-5, Sat. 10-5. SIZE: Large. *STOCK: Oak furniture, £100-£10,000; accessories, £50-£2,500; both pre-1720.* Not Stocked: 18th C mahogany. LOC: Between A303 and M5, 5 miles north-east of Ilminster. House is National Trust property, signposted in area. PARK: Easy. TEL: 01460 240349. SER: Valuations; buys at auction (early oak furniture and accessories, interior design and architectural items including oak panelling). VAT: Spec.

BATH

"27A" "27B"

27a 27b Belvedere, Lansdown. BA1 5HR. (Paul Michael Farnham and Asociates). Est. 1970. Open 10-6. SIZE: Large. *STOCK: Interesting furniture and objects from all periods.* PARK: Easy. TEL: 01225 428256; fax - same; e-mail - pmfarnham@ aol.com.

4 Miles Buildings - Nick Kuhn

4 Miles Buildings, Off George St. BA1 2QS. BABADA. Est. 1992. Always open Sat. 10-5, other times by chance or appointment. SIZE: Small. *STOCK: 20th C furniture and design, British fine art, naïve art, hooked rugs, country pottery, £30-£2,000.* LOC: City centre, near Bartlett Street Antiques Centre. PARK: Nearby. TEL: 01225 425486. FAIRS: Bath & Bradford-on-Avon Antique Dealers.

Abbey Galleries

9 Abbey Churchyard. BA1 1LY. (R. Dickson). Est. 1930. Open 10.30-5.30. *STOCK: Jewellery, £50; Oriental, £100; both 18th-19th C; silver, 18th C, £100.* Not Stocked: Furniture. TEL: 01225 460565. SER: Valuations; restorations (jewellery and clocks); buys at auction. VAT: Stan.

Adam Gallery

13 John St. BA1 2JL. (P. and P. Dye). Open 9.30-5.30 or by appointment. *STOCK: Late Victorian and Modern British oil paintings and water-colours, especially figurative and landscape, and Glasgow and Newlyn Schools, £200-£20,000.* TEL: 01225 480406; fax - same. SER: Contemporary exhibitions.

A J Antiques

13 Broad St. BA1 5LJ. BABADA. (Patrick Anketell-Jones). Open 10-6 or by appointment. *STOCK: Furniture, Georgian to Art Deco.* PARK: At rear. TEL: 01225 447765.

Alderson BADA

2 Princes Buildings, George St. BA1 2ED. BABADA. (C.R. Alderson). Est. 1976. Open 9.30-1 and 2-5.30, Sat 9.30-1, or by appointment. *STOCK: Furniture and accessories, 17th-18th C.* LOC: Central. TEL: 01225 421652; fax - same. VAT: Spec.

Antique Linens and Lace

11 Pulteney Bridge. BA2 4AY. BABADA. (Mrs R. Mellor). Est. 1971. Open 10-5.30 including Sun. SIZE: Small. *STOCK: Quality linens and lace, bedspreads, sheets, tablecloths, pillow cases, christening gowns, baby bonnets, collars, veils and shawls, 1850-1920, £10-£600.* LOC: City centre. PARK: Great Pulteney St.- 100 yards. TEL: 01225 465782; fax - 01225 754067. VAT: Stan/Spec.

Bath continued

Antique Textiles

34 Belvedere, Lansdown Rd. BA1 5HR. BABADA. (Joanna Proops). Open Tues.-Sat. 10-5 or by appointment. *STOCK: Tapestries, paisleys, beadwork, fans, samplers, bellpulls, linen and lace.* TEL: 01225 310795; mobile - 0378 634627.

The Antiques Warehouse

57 Walcot St. BA1 5BN. BABADA. Open 10.30-5.30. SIZE: Medium. *STOCK: 19th C mahogany furniture, £300-£2,000 and decorative objects, £20-£200.* LOC: From J18, M4 along A46 then A4, at first mini-roundabout veer left into Walcot St. Shop 300yds on right. PARK: Easy. TEL: 01225 444201; mobile - 0836 338131. VAT: Stan/Spec.

Arkea Antiques

10A Monmouth Place. (G. Harmandian). Est. 1972. *STOCK: Furniture and china.* TEL: 01225 429413/835382. SER: Repairs (antiques); traditional French polishing.

Assembly Antiques Centre

5/8 Saville Row. BA1 2QP. BABADA. Open 10-5, Wed. 8.15-5. *STOCK: Wide range of general antiques including maps and prints, period costume, decorative items and small collectables.* LOC: Near the Assembly Rooms. TEL: 01225 426288; fax - 01225 429661.

Bartlett Street Antique Centre

5-10 Bartlett St. BA1 2QZ. BABADA. Open 9.30-5, Wed. 8-5. SIZE: 60 dealers. *STOCK: Wide range of general antiques.* TEL: 01225 466689; stallholders - 01225 310457/446322; fax - 01225 444146.

Bath Antiques Market

Guinea Lane, Off Lansdown Rd. BA1 5NB. BABADA. Est. 1968. Open Wed. only 6.30-2.30. SIZE: 60 dealers. *STOCK: General antiques and collectables.* LOC: From London A4 across two sets of traffic lights after entering Bath. Right at third set (Lansdown Rd.) and first right again. PARK: Nearby. TEL: 01225 337638; enquiries - 0171 351 5353; fax - 01225 422510. SER: Valuations.

Bath Galleries

33 Broad St. BA1 5LP. BABADA. J. Griffiths). Open 9.30-5. SIZE: Medium. *STOCK: Always 50 clocks in stock, furniture, paintings, porcelain, jewellery, barometers, silver.* LOC: 50yds. from Central Post Office. PARK: Walcot St. multi-park, 30yds. TEL: 01225 462946. SER: Valuations; restorations; buys at auction. VAT: Stan/Spec.

Bath Saturday Antiques Market

Walcot St. (J. Whittingham). Est. 1978. Open Sat. 7-5. SIZE: 100 stalls. *STOCK: Wide variety of general antiques, £1-£4,000.* LOC: Close to Hilton Hotel. PARK: Multi-storey. TEL: Mobile - 0836 534893.

Bath continued

Bath Stamp and Coin Shop

Pulteney Bridge. BA2 4AY. (H. and A. Swindells). Est. 1946. Open 9.30-5.30. *STOCK: Coins - Roman, hammered, early milled, G.B. gold, silver and copper, some foreign; literature and accessories; banknotes, medals, stamps and postal history.* PARK: Laura Place; Walcott multi-storey. SER: Valuations. VAT: Stan.

George Bayntun

Manvers St. BA1 1JW. BABADA. (H.H. Bayntun-Coward). Est. 1829. Open 9-1 and 2-5.30, Sat. 9.30-1. SIZE: Large. *STOCK: Rare books. First or fine editions of English literature, standard sets, illustrated and sporting books, poetry, biography and travel, mainly in new leather bindings; also large stock of antiquarian books in original bindings.* LOC: By railway and bus stations. PARK: 50 yds. by station. TEL: 01225 466000; fax - 01225 482122. SER: Restorations (rare books). VAT: Stan.

Beau Nash Antiques LAPADA

1st Floor, Beau Nash House, Union Passage. BA1 1RD. CINOA. Est. 1973. Open 10-5. SIZE: Large. *STOCK: English furniture, 1700-1840, £1,000-£25,000; oil paintings, 1800-1890, £750-£10,000; decorative objects, 1760-1890, £150-£1,500.* LOC: 75 yds. from Guildhall in lanes opposite. PARK: Waitrose public. TEL: 01225 447806; fax - same. VAT: Spec.

Bladud House Antiques

8 Bladud Buildings. BA1 5LS. (Mrs E. Radosenska). Open 9.30-1 and 2-4.30. CL: Mon. and Thurs. *STOCK: Jewellery and small items.* Not Stocked: Furniture. TEL: 01225 462929.

Blyth Antiques

28 Sydney Buildings. BA2 6BZ. Resident. (B. Blyth). Est. 1971. Open by appointment. *STOCK: Small furniture, samplers, brass and unusual decorative items.* LOC: Off Bathwick Hill. PARK: Easy. TEL: 01225 469766.

Lawrence Brass

PO Box 1942. BA1 3SD. BAFRA: UKIC. Est. 1973. Open by appointment. SIZE: Small. *STOCK: Furniture, 16th-19th C, £50-£5,000.* Not Stocked: Ceramics, silver, glass. LOC: Main road into town centre. PARK: Easy. TEL: 01225 852222. SER: Restorations (furniture, clocks and barometers). VAT: Stan/Spec.

Geoffrey Breeze LAPADA

6 George St. BA1 2EH. BABADA. Open 10-5. *STOCK: Furniture, 18th-20th C.* TEL: 01225 466499.

David Bridgwater

Heather Cottage, Lansdown. BA1 9BL. Open by appointment. *STOCK: Traditional garden architecture, sculpture, pots, watering cans, implements and decorative items for the period garden and conservatory.* TEL: 01225 463435.

Bath continued

Bruton Gallery

35 Gay St., Queen Sq. BA1 2NT. Est. 1975. SIZE: Medium. *STOCK: European sculpture, 19th-20th C; contemporary paintings and sculpture.* PARK: Nearby. TEL: 01225 466292; fax - 01225 461294. VAT: Stan/Spec.

Bryers Antiques

Entrance to the Guildhall Market, High St. BA1 1JQ. (S. Bryers). Est. 1940. *STOCK: Furniture, decorative items, porcelain, glass, silver and Victorian plate.* TEL: 01225 466352/460535. VAT: Stan/Spec.

Sheila Cooper t/a Sheila Smith Antiques

Stand 61, Bartlett St. Antique Centre, 5-10 Bartlett St. BA2. (S.M. Cooper). Est. 1967. Open 9.30-5. *STOCK: Fans, needlework tools and accessories, collectors' items.* LOC: A4 into city. At 3rd set of traffic lights, turn right into Lansdown then 2nd left into Alfred St. TEL: 01225 442730.

Corridor Stamp Shop

7a The Corridor. BA1 5AP. (G.H. and S.M. Organ). Est. 1970. Open 9.30-5.30. CL: Mon. SIZE: Small. *STOCK: Stamp and postal history, 1700 to date, 5p-£500; albums, reference books; picture postcards, cigarette cards, 1895-1940.* LOC: Within 200yds. of Abbey. PARK: Walcot St. TEL: 01225 463368; home - 01225 316445. SER: Valuations.

Country Interiors

Bartlett St. Antique Centre, 5-10 Bartlett St. (L. Macrae-Stewart). Open 9-5. SIZE: Small. *STOCK: Pine sleigh beds, quilts and cushions, 19th C, unusual pine and decorative items, £10-£500; prior telephone advisable to check stock availability.* LOC: 1st left into Alfred St., off Lansdown Rd. and short walk down slipway. PARK: Easy - Alfred St. TEL: 01380 722365; home/fax - same. FAIRS: Shepton.

Brian and Caroline Craik Ltd

8 Margaret's Buildings. BA1 2LP. *STOCK: Decorative items, mainly 19th C; metalwork, treen, glass and pewter.* TEL: 01225 337161.

Mary Cruz LAPADA

3 George St. BA1 2EH. BABADA. CINOA. Est. 1974. Open 10-6.30, Sun. by appointment. IZE: Medium. *STOCK: 17th-19th C furniture and decorative items; 19th-20th C paintings and bronzes.* PARK: Easy. TEL: 01225 334174; home - 01225 858000. SER: Valuations; restorations. VAT: Stan/Spec.

Bath continued

Andrew Dando BADA

4 Wood St., Queen Sq. BA1 2JQ. BABADA. (A.P. and J.M. Dando). Est. 1915. Open 9.30-5.30, Sat. 10-1. SIZE: Large. *STOCK: English, Continental, Oriental porcelain and pottery, 17th to mid-19th C; local topographical and decorative antique prints; some furniture, 18th to mid-19th C.* LOC: 200yds. from bottom of Milsom St. towards Queen Sq. TEL: 01225 422702. SER: Valuations. VAT: Stan/Spec.

D. and B. Dickinson BADA

22 New Bond St. BA1 1BA. BABADA. (S.G., D. and N.W. Dickinson and Mrs E.M. Dickinson). Est. 1917. Open 9.30-1 and 2-5. CL: Sat. pm. SIZE: Small. *STOCK: Jewellery, 1770-1900, £20-£2,000; silver, 1750-1900, £25-£3,000; Sheffield plate, 1770-1845, £50-£1,000.* LOC: Next to Post Office. PARK: 100yds. at bottom of street, turn left then right for multi-storey. TEL: 01225 466502. VAT: Stan/Spec.

Frank Dux Antiques

33 Belvedere, Lansdown Rd. BA1 5HR. Resident. BABADA. (F. Dux and M. Hopkins). Open 10-6. SIZE: Medium. *STOCK: Georgian and earlier furniture (mainly oak), £250-£5,000; 18th C and later glass, £10-£1,000; unusual decorative items - pottery, pewter, pictures, rugs.* LOC: From Broad St. up Lansdown Hill, on right 100yds. past Guinea Lane. PARK: Easy. TEL: 01225 312367; fax - same. SER: Restorations (furniture); replicas made to order; search service. VAT: Spec.

Fountain Antiques Centre

3 Fountain Buildings, Lansdown Rd. BABADA. (Maggie Adams and Ken Jones). Open 10-5, Wed. 7.30-5, Sat. 9.30-5. SIZE: Medium. *STOCK: General antiques including jewellery, furniture, porcelain, collectables, vintage and antique clothing, textiles, linen, lace and costume jewellery.* LOC: At the crossroads with the Paragon, George St. PARK: Nearby. TEL: 01225 428731/471133. SER: Valuations (jewellery).

The Galleon

33 Monmouth St. BA1 2AN. (D.L. Gwilliam and M.J. Wren). Est. 1972. Open Tues.-Sat. 10-5.30 or by appointment. SIZE: Medium. *STOCK: Furniture, jewellery, silver, china, copper, brass, general collectables and antiques, Georgian to Art Deco, £5-£1,500.* LOC: Near rear of Theatre Royal. PARK: Easy. TEL: 01225 312330. VAT: Stan/Spec.

George Gregory

Manvers St. BA1 1JW. (H.H. Bayntun-Coward). Est. 1845. Open 9-1 and 2-5.30, Sat. 9.30-1. SIZE: Large. *STOCK: Books, 1600 to date; engravings.* LOC: By rail station. PARK: By rail station. TEL: 01225 466055. SER: Restorations (fine books). VAT: Stan.

Bath continued

Haliden Oriental Rug Shop

98 Walcot St. BA1 5BG. BABADA. (Andrew Lloyd, Craig Bale and Owen Parry). Est. 1963. Open 10-5. SIZE: Medium. *STOCK: Caucasian, Turkish, Persian, Chinese, Afghan, Turcoman and tribal rugs and carpets, 19th C, £50-£3,000; some Oriental textiles - coats, embroideries, wall hangings, 19th C, £50-£750.* LOC: Off main London road, into town by Walcot Reclamation. PARK: Walcot St. or multi-storey. TEL: 01225 469240. SER: Valuations; cleaning; restorations (as stock); buys at auction (as stock).

Anthony Hepworth Fine Art

Ivy House, Cavendish Rd., Sion Hill. BA1 2UE. BABADA. Open Thurs., Fri. and Sat. 11-5 or by appointment. *STOCK: Mainly 20th C British paintings, ceramics and sculpture; 19th C prints; African tribal art.* LOC: Western end of Lansdown Crescent on crossroads. PARK: Free. TEL: 01225 442917; fax - same. mobile - 0370 920599 (fairs only). SER: Exhibitions Bath and London. FAIRS: Islington, Olympia and 20th C British Art.

Helena Hood and Co

3 Margarets Buildings, Brock St. BA1 2LP. BABADA. (Mrs L.M. Hood). Est. 1973. Open 9.30-1 and 2.15-5.30, Sat. 10.30-1. CL: Mon. SIZE: Medium. *STOCK: Decorative items - furniture, prints, paintings and porcelain, 18th-19th C, £50-£2,500.* LOC: Pedestrian walkway running north from Brock St. PARK: Easy. TEL: 01225 424438. SER: Restorations. VAT: Stan/Spec.

Jadis Ltd

The Old Bank, 17 Walcot Buildings, London Rd., BA1 6AD. BABADA. (S.H. Creese-Parsons and N.A. Mackay). Est. 1970. Open 9.30-6, Sun. by appointment. SIZE: Medium. *STOCK: Furniture, English and European, 18th-19th C; decorative items.* LOC: On left hand side of A4 London Rd., entering Bath. PARK: At rear. TEL: 01225 338797; fax - same; mobile - 0468 232133. VAT: Stan/Spec.

Orlando Jones

10b Monmouth Place, Upper Bristol Rd. BA1 2AX. Open 9.30-5.30. *STOCK: Victorian and Edwardian brass bedsteads.* TEL: 01225 422750.

K & D Antique Clocks

Bartlett Street Antique Centre, 5 Bartlett St. BA1 2QZ. (E. Kembery). Est. 1993. Open 10-5. *STOCK: Longcase, bracket, mantel, wall and carriage clocks and barometers, 18th-19th C, £200-£10,000.* TEL: 0117 956 5281. SER: Valuations; restorations. VAT: Spec.

Ann King

38 Belvedere, Lansdown Rd. BA1 5HR. Est. 1977. Open 10-5. SIZE: Small. *STOCK: Period clothes, 19th C to 1960; baby clothes, shawls, bead dresses, linen, lace, curtains, cushions,*

Bath continued

quilts and textiles. LOC: Around corner from Guinea Lane Antique Market. PARK: Easy. TEL: 01225 336245.

Kingsley Gallery

16 Margarets Buildings, Brock St. BA1 2LP. BABADA. Open 10.30-5.30 including Sun., or by appointment. SIZE: Medium. *STOCK: 19th-20th C furniture, paintings, silver and decorative items.* LOC: Off Brock St. between The Circus and Royal Crescent. PARK: Nearby. TEL: 01225 448432.

Lansdown Antiques

23 Belvedere, Lansdown Rd. BA1 5ED. BABADA. (Chris and Ann Kemp). Open 9.30-6, Sat. 9.30-5.30, Sun. by appointment. *STOCK: Painted pine and country furniture, 17th-19th C; metalware, unusual and decorative items.* LOC: From A4/A46 roundabout across 2 sets of traffic lights, right at mini roundabout, right at next traffic lights, shop 350yds. on left. PARK: Easy. TEL: 01225 313417; home - same. VAT: Stan/Spec.

Looking Glass of Bath

96 Walcot St. BA1 5BG. (Anthony Reed). Est. 1972. Open 9-6. SIZE: Small. *STOCK: Large mirrors and picture frames, 18th-19th C, £50-£5,000; decorative prints, 18th-20th C.* PARK: Easy. TEL: 01225 461969; home - 01275 333595. SER: Valuations; restorations (re-gilding, gesso and compo work, re-silvering and bevelling glass); manufactures arched top overmantel, pier, convex and triptych mirrors; old mirror plates supplied; buys at auction (mirrors and pictures). VAT: Stan/Spec.

E.P. Mallory and Son Ltd — BADA

1-4 Bridge St. and 5 Old Bond St. BA2 4AP. BABADA. Est. 1856. Open 10-5. *STOCK: Period silver and Sheffield plate, jewellery, objets de vertu, £50-£5,000.* TEL: 01225 465885; fax - 01225 442210. VAT: Stan/Spec.

Mayfly

5 London St. BABADA. (Alistair Henderson). Open 10-5.30. *STOCK: English and Continental furniture, garden objects, decorative and antique lighting.* PARK: Loading in front of shop. TEL: 01225 428908; mobile - 0802 313526.

Montague Antiques

16 Walcot Buildings, London Rd. BA1 6AD. BABADA. Resident. (A. R. Schlesinger and D.K. Moore). Est. 1986. Open 10-6, Sun.11-4. CL: Thurs. SIZE: Medium. *STOCK: Furniture, 17th C to 1920, £50-£1,000; collectables, Oriental rugs, ceramics, glass, £1-£500; glass light shades and fittings, to 1939, £5-£1,500.* Not Stocked: Weapons and jewellery. LOC: A4. Shop near pedestrian crossing past bus depot. PARK: Own at rear, via Bedford St. TEL: 01225 469282; home - same. SER: Valuations.

Number Twelve Queen Street

12 Queen St. BABADA. *STOCK: Small oak and country furniture, 17th-19th C; cushions, tapestries, needlework, decorative items and papiér mâche.* TEL: 01225 462363; evenings - 01225 314846. SER: Interior design and decoration.

Paragon Antiques and Collectors Market

3 Bladud Buildings, The Paragon. BA1 5LS. (T.J. Clifford and Son Ltd). Est. 1978. Open Wed. 6.30-3.30. SIZE: Large. LOC: Milsom St./Broad St. PARK: 50yds. TEL: 01225 463715.

Patterson Liddle

10 Margaret's Buildings, Brock St. BA1 2LP. ABA, PBFA. Open 10-5.30. *STOCK: Antiquarian books and prints especially art and architecture, illustrated and transport history, travel, English literature, maps.* PARK: Nearby. TEL: 01225 426722; fax - same. SER: Catalogues issued.

Pennard House Antiques — LAPADA

3/4 Piccadilly, London Rd. BA1 6PL. BABADA. (M. and S. Dearden). Est. 1966. Open 9.30-5.30. SIZE: Large. *STOCK: Pine, 18th-19th C, £100-£2,000; French provincial furniture, 17th-19th C; £500-£2,500; decorative items, 19th C, £30-£350.* LOC: On A4 from east when entering city. PARK: Easy and at rear. TEL: 01225 313791; fax - 01225 448196; home - 01749 860266. SER: Valuations; restorations (furniture). VAT: Stan/Spec. The following dealers are also trading from these premises.

Robin and Jan Coleman Antiques

BABADA. *Interesting and decorative items.* VAT: Stan/Spec.

John Davies

18th-19th C furniture especially country and Gothic oak, and decorative smalls. TEL: Home - 01225 852103.

Gene and Sally Foster (Antiques)

BABADA. *Decorative and unusal items, 17th-19th C; Continental and English painted furniture, paintings, needlework, prints and metalware, £25-£2,500.* VAT: Stan/Spec.

John Holden

Furniture and decorative accessories, 18th -19th C.

Mike Holt

BABADA. *19th C decorative metalware.*

Denny Leroy

Country furniture, primitive and naïve artefacts, samplers and quilts.

Bath continued

Penny Philip and David Lewin
4 London St. BA1 5BU. BABADA. Open 10-5 or by appointment. *STOCK: Decorative and garden furniture, textiles, pottery and decorative items.* TEL: 01225 469564; mobile - 0966 172294; evenings - 01225 427406; e-mail - d.lewin@btinternet.com.

Quiet Street Antiques
3 Quiet St. and 14/15 John St. BA1 2JS. BABADA. (K. Hastings-Spital). Est. 1985. Open 10-6. SIZE: Large - 8 showrooms. *STOCK: Furniture, 1750-1870, £250-£8,000; objects including bronzes, caddies, boxes, mirrors, £50-£2,000; Royal Worcester porcelain, £30-£2,000; clocks including longcase, wall, bracket and carriage, 1750-1900, £150-£6,000.* LOC: 25yds. from Milsom St. PARK: Nearby. TEL: 01225 315727; fax - 01225 448300. SER: Buys at auction (furniture and clocks); upholstery; free delivery service 100 mile radius of Bath.

P.R. Rainsford
23a Manvers St. BA1 1JW. Est. 1967. *STOCK: Architecture, fine and applied art.* TEL: 01225 445107; fax - 01225 482122. VAT: Stan.

T.E. Robinson — BADA
3 and 4 Bartlett St. BA1 2QZ. Est. 1957. *STOCK: Period furniture, unusual and rare items.* TEL: 01225 463982; fax - same; home - 01225 832307. VAT: Spec.

Sarah Russell Rare Antiquarian Prints
6 Margaret Buildings, Brock St. BA1 2LP. BABADA. *STOCK: Unusual antiquarian prints including architecture, flower, portraits, landscapes and Bath views, many in original frames.* TEL: 01225 466335; fax - 01225 427594; e-mail - sprint@nildram.co.uk. SER: Framing.

Michael and Jo Saffell
3 Walcot Buildings, London Rd. BA1 6AD. Est. 1975. Open 9.30-5, Sat. by appointment. SIZE: Small. *STOCK: British tins and other advertising material including showcards and enamels, 1870-1939; decorative items; all £5-£500.* LOC: A4 - main road into city from M4. PARK: Side streets opposite. TEL: 01225 315857; fax - same; home - same.

Tim Snell Antiques
5 Cleveland Terrace, London Rd. BA1 5DF. BABADA. Open 10-6 including Sun. *STOCK: Fully restored golden oak, mahogany and walnut, late 19th to early 20th C.* TEL: 01225 423045.

Source
93-95 Walcot St. BA1 3SD. BABADA. (Roderick I. Donaldson). *STOCK: Period architectural materials, church and bar fittings, mirrors, lighting, decorative items, metalware, ironwork and garden furniture.* PARK: Nearby and limited. TEL: 01225 469200. SER: Worldwide search and supply.

Bath continued

Susannah
142/144 Walcot St. BA1 5BC. BABADA. (Susan M. Holley). Open 10-5. *STOCK: Decorative textiles and antiques.* TEL: 01225 445069; fax - 0117 932 2635.

James Townshend Antiques
1 Saville Row. BA1 2QP. BABADA. *STOCK: Furniture, china, unusual decorative items, mainly 19th C.* PARK: Easy. TEL: 01225 332290; home - 01225 421730; mobile - 07970 779482. SER: Deliveries arranged.

Bruce Tozer Rugs & Antiques
4 Cleveland Terrace, London St. BA1 5DF. BABADA. (Bruce and Jan Tozer). Open 10-5.30, or by appointment. SIZE: Small. *STOCK: Tribal rugs, room size carpets, kilims, textile fragments, saddle bags and trappings; tables, cupboards, chests, from £20.* LOC: On A4 into Bath, 5 mins. from city centre. PARK: Easy. TEL: 01225 420875; home - same. SER: Valuations; cleaning; restoration. FAIRS: BABADA.

Trimbridge Galleries
2 Trimbridge. BA1 1HD. (Mr and Mrs A. Anderson). Est. 1973. SIZE: Medium. *STOCK: Watercolours and drawings, £50-£3,000; prints and oil paintings; all 18th to early 20th C.* LOC: Just off lower end of Milsom St. PARK: Easy. TEL: 01225 466390.

Walcot Reclamation
108 Walcot St. BA1 5BG. BABADA. Est. 1977. Open 8.30-5.30, Sat. 9-5. SIZE: Large. *STOCK: Architectural items - chimney pieces, ironwork, doors, fireplaces, garden statuary, period baths and fittings and traditional building materials.* PARK: Own and multi-storey nearby. TEL: 01225 444404/335532. SER: Valuations; restorations; brochure available. VAT: Stan.

BISHOPSWOOD, Nr. Chard

M. Wood
Est. 1980. Open by appointment. SIZE: Medium. *STOCK: 18th-19th C pottery, porcelain and glass.* LOC: 1 mile off A303 and 1 mile off B3170. PARK: Easy. TEL: 01460 234639.

BRUTON

Michael Lewis Gallery
17 High St. BA10 0AB. Open 9.30-5.30, or by appointment. CL: Thurs. pm. SIZE: Large. *STOCK: Maps, 17th-19th C; prints, mostly 18th-19th C.* LOC: A359. PARK: High St. TEL: 01749 813557; home - same. SER: Picture framing.

M.G.R. Exports
Station Rd. BA10 0EH. Open 8.30-5.30 or by appointment. SIZE: Large. *STOCK: Georgian, Victorian, Edwardian and decorative items, carved oak, barley twist and shipping goods,*

Bath continued

Continental furniture. PARK: Easy. TEL: 01749 812460; fax - 01749 812882; e-mail - antiques@ mgr.exports.co.uk. SER: Packing and shipping by Camion 01749 813726.

BUCKLAND ST. MARY, Nr. Chard

Combesbury Antiques

Comesbury Farm. TA20 3ST. (Susan and Trevor Micklem). Est. 1962. Appointment preferred. *STOCK: Fine early furniture, antiques and works of art.* TEL: 01460 234323; home - same.

BURNHAM-ON-SEA

Adam Antiques

30 Adam St. TA8 1PQ. (R. Coombes). Open 9-5. SIZE: Large. *STOCK: Furniture, clocks, brass, porcelain and shipping goods.* PARK: Easy. TEL: 01278 783193.

Castle Antiques

Victoria Court, Victoria St. TA8 1AL. (T.C. Germain). Open daily except Wed. *STOCK: Jewellery, silver, 18th-19th C furniture, porcelain, clocks.* TEL: 01278 785031.

Heape's Antiques

39 Victoria St. TA8 1AN. FATG. (Mrs M.M. Heap). Open 10-1 and 2.30-4.30. *STOCK: Small furniture, fine arts, porcelain, glass, memorabilia.* TEL: 01278 782131.

CARHAMPTON

Chris's Crackers

Open 11-5.30 including Sun. SIZE: Large warehouses. *STOCK: Mainly 18th-19th C furniture, iron and stone-work, general building reclamation materials and country artefacts.* LOC: A39 coast road. TEL: 01643 821873. SER: Pine-stripping.

CASTLE CARY

Cary Antiques Ltd

2 High St. (Mrs. J.A. Oldham). Est. 1977. Open 10.30-5. CL: Mon. and Wed. SIZE: Small. *STOCK: Furniture, Victorian and Edwardian, £30-£500; china, brass and copper, glass, bric-a-brac, pictures, 18th-19th C, £5-£150.* LOC: Town centre, B3152. PARK: Easy. TEL: 01963 350437. SER: Valuations; picture framing; caning and rushing; repairs (china).

CHARD

Guildhall Antique Market

The Guildhall. TA20 1PH. Open Thurs. 9-2. SIZE: 26 dealers. *STOCK: General antiques and collectables.*

CHILCOMPTON, Nr. Bath

Billiard Room Antiques

The Old School, Church Lane. BA3 4HP. BABADA. (Mrs J. McKeivor). Est. 1992. Open

Chilcompton continued

by appointment. SIZE: Small. *STOCK: Billiard, snooker and pool tables and accessories, 19th C, £100-£10,000.* PARK: Easy. TEL: 01761 232839; home and fax - same. SER: Valuations; restorations; buys at auction; search.

CLEVEDON

Beach Antiques

Adelaide House, 13 The Beach. BS21 7QU. (D.A. Coles). Open 2-5, Sat. and Sun. 11-5. CL: Mon. and Fri. *STOCK: Jewellery, silver frames, china, brass, glass, mainly small items.* PARK: Easy. TEL: 01275 876881.

Clevedon Antiques Centre

1 East Clevedon Triangle. BS21 6BQ. (Richard Dawes). 1987. Open Tues.-Fri. 10-4, Sat. 10-5, Sun. 11-5. CL: Mon. SIZE: Medium. *STOCK: Furniture, pre-1930, £50-£1,000; china.* PARK: Nearby. TEL: 01275 792283. SER: Restorations (furniture); re-caning; re-upholstery.

CLUTTON

Ian McCarthy

Arcadian Cottage, 112 Station Rd. BS18 4RA. Resident. Est. 1958. Open by appointment. SIZE: Medium. *STOCK: Lamps - oil, gas, electric for domestic, industrial, shipping and transport usage; unusual candle lamps; copper and brassware, 17th C to 1920, £5-£2,000.* PARK: Easy and opposite. TEL: 01761 453188. SER: Valuations; restorations (metalware); cleaning; spares and lamp-shades. *Trade Only.*

COXLEY, Nr. Wells

Wells Reclamation Company

The Old Cider Farm. BA5 1RQ. (H. Davies). Est. 1984. Open 9-5.30. SIZE: Large. *STOCK: Architectural items, 18th-19th C.* LOC: A39 towards Glastonbury from Wells. PARK: Easy. TEL: 01749 677087. SER: Valuations. VAT: Stan.

CREWKERNE

Antiques and Country Pine

14 East St. TA18 7AG. (M.J. Wheeler). Open Tues.-Sat. 10-5 or by appointment. *STOCK: Country pine and decorative items.* TEL: 01460 75623.

Julian Armytage

TA18 8QG. Open by appointment only. *STOCK: Fine sporting, marine and decorative prints, 18th-19th C.* TEL: 01460 73449; fax - same.

Crewkerne Furniture Emporium

Viney Bridge, South St. TA18 8AE. (A.P. and J.F. Bucke). Est. 1974. Open 8.30-5.30, Sun. 11-5. *STOCK: Furniture, shipping goods, collectors' items, agricultural bygones.* TEL: 01460 75319.

Crewkerne continued

East St Antiques

42 East St. TA18 7AG. Open 10-5, Sun. and other times by appointment. SIZE: Warehouse - 6 dealers. *STOCK: Furniture - pine, oak, fruitwood, painted and decorative from UK, France and central Europe.* LOC: A30 from Yeovil. PARK: Easy. TEL: 01460 78060; fax - 01460 78600. VAT: Stan/Spec.

David Gibson BADA LAPADA

5 Church St. TA18 7HR. Est. 1975. Open by appointment. SIZE: Medium. *STOCK: Longcase clocks, £3,000-£28,000; barometers.* PARK: Easy. TEL: 01460 76667. SER: Valuations; restorations. FAIRS: BADA; NEC; Harrogate. VAT: Spec.

Hennessy LAPADA

42 East St. TA18 7AG. (Carl Hennessy). Est. 1977. Open Tues., Wed., Fri. and Sat. 10-5, other times by appointment. SIZE: Large. *STOCK: Furniture - pine, country, painted and French provincial; related decorative items.* LOC: A30 from Yeovil. PARK: Easy. TEL: 01460 78060; fax - 01460 78600. VAT: Stan/Spec.

Octopus Antique Centre

16 Market St. TA18 7LA. (F. Martin). Est. 1987. Open 9.30-4.30. CL: Mon. SIZE: Large. *STOCK: Furniture, £25-£1,500; collectables, £5-£500; pictures, £5-£500; all 18th-20th C.* LOC: A303 westward, A359 to Crewkerne, Chard road through town. PARK: Easy. TEL: 01460 77111. SER: Valuations; restorations.

Oscars Antiques

13-15 Market Sq. and North St. TA18 7LE. (B.J. and H.M. Hall). Est. 1966. Open 10-5. SIZE: Large. *STOCK: Victoriana, shipping goods, china and books.* LOC: Centre of the square on A30. PARK: Easy. TEL: 01460 72718. VAT: Stan/Spec.

DOWLISH WAKE, Nr. Ilminster

Dowlish Wake Antiques

TA19 0NY. (Mrs G. Estling). Est. 1973. Open 1 and 2.30-5.30. SIZE: Medium. *STOCK: Ceramics*

Dowlish Wake continued

only - English porcelain and pottery, late 18th C to early 20th C. LOC: Take Ilminster/ Crewkerne road and turn off at Kingstone corner, downhill to village. PARK: Easy. TEL: 01460 52784; fax - same. VAT: Stan/Spec.

DULVERTON

Acorn Antiques

39 High St. TA22 9DW. (P. Hounslow). Est. 1988. Open 9.30-5.30. SIZE: Medium. *STOCK: Country furniture, 18th-19th C; fine art, textiles, works of art, £5-£5,000.* LOC: Town centre. PARK: Nearby. TEL: 01398 323286; home - same. SER: Interior design.

Guy Dennler Antiques

The White Hart, 23 High St. TA22 9HB. Open 10-5. CL: Thurs. pm. *STOCK: Fine 18th to early 19th C English furniture and decorative objects.* TEL: 01398 324300; fax - 01398 324301.

Faded Elegance

39 High St. TA22 9DW. (M. Delbridge). Open 9.30-5.30. *STOCK: 18th-19th C decorative antiques, textiles, upholstery.* TEL: 01398 323286.

Rothwell and Dunworth

2 Bridge St. TA22 9HJ. ABA. (Mrs C. Rothwell and Mr M. Rothwell). Est. 1975. Open 10.30-1 and 2.15-5, including Sun. May-Sept. SIZE: Medium. *STOCK: Antiquarian and secondhand books especially on hunting and horses.* LOC: 1st shop in village over River Barle. PARK: 100yds. TEL: 01398 323169; fax - 01398 331161. SER: Valuations.

EAST PENNARD, Nr. Shepton Mallet

Pennard House

BA4 6TP. Resident. (M. and S. Dearden). Est. 1979. Open by appointment. SIZE: Large. *STOCK: Pine furniture, 18th-19th C, £100-£2,000; French provincial tables, armoires, buffets, £300-£3,000.* LOC: From Shepton Mallet, 4 miles south off A37. PARK: Easy. TEL: 01749 860266; home - same. SER: Valuations; restorations (pine and country furniture). VAT: Stan/Spec. *Trade Only.*

FRESHFORD, Nr. Bath

Janet Clarke

3 Woodside Cottages. BA3 6EJ. Open by appointment. *STOCK: Antiquarian books on gastronomy, cookery and wine.* TEL: 01225 723186. SER: Catalogue issued.

FROME

Antiques & Country Living

43-44 Vallis Way, Badcox. BA11 3BA. (Mrs D.M. Williams). Open 9.30-5.30 including Sun. SIZE: Medium. *STOCK: Furniture including country, 19th-20th C, £15-£1,000; porcelain, 18th-19th C, £5-£500.* LOC: A362 Frome to Radstock road. PARK: Free opposite. TEL: 01373 463015.

Sutton and Sons

15 and 33 Vicarage St. BA11 1PX. *STOCK: Furniture, 18th-19th C; clocks, pictures, decorative pieces.* TEL: 01373 462062/462526. SER: Restorations and upholstery. VAT: Stan/Spec.

GLASTONBURY

Abbey Antiques

51 High St. BA6 9DS. (G.E. Browning and Son). Est. 1952. Open 8-5. CL: Sat. SIZE: Small. *STOCK: Glass and furniture.* TEL: 01458 831694. VAT: Stan.

HIGHBRIDGE

C.W.E. and R.I. Dyte Antiques LAPADA

The Old Bacon Factory, Huntspill Rd. TA9 3DE. Open 8-5.30 or by appointment. SIZE: Large. *STOCK: Mahogany, oak, walnut, 18th-20th C, shipping goods.* PARK: Easy. TEL: 01278 788590/788603; home - 01278 683761. SER: Packing; transport; documentation.

T.M. Dyte Antiques

1 Huntspill Rd. Open 8.30-5.30. CL: Sat. *STOCK: Shipping goods.* TEL: 01278 786495.

Terence Kelly Antiques

Huntspill Court, West Huntspill. TA9 3QZ. Open by appointment. *STOCK: Furniture, decorative and collectors' items.* TEL: 01278 785052.

The Treasure Chest

The Jays, 19 Alstone Lane. TA9 3DS. (R.J. and V. Rumble). Est. 1964. CL: Sun., except by appointment. SIZE: Medium. *STOCK: General antiques including furniture, 17th-20th C; smalls especially silver plate, glass, clocks and musical boxes.* LOC: Off A38 down lane by Royal Artillery public house, 200yds. on left. PARK: Easy. TEL: 01278 787267. SER: Valuations; restorations (pictures); buys at auction. VAT: Stan/Spec. *Trade Only.*

ILCHESTER

Gilbert & Dale

The Old Chapel, Church St. Est. 1965. Open 9-5.30 or by appointment. SIZE: Large. *STOCK: English and French country furniture and accessories.* LOC: Centre of village on A37. PARK: Easy. TEL: 01935 840464; fax - 01935 841599; home - 01458 250193.

ILMINSTER

County Antiques Centre

17 Court Barton. TA19 0DU. Resident. (Mrs J.P. Barnard). Est. 1981. Open Mon., Thurs., Fri. and Sat. 10.30-5.30, or by appointment. SIZE: Medium - 12 dealers. *STOCK: 18th-19th C pottery, porcelain, metalwork, furniture and decorative antiques.* TEL: 01460 54151; home - 01460 52269; mobile - 0378 371967.SER: Upholstery.

James Hutchison

5 West St. TA19 9AA. *STOCK: Pictures, frames, china and glass, collectables, furniture.*

West End House Antiques

34-36 West St. TA19 9AB. (T.H. Sabine). Est. 1964. Open 9.30-5. SIZE: Large. *STOCK: Furniture, 18th to early 20th C, £50-£700; Art Deco china including Clarice Cliff, £5-£1,000; pictures, 19th-20th C, £10-£500.* LOC: Old A303. PARK: Easy. TEL: 01460 52793; home - 01404 42140. SER: Valuations; buys at auction.

LITTLETON, Nr. Somerton

Westville House Antiques

TA11 6NP. (D. and M. Stacey). Est. 1986. Open daily, Sun. by appointment. SIZE: Large. *STOCK: 18th-19th C pine furniture, £100-£5,000, country antiques.* LOC: B3151 approximately 1.5 miles north of Somerton. PARK: Own. TEL: 01458 273376; fax - same. SER: Valuations; buys at auction. VAT: Stan/Spec.

MARTOCK

Castle Reclamation

Parrett Works. TA12 6AE. (T.A.B. Dance and A.J. Wills). Est. 1986. Open daily, Sat. 10-1. SIZE: Large. *STOCK: Architectural antiques.* LOC: 2 miles off A303 between Martock and South Petherton. PARK: Easy. TEL: 01935 826483; fax - same. SER: Restorations (stone). FAIRS: Bath and West. VAT: Stan.

MEARE, Nr. Glastonbury

Borough Antiques

St. Mary's Rd. BA6 9SP. Resident. (R.C. and L. Tincknell). Open by appointment only. *STOCK: Town and country furniture, decorative accessories and 19th C brass.* LOC: B3151 between Glastonbury and Wedmore. TEL: 01458 860701.

MERRIOTT, Nr. Crewkerne

Chez Chalon

Sockety Farm, Sandy Hole. TA16 5QS. (Jake and Nick Chalon). Est. 1973. Open 9-6, Sat. 9-1, Sat. pm. and Sun. by appointment. SIZE: Medium. *STOCK: Country furniture and pine, 18th-19th C, £100-£3,000.* LOC: 5 minutes from A303 (Lopen Head), 10 minutes from Crewkerne. PARK: Easy.TEL: 01460 77397; home/fax - 01460 68679. SER: Restorations (country furniture); buys at auction (country furniture). VAT: Stan.

MIDSOMER NORTON

Somervale Antiques BADA LAPADA

6 Radstock Rd. BA3 2AJ. BABADA. CINOA. Resident. (Wing Cdr. R.G. Thomas). Open by appointment only. *STOCK: English drinking glasses, decanters, cut and coloured; "Bristol" and "Nailsea"glass; bijouterie; glass scent bottles, 18th to early 19th C.* LOC: On A362 on Radstock side of town. PARK: Easy. TEL: 01761 412686 (24hrs); fax - same; mobile - 0585 088022; internet - http://www.lapada. co.uk/lapada and http://www.thesaurus.co.uk/. SER: Valuations; buys at auction; trains to Bath met by arrangement. VAT: Stan/Spec.

MILVERTON, Nr. Taunton

Milverton Antiques

Fore St. TA4 1JU. (A. Waymouth). Est. 1972.

Milverton continued

Resident, open any time. SIZE: Medium. *STOCK: Pine and oak country furniture, longcase clocks, interesting china, copper, brass and treen.* LOC: 8 miles from Taunton on B3227 Barnstaple road. PARK: 50yds. TEL: 01823 400597. VAT: Stan/Spec.

J.C. White

The Granary, Fitzhead. TA4 3JT. Est. 1960. *STOCK: Country furniture and clocks.* TEL: 01823 400427.

MONTACUTE, Nr. Yeovil

Montacute Antiques

April Cottage, 12 South St. TA15 6XD. (E.M. and J.K. Warrick). Open 9-6 including Sun. *STOCK: Oak country furniture and pewter; porcelain and glass.* PARK: Easy. TEL: 01935 824786.

NETHER STOWEY, Nr. Bridgwater

The Court Gallery

2 Lime St. TA5 1NG. (John Wilcox). Est. 1990. Open Wed.- Sat. 10-1 and 2-5, or by appointment. SIZE: Medium. *STOCK: British paintings, 1880-1939, especially Newlyn, St Ives and London Group, £50-£15,000.* LOC: Bridgwater turn off M5, then A39 towards Minehead. PARK: Easy. TEL: 01278 732539; home - same. SER: Valuations; restorations; buys at auction.

Nether Stowey continued

House of Antiquity

St. Mary St. TA5 1LJ. (M.S. Todd). Est. 1967. Open 10-5 or by appointment. SIZE: Medium. *STOCK: Philatelic literature, world topographical, maps, handbooks, postcards, ephemera, postal history.* LOC: A39. PARK: Easy. TEL: 01278 732426; fax - same. SER: Valuations; buys at auction. VAT: Stan.

NORTH PETHERTON, Nr. Taunton

Harrison House Antiques

60 Fore St. TA6 6QA. (James and Janya Yarrow). Open by appointment. SIZE: Large. *STOCK: Architectural features, furniture and furnishings.* LOC: Off junction 24, M5. PARK: Own. TEL: 01278 662535. *Trade Only.*

QUEEN CAMEL, Nr. Yeovil

Steven Ferdinando

The Old Vicarage. BA22 7NG. Open by appointment. *STOCK: Antiquarian and secondhand books.* TEL: 01935 850210.

RODE

The Chapel at Rode

16a High St. BA3 6NZ. BABADA. (Dominic O'Dwyer, Richard Nadin and Richard Cornish). Open Mon.-Fri. 10-5 or by appointment. *STOCK: Mainly English and Continental furniture, to Art Deco.* LOC: 20 minutes south of Bath. PARK: Easy. TEL: 01373 830531; fax - 01373 830792; mobile - 0802 884133; e-mail - anyone@fod-ant.prestel.co.uk. SER: Restorations.

SOMERTON

John Gardiner Antiques

Monteclefe House. TA11 7NL. Appointment advisable. *STOCK: General antiques; decorative Edwardian, Georgian and quality old reproduction furnishings.* LOC: A303, close to M5. TEL: 01458 272238; fax/answerphone - 01458 274329; mobile - 0831 274427.

The London Cigarette Card Co. Ltd

West St. TA11 6NB. (I.A. and E.K. Laker, F.C. Doggett and Y. Berktay). Est. 1927. Open daily. SIZE: Medium. *STOCK: Cigarette and trade cards, 1885 to date; sets from £1.50; other cards, from 15p; frames for mounting cards and special albums.* PARK: Easy. TEL: 01458 273452. SER: Publishers of catalogues, reference books and monthly magazine; mail order.

Times Past

(Above Rocking Horse Children's Shop), Market Place. TA11 7NB. (D. and G. Rogers). *STOCK: Linen, lace, samplers, quilts, textiles, watercolours, metalware, treen, period oak and country furniture.* LOC: 1.5 miles off A303 at Podimore. 10 minutes from Clark's Village, Street. PARK: Easy. TEL: 01458 274393.

TAUNTON

East Reach Antiques

38 East Reach. TA1 3ES. (R.E. and C.S. Salmon). Open 9-5. SIZE: Medium. *STOCK: Furniture, 19th to early 20th C, £50-£1,000; porcelain and glass, 19th C, £25-£500; watercolours and etchings, £50-£1,000; silver, £20-£250; marine and scientific instruments, £10-£1,500.* LOC: From junction 25, M5 into town centre. PARK: Easy. TEL: 01823 322432; fax - same. SER: Valuations. FAIRS: ICAF.

Lords Antiques

8 East Reach. TA1 3EN. (J.R. and A.A. Lord). Open 10-4. SIZE: Medium. *STOCK: Metalware, 19th to early 20th C, £50-£100.* PARK: Easy. TEL: 01823 275641. VAT: Global.

Selwoods

Queen Anne Cottage, Mary St. TA1 3PE. Est. 1927. Open 9.30-5. SIZE: Large. *STOCK: Furniture, including Victorian and Edwardian.* TEL: 01823 272780.

Staplegrove Lodge Antiques

East Criddles Farm, Tolland, Lydeard St. Lawrence. TA4 3PW. (T. Atkins). Est. 1958. Open by appointment only. SIZE: Medium. *STOCK: Porcelain and pottery including Prattware, 18th-19th C.* TEL: 01984 667310.

Taunton Antiques Market - Silver Street

27/29 Silver St. TA1 3DH. (Bath Antiques Market td.). Est. 1978. Open Mon. 9-4 including Bank Holidays. SIZE: 100+ dealers. *STOCK: General antiques and collectables, including specialists in most fields.* LOC: 2 miles from M5 Junc. 25, to town centre, 100yds. from Sainsburys car park across lights. PARK: Easy - Sainsburys (town centre branch). TEL: 01823 289327; fax - same; enquiries - 0171 351 5353. SER: Valuations.

WATCHET

Clarence House Antiques

41 Swain St. TA23 0AE. Est. 1970. Open 10-6.30. CL: Sun. in winter. SIZE: Medium. *STOCK: General antiques, pine, brass, copper, bric-a-brac, upholstered furniture.* TEL: 01984 631389. VAT: Stan.

Nick Cotton Fine Art

Beachstone House, 46/47 Swain St. TA23 0AG. Est. 1970. Open by appointment only. SIZE: Large. *STOCK: Paintings, 1800-1970; some period furniture.* TEL: 01984 631814. SER: Restorations; conservation; research. VAT: Spec.

WELLINGTON

Michael and Amanda Lewis Oriental Carpets and Rugs LAPADA

8 North St. TA21 8LT. UKIC. Est. 1982. Open 10-1 and 2-5.30, Mon. and weekends by appointment. SIZE: Medium. *STOCK: Oriental carpets and rugs, mainly 19th-20th C, £25-£25,000.* PARK: 100yds. TEL: 01823 667430. SER: Valuations; restorations; repairs and cleaning; courses.

WELLS

Courtyard Antiques

Palace Courtyard, Priory Rd. BA5 2SY. (Mr and Mrs M.J. Mitchell). Est. 1985. Open 9-5, Sun by appointment. SIZE: Medium. *STOCK: Furniture, £100-£300; smalls, £10-£50; both 19th-20th C.* LOC: Just off High St., towards Glastonbury. PARK: Easy. TEL: 01749 679533; home - 01749 675028. SER: Valuations; restorations (upholstery, cane and rush work, china and furniture). FAIRS: Bath and West Showground, Shepton Mallet, Newark, Ardingly.

Bernard G. House

Market Place. BA5 2RF. Est. 1963. Open 9.30-5.30. SIZE: Medium. *STOCK: Barometers and scientific instruments, barographs, telescopes, tripod and hand held; furniture including miniatures and apprentice pieces, 18th-19th C; longcase and bracket clocks, metalware, decorative and architectural items.* PARK: Opposite shop. TEL: 01749 672607. SER: Repairs; restorations. VAT: Stan/Spec.

Edward A. Nowell BADA

12 Market Place. BA5 2RB. Est. 1952. Open 9.15-5. SIZE: Large. *STOCK: Furniture, clocks, barometers, 17th to early 19th C; jewellery, silver, porcelain, English and Continental, all prices.* Not Stocked: Victoriana, bric-a-brac, curios, weapons, books. LOC: From any direction, turn left into Market Place (one-way system). PARK: 20yds. facing shop. TEL: 01749 672415; fax - 01749 673519. SER: Valuations; restorations (furniture, silver, clocks and jewellery); re-upholstery. VAT: Stan/Spec.

Sadler Street Gallery,

7a Sadler St. BA5 2RR. Open 10-5.30. CL: Mon. *STOCK: Watercolours and oils, mainly contemporary; antique prints and engravings.* SER: Framing.

WEST BUCKLAND, Nr. Taunton

Tim Everett

Pitminster Studio, Budleigh. Open by appointment. *STOCK: 19th-20th C paintings and sculpture, £200-£10,000.* PARK: Easy. TEL: 01823 421710. SER: Restorations; conservation (paintings and frames). VAT: Stan/Spec.

WEST HARPTREE, Nr. Bristol

Tilly Manor Antiques

Tilly Manor. BS40 6EB. (J.D. Scott). Est. 1978. Open Thurs.-Sat. 10-5, other times by appointment. SIZE: Large. *STOCK: Town and country furniture, 18th-19th C, £100-£5,000; brass, copper and metalware, 17th-19th C, decorative collectors items, 18th-19th C; all £5-£500.* LOC: Next to church on A368. PARK: Own. TEL: 01761 221888; home - same. SER: Restorations.

WESTON-SUPER-MARE

Bay Tree House Antiques

Stevens Lane, Lympsham. BS24 0BY. (N.W. and S.M. Adams). Est. 1982. Open 10-5.30 including Sun. SIZE: Warehouse. *STOCK: Stripped pine, satin walnut and mahogany furniture, some smalls, £25-£2,000.* LOC: Off A370 - turn left immediately after first Jeff Brown garage, premises about 3/4 mile on right. PARK: Easy. TEL: 01934 750367; home - same. VAT: Stan/Spec.

D.M. Restorations

3 Laburnum Rd. (D. Pike). Open 9-5. *STOCK: Small mahogany furniture.* PARK: Easy. TEL: 01934 811120.

Sterling Books

43A Locking Rd. BS23 3DG. Est. 1966. Open 9-6. *STOCK: Books, antiquarian and secondhand, some new; ephemera and prints.* TEL: 01934 625056. SER: Bookbinding and picture framing.

Toby's Antiques

47 Upper Church Rd. BS23 2DY. (D. White). Open by appointment only. *STOCK: Furniture and general antiques.* TEL: 01934 623555.

Winter's Antiques LAPADA

62 Severn Rd. BS23 1DT. (R.N. and E.P. Winters). Open 9-12 and 2-3.30. CL: Sat. pm. and Thurs. SIZE: Large. *STOCK: Furniture, clocks, smalls and fine art, all periods.* Not Stocked: Coins, stamps. LOC: Off sea front. PARK: Easy. TEL: 01934 620118/81460.

WILLITON

Edward Venn

Unit 3, 52 Long St. TA4 4QU. Est. 1979. Open 10-5. *STOCK: Furniture, clocks.* TEL: 01984 632631; fax - same. SER: Restorations (furniture, barometers and clocks).

WINCANTON

Green Dragon Antiques Centre

24 High St. BA9 9DH. (Mrs Sally Denning). Est. 1986. Open 9-5.15, Sun. 1.30-5. SIZE: 46 dealers. *STOCK: Wide variety of general antiques and collectables, £1-£1,000.* TEL: 01963 34111. SER: Valuations.

Wincanton continued

Barry M. Sainsbury

17 High St. BA9 9JT. Est. 1958. *STOCK: Oak and mahogany furniture, china, glass, pictures, decorative items.* TEL: 01963 32289. SER: Restorations; cabinet makers. VAT: Stan/Spec.

WIVELISCOMBE

J.C. Giddings

TA4 2SN. Open by appointment only. SIZE: Large warehouses. *STOCK: Mostly 18th-19th C furniture, iron-work and general building reclamation materials.* TEL: 01984 623703. VAT: Stan. *Mainly Trade.*

Heads 'n' Tails

Bournes House, 41 Church St. TA4 2LT. Resident. (D. McKinley). Open by appointment. *STOCK: Taxidermy including Victorian cased and uncased birds, mammals and fish, £5-£2,000; decorative items, glass domes.* LOC: Opposite church. PARK: Easy. TEL: 01984 623097; fax - 01984 624445. SER: Taxidermy; restorations; commissions; hire. VAT: Spec.

YATTON, Nr. Bristol

Glenville Antiques LAPADA

120 High St. BS49 4DH. (Mrs S.E.M. Burgan). Est. 1969. Open 10.30-5. CL: Sun. except by appointment. SIZE: Small. *STOCK: Glass, £5-£750; small furniture, £25-£2,500; pottery and porcelain, £5-£1,500, all mainly 19th C; collectors' items, sewing items.* Not Stocked: Pewter, guns, antique foreign curios, coins, stamps. LOC: On B3133. PARK: Easy. TEL: 01934 832284. VAT: Stan/Spec.

YEOVIL

John Hamblin

Unit 6, 15 Oxford Rd., Penn Mill Trading Estate. BA21 5HR. (J. and M. A. Hamblin). Est. 1980. Open 8.30-5. CL: Sat. SIZE: Small. *STOCK: Furniture, 1750-1900, £300-£3,000.* PARK: Easy. TEL: 01935 471154; home - 01935 476673. SER: Restorations (furniture); cabinet work. VAT: Stan.

The Somerset and Dorset Antique Centre

Main Hall, Main St, Mudford. BA21 5TE. (Michael Shortall). Open 10-5, Sun. 1-4. *STOCK: General antiques including furniture, ceramics, silver, jewellery and collectors' items.* TEL: 01935 851511.

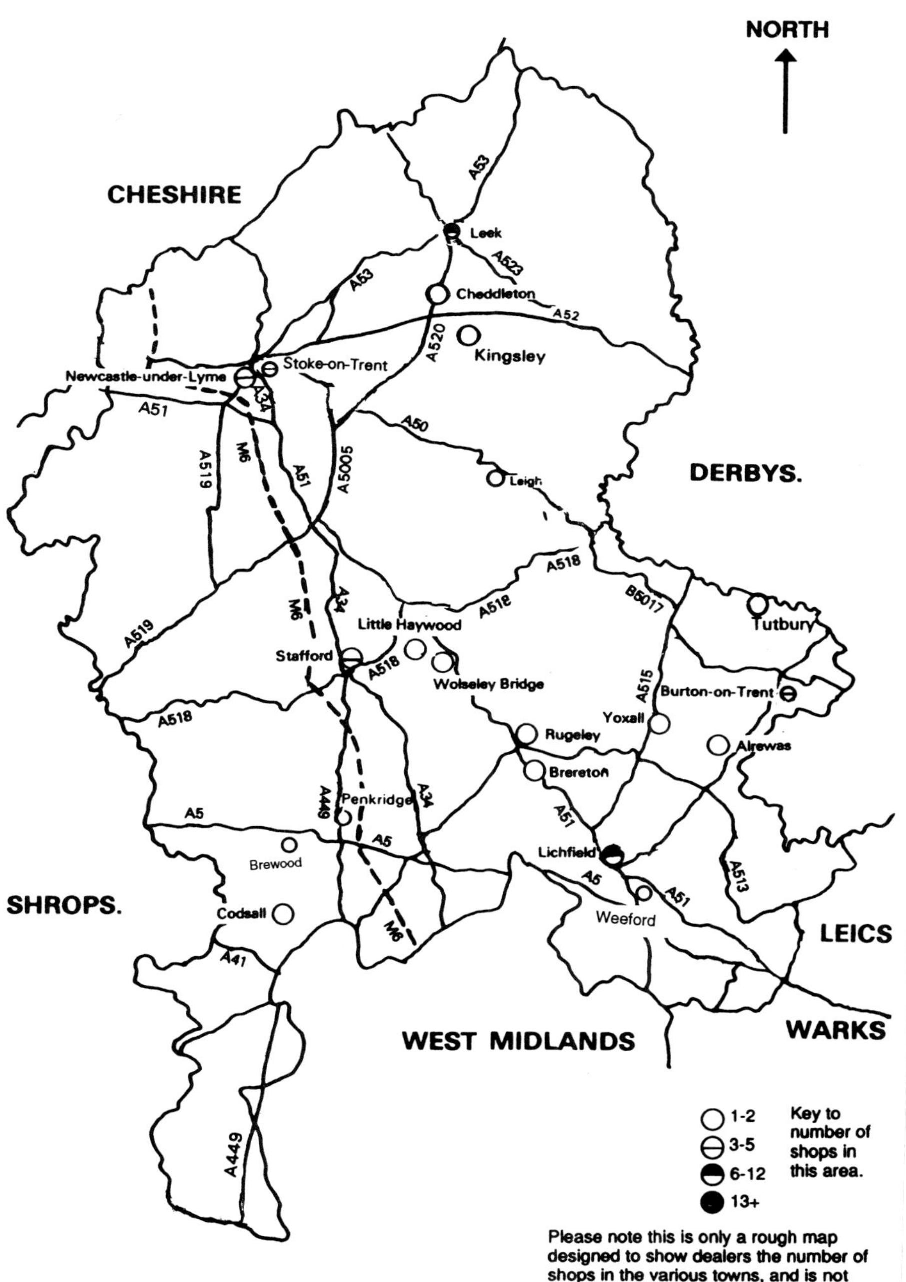

Please note this is only a rough map designed to show dealers the number of shops in the various towns, and is not necessarily totally accurate.

ALREWAS, Nr. Burton-on-Trent

Poley Antiques

5 Main St. DE13 7AA. (D.T. and A.G. Poley). Est. 1977. Open Thurs., Fri. and Sat. 10-5, other times by arrangement. SIZE: Small. *STOCK: General antiques, furniture, silver, china, glass, copper, brass.* Not Stocked: Stamps, coins and militaria. LOC: 20yds. from A38, between Lichfield and Burton. PARK: Own. TEL: 01283 791151; home - same; fax - same.

BRERETON, Nr. Rugeley

Rugeley Antique Centre

161-3 Main Rd. WS15 1DX. Open 9-5, Sun. 12-4.30. SIZE: Large - 40 units. *STOCK: China, glass, pottery, pictures, furniture, pine, treen, linen and shipping goods.* LOC: A51, one mile south of Rugeley town, opposite Cedar Tree Hotel. PARK: Own. TEL: 01889 577166. VAT: Stan/Spec.

BREWOOD

Passiflora

25 Stafford St. ST19 9DX. (David and Paula Whitfield). Est. 1988. Open Thurs., Fri., Sat. and Bank Holidays Sun. and Mon. 10-4ish, other times by appointment. SIZE: Medium. *STOCK: General antiques, collectables and curios, Victorian to 1950's, £1-£300; early children's book and Mabel Lucie Atwell corner, 1900-1980, £1-£100.* LOC: Off A5 and A449 near Gailey roundabout, village on Shropshire Union canal. PARK: Free opposite. TEL: 01902 851557 (answerphone). SER: Valuations. FAIRS: Bingley Hall.

BURTON-ON-TRENT

Burton Antiques

1 and 2 Horninglow Rd. (C.H. Armett). Est. 1977. Open 10-5 every day. SIZE: Large. *STOCK: Shipping and pine furniture.* LOC: A50. PARK: Nearby. TEL: 01283 542331. SER: Valuations; pine stripping; buys at auction.

Justin Pinewood Ltd

The Maltings, Wharf Rd. DE14 1PZ. (S. Silvester). Open 9-5.30, including Sun. *STOCK: Stripped pine furniture and decorative accessories.* TEL: 01283 510860.

C. and R. Scattergood LAPADA

132 Branston Rd. DE14 3DQ. Open 9-6. *STOCK: Fine English and Continental glass.* TEL: 01283 546695.

CHEDDLETON, Nr. Leek

Jewel Antiques

'Whitegates', 63 Basford Bridge Lane. ST13 7EQ. (B. and D.J. Smith). Est. 1967. Open by

Cheddleton continued

appointment. *STOCK: Paintings, prints, jewellery, oil lamps, small furniture and clocks, 18th-19th C, £25-£2,000.* PARK: Easy. TEL: 01538 360744/361247.

CODSALL

Dam Mill Antiques

Birches Rd. WV8 2JR. (H. Bassett). Est. 1977. Open 10-1 and 2.30-5.30. CL: Tues. and Thurs. SIZE: Small. *STOCK: General antiques, small furniture, china, glass, copper, brass, silver and jewellery.* PARK: Easy. TEL: 01902 843780.

KINGSLEY, Nr. Leek

Country Cottage Interiors

Newhall Farmhouse, Hazels Crossroads. ST10 2AY. Resident. (L. Salmon). Est. 1972. Open 10-5. SIZE: Medium. *STOCK: Pine, £5-£500; kitchenalia, 25p-£100.* LOC: Off A52. PARK: Own. TEL: 01538 754762; mobile - 0378 062297.

LEEK

Antiques and Objets d'Art of Leek

70 St. Edwards St. ST13 5DL. Est. 1955. Open 10-6. CL: Thurs. *STOCK: English and Continental furniture; porcelain, silver, glass, oil paintings.* TEL: 01538 382587. FAIRS: Buxton. VAT: Spec.

Anvil Antiques Ltd

Cross Mills, Cross St. ST13 6BL. (J.S. Spooner and N.M. Sullivan). Est. 1975. Open 9-6. SIZE: Large. *STOCK: Stripped pine, architectural and oak, mahogany, bric-a-brac, decorative items and painted furniture, prints and art.* LOC: Ashbourne Rd., from town centre roundabout, turn first left, Victorian mill on right. PARK: Easy. TEL: 01538 371657. VAT: Stan.

Sylvia Chapman Antiques

56 St. Edward St. ST13 5DL. Est. 1983. Open 10-5.30. CL: Thurs. SIZE: Medium. *STOCK: Small oak, mahogany and country furniture; general antiques and collector's items, especially 19th to early 20th C pottery and porcelain, Staffordshire jugs, Victorian coloured glass, copper, brass and kitchenalia.* PARK: Outside. TEL: 01538 399116.

England's Gallery

Ball Haye House, 1 Ball Haye Terr. ST13 6AP. (F.J. and S. England). Est. 1968. Open 10-5.30. CL: Mon. SIZE: Large. *STOCK: Oils and watercolours, 18th-19th C, £500-£10,000; etchings, engravings, lithographs, mezzotints, £50-£4,000.* LOC: Towards Ball Haye Green from A523 turn at lights. PARK: Nearby. TEL: 01538 373451; home - 01538 386352. SER: Valuations; restorations (cleaning, relining, regilding); framing, mount cutting; buys at auction (paintings). VAT: Stan.

Leek continued

Gemini Trading

Limes Mill, Abbotts Rd. ST13 6EY. (T.J. Lancaster and Mrs Y.A. Goldstraw). Est. 1981. Open Mon.-Fri. 9-5, other times by appointment. SIZE: Large. *STOCK: Pine, £25-£850; kitchenalia, £5-£35; both 19th C.* LOC: Turn off A53 along Abbotts Rd. before town centre. PARK: Easy. TEL: 01538 387834; fax - 01538 399819. VAT: Stan.

Gilligans Antiques

59 St. Edward St. ST13 5DN. (M.T. Gilligan). Est. 1977. *STOCK: Victorian and Edwardian furniture.* TEL: 01538 384174.

Grosvenor Clocks

Overton Bank House. ST13 5ES. Open 9-4.30. *STOCK: Clocks, watches and barometers; some furniture.* TEL: 01538 385669.

Roger Haynes - Antiques Finder

31 Compton. ST13 5NJ. Open by appointment. *STOCK: Pine, smalls and decorative items.* TEL: 01538 385161.

Johnson's

120 Mill St. ST13 8HA. Est. 1976. Open 9-5.30. SIZE: Large. *STOCK: 18th-19th C English, Irish and French country furniture, £50-£2,000; decorative accessories, £10-£500.* PARK: Own. TEL: 01538 386745; fax - same.

Leek continued

The Leek Antiques Centre

Barclay House, 4-6 Brook St. ST13 5JE. Est. 1977. Open 10-5, Sun. by appointment. *STOCK: Furniture including sets of chairs and extending dining tables; pottery, oils, watercolours, prints; pine.* TEL: 01538 398475; home - 01782 394383. SER: Valuations; restorations (furniture). FAIRS: Bowman's - Staffordshire Showground and NEC. VAT: Stan/Spec.

Molland Antique Mirrors

40 Compton. ST13 5NH. (John and Karen Molland). Est. 1980. Open 7.30-6. SIZE: Medium. *STOCK: Mirrors - gilt, painted and wooden, 19th C, £200-£3,500.* LOC: From Stoke-on-Trent, right at 1st traffic lights, shop 200 yards on right. PARK: Easy. TEL: 01538 372553. SER: Export packing. FAIRS: NEC (Aug). VAT: Stan/Spec.

Odeon Antiques

76-78 St. Edward St. ST13 5PA. (Steve Ford). Open 10-5. *STOCK: Lighting, beds, pine and general antiques.* TEL: 01538 387188; fax - same. SER: Restorations (lighting).

LEIGH, Nr. Stoke-on-Trent

John Nicholls

Open by appointment only. *STOCK: Oak furniture and related items, 17th-18th C.* LOC: 2 miles from Uttoxeter, just off A50 towards Stoke-on-Trent. TEL: 01889 502351; mobile - 0836 244024.

A collection of 18th century English porcelain: largely Worcester, but also including Liverpool, Vauxhall and Lowestoft. Collections of this type may require a specialist's eye and be beyond the scope of a generalist.

Like most people involved in the business of antiques and fine art, *Paul Davidson* is often asked the 'value' of a particular item. Such an apparently straightforward question does not usually yield such a straightforward answer. From an article entitled "What is a Valuation Worth?" which appeared in the November 1997 issue of **Antique Collecting.**

LICHFIELD

Mike Abrahams Books

9 Burton Old Rd., Streethay. WS13 8LJ. Est. 1975. Open by appointment. SIZE: Large. *STOCK: Books and ephemera especially Midlands topography, sport, transport, childrens, illustrated, military and antiquarian, 17th C to date, £2-£1,000.* LOC: Last but one R/H turn A5127 Lichfield to Burton-on-Trent before road joins A38 by-pass, house on left near corner. PARK: Easy. TEL: 01543 256200; home - same. SER: Valuations. FAIRS: Stafford, Bingley Hall and Pavillion; Midland Antiquarian Book (organiser).

The Bournemouth Gallery Ltd

P.O Box 23. WS14 ODQ. *STOCK: Limited edition prints.* TEL: 01543 481880. SER: Mail order.

Cordelia and Perdy's Antique Junk Shop

53 Tamworth St. WS13 6JW. (C.R.J. and P.J. Mellor). *STOCK: General antiques and trade shipping goods.* TEL: 01543 263223.

Images - Peter Stockham

at The Staffs Bookshop, 4 & 6 Dam St. WS13 6AA. Open 9.30-5. *STOCK: Early children's books, art and illustrated books, printed ephemera; antique toys, mainly wooden; games and associated items; fine printing; prints and wood engravings.* TEL: 01543 264093.

James A. Jordan

7 The Corn Exchange. CMBHI. Open 9-5.30. *STOCK: Clock, especially longcase; watches and barometers.* TEL: 01543 416221; fax - 0121 522 2004. SER: Valuations; restorations (clocks and chronometers).

Milestone Antiques LAPADA

5 Main St., Whittington. WS14 9JU. Resident. (H. and E. Crawshaw). Est. 1988. Open Thurs.-Sat. 10-6, Sun. 11-3, other times by appointment. *STOCK: Furniture, porcelain, pottery, pictures, brass and copper, 18th-19th C.* LOC: A51 Lichfield/Tamworth road, turn north at Whittington Barracks, shop 50yds. past crossroads in village. PARK: Outside. TEL: 01543 432248. VAT: Stan/Spec.

L. Royden Smith

Church View, Farewell Lane, Burntwood. WS7 9DP. Est. 1972. Open Sat. 10-4 or by appointment. *STOCK: Secondhand books, general antiques, bric-a-brac.* TEL: 01543 682217.

The Staffs Bookshop

4 & 6 Dam St. WS13 6AA. Open 9.30-5. *STOCK: Rare, secondhand, antiquarian and collectors books, especially 18th-19th C.* TEL: 01543 264093.

Lichfield continued

The Tudor of Lichfield Antiques Centre

Bore St. WS13 6LL. (Miss S. Burns-Mace). Est. 1992. Open 10-5. SIZE: 5 rooms. *STOCK: Furniture, clocks, jewellery, china, collectables, 50p-£2,500.* LOC: Above tea rooms. TEL: 01543 263951. SER: Buys at auction.

LITTLE HAYWOOD, Nr. Stafford

Jalna Antiques

Coley Lane. ST18 0UP. Resident. Est. 1974. Open most times. *STOCK: Furniture, pre-1900.* Not Stocked: Shipping goods. LOC: 1/2 mile off A51, 12 miles north of Lichfield. TEL: 01889 881381. SER: Restorations; re-upholstery. VAT: Spec.

NEWCASTLE-UNDER-LYME

Antique Market

The Stones. ST5 2AG. (Antique Forum). Every Tues. 9-4. SIZE: 70 dealers. *STOCK: General antiques.* TEL: 01782 595805; mobile - 0836 322343.

Errington Antiques

63 George St. ST5 1JT. (G.K. Errington). Open 10-12.30 and 1.30-4.30 CL: Thurs. *STOCK: Oriental items, English furniture, general antiques, lamps.* LOC: Corner of George and Albert St. PARK: Easy. TEL: 01782 632822.

Richard Midwinter Antiques

31 Bridge St. ST5 2RY. (Mr and Mrs R. Midwinter). Est. 1987. Open 10-5, Thurs. by appointment. SIZE: Medium. *STOCK: Furniture, oak, walnut, mahogany, 17th-19th C, £50-£10,000; textiles, samplers and embroideries; longcase, mantel and wall clocks, £150-£4,000; paintings, £35-£3,000, both 18th-19th C; ceramics and watercolours, 19th C, £15-£1,500.* Not Stocked: Pine and ephemera. LOC: Close to Sainsburys and the Magistrates Courts. TEL: 01782 712483; home - 01630 672289. SER: Valuations; restorations (framing, clock repair). VAT: Spec.

PENKRIDGE, Nr. Stafford

Golden Oldies

1 and 5 Crown Bridge. ST19 5AA. (W.A. and M.A. Knowles). Open 10-5.30, Mon. 10-2. *STOCK: Victorian, Edwardian and later furniture; paintings, decorative items.* PARK: Easy. TEL: 01785 714722.

RUGELEY

Eveline Winter

1 Wolseley Rd. WS15 2QH. (Mrs E. Winter). Est. 1962. Open Thurs.-Sat. 10.30-5 appointment advisable. SIZE: Small. *STOCK: Staffordshire figures, pre-Victorian, from £90; Victorian, £30-£500; copper, brass, glass and general antiques.* Not Stocked: Coins and weapons. LOC: Coming from Lichfield or Stafford stay on A51 and avoid town by-pass. PARK: Easy and at side of shop. TEL: 01889 583259.

STAFFORD

The Antique Restoration Studio

1 Newport Rd. ST18 9JH. GADAR. (P. Albright). Est. 1989. Open 9-5. *STOCK: General antiques.* LOC: Main road. TEL: 01785 780424; e-mail - ars@uk-hq.demon.co.uk. SER: Valuations; repair and restoration (furniture, ceramics, glassware and paintings). VAT: Stan.

Browse

127 Lichfield Rd. ST17 4LF. (H. Barnes). Est. 1981. Open 9.30-5. SIZE: Large. *STOCK: Furniture, 1860-1940 and reproduction.* LOC: Outskirts of town. PARK: Easy. TEL: 01785 241097; home - 01785 660336. SER: Valuations; restorations.

Windmill Antiques

9 Castle Hill, Broadeye. ST16 2QB. Open 10-5. SIZE: Medium - several dealers. *STOCK: General antiques and decorative items.* PARK: Easy. TEL: 01785 228505.

STOKE-ON-TRENT

Ann's Antiques

24/26 Leek Rd., Stockton Brook. ST9 9MN. Open 10-5. CL: Thurs. *STOCK: Victorian furniture, brass, copper, jewellery, paintings, pottery and unusual items.* TEL: 01782 503991. VAT: Stan.

Ceramic Search - Top of the Hill

14/14a Nile St., Burslem. (A. Phillips and E.J. Butterton). Est. 1995. Open 9.30-5, Sun. by appointment. SIZE: Medium. *STOCK: Staffordshire ceramics especially Doulton and Beswick, £5-£500; furniture, £30-£1,000; architectural items, £10-£1,000; all 19th-20th C.* LOC: Follow Doulton signs from A500, premises opposite factory shop. PARK: Easy. TEL: 01782 834506. SER: Valuations; buys at auction (Staffordshire pottery). FAIRS: Bingley; International.

Five Towns Antiques

17 Broad St., Hanley. ST1 4HS. (B. and B. Arkinstall). Open 10-5.30. CL: Thurs. SIZE: Small. *STOCK: 1930's pottery and porcelain, general antiques.* PARK: Nearby. TEL: 01782 272930.

Manor Court Antiques

4 Manor Court St., Penkhull. (R. Broad). Est. 1995. Open 10-5. SIZE: Medium. *STOCK: Edwardian and Victorian furniture, Art Deco, clocks, pottery.* LOC: Opposite church, next door to Greyhound public house. PARK: Outside. TEL: 01782 410140.

The Potteries Antique Centre

271 Waterloo Rd., Cobridge. ST6 3HR. (W. Buckley). Est. 1972. Open 9-6 including Sun. SIZE: Large+ trade and export warehouse. *STOCK: Furniture including pine and shipping, 18th-20th C; pottery and porcelain including Doulton, Moorcroft, Beswick, Wedgwood,*

Stoke-on-Trent continued

Coalport, Shelley, 19th-20th C; collectors' items, silver plate, clocks, brass, jewellery, pictures, 18th-20th C; all £1-£5,000. LOC: Off M6, junction 15 or 16 on to A500, follow signs for Festival Park or Potteries Shopping Centre. PARK: Easy. TEL: 01782 201455; fax - 01782 201518. SER: Valuations; export facilities - supply and packing; buys at auction (pottery and collectors' items). VAT: Stan/Spec.

TUTBURY, Nr. Burton-on-Trent

Old Chapel Antique & Collectables Centre

31 High St. Open 10-5, including Sun., other times by appointment. *STOCK: China, glass, furniture.* PARK: Easy. TEL: 01283 815255; mobiles - 0421 438803/0374 238775.

Tutbury Mill Antiques Centre

Tutbury Mill Mews, Lower High St. DE13 9LU. (Richardson & Linnell Properties). Open 9.30-5.30, Sun. 12-5. SIZE: Large. *STOCK: General antiques including collectables, china and pine, from 18th C, £10-£1,000.* PARK: Easy. TEL: 01283 520074. SER: Valuations. VAT: Stan/Spec.

WEEFORD, Nr. Lichfield

Blackbrook Antiques Village

London Rd. WS14 0PS. Open 10-6 including Sun. SIZE: Large - 20 dealers. *STOCK: General antiques including furniture, fireplaces, architectural antiques, statuary, terracotta.* PARK: Own. TEL: 01543 481450; fax - same.

WOLSELEY BRIDGE, Nr. Rugeley

Jalna Antiques

The Old Barn. ST18 0UP. (G. and D. Hancox). Open 10-5. *STOCK: Furniture and smalls.* LOC: Junction A51/A513. TEL: 01889 882125.

YOXALL, Nr. Burton-on-Trent

Armson's of Yoxall Antiques LAPADA

The Hollies. DE13 8NH. (F.R.B. and P.K. Armson). Est. 1955. Open 9-5, Sat. 9-12, other times by appointment. SIZE: Large. *STOCK: Period furniture and shipping goods.* LOC: On A515. TEL: 01543 472352; fax - same. VAT: Stan/Spec.

H.W. Heron and Son Ltd LAPADA

The Antique Shop, 1 King St. DE13 8NF. (H.N.M. and J. Heron). Est. 1949. Open 9-6, Sat. 9-5.30, Sun. 2-6, Bank Hols. 10.30-5.30. SIZE: Medium. *STOCK: 18th-19th C furniture, ceramics and decorative items.* LOC: A515 village centre, opposite church. PARK: Easy. TEL: 01543 472266; home - same. SER: Valuations. VAT: Spec.

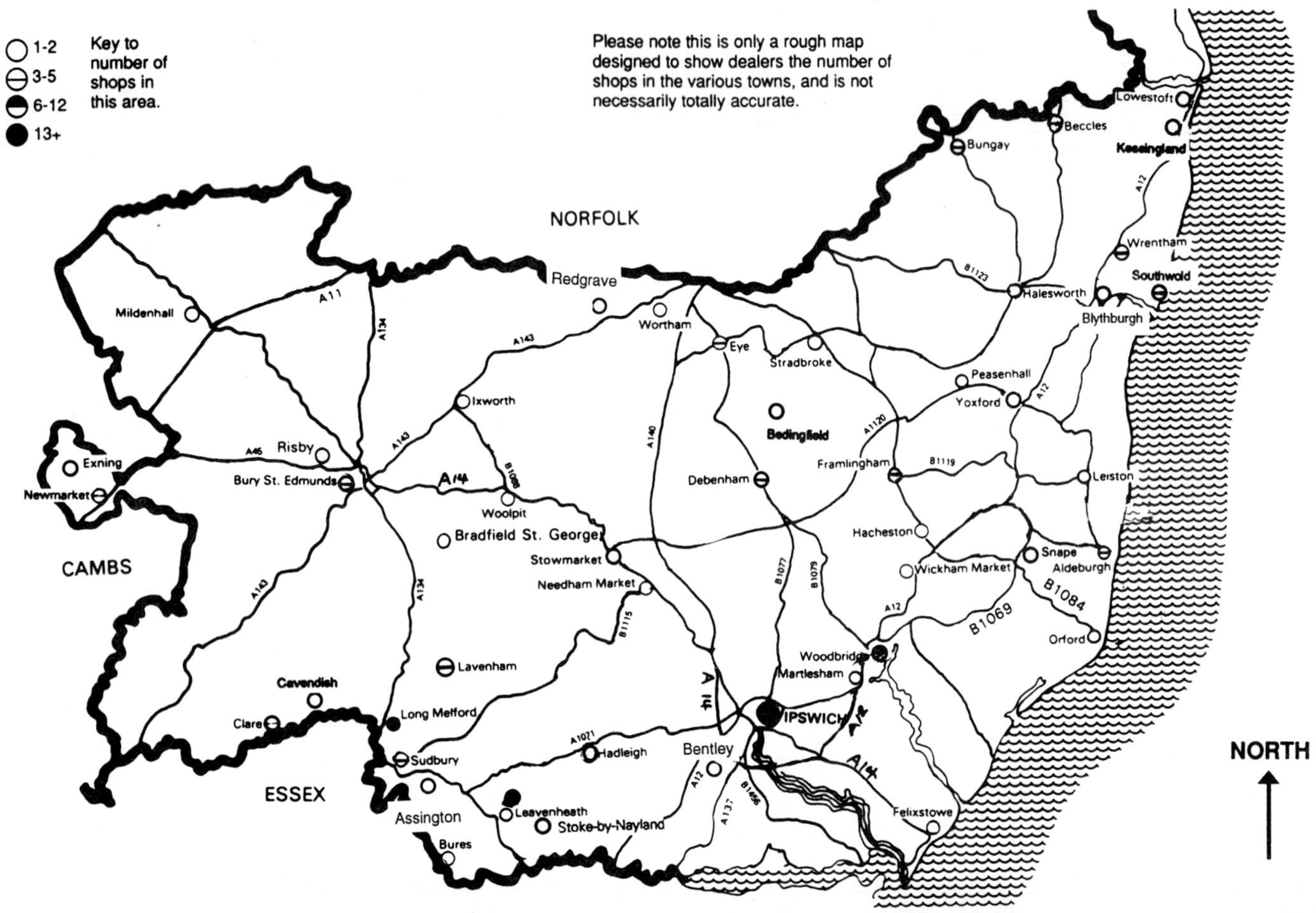
1-2
3-5
6-12
13+
Key to number of shops in this area.
Please note this is only a rough map designed to show dealers the number of shops in the various towns, and is not necessarily totally accurate.
NORFOLK
CAMBS
ESSEX
NORTH
Lowestoft
Kessingland
Beccles
Bungay
Wrentham
Southwold
Halesworth
Blythburgh
Redgrave
Wortham
Mildenhall
Eye
Stradbroke
Peasenhall
Yoxford
Ixworth
Bedingfield
Risby
Exning
Newmarket
Bury St. Edmunds
Woolpit
Debenham
Framlingham
Leiston
Bradfield St. George
Stowmarket
Needham Market
Hacheston
Wickham Market
Snape
Aldeburgh
Orford
Woodbridge
Martlesham
IPSWICH
Lavenham
Cavendish
Clare
Long Melford
Sudbury
Hadleigh
Bentley
Leavenheath
Stoke-by-Nayland
Assington
Bures
Felixstowe
A11
A134
A143
A45
A14
A140
A1120
A12
A1071
A137
B1123
B1119
B1088
B1077
B1079
B1115
B1084
B1069
B1456

ALDEBURGH

Aldeburgh Galleries

132 High St. IP15 5AQ. (Mrs K. Dandy and S. Haslam). Open 10-5, Sun. 2-4.30. *STOCK: Jewellery, silver, glass, studio pottery, books, furniture, pictures, collectables and general antiques.* TEL: 01728 453963.

Guillemot

134-136 High St. IP15 5AQ. (Lisabeth Hoad). Est. 1973. Open 10-1 and 2-5, Wed. 10-1, or by a appointment. SIZE: Medium. *STOCK: Country furniture, pine, elm, oak and fruitwood.* LOC: Town centre. PARK: Easy. TEL: 01728 453933.

Mole Hall Antiques

102 High St. IP15 5AB. (Peter Weaver). Est. 1976. Open 10-5, Sun. by appointment. SIZE: Small. *STOCK: Paintings, prints, unusual decorative items and country furniture.* PARK: Easy. TEL: 01728 452361; home - same.

Thompson's Gallery

175 High St. IP15 5AN. (J. and S. Thompson). Open 10-5 or by appointment. SIZE: Medium. *STOCK: Oils and watercolours, 18th-19th C; furniture, 18th to early 20th C; both £300-£10,000.* PARK: Easy. TEL: 01728 453743. SER: Valuations; restorations; framing; buys at auction. VAT: Spec.

ASSINGTON

Galleries Antique Warehouse

Glebe House Barn, Aveley Hall Lane. CO10 5LG. (Roland S. Strickland). Est. 1992. Open 10-5 including Sun. SIZE: Medium. *STOCK: Furniture, £100-£1,000; china, glass, £5-£250; all 19th-20th C.* LOC: A134 between Colchester and Sudbury. PARK: Easy. TEL: 01787 211685. SER: Valuations; restorations (furniture). VAT: Stan/Spec.

BECCLES

Besleys Books

4 Blyburgate. NR34 9TA. ABA, PBFA. (P.A. and P.F. Besley). Est. 1978. Open 9.30-1 and 2-5. CL: Wed. SIZE: Medium. *STOCK: Books, 50p-£1,000; prints, £7-£50; maps, £3-£100; all 17th-20th C.* LOC: Town centre. PARK: Nearby. TEL: 01502 715762; home - 01502 675649. SER: Valuations; restorations (book binding); buys at auction (books). FAIRS: Various PBFA.

Saltgate Antiques

11 Saltgate. NR34 9AN. Resident. (A.M. Ratcliffe). Est. 1971. Open 10-5. CL: Wed. pm. SIZE: Medium. *STOCK: Furniture, 17th-19th C, £100-£4,500; clocks, collectors' items, brass, copper, Staffordshire figures, paintings and prints, 19th C bric-a-brac, £5-£300.* LOC: Town centre opposite bus station. PARK: Easy. TEL: 01502 712776.

Beccles continued

Waveney Antiques Centre

Peddars Lane. Open 10-5.30. SIZE: Several dealers. *STOCK: General antiques, books, furniture, jewellery, silver, clocks and collectors' items.* PARK: Easy. TEL: 01502 716147.

BEDINGFIELD, Nr. Eye

The Olde Red Lion

The Street. IP23 7LQ. Est. 1973. Open by appointment. *STOCK: Furniture and general antiques.* LOC: 3 miles from Eye, 2 miles from Debenham. TEL: 01728 628491. SER: Restorations (furniture, oil paintings, ceramics, snuff boxes, wood carvings).

BENTLEY, Nr. Ipswich

P. Dawson Furniture Restorers

Unit O, Dodnash Priory Farm. IP9 2DF. Est. 1996. Open 8-6, Sun. by appointment. SIZE: Small. *STOCK: Mahogany, 18th-19th C, £50-£3,000; walnut and rosewood, 17th to late 19th C, £50-£3,000; oak, 17th to late19th C, £50-£1,500.* LOC: Take Bentley turning off the A12 outside Ipswich, 1st right into Bergholt road, next left and follow the road round to farm estate. TEL: 01473 462397; fax - 01473 449388; workshop - 01473 311947. SER: Restorations (furniture).

BLYTHBURGH, Nr. Halesworth

E.T. Webster

Westwood Lodge. IP19 9NB. Open by appointment. *STOCK: Ancient oak beams, oak ceilings, panelling, quality reproduction oak furniture, doors, mullioned windows.* TEL: 01502 478539.

BRADFIELD ST. GEORGE, Nr. Bury St. Edmunds

Denzil Grant Antiques BADA LAPADA

Hubbards Corner. IP30 0AQ. Est. 1979. Open anytime by appointment. *STOCK: Furniture, 16th to early 19th C; tapestry, metalware.* LOC: Off A14 between Bury St. Edmunds and Ipswich. PARK: Easy. TEL: 01449 736576; fax - 01449 737679.

BUNGAY

Black Dog Antiques

51 Earsham St. NR35 2PB. (K. Button). Est. 1986. Open seven days a week. *STOCK: General antiques including oak, mahogany and pine, china, linen and collectables, antiquities, Saxon and Roman, £1-£1000.* LOC: Opposite Post Office. PARK: Easy. TEL: 01986 895554; home - 01986 894489. SER: Valuations.

Broadly Antiques

30A Broad St. NR35 1EE. (Patricia Walker and Joan Gibson). Est. 1971. Open 10.30-5. CL: Wed. SIZE: Medium. *STOCK: General antiques*

Bungay continued

including furniture, ceramics, pictures, costume jewellery. LOC: A143. PARK: Easy.TEL: 01986 894692. SER: Valuations.

Cork Brick Antiques

6 Earsham St. NR35 1AG. (G. and K. Skipper). Open 10.30-5.30. CL: Mon. *STOCK: Country and decorative antiques; architectural decoration.* PARK: Easy. TEL: 01986 894873; home - 01502 712646.

Country House Antiques

30 Earsham St. Est. 1979. CL: Wed., and Sat. pm. except by appointment. SIZE: Medium and trade warehouse. *STOCK: Mahogany, inlaid, oak and walnut furniture, 18th-19th C; 19th C porcelain and collectables, £1-£5,000.* LOC: Near Post Office. PARK: Easy. TEL: 01986 892875; home and warehouse - 01508 558144.

BURES

Foord Antiques and Restoration

CO8 5EW. (C.G. and E.S. Foord). By appointment only. *STOCK: Furniture, boxes, treen, metalware, decorative items.* TEL: 01787 227268; mobile - 0836 533655. SER: Restorations; valuations.

BURY ST. EDMUNDS

Corner Shop Antiques

1 Guildhall St. IP33 1PR. Open 10-4.30. CL: Thurs. *STOCK: Victoriana, porcelain, jewellery, silver, glass and collectors' items.* LOC: Corner of Abbeygate St., opposite Corn Exchange. TEL: 01284 701007.

The Enchanted Aviary

Lapwings, Rushbrooke Lane. IP33 2RS. (C.C. Frost). Est. 1970. Open by appointment only. *STOCK: Cased and uncased mounted birds, animals and fish, mostly late Victorian, £15-£800.* PARK: Easy. TEL: 01284 725430.

Guildhall Street Antiques LAPADA

27 Guildhall St. IP33 1QD. (Mrs T. Cutting). Est. 1965. Open 9.30-5.30. CL: Mon. am. and Thurs. SIZE: Medium. *STOCK: General antiques, bric-a-brac, £25-£2,500.* LOC: From town centre down Guildhall St. to below Churchgate St. junction. PARK: Easy. TEL: 01284 703060/735278.

Peppers Period Pieces

23 Churchgate St. IP33 1RG. (M.E. Pepper). Est. 1975. Open 10-5. *STOCK: Furniture, oak, elm, yew, fruitwood, mahogany, 16th-19th C; English domestic implements in brass, copper, lead, tin, iron, pewter and treen, 16th to early 20th C; some pottery and porcelain, bygones and collectables, late 19th to early 20th C.* Not Stocked: Reproductions. PARK: Easy. TEL: 01284 768786; home - 01359 250606. SER: Valuations; repairs and polishing.

Bury St. Edmunds continued

Winston Mac (Silversmith)

65 St. John's St. IP33 1SJ. (E.W. McKnight). Est. 1978. Open 9-5. CL: Sun. except by appointment and Sat. SIZE: Small. *STOCK: Silver tea services, creamers, salts.* PARK: Easy. TEL: 01284 767910. SER: Restorations (silver and plating). VAT: Stan/Spec.

CAVENDISH

Cavendish Rose Antiques

High St. and Lower St. (T. Patterson). Est. 1972. Open 10.30-5. SIZE: Large. *STOCK: Furniture, 18th-19th C mahogany, £500-£2,500.* PARK: Easy. TEL: 01787 280332/282133. VAT: Spec.

CLARE, Nr. Sudbury

Clare Antique Warehouse

The Mill, Malting Lane. CO10 8NW. (D. Edwards and J. Tanner). Est. 1989. Open 9.30-5.30, Sun. 1-5. SIZE: Large - over 40 dealers. *STOCK: 17th-20th C furniture, textiles, pictures, porcelain, glass, silver, decorative items.* LOC: 100yds. from High St. Follow signs for Clare Castle, Country Park. PARK: Easy. TEL: 01787 278449. SER: Valuations; restorations. VAT: Stan/Spec.

J. de Haan & Son BADA

Market Hill. CO10 8NN. Est. 1905. Open Mon.-Wed. by appointment, Thurs. and Fri. 10-5, Sat., 10-1. SIZE: Medium. *STOCK: English furniture, barometers, gilt mirrors and fine tea caddies, all 18th-19th C.* LOC: Corner of Market Hill. PARK: Easy. TEL: 01787 278870; home - 01787 277304. VAT: Stan/Spec.

Granny's Attic

22 High St. CO10 8NY. (M. Sadler-Chapman). Est. 1972. Open Sat. only 10.30-5. *STOCK: Victorian to 1940's cottage bygones.* LOC: Off main road, opposite church tower doorway. PARK: Easy.

F.D. Salter Antiques

1-2 Church St. CO10 8NN. Est. 1959. Open 9-5. CL: Wed. pm. SIZE: Medium. *STOCK: 18th to early 19th C English furniture, porcelain and glass.* LOC: A1092. PARK: Easy. TEL: 01787 277693. SER: Valuations; restorations (furniture). FAIRS: Harrogate (April); Barbican. VAT: Stan/Spec.

Trinders' Fine Tools

Malting Lane. CO10 8NW. (P. and R. Trinder). Est. 1975. Open Sat. 10-1 and 2-5, Sun. 2-5, weekdays telephone or ring the doorbell. SIZE: Medium. *STOCK: Woodworking and metalworking books, some art and antiques reference books; hand tools for craftsmen and collectors.* PARK: Nearby. TEL: 01787 277130; home - same; fax - 01787 277677; e-mail - finetools@dial.pipex.com; internet - http:// dialspace.dial.pipex.com/finetools/.

DEBENHAM

Gil Adams Antiques
Foresters Hall, High St. IP14 6QW. (Phil Massey and Gil Adams). Open 10-5 and by appointment. SIZE: Large - 2 floors. *STOCK: 18th-20th C English and Continental furniture and decorative antiques.* PARK: Opposite. TEL: 01728 860777; fax - 01728 860142. SER: Restorations (furniture). VAT: Stan/Spec.

C. & A.C. Bigden Antiques
No. 1 High St. IP14 6QL. Est. 1969. Open 10-5. SIZE: Large. *STOCK: 17th-19th C furniture and paintings, £50-£10,000.* PARK: Easy. TEL: 01728 860707; fax - 01728 860333. VAT: Stan/Spec.

Ian Collins Antiques
73 High St. IP14 6QW. Open 10-5.30, Sun. 12-5. *STOCK: Furniture, mainly mahogany and oak, 17th-18th C; decorative works of art.* TEL: 01728 861450; fax - 01728 861297; mobile - 0802 492153. SER: Buys at auction. VAT: Stan/Spec.

N.A.J. Lanchester
21 High St. IP14 6QL. Open every day. *STOCK: General antiques, 18th-19th C shipping goods and smalls.* TEL: 01728 860756.

Quercus
4 High St. IP14 6QH. Resident. (Peter Horsman and Bill Bristow-Jones). Est. 1972. Open by appointment. SIZE: Medium. *STOCK: Oak furniture, 17th-18th C, £1,000-£5,000.* PARK: Easy. TEL: 01728 860262; home - same. SER: Valuations; restorations (17th C oak furniture). VAT: Spec.

EXNING, Nr. Newmarket

Derby Cottage Collectables
Fordham Rd. CB8 7LG. (V. Cole). Open 9-6 including Sun. SIZE: Medium. *STOCK: Furniture and ceramics especially Derby porcelain, 19th to early 20th C, £5-£1,500; bygones and collectors' items, £1-£300.* LOC: Just off A14 Newmarket by-pass on A142 to Ely. PARK: Easy. TEL: 01638 578422; home - same. VAT: Stan/Spec.

EYE

Allsorts
3 Castle St. IP23 7AN. (David, Melvin and Joy Fielding-Gooderham). Est. 1994. Open 11-6. SIZE: Small. *STOCK: Memorabilia, 19th C; collectibles and bric-a-brac, 19th C to 1960's, £5-£200.* PARK: Nearby. TEL: 01379 871492; mobile - 0468 155971. SER: Valuations.

Bramley Antiques
4 Broad St. (C. Grater). Open Wed.-Sat. 9.30-5, other times by appointment. SIZE: Medium. *STOCK: Furniture, £20-£5,000; glass, £5-£500; boxes, pictures, general antiques, all 18th-early 20th C.* PARK: Easy. TEL: 01379 871386. SER: Valuations; restorations.

English and Continental Antiques
1 Broad St. IP23. (Roger Ford). Est. 1977. Open 9-5.30. CL: Mon. SIZE: Large. *STOCK: Furniture, 17th-19th C, £50-£4,000.* PARK: Easy. TEL: 01379 871199. *Trade Only.*

Eye continued

Laburnum Cottage Antiques LAPADA
Laburnum Cottage, 2 Broad St. Resident. (S. Grater). Est. 1978. Open Wed.-Sun. 9.30-5, other times by appointment. SIZE: Small. *STOCK: Porcelain and glass, £5-£250; furniture, £30-£2,500; linen, silver, jewellery, £2.50-£500; all 18th to early 20th C.* PARK: Easy. TEL: 01379 871386. SER: Valuations; restorations. VAT: Global.

Jennifer and Raymond Norman Antiques
Home Farm, South Green. IP23 7NW. Resident. Est. 1974. Open by appointment. *STOCK: Clocks especially longcase, dolls, mechanical music.* LOC: From A140 take B1117 to Eye, then towards Stradbroke for 2 miles, turn left to Hoxne, after half mile South Green is on right, Home Farm at very end of lane. PARK: Easy. TEL: 01379 870040; mobile - 0374 887045. SER: Valuations; restorations (furniture, clocks and musical boxes); finder (specialist pieces of period and Victorian furniture). VAT: Stan/Spec.

FELIXSTOWE

George Eliot Antique and Country Things
10 Orwell Rd. IP11 7HN. (George Eliot and Partners). Est. 1994. Open 10-5. CL: Mon. SIZE: Small. *STOCK: General antiques, collectables and country things, 19th-20th C, £25-£1,000.* LOC: Down Hamilton Rd. towards sea, turn left at crossroads (Lloyds Bank and church). PARK: End of Orwell Rd. TEL: 01394 275577. SER: Buys at auction. FAIRS: IACF, Tradex and R & S.

John McCulloch Antiques
1a Hamilton Rd. IP11 7HN. Open 9.30-5, Wed. 9.30-1. *STOCK: Furniture, copper, brass, pictures, clocks and bric-a-brac.* LOC: Main street, sea front end at top of Bent Hill. PARK: Around corner. TEL: 01394 283126; home - 01394 272179.

FRAMLINGHAM

Antiques Warehouse
The Old Station. IP13 9EE. (Bed Bazaar and Richard Goodbrey). Est. 1992. Open 10-5, Sun. 2-5. *STOCK: Decorative furniture and Victorian brass and iron bedsteads.* PARK: Easy. TEL: 01728 723756; fax - 01728 724626. SER: Restorations (beds); mattresses and bases made-to-measure.

Dix-Sept
17 Station Rd. IP13. (S. Goodbrey and M. Cluzan). Est. 1996. Open Sat. 10-1 and 2-5, other times by appointment. *STOCK: French country furniture and decoration, pottery, garden furniture, mirrors.* LOC: On approach road from A12. PARK: Easy. TEL: 01728 621505. VAT: Global.

Framlingham continued

Goodbreys

29 Double St. IP13 9BN. (R. and M. Goodbrey). Est. 1965. Open Sat. 9-5.30, other times by appointment. SIZE: Large. *STOCK: Decorative items including sleighbeds, upholstery, Biedermeier, simulated bamboo, painted cupboards, garden furniture, country pieces; pottery, glass, textiles, mirrors, bric-a-brac.* LOC: Up Church St. towards Framlingham Castle. Opposite church gates turn right into Double St. PARK: Easy. TEL: 01728 621191; fax - 01728 724626. VAT: Mainly Spec. *Mainly Trade.*

HACHESTON, Nr. Wickham Market

Joyce Hardy Pine and Country Furniture

IP13 0DS. Resident. Open 9.30-5.30, Sun. 9.30-12. *STOCK: Pine - dressers, corner cupboards, butcher's blocks, farmhouse tables.* LOC: B1116, Framlingham Rd. PARK: Easy. TEL: 01728 746485. SER: Hand-made furniture from old pine.

HADLEIGH, Nr. Ipswich

Randolph BADA

97 and 99 High St. IP7 5EJ. (B.F. and H.M. Marston). Est. 1921. Open 9.30-5.30, appointment advisable. Sun. by appointment only. SIZE: Medium. *STOCK: Furniture, 1600-1830, £50-£25,000; brass, copper, porcelain, delftware, treen.* Not Stocked: Silver. PARK: Easy. TEL: 01473 823789; fax - 01473 823867. SER: Valuations; restorations (furniture). FAIRS: BADA. VAT: Spec.

Tara's Hall

Victoria House, Market Place. IP7 5DL. (B. O'Keefe). Est. 1977. Open 10-5. CL: Wed. SIZE: Medium. *STOCK: Textiles and linen, jewellery, Art Nouveau and Art Deco, small items.* PARK: Easy. TEL: 01473 824031. SER: Valuations; buys at auction (jewellery, Art Nouveau objects).

HALESWORTH

Halesworth Antiques Market

3A Bridge St. IP19 8AB. (Tony Hull and Miles Fairhurst). Est. 1994. Open 10-5, Thurs. 10-1. SIZE: Medium. *STOCK: Victorian furniture, £50-£1,500; Victorian china, £5-£150; general small antiques, 20th C, £5-£1,000.* PARK: Easy. TEL: 01986 875599.

IPSWICH

A. Abbott Antiques

757 Woodbridge Rd. IP4 4NE. (C. Lillistone). Est. 1965. Open 10.30-5. CL: Wed. SIZE: Medium. *STOCK: Small items, especially clocks and jewellery; Victorian, Edwardian and shipping furniture, £5-£1,000.* PARK: Easy. TEL: 01473 728900; fax - same; mobile - 0802 813848.

Ipswich continued

Tony Adams Wireless & Bygones Shop

175 Spring Rd. IP4 5NG. Open 10-5. CL: Wed. and Thurs. *STOCK: Bygones, especially wireless sets; toy trains, cameras.*

Ashley Antiques

20A Fore St. IP4 1JU. (A.M. Warren). Open by appointment only. SIZE: Medium. *STOCK: Furniture, 18th-19th C, £200-£4,000; 19th C barometers, £300-£1,000; Victorian coloured glass, £30-£200.* Not Stocked: Silver and jewellery. LOC: Off Star Lane. PARK: Easy. TEL: 01473 251696/444054. SER: Restorations (furniture). FAIRS: NEC (Aug.).

Atfield and Daughter

17 St. Stephen's Lane. IP1 1DP. (D.A. and Miss S.F. Atfield). Est. 1920. Open 9.30-5.30. SIZE: Medium. *STOCK: Furniture, clocks, metal, pottery, china, £5-£500; pistols, swords, guns, militaria, £25-£1,000; books on collecting, local history, military history and all kinds of transport, £5-£75.* LOC: Opposite bus station, Old Cattle Market. PARK: Very nearby. TEL: 01473 251158. SER: Restorations (cabinet work). VAT: Stan.

Paul Bruce Antiques

Frobisher Rd. IP3 0HR. Est. 1972. Open by appointment. SIZE: Warehouse. *STOCK: Oak, walnut and mahogany, paintings, general antiques, £20-£6,500.* TEL: 01473 255400/233671; fax - 01473 233656.

Claude Cox at College Gateway Bookshop

3 Silent St. IP1 1TF. Open 10-5. CL: Wed. SIZE: Medium. *STOCK: Books, from 1470; some local maps and prints.* LOC: Leave inner ring road at Novotel double roundabout, turn into St. Peters St. PARK: Cromwell Square and Buttermarket Centre. TEL: 01473 254776; fax - same. SER: Valuations; restorations (rebinding); buys at auction; catalogue available.

The Edwardian Shop

556 Spring Rd. IP4 4NT. Est. 1979. Open 9-5. *STOCK: Victorian, Edwardian and 1920's shipping goods, £10-£400.* LOC: Half-mile from hospital. PARK: Own. TEL: 01473 716576.

The Fortescue Gallery

27 St. Peter's St. IP1 1XF. (L. Fortescue). Open Tues.-Fri. 10-3. *STOCK: 19th C pictures.* PARK: Easy. TEL: 01473 251342.

Hubbard Antiques

16-18 St. Margarets Green. IP4 2BS. Est. 1964. Open 9-6 and by appointment. SIZE: Large. *STOCK: Furniture and decorative items, 18th-19th C.* PARK: Easy. TEL: 01473 226033/233034; fax - 01473 212726. SER: Valuations; restorations. VAT: Stan/Spec. *Trade & Export.*

Ipswich continued

Hyland House Antiques

45 Felixstowe Rd. IP3 8DX. (J. Burton). Open 9.30-5. CL: Wed. and Thurs. SIZE: Large. *STOCK: Pre-war furniture and bric-a-brac.* TEL: 01473 210055/445403.

Orwell Pine Co Ltd

Halifax Mill, 427 Wherstead Rd. IP2 8LH. (M. Weiner). Open 8.30-5.30, Sat. 8.30-4. *STOCK: Pine.* TEL: 01473 680091. SER: Restorations; stripping; pine furniture and kitchens made to order from old wood.

Tom Smith Antiques

33A St. Peter's St. IP1 1XF. Est. 1959. *STOCK: Period furniture, silver and plate, china, pine and gifts, £2-£1,000.* TEL: 01473 210172.

Thompson's

418 Norwich Rd. IP1 5DX. (D. and Mrs S. Thompson). Est. 1978. Open 9-5. CL: Sun. except by appointment. SIZE: Medium. *STOCK: Furniture, mainly late Victorian and shipping, 1870 to date, £10-£1,000.* LOC: 1 mile from town centre, on corner at traffic lights next to railway bridge. PARK: Own, at side of premises. TEL: 01473 747793; fax - same. SER: Valuations; buys at auction (shipping items). VAT: Stan/Spec.

IXWORTH, Nr. Bury St. Edmunds

E.W. Cousins and Son LAPADA

27 High St. and The Old School. IP31 2HJ. CL: Sat. pm. SIZE: Large and warehouse. *STOCK: General antiques, 18th-19th C, £50-£6,000; shipping items.* LOC: A143. PARK: Easy. TEL: 01359 230254; fax - 01359 232370. SER: Valuations; restorations. VAT: Stan/Spec.

Ixworth Antiques

17 High St. IP31 2HH. (M. Ginders). Open 10-5, Sat. 10-1. *STOCK: Victorian and Edwardian furniture, brass and silver plate.* PARK: Easy. TEL: 01359 231691. SER: Polishing (brass); plating (silver).

KESSINGLAND

Kessingland Antiques

36A High St. NR33 7QQ. Est. 1976. Open 10-5.30. SIZE: Large. *STOCK: Edwardian, Victorian furniture, general antiques and collectables, watches, clocks, jewellery, shipping goods.* LOC: On A12, 3 miles south of Lowestoft. PARK: On forecourt and own. TEL: 01502 740562.

LAVENHAM, Nr. Sudbury

R.G. Archer

7 Water St. CO10 9RW. Est. 1970. Open 9-5, Sun. 10-5. CL: Wed. *STOCK: Antiquarian and secondhand books.* TEL: 01787 247229.

Lavenham continued

J. and J. Baker
12-14 Water St. and 3a High St. CO10 9RW. (C.J. and Mrs B.A.J. Baker). Est. 1960. Open 9-1 and 2-5.30. SIZE: Medium. *STOCK: Oak and mahogany furniture, 1600-1870, £100-£10,000; oils and watercolours, 19th C, £150-£5,000; English porcelain and metalware, 18th-19th C, £20-£1,000; collectors' items, £20-£1,000.* LOC: Below Swan Hotel at T junction of A1141 and B1071. PARK: Easy. TEL: 01787 247610. VAT: Stan/Spec.

One Bell
46 High St. CO10 9PY. (J.F. and M.A. Tinworth). Open 11-4.30, Sat. 10.30-5, Sun. 11-5. CL: Wed. and Thurs. SIZE: Small. *STOCK: Militaria and collectables.* LOC: A134. PARK: Easy. TEL: 01787 248206; home - same.

Tom Smith Antiques
36 Market Place. Est. 1959. SIZE: Large and warehouse. *STOCK: Furniture, early Staffordshire figures, rugs, early maps and decorative prints.* TEL: 01787 247463. SER: Valuations; restorations. VAT: Stan/Spec.

The Timbers
Antique & Collectables Centre, High St. Resident. (B.A. Preece and A.M. Trodd). Est. 1996. CL: Wed. SIZE: Medium. *STOCK: Smalls and small furniture, £5-£500.* PARK: Easy. TEL: 01787 247218; home - same.

LEAVENHEATH

Clock House
Locks Lane. CO6 4PF. (A.G. Smeeth). Est. 1983. Open by appointment. SIZE: Small. *STOCK: English clocks, 17th to early 19th C, £1,500-£6,000; French and English clocks, Victorian and Edwardian, £300-£2,000.* PARK: Easy. TEL: 01206 262187; home - same. SER: Valuations; restorations (clocks and furniture); buys at auction (clocks and furniture).

The Persian Carpet Studio
Harrow St. CO6 4PN. (Sara Barber). Est. 1990. Open 9-5, Sun. morning by appointment. SIZE: Medium. *STOCK: Antique and decorative Oriental carpets and rugs, from 1860, from £50.* LOC:.75 mile off A134. PARK: Easy. TEL: 01787 210034; fax - same. SER: Valuations; repairs and hand-cleaning (Oriental rugs); buys at auction (Oriental carpets, rugs and textiles). Exhibitions held. FAIRS: Snape. VAT: Stan/Spec.

LEISTON

Leiston Trading Post
13a High St. IP16 4EL. (A.E. Moore). Est. 1967. Open 10-1 and 2-5, other times by appointment. CL: Wed. pm. *STOCK: Bric-a-brac, Victoriana, Victorian and Edwardian furniture.* PARK: Easy. TEL: 01728 830081; home - 01728 830281. VAT: Stan.

Warrens Antiques Warehouse
High St. IP16 4EL. (J.R. Warren). Est. 1980. CL:

Leiston continued

Wed. and Sat. pm. except by appointment. SIZE: Medium. *STOCK: Furniture, Georgian, Victorian, Edwardian and shipping oak, £20-£2,000.* LOC: Off High St., driveway beside Geaters Florists. PARK: Easy. TEL: 01728 831414; home - same; mobile - 0385 564905. SER: Valuations; restorations (furniture). VAT: Stan/Spec.

LONG MELFORD

Antique Clocks by Simon Charles
Little St. Mary's Court, Hall St. CO10 9LQ. Est. 1970. Open 10.30-5.30, Sun. by appointment only. SIZE: Medium. *STOCK: Clocks - especially longcase, lantern and early bracket, 17th-19th C, £150-£10,000; barometers, 18th-19th C, £150-£1,000.* LOC: Opposite fire station on main road. PARK: Easy. TEL: 01787 880040; home - 01787 375931. SER: Valuations; restorations (clock movements and cases); buys at auction (clocks). FAIRS: Snape and Bury St. Edmunds. VAT: Stan/Spec.

Ashley Gallery
Belmont House, Hall St. CO10 9JF. Est. 1965. Open 9.30-5.30 or by appointment. SIZE: Medium. *STOCK: Paintings, watercolour drawings, furniture, porcelain.* LOC: A134, opposite Crown Hotel. PARK: Easy. TEL: 01787 375434.

Karen Bryan Antiques
Little St. Mary's Court. CO10 9LQ. Est. 1975. Open 10.30-5. SIZE: Medium. *STOCK: Mahogany, walnut and satinwood furniture, 18th-19th C, £200-£8,000; prints, paintings, mirrors and lighting, 19th C, £30-£700; objects of vertu, 19th to early 20th C, £20-£400.* PARK: Easy. TEL: 01787 312613. SER: Valuations. VAT: Spec.

Roger Carling and Tess Sinclair LAPADA
Coconut House, Hall St. CO10 9JQ. Resident. Usually open 10-1 and 2-5, other times by appointment. *STOCK: Furniture, mahogany and oak, 18th-19th C; general antiques, metalware, clocks, barometers, textiles, mirrors, decorative items.* TEL: 01787 312012.

Charles Antiques
Little St. Marys. (Meg Charles). Est. 1992. Open 11-5. SIZE: Medium. *STOCK: Georgian furniture including bureaux, dining tables and chairs, to £5,000; period pieces, £85-£1,000; marine oils, £250-£1,000; both Georgian and Victorian.* LOC: Sudbury end of village, opposite fire station. PARK: Easy. TEL: 01787 880040; home - 01787 375931; fax - same. SER: Restorations (period furniture).

Sandy Cooke Antiques
Hall St. CO10 9JQ. Est. 1982. Open Mon., Fri. and Sat. 10-1 and 2-5. SIZE: Large. *STOCK: Furniture, 17th to early 19th C, £100-£40,000.* Not Stocked: Silver and glass. LOC: A134. PARK: Easy. TEL: 01787 378265; fax - 01284 830935. SER: Valuations; restorations; buys at auction (furniture). VAT: Stan/Spec.

Long Melford continued

Country Antiques

10 Westgate St. CO10 9DS. (Mrs E. Pink). Est. 1984. Open 11-5. CL: Mon. and Thurs. SIZE: Small. *STOCK: Objects and jewellery; small furniture, £50-£2,000; toys and unusual objects, £50-£500; all 18th-19th C.* LOC: Outskirts of village, on Clare road. PARK: Easy. TEL: 01787 310617.

Long Melford Antique Centre

Chapel Maltings and the adjacent White Hart Annexe. CO10 9HX. (Baroness V. von Dahlen). Est. 1984. Open 9.30-5.30 or by appointment. SIZE: Large - 42 dealers. *STOCK: Furniture - oak, Georgian, Edwardian and Victorian; silver, china, glass, clocks and decorators' items.* LOC: A134, Sudbury end of village. PARK: Ample, behind White Hart. TEL: 01787 379287/310316. SER: Packing and shipping. VAT: Stan/Spec.

Alexander Lyall Antiques

Belmont House, Hall St. CO10 9JF. (A.J. Lyall). Est. 1977. Open 9.30-5.30. SIZE: Medium. *STOCK: Furniture, 18th-19th C.* LOC: A134 opposite Crown Hotel. PARK: Easy. TEL: 01787 375434; home - same. SER: Restorations (furniture); buys at auction (English furniture). VAT: Stan/Spec.

Magpie Antiques

Hall St. CO10 9JT. (Mrs P. Coll). Est. 1985. Open

Long Melford continued

10.30-1 and 2.15-5, Sat. 10.30-5. CL: Mon. and Wed. SIZE: Small. *STOCK: Smalls including hand-painted china; furniture, Victorian and stripped pine.* LOC: Main street. PARK: Easy. TEL: 01787 310581; home - same.

Patrick Marney

The Gate House, Melford Hall. CO10 9AA. Est. 1964. Open by appointment. SIZE: Small. *STOCK: Fine barometers, 18th-19th C, £1,000-£5,000; pocket aneroids, 19th C, £150-£1,000; scientific instruments, 18th-19th C, £250-£2,000; all fully restored.* LOC: A134. PARK: Easy. TEL: 01787 880533. SER: Valuations; restorations (mercury barometers). VAT: Stan.

Melford Antique Warehouse

Hall St. (D. Edwards and J. Tanner). Open 9.30-5.30, Sun. 1-5. SIZE: 90 dealers on four floors. *STOCK: General antiques, 17th-20th C.* TEL: 01787 379638; fax - 01787 311788; home - same.

Noel Mercer Antiques

Aurora House, Hall St. CO10 9RJ. Est. 1990. Open 10-5. SIZE: Large. *STOCK: Early oak, walnut and country furniture and works of art, £500-£20,000.* LOC: Centre of Hall St. PARK: Easy. TEL: 01787 311882.

Seabrook Antiques

Hall St. CO10 9JG. (J. Tanner). Est. 1965. Open 9.30-5.30, Sun. 1-5. SIZE: Large - 10 showroms.

Long Melford continued

STOCK: Furniture, £500-£15,000; objects, £100-£2,000; both 17th-18th C. LOC: A134 near Bull Hotel. TEL: 01787 375787; fax - same; home - 01787 311788. SER: Valuations; restorations (17th-18th C furniture); buys at auction (17th-18th C furniture). FAIRS: International.

Oswald Simpson BADA

Hall St. CO10 9JL. Est. 1971. Open 10-5.30, other times by appointment. *STOCK: Early oak and country furniture, £25-£10,000; brass, copper, pewter and country items, £10-£500; all 17th-19th C; samplers and needlework, 17th-20th C, £25-£1,000; Staffordshire figures, £100-£1,000.* PARK: Easy. TEL: 01787 377523; home - 01449 740030. SER: Valuations; restorations. VAT: Spec.

Suthburgh Antiques

Red House, Hall St. CO10 9JQ. (R.P. Alston). Est. 1977. Open by appointment. SIZE: Medium. *STOCK: Furniture, 17th C oak, 18th C walnut and mahogany, £500-£5,000; portraits, 17th-19th C, £2,000-£10,000; Georgian barometers and clocks, £400-£15,000; small collectors' items, boxes, glass, brass, copper, oak carvings and panels, £50-£600; English county maps and prints, £40-£500.* Not Stocked: Victorian furniture and later items. LOC: Opposite Bull Hotel, A134. PARK: Easy. TEL: 01787 374818; fax - same; home - same. SER: Valuations; restorations (furniture, barometers); buys at auction. VAT: Stan/Spec.

Trident Antiques LAPADA

2 Foundry House, Hall St. CO10 9JR. (Thomas McGlynn). Est. 1989. Open 10-5.30, Sat. 10-6, Sun. by appointment. SIZE: Medium. *STOCK: Oak furniture, 17th C, £250-£10,000; barometers, 19th C, £450-£2,500; paintings, 17th-18th C, £2,000-£6,000; objects including bottles, spoons and carvings, 17th-18th C, £100-£600.* LOC: Next to Cock and Bell Inn. PARK: Easy. TEL: 01787 883388; home - 01787 371867. SER: Valuations; restorations (early English oak); buys at auction (oak furniture). FAIRS: LAPADA (NEC); Kenilworth (Mar. and Oct); City of London. VAT: Spec.

Tudor Antiques

Little St. Marys. CO10 9HY. (A.H. Denton-Ford). Est. 1974. Open 9.30-5.30. SIZE: Large + warehouse. *STOCK: General antiques, £5-£5,000; curios, silver, objets d'art, furniture, bygones, books on antiques.* LOC: Sudbury end of Long Melford, shop with yellow blind. PARK: Easy. TEL: 01787 375950; mobile - 0467 265436; e-mail - sford@antiqueandsilver.demon.co.uk. SER: Valuations; metal polishing; repairs (metal, clocks, barometers); mail-order catalogue. VAT: Stan/Spec.

Village Clocks

Little St. Mary's. CO10 9LQ. (J.C. Massey). Est. 1975. Open 10-5, Sat. 9.30-5. CL: Wed. SIZE: Small. *STOCK: Clocks - longcase, bracket, wall and mantle, 18th-19th C, £500-£5,000+; carriage, 19th C, £500-£2,000+.* PARK: Easy. TEL: 01787 375896. SER: Valuations; restorations (as stock); buys at auction (clocks). FAIRS: Uxbridge Horological, Brunel University.

LOWESTOFT

Carlton Road Antiques

1 Carlton Rd. NR34 7PF. (A. and I. Murray). Est. 1983. Open 9.30-5, Sat. 9.30-5.30. SIZE: Large. *STOCK: Stripped pine, £25-£1,000; Victorian furniture, £100-£2,000; china, paintings, mirrors, silver and collectables, £25-£100; all 18th-20th C.* LOC: From A12 into Lowestoft, approximately 2 miles from Bloodmoor Lane roundabout, turn left into Carlton Road. PARK: Easy. TEL: 01502 512946; home - 01502 713896.

North End Antiques

56-57 High St. NR32 1JA. (Mr and Mrs Fletcher). Open 9-5.30. *STOCK: Victorian furniture and collectables.* TEL: 01502 568535.

MARTLESHAM, Nr. Woodbridge

Martlesham Antiques

The Thatched Roadhouse. IP12 4RJ. (R.F. Frost). Est. 1973. Open daily, Sun. by appointment. SIZE: Large. *STOCK: Furniture and decorative items, 17th-20th C, £25-£3,000.* LOC: A1214 opposite Red Lion public house. PARK: Own. TEL: 01394 386732; fax - 01394 382959.

John Read

29 Lark Rise, Martlesham Heath. IP5 3SA. Est. 1992. By appointment. *STOCK: Pre. 1840 Staffordshire figures, animals and English pottery, including Delft, salt glaze, creamware and pearlware, coloured glazed, underglazed (Pratt) and enamel decoration, 1750-1840, £100-£4,000.* LOC: A12 Ipswich bypass, opposite B.T. tower. PARK: Easy. TEL: 01473 624897; home - same. SER: Valuations; restorations (as stock).

MILDENHALL

Mildenhall Antiques

10 North Terrace. IP28 7AA. Open 10-5. SIZE: Large. *STOCK: Restored English and Continental pine furniture and bric-a-brac.* TEL: 01638 718025.

NEEDHAM MARKET

Roy Arnold

77 High St. IP6 8AN. Est. 1974. Open 9.30-5.30 appointment advisable, Sun. by appointment. SIZE: Medium. *STOCK: Woodworkers' and craftsmen's tools; scientific instruments; books - new, secondhand and antiquarian - on tools; all £10-£5,000.* LOC: A14, centre of High St. PARK: Easy. TEL: 01449 720110; fax - 01449 722498; e-mail - Roy.Arnold@btinternet.com. VAT: Stan/Spec.

The Old Town Hall Antique Centre

High St. IP6 8AL. (S. and R. Abbott). Open 10-5. SIZE: Several dealers. *STOCK: General antiques.* TEL: 01449 720773. SER: Repairs (jewellery).

NEWMARKET

Equus Art Gallery

Sun Lane. CB8 8EW. (Mr and Mrs T. Minahan). Est. 1989. Open 9.30-4.30. CL: Wed. pm. SIZE: Medium. *STOCK: Equine oils, watercolours and sculpture, 19th-20th C, £300-£1,000; equine prints, 18th-20th C, £50-£2,000.* LOC: Off High St. PARK: Nearby. TEL: 01638 560445; home - 01638 666637. VAT: Stan.

Jemima Godfrey

5 Rous Rd. CB8 8DH. (Miss A. Lanham). Est. 1968. Open Thurs. and Fri. 10-1 and 2-4.30. SIZE: Small. *STOCK: Small antiques, jewellery and linen, 19th C.* LOC: Just off High St., near clock tower. PARK: Easy. TEL: 01638 663584.

R.E. and G.B. Way

Brettons, Burrough Green. CB8 9NA. Open 8.30-5 appointment advisable. *STOCK: Antiquarian and secondhand books on shooting, fishing, horses, racing and hunting and small general section.* TEL: 01638 507217; fax - 01638 508058.

ORFORD

Castle Antiques

Market Sq. IP12 2LH. (S. Simpkin). Est. 1969. Open daily including Sun. 11-4.30. SIZE: Medium. *STOCK: Furniture, general small antiques, bric-a-brac, glass, china, clocks.* TEL: 01394 450100.

PEASENHALL, Nr. Saxmundham

Peasenhall Art and Antiques Gallery

The Street. IP17 2HJ. Resident. (A. and M. Wickins). Est. 1972. Open every day. *STOCK: 19th C watercolours and oils; country furniture, all woods; walking sticks.* TEL: 01728 660224; home - same. SER: Restorations (oils, watercolours, furniture).

REDGRAVE

Abington Books

Rockhols, Half Moon Lane. IP22 1RU. (J. Haldane). Est. 1971. By appointment only. SIZE: Small. *STOCK: Books on Oriental rugs, from 1877, £1-£5,000; books on classical tapestries, from 17th C, £1-£3,000.* PARK: Easy. TEL: 01379 898240; fax - 01379 898377. SER: Valuations; book binding.

RISBY, Nr. Bury St. Edmunds

The Risby Barn

IP28 6QU. (R. and S. Martin). Open 9-5.30, Sun. and Bank Holidays 10-5. SIZE: 24 dealers. *STOCK: Furniture, porcelain, metalware, tools, pine, Art Deco.* LOC: Just off A14 west of Bury St. Edmunds. TEL: 01284 811126; fax - 01284 810783.

SNAPE

Snape Antiques and Collectors Centre

Snape Maltings. IP17 1SR. Est. 1992. Open 7 days 10-6 or until dusk in winter. SIZE: 30 dealers. *STOCK: Antiques and collectables, especially smalls - sewing, silver, jewellery, ceramics from 18th C-Doulton-Deco-Studio, glass, maps, prints, paintings, textiles, country, decorative and useful furniture, stamps, costume jewellery.* LOC: Next to the Concert Hall. PARK: Easy. TEL: 01728 688038.

SOUTHWOLD

The Emporium Antiques and Collectors Centre

70 High St. IP18 6DN. (Michael Brown). Est. 1992. Open 10-5.30, Sun. 12-5. SIZE: Over 40 dealers. *STOCK: Wide range of general antiques and collectables.* PARK: Nearby. TEL: 01502 723909.

Robinson & Munday Antiques

Basement, 39 High Street. IP18 6AB. (E. Robinson and Ms. S. Munday). Est. 1994. Open 10-5, Sun. (April-Dec.) 12-4. CL: Wed. SIZE: Small. *STOCK: Glass, late 18th-19th C, £75-£150; ceramics and silver, 19th to early 20th C, £50-£100; furniture, 19th to early 20th C, £200-£500.* PARK: Easy. TEL: 01502 722630. SER: Valuations; restorations (glass); buys at auction (glass and ceramics).

T. Schotte Antiques

The Old Bakehouse, Black Mill Rd. IP18 6AQ. (T. and J. Schotte). Open 10-1 and 2-4. CL: Wed. SIZE: Small. *STOCK: Small furniture, £25-£500; decorative objects, £5-£250; both 18th-19th C. Unusual collectables, £5-£100.* LOC: Turn right at the King's Head, then first left. TEL: 01502 722083. FAIRS: Snape Summer; Long Melford monthly; Adams, Horticultural Hall, London.

S. J. Webster-Speakman BADA

Open by appointment only. *STOCK: English furniture, clocks, Staffordshire pottery, general antiques.* TEL: 01502 722252. SER: Valuations; restorations (clocks, furniture, ceramics). FAIRS: Various.

STOKE BY NAYLAND, Nr. Colchester

Suffolk Antique Connection LAPADA

Scotland Place, Scotland St. CO6 4QG. (Julia Pike). *STOCK: 17th-19th C country furniture, especially English and French farmhouse and refectory tables.* TEL: 01206 262098; fax - 01206 263339. FAIRS: London; Boston USA.

STOWMARKET

Trench Puzzles

Three Cow Green, Bacton. IP14 4HJ. *STOCK: Antique, old jigsaw and mechanical puzzles.* TEL: 01449 781178. *Mail Order Only.*

STRADBROKE, Nr. Eye

Mary Palmer Antiques

The Cottage Farm, New St. IP21 5JG. Resident. (Mrs M. Palmer Stones). Est. 1980. Open 9-9, Sun. by appointment. SIZE: Small. *STOCK: English glass, 1750-1850; furniture, 1700-1900.* LOC: B1117. PARK: Easy. TEL: 01379 388100. SER: Valuations.

SUDBURY

Antique Clocks by Simon Charles

The Limes, 72 Melford Rd. CO10 6LT. Est. 1970. Open by appointment only. *STOCK: Interesting clocks especially English longcase, lantern and unusual skeleton clocks, 17th-19th C.* TEL: 01787 375931. SER: Valuations; free estimates; restorations; repairs.

Napier House Antiques

Church St. CO10 6BJ. Est. 1977. Open 10-4.30 and by appointment. SIZE: Large. *STOCK: 18th-19th C mahogany furniture, especially larger items - linen presses, wardrobes, desks, bureaux, bookcases, dining tables, sideboards, wing chairs, £150-£2,700.* PARK: Easy. TEL: 01787 375280; fax - 01787 478757. SER: Free delivery (UK).

Sudbury continued

Neate Militaria & Antiques

PO Box 3794, Preston St Mary. CO10 9PX. OMRS, OMSA, MMSSA. MCCofC. (Gary C. Neate). Open Mon.-Fri. 9-6. *STOCK: Orders, decorations and medals of the world, £5-£15,000.* TEL: 01787 248168; fax - 01787 248363. SER: Valuations. FAIRS: Brittania Medal; Aldershot Medal & Militaria; OMRS Convention. VAT: Spec. *Mail order only.*

WICKHAM MARKET

Crafers Antiques

The Hill. IP13 0QS. (Mrs Elizabeth Davies). Est. 1970. Open Tues.-Sat. 10-5. *STOCK: 18th-19th C porcelain and pottery, glass, silver, jewellery, small furniture and collectors' items.* LOC: Corner of Square, opposite church. PARK: Easy. TEL: 01728 747347.

Greystone Antiques

87 High St. (M.W. and L.D. Turner). Est. 1989. Open Fri., Sat., and Sun. a.m, other times by appointment. SIZE: Small. *STOCK: Victorian and Edwardian pine and satin walnut, £100-£300; Art Deco clocks and figures, £80-£120; enamel stoves, £100-£400.* PARK: Market Sq. TEL: 01728 746654.

A strawberry leaf soup plate, c.1755, painted by the 'Trembly Rose Painter', 8¾in. £950 with restored chip.

From an article entitled "Factory Fact File: Longton Hall c.1750-60, West Pans c.1764-77" by David Battie of Sotheby's which appeared in the October 1997 issue of **Antique Collecting.**

Wickham Market continued

Roy Webb

179 & 181 High St. Open Mon., Thurs. and Sat. 10-6 or by appointment. *STOCK: Furniture, 18th-19th C; clocks.* TEL: 01728 746077; home - 01394 382697. VAT: Stan.

WOODBRIDGE

Ancient and Modern

The Old Brewery, Melton Rd., Melton. (Mrs. E.M. Highmoor). Open 10-5, Sat. 9.30-5.30, Sun. pm. *STOCK: Collectors' items, pine, mirrors, prints, furniture, £1-£800.* LOC: Next to Coach & Horses pub.

Antique Furniture Warehouse

Old Maltings, Crown Pl. IP12 1BU. (H.T. and R.E. Ferguson). Est. 1976. Usually open 9-5, but prior 'phone call advisable. CL: Sat. and Sun. except by appointment. SIZE: Medium. *STOCK: Furniture, 17th to early 20th C, £200-£10,000; small items.* LOC: In centre of town, off Quay St. First warehouse in Crown Place. TEL: 01394 387222; fax - 01394 383832. VAT: Stan/Spec. *Trade and Export Only.*

Bagatelle

40 Market Hill. IP12 4LU. (N. Lambert). Est. 1990. Open 10.30-3.30, Wed. 10.30-1. CL: Thurs. SIZE: Medium. *STOCK: Orientalia, water-colours, oils and engravings, furniture, china, glass and collectables, 18th-20th C, £10-£2,000.* PARK: Nearby. TEL: 01394 380204.

David Gibbins Antiques BADA

21 Market Hill. IP12 4LX. Est. 1964. Open 9.30-5.30, Wed. 9.30-1. *STOCK: English furniture, late 16th to early 19th C, £300-£15,000; English pottery and porcelain, metalwork.* PARK: Own in Theatre St. TEL: 01394 383531; fax - same; home - 01394 382685; mobile - 0402 306914. SER: Valuations; buys at auction. VAT: Spec.

Hamilton Antiques LAPADA

5 Church St. IP12 1DH. (H.T. and R.E. Ferguson). Est. 1976. Open 10-5. *STOCK: Furniture - mahogany, walnut, oak, fruitwood, 17th-20th C, £200-£10,000.* TEL: 01394 387222; fax - 01394 383832. VAT: Stan/Spec.

Anthony Hurst Antiques LAPADA

13 Church St. IP12 1DS. (C.G.B. Hurst). Est. 1957. Open 9.30-1 and 2-5.30. CL: Wed. and Sat. pm. SIZE: Large. *STOCK: English furniture, oak, walnut and mahogany, 1600-1900, £100-£5,000.* PARK: Easy. TEL: 01394 382500. SER: Valuations; restorations (furniture); buys at auction. VAT: Stan/Spec.

Lambert's Barn

24A Church St. Open 9.30-1 and 2-5. CL: Wed. pm. SIZE: Large. *STOCK: Mainly Victorian and 20th C furniture, miscellaneous items.* PARK: Easy. TEL: 01394 382380.

Woodbridge continued

Edward Manson (Clocks)
8 Market Hill. IP12 4LU. Open 10-5.30, Wed. 10-1. *STOCK: Clocks.* TEL: 01394 380235. SER: Restorations (clocks).

Melton Antiques
Kingdom Hall, Melton Rd., Melton. (A. Harvey-Jones). Est. 1975. Open 9.30-5. SIZE: Small. *STOCK: Silver, collector's items, £5-£500; decorative items and furniture, £15-£500; both 18th-19th C; Victoriana and general antiques, 19th C, £5-£500.* LOC: On right hand-side coming from Woodbridge. PARK: Easy. TEL: 01394 386232.

Sarah Meysey-Thompson Antiques
10 Church St. IP12 1DH. Est. 1962. Open 10-5., Sun. by appointment. SIZE: Medium. *STOCK: Small furniture, late 18th to early 19th C; china, glass, decorative items, 19th C; textiles and curtains.* PARK: Easy. TEL: 01394 382144. VAT: Spec.

Isobel Rhodes
10-12 Market Hill. *STOCK: Furniture, oak, country, mahogany; brassware.* PARK: Easy. TEL: 01394 382763. VAT: Spec.

Woodbridge continued

A.G. Voss
24 Market Hill. IP12 4LU. Est. 1965. Open 10-1 and 2.15-5. CL: Wed. *STOCK: Furniture, glass, late 17th to early 20th C.* PARK: Nearby. TEL: 01394 385830. SER: Valuations; restorations.

WOOLPIT, Nr. Bury St. Edmunds

J.C. Heather
The Old Crown. IP30 9SA. Est. 1946. Open every day 9-8. SIZE: Large. *STOCK: Furniture, 18th-19th C, £20-£1,000.* Not Stocked: China. LOC: Near centre of village on right. PARK: Easy. TEL: 01359 240297. VAT: Stan/Spec.

WORTHAM, Nr Eye

The Falcon Gallery
Honeypot Farm. IP22 1PW. (N. Smith). Est. 1974. Open by appointment seven days. SIZE: Medium. *STOCK: Watercolours and oils especially animal paintings and primitives, 19th C.* LOC: South side of A143 in village centre, overlooking village green, 4 miles west of Diss. PARK: Easy. TEL: 01379 783312; fax - 01379 783293; e-mail - smith@macserious.source.co.uk. SER: Valuations; restorations (oils, watercolours); framing. VAT: Stan/Spec.

WRENTHAM, Nr. Beccles

Wren House Antiques

1 High St. NR34 7HD. (Valerie and Tony Kemp). Open Thurs.-Sat. 10.30-5, Sun. 11-4, or by appointment. SIZE: Medium. *STOCK: Furniture, china and collectables.* LOC: A12 village centre, Fiveways junction. TEL: 01502 675276.

Wrentham Antiques

40-44 High St. NR34 7HB. (B. Spearing). Always open. SIZE: Large. *STOCK: Victorian, Georgian, Edwardian and decorative furniture.* LOC: A12. PARK: Easy.TEL: 01502 675583; fax - 01502 675707; home - 01502 513633. SER: Buys at auction. VAT: Stan/Spec.

Wrentham Antiques Centre

The Old Reading Rooms, 7 High St. (Anthony Rush). Open 10-5, Sun. 11-4. CL: Mon. *STOCK: Furniture, china, glass, jewellery, pictures, prints and bric-a-brac.* TEL: 01502 675376.

YOXFORD

Red House Antiques

The Red House, Old High Rd. IP17 3HW. (J. and Mrs M. Trotter). Est. 1987. Open by appointment only. *STOCK: 18th and early 19th C ceramics, £20-£1,000.* Not Stocked: Stamps, arms, silver, pictures, furniture and clocks. LOC: Off either A1120 or A12, opposite churchyard. PARK: Easy. TEL: 01728 668615.

Suffolk House Antiques BADA

High St. IP17 3EP. (A. Singleton). Open 10-1 and 2.15-5.15. CL: Wed. SIZE: Large. *STOCK: 17th-18th C oak and country furniture, works of art, paintings, clocks, delftware and metalware.* LOC: A1120, just off A12. PARK: Easy. TEL: 01728 668122; fax - same; mobile - 0860 521583.

Figure 1 (Left). A Hornby-Dublo 'Barnstable' locomotive and tender – the direct equivalent of the Wrenn locomotive in figure 2, and worth around £120.

Figure 2 (Right). A Wrenn rebuilt West Country class 'Lyme Regis' locomotive and tender, sold with a 'Golden Arrow' coach for £161.

From an article entitled "Which Locomotive?" by Hugo Marsh which appeared in the December 1997/January 1998 issue of **Antique Collecting.**

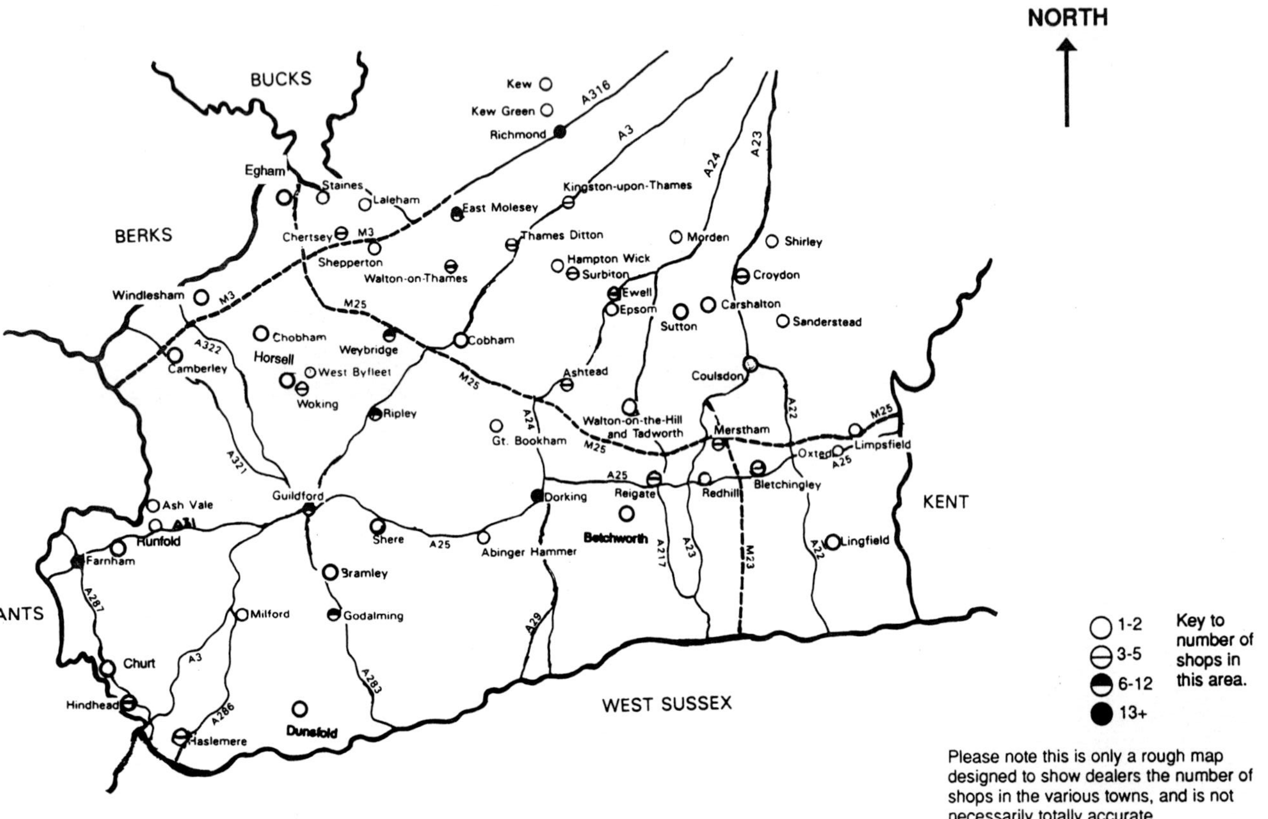
NORTH
BUCKS
BERKS
HANTS
KENT
WEST SUSSEX
Kew
Kew Green
Richmond
Egham
Staines
Laleham
East Molesey
Kingston-upon-Thames
Chertsey
Shepperton
Walton-on-Thames
Thames Ditton
Morden
Shirley
Hampton Wick
Surbiton
Croydon
Windlesham
Ewell
Epsom
Sutton
Carshalton
Sanderstead
Chobham
Horsell
Weybridge
Cobham
Camberley
West Byfleet
Woking
Ashtead
Coulsdon
Ripley
Gt. Bookham
Walton-on-the-Hill and Tadworth
Merstham
Limpsfield
Oxted
Bletchingley
Redhill
Reigate
Guildford
Dorking
Ash Vale
Runfold
Farnham
Shere
Abinger Hammer
Betchworth
Lingfield
Bramley
Milford
Godalming
Churt
Hindhead
Haslemere
Dunsfold
A316
A3
A24
A23
A22
A25
A217
M23
M25
M3
A29
A283
A286
A287
A31
A321
A322
1-2
3-5
6-12
13+
Key to number of shops in this area.
Please note this is only a rough map designed to show dealers the number of shops in the various towns, and is not necessarily totally accurate.

ABINGER HAMMER

Abinger Bazaar

Guildford Rd. RH5 6SA. Est. 1978. Open Thurs., Fri., Sat. and Sun. 11-5. SIZE: Medium. *STOCK: Collectables, books, junk and wine by the case.* LOC: A25 next to Mad Dog's Restaurant. PARK: Nearby. TEL: 01306 730756.

Stirling Antiques

Aberdeen House. RH5 6RY. (V.S. Burrell). Est. 1968. Open 9.30-6.30. CL: Thurs. *STOCK: Stained glass, furniture, copper, brass, jewellery, silver, curios, dolls.* PARK: Easy. TEL: 01306 730706. VAT: Stan.

ASH VALE, Nr. Aldershot (Hants)

House of Christian

5-7 Vale Rd. GU12 5HH. (A. Bail). Est. 1978. Open 10-5.30, Sat. 10-4. SIZE: Medium. *STOCK: Pine, 19th-20th C, £30-£1,500; some mahogany, oak, 19th-20th C.* LOC: On A321 between Ash and Mytchett. From Ash Wharf over canal bridge, shop (bright green) on left on hill. PARK: Easy - opposite. TEL: 01252 314478. SER: Valuations; restorations (including stripping, waxing, staining); stockists of Briwax and Liberon wax/stain, etc.

ASHTEAD

Bumbles

90 The Street. KT21 1AW. (Bob and Barbara Kay). Open 9.30-5.30. *STOCK: Furniture, lighting, clocks and barometers, oil lamps and general antiques.* PARK: Easy. TEL: 01372 276219. SER: Restorations; silver plating.

Memory Lane Antiques

102 The Street. KT21 1AW. (J. Westwood). Est. 1984. Open 10-5. CL: Wed. *STOCK: Toys and general antiques, pre-1920, £5-£1,000.* PARK: Easy. TEL: 01372 273436.

Temptations

88 The Street. KT21 1AW. FGA, NAG. (Pauline Watson). Open 10-5. *STOCK: Jewellery and silver.* LOC: Main street. PARK: Easy. TEL: 01372 277713. SER: NAG registered valuer; security photography; lecturer. VAT: Stan/Spec.

BETCHWORTH, Nr. Dorking

Stoneycroft Farm

Reigate Rd. RH3 7EY. (J.G. Elias). Open Mon.-Fri. 8-5.30, evenings and weekends by appointment. *STOCK: Large oak and country furniture, library bookcases, dining tables and chairs, special writing furniture.* TEL: 01737 845215.

BLETCHINGLEY

Cider House Galleries Ltd

Norfolk House, 80 High St. RH1 4PA. (T. Roberts). Est. 1967. Open 9.30-5.30. CL: Sat. pm. and Sun. except by appointment. SIZE: Large. *STOCK: Paintings, 17th-20th C, from £200.* LOC: A25, behind F.G. Lawrence Auctioneers. PARK: Own. TEL: 01883 742198; fax - 01883 744014. SER: Valuations. VAT: Stan/Spec.

John Anthony Antiques

71 High St. RH1 4LJ. Resident. (J.A. and N. Hart). Open by appointment only. *STOCK: 18th to early 19th C furniture.* TEL: 01883 743197; fax - 01883 742108.

Simon Marsh

The Old Butchers Shop, High St. RH1 4PA. BAFRA. Est. 1970. Open by appointment. *STOCK: Grandfather clocks; 18th-19th C furniture.* PARK: Easy. TEL: 01883 743350; fax - 01883 744844. SER: Restorations (furniture and clocks).

Post House Antiques

32 High St. RH1 4PE. (P. and V. Bradley). Open daily, Sun. by appointment. *STOCK: Antique lighting; general antiques including mirrors, fenders, decorative items.* LOC: A25. PARK: Easy. TEL: 01883 743317. VAT: Stan/Spec.

Quill Antiques

86 High St. RH1 4PA. (Mrs J. Davies). Est. 1971. Open 10-1 and 2-5.30, other times by appointment. CL: Wed. pm. *STOCK: General antiques including copper, brass, china, farming bygones, kitchenalia, linen and lace, 50p-£500.* LOC: A25. PARK: Easy. TEL: 01883 743755; home - same.

BRAMLEY, Nr. Guildford

Drummonds of Bramley Architectural Antiques Ltd

Birtley Farm. GU5 0LA. Est. 1988. Open 9-6 including Sun. SIZE: Very large. *STOCK: Architectural and decorative antiques, garden statuary and furniture, salvaged building materials, especially period bathroom equipment, 1800-1950, £30-£30,000.* LOC: 1 mile south of Bramley on A281, on left. PARK: Easy. TEL: 01483 898766; fax - 01483 894393. SER: Restorations (stonework and gates); vitreous re-enamelling of baths. VAT: Stan/Spec.

Memories

High St. GU5 0HB. (P. Kelsey). Est. 1984. Open 10-5. SIZE: Small - 7 dealers. *STOCK: Victorian and Edwardian furniture, china and glass, silver, linen and lace, collectables and bygones, kitchenalia, stripped pine furniture, Art Deco.* LOC: South of Guildford on A281. PARK: Easy. TEL: 01483 892205.

CAMBERLEY

235 Antiques

235 London Rd. GU17 9ED. (R.G. and P.T. Ellis). Est. 1977. Open 10-1 and 2-4. CL: Mon. and Wed. SIZE: Small. *STOCK: Furniture, clocks and silver, 19th-20th C, from £20.* LOC: A30. PARK: Easy. TEL: 01276 24071/32123. SER: Restorations (furniture and clocks).

CARSHALTON

Carshalton Antique Galleries

5 High St. SM5 3AP. (B.A. Gough). Est. 1968. Open 9-4. CL: Wed. SIZE: Large. *STOCK: General antiques, furniture, clocks, glass, china, pictures.* Not Stocked: Silver, jewellery, bronze, firearms. PARK: Nearby. TEL: 0181 647 5664; home - 01306 887187. VAT: Stan/Spec.

Cherub Antiques

312 Carshalton Rd. SM5 3QB. (M. Wisdom). Open 10.30-5.30. CL: Wed. *STOCK: Pine and general antiques.* TEL: 0181 643 0028.

CHERTSEY

Chertsey Antiques

10 Windsor St. KT16 8AS. Open 8-5, Sun 11-4. SIZE: 8 dealers. *STOCK: Furniture, jewellery, glass, pottery and porcelain, silver, silver plate, pictures, kitchenalia, memorabilia, books, linen, clocks.* TEL: 01932 563313; fax - 01753 682082.

Mister Sun Antiques

96 Guildford St. KT16 9AD. (R. Lee). Open 10-5.30. *STOCK: General antiques and pine furniture.* TEL: 01932 566323.

CHOBHAM

Greengrass Antiques LAPADA

Hookstone Farm, Hookstone Lane, West End. GU24 9QP. (D. Greengrass). Open by appointment only. *STOCK: Decorative items; furniture, 19th C; works of art; shipping goods.* TEL: 01276 857582; fax - 01276 855289.

CHURT, Nr. Farnham

Churt Curiosity Shop

Crossways. GU10 2JE. (Mrs G. Gregory). Est. 1996. Open Tues., Thurs., Fri. and Sat. 10-4. SIZE: Small. *STOCK: Pottery, porcelain and collectables, Victorian and Edwardian furniture.* LOC: A287 Farnham to Hindhead road. PARK: Easy. TEL: 01428 714096.

COBHAM

Cobham Galleries LAPADA

65 Portsmouth Rd. KT11 1JQ. (Mrs Jerry Burkard). Open Mon. by appointment, Tues.-Sat. 10-5, Sun. 11-5. SIZE: Medium. *STOCK: Period and country furniture, 19th to early 20th C oils and watercolours.* LOC: South off A3, on second roundabout. 5 minutes from M25.

Cobham continued

PARK: Driveway beside shop. TEL: 01932 867909; mobile - 0850 651743; home - 01932 845360. SER: Buys at auction; searches.

COULSDON

Decodream

233 Chipstead Valley Rd. CR5 3BY. Open by appointment only. *STOCK: Pottery - Clarice Cliff, Shorter, Shelley, Foley, F. and C. Rhead and Carlton ware.* PARK: Free. TEL: 0181 668 5534.

D. Potashnick Antiques

7 Stoats Nest Parade, 73 Stoats Nest Rd. CR5 2JJ. Open 9-5.30, Sat. 9-12 or by appointment. *STOCK: General antiques.* TEL: 0181 660 8403. SER: Restorations (furniture).

CROYDON

Oscar Dahling Antiques

87 Cherry Orchard Rd. CR0 6BE. (Oscar Dahling and Liz Lancaster). Est. 1988. Open Mon.-Fri. 10.30-6, Sun. 10.30-3.30 and other times by appointment only. SIZE: Medium. *STOCK: Furniture, £50-£2,500; ceramics, £10-£250; jewellery and costume, £10-£500; all 18th-20th C.* LOC: Ist left after leaving East Croydon B.R. station. shop 300 yards, near Grouse and Claret public house. PARK: Easy. TEL: 0181 681 8090; home - same. SER: Valuations.

G.E. Griffin

43a Brighton Rd., South Croydon. CR2 6EB. (E.J.H. Robinson). Est. 1896. Open 8-5.30, Sat. 10-4.30. SIZE: Large. *STOCK: General antiques.* TEL: 0181 688 3130. SER: Restorations; upholstery.

Trengove

46 South End. CR0 1DP. Est. 1890. SIZE: Large. *STOCK: General antiques, Victoriana; oils, watercolours, 18th-19th C.* LOC: On main road through Croydon. TEL: 0181 688 2155. SER: Valuations. VAT: Stan/Spec.

The Whitgift Galleries

77 South End. CR0 1BF. FATG. Est. 1945. *STOCK: Paintings, 19th-20th C.* TEL: 0181 688 0990. SER: Restorations; conservation, framing. VAT: Spec.

DORKING

Antique Clocks by Patrick Thomas

62A West St. RH4 1BS. Open 9.30-5.30, Sun. 11-4. SIZE: Medium. *STOCK: Clocks, 18th-19th C, £50-£5,000; optical antiques, 19th-20th C, £50-£3,000; paintings, 19th-20th; furniture, 18th-19th C; both £200-£2,000.* TEL: 01306 743661; fax - 01483 715289. SER: Valuations; restorations (clock and furniture). VAT: Spec.

Dorking continued

Howard Blay Antiques

56 West St. RH4 1BS. Open 10-5. SIZE: Medium. *STOCK: English walnut, oak and mahogany furniture, pre 1800, £500-£10,000.* TEL: 01306 743398.

T. M. Collins

70 High St. RH4 1AY. Est. 1963. SIZE: Medium. *STOCK: Jewellery, 1800-1900, £25-£3,000.* LOC: Opposite Boots chemist. PARK: Behind shop. TEL: 01306 880790. SER: Valuations; restorations (jewellery). VAT: Stan.

J. and M. Coombes

44 West St. RH4 1BU. Est. 1965. Open 9-5, Sun. 11-4. *STOCK: General antiques.* TEL: 01306 885479. VAT: Stan.

Dolphin Square Antiques

42 West St. RH4 1BU. (Mr and Mrs N. James). Est. 1995. Open 10-5.30. SIZE: Medium. *STOCK: Furniture, £300-£15,000; china and glass, £50-£2,000; antique maps and Staffordshire pottery, all 18th-19th C.* LOC: Western end of High St. PARK: Nearby. TEL: 01306 887901. SER: Valuations.

Dorking Antique Centre

17/18 West St. RH4 1BS. (Mrs G.D. Emburey). Est. 1989. Open 10-5. SIZE: 30 dealers. *STOCK: Period and pine furniture, silver, porcelain, jewellery, copper and brass, pictures and prints, decorative and collectors' items.* LOC: Continuation of High St. into one-way system. PARK: Opposite. TEL: 01306 740915. SER: Restorations.

Dorking Desk Shop LAPADA

41 West St. RH4 1BU. (J.G. Elias). Est. 1969. Open 8-1 and 2-5.30, Sat. 10.30-1 and 2-5. SIZE: Large. *STOCK: Desks, especially partners, cylinder bureaux, davenports, kneehole and pedestal, 18th to mid-20th C, £100-£60,000.* PARK: Nearby. TEL: 01306 883327; fax - 01306 875363. VAT: Stan/Spec.

Dorking Emporium Antiques Centre

1A West St. RH4 1BL. (Mrs S.M. Kenny). Est. 1982. Open 10-5. SIZE: Medium. *STOCK: Furniture, mainly mahogany, 18th-19th C; British and Continental ceramics, country bygones, books and collectables; Art Deco ceramics including Clarice Cliff, Shelley, Susie Cooper, £5-£5,000.* LOC: A25. PARK: Nearby. TEL: 01306 876646; home - 01883 627270.

Hampshires of Dorking LAPADA

50-52 West St. RH4 1BU. Open 9.30-1 and 2.15-5.30. SIZE: Large. *STOCK: Fine English walnut, mahogany, rosewood and satinwood furniture, 18th-19th C, £500-£70,000.* PARK: Own. TEL: 01306 887076; fax/ansaphone - 01306 881029. VAT: Spec.

Dorking continued

Harman's Antiques LAPADA

19 West St. RH4 1QH. (Paul and Nicholas Harman). Est. 1953. Open 10-5. SIZE: Large. *STOCK: Furniture including tables, linen presses, sideboards, bookcases, 18th-19th C, £1,500-£10,000.* PARK: Nearby. TEL: 01306 743330; home - same; fax - 01306 742593. SER: Restorations (polishing and repairs). VAT: Stan/Spec.

Hebeco

47 West St. RH4 1BU. Est. 1982. Open 10.30-5. SIZE: Small. *STOCK: Silver and plate, antique and 20th C, £5-£1,000; glass, 18th-20th C, £5-£300; pewter, 17th-19th C; blue and white porcelain, 18th-19th C.* LOC: Off High St. PARK: Nearby. TEL: 01306 875396 (answerphone). SER: Valuations. FAIRS: Country Houses. VAT: Stan.

Holmwood Antiques

Norfolk Rd., South Holmwood. RH5 4LA. (R. Dewdney). Open 9-6.30, evenings and weekends by appointment. *STOCK: Georgian and Victorian furniture.* TEL: 01306 888174/888468.

The House of Bulow Antiques

5 West St. RH4 1BL. (Karen E. von Bülow). Est. 1989. Open 10.30-5. SIZE: Medium. *STOCK: Furniture, 19th C, £100-£2,000; British Victorian porcelain and pottery, especially jugs, £10-£500; paintings, £100-£500; small collectibles, £5-£200.* LOC: Town centre. PARK: Nearby. TEL: 01306 877767; e-mail - antiques@vonbulow. demon. co.uk.

King's Court Galleries

54 West St. RH4 1BS. (Mrs J. Joel). Open 9.30-5.30. *STOCK: Antique maps, engravings, decorative and sporting prints.* TEL: 01306 881757. SER: Framing.

Mayfair Antiques

43 West St. (R.G. Dewdney). Est. 1963. Open 9-1 and 2-5. SIZE: Large. *STOCK: Furniture, mainly 18th-19th C, to £500+.* LOC: Opposite Junction Rd. PARK: Nearby. TEL: 01306 885007. VAT: Spec.

Norfolk House Galleries

48 West St. RH4 1BU. Open 10-5. *STOCK: 18th-19th C furniture, especially dining tables and chairs; period antique clocks, longcase always in stock.* TEL: 01306 881028.

Pilgrims Antique Centre

7 West St. RH4 1BL. Resident. (Jo F. Pritchard). Est. 1974. Open 10-5.30. SIZE: 10 dealers. *STOCK: Furniture, 18th to early 20th C, £65-£2,000; paintings, 18th-20th C, £50-£1,200; smalls, 17th-20th C, £5-£1,000.* LOC: A25 through town, just off High St. PARK: Opposite. TEL: 01306 875028. SER: Valuations; restorations (furniture); buys at auction.

Dorking continued

Elaine Saunderson Antiques BADA.

18/18a Church St. RH4 1DW. (Mrs E.C. Saunderson). Est. 1988. Open 10-1 and 2-5.30, Sat. 9.30-6, other times by appointment. SIZE: Medium. *STOCK: Furniture, late 18th to early 19th C, £50-£10,000; decorative items.* Not Stocked: Silver and jewellery. LOC: Turn left into North St. at end of West St. one-way. 100yds. up North St., opposite junction with Church St. PARK: Easy. TEL: 01306 881231/ 886082; home - same; mobile - 0836 597485. SER: Valuations; restorations (furniture). VAT: Spec.

Michael Schryver Antiques Ltd

The Granary, 10 North St. RH4 1DN. Est. 1964. Open 8.30-1 and 2-5.30, Sat. 8-12. *STOCK: Furniture.* LOC: Turn left at top of West St., business at end on right. PARK: Own. TEL: 01306 881110. SER: Valuations; restorations (cabinet work, polishing and upholstery). VAT: Stan/Spec.

Surrey Antiques

11 West St. RH4 1BL. Open 10-5.30, Sun. 11-4. SIZE: Large. *STOCK: Furniture, Georgian and early Victorian, from £500; smalls including clocks and pictures, 17th-19th C.* PARK: Opposite. TEL: 01306 881777; fax - same; mobile - 0860 896171. SER: Valuations.

Thorpe and Foster Ltd LAPADA

51 West St. RH4 1BU. Open 9.30-1 and 2.15-5.30. SIZE: Large. *STOCK: Fine English walnut, mahogany, rosewood and satinwood furniture, 18th-19th C, £500-£70,000.* LOC: On A24. PARK: Own. TEL: 01306 887076; fax - 01306 881029. VAT: Spec.

Victoria and Edward Antiques Centre

61 West St. RH4 1BS. Est. 1972. Open 9.30-5.30. SIZE: Medium - 28 dealers. *STOCK: General antiques.* PARK: Nearby. TEL: 01306 889645.

Pauline Watson

Old King's Head Court. RH5 1AR. FGA, NAG. Est. 1960. Open 9.30-5. SIZE: Small. *STOCK: Jewellery and silver especially Victorian.* LOC: In the High Street at the top of West Street. PARK: Behind shop in North St. TEL: 01306 885452. SER: NAG registered valuer; lecturer. VAT: Stan/Spec.

West Street Antiques

63 West St. RH4 1BS. (J.G. Spooner, R.A. Ratner and P.J. Spooner). Est. 1980. Open 9.30-1 and 2.15-5.30. SIZE: Medium. *STOCK: Furniture, 17th to early 20th C, £100-£10,000; arms and armour, 17th-19th C, £100-£20,000; brass and copper, ceramics, paintings and collectors' items.* Not Stocked: Jewellery and carpets. LOC: A25,

Dorking continued

one-way system. PARK: Nearby. TEL: 01306 883487; fax - same; home - 01306 730182 or 01372 452877. VAT: Spec.

DUNSFOLD, Nr. Godalming

Antique Buildings Ltd

GU8 4NP. Resident. (Peter Barker). Est. 1975. Open daily, Sat. and Sun. by appoint. SIZE: Large. *STOCK: Oak timbers, 17th C, £25-£1,000; architectural items, 15th-18th C, £25-£500; barn frames, 17th C, £2,000-£50,000.* LOC: From Sun public house 500 yards down Alford road, row of white posts, premises up tarmac drive between last two. PARK: Easy. TEL: 01483 200477; fax - 01483 200752. SER: Valuations; restorations (ancient oak framed buildings); buys at auction (buildings and architectural items). VAT: Stan.

EAST MOLESEY

Abbott Antiques

75 Bridge Rd. KT8 9HH. Est. 1970. *STOCK: Clocks.* TEL: 0181 941 6398.

The Antiques Arcade

77 Bridge Rd. KT8 9HH. (Mrs Sarah Simons). Open 10-5.30. SIZE: 10 dealers. *STOCK: 18th-20th C furniture, ceramics, silver, glass and collectables.* LOC: Turn down Creek Rd., opposite Hampton Court station, over mini roundabout into Bridge Rd. TEL: 0181 979 7954. SER: Valuations.

The Court Gallery

16 Bridge Rd. KT8 9HA. (J. Clark). Est. 1980. Open 8.30-4.30. CL: Mon. *STOCK: Oils, watercolours, drawings and engravings, 18th-20th C, £35-£2,000.* LOC: From Scilly Isles roundabout turn into Hampton Court Way, Bridge Rd. is on left by Hampton Court Bridge. PARK: Easy. TEL: 0181 941 2212. SER: Valuations; restorations (oils and watercolours); framing.

The Gooday Shop and Studio

48-50 Bridge Rd., Hampton Court. KT8 9EU. (R. Gooday). Open Sat. afternoon. *STOCK: Arts and crafts, 1950's and 1960's.* TEL: 0181 979 9971.

Hampton Court Antiques

75 Bridge Rd., Hampton Court. KT8 9HH. (H. Abbott). Open 10-5. *STOCK: General antiques including clocks, furniture, lamps and decorative objects.* TEL: 0181 941 6398.

Hampton Court Emporium

52-54 Bridge Rd., Hampton Court. KT8 9HA. Open 9.30-5.30, Sun 10-5. SIZE: Medium. *STOCK: Furniture, paintings, silver, jewellery, mirrors, books, clocks, brass and copper, objets d'art, lamps, china and porcelain, collector's cameras, Art Deco.* PARK: Palace Rd. station. TEL: 0181 941 8876. SER: Valuations; restorations. VAT: Stan/Spec.

East Molesey continued

Howard Hope Phonographs and Gramophones
21 Bridge Rd. KT8 9EU. Open Fri. and Sat. 10-5 and by appointment. *STOCK: Mechanical and musical items.* LOC: Close by Hampton Court Palace. TEL: 0181 941 2472; 0181 398 7130. SER: Spare parts.

Nicholas Antiques
31 Bridge Rd. KT8 9ER. Open 9.30-5. *STOCK: Furniture, general antiques and decorative items.* TEL: 0181 979 0354. VAT: Stan/Spec.

The Sovereign Antique Centre
53B Bridge Rd. KT8 9ER. SIZE: 11 dealers. *STOCK: Furniture, cigarette cards, silver, jewellery, glass, pictures and collectables.* LOC: Near Hampton Court. TEL: 0181 783 0595.

EGHAM

The Pine Warehouse
195 High St. (A. and C. Perry). Open 10-5. CL: Mon. *STOCK: Old and new pine.* TEL: 01784 472621.

EPSOM

Vandeleur Antiquarian Books
6 Seaforth Gdns. KT19 0NR. (E.H. Bryant). By appointment only. *STOCK: Antiquarian and secondhand books on all subjects; prints including rowing, and maps.* TEL: 0181 393 7752 (24 hrs). SER: Valuations; catalogues issued; searches undertaken. FAIRS: Various book fairs. VAT: Stan.

EWELL

A. E. Booth & Son
9 High St. KT17 1SG. BAFRA, Assn. Master Upholsterers. (David J. and Mrs Ann Booth). Est. 1934. Open 9-5. SIZE: Large. *STOCK: Furniture, 1700-1900, £200-£2,000; porcelain, from 1800, £20-£200.* LOC: A24 to Ewell village. PARK: Own - through gates beside shop. TEL: 0181 393 5245; fax - same; home - 0181 391 0705. SER: Restorations (furniture including polishing, repairs and upholstery). VAT: Stan/Spec.

J.W. McKenzie
12 Stoneleigh Park Rd. KT19 0QT. Est. 1971. Appointment advisable. *STOCK: Old and new books on cricket.* TEL: 0181 393 7700.

Token House Antiques
7 Market Parade, High St. KT17 1SL. (Mrs D. Walker). Est. 1966. Open 11-5. CL: Wed. *STOCK: Furniture, 18th-19th C; porcelain, decorative items, metalware and general antiques.* LOC: Opposite post office. PARK: At rear. TEL: 0181 393 9654. VAT: Stan/Spec.

FARNHAM

Annie's Antiques
1 Ridgway Parade, Frensham Rd. GU9 8UZ. Est. 1982. Open 9.30-5.30, Fri. 10.30-5.30, Sun. by appointment. SIZE: Medium. *STOCK: Furniture, bric-a-brac, jewellery, 19th to early 20th C, £5-£1,000; general antiques.* LOC: 1 mile out of Farnham on A287 towards Hindhead. PARK: Easy. TEL: 01252 713447; home - 01252 723217.

The Antiques Warehouse
Badshot Farm, St George's Rd., Runfold. GU9 9HY. (Hilary Burroughs). Est. 1995. Open 10-5.30, including Sun. SIZE: Large - 2 barns. *STOCK: Furniture, 19th C to 1930's, £75-£2,000; china, pictures and interesting collectables, 19th C to 1940's, £5-£200.* LOC: A31 from Farnham towards Guildford, 1st exit (signed Runfold), left at end of slip road towards Badshot Lea, premises 200 yds on left. PARK: Easy. TEL: 01252 317590; fax - 01252 879750. SER: Restorations (woodwork including dipping, veneering, caning).

Bits and Pieces Antiques
82 West St. GU9 7EN. (Mrs C.J. Wickins). *STOCK: Victoriana, chandeliers, furniture, Art Nouveau, Art Deco and costume.* TEL: 01252 722355/715043.

Bourne Mill Antiques
39-43 Guildford Rd. GU9 9PY. Est. 1960. Open 10-5.30 every day. SIZE: Large - 83 dealers. *STOCK: Antique and reproduction furniture in oak, walnut, mahogany, yew and pine; china, glass, pictures, jewellery, fireplaces, beds, kitchenalia, bespoke furniture, collectors' items, books, bric-a-brac; garden ornaments, furniture and buildings.* PARK: Own. TEL: 01252 716663.

Casque and Gauntlet Militaria
55/59 Badshot Lea Rd., Badshot Lea. GU9 9LP. (R. Colt). Est. 1957. SIZE: Large. *STOCK: Militaria, arms, armour.* LOC: On Aldershot to Farnham road. PARK: Easy. TEL: 01252 20745; fax - same. SER: Restorations (metals); re-gilding.

Childhood Memories
27a South St. GU9 7QU. (Miss M.A. Stanford). *STOCK: Teddy bears, dolls, Dinky and Britains toys, games and childhood collectables.* TEL: 01252 724475.

Christopher's Antiques
Sandford Lodge, 39a West St. GU9 7DX. Resident. (Mr and Mrs C.M. Booth). Est. 1972. Open 8-1 and 2-5.30, weekends by appointment. SIZE: Large. *STOCK: Fruitwood country and mahogany furniture, 18th-19th C; walnut furniture, 17th-18th C.* LOC: From Guildford on the A31, turn right at second roundabout. PARK: Easy. TEL: 01252 713794. SER: Valuations; restorations (furniture). VAT: Stan/Spec.

Farnham continued

Farnham Antique Centre

27 South St. GU9 7QU. (Miss M.A. Stanford). Est. 1976. Open 9.30-5. SIZE: 6 dealers. *STOCK: General antiques including silver, jewellery, porcelain, brass and copper, clocks, small furniture and collectors' items.* LOC: On the one-way system into Farnham, large corner site. PARK: At rear. TEL: 01252 724475.

Heytesbury Antiques BADA LAPADA

P.O. Box 222. GU10 5HN. (I. and S. Ingall). Est. 1974. Open by appointment only. SIZE: Medium. *STOCK: Pre-1830 mahogany, walnut and rosewood furniture, and 19th C decorative furniture, textiles and associated items, £200-£12,000; paintings and bronzes, 19th C, £100-£2,000.* TEL: 01252 850893; mobile - 0836 675727; fax - 01252 850828. FAIRS: West London, Olympia, Kensington, Decorators and others. VAT: Mainly Spec.

Maltings Monthly Market

Bridge Sq. GU9 7QR. Est. 1969. First Sat. monthly. SIZE: 200+ stalls. *STOCK: 60% of the dealers sell a wide variety of antiques, bric-a-brac, postcards and collectables.* LOC: Follow signs to Wagon Yard car park, Maltings over footbridge. TEL: 01252 717434; fax - 01252 718177.

Karel Weijand Fine Oriental Carpets

LAPADA

Lion and Lamb Courtyard. GU9 7LL. Est. 1975. Open 9.30-5.30. SIZE: Large. *STOCK: Fine antique and contemporary Oriental rugs and carpets, from £150.* LOC: Off West St. PARK: Easy. TEL: 01252 726215. SER: Valuations; restorations; cleaning. VAT: Stan/Spec.

GODALMING

The Antique Shop

72 Ockford Rd. (G. Jones). Open 10.30-4.30, Sat. 10.30-5. CL: Mon. *STOCK: General antiques including furniture, light fittings.* PARK: Opposite. TEL: 01483 414428.

Church Street Antiques

10 Church St. GU7 1EH. (L. Bambridge). Est. 1985. Open 10-5, Wed. 10-1. SIZE: Medium. *STOCK: British ceramics, 1800-1930, £5-£1,000; glass, 1800-1930, £5-£200; silver, 1750-1930, £20-£500.* LOC: Off A3. PARK: Easy and behind shop. TEL: 01483 860894. SER: Valuations; commission buying. VAT: Stan/Spec.

Heath-Bullocks BADA

8 Meadrow. GU7 3HN. (R.J. and M.E. Heath-Bullock). Est. 1926. Open 10-5. SIZE: Large. *STOCK: English and Continental furniture, upholstered seat furniture, works of art, fine art.* LOC: A3100. From Guildford on the left side approaching Godalming. PARK: Own. TEL:

Godalming continued

01483 422562; fax - 01483 426077. SER: Valuations; restorations; upholstery. FAIRS: Exhibitors at and Organisers of Buxton and Surrey.

The Olde Curiosity Shoppe

99 High St. GU7 1AQ. *STOCK: Silver, brass, copper, china, collectables and jewellery.* TEL: 01483 415889.

Priory Antiques

29 Church St. (P. Rotchell). Open 10-4. CL: Wed. *STOCK: General antiques.* TEL: 01483 421804.

Barbara Rubenstein Fine Art

at Heath-Bullocks, 8 Meadrow. GU7 3HN. Open 10-5. *STOCK: Watercolours and some oils, 19th-20th C, £250-£10,000.* TEL: 01483 422562.

GREAT BOOKHAM, Nr. Leatherhead

Roger A. Davis Antiquarian Horologist

19 Dorking Rd. KT23 4PU. Est. 1971. Open 9.30-12.30 and 2-5.30. CL: Mon. and Wed., Fri. pm. and Sun. am. except by appointment. SIZE: Small. *STOCK: Clocks, 18th-19th C, £100-£4,000.* LOC: From Leatherhead A246 to centre of village, turn left at sign for Polesden Lacey, shop 1/4 mile along Dorking Rd. PARK: Easy. TEL: 01372 457655; home - 01372 453167. SER: Valuations; restorations (mechanical and case work); buys at auction (antique clocks).

GUILDFORD

The Antiques Centre

22 Haydon Place, Corner of Martyr Rd. GU1 4LL. (Mrs J. Carter). Est. 1969. Open 10-4. CL: Mon. and Wed. *STOCK: Wide range of general antiques.* LOC: Close to Surrey Advertiser. PARK: 100yds. on left from North St. Below are listed the dealers at this centre. TEL: 01483 567817.

Jennifer Carter
China, collectables, bygones.

Joan Goggin
China, collectables, bygones.

Jony's
Pictures, linens, costume and small furniture.

Sylvia Pullen
Silver, jewellery, Devon ware.

Cry for the Moon

17 Tunsgate. GU1 3QT. (J.L. Ackroyd). Est. 1977. Open 9.30-5.30. SIZE: Medium. *STOCK: Mainly jewellery, £30-£20,000; silver and objets d'art.* TEL: 01483 306600; fax - 01483 306300. SER: Valuations; repairs; jewellery commissions undertaken. VAT: Stan/Margin.

Guildford continued

Denning Antiques
1 Chapel St. GU1 3UA. Open 10-5. *STOCK: Silver, jewellery, lace, linen, and collectors' items.* LOC: Off High St. PARK: Nearby. TEL: 01483 539595.

Horological Workshops BADA
204 Worplesdon Rd. GU2 6UY. (M.D. Tooke). Est. 1968. Open 8.30-5.30, Sat. 9-12.30 or by appointment. *STOCK: Clocks, watches, barometers.* TEL: 01483 576496.

Manor House
96 Stoke Rd. Est. 1952. *STOCK: Furniture, 18th C; copper and brass, 18th-19th C; clocks, prints - mainly sporting and military; china and glass.* TEL: 01483 574740. VAT: Stan/Spec

Oriental Rug Gallery
230 Upper High St. GU1 3JD. (R. Mathias and J. Blair). *STOCK: Russian, Afghan, Turkish and Persian carpets, rugs and kelims; Oriental objets d'art.* TEL: 01483 457600.

Thomas Thorp Bookseller
170 High St. GU1 3HP. Est. 1883. Open 9-5, 5.30 on Sat. SIZE: Large. *STOCK: Books including antiquarian and out-of-print.* LOC: At traffic lights at top of High St. PARK: Road running parallel High St. 200yds. away. TEL: 01483 562770. SER: Buys at auction (antiquarian books); private collections bought.

Tramp Jewellers
14 Swan Lane. GU1 4EQ. (Mrs N. Harper). Est. 1968. Open daily 10-5.30. *STOCK: Jewellery.* TEL: 01483 504138. VAT: Stan.

Charles W. Traylen
Castle House, 49/50 Quarry St. GU1 3UA. Est. 1945. Open 9-5. CL: Mon. SIZE: Large. *STOCK: Fine books and manuscripts, 13th C to date.* PARK: 200yds. TEL: 01483 572424; fax - 01483 450048. SER: Valuations; restorations (bindings); catalogues issued. VAT: Stan.

HAMPTON WICK

Hampton Wick Antiques
48 High St. KT1 4DB. Est. 1957. Open 11-6. *STOCK: Furniture including pine; religious items and statues.* TEL: 0181 977 3178.

HASLEMERE

Allen Avery Interiors
1 High St. Est. 1971. Open 9-1 and 2.15-5. CL: Sat. pm. and Wed. *STOCK: English furniture.* TEL: 01428 643883.

Haslemere Antique Market
1A Causewayside, High St. GU27 2JZ. Est. 1990. Open 9.30-5. SIZE: Large. *STOCK: Wide variety of general antiques.* LOC: Off High St. (A286). PARK: Easy. TEL: 01428 643959. SER: Valuations; restorations; buys at auction.

Haslemere continued

Surrey Clock Centre
3 Lower St. GU27 2NY. (J.P. Ingrams and S. Haw). Est. 1962. Open 9-1 and 2-5. SIZE: Large. *STOCK: Clocks and barometers.* PARK: Easy. TEL: 01428 651313. SER: Restorations; hand-made parts; shipping orders; clocks made to order. VAT: Stan/Spec.

Wood's Wharf Antiques Bazaar
56 High St. GU27 2LA. SIZE: 12 dealers. *STOCK: A wide selection of antiques.* LOC: Opposite The Georgian Hotel. TEL: 01428 642125; fax - same.

HINDHEAD

Albany Antiques Ltd
8-10 London Rd. GU26 6AF. (T. Winstanley). Est. 1965. Open 9-6. CL: Sun. except by appointment. *STOCK: Furniture, 17th-18th C, £20-£400; china including Chinese, £5-£400; metalware, £7-£50; both 18th-19th C.* Not Stocked: Silver. LOC: A3. PARK: Easy. TEL: 01428 605528. VAT: Stan/Spec.

M. J. Bowdery BADA
12 London Rd. GU26 6AF. Est. 1970. Always available, prior telephone call advisable. *STOCK: Furniture, 18th-19th C.* TEL: 01428 606376; mobile - 0374 821444. VAT: Stan/Spec.

Oriel Antiques
3 Royal Parade, Tilford Rd. GU26 6TD. (J. Gear). Est. 1974. Open 9-5. CL: Wed. pm. *STOCK: Furniture and pictures, 18th-19th C.* TEL: 01428 606281.

"Second Hand Rose"
Portsmouth Rd., Bramshott Chase. GU26 6DB. (S.J. Ridout). Est. 1980. Open 10-5.30 and by appointment. SIZE: Large. *STOCK: Furniture, paintings, bric-a-brac, 18th-20th C.* LOC: On A3, 1 mile S.W. of Hindhead. PARK: Easy. TEL: 01428 604880; home - same. VAT: Stan/Spec.

What Not Antiques
Crossways Rd., Grayshot. (Mrs M. Wylie). Open 9-5.30. *STOCK: General antiques and pine.* TEL: 01428 604871.

HORSELL, Nr. Woking

Horsell Antiques
77 High St. GU21 4UA. (Philip Gilbert). Est. 1974. Open 10-5. SIZE: Small. *STOCK: Brown furniture, 18th-19th C, £100-£3,000; pictures and china, 18th-20th C, £5-£600; small collectables, 19th-20th C, £5-£50.* LOC: From A322 along Knaphill High St. At roundabout turn right into Horsell High St. PARK: High St. TEL: 01483 756807. SER: Restorations (French polishing, cabinet work, upholstery); buys at auction (furniture). VAT: Spec.

KEW

Lloyds of Kew

9 Mortlake Terrace. TW9 3DT. (S. Cobley). Open Tues.-Sat. 10-6. *STOCK: Out-of-print books on gardening, botany and some general.* LOC: Junction of Kew and Mortlake Roads, 10 mins walk from Kew Gardens Station (District line). PARK: Easy. TEL: 0181 940 2512. SER: Annual catalogues (Oct.).

Dennis Woodman Oriental Carpets

105 North Rd. TW9 4HJ. Est. 1991. Open Wed.-Sun. 10-6. SIZE: Medium. *STOCK: Islamic carpets, rugs, kilims, embroideries and weavings.* LOC: At Kew Gardens station. PARK: Easy. TEL: 0181 878 8182. SER: Valuations; restorations; buys at auction. VAT: Stan/Spec.

KEW GREEN

Andrew Davis

6 Mortlake Terrace. TW9 3DT. Resident. Est. 1969. *STOCK: Decorative and functional items of all periods, including furniture, ceramics, glass, pictures, clocks, garden and architectural items.* TEL: 0181 948 4911. SER: Valuations; restorations.

KINGSTON-UPON-THAMES

Glencorse Antiques LAPADA

321 Richmond Rd., Ham Parade, Ham Common. KT2 5QU. (M. Igel and B.S. Prydal). Open 10-5.30. *STOCK: 18th-19th C furniture; 19th C oils and modern British watercolours.* PARK: Own. TEL: 0181 541 0871.

Glydon and Guess Ltd

14 Apple Market. KT1 1JE. Est. 1940. Open 9.30-5. CL: Wed. *STOCK: Jewellery, small silver, £100-£5,000.* LOC: Town centre. TEL: 0181 546 3758. SER: Valuations; restorations.

Kingston Antique Market

29-31 London Rd. KT2 6ND. (Reflections Ltd). Est. 1995. Open daily including Sun. SIZE: 80 dealers. *STOCK: Antique and period furniture, Art Deco, Art Nouveau, exotic, glass, fabrics, jewellery, objets d'art, pine, clocks, militaria, books.* LOC: Off Clarence St. PARK: Easy. TEL: 0181 549 2004. SER: Valuations; restorations; buys at auction.

LALEHAM, Nr. Staines

Laleham Antiques

23 Shepperton Rd. TW18 1SE. (E. Potter). Est. 1970. Open 10.30-5. SIZE: Medium. *STOCK: Furniture, porcelain, mirrors, pine, antique lighting, silver, general and trade antiques.* LOC: B376. PARK: Easy. TEL: 01784 450353; mobile - 0589 951652.

LIMPSFIELD

Limpsfield Watercolours

High St. RH8 0DT. FATG. (Mrs C. Reason). Est. 1985. Open Tues.-Fri. 10.30-4, Sat. 10-5. SIZE: Small. *STOCK: Watercolours, £15-£5,000; prints and etchings, £5-£200; all 1850-1940 and contemporary.* Not Stocked: Oils. LOC: From junction 6, M25 on B269. PARK: Easy. TEL: 01883 717010. SER: Valuations; restoration and cleaning of watercolours, prints and oils; framing including conservation. VAT: Spec.

LINGFIELD

Browsers

7 East Grinstead Rd. (S. Robbins). Open 10-5. SIZE: Small. *STOCK: Collectables including stamps, books.* LOC: Between East Grinstead and Lingfield Race Course. PARK: Easy. TEL: 01342 834881. SER: Valuations.

I.O.U. (Interesting, Old & Unusual)

Paris House, 52/56 High St. RH7 6AA. (Keith Wheeler and Emma Tingley). Est. 1979. Open 9.30-5, Mon. 9.30-4.30. SIZE: Large. *STOCK: Victorian, Edwardian and traditional furniture; collectors' items, ephemera, china.* LOC: Southbound A22 turn east to Lingfield, follow signs for racecourse - 4th to last shop out of village at corner of Talbot Rd. PARK: Easy. TEL: 01342 836565; home - 01732 865651. SER: Valuations; commission sales.

MERSTHAM

Elm House Antiques

3 High St. RH1 3BA. (Robert Black). Est. 1995. Open 10.30-5.30. SIZE: Medium. *STOCK: Georgian to Edwardian town and country furniture, mahogany, oak and decorative items, £50-£5,000; country furniture, pine, kitchenalia, decorative items, textiles, £5-£500; brass and copper, £5-£100; period cabinet fittings.* LOC: A23 just past beginning of M23. PARK: Own. TEL: 01737 643983. SER: Valuations; restorations (textiles, boxes, inlay, gesso work, furniture including French polishing, upholstery).

MILFORD, Nr. Godalming

Michael Andrews Antiques

Portsmouth Rd. GU8 5AU. Est. 1974. Open daily, Thurs. and Sun. by appointment. SIZE: Medium. *STOCK: Furniture, 18th-19th C.* LOC: Corner of Cherry Tree Rd. (on traffic lights, from A3 slip road to Petworth). PARK: Own. TEL: 01483 420765; home - same. VAT: Stan/Spec.

E. Bailey

Portsmouth Rd. GU8 5DR. (Eric Bailey). Est. 1979. Open 9-5. CL: Thurs. SIZE: Small. *STOCK: Furniture and tools, from Victorian, £5-£100; china, £5-£25.* LOC: Main road. PARK: Easy. TEL: 01483 422943.

MORDEN

A. Burton-Garbett

35 The Green. SM4 4HJ. Est. 1959. By appointment only. Prospective clients met (at either Morden or Wimbledon tube station) by car. *STOCK: Books on travel, the arts, antiquities of South and Central America, Mexico and the Caribbean, 16th-20th C, £5-£5,000.* TEL: 0181 540 2367; fax - 0181 540 4594. SER: Buys at auction (books, pictures, fine arts, ethnographica). VAT: Stan.

OXTED

Antiques Centre

80-84 Station Rd. East. RH8 0PG. (D. Quigley and Mrs J. Wagstaff). Est. 1992. Open 9.45-5.30. SIZE: Large. *STOCK: Furniture, Georgian, Victorian, Edwardian and 30's, £50-£3,500; clocks, barometers and watches, 19th C, £50-£3,000; metalware, fire accessories, china and porcelain, £1-£1,000; silver and jewellery, £20-£1,000; second-hand books.* LOC: 3 miles south junction 6, M25; off A25. Almost opposite railway station. PARK: Easy and at rear. TEL: 01883 712806; restorations - 01474 872307. SER: Restorations (upholstery).

REDHILL

F.G. Lawrence and Sons

89 Brighton Rd. RH1 6PS. Est. 1891. Open 9-5, Sat. 9-1. SIZE: Large. *STOCK: Edwardian, Victorian and Georgian furniture.* LOC: On A23. PARK: Own. TEL: 01737 764196. SER: Valuations. VAT: Stan.

REIGATE

Bourne Gallery Ltd LAPADA

31/33 Lesbourne Rd. RH2 7JS. (J. Robertson). Est. 1970. Open 10-1 and 2-5. CL: Mon. SIZE: Large. *STOCK: 19th-20th C oils and watercolours, £250-£25,000.* PARK: Easy. TEL: 01737 241614. SER: Restorations (oil paintings). VAT: Spec.

The Gallery

3/5 Church St. RH2 0AA. (Jeffrey S. Cohen). Open 10-6. SIZE: Medium. *STOCK: 19th-20th C oil paintings and watercolours, especially Modern British artists post 1850, £250-£15,000; 18th-19th C furniture and mirrors, especially small decorative pieces, £500-£10,000.* LOC: Town centre. PARK: Easy and opposite. TEL: 01737 242813; fax - 01737 362819. SER: Valuations; restorations (paintings and furniture). VAT: Stan/Spec.

Bertram Noller (Reigate)

14a London Rd. RH2 9HY. (A.M. Noller). Est. 1970. Open 9.30-1 and 2-5.30. CL: Tues. and Wed. SIZE: Small. *STOCK: Collectors' items, furniture, grates, fenders, mantels, copper, brass, glass, pewter, £1-£500.* LOC: West side of one-way traffic system. Opposite Upper West St. car

Reigate continued

park. PARK: Opposite. TEL: 01737 242548. SER: Valuations; restorations (furniture, clocks, bronzes, brass and copper, marble).

Reigate Galleries Ltd

45a Bell St. RH2 7AQ. (J.S. Morrish). Est. 1958. Open 9-5.30, Wed. 9-1. SIZE: Large. *STOCK: Old prints, engravings, antiquarian books.* PARK: Opposite. TEL: 01737 246055. SER: Picture framing. VAT: Stan.

RICHMOND

Antique Mart

72-74 Hill Rise. TW10 6UB. (G. Katz). Open Thurs., Fri., Sat. and Sun. 2-6, otherwise by appointment. SIZE: Large. *STOCK: Furniture, 18th-19th C; French and English oils and watercolours, 19th and 20th C.* TEL: 0181 940 6942; mobile - 0498 678291. SER: Buys at auction. VAT: Stan/Spec.

The Chair Set - Antiques

84 Hill Rise. TW10 6UB. (Allan James). Est. 1982. Open Mon. 12-4, Sat. 10-5, Sun. 2-5.30, other times by appointment. SIZE: Medium. *STOCK: Sets of chairs, £1,000-£8,000; single and pairs of chairs, £200-£3,000; dining tables and accessories, £800-£5,000; all early 18th to late 19th C.* LOC: 2 minutes walk from Richmond Bridge. PARK: Meters nearby. TEL: 0181 332 6454; fax - same. SER: Valuations; restorations (woodwork and upholstery); buys at auction (sets of chairs). VAT: Spec.

Richmond continued

Court Antiques (Richmond)

12/14 Brewers Lane. (A. and L. Coombs). Est. 1958. Open 9.30-5.30. SIZE: Small. *STOCK: General antiques, jewellery, furniture, silver.* Not Stocked: Coins and stamps. LOC: From Richmond station turn left along the Quadrant into George St., Brewers Lane is on the right. PARK: 30yds. turn left. TEL: 0181 940 0515. VAT: Stan.

Mollie Evans

82 Hill Rise. TW10 6UB. Est. 1965. Open Thurs. and Sat. 10.30-5.30, Sun. 2.30-5.30 other times by appointment. SIZE: Medium. *STOCK: Early country and painted furniture, interesting bygones, unusual bold decorative items, original works of art, bronzes and sculpture, £50-£5,000.* LOC: From centre of Richmond, take A307 towards Kingston (Petersham Rd.). Fork left up hill immediately after passing Richmond Bridge on right. PARK: Meters. TEL: 0181 948 0182; fax/answerphone - same; e-mail - antiques.info @all-about-antiques.co.uk. SER: Buys at auction. VAT: Spec.

The Gooday Gallery

20 Richmond Hill. TW10 6QX. (Debbie Gooday). Est. 1971. Open Thurs.-Sat. 11-5. SIZE: Medium. *STOCK: Decorative and applied design, 1880-1980, Arts & Crafts, Art Nouveau - especially Liberty pewter, Art Deco, furniture, pictures,*

Richmond continued

ceramics, metalwork, jewellery; African and oceanic tribal artefacts; all £20-£5,000. LOC: 100yds. from Richmond Bridge. PARK: Easy. TEL: 0181 940 8652. SER: Buys at auction.

Roland Goslett Gallery

139 Kew Rd. TW9 2PN. Est. 1974. Open Thurs. and Fri. 10-6, Sat. 10-2; or by appointment. SIZE: Small. *STOCK: English watercolours and oil paintings, 19th to early 20th C, £100-£5,000.* PARK: Meters. TEL: 0181 940 4009. SER: Valuations; restorations (oils, watercolours and frames); framing. VAT: Spec.

Hill Rise Antiques LAPADA

26 Hill Rise. TW10 6UA. (P. Hinde and D. Milewski). Est. 1978. Open 10.30-5.30, Sun. 2.30-5.30. CL: Wed. SIZE: Large. *STOCK: 18th-19th C walnut and mahogany furniture and longcase clocks, £100-£10,000; silver and plate, mirrors, boxes and glassware.* LOC: 1 mile from A316 (M3). PARK: At rear by arrangement. TEL: 0181 332 2941; home - same. FAIRS: Olympia (June). VAT: Stan/Spec.

Horton's LAPADA

2 Paved Court, The Green. TW9 1LZ. FGA. (D. and R. Horton). *STOCK: Jewellery and silver, 18th-20th C, £500-£2,000.* TEL: 0181 332 1775.

Lionel Jacobs

16 Brewers Lane. TW9 1HH. Open 9-5. *STOCK: Silver and jewellery.* TEL: 0181 940 8069.

Robin Kennedy

P.O Box 265. TW9 1UB. Open by appointment. *STOCK: Japanese prints, £50-£5,000.* TEL: 0181 940 5346; fax - same; e-mail - 106025.2327@ compuserve.com.

F. and T. Lawson Antiques

13 Hill Rise. TW10 6UQ. Resident. Est. 1965. Open 10-5.30, Sat. 10-5. CL: Wed. and Sun. am. SIZE: Medium. *STOCK: Furniture, 1680-1870; paintings and watercolours; both £30-£1,500; clocks, 1650-1930, £50-£2,000; bric-a-brac, £5-£300.* LOC: Near Richmond Bridge at bottom of Hill Rise on the river side, overlooking river. PARK: Limited and further up Hill Rise. TEL: 0181 940 0461. SER: Valuations; buys at auction.

Marryat LAPADA

88 Sheen Rd. TW9 1AJ. (Marryat (Richmond) Ltd.). Est. 1990. Open 10-5.30. SIZE: Large. *STOCK: English and Continental furniture, watercolours and oils, £100-£5,000; ceramics, glass, silver, objets and decorative antiques, £5-£500; all 18th-19th C.* LOC: Follow M3/A316 towards Richmond, first left into Church Rd. then left again. PARK: Easy. TEL: 0181 332 0262. SER: Valuations; restorations. VAT: Stan/Spec.

Richmond continued

Palmer Galleries
10 Paved Court. TW9 1LZ. (C.D. and V.J. Palmer). Est. 1984. Open 10-5. SIZE: Medium. *STOCK: Prints, watercolours and engravings, 19th-20th C, £50-£1,000.* PARK: Richmond Green. TEL: 0181 948 2668. VAT: Stan/Spec.

Piano Nobile Fine Paintings
26 Richmond Hill. TW10 6QX. (Dr. Robert A. Travers). Est. 1986. Open Tues.-Sat. 10-5.30. SIZE: Medium. *STOCK: Fine 19th C Impressionist and 20th C Post-Impressionist and Modernist British and Continental oil paintings and sculpture, especially Les Petit Maitres of the Paris Schools, £500-£50,000.* PARK: Easy. TEL: 0181 940 2435; fax - same. SER: Valuations; restorations (paintings and sculpture); framing; buys at auction (19th-20th C oil paintings). FAIRS: Grosvenor; 20th C British Art & London Contemporary. VAT: Stan/Spec.

Richmond Antiques
28, 30/32 Hill Rise. Open 10.30-5.30, Sun. 2-5. CL: Wed. SIZE: 10 dealers. *STOCK: General antiques.* TEL: 0181 948 4638.

Roderic Antiques
6/8 Richmond Hill. (R. Arnoldi and E. Gunawardena). Est. 1971. Open 10-5.30, Sun. 2-5.30. CL: Wed. SIZE: Large. *STOCK: Furniture including colonial, and decorative items, 18th-19th C, £200-£10,000.* PARK: Nearby. TEL: 0181 332 6766; mobile - 0831 385634. FAIRS: Olympia (June); City of London. VAT: Stan/Spec.

RIPLEY

Cedar House Gallery LAPADA
High St. GU23 6AE. Resident. Est. 1987. *STOCK: Watercolours and oils, 19th to early 20th C, £500-£10,000.* LOC: 1/2 mile M25/A3 junction. PARK: Easy. TEL: 01483 211221. SER: Restorations.

J. Hartley Antiques Ltd LAPADA
186 High St. GU23 6BB. Est. 1949. Open 8.45-5.45, Sat. 9.45-4.45. *STOCK: Queen Anne, Georgian and Edwardian furniture.* TEL: 01483 224318. VAT: Stan.

Ripley Antiques LAPADA
67 High St. GU23 6AN. (H. Denham). Est. 1960. Open 9.30-5.30, Sun. by appointment. SIZE: Large. *STOCK: Furniture, English and French, 18th-19th C; decorative items - mirrors and chandeliers.* LOC: 2 mins. from junction 10 at M25/A3 interchange. Between Heathrow and Gatwick Airports. PARK: Easy. TEL: 01483 224981; fax - 01483 224333. SER: Valuations; restorations. VAT: Stan/Spec.

Ripley continued

Sage Antiques and Interiors LAPADA
High St. GU23 6BB. GMC. (H. and C. Sage). Est. 1971. Open 9.30-5.30. SIZE: Large. ***STOCK: Furniture, mahogany, oak, walnut, 1600-1900, £150-£8,000; oil paintings, £100-£5,000; watercolours, £50-£1,000, china, £2-£500, all 18th-19th C; silver, Sheffield plate, brass, pewter, decorative items, 18th-19th C, £50-£1,000.*** **LOC: Village centre, on main road. PARK: Easy. TEL: 01483 224396; fax - 01483 211996. SER: Restorations (furniture, pictures); interior furnishing. VAT: Stan.**

Sweerts de Landas BADA
Dunsborough Park, Newark Lane. GU23 6AL. (A.J.H. and A.C. Sweerts de Landas). Est. 1979. Open by appointment only. SIZE: Large. ***STOCK: Garden ornaments and statuary, 17th-20th C, £250-£150,000.*** **LOC: From High St. turn into Newark Lane (between estate agent and Suzuki garage), continue 400 yds, go through archway on right, follow drive to end. PARK: Easy. TEL: 01483 225366; home - same. SER: Valuations; restorations (stone, lead, cast iron, marble); buys at auction (as stock). FAIRS: Olympia, Maastricht, Basle. VAT: Stan/Spec.**

Ripley continued

Anthony Welling Antiques BADA
Broadway Barn, High St. GU23 6AQ. Est. 1970. Open 9-1 and 2-5.30. Sun. and evenings by appointment. SIZE: Large. ***STOCK: English oak, 17th-18th C, £250-£8,000; country furniture, 18th C, £200-£6,000; brass, copper, pewter, 18th C, £100-£750.*** **Not Stocked: Glass, china, silver. LOC: Turn off A3 at Ripley, shop in village centre on service road. PARK: Easy. TEL: 01483 225384; fax - same. VAT: Spec.**

RUNFOLD, Nr. Farnham

The Packhouse
Hewetts Kilns, Tongham Rd. GU10 1PQ. (Mr and Mrs P. Hewett). Est. 1991. Open 10.30-5.30 including Sun. SIZE: Large. *STOCK: Furniture, including period, 1930's, country pine; garden statuary, architectural items.* LOC: Off A31 (Hogs Back). PARK: Easy. TEL: 01252 781010; fax - 01252 783876.

SANDERSTEAD

Raymond Slack FRSA & Shirley Warren
CR2 9DQ. *STOCK: Reference books on antique collecting, emphasis on glass.* TEL: 0181 657 1751. FAIRS: London and Birmingham Glass Fairs. Mail Order.

SHEPPERTON

Rickett & Co. Antiques

Church Sq. TW17 9JY. (A.L. Spencer). Est. 1968. Open 10-5, Wed. 10-1, prior telephone call advisable. *STOCK: Brass and copper, 18th-19th C, £100-£300; fenders and fire tools, oil lamps, inkwells, chandeliers, grandfather clocks.* LOC: 10 mins. from London airport. PARK: Easy. TEL: 01932 243571; home - 01932 222508. SER: Restorations (metal repairs and polishing). VAT: Spec.

SHERE, Nr. Guildford

Shere Antiques Centre

Middle St. GU5 9HL. (Jean Watson). Est. 1983. Open 10-5, Sun. 11-5. SIZE: Large. *STOCK: Victorian and Edwardian items, £5-£500.* LOC: A25 - between Dorking and Guildford. PARK: Easy. TEL: 01483 202846. VAT: Stan/Spec.

Yesterdays Pine

Parklands Farm, Hound House Rd. GU5. (J. Stuart). Est. 1985. Open 10-5. CL: Mon. *STOCK: Victorian and Continental pine.* LOC: Midway between Guildford and Dorking off A25. PARK: Easy. TEL: 01483 203198.

SHIRLEY

Norman Witham

217 Wickham Rd. Est. 1959. Open Mon.-Sat. *STOCK: Porcelain, glass, small furniture, mainly Victorian, £5-£500.* TEL: 0181 655 4445; evenings - 0181 650 4651. SER: Valuations.

STAINES

K.W. Dunster Antiques

23 Church St. TW18 4EN. Open 9-4.30. CL: Thurs. SIZE: Medium. *STOCK: Clocks, furniture, general antiques, interior decor, jewellery, nautical items.* TEL: 01784 453297; fax - 01784 483146. VAT: Stan/Spec.

Margaret Melville Watercolours

LAPADA

11 Colnebridge, Market Sq. TW18 4RZ. TVADA. Est. 1980. Open by appointment only. *STOCK: English watercolours, 1850-1950, £75-£7,000.* TEL: 01784 455395. SER: Valuations; commissions. FAIRS: Earls Court (Aug.); Chester (Feb. and Nov.); Eton College (Easter); Oxford (Oct); LAPADA; NEC (Jan.); Penman Fairs ('phone for tickets). VAT: Spec.

SURBITON

Cockrell Antiques

278 Ewell Rd. KT6 7AG. Resident. (Sheila and Peter Cockrell). Est. 1982. Open Thurs., Fri. and Sat. 9-6, other days by appointment. SIZE: Medium. *STOCK: Furniture including Art Deco, from 18th C, £50-£3,000+; decorative items, £50-£500.* LOC: Off A3 at Tolworth Tower on A240.

Surbiton continued

PARK: Easy. TEL: 0181 390 8290; home - same; e-mail - antiques@cockrell.co.uk; internet - http://www.cockrell.co.uk. FAIRS: IACF and Kempton Park. VAT: Stan/Spec.

House of Mallett

77 Brighton Rd. KT6 5NF. (K. Mallett). Est. 1974. Open Mon., Fri. and Sat. 10-5, Sun. (trade only) 10-1. SIZE: Large. *STOCK: Mahogany furniture, general antiques and art pottery, arts and crafts.* PARK: Easy. TEL: 0181 390 5973.

B. M. and E. Newlove

139-141 Ewell Rd. KT6 6AL. Est. 1958. Open 9.30-5.30, Sat. by appointment. CL: Wed. SIZE: Medium and store. *STOCK: Furniture especially early oak and Georgian mahogany, 17th-19th C, £200-£5,000; china, 18th-19th C, £75-£200; paintings, all periods, £50-£2,000; longcase clocks, Georgian barometers.* Not Stocked: Pot-lids, fairings. LOC: Down Kingston by-pass at Tolworth underpass, turn right into Tolworth Broadway, then into Ewell Rd. Shop one mile on. PARK: Easy. TEL: 0181 399 8857. VAT: Stan/Spec.

Laurence Tauber Antiques

131 Ewell Rd. KT6 6AL. Open 10-5. CL: Wed. pm. *STOCK: General antiques, especially for Trade.* PARK: Easy. TEL: 0181 390 0020. VAT: Stan/Spec.

SUTTON

Euro-Pine

Spring House, Benhill Rd. SM1 3RN. (M.A. Wisdom). Est. 1993. Open 9-5.30. SIZE: Large. *STOCK: Continental and English painted, stripped and restored pine, £10-£1,000.* PARK: Easy. TEL: 0181 661 7427; home - 0181 643 0028. SER: Restorations (stripping, polishing and repairs). FAIRS: Ardingly. VAT: Stan/Spec. *Trade Only.*

S. Warrender and Co

4 and 6 Cheam Rd. (F.R. Warrender). Est. 1953. Open 9-5.30. CL: Wed. SIZE: Medium. *STOCK: Jewellery, 1790 to date, £10-£1,500; silver, 1762 to date, £10-£1,000; carriage clocks, 1860-1900, £115-£800.* TEL: 0181 643 4381. SER: Valuations; restorations (jewellery, silver, quality clocks). VAT: Stan.

THAMES DITTON

Clifford and Roger Dade **LAPADA**

Boldre House, Weston Green. KT7 0JP. Resident. Est. 1937. Open 9.30-6. SIZE: Large. *STOCK: Mahogany furniture, 18th to early 19th C, £500-£5,000.* LOC: A309 between Esher and Hampton Court, near Sandown Park Racecourse. PARK: Outside shop. TEL: 0181 398 6293; fax - same; mobile - 0402 014222. VAT: Spec.

Thames Ditton continued

Fern Cottage Antiques

28/30 High St. KT7 0RY. Est. 1960. Open 10-5.30. CL: Wed. SIZE: Large. *STOCK: General antiques, 18th-19th C furniture, prints, porcelain, Art Deco, Clarice Cliff, Shelley, Susie Cooper, Royal Doulton and Beswick figurines and silver.* TEL: 0181 398 2281.

Elizabeth Gant

52 High St. KT7 0SA. ABA. PBFA. Est. 1981. CL: Wed. SIZE: Small. *STOCK: Antiquarian, second-hand and illustrated books, especially childrens; ephemera, 10p-£1,000.* PARK: Nearby. TEL: 0181 398 0962; 0181 398 5107; fax - 0181 398 5107. SER: Valuations; buys at auction (books). FAIRS: PBFA (London); ABA (Chelsea); Grosvenor House.

WALTON-ON-THAMES

Antique Church Furnishings

Rivernook Farm, Sunnyside. KT12 2ET. (L. Skilling and S. Williams). Est. 1989. Open Mon.-Fri. 10-6. SIZE: Large. *STOCK: Church chairs and pews, £10-£750; altar tables and screens, pulpits, lecterns, reredos, pine and architectural items, £20-£2,000; all late 19th C to early 20th C.* LOC: Between A3050 and River Thames. PARK: Easy. TEL: 01932 252736; fax - same. SER: Valuations; buys at auction (church fixtures and furnishings, stained glass). FAIRS: Newark. VAT: Stan/Spec.

Susan Becker — LAPADA

P O Box 160. KT12 3HJ. (S. Becker Fleming). Est. 1959. Open by appointment only. *STOCK: English (especially Royal Worcester), and Continental porcelain, 18th-20th C, £200-£25,000; glass and fine objects.* LOC: 10 minutes A3, M25, M4. PARK: Easy. TEL: 01932 227820. SER: Valuations. VAT: Spec.

Boathouse Gallery

The Towpath, Manor Rd. KT12 2PG. (B.E. Clark). CL: Mon. *STOCK: Oil paintings, watercolours, engravings.* TEL: 01932 242718. SER: Picture framing, mounting and restorations. VAT: Stan.

WALTON-ON-THE-HILL AND TADWORTH

Ian Caldwell — LAPADA

9a Tadworth Green, Dorking Rd. KT20 5SQ. Est. 1978. Open 10-5. CL: Wed. SIZE: Medium. *STOCK: Oak, walnut and mahogany furniture especially Georgian.* LOC: 2 miles from M25, 1/4 mile from A217 on B2032 in Dorking direction. PARK: Easy. TEL: 01737 813969. SER: Valuations; restorations. VAT: Stan/Spec.

WEST BYFLEET

Academy Billiard Company

5 Camphill Industrial Estate. KT14 6EW. (R.W. Donnachie). Est. 1975. Open anytime by appointment. SIZE: Large warehouse and showroom. *STOCK: Period and antique billiard/snooker tables, all sizes, 1830-1920; combined billiard/*

West Byfleet continued

dining tables, period accessories including lighting. LOC: On A245, 2 miles from M25/A3 junction. PARK: Easy. TEL: 01932 352067; mobile - 0860 523757; fax - 01932 353904. SER: Valuations; restorations; removals; structural advice. VAT: Stan/Spec.

WEYBRIDGE

Brocante

120 Oatlands Drive, Oatlands Village. (Barry Dean and Ray Gwilliams). Est. 1988. Open 10-5.30, Sun. 10-5. CL: Mon. and Wed. SIZE: Small. *STOCK: Furniture, 19th C, £300-£1,500; porcelain, 19th C, £10-£250; Sheffield plate, 18th-19th C, £10-£300.* PARK: Easy. TEL: 01932 857807; home - 01932 345524. SER: Valuations. FAIRS: Oatlands Park Hotel; Seven Hills Hilton, Cobham.

Church House Antiques — LAPADA

42 Church St. KT13 8DP. (M.I. Foster). Est. 1886. Open Thurs., Fri., Sat. 10-5.30. SIZE: Medium. *STOCK: Furniture, 18th-19th C, £95-£7,000; jewellery, 18th-19th C, some modern, £30-£5,000; pictures, silver, plate, decorative items.* Not Stocked: Coins and stamps. PARK: Behind library. TEL: 01932 842190. VAT: Stan/Spec.

The Clock Shop Weybridge

64 Church St. KT13 8DL. Est. 1970. Open 10-6. SIZE: Medium. *STOCK: Clocks, 1685-1900, from £500; French carriage clocks, from £300.* LOC: Opposite Midland Bank on corner. PARK: Easy. TEL: 01932 840407/855503. SER: Valuations; restorations (clocks). VAT: Stan/Spec.

Edward Cross - Fine Paintings

128 Oatlands Drive. KT13 9HL. Est. 1973. Open Fri. 10-12.30 and 2-4, Sat. 10-12.30. SIZE: Medium. *STOCK: Fine paintings and bronzes, 19th-20th C, £500-£30,000.* LOC: A3050. PARK: Opposite. TEL: 01932 851093. SER: Valuations; restorations (watercolours and oil paintings); buys at auction (pictures). VAT: Spec.

Not Just Silver

16 York Rd. KT13 9DT. (Mrs S. Hughes). Est. 1969. Open 9.30-5.30, Sun. by appointment. *STOCK: Silver, Georgian to Modern.* LOC: Opposite car park, just off Queens Rd. TEL: 01932 842468; fax - 01932 830054; mobile - 0374 298151. SER: Valuations.

Olde Forge Antiques

37 St Mary's Rd., Oatlands Village. KT13 9PC. (Ian and Joan Porter). Est. 1976. Open Tues.-Sat. 11-4.30, or any time by prior appointment. SIZE: Small. *STOCK: Edwardian, Victorian and later furniture, £500-£1,500; motoring and sporting memorabilia, £25-£50; old radios and gramophones.* LOC: Off Oatlands Drive. PARK: Easy. TEL: 01932 828789; fax - 01932 253686. SER: Valuations; restorations (furniture including French polishing and upholstery).

Weybridge continued

R. Saunders

71 Queen's Rd. KT13 9UQ. (J.B. Tonkinson). Est. 1878. Open 9.30-1 and 2.30-5. CL: Wed. SIZE: Medium. *STOCK: English mahogany, oak and walnut furniture, wheel and stick barometers, 1650-1830, £50-£5,000; glass, porcelain, silver, watercolours, pewter and brass.* Not Stocked: Reproductions. PARK: 150yds. in York Rd. TEL: 01932 842601. SER: Valuations; restorations (furniture). VAT: Spec.

Village Antiques

39 St Mary's Rd., Oatlands Village. KT13 9PT. (B. Mulvany). Est. 1976. Open 10-4.30. CL: Wed. SIZE: Small. *STOCK: Furniture, small silver and china, 19th-20th C, £50-£100.* LOC: Off Oatlands Drive. PARK: Easy. TEL: 01932 846554. SER: Valuations; restorations (French polishing, small furniture repairs). FAIRS: Ardingly.

Weybridge Antiques

43 Church St., The Quadrant. KT13 8XD. (P. Pocock). Est. 1974. Open 10-5.30. SIZE: Large. *STOCK: Furniture, 18th-19th C; paintings, objects.* LOC: From M25 into town, Church St. is first right. PARK: Opposite in Mayfield Road. TEL: 01932 852503. SER: Restorations (oil paintings, porcelain, furniture, leathering). VAT: Spec.

Willow Gallery BADA LAPADA

75 Queens Rd. KT13 9UQ. (Andrew and Jean Stevens). Est. 1987. Open 10-6, Sun. by appointment. SIZE: Medium. *STOCK: British and European oil paintings, 19th C, £1,000-£40,000; furniture, 1750-1900, £500-£5,000.* LOC: Near town centre. PARK: Easy and nearby. TEL: 01932 846095/6; fax and home - 01932 846095. SER: Valuations; restorations; conservation; framing; catalogue available. FAIRS: BADA; LAPADA; Royal College of Art; NEC. VAT: Spec.

WINDLESHAM

Country Antiques

Country Gardens Garden Centre, London Rd. GU20 6LL. (S. Sommers and C. Martin). Est. 1990. Open 10-5 including Sun. SIZE: Large. *STOCK: Victorian and Edwardian, some Georgian, furniture, £50-£2,000; china and glass, collectables including lace and prints, Victorian to 1930's, £2-£100.* LOC: A30, between Sunningdale and Bagshot; off M3, junction 3. PARK: Easy. TEL: 01344 873404.

Richard Kimbell Antiques

Country Gardens Garden Centre, London Rd. GU20 6LL. Open 9-6. *STOCK: Antique pine.* LOC: A30 between Sunningdale and Bagshot; off M3, junction 3. PARK: Easy. TEL: 01344 875168; fax - 01344 875172.

WOKING

Alan's Antique Restorations

P O Box 355. GU22 9QE. (A.V. Wellstead). Open by appointment. *STOCK: General antiques, pine.* TEL: 01483 724666; fax - 01483 750366; mobile - 0860 851956. SER: Valuations; restorations (furniture, clocks and pictures); picture framing; caning and re-rushing; woodturning.

Keith Baker

42 Arnold Rd. GU21 5JU. (K.R. Baker). *STOCK: General antiques.* TEL: 01483 767425.

Chattels Antiques

156 High St., Old Woking. GU22 9JH. (John Kendall). Open by appointment only. SIZE: Small. *STOCK: Clocks, barometers, some small furniture.* LOC: Two miles off A3 at Ripley. PARK: Own. TEL: 01483 771310. SER: Restorations (English clocks, furniture).

Wych House Antiques

Aberdeen House, Wych Hill. GU22 0EU. (A. and C. Perry). Est. 1965. Open Tues., Thurs. and Sat. 10-5. SIZE: Large warehouses. *STOCK: Continental and English furniture, pine, decorative items, paintings, kitchenalia.* TEL: 01483 764636. SER: Interior design. VAT: Stan/Global.

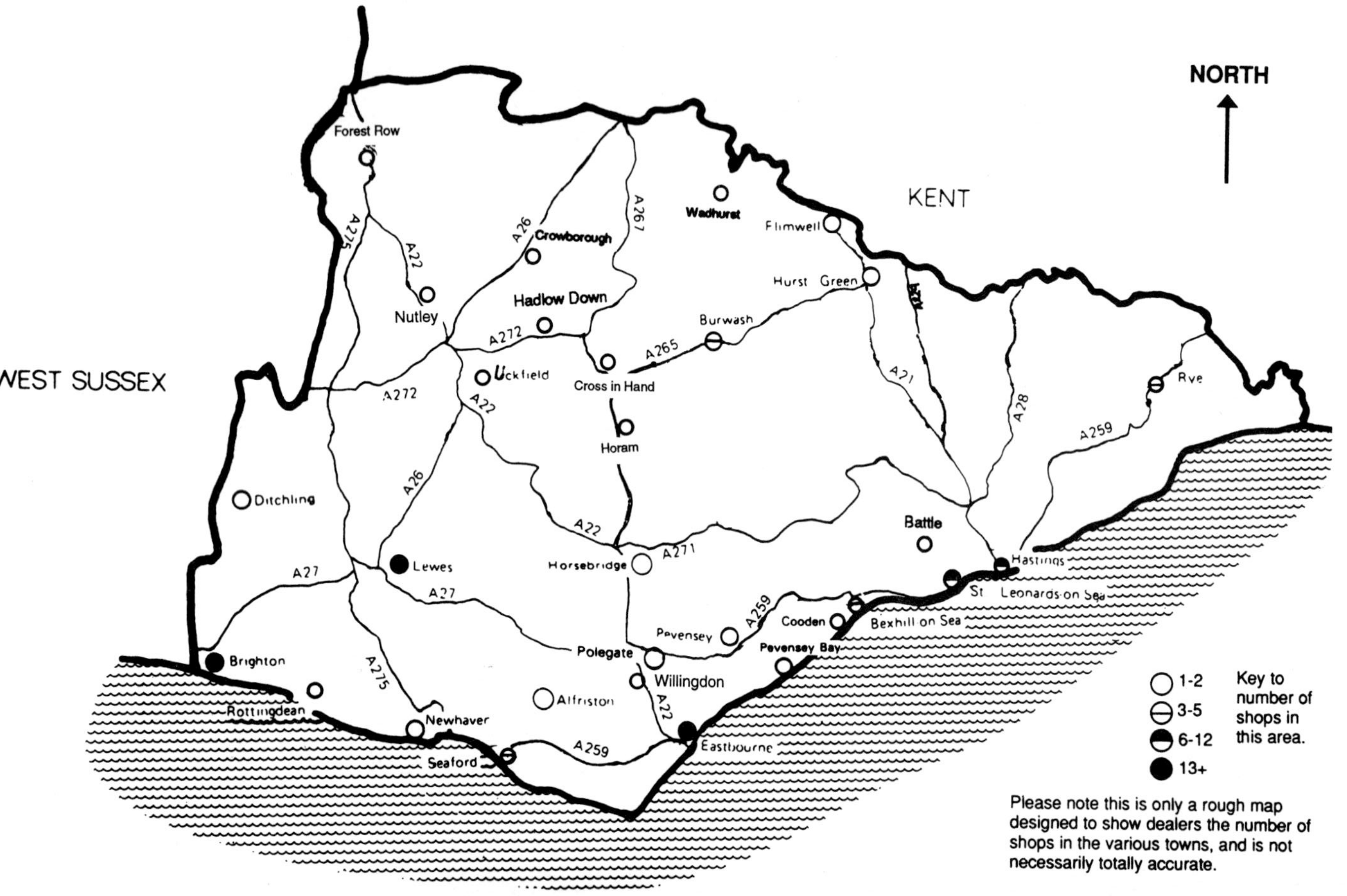
NORTH
KENT
WEST SUSSEX
Forest Row
A275
A22
Nutley
A26
Crowborough
A267
Wadhurst
Flimwell
Hurst Green
Hadlow Down
A272
Burwash
A265
Cross in Hand
Uckfield
A272
A22
Horam
A21
A28
Rye
A259
Ditchling
A26
A22
Battle
Lewes
Horsebridge
A271
Hastings
A27
A27
St Leonards-on Sea
Bexhill on Sea
Cooden
Pevensey
A259
Pevensey Bay
Polegate
Willingdon
Brighton
Rottingdean
A275
Alfriston
A22
Newhaven
Eastbourne
A259
Seaford
1-2
3-5
6-12
13+
Key to number of shops in this area.
Please note this is only a rough map designed to show dealers the number of shops in the various towns, and is not necessarily totally accurate.

ALFRISTON, Nr. Polegate

Alfriston Antiques

The Square. BN26 5UD. (J. Tourell). Est. 1967. Open Wed.-Sat. 11-5, Sun. 2.30-5. SIZE: Small. *STOCK: Collectors' items, vinaigrettes, snuff boxes, caddy spoons, silver, plate, carriage and other clocks, jewellery, paintings, pot-lids, copper, brass, books.* PARK: Easy. TEL: 01323 870498; fax - same. VAT: Stan/Spec.

BATTLE

Tymes Past Antiques

46 High St. (Mrs S. Fasey). Open 10-5, Sun. by appointment. SIZE: Medium. *STOCK: Mainly 18th and 19th C furniture, some Edwardian inlaid; general antiques - clocks, boxes, treen, gramophones, porcelain, glass, silver, games, commemorative ware and linen.* LOC: Near the roundabout. PARK: Nearby. TEL: 01424 774404.

BEXHILL-ON-SEA

Bexhill Antique Exporters

56 Turkey Rd. and Quakers Mill, Old Town. BN40 2HA. (H. and K. Abbott). Open 8-5.30, Sun. by appointment. SIZE: Warehouse. *STOCK: Antique and shipping furniture.* TEL: 01424 225103/210182; fax - 01424 731430. SER: Container packing.

The Old Mint House LAPADA

45 Turkey Rd. TN39 5HB. (J.C. and A.J. Nicholson). Est. 1960. Open 9-5.30. CL: Sat. SIZE: Large. *STOCK: Furniture - Victorian, Edwardian and shipping, some period; clocks, barometers and porcelain, 18th-19th C, £20-£10,000.* PARK: Easy. TEL: 01424 216056; 01323 762337; fax - 01323 762337. SER: Buys at auction; worldwide container packing. VAT: Stan.

Recollections

57 St. Leonards Rd. TN40 1JA. (A.R. Harmer). Est. 1993. Open 10-1 and 2-5. CL: Mon. SIZE: Medium. *STOCK: Decorative objects, £5-£300; old and new pine, all hand finished, £10-£500; restored Victorian and Edwardian baths, taps and accessories; architectural salvage items.* LOC: Town centre, near station. TEL: 01424 730650; home - 01424 892357. FAIRS: Newark; Ardingly. VAT: Spec.

BRIGHTON

Alexandria Antiques

3 Hanover Place, Lewes Rd. BN2 2SD. (A.H. Ahmed). Open 9.30-6, Sat. morning by appointment. *STOCK: Georgian and Victorian furniture; Oriental and European porcelain; oil and watercolour paintings; Oriental carpets, objets d'art.* TEL: 01273 688793.

Brighton continued

Alexandria Antiques

33 Upper North St. BN1 3FG. (A.H. Ahmed). Open 9.30-5 or by appointment. *STOCK: Georgian and Victorian furniture, glassware and porcelain, Oriental and European bronzes, works of art.* TEL: 01273 328072.

Art Deco Etc.

73 Upper Gloucester Rd. BN1 3LQ. (John Clark). Est. 1979. Open 12-5.30, Sun. and other times by appointment. SIZE: Medium. *STOCK: Pottery, especially Poole; glass, furniture, lighting, mirrors, pictures and collectors' items, Art Deco, Art Nouveau, Arts and Crafts, 1950's, £5-£2,000.* LOC: From Brighton station down Queens Rd., first on right. PARK: Easy. TEL: 01273 329268; home - 01273 202937. SER: Valuations. FAIRS: Decorative Arts, Kensington; Art Deco, Battersea; Alexandra Palace; Ardingly and Newark.

Ashton's Antiques

1-3 Clyde Rd., Preston Circus. BN1 4NN. (R. Ashton). Open 9.30-5.30. CL: Wed. SIZE: 4 showrooms. *STOCK: Victorian and Edwardian furniture, upholstery and decorative items.* TEL: 01273 605253; fax - same. VAT: Stan/Spec.

Attic Antiques

23 Ship St. BN1 1AD. (F.B. and M.J. Moorhead). Est. 1965. Open 11-1 and 2.15-5, Sat. 12-1, prior telephone call advisable. *STOCK: General antiques, 1720-1920, £15-£1,500; English and Continental paintings, mainly Victorian and Georgian; clocks, barometers, Oriental antiques, bronzes, English and continental china, tantalus, Victorian oil lamps, copper, brass, pewter; Imari, Canton, Satsuma and Worcester china; Georgian, Victorian, Edwardian and Continental furniture.* TEL: 01273 326378. VAT: Stan. *Mainly Trade.*

Bears and Friends

41 Meeting House Lane, The Lanes. BN1 1HB. (P. Goble). Est. 1989. Open 9-5.30, Sat. 9-6, Sun. 10-6 or by appointment. *STOCK: Teddy bears and bear related items; antique dolls and miniatures.* TEL: 01273 208940; fax - 01273 202736. SER: Valuations; export; mail order; museum of childhood. FAIRS: Major London Hugglетts Teddy Bear fairs. VAT: Stan/Spec.

Brighton Antique Wholesalers

39 Upper Gardner St. SIZE: Several dealers. *STOCK: 18th-19th C furniture, £50-£5,000.* LOC: Off North Rd. PARK: Easy. TEL: 01273 695457.

Brighton Architectural Salvage

33-34 Gloucester Rd. BN1 4AQ. (L. F. Moore). Open 10-5. *STOCK: Restored architectural items including pine furniture; fireplaces and surrounds - marble, pine, mahogany, cast-iron, Victorian tiled and cast inserts and over-mantels; doors, stained glass, panelling; cast-iron balcony and street railings, gas coal fires, light fittings; garden seats and ornaments.* TEL: 01273 681656.

Brighton continued

Brighton Flea Market
31A Upper St. James's St. BN2 1JN. (A. Wilkinson). Est. 1990. Open seven days. SIZE: Large. *STOCK: Bric-a-brac, furniture and collectables, 19th-20th C, £5-£1,000.* LOC: 50 yards from coast road, Kemp Town. TEL: 01273 624006.

Mary Brown
42 Surrey St. BN1 3PB. Open 11-5.30. *STOCK: Period clothes, linen and lace, costume jewellery.* LOC: Near station and CAB office. TEL: 01273 721160.

C.A.R.S. (Classic Automobilia & Regalia Specialists)
4-4a Chapel Terrace Mews, Kemp Town. BN2 1HU. (G.G. Weiner). *STOCK: Collectors' car badges, mascots and associated automobilia and related motoring memorabilia; children's pedal cars, electric cars, collectors' veteran and vintage pedal cars, 1930's-1970's.* TEL: 01273 601960; fax - same. SER: Catalogue/price list on receipt of SAE.

Sheila Cashin Antiques
40 Upper North St. BN1 3FH. Est. 1982. Open 10-5, Sat. and Sun. by appointment. SIZE: Small. *STOCK: Restored decorative Victorian bamboo and lacquer furniture, £50-£1,000; painted and faux-bamboo furniture and decorative items, especially mirrors.* PARK: Voucher parking nearby. TEL: 01273 326619.

Connoisseur Antique Gallery
113 Church Rd., Hove. BN3 2AF. *STOCK: General antiques.* TEL: 01273 777398.

Harry Diamond and Son
9 Union St., The Lanes. BN1 1HA. (R. and H. Diamond). Est. 1937. Open 9-5. *STOCK: Diamond jewellery, antique silver, £50-£20,000.* Not Stocked: Coins, furniture. TEL: 01273 329696. VAT: Stan.

James Doyle Antiques
10 Union St., The Lanes. BN1 1HA. (J.R. Doyle). Est. 1975. Open 9.30-6. *STOCK: Jewellery, silver.* TEL: 01273 323694; fax - 01273 324330.

D.H. Edmonds Ltd
28 Meeting House Lane, The Lanes. BN1 1HB. Est. 1965. Open 10-5.30. SIZE: Large. *STOCK: Jewellery, silver, objets d'art, watches, £50-£20,000.* TEL: 01273 327713/328871. VAT: Stan.

Faques Gallery
32 Upper St James's St., BN2 1JN. Est. 1962. Open 10-5.30. SIZE: Large. *STOCK: Reproduction oil paintings.* LOC: Kemp Town area. PARK: Side roads. TEL: 01273 624432; fax - 01273 683692. VAT: Stan.

Brighton continued

Alan Fitchett Antiques
5-5A Upper Gardner St. BN1 4AN. Est. 1969. Open 9-5.30. CL: Sat. SIZE: Large. *STOCK: Furniture, 18th-20th C, £50-£10,000; works of art.* LOC: North Laines (Station area). PARK: Easy. TEL: 01273 600894; fax - same. SER: Valuations; restorations. VAT: Stan.

Furniture Finders Ltd
156 Lewes Rd. BN2 3LH. *STOCK: 1930's and older furniture.* TEL: 01273 705004; fax - 01273 705005.

Paul Goble
44 Meeting House Lane, The Lanes. BN1 1HB. Est. 1965. Open 9-5.30, Sun. 10-5.30 or by appointment. *STOCK: Jewellery, watches, silver, pictures and prints, teddy bears and dolls.* TEL: 01273 202801; fax - 01273 202736. SER: Trade/export valuation. VAT: Stan/Spec.

The Gold and Silversmiths of Hove
3 Planet House, 1 The Drive, Hove. BN3 3JE. Open 8.45-5. *STOCK: Jewellery and silver.* TEL: 01273 738489.

Douglas Hall Ltd
23 Meeting House Lane. BN1 1HB. (K.J. Longthorne). Est. 1968. Open 9.30-5. *STOCK: Silver, jewellery.* TEL: 01273 325323. VAT: Stan.

Hallmarks
4 Union St., The Lanes. BN1 1HA. (J. Hersheson). Est. 1966. Open 9-5. SIZE: Small. *STOCK: Silver and plate, jewellery and clocks, collectables.* TEL: 01273 725477. VAT: Stan/Spec.

Mark and David Hawkins
The Lanes Armoury, 27 Meeting House Lane, The Lanes. BN1 1HB. Open 9-5.30, Sun. by appointment. *STOCK: General antiques, militaria, arms and armour, £10-£7,500.* TEL: 01273 321357.

Holleyman and Treacher Ltd
21a and 22 Duke St. BN1 1AH. Est. 1937. Open 9-5. CL: Mon. *STOCK: Books including antiquarian, music.* TEL: 01273 328007.

The House of Antiques — LAPADA
17 Prince Albert St. BN1 1HF. (A. Margiotta). Open 10-5.30. *STOCK: Jewellery and silver.* TEL: 01273 327680/324961. VAT: Stan.

Dudley Hume
46 Upper North St. BN1 3FH. Est. 1973. CL: Sat. pm. and Sun., except by appointment. SIZE: Medium. *STOCK: Period and Victorian furniture, metal, light fittings, decorative items.* LOC: Parallel to the Western Rd., one block to the north. TEL: 01273 323461; fax - same. VAT: Stan/Spec.

Brighton continued

Hyndford Antiques

143 Edward St. BN2 2JG. (Mrs M.C. Skelson). Est. 1968. Open Thurs.-Sat. 10.30-4.30 or by appointment. SIZE: Small. *STOCK: Bygones, china, collectables, Oriental carvings, £1-£150; prints, ephemera, postcards, 50p-£75; small furniture, £10-£250; all 19th-20th C.* LOC: Edward St. east at right angles to Brighton Pavilion. PARK: Vouchers near shop, NCP in High St. TEL: 01273 679936/602220. FAIRS: Hove Town Hall; Brighton Centre.

Leoframes

70 North Rd. BN1 1YD. (H. and Mrs A. Schofield and S. Round). Open 9-5.30. *STOCK: Prints and maps.* TEL: 01273 695862. SER: Restorations; framing.

Harry Mason

P O Box 687, Hove. BN3 6JY. Est. 1954. Open by appointment. *STOCK: Silver and plate, 18th-20th C; jewellery, 19th-20th C.* TEL: 01273 500330; fax - 01273 553300; e-mail - mason@fastnet.co.uk. SER: Valuations; restorations (silver and jewellery); buys at auction (as stock); buyers of scrap silver and gold. FAIRS: Sunday London Hotel. VAT: Stan/Spec.

Patrick Moorhead Antiques

15B Prince Albert St. BN1 1AD. Open 10-5.30 or by appointment. CL: Sat. SIZE: Shop and large trade warehouse (Spring Gardens/Church Street). *STOCK: Victorian and Georgian furniture; French, Oriental and English porcelain; clocks, pictures, bronzes, metalware, objets d'art.* TEL: 01273 779696; fax - 01273 220196.

Michael Norman Antiques Ltd BADA

Palmeira House, 82 Western Rd., Hove. BN3 1JB. Est. 1965. Open 9-1 and 2-5.30, other times by appointment. *STOCK: English furniture.* TEL: 01273 329253 or 01273 326712; fax - 01273 206556. VAT: Stan/Spec.

Oasis Antiques

39 Kensington Gdns. BN1 4AL. (I. and A. Stevenson). Est. 1970. Open 10-5, Mon. 11-5, Sat. 8-5. SIZE: Medium. *STOCK: Lighting and furniture, to 1930, £1-£5,000; European and Oriental items including bronzes, art glass, period clothes, linen and lace, gramophones, radios, telephones, collectable modern design, Art Nouveau, Art Deco.* LOC: Off North Road from railway station, centre of North Laines. PARK: Nearby. TEL: 01273 683885. SER: Restorations (radios, telephones, furniture, metals, ceramics); polishing.

Colin Page Antiquarian Books

36 Duke St. BN1 1AG. (C.G. Page). Est. 1971. Open 9-5.30. *STOCK: Antiquarian and second-hand books, especially topography, travel, natural history, illustrated and leather bindings, 16th-20th C, £1-£5,000.* LOC: Town centre. PARK: Multi-storey nearby. TEL: 01273 325954; fax - 01273 746246; e-mail - cpage@pavilion. co.uk.

Brian Page Antiques

18 Regent Arcade, East St. BN1 1HR. Open 10-5.30. *STOCK: Chinese and Japanese antiques and works of art, BC3000-20th C; antiquarian and rare books.* LOC: Adjacent to Town Hall. TEL: 01273 723956; fax - 01273 746246.

Dermot and Jill Palmer Antiques

7-8 Union St., The Lanes. BN1 1HA. Resident. Est. 1968. Open 9-6, Sun. by appointment. *STOCK: French and English furniture, objects, pictures, mirrors, screens, garden furniture and ornamental pieces, textiles, £50-£5,000.* TEL: 01273 328669 (2 lines); fax - 01273 777641. FAIRS: Olympia; Decorative Antique & Textile. VAT: Stan/Spec.

Sue Pearson

13 1/2 Prince Albert St. BN1 1HE. Open 10-5. SIZE: Small. *STOCK: Antique dolls, teddy bears, dolls' house miniatures.* LOC: Lanes area. PARK: NCP. TEL: 01273 329247. SER: Valuations; restorations; buys at auction (dolls and bears). FAIRS: Major London Doll and Bear. VAT: Stan/Spec.

Ben Ponting Antiques

53 Upper North St. Open 9.30-5.30, Sat. 10-1. *STOCK: Furniture, 18th-19th C.* TEL: 01273 329409.

Recollections

1a Sydney St. BN1 4EN. (B. Bagley). Est. 1973. Open Tues., Thurs., Fri. and Sat. 10.30-4.30. SIZE: Small. *STOCK: Small collectable items, 19th-20th C, £5-£250; brass and copper especially fireplace furniture; Victorian oil lamps.* LOC: From railway station down Trafalgar St. last turning on right. PARK: Opposite in Belmont St. TEL: 01273 681517. SER: Valuations; restorations (metal, china, oil lamps).

Ruddy Antiques

39 Upper North St. (Paula Ruddy). Est. 1994. Open 10-5. CL: Sat. SIZE: Medium. *STOCK: Interesting decorative English and Continental furniture, 18th-19th C, £100-£2,000; mirrors and decorative objects, £100-£500.* LOC: Parallel to Western Rd., north side. PARK: Easy. TEL: 01273 772060.

Rutland Antiques

48 Upper North St. BN1 3FH. Open 10.30-5.30. SIZE: Small. *STOCK: Porcelain, china, textiles, clocks and watches and general antiques.* LOC: North of and parallel to Western Rd. PARK: Reasonable. TEL: 01273 329991.

Brighton continued

Savery Antiques
257 Ditchling Rd., (Fiveways). BN1 1JH. Resident. (J. and H. Savery). Est. 1968. Open 9-5. CL: Wed. SIZE: Small. *STOCK: Glass and china, £5-£500; copper and brass, £20-£200; all 19th-20th C.* LOC: Near Midland Bank. TEL: 01273 564899. FAIRS: Ardingly; Sandown Park.

S.L. Simmons
9 Meeting House Lane, The Lanes. BN1 1HB. NAG. Est. 1948. Open 9.30-5.30. *STOCK: Jewellery and silver, 19th C.* TEL: 01273 327949. VAT: Stan.

Sleeping Beauty Antique Beds
212 Church Rd., Hove. BN3 2DT. (Mr and Mrs Roberts). Est. 1975. Open 10-5 including Sun. SIZE: Medium. *STOCK: Brass, iron and French wooden beds, 19th C, £500-£1,000.* LOC: Continuation of Western Rd. PARK: Nearby. TEL: 01273 205115; home - same. SER: Valuations; restorations; buys at auction (beds).

Tapsell Antiques LAPADA
59 and 59a Middle St. and 10 Ship St. Gdns. BN1 1AL. Est. 1948. Open 9-5.30, other times by appointment. SIZE: Large. *STOCK: English and Continental furniture, clocks, bronzes, general antiques; Oriental ceramics, lacquer, furniture and bronzes.* TEL: 01273 328341; fax - 01273 775245. VAT: Stan/Spec.

Michael Tidey Antiques
87 St. Georges Rd., Kemp Town. BN2 1EE. Resident. *STOCK: English furniture.* TEL: 01273 602389.

Timewarp
6 Sydney St. BN1 4EN. (Miss J. Whiskin). Est. 1982. Open 10.30-5.45, Sat. 9-6, Sun. by appointment. SIZE: Large. *STOCK: Lamps and shades, Art Deco to 1960's, £15-£55; Victorian oil lamps and spare parts, to £250; bakelite, furniture, 1930-1940, £2-£300.* LOC: 5 minutes from station, turn right off Trafalgar St. TEL: 01273 607527. SER: Restorations (oil lamps).

Graham Webb
59A Ship St. BN1 1AE. Est. 1961. Open 10-5, prior telephone call advisable. SIZE: Small. *STOCK: Cylinder and disc musical boxes, all mechanical musical instruments, £650-£45,000.* LOC: Close to the Lanes. PARK: Middle St. TEL: 01273 321803; fax - same; home - 01273 772154. VAT: Stan/Spec.

Stephen Welbourne
20 Bond St. BN1 1RD. Resident. Est. 1977. Open 11-5. SIZE: Medium. *STOCK: 19th C oil paintings, watercolours and prints; decorative antiques and light fittings.* LOC: Off Church St. PARK: Easy. TEL: 01273 694464; fax - 01273 620021. SER: Valuations; buys at auction. VAT: Spec.

Brighton continued

E. and B. White
43 & 47 Upper North St. BN1 3FH. Est. 1962. Open 9.30-5. CL: Sat. pm. SIZE: Medium. *STOCK: Oak and country furniture and decorative items, £50-£2,000.* LOC: Upper North St. runs parallel to and north of Western Rd. (the main shopping street). TEL: 01273 328706; fax - 01273 207035. VAT: Spec.

Wilkinsons
11 Church St. Est. 1985. Open Mon.-Sat. SIZE: Small. *STOCK: Furniture and collectables, 18th-20th C, £50-£2,000.* LOC: 200 m. north of Brighton Pavilion. TEL: 01273 328665.

The Witch Ball
48 Meeting House Lane. BN1 1HB. (Mrs Gina Daniels). Est. 1967. Open 10.30-6. *STOCK: 18th-19th C topographical and decorative engravings; 16th-19th C maps.* TEL: 01273 326618. VAT: Stan/Spec.

Witney & Airault
The Lanes Gallery, 32 Meeting House Lane. BN1 1HB. Open 11-4. *STOCK: Art Deco including Clarice Cliff, Susie Cooper.* TEL: 01273 735479.

Yellow Lantern Antiques Ltd LAPADA
34 Holland Rd., Hove. BN3 1JL. (B.R. and E.A. Higgins). Est. 1950. Open 10-1 and 2.15-5.30, Sat. 10-4. SIZE: Medium. *STOCK: Mainly English furniture, £50-£3,000; French and English clocks; both to 1850; bronzes, 19th C, £100-£1,500; Continental porcelain, 1820-1860, £50-£1,000.* Not Stocked: Pottery, oak, 18th C porcelain. LOC: From Brighton seafront to Hove, turn right after parade of Regency houses, shop 100yds. on left past traffic lights, opposite Michael Norman Antiques. PARK: Easy. TEL: 01273 771572; mobile - 0860 342976; home - 01273 455476. SER: Valuations; restorations; buys at auction. FAIRS: Buxton; Harrogate; NEC; Olympia; Guildford; Kensington; Chester. VAT: Spec.

BURWASH, Nr. Etchingham

Chateaubriand Antiques Centre
High St. TN19 7ES. Open 10-5.30, Sun. 12-5.30. SIZE: 8 dealers. *STOCK: Linen, furniture, country oak, glass, paintings, smalls.* LOC: A265. PARK: Nearby. TEL: 01435 882535. SER: Shipping; framing.

Chaunt House
High St. TN19 7ES. (M. Walsh). Est. 1976. Open Thurs.-Sat. SIZE: Small. *STOCK: Clocks, 19th C, £50-£1,000; watches and barometers.* LOC: A265. PARK: Easy. TEL: 01435 882221; home - same. SER: Valuations; restorations; buys at auction (as stock). VAT: Stan/Spec.

COODEN

Annies

4 Bixlea Parade, Little Common Rd. TN39 4SD. (P.A. Rose). Est. 1990. Open 10-5, Wed. and Sun. by appointment. SIZE: Small. *STOCK: China, glass, porcelain and linen, 1800-1930, £5-£500; furniture, from 1880, £50-£750; silver plate, kitchenalia, copper, brass and clocks, from 1800, £5-£150.* LOC: A259 between Bexhill and Eastbourne by Little Common roundabout. PARK: Easy. TEL: 01424 846966. SER: Valuations; buys at auction. FAIRS: De La Warr, Bexhill. VAT: Stan/Spec.

CROSS IN HAND, Nr Heathfield

Colonial Times

Lewes Rd. TN21 0TA. (A.P. Skinner). Open Tues., Fri. and Sat. 10-5, other days (including Sun.) by appointment. SIZE: Medium + barns. *STOCK: Colonial furniture, Victorian and Edwardian, £50-£2,500; china, including Staffordshire, £20-£300; clocks, Edwardian, £40-£125.* LOC: A267 from Tunbridge Wells to Eastbourne, opposite Esso garage. PARK: Easy. TEL: 01435 862962; fax and home - same. FAIRS: Newark; Ardingly. VAT: Stan.

CROWBOROUGH

Broadway Hall Antiques

The Broadway. (B. Ross). Open 10-5. SIZE: 8+ dealers. *STOCK: Furniture, pine, oak and mahogany; lighting, metalware, collectables, postcards and topographical prints.* LOC: Top of Crowborough Hill, opposite the Town Hall. PARK: Easy - nearby. TEL: 01892 664225; fax - 01892 740264.

DITCHLING

Dycheling Antiques

34 High St. BN6 8TA. (E.A. Hudson). Est. 1977. Open 10.30-5.30. CL: Wed. SIZE: Large - shop and showroom. *STOCK: Georgian, Victorian and Edwardian furniture, especially dining and armchairs, £25-£5,000.* LOC: Off A23 on A273-B2112 north of Brighton. PARK: Easy. TEL: 01273 842929; home - same; mobile - 0585 456341. VAT: Spec.

Jonathan Holley Antiques

8 West St. BN6 8TS. Est. 1983. SIZE: Medium. *STOCK: Furniture, copper and brass, glass and decorative items.* TEL: 01273 843290. VAT: Stan/Spec.

EASTBOURNE

Bell Antiques

47 South St. BN21 4UT. (Mrs M.J. Everett). Open 10-1 and 2-4.30. SIZE: Small. *STOCK: Porcelain and small bijou items, 18th-19th C, £10-£300; furniture, Victorian and Edwardian, £50-£400; paintings and prints, to 1930, £10-£150.* LOC: Road opposite Town Hall. PARK: Easy. TEL: 01323 641339. SER: Valuations.

Eastbourne continued

Wm. Bruford and Son Ltd 11/13

Cornfield Rd. BN21 3NA. Est. 1883. Open 9.30-5.15. SIZE: Medium. *STOCK: Jewellery, Victorian, late Georgian; some silver, clocks (bracket, carriage).* Not Stocked: China, glass, brass, pewter, furniture. TEL: 01323 725452. SER: Valuations; restorations (clocks and silver). VAT: Stan/Spec.

Camilla's Bookshop

57 Grove Rd. BN21 4TX. (C. Francombe and S. Broad). Est. 1976. Open 10-6. *STOCK: Books including antiquarian and on art, antiques and collectables, and especially naval, military, aviation, technical, needlework, broadcasting.* LOC: Next to police station. TEL: 01323 736001. SER: Valuations; book search; postal service; own book tokens.

John Cowderoy Antiques LAPADA

42 South St. BN21 4XB. GMC. (R., D.J. and R.A. Cowderoy). Est. 1973. Open 9.30-5. CL: Wed. pm. and Sat. pm. SIZE: Large. *STOCK: Clocks, musical boxes, furniture, porcelain, silver and plate, jewellery, copper, brass, paintings.* LOC: 150yds. from Town Hall. PARK: Easy. TEL: 01323 720058. SER: Restorations (clocks, barometers, music boxes and furniture). VAT: Stan/Spec.

Crest Collectables

54 Grove Rd. BN21 4UD. (C. Powell). Open 10-6. *STOCK: General antiques and collectables.* TEL: 01323 721185.

John Day of Eastbourne Fine Art

9 Meads St. BN20 7QY. Est. 1964. Open 9.30-1 and 2-5 (prior 'phone call advisable). CL: Wed. and Sat. pm. SIZE: Medium. *STOCK: English, especially East Anglian, and Continental paintings and watercolours, 19th C.* LOC: Meads village, west end of Eastbourne. PARK: Easy. TEL: 01323 725634; mobile - 0860 466197. SER: Restorations; framing (oils and watercolours).

Roderick Dew

10 Furness Rd. BN21 4EZ. Est. 1971. *STOCK: Antiquarian books, especially on art and antiques.* TEL: 01323 720239. *Postal Only.*

Eastbourne Antiques Market

80 Seaside. BN22 7QP. Est. 1969. Open 10-5.30, Sat. 10-5. SIZE: Large - 30+ stalls. *STOCK: A wide selection of general antiques and collectables.* PARK: Easy. TEL: 01323 642233.

Elliott and Scholz Antiques

12 Willingdon Rd. BN21 1TH. (C.R. Elliott and K.V. Scholz). Est. 1981. Open 9.30-4.30, Wed. and Sat. 9.30-1. SIZE: Small. *STOCK: Small furniture, £100-£500; clocks, £20-£300; bric-a-brac, £10-£100; all 19th-20 C.* LOC: A22. PARK: Easy. TEL: 01323 732200. SER: Valuations.

Eastbourne continued

Enterprise Collectors Market

The Enterprise Centre, Station Parade. Est. 1989. Open 9.30-5. SIZE: Medium. *STOCK: Wide range of general antiques and collectables.* LOC: Next to railway station. PARK: Easy. TEL: 01323 732690. SER: Valuations.

A. & T. Gibbard

(formerly Raymond Smith). 30 South St. BN21 4XB. Open 9-5.30. SIZE: Large. *STOCK: Secondhand and antiquarian books, 16th-20th C, £1-£1,000; publishers' remainders, 75p-£30; maps and prints, 17th-20th C, 50p-£350.* LOC: 200yds. east of Town Hall. PARK: Easy. TEL: 01323 734128. SER: Valuations. VAT: Stan.

The Old Town Antiques Centre

52 Ocklynge Rd. BN21 1PR. (V. Franklin). Est. 1990. Open 9.30-5. SIZE: Medium. *STOCK: General antiques.* LOC: East Dean coast road. PARK: Easy. TEL: 01323 416016. FAIRS: Ardingly.

Timothy Partridge Antiques

46 Ocklynge Rd. Open 10-1. *STOCK: Victorian, Edwardian and 1920's furniture.* LOC: In old town, near St. Mary's Church. PARK: Easy. TEL: 01323 638731.

Pharoahs Antiques Centre

28 South St. BN21 4UJ. (W. and J. Pharoah). Est. 1973. Open 10-5. SIZE: Medium. 14 stallholders. *STOCK: A wide range of antiques including jewellery, pine, kitchenalia, china, curios, lace, linen, Victorian furniture, original light fittings and lamps.* LOC: Near Town Hall. PARK: Easy. TEL: 01323 738655. FAIRS: Ardingly.

Ernest Pickering

44 South St. BN21 4XB. Est. 1946. Open 9-5. CL: Wed. pm. and Sat. pm. *STOCK: Furniture, porcelain, grandfather clocks.* TEL: 01323 730483. VAT: Stan/Spec.

Premier Gallery & Bookshop

24 South St. BN21 4XB. (D. Mazzoli). Est. 1983. Open 10-5, Sun. by appointment. SIZE: Large. *STOCK: Antiquarian and second-hand books, antiquarian prints, watercolours, modern British paintings (John Bratby RA).* LOC: Near station. PARK: Easy. TEL: 01323 736023. SER: Valuations; restorations (oil paintings, watercolours and prints). VAT: Stan.

Stewart Gallery

25 Grove Rd. BN21 4TT. (Gallery Laraine Ltd). Est. 1970. Open 9-5.30. SIZE: Large. *STOCK: Paintings and ceramics, 19th-20th C, £5-£25,000.* LOC: Next to library, 150yds. from station. PARK: Easy. TEL: 01323 729588; fax - 01323 412900. SER: Valuations; restorations (paintings and frames). VAT: Stan/Spec.

Eastbourne continued

Wellers Restoration Centre

12 North St. BN21 3HG. (D. Ricketts). Est. 1892. Open 9.15-4.45. *STOCK: Trophies, silver, pewter, brass.* TEL: 01323 723592. SER: Restorations; polishing; silver plating; engraving; repairs; plaques, hardwood bases, etc.

Lloyd Williams - Antique Anglo Am Warehouse

2a Beach Rd. BN22 7EX. Est. 1976. Open 9.30-5, Sat. and Sun. by appointment. SIZE: Large. *STOCK: Shipping furniture, 1850-1920, £50-£3,000; period furniture, pre 1850, £500+; general antiques.* LOC: Off Seaside Rd. PARK: Easy. TEL: 01323 648661; fax - 01323 648658; home - 01435 872566. SER: Restorations; containers. VAT: Stan. *Trade Only.*

FLIMWELL

Graham Lower

Stonecrouch Farmhouse. TN5 7QB. Open by appointment. *STOCK: English and Continental 17th-18th C oak furniture.* LOC: A21. TEL: 01580 879535. SER: Valuations. VAT: Spec.

FOREST ROW

Aspidistra Antiques

16 Hartfield Rd. RH18 5ND. (Trudy and Jeroen Markies). Est. 1980. Open 10-5, Wed. 10-1, Sat. 9.30-5. *STOCK: Furniture, 18th-19th C, £1,000-£3,500; silver, Oriental and European ceramics, linen, 19th-20th C, £20-£500.* LOC: 3 miles south of East Grinstead, 100 yards down Hartfield Rd. PARK: Behind shop. TEL: 01342 824980; fax - 01342 823677. SER: Valuations; restorations (furniture and silver); buys at auction. VAT: Spec.

HADLOW DOWN, Nr. Uckfield

Hadlow Down Antiques

Hastingford Farm, School Lane. TN22 4DY. (Adrian Butler). Est. 1989. Open 10-5 including Sun., Mon. and Wed. by appointment. SIZE: Large. *STOCK: Country and formal furniture, 17th-20th C, £25-£2,500; stripped pine, 19th C, £15-£900; decorative accessories, 19th C, £5-£500.* LOC: 2 mins. down School Lane from A272 in village. PARK: Easy. TEL: 01825 830707; home - same. SER: Valuations; restorations (furniture).

HASTINGS

Coach House Antiques

48 George St. TN34 3EG. (R.J. Luck). Est. 1972. Open 10-5 including Sun. SIZE: Medium. *STOCK: Longcase clocks, 18th-19th C, £1,000+; furniture, 19th C, £100+; collectables including Dinky toys, trains, dolls houses.* PARK: Nearby. TEL: 01424 461849. SER: Valuations; restorations (clocks and furniture); buys at auction (clocks and furniture). VAT: Spec.

Hastings continued

George Street Antiques Centre
47 George St. TN34 3EA. (F. Stanley and P. Heuduk). Est. 1969. Open 9-5, Sun. 11-4. SIZE: Medium - 20 dealers. *STOCK: Small items, 19th-20th C, £5-£500.* LOC: In old town, parallel to seafront. PARK: Seafront. TEL: 01424 429339; home - 01424 813526/713300.

Howes Bookshop
Trinity Hall, Braybrooke Terrace. TN34 1HQ. ABA. Est. 1920. Open 9.30-1 and 2.15-5. CL: Sat. pm. *STOCK: Antiquarian and academic books in literature, history, arts, bibliography.* TEL: 01424 423437; fax - 01424 460620. FAIRS: ABA.

Nakota Curios
12 Courthouse St. TN35 3AU. (D.H. Brant). Est. 1964. Open 10.30-1 and 2-5. SIZE: Medium. *STOCK: General trade items, decorative china, Victoriana, jewellery, pictures, lighting.* Not Stocked: Coins, medals. PARK: Easy. TEL: 01424 438900.

J. Radcliffe
40 Cambridge Rd. TN34 1DT. Open 10-1 and 2-5. CL: Wed. pm. *STOCK: General antiques, trade goods.* TEL: 01424 426361.

Spice
Samphire House, 75 High St., Old Town. TN34 3EL. (S. Dix). Open by appointment. *STOCK: Early furniture and decorative items.* TEL: 0410 209556.

HORAM, Nr. Heathfield

John Botting Antiques
Winstan House, High St. TN21 0ER. Open by appointment only. SIZE: Small. *STOCK: Victorian and Edwardian mahogany, oak and pine; French furniture.* PARK: Easy, on forecourt. TEL: 01435 813553.

Sussex Antiques
Whatleys House, High St. TN21. (Victor Haynes). Open Tues., Thurs., Fri. and Mon. Wed. and Sat. mornings, other times by appointment. SIZE: Medium. *STOCK: Victorian oil lamps, china, glass, furniture, clocks, silver and plate.* PARK: Easy. TEL: 01435 812105; home - 01825 872222.

HORSEBRIDGE, Nr. Hailsham

Horsebridge Antiques Centre
1 North St. BN27 4DJ. Resident. (R. Lane). Est. 1978. Open 10-1 and 1.30-5. SIZE: Large. *STOCK: General antiques including furniture, silver, glass, pottery, brass and copper.* LOC: A271. PARK: Easy. TEL: 01323 844414; fax - 01323 844000; e-mail - leung@enterprise.net. SER: Valuations.

HURST GREEN

Delmas
Little Bernhurst. TN19 7PN. (P.D. Stimpson). Est. 1973. Open 10-6.30. CL: Wed. *STOCK: English and Continental furniture and paintings.* TEL: 01580 860345. VAT: Stan/Spec.

Libra Antiques
81 London Rd. TN19 7PN. Resident. (Janice Hebert). Est. 1976. Open 9.30-6, Sun. and Mon. by appointment. SIZE: Medium. *STOCK: Lighting, 19th to early 20th C, £100-£400; pine furniture, £50-£500; decorative items, £10-£200; both 18th-19th C.* LOC: A21. PARK: Easy. TEL: 01580 860569; home - same.

LEWES

Ashcombe Coach House BADA
BN7 3JR. Open by appointment only. *STOCK: Furniture and objects, 17th to early 19th C.* TEL: 01273 474794; fax - 01273 705959; mobile - 0860 720731.

John Bird and Annette Puttnam Antiques
Norton House, Iford. BN7 3EJ. Est. 1970. Open anytime by appointment. *STOCK: Furniture - country, pine, oak, fruitwood, mahogany, painted, architectural, garden and upholstery.* TEL: 01273 483366; mobiles - 0973 421070/0802 803440.

Bow Windows Book Shop
175 High St. BN7 1YE. (A. and J. Shelley). Open 9.30-5. SIZE: Large. *STOCK: Books including natural history, English literature, travel, topography.* LOC: Off A27. TEL: 01273 480780; fax - 01273 486686. FAIRS: Antiquarian Book.

Castle Antiques
163a High St. (C. J. Harris). Est. 1984. Open 10-5, Sun. 2-5. SIZE: Medium. *STOCK: Pine furniture, late 19th C, £80-£120; kitchenalia, late 19th C, £5-£25; bric-a-brac, late 19th to early 20th C, £5-£25.* LOC: Top part of High St., down a twitten, opposite Lloyds Bank. TEL: 01273 475176.

Church-Hill Antiques Centre
6 Station St. BN7 2DA. (S. Miller and S. Ramm). Est. 1970. Open 9.30-5. SIZE: 60 stalls and cabinets. *STOCK: Wide range of general antiques including furniture, china, silver, jewellery, clocks, lighting, paintings and decorative items.* LOC: From railway station, in town centre. PARK: Easy, own. TEL: 01273 474842; fax - 01273 846797. VAT: Stan.

Cliffe Antiques Centre
47 Cliffe High St. BN7 2AN. (M. Nash). Est. 1984. Open 9.30-5. SIZE: Medium - 16 dealers. *STOCK: General antiques, £5-£1,000.* LOC: Follow town centre signs, turning left 200 yds. past Safeways. PARK: Easy. TEL: 01273 473266.

Lewes continued

Cliffe Gallery Antiques
39 Cliffe High St. BN7 2AN. (Grimes & Hayward). Open 9.30-5. *STOCK: 18th-20th C furniture and objects, including pine, mahogany, oak, china and lighting.* TEL: 01273 471877.

A. & Y. Cumming
84 High St. BN7 1XN. Est. 1976. Open 10-5, Sat. 10-5.30. *STOCK: Antiquarian and out of print books.* TEL: 01273 472319. SER: Buys at auction.

The Drawing Room
53 High St. BN7 1XE. Open 9.30-5.30. SIZE: Medium. *STOCK: Furniture, pictures, objets d'art.* TEL: 01273 478560.

The Emporium Antique Centre
42 Cliffe High St. (Doyle and Madigan). Open 9.30-5, Sun. (Easter-Christmas) 11-4. SIZE: 48 dealers. *STOCK: Furniture, pictures, clocks, collectables, books, jewellery, Art Nouveau and Deco, decorative arts, vintage and collector's toys, Royal Winton.* TEL: 01273 486866.

Felix Gallery
Corner of Sun St. and Lancaster St. BN7 2QB. (W.S.H. and Mrs M.M. Whitehead). Est. 1981. Open 10-6, Sun. 12-6. SIZE: Small. *STOCK: Cats only - pottery, porcelain, bronze and silver, pictures, general objets d'art, English and Continental.* LOC: 2 mins. from town centre. PARK: Nearby. TEL: 01273 472668; home - same.

Fifteenth Century Bookshop
99 High St. BN7 1XH. (S. Mirabaud). Est. 1938. Open 10-5.30. *STOCK: Antiquarian and general secondhand books, especially children's and illustrated; prints and teddies.* TEL: 01273 474160.

Bob Hoare Pine Antiques
Unit Q, Phoenix Place, North St. BN7 2DQ. Open 8-6, Sat. 9-2. *STOCK: Pine.* TEL: 01273 480557; fax - 01273 471298.

Lewes Antique Centre
20 Cliffe High St. BN7 2AH. (Jamie Pettit). Est. 1968. Open 9.30-5. SIZE: Large - 59 stallholders. *STOCK: Furniture, china, copper and metalware, glass, clocks, architectural salvage.* LOC: A27 from Brighton, 2nd roundabout into Lewes, end of tunnel turn left, then next left, next right into Phoenix car park. 100m. walk to Cliffe High Street. PARK: Easy. TEL: 01273 476148/472173. SER: Shipping; stripping; restoration; valuation.

Lewes Flea Market
14a Market St. Est. 1995. Open daily including Sun. SIZE: Large. *STOCK: Bric-a-brac, furniture, collectables, 18th-20th C, £5-£1,000.* LOC: 50 metres north of monument. TEL: 01273 480328.

Lewes continued

Pastorale Antiques
15 Malling St. and 33 Cliffe High St. BN7 2RA. (O. Soucek). Open 9.30-6 or by appointment. SIZE: Large. *STOCK: Pine and European country furniture, Georgian and Victorian mahogany and decorative items and garden items.* TEL: 01273 473259; home - 01435 863044; fax - 01273 473259.

Southdown Antiques
48 Cliffe High St. BN7 2AN. (Miss P.I. and K.A. Foster). Est. 1969. Open by appointment. SIZE: Medium. *STOCK: Small antiques, especially 18th-19th C English, Continental and Oriental porcelain, objets d'art, works of art, glass, papier mâché trays, silver plate, £50-£350,000; reproduction and interior decor items.* LOC: A27. One-way street north. PARK: Easy. TEL: 01273 472439. VAT: Stan/Spec.

NEWHAVEN

Newhaven Flea Market
28 South Way. BN9 9LA. (R. Mayne and A. Wilkinson). Est. 1971. Open every day 10-5.30 except 25th Dec. *STOCK: Victoriana, Edwardian, bric-a-brac.* TEL: 01273 517207/516065.

Leonard Russell
21 Kings Ave., Mount Pleasant. BN9 0NB. Resident. Est. 1981. Open by appointment. SIZE: Small. *STOCK: English pottery figures, groups, animals, Toby jugs, 1750-1830.* LOC: 500 yards from A259 South Coast Rd., 3/4 mile from town centre. PARK: Easy. TEL: 01273 515153. SER: Valuations; buys at auction (pottery).

NUTLEY

Nutley Antiques
Libra House, High Street. TN22 3NF. (Liza Hall and Anne-Marie Dickinson). Open 10-5, Sun. and Bank Hols. 1.30-5. SIZE: Small. *STOCK: Country and cottage furniture, £10-£1,000; decorative items, £1-£400; prints, oils, watercolours, £5-£500; all 19th C to 1930.* LOC: A22 between East Grinstead and Uckfield. PARK: Easy. TEL: 01825 713220. VAT: Stan.

PEVENSEY

The Old Mint House LAPADA
High St. BN24 5LF. (J.C. and A.J. Nicholson). Est. 1901. Open 9-5.30, Sat. by appointment. SIZE: Large + export warehouse. *STOCK: Furniture - period, Victorian, Edwardian and shipping; porcelain, clocks, barometers, 18th-19th C, £20-£10,000.* LOC: A259 coast road, 1 mile from Eastbourne. PARK: Easy. TEL: 01323 762337; fax - 01323 762337; e-mail - minthouse@mistral.co.uk. SER: Worldwide container packing; Victoria trains met at Polegate station. VAT: Stan/Spec.

PEVENSEY BAY

Murray Brown

The Studio, Norman Rd. BN24 6JE. (G. Murray-Brown). Open by appointment only. *STOCK: Paintings and prints.* TEL: 01323 764298. SER: Valuations; restorations; cleaning; conservation.

POLEGATE

Graham Price Antiques Ltd

4 Chaucer Industrial Estate, Dittons Rd. BN26 6JD. Open 9-6. SIZE: Large. *STOCK: Mainly furniture - pine, country, decorative, French, Irish, European, period and Victorian oak, mahogany and walnut; bric-a-brac and kitchen-alia.* LOC: Between Hastings and Brighton on A27. TEL: 01323 487167; fax - 01323 483904. SER: Export, packing, shipping and courier; restorations.

E. Stacy-Marks Limited BADA

"The Flint Rooms", P O Box 808. BN26 5ST. Est. 1889. SIZE: Large. *STOCK: Paintings, English, Dutch and Continental schools, 18th-20th C.* TEL: 01323 482156; fax - 01323 482513. VAT: Stan.

ROTTINGDEAN

Trade Wind

Little Crescent. BN2 7GF. (R. Morley Smith). Est. 1974. Open by appointment only. *STOCK: Caddy and sifter spoons, wine labels and other interesting items, including coloured glass, Bristol blue, green and amethyst; small furniture, George III to Victoria.* TEL: 01273 301177.

RYE

Bragge and Sons

Landgate House. TN31 7LH. (N.H. and J.R. Bragge). Est. 1840. Open 9-5. CL: Tues. *STOCK: 18th C furniture and works of art.* LOC: Entrance to town - Landgate. TEL: 01797 223358. SER: Valuations; restorations. VAT: Spec.

Herbert Gordon Gasson

The Lion Galleries, Lion St. TN31 7LB. (T.J. Booth). Est. 1909. Open 9-1 and 2-5.30. CL: Tues. pm. SIZE: Large. *STOCK: 17th-18th C oak and walnut; Staffordshire and Chinese porcelain.* Not Stocked: Silver and glass. PARK: Easy. TEL: 01797 222208. SER: Restorations. VAT: Stan/Spec.

Landgate Antiques

22 Landgate. TN31 7LH. Resident. (J. Jones). Est. 1974. Open 10-5.30. *STOCK: Furniture, decorative items, clocks, desks.* TEL: 01797 224746.

Rye continued

Ann Lingard - Rope Walk Antiques

LAPADA

18-22 Rope Walk. TN31 7NA. Est. 1972. SIZE: Large. ***STOCK: English antique pine furniture and accessories; kitchen shop; garden tools and accessories, some architectural items.*** **Not Stocked: Jewellery, silver and plate. PARK: Own, and public next door. TEL: 01797 223486; fax - 01797 224700. VAT: Stan.**

Rye Antiques

93 High St. TN31 7JN. (Mrs D. Turner). Est. 1966. Open 9.30-5.30. CL: Sun. except by appointment. SIZE: Small. *STOCK: Small oak, walnut and mahogany furniture, 17th-19th C, £50-£1,000; metalware, jewellery, silver and plate, 18th-19th C, £5-£1,000.* Not Stocked: Coins, bric-a-brac. PARK: Easy. TEL: 01797 222259.

SEAFORD

Molly Alexander

Crouch House, Crouch Lane. BN25 1PX. Est. 1967. *STOCK: Paintings, watercolours and antiquities.* LOC: Opposite new Constitutional Club. PARK: Opposite. TEL: 01323 896577.

The Courtyard Antiques Market

15 High St. BN25 1PD. (Mrs V.E. Finch). Open 9-5, Wed. 9-1. SIZE: Medium - 13 dealers. *STOCK: General antiques and collectables.* TEL: 01323 892091.

The Old House

15/17 High St. BN25 1PD. (S.M. Barrett). Est. 1928. Open 9-5, Wed. 9-1. SIZE: Large. *STOCK: 18th-20th C furniture, china and glass, £5-£5,000.* LOC: Near railway station. PARK: Opposite in Pelham Yard. TEL: 01323 892091/893795. SER: Valuations; restorations (furniture); shippers. VAT: Stan/Spec.

Seaford continued

Seaford's "Barn Collectors' Market" and Studio Bookshop

The Barn, Church Lane. BN25 1HL. Est. 1967. Open 9.30-5. SIZE: Several dealers. *STOCK: Collectables, ephemera, books, post and cigarette cards.* LOC: Off High St. TEL: 01323 890010.

ST. LEONARDS-ON-SEA

Aarquebus Antiques

37 & 46 Norman Rd. TN38 0EJ. Resident. (Mr and Mrs G. Jukes). Est. 1957. Open 9.30-5, Sat. 9.30-1. CL: Wed. SIZE: Medium. *STOCK: Furniture, 18th C, £500-£1,000; shipping goods, Victorian to 1930, £5-£500; glass, gold and silver, 18th-19th C, £5-£1,000.* LOC: Take A2100 to St. Leonards-on-Sea, turn right after main P.O. PARK: Easy. TEL: 01424 433267; mobile - 0410 630486. SER: Valuations.

The Book Jungle

24 North St. TN38 0EX. (M. Gowen). Est. 1988. Open 10-5. CL: Wed. SIZE: Medium. *STOCK: Secondhand books.* LOC: Just off seafront. PARK: Nearby. TEL: 01424 421187.

Chapel Antiques

1 London Rd. TN37 6AE. (Mrs. Gordana). Est. 1946. Open 10-5. *STOCK: Furniture, paintings, militaria, decorative items, 18th-19th C, £20-£10,000.* PARK: Easy. TEL: 01424 440025. SER: Valuations; restorations (furniture).

Nicholas Cole Antiques

7 Grand Parade. TN38 0DA. Est. 1973. Open 9-6, Sat. 9-1 or by appointment, Sun. by appointment. SIZE: Medium. *STOCK: Victorian, Edwardian and 1920's oak and mahogany furniture, £50-£500.* LOC: A259 junction with A21. PARK: Easy. TEL: 01424 420671; home - 01424 461031. SER: Valuations; restorations. VAT: Stan.

Gensing Antiques

70 Norman Rd.TN38 0EJ. (Peter Cawson). Open normal shop hours and by appointment. *STOCK: General antiques especially early Chinese furniture and other Oriental items.* TEL: 01424 424145/714981.

St. Leonards-on-Sea continued

The Hastings Antique Centre

59-61 Norman Rd. TN38 0EG. (R.J. Amstad). Open 10-5.30, Sun. by appointment. TEL: 01424 428561. Below are listed some of the dealers at this centre.

R. J. Amstad
Furniture.

Sarah Brixton
Lace and linen, jewellery.

Clive Brown
Pictures, prints, decorative furniture.

Terry Cuthbert
Furniture.

S. Dahms
Clocks.

Dee's Antiques
Decorative items.

P. Few
Decorative French items.

Brenda Fox and Bridget Howett
Decorative items.

P. Grant
French furniture, decorative items and pine.

K. Gumbrell
Decorative items.

G. Mennis
Sporting, leather goods.

Steven Owen
Period furniture.

Robert Paul Antiques
Furniture and shipping goods.

V. Russell
Gold and silver.

Tiffany Antiques
Furniture.

S. Young
Furniture and smalls.

Helgato

121 Bohemia Rd. TN37 6RL. (Helga E. and R.J. Nicholls). Est. 1961. Open by appointment only. SIZE: Medium. *STOCK: Porcelain, glass, objects of vertu and art, books, prints and maps, 1650-1890, £2-£500.* LOC: A21. TEL: 01424 423049.

St. Leonards-on-Sea continued

Monarch Antiques

5, 6, 9 and 19 Grand Parade. TN38 0DD. (J.H. King). Est. 1983. Open Mon.-Fri. 9-5, or any other time by appointment. SIZE: Large. *STOCK: General furniture, especially 1930's oak furniture for the European and Japanese markets.* LOC: A259. PARK: Easy. TEL: Home - 01424 214158/ 460010; mobiles - 0802 217842/213081; pager - 01425 253204. SER: Restorations.

K. Nunn

at Chapel Antiques, Chapel House, 1 London Rd. TN37 6RN. Open 9.30-5.30. *STOCK: General antiques, weapons, ship and aero models, toys and unusual items.* TEL: 01424 431093. SER: Buys at auction.

John H. Yorke Antiques

Filsham Farmhouse, 111 Harley Shute Rd. TN38 8BY. (J.H. Yorke). Open 9-5.30. *STOCK: Furniture for trade, export and shipping.* TEL: 01424 433109. VAT: Stan.

UCKFIELD

Ivan R. Deverall

Duval House, The Glen, Cambridge Way. TN22 2AB. *STOCK: Maps.* TEL: 01825 762474. SER: Catalogue available; colouring.

Ringles Cross Antiques

Ringles Cross. TN22 1HF. Resident. (C. and J. Dunford). Est. 1965. Open 9.30-6 or by appointment. *STOCK: English furniture, 17th-18th C and accessories; Oriental items.* LOC: 1 mile north of Uckfield. PARK: Own. TEL: 01825 762909.

WADHURST

Park View Antiques

High St., Durgates. TN5 6DE. (B. Ross). Est. 1985. Open 10-5. CL: Wed. SIZE: Medium. *STOCK: Pine, oak and country furniture, 17th-19th C, £100-£1,500; decorative items, 1930's, £25-£150; iron and metalware, 17th-19th C, £25-£250.* LOC: On B2099 Frant-Hurst Green road. PARK: Easy. TEL: 01892 783630; fax - 01892 740264; home - 01892 740264. SER: Valuations; restorations (furniture).

WILLINGDON, Nr. Eastbourne

Skyline Interiors

122-124 Wish Hill. BN22 0LN. (Mrs J. Innes). Open Mon., Tues., Thurs. 9.30-1 and 2-4, Wed. 9.30-12, Fri. 9.30-1, Sat. 10-4.30, Sun. 2-4.30. SIZE: Medium. *STOCK: Art Deco, £5-£2,000.* LOC: Between Polegate and Eastbourne on the A22. PARK: Easy. TEL: 01323 504600; fax - same; home - 01323 501923. SER: Valuations; buys at auction. FAIRS: Ardingly.

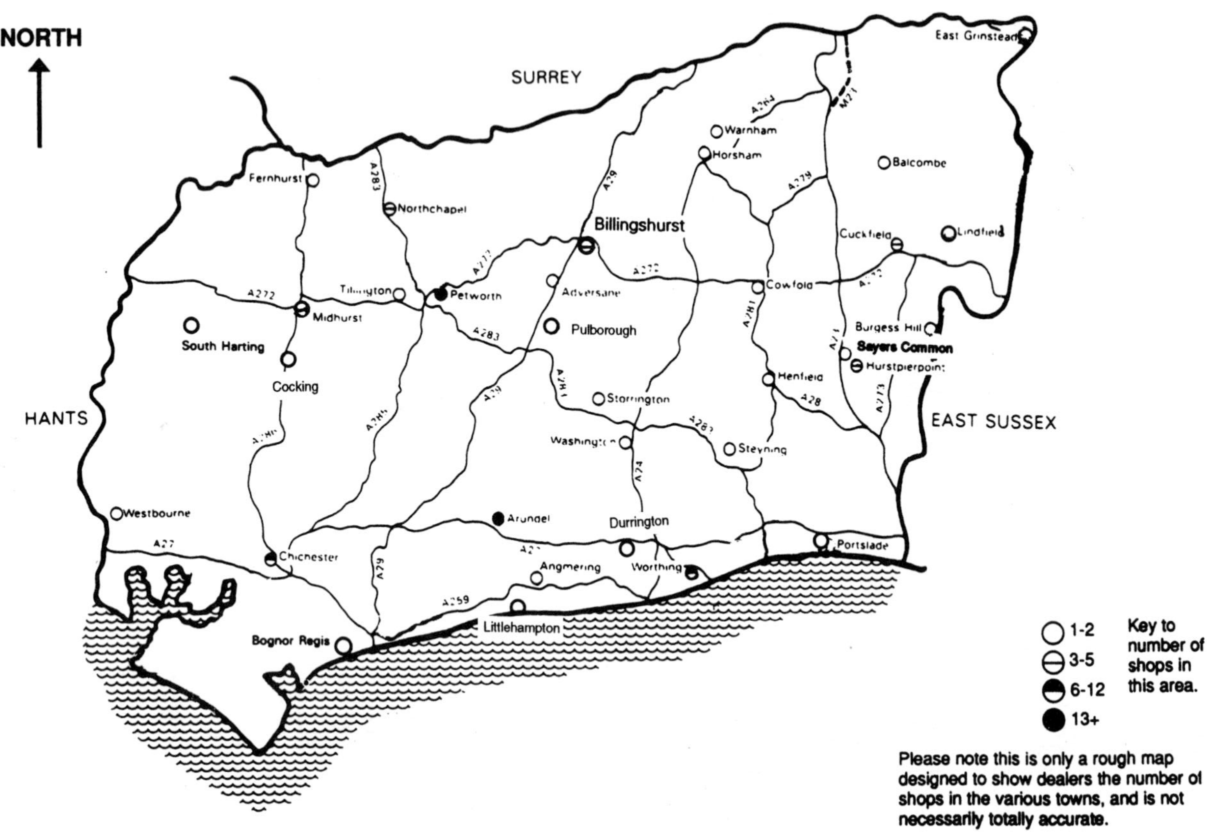
NORTH
SURREY
EAST SUSSEX
HANTS
East Grinstead
Warnham
Horsham
Balcombe
Fernhurst
Northchapel
Billingshurst
Cuckfield
Lindfield
Petworth
Adversane
Cowfold
Midhurst
South Harting
Pulborough
Burgess Hill
Sayers Common
Hurstpierpoint
Cocking
Henfield
Storrington
Washington
Steyning
Westbourne
Arundel
Durrington
Portslade
Chichester
Angmering
Worthing
Littlehampton
Bognor Regis
A283
A272
A29
A281
A279
A24
A27
A259
A28
M23
1-2
3-5
6-12
13+
Key to number of shops in this area.
Please note this is only a rough map designed to show dealers the number of shops in the various towns, and is not necessarily totally accurate.

ADVERSANE, Nr. Billingshurst

Old House Antique Centre

Old House. RH14 9JJ. Open daily including Sun. SIZE: 30+ stallholders. *STOCK: General antiques and collectors' items.* PARK: Easy. TEL: 01403 782186/783594.

ANGMERING

Bygones

The Square. BN16 4EQ. (R.A. and Mrs L.R. Whittaker). Est. 1965. Open Tues. and Thurs. 10-1 and 2.15-5, Sat. 10-12. SIZE: Medium. *STOCK: Furniture, £50-£2,500; china, £5-£750; silver, £10-£250; linen, £5-£75; all 1790-1940.* LOC: A280. PARK: Easy. TEL: 01903 786152; home - same. SER: Valuations; buys at auction (furniture).

ARUNDEL

Antiquities

5 Tarrant St. BN18 9DG. (Ian and Christina Fenwick). Est. 1990. Open 10-5 or by appointment. SIZE: Medium + 3 warehouses. *STOCK: English, French and Irish country furniture, 19th C, some mahogany and fruitwood; unusual, decorative and painted items, majolica, French mirrors, pond yachts, luggage.* LOC: Just off town square. PARK: Nearby. TEL: 01903 884355; fax - same. SER: Shipping. VAT: Stan/Spec.

Arundel Clocks

Lasseters Corner, High St. BN18 9AB. (F.M. Henderson). Open 9.30-1 and 2-5. SIZE: Small. *STOCK: Longcase clocks, £1,500-£6,000; dial clocks, £300-£4,000; mantel clocks, £250-£1,500.* LOC: Corner of High St. and Mill Lane. PARK: Easy. TEL: 01903 884525; fax - same. SER: Valuations; restorations (clocks including dials). VAT: Spec.

Baynton-Williams

37A High St. BN18 9AG. (R.H. and S.C. Baynton-Williams). Est. 1946. Open 10-6. *STOCK: Maps, views, sporting, marine and decorative prints.* TEL: 01903 883588; fax - same. SER: Valuations; cataloguing. VAT: Stan/Spec.

Richard Davidson Antiques

Romsey House, 51 Maltravers St. BN18 9BQ. Open by appointment only. *STOCK: Fine furniture, decorative accessories.* TEL: 01903 883141; fax - 01903 883914. SER: Interior decoration. VAT: Spec.

Faringdon Gallery

27 Tarrant St. BN18 9DG. (Mr and Mrs G.E. Lott). Est. 1970. Open 10-5, Sun. and Mon. by appointment. SIZE: Small. *STOCK: Watercolours and etchings, late 19th C to contemporary, £100-£3,000.* LOC: From A27, first right down High St. hill. PARK: 100 yards at rear. TEL: 01903 882047; home - 01243 554572. SER: Valuations; restorations; buys at auction (watercolours and etchings).

Arundel continued

Pat Golding

6 Castle Mews, Tarrant St. BN18 9DG. Open 10-1 and 2-5. *STOCK: Ceramics and glass, 18th-20th C.*

Phyllis Gordon

BN18 9DW. Est. 1972. Open by appointment only. *STOCK: Georgian and Victorian furniture; button back chairs, porcelain, silver, glass and clocks.* TEL: 01903 885064.

Tom Littlefair Antiques

5 River Rd. BN18 9DG. Open: Winter - 10.30-4.30, Sun. 11-4; Summer - every day 10.30-5.30. *STOCK: Furniture, decorative fine art.* PARK: Easy. TEL: 01903 884774.

Sussex Fine Art

7 Castle Mews, Tarrant St. BN18 9DG. (G.C. and P.A. Miller). Est. 1987. Open Fri. and Sat. 10.30-5.30, Sun. 12-5, other days by appointment. SIZE: Small. *STOCK: English watercolours, 1760-1930, from £200.* LOC: Off High St. PARK: 50yds. TEL: 01903 884055. SER: Framing; buys at auction. VAT: Spec.

Spencer Swaffer — LAPADA

30 High St. BN18 9AB. Est. 1974. Open 9-6, other times by appointment. SIZE: Large. *STOCK: Unusual decorative and traditional items, brass, blue and white, Staffordshire, dinner services, pine, oak dressers, marble tables, bamboo, shop fittings, candlesticks, majolica, French, English, painted and garden furniture.* PARK: Easy. TEL: 01903 882132; fax - 01903 884564. VAT: Stan/Spec.

Tarrant Street Antique Centre

Nineveh House, Tarrant St. BN18 9DG. (Miss J. Millar). Open 10-5, Sun. 11-5. SIZE: Large - 25 dealers. *STOCK: Wide range of general antiques including Edwardian and Victorian, country and pine furniture, jewellery and silver, paintings and prints, china and glass, luggage and Oriental rugs.* LOC: Off A27 and A29 into town then second left off High St. PARK: Own forecourt. TEL: 01903 884307. SER: Valuations; restorations.

Treasure House Antiques and Collectors Market

31b High St. and Crown Yard Car Park. BN18 9AG. Est. 1972. Open 9-5; Crown Yard Sat. 9-5 only. CL: Wed. *STOCK: Victoriana, domestic bygones, porcelain, Goss and crested china models, toys, Royal commemoratives, lace, lamps, curios, metalware, small furniture.* PARK: Easy. TEL: 01903 507446/883101/882908.

The Walking Stick Shop

Stuart Thompson (Fine Canes) 39 Tarrant St. BN18 9DG. Est. 1981. Open 8.30-5.30, Wed. 8.30-1, Sun. pm. by appointment. SIZE: Medium. *STOCK: Walking sticks and canes, 1620 to date, £10-£2,000.* LOC: Off High St. PARK: Easy. TEL: 01903 883796; home - 01903 882713; fax - 01903 884491. SER: Valuations; buys at auction (canes). VAT: Stan.

Arundel continued

Whitehouse Antique Interiors
4 Tarrant Square, Tarrant St. BN18 9DE. (G.G. Cross). Open 10-5. *STOCK: Furniture, porcelain, decorative items.* TEL: 01903 882443.

BALCOMBE

Woodall and Emery Ltd
Haywards Heath Rd. RH17 6PG. Est. 1884. TEL: 01444 811608. VAT: Stan.

BILLINGSHURST

Susan and Robert Botting LAPADA
Great Grooms Antiques Centre, Great Grooms, Parbrook. RH14 9EU. Est. 1979. Open every day. SIZE: Medium. *STOCK: Oil paintings and watercolours, 19th and 20th C, £100-£25,000.* LOC: Half-mile south of Billingshurst on A29. TEL: 01243 584515; home - same. SER: Valuations; restorations. FAIRS: NEC; LAPADA; Claridges; Petworth.

Great Grooms Antique Centre
Great Grooms, Parbrook. RH14 9EU. Est. 1983. Open Mon.-Sat. 9.30-5.30, Sun. 10-6. SIZE: 50 dealers. *STOCK: Wide variety of specialist dealers in 18th-19th C English and Continental town and country furniture, pottery and porcelain, silver and plate, works of art, metalware, glass, clocks, Oriental, oils and watercolours, prints, arms and armour, books, clocks and watches, scientific instruments.* LOC: A29 south of Billingshurst. PARK: Easy. TEL: 01403 786202; fax - 01403 786224. SER: Valuations; restorations (furniture, pictures, silver and jewellery); buys at auction. VAT: Spec.

Lannards Gallery
Okehurst Lane. RH14 9HR. (Mr and Mrs Derek Sims). Open by appointment; open every day during exhibitions. *STOCK: Watercolours, oils and furniture, from 1850.* TEL: 01403 782692. SER: Exhibitions held, please telephone for details.

Michael Wakelin and Helen Linfield BADA LAPADA
P.O Box 48. RH14 0YZ. Est. 1968. Open any time by appointment only. *STOCK: Fine English and Continental formal and country furniture - walnut, fruitwoods, faded mahogany and other exotic woods; early brass, bronze, iron and steel; wood carvings, treen, needlework, naïve pictures and lighting.* TEL: 01403 700004; fax - same. VAT: Stan/Spec.

BOGNOR REGIS

Gough Bros. Art Shop and Gallery
71 High St. PO21 1RZ. (S. Neal). Est. 1916. CL: Wed. pm. SIZE: Medium. *STOCK: Watercolours, £50-£1,000; oils, £100-£1,500; miniatures, £150-£400; all 19th-20th C.* LOC: Off High St., behind Unicorn public house. PARK: Nearby. TEL: 01243 823773. SER: Valuations; restorations (oils and watercolours, frames and gilding). VAT: Stan/Spec.

Bognor Regis continued

BURGESS HILL

British Antique Replicas LAPADA
School Close, Queen Elizabeth Ave. RH15 9RX. Est. 1962. Open 9-5.30. SIZE: Large. *STOCK: Furniture, £100-£20,000.* LOC: 3 miles west A23. PARK: Easy. TEL: 01444 245577. SER: Bespoke furniture. VAT: Stan.

CHICHESTER

Almshouses Arcade
19 The Hornet. Est. 1983. Open 9.30-4.30. LOC: 200yds. from Cattle Market at eastern end of city. On one-way system (A286) just before traffic lights at Market Ave. PARK: Easy. Below are listed the dealers at these premises.

Antics
(P. German). *General antiques and collectables.* TEL: 01243 786327.

R.K. Barnett
Antiques and collectables, furniture. TEL: 01243 528089.

Helter Skelter
Records, tapes, CDs. TEL: 01243 771744.

Overlord
(D. Rowe). *Militaria, toys and general antiques, £5-£100.* TEL: 01243 774613.

Panormo Antiques
(M. Panormo) *General antiques and collectables.*

Squirrel Antiques
(L. Hampshire) *Small antiques, toys, collectables, etc.*

Yesteryears
(J.A. Cook) *Lighting (oil), general antiques and collectables.* TEL: 01243 771994.

Chichester Antiques Centre
46-48 The Hornet. PO10 4JG. (Andrew Davies). Est. 1994. Open 10-5, Sun. 11-5. SIZE: 50 stalls. *STOCK: General antiques and collectables, 50p to £10,000.* LOC: M27 onto A27 to town. PARK: Loading only and nearby. TEL: 01243 530100. SER: Clock restoration on premises.

County Place Antiques
9 South St. PO19 1EH. (G. Hawkins). Est. 1991. Open 9.30-5. SIZE: Large. *STOCK: Furniture, porcelain and fine art, 18th C to 1945, £100-£15,000.* LOC: 50 yards from Market Cross, near cathedral. PARK: South St. TEL: 01243 537699. SER: Valuations; restorations (furniture and porcelain); buys at auction.

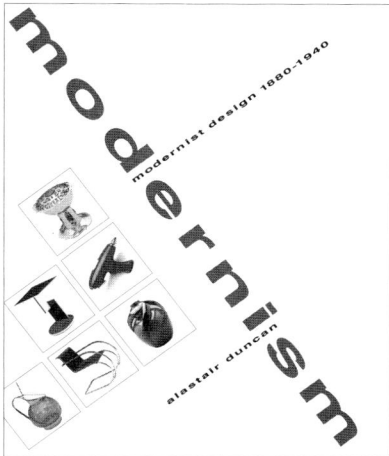

Chichester continued

The Delightful Muddle
82 Fishbourne Rd. West. PO19 3JL. Open Wed. 1-5, Thurs.-Sat. 10-5. *STOCK: China, glass, objets d'art, Victorian and Edwardian, £1-£100; lace £1-£50; linen, general antiques and bric-a-brac, £3-£65.* LOC: 1 mile west of Chichester on A259, opposite Fishbourne P.O & Stores. PARK: Easy.

Frensham House Antiques
Hunston. PO20 6NX. (J. and M. Riley). Est. 1966. Open 9-6. *STOCK: English furniture, 1700-1830, £500-£6,000; clocks, paintings, copper.* LOC: One mile south of Chichester by-pass on B2145. PARK: Easy. TEL: 01243 782660.

Gems Antiques
39 West St. PO19 1RP. (M.L. Hancock). Open 10.30-1 and 2.30-5.30. *STOCK: Period furniture, Staffordshire and porcelain figures, glass and pictures.* TEL: 01243 786173.

Peter Hancock Antiques
40-41 West St. PO19 1RP. Articles on coins. Est. 1950. Open 10.30-1 and 2.30-5.30. SIZE: Medium. *STOCK: Silver, jewellery, porcelain, furniture, £20-£2,000; pictures, glass, clocks, books, £20-£1,500; all 18th-19th C; enthnographica, Art Nouveau, Art Deco, 19th-20th C, £5-£500.* LOC: From Chichester Cross, 17 doors past Cathedral. PARK: Easy. TEL: 01243 786173. SER: Valuations. VAT: Stan/Spec.

Heritage Antiques
77D, 83 and 84 St. Pancras. PO19 4LS. (D.R. and D.A. Grover). Open 9.30-5.30. *STOCK: Furniture and decorative items.* TEL: 01243 783796.

W.D. Priddy Antiques
Unit 6 Terminus Mill, Terminus Rd. PO19 2UN. Open 9.30-5 by appointment. SIZE: Large. *STOCK: Oak, mahogany and walnut furniture, mid-19th C to pre-war and shipping, £500-£1,000.* LOC: Runs off A27 Chichester bypass. PARK: Easy. TEL: 01243 783960; fax - same; home - 01705 667436. FAIRS: Newark; Ardingly. VAT: Stan.

St. Pancras Antiques
150 St. Pancras. PO19 1SH. (R.F. and M. Willatt). Est. 1980. Open 9.30-1 and 2-5. CL: Thurs. pm. SIZE: Small. *STOCK: Arms and armour, militaria, medals, documents, uniforms and maps, 1600-1914, £5-£3,000; china, pottery and ceramics, 1800-1930, £2-£500; small furniture, 17th-19th C, £20-£1,000; coins, ancient to date.* Not Stocked: Silver and carpets. TEL: 01243 787645. SER: Valuations; restorations (arms and armour); buys at auction (militaria).

COCKING, Nr. Midhurst

The Victorian Brass Bedstead Company
Hoe Copse. GU29 0HL. Resident. (David Woolley). Est. 1970. Open by appointment. SIZE: Large. *STOCK: Victorian and Edwardian brass and iron bedsteads, bases and mattresses, 19th-20th C, £300-£3,5000.* LOC: Right behind village Post Office, 3/4 mile left turning to Hoe Copse. PARK: Easy. TEL: 01730 812287. SER: Valuations; restorations (brass and iron bedsteads). VAT: Stan.

COWFOLD

Squire's Pantry Pine and Antiques
Station Rd. RH13 8DA. (L.M. Lasham). Open 10-1 and 2-5. *STOCK: Pine.* TEL: 01403 864869; fax - 01403 865283. VAT: Stan/Spec.

CUCKFIELD

David Foord-Brown Antiques **BADA LAPADA**
High St. RH17 5JU. Est. 1988. Open 10-5.30. SIZE: Medium. *STOCK: Furniture, 1750-1880, £500-£10,000; decorative objects.* Not Stocked: Country furniture. LOC: A272. PARK: Easy. TEL: 01444 414418.

Richard Usher Antiques
23 South St. RH17 5LB. Est. 1978. Open 10-5.30 and at other times by appointment. CL: Wed. pm. and Sat. pm. SIZE: Medium. *STOCK: Furniture, 17th-19th C, £50-£3,000; decorative items.* LOC: A272. PARK: Easy. TEL: 01444 451699. SER: Valuations; restorations.

DURRINGTON

Mary Gregory's
9 Manor Parade, Farthington Rd. BN13 2JP. Est. 1990. Open 10-4, Sat. 9-3. CL: Wed. *STOCK: Furniture, Royal Doulton.* TEL: 01903 264922.

EAST GRINSTEAD

The Antique Atlas
31A High St. RH19 3AF. View by appointment. *STOCK: Maps, charts, plans and views worldwide.* LOC: Entrance Cantelupe Rd. TEL: 01342 315813.

The Antique Print Shop
11 Middle Row. RH19 3AX. (A.A.W. Daszewski and Mrs A.C. Keddie). Est. 1988. Open 9.30-6. SIZE: Small. *STOCK: Prints, pre-1880, £10-£200; maps especially British county, 1500-1870, £20-£1,000; English watercolours and drawings, 1700-1880, £100-£1,000.* LOC: On island in middle High St., opposite St. Swithins church. PARK: Lewes Rd. TEL: 01342 410501; fax - 01342 410795. SER: Restorations; framing. FAIRS: Park Lane Hotel, London (Sundays); NEC. VAT: Stan.

FERNHURST, Nr. Haslemere

Sheelagh Hamilton

9b Midhurst Rd. GU27 3EE. Open 9-5, Sat. 9-1, Sun. by appointment. *STOCK: Period furniture, pictures.* LOC: A286 village centre. TEL: 01428 653253.

HENFIELD

Alexander Antiques

Post House, Small Dole. BN5 9XE. (Mrs J.A. Goodinge). Est. 1971. CL: Sun. except by appointment. SIZE: Medium. *STOCK: Country furniture, brass, copper, pewter, samplers, small collectors' and decorative items, treen.* LOC: A2037. PARK: Easy. TEL: 01273 493121; home - same. VAT: Stan/Spec.

HORSHAM

L.E. Lampard and Sons

23-25 Springfield Rd. RH12 2PG. Est. 1920. Open 8-1 and 2-5. SIZE: Medium. *STOCK: Mahogany and oak furniture, firebacks, grates.* TEL: 01403 254012. VAT: Stan/Spec.

HURSTPIERPOINT

The Clock Shop LAPADA

34-36 High St. Open 9-6, or by appointment. CL: Sat. *STOCK: 18th-19th longcase and table clocks.* TEL: 01273 832081; mobile - 0860 230888. SER: Restorations (clocks and furniture).

Julian Antiques

124 High St. BN6 9DX. Est. 1964. Open 9-6. CL: Sat. *STOCK: French 19th C clocks, bronzes, Art Deco, fireplaces, mirrors, furniture.* TEL: 01273 832145.

Michael Miller

The Lamb, 8 Cuckfield Rd. BN6 9RU. (M. and V. Miller). Est. 1880. Open Sat. 9.30-5, other times appointment advisable. *STOCK: Arms and armour, post-1460, from £5; general antiques.* TEL: 01273 834567. SER: Buys at auction; exporters.

LINDFIELD

Lindfield Galleries - David Adam BADA

62 High St. RH16 2HL. Est. 1972. Open 9.30-5.30. *STOCK: Oriental carpets.* TEL: 01444 483817. VAT: Stan/Spec.

LITTLEHAMPTON

The Round Pond

Faux Cottage, 4a Selborne Rd. BN17 5NN. (John Haynes and Kay Meader). Est. 1962. Open by appointment. SIZE: Small. *STOCK: Vintage model boats especially yachts, 19th C to 1950's, £50-£2,000.* PARK: Easy. TEL: 01903 714261; home - same. SER: Valuations.

MIDHURST

Churchill Clocks

Rumbolds Hill. GU29 9BZ. (W.P. and Dr. E. Tyrrell). Open 9-5, Wed. 9-1. *STOCK: Clocks and furniture.* LOC: Main street. TEL: 01730 813891; fax - same. SER: Clock restoration.

Curfew Antiques Centre

Knockhundred Row. GU29 9DQ. (D.M. Brindle-Wood-Williams). Est. 1974. Open 9.30-5. TEL: 01730 814231.

The Old Town Hall Gallery

Market Square. GU29 9NJ. (W.J. Pannett). Opening hours are variable, prior telephone call advisable. SIZE: Medium. *STOCK: Furniture, paintings, Art Deco, china, vintage toys.* PARK: Easy. TEL: 01730 817166.

West Street Antiques & Presents

West St. (Janet Lintott and Angela Campbell). Est. 1984. Open 9.30-1 and 2-4.30. SIZE: Medium. *STOCK: Decorative and country furniture, brass, pottery and porcelain; quilts, rugs, £5-£1,000.* PARK: Easy. TEL: 01730 815232. SER: Buys at auction.

NORTHCHAPEL, Nr. Petworth

Callingham Antiques

GU28 9HL. Est. 1979. Open 9-5.30. CL: Wed. SIZE: Medium. *STOCK: Furniture, 1700-1900, £10-£10,000.* LOC: London Road 5 miles north of Petworth. PARK: Easy. TEL: 01428 707379. SER: Valuations; restorations.

Expect to pay £300-£500 for the Returning Woodman pattern when it comes under Bonhams Knightsbridge sale of blue printed pottery on 21st April.

From an "Auction Preview" which appeared in the April 1998 issue of **Antique Collecting.**

PETWORTH

Majid Amini - Persian Carpet Gallery

LAPADA

Church St. GU28 0AD. Open 9.30-5. *STOCK: Old and new Oriental rugs and carpets.* LOC: A272. PARK: Nearby. TEL: 01798 343344; fax - 01798 342673. SER: Valuations; restorations; hand cleaning.

Angel Antiques

Church St. GU28 0AD. (Nick and Barbara Swanson). Open 10-5.30, Sun. by appointment. SIZE: Medium. *STOCK: Country furniture and associated items, 17th-19th C, £100-£6,000.* LOC: Opposite Petworth House and church. TEL: 01798 343306; fax - 01798 342665. VAT: Spec.

Bacchus Gallery

Lombard St. GU28 0AG. (R. and A. Gillett). Est. 1988. Open 10-1 and 2.30-5. SIZE: Small. *STOCK: Wine related items.* LOC: Cobbled street leading off town square. PARK: Town square. TEL: 01798 342844; fax - 01798 342634. SER: Buys at auction (as stock). VAT: Stan/Spec.

Baskerville Antiques BADA

Saddlers House, Saddlers Row. GU28 0AN. (A. and B. Baskerville). Est. 1978. Open 9.30-6, Sun. by appointment. SIZE: Medium. *STOCK: English clocks, barometers and furniture, £1,000-£20,000; decorative items and instruments, £500-£5,000; all 18th-19th C.* LOC: Town centre. PARK: Public, adjoining shop. TEL: 01798 342067; home - same; fax - 01798 343956. VAT: Spec.

Lesley Bragge Antiques LAPADA

Fairfield House, High St. GU28 0AU. Est. 1974. Open 10-1 and 2-5.30. SIZE: Medium. *STOCK: Decorative furniture, 18th-19th C; silver and plate, porcelain, textiles, ormolu, brass, copper, objets d'art, garden furniture.* LOC: Off Golden Square. PARK: Nearby. TEL: 01798 342324. SER: Valuations; restorations; upholstery. VAT: Stan/Spec.

The Canon Gallery BADA LAPADA

New St. (Jeremy Green and James Fergusson). Open 10-5.30. SIZE: Medium. *STOCK: Oils and watercolours, 18th-20th C, £500-£25,000.* LOC: Main road. PARK: Easy. TEL: 01798 344422. SER: Valuations; restoration. FAIRS: World of Watercolours; NEC; Harrogate; Olympia; New York; BADA. VAT: Spec.

J. Du Cros Antiques

1 Pound St. GU28 0DX. (J. and P. Du Cros). Est. 1982. Open 10-5.30, sometimes closed Wed. p.m. SIZE: Medium. *STOCK: English furniture, 1660-1900, £100-£5,000; treen, metalware, some glass.* LOC: Corner of Sadlers Row. PARK: Nearby. TEL: 01798 342071. VAT: Stan/Spec.

Petworth continued

The French Room

5 High St. Open 10-5.30, Sun. by appointment. *STOCK: 19th-20th C French furniture and decorative antiques.* TEL: 01798 344454.

Richard Gardner Antiques

Millhouse, Market Sq. and Swan House, Saddlers Row. GU28 0AN. PAADA. Resident. (Richard and Janice Gardner). Est. 1992. Open 10-5.30 including Sun. SIZE: Medium. *STOCK: Fine period furniture and works of art, up to £40,000; English and Continental porcelain, 18th-19th C, £500-£5,000; associated items, £50-£2,000.* PARK: 50 yards. TEL: 01798 343411/344463. VAT: Spec.

George House Gallery

George House, East St. GU28 0AB. (John Morgan). Est. 1993. Open 10-6, Sun. by appointment. CL: Some Mon. SIZE: Small. *STOCK: Prints and engravings, 18th-20th C, £5-£50; oils and watercolours, £50-£1,000; cartoons - country, sporting and fishing, to £50.* LOC: Opposite Petworth House and church. PARK: Easy. TEL: 01798 342312; fax/home - same. SER: Restorations; buys at auction.

Granville Antiques BADA

High St. GU28 0AU. (I.E.G. Miller). Est. 1979. Open 10-5.30, Wed. 10-2.30 or by appointment. SIZE: Medium. *STOCK: Period furniture, pre-1840, £50-£15,000; accessories and pictures.* Not Stocked: Militaria and jewellery. LOC: 100yds. from market square. PARK: Nearby. TEL: 01798 343250; mobile - 0966 279761. SER: Valuations (furniture); restorations (furniture); buys at auction. FAIRS: BADA. VAT: Spec.

William Hockley Antiques LAPADA

East St. GU28 0AB. (D. and V. Thrower). Est. 1974. *STOCK: Fine 18th to early 19th C furniture and decorative items; early English pottery.* TEL: 01798 343172.

Lombard Gallery

Lombard St. GU28 0AG. Est. 1974. Open 10-1 and 2-5. CL: Mon. *STOCK: Oils and watercolours, 1880-1930, £50-£2,500; illustrated art, travel and motoring books.* TEL: 01798 342040. VAT: Spec.

The Madison Gallery

Swan House, Market Sq. GU28 0AH. (L.A. Long). Open 10-5.30 including Sun. SIZE: Large. *STOCK: Furniture including decorative; pictures, accessories.* PARK: Easy. TEL: 01798 343638. SER: Restorations; upholstery. VAT: Stan/Spec.

Petworth Antique Market

East St. GU28 0AB. (D.M. Rayment). Est. 1968. Open 10-5.30. SIZE: Large - 36 dealers. *STOCK: General antiques, books, furniture, brass, copper, pictures, textiles.* LOC: Near church. PARK: Adjoining. TEL: 01798 342073. VAT: Stan/Spec.

Petworth continued

Red Lion Antiques

New St. GU28 0AS. (R. Wilson and D. Swanson). Est. 1981. Open 10-5.30. SIZE: Large. *STOCK: Antiques for the country home, oak, walnut and pine furniture, 17th-19th C, £100-£10,000.* LOC: Town centre. PARK: Easy. TEL: 01798 344485; fax - 01798 342367; e-mail - redlion@tangent.demon.co.uk; Web - http://.www.co.uk/ tangent/redlion. VAT: Spec.

Stewart Antiques

High St. GU28 0AU. (John and Sandra Moore). Est. 1984. Open 10-5.30, Sun. by appointment. SIZE: Medium. *STOCK: Stripped pine, Victorian, £25-£2,000; kitchenalia, Victorian, £5-£100; collectables, 19th-20th C, £1-£50.* LOC: Town centre. PARK: Easy. TEL: 01798 342136. SER: Valuations. VAT: Spec.

J.C. Tutt Antiques

Angel St. GU28 0BQ. Open 10-5. CL: Some Mon. SIZE: Large. *STOCK: Mahogany and country furniture and accessories.* PARK: Nearby. TEL: 01798 343221.

T.G. Wilkinson Antiques Ltd BADA

Lombard St. GU28 0AG. (T. and S. Wilkinson). Est. 1979. Open 10-5.30. SIZE: Medium. *STOCK: English and Continental furniture, paintings and works of art, 17th-19th C, £500-£15,000.* PARK: Town centre. TEL: 01798 344443. VAT: Stan/Spec.

PORTSLADE

J. Powell (Hove) Ltd LAPADA

20 Wellington Rd. BN4 1DN. Est. 1949. Open 7.30-5.30. CL: Sun. and Sat. pm. except by appointment. SIZE: Large. *STOCK: Bookcases, display cabinets, £110-£1,500; writing tables and desks, £120-£1,200; longcase and bracket clocks, £50-£2,000; general furniture, shipping goods, 18th-20th C, £5-£1,500.* Not Stocked: Porcelain, jewellery, silver. LOC: 150yds. west of Boundary Rd., on seafront. PARK: Easy. TEL: 01273 411599; fax - 01273 421591. SER: Restorations (furniture). VAT: Stan.

PULBOROUGH

Thakeham Furniture

Marehill Rd. RH20 2DY. (T.J.G. Chavasse). Est. 1988. Open Mon.-Fri. 9-5. SIZE: Medium. *STOCK: Furniture and clocks, 1750-1880, £100-£5,000.* LOC: 1 mile east of Pulborough on A283. PARK: Easy. TEL: 01798 872006. SER: Restorations (furniture); buys at auction (furniture). VAT: Stan/Spec.

SAYERS COMMON

Recollect Studios

The Old School, London Rd. BN6 9HX. (P. Jago). Est. 1970. Open 10-4. CL: Mon. and Sat. *STOCK: Dolls, dolls house miniatures, doll restoration materials.* LOC: B2118. PARK: Own. TEL: 01273 833314. SER: Restorations (dolls); catalogues available (£2.75 cash/stamps).

SOUTH HARTING, Nr. Petersfield (Hants.)

Julia Holmes Antique Maps and Prints

South Gardens Cottage. GU31 5QJ. By appointment only. SIZE: Medium. *STOCK: Maps, 1600-1850, £10-£1,000; prints, especially sporting, all periods, to £500.* LOC: End of main street, on the Chichester road. PARK: Opposite. TEL: 01730 825040. SER: Valuations; restorations (cleaning and colouring maps and prints); framing; buys at auction; catalogues. FAIRS: Local and major sporting events. VAT: Stan.

STEYNING

David R. Fileman

Squirrels, Bayards. BN44 3AA. Open daily. *STOCK: Table glass, £20-£1,000; chandeliers, candelabra, £500-£20,000; all 18th-19th C. Collectors' items, 17th-19th C, £25-£2,000; paperweights, 19th C, £50-£5,000.* LOC: A283 to north of Steyning village. TEL: 01903 813229. SER: Valuations; restorations (chandeliers and candelabra). VAT: Stan/Spec.

STORRINGTON

Stable Antiques

46 West St. RH20 4EE. (Ian J. Wadey). Est. 1993. Open 10-6 including Sun. SIZE: Large. *STOCK: General antiques, furniture and bric-a-brac, £1-£1,000.* LOC: A283 west of A24 towards Pulborough, just before Amberley turn. PARK: Easy. TEL: 01903 740555; home - 01903 740441.

TILLINGTON, Nr. Petworth

Loewenthal Antiques

Tillington Cottage. GU28 0RA. CL: Wed. *STOCK: 18th C furniture and objets d'art.* LOC: A272, 1 mile west of Petworth. TEL: 01798 342969.

WARNHAM, Nr Horsham

Sayer Antiques

Bailing Hill Farmhouse. Est. 1971. Open by appointment, including Sun. *STOCK: 19th-20th C French furniture and decorative antiques.* PARK: Easy. TEL: 01403 257546; fax - 01403 269880; mobile - 0585 191652. SER: Containers. VAT: Margin. *Trade Only.*

WASHINGTON

Chanctonbury Antiques

Clematis Cottage. RH20 4AP. (G. D. Troche). Est. 1961. Open by appointment only. SIZE: Small. *STOCK: Pottery, porcelain, needlework, small furniture and collectables.* LOC: Just off A24. PARK: Easy. TEL: 01903 892233.

WESTBOURNE, Nr. Emsworth

Westbourne Antiques

3 Lamb Buildings, The Square. PO10 8SH. (H.J. and V.J. Lain). Est. 1951. Open Thurs., Fri. and Sat. 9-5. SIZE: Large. *STOCK: Silver, jewellery, collectors' items.* PARK: Nearby. TEL: 01243 373711. SER: Valuations; repairs (jewellery and watches).

WORTHING

A. Biscoe

122 Montague St. BN11 3HG. (L. Byskou). Open 10-5. *STOCK: Mirrors, furniture, silver, porcelain, jewellery, clocks and objets d'art, 18th-19th C.* TEL: 01903 202489.

Chloe Antiques

61 Brighton Rd. BN11 3EE. (Mrs D. Peters). Est. 1960. Open 10-12.30 and 1.30-4.30. CL: Wed. SIZE: Small. *STOCK: General antiques, furniture, jewellery, china, glass, bric-a-brac.* LOC: From Brighton, on main rd. just past Beach House Park on corner. PARK: Opposite. TEL: 01903 202697.

Worthing continued

Rathbone Law Antiques

7 The Arcade. BN11 3AY. (R. Law). Open 10-5. CL: Some Wed. *STOCK: Victorian and Edwardian fine jewellery, silver, objets d'art, porcelain dolls.* TEL: 01903 200274.

Rococo Antiques

21 Warwick Rd. BN11 3ET. (K.P. Jakes). Open 11-5. CL: Fri. *STOCK: General antiques.* TEL: 01903 235896.

Robert Warner and Son Ltd

1-13 South Farm Rd. BN14 7AB. Est. 1940. CL: Wed. pm. SIZE: Large. *STOCK: Furniture, bric-a-brac.* TEL: 01903 232710; fax - 01903 217515. VAT: Stan.

Wilsons Antiques LAPADA

57/59 Broadwater Rd. BN14 8AH. (F. Wilson). Est. 1936. Open 10-5. SIZE: Large. *STOCK: Period furniture, 18th-19th C, £100-£10,000; Edwardian furniture, £50-£4,000; decorative items, 19th C, £10-£750; watercolours and oil paintings, 19th-20th C.* Not Stocked: Pine. PARK: At rear. TEL: 01903 202059; fax - 01903 206300; mobile - 0378 813395. SER: Valuations; restorations (furniture). FAIRS: Olympia (June); Goodwood House. VAT: Stan/Spec/Global.

A lively carved and painted cantering zebra, with leather tack and brass detail by the House of Gustave Bayol. The firm was established in 1884 in Augers and became the centre of the French industry. One of the firm's specialities was theme carousels, that concentrated on a single species of animal, or even fish c.1890. Length 52in. Sold for £8,625. (Christie's South Kensington)

From an article entitled "Collecting Fairground Art" by Constance King which appeared in the February 1998 issue of **Antique Collecting.**

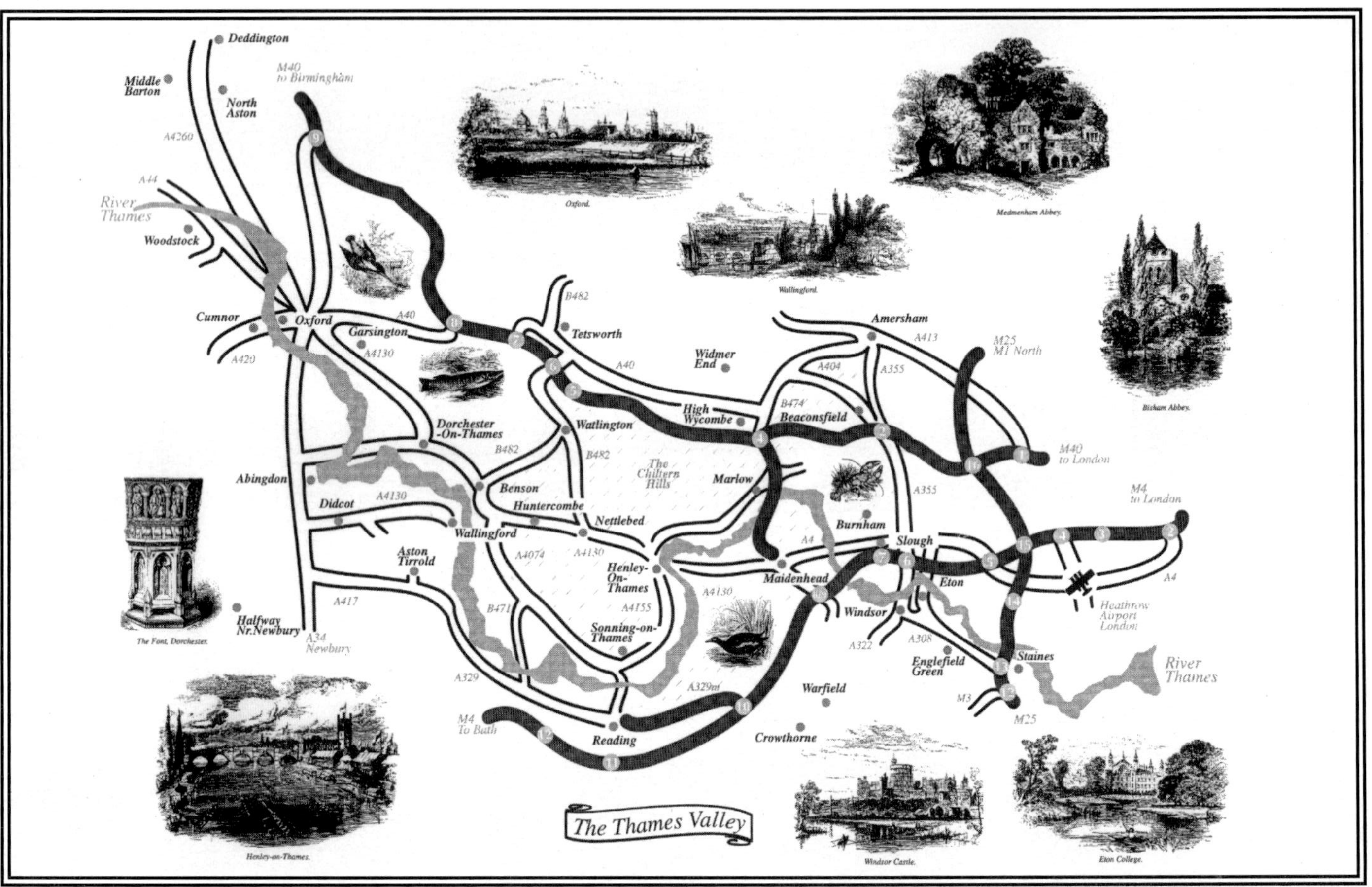
The Thames Valley
Deddington
Middle Barton
North Aston
M40 to Birmingham
A4260
A44
River Thames
Woodstock
Cumnor
Oxford
A420
Garsington
A4130
A40
B482
Tetsworth
Widmer End
Amersham
A413
M25 M1 North
A404
A355
Dorchester -On-Thames
Watlington
High Wycombe
B474
Beaconsfield
M40 to London
Abingdon
B482
B482
The Chiltern Hills
Marlow
A355
M4 to London
Didcot
A4130
Benson
Huntercombe
Nettlebed
Burnham
Slough
A4
Wallingford
A4074
A4130
Aston Tirrold
Henley-On-Thames
Maidenhead
Eton
A4
A417
A4130
Windsor
Heathrow Airport London
B471
A4155
Halfway Nr.Newbury
A34 Newbury
Sonning-on-Thames
A322
A308
Englefield Green
Staines
River Thames
A329
A329m
Warfield
M3
M25
M4 To Bath
Reading
Crowthorne
Oxford.
Medmenham Abbey.
Wallingford.
Bisham Abbey.
The Font, Dorchester.
Henley-on-Thames.
Windsor Castle.
Eton College.

THAMES VALLEY ANTIQUE DEALERS ASSOCIATION

T.V.A.D.A.

The Thames Valley Antique Dealers Association has over 40 members offering a vast range of antiques and services to all its customers. The area covered by the T.V.A.D.A. stretches from **Windsor** to **Woodstock.** The eastern end of the area is conveniently close to London (less than 20 minutes drive from Heathrow Airport) and is served by the major routes of the M4, M25 and M40.

The Thames Valley area is one of outstanding natural beauty. From the magnificent castle at **Windsor,** following the river you travel through many historic and picturesque towns and villages along the way - past **Eton College,** through Marlow and **Henley,** then the busy town of **Reading,** on to Pangbourne, through Goring Gap, where the river cuts through the Chiltern Hills to **Wallingford,** where the Norman invaders crossed the river on their way to London in 1066, and on again to the pretty village of **Dorchester-on-Thames.** Here the river goes into a big sweeping bend and you can follow this bend through the pictureque village of Clifton Hampden to Culham and the market town of Abingdon, then turning northwards, approach the dreaming spires of **Oxford.** From here it is just a short step to the pretty **Woodstock** and Blenheim Palace, with a visit to Churchill's burial place at Bladon to round off your visit.

Throughout the area you will find our members - see the gold and black T.V.A.D.A. sign in the windows of their shops, showing our Logo (as above), Old Father Thames (Tamesis), taken from the stone sculpture to be found on Henley Bridge.

You will be welcomed by T.V.A.D.A. members and will find them anxious to give help in finding whatever antique pieces you seek. If the shop in question does not have exactly what you require they will look for it amongst other members of the group. A courier service is available by contacting our office (details below).

The route has a wide variety of antique shops offering an infinite choice of antiques from paintings to furniture, silver to porcelain, collectables and decorative objects for inside and out. For collectors, exporters, trade and tourists alike this is an Aladdin's cave where simple small items or whole consignments can be purchased with ease.

So come and spend some time in the land of 'Three Men in a Boat' and see for yourselves the countryside described by Jerome K. Jerome. Sit in a riverside pub or go to a friendly local hotel and browse amongst the treasures this area holds.

For further details please contact the Secretary, T.V.A.D.A., The Old College, Queen Street, Dorchester-on-Thames, Oxon OX10 7HL.
Tel/Fax: 01865 341639 E-Mail: tvada@btinternet.com

AMERSHAM

The Cupboard Antiques LAPADA
80 High St., Old Amersham. HP7 0DS. TVADA. (N. Lucas). Open 10-5. CL: Fri. SIZE: 4 showrooms. *STOCK: Georgian, Regency and early Victorian furniture and decorative items.* PARK: Easy. TEL: 01494 722882.

ASTON TIRROLD, Nr. Didcot

John Harrison Fine Art
Skirmers, Aston St. OX11 9DQ. TVADA. (J.M.C. Harrison). Strictly by appointment. *STOCK: Drawings and watercolours, 18th-19th C.* TEL: 01235 850260. SER: Commissions undertaken.

BEACONSFIELD

Period Furniture Showrooms
49 London End. HP9 2HW. TVADA. (R.E.W. Hearne and N.J. Hearne). Est. 1965. Open 9-5.30. SIZE: Large. *STOCK: Furniture, 1700-1900, £50-£3,000.* LOC: A40 Beaconsfield Old Town. PARK: Own. TEL: 01494 674112; fax - 01494 681046. SER: Restorations (furniture). VAT: Stan/Spec.

BENSON, Nr. Wallingford

Benson Antiques Centre & Gallery
The Old Bakehouse, Castle Sq. OX10 6SD. TVADA. (Dane Clouston). Est. 1978. Open 10-5, Sun. 2-5. CL: Mon. SIZE: Medium. *STOCK: Furniture, 17th to early 20th C, £100-£5,000; ceramics, glass, silver, 18th to early 20th C, £5-£1,000; bronze, pewter, oils and watercolours, 19th-20th C, £25-£5,000.* LOC: Village centre. PARK: Easy. TEL: 01491 832525. SER: Valuations. FAIRS: TVADA.

BURNHAM

H. Edwards - The Treasure Chest
17 Britwell Road. SL1 8AQ. TVADA. Open by appointment only. *STOCK: Porcelain and jewellery.* TEL: 01628 603510. FAIRS: Oxford; Blue Coat School, (Reading); Thame.

CAVERSHAM, Nr. Reading

The Clock Workshop LAPADA
17 Prospect St. RG4 8JB. FBHI, TVADA. (J. M. Yealland). Est. 1980. Open 9.30-5.30, Sat. 10-1. SIZE: Small. *STOCK: Clocks, late 17th to late 19th C, £350-£60,000; barometers, 18th-19th C, £500-£8,000.* LOC: Prospect St. is the beginning of main Reading to Henley road. PARK: North St. TEL: 01734 470741. SER: Valuations; restorations (clocks and barometers); buys at auction. FAIRS: TVADA; LAPADA; Olympia. VAT: Stan/Spec.

DEDDINGTON

Deddington Antiques Centre
Laurel House, Bull Ring, Market Sq. OX15 0TT. TVADA. (Mrs B. J. Haller). Est. 1972. Open 10-5, including Sun. SIZE: 27 dealers. *STOCK: Furniture, Georgian to 1930's, £40-£4,000; porcelain, silver, pictures, jewellery, 1700-1930, £5-£500; collectables, £10-£200.* LOC: Off A4260 Oxford-Banbury road at Deddington traffic lights. PARK: Easy, free. TEL: 01869 338968; fax - 01869 338916. SER: Valuations. FAIRS: NEC; Oxford; Eton; Goodwood House.

DIDCOT

Didcot Antiques Centre
220 The Broadway. OX11 8RS. TVADA. (Dr. A. Vetta). Est. 1995. Open 10-5, Sun. 11-4. CL: Mon. SIZE: Large. *STOCK: Furniture, £50-£1,000; silver and plate, books and ephemera, all 19th-20th C.* PARK: Own. TEL: 01235 510819; fax - 01235 512178. SER: Valuations.

DORCHESTER-ON-THAMES

Dorchester Antiques LAPADA
(formerly The Shambles), The Barn, 3 High St. OX10 7HH. TVADA. (J. and S. Hearnden). Est. 1992. Open Tues.-Sat. 10-5. SIZE: Medium. *STOCK: Furniture including chairs and decorative country pieces, 18th-19th C.* LOC: Opposite Abbey. PARK: Easy. TEL: 01865 341373. SER: Restorations; upholstery; finder.

Hallidays (Fine Antiques) Ltd LAPADA
The Old College, High St. OX10 7HL. TVADA. Est. 1950. Open 9-5, Sat. 10-1 and 2-4. SIZE: Large. *STOCK: Furniture, 17th-19th C, £100-£40,000; paintings, 18th-19th C, £100-£20,000; decorative and small items, pine and marble mantelpieces, firegrates, fenders, 18th-20th C; room panelling.* PARK: At rear. TEL: 01865 340028; fax - 01865 341149. FAIRS: Olympia. VAT: Stan/Spec.

HALFWAY, Nr. Newbury

Alan Walker BADA

Halfway Manor. RG20 8NR. TVADA. Open by appointment. *STOCK: Fine barometers and weather instruments.* TEL: 01488 657670; mobile - 0831 147480. SER: Restorations.

HENLEY-ON-THAMES

The Barry M. Keene Gallery

12 Thameside. RG9 1BH. TVADA, FATG. (B.M. and J.S. Keene). Est. 1971. Open 9.30-5.30, Sun. 11-5.30, and by appointment. *STOCK: Paintings, watercolours, drawings, etchings, prints, 18th C to 1998; modern sculpture.* LOC: Junction 8/9 M4, over bridge, immediate left, 5th building on right. TEL: 01491 577119. SER: Restorations; framing, cleaning, relining, gilding, export. VAT: Stan/Spec.

Richard J. Kingston BADA

95 Bell St. RG9 2BD. TVADA. Open 9.30-5 or by appointment. SIZE: Medium. *STOCK: Furniture, 17th to early 19th C; silver, porcelain, glass, paintings, antiquarian and secondhand books.* PARK: Easy. TEL: 01491 574535; home - 01491 573133. SER: Restorations. FAIRS: Surrey, Buxton, Snape. VAT: Stan/Spec.

Thames Gallery

Thameside. RG9 2LJ. TVADA. (S. Came). Open 10-5. *STOCK: Georgian and Victorian silver; paintings, 19th C.* TEL: 01491 572449; fax - 01491 410273.

HIGH WYCOMBE

Windmill Fine Art

Widmer End. TVADA. (Ray and Carol White). Open by appointment only. *STOCK: Fine Victorian and early 20th C watercolours.* TEL: 01494 713757; fax - same; mobile - 0585 370408. SER: Valuations; commission search. FAIRS: Most major.

HUNTERCOMBE

The Country Seat LAPADA

Huntercombe Manor Barn. RG9 5RY. TVADA. (Harvey Ferry and William Clegg). Est. 1965. Open 9-5.30, Sun. by appointment. SIZE: Large. *STOCK: Furniture - signed and designed, 1700-1910, Chinese, 19th C; garden statuary, panelled rooms, metalwork and art pottery, upholstered furniture and ancient artefacts.* LOC: 200 yds down right-hand turn off A4130 Nettlebed-Wallingford. PARK: Easy. TEL: 01491 641349; fax - 01491 641533. SER: Restorations. VAT: Spec.

MARLOW

Glade Antiques LAPADA

CINOA, TVADA. (Sonia Garry). Open by appointment only. *STOCK: Fine Oriental ceramics, bronzes and jades: Chinese items from Han, Tang, Song, Ming and Quing periods; Japanese items - mainly Kakiemon, Nabeshima, Kutani, Satsuma and Imari; also Korean Koryo, Yi and Choson periods.* TEL: 01628 487255; fax - 01628 476601; mobile - 0976 159669.

Marlow Antique Centre

35 Station Rd. SL7 1NW. TVADA. (Kay Darby and Keith Hill). SIZE: 30+ dealers. *STOCK: Wide range of general antiques and collectables including Georgian, Victorian and Edwardian furniture, country pine, silver, glass, china, bedsteads, clocks, old tools and garden items, cameras, books, jewellery.* TEL: 01628 473223; fax - 01628 778834.

NETTLEBED, Nr. Henley-on-Thames

Willow Antiques and the Nettlebed Antique Merchants

The Barns, 1 High St. RG9 5DA. TVADA. (Willow Bicknell, Michael Plummer, Gregory Cupitt-Jones and Robert Wookey). Open Tues.-Sat 10-5.30, Sun. 11-4, other times by appointment. SIZE: Large. *STOCK: Decorative, fine and unusual furniture, objects and decorations, including architectural items, original painted or stripped and wax finished pine.* LOC: Between Wallingford and Henley on A4031. PARK: Easy. TEL: 01491 642062; fax - same; mobile - 0370 554559. SER: Cottage Upholstery - fabrics; upholstery.

NORTH ASTON

Elizabeth Harvey-Lee

1 West Cottages, Middle Aston Lane. OX6 3QB. TVADA. Est. 1986. Open by appointment. *STOCK: Original prints, 15th-20th C; artists' etchings, engravings, lithographs, £100-£6,000.* LOC: 6 miles from junction 10, M40, 15 miles north of Oxford. TEL: 01869 347164. SER: Illustrated catalogue available twice yearly (£12 p.a.). FAIRS: London Original Print, Royal Academy; Olympia (June and Nov).VAT: Spec.

OXFORD

Magna Gallery

41 High St. OX1 4AP. TVADA. (Martin J. Blant). Est. 1969. Open 10-5.30. SIZE: Medium. *STOCK: Maps especially Oxfordshire, general topography, prints including botanical, caricatures, 1550-1895.* TEL: 01865 245805. SER: Valuations; framing. VAT: Stan.

READING

Blond Fine Art

Barnat Works, 1a Upper Redlands Rd. RG1 5JJ. TVADA. (Simon Blond). Open by appointment only. *STOCK: British original prints, 1920-1980; Art Deco ceramics.* TEL: 0118 9260880.

P.D. Leatherland Antiques

68 London St. RG1 4SQ. TVADA. Est. 1970. Open 9-5. *STOCK: Furniture, 18th C to 1920's; decorative china, clocks, metalware, mirrors and pictures, £5-£4,000.* PARK: Easy. TEL: 0118 9581960. VAT: Stan/Spec.

SONNING-ON-THAMES

Cavendish Fine Arts LAPADA

The Dower House. RG4 6UL. TVADA. (Janet Middlemiss and Guy Hazel). Open by appointment only. *STOCK: Fine Queen Anne and English Georgian furniture, glass and porcelain.* TEL: 01189 691904; mobile - 0831 295575. VAT: Stan/Spec.

STAINES

Margaret Melville Watercolours LAPADA

11 Colnebridge, Market Sq. TW18 4RZ. TVADA. Est. 1980. Open by appointment only. *STOCK: English watercolours, 1850-1950, £75-£7,000.* TEL: 01784 455395. SER: Valuations; commissions. FAIRS: Earls Court (Aug.); Chester (Feb. and Nov.); Eton College (Easter); Oxford (Oct); LAPADA; NEC (Jan.); Penman Fairs ('phone for tickets). VAT: Spec.

TETSWORTH, Nr. Thames

The Swan at Tetsworth

High St. OX9 7AB. TVADA. Est. 1995. Open every day including Sun. LOC: A40, 5 minutes from junctions 6 and 8, M40. PARK: Own large. TEL: 01844 281777; fax - 01844 281770. SER: Valuations; restorations (clocks, cabinet work and gilding).

WALLINGFORD

The Lamb Arcade

83 High St. OX10 0BX. TVADA. Open 10-5, Sat. 10-5.30. TEL: 01491 835166. SER: Restorations (furniture).

Summers Davis Antiques Ltd LAPADA

Calleva House, 6 High St. OX10 0BP. CINOA, TVADA. (Graham Wells). Est. 1917. Open 8.30-5.30, Sat. 9-5, Sun. 11-5. SIZE: Large. *STOCK: English and Continental furniture, decorative items and objects.* Not Stocked: Silver, shipping goods. LOC: From London, shop is on left, 50yds. from Thames Bridge. PARK: Opposite, behind castellated gates. TEL: 01491 836284; fax - 01491 833443; e-mail - summersdavisantiques@msn.com VAT: Spec.

WARFIELD

Moss End Antique Centre

Moss End Garden Centre. RG12 6EJ. TVADA. Open 10.30-5. CL: Mon. SIZE: Large - 25 dealers. *STOCK: General antiques and collectables.* LOC: A3095. PARK: Own. TEL: 01344 861942.

WATLINGTON, Nr. Oxford

Cross Antiques

37 High St. OX9 5PZ. TVADA. (R.A. and I.D. Crawley). Est. 1986. Open 10-6, Sun. and Wed. by appointment. SIZE: Small. *STOCK: Furniture, £100-£5,000; decorative smalls, clocks and garden items, £50-£2,000; all 1600-1900.* LOC: Off B4009 in village centre. PARK: Easy and at rear. TEL: 01491 612324; home - same.

Stephen Orton Antiques

The Antiques Warehouse, Shirburn Rd. OX9 5BZ. TVADA. Open Mon.-Fri. 9-5, other times by appointment. SIZE: Warehouse. *STOCK: 18th-19th C furniture, some decorative items.* LOC: 2 mins. from exit 6, M40. TEL: 01491 613752; fax - 01491 613875. SER: Valuations; restorations; buying agent. VAT: Stan/Spec.

Mark Shanks BADA

The Royal Oak, High St. OX9 5QB. TVADA. Est. 1960. Open Tues.-Sat. 10-5, or by appointment. *STOCK: Furniture, £100-£20,000; barometers, £100-£10,000; both mainly 18th-19th C. Decorative items, £50-£5,000.* Not Stocked: Silver, jewellery, coins. LOC: 3 miles from junction 6, M40. Turn right into High St. (one-way). PARK: Own. TEL: 01491 613317; fax - 01491 613318.

WINDSOR & ETON

Country Furniture

79 St. Leonards Rd., Windsor. SL4 3BZ. TVADA. (Jan Hicks and Austin Maude). Open 9.30-5.30. *STOCK: French provincial furniture and unusual decorative items.* TEL: 01753 830154; fax - same.

Dee's Antique Pine

89 Grove Rd. SL4 1HT. TVADA. (Dee Waghorn). Open 10.30-6, other times by appointment. *STOCK: 19th C pine furniture.* TEL: 01753 865627; fax - 01753 850926.

Eton Gallery LAPADA

TVADA. (Josephine Smith). Open by appointment only. *STOCK: 18th to early 19th C furniture, specialising in dining tables and sets of chairs.* TEL: 01753 860963.

Shirley Hayden Antiques

79 High St., Eton. SL4 6AF. TVADA. Est. 1980. Open 10-5.30, Sun. 11.30-5. SIZE: Small. *STOCK: English mahogany furniture, 18th-19th C, £350-£4,500; decorative items - pictures, mirrors, lamps and porcelain.* LOC: First antiques shop on left over the bridge from Windsor. PARK: Meadow Lane. TEL: 01753 833085; home - 01753 540203. FAIRS: TVADA. VAT: Spec.

Peter J. Martin

40 High St., Eton. SL4 6BD. TVADA. Est. 1963. Open 9-1 and 2-5. CL: Sun. SIZE: Large and warehouse. *STOCK: Period, Victorian and decorative furniture and furnishings, £50-£5,000; metalware, £10-£500, all from 1800.* PARK: 50yds. opposite. TEL: 01753 864901; home - 01753 863987. SER: Restorations; shipping arranged; buys at auction. VAT: Stan/Spec.

Morgan Stobbs

17 High St., Eton. SL4 6AX. TVADA. (Glenn Morgan). Open 10.30-5.30, Sun. 1-5. *STOCK: Arts & Crafts, Art Deco furniture and objects, 1880-1940.* TEL: 01753 840631.

Oriental Rug Gallery Ltd

115-116 High St., Eton. SL4 6AN. TVADA, BORDA. (Richard Mathias and Julian Blair). Open 10-5.30. *STOCK: Russian, Afghan, Turkish and Persian carpets, rugs and kelims; Oriental objets d'art.* PARK: Behind showroom. TEL: 01753 623000; fax - same.

Rules Antiques

62 St Leonard's Rd. SL4 3BY. TVADA. (Sue Rule and Kathryn Cale). Open 10.30-6.*STOCK: Fixtures and fittings; brass, metalwork; unusual small furniture; lighting.* TEL: 01753 833210.

Windsor & Eton continued

Woodage Antiques

4 High St., Eton. SL4 6AS. TVADA. Open daily, prior telephone call advisable. *STOCK: Mainly 18th-19th C furniture and associated decorative items; samplers, marble, gilt mirrors.* LOC: Close to college. PARK: Easy. TEL: 01753 863016; fax - same.

WOODSTOCK

Chris Baylis Country Chairs

Minstrel House, 60 Oxford St. OX20 1TT. TVADA. Open 10.30-5.30 including Sun. *STOCK: English country chairs, from 1780; Windsors, ladder and spindlebacks, kitchen chairs; also good country furniture and reproductions including farm tables and chairs.* TEL: 01993 813887; fax - 01993 812379.

Bees Antiques

30 High St. OX20 1TG. TVADA. (Jo and Jim Bateman). Est. 1991. Open 10-1 and 1.30-5, Sun. 11-5. CL: Tues. SIZE: Small. *STOCK: Pottery, porcelain and glass, 18th-20th C, £30-£1,500; small furniture, 19th to early 20th C, £50-£2,000; metalware, 19th C, £30-£200; jewellery, 19th-20th C, £30-£1,000.* LOC: Just off A3440 Oxford/Stratford-on-Avon road, in town centre. PARK: Opposite. TEL: 01993 811062; home - 01993 771593. SER: Valuations; buys at auction (as stock). FAIRS: TVADA.

Span Antiques

6 Market Place. OX20 1TA. TVADA. Est. 1978. Open 10-1 and 2-5, Sun 1-5. SIZE: Medium. LOC: Near Town Hall. PARK: Easy. TEL: 01993 811332.

Saladware, Chequers, Melody and Nature Study, all by Sir Terence Conran for Midwinter, 1955-58. From an exhibition at The Richard Dennis Gallery.

From a feature entitled "What's on in London" which appeared in the June 1997 issue of **Antique Collecting.**

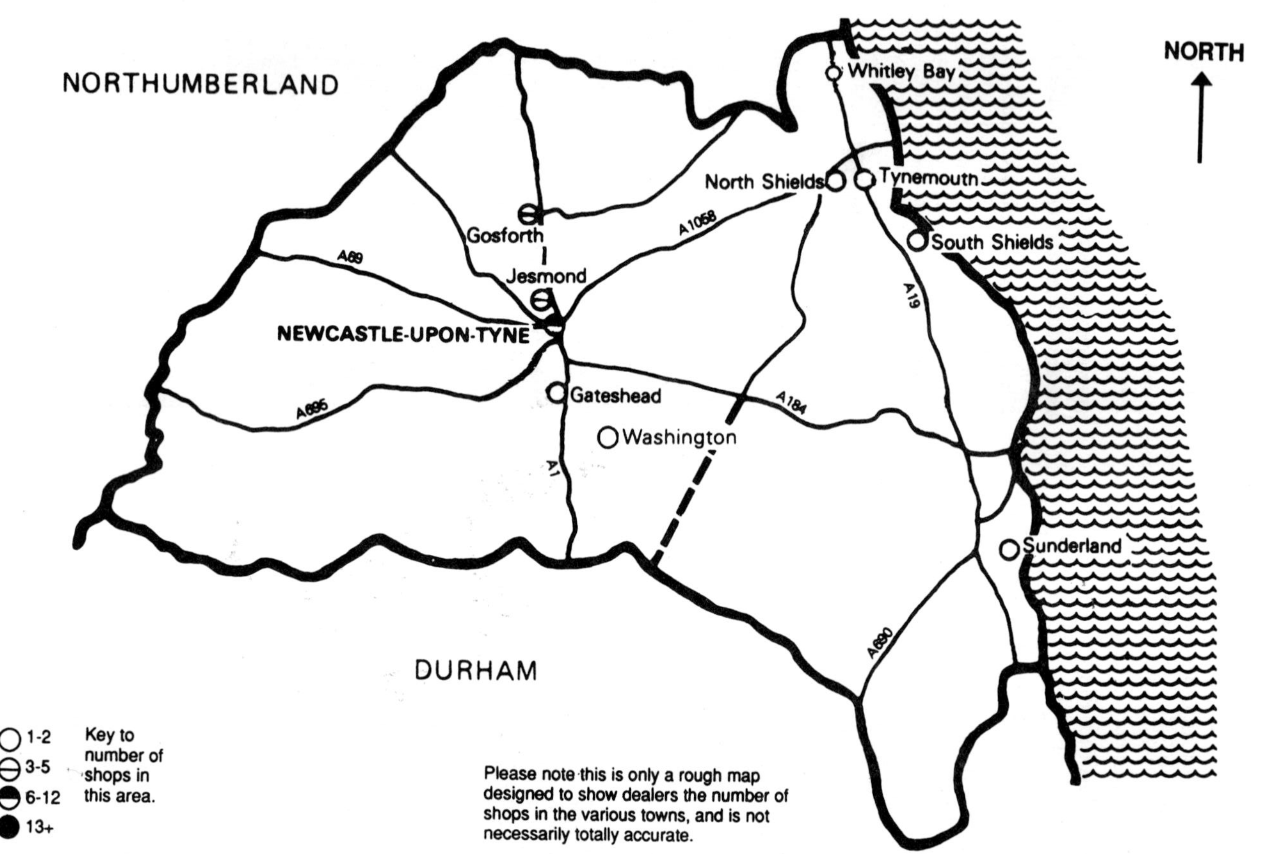
NORTH
NORTHUMBERLAND
Whitley Bay
North Shields
Tynemouth
South Shields
Gosforth
Jesmond
NEWCASTLE-UPON-TYNE
A69
A1058
A19
A695
Gateshead
A184
Washington
A1
Sunderland
A690
DURHAM
1-2
3-5
6-12
13+
Key to number of shops in this area.
Please note this is only a rough map designed to show dealers the number of shops in the various towns, and is not necessarily totally accurate.

GATESHEAD

Sovereign Antiques

35 The Boulevard, Antique Village, Metrocentre. NE11 9YN. Open Mon.-Wed. 10-8, Thurs. 10-9, Sat. 9-6. *STOCK: Fine antique and modern jewellery, diamonds, silver, original prints and maps.* TEL: 0191 460 9604; fax - 0191 460 7600.

GOSFORTH, Nr. Newcastle-upon-Tyne

Causey Antique Shop

Causey St. NE3 4DL. *STOCK: Silver, Victoriana and collectors' items.*

H & S Collectables

1-3 Ashburton Rd. NE3 4XN. (Harry and Mrs Sheila Shorrick). Est. 1986. Open 10-5, Sun. by appointment. SIZE: Small. *STOCK: China, porcelain, figurines, Tyneside Malingware, spelter, silver, Sheffield plate, Cranberry glass, prints, armchairs and small occasional furniture, all £5-£900.* LOC: Corner of Salters Road/Ashburton Road. TEL: 0191 284 6626; home - 0191 286 3498. SER: Valuations. VAT: Stan.

Anna Harrison Antiques Centre LAPADA

Grange Park, Great North Rd. NE3 2DQ. Est. 1976. Open 10-5, Sat. 10.30-5. SIZE: Large. *STOCK: Furniture and porcelain, 18th-20th C, £20-£2,000; paintings and prints, 19th-20th C, £50-£2,000.* LOC: B1318 through Gosforth. PARK: Easy. TEL: 0191 284 3202. SER: Valuations; restorations (upholstery, French polishing, cabinet making, china). VAT: Stan/Spec.

Anna Harrison Fine Antiques LAPADA

Grange Park, Great North Rd. NE3 2DQ. Est. 1976. Open 9-5. SIZE: Large. *STOCK: English furniture, porcelain, oils and watercolours.* LOC: A6125, 3 miles north of city centre, near Regent Centre. PARK: Forecourt. TEL: 0191 284 3202. SER: Valuations; restorations. VAT: Stan/Spec.

MacDonald Fine Art

6 Ashburton Rd. NE3 4JB. (T. and C. MacDonald). Est. 1976. Open 10-1 and 2.30-5.30. CL: Wed. SIZE: Medium. *STOCK: Watercolours and oils, mainly north-eastern artists, English and Scottish, 18th-20th C.* LOC: 1 mile west of A1. PARK: Easy. TEL: 0191 284 4214; home - 0191 285 6188. SER: Valuations; restorations (watercolours and oils); framing; buys at auction (watercolours and oils). VAT: Spec.

JESMOND, Nr. Newcastle-upon-Tyne

Geoffrey Hugall

19 Clayton Rd. NE2 4RP. Est. 1970. Open 10-5 or by appointment. SIZE: Medium. *STOCK: General antiques, furniture, china, silver, period and decorative items.* Not Stocked: Weapons, musical instruments, books. PARK: Easy. TEL: 0191 281 8408. SER: Valuations. VAT: Stan/Spec.

Jesmond continued

Owen Humble LAPADA

11-12 Clayton Rd. NE2 4RP. Est. 1958. Open 6 days. SIZE: Large and warehouse. *STOCK: Furniture, general antiques.* PARK: Easy. TEL: 0191 281 4602; fax - 0191 281 9076. SER: Restorations. VAT: Stan/Spec.

Osborne Art and Antiques

18c Osborne Rd. NE2 2AD. (F.T. and J. Jackman). Est. 1974. Open 10-5.15. *STOCK: Victorian oil paintings and watercolours, drawings, topographical engravings and antiquarian maps, etchings, marine etchings, 19th-20th C.* TEL: 0191 281 6380. SER: Restorations (oil paintings, ornate Victorian frames); paper conservation (watercolours, maps, etchings, documents); bespoke picture-framing. VAT: Stan/Spec.

NEWCASTLE-UPON-TYNE

Davidson's The Jewellers Ltd

94 and 96 Grey St. NE1 6AG. Open 9-5. *STOCK: Jewellery, silver.* TEL: 0191 232 2551/232 2895.

The Dean Gallery Ltd

42 Dean St. NE1 1PG. Est. 1970. Open 10-5. CL: Sat. pm. SIZE: Large. *STOCK: Oils, watercolours, local and national, 18th to early 20th C, £500-£10,000.* LOC: Going north over Tyne Bridge, turn left, and left again. PARK: Easy. TEL: 0191 232 1208. SER: Valuations; restorations; framing. VAT: Stan/Spec.

Intercoin

103 Clayton St. NE1 5PZ. Open 9-4.30. *STOCK: Coins and items of numismatic interest; jewellery, silver.* LOC: City centre. TEL: 0191 232 2064.

Steve Johnson Medals & Militaria

P O Box 1SP. NE99 1SP. *STOCK: Medals and militaria.* TEL: Fax - 01207 545073. *Mail Order Only*

Owen's Jewellers

14 Shields Rd., Byker. NE6 1DR. (D.W. Robertson). Est. 1968. Open 9-5. *STOCK: Jewellery.* TEL: 0191 265 4332.

Shiners Architectural Reclamation

123 Jesmond Rd. NE2 1JY. (B. and A. Lawson). Open 9-5. SIZE: Large. *STOCK: Architectural items including Victorian and Edwardian fireplaces.* LOC: On main road. PARK: Easy. TEL: 0191 281 6474. SER: Valuations; metal polishing.

R.D. Steedman

9 Grey St. NE1 6EE. Est. 1907. CL: Sat. pm. *STOCK: Rare books.* TEL: 0191 232 6561.

NORTH SHIELDS

Maggie May's

(Incorporating Tynemouth Fine Art) 49 Kirton Park Terrace. NE29 0LJ. (Miss M.L. Hayes). Est. 1960. Open Thurs.-Sat. 11-5.30. SIZE: Medium. *STOCK: General antiques and collectors' items, Art Deco, Victorian and Edwardian furniture, china, glass; paintings and watercolours, especially Northumbrian artists, 1800-1950; Continental furniture, glassware, porcelain, decorative items, gramophones.* LOC: Opposite The Gunner Inn. TEL: 0191 237 6933. SER: Valuations; restorations; framing; French polishing; buys at auction.

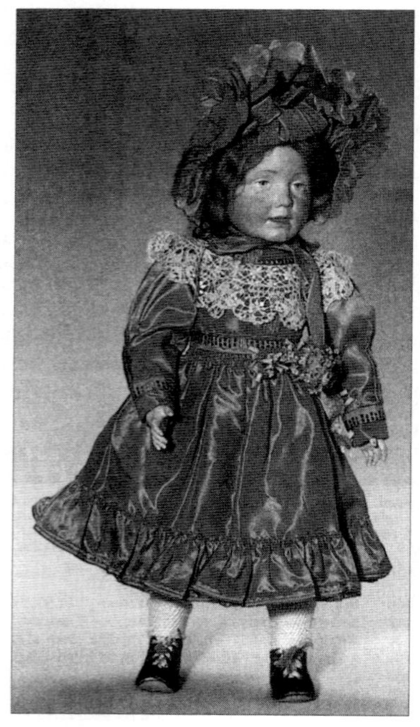

A rare Kämmer and Reinhardt bisque headed German character, the head incised '105' with the 55 cm. size. She has painted eyes and an open-closed mouth. Despite the unsympathetic French style costume, she sold for £108,000. (Sotheby's London)

From an article entitled "Dolls" by Constance King which appeared in the July/August 1997 issue of **Antique Collecting.**

SOUTH SHIELDS

The Curiosity Shop

16 Frederick St. NE33 5EA. Est. 1969. CL: Wed. *STOCK: General antiques, paintings, jewellery, furniture, Royal Doulton.* TEL: 0191 456 5560.

SUNDERLAND

Peter Smith Antiques LAPADA

12-14 Borough Rd. SR1 1EP. Est. 1968. Open 9.30-4.30, Sat. 10-1, other times by appointment. SIZE: Warehouse. *STOCK: Georgian, Victorian, Edwardian longcase clocks, shipping goods, £5-£15,000.* LOC: 10 miles from A1(M); towards docks/Hendon from town centre. PARK: Easy. TEL: 0191 567 3537/567 7842; fax - 0191 514 2286; home - 0191 514 0008. SER: Valuations; restorations; some shipping; containers packed; buys at auction. VAT: Stan/Spec.

TYNEMOUTH

Ian Sharp Antiques

23 Front St. NE30 4DX. Open 10-5.30 or by appointment. *STOCK: Furniture, 18th to early 20th C; British pottery including northern especially Sunderland and Tyneside lustreware, 18th to early 20th C.* TEL: 0191 296 0656; e-mail - iansharp@sharpantiques.demon.co.uk; internet - www.sharpantiques.demon.co.uk.

WASHINGTON

Harold J. Carr Antiques

Field House, Rickleton. NE38 9HQ. Open by appointment. *STOCK: General antiques and furniture.* TEL: 0191 388 6442. SER: Shippers.

Grate Expectations (Fireplaces)

Unit 6, Lee Close, Pattinson North Industrial Estate. NE38 8QA. (Geoffrey Moore). Est. 1983. Open 9-5. SIZE: Large. *STOCK: Fireplaces, £95-£550; fireplace accessories, £10-£125; both 19th C.* LOC: Close to A1 and A19. PARK: Easy. TEL: 0191 416 0609. SER: Restorations (cast-iron refurbishment, repair and welding). VAT: Stan.

WHITLEY BAY

Northumbria Pine

54 Whitley Rd. NE26 2NF. (C. and V. Dowland). Est. 1979. Open 9-5.30. SIZE: Medium. *STOCK: Stripped pine and reproduction items.* LOC: Cullercoats end of Whitley Rd., behind sea front. PARK: Easy. TEL: 0191 252 4550. VAT: Stan.

Treasure Chest

2 and 4 Norham Rd. Est. 1974. Open 10.30-1 and 2-4. CL: Wed. and Thurs. SIZE: Small. *STOCK: General antiques.* LOC: Just off main shopping area of Park View, leading to Monkseaton Railway Station. PARK: Easy. TEL: 0191 251 2052.

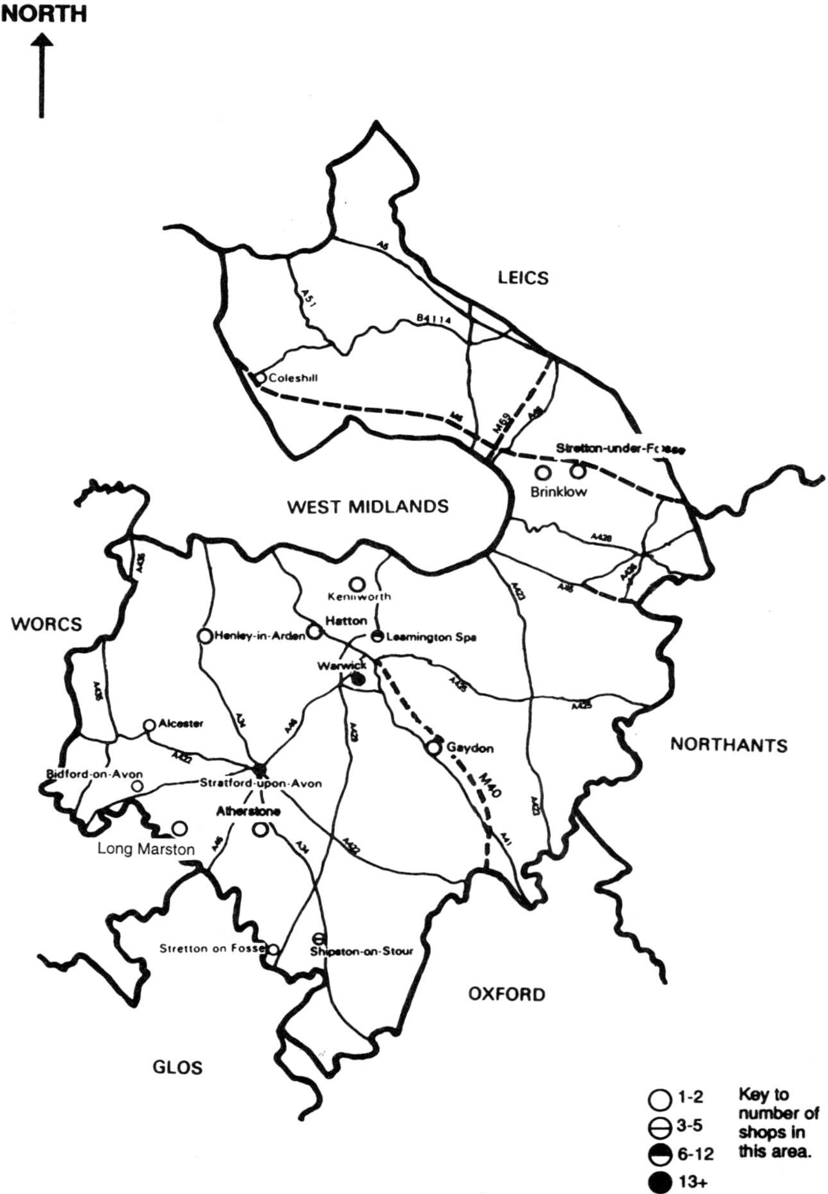

1-2
3-5
6-12
13+
Key to number of shops in this area.

Please note this is only a rough map designed to show dealers the number of shops in the various towns, and is not necessarily totally accurate.

ALCESTER

High St. Antiques

11A High St. B49 5AE. (B.J. Payne). Est. 1979. Open Tues. 11-1 and 2.30-4.30, Fri. 11-1, Sat. 11-1 and 2.30-5. SIZE: Small. *STOCK: Glass and china, 18th-20th C, £5-£200; brass, copper and silver, 19th-20th C, £5-£100+; postcards and Art Deco china.* LOC: On left-hand side near church coming from Stratford-on-Avon road. PARK: Rear of High St. TEL: 01789 764009; home - same. SER: Valuations.

Malthouse Antiques Centre

Market Place. B49 5AE. (J. and P. Allcock). Est. 1982. Open 10-5, Sun. 1-4. SIZE: Large. *STOCK: Furniture, china, silver, collectables and objets d'art, 18th-20th C, £1-£2,000.* LOC: Adjacent to free town car park. TEL: 01789 764032.

ATHERSTONE

Down Memory Lane

18-20 Church St. (Mrs Lynne Robinson). Est. 1989. Open 10-5. CL: Thurs. SIZE: Large. *STOCK: Oak and country furniture, 17th-18th C, £50-£1,000; Victorian and Edwardian furniture, £50-£500; clocks, 1720's to 1930's, £30-£1,500; smalls including china.* LOC: Off A5, shop on market square. PARK: Easy, at rear. TEL: 01827 7133335. SER: Valuations; buys at auction.

BIDFORD-ON-AVON

Bidford Antiques Centre

High St. Est. 1983. Open 10-5, Tues. until 7, Sun. 2-5. SIZE: 12 dealers. *STOCK: Furniture, china, glass, jewellery, pictures, books, records, linen, collectables.* PARK: Easy. TEL: 01789 773680.

BRINKLOW, Nr. Rugby

Cottage Pine Antiques

19 Broad St. CV23 0LS. (Chris and Jill Peters). Est. 1987. Open 10-5.30, Sun. by appointment. SIZE: Medium. *STOCK: Painted pine and country furniture, including kitchen, and decorative items, £50-£7,500.* LOC: B4455 Fosseway; 15 minutes M40, M1, M6. PARK: Easy. TEL: 01788 832673; home - 01926 632517. SER: Valuations; restorations (pine stripping and repairs); buys at auction (period oak and pine). VAT: Stan/Spec.

COLESHILL

Coleshill Antiques and Interiors Ltd

12 and 14 High St. B46 1AZ. (A.J. Webster). Est. 1958. Open Tues.-Sat. 9.30-5, or by appointment. SIZE: Large. *STOCK: Porcelain, furniture, jewellery and silver, £100-£10,000.* LOC: 1 mile from NEC. PARK: Easy. TEL: 01675 462931; 01675 467416. SER: Valuations; restorations; repairs. VAT: Stan/Spec.

GAYDON

MPA Warwick Ltd — LAPADA

(Martin Payne). Est. 1971. Open by appointment only. *STOCK: Silver especially cutlery including canteens, 18th-19th C.* TEL: 01926 641109; mobile - 0850 494948. SER: Valuations; restorations. FAIRS: Most major. VAT: Spec.

HATTON, Nr. Warwick

The Stables Antique Centre

Hatton Country World, Dark Lane. CV35 7LD. (John and Margaret Colledge). Est. 1990. Open 10-5 including Sun. SIZE: Large - 25 units. *STOCK: Furniture, 18-19th C, £50-£3,000; china, 19th-20th C, £5-£200; clocks, 18th-19th C, £200-£4,000; linen, glass,brass and copper, paintings and prints, kitchenalia and jewellery.* LOC: Just off A4177 Solihull-Warwick road, 5 minutes from junction 15, M40. PARK: Own. TEL: 01926 842405. SER: Valuations.

HENLEY-IN-ARDEN

Arden Gallery

B95 5AN. (G.B. Horton). Est. 1963. Open 1-6. CL: Sat. SIZE: Medium. *STOCK: Oil paintings, Victorian, £20-£1,000; watercolours, all periods, to £1,500; portrait miniatures.* LOC: A3400. PARK: Easy. TEL: 01564 792520. VAT: Spec.

Colmore Galleries Ltd — LAPADA

52 High St. B95 5AN. Open 11-5.30, Sat. 11-4.30. *STOCK: Pictures, 19th-20th C.* TEL: 01564 792938; fax - same. SER: Valuations; restorations; framing.

KENILWORTH

Janice Paull Antiques — BADA LAPADA

PO Box 100. CV8 1JR. Est. 1965. Open by appointment. SIZE: Medium. *STOCK: Mason's Ironstone, 1813-1880; pottery.* TEL: 01926 855253; fax - 01926 863384; mobile - 0831 691254. FAIRS: Olympia (June/Nov); Kenilworth (March/Oct). VAT: Spec.

LEAMINGTON SPA

David & Karol Hooper Antiques

The Elephant House, 38-40 Morton Street. CV32 5SY. Open Tues.-Sat. 10-4 or by appointment. *STOCK: General antiques, fairground, circus and unusual items.* TEL: 01926 429679.

The Incandescent Lighting Company

36 Regent St. CV32 5EG. (Mrs Patricia Cunningham). Est. 1988. Open 9.30-5.30, Sat. 9-6. SIZE: Medium. *STOCK: Lighting and especially glass shades, 19th to early 20th C, £25-£2,500; reproduction period-style lighting, shades and components, £2-£1,000.* LOC: Town centre. PARK: Easy. TEL: 01926 422421. SER: Valuations. VAT: Stan.

Leamington Spa continued

King's Cottage Antiques LAPADA

4 Windsor St. CV32 5EB. (G. and A. Jackson). Open 9.30-5. *STOCK: Early oak and country furniture, 16th-18th C.* TEL: 01926 422927.

R.J. Antiques

6 Southborough Terrace, Brunswick Street. CV32. (R.J. Salt). Open every day except Thurs., Sun. by appointment. SIZE: Small. *STOCK: Furniture, £50-£500; porcelain, pottery, postcards, collectibles, £10-£200; all 19th-20th C.* LOC: Continuation of Parade in Leamington Old Town. PARK: Easy. TEL: 01926 887553. SER: Valuations; restorations (furniture).

Yesterdays

21 Portland St. CV32 5EY. (Shona Caldwell). Est. 1986. Open Tues.-Sat. 10-5. SIZE: Medium. *STOCK: Furniture, George III to Edwardian, £75-£3,500; china, prints, 1850-1910, £10-£200.* Not Stocked: Pine. LOC: Parallel to The Parade. PARK: Easy. TEL: 01926 450238.

LONG MARSTON
Nr Stratford-upon-Avon

Barn Antiques Centre

Station Rd. CV37 8RB. (Bev and Graham Simpson). Open 10-5. SIZE: Large. *STOCK: Furniture, collectables, silver, porcelain, china, kitchenalia, fireplaces, linen, pictures, 18th C-1950, £5-£2,000.* LOC: Take B4632 from Stratford-upon-Avon to Broadway, brown heritage signs en route. PARK: Easy. TEL: 01789 721399; fax - 01789 721390.

SHIPSTON-ON-STOUR

Fine-Lines (Fine Art) LAPADA

The Old Bake House Gallery, at The Old Rectory Lodge, West St. CV36 4HD. (L.W. and R.M. Guthrie). Est. 1975. Open seven days by appointment only. SIZE: Medium. *STOCK: British and European watercolours, pastels, drawings and selected oils, from 1850, £300-£20,000.* PARK: Easy and nearby. TEL: 01608 662323 (answerphone). SER: Valuations; restorations, cleaning and framing; buys at auction (paintings, watercolours and drawings). VAT: Spec.

The Grandfather Clock Shop

2 Bondgate House, West St., Granville Court. CV36 4AL. (M.S. Chambers). Est. 1978. Open 9.30-5. CL: Mon. and Thurs. pm. SIZE: Medium. *STOCK: Clocks - longcase, pre-1800, £1,000-£4,000; wall, £250-£1,000; mantle and bracket, 1790-1890, £200-£2,000; barometers, 1790-1860, £350-£1,000; furniture including oak, 17th-18th C.* PARK: Easy. TEL: 01608 662144; home - 01926 857487.

Shipston-on-Stour continued

Halford Bridge Antiques

Halford Bridge. CV36 5BN. Open Tues., Thurs. and Sat. 12-5, or by appointment. SIZE: Small. *STOCK: Furniture, paintings, silver and EPNS, clocks, rugs, prints, copper, brass, pewter, ivory, statuary, garden ornaments, watercolours and etchings, 18th-20th C.* LOC: On Fosse Way, near Tredington roundabout. PARK: Fairly easy. TEL: 01789 740063.

Pine and Things

Portobello Farm, Campden Rd. CV36 4PY. (John Hudson). Est. 1991. Open 9-5. SIZE: Large. *STOCK: Pine, 18th-19th C, £50-£1,000.* LOC: A429. PARK: Easy. TEL: 01608 663849; home - same. VAT: Stan/Spec.

'Time in Hand'

11 Church St. CV36 4AP. (F.R. Bennett). Open 9-1 and 2-5.30 or by appointment. SIZE: Large. *STOCK: Longcase, carriage and wall clocks, barometers.* PARK: Town centre. TEL: 01608 662578. SER: Restorations (clocks, watches, barometers and mechanical instruments).

Liverpool. (Left to right) John Pennington milk jug, £207; Philip Christian teapot, £414; Chaffers coffee can, £529; Seth Pennington coffee pot, £172; John Pennington teapot, £265; Philip Christian sauceboat, £276; Christian's teapot, £483; Chaffers coffee can, £414. (Phillips)

From an article entitled "18th Century English Porcelain" by Simon Spero which appeared in the July/August 1997 issue of **Antique Collecting.**

STRATFORD-UPON-AVON

Abode
Shrieve's House, 40 Sheep St. CV37 6EE. (Mrs A. and Miss J. Bannister). Est. 1975. Open 9-5.30. SIZE: Large. *STOCK: Furniture, pine, interior design items.* LOC: Town centre. TEL: 01789 268755. SER: Buys at auction (furniture). VAT: Stan/Spec.

Arbour Antiques Ltd
Poet's Arbour, Sheep St. CV37 6EF. (R.J. Wigington). Est. 1952. Open 9-5, Sat. by appointment. *STOCK: Arms, armour.* LOC: From town centre towards Theatre and River, behind Lamb's Café through archway at right. PARK: Easy. TEL: 01789 293453. VAT: Spec.

Bow Cottage Antiques
30 Henley St. CV37. (R. Harvey-Morgan). Open 10-5.30. *STOCK: English porcelain, glass, silver, paintings, engravings, maps, books; general antiques, all 18th-20th C, £5-£150+.* TEL: 01789 205883. FAIRS: Classic.

Burman Antiques
34 College St. CV37 6DBW. (J. and J. Burman Holtom). Est. 1973. Open by appointment only. *STOCK: Ruskin ware, pot-lids, fishing tackle.* TEL: 01789 295164. SER: Restorations (clocks).

Greenhill Antiques
35 Greenhill St. CV37 6LE. (Martin Prokain). Est. 1997. Open 9.30-5.30. SIZE: Medium. *STOCK: Furniture, 18th-20th C, £50-£1,000; pictures, ceramics and glass, 19th-20th C, £10-£500.* LOC: A422 from Worcester, over lights, 50 yards on right. PARK: Easy. TEL: 01789 295422; home - same. SER: Restorations (furniture).

Howards Jewellers
44a Wood St. CV37 6JG. (Howards of Stratford Ltd). Est. 1985. Open 9.30-5.30. *STOCK: Jewellery, silver, objets d'art, 19th C.* LOC: Town centre. PARK: Nearby. TEL: 01789 205404. SER: Valuations; restorations (as stock); buys at auction (as stock). VAT: Stan/Spec.

The Loquens Gallery
The Minories, Rother St. CV37 6NE. (S. and J. Loquens). Est. 1975. Open 9.30-5, Sun. by appointment. SIZE: Medium. *STOCK: English watercolours, some oil paintings, late 18th to early 20th C, to £5,000.* LOC: From island in town centre, follow Wood St. to Rother St. junction, entrance to Minories is on right. PARK: Easy. TEL: 01789 297706. SER: Valuations; restorations (cleaning watercolours, relining oils); framing. VAT: Stan/Spec.

Stratford Antique Centre
Ely St. CV37 6LN. (N. Sims). Open 10-5.30 every day. SIZE: 60 dealers. *STOCK: General antiques.* TEL: 01789 204180.

Stratford-upon-Avon continued

The Stratford Antiques and Interiors Centre Ltd
Dodwell Industrial Park, Evesham Rd. CV37 9ST. (Andrew and Suszanna Kerr). Est. 1980. Open 10-5 including Sun., evenings by appointment. SIZE: 25+ dealers. *STOCK: Georgian, Victorian, Edwardian and shipping furniture, £100-£2,000; china and smalls, 19th-20th C, £5-£300; reclaimed pine, £50-£2,000.* LOC: B439. PARK: Easy. TEL: 01789 297729; fax - 01789 297710; home - 01386 765122. SER: Valuations; restorations; buys at auction. FAIRS: Newark and Ardingly.

The Stratford Bookshop
45A Rother St. CV37 6LY. (J. and S. Hill). Est. 1993. Open 10-6. SIZE: Medium. *STOCK: Secondhand and out-of-print books.* LOC: From island in town centre follow Wood St., shop opposite police station. PARK: Easy. TEL: 01789 298362.

Robert Vaughan
20 Chapel St. CV37 6EP. ABA. (C.M. Vaughan). Est. 1953. Open 9.30-5.30. SIZE: Medium. *STOCK: Antiquarian and out-of-print books, maps and prints.* LOC: Town centre. PARK: Easy. TEL: 01789 205312. SER: Valuations; buys at auction (books). VAT: Stan.

James Wigington Arms and Armour
'Winchester 73', 276 Alcester Rd. CV37 9QX. Open by appointment. *STOCK: General antiques, arms and armour, cannons, early fishing tackle.* TEL: 01789 261418; fax - 01789 261600.

STRETTON-ON-FOSSE Nr. Moreton-in-Marsh

Astley House - Fine Art LAPADA
The Old School. GL56 9SA. CADA. (D. and N. Glaisyer). Est. 1974. Open by appointment. SIZE: Large. *STOCK: Large decorative oil paintings, 19th-20th C.* LOC: Village centre. PARK: Easy. TEL: 01608 650601; fax - 01608 651777. SER: Restorations; framing; exhibitions; mailing list. VAT: Spec.

STRETTON-UNDER-FOSSE, Nr. Rugby

The Old Forge
29 Main St. CV23. (C.J. Hall). Est. 1991. Open 10-1 and 2-5, Sat. and Sun. 11-1 and 2-4.30. CL: Thurs. SIZE: Large. *STOCK: Hardwood furniture, £50-£5,000; pine, £50-£1,000; ceramics, £5-£300; glass, £5-£100.* LOC: Half mile from Fosse Way, 2 miles north of Brinklow and 8 miles north east of Coventry. PARK: Easy. TEL: 01788 832191/833161. SER: Buys at auction (furniture).

WARWICK

Duncan M. Allsop

26 Smith St. CV34 4HS. ABA. Est. 1965. Open 9.30-5.30. SIZE: Medium. *STOCK: Antiquarian and modern books.* PARK: Nearby. TEL: 01926 493266; fax - same; mobile - 0370 895924.

Apollo Antiques Ltd LAPADA

The Saltisford, Birmingham Rd. CV34 4TD. (R.H. Mynott). Est. 1968. Open 9-6, Sat. 9.30-12.30. SIZE: Large. *STOCK: Period, decorative English and Continental furniture, sculpture, paintings, decorative objects; Victorian, Arts & Crafts and unrestored furniture.* PARK: Easy. TEL: 01926 494746; fax - 01926 401477. VAT: Stan/Spec

Eastgate Fine Arts

6 Smith St. CV34 4HH. (K. Pittaway). Open 10-5.30. *STOCK: Original maps, prints, paintings.* TEL: 01926 499777.

Fynewood Antiques

25-27 Jury St. CV34 4EH. (R. and C. Haynes). Est. 1976. Open 10-5. SIZE: 4 showrooms. *STOCK: Furniture, 18th-19th C, Edwardian, inlaid, £100-£10,000.* LOC: Adjoining High St. PARK: Easy. TEL: 01926 491122; home - same. SER: Valuations; buys at auction (furniture). FAIRS: Newark, NEC. VAT: Stan/Spec.

Warwick continued

John Goodwin and Sons

38 West St., Westgate. CV34 6AN. Open 8.30-5.30, Sat. 10-4 or by appointment. SIZE: Shop + warehouse 20 mins. away. *STOCK: Victorian and Edwardian furniture, paintings, pottery and porcelain, books and collectables.* TEL: 01926 491191; fax - same. SER: Restorations (furniture).

Russell Lane Antiques

2-4 High St. CV34 4AP. (R.G.H. Lane). Open 10-5. *STOCK: Fine jewellery and silver.* TEL: 01926 494494.

Patrick and Gillian Morley Antiques

LAPADA

62 West St. CV34 6AW. Est. 1968. Open 9-5.30, Sat. and Sun. by appointment. SIZE: Large. ***STOCK: Furniture, 17th to late 19th C; unusual and decorative items, sculpture, carvings and textiles; all £50-£20,000.*** **LOC: Almost opposite Warwick Castle 2nd car park. PARK: Easy. TEL: 01926 494464; home - 01926 54191; mobile - 0468 835040; fax - 01926 400531. SER: Valuations; buys at auction. VAT: Mainly Spec.**

The Old Cornmarket Antiques Centre

70 Market Place. CV34 4SO. (Jonathan Lysaght). Est. 1993. Open 10-5, Sat. 9.30-5.30. LOC: Town centre. TEL: 01926 419119. FAIRS: Below are listed the dealers at this Centre:

Warwick continued

Cliffe Antiques

Est. 1973. *Antique jewellery, silver and porcelain.*

J & S Antiques

(J. Lysaght) *Clocks, from carriage to bracket.*

Midland Goss and Commemoratives

Est. 1978. *Ceramics especially Goss and crested ware.*

Richmond Antiques

(Terry Hare-Walker). Est. 1981. *Period jewellery, wooden boxes, barometers and porcelain.*

James Reeve

at Quinneys of Warwick, 9 Church St. CV34 4AB. Est. 1865. Open 9.30-5.30. CL: Sat. pm. *STOCK: Furniture, mahogany, oak, and rosewood, 17th-18th C, £80-£8,000; furniture, 19th C, £50-£3,500; glass, copper, brass, pewter, china.* TEL: 01926 498113. VAT: Stan/Spec.

Don Spencer Antiques

36a Market Place. CV34 4SH. Est. 1963. Open daily. SIZE: Large. *STOCK: Desks, 1850-1920, £500-£5,000; dining furniture and bookcases, 1800-1920, £500-£3,000.* PARK: Easy. TEL: 01926 499857/407989; home - 01564 775470; internet - www.antique-desks.co.uk. VAT: Stan/Spec.

Summersons

172 Emscote Rd. CV34 5QN. CMBHI. (Peter Lightfoot). Open 10-5, Sat. 10-1. *STOCK: Clocks and barometers.* TEL: 01926 400630; fax - same. SER: Restorations; horological and barometer materials supplied.

Vintage Antiques Centre

36 Market Place. CV34 4SH. (Peter Sellors). Est. 1977. Open 10-5.30, Sun. 11.30-4.30. SIZE: 15 dealers + cabinets. *STOCK: Ceramics, glass, collectables and small furniture, 19th-20th C.* PARK: Easy. TEL: 01926 491527.

The Warwick Antique Centre

20-22 High St. CV34 4AP. Est. 1973. Open 10-5. SIZE: 25 dealers. *STOCK: Porcelain, silver and plate, jewellery, coins, militaria, books, furniture, stamps, metalware, toys, collectables, postcards, glass.* TEL: 01926 491382/495704..

Warwick Antiques

16-18 High St. CV34 4AP. (M. Morrison). Est. 1969. Open 9-5, Sat. 10-5. SIZE: Large and warehouses. *STOCK: Furniture, mahogany, oak, Chinese; metalware, copper, brass, pewter, glass, china, bygones, curios, statuary, garden furniture, shipping goods.* LOC: Midway between E. and W. Gate clock towers. PARK: At rear. TEL: 01926 492482; fax - 01926 492482. SER: Restorations (furniture). VAT: Stan/Spec.

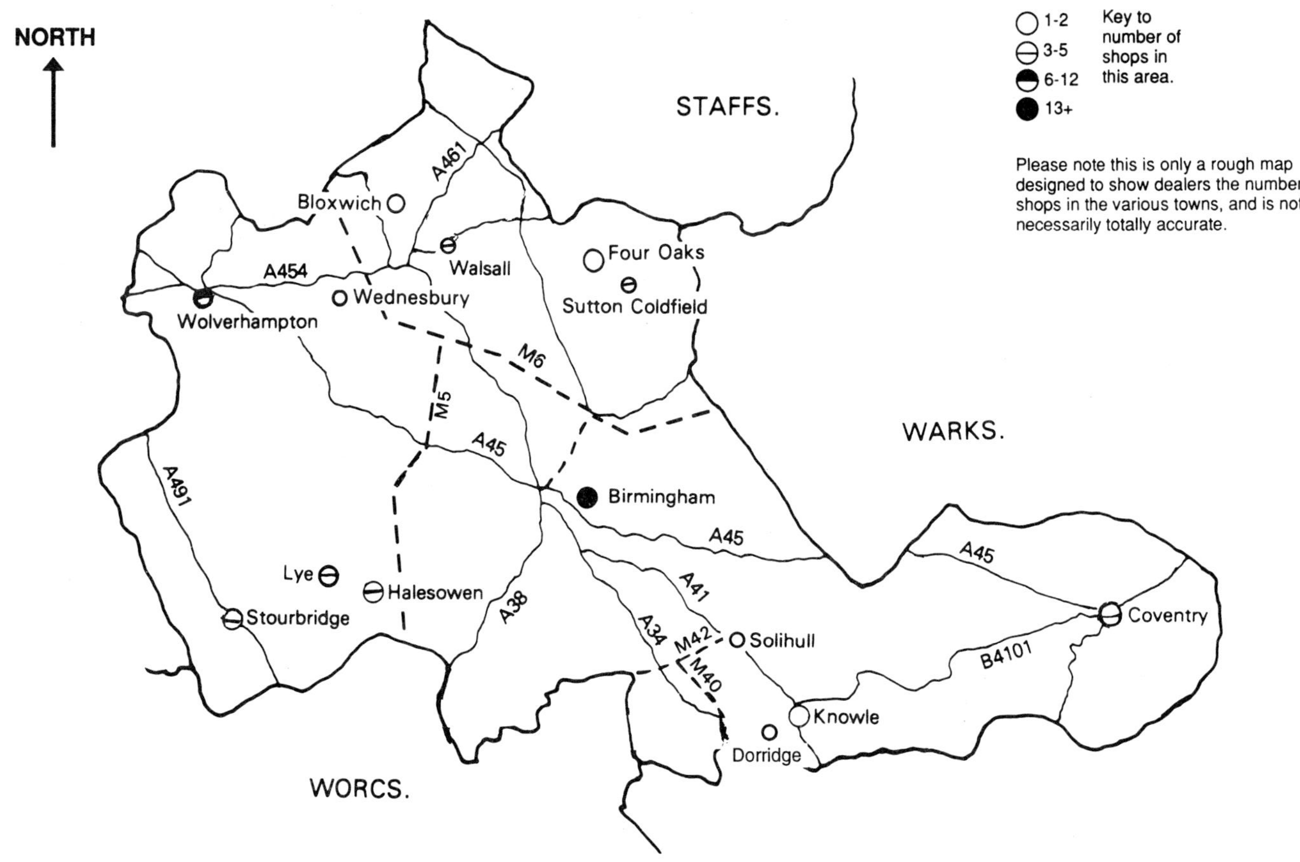

NORTH
STAFFS.
WARKS.
WORCS.
Bloxwich
Walsall
Four Oaks
Sutton Coldfield
Wolverhampton
Wednesbury
Birmingham
Lye
Halesowen
Stourbridge
Solihull
Knowle
Dorridge
Coventry
A461
A454
M6
M5
A45
A491
A45
A45
A38
A41
A34
M42
M40
B4101
1-2
3-5
6-12
13+
Key to number of shops in this area.
Please note this is only a rough map designed to show dealers the number of shops in the various towns, and is not necessarily totally accurate.

BIRMINGHAM

Always Antiques
285 Vicarage Rd., Kings Heath. B14 7NE. (R. and D. Messenger). Open Thurs.-Sat. 9-6, other times by appointment. *STOCK: Victorian and Edwardian furniture, dolls, linen, lace and curios.* TEL: 0121 444 8701.

Archives
496 Bristol Rd., Selly Oak. B29 6BD. (S.D. and I.J. Healey). Open 9.30-5.30. *STOCK: Victorian and Edwardian furniture; clocks and upholstery, to 1930.* TEL: 0121 472 4026.

Peter Asbury Antiques
Greenfield House Farm, 6 Hales Lane, Smethwick, Warley. B67 6RS. Open 9.30-5. *STOCK: General antiques.* TEL: 0121 558 0579. SER: Doll repairs.

Paul Baxter
B47 6LS. Open by appointment only. *STOCK: Oriental ceramics and general antiques.* TEL: 01564 824920.

The Birmingham Antique Centre Ltd
1403-1407 Pershore Rd., Stirchley. B30 2JR. Est. 1960. Open 9-5.30, Sun. 10-5. *STOCK: General antiques; shipping furniture; trade display cabinets.* TEL: 0121 459 4587/689 6565.

Birmingham Piano Warehouse
Unit L, 68 Wyrley Rd., Witton. B6 7BN. (Gavin Burrell). Open 10-2, Fri. and Sat. 9-4. SIZE: Warehouse. *STOCK: Upright and grand pianos.* LOC: 3 minutes from Spaghetti junction (M6, junction 6). PARK: Easy. TEL: 0121 327 2701; mobile - 0831 560518.

Carleton Gallery
91 Vivian Rd., Harborne. B17 0DR. (D. Dunnett). Open 9-5.30, Wed. 9-1. *STOCK: Maps and prints.* TEL: 0121 427 2487.

Chesterfield Antiques
181 Gravelly Lane. B23 5SG. (Mara Cirjanic). Est. 1977. Open 9.30-5.30. *STOCK: General antiques and fine art.* TEL: 0121 373 3876.

Peter Clark Antiques LAPADA
36 St. Mary's Row, Moseley. B13 8JG. Open 9-5.30. SIZE: Medium. *STOCK: Furniture, mid-17th C to early 20th C, £175-£2,500; silver, early 19th C to early 20th C, £100-£500.* LOC: Centre of Moseley. PARK: At rear. TEL: 0121 449 8245. SER: Valuations; restorations (furniture). VAT: Stan/Spec.

R. Collyer
185 New Rd., Rubery. B45 9JP. Open 9-5.30. *STOCK: Clocks including longcase; watches, barometers, secondhand jewellery.* LOC: 1 mile from Lydiate Ash roundabout. TEL: 0121 453 2332. SER: Valuations; restorations.

Birmingham continued

Dolly Mixtures
B68 0AU. Open by appointment. *STOCK: Dolls and teddies.* TEL: 0121 422 6959. SER: Restorations.

Maurice Fellows
21 Vyse St., Hockley. B18 6LE. *STOCK: Objets d'art, jewellery.* TEL: 0121 554 0211. SER: Valuations; restorations.

Format of Birmingham Ltd
18 Bennetts Hill. B2 5QJ. (G. Charman and D. Vice). Open 9.30-5. CL: Sat. *STOCK: Coins, medals.* PARK: New St. station. VAT: Stan/Spec.

Garratt Antiques
22 Great Western Arcade. Est. 1958. *STOCK: Jewellery, clocks, brass, silver, copper, pewter, silver plate, china, crystal, dolls and bric-a-brac.* TEL: 0121 212 1248; fax - 0121 236 0848. SER: Valuations; restorations. VAT: Stan/Spec.

A.W. Hone and Son Oriental Carpets
1486 Stratford Rd., Hall Green. B28 9ET. (Ian Hone). Est. 1949. Open 9.30-5.30, Sun. by appointment. SIZE: Medium. *STOCK: Persian rugs and carpets, late 19th C to date.* LOC: A34 south of city on Robin Hood Island. PARK: Own forecourt. TEL: 0121 744 1001; fax - same. SER: Valuations; restorations; finder service. VAT: Stan.

John Hubbard Antiques and Fine Art
LAPADA

224-226 Court Oak Rd., Harborne. B32 2EG. Est. 1968. Open 9-6. SIZE: Large. *STOCK: Furniture, 18th-19th C; paintings and watercolours, all £50-£15,000; lighting, silver, plate and decorative items.* LOC: 3 miles from city centre. PARK: Outside. TEL: 0121 426 1694. SER: Valuations; restorations; leather linings. VAT: Stan/Spec.

James Antiques
1053 Pershore Rd., Stirchley. B30 2YH. (P. and D. James). Est. 1969. Open afternoons or by appointment. SIZE: Small. *STOCK: Decorative antiques, country furniture, stained glass, painted goods, folk art, general, some 18th, mainly 19th C, to £500; architectural items.* TEL: 0121 444 4628/415 4229. SER: Valuations; restorations; stained glass design and manufacture; buys at auction.

Rex Johnson and Sons
8 Corporation St. B2 4RN. (D. Johnson). Open 9.15-5.15. *STOCK: Gold, silver, jewellery, porcelain and glass.* TEL: 0121 643 9674.

March Medals
113 Gravelly Hill North, Erdington. B23 6BJ. (M.A. March). Est. 1975. Open 10-5, Sat. 10-2. *STOCK: Orders, decorations, campaign medals, militaria and military books.* TEL: 0121 384 4901. SER: Catalogues issued. VAT: Stan/Spec.

Birmingham continued

F. Meeks & Co

197 Warstone Lane, Hockley. B18. (M.L. and S.R. Durham). Open 9-5, Sat. 9-12. *STOCK: Clocks especially longcase, mantle and wall; vintage wrist watches and antique pocket watches; all £100-£10,000.* TEL: 0121 236 9058. SER: Valuations; restorations (clocks); clock and watch parts supplied. VAT: Stan/Spec.

The Old Bakehouse

71 Station Rd., Harborne. B17 9LR. (Andrew Brooker-Carey). Est. 1989. Open Tues.-Sat. 11-5.30. SIZE: Medium. *STOCK: Pine furniture, fireplaces and mirrors, Georgian-Victorian, £50-£1,000; lighting, Victorian to 1920's, £50-£500; garden furniture, from Victorian, £10-£500; Victorian beds, £200-£600; furniture, Georgian to 1920's, £50-£800.* LOC: Parallel to High St. PARK: Easy. TEL: 0121 428 1928. SER: Valuations; restorations (wood and metal including polishing and painting). VAT: Stan/Spec.

The Original Choice Ltd

1340 Stratford Rd., Hall Green. B28 9EH. (J. Ellis). Open 10-6. *STOCK: Fireplaces, tiles, stained glass windows.* TEL: 0121 7783821.

Piccadilly Jewellers

105 New St. B2 4HD. (R. and R. Johnson). Open 10-5. *STOCK: Jewellery, silver and objects.* TEL: 0121 643 5791.

Alan Richards Brocante

168 Gravelly Lane, Erdington. B23 5SN. Open 10-5.30. *STOCK: French 19th-20th C furniture, Art Deco and books.* TEL: Mobile - 0410 202909; fax - 0121 384 6831.

S.R. Furnishing and Antiques

18 Stanley Rd., Oldbury. B68 0DY. (S. Willder). Est. 1975. *STOCK: General antiques and shipping furniture.* TEL: 0121 422 9788.

David Temperley Fine and Antiquarian Books

19 Rotton Park Rd., Edgbaston. B16 9JH. Resident. (D. and R.A. Temperley). Est. 1967. Open 9.30-5.30 by prior appointment. SIZE: Small. *STOCK: Fine antiquarian and rare books especially fine bindings, illustrated and press; fine colour plate books - natural history, costume, travel, topography and atlases, 16th-20th C; early and rare English and European playing cards.* LOC: 150 yards off Hagley Rd. (A456) and under 2 miles from city centre. 4 miles junction 3, M5. PARK: Easy. TEL: 0121 454 0135; fax - 0121 454 1124. SER: Valuations; restorations (book binding and paper); buys at auction (antiquarian books).

Warley Antique Centre

146 Pottery Rd., Warley Woods. B68 9HD. Open seven days. SIZE: 50+ cabinets and 4 furniture showrooms. *STOCK: General antiques and furniture, mainly 19th-20th C, including Ruskin pottery, silver, Worcester, Doulton, Moorcroft,*

Birmingham continued

clocks, bisque dolls, shipping items, etc. LOC: Off the A456 or A4123, J2/3 M5. PARK: Easy. TEL: 0121 434 3813; home - 0121 552 1525.

The Windmill Gallery

6 Ernest St., Holloway Head. B1 1NS. (M. and C. Ashton). Est. 1985. Open 9-5.30, Sat. and Sun. by appointment. SIZE: Medium. *STOCK: Watercolours and drawings, 18th-20th C, £100-£3,000+.* LOC: City centre. PARK: Easy. TEL: 0121 622 3986; fax - 0121 666 6630. SER: Valuations; restorations; mounting, framing. VAT: Spec.

BLOXWICH, Nr. Walsall

Cobwebs

639d Bloxwich Rd., Leamore. WS3 2BQ. (Mrs M. Hannaway). Open 10.30-4.30. CL: Mon. and Thurs. *STOCK: Bric-a-brac.* PARK: Easy. TEL: 01922 493670.

COVENTRY

The Antique Shop

107 Spon End. CV1 3HF. (J. Branagh). Open 10-5. *STOCK: General antiques, oils and 19th C watercolours.* TEL: 01203 525915.

Nicholas Green's Antiques

The Antique Warehouse, Rugby Rd., Binley Woods. Est. 1964. Open 9-5, Sun. 12-4. SIZE: Large. *STOCK: Furniture, 18th-20th C, £30-£3,000.* LOC: 2 minutes from M6 and A45 on A46 Coventry by-pass. PARK: Easy. TEL: 01203 453878. SER: Buys at auction. FAIRS: Newark. VAT: Stan.

Memories Antiques

400A Stoney Stanton Rd. CV6 5DH. (R.D. Seymour). Est. 1964. Open 10.30-1.30. CL: Wed. *STOCK: General antiques, Victorian and Edwardian furniture, shipping goods, stripped pine, china, gold, silver, paintings and collectors' items; Royal Doulton.* TEL: 01203 687994.

DORRIDGE, Nr Solihull

Dorridge Antiques & Collectables

7 Forest Court. (M. Kentish and C. Swift). SIZE: Medium. *STOCK: Furniture, £5-£1,500, ceramics, £5-£1,100, arms and armour, £5-£750, all from 18th C.* PARK: Easy. TEL: 01564 779336; home - 01564 779768; fax - same.

FOUR OAKS, Nr. Sutton Coldfield

M. Allen Watch and Clockmaker

76A Walsall Rd. B74 4QY. (M.A. Allen). Est. 1969. Open 9-5.30, Sun. by appointment. SIZE: Small. *STOCK: Vintage wristwatches - Omega, Longines, Girard, Perregaux and Jaeger le Coultre; clocks - Vienna regulators, 1820-1880, mantle and wall clocks.* LOC: By Sutton Park, close to television mast. PARK: Easy. TEL: 0121 308 6117; home - 0121 308 8134. SER: Valuations; restorations (clocks and watches). VAT: Stan/Spec.

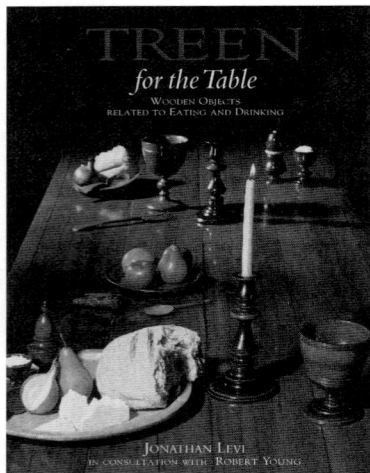

Four Oaks continued

Robert Taylor

Windy Ridge, Worcester Lane. B75 5QS. Est. 1983. Open 9-6.30 by appointment only, including Sun. *STOCK: Old collectable toys, including Dinky, Corgi, clockwork, tinplate, £5-£1,000.* PARK: Easy. TEL: 0121 308 4209; fax - 0121 323 3473. SER: Valuations; buys at auction. FAIRS: NEC; Donnington; Windsor.

HALESOWEN, Nr. Birmingham

Martyn Brown Antiques

130 Hagley Rd., Hayley Green. B63 1DY. Open 10-1. CL: Wed. *STOCK: Furniture, clocks, paintings and collectables.* TEL: 0121 585 5758.

Tudor House Antiques

68 Long Lane. B62 9LS. (D. Taylor). Open 9.30-5.30. *STOCK: Doors, fireplaces, pine including kitchens and furniture.* TEL: 0121 561 5563.

Robert Withers Antiques & Paintings

242 Hagley Rd., Hasbury. B63 4QQ. Open 9.30-6. *STOCK: Oils, watercolours, furniture, all 19th C.* PARK: At rear of gallery. TEL: 0121 585 0513; home - 0121 550 9033.

KNOWLE

Chadwick Antiques

Chadwick End. B93 0BP. Resident. (Mrs P. Tibenham). Est. 1973. Open 10-5, also some Sun. SIZE: Medium. *STOCK: Country furniture, 17th-19th C; interior decorating items.* Not Stocked: Oil paintings. LOC: A4141 mid-way between Warwick and Solihull. PARK: Easy. TEL: 01564 782096. SER: Valuations.

Tango Art Deco

22 Kenilworth Rd. B93 0JA. (Jenny and Martin Wills). Open Fri. and Sat. 9-6. SIZE: Small. *STOCK: Art Deco ceramics including Clarice Cliff, Susie Cooper, Shelley: small furniture, 1930's, £50-£500.* LOC: From M42, junction 5, take A4141 for 1 mile to end of Knowle High St., left on to A4101 (signposted Balsall Common), shop is 120yds on right. PARK: Free nearby.TEL: 01564 776669; home - 0121 704 4969; fax - same. FAIRS: NEC; Stafford; Thornbury; Deco at Warwick, Loughborough, Chester, Leeds, Syon Park. VAT: Spec.

LYE, Nr. Stourbridge

Lye Antique Furnishings

181 High St. DY9 8LH. (Mr and Mrs P. Smith). Est. 1979. Open 9-5. SIZE: Medium. *STOCK: Furniture, china, glass, metalware and collectors' items.* PARK: Easy. TEL: 01384 897513; mobile - 0976 765142. SER: Valuations.

Retro Products

Antique Warehouse, The Yard, Star St. DY9 8TU. (M. McHugo). Est. 1980. Open Mon., Wed. and Fri. 10-5. SIZE: Large. *STOCK: Furniture - Victorian, Edwardian, garden and shipping, £5-£1,000; cast iron metalwork; architectural items.* LOC: Off Stourbridge to Birmingham Rd. PARK: Easy. TEL: 01384 894042; home - 01384 373332. FAIRS: Ardingly and Newark. VAT: Stan.

Lye continued

Smithfield Antiques

20 Stourbridge Rd. DY9 7DL. (R. Harling). Open 9-5.30, other times by appointment. *STOCK: General antiques and shipping goods.* TEL: 01384 897821.

SOLIHULL

Renaissance

18 Marshall Lake Rd., Shirley. B90 4PL. MGMC. (S.K. Macrow). Est. 1981. Open 9-5. SIZE: Small. *STOCK: General antiques.* LOC: Near Stratford Rd. TEL: 0121 745 5140. SER: Restorations (repairs, re-upholstery and polishing).

Tilleys Antiques LAPADA

B91 2ES. (S.A. Alpren). Open by appointment only. *STOCK: British glass, Oriental pottery, porcelain, shipping goods; silver, 19th C; Worcester.* TEL: 0121 704 1813. SER: Valuations; restorations (jewellery, silver); repairs (clock, watch).

STOURBRIDGE

Oldswinford Gallery

106 Hagley Rd., Oldswinford. DY8 1QU. (A.R. Harris). Open 9.30-5. CL: Mon. and Sat. p.m. *STOCK: 18th-20th C oil paintings, watercolours and prints.* TEL: 01384 395577. SER: Restorations; framing.

Regency Antique Trading Centre

116 Stourbridge Rd. DY9 7BU. (D. Bevan). Open 9.30-5. SIZE: Several dealers. *STOCK: General antiques and collectables, fireplaces and pine.* TEL: 01384 868778.

Retro

48 Worcester St. DY8 1AS. (M. McHugo). Open Tues., Thurs., Sat. 9.30-5. *STOCK: Furniture.* TEL: 01384 442065.

SUTTON COLDFIELD

Thomas Coulborn and Sons BADA

Vesey Manor, 64 Birmingham Rd. B72 1QP. (P. Coulborn). Est. 1939. Open 9.15-5.30 (1hr. lunch). SIZE: Medium. *STOCK: General antiques, 1600-1830; fine English furniture, 17th-18th C; paintings and clocks.* LOC: 3 miles from Spaghetti Junction. From Birmingham A5127 through Erdington, premises on main road opposite cinema. PARK: Easy. TEL: 0121 354 3974; fax - 0121 354 4614. SER: Valuations; restorations (furniture and paintings); buys at auction. VAT: Spec.

Sutton Coldfield continued

Driffold Gallery
78 Birmingham Rd. B72 1QR. (David Gilbert). Open 10.30-5.30. CL: Thurs. *STOCK: Oil paintings and watercolours, 19th-20th C.* TEL: 0121 355 5433.

Kelford Antiques
14a Birmingham Rd. B72 1QG. (E.S. Kelsall). Est. 1968. Open 9-5. CL: Thurs. *STOCK: General antiques, Georgian and Victorian furniture, silver, porcelain, Staffordshire figures, pot-lids, jewellery.* TEL: 0121 354 6607. VAT: Stan/Spec.

Osborne Antiques
91 Chester Rd., New Oscott. B73 5BA. (C. Osborne). Est. 1976. Open 9-5, Sat. 9.15-12.15. CL: Mon. *STOCK: Barometers and clocks.* TEL: 0121 355 6667. SER: Restorations; spares (clocks, barometers); glass-blowers (barometers).

H. and R.L. Parry Ltd
23 Maney Corner. B72 1QL. (H. Parry). Est. 1925. Open 9.30-5.30. CL: Wed. SIZE: Medium. *STOCK: Porcelain, silver and jewellery, all periods; metalware, paintings.* LOC: A38 from Birmingham road into Sutton. Cinema on right, on corner of service road in which premises are situated. TEL: 0121 354 1178. SER: Valuations. VAT: Stan/Spec.

WALSALL

The Doghouse
309 Bloxwich Rd. WS2 7BD. Open 9-5.30, Sun. (Oct.-March) 2-5.30. SIZE: Large. *STOCK: General antiques.* TEL: 01922 30829. VAT: Stan.

Hardwick Antiques
317B Chester Rd., Aldridge. WS9 0PH. (P. Chatfield). Open 11-6. CL: Wed. am. *STOCK: Jewellery, silver, porcelain, furniture.* LOC: Opposite Ruby Rest. TEL: 0121 353 1489.

L.P. Antiques (Mids) Ltd
The Old Brewery, Short Acre St. WS2 8HW. (Pierre Farouz). Est. 1982. Open daily, Sun. by appointment. SIZE: Warehouse. *STOCK: French and Continental decorative furniture, period armoires, farm and rustic furniture, parquet tables, rush chairs.* LOC: Junction 10, M6, take A34 towards Cannock. PARK: Easy. TEL: 01922 746764; fax - 01922 611316; mobile - 0860 249097. SER: Packing, shipping. VAT: Stan.

Nicholls Jewellers and Antiques
57 George St. WS1 3RS. (R. Nicholls). Open 9-5. *STOCK: Jewellery; dolls by Gotz, Zapf, Alberon and Fair Lady.* TEL: 01922 641081. SER: Repairs.

WEDNESBURY

Brett Wilkins Antiques
81 Holyhead Rd. WS10 7PS. Est. 1983. Open Fri. and Sat., other days (including Sun.) by appointment. SIZE: Medium. *STOCK: Shipping items, 1900-1940, £5-£250; Victorian mahogany, 19th C, £100-£500; some pine, 19th-20th C, £100-£500.* LOC: 2 miles off M6, junction 9 on A41. PARK: Easy. TEL: 0121 502 0720; mobile - 0860 541260. FAIRS: All major. VAT: Stan.

Wednesbury continued

WOLVERHAMPTON

Antiquities
75-76 Dudley Rd. Est. 1968. Open 10-6. *STOCK: General antiques.* TEL: 01902 459800.

Alan M. France
WV11 1PE. Open by appointment only. *STOCK: Clocks, wrist and pocket watches.* TEL: 01902 731167.

Golden Oldies
5 St. Georges Parade. WV2 1AZ. (W.A. and M.A. Knowles). Open 10-5.30. CL: Mon. *STOCK: Victorian, Edwardian and later furniture, £25-£2,000; paintings, decorative items.* PARK: Easy. TEL: 01902 422397.

Kimber & Son
at Martin Taylor Antiques, 140b Tettenhall Rd. *STOCK: 18th-20th C antiques for the English, Continental and American markets.* PARK: Easy. TEL: 01902 751166; home - 01684 572000. VAT: Stan/Spec.

Martin-Quick Antiques LAPADA
323 Tettenhall Rd. WV6 0JZ. Est. 1965. Open 9-6, Sat. 9.30-4. SIZE: Large. *STOCK: 18th-19th C furniture including French and upholstered, shipping goods, stripped pine,* LOC: One mile from town centre on A41. PARK: Easy. TEL: 01902 754703; home - 01902 752908; fax - 01902 756889. SER: Packing and shipping. VAT: Stan/Spec.

Pendeford House Antiques
1 Pendeford Ave., Claregate, Tettenhall. WV6 9EG. (Mrs B. Tonks). Est. 1980. Open 10.30-5. CL: Thurs. SIZE: Medium. *STOCK: China and porcelain, £5-£500; furniture and clocks, £50-£1,500; oil paintings and watercolours, £50-£500; all 19th-20th C; glass, linen, brass and copper, jewellery and silver.* LOC: From main Tettenhall Rd., turn at traffic lights towards Codsall. At first small traffic island, take 3rd exit, shop next to Jet Garage. PARK: Easy. TEL: 01902 756175; home - 01902 752650.

The Red Shop
7 Hollybush Lane, Penn. (B. Savage). Open 9.30-5.30. *STOCK: Furniture including pine.* TEL: 01902 342915.

Martin Taylor Antiques LAPADA
140b Tettenhall Rd. WV6 0BQ. Est. 1967. Open 8.30-5.30, Sat. 9.30-1.30. SIZE: Large. *STOCK: Furniture, mainly 1800-1930 especially for USA, Australian, South African and European markets, £50-£10,000.* LOC: One mile from town centre on A41. PARK: Easy. TEL: 01902 751166; fax - 01902 746502; mobile - 0836 636524; home - 01785 284539. VAT: Stan/Spec

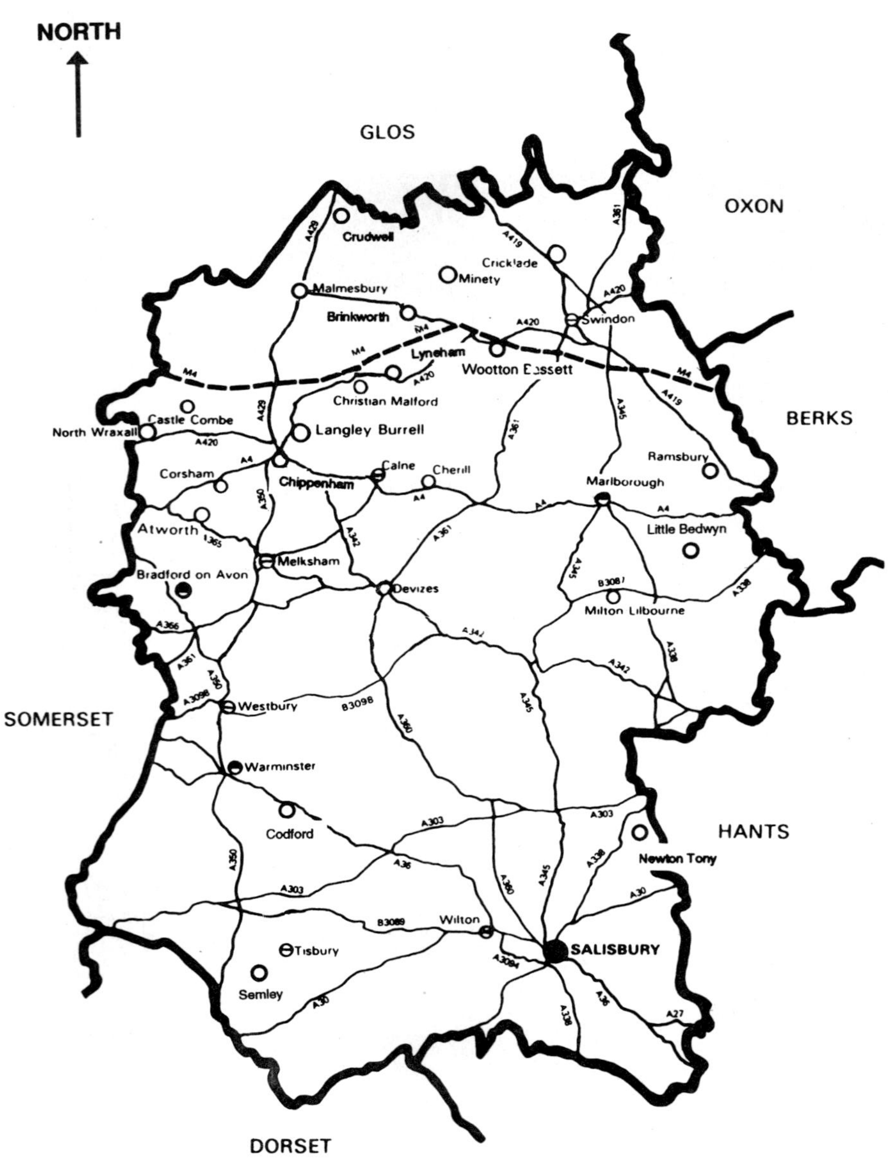

	Key to number of shops in this area.
○ 1-2	
⊖ 3-5	
◒ 6-12	
● 13+	

Please note this is only a rough map designed to show dealers the number of shops in the various towns, and is not necessarily totally accurate.

ATWORTH, Nr. Melksham

Peter Campbell Antiques

59 Bath Rd. SN12 8JY. BABADA. (P.R. Campbell). Est. 1976. Open 10-5, Sun. and Thurs. by appointment. SIZE: Medium. *STOCK: General antiques and decorative items, 18th-19th C.* Not Stocked: Silver and jewellery. LOC: Between Bath and Melksham on A350. PARK: Easy. TEL: 01225 709742; home - same. VAT: Stan/Spec.

BRADFORD-ON-AVON

Audley House Antiques

5 Woolley St. BA15 1AD. BABADA. (David, Joyce and Richard Brown). Open 9-6 or by appointment. *STOCK: Quality furniture, mainly Victorian and Edwardian; watercolours, prints, small silver, porcelain and interesting small items.* TEL: 01225 862476. SER: Framing.

Avon Antiques BADA

25, 26 and 27 Market St. BA15 1LL. BABADA. (V. and A. Jenkins BA). Est. 1963. Open 9.45-5.30, Sun. by appointment. SIZE: Large. *STOCK: English and some Continental furniture, 1600-1880; metalwork, treen, clocks, barometers, some textiles, painted and lacquer furniture.* LOC: A363, main street of town. PARK: Ask at shop for key to private parking opposite. TEL: 01225 862052; fax - 01225 868763. FAIRS: Grosvenor House. VAT: Spec.

Mac Humble Antiques BADA

7-9 Woolley St. BA15 1AD. BABADA. (W. Mc. A. and B.J. Humble). Open 9-6. SIZE: Medium. *STOCK: 17th-19th C oak, mahogany, fruitwoods, metalware, treen, samplers, silkwork pictures, decorative objects.* TEL: 01225 866329; fax – same. SER: Valuations; restorations. VAT: Stan/Spec.

Moxhams Antiques LAPADA

17, 23 and 24 Silver St. BA15 1JZ. BABADA. (R., J. and N. Bichard). Est. 1966. Open 9-5.30 or by appointment. SIZE: Large. *STOCK: English and Continental furniture, clocks, 1650-1850; European and Oriental pottery and porcelain, 1700-1850; decorative items, 1600-1900, all £50-£50,000.* PARK: Own, at rear. TEL: 01225 862789; fax - 01225 867844; home - 01380 828677. VAT: Spec.

Paul Nash Antiques LAPADA

11 Silver St. BA15 1JY. Est. 1961. Open Mon.-Sat., otherwise by appointment. *STOCK: Period furniture.* TEL: 01225 866561; mobile - 0385 570701; fax - 01225 867455. VAT: Spec.

Town and Country Antiques

34 Market St. BA15 1LL. BABADA. (Rosemary Drewett and Michael Hughes). Open 10.15-5, other times by appointment. *STOCK: Fine period furniture, metalware, caddies, boxes and period decorative items.* PARK: Nearby. TEL: 01225 867877; fax - same. VAT: Spec.

BRADFORD ON AVON

Probably the best town for period antique furniture outside of LONDON

AVON ANTIQUES

Established 1963

25-26-27 Market Street, Bradford on Avon, Wiltshire BA15 1LL
Telephone: (01225) 862052 Andrew & Vibeke Jenkins

TOWN & COUNTRY ANTIQUES

34 Market Street, Bradford-on-Avon, Wilts. BA15 1LL
Tel. & Facsimile: (01225) 867877

ROSEMARY DREWETT & MICHAEL HUGHES

Fine Period Furniture, Country Furniture, Metalware and Decorative Items

MOXHAMS ANTIQUES

17, 23 & 24 Silver Street, Bradford on Avon, Wiltshire BA15 1JZ
Tel: (01225) 862789 Fax: (01225) 867844 Home: (01380) 828677
Roger, Jill and Nicholas Bichard
Open Mon - Sat 9 - 5.30 or by appointment
Period furniture, ceramics, metalware
Needlework, decorative & garden items

AUDLEY HOUSE ANTIQUES

5 Woolley Street, Bradford-on-Avon, Wiltshire BA15 1AD

Tel: (01225) 862476

MAC HUMBLE
ANTIQUES

18th & 19th Century Furniture, Metalware, Treen and Needlework.
Decorative items. Valuations & Restorations.

7-9 Woolley Street, Bradford-on-Avon, Wiltshire BA15 1AD
Telephone: (01225) 866329 Facsimile: (01225) 866329

An excellent place to stop for lunch with good pubs, cafes and restaurants in the centre of this beautiful Wiltshire town.

Bradford-on-Avon continued

Trevor Waddington Antique Clocks

5 Trowbridge Rd. BA15 1EE. MBHI. Est. 1996. Strictly by appointment. SIZE: Small. *STOCK: 18th-19th C clocks - longcase, £2,000-£8,000; wall, £750-£2,000; carriage, bracket and mantel, £500-£5,000.* LOC:.25 mile south of town bridge on A363. PARK: Easy. TEL: 01225 862351; home/fax - same. SER: Valuations; restorations (BADA/West Dean Dip. conservator); buys at auction (as stock).

BRINKWORTH, Nr. Malmesbury

North Wilts Exporters

Farm Hill House. SN15 5AJ. (M. Thornbury). Est. 1972. Open Mon.-Sat. or by appointment. *STOCK: Imported Continental pine, 18th-19th C; shipping goods.* LOC: Off M4, junction 16 Malmesbury road. TEL: 01666 510876; mobile - 0836 260730. SER: Valuations; shipping; import and export. VAT: Stan.

CALNE

Calne Antiques

London Rd. SN11 0AB. (M. Blackford). Open 9-5 including Sun. *STOCK: Victorian and Edwardian furniture including pine; shipping goods and smalls.* LOC: Next to White Hart Hotel. TEL: 01249 816311.

Clive Farahar and Sophie Dupré - Rare Books, Autographs and Manuscripts

Horsebrook House, 15 The Green. SN11 8DQ. Open by appointment. SIZE: Medium. *STOCK: Rare books on voyages and travels, autograph letters and manuscripts, 15th-20th C, £5-£5,000.* LOC: Off A4 in town centre. PARK: Easy. TEL: 01249 821121; fax - 01249 821202. SER: Valuations; buys at auction (as stock). FAIRS: ABA; Universal Autograph Collectors' Club. VAT: Stan.

Calne continued

Hilmarton Manor Press

Hilmarton Manor. SN11 8SB. (H. Baile de Laperriere). Est. 1967. Open 9-6. SIZE: Medium. *STOCK: New and out-of-print art and photography reference books, some antiquarian.* LOC: 3 miles from Calne on A3102 towards Swindon. PARK: Easy. TEL: 0124 976 208. SER: Buys at auction.

CASTLE COMBE, Nr. Chippenham

Combe Cottage Antiques

SN14 7HU. (B. and A. Bishop). Est. 1960. Open 10-1 and 2-6, prior telephone call advisable. SIZE: Medium. *STOCK: Country furniture, £20-£5,000; metalware, £10-£2,000; both 17th to early 19th C; treen, pottery, 18th-19th C, £5-£500; early lighting devices.* Not Stocked: Mahogany furniture, glass, silver, Victoriana. LOC: A420 from Chippenham towards Bristol. After 3 miles bear right on B4039. PARK: 20yds. TEL: 01249 782250; fax - 01249 782250. SER: Valuations; specialists in cottage furnishings. VAT: Spec.

CHERHILL, Nr. Calne

P.A. Oxley Antique Clocks and Barometers

LAPADA

The Old Rectory, Main Rd. SN11 8UX. Est. 1971. Open 9.30-5, other times by appointment. CL: Wed. SIZE: Large. *STOCK: Longcase, bracket, carriage clocks and barometers, 17th-19th C, £500-£30,000.* LOC: A4, not in village. PARK: Easy. TEL: 01249 816227; fax - 01249 821285. VAT: Spec.

CHIPPENHAM

Lucy Cope Designs

Foxhill House, Allington. SN14 6LL. Resident. (G.E. and L. Cope). Est. 1986. Open 7 days 9-6 by appointment. SIZE: Medium. *STOCK: Lamps, small decorative accessories and paintings.* LOC: Off A420 towards Bath, 2 miles from Chippenham. PARK: Easy. TEL: 01249 650446; fax - 01249 444936. SER: Restorations (period lampshades); lampshade makers. *Trade Only.*

CHRISTIAN MALFORD, Nr. Chippenham

Harley Antiques

The Comedy. SN15 4BS. (G.J. Harley). Est. 1959. Open 9-6 including Sun., or later by appointment. SIZE: Large. *STOCK: Furniture, 18th-19th C, £150-£3,000; decorative objects, £30-£1,000.* LOC: B4069, 4 miles off M4, junction 17. PARK: Own. TEL: 01249 720112; home - same; fax - 01249 720553. SER: Colour brochure available (export only). VAT: Stan. *Trade Only.*

CODFORD, Nr. Warminster

Tina's Antiques

75 High St. BA12 0ND. (T.A. Alder). Open 9-6, Sat. 9-1. *STOCK: General antiques.* TEL: 01985 850828.

CORSHAM

Matthew Eden

Pickwick End. SN13 0JB. Resident. Est. 1951. SIZE: Large. *STOCK: Country house furniture and garden items, 17th-19th C.* TEL: 01249 713335; fax - 01249 713644. VAT: Spec.

A Sèvre seau dating from around 1753, originally decorated in bleu lapis with gilt panels and birds and later decorated in the mid 19th century with a repellent inflatable-rubber putto on an appalling mixture of pink and bleu céleste grounds. Under the handles traces of the bleu lapis ground which was etched off with hydrofluoric acid can be detected. 6in. £120.

From an article entitled "Sèvres or What?" by David Battie which appeared in the December 1997/January 1998 issue of **Antique Collecting.**

CRICKLADE, Nr. Swindon

Edred A.F. Gwilliam

Candletree House, Bath Rd. SN6 6AX. Est. 1976. Open by appointment. SIZE: Medium. *STOCK: Arms and armour, swords, pistols, long guns, £50-£20,000+.* PARK: Easy. TEL: 01793 750241; fax - 01793 750359. SER: Valuations; buys at auction. FAIRS: Major arms. VAT: Stan/Spec.

Robin Shield Antiques BADA LAPADA

23 High St. SN6 6AP. Est. 1974. Open 9.30-5.30, but appointment advisable. SIZE: Medium. *STOCK: Furniture and paintings, £200-£20,000; works of art, £100-£5,000; all 17th-19th C.* PARK: Easy. TEL: 01793 750205; fax - 01793 752010; mobile - 0860 520391. SER: Valuations; buys at auction. VAT: Stan/Spec.

CRUDWELL

Crudwell Furniture

Odd Penny Farm. SN16 9SJ. TADA. (Philip A. Ruttleigh). Est. 1990. Open 9-5 and by appointment. CL: Sat. SIZE: Small. *STOCK: Furniture including pine in the paint, and decorative items, £10-£2,000.* LOC: Next to RAF Kemble on A429, 5 minutes from Cirencester, 15 mins from junction 17, M4. TEL: 01285 770970. SER: Furniture restoration, including stripping; bead blasting for architectural antiques.

DEVIZES

Cross Keys Jewellers

The Ginnel, Market Pl. SN10 1HN. (D. and D. Pullen). Est. 1967. Open 9.15-5.15. *STOCK: Jewellery, silver.* LOC: Alley adjacent Nationwide Building Society. PARK: Easy. TEL: 01380 726293. VAT: Stan.

St Mary's Chapel Antiques

Northgate St. BABADA. (Richard Sankey). *STOCK: Painted and Continental country furniture, decorative accessories and garden items.* TEL: 01380 721399.

LANGLEY BURRELL, Nr. Chippenham

Harriet Fairfax Fireplaces and General Antiques

Langley Green. Open by appointment only. *STOCK: China, glass, dolls, furniture, fabrics and needlework; architectural items and fittings, brass and iron knobs, knockers; fireplaces, pine and iron, 1780-1950.* TEL: 01249 652030. SER: Polishing; welding; design consultancy.

LITTLE BEDWYN, Nr. Marlborough

Turpin's Antiques BADA

Old Manor Cottage. SN8 3JG. (Jane Sumner). Open by appointment. SIZE: Large. *STOCK: 17th-18th C walnut, oak and mahogany, metalware.* TEL: 01672 870727. SER: Restorations. VAT: Spec.

LYNEHAM, Nr. Chippenham

Pillars Antiques

10 The Banks. Resident. (K. Clifford). Est. 1986. Open 10-5, including Sun. CL: Thurs. SIZE: Medium. *STOCK: Victorian and Edwardian pine, £5-£1,000; shipping oak, 1900-1940's, from £15.* LOC: B4069 Chippenham road, 1 mile from village. PARK: Easy. TEL: 01249 890632; home - same.

MALMESBURY

Antiques - Rene Nicholls

56 High St. SN16 9AT. (Mrs. R. Nicholls). Est. 1980. Open 10-5.30, Sun. by appointment. SIZE: Small. *STOCK: English pottery and porcelain, 18th to early 19th C, £50-£900; small furniture.* PARK: Opposite. TEL: 01666 823089; home - same.

Andrew Britten Antiques

48 High St. SN16 9AT. (T.M. Tyler and T.A. Freeman). Est. 1975. Open 9.30-6, Sun. by appointment. SIZE: Medium. *STOCK: Furniture, 1700-1900, £100-£1,500; decorative brass, wood, glass and porcelain items, £15-£500.* PARK: Opposite. TEL: 01666 823376. VAT: Spec.

Cross Hayes Antiques LAPADA

The Antique and Furniture Warehouse, 19 Bristol St. SN16 0AY. (D. Brooks). Est. 1975. Open 9-5 or by appointment. SIZE: Warehouse. *STOCK: Shipping oak, plus Victorian and Edwardian mahogany and walnut, French furniture, 1850-1920's; bric-a-brac.* TEL: 01666 824260; home - 01666 822062; fax - 01666 823020. SER: Valuations. VAT: Stan/Spec.

MARLBOROUGH

The Antique and Book Collector

Katharine House, The Parade. SN8 1NE. (C.C. Gange). Est. 1983. Open 9.45-5.30. SIZE: Medium. *STOCK: Furniture, 17th-19th C, £200-£2,000; decorative items, £100-£1,000; Chinese, Roman and Greek antiquities, 2000BC-1000AD, £100-£1,000; paintings and prints, £10-£1,000; books, £5-£500.* PARK: Easy. TEL: 01672 514040; home - same. FAIRS: PBFA monthly. VAT: Stan/Spec.

Bona Art Deco Store

Bizarre House, 124 High Street. SN8 1LZ. ADDA. Open 10-5 including Sun. SIZE: Large. *STOCK: Decorative arts, 1925-1942, £5-£20,000.* PARK: Easy. TEL: 01252 372188; fax - 01672 514100. SER: Valuations; restorations (ceramics, bronze, spelter). VAT: Stan.

Cook of Marlborough Fine Art Ltd

LAPADA

High Trees House, Savernake Forest. SN8 4NE. BAFRA. (W.J. Cook). Est. 1963. Open 10-5, Sat. and Sun. by appointment. SIZE:

Marlborough continued

Medium. *STOCK: Furniture, 18th to early 19th C; objets d'art, 18th-19th C; pictures, 19th-20th C.* LOC: 1.5 miles from Marlborough on A346 towards Burbage. PARK: Easy. TEL: 01672 513017; fax - 01672 514455. SER: Valuations; restorations (furniture including polishing and gilding); buys at auction (furniture). FAIRS: Café Royal; Olympia; Barbican; Harrogate. VAT: Stan/Spec.

Cross Keys Jewellers

21a High St. SN8 1LW. (D. and D. Pullen). Est. 1967. Open 9.30-5.30. *STOCK: Jewellery, silver.* LOC: Entrance to Waitrose car park. TEL: 01672 516260. VAT: Stan.

Robert Kime Antiques

PO Box 454 SN8 3UR. Est. 1968. Open by appointment only. *STOCK: Decorative, period furniture.* TEL: 01264 731268. VAT: Spec.

The Marlborough Parade Antique Centre

The Parade. SN8 1NE. (T. Page and N. Cannon). Est. 1985. Open 10-5 including Sun. SIZE: 57 dealers. *STOCK: Good quality furniture, paintings, silver, porcelain, glass, clocks, jewellery, copper, brass and pewter, £5-£5,000.* LOC: Adjacent A4 in town centre. PARK: Easy. TEL: 01672 515331. SER: Valuations; restorations (furniture, porcelain, copper, brass). VAT: Spec.

The Military Parade Bookshop

The Parade. SN8 1NE. (G. and P. Kent). *STOCK: Military history books especially regimental histories and the World Wars.* LOC: Next to The Lamb. TEL: 01672 515470; fax - 01980 630150.

Principia Arts and Sciences

5 London Rd. SN8 1PH. (M.D.C. Forrer). Open 9-6, Sun. 10-5. *STOCK: Collectors' items, scientific instruments, country furniture, treen, pictures, clocks, china, porcelain and books.* TEL: 01672 512072; fax - 01672 511551.

Stuart Gallery

4 London Rd. SN8 1PH. (A.B. Loncraine). Est. 1968. Open Thurs., Fri. and Sat. 9-6.30. *STOCK: General antiques especially small collectables, watercolours, oils and prints, china, glass, interior design pieces, books, garden items.* PARK: Easy. TEL: 01672 513593.

Annmarie Turner Antiques

22 Salisbury Rd. SN8 4AD. Resident. Est. 1960. Open 10-6, Sun. by appointment. SIZE: Small. *STOCK: British oak, fruitwood, pine and primitive country furniture, £50-£1,500; treen and kitchenalia, £5-£100; allied decorative items and the unusual, £20-£500, 17th C-1920's.* Not Stocked: Mahogany, jewellery, silver, reproduction. LOC: Left side of first roundabout approaching town centre from Hungerford on A4. PARK: Easy and at rear. TEL: 01672 515396; home - same. SER: Valuations. VAT: Spec.

MELKSHAM

Dann Antiques Ltd

Unit 1, Avonside Enterprise Park, New Broughton Rd. SN12 8BS. BABADA. Open 9-5.30, Sat. 9-1. SIZE: Large. *STOCK: 18th-19th C mahogany and walnut furniture and accessories including majolica, Masons and Staffordshire.* TEL: 01225 707329; fax - 01225 790120; home - 01380 812228.

Alan Jaffray

16 Market Place. SN12 6EX. BABADA. Est. 1956. Open Mon-Fri. 9-5. SIZE: Large. *STOCK: Furniture and smalls, 18th-19th C, £50-£2,000.* LOC: Main Bath to Devizes Rd. PARK: On premises. TEL: 01225 702269; fax - 01225 790413. VAT: Stan/Spec.

King Street Curios

8 King St. SN12 6HD. Est. 1991. SIZE: 20 units. *STOCK: China, Denby, Goss, glass, jewellery, Art Deco, kitchenalia, furniture.* LOC: A350. PARK: Own at rear. TEL: 01225 790623. FAIRS: Oasis, Swindon; Neeld Hall, Chippenham; Templemeads (Brunel), Bristol.

MILTON LILBOURNE, Nr. Pewsey

Rupert Gentle Antiques BADA

The Manor House. SN9 5LQ. Est. 1954. Open 9.15-6. SIZE: Medium. *STOCK: English and*

Milton Lilbourne continued

***Continental domestic metalwork, 1650-1850; treen, decorative objects, needlework and domestic accessories.* LOC: From Hungerford on A4 take A338 for Pewsey. PARK: Easy. TEL: 01672 563344; fax - 01672 564136. SER: Valuations; buys at auction. VAT: Stan/Spec.**

MINETY, Nr. Malmesbury

Sambourne House Antiques

Sambourne House. SN16 9RQ. (T. Cove). Est. 1984. Open daily, Sun. by appointment. SIZE: Large. *STOCK: Pine, 19th C, £75-£1,000; furniture, 20th C, £20-£1,000; containers from Eastern Europe.* LOC: 10 mins. from M4, junction 16. PARK: Easy. TEL: 01666 860288; home - 01666 822271. SER: Valuations; restorations (pine, renovating, stripping and finishing); furniture made from reclaimed pine; export arranged. VAT: Stan.

NEWTON TONY, Nr Salisbury

Ray Best Antiques LAPADA

Owl Cottage SP4 0HF. Est. 1964. Open by appointment. *STOCK: Period furniture and decorative objects.* TEL: 01980 629528; mobile - 0831 766340. *Trade Only.*

NORTH WRAXALL, Nr. Chippenham

Delomosne and Son Ltd BADA

Court Close. SN14 7AD. BABADA. Articles on chandeliers, glass and porcelain. (T.N.M. Osborne and M.C.F. Mortimer). Est. 1905. Open 9.30-5.30; Sat. 9.30-1 (except Bank Holiday weekends). SIZE: Large. *STOCK: English and Irish glass, pre-1830, £20-£20,000; glass, chandeliers, English and European porcelain, needlework, papier mâché and treen.* LOC: Off A420 between Bath and Chippenham. PARK: Easy. TEL: 01225 891505; fax - 01225 891907. SER: Valuations; buys at auction. FAIRS: International Ceramic. VAT: Spec.

RAMSBURY, Nr. Marlborough

Heraldry Today

Parliament Piece. SN8 2QH. Est. 1954. Open 9.30-4.30. CL: Sat. *STOCK: Heraldic and genealogical books and manuscripts, £3-£6,000.* TEL: 01672 520617; fax - 01672 520183; e-mail - heraldry@heraldrytoday.co.uk; internet - http://www.heraldrytoday.co.uk.

Inglenook Antiques

59 High St. SN8 2QN. (D. White). Est. 1969. Open 10-5. CL: Mon. and Wed. except by appointment. *STOCK: Oil lamps, clocks, barometers and spare parts, some furniture.* LOC: Off A4. TEL: 01672 520261. SER: Restorations (longcase clock movements and barometers).

SALISBURY

Antique and Collectors Market

37 Catherine St. SP1 2DH. Open 9-5. SIZE: Large. *STOCK: Silver, plate, china, glass, toys, books, taxidermy, postcards, pens and furniture.* TEL: 01722 326033.

The Avonbridge Antiques and Collectors Market

United Reformed Church Hall, Fisherton St. Open Tues. 9-3.30. SIZE: 15 dealers. *STOCK: General antiques.*

The Barn Book Supply

88 Crane St. SP1 2QD. (J. and J. Head). Est. 1958. Open 9.30-5. CL: Sat. *STOCK: Antiquarian books on angling, shooting, horses, deerstalking.* TEL: 01722 327767; fax - 01722 339888.

D.M. Beach

52 High St. SP1 2PG. (A. Beach). Est. 1930. Open 9-5.30. SIZE: Large. *STOCK: Antiquarian books, 1500 to date, 5p-£1,000; maps, prints, oils and watercolours, to £1,500.* LOC: From Bournemouth into city, take first possible turn left. Shop is on next corner. PARK: 120yds. down Crane St. TEL: 01722 333801: fax - 01722 333720. SER: Valuations; restorations (leather bindings); buys at auction.

Salisbury continued

Derek Boston Antiques

223 Wilton Rd. and warehouse at Wilton. SP2 7JY. Est. 1964. Open 9.30-5. *STOCK: 18th-19th C furniture.* TEL: 01722 322682; home - 01722 324426. VAT: Stan/Spec.

Robert Bradley Antiques

71 Brown St. SP1 2BA. Est. 1970. Open 9.30-5.30. CL: Sat. *STOCK: Furniture, 17th-18th C; decorative items.* TEL: 01722 333677; fax - 01722 339922. VAT: Spec.

Ronald Carr

6 St. Francis Rd. SP1 3QS. (R.G. Carr). Est. 1983. Open by appointment. SIZE: Small. *STOCK: Modern British etchings, wood engravings and colour wood cuts, £5-£1,000.* LOC: 1 mile north of city on A345. PARK: Easy. TEL: 01722 328892; home - same. SER: Buys at auction.

Castle Galleries

81 Castle St. SP1 3SP. (John C. Lodge). Est. 1971. Open 9-5, Sat. 9-1. CL: Mon. and Wed. *STOCK: General antiques, coins and medals.* PARK: Easy. TEL: 01722 333734.

Jonathan Green Antiques

87 Castle St. SP1 3SP. Est. 1975. Open 9.30-4.30, Sat. 9.30-12.30. CL: Mon. SIZE: Small. *STOCK: Silver and plate, Georgian to modern, £5-£5,000.* PARK: Easy. TEL: 01722 332635. SER: Valuations; restorations (silver including re-plating). VAT: Stan/Spec.

Edward Hurst Antiques

The Garden Room, Netherhampton. SP2 8PU. Est. 1983. Open 9.30-5.30, Sat. by appointment. SIZE: Medium. *STOCK: English furniture and associated works of art, 1650-1820.* LOC: Just west of Salisbury. PARK: Easy. TEL: 01722 743042. VAT: Spec.

The Jerram Gallery LAPADA

7 St John St. SP1 2SB. (Mark Jerram). Open Tues., Thurs., Fri. 10-5. SIZE: Medium. *STOCK: British oil paintings and watercolours, 1850-1950; 20th C etchings, contemporary pictures and sculptures, £100-£15,000.* LOC: St John St. is an extension of Exeter St., opposite Queen Anne's Gate. PARK: Loading and unloading, or nearby. TEL: 01722 412310; fax - 01722 323577. SER: Valuations; restorations; framing; finder; buys at auction.

Salisbury Antiques Warehouse LAPADA

94 Wilton Rd. SP2 7JJ. (Chris Watts). Est. 1964. Open 9.30-5.30, Sat. and Sun. by appointment. SIZE: Large. *STOCK: Furniture, clocks and shipping goods, 18th-19th C, £50-£3,000; paintings, 19th C, £100-£2,000.* LOC: A36 Warminster-Southampton road. PARK: Easy. TEL: 01722 410634; mobile - 0802 635055. VAT: Stan/Spec.

Salisbury continued

William Sheppee

Old Sarum Airfield. SP4 6BJ. (W. Hiley and A. Cox). Est. 1989. Open Mon.-Fri. 9-5.30 by appointment only. SIZE: Large. *STOCK: Anglo-Indian and Indian furniture, 19th C, £500-£6,000; treen, £50-£250.* TEL: 01722 334454; fax - 01722 337754. SER: Valuations; export. VAT: Stan.

Chris Wadge Clocks

83 Fisherton St. SP2 7ST. Open 9-5. CL: Mon. *STOCK: Clocks, movements and spare parts.* TEL: 01722 334467. SER: 400 day specialist.

SEMLEY, Nr. Shaftesbury

May and May Ltd

Whitebridge. SP7 9QP. Est. 1963. Open by appointment. *STOCK: Antiquarian music and music literature.* TEL: 01747 830034; fax - 01747 830035. SER: Buys at auction.

SWINDON

Antiques and All Pine

11 Newport St., Old Town. SN1 3DX. (J. and M. Brown). Open 10-5.30. CL: Wed. SIZE: Medium. *STOCK: Pine, traditional brass and iron beds, china, lace, linen and costume jewellery.* LOC: From M4, junction 15 or 16 follow signs to Old Town. PARK: 100yds. TEL: 01793 520259. VAT: Stan/Spec.

Savernake Antiques Arcade

Victoria Centre, 138/9 Victoria Rd., Old Town. SN1 3BU. (Peter and Carol Dent). Est. 1977. Open 10-5, Sun. 11-4. SIZE: Large. *STOCK: Furniture, £50-£1,500; china and porcelain, £20-£100; jewellery and silver, £10-£300.* LOC: On left on hill between Old Town and college. PARK: Prospect Place. TEL: 01793 536668; fax - 01488 684004; home - 01488 686800. SER: Restorations (furniture); buys at auction. VAT: Stan.

Allan Smith Antique Clocks

162 Beechcroft Rd., Upper Stratton. SN2 6QE. Est. 1988. Open by appointment. SIZE: Medium. *STOCK: 50+ longcase clocks, including automata, moonphase, painted dial, brass dial, 30 hour, 8 day, London and Provincial, £1,650-£9,750; occasionally stick and banjo barometers, mantel, wall, bracket, Vienna and lantern clocks.* LOC: Near Bakers Arms Inn. PARK: Own. TEL: 01793 822977; mobile - 0378 834342. VAT: Spec.

Victoria Bookshop

30 Wood St., Old Town. SN1 4AB. (S. Austin). Est. 1965. Open 9-5.30. SIZE: Large. *STOCK: Books, most subjects, old postcards.* LOC: Middle of Old Town shopping area. PARK: Nearby. TEL: 01793 527364.

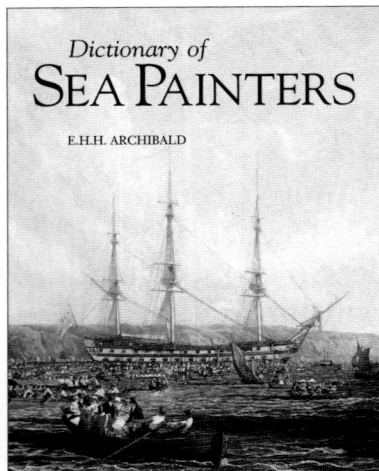

TISBURY

Edward Marnier Antiques

17 High St. SP3 6HF. Resident. (E.F. Marnier). Est. 1989. Open 10-6, Sun. and Wed. by appointment. *STOCK: English and Continental furniture, pictures, rugs, carpets and interesting decorative objects, 17th-20th C, £5-£5,000.* PARK: Easy. TEL: 01747 870213; fax - same. SER: Valuations; buys at auction. VAT: Spec.

WARMINSTER

Bishopstrow Antiques

55 East St. BA12 9BZ. (J.M. Stewart Cox). Est. 1974. Open 10-1 and 2-5.30. SIZE: Medium. *STOCK: 18th-19th C mahogany, oak and painted furniture; pottery and porcelain, boxes, small silver and decorative items.* LOC: On left of old A36 leaving Warminster on Salisbury road, opposite Esso garage. PARK: Easy. TEL: 01985 212683; home - 01985 840877. VAT: Spec.

Choice Antiques

4 Silver St. BA12 8PS. (Avril Bailey). Open 10-1 and 2-5.30. SIZE: Medium. *STOCK: General antiques and decorative items, 18th-19th C, £25-£2,000.* PARK: Easy. TEL: 01985 218924. VAT: Stan/Spec.

Emma Hurley Antiques and Textiles

3 Silver St. BA12 8PS. (Emma and John Hurley). Est. 1970. Usually open 10-5. SIZE: Medium. *STOCK: Decorative furnishings, 19th C; textiles, 18th-19th C; both £25-£1,000.* LOC: From Bath or Frome road, 200 yards past obelisk monument on right. PARK: Nearby. TEL: 01985 219726; home - 01985 847021. FAIRS: Shepton Mallet; Bath Decorative.

Isabella Antiques

11 Silver St. BA12 8PS. (B.W. Semke). Est. 1990. Open 10-5.30. SIZE: Medium. *STOCK: Furniture, late 18th C to late 19th C, £100-£5,000; boxes and mirrors, 19th C, £50-£500.* LOC: Main road. PARK: Easy. TEL: 01985 218933. SER: Buys at auction (furniture). VAT: Spec.

Number 9

9 Silver St. BA12 8PS. *STOCK: French and English country and garden furniture; decorative items.* LOC: Main road. PARK: Easy. TEL: 01985 214576.

Obelisk Antiques LAPADA

2 Silver St. BA12 8PS. (P. Tanswell). Open 10-1 and 2-5.30. SIZE: Large. *STOCK: English and Continental furniture, 18th-19th C; decorative items, objets d'art.* TEL: 01985 846646; fax - 01985 219901.

Tristram Latimer Sayer

8 Silver St. BA12 8PS. *STOCK: Early furniture, lighting and effects.* LOC: Main road. PARK: Easy. TEL: 01985 847230.

Warminster continued

K. and A. Welch

1A Church St. BA12 8PG. Est. 1967. Open 8-6, Sat. 9-1. SIZE: Large. *STOCK: Shipping furniture, 18th-19th C, £10-£2,000.* LOC: A36 west end of town. PARK: Own. TEL: 01985 214687; home - 01985 213433. VAT: Stan/Spec.

WEST YATTON, Nr. Chippenham

Heirloom & Howard Limited

Manor Farm. SN14 7EU. BABADA. (D.S. Howard). Est. 1972. Open 9.30-5.30, Sat. 11-5 or by appointment. SIZE: Medium. *STOCK: Porcelain mainly Chinese armorial and export, 18th C, £100-£5,000; heraldic items, 18th-19th C, £10-£1,000; portrait engravings, 17th-19th C, £10-£50.* LOC: 10 miles from Bath, 1/4 mile off A420 Chippenham/Bristol road. Transport from Chippenham station (4 miles) if required. PARK: Own. TEL: 01249 783038; fax - 01249 783039. SER: Valuations; buys at auction (Chinese porcelain). VAT: Spec.

WESTBURY

Ray Coggins Antiques

1 Fore St. BA13 3AU. Open 9-5.30. *STOCK: Antique and decorative furniture and architectural fittings.* TEL: 01373 826574.

WILTON, Nr. Salisbury

Hingstons of Wilton

36 North St. SP2 0HJ. Open 9-5, Sat. 10-4. SIZE: Large. *STOCK: Mainly furniture, Victorian-1930's.* TEL: 01722 742263; home - 01703 812143.

Pamela Lynch

18 West St. SP2 0DF. Resident. Open Tues., Wed. and Thurs. 10-5, other times by appointment. *STOCK: Small furniture, needlework pictures, decorative items, objets de vertu.* TEL: 01722 744113.

Mark Patterson Antiques

26 North St. SP2 0HJ. Open 9-5 or by appointment. SIZE: Shop + warehouse. *STOCK: General antiques, specialising in period English furniture.* TEL: 01722 743392; mobile - 0973 551519. VAT: Spec.

A.J. Romain and Sons

The Old House, 11 and 13 North St. SP2 0HA. *STOCK: Furniture, mainly 17th-18th C; early oak, walnut and marquetry; clocks, copper, brass and miscellanea.* TEL: 01722 743350. VAT: Stan/Spec.

WOOTTON BASSETT, Nr. Swindon

Tubbjoys Antique Market

118 High St. SN4 7AU. (Charles and Bridget Tubb). Est. 1992. Open 10-5. SIZE: 15 units. *STOCK: Midwinter Poole pottery and Whitefriars glass.* LOC: 2 miles off M4, junction 16. PARK: Easy and at rear. TEL: 01793 849499; home - same; fax - same.

Worcestershire

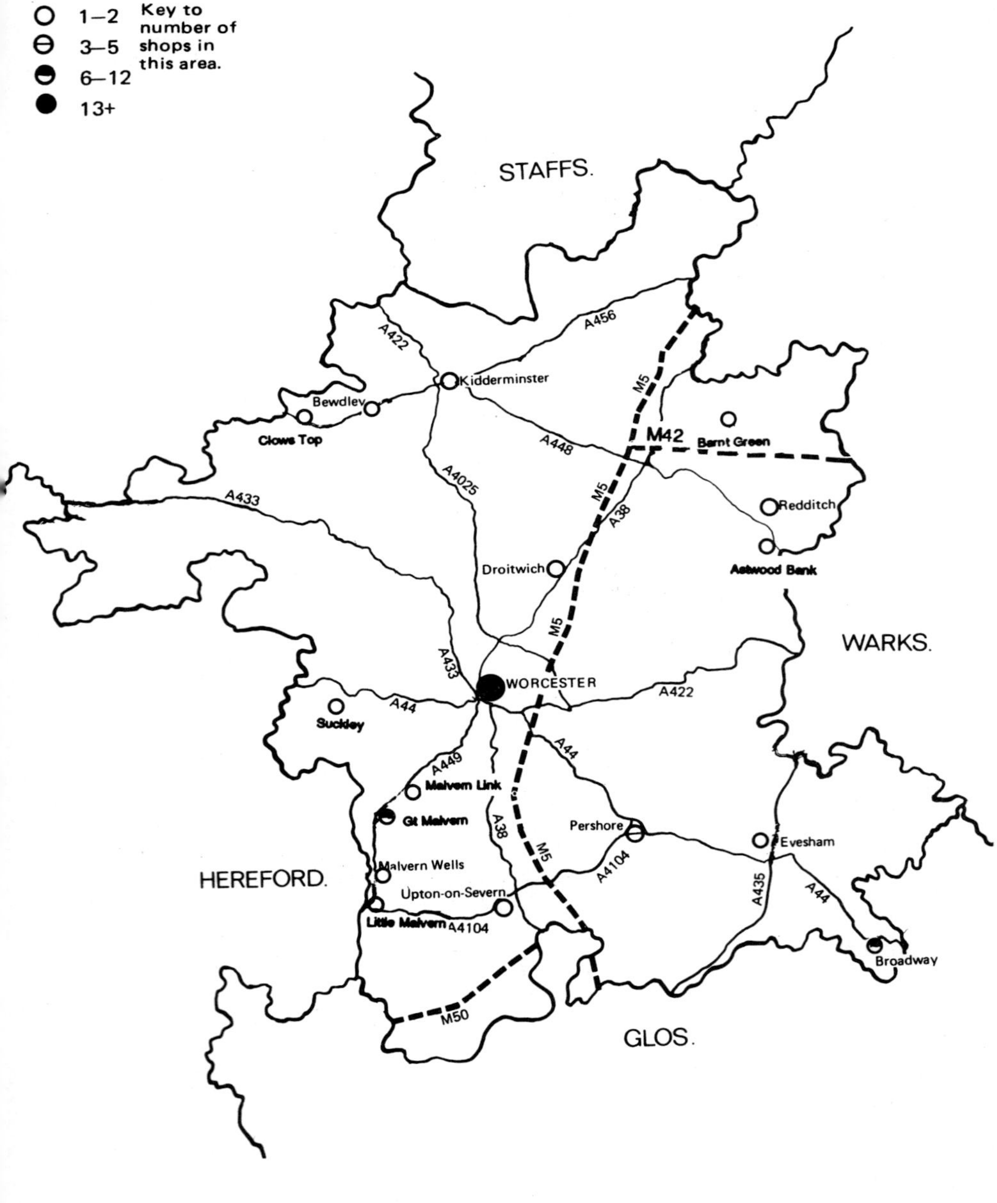

○ 1–2 Key to number of shops in this area.
⊖ 3–5
◒ 6–12
● 13+

STAFFS.

A422
A456
M5
Kidderminster
Bewdley
Clows Top
A448
M42
Barnt Green
A4025
A433
M5
A38
Redditch
Astwood Bank
Droitwich
M5
WARKS.
A433
WORCESTER
A422
A44
Suckley
A44
A449
Malvern Link
Gt Malvern
A38
M5
Pershore
Evesham
A4104
HEREFORD.
Malvern Wells
Upton-on-Severn
A435
A44
Little Malvern
A4104
Broadway
M50
GLOS.

N

Please note this is only a rough map designed to show dealers the number of shops in the various towns, and is not necessarily totally accurate.

ASTWOOD BANK, Nr. Redditch

Bracebridge Fine Art

The Old Bakehouse, 1242 Evesham Rd. B96 6AA. Est. 1987. Open by appointment only. *STOCK: 18th-20th C oil paintings, and rare signed limited edition prints.* TEL: 01527 893444.

BARNT GREEN, Nr. Birmingham

Barnt Green Antiques

93 Hewell Rd. B45 8NL. BAFRA. (N. Slater). Est. 1965. Open 9-5.30. SIZE: Medium. *STOCK: Furniture, 17th-19th C, £100-£5,000.* PARK: Easy. TEL: 0121 445 4942. SER: Restorations (furniture, gilt frames, clocks, oils). VAT: Stan/Spec.

BEWDLEY

Clent Books

Rose Cottage, Habberley Rd. DY12 1JA. (Ivor Simpson). Open by appointment. *STOCK: Midlands topography and history, antiquarian, military, fine and rare, £20-£200.* TEL: 01299 401090; e-mail - clent.books@btinternet.com. SER: Valuations. FAIRS: Waverley Antique and Book (Organiser).

BROADWAY

Broadway Bears & Dolls

76 High St. WR12 7AJ. (Janice Longhi). Open 9-6. *STOCK: Antique and modern artist's dolls and teddy bears.* TEL: 01386 858323. SER: Teddy bear museum; restoration (bears and dolls).

Broadway Clocks

Kennel Lane, High St. WR12 7DP. FBHI. (R.J. Kemp). Est. 1992. Open 10-1 and 2.15-5. CL: Thurs. *STOCK: Longcase clocks, 17th-19th C, £1,500-£6,000; also bracket, French mantel, carriage and wall clocks.* LOC: 30 yds up lane next to Lloyds Bank. TEL: 01386 852458. SER: Clock restoration and repairs. VAT: Stan/Spec.

Fenwick and Fenwick Antiques

88-90 High St. WR12 7AJ. CADA. Est. 1980. Open 10-6, and by appointment. SIZE: Large. *STOCK: Furniture, oak, mahogany and walnut, 17th to early 19th C; samplers, boxes, treen, Tunbridgeware, Delft, decorative items and corkscrews.* TEL: 01386 853227; after hours - 01386 841724; fax - 01386 858504.

Richard Hagen

Yew Tree House. WR12 7DT. Open 9.30-5.30, Sun. by appointment. *STOCK: 20th C oils, watercolours and bronzes.* TEL: 01386 853624/858561; fax - 01386 852172. SER: Valuations; restorations; framing. VAT: Spec.

Hay Loft Gallery

Berry Wormington. WR12 7NH. Resident. (Mrs J.R. Pitt and Miss S.A. Pitt). Est. 1984. Open 10.30-5.30 or by appointment. SIZE: Medium. *STOCK: Victorian paintings, £250-£15,000; Victorian watercolours, £250-£3,000.* LOC: From Broadway,

Broadway continued

4 miles on B4632 towards Cheltenham, farm on right hand side. PARK: Easy. TEL: 01242 621202/511324. SER: Restorations. VAT: Spec.

Haynes Fine Art of Broadway BADA LAPADA

The Bindery Galleries, 69 High St. WR12 7DP. Est. 1971. Open 9-6. SIZE: Large. *STOCK: 16th-20th C paintings.* LOC: From Moreton, 50yds. past the Stratford turn off on the left. PARK: Easy. TEL: 01386 852649; fax - 01386 858187. SER: Valuations; restorations; framing; catalogue. VAT: Spec.

Haynes Fine Art of Broadway Picton House Galleries BADA

42 High St. Open 9.30-6. SIZE: Large. *STOCK: 19th-20th C watercolours and 20th C paintings.* LOC: From Lygon Arms, 100 yds up High St. on left. PARK: Easy. TEL: 01386 858889; fax - 01386 858882. SER: Valuations; restorations; framing; catalogue available (£4). VAT: Spec.

Howards of Broadway

27a High St. WR12 7DP. Open 9.30-5.30. SIZE: Small. *STOCK: Jewellery, 1750 to modern, £20-£5,000; silver, 1700 to modern, £20-£5,000; objects of vertu, 1700-1900, £50-£500.* PARK: Easy and nearby. TEL: 01386 858924. SER: Valuations; restorations. VAT: Stan/Spec.

H.W. Keil Ltd BADA

Tudor House. WR12 7DP. CADA. (V.M. Keil). Est. 1925. Open 9-5.30. CL: Thurs. pm. SIZE: Large. *STOCK: Walnut, oak, mahogany and rosewood furniture; early pewter, brass and copper, tapestry, glass and works of art, 17th-18th C.* LOC: By village clock. TEL: 01386 852408; fax - 01386 852069. VAT: Spec.

John Noott Galleries BADA LAPADA

58 High St., 14 Cotswold Court, and at The Lygon Arms, High St. WR12 7AA. CADA. Est. 1972. Open 9.30-1 and 2-5. SIZE: Large. *STOCK: Paintings, watercolours and bronzes, 19th C to Contemporary.* PARK: Easy. TEL: 01386 852787/858969; fax - 01386 858348. SER: Valuations; restorations; framing. VAT: Stan/Spec.

Olive Branch Antiques

80 High St. WR12 7AJ. Resident. (P. and S. Riley). Est. 1977. Open 9-5.30 including Sun. SIZE: Small. *STOCK: Furniture, to 1900, from £100; clocks, £90-£800; pottery, £5-£150.* LOC: Top end of High St. PARK: Easy and at rear. TEL: 01386 853831. SER: Silver repairs; silver plating. VAT: Stan/Spec.

DROITWICH

Grant Fine Art

The Coach House, New Rd., Cutnall Green. WR9

Droitwich continued

0PQ. Est. 1976. Open 9-5 or by appointment. CL: Sat. SIZE: Small. *STOCK: Golfiana, books, prints, pictures, clubs, £5-£1,000.* TEL: 01299 851588; fax - 01299 851446.

High Park Antiques Ltd

10 High St. Est. 1973. Open Tues., Fri. and Sat. 10-5. *STOCK: Furniture, early 19th C; silver, china, porcelain, paintings.* TEL: 01905 796989; home - 01905 772163.

EVESHAM

Magpie Jewellers and Antiques and Magpie Arms & Armour LAPADA

2 Port St. and 61 High St. (R.J. and E.R. Bunn). Est. 1975. Open 9-5.30. SIZE: Large. *STOCK: Silver, jewellery, furniture, general antiques, arms and armour, books, stamps and coins.* TEL: 01386 41631.

GREAT MALVERN

Carlton Antiques

43 Worcester Rd. WR14 4RB. (Dave Roberts). Open 10-5. *STOCK: Edwardian postcards and cigarette cards; Victorian and Edwardian furniture, stripped pine; oil paintings, watercolours and prints.* TEL: 01684 573092; internet - www. malvern.net.carlton-antiques. SER: Valuations.

Joan Coates of Malvern

26 St. Ann's Rd. WR14 4RG. Resident. Est. 1969. Open Thurs. and Fri. 10-1 and 2.30-5.30, Sat. 10-1. SIZE: Small. *STOCK: Silver, £10-£250; small furniture, £50-£800; both 18th-20th C; small items.* LOC: From Worcester take A449, in town Foley Arms Hotel on left-hand side, take first right. PARK: Easy. TEL: 01684 575509.

Foley Furniture

Foley Bank. (Dave Roberts). *STOCK: Furniture - shipping, modern and old; postcards, cigarette cards, books, pictures, sheet music and general collectables.* TEL: 01684 891255.

Malvern Antiques Centre

3 Edith Walk. WR14 4QH. (Kerry Tombs). Open 9.30-5, Sat. 9.30-5.30. SIZE: Medium - 14 dealers. *STOCK: General antiques including pictures, Art Deco lamps, books, records, Victorian prints, porcelain, jewellery, silver, etc, £5-£500.* LOC: 10yds from main Worcester-Ledbury road. PARK: Limited outside and nearby. TEL: 01531 633902; home - same.

Malvern Arts

43 Worcester Rd. WR14 4RB. (S.A. Conein-Veber). Est. 1988. Open 10-5. SIZE: Small. *STOCK: Watercolours, Victorian and Edwardian, £50-£500; oil paintings, 19th-20th C; £80-£1,000+.* LOC: Town centre. PARK: Easy. TEL: 01684 575889. SER: Valuations; restorations (pictures).

Great Malvern continued

Malvern Bookshop

7 Abbey Rd. WR14 3ES. (J.P. and A.M. Gibbs). Open 9.15-5.30 (Nov.-Feb. 9.15-5). *STOCK: Antiquarian, secondhand books and remainders.* LOC: Near GPO by Priory steps. PARK: Short stay on road above. TEL: 01684 575915.

Malvern Studios

56 Cowleigh Rd. WR14 1QD. BAFRA. (L.M. Hall). Open 9-5.15, Fri. and Sat. 9-4.45. CL: Wed. *STOCK: Period, Edwardian painted and inlaid furniture, general furnishings.* TEL: 01684 574913; fax - 01684 569475. SER: Restorations; woodcarving; polishing; interior design. VAT: Stan/Spec.

Miscellany Antiques

20 Cowleigh Rd. WR14 1QD. Resident. (Ray and Liz Hunaban). Est. 1974. SIZE: Medium showroom + large trade warehouse. *STOCK: Victorian, Edwardian and Georgian furniture, including shipping goods, £300-£20,000; some porcelain, silver, bronzes and jewellery.* LOC: B4219 to Bromyard. PARK: Own. TEL: 01684 566671; fax - 01684 560562; mobile - 0836 507954. SER: Valuations. VAT: Stan/Spec.

Promenade Antiques

41 Worcester Rd. WR14 4RB. (Mark Sylvester). Open 10-5, Sun. 12-5. CL: Tues. *STOCK: General antiques, including Victorian and Edwardian furniture, bric-a-brac and books.* TEL: 01684 566876.

Whitmore

Teynham Lodge, Chase Rd., Upper Colwall. WR13 6DT. *STOCK: British and foreign coins, 1700-1950, £1-£500; trade tokens, 1650-1900, £1-£200; commemorative medallions, 1600-1950, £1-£200.* TEL: 01684 540651. *Postal Only.*

KIDDERMINSTER

B.B.M. Jewellery and Antiques

8 and 9 Lion St. DY10 1PT. (W.V. and A. Crook). Est. 1977. Open 10-5. CL: Tues. SIZE: Medium. *STOCK: Jewellery, 19th C, £50-£3,000; coins, £5-£1,000; general antiques, £5-£500.* LOC: Adjacent Youth Centre, off ring road. PARK: Easy. TEL: 01562 744118. SER: Valuations; restorations (jewellery, porcelain, silver). VAT: Stan/Spec/Global.

LITTLE MALVERN

St. James Antiques

De Lys Wells Rd. WR14 4JL. (H. Van Wyngaarden). Open 10-5 or by appointment. *STOCK: Continental pine furniture.* PARK: Easy. TEL: 01684 563404. SER: Restorations. VAT: Stan.

MALVERN LINK

Kimber & Son

6 Lower Howsell Rd. WR14 1EF. Est. 1956. Open 9-6, Sat. 9-1. *STOCK: 18th-20th C antiques for English, Continental and American markets.* TEL: 01684 574339; home - 01684 572000. VAT: Stan/Spec.

Malvern Link Antiques Centre

154 Worcester Rd. (Trevor and Paul Guiver, Roger Hales and Charles Harries). Open 10-5.30, Sun. 11-5. SIZE: Large. *STOCK: General furnishings and beds, 19th to early 20th C, £100-£2,000; collectables, china, £5-£100; fireplaces, from 19th C, £75-£2,000.* LOC: A449 entering Malvern Link. PARK: Easy. TEL: 01684 575750; home - 01684 575904/572491. SER: Valuations; restorations; French polishing; buys at auction. VAT: Stan/Spec.

MALVERN WELLS

Gandolfi House

211-213 Wells Rd. WR14 4HF. (P. and R. Weller). Open 10-5.30 or by appointment. CL: Mon. *STOCK: Paintings, watercolours, prints, 19th-20th C; country furniture and smalls.* TEL: 01684 569747.

PERSHORE

Hansen Chard Antiques

126 High St. WR10 1EA. (P.W. Ridler, LBHI). Est. 1984. Open 10-5, Thurs. 10-12 but appointment advisable. CL: Mon. SIZE: Large. *STOCK: Clocks, pre-1940; longcase clocks, pre-1850, £10-£3,000; barometers, £50-£3,000.* LOC: On A44. PARK: Easy. TEL: 01386 553423; home - same. SER: Valuations; restorations (as stock); buys at auction (as stock). VAT: Spec.

Penoyre Antiques

9 and 11 Bridge St. WR10 1AJ. Est. 1969. Open 10-5, other times by appointment. CL: Thurs. SIZE: Medium. *STOCK: 18th-19th C mahogany, rosewood and satinwood furniture, especially dining; giltwood mirrors, framed prints and engravings, £20-£20,000.* PARK: Easy (in main square or opposite). TEL: 01386 553522; fax - 01905 754129; home - 01386 710214. SER: Valuations. VAT: Stan/Spec.

S.W. Antiques

Abbey Showrooms, Newlands. WR10 1BP. (R.J. Whiteside). Est. 1978. Open 9-5, Sun. 10.30-4. SIZE: Large. *STOCK: 19th-20th C furniture including beds and bedroom furniture, to £4,000.* Not Stocked: Jewellery, small items. LOC: 2 mins. from Abbey. PARK: Own. TEL: 01386 555580; fax - 01386 556205. VAT: Stan/Spec.

REDDITCH

Lower House Fine Antiques

Lower House, Far Moor Lane, Winyates Green. B98 0QX. (Mrs J.B. Hudson). Est. 1987. Usually open but prior appointment advisable. SIZE: Small. *STOCK: Furniture, 17th to early 20th C, £100-£4,000; silver and plate, 18th to early 20th C, £10-£1,000; oil lamps, 19th C, £50-£500.* Not Stocked: Pine furniture. LOC: 3 miles due east Redditch town centre and half a mile from Coventry Highway island, close to A435. PARK: Own. TEL: 01527 525117; home - same. SER: Valuations; restorations (including porcelain).

SUCKLEY

Holloways

Lower Court. WR6 5DE. (Edward and Diana Holloway). SIZE: Large. *STOCK: Garden statuary, £50-£3,000; garden salvage, £20-£300; architectural antiques, £20-£3,000; all 18th-20th C.* LOC: A44 from Worcester towards Leominster, left to village, premises next to church. PARK: Easy. TEL: 01886 884665; home - same. SER: Valuations; restorations; buys at auction. VAT: Stan/Spec.

UPTON-UPON-SEVERN

The Highway Gallery

40 Old St. WR8 0HW. (J. Daniell). Est. 1969. Open 10.30-5, but appointment advisable. CL: Thurs. and Mon. SIZE: Small. *STOCK: Oils, watercolours, 19th-20th C, £100-£10,000.* Not Stocked: Prints. LOC: 100yds. from crossroads towards Malvern. PARK: Easy. TEL: 01684 592645; home - 01684 592909. SER: Valuations; restorations (reline and clean); buys at auction (pictures).

WORCESTER

Antique Map and Print Gallery

61 Sidbury. WR1 2HU. (M. Nichols). Open 9-5.30. *STOCK: Antiquarian maps, prints and books, Baxter and Le Blond prints.* TEL: 01905 612926. SER: Framing.

Antique Warehouse

Rear of 74 Droitwich Rd, Barbourne. WR3 8BW. (D. Venn). Open 9-5, Sat. 10-4.30. *STOCK: General antiques, shipping, restored pine and satin walnut, also door furniture.* PARK: Easy. TEL: 01905 27493. SER: Stripping pine, walnut and metal.

Antiques and Curios

50 Upper Tything. WR1 1JZ. Open 9.30-5.30. SIZE: Large - 6 dealers on three floors. *STOCK: 18th to early 20th C furniture, oak, mahogany, walnut, especially Victorian and Edwardian desks, dining and bedroom, decorative and upholstered, furnishings, mirrors, pictures, clocks, curios, treen, objects d'art.* LOC: From Birmingham A38 into Worcester on right-hand side. PARK: Easy. TEL: 01905 25412/764547. SER: Restorations; re-polishing; upholstery; valuations.

Bygones by the Cathedral LAPADA

Cathedral Sq. FGA DGA. (Gabrielle Doherty Bullock). Est. 1946. Open 9.30-5.30, Sat. 9.30-1 and 2-5.30. *STOCK: Furniture, 17th-19th C;*

Worcester continued

***silver, Sheffield plate, jewellery, paintings, glass; English and Continental pottery and porcelain especially Royal Worcester.* LOC: Adjacent main entrance to Cathedral. TEL: 01905 25388.**

Bygones (Worcester) LAPADA

55 Sidbury. WR1 2HU. FGA. (Gabrielle Bullock). Est. 1946. Open 9.30-1 and 2-5.30. *STOCK: Furniture, 17th-19th C; silver, Sheffield plate, jewellery, paintings, glass; English and Continental porcelain and pottery especially Royal Worcester.* LOC: Opposite car park in Sidbury and adjacent to the City Walls road junction. TEL: 01905 23132. VAT: Stan/Spec.

D & J Lines Antiques

Tything House, 35 The Tything. WR1 1JL. (Derek and Jill Lines). Open 10-5, Sun. by appointment. SIZE: Medium. *STOCK: Oak and country furniture, 17th-18th C, £500-£8,000; metalware, 18th-19th C, £50-£500; Persian carpets, 19th-20th C, £50-£1,000.* LOC: A38 (Worcester city north). PARK: Own. TEL: 01905 724546; home - 01527 861282. SER: Valuations; restorations; desk re-leathering..

John Edwards Antiques

Worcester Antiques Centre, 15 Reindeer Court, Mealcheapen St. WR1 4DF. *STOCK: English majolica and porcelain, Royal Worcester and Doulton.* TEL: 01905 610680; home - 01905 353840; mobile - 0589 468934; fax - 01905 764370.

Gray's Antiques of Worcester

49 and 50a Upper Tything. (D. and M. Gray). Open 8.30-5.30. *STOCK: General antiques and soft furnishings.* TEL: 01905 724456; fax - same.

Gray's Antiques of Worcester

58 Lowesmoor. (D. and M. Gray). Open 8.30-5.30. *STOCK: Antiques and shipping goods.* TEL: 01905 616868.

Heirlooms

46 Upper Tything. WR1 1JZ. (W. MacMillan, D. Tarran and L. Rumford). Open 9.30-4.30. *STOCK: General antiques, objets d'art, Royal Worcester porcelain and prints.* TEL: 01905 23332.

Jean Hodge

Peachley Manor, Hallow Lane, Lower Broadheath. WR2 6QL. Resident. Est. 1969. Open daily including Sunday. SIZE: Large. *STOCK: Furniture, 18th-19th C; general antiques, all £30-£4,000.* LOC: Off B4204 3 miles NW Worcester. PARK: Easy. TEL: 01905 640255.

Sarah Hodge

Peachley Manor, Hallow Lane, Lower Broadheath. WR2 6QL. Resident. Est. 1985. Open daily including Sun. SIZE: Large. *STOCK: General antiques, country bygones, pine and kitchenalia.* LOC: Off B4204, 3 miles N.W. Worcester. PARK: Easy. TEL: 01905 640255.

M. Lees and Sons LAPADA

Tower House, Severn St. WR1 2NB. Resident. Est. 1955. Open 9.15-5.15, Sat. by appointment. CL: Thurs. pm. SIZE: Medium. *STOCK: Furniture, 1780-1880; porcelain, 1750-1920.* LOC: At southern end of Worcester Cathedral adjacent to Edgar Tower; near Royal Worcester Porcelain Museum and factory. PARK: Easy. TEL: 01905 26620; home - 01905 427142. VAT: Stan/Spec.

Peachley Antiques

47b Upper Tything. WR1 1JZ. (Sarah Hodge). Est. 1985. Open Tues.-Sat. 10-4. *STOCK: Furniture, 18th-19th C; general antiques, all £30-£4,000.* LOC: Opposite Boys Grammar School. PARK: Easy. TEL: 01905 29014.

Round the Bend

1 Deansway. FGA DGA. (Gabrielle Doherty Bullock). Open 10-5.30. *STOCK: Eccentricities, brocante-type goods and jolly junk.* TEL: 01905 616516.

St. Georges Antiques

31B Barbourne Rd. WR1 1SA. Open 10-5.30. TEL: 01905 25915. The following dealers trade from this address.

Collectors World

Coins, militaria, cameras and Royal Worcester porcelain.

Yestertime Antiques

Clocks, barometers, furniture and small boxes. SER: Restorations.

Long Tran Antiques LAPADA

WR9 9EW. (L. Tran). Open by appointment only. *STOCK: Fine porcelain and pottery, English and Continental.* TEL: 01905 776685; mobile - 0831 400685.

The Tything Antique Centre

39 The Tything. WR1 1KX. Open 10-5. SIZE: Medium - 30 units. *STOCK: Wide variety of general antiques.* PARK: Easy. TEL: 01905 610597.

Worcester Antiques Centre

15 Reindeer Court, Mealcheapen St. WR1 4DF. (Stephen Zacaroli). Est. 1992. Open 10-5. SIZE: Large. *STOCK: Pottery and porcelain, 1750-1940, £10-£2,000; silver, 1750-1940, £10-£3,000; jewellery, 1800-1940, £5-£2,000; furniture, 1650-1930, £50-£5,000.* PARK: Loading only or 50 yards. TEL: 01905 610680/1; fax (after 5 p.m.) - 01905 610681. SER: Valuations; restorations. FAIRS: NEC (April and Aug); East Berkshire (May and Oct). VAT: Stan/Spec.

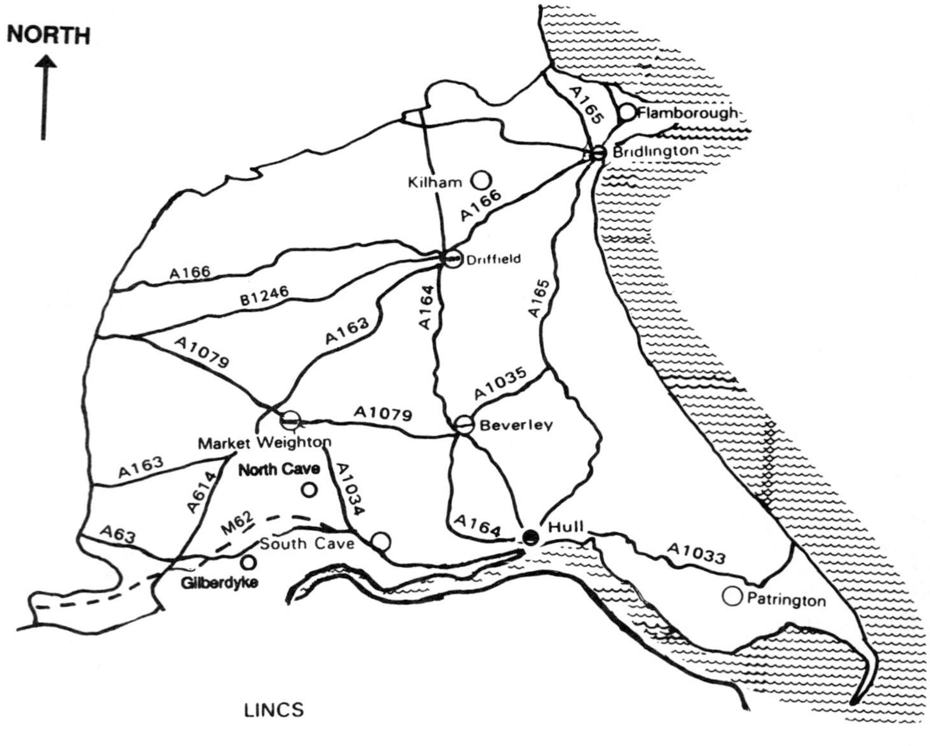

○ 1-2
⊖ 3-5
◓ 6-12
● 13+

Key to number of shops in this area.

Please note this is only a rough map designed to show dealers the number of shops in the various towns, and is not necessarily totally accurate.

BEVERLEY

Bridge House Antiques (formerly Avenue Antiques of Hull)

Hull Bridge, Tickton. HU17 9RY. Resident. (Peter White and Adele Wilkinson). Est. 1988. Open 10-5. CL: Mon. SIZE: Medium. *STOCK: Art Deco ceramics and collectables, general furniture, paintings and costume jewellery, £5-£500.* LOC: 2 miles east of Beverley on A1035. Turn right at 2nd sign for Hull Bridge - shop opposite Crown & Anchor. PARK: Own. TEL: 01964 542355. SER: Valuations. FAIRS: Hessle Foreshore and Grange Park, Willerby.

Karen Guest Antiques

24 Saturday Market Place. NAG registered Valuer and Jeweller. HRD Dip. of Diamond Grading. Open 9.15-5. SIZE: Small. *STOCK: Jewellery and silver, 18th-20th C, £50-£1,000.* PARK: Easy. TEL: 01482 882334; fax - same. SER: Valuations; restorations. VAT: Stan/Spec.

Hawley Antiques LAPADA

5 North Bar Within. HU17 8AP. Open 9.30-4, Sat. 9.30-5. *STOCK: General antiques, furniture, pottery, porcelain, glass, oil paintings, watercolours, silver.* TEL: 01482 868193. SER: Restorations (fine furniture). VAT: Stan/Spec.

James H. Starkey Galleries

49 Highgate. HU17 0DN. Est. 1968. Open 10-5, Sat. 10-1 or by appointment. SIZE: Medium. *STOCK: Oil paintings, 16th-19th C; drawings and watercolours, 17th-19th C.* LOC: Opposite minster. PARK: Easy. TEL: 01482 881179; fax - 01482 861644. SER: Valuations; restorations (paintings); buys at auction. VAT: Stan/Spec.

Time and Motion

1 Beckside. HU17 0PB. FBHI. (Peter A. Lancaster). Est. 1977. Open 10-5, Thurs. and Sun. by appointment. SIZE: Medium. *STOCK: English longcase clocks, 18th-19th C, £1,500-£8,000; English, German and French mantel and wall clocks, 19th C, £300-£3,500; aneroid and mercurial barometers, 18th-19th C, £150-£3,000.* LOC:.25 mile from town centre and minster, 300 yards from Army Museum of Transport. PARK: Easy. TEL: 01482 881574; home - same. SER: Valuations; restorations (clocks and barometers). VAT: Stan/Spec.

BRIDLINGTON

C.J. and A.J. Dixon Ltd

1st Floor, 23 Prospect St. YO15 2AE. Est. 1969. Open 10-4.30. SIZE: Large. *STOCK: War medals and decorations, British and foreign.* LOC: Town centre. PARK: Easy. TEL: 01262 676877/603348; fax - 01262 606600. SER: Valuations; renovations. VAT: Stan/Spec.

Priory Antiques

47-49 High St. YO16 4PR. (P.R. Rogerson). Est. 1979. Open 10-5. CL: Thurs. *STOCK: Georgian and Victorian furniture.* TEL: 01262 601365.

Bridlington continued

Sedman Antiques

106 Cardigan Rd. YO15 3LR. (R.H.S. and M.A. Sedman). Est. 1971. Open 10-5.30, Sun. by appointment. *STOCK: General antiques, period and shipping furniture, Oriental porcelain, Victorian collectors' items.* TEL: 01262 675671.

G. M. Wheeler Antiques: Style & Design

53 Flamborough Rd. YO16 2JH. Est. 1989. Open 1.30-5.30. CL: Thurs. SIZE: Small. *STOCK: Furniture including stripped pine, country oak, period and decorative pieces; curios, pictures, collectables.* PARK: Easy. TEL: 01262 604308. SER: Valuations; restorations.

DRIFFIELD

The Antique Pine & Country Furniture Shop

58A Middle St. North. YO25 7SU. (D. A. Smith and A.E. Gravells). Est. 1977. Open 9.30-5.30, Sat. 9.30-5, Sun. by appointment. SIZE: Medium + warehouse. *STOCK: Furniture including pine and country, 18th to early 20th C, £50-£2,000; furniture designed and made to order, from £50+.* LOC: Main street. PARK: Easy. TEL: 01377 256321; home - same; e-mail - antique@ssdesign.demon.co.uk. SER: Restorations.

Driffield continued

The Crested China Co

Station House. YO25 7PY. (D. Taylor). Est. 1978. Open Mon.-Fri. 9-4.30, other times by appointment or by chance. *STOCK: Goss and crested china.* PARK: Easy. TEL: 01377 257042 (24 hr.). SER: Sales catalogues.

Karen Guest Antiques

80A Middle Street South. YO25 7QE. NAG registered Valuer and Jeweller. HRD Diploma of Diamond Grading. Open 9.15-5. SIZE: Small. *STOCK: Jewellery and silver, 18th-20th C, £50-£1,000.* TEL: 01377 241467. SER: Valuations; restorations. VAT: Stan/Spec.

FLAMBOROUGH, Nr. Bridlington

Lesley Berry Antiques

The Manor House. YO15 1PD. Resident. (Mrs L. Berry). Est. 1972. Open 9.30-5.30, other times by appointment. SIZE: Small. *STOCK: Furniture, silver, jewellery, amber, Whitby jet, oils, watercolours, prints, copper, brass, textiles, fountain pens.* Not Stocked: Shipping goods. LOC: On corner of Tower St. and Lighthouse Rd. PARK: Easy. TEL: 01262 850943. SER: Buys at auction.

GILBERDYKE, Nr. Howden

Lewis E. Hickson FBHI

Antiquarian Horologist, Sober Hill Farm. HU15 2TB. Est. 1965. Open by appointment only. SIZE: Small. *STOCK: Longcase, bracket clocks, barometers and instruments.* TEL: 01430 449113. SER: Restorations; repairs.

HULL

De Grey Antiques

96 De Grey St., Beverley Rd. HU5 2SB. (G. Dick). Est. 1962. Open 10.30-1 and 2-5.45. SIZE: Medium. *STOCK: Furniture, clocks, paintings and watercolours, Victorian; glass, china, pewter, brass, copper and oil lamps.* LOC: Off main Beverley Rd., near overhead railway bridge. PARK: Easy. TEL: 01482 442184. SER: Valuations; buys at auction.

Steven Dews Fine Art

66-70 Princes Ave. HU5 3QJ. Open 9-6. CL: Sat. SIZE: Medium. *STOCK: Paintings, 19th-20th C.* TEL: 01482 345345; fax - 01482 447928. SER: Valuations; restorations; framing. VAT: Spec.

Grannie's Parlour

33 Anlaby Rd. HU1 2PG. (Mrs N. Pye). Open 11-5. *STOCK: General antiques, ephemera, Victoriana, dolls, toys, kitchenalia.* TEL: 01482 228258; home - 01482 341020.

Grannie's Treasures

1st Floor, 33 Anlaby Rd. HU1 2PG. (Mrs N. Pye). Open 11-5. *STOCK: Advertising items, dolls prams, toys, small furniture, china and pre-1940s clothing.* TEL: 01482 228258; home - 01482 341020.

Hull continued

David K. Hakeney Antiques LAPADA

The Mall Antique Centre, 400 Wincolmlee. HU2 0QL. Est. 1971. Open 10.30-5, Sun. 12-4. *STOCK: Georgian, Victorian, Edwardian furniture, smalls, shipping goods.* PARK: Easy. TEL: 01482 228190; mobile - 0860 507774. VAT: Stan/Spec.

Imperial Antiques

397 Hessle Rd. HU3 4EH. (M. Langton). Est. 1982. Open 9-5.30. *STOCK: British stripped pine furniture, antique, old and reproduction.* TEL: 01482 327439; fax - same. FAIRS: Newark. VAT: Stan.

Lesley's Antiques

329 Hessle Rd. HU3 4BL. Est. 1967. Open 10-5.30. SIZE: Medium. *STOCK: General antiques, shipping goods; collectors' items, mostly under £25.* LOC: On main Hull to Hessle Rd. PARK: Easy. TEL: 01482 323986; home - 01482 646280. SER: Restorations; hire.

The Mall Antique Centre & Geoffrey Mole Antiques

400 Wincolmlee. HU2 0QL. Est. 1974. Open 9-5, Sat. and Sun. 10-4. SIZE: Large. *STOCK: Silver, china, hardware, period and later furniture, rugs, architectural collectables and shipping goods.* LOC: Half mile east of main Beverley Rd. PARK: Easy. TEL: 01482 327858; fax - 01482 218173.

Kevin Marshall's Antiques Warehouse

17-20A Wilton St., (Off Dansom Lane South), Holderness Rd. HU8 7LG. Est. 1981. Open 10-5, Sun. by appointment. SIZE: Large. *STOCK: Bathroom ware, architectural items, fires, lighting, furniture and reproductions, 19th C, £5-£5000.* LOC: 1st right off Dansom Lane South. PARK: Easy. TEL: 01482 326559; fax - same. SER: Valuations; restorations; boardroom tables made to order. VAT: Stan/Spec.

Pearson Antiques

The Warehouse, 6 Dalton St. HU17 0RR. (W.B.T. Grozier). Est. 1972. Open 10-5, Sat. by appointment. SIZE: Large. *STOCK: Furniture, pottery, brass, silver and plate, stuffed birds, stone figures, late 17th C to Edwardian, £50-£1,000.* LOC: Off Cleaveland St. PARK: Easy. TEL: 01482 329647; home - 01482 862927. SER: Valuations. VAT: Spec. *Trade Only.*

Sandringham Antiques

64a Beverley Rd. HU5 1NE. (P. and P. Allison). Est. 1968. *STOCK: General antiques.* TEL: 01482 847653/320874.

KILHAM, Nr. Driffield

The Old Ropery Antique Clocks

East St. YO25 0SG. *STOCK: Clocks - longcase, bracket, carriage and French, Vienna regulator, fusee and wall.* LOC: Village centre, near PO. PARK: Easy. TEL: 01262 420233. SER: Valuations; restorations (furniture and clocks); spares.

MARKET WEIGHTON, Nr. York

Garforth Gallery

57 Market Place. YO4 3AJ. Est. 1956. Open 9-5, Sat. 9-4. SIZE: Small. *STOCK: Paintings, prints, maps, clocks, jewellery, silver, £20-£600.* Not Stocked: Porcelain. LOC: On main road in town centre. TEL: 01430 872391. SER: Valuations; restorations.

Houghton Hall Antiques

Cliffe/North Cave Rd. YO4 3RE. (M.E. Watson). Est. 1965. Open daily 8-4, Sun. 11-4. SIZE: Large. *STOCK: Furniture, 17th-19th C, £5-£8,000; china, 19th C, £1-£600; paintings and prints, £20-£1,000; objets d'art.* Not Stocked: Coins, guns. LOC: Turn right on new by-pass from York (left coming from Beverley), 3/4 mile, signposted North Cave - sign on entrance. PARK: Easy. TEL: 01430 873234. SER: Valuations; restorations (furniture); buys at auction. FAIRS: New York (USA). VAT: Stan/Spec.

Pieter Plantenga

49 Holme Rd. YO4 3EW. Open 9-4.30. *STOCK: Stripped pine, general furniture.* TEL: 01430 872473.

NORTH CAVE

Penny Farthing Antiques

Albion House, 18 Westgate. (C.E. Dennett). Est. 1987. Open 9.30-6. SIZE: Medium. *STOCK:*

North Cave continued

Furniture, 19th-20th C, Victorian brass and iron bedsteads, £25-£2,000; linen, textiles and samplers, 18th-20th C, £5-£500; general collectables, china and glass, 19th-20th C, £5-£500. LOC: Main road (B1230). PARK: Easy. TEL: 01430 422958. SER: Valuations; buys at auction. FAIRS: Newark.

PATRINGTON

Clyde Antiques

12 Market Place. HU12 0RB. (S. M. Nettleton). Est. 1978. Open 10-5. CL: Sun., Mon. and Wed. except by appointment. SIZE: Medium. *STOCK: General antiques.* PARK: Easy. TEL: 01964 630650; home - 01964 612471. SER: Valuations. VAT: Stan.

SOUTH CAVE

The Old Copper Shop and Post House Antiques

69 and 75 Market Place. HU15 2AS. (Mrs E.A. Featherstone). Est. 1986. Open 9.30-4.30. SIZE: Medium. *STOCK: Furniture, 19th-20th C; linen, general antiques and collectors' items.* Not Stocked: Militaria, coins. LOC: A1034. PARK: Easy. TEL: 01430 423988; home - 01482 631110. SER: Valuations.

Boo Boos by Mabel Lucie Attwell. Shelley Potteries, c.1925.

From an article entitled "Gifts for Good Children" by Maureen Batkin which appeared in the May 1997 issue of **Antique Collecting.**

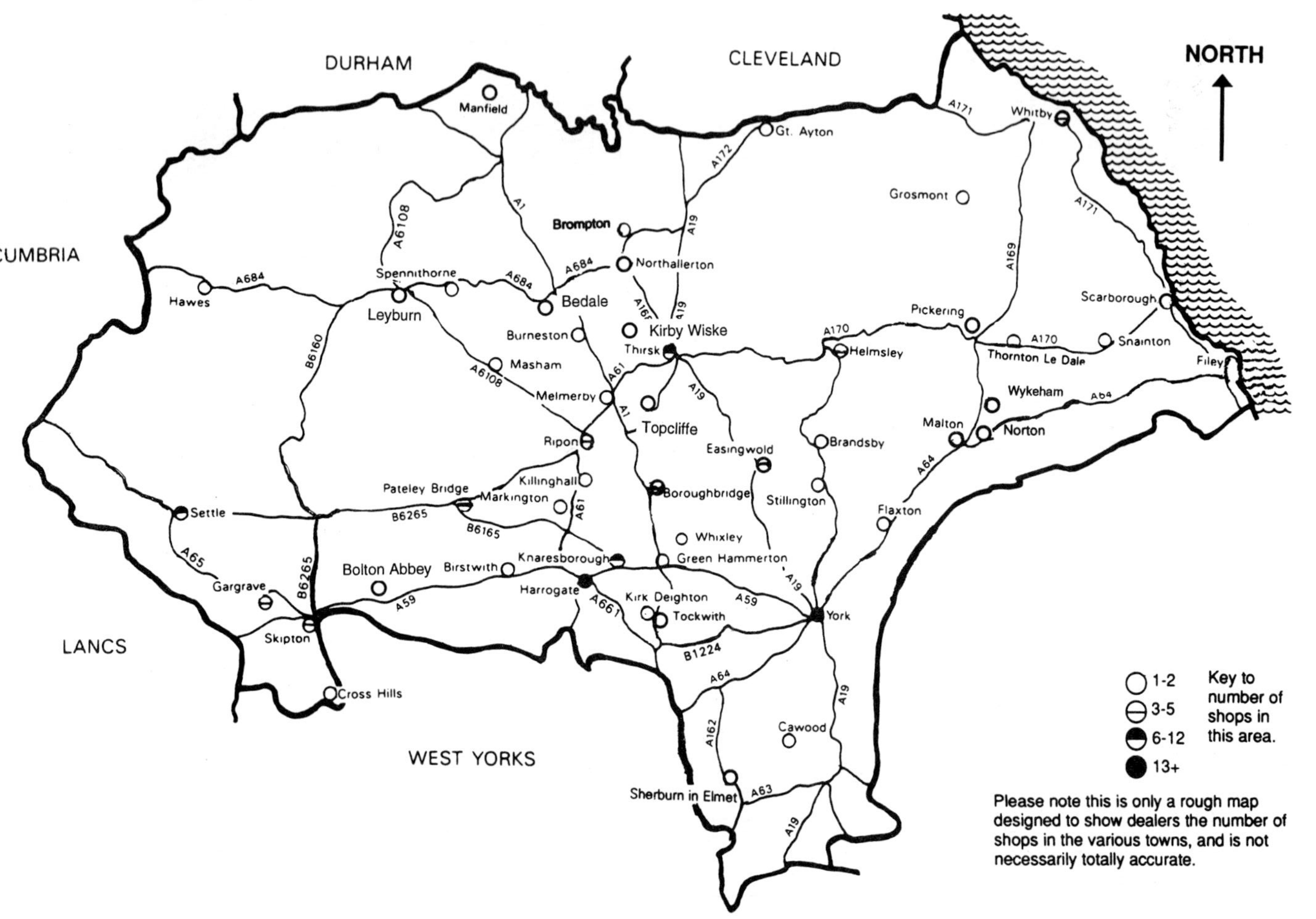

DURHAM
CLEVELAND
NORTH
CUMBRIA
LANCS
WEST YORKS
Manfield
Gt. Ayton
Whitby
Grosmont
Brompton
Northallerton
Spennithorne
Hawes
Leyburn
Bedale
Kirby Wiske
Thirsk
Burneston
Masham
Melmerby
Topcliffe
Ripon
Easingwold
Boroughbridge
Stillington
Whixley
Green Hammerton
Killinghall
Pateley Bridge
Markington
Settle
Knaresborough
Bolton Abbey
Birstwith
Harrogate
Gargrave
Kirk Deighton
Tockwith
Skipton
York
Cross Hills
Cawood
Sherburn in Elmet
Scarborough
Pickering
Snainton
Thornton Le Dale
Helmsley
Filey
Wykeham
Malton
Norton
Brandsby
Flaxton
A171
A172
A19
A1
A6108
A684
A168
A170
A169
A64
A61
B6160
B6265
B6165
A65
A59
A661
B1224
A162
A63
Key to number of shops in this area.
1-2
3-5
6-12
13+
Please note this is only a rough map designed to show dealers the number of shops in the various towns, and is not necessarily totally accurate.

BEDALE

Bennett's Antiques & Collectables

7 Market Place. DL8 1ED. (Paul and Kim Bennett). Est. 1996. Open 9-5, Sun. by appointment. SIZE: Medium. *STOCK: Furniture, 18th to early 20th C, £100-£3,000; fine art, 19th to early 20th C, £100-£500; collectables, 19th-20th C, £20-£200; local works of art, 20th C, £80-£300.* PARK: Easy. TEL: 01677 427900; fax - 01677 426858; home - 01677 424950. SER: Restorations. VAT: Spec.

BIRSTWITH, Nr. Harrogate

John Pearson Antique Clock Restoration

Church Cottage. HG3 2NG. Est. 1978. Open by appointment. *STOCK: Longcase, bracket and wall clocks, 18th C.* LOC: Off A59. PARK: Easy. TEL: 01423 770828; home - same. SER: Restorations (clocks, cases, movements and especially dials).

BOLTON ABBEY

The Grove Country Bookshop with Coopers of Ilkley LAPADA

The Old Post Office. PBFA. (Andrew and Janet Sharpe). Open 10-5 (summer) including Sun. *STOCK: Antiquarian and rare books, maps, prints, country furniture, metalware, glass, clocks, etc.* PARK: Own. TEL: 01756 710717; fax - 01943 817086. SER: Valuations; book-binding; restorations (furniture); buys at auction (as stock).

BOROUGHBRIDGE

Country Antiques

38 High St. YO5 9AW. Resident. (P.W. Raine). Est. 1969. Open 10-4, prior telephone call advisable. CL: Thurs. and Fri. SIZE: Small. *STOCK: Silver, 17th-20th C, £25-£500; metalware, small furniture, 18th-19th C, and objet d'art.* PARK: Easy. TEL: 01423 324017. SER: Buys at auction (silver).

Anthony Graham Antiques

Aberure, Bridge St. YO5 9LA. Resident. Est. 1985. Open 9.30-5, or by appointment. SIZE: Medium. *STOCK: Period decorative antiques and accessories, pictures, furniture and collectors items, 18th-19th C, £5-£5,000.* LOC: Off A1. PARK: Easy. TEL: 01423 323952; fax - same; mobile - 0860 785687. SER: Valuations.

St. James House Antiques LAPADA

St. James Sq. YO5 9AR. (J.D. Wilson). Est. 1989. Open 9-5.30, Sun. by appointment. SIZE: Medium. *STOCK: Period and later furniture, brass, copper and china.* LOC: Town centre. PARK: Own. TEL: 01423 322508; home - same. SER: Valuations; restorations; upholstery. VAT: Stan/Spec.

Boroughbridge continued

R.S. Wilson and Sons

4 Hall Square. YO5 9AN. Est. 1917. Open 9-5.30, Thurs. 9-12.30. *STOCK: 17th-19th C furniture and accessories.* TEL: 01423 322417; fax - same. VAT: Stan/Spec.

BRANDSBY

L.L. Ward and Son

Bar House. YO6 4RQ. (R. Ward). Est. 1970. Open 8.30-5. *STOCK: Antique pine.* TEL: 01347 888651

BROMPTON Nr. Northallerton

Country Pine Antiques

Unit 45, The Old Mill. DL6 2UP. (C. Tindle). Open 9-5, Sat. by appointment. *STOCK: Victorian pine.* TEL: 01609 774322.

BURNESTON, Nr. Bedale

W. Greenwood (Fine Art)

Oak Dene, Church Wynd. DL8 2JE. Est. 1978. Open by appointment. *STOCK: Paintings and watercolours, 19th-20th C, £100-£5,000; frames, £20-£500; mirrors.* LOC: Take B6285 left off A1 northbound, house 1/4 mile on right. PARK: Easy. TEL: 01677 424830; home - 01677 423217. SER: Valuations; restorations (paintings and frames); framing.

CAWOOD, Nr. Selby

Cawood Antiques

Sherburn St. YO8 0SS. (J.E. Gilham). Open 9-6 including Sun. *STOCK: General antiques, shipping, furniture, copper, brass, porcelain, pictures, collectors' items.* PARK: Easy. TEL: 01757 268533.

CROSS HILLS, Nr. Keighley

Heathcote Antiques

Skipton Rd. Junction. BD20 7RT. Resident. (M. Webster). Est. 1979. Open 10-5.30, Sun. 12.30-4.30. CL: Mon. and Tues. SIZE: Large showroom + warehouse. *STOCK: Furniture, including pine especially unstripped; smalls.* PARK: Own. TEL: 01535 635250; fax - 01535 637205; mobile - 0836 259640.

EASINGWOLD

Fox's Antique Pine

108 Long St. YO6 3HY. (M.J. Fox). Est. 1958. Open 10-5.30. *STOCK: Pine and country furniture including kitchenalia and collectables.* Not Stocked: Reproduction. PARK: Easy. TEL: 01347 822977.

Easingwold continued

Milestone Antiques

Farnley House, 101 Long St. (A.B. and S.J. Streetley). Open daily, Sun. by appointment. SIZE: Medium. *STOCK: Mahogany and oak furniture, £100-£2,000; longcase and wall clocks, upholstered and pine furniture, pictures, prints. oils and watercolours, £100-£800; all 18th to early 20th C.* LOC: A19, village centre. PARK: Easy. TEL: 01347 821608; home - same. SER: Valuations. VAT: Stan/Spec.

Old Flames

30 Long St. YO6 3HT. (P. Lynas and J.J. Thompson). Est. 1988. Open 10-5. SIZE: Medium. *STOCK: Fireplaces, 18th-19th C, £100-£1,000; lighting, 19th C, £25-£250; architectural items, 18th-19th C, £50-£500.* PARK: Easy. TEL: 01347 821188. SER: Valuations. FAIRS: Newark. VAT: Stan/Spec.

Mrs B.A.S. Reynolds

42 Long St. *STOCK: General antiques, Victorian.* TEL: 01347 821078.

White House Farm Antiques

Thirsk Rd. YO6 3NF. Resident. (G. Hood). Est. 1960. Usually open but prior 'phone call advisable. *STOCK: Rural and domestic bygones, stone troughs, architectural reclamation and garden ornaments.* LOC: 1 mile north of Easingwold, 200 yds from northern junction of bypass (A19). PARK: Easy. TEL: 01347 821479.

FILEY

Cairncross and Sons

31 Bellevue St. YO14 9HU. (G. Cairncross). Open 9.30-12.45 and 2-4.30. CL: Wed. (Oct.-March). *STOCK: Medals, uniforms, insignia, cap badges.* Not Stocked: Weapons. TEL: 01723 513287.

Filey Antiques

1 Belle Vue St. YO14 9HU. Est. 1970. Open daily 11-4.30; Thurs. to Sat. 11-4 in winter. SIZE: Small. *STOCK: Small furniture, prints, china, bric-a-brac, jewellery.* Not Stocked: Coins, militaria. LOC: Town centre, at corner of West Ave. PARK: Easy. TEL: 01723 513440.

FLAXTON, Nr. York

Elm Tree Antiques

YO6 7RJ. (R. and J. Jackson). Est. 1975. Open 9-5, Sun. 10-5. SIZE: Large. *STOCK: Furniture, 17th C to Edwardian; small items, £5-£5,000, Staffordshire figures.* LOC: 1 mile off A64. PARK: Easy. TEL: 01904 468462; home - same; fax - 01904 468728. SER: Valuations; restorations (cabinet making, polishing and upholstery).

GARGRAVE, Nr. Skipton

Antiques at Forge Cottage

22A High St. BD23 3RB. Est. 1979. Open Tues., Thurs., 11-4.30, Wed., Fri. 2-4.30, Sat. 10-1, or by appointment. *STOCK: Porcelain, small silver, glass, collectables, brass.* LOC: A65. PARK: Easy. TEL: 01756 748272.

Bernard Dickinson

Estate Yard, West St. BD23 3PH. Resident. (H.H. and A.E. Mardall). Est. 1958. Open 9-5.30 or by appointment. *STOCK: Early English furniture.* LOC: Just off A65 Skipton-Settle road. PARK: Easy. TEL: 01756 748257. VAT: Spec.

Gargrave Gallery

48 High St. BD23 3RB. (B. Herrington). Appointment advisable. *STOCK: General antiques, oak, mahogany, metal, 18th to early 20th C.* PARK: Easy. TEL: 01756 749641.

R.N. Myers and Son — BADA

Endsleigh House, High St. BD23 3LX. Est. 1890. Open 9-5.30 or by appointment. SIZE: Medium. *STOCK: Furniture, oak, mahogany, 17th to early 19th C; pottery, porcelain and metalware.* Not Stocked: Victoriana, weapons, coins, jewellery. LOC: A65. Skipton-Settle road. PARK: Behind shop and opposite. TEL: 01756 749587. SER: Valuations. VAT: Spec.

GREAT AYTON

The Great Ayton Bookshop

47 & 53 High St. TS9 6NH. (M.S. Jones). Est. 1978. Open 10-5.30, Wed. 10-2, Sun. 2-5.30. CL: Mon. SIZE: Medium. *STOCK: Books, rare and secondhand, 50p-£100; postcards, pre-1930, 10p-£20; prints, 10p-£50.* LOC: 7 miles south of Middlesbrough off Stokesley road. PARK: Easy. TEL: 01642 723358. SER: Valuations. FAIRS: PBFA. VAT: Stan.

GREEN HAMMERTON, Nr. York

The Main Pine Co

Grangewood, The Green. YO5 8DB. (C. and K.M. Main). Est. 1976. Open 9-5, Sun. 11-4. SIZE: Large. *STOCK: Pine furniture, 18th-19th C, £100-£1,500; reproductions from old pine.* LOC: Just off A59. PARK: Easy. TEL: 01423 330451; home - 01423 331078; fax - 01423 331278; e-mail - mainpine@onyxnet.co.uk; internet - http://www.activ.co.uk/mainpine/. SER: Export; containers packed. VAT: Stan.

GROSMONT, Nr. Whitby

Country Connections (Esk House Arts)

Front St. Workshop and Framing Dept., Esk House, Grosmont. YO22 5PF. (J.M. Stonehouse). Open 11-5 including Sun. *STOCK: Fine art, prints especially sporting, steam engine and landscapes, some originals by local artists; china and pottery by local craftsmen.* LOC: First floor, above the Co-op. TEL: 01947 895319; fax - same; home - 01947 895469.

HARROGATE

Alexander Adamson LAPADA

Flat 1, 19 Parkview. HG1 5LY. (N.J.G. Adamson). Est. 1863. Open by appointment only. *STOCK: Furniture, 17th to early 19th C; porcelain.* TEL: 01423 528924; mobile - 0831 552741. SER: Valuations; restorations (furniture, porcelain). VAT: Spec.

Ann-tiquities

12 Cheltenham Parade. (Mrs A. Wilkinson). Open 12-4. CL: Wed. *STOCK: Antique linen and small collectables.* TEL: 01423 503567.

Armstrong BADA LAPADA

10-11 Montpellier Parade. HG1 2TJ. (M.A. Armstrong). Est. 1976. Open 10-5.30. SIZE: Medium. *STOCK: Fine English furniture, 18th to early 19th C; glasses and works of art, 18th C.* PARK: Easy. TEL: 01423 506843. FAIRS: Olympia (Feb., June, Nov.); BADA; Chelsea. VAT: Spec.

Bill Bentley

16 Montpellier Parade. HG1 2TG. Open 9.30-5.30 or by appointment. SIZE: Large. *STOCK: Oak furniture, 1600-1800; country furniture, 1700-1800; period metalwork and treen.* PARK: Easy. TEL: 01423 564084; home - 01423 564564. VAT: Spec.

Bryan Bowden

Oakleigh, 1 Spacey View, Leeds Rd., Pannal. HG3 1LQ. Est. 1969. By appointment only. SIZE: Small. *STOCK: English pottery and porcelain, 1750-1850; small Georgian furniture.* LOC: 2.5 miles south of Harrogate on Leeds road. PARK: Easy. TEL: 01423 870007; home - same. SER: Valuations; restorations (pottery and porcelain); buys at auction (English pottery and porcelain). FAIRS: Northern; Buxton; Wakefield Ceramic. VAT: Spec.

Derbyshire Antiques Ltd

27 Montpellier Parade. HG1 2TG. (R.C. and M.T. Derbyshire). Est. 1960. Open 10-5.30. SIZE: Medium. *STOCK: Early oak and walnut, 16th-18th C; Georgian furniture to 1820; decorative items.* TEL: 01423 503115/564242. VAT: Spec.

Harrogate continued

Dragon Antiques

10 Dragon Rd. HG1 5DF. Resident. (P.F. Broadbelt). Est. 1954. Open 11-6. Always available. SIZE: Small. *STOCK: Victorian art glass, £30-£300; art pottery, postcards, G.B. and foreign.* LOC: 5 mins. from town centre, opposite Dragon Road car park. PARK: Easy. TEL: 01423 562037.

Garth Antiques LAPADA

2 Montpellier Mews. HG1 2TQ. (I. Chapman). Open 10-5.30. SIZE: Small. *STOCK: Furniture, 18th-19th C, £50-£3,000; brass and copper, 19th C, £1-£500; oils and watercolours, £5-£3,000.* LOC: Turn left from Montpellier Parade at Montpellier public house. TEL: 01423 530573. VAT: Stan/Spec.

The Ginnel

Harrogate Antique Centre, The Ginnel. HG1 2RB. (P. Stephenson). Open 9.30-5.30. *STOCK: All date-lined and vetted - see individual entries.* LOC: Off Parliament St. opposite Debenhams. PARK: Nearby. TEL: 01423 508857. SER: Courier. Below are listed the specialist dealers at this centre.

Anglo-Scandinavian

Cutlery, silver plate, inkwells, collectors' and decorative items.

Appleton Antiques

Art pottery - Moorcroft, Carlton ware specialist. TEL: Home - 01642 316417. SER: Valuations.

Fiona Aston

Objets d'art including porcelain and miniatures.

J. Bottomley

Victorian jewellery and silver items.

Brackmore Antiques

Silver, porcelain and objets d'art.

Bygones

Objets d'art including dolls, small silver, porcelain and jewellery.

Harrogate continued

Mary Cooper
Antique costumes and textiles to 1929, including lace, fans, shawls, linen, quilts, samplers, woolwork and beadwork. TEL: 01423 567182.

A. & A. Cox
Period pottery and porcelain.

Dale Antiques
Silver and objet d'art.

Richard Freeman
British, Oriental and Continental ceramics, 18th to early 19th C. TEL: Mobile - 0421 645788.

Georgian House
Victorian and Edwardian furniture.

R. Gillingham
Small 19th C furnishings and general works of art.

Jeffrey and Pauline Glass
Porcelain and glass, objets d'art, 19th to early 20th C.

M. Hawkridge
(Corn Mill Antiques) *English china and glass.*

Ian Legard
18th and 19th C silver and works of art.

Libra Antiques
Georgian, Victorian and Edwardian furniture and decorative items, including cranberry glass.

Brian Loomes
Longcase clocks, small period furniture.

Catherine Lough
Small 19th C furniture and furnishings, French influence.

M.S. Antiques Ltd
(M. Swycher) *Fine quality china, specialising in Meissen and Staffordshire pottery.*

Brian Naylor
Pottery including Mason's and Staffordshire figures; boxes; all 18th-19th C.

Parker Gallery
19th to early 20th C oils and watercolours, £100-£3,000.

Past Reflections
Victorian and Edwardian furniture, porcelain and silver.

Jane Robson
Collectables.

Ian Sharp
Early 19th C furniture and quality porcelain.

Beverley Shaw
Fine period silver and cutlery.

Harrogate continued

Shire Antiques
19th C furniture and pictures.

J. Steele
Victorian and Edwardian silver.

Stella-Mar
Fine quality 19th C furniture and furnishings, wide variety of object d'art.

Terry's Art Co
18th and 19th C Chinese works of art.

Chris Wilde
18th and 19th C furniture including long case clocks.

Ann Wilkinson
Silver, porcelain and jewellery.

Wycliffe Antiques
19th C pottery and porcelain.

Michael Green Traditional Interiors
Library House, Regent Parade. HG1 5AN. Est. 1976. Open 8.30-5.30, Sat. 8.45-4, Sun. by appointment. SIZE: Medium. *STOCK: Pine furniture, Georgian, Victorian, Edwardian, £5-£2,000; treen, kitchenalia and collectors' items.* LOC: Overlooking the Stray. PARK: Easy. TEL: 01423 560452. SER: Valuations; restorations; stripping. VAT: Stan/Spec.

Havelocks
15-17 Westmoreland St. HG1 5AY. (Philip Adam). Est. 1989. Open 10-5, Wed. 10-1. SIZE: Large. *STOCK: Original pine, oak, general antique furniture.* LOC: A59 towards Skipton, turn left into Westmoreland St. TEL: 01423 506721. SER: Valuations; restorations; stripping and finishing; buys at auction.

Haworth Antiques
26 Cold Bath Rd. HG2 0NA. (G. and J. White). Open 10-5 or by appointment. CL: Mon. SIZE: Medium. *STOCK: Clocks, 18th-19th C, £100-£3,000; small furniture, Georgian and Victorian, £50-£1,000.* LOC: 300yds. from Crown Hotel. PARK: Easy. TEL: 01423 521401; mobile - 0831 692263. SER: Restorations (clocks, dials, re-painted and re-silvered). VAT: Stan/Spec.

London House Oriental Rugs and Carpets
9 Montpellier Parade. HG1 2TJ. Est. 1981. Open 10-5.30. SIZE: Medium. *STOCK: Persian, Turkish, Indian, Tibetan, Nepalese, Afghan, Chinese and Rumanian rugs and carpets, 19th-20th C, £25-£5,000; kelims and camel bags, 19th-20th C, £25-£2,000.* LOC: Town centre on The Stray. PARK: Easy. TEL: 01423 567167; home - 01937 845123. SER: Valuations; restorations (handmade rugs). VAT: Stan.

Harrogate continued

David Love BADA

10 Royal Parade. HG1 2SZ. Est. 1969. Open 9-1 and 2-5.30. SIZE: Large. *STOCK: Furniture, English, 17th-19th C; pottery and porcelain, English and Continental; decorative items, all periods.* LOC: Opposite Pump Room Museum. PARK: Easy. TEL: 01423 565797. SER: Valuations; buys at auction. VAT: Stan/Spec.

Charles Lumb and Sons Ltd BADA

2 Montpellier Gardens. HG1 2TF. (F. and A.R. Lumb). Est. 1920. Open 9-1 and 2-6. SIZE: Medium. *STOCK: Furniture, 17th to early 19th C; metalware, period accessories.* PARK: 20yds. immediately opposite. TEL: 01423 503776; home - 01423 863281; fax - 01423 530074. VAT: Spec.

D. Mason & Son

7/9 Westmoreland St. HG1 5AY. FGA, NAG. Open 9-5. *STOCK: Victorian, Edwardian and secondhand jewellery; clocks.* TEL: 01423 567305. SER: Repairs (clocks and jewellery).

McTague of Harrogate

17/19 Cheltenham Mount. HG1 1DW. (P. McTague). Open 9.30-1 and 2-5. SIZE: Medium. *STOCK: Prints, watercolours, some oil paintings, mostly 18th to early 20th C.* LOC: From Conference Centre on Kings Rd., go up Cheltenham Parade and turn first left. PARK: Easy. TEL: 01423 567086. VAT: Stan/Spec.

Montpellier Mews Antique Market

Montpellier St. HG1 2TG. Open 10-5. SIZE: Various dealers. *STOCK: General antiques - porcelain, jewellery, furniture, paintings, interior decor, linen, glass and silver.* LOC: Behind Weatherells. TEL: 01423 530484.

Ogden of Harrogate Ltd BADA

38 James St. HG1 1RQ. Est. 1893. Open 9.15-5. SIZE: Large. *STOCK: Jewellery, English silver and plate.* TEL: 01423 504123; fax - 01423 522283. VAT: Stan/Spec.

Omar (Harrogate) Ltd

The Smithy, Haggs Farm, Haggs Rd., Follifoot. Est. 1946. Open by appointment. SIZE: Medium. *STOCK: Persian, Turkish, Caucasian rugs and carpets.* PARK: Easy. TEL: 01423 873796/863199. SER: Cleaning and restoration. VAT: Stan.

Paraphernalia

38A Cold Bath Rd. HG2 0NA. (P.F. Hacker). Open 10-5. *STOCK: Wallplates, crested and commemorative china, cutlery, glass, bric-a-brac, small furniture.* TEL: Evenings - 01423 567968.

Paul M. Peters Antiques LAPADA

15a Bower Rd. HG1 1BE. Est. 1967. Open 10-5. CL: Sat. SIZE: Medium. *STOCK: Chinese and Japanese ceramics and works of art, 17th-19th C; European ceramics and glass, 18th-19th C;*

Harrogate continued

***European metalware, scientific instruments and unusual objects.* LOC: Town centre, at bottom of Station Parade. PARK: Easy. TEL: 01423 560118. SER: Valuations. VAT: Stan/Spec.**

Elaine Phillips Antiques Ltd BADA

1 and 2 Royal Parade. HG1 2SZ. Open 9.30-5.30, other times by appointment. SIZE: Large. *STOCK: Oak furniture, 1600-1800; country furniture, 1700-1840; some mahogany, 18th to early 19th C; period metalwork and decoration.* LOC: Opposite Crown Hotel. TEL: 01423 569745. VAT: Spec.

Smith's (The Rink) Ltd

Dragon Rd. HG1 5DR. Est. 1906. Open 9-5.30. SIZE: Large. *STOCK: General antiques, 1750-1820, £150; Victoriana, 1830-1900, £50.* LOC: From Leeds, right at Prince of Wales crossing, left at Skipton Rd. and left before railway bridge. PARK: Easy. TEL: 01423 567890. VAT: Stan/Spec.

Sutcliffe Galleries BADA

5 Royal Parade. HG1 2SZ. Est. 1947. Open 10-5. CL: Mon. *STOCK: Paintings, 19th C.* LOC: Opposite Crown Hotel. TEL: 01423 562976; fax - 01423 528729. SER: Valuations; restorations; framing.

Harrogate continued

Thorntons of Harrogate LAPADA

1 Montpellier Gdns. HG1 2TF. Open 9.30-5.30. ***STOCK: 17th-19th C furniture, metalware, clocks, paintings, porcelain, arms and armour, scientific instruments.*** **TEL: 01423 504118; fax - 01423 528400. VAT: Spec.**

Walker Galleries Ltd BADA LAPADA

6 Montpellier Gdns. HG1 2TF. Est. 1972. Open 9.30-1 and 2-5.30. SIZE: Medium. ***STOCK: Oil paintings and watercolours, 18th C furniture.*** **TEL: 01423 567933. SER: Valuations; restorations; framing. FAIRS: Chelsea, Harrogate, Olympia. VAT: Spec.**

Weatherell's of Harrogate Antiques and Fine Arts LAPADA

29 Montpellier Parade. HG1 2TG. Open 9-5.30. SIZE: Large. ***STOCK: Period and fine decorative furniture.*** **TEL: 01423 507810/ 525004; fax - 01423 520005.**

Chris Wilde Antiques LAPADA

The Courtyard, Mowbray Sq., Westmoreland St. HG1 5AU. (C.B. Wilde). Est. 1996. Open Mon.-Fri. 10-4, or by appointment. SIZE: Large. ***STOCK: Furniture, 1730-1920, £300-£3,000; longcase clocks, 1750-1920, £250-£2,500.*** **LOC: North side of town. PARK: Easy. TEL: Mobile - 0831 543268; fax - 01423 506030. SER: Valuations. VAT: Stan/Spec.**

HAWES

Sturman's Antiques LAPADA

Main St. DL8 3QW. Open 10-5 including Sun. ***STOCK: Georgian and Victorian furniture; porcelain, silver plate, paintings; longcase, wall and mantel clocks.*** **TEL: 01969 667742.**

HELMSLEY

E. Stacy-Marks Limited

10 Castlegate. YO6 5AB. Est. 1889. *STOCK: Paintings, English, Dutch and Continental schools, 18th-20th C.* TEL: 01439 771950; fax - 01439 771859.

Westway Pine

Carlton Lane. YO6 5HB. (J. and J. Dzierzek). Est. 1987. Open 9-5, Sat. 10-5, other times by appointment. SIZE: Medium. *STOCK: Pine furniture, 19th C, £20-£2,000.* LOC: From A170 from Scarborough, first right into town, first left, then left again 100m. PARK: Easy. TEL: 01439 771399. SER: Valuations; restorations (pine).

York Cottage Antiques LAPADA

7 Church St. YO6 5AD. (G. and E.M. Thornley). Est. 1976. Open May-Oct. Thurs., Fri. and Sat.; Nov.-April Fri. and Sat. 10-4 or

Helmsley continued

by appointment. ***STOCK: Early oak and country furniture; 18th-19th C metalware; drinking glasses, pottery and porcelain especially Ironstone, Staffordshire figures, lustre and blue and white; cranberry glass.*** **LOC: Opposite church. PARK: Adjacent. TEL: 01439 770833; home - same.**

KILLINGHALL, Nr. Harrogate

Norwood House Antiques

88 Ripon Rd. HG3 2DH. Resident. (R.M. Mallaby). Est. 1981. Open 10-4. CL: Wed. *STOCK: English and Continental furniture, 19th C; porcelain, clocks, silver, decorative items.* PARK: Easy. TEL: 01423 506468.

KIRBY WISKE, Nr. Thirsk

Sion Hill Hall Antique Centre

Sion Hill Hall. (Sheila Kindon). Est. 1971. SIZE: Medium. *STOCK: Furniture and furnishings, collectable, china, mirrors, pictures and kitchenalia.* LOC: A167. PARK: Easy. TEL:01845 587071. SER: Valuations; restorations (furniture).

KIRK DEIGHTON, Nr. Wetherby

Elden Antiques

23 Ashdale View. LS22 4DS. (E. and D. Broadley). Est. 1970. Open 9-6, Sat. 12-5.30. SIZE: Medium. *STOCK: General antiques including furniture.* LOC: Main road between Wetherby and Knaresborough. PARK: Easy. TEL: 01937 584770; home - same.

KNARESBOROUGH

Robert Aagaard & Co

Frogmire House, Stockwell Rd. HG5 0JP. Est. 1961. Open 9-5, Sat. 10-4. SIZE: Medium. *STOCK: Chimney pieces, marble fire surrounds and interiors.* LOC: Town centre. PARK: Own. TEL: 01423 864805. VAT: Stan.

Bowkett

9 Abbey Rd. HG5 8HY. Resident. (E.S. Starkie). Est. 1919. Open 9-6. SIZE: Medium. *STOCK: Chairs, small furniture, brass, copper, pot-lids, Goss, books.* LOC: By the river at the lower road bridge. PARK: Easy. TEL: 01423 866112. SER: Restorations (upholstery and small furniture).

Cheapside Antiques

4 Cheapside. (Mrs M.E. Hanson). Open 10.30-5. CL: Mon. and Thurs. *STOCK: Furniture, porcelain, metalware and small collectors' items, 1750-1900.* TEL: 01423 867779. VAT: Spec.

Knaresborough continued

The Emporium

Market Flat Lane, Lingerfield. HG5 9JA. (N. Wadley). Open by appointment. SIZE: Medium and warehouse. *STOCK: Pine and general antiques.* PARK: Easy. TEL: 01423 868539. SER: Packing; shipping; courier. VAT: Stan.

Milton J. Holgate BADA

36 Gracious St. HG5 8DS. Est. 1972. Open 9-5.30 or by appointment. CL: Thurs. *STOCK: Fine English furniture, 17th-19th C, antique accessories.* PARK: Easy. TEL: 01423 865219. VAT: Mainly Spec.

The Gordon Reece Gallery

24 Finkle St. HG5 8AA. Open 10.30-5, Sun. 2-5. CL: Thurs. SIZE: Large. *STOCK: Flat woven rugs and nomadic carpets, tribal sculpture, jewellery, furniture, decorative and non-European folk art especially ethnic and Oriental ceramics.* TEL: 01423 866219; fax - 01423 868165. SER: Restorations.

Reflections

23 Waterside. HG5 8DE. Resident. (J. and M.V. McNamara). Est. 1977. Open Tues.-Sun. 9.30-6, other times by appointment. SIZE: Small. *STOCK: Furniture, 19th C; paintings, 19th to early 20th C, both £50-£1,000; bric-a-brac and brassware.* LOC: Turn off A59 at World's End Inn. PARK: Easy. TEL: 01423 862005.

John Thompson Antiques LAPADA

Swadforth House, Gracious St. HG5 8DT. Est. 1968. *STOCK: 18th-19th C furniture and related decorative objects.* TEL: 01423 864698. VAT: Spec.

LEYBURN

Thirkill Antiques

Newlands, Worton. DL8 3ET. Est. 1963. *STOCK: Musicals, pottery, porcelain, small furniture, 18th-19th C.* TEL: 01969 650725.

LONG PRESTON

Gary K. Blissett

3 Station Rd. BD23 4NH. Open by appointment only. *STOCK: 19th-20th C paintings and watercolours.* TEL: 01729 840384.

MALTON

Malton Antique Market

2 Old Maltongate. YO17 0EG. (Mrs M.A. Cleverly). Est. 1970. Open 9.30-12.30 and 2-5. CL: Thurs. SIZE: Medium. *STOCK: Furniture, Georgian to Victorian, to £1,500; glass, bric-a-brac, porcelain, pottery, copper and brass.* LOC: From York take A64, shop is at main traffic light junction in Malton. PARK: 20yds. further. TEL: 01653 692732. SER: Commission sales.

Malton continued

Talents Fine Arts Ltd

7 Market Place. YO17 0LP. (J. Burrows). Est. 1986. Open daily. SIZE: Medium. *STOCK: Oils, watercolours and prints, 19th C, £500-£3,000; contemporary local artists.* LOC: A64 near church. PARK: Easy. TEL: 01653 600020. SER: Restorations; framing.

MANFIELD, Nr. Darlington

Trade Antiques - D.D. White

Lucy Cross Cottage. DL2 2RJ. Est. 1975. Open after prior telephone call. *STOCK: Georgian, Victorian and export furniture.* LOC: B6275, Scotch Corner to Piercebridge road, on left 3 miles after leaving A1. PARK: Easy. TEL: 01325 374303; 01833 638329. VAT: Stan/Spec.

MARKINGTON, Nr. Harrogate

Daleside Antiques

Hinks Hall Lane. HG3 3NU. Est. 1978. Open 8-5, Sat. and Sun. by appointment. *STOCK: Pine furniture, decorative items, architectural features and fittings, 18th-19th C, £50-£3,500; Georgian mahogany furniture; Victorian shop fittings.* TEL: 01765 677888; fax - 01765 677886. SER: Containers; courier; restorations. VAT: Stan.

MASHAM, Nr. Ripon

Aura Antiques

1-3 Silver St. HG4 4DX. (R. and R. Sutcliffe). Est. 1985. Open 9.30-5, Sun. by appointment. SIZE: Medium. *STOCK: Furniture especially period mahogany dining furniture, 18th to mid-19th C, £50-£5,000; metalware - brass and copper, fenders, £5-£250; china, glass, silver and decorative objects, £5-£1,000; all 18th-19th C.* LOC: Corner of Market Sq. PARK: Easy. TEL: 01765 689315; home - 01765 658192. SER: Valuations; delivery throughout UK. VAT: Spec.

MELMERBY, Nr. Ripon

Kindon Antiques Ltd

Unit 23 Melmerby Industrial Estate, Green Lane. Open 9.30-5, other times by appointment. CL: Sat. *STOCK: Large and unusual pine.* TEL: 01765 640522. SER: Containers. *Trade Only.*

NORTHALLERTON

The Antique and Art

7 Central Arcade. DL7 8PY. (Mrs J. Willoughby). Open 10-4. CL: Thurs. *STOCK: Porcelain, pottery, silver, jewellery, glass, prints and paintings.* TEL: 01609 772051; home - 01609 774157.

Collectors Corner

145/6 High St. DL7 8SL. (J. Wetherill). Est. 1972. Open 10-4, Sat. 10-5, or by appointment. CL: Thurs. *STOCK: General antiques, collectors' items.* LOC: Opposite GPO. TEL: 01609 777623; home - 01609 775199.

NORTON, Nr. Malton

Northern Antiques Company

2 Parliament St., Scarborough Rd. YO17 9HE. (Sara Ashby-Arnold). Est. 1991. Open 9-1 and 2-5, Sat. 9.30-12.30, Sun. and evenings by appointment. SIZE: Medium. *STOCK: Country oak furniture, from 17th C, £200-£2,000; pine, Georgian to Victorian, to £1,000; upholstered sofas and chairs, cast-iron and wooden beds, decorative items and prints, from 19th C, to £800; some contemporary interior design items.* LOC: From Malton town centre on old Scarborough Rd., through Norton, shop on right above Aga shop. PARK: Easy. TEL: 01653 697520; home - 01423 340398.

PATELEY BRIDGE

Cat in the Window Antiques

22 High St. HG3 5JU. (Mrs S. Morgan). Est. 1976. Open 2.30-5 and by appointment. CL: Mon. and Wed. *STOCK: Small furniture, metalware, glass, ceramics, Art Nouveau, Art Deco, amber, coral, jet, pictures, sewing items, linen, lace and collectors' items.* PARK: Easy. TEL: 01423 711343.

Brian Loomes

Calf Haugh Farm. HG3 5HW. (Author of clock reference books). Est. 1966. Open 9-5 by appointment. SIZE: Medium. *STOCK: British*

Pateley Bridge continued

clocks especially longcase, wall, bracket and lantern, pre-1840, £500-£15,000. Not Stocked: Foreign clocks. LOC: From Pateley Bridge, first private lane on left on Grassington Rd. (B6265). PARK: Own. TEL: 01423 711163; home and fax - same. VAT: Spec.

Pateley Bridge Antiques

The Apothecary's House, 35 High St. HG3 5QG. (A.D. Gora and Ms C. Simmons). Est. 1995. Open Wed.-Sat. 1.30-5, other times by appointment (including Sun.). SIZE: Medium. *STOCK: Oak and country furniture, 17th-18th C, £100-£3,000; longcase clocks and Windsor chairs, 18th-19th C, £250-£2,000; metalware including copper and pewter, 17th-19th C, £30-£300.* LOC: Ripon-Grassington road. PARK: Almost opposite. TEL: 01423 711004; home - 01423 711517. SER: Valuations.

PICKERING

Country Collector

11-12 Birdgate. Y018 7AL. (G. and M. Berney). Est. 1991. Open 10-5. CL: Wed. SIZE: Small. *STOCK: Ceramics, including blue and white and Art Deco pottery, and collectables, 1800-1940, £5-£500.* LOC: Top of the Market Place, at crossroads of A169 and A170. PARK: Eastgate. TEL: 01751 477481. SER: Valuations; buys at auction (ceramics). VAT: Stan.

C.H. Reynolds Antiques

The Old Curiosity Shop, 122 Eastgate. YO18 7DW. Est. 1947. Open 9.30-5.30, Sun. by appointment. *STOCK: General antiques.* TEL: 01751 472785.

RIPON

Balmain Antiques

13 High Skellgate. HG4 1BA. Open 10-4. *STOCK: Fine furniture, paintings, silver and porcelain.* TEL: 01765 601294.

Rose Fine Art and Antiques

13 Kirkgate. HG4 1PA. (Mr and Mrs S. Rose). Est. 1984. Open daily, Sun. by appointment. CL: Wed. SIZE: Medium. *STOCK: Pictures, 18th to early 20th C, £5-£2,000; furniture, £50-£1,000; porcelain and glass, £5-£500; both 19th to early 20th C.* LOC: Between Market Place and cathedral. PARK: Nearby. TEL: 01765 690118; home - same. SER: Valuations; restorations (pictures); buys at auction (pictures and prints); framing. VAT: Stan.

Sigma Antiques and Fine Art

Water Skellgate. HG4 1BQ. (D. Thomson). Est. 1963. Open 10.30-5, other times by appointment. *STOCK: 17th-20th C furniture, furnishing items, pottery, porcelain, objets d'art, paintings, jewellery and collectors' items.* PARK: Nearby. TEL: 01765 603163; fax - 01765 690933.

Ripon continued

Skellgate Curios

2 Low Skellgate. HG4 1BE. (J.I. Wain and P.S. Gyte). Est. 1974. Open 11-5. CL: Wed. *STOCK: General antiques, silver, jewellery and curios.* TEL: 01765 601290; home - 01765 635336/01748 812140.

SCARBOROUGH

Hanover Antiques & Collectables

33 St Nicolas Cliff. YO11 2ES. Est. 1976. Open 11-4. CL: Wed. p.m. *STOCK: Small collectables, medals, badges, toys, 50p-£500.* PARK: Nearby. TEL: 01723 374175.

Shuttleworths

7 Victoria Rd. YO11 1SB. (L.R. Shuttleworth). Open 10-4. CL: Wed. *STOCK: General antiques.* TEL: 01723 366278.

SCARTHINGWELL, Nr. Tadcaster

Scarthingwell Arcades

Scarthingwell Centre, Scarthingwell Farm. LS24 9PG. (Mrs G. Brier). Est. 1990. Open 10-5 including Sun. SIZE: Large. *STOCK: General antiques - bric-a-brac, pine, small period furniture, from £5.* LOC: Off A162 between Sherburn-in-Elmet and Tadcaster. PARK: Easy. TEL: 01937 557877. SER: Valuations; restorations (furniture); buys at auction.

SETTLE

Benita - Antique Textiles and Interiors

King William House, High St. BD24 9EX. Est. 1987. Open 9-5.30. CL: Wed. SIZE: Large. *STOCK: Period textiles, cushions, curtains, needlework pictures and tapestries, 17th-20th C; Old Master drawings, French decorative objects, some period furniture and smalls.* LOC: Opposite Post Office, on old High St. PARK: Easy. TEL: 01729 822085; fax - 01729 824179. SER: Full interior design; suppliers of National Trust paints and quality modern fabrics and wallpapers. VAT: Stan/Spec.

Mary Milnthorpe and Daughters Antique Shop

Market Place. BD24 9DX. Est. 1958. Open 9.30-5. CL: Wed. SIZE: Small. *STOCK: Antique and 19th C jewellery and English silver.* LOC: Opposite Town Hall. PARK: Easy. TEL: 01729 822331. VAT: Stan/Spec.

Nanbooks

Roundabout, 41 Duke St. BD24 9AJ. Resident. (J.L. and N.M. Midgley). Est. 1955. Open Tues., Fri. and Sat. 11-12.30 and 2-5.30. CL: Jan., Feb. and Mar. SIZE: Small. *STOCK: English pottery, porcelain including Oriental, glass, general small antiques, 17th-19th C, to £250.* Not Stocked: Jewellery. LOC: A65. PARK: Easy. TEL: 01729 823324; home - 01729 823856.

Settle continued

Roy Precious

King William House, High St. BD24 9EX. Resident. Est. 1972. Open 10-5.30 or by appointment. CL: Wed. SIZE: Large. *STOCK: Oak, walnut, mahogany and country furniture, 17th-19th C, £30-£6,000; oil paintings, mainly portraits, 17th-19th C, £300-£10,000; pottery and prints; textiles, needlework pictures and tapestries, 17th-19th C.* LOC: Near the Talbot Inn on the old High St. PARK: Easy. TEL: 01729 823946; fax - 01729 824179. SER: Valuations. VAT: Stan/Spec.

Anderson Slater Antiques

6 Duke St. BD24 7DW. (K.C. Slater). Est. 1962. Open 10-1 and 2-5. CL: Wed. SIZE: Medium. *STOCK: Furniture, 18th-19th C, £200-£4,000; porcelain, 18th-19th C, £25-£500; pictures, 19th-20th C, £200-£1,500.* LOC: Main street out of Market Place. PARK: Nearby. TEL: 01729 822051. SER: Valuations; restorations (furniture and porcelain); buys at auction. VAT: Stan/Spec.

E. Thistlethwaite

The Antique Shop, Market Sq. BD24 9EF. Est. 1972. Open 9-5. CL: Wed. SIZE: Medium. *STOCK: Country furniture and metalware, 18th-19th C.* LOC: Town centre, A65. PARK: Forecourt. TEL: 01729 822460. VAT: Stan/Spec.

SHERBURN IN ELMET

Drey Antique Centre

56 Low St. LS25 6BA. (Valerie L. Keates). Est 1979. Usually 10-5 including Sun. CL: Wed. SIZE: Medium. *STOCK: Country furniture, 18th-19th C, £150-£1,000; collectables and Doulton figures, £2-£200; paintings and prints, £5-£1,000; books on Yorkshire.* LOC: 3 miles east A1 between Leeds and Selby. PARK: Easy. TEL: 01977 681404. SER: Valuations; restorations (furniture, clocks, pictures including framing); buys at auction. FAIRS: Local and Newark.

SKIPTON

Adamson Armoury

Otley Rd. BD23 1ET. (J.K. Adamson). Est. 1975. Open 10-4.15, Mon. 10-12. SIZE: Medium. *STOCK: Weapons, 17th-19th C, £10-£1,000.* LOC: A65, 200yds. from town centre. PARK: Rear. TEL: 01756 791355. SER: Valuations. FAIRS: London.

Corn Mill Antiques

High Corn Mill, Chapel Hill. BD23 1NL. (Mrs M. Hawkridge). Est. 1984. Open 10-4. CL: Tues. and Wed. SIZE: Medium. *STOCK: Oak, mahogany and walnut furniture, £100-£2,000; porcelain, silver plate, prints, pictures, brass and copper, £5-£500; all Georgian to 1920's.* Not Stocked: Jewellery, gold and silver. LOC: From town centre take Grassington Road, Chapel Hill is first right. PARK: Easy. TEL: 01756 792440; home - 01729 830489. SER: Valuations. VAT: Spec.

Skipton continued

Old Co-op

Off Main St., Hellifield. (Graham Coles). Est. 1988. Usually open daily but prior 'phone call advisable. SIZE: Large. *STOCK: 17th-19th C furniture and railwayana.* TEL: 01729 850573. SER: Restorations (furniture); polishing.

SNAINTON, Nr. Scarborough

D. & E.A. Shackleton Antiques

19 & 72/3 High St. YO13 9AE. Resident. (Mrs E.A. Shackleton). Est. 1984. CL: Sat. pm. SIZE: Medium. *STOCK: Longcase clocks, Victorian rocking horses, Georgian and Victorian furniture, collectables, £1-£3,500.* LOC: A170, equidistant Scarborough and Pickering. PARK: Easy. TEL: 01723 859577. SER: Restorations (furniture, longcase clocks, rocking horses).

SPENNITHORNE, Nr. Leyburn

N.J. and C.S. Dodsworth

Thorney Hall. DL8 5PW. Est. 1973. Open by appointment. SIZE: Medium. *STOCK: Furniture, clocks and small items, 17th-19th C.* LOC: Off A684. TEL: 01969 622277. VAT: Margin.

STILLINGTON

Pond Cottage Antiques

Brandsby Rd. YO6 1NY. Resident. (C.M. and D. Thurstans). Est. 1972. *STOCK: Pine, kitchenalia, country furniture, treen, metalware, brass, copper.* TEL: 01347 810796.

THIRSK

Richard Bennett

18 Kirkgate. Est. 1979. Open by appointment. SIZE: Small. *STOCK: Oil paintings, £50-£2,000; watercolours, £50-£500; both 19th to mid-20th C.* LOC: Joins Market Place. PARK: Nearby. TEL: 01845 524085; home - same. SER: Restorations (oil paintings); buys at auction; framing.

Cottage Antiques and Curios

1 Market Place. YO7 1HQ. (Mrs E.H. and S.R. Ballard). Est. 1970. Open 9-5. CL: Wed. *STOCK: Victorian porcelain and glass, £5-£500; paintings, £20-£1,000, furniture, from 1750, £20-£1,000; brass, copper, silver and plated ware, £5-£500.* PARK: Easy. TEL: 01845 522536/523212; home - 01845 577461.

Millgate Pine & Antiques

17-19 Millgate. YO7 1AA. (Mr. Parvin). Open 11-5, Sat. 9.30-5, Sun. 10.30-5. *STOCK: Mainly antique pine.* TEL: 01845 523878.

Thirsk continued

Barry Alexander Ogleby (Jnr) Antiques

St James' House. YO7 1AQ. Open every day 10-5 and by appointment. SIZE: Medium - shop and workshop. *STOCK: Mainly period oak and country furniture, also Georgian and Victorian mahogany.* LOC: A1, A168 to Thirsk. TEL: 01845 526565/524120. SER: Restorations (furniture).

B. Ogleby - St James' House Antiques

35-37 St James' Green. YO7 1AQ. Est. 1966. Open 10-5 and by appointment. SIZE: Large. *STOCK: Mahogany, oak, walnut, rosewood and pine furniture, 17th-20th C.* LOC: A1, A168 to Thirsk 6 minutes. TEL: 01845 526565; fax - same; mobile - 0410 353534. SER: Packing; shipping. VAT: Stan/Spec.

Potterton Books

The Old Rectory, Sessay. YO7 3LZ. (Clare Jameson). Open 9-5. SIZE: Large. *STOCK: Classic reference works on art, architecture, interior design, antiques and collecting.* TEL: 01845 501218; fax - 01845 501439. SER: Book search; catalogues. FAIRS: London; Frankfurt; Paris; New York; Milan; Dubai.

Windmill Antiques

(B. and J. Tildesley). Est. 1980. Open by appointment only. *STOCK: Restored antique rocking horses, children's chairs and reproductions of horses, £400-£5,000.* TEL: 01845 501330; fax - 01845 501700.

THORNTON LE DALE, Nr. Pickering

Stable Antiques

4 Pickering Rd. YO18 7LG. (Mrs S. Kitching Walker). Open 2-5, mornings by appointment. CL: Mon. SIZE: Medium. *STOCK: Porcelain, £5-£500; furniture, £20-£700; silver, glass, brass, plate, copper, collectors' items, £5-£150, all 19th C to 1930's.* LOC: A170. PARK: Easy. TEL: 01751 474332; home - 01751 474435. SER: Valuations.

TOCKWITH, Nr. York

Tomlinson (Antiques) Ltd. & Period Furniture Ltd LAPADA

Moorside. YO5 8QG. Est. 1971. Open 8-5, Sat. 9-4.30 or by appointment. SIZE: Large. *STOCK: Furniture, £5-£12,000; clocks, £10-£3,000.* LOC: A1 Wetherby take B1224 towards York. After 3 miles turn left on to Rudgate. At end of this road turn left, business 200m on left. PARK: Easy. TEL: 01423 358833; fax - 01423 358188. SER: Export; restorations; container packing. VAT: Stan/Spec. *Trade Only (Mon-Fri.).*

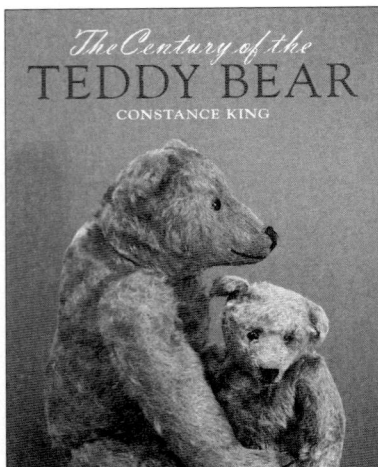

TOPCLIFFE, Nr. Thirsk

Chattels Antiques

19 Church St. YO7 3PA. (M. Pitman and A. Walton). Est. 1984. Open 10-5.30 including Sun; Fri. 10-1, Wed. and Sat. by appointment. *STOCK: Pre 1830 oak and country furniture, longcase clocks, curios, £150-£6,000.* LOC: Off the A1 at Dishforth. PARK: Easy. TEL: 01845 578644; fax/home - same.

WHITBY

Aird-Gordon Antiques

15 Baxtergate. Open Mon.-Sat. *STOCK: Glass, jewellery, jet, china, small furniture.* TEL: 01947 601515.

The Bazaar

7 Skinner St. YO21 3AH. (F.A. Doyle). Est. 1970. Open 10.30-5.30. *STOCK: Jewellery, furniture, general antiques, 19th C.* TEL: 01947 602281.

'Bobbins' Wool, Crafts, Antiques

Wesley Hall, Church St. YO22 4DE. (D. and P. Hoyle). Open 10-5 every day. SIZE: Small. *STOCK: General antiques especially oil lamps, bric-a-brac, kitchenalia, 19th-20th C.* LOC: Between Market Place and steps to Abbey on cobbled East Side. PARK: Nearby (part of Church St. is pedestrianised). TEL: 01947 600585 (answerphone). SER: Repairs and spares (oil lamps). VAT: Stan.

Caedmon House

14 Station Sq. YO21 1DU. (E.M. Stanforth). Est. 1977. Open 10-5. SIZE: Medium. *STOCK: General, mainly small, antiques including jewellery, dolls, Disney and china, especially Dresden, to £1,200.* PARK: Easy. TEL: 01947 602120; home - 01947 603930. SER: Valuations; restorations (china); repairs (jewellery). VAT: Stan/Spec.

Coach House Antiques

75 Coach Rd., Sleights. YO22 5BT. Resident. (C.J. Rea). Est. 1973. Open by appointment. SIZE: Small. *STOCK: Furniture, especially oak and country; glass, metalware, paintings, porcelain, pottery, unusual and decorative items.* LOC: On A169, 3 miles south west of Whitby. PARK: Easy, opposite. TEL: 01947 810313.

WHIXLEY

Garth Antiques

The Old School, Franks Lane. YO5 8AP. (I. Chapman). Est. 1978. Open Tues-Sat. 10-5. SIZE: Medium. *STOCK: Furniture, 18th-19th C, £50-£3,000; brass and copper, 19th C, £1-£500; oils and watercolours, £5-£3,000.* LOC: A59, turn towards Whixley at the Cattle/Whixley junction, then left opposite The Anchor into old village, next to Village Hall. PARK: Easy. TEL: 01423 331055. VAT: Stan/Spec.

WYKEHAM, Nr. Scarborough

Village Farm Antiques
30 The Village. YO13 9QP. (J.D. and C. Vance). Est. 1996. Open 10.30-5, Sun. 12-5. CL: Mon. SIZE: Medium. *STOCK: Antique bedsteads, furniture, china, metalware.* LOC: Off A170, turn opposite Downe Arms Hotel in village. PARK: Easy. TEL: 01723 865427; home - same. SER: Restorations (metalware).

YORK

Barbican Bookshop
24 Fossgate. YO1 2TA. Est. 1961. Open 9.15-5.30. *STOCK: Antiquarian books.* TEL: 01904 653643; fax - 01904 653643. VAT: Stan.

Barker Court Antiques and Bygones
44 Gillygate. YO3 7EQ. (Mrs D. Yates). Est. 1970. Open 10.30-5.30. SIZE: Small. *STOCK: Pottery and porcelain, glass, flatware, jewellery, Victorian to 1970, £3-£100.* LOC: 3 mins. walk from minster. PARK: Nearby. TEL: 01904 622611.

Bishopsgate Antiques
23/24 Bishopsgate St. YO2 1JH. (R. Wetherill). Open 9.15-6. *STOCK: General antiques.* TEL: 01904 623893; fax - 01904 626511.

Barbara Cattle BADA
45 Stonegate. YO1 2AW. Open 9-5.30. *STOCK: Jewellery and silver, Georgian to date.* TEL: 01904 623862.

Coulter Galleries
YO2 2LX. Open by appointment only. *STOCK: Watercolours and oils, pre-1900; frames.* TEL: 01904 702101.

The Emporium
77 Walmgate. YO1 2TZ. Open 10-5. CL: Tues. *STOCK: General antiques, including furniture and fireplaces, and collectables.* PARK: Nearby. TEL: 01904 634124.

Ruth Ford Antiques
39 Fossgate. Est. 1976. Open 11.30-4.30. CL: Wed. SIZE: Small. *STOCK: 18th-19th C country furniture, pine, treen and collectables, £5-£1,000.* LOC: Near Merchant Adventurers Hall. PARK: Nearby. TEL: Home - 01904 632864.

Golden Memories of York
14 Newgate. YO1 2LA. NAG. (M.S. and D.J. Smith). Est. 1991. Open 9-5.30. SIZE: Small. *STOCK: Antique and secondhand jewellery and silver, £5-£3,000.* LOC: Adjacent York market, off Parliament St. PARK: Multi-storey. TEL: 01904 655883. VAT: Stan/Spec.

Robert M. Himsworth
28 The Shambles. YO1 2LX. Est. 1949. Open 9-5. SIZE: Small. *STOCK: Antique jewellery.* TEL: 01904 625089. VAT: Stan/Spec.

York continued

Holgate Antiques
Holgate Rd. YO2 4AB. (E.J.W. Mellors and A.C.R. Kent). Est. 1980. Open 10-5. *STOCK: Furniture and general antiques.* TEL: 01904 630005.

Minster Antiques
24 Goodramgate. YO1 2LG. (M. Tanner and K. Nevens). Est. 1982. Open daily. SIZE: Small. *STOCK: Brass and copper, silver, scientific instruments, 19th C, £5-£500.* LOC: 2 minutes from Minster, past St. William's College towards Monk Bar. PARK: Loading only. TEL: 01904 655481. SER: Valuations.

Minster Gate Bookshop
8 Minster Gates. YO1 2HL. (N. Wallace). Est. 1970. Open 9.30-5.30. SIZE: Large. *STOCK: Antiquarian and secondhand books; old maps and prints.* LOC: Opposite south door of minster. PARK: Nearby. TEL: 01904 621812. SER: Valuations; restorations; book finding.

Robert Morrison and Son BADA
Trentholme House, 131 The Mount. YO2 2DA. (C. Morrison). Est. 1890. Open 9-5. SIZE: Large. *STOCK: English furniture, 1700-1900; porcelain and clocks.* LOC: Near racecourse, one mile from city centre on Leeds Rd. From A1, take A64 to outskirts of York, then take A1036 York west road. PARK: Easy. TEL: 01904 655394. VAT: Stan/Spec.

Ken Spelman
70 Micklegate. YO1 1LF. ABA. (P. Miller and A. Fothergill). Est. 1948. SIZE: Large. *STOCK: Secondhand and antiquarian books especially fine arts and literature, 50p-£10,000; early English watercolours.* PARK: Easy. TEL: 01904 624414; fax - 01904 626276; e-mail - spelman.@dial.pipex.com; internet (rare books viewable on-line) - http://dspace.dial,pipex.com/ spelman/. SER: Valuations; buys at auction (books); catalogues issued. FAIRS: Bath, Oxford, York, Harrogate, Cambridge, Edinburgh and London PBFA and ABA. VAT: Spec.

St. John Antiques
26 Lord Mayor's Walk. YO3 7HA. (R. and N. Bell). Open 10-5. CL: Mon. *STOCK: Victorian stripped pine, curios, blue and white pottery.* PARK: At rear. TEL: 01904 644263.

York Antiques Centre
2 Lendal. YO1 2AA. Open 9.30-5.30, winter 10-5. SIZE: 20 dealers. *STOCK: Antiques and collectable items, 18th-20th C.* LOC: Opposite the museum gardens. PARK: Easy. TEL: 01904 641445/641582.

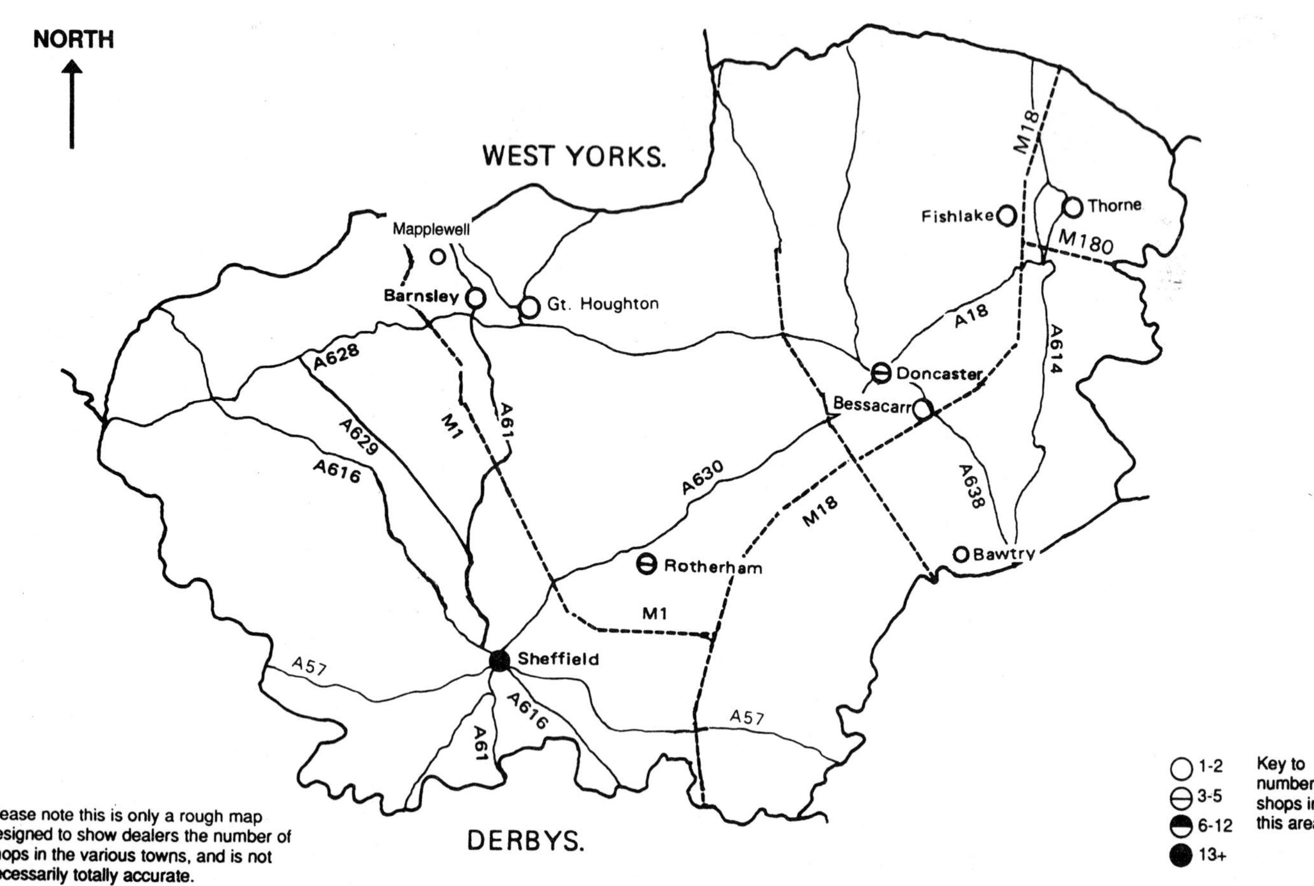
NORTH
WEST YORKS.
Mapplewell
Barnsley
Gt. Houghton
Fishlake
Thorne
M18
M180
A18
A614
Doncaster
Bessacarr
A628
A629
A616
M1
A61
A630
M18
A638
Bawtry
Rotherham
M1
Sheffield
A57
A616
A61
A57
DERBYS.
Please note this is only a rough map designed to show dealers the number of shops in the various towns, and is not necessarily totally accurate.
1-2
3-5
6-12
13+
Key to number of shops in this area.

BARNSLEY

Charisma Antiques Trade Warehouse
St. Paul's former Methodist Chapel, Market St., Hoyland. S74 9QR. (J.C. Simmons). Est. 1980. Open 10-5. SIZE: Large. *STOCK: Furniture, shipping goods, pictures.* LOC: 1.5 miles off M1, exit 36. PARK: Easy. TEL: 01226 747599; home - 01226 790482.

Christine Simmons Antiques
St. Paul's Former Methodist Chapel, Market St., Hoyland. S74 9QR. Est. 1976. Open 10-4. SIZE: Medium. *STOCK: Smalls and pictures.* LOC: 1.5 miles from exit 36, M1. PARK: Easy. TEL: 01226 747599/790482.

BAWTRY, Nr. Doncaster

Swan Antiques
2 Swan St. DN10 6JQ. Open 10-5. CL: Wed. SIZE: Large. *STOCK: Furniture, silver, ceramics, collectables, costume jewellery.* PARK: Easy. TEL: 01302 710301.

Treasure House Antiques Centre
4-10 Swan St. DN10 6JR. Est. 1982. Open 10-5 including Sun. CL: Wed. SIZE: Large - various dealers. *STOCK: Silver, porcelain, furniture, carnival glass, postcards, toy trains and general antiques.* PARK: Easy. TEL: 01302 710621.

BESSACARR, Nr. Doncaster

Keith Stones Grandfather Clocks
5 Ellers Drive. DN4 7DL. Est. 1988. Open by appointment. SIZE: Small. *STOCK: Grandfather clocks especially painted dial with 30 hour and 8 day movements, Georgian to early 19th C, £750-£2,000.* LOC: Take A638 Bawtry road off racecourse roundabout, through traffic lights after 3/4 mile, take second right into Ellers Rd. then second left. PARK: Easy. TEL: 01302 535258; home - same. SER: Valuations.

DONCASTER

Doncaster Sales and Exchange
20 Copley Rd. DN1 2PF. Open 9.30-5. CL: Thurs. *STOCK: General small antiques.* TEL: 01302 344857. VAT: Stan.

FISHLAKE

Fishlake Antiques
Pinfold Lane. DN7 5LA. Resident. Est. 1972. Open Sat. 1-5, and by appointment. SIZE: Medium. *STOCK: Rural furniture especially stripped pine; clocks including longcase and wall clocks, Victorian to mid-19th C, £30-£1,000; smalls, £3-£70.* LOC: Off A63. PARK: Own. TEL: 01302 841411.

GREAT HOUGHTON, Nr. Barnsley

Rebecca L. Calvert t/a Farmhouse Antiques
7 High St. S72 0AA. Open 10-12 and 1-5, Sun. by appointment. CL: Wed. and Fri. *STOCK: Furniture including pine; pottery, porcelain, Susie Cooper, linen, jewellery, pictures and decorators items.* TEL: 01226 754057; mobile - 0370 978501.

MAPPLEWELL, Nr. Barnsley

A Maze of Pine and Roses
1 Blacker Rd. S75 6BW. (Mrs Gioia L. Padgett). Est. 1983. Open Mon. and Fri. 10-5, Tues. and Thurs. 10-4, Sun. 2-4. SIZE: Small. *STOCK: Pine, walnut and mahogany furniture and doors.* LOC: Off M1, exit 38, head back towards Barnsley, turn into Darton at the church, carry on to Mapplewell, premises on crossroads. PARK: Easy. TEL: 01226 388014; fax and ansaphone - 01226 282992. SER: Valuations; curtains, loose covers, bedspreads made to order from designer fabrics.

ROTHERHAM

Roger Appleyard Ltd LAPADA
Fitzwilliam Rd., Eastwood Trading Estate. S65 1SL. Open 8-5, Sat. 8-12. SIZE: Large. *STOCK: General antiques, £5-£1,500.* LOC: A630. PARK: Easy. TEL: 01709 367670/ 377770; fax - 01709 829395. SER: Packing and shipping. VAT: Stan/Spec. *Trade Only.*

Foster's Antique Centre
Foster's Garden Centre, Doncaster Rd., Thrybergh. S65 4BE. (The Foster Family). Est. 1996. Open 10-4.30, Sun. 11-5. SIZE: 20 dealers. *STOCK: Wide range of general antiques and collectables including furniture, jewellery, Rockingham china.* LOC: A630 between Rotherham and Doncaster. PARK: Own large. TEL: 01709 850337; fax - 01709 851905.

John Mason Jewellers Ltd
36 High St. S60 1PP. Open 9-5.30. *STOCK: Silver, jewellery.* TEL: 01709 382311. SER: Valuations; repairs. VAT: Spec.

South Yorkshire Antiques
88-94 Broad St. S62 6DZ. (A. Swindells). Est. 1955. Open 9.30-4.30. *STOCK: General antiques and shipping furniture.* PARK: Easy. TEL: 01709 526514/582688 (ansaphone); mobile - 0378 46154. SER: Valuations; restorations.

Philip Turnor Antiques
94a Broad St., Parkgate. Open 9-5, Sat. 10-4. *STOCK: Shipping furniture including oak, 1880-1940.* PARK: Easy. TEL: 01709 524640. SER: Export.

SHEFFIELD

A. and C. Antiques

239 Abbeydale Rd. S7 1FJ. (C.E. Maltby). Est. 1984. Open 10.30-5. SIZE: Medium. *STOCK: General antiques, smalls, jewellery, £30-£500.* LOC: Main road south of city centre, towards Chesterfield. PARK: Easy. TEL: 0114 2589161.

Anita's Holme Antiques

144 Holme Lane, Hillsborough. S6 4JW. (A.L. Spalton). Est. 1986. Open 9-5. SIZE: Medium. *STOCK: General antiques, 19th C, £50-£100.* LOC: A61, turn left at traffic lights opposite Owlerton Sports Stadium, shop 1.5 miles on right. PARK: Easy. TEL: 0114 2336698.

The Basement Gallery at Fulwood Antiques

7 Brooklands Ave. S10 4GA. (S.R. & H.J. Wills). Est. 1977. Open Wed. and Fri. 10-5, Sat. 10-1. SIZE: Medium. *STOCK: Oil paintings and watercolours, specialising in Sheffield Artists, 19th-20th C, £50-£10,000; some furniture and silver.* LOC: From city centre towards Broomhill, Fulwood Rd., Nethergreen and straight on for Fulwood. PARK: Easy. TEL: 0114 2307387; home - 0114 2301346. SER: Valuations; restorations.

Chimney Piece Antique Fires

262 South Rd., Walkley. S6 3TB. (J. Young). Open 9.30-5. CL: Wed. *STOCK: Fireplaces.* TEL: 0114 2346085.

Sheffield continued

Court House Antique Centre

2-6 Town End Rd., Ecclesfield. S35 9YY. (J.P. & K.E. Owram). Open 10.30-5, Sun. 11.30-5. SIZE: Large. *STOCK: Town and country furniture, £5-£2,500; ceramics, glass, clocks, barometers, kitchenalia, militaria, books.* LOC: 2 miles from M1, junction 35. Down hill, bear left into Nether Lane, through lights to church, turn left 250 yards on right. PARK: Easy. TEL: 0114 257 0641.

Dronfield Antiques

375-377 Abbeydale Rd. S7 1FS. (H.J. Greaves). Est. 1968. Open 10.30-5.30. CL: Thurs. and Sat. except by appointment. SIZE: Large + warehouses. *STOCK: Trade and shipping goods, Victoriana, glass, china.* LOC: A621, 1 mile south of city centre. PARK: Easy. TEL: 0114 2550172/2581821; home and fax - 0114 2556024. VAT: Stan.

Ellis's

144 Whitham Rd. S10 2SR. Est. 1943. Open 10-6. *STOCK: Oriental carpets and rugs.* TEL: 0114 2662920. VAT: Stan.

F S Antiques

Court House Antiques Centre, 2-6 Town End Rd., Ecclesfield. 10.30-5, Sun. 11.30-4.30. SIZE: Small. *STOCK: Longcase, wall and mantel clocks and barometers, 1790-1920, £60-£2,500.* LOC: 2 miles from M1, junction 35. PARK: Easy. TEL: 0114 257 0641; home - 01226 382805. SER: Restorations.

Fun Antiques

72 Abbeydale Rd. S7 1FD. (B. Harrap). Est. 1978. Open by appointment. SIZE: Medium. *STOCK: Unusual and collectable items including sporting items, toys, advertising, Christmas, arcade and fairground items, 20th C, £5-£1,000.* PARK: Easy. TEL: 0114 2553424. SER: Valuations; installations. FAIRS: Harrow, Ardingly, Newark, Stoneleigh. VAT: Stan. *Trade Only.*

Julie Goddard Antiques

Court House Antiques Centre, Town End Rd., Ecclesfield. S35 9YY. Est. 1982. Open 10.30-5, Sun. 11.30-4.30. SIZE: Small. *STOCK: Furniture, Georgian to Edwardian, oak and mahogany.* LOC: 5 mins from J36 M1, next to St. Mary's Church. PARK: Easy. TEL: 0114 257 0641; mobile - 0410 098748. SER: Buys at auction. VAT: Spec.

Hibbert Brothers Ltd

117 Norfolk St. S1 2JE. (Paul Hibbert-Greaves). Est. 1834. Open 9-5. SIZE: Large. *STOCK: 19th-20th C paintings, £500-£10,000.* LOC: City centre, next to town hall. PARK: Easy. TEL: 0114 2722038. SER: Restorations; framing. FAIRS: NEC. VAT: Stan/Spec.

Sheffield continued

Alan Hill Books, Sheffield
261 Glossop Rd. S10 2GZ. Est. 1980. Open 10.30-5.30. *STOCK: Antiquarian books, maps and prints.* TEL: 0114 2780594.

Peter James Antiques
336 Abbeydale Rd. S7 1FN. (P.J. Conboy). Est. 1980. Open 9.30-4.30. SIZE: Medium. *STOCK: Georgian, Victorian and Edwardian mahogany, walnut, oak and pine furniture.* PARK: Easy. TEL: 0114 2551554. SER: Restorations. VAT: Stan/Spec.

A.E. Jameson and Co LAPADA
257 Glossop Rd. S10 2GZ. (P. Jameson). Est. 1883. Open 9-5.45. SIZE: Large. *STOCK: Furniture, pre-1820, £20-£15,000; glass, china, weapons.* LOC: A57. TEL: 0114 2723846; home - 0114 2726189. SER: Valuations; restorations (furniture); buys at auction. VAT: Stan/Spec.

Nichols Antique Centre
The Nichols Building, Shalesmoor. S3 8UJ. (T. and M. Vickers.). Est. 1994. Open 10-5, Sat. and Sun. 10.30-4.30. SIZE: Large. *STOCK: Ceramics, furniture, clocks and collectables, mainly 19th-20th C, £50-£1,000.* LOC: A61,.50 mile from city centre. PARK: Easy. TEL: 0114 281 2811; fax - 0114 281 2812. SER: Valuations; restorations; re-upholstery. VAT: Stan.

The Oriental Rug Shop
763 Abbeydale Rd. S7 2BG. (Kian A. Hezaveh). Open 10-5. *STOCK: Handmade rugs and carpets.* TEL: 0114 2552240/2589821; fax - 0114 2509088.

Paraphernalia
66/68 Abbeydale Rd. Est. 1972. *STOCK: General antiques, stripped pine, lighting, brass and iron beds.* TEL: 0114 2550203. VAT: Stan.

Renishaw Antiques
32 Main Rd., Renishaw. S31 9UT. (B. Findley). Open by appointment. *STOCK: Architectural antiques, old doors.* TEL: 01246 435521. SER: Door stripping.

N.P. and A. Salt Antiques LAPADA
Unit 2, Barmouth Rd. S7 2DH. Open 9.30-4.30. CL: Sat. SIZE: Large. *STOCK: Victorian furniture, shipping goods, smalls and toys.* TEL: 0114 2582672. SER: Valuations; packing; shipping; courier. *Trade Only.*

Sheffield Antiques Emporium
15 Clyde Rd., (Off Broadfield Rd.), Heeley and the Chapel, 99 Broadfield Rd. Open 10-5, Sun. 11-5. SIZE: 70+ dealers. *STOCK: Furniture, collectables, jewellery, linens, glass, china, books, £1-£5,000.* LOC: Clyde Rd 1st right off Broadfield Rd., which is opposite Broadfield public house on Abbeydale Rd. PARK: Easy. TEL: 0114 258 4863/258 8288. SER: Valuations; restorations (furniture and pottery).

Sheffield continued

Tilley's Vintage Magazine Shop
281 Shoreham St. (A.G.J. and A.A.J.C. Tilley). Est. 1979. Open Tues.-Sat. 9.30-4.30, other times by appointment. SIZE: Large. *STOCK: Magazines, comics, newspapers, books, postcards, programmes, posters, cigarette cards, prints, ephemera.* LOC: Opposite Sheffield United F.C. PARK: Easy. TEL: 0114 2752442; fax - same; e-mail - atilley437@aol.com. SER: Mail order; valuations.

Top Hat Antique Centre
529 Eccesall Rd. (Richard Crabtree). Est. 1978. Open 10-5. CL: Thurs pm. SIZE: Large - 5 showrooms. *STOCK: Furniture, 18th-19th C, £200-£2,000; clocks, £200-£5,000; porcelain, £100-£5,500; both 19th C.* LOC: Main road from city centre. PARK: Easy. TEL: 0114 2666876. SER: Valuations; restorations (clocks and barometers, re-upholstery, rush and cane work). FAIRS: Newark, Ardingly.

Paul Ward Antiques
Owl House, 8 Burnell Rd., Owlerton. S6 2AX. Resident. Est. 1976. Open by appointment. SIZE: Large. *STOCK: Matched sets of Victorian dining and kitchen chairs, country chairs, general antiques.* LOC: 2 miles north of city on A61. TEL: 0114 2335980. VAT: Stan/Spec.

THORNE, Nr. Doncaster

Canterbury House
24 Finkle St. DN8 5DE. Est. 1977. Open 9-5. *STOCK: Jewellery and watches.* TEL: 01405 812102.

(Left) A Roullet et Decamps pouncing tiger, c.1910, 35cm long, £782. (Right) A Roullet et Decamps drinking bear, c.1910, 34cm high, £345. Sotheby's, Billingshurst.

From a feature on Saleroom Prices which appeared in the May 1997 issue of **Antique Collecting.**

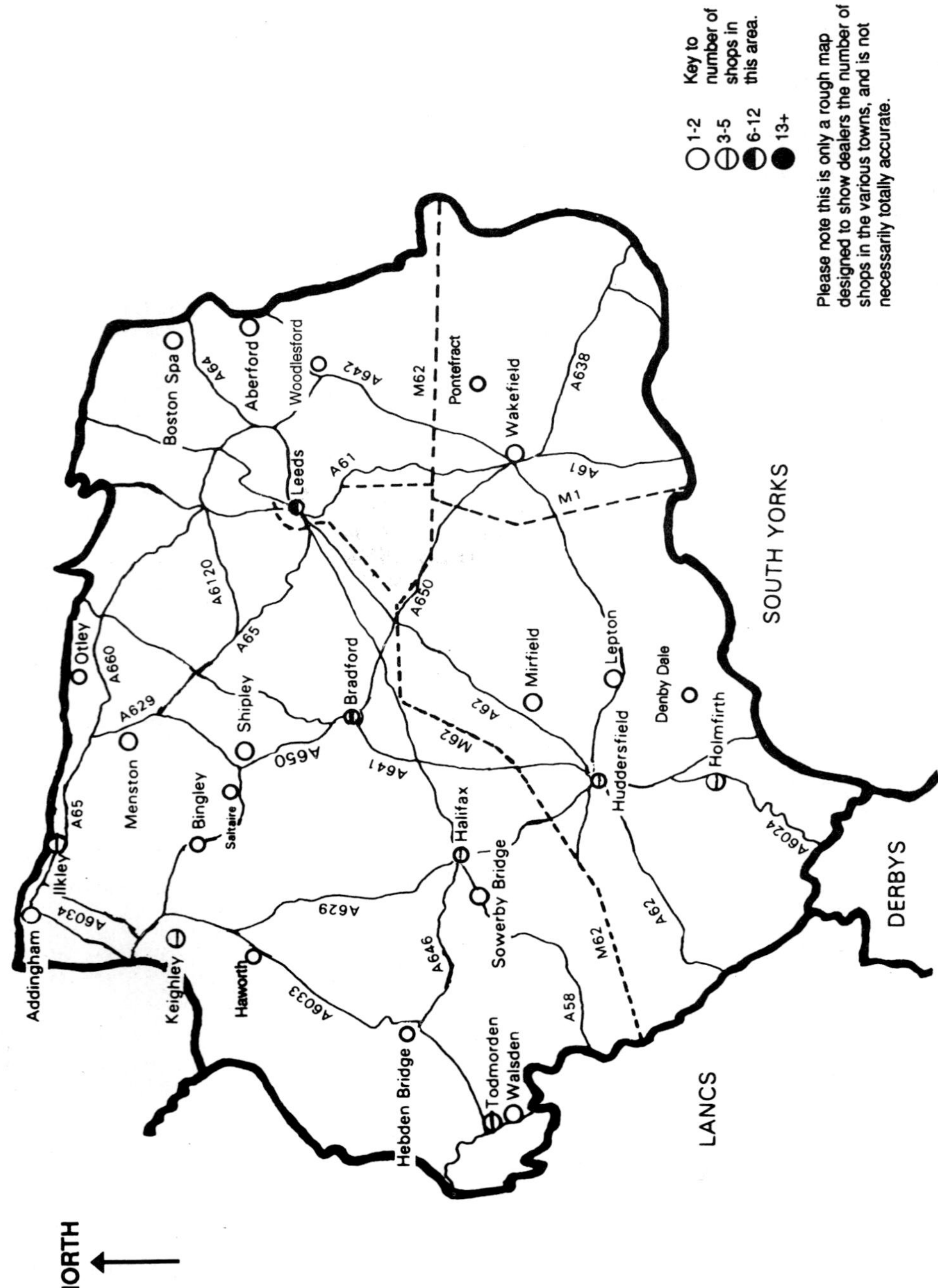
NORTH
Key to number of shops in this area.
1-2
3-5
6-12
13+
Please note this is only a rough map designed to show dealers the number of shops in the various towns, and is not necessarily totally accurate.
Addingham
Ilkley
Keighley
Haworth
Hebden Bridge
Todmorden
Walsden
Otley
Menston
Bingley
Saltaire
Shipley
Bradford
Halifax
Sowerby Bridge
Leeds
Boston Spa
Aberford
Woodlesford
Pontefract
Wakefield
Mirfield
Lepton
Huddersfield
Denby Dale
Holmfirth
LANCS
SOUTH YORKS
DERBYS
A65
A6034
A6033
A660
A629
A65
A6120
A650
A641
A646
A629
A58
M62
A62
A6024
A64
A642
M62
A61
A638
A61
M1
A650
A62

ABERFORD

Aberford Antiques Ltd

Hicklam House. LS25 3DP. (J.W.H. Long and C.A. Robinson). Est. 1973. Open 9-5.30, Sundays 10-5.30. SIZE: Large. *STOCK: Stripped pine, oak and mahogany, Victorian and period, £10-£1,500; Victoriana, collectables and memorabilia, £5-£1,000; local prints and maps.* LOC: Opposite Almshouses at southern end of village. PARK: Easy. TEL: 0113 2813209; fax - 0113 2813121. SER: Fitted pine kitchens. VAT: Stan/Spec.

ADDINGHAM, Nr. Ilkley

Manor Barn

Burnside Mill, Main St. LS29 0PJ. (Whiteley Wright Ltd). Est. 1972. Open 9-5. SIZE: Warehouse. *STOCK: Pine, 17th-19th C and reproduction; oak and shipping goods.* PARK: Easy. TEL: 01943 830176. VAT: Stan/Spec.

BINGLEY

E. Carrol

5 Ryshworth Hall, Keighley Rd., Crossflatts. BD16 2EL. Est. 1970. Open by appointment. SIZE: Small. *STOCK: Oil paintings, watercolours.* LOC: A650. PARK: Easy. TEL: 01274 568800. VAT: Stan.

BOSTON SPA, By Wetherby

London House Oriental Rugs and Carpets

London House, High St. LS23 6AD. (M.A. and Mrs I.T.H. Ries). Open 10-5.30 including Sun. CL: Mon. SIZE: Large. *STOCK: Caucasian, Turkish, Afghan and Persian rugs, runners and carpets, £50-£10,000; kelims, tapestries and textiles.* LOC: Off A1, south of Wetherby. PARK: Easy. TEL: 01937 845123; home - same. SER: Valuations; restorations (Oriental carpets and rugs); buys at auction (Oriental carpets and rugs). VAT: Stan.

BRADFORD

The Corner Shop

89 Oak Lane. BD9 4QU. (Miss Badland). Est. 1961. Open Tues., Thurs. and Fri. 2-5.30, Sat. 11-5.30. *STOCK: Pottery, small furniture, clocks and general items.*

Cottingley Antiques

286 Keighley Rd., Frizinghall. (Peter and Barbara Nobbs). Est. 1981. Open 9-5. SIZE: Medium. *STOCK: Victorian stripped and restored pine, £100-£500.* LOC: Right hand side of A650 from Keighley. PARK: Easy. TEL: 01274 545829; home - 01274 569091. SER: Restorations (furniture).

Bradford continued

Heaton Antiques

1 Hammond Place, Emm Lane, Heaton. BD9 4AN. (T. Steward). Est. 1991. Open 10-5. CL: Mon. SIZE: Medium. *STOCK: Furniture, silver plate and bric-a-brac, pre 1930, £10-£1,000.* LOC: Near A650. PARK: Easy. TEL: 01274 480630. SER: Valuations. FAIRS: NEC; Yorkshire Showground, Harrogate; Newark.

Langley's (Jewellers) Ltd

59 Godwin St. BD1 2SH. TEL: 01274 722280. VAT: Stan.

DENBY DALE, Nr. Huddersfield

Joan's Antiques

1A Denby Dale Industrial Park, Wakefield Rd. (Mrs J.M. Hirst). Est. 1988. Open 10-4.30, Sun. 1-4. SIZE: Medium. *STOCK: Victorian and Edwardian furniture, to £2,500.* LOC: Off M1. PARK: Easy. TEL: 01484 864209; home - same; mobile - 0410 777137. SER: Restorations; waxing and stripping; French polishing. FAIRS: Wentworth Village Hall, Rockingham.

HALIFAX

Collectors Old Toy Shop and Antiques

89 Northgate. HX1 1XF. (S. Haley). Open 10.30-4.30. CL: Thurs. *STOCK: Collectors toys, clocks and antiques.* TEL: 01422 360434/822148.

Halifax Antiques Centre

Queens Rd. HX1 4LR. Est. 1981. Open Tues.-Sat. 10-5. SIZE: Large - 30 dealers. *STOCK: Art Deco, jewellery, porcelain, linen, costume, pine, oak, mahogany, French furniture, kitchenalia, decorative collectables.* LOC: Follow A58 to King Cross, turn at Trafalgar Inn into Queens Rd. corner, 3rd set of lights. PARK: Own. TEL: 01422 366657.

Muir Hewitt Art Deco Originals

Halifax Antiques Centre, Queens Rd. Open 10-5. CL: Mon. *STOCK: Pottery including Clarice Cliff, Susie Cooper, Charlotte Rhead; Shelley ceramics; furniture, lighting and mirrors.* LOC: 1 mile west of town centre on the A58 (A646), turn right into Queens Rd. at Trafalgar Inn traffic lights, centre is at next traffic lights, opposite Lloyds Bank. PARK: Easy. TEL: 01422 347377; fax - same; home - 01274 882051; internet - www.muir-hewitt.com/hewitt. VAT: Stan.

Andy Thornton Architectural Antiques Ltd

Victoria Mills, Stainland Rd., Greetland. HX4 8AD. Est. 1973. Open 8-5.30, Sat. 9-5, Sun. 11-5. SIZE: Large. *STOCK: Architectural antiques - doors, stained glass, fireplaces, panelling, garden furniture, light fittings, pews and decor items.* PARK: Easy. TEL: 01422 377314; fax - 01422 310372. VAT: Stan.

HAWORTH, Nr. Keighley

Bingley Antiques

Springfield Farm Estate, Flappit. BD21 5PT. (J.B. and J. Poole). Est. 1965. Open 8.30-5. SIZE: Large. *STOCK: Furniture, 18th-19th C; shipping goods, porcelain, architectural antiques.* LOC: Near Haworth. PARK: Easy. TEL: 01535 646666. SER: Valuations. VAT: Stan/Spec.

HEBDEN BRIDGE, Nr. Halifax

Cornucopia Antiques

9 West End. HX7 8JP. (C. Nassor). Open Thurs., Fri. and Sun. 1-5, Sat. 11-5. *STOCK: Furniture including pine, stoves, lighting, bric-a-brac.* LOC: Town centre behind Pennine Information Centre. PARK: Easy. TEL: 01422 844497.

HOLMFIRTH, Nr. Huddersfield

Andrew Spencer Bottomley

The Coach House, Huddersfield Rd. HD7 2TT. Open by appointment. *STOCK: Arms and armour including pistols, swords, daggers, helmets and suits of armour.* TEL: 01484 685234; fax - 01484 681551. SER: Valuations; catalogues available. *Mail order only.*

Chapel House Fireplaces

Netherfield House, St. Georges Rd., Scholes. HD7 1UH. Open strictly by appointment Tues. 9-7, Wed.-Sat. 9-5. SIZE: Large. *STOCK: Georgian, Victorian and Edwardian grates and mantels; French chimneypieces.* TEL: 01484 682275.

The Toll House Bookshop

32/34 Huddersfield Rd. (E.V. Beardsell). Est. 1978. Open 10-5. *STOCK: Books including antiquarian.* TEL: 01484 686541.

Upperbridge Antiques

9 Huddersfield Rd. HD7 1JR. (Mrs M. Coop and I. Ridings). Open 1-5, Sun. 2-5. CL: Tues. SIZE: Small. *STOCK: Pottery, linen, metalware, interesting items, Victorian to Art Deco, £5-£150.* Not Stocked: Jewellery. LOC: A635. PARK: Nearby. TEL: 01484 687200.

HUDDERSFIELD

Beau Monde Antiques

343a Bradford Rd., Fartown. HD2 2QF. (R.M. Schofield). Est. 1963. Open 9.30-6, Sat. 9.30-5. CL: Wed. pm. SIZE: Medium. *STOCK: Furniture, general antiques, bric-a-brac, £5-£500.* LOC: On A641, 1 mile from town centre. PARK: Easy. TEL: 01484 427565.

D.W. Dyson (Antique Weapons)

Wood Lea, Shepley. HD8 8ES. Est. 1974. Open by appointment only. *STOCK: Antique weapons including cased duelling pistols, armour, miniature arms, cigar and smoking related accessories, rare and unusual items.* LOC: Off A629. PARK: Easy. TEL: 01484 607331; home - same.

Huddersfield continued

SER: Valuations; buys at auction (antique weapons); special presentation items made to order in precious metals; restoration; interior design; finder (film props). FAIRS: Dorchester Hotel, London; Dortmund, Stuttgart and other major foreign. VAT: Spec.

Huddersfield Antiques

170 Wakefield Rd., Moldgreen. HD5 9AW. Est. 1971. Open 10.30-4.30 or by appointment. SIZE: Medium. *STOCK: Victoriana, bric-a-brac, collectors' items, postcards; warehouse of trade and shipping goods.* PARK: Easy. TEL: 01484 539747. SER: Valuations; buys at auction.

Geoff Neary (incorporating Fillans Antiques Ltd)

2 Market Walk. HD1 2QA. NAG, FGA. Est. 1852. Open 9.30-5.15. SIZE: Small. *STOCK: English silver, 1700-1980; Sheffield plate, 1760-1840, £10-£500; jewellery, £50-£10,000.* Not Stocked: Other than above. PARK: Town centre multi-storey. TEL: 01484 531609. SER: Valuations; restorations; buys at auction (English silver and jewellery). VAT: Stan/Spec.

ILKLEY

Coopers of Ilkley LAPADA

46-50 Leeds Rd. LS29 8EQ. Est. 1910. Open 9-1 and 2-5.30. SIZE: Large. *STOCK: English furniture, pre-1830, £100-£10,000; porcelain and silver, pictures.* LOC: A65. PARK: Own. TEL: 01943 608020. SER: Valuations; restorations (furniture); buys at auction. VAT: Stan/Spec.

The Grove Bookshop

10 The Grove. LS29 9EG. PBFA. (Andrew and Janet Sharpe). Open 9-5.30. SIZE: Medium. *STOCK: Antiquarian books and maps; topographical and sporting prints.* LOC: 200 yards from A65. PARK: Easy. TEL: 01943 609335. SER: Valuations; restorations (book-binding and framing); buys at auction (as stock).

Jack Shaw and Co

The Old Grammar School, Skipton Rd. LS29 9EJ. Est. 1945. Open 9.30-12.45 and 2-5.30, Thurs.-Sat. *STOCK: Silver especially cutlery and 18th C domestic; furniture.* TEL: 01943 609467. VAT: Spec.

KEIGHLEY

Barleycote Hall Antiques

2 Janet St., Crossroads. BD22 9ET. Resident. (R. Hoskins). Est. 1968. Open most days 11-5. *STOCK: Georgian and Victorian furniture, porcelain, metalwork, paintings, jewellery, Victorian and Edwardian clothing, clocks of all types.* LOC: A629, turn right towards Haworth, 600yds. on right. TEL: 01535 644776. VAT: Stan/Spec.

Keighley continued

Keighleys of Keighley
153 East Parade. BD21 5HX. (B. Keighley and Son). Est. 1939. Open 9-5. CL: Tues. *STOCK: Furniture, jewellery, gold and silver, china.* LOC: Next to the Victoria Hotel. PARK: Easy. TEL: 01535 663439; home - 01535 607180. VAT: Stan.

Real Macoy
2 Janet St. BD22 9ET. (D. Seal). Open most days 11-5. *STOCK: Quilts, textiles, period clothing.* TEL: 01535 644776.

D. Richardson Antiques
72 Haworth Rd., Crossroads. Open 9-5. CL: Sat. *STOCK: General antiques and shipping goods.* PARK: Easy at rear. TEL: 01535 644982.

LEEDS

Aladdin's Cave
19 Queens Arcade. LS1 6LF. (P. D. and S. Isaacs). Est. 1954. CL: Mon. SIZE: Small. *STOCK: Jewellery, £15-£250; collectors' items; all 19th-20th C.* LOC: Town centre. PARK: 100 yards. TEL: 0113 2457903; 0113 2842425. SER: Valuations. VAT: Stan.

The Antique Exchange
400 Kirkstall Rd. LS4 2JX. (S. Wood). Est. 1976. Open 10.30-3. CL: Tues. and Wed. *STOCK: Furniture including satin walnut, ash and oak, 19th-20th C, £195-£3,000.* LOC: Kirkstall Rd. is 1/2 mile west of Yorkshire Television Studios. PARK: Easy. TEL: 0113 2743513. VAT: Stan/Spec.

Coins International and Antiques International
1 and 2 Melbourne St. LS2 7PS. (J.M. Harrison). Open 9-5. CL: Sat. *STOCK: Coins, banknotes, medals, silver, gold, general antiques, jewellery, crested china, cigarette cards.* PARK: Easy. TEL: 0113 2434230; fax - 0113 2345544.

Geary Antiques
114 Richardshaw Lane, Stanningley, Pudsey. LS28 6BN. (J.A. Geary). Est. 1933. Open 10-5.30, Sun. 12-4. SIZE: Warehouse. *STOCK: Furniture, Georgian, Victorian and Edwardian; copper and brass.* LOC: 500 yds. from West Leeds Ring Rd. PARK: Easy. TEL: 0113 2564122. SER: Restorations (furniture); interior design. VAT: Stan/Spec.

Headrow Antiques Centre
Level 3 Headrow Shopping Centre, The Headrow. (Pat Cooper and Sally Hurrell). Est. 1981. Open 10-5, Sun. (Oct-Dec) 11-4. SIZE: 14 dealers. *STOCK: Ceramics, jewellery and furniture, £5-£2,000.* LOC: City centre. PARK: NCP Albion St. TEL: 0113 2455344; home - 0113 2749494.

Leeds continued

J. Howorth Antiques/Swiss Cottage Furniture

85 Westfield Crescent, Burley. LS3 1DJ. Est. 1986. Open 10-5.30, Sun. 1-5.30. CL: Tues. SIZE: Warehouse. *STOCK: Collectables, furniture, architectural items, £5-£3,000.* LOC: Town hall to Burley Rd., road opposite YTV. PARK: Easy. TEL: 0113 2306268/2429994. SER: Prop. hire for film and TV. FAIRS: Newark. VAT: Stan/Spec.

Leeds Antiques Centre

16 Globe Rd. LS11 5QG. Open 10-5. CL: Mon. SIZE: 40 dealers. *STOCK: General antiques.* LOC: On the Canal Basin, M1 to Leeds Hilton, turn left, 170 mtrs on right. TEL: 0113 2423194.

Oakwood Gallery

613 Roundhay Rd., Oakwood. Open 9-6. *STOCK: Fine paintings and prints.* PARK: Easy. TEL: 0113 2401348. SER: Framing; restorations; conservation.

The Piano Shop

39 Holbeck Lane. LS11 9XE. (B. Seals). Open 9-5. *STOCK: Pianos, especially decorated cased grand.* TEL: 0113 2443685. SER: Restorations; French polishing; hire.

Windsor House Antiques (Leeds) Ltd.

LAPADA

18-20 Benson St. LS7 1BL. (D.K. Smith). Est. 1959. Open 9-5. CL: Sat. SIZE: Large. *STOCK: English furniture, 18th-19th C; paintings, objects.* PARK: Easy. TEL: 0113 2444666; fax - 0113 2426394. VAT: Stan/Spec.

Year Dot

16 Market St. Arcade. LS1 6EN. (A. Glithro). Open 9.30-5. *STOCK: Jewellery, watches, silver, pottery, porcelain, glass, clocks, prints, paintings, bric-a-brac.* TEL: 0113 2460860.

LEPTON, Nr. Huddersfield

K.L.M. & Co. Antiques

The Antique Shop, Wakefield Rd. HD8 0EL. (K.L. & J. Millington). Est. 1980. Open 10.30-5, other times by appointment. SIZE: 8 showrooms and warehouse. *STOCK: Furniture including stripped pine, satin walnut, to 1940's; pianos, all £25-£1,500.* LOC: A642 Wakefield road from Huddersfield, shop opposite village church. PARK: Easy and at rear. TEL: 01484 607763; home - 01484 607548. SER: Valuations. VAT: Stan.

MENSTON

Antiques

101 Bradford Rd. (W. and J. Hanlon). Est. 1974. Open 2.30-5. CL: Tues. and Wed. *STOCK: Handworked linen, textiles, pottery, porcelain, Art Nouveau, Art Deco, silver, plate, jewellery, small furniture, collectors items, barometers.* PARK: Forecourt. TEL: 01943 877634; home - 01943 463693.

Park Antiques

2 North View, Main St. LS29 6JU. Resident. Est. 1975. Open 10-6.30, Sun. 10-5.30. CL: Mon. and Tues. SIZE: Medium. *STOCK: Furniture, Georgian to Edwardian, £500-£5,000; decorative items, £100-£1,000, soft furnishings, £500-£2,000.* Not Stocked: Pine, silver. LOC: Opposite the park. PARK: Easy. TEL: 01943 872392. VAT: Stan/Spec.

MIRFIELD

Lawn and Lace

5 Knowl Rd. WF14 9NQ. (G.D. Hurst and Mrs N. Gunson). Est. 1988. Open Wed.-Sat. 9.30-5.30. SIZE: Small. *STOCK: Textiles including linen and lace, 17th-20th C, £5-£250; dolls and ceramics, £5-£300; small furniture, £15-£500; both 19th-20th C.* LOC: 2 miles east of junction 25, M62. Just off main Huddersfield to Dewsbury road. PARK: Easy. TEL: 01924 491083. SER: Valuations; restorations (textiles and dolls). FAIRS: Newark.

OTLEY, Nr. Leeds

Martin-Clifton Antiques

28 Westgate. LS21 3AS. (A.S. Ambler). Est. 1972. Open 10-5.30. CL: Wed. and Thurs. SIZE: Medium. *STOCK: Furniture, china, copper and brass, barometers, mirrors.* LOC: A650. PARK: Easy. TEL: 01943 851117. SER: Restorations and repairs (furniture); polishing.

PONTEFRACT

Cottage Antiques

5 Ropergate End. (Sheila Whittaker). Est. 1987. Open 12-4. CL: Thurs. SIZE: 3 rooms. *STOCK: Pine and antique furniture, 19th C, £150-£450; Victorian pottery, £50-£150; linen and kitchenalia, 19th-20th C, £20-£100.* LOC: Town centre. PARK: Easy. TEL: 01977 611146. SER: Restorations (furniture). FAIRS: Newark (Stand F32).

D. Turner Antiques

The Old Coach House, Bondgate. (Dennise Turner). Est. 1988. Open 11-5. CL: Thurs. SIZE: Medium. *STOCK: Furniture, £30-£300; pottery, £20-£100, both late 19th to early 20th C; collectables, £5-£25.* LOC: Just off A1 towards town. PARK: Easy. TEL: 01977 798818; home - 01226 751802. SER: Valuations; buys at auction (furniture). FAIRS: Newark, Harrogate and Ardingly.

SALTAIRE, Nr Shipley

The Victoria Centre

3-4 Victoria Rd. BD18 3LA. (Margaret and Malcolm Gray). Est. 1995. Open 10-5.30. CL: Mon. and Tues. SIZE: Large - 36 units. *STOCK: Wide range of general antiques including fine furniture, paintings, silver, clocks, porcelain, pine and collectables, £5-£10,000.* PARK: Nearby. TEL: 01274 530611. SER: Valuations. VAT: Stan/Spec.

SHIPLEY

Paul Graham Antiques

Dock Mill, Dockfield Terrace. BD17 3JH. (Mastermark Ltd). Est. 1985. Open 9.30-6. SIZE: Large. *STOCK: Shipping furniture, 19th C to 1930's, £50-£2,000.* LOC: A650 from Bradford. PARK: Easy. TEL: 01274 584594; fax - 01274 594594. SER: Buys at auction (as stock). VAT: Stan. *Trade Only*

Price-Less Antiques

2 Gaisby Lane. BD18 1AZ. (Mrs P. Lee). Open 11-6. *STOCK: China, bric-a-brac, general antiques.* TEL: 01274 581760.

The Titus Gallery

1 Daisy Place, Saltaire Rd. BD18 4NA. (C.A. Grice). Est. 1975. Open 10-5.30, Sun. 11-5.30 or by appointment. SIZE: Medium. *STOCK: Oil paintings and watercolours, 17th-20th C, £100-£55,000; occasional furniture, 18th-19th C, £400-£5,000; objets d'art, 18th-20th C, £50-£7,000.* LOC: Near roundabout, at junction of A650 and A657. PARK: Own. TEL: 01274 581894; home - same. SER: Valuations; restorations (oil paintings, watercolours and frames). VAT: Stan/Spec.

SOWERBY BRIDGE, Nr. Halifax

Memory Lane

69 Wakefield Rd. HX6 2UX. (L. Robinson). Open 10.30-5. SIZE: Warehouse. *STOCK: Pine, oak, dolls and teddies.* TEL: 01422 833223.

Talking Point Antiques

66 West St. HX6 3AP. (P. and L. Austwick). Open Thurs., Fri., Sat. 10.30-5.30, other days by appointment. *STOCK: Restored gramophones and phonographs, 78rpm records, gramophone accessories and related items; small furniture; pottery, porcelain and curios.* TEL: 01422 834126.

TODMORDEN

Echoes

650a Halifax Rd., Eastwood. OL14 6DW. (P. Oldman). Est. 1980. CL: Tues. SIZE: Medium. *STOCK: Costume, textiles, linen and lace, £5-£500; jewellery, £5-£150; all 19th-20th C.* LOC: A646. PARK: Easy. TEL: 01706 817505; home - same. SER: Valuations; restorations (costume); buys at auction (as stock).

Todmorden continued

Fagin & Co.

54-56 Burnley Rd. OL14 5EY. (J. Ratcliff). Est. 1982. Open 10-5, Sun. by appointment. SIZE: Medium + warehouse. *STOCK: Country, antique and quality furniture, £50-£2,000; small architectural items and curiosities.* LOC: A646 Burnley road. PARK: Easy. TEL: 01706 819499; home - 01706 814773. SER: Valuations.

Todmorden Antiques Centre

Sutcliffe House, Halifax Rd. OL14 5DG. (Mr and Mrs Hoogeveen). Open 10-5, Sat. 10-4, Sun. 1-4. SIZE: 20 dealers. *STOCK: General antiques, furniture and jewellery.* TEL: 01706 818040.

Todmorden Fine Art

27 Water St. OL14 5AB. (Mr Gunning and Mr Middleton). Est. 1981. Usually open 7 days but prior telephone call advisable. SIZE: Small. *STOCK: Contemporary collectable oil paintings, £100-£1,000.* LOC: Off M62, Junction 20. PARK: Hall St. opposite. TEL: 01706 814723; home - same. SER: Valuations; restorations; framing. VAT: Spec.

WAKEFIELD

Robin Taylor Fine Arts

36 Carter St. WF1 1XJ. Open 9.30-5.30. *STOCK: Oils and watercolours.* TEL: 01924 381809.

WALSDEN, Nr. Todmorden

Cottage Antiques (1984) Ltd

788 Rochdale Rd. OL14 7UA. Resident. (G. Slater). Est. 1978. Open Tues.-Sun. SIZE: Medium. *STOCK: Pine furniture, kitchenalia, 19th C, £5-£1,000; general antiques.* PARK: Easy. TEL: 0170 681 3612. SER: Restorations; pine stripping; import and export of Continental pine.

WOODLESFORD, Nr. Leeds

Harrington Antiques Centre

Trafalgar Works, Astley Lane. LS26 8AN. (Rodger Wood and June Harrington). Est.1968. Open daily and Sun. from 11. SIZE: Large - 6 dealers. *STOCK: Mahogany, walnut and oak, 18th to early 20th C.* LOC: Off M62, junction 30 towards Garforth, into Swillington, look for Astley Lane. PARK: Own. TEL: 01132 875955; fax - 01132 875966; mobile - 0976 429863. SER: Valuations; restorations. VAT: Stan/Spec

Guernsey

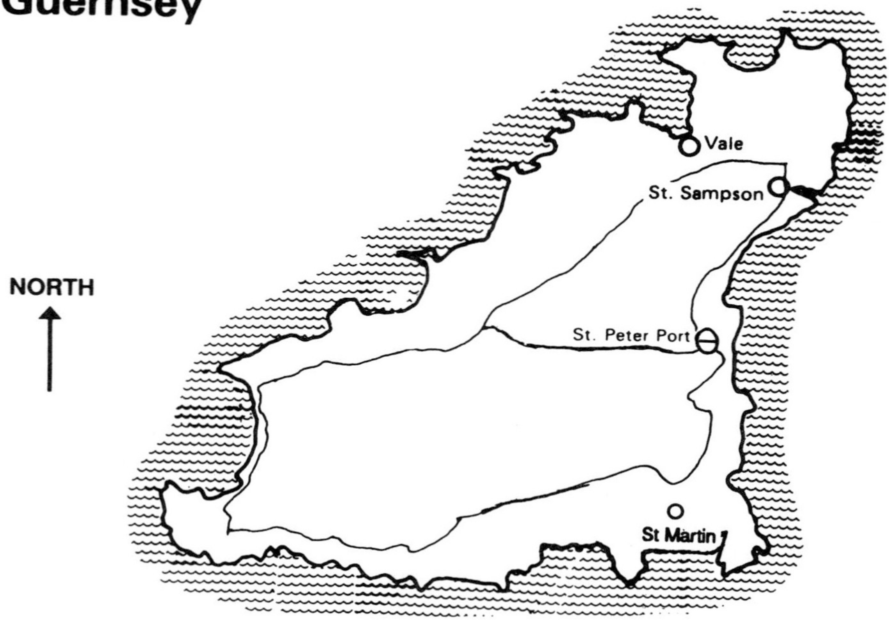

Vale

St. Sampson

NORTH

St. Peter Port

St Martin

Jersey

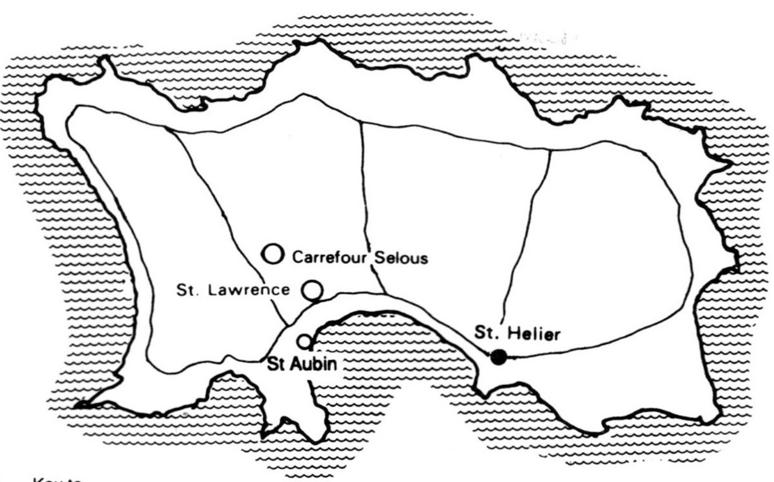

Key to number of shops in this area.

- 1-2
- 3-5
- 6-12
- 13+

Please note this is only a rough map designed to show dealers the number of shops in the various towns, and is not necessarily totally accurate.

Alderney

Beverley J. Pyke - Fine British Watercolours

22 Victoria St. Open by appointment only. *STOCK: 20th C watercolours, £150-£2,000.* TEL: 01481 824092.

Victoria Antiques

St. Catherine's, Victoria St. (P.A. Nightingale). Open 10-12.30 and 2.30-4.30. *STOCK: Period and Victorian furniture, glass, silver, china, jewellery, small objets d'art.* TEL: 01481 823260. SER: Valuations.

Guernsey

ST. MARTIN

Mark Blower Antiques

Les Chenes, Rue de Putron. Est. 1978. Open by appointment only. SIZE: Small. *STOCK: Furniture, 18th C, £1,000-£10,000; pictures, 18th-19th C, £500-£5,000.* PARK: Easy. TEL: 01481 39098. SER: Valuations; restorations (furniture and pictures); fine art packing and shipping; buys at auction.

ST. PETER PORT

The Antique Centre

12 Mansell St. Est. 1973. Open 10-1 and 2-5. CL: Thurs. pm. SIZE: 5 dealers. *STOCK: Period, Victorian and Edwardian furniture, clocks, nautical items, oils, watercolours, silver and plate, items of local interest.* PARK: Nearby. TEL: 01481 726808; home - 01481 46025.

Channel Islands Galleries Ltd

Trinity Sq. Centre, Trinity Sq. GY1 1LX. (G.P. and Mrs C. Gavey). Est. 1967. Open 10-12.30 and 2-5, or by appointment. CL: Thurs. pm. *STOCK: Antique maps, sea charts and prints of the Channel Islands; oil paintings, watercolours, Channel Islands' books, illustrated, historical, social, geographical and natural history.* Not Stocked: General antiques. TEL: 01481 723247; home - 01481 47337.

Grange Antiques

7/8 The Grange. GY1 2PX. (Mrs K.M. Carré). Est. 1968. Open 9.30-5. CL: Sat. pm., Thurs. and Sun. except by appointment. SIZE: Medium. *STOCK: Objets d'art, and small furniture, 18th-19th C, £25-£1,000; pottery and porcelain, 18th C to Art Deco, £5-£500; linens, silver and plate.* LOC: One of main roads from harbour going inland, shop opposite the Elizabeth College. PARK: 50yds. on right. TEL: 01481 721480. SER: Valuations; buys at auction.

St. Peter Port continued

The Pine Collection

La Route de la Garenne, Pitronnerie Road Industrial Estate, GY1 2RL. (P. Head). Est. 1986. Open 9.30-5.30. *STOCK: Pine.* TEL: 01481 726891.

St. James's Gallery Ltd

18-20 Smith St and 18-20 The Bordage. GY1 2JQ. (C.O. Whittam). Est. 1945. CL: Lunch times. SIZE: Large. *STOCK: Furniture, £100-£20,000; porcelain, both 18th-19th C; paintings, 18th-20th C.* TEL: 01481 720070; home - 01481 723999. SER: Valuations.

ST. SAMPSON

The Old Curiosity Shop

Commercial Rd. GY2 4QP. Est. 1978. CL: Mon. and Thurs. *STOCK: Old and antiquarian books, prints, postcards, coins, ephemera, paintings, small furniture, china, glass, silver, brass, £1-£5,000.* TEL: 01481 45324. FAIRS: Organiser.

VALE

Geoffrey P. Gavey

Les Clospains, Rue de L'Ecole. GY3 5LL. Est. 1967. Open by appointment. *STOCK: Maps, sea charts and prints of the Channel Islands; oil and watercolour paintings; Channel Islands books, illustrated, historical, social, geographic and natural history.* Not Stocked: General antiques. TEL: 01481 47337.

Jersey

CARREFOUR SELOUS, ST. LAWRENCE

David Hick Antiques

Alexandra House. Est. 1977. Open Wed., Fri. and Sat. 9.30-5. SIZE: Large and warehouse. *STOCK: Furniture and small items.* TEL: 01534 865965; fax - 01534 865448.

ST AUBIN

Boulevard Antiques

Charing Cross House. JE3 8AA. (Veronica Mileti). Est. 1996. Open 10-5.30 (late night opening in summer). SIZE: Small. *STOCK: French and Italian gilt small furniture; European interesting and unusual items.* PARK: Parish Hall near Marina. TEL: 01534 45753; fax - 01534 498037.

ST. HELIER

John Blench & Son

50 Don St. JE2 4TR. *STOCK: Fine books, bindings, local maps and prints.* TEL: 01534 25281.

St. Helier continued

John Cooper Antiques
16 The Market. *STOCK: General antiques.* TEL: 01534 23600.

Falle Fine Art Limited LAPADA
The Napier Gallery, 86 Halkett Place. JE2 4WH. (John Falle). Open Tues.-Fri. 11-5, Sat. 9.30-1, Mon. by appointment. SIZE: Medium. *STOCK: British paintings, watercolours and bronzes, 20th C, £250-£25,000.* LOC: Opposite Public Library. PARK: Easy. TEL: 01534 887877; fax - 01534 23459. SER: Valuations; restorations (as stock); exhibitions.

Falle Fine Art Limited
PO Box 562. (John Falle). Open by appointment. *STOCK: Paintings, watercolours, bronzes, especially Channel Islands and 19th C.* TEL: 01534 854845; fax - 01534 89690.

Grange Gallery and Fine Arts Ltd
39 New St. JE2 3RA. (G.J. Morris). Est. 1974. Open 9-5.30. CL: Sun., Tues. and Thurs. except by appointment. SIZE: Medium. *STOCK: Oil paintings, 18th-19th C, local prints, 19th C; all £100-£9,000.* LOC: Antique area of St. Helier. PARK: Multi-storey 100yds. TEL: 01534 616810; fax - 01534 880460. SER: Valuations; restorations (pictures); buys at auction; framing.

David Hick Antiques
45 Halkett Place. JE2 4WG. Open 10-5, Thurs. 10-1. *STOCK: Furniture and smalls.* TEL: 01534 21162; fax - same.

St. Helier continued

Jeremiah's Antiques
14 1/2 Queen St. (K.J. O'Keeffe). Est. 1981. Open 10-5. CL: Mon. SIZE: Small. *STOCK: Fine wrist and pocket watches, clocks; silver, porcelain, bronzes, jewellery, small furniture.* LOC: Main shopping area. PARK: Nearby. TEL: 01534 23153. SER: Valuations; restorations (clocks and watches); buys at auction (clocks and watches). FAIRS: Miami, Munich, London. *Trade Only.*

Rae Antiques
Savile St. JE2 3XF. Est. 1946. Open daily. SIZE: Large. *STOCK: General antiques, furniture, pictures, clocks and silver.* TEL: 01534 32171

Sheila Rae Antiques
Clare St. and Savile St. JE2 3XF. *STOCK: Clocks, paintings, silver, porcelain and furniture.* TEL: 01534 58071/32171.

A. & R. Ritchie
7 Duhamel Place. Open 9.30-4.30. *STOCK: Militaria and jewellery.* TEL: 01534 873805.

The Selective Eye Gallery
50 Don St. JE2 4TR. (J. and P. Blench). Est. 1958. Open 9-5. CL: Thurs. and Sat. pm. SIZE: Medium. *STOCK: Oil paintings, 19th-20th C; maps, prints and antiquarian books, 16th-20th C.* Not Stocked: General antiques. LOC: Town centre. PARK: Multi-storey 100yds. TEL: 01534 25281. SER: Valuations; restorations (pictures). FAIRS: Jersey.

Thesaurus (Jersey) Ltd
3 Burrard St. JE2 4WS. (I. Creaton). Est. 1973. Open 8.30-6. SIZE: Large. *STOCK: Antiquarian and out of print books, £1-£2,000; maps and prints.* Not Stocked: General antiques. LOC: Town centre. PARK: 100yds. TEL: 01534 37045. SER: Buys at auction. VAT: Spec.

Joan Thomson Antiques
12 Burrard St. Est. 1967. Open 10-4. CL: Mon. and Thurs. SIZE: Medium. *STOCK: Smalls, £10-£500, jewellery, linen, collectors' items, Oriental.* PARK: Nearby. TEL: 01534 37206; home - 01534 856908.

Thomson's
60 Kensington Place and 4 Wharf St., St. Helier. JE2 3PA. Est. 1967. Open 10-5. CL: Tues. SIZE: Large. *STOCK: General antiques mainly furniture.* LOC: Side of Grand Hotel and rear of Pomme d'Or Hotel. PARK: Easy and Pier Road. TEL: 01534 23673/601081. SER: Valuations.

ST. LAWRENCE

I.G.A. Old Masters Ltd
5 Kimberley Grove, Rue de Haut. (I.G. and Mrs C.B.V. Appleby). Est. 1953. Open by appointment. *STOCK: Old Master and 19th C paintings.* LOC: Near glass church. PARK: Easy. TEL: 01534 24226; home - same.

NORTHERN IRELAND

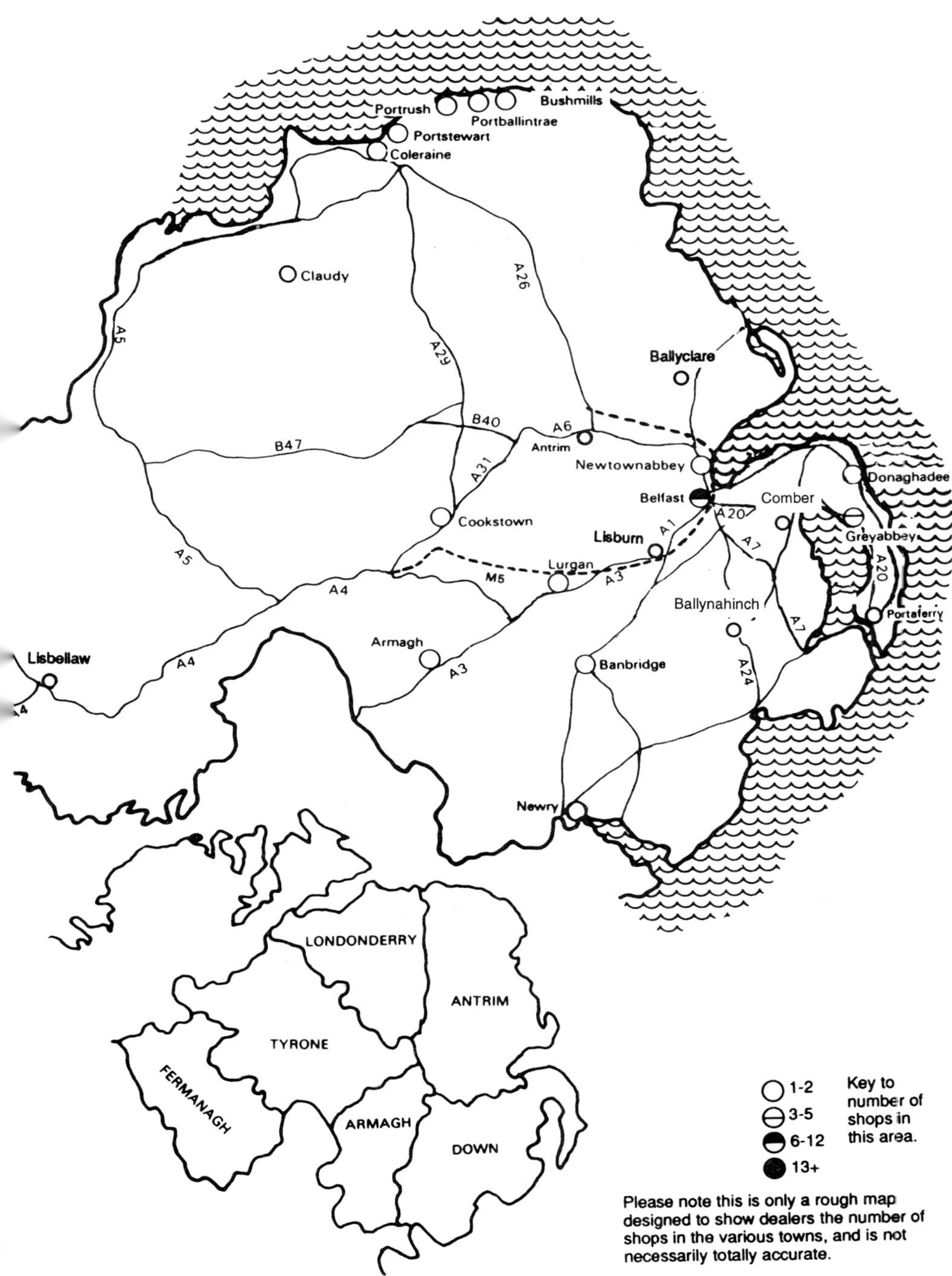

Please note this is only a rough map designed to show dealers the number of shops in the various towns, and is not necessarily totally accurate.

BELFAST

The Bell Gallery

13 Adelaide Park. BT9 6FX. (J.N. Bell). Est. 1964. Open 10-6. SIZE: Medium. *STOCK: British and Irish art, 19th-20th C.* LOC: Off Malone Rd. TEL: 01232 662998. SER: Valuations; restorations (paintings); buys at auction. VAT: Stan/Spec.

Emerald Isle Books

539 Antrim Rd. BT15 3BU. Est. 1966. Open by appointment. *STOCK: Travel, Ireland, theology.* TEL: 01232 370798; fax - 01232 777288. SER: Catalogues available.

Hearth and Home

29 Howard St. BT1 6DN. (C. Heath and M.P.W. Smith). Open 10-5.30. *STOCK: Pine furniture, Mexican rustic furniture and decorative items.* LOC: City centre. PARK: Easy. TEL: 01232 322355; fax - same.

T.H. Kearney & Sons

Treasure House, 123 University St. BT7 1HP. Resident. *STOCK: Small antiques.* TEL: 01232 231055. SER: Restorations and upholstery. VAT: Stan.

Charlotte and John Lambe

41 Shore Rd. BT15 3PG. Open 10-5. CL: Sat. *STOCK: English and French furniture, 19th C; pictures and works of art.* TEL: 01232 370761.

Mews Antique and Reproduction Fireplaces & Architectural Salvage

The Gate Lodge, 260 Antrim Rd. BT15 2AT. (P. O'Flaherty). Open 10.30-5. CL: Mon. *STOCK: Restored Victorian fireplaces, wood flooring and miscellaneous items.* TEL: 01232 751319.

Sinclair's Antique Gallery

19 Arthur St. BT1 4GA. Est. 1900. Open 9-5.30. CL: Sat. SIZE: Small. *STOCK: Victorian jewellery, china, glass, £10-£1,000; silver, coins.* LOC: 100yds. from city centre. TEL: 01232 322335. VAT: Stan.

Co. Antrim

ANTRIM

The Country Antiques LAPADA

219B Lisnevenagh Rd. BT41 2JT. (David Wolfenden). Open 10-6. SIZE: Large. *STOCK: Furniture, £200-£5,000; jewellery and porcelain, £100-£3,000; all 19th C.* LOC: Main Antrim-Ballymena line. PARK: Easy. TEL: 01849 429498. SER: Valuations; restorations. VAT: Stan/Spec.

BALLYCLARE

Robert Christie Antiques

20 Calhame Rd., Straid. IADA. Est. 1976. Usually open, prior telephone call appreciated. SIZE: Medium. *STOCK: Furniture, 1750-1900, £200-£3,000; clocks, 1750-1900, £500-£2,000; decorative objects, 1800-1900, £50-£500.* LOC: 1/4 mile off A8 Belfast-Larne road. PARK: Easy. TEL: 01960 341149; home - same; mobile - 0802 968846. SER: Valuations. FAIRS: Templeton Hotel, Templepatrick; Culloden Hotel, Holywood.

BUSHMILLS

Dunluce Antiques

33 Ballytober Rd. BT57 8UU. (Mrs C. Ross). Est. 1978. Open 2-6 or by appointment. CL: Fri. SIZE: Small. *STOCK: Furniture, £50-£1,000; porcelain and glass, £1-£1,000; silver, £5-£5000; all Georgian to 1930's; paintings, mainly Irish, £50-£10,000.* LOC: 1.5 miles off Antrim coast rd. at Dunluce Castle. PARK: Easy. TEL: 012657 31140. SER: Restorations (porcelain).

LISBURN

Parvis Sigaroudinia

Mountainview House, 40 Sandy Lane, Ballyskeagh. BT27 5TL. IADA. Est. 1974. Open by appointment at any time. *STOCK: Oriental and European carpets and tapestries (extra large sizes stocked).* LOC: Take Malone Road from Belfast, then Upper Malone Road towards Lisburn, cross Ballyskeagh bridge over M1, 1st left into Sandy Lane. PARK: Easy. TEL: 01232 621824; home - same. SER: Valuations; buys at auction; exhibitions held in Belfast. FAIRS: Culloden, Belfast; IADA in RDS Dublin. VAT: Stan.

NEWTOWNABBEY

MacHenry Antiques

Caragh Lodge, Glen Rd., Jordanstown. BT37 0RY. IADA. (A. MacHenry). Est. 1964. Open 2-7, or by appointment. SIZE: Medium. *STOCK: Georgian and Victorian furniture and objects.* LOC: 6 miles from Belfast to Whiteabbey village, left at traffic lights at Woody's, then left into Old Manse Rd. and continue into Glen Rd. PARK: Easy. TEL: 01232 862036; fax - 01232 853281. SER: Valuations. FAIRS: Dublin, Belfast and Irish. VAT: Stan/Spec.

PORTBALLINTRAE, Nr. Bushmills

Brian R. Bolt Antiques

88 Ballaghmore Rd. BT57 8RL. IADA. Open 11-5.30, and by appointment. CL: Wed. and Fri. *STOCK: Silver - small and unusual items, objects of vertu, snuff boxes, vesta cases, table, Scottish and Irish provincial; treen; English and Continental glass, antique and 20th C; art and studio glass and ceramics; Arts and Crafts, Art Nouveau and Art Deco jewellery and metalwork; vintage fountain pens.* TEL: 012657 31129. SER: Search; illustrated catalogues available; worldwide postal service; valuations.

PORTRUSH

Alexander Antiques
108 Dunluce Rd. BT56 8NB. (Mrs M. and D. Alexander). Est. 1974. Open 10-6. CL: Sun. except by appointment. SIZE: Large. *STOCK: Furniture, silver, porcelain, fine art, 18th-20th C; oils and watercolours, 19th-20th C.* Not Stocked: Militaria, jewellery, coins. LOC: 1 mile from Portrush on A2 to Bushmills. PARK: Easy. TEL: 01265 822783. SER: Valuations; buys at auction. VAT: Stan/Spec.

Co. Armagh

ARMAGH

The Hole-in-the-Wall
Market St. BT61 7BW. (I. Emerson). Est. 1953. *STOCK: General antiques.* LOC: City centre. VAT: Stan/Spec.

LURGAN

Charles Gardiner Antiques
48 High St. BT66 8AU. Est. 1968. Open 9-1 and 2-6. CL: Wed. *STOCK: Clocks, furniture and general antiques.* PARK: Own. TEL: 01762 323934.

PORTADOWN

Moyallon Antiques
54 Moyallon Rd. Est. 1975. Usually open. SIZE: Medium. *STOCK: Furniture, 19th C, £50-£1,000; pine and country furniture, 18th-19th C, £50-£500; ceramics and bric-a-brac, £5-£100.* LOC: Portadown - Gilford Rd., 1 mile from Gilford on right-hand side. PARK: Easy. TEL: 01762 831615.

Co. Down

BALLYNAHINCH

Riverside Antiques
55 Dromore St. (John Cousans). Open 9.30-5.30. SIZE: Large. *STOCK: Marble chimney pieces, early 18th to late 19th C, £5-£1,000; period panelling and pine pews, stained glass, Victorian bathrooms, decorative architectural items.* TEL: 01238 561330. SER: Valuations; restorations (marble); pine stripping; French polishing; buys at auction. VAT: Stan.

BANBRIDGE

Cameo Antiques
41 Bridge St. BT32 3LY. (D. and J. Bell). Est. 1966. TEL: 0182 06 23241.

COMBER

Bobby Douglas Antiques
9 Killinchy St. BT23 5SD. (B. and N.R.G. Douglas). Open by appointment only. SIZE: Medium shop + Trade barn. *STOCK: Irish furniture, 18th-19th C, £1,000-£25,000; unusual collectors' items, 19th C, under £1,000.* PARK: Easy. TEL: 01238 528351. SER: Valuations. VAT: Stan/Spec. *Trade only.*

DONAGHADEE

Furney Antiques and Interiors
3-4 Shore St. BT21 0DG. (The Furney Family). Est. 1976. Open Fri. and Sat. 11-1 and 2-5.30, or by appointment. *STOCK: Period furniture and decorative items.* TEL: 01247 883887/883517; fax - 01247 883887.

GREYABBEY, Nr. Newtownards

Phyllis Arnold Gallery Antiques
Hoops Courtyard. BT22 2NE. Est. 1968. Open Wed., Fri. and Sat. 11-5. *STOCK: General antiques, jewellery, small furniture, 19th-20th C watercolours, portrait miniatures, maps and prints of Ireland.* TEL: 012477 88199; home - 01247 853322; fax - same. SER: Restorations (maps, prints, watercolours, portrait miniatures); conservation framing. FAIRS: Culloden.

Marjorie McAuley - The Antique Shop
9 Main St. BT22 2NE. Est. 1968. *STOCK: General antiques.* TEL: Home - 012477 38333.

Old Priory Antiques LAPADA
3-5 Main St. BT22 2NE. (Patty Loane). Est. 1983. Open 11.30-5.30, other times by appointment. CL: Tues. *STOCK: Jewellery, 1780-1930; silver and furniture, 1750-1930.* Not Stocked: Books, stamps, coins, medals. LOC: Village centre. PARK: Easy. TEL: 012477 88346.

HOLYWOOD

Herbert Gould and Co.
21-23 Church Rd. BT18 9BU. (Robert Brown). Est. 1897. Open 9.15-5.30. SIZE: Medium.. *STOCK: Pine, 19th C, £75-£200; collectables, architectural antiques, 19th-20th C, £10-£100.* LOC: 20 yards from maypole in town centre. PARK: Opposite. TEL: 01232 427916. SER: Valuations; pine stripping; buys at auction (as stock). VAT: Stan.

NEWRY

Downshire House Antiques
62 Downshire Rd. (H. and R. McCabe). Open 9-5.30. *STOCK: General antiques including furniture and porcelain, 18th-19th C, £50-£10,000.* TEL: 01693 66689/69199. SER: Valuations; restorations (furniture); deliveries.

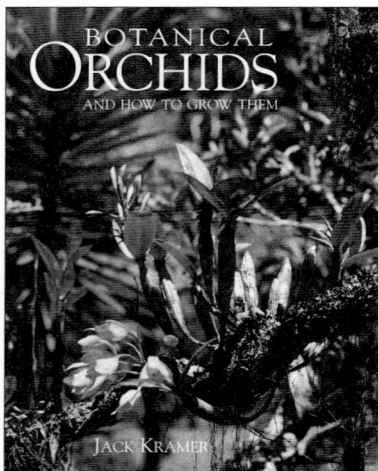

Newry continued

McCabe's Antique Galleries

62 Downshire Rd. (R. McCabe). Est. 1910. Open 9-5.30, Wed., Sun. and evenings by appointment. SIZE: Large and warehouse. *STOCK: General antiques including furniture and porcelain, 18th-19th C.* PARK: Own. TEL: 01693 62695/ 66689/69199. SER: Valuations; restorations (furniture). FAIRS: Conway Hotel, Lisburn; Drumkeen Hotel, Belfast. VAT: Stan.

PORTAFERRY

Time & Tide Antiques

2 Ferry St. BT22 1PB. (D. Dunlop). Open Wed., Fri., Sat. and Sun. 12-5.30, or by appointment. SIZE: Medium. *STOCK: Clocks, barometers, marine instruments, pictures and nautical memorabilia and small furniture, £50-£2,500.* LOC: A20 from Newtownards through Greyabbey. PARK: Easy. TEL: 012477 28935; home - same. SER: Valuations; restorations and repairs.

WARRENPOINT

Antiques and Fine Art Gallery

3 Charlotte St. BT34 3LF. (B. Woods). Est. 1991. Open 10.30-1 and 2.30-5.30. CL: Mon. and Wed. SIZE: Medium. *STOCK: Furniture, Georgian to Edwardian, £50-£5,000; paintings especially Irish, 20th C, £50-£10,000.* LOC: Turn off main road at Newry. PARK: Easy. TEL: 016937 52905. SER: Valuations.

Co. Fermanagh

LISBELLAW

Forge Antiques

Brooke St. (Mrs I. Burton and K. Johnston). Est. 1989. Open 2-5.30, Sat. 9.30-5.30. SIZE: Medium. *STOCK: Georgian, Victorian and Edwardian furniture, £50-£3,000; porcelain and ceramics including Belleek, pictures and glass.* LOC: 5 miles from Enniskillen, off A4 Belfast road. PARK: Easy. TEL: 01365 387777; home - 01365 387774. SER: Valuations. FAIRS: Major Northern Ireland.

Co. Londonderry

CLAUDY

K.O. Hagan

'Bensara', 162 Foreglen Rd. BT47 4ED. *STOCK: Georgian, Victorian and Edwardian furniture, especially pine.* TEL: 01504 338506.

COLERAINE

The Forge Antiques

24 Long Commons. BT52 1LH. (M.W. Walker). Est. 1977. Open 10-5.30. CL: Thurs. *STOCK: General antiques, silver, clocks, jewellery, porcelain, paintings.* TEL: 01265 51339. VAT: Stan.

Homes, Pubs and Clubs

1-5 Portrush Rd. Resident. (McNulty Wholesalers). Est. 1983. Open 9-6, Sun. 2.30-6. SIZE: Large. *STOCK: Pine and mahogany, small interesting items.* LOC: Main Portrush road, near traffic lights. PARK: At rear of premises. TEL: 01265 55733. SER: Valuations; restorations. FAIRS: Newark. VAT: Stan.

PORTSTEWART

Harbour Antiques

16 Harbour Rd. BT55 7AX. (Mrs Bea Macafee). Est. 1981. Open 2-5. SIZE: Small. *STOCK: Porcelain, furniture, silver, jewellery, glass, collectables.* LOC: 100 yards from Portstewart Harbour on way to Portrush. TEL: 01265 832209; home - 01265 52153.

Co. Tyrone

COOKSTOWN

Cookstown Antiques

16 Oldtown St. BT80 8EF. (G. Jebb). Est. 1976. Open Thurs. and Fri. 2-5.30, Sat. 10.30-5.30. SIZE: Small. *STOCK: Jewellery, silver, £10-£2,000; coins, £25-£200; pictures, ceramics and militaria, £5-£1,000; general antiques, all 19th-20th C.* Not Stocked: Large furniture. LOC: Going north, through both sets of traffic lights, on left at rear of estate agency. PARK: Easy. TEL: 016487 65279; fax - 016487 62946; home - 016487 62926. SER: Valuations; buys at auction.

The Saddle Room Antiques

4 Coagh St. BT80 8NG. (C.J. Leitch). Est. 1968. Open 10-5.30. CL: Mon. and Wed. *STOCK: China, silver, furniture, glass, jewellery.* TEL: 016487 64045.

SCOTLAND NORTH

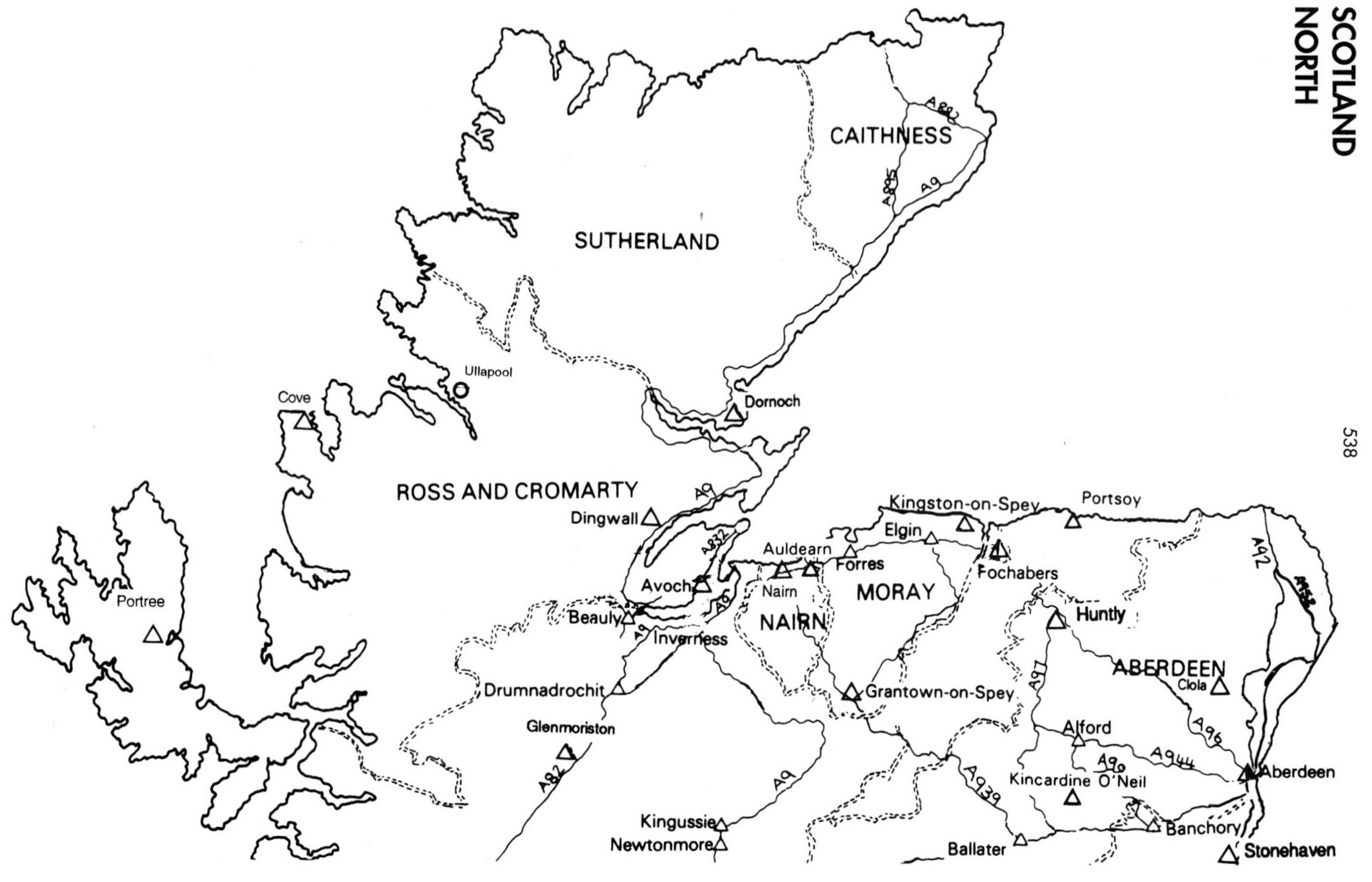

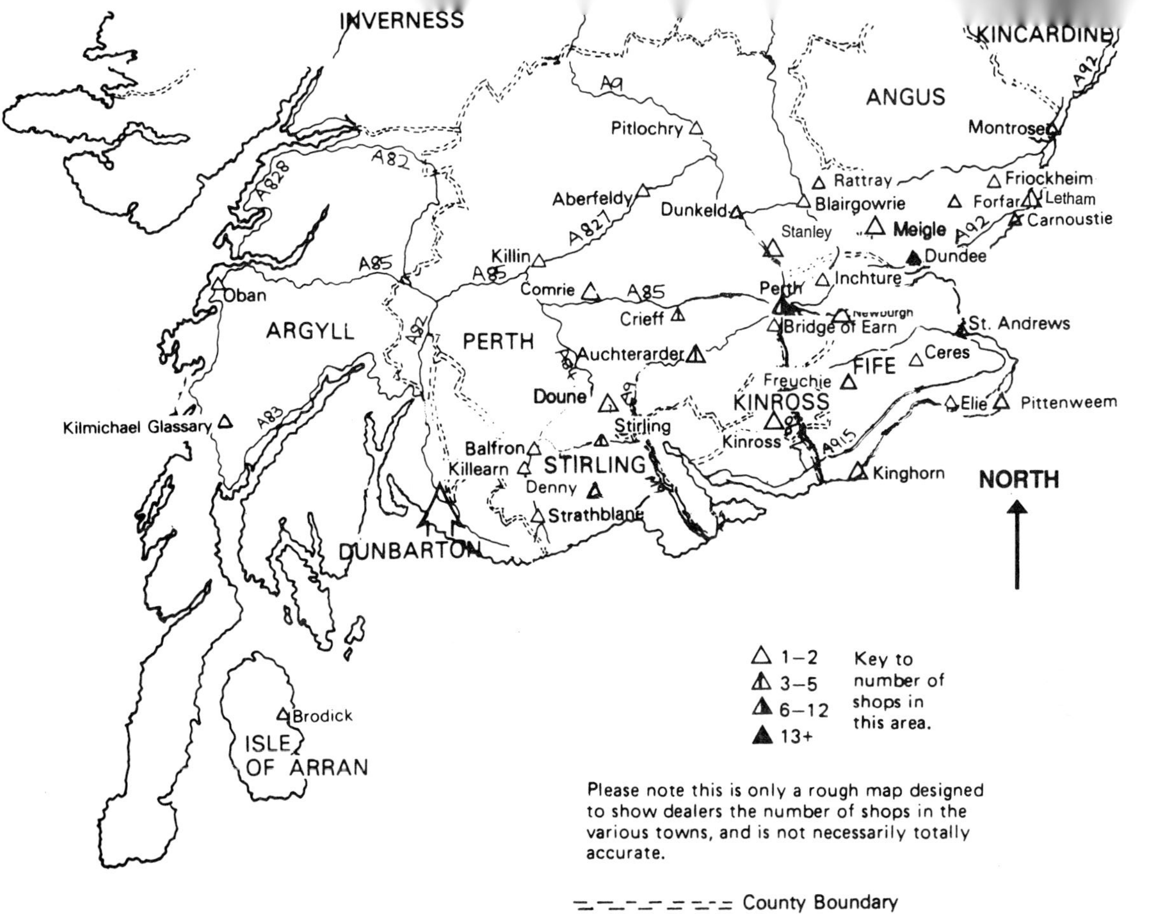
INVERNESS
KINCARDINE
A92
ANGUS
Montrose
A9
Pitlochry
A82
A828
Aberfeldy
Dunkeld
Rattray
Blairgowrie
Friockheim
Forfar
Letham
Carnoustie
Stanley
Meigle
Dundee
A827
Killin
A85
Oban
Comrie
Inchture
Perth
Newburgh
Bridge of Earn
St. Andrews
ARGYLL
A82
PERTH
Crieff
Auchterarder
FIFE
Ceres
Freuchie
Doune
KINROSS
Elie
Pittenweem
Kilmichael Glassary
A83
Stirling
Kinross
A915
Balfron
Killearn
STIRLING
Kinghorn
NORTH
Denny
Strathblane
DUNBARTON
Brodick
ISLE OF ARRAN
1–2
3–5
6–12
13+
Key to number of shops in this area.
Please note this is only a rough map designed to show dealers the number of shops in the various towns, and is not necessarily totally accurate.
County Boundary
Motorway

SCOTLAND SOUTH

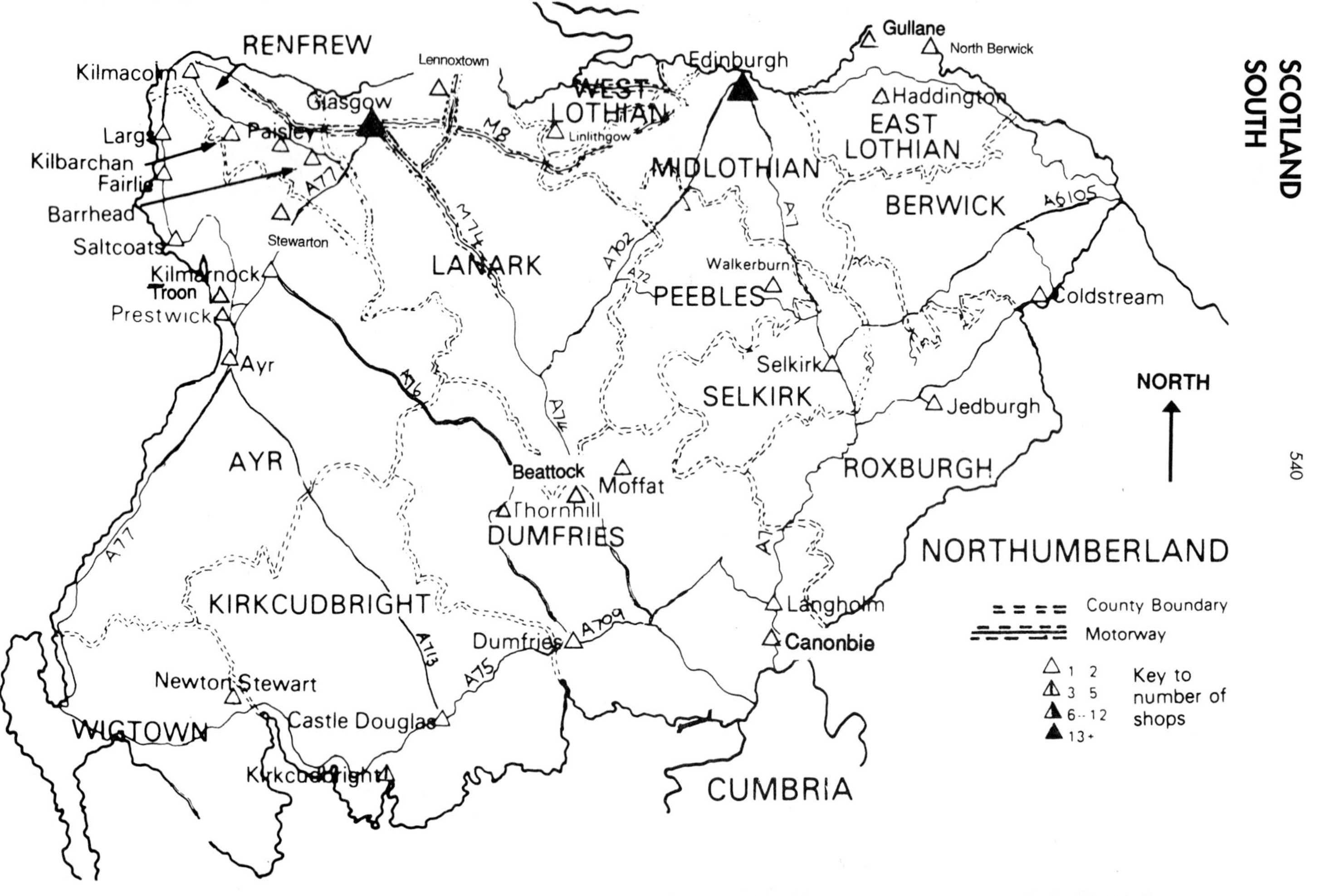
RENFREW
Kilmacolm
Largs
Kilbarchan
Fairlie
Barrhead
Saltcoats
Kilmarnock
Troon
Prestwick
Ayr
Stewarton
Paisley
Glasgow
Lennoxtown
M8
WEST LOTHIAN
Linlithgow
Edinburgh
Gullane
North Berwick
Haddington
EAST LOTHIAN
MIDLOTHIAN
BERWICK
A6105
A77
M74
LANARK
A702
A72
A7
Walkerburn
PEEBLES
Coldstream
Selkirk
SELKIRK
NORTH
Jedburgh
A76
A74
AYR
Beattock
Moffat
ROXBURGH
Thornhill
DUMFRIES
NORTHUMBERLAND
KIRKCUDBRIGHT
A713
A709
A75
Dumfries
Langholm
Canonbie
Newton Stewart
Castle Douglas
WIGTOWN
Kirkcudbright
CUMBRIA
County Boundary
Motorway
1 2
3 5
6–12
13+
Key to number of shops

SCOTTISH COUNTY BOUNDARIES

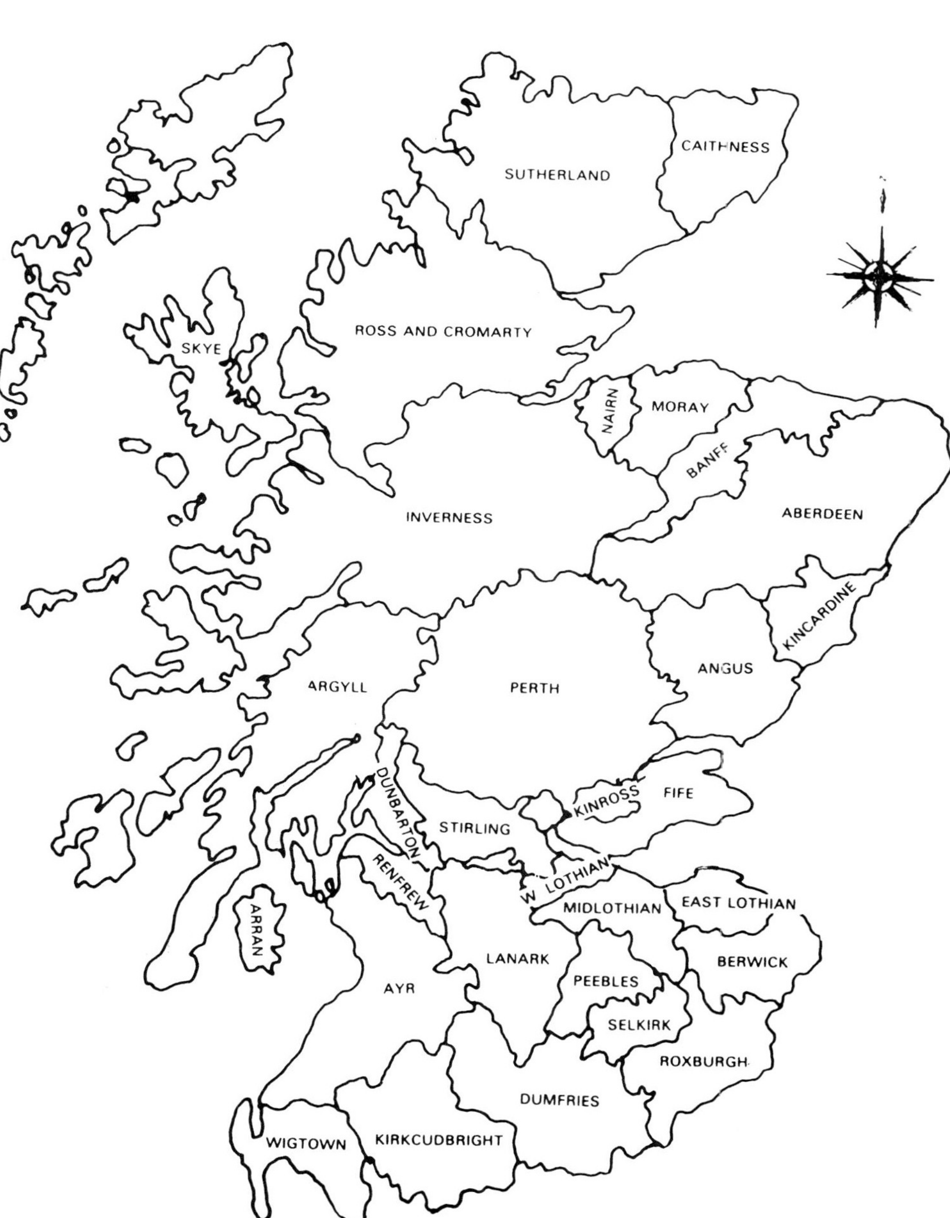
SUTHERLAND
CAITHNESS
ROSS AND CROMARTY
SKYE
NAIRN
MORAY
BANFF
INVERNESS
ABERDEEN
KINCARDINE
ANGUS
ARGYLL
PERTH
DUNBARTON
KINROSS
FIFE
STIRLING
RENFREW
W LOTHIAN
MIDLOTHIAN
EAST LOTHIAN
ARRAN
LANARK
BERWICK
AYR
PEEBLES
SELKIRK
ROXBURGH
DUMFRIES
WIGTOWN
KIRKCUDBRIGHT

ABERDEEN

Atholl Antiques
322 Great Western Rd. AB10 6PL. Open 10.30-1 and 2.30-6 or by appointment. *STOCK: Scottish paintings and furniture.* TEL: 01224 593547. VAT: Stan/Spec.

Burning Embers
165-167 King St. AB2 3AE. (J. Bruce). Open 10-5. *STOCK: Fireplaces, bric-a-brac and pine.* TEL: 01224 624664.

Gallery
239 George St. (M. Gray). Est. 1981. Open 9-5.30. SIZE: Large. *STOCK: Jewellery, post 1850; curios and Victoriana, paintings and prints, post 1800.* TEL: 01224 632522. SER: Valuations; repairs (jewellery and clocks).

McCalls (Aberdeen)
90 King St. AB1 2JH. (B. McCall). Est. 1948. Open 10-5.30. *STOCK: Jewellery.* PARK: Nearby. TEL: 01224 641916.

McCalls Limited
11 Bridge St. AB1 2JL. Open 9.30-5.30, Thurs. 9.30-8. *STOCK: Jewellery.* TEL: 01224 584577.

The Rendezvous Gallery
100 Forest Ave. AB15 6TL. Est. 1973. Open 10-1 and 2.30-6. CL: Fri. SIZE: Medium. *STOCK: Art Nouveau, Art Deco, glass, jewellery, bronzes,*

Aberdeen continued

urniture, £100-£5,000; paintings, watercolours, Scottish School, £200-£5,000. LOC: Just off Great Western Rd. to Braemar. PARK: Easy. TEL: 01224 323247. VAT: Stan/Spec.

Mr Reynolds
162/164 Skene St. AB1 1TP. Resident. *STOCK: General antiques.* SER: Restorations.

Thistle Antiques LAPADA
28 Esslemont Ave. AB2 4SN. Est. 1967. TEL: 01224 634692. VAT: Spec.

Colin Wood (Antiques) Ltd
25 Rose St. AB1 1TX. Est. 1968. Open 9.15-5, Wed., Thurs., Sat. 10-1 and 2-5. SIZE: Medium. *STOCK: Furniture, 17th-19th C; works of art, Scottish paintings and silver.* PARK: Multi-storey in Chapel St. TEL: 01224 644786 (answerphone); fax - same. VAT: Stan/Spec.

Michael Young
262 Great Western Rd. AB10 6PJ. Est. 1887. Open by appointment. *STOCK: 17th-19th C furniture, paintings and silver.* TEL: 01224 574486.

ABERFELDY (Perthshire)

Sonia Cooper
19 Bridgend. PH15 2DF. Est. 1983. Open Fri. and Sat. 11-5, Thurs. 11-4; Mon. 11-5 in summer. SIZE: Medium. *STOCK: China and glass, wood and metal, from 18th C, £1-£100.* LOC: 10 miles from A9. PARK: Easy. TEL: 01887 820266. SER: Buys at auction.

ABERNYTE (Perthshire)

Fine Antique Glass
Smithy Cottage. PH14 9ST. (S.D. Hole). Open by appointment. SIZE: Small. *STOCK: Decanters and bowls, £40-£1,500; drinking glasses, £20-£1,000; candelabra and chandeliers, £200+; all 1750-1900.* LOC: A90 from Perth, then north on B953. Cottage has stone pillars and is opposite duck pond. TEL: 01828 686350.

Scottish Antique & Arts Centre
PH14 9SJ. (Templemans). Open 10-5 including Sun. SIZE: Large. *STOCK: Furniture, £50-£5,000; accessories, £5-£2,000; collectibles, £5-£50; all 18th-19th C.* LOC: 1.5 miles from A90 Perth-Dundee link road. PARK: Own. TEL: 01828 686401; fax - 01828 686199. SER: Valuations; restorations. VAT: Stan/Spec/Global.

ALFORD (Aberdeenshire)

R.S. Gordon Antiques
Main St. AB33 8AA. (R. and J. Gordon). Est. 1959. Open 9-5.30. *STOCK: Furniture, clocks, Victoriana, bric-a-brac.* LOC: A944 between Aberdeen and Huntly. TEL: 01975 562404. VAT: Stan/Spec.

AUCHTERARDER (Perthshire)

Paul Hayes Gallery

71 High St. PH3 1BN. PADA. Est. 1962. Open 10-1 and 2-5 or by appointment. CL: Wed. *STOCK: Fine paintings, especially Scottish landscapes, marine and Scottish post-impressionist, 18th-20th C.* TEL: 01764 662320/663442; fax - 01764 664179. VAT: Spec.

Times Past Antiques

Broadfold Farm. PH3 1DR. (J.M. Brown). Est. 1970. Open 8-5, weekends and holidays 10-4. SIZE: Large. *STOCK: Stripped pine, 19th-20th C, from £50; shipping goods, £5-£500.* LOC: From town centre take Abbey Rd. to flyover A9 at T junction. Turn left, 1st farm on left. PARK: Easy. TEL: 01764 663166; home - same. SER: Restorations (pine); courier; container-packing. VAT: Stan.

John Whitelaw and Sons Antiques

LAPADA

120 & 125 High St. PH3 1AA. Open 9-5, Sat. 10-1 and 2-5. *STOCK: General antiques; furniture, 17th-19th C.* PARK: Easy. TEL: 01764 662482; fax - same. VAT: Stan/Spec.

AULDEARN, Nr. Nairn (Nairnshire)

Auldearn Antiques

Dalmore Manse, Lethen Rd. IV12 5HZ. Est. 1980. Open 10-6 including Sun. SIZE: Medium. *STOCK: Victorian linen and lace, kitchenalia, china, furniture, architectural items.* LOC: 1 mile from village. TEL: 01667 453087; home - same.

AVOCH (Ross-shire)

Highland Antiques

The Old Post Office. IV9 8RQ. HADA. (J. and H. Hesling). Est. 1962. Open 10.30-5. CL: Thurs. and Mon. (winter). *STOCK: Furniture, £100-£1,000; paintings, £50-£1,000; both 19th C; general antiques, 18th-19th C, £20-£1,000; antiquarian books especially of Scottish interest.* LOC: Village centre. PARK: Easy. TEL: 01381 621000; home - 01463 772250. SER: Valuations; buys at auction.

AYR (Ayrshire)

Antiques

39 New Rd. KA7 2PL. (T. Rafferty). Est. 1970. Open 10-5. *STOCK: General antiques.* TEL: 01292 265346.

Mansfield Antiques

27-29 Crown St. KA8 8AG. (J. Kelly). Est. 1987. Open 9-5, Sat. 9-3. SIZE: Medium. *STOCK: Furniture, smalls, paintings, £10-£2,000.* LOC: Cross 'Auld Brig' leaving Ayr for Prestwick, 1st left after traffic lights. PARK: Easy. TEL: 01292 266284. SER: Valuations; restorations; French polishing.

BALFRON (Stirlingshire)

Amphora Galleries

16-18 Buchanan St. G63 0TT. Resident. (L Ruglen). Est. 1961. Open 10-5.30 and by appointment. SIZE: Large. *STOCK: General antiques, furniture, decorative items.* LOC: On A81. TEL: 01360 440329.

BALLATER (Aberdeenshire)

The McEwan Gallery

LAPADA

Bridge of Gairn. AB35 5UB. (D., P. and R. McEwan). Est. 1968. Open 10-5, Sun. 2-5, prior telephone call advisable during winter. SIZE: Medium. *STOCK: 18th-20th C British and European paintings, specialising in Scottish; rare and elusive Scottish, sporting and natural history books.* LOC: First house on the east side of A939 after its junction with A93 outside Ballater. PARK: Easy. TEL: 013397 55429; fax - 013397 55995. SER: Valuations; restorations (framing); buys at auction (paintings, watercolours, books); golf catalogues. VAT: Spec.

BANCHORY (Kincardineshire)

Bygones

6 Dee St. AB31 3ST. (V. Watt). Est. 1983. Open 10-1 and 2-5, Sat. 10-5. SIZE: Medium. *STOCK: Victoriana, bric-a-brac, small furniture, to £500.* LOC: Town centre. PARK: Easy. TEL: 01330 823095. SER: Valuations. VAT: Global.

BARRHEAD, Nr. Glasgow (Renfrewshire)

C.P.R. Antiques and Services

96 Main St. G78 1SE. (Mr and Mrs Porterfield). Est. 1965. Open 10-1 and 1.30-5. CL: Tues. SIZE: Medium. *STOCK: Brass, furniture and curios, 19th-20th C, to £5,000.* PARK: Easy. TEL: 0141 881 5379.

BEATTOCK (Dumfriesshire)

T.W. Beaty

Lochhouse Farm. DG10 9SG. Open 9.30-5; trade any time by appointment. SIZE: Large and warehouse. *STOCK: Furniture, china, glass, brass, pictures, 18th-20th C.* TEL: 01683 300451. VAT: Stan/Spec.

BEAULY (Inverness-shire)

Iain Marr Antiques

3 Mid St. IV4 7DP. HADA. (I. and A. Marr). Est. 1975. Open 10.30-1 and 2-5.30. CL: Thurs. *STOCK: Silver, jewellery, clocks, porcelain, scientific instruments, arms, oils, watercolours, small furniture.* LOC: Off Square, on left going north, next to Gael's Coffee Shop. TEL: 01463 782372. VAT: Stan/Spec/Global.

BLAIRGOWRIE (Perthshire)

Roy Sim Antiques

The Granary Warehouse, Lower Mill St. PH10 6AQ. Est. 1977. Open 9-5.30, Sun. 12-5. SIZE: Large. *STOCK: Furniture, clocks, silver and plate, collectables.* TEL: 01250 873860.

BRIDGE OF EARN (Perthshire)

Imrie Antiques LAPADA

Back St. PH2 9AE. (Mr and Mrs I. Imrie). Est. 1969. Open 10-1 and 2-5.30. SIZE: Large. *STOCK: Victorian and 18th C shipping goods.* PARK: Easy. TEL: 01738 812784. VAT: Stan.

BRODICK AND WHITING BAY (Isle of Arran)

Kames Antiques & Jewellery and Kames Antiques & Furnishings

Kames Cottage, Shore Rd. KA27 8AS. (C.J. and J.M. Fieldhouse). Open 10-5. SIZE: 2 shops. *STOCK: Furniture, porcelain, paintings, jewellery, collectables, objets d'art, silver and artists' materials.* TEL: 01770 302213/700201.

CANONBIE (Dumfreisshire)

John Mann Antique Clocks

The Clock Showroom. DG14 0RY. MBHI. (John R. Mann). Est. 1987. Open by appointment. SIZE: Large. *STOCK: Clocks - over 70 longcase, 17th-19th C, £2,000-£20,000; bracket, 17th-19th C, £3,500-£14,500; wall, 19th C, £500-£2,000.* LOC: Leave M6, junction 44, A7 north through Longtown, follow sign to village, premises next to Cross Keys Hotel. PARK: Easy. TEL: 013873 71337/71827; fax - 013873 71337; mobile - 0850 606147. SER: Valuations; restorations (clock movements, cases and dials); buys at auction (clocks).

CASTLE DOUGLAS (Kirkcudbrightshire)

Bendalls Antiques LAPADA

221-223 King St. DG7 1DT. (R.A. Mitchell). Est. 1949. Open 9.30-12.30 and 1.30-5. CL: Thurs. pm. and Sat. pm. TEL: 01556 502113. VAT: Stan/Spec.

CERES (Fife)

Ceres Antiques

1 High St. (Mrs E. Norrie). SIZE: Medium. *STOCK: General antiques, china.* PARK: Easy. TEL: 01334 828384.

Steeple Antiques

38 Main St. KY15 5NH. (Mrs Elizabeth Hart). Est. 1980. Open 2-5 including Sun., mornings by appointment. CL: Wed. pm. SIZE: Medium. *STOCK: Porcelain including some Wemyss, 1800-1950, £5-£500; cutlery, silver and plate, £5-£200+; Victorian linen, some furniture, £50-£400.* LOC: 3 miles from Cupar. PARK: Easy. TEL: Home - 01334 828553. SER: Valuations; buys at auction (silver, china and furniture).

CLOLA BY MINTLAW Nr. Peterhead (Aberdeenshire)

Clola Antiques Centre

Shannas School House. AB42 8AE. (Joan and David Blackburn). Est. 1985. Open 10-5, Sun. 11-4.30 or by appointment. SIZE: Large - 10 dealers. *STOCK: Victorian and Edwardian furniture, antique and modern jewellery, collectables, china and militaria.* LOC: 3 miles south of Mintlaw and 25 miles north of Aberdeen on A952. PARK: Own. TEL: 01771 624584; fax - same. FAIRS: Aberdeen

COLDSTREAM (Berwickshire)

Coldstream Antiques

44 High St. TD12 4AS. Resident. (Mr and Mrs J. Trinder). Open daily. SIZE: Large. *STOCK: Furniture, 17th-20th C; general antiques, clocks, silver and shipping goods, 17th-19th C.* LOC: A697. TEL: 01890 882552. VAT: Stan/Spec.

Fraser Antiques

65 High St. TD12 4DL. Est. 1968. Open Tues.-Fri. 10-5, other times by appointment. SIZE: Medium. *STOCK: Porcelain, glass, pictures, silver, small furniture, general antiques.* TEL: 01890 882450. SER: Restorations.

COLLESSIE By Cupar (Fife)

Collessie Antiques

The Glebe. KY7 7RQ. (Mary Malocco). Est. 1989. Open Fri., Sat. and Sun 2-5, other times by appointment. SIZE: Small. *STOCK: Porcelain, small furniture, 19th C, £5-£500; Paisley shawls and rugs, 19th C, £100-£600.* LOC: Just off A91. PARK: Easy. TEL: 01337 810338; home - same. FAIRS: Aberdeen.

COVE (Argyll & Bute)

Cove Curios

Shore Rd. G84 0LR. (R. and K.J. Young). Open daily May-Sept., other times by appointment. *STOCK: General antiques.* TEL: 01436 842222.

CRIEFF (Perthshire)

Antiques and Fine Art

11 Comrie St. PH7 4AX. (Mrs S. Drysdale). Open 10-1 and 2-5. CL: Wed. pm. SIZE: Medium. *STOCK: Furniture, paintings, silver, general antiques, French paperweights.* LOC: A85. PARK: Easy. TEL: 01764 654496; home - 01764 652653. VAT: Spec.

DENNY (Stirlingshire)

Ian Burton

Viewfield, 74 Glasgow Rd. FK6 5DN. Open by appointment only anytime. *STOCK: Mainly clocks.* LOC: From M80, junction 4 or junction 9, M9, on main road through village, corner house opposite fire station. PARK: Easy. TEL: 01324 823333; fax - 01324 825207; mobile - 0385 114800. VAT: Stan/Spec.

DINGWALL (Ross-shire)

Mercat Antiques

6 Church St. IV15 9SB. (Hazel Macmillan). Est. 1988. Open 10-5. SIZE: Medium. *STOCK: Books, secondhand; china and glass, linen, £1-£200.* PARK: Easy. TEL: 01349 865593. VAT: Stan.

DORNOCH (Sutherland)

Castle Close Antiques

Castle Close. IV25 3SN. (Mrs J. Maclean). Est. 1982. Open 10-1 and 2-5, Thurs. 10-1. SIZE: Medium. *STOCK: General antiques including, furniture, stripped pine, porcelain, jewellery and silver, paintings.* PARK: Easy. TEL: 01862 810405; home - 01862 81057. VAT: Spec.

DRUMNADROCHIT (Inverness-shire)

Joan Frere Antiques

Drumbuie House. (Mrs J. Frere). Open daily 9-8 May-October, other times by appointment. SIZE: Medium. *STOCK: Furniture especially English oak, pre-1800.* Not Stocked: Victoriana, reproductions. LOC: On Loch Ness just before Drumnadrochit village, on A82. PARK: Easy. TEL: 01456 450210; home - same.

DUMFRIES (Dumfriesshire)

Cairnyard Antiques

Cairnyard House, Beeswing. DG2 8JE. (B. Farnell). Est. 1971. Open daily or by appointment. SIZE: Medium. *STOCK: General antiques, furniture and clocks.* LOC: A711, 5 miles S.W. of Dumfries (follow Dalbeattie signs). PARK: Easy. TEL: 01387 730218; home - same.

Vennel Antiques

15 Friars Vennel. (Mr and Mrs T.L. Burford). Est. 1987. Open 10-4.30. SIZE: Small. *STOCK: General antiques, furniture and collectors' items, 18th-20th C.* PARK: Easy. TEL: 01387 247929. SER: Buys at auction; restoration (furniture); upholstery.

DUNDEE (Angus)

Angus Antiques

4 St. Andrews St. DD1 2BY. Est. 1964. Open 10-4. CL: Sat. *STOCK: Militaria, badges, medals, swords, jewellery, silver, gold, collectors items, Art Nouveau, Art Deco, advertising and decorative items, tins, toys, teddy bears.* TEL: 01382 322128.

Neil Livingstone **LAPADA**

Unit 9 South Grove Works, Lower Pleasance/ Brewery Lane. Open any time by appointment. SIZE: Large. *STOCK: Furniture and decorative items, 18th-20th C.* TEL: 01382 667454/ 221618/221751; fax - 01382 566332. SER: Packing and shipping.

McLaren's Antiques

4 Johnston's Lane, Westport. DD1 5ET. (Jean McLaren). Est. 1994. Open 9.30-5 or by appointment. SIZE: Small. *STOCK: Jewellery, ceramics, silverware, collectables.* LOC: Small lane off Westport. PARK: Easy. TEL: 01382 206888; fax - 01382 566332; home - 01382 450032. SER: Valuations; restorations; repairs; buys at auction.

Westport Fine Art

3 Old Hawkhill. Est. 1975. Open 9-5. SIZE: Medium. *STOCK: 18th-19th C furniture, paintings and works of art.* LOC: Near Westport. TEL: 01382 322033. SER: Valuations; restorations. VAT: Stan/Spec

Westport Gallery

48 Westport. DD1 5ER. Est. 1976. Open 9-5. SIZE: Medium. *STOCK: Decorative items and antique jewellery.* LOC: At city centre end of Perth Road, turn into Tay St. and bear left, shop on the right. PARK: Easy. TEL: 01382 221751. SER: Valuations; restorations (jewellery, furniture, ceramics). VAT: Stan/Spec.

DUNKELD (Perthshire)

Dunkeld Antiques LAPADA

Tay Terrace. PH8 0AQ. (D. Dytch). Est. 1986. Open 10-5.30, Sun. 12-5.30. SIZE: Large. *STOCK: 18th-19th C items especially dining furniture, decorative boxes and clocks, Japanese ceramics, shooting and fishing memorabilia, out of print books.* LOC: Overlooking River Tay, premises are a converted church. PARK: Easy. TEL: 01350 728832; fax - 01350 727008. VAT: Spec.

Dunkeld Interiors

14 Bridge St. PH8 0AH. (Mrs B. Cowe). Est. 1984. Open 10-5. CL: Thurs. *STOCK: Furniture, 18th-19th C, £500-£6,000; decorative items, 19th-20th C.* LOC: 2 mins. off A9, Perth to Inverness road. PARK: Easy. TEL: 01350 727582; home - same. SER: Finder. VAT: Stan/Spec.

EDINBURGH (Midlothian)

Another World

25 Candlemaker Row. EH1 2QG. (D. Harrison). Est. 1974. Open Fri. and Sat. 1-4.30 or by appointment. *STOCK: Netsuke and Oriental art.* TEL: 0131 225 1988. VAT: Spec.

Antiques

48 Thistle St. EH2 1EN. (E. Humphrey). Est. 1946. Open 10-4, Sat. 10-12.30 or by appointment. *STOCK: Paintings, glass, china, curios, postcards.* TEL: 0131 226 3625.

Paddy Barrass

15 The Grassmarket. EH1 2HS. Est. 1974. Open 12-6, Sat. 10.30-5.30, Sun. in Aug. 2-7. SIZE: Small. *STOCK: Period clothing and household linen, 19th-20th C, £5-£100.* LOC: South side of High St., directly below castle. PARK: Easy. TEL: 0131 226 3087. SER: Valuations.

Berland's of Edinburgh

143 Gilmore Place. EH3 9PW. (R. Melvin). Open 9-5. *STOCK: Restored antique light fittings.* TEL: 0131 228 6760.

Laurance Black Ltd BADA

60 Thistle St. EH2 1EN. Est. 1967. Open 10.15-5, Sat. 10.15-3. SIZE: Small. *STOCK: Scottish furniture and decorative items, £50-£5,000; pottery and porcelain, £5-£1,000; paintings and prints, £50-£20,000; all 18th-19th C.* TEL: 0131 220 3387. VAT: Spec.

Joseph Bonnar, Jewellers

72 Thistle St. EH2 1EN. Open 10.30-5 or by appointment. SIZE: Medium. *STOCK: Antique and period jewellery.* LOC: Parallel with Princes St. TEL: 0131 226 2811; fax - 0131 225 9438. VAT: Stan/Spec.

Edinburgh continued

Bourne Fine Art Ltd

6 Dundas St. EH3 6HZ. (P. Bourne). Est. 1978. Open 10-6, Sat. 10-1. SIZE: Medium. *STOCK: British paintings, 1700-1950.* PARK: Easy. TEL: 0131 557 4050. SER: Valuations; restorations; buys at auction; framing. VAT: Stan/Spec.

Bruntsfield Antiques

1 Viewforth Gardens. EH10 4ET. (Robert Sinclair). Est. 1995. Open 10-6. SIZE: Small. *STOCK: British and Oriental ceramics, 16th-20th C, £50-£1,000; furniture, 18th-19th C, £150-£1,500; musical instruments, 18th-20th C, £150-£750.* LOC: Just off Bruntsfield Place, uphill from Bruntsfield Hotel. PARK: Easy. TEL: 0131 229 8180. SER: Valuations; buys at auction.

Calton Gallery BADA

10 Royal Terr. EH7 5AB. (A. and S. Whitfield). Est. 1979. Open 10-6, Sat. 10-1. SIZE: Large. *STOCK: Paintings, especially Scottish marine and watercolours, £100-£100,000; prints, £10-£1,000; sculpture, to £20,000; all 19th to early 20th C.* PARK: Easy. TEL: 0131 556 1010; home - same; fax - 0131 558 1150. SER: Valuations; restorations (oils, watercolours, prints); buys at auction (paintings). VAT: Stan/Spec.

The Carson Clark Gallery - Scotland's Map Heritage Centre

181-183 Canongate, The Royal Mile. EH8 8BN. FRGS., FBCartS. (A.Carson Clark). Est. 1969. Open 10.30-5.30. *STOCK: Maps, sea charts and prints.* TEL: 0131 556 4710; fax - same. SER: Collections valued and purchased.

Collector Centre

127 Gilmore Place. EH3 9PP. (Mrs Katharine M. Chalmers). Est. 1983. Open 10-6. CL: Wed. SIZE: Small. *STOCK: General antiques and collectors' items including silver spoons, glass, pottery and porcelain, jewellery, militaria and kitchenalia, from late 17th C, £1-£1,000.* LOC: From King's Theatre to Gilmore Place, on left about 50 yds before traffic lights. PARK: Meters in Viewforth (except Sat.). TEL: 0131 229 1059. SER: Valuations; advice; research.

The Collectors Shop

49 Cockburn St. EH1 1BS. (D. Cavanagh). Est. 1960. Open 11-5. *STOCK: Coins, medals, militaria, cigarette and postcards, small collectors' items, jewellery, silver and plate.* Not Stocked: Postage stamps. TEL: 0131 226 3391. SER: Buys at auction.

Craiglea Clocks

88 Comiston Rd. EH10 5QJ. (R.J. Rafter). Est. 1978. Open 10-5. CL: Wed. SIZE: Small. *STOCK: Antique clocks and barometers.* LOC: On Biggar road from Morningside. PARK: Adjacent streets. TEL: 0131 452 8568. SER: Restorations (clocks and barometers).

Edinburgh continued

Alan Day Antiques LAPADA

3 Ravelston Place. EH3 4DT. By appointment only. *STOCK: Furniture, 19th C; general antiques.* TEL: 0131 667 7120.

A.F. Drysdale Ltd

20 and 35 North West Circus Place. EH3 6JW. Est. 1974. Open 10-1 and 2-6, Sat. 10-1. *STOCK: Quality Continental reproduction lamps, decorative furniture; antique prints.* TEL: 0131 225 4686/220 1903. VAT: Stan.

George Duff Antiques

254 Leith Walk. Open by appointment. *STOCK: Shipping goods, pre-1940.* TEL: 0131 554 8164; home - 0131 337 1422. VAT: Stan. *Export Only.*

Dunedin Antiques Ltd

4 North West Circus Place. EH3 6ST. (D. Ingram and Theresa Ingram). Est. 1973. Open 10.30-1 and 2.30-5. SIZE: Large. *STOCK: Furniture, period items, chimney pieces, architectural fittings, 18th-19th C, £100-£15,000.* LOC: From Princes St. down Frederick St. PARK: Easy. TEL: 0131 220 1574; fax - 0131 556 4423; home - 0131 556 8140. SER: Valuations; buys at auction (furniture, weapons). VAT: Stan/Spec.

EASY - Edinburgh & Glasgow Architectural Salvage Yards

Unit 6, Couper St., Off Coburg St., Leith. EH6 6HH. Est. 1985. Open 9-5. SIZE: Large. *STOCK: Fireplaces, stained glass, roll-top baths etc.* TEL: 0131 554 7077.

Edinburgh Coin Shop

11 West Crosscauseway. EH8 9JW. (T.D. Brown). Open 10-5. CL: Sun. *STOCK: Coins, medals, badges, militaria, postcards, cigarette cards, stamps, jewellery, clocks and watches, general antiques, bullion dealers.* TEL: 0131 668 2928/667 9095; fax - 0131 668 2926. VAT: Stan.

Donald Ellis incorporating Bruntsfield Clocks

7 Bruntsfield Place. (D.G. and C.M. Ellis). Est. 1970. Open 9.30-5.30. CL: Wed. pm. *STOCK: Clocks.* LOC: Opposite Links Garage at Bruntsfield Links. PARK: Nearby. TEL: 0131 229 4720. SER: Clock repairs.

A. Essex & Co

1 Hope Park Terrace. EH8 9LZ. (M. and R.K. Dorfman). Open 9-6, Mon. and Fri. 9.30-6, Sat. 9.30-12.30 and 1-5. SIZE: Medium. *STOCK: Furniture, 19th C, £60-£3,000; porcelain, china, 19th-20th C, £15-£450; silver and crystal, 19th-20th C, £10-£1,500.* LOC: Off Clerk Street, opposite college. PARK: Easy. TEL: 0131 667 5387. SER: Valuations; restorations (furniture, porcelain, glass). VAT: Stan/Spec.

Edinburgh continued

Tom Fidelo

49 Cumberland St. EH3 6RA. Open 2-6. *STOCK: Paintings, works of art, 18th-20th C.* LOC: Left at corner of Dundas St. and Cumberland St. PARK: Easy. TEL: 0131 557 2444.

Pamela George Antiques

37 Thistle St. EH2 1DY. Est. 1986. Open 11-3, Sat. 10-3. SIZE: Small. *STOCK: Blue and white ceramics, Scottish pottery, horse harness and brasses, collectables, clocks, Staffordshire figures and small furniture, all 19th C.* LOC: 400 metres north of Princes St. PARK: Easy. TEL: 0131 225 6350; home - 0131 225 2159. SER: Valuations. FAIRS: Mammoth. VAT: Spec.

Georgian Antiques LAPADA

10 Pattison St., Leith Links. EH6 7HF. Est. 1976. Open 8.30-5.30, Sat. 10-2. SIZE: Large - 2 warehouses. *STOCK: Furniture, Georgian, Victorian, inlaid, Edwardian; shipping goods, smalls, £10-£10,000.* LOC: Off Leith Links. PARK: Easy. TEL: 0131 553 7286 (24 hrs.); fax - 0131 553 6299. SER: Valuations; restorations; buys at auction; packing; shipping; courier. VAT: Stan/Spec.

Gladrags

17 Henderson Row. EH3 5DH. (Kate Cameron). Est. 1977. Open Tues.-Sat. 10.30-6. *STOCK: Period clothes, linen, lace, beadwork, silk and paisley shawls, costume jewellery, silks and satins, cashmeres and accessories.* TEL: 0131 557 1916.

Goodwin's Antiques Ltd

15-16 Queensferry St. and 106A-108A Rose St. EH2 4QW. Est. 1952. Open 9.30-5.30, Sat. 9.30-1. SIZE: Medium + units in Inverlochy Castle Hotel and The Sheraton Grand, 1 Festival Sq. *STOCK: Jewellery, silver.* LOC: Off Princes St., West end. TEL: 0131 225 4717/229 9131 Ext. 5808. VAT: Stan/Spec.

Hand in Hand

3 North West Circus Place. EH3 6ST. (Mr and Mrs O. Hand). Est. 1969. Open 10-5.30. CL: Mon. *STOCK: Victorian linen, embroidery, furnishings, lace, Paisley shawls; period costume and accessories including jewellery.* TEL: 0131 226 3598; fax - same. VAT: Stan/Spec.

Tim Hardie Antiques

36 Bruntsfield Place. EH10 4HJ. Est. 1991. Open 10-1 and 2-5.30. SIZE: Small. *STOCK: Victorian and upholstered furniture, also country home pieces.* LOC: 300 yards from Tollcross, near King's Theatre. PARK: Nearby. TEL: 0131 229 1819. VAT: Spec.

Malcolm Innes Gallery

4 Dundas St. EH3 6HZ. Est. 1981. Open 9.30-6, Sat. 10-1. *STOCK: Scottish landscape, sporting and military pictures.* TEL: 0131 558 9544/5; fax - 0131 558 9525. SER: Valuations; restorations; buys at auction; framing. VAT: Spec.

Edinburgh continued

Kaimes Smithy Antiques
79 Howdenhall Rd. EH14 2LQ. (J. Lynch). Est. 1972. Open 1.30-5.30. SIZE: Medium. *STOCK: Furniture, clocks, porcelain, glass, paintings, curios, 18th-20th C, £10-£3,000.* LOC: From City bypass take A701 (at Straiton junction) into city centre, located at 1st set of traffic lights. PARK: Easy. TEL: 0131 441 2076/664 0124. SER: Valuations; restorations.

London Road Antiques
15 Earlston Place, London Rd. EH7 5SU. (R. and C. Forrest). Open Thurs.-Sat. 11-5, Sun. 1-5, other times by appointment. SIZE: Large + trade store. *STOCK: Georgian, Victorian and stripped pine furniture.* TEL: 0131 652 2790.

John Mathieson and Co
48 Frederick St. EH2 1EX. Open 9-5.30, Sat. 9-4.30. *STOCK: Paintings, watercolours, prints.* TEL: 0131 225 6798. SER: Restorations (framing, gilding). VAT: Stan/Spec.

McNaughtan's Bookshop
3a and 4a Haddington Place. EH7 4AE. Est. 1957. Open 9.30-5.30. CL: Mon. *STOCK: Antiquarian books.* TEL: 0131 556 5897; fax - 0131 556 8220.

Montresor
35 St. Stephen St. EH3 5AH. (Pierre De Fresne and Gareth Jones). Est. 1989. Open 10.30-1 and 2-6. SIZE: Small. *STOCK: Costume and designer jewellery, 1850-1950, £50-£200; Art Deco and Art Nouveau lighting, china and glass, £50-£1,000.* LOC: North from Princes St. to Stockbridge. PARK: Easy. TEL: 0131 220 6877. SER: Valuations; restorations (paste jewellery).

T. and J. W. Neilson Ltd
76 Coburg St., Leith. EH6 6HJ. (J. and A. Neilson). Est. 1932. Open 9.30-5. SIZE: Large. *STOCK: Fireplaces, 18th-20th C, £100-£20,000; interiors, stoves, fenders, fire irons; marble (including French), wood and stone chimney pieces.* LOC: Continuation of Ferry Rd. PARK: Own. TEL: 0131 554 4704; fax - 0131 555 2071. SER: Installations (fireplaces). VAT: Stan.

Now and Then (Toy Centre)
7 and 9 West Crosscauseway. EH8 9JW. Open 11-6, Sat. 10-6. *STOCK: Telephones, tin and diecast toys, clockwork and electric model trains, collectable mechanical ephemera, automobilia, juvenalia, clocks, gold and silver watches, small furniture, old advertisements, bric-a-brac.* LOC: City centre off A68. PARK: Nearby. TEL: 0131 668 2927; 0131 226 2867 (answerphone). SER: Valuations; buys at auction.

Open Eye Gallery Ltd
75/79 Cumberland St. EH3 6RD. (T. and P. Wilson). Est. 1976. Open 10-6, Sat. 10-4. SIZE: Medium. *STOCK: Early 20th C etchings, contemporary paintings, ceramics and jewellery.* LOC: From Princes St. go east, left into Frederick St.

Edinburgh continued

right at bottom of hill. PARK: Easy. TEL: 0131 557 1020. SER: Valuations; restorations (paintings and ceramics); buys at auction. VAT: Mainly Spec.

H. Parry
Castle Antiques, 330 Lawnmarket. EH1 2PN. *STOCK: Silver, porcelain, English and Continental furniture, clocks.* TEL: 0131 225 7615.

Present Bygones
61 Thistle St. EH2 1DY. (Pat and Simon McIntyre). Est. 1982. Open 10-5, other times by appointment. SIZE: Small. *STOCK: Ceramics, 18th-20th C, £25-£1,000; samplers, fans and sewn work, 18th-19th C, £100-£1,000; small period and later furniture, £100-£2,000; silver, 18th-20th C, £10-£1,000.* LOC: City centre, between George St. and Queen St. PARK: Meters. TEL: 0131 226 7646. SER: Buys at auction. VAT: Stan/Margin.

Alan Rankin
72 Dundas St. EH3 6QZ. Est. 1964. Open by appointment. SIZE: Small. *STOCK: Antiquarian books, £5-£500; out-of-print scholarly books from 1850, £1-£40; prints, maps from earliest times to 1860, £1-£200.* LOC: From Princes St., down Hanover St. to first block on left past Gt. King St. PARK: Easy. TEL: 0131 556 3705; home - same. SER: Valuations; buys at auction.

R.L. Rose Ltd
12 McDonald Rd. EH7 4LZ. Open Tues.-Sat. 10-5 and by appointment. *STOCK: Oriental and decorative carpets and rugs (large and unusual sizes).* TEL: 0131 556 7171; fax - 0131 556 7179. SER: Repair; cleaning.

Royal Mile Curios
363 High St. EH1 1PW. (L. Bosi and R. Eprile). Open 10.30-5. *STOCK: Jewellery and silver.* TEL: 0131 226 4050.

James Scott
43 Dundas St. EH3 6JN. Est. 1964. Open 11.30-1 and 2-5.30. CL: Thurs. pm. *STOCK: Curiosities, unusual items, silver, jewellery, small furniture.* TEL: 0131 556 8260; home - 0131 332 0617. VAT: Stan.

The Scottish Gallery
16 Dundas St. EH3 6HZ. (Aitken Dott Ltd.). Est. 1842. Open 10-6, Sat. 10-4. *STOCK: 20th C and contemporary Scottish paintings and contemporary crafts.* LOC: New Town. TEL: 0131 558 1200. VAT: Stan/Spec.

Stockbridge Antiques and Fine Art
8 Deanhaugh St., Stockbridge. EH4 1LY. Est. 1988. Open 2-5.30. CL: Mon. SIZE: Small. *STOCK: Fine French and German dolls, 19th to early 20th C; fine small furniture, Georgian to Edwardian; paintings and prints, some textiles, Oriental items, ceramics, glass and brass, early teddy bears and juvenilia.* Not Stocked: Silver, jewellery and militaria. LOC: 1/2 mile north of Princes St. PARK: Easy. TEL: 0131 332 1366. SER: Restorations (doll and teddy repair and re-costuming).

Edinburgh continued

James Thin (Booksellers)

53-59 South Bridge. EH1 1YS. Est. 1848. Open seven days, weekdays until 10pm (Antiquarian Section not available evenings/Sundays). *STOCK: Antiquarian and secondhand books.* TEL: 0131 556 6743. SER: Catalogues (3 per year).

This and That Antiques and Bric-a-Brac

22 Argyle Place. EH9 1JJ. Open 11-1 and 2.30-5, Sat. 10.30-2, or by appointment. *STOCK: Porcelain, silver, furniture, Scottish pottery, bric-a-brac.* TEL: 0131 229 6069; home - 0131 447 1309/229 7161.

The Thrie Estaits

49 Dundas St. EH3 6RS. Est. 1970. Open Tues.-Sat. *STOCK: Pottery, porcelain, glass, paintings and prints, unusual and decorative items, some furniture.* TEL: 0131 556 7084.

The Thursday Shop

5 Clermiston Rd., Corstorphine. (Mrs I.J. Robertson). Est. 1982. Open 10.30-5, Sat. 10-5. CL: Mon. and Wed. SIZE: Small. *STOCK: General antiques and bric-a-brac especially unusual items, £5-£500.* LOC: Near St. John's Rd. PARK: Nearby. TEL: 0131 334 3696. SER: Valuations. FAIRS: Scotfairs, Edinburgh, Ingliston.

Unicorn Antiques

65 Dundas St. EH3 6RS. (N. Duncan). Est. 1967. Usually open 11-6. SIZE: Medium. *STOCK: Architectural and domestic brassware, lights, mirrors, glass, china, cutlery and bric-a-brac.* Not Stocked: Weapons, coins, jewellery. LOC: From Princes St. turn into Hanover St. Dundas St. is a continuation of Hanover St. TEL: 0131 556 7176; home - 0131 332 9135.

John Whyte

116b Rose St. EH2 3JF. Est. 1928. Open 9.30-5.15, Sat. 9.30-5. *STOCK: Jewellery, watches, clocks and silver.* TEL: 0131 225 2140. VAT: Stan.

Whytock and Reid

Sunbury House, Belford Mews. EH4 3DN. (D.C. Reid). Est. 1807. Open 9-5.30, Sat. 10-2. SIZE: Large. *STOCK: Furniture, English and Continental, 18th-19th C, £50-£20,000; Eastern rugs, carpets, £50-£10,000.* LOC: 1/2 mile from West End, off Belford Rd. PARK: Own. TEL: 0131 226 4911; fax - 0131 226 4595. SER: Restorations (furniture, rugs); buys at auction; interiors. VAT: Stan/Spec.

Wild Rose Antiques

15 Henderson Row. EH3 5DH. (K. and E. Cameron). Est. 1975. Open Tues.-Sat. 10.30-6. *STOCK: General antiques - silver, jewellery, glass, pottery, porcelain, small furniture, objects, Paisley shawls, brassware.* TEL: 0131 557 1916.

Edinburgh continued

Aldric Young

49 Thistle St. *STOCK: General antiques; English and Continental furniture, paintings, 18th-19th C.* TEL: 0131 226 4101/01506 882121. VAT: Spec.

Young Antiques

185 Bruntsfield Place. EH10 4DG. (T.C. Young). Est. 1979. Open 10.30-1.30 and from 2.30. CL: Wed. pm. SIZE: Medium. *STOCK: Victorian and Edwardian furniture, £50-£1,000; ceramics, £20-£2,000; Persian rugs, oils and watercolours, £50-£1,500.* LOC: Bruntsfield. PARK: Easy. TEL: 0131 229 1361. SER: Valuations; buys at auction (Persian rugs, art pottery).

ELGIN (Morayshire)

Antiques and Interior Design

51 Mayne Rd. IV30 1PF. (B. Alexander-Forsyth). Open by appointment only. *STOCK: Furniture and paintings.* TEL: 01343 549313.

West End Antiques

35 High St. IV30 1EE. HADA. (F. Stewart). Est. 1969. Open daily 9-5.30, Wed. 9-1. *STOCK: Silver, clocks and watches, Victorian jewellery, bric-a-brac.* TEL: 01343 547531; home - 01343 813019. VAT: Stan/Spec.

ELIE (Fife)

Malcolm Antiques

5 Bank St. KY9 1BW. Est. 1965. *STOCK: Victoriana, collectors' items, curios, clocks.* TEL: 01333 330116.

FAIRLIE (Ayrshire)

Fairlie Antique Shop

86 Main Rd. KA29 0AD. (Mrs. Alvarino). Est. 1976. Open 11-5. CL: Mon. SIZE: Small. *STOCK: Ornaments, £10-£500; small furniture, clocks and silver, £10-£500; jewellery; all Victorian or Edwardian.* LOC: A78. PARK: 25yds. TEL: 01475 568613. SER: Valuations.

FOCHABERS (Morayshire)

Antiques (Fochabers)

22 The Square. (J. and M.L. Holstead). Est. 1983. Open 10-1 and 2-5. SIZE: Medium. *STOCK: General collectables, Oriental, clocks including longcase, from 18th C oak to 1930's.* PARK: Easy. TEL: 01343 820838; home - 01343 820572. FAIRS: Tree Tops.

Country Collectables

22 The Square. (A. Holstead). Open 10-1 and 2-5. *STOCK: Pine furniture and collectables.* PARK: Easy. TEL: 01303 820838; home - 01542 836140. FAIRS: Dee; Aberdeen; Drummossie; Inverness; Amatola.

Fochabers continued

Pringle Antiques
High St. IV32 7EP. (G. A. Christie). Est. 1983. Open 9.30-1 and 2-6 (5 in winter) every day. SIZE: Medium. *STOCK: Furniture, Victorian, £20-£5,000; general antiques, pictures, brass, pottery, silver and jewellery.* Not Stocked: Books and clothing. LOC: A96, premises are a converted church. PARK: Easy. TEL: 01343 821204; home - 01343 820599. VAT: Stan/Spec.

Marianne Simpson
61/63 High St. IV32 7DU. (M.R. Simpson). Est. 1990. Open Easter-Oct: Mon.-Sat. 10-1 and 2-4; Oct.-Easter: Tues., Thurs., Sat. 10-1 and 2-4, or by appointment. SIZE: Small. *STOCK: Books and ephemera, 19th-20th C, £1-£100.* LOC: A96. PARK: Easy. TEL: 01343 821192; home - same.

FORFAR (Angus)

Gow Antiques
Pitscandly Farm. DD8 3NZ. (Jeremy Gow). Est. 1986. Open all hours (prior telephone call advisable). SIZE: Small. *STOCK: 17th-18th C furniture, £50-£5,000.* LOC: Take B9134 out of Forfar, through Lunenhead, then first right marked Myreside, premises next left, 3 miles off A90. PARK: Easy. TEL: 01307 465342; mobile - 0411 416986; home - 01307 465342. SER: Valuations; restorations (17th-18th C furniture especially marquetry); buys at auction (furniture). FAIRS: Scone Game.

FORRES (Morayshire)

Michael Low Antiques
45 High St. IV36 0PB. Est. 1967. TEL: 01309 673696. VAT: Stan.

FREUCHIE (Fife)

Freuchie Antiques
Oxley House, Main St. KY15 7EY. (C.P. Wakefield). Est. 1980. Sometimes open, prior telephone call advisable. CL: Mainly Fri., Sat. and Sun. and Mon. SIZE: Medium. *STOCK: Small collectables and postcards, local and Scottish framed prints, £5-£100.* PARK: Easy. TEL: 01337 857348.

FRIOCKHEIM Nr. Arbroath (Angus)

M.J. and D. Barclay
29 Gardyne St. DD11 4SQ. Est. 1965. Open 11-1 and 2-5.30. CL: Thurs. *STOCK: General antiques including furniture, jewellery, silver, porcelain and clocks.* Not Stocked: Stamps, books, coins. PARK: Easy. TEL: 01241 828265. VAT: Stan.

GLASGOW (Lanarkshire)

Albany Antiques LAPADA
1347 Argyle St. G3 8AD. (P.J. O'Loughlin). Est. 1969. Open 9.30-5.30 or by appointment.

Glasgow continued

CL: Sat. *STOCK: Chinese and Japanese porcelain, Georgian, Victorian and Edwardian furniture, shipping goods.* TEL: 0141 339 4267. VAT: Stan/Spec.

All Our Yesterdays
6 Park Rd., Kelvinbridge. G4. (Susie Robinson). Est. 1989. Open 11.30-5.30. SIZE: Small. *STOCK: Kitchenalia, mainly 1850-1949, £5-£500; smalls, especially decorative arts, advertising related items, books, etchings and postcards, mechanical items, smokers sundries and oddities, to £500.* LOC: Near junction of Gt. Western Rd. and Park Rd. and university. PARK: Easy. TEL: 0141 334 7788; fax - 0141 339 8994. SER: Valuations; buys at auction; search and hire.

E.A. Alvariño - Antiques
13 Radnor St., Kelvingrove. G3 7UA. Est. 1976. Open Mon.-Fri. 1-5. *STOCK: Furniture, 18th-19th C, £50-£5,000; silver and ornaments, pictures, jewellery, clocks and instruments.* LOC: Near Kelvingrove Art Gallery & Museum. PARK: Easy. TEL: 0141 334 1213. SER: Valuations; restoration; buys at auction.

The Roger Billcliffe Fine Art
134 Blythswood St. G2 4EL. Est. 1876. Open 9.30-5.30, Sat. 10-1. SIZE: Large. *STOCK: British paintings, watercolours, drawings, sculpture, especially Scottish, from 1850; jewellery, metalwork, glass and woodwork.* TEL: 0141 332 4027; fax - 0141 332 6573. VAT: Spec.

Brown's Clocks
13 Radnor St., Kelvingrove. G3 7UA. (J. Wilson and J. Cairns). Est. 1933. Open 9.30-5, Sat. 10.30-12.30. *STOCK: Fine clocks and barometers.* TEL: 0141 334 6308. SER: Restorations.

Butler's Furniture Galleries Ltd
24-26 Millbrae Rd., Langside. G42 9TU. (L. Butler). Open 9.30-5.30 or by appointment. CL: Sat. *STOCK: Furniture, Georgian, Victorian, Edwardian; small decorative items.* TEL: 0141 632 9853/639 3396. SER: Valuations.

The Den of Antiquity
Langside Lane, 539 Victoria Rd., Queenspark. G42 8BH. Est. 1960. Open 9.30-5.30, Sun. 12-5. *STOCK: General antiques.* TEL: 0141 423 7122; evenings - 0141 644 5860. VAT: Stan/Spec.

EASY - Edinburgh and Glasgow Architectural Salvage Yards
G40 4DU. (Neil Barrass). Open by appointment 9-5. *STOCK: Fireplaces, doors, radiators, baths, etc.* TEL: 0141 556 7772. VAT: Stan.

James Forrest and Co (Jewellers) Ltd
53 West Nile St. G1 2QB. Est. 1957. CL: Sat. pm. *STOCK: Silver, jewellery, clocks.* LOC: City centre. TEL: 0141 221 0494. VAT: Stan.

Glasgow continued

A.D. Hamilton and Co

7 St. Vincent Place. G1 2DW. (Jeffrey Lee Fineman). Est. 1890. Open 9-5.15. SIZE: Small. *STOCK: Jewellery and silver, 19th to early 20th C, £100-£3,000; British coins, medals and banknotes, £10-£1,000.* LOC: City centre, next to George Square. PARK: Meters. TEL: 0141 221 5423; fax - 0141 248 6019. SER: Valuations. VAT: Stan/Spec.

Heritage House Antiques

Unit 3b, Yorkhill Quay. G3 3QE. (P. Mangan). Open 9-5, Sat. 10-5, Sun. 12-5. SIZE: 19 dealers. *STOCK: Antique pine, Oriental rugs and carpets, general antiques, furnishings, smalls and fine arts.* TEL: 0141 334 4924. SER: Import and export worldwide.

King's Court Antique Centre

Units 1-4, King's Court, King St. (King's Court Traders Assn). Open 10-5 including Sun. CL: Mon. SIZE: 6 dealers. *STOCK: Furniture, silver and general antiques, pre-1940.* LOC: Opposite King St. car park, behind St. Enoch shopping centre. PARK: Easy. TEL: 0141 552 7854/7856. SER: Valuations; buys at auction.

Mercat-Hughes Antiques

85 Queen St., 1 Royal Exchange Court. G2 4QY. (P. Hughes and C. Forrester). Open 10-5.30 or by appointment. CL: Sat. *STOCK: Small furniture, brass, ceramics, clocks, watches, E.P. and silver, jewellery and trade items.* TEL: 0141 204 0851; home - 0141 770 4572.

Muirhead Moffat and Co

182 West Regent St. G2 4RU. (D.J. Brewster and J.D. Hay). Est. 1896. Open 10-12.30 and 1.30-5. CL: Sat. and Sun. except by appointment. SIZE: Medium. *STOCK: Period furniture, barometers and jewellery; clocks, silver, weapons, porcelain, tapestries and pictures.* LOC: Off Blythswood Sq. PARK: Easy. TEL: 0141 226 4683/226 3406. SER: Valuations; restorations (furniture, clocks, barometers and jewellery); buys at auction. VAT: Stan/Spec.

Ewan Mundy Fine Art Ltd

Lower Ground Floor, 211 West George St. G2 2LW. Est. 1981. Open daily. SIZE: Medium. *STOCK: Fine Scottish, English and French oils and watercolours, 19th-20th C, from £250; Scottish and English etchings and lithographs, 19th-20th C, from £100; Scottish contemporary paintings, from £50.* LOC: City centre. PARK: Nearby. TEL: 0141 248 9755. SER: Valuations; restorations arranged; buys at auction (pictures). FAIRS: New York. VAT: Stan/Spec.

Nice Things Old and New

1010 Pollokshaws Rd. G41 2HG. (Mrs. E.Q. Lake). Est. 1962. Open 12-6. *STOCK: Interesting and unusual pieces.* LOC: Facing Langside Halls and Marlborough House (Shawlands). TEL: 0141 649 3826. FAIRS: Organiser.

Glasgow continued

Pastimes Vintage Toys

126 Maryhill Rd. G20 7QS. (Gordon and Anne Brown). Est. 1980. Open 10-5. SIZE: Medium. *STOCK: Vintage toys, die-cast, railways and dolls' houses, from 1910, £1-£300.* LOC: From west off junction 17, M8; from east junction 16, M8. PARK: Easy. TEL: 0141 331 1008. SER: Valuations. FAIRS: Toy & Collectors auctions - 3 annually. VAT: Stan.

The Renaissance Furniture Store

103 Niddrie Rd., Queens Park. G42 8PR. (Caroline Kerr). Open 10.30-5, Sat. and Sun. 12.30-5. CL: Mon. *STOCK: General antiques; Arts & Crafts and Art Nouveau furniture; fire inserts and surrounds.* PARK: Easy. TEL: 0141 423 0022. SER: Buys at auction.

R.L. Rose Ltd

Unit 3b, Yorkhill Quay. G3 8QE. Open 9-5, Sat. 10-5, Sun. 12-5. *STOCK: Oriental and decorative carpets and rugs (large and unusual sizes).* TEL: 0141 339 7290; fax - 0141 334 1499. SER: Repair; cleaning.

Jeremy Sniders Antiques

158 Bath St. G2 4TB. Est. 1983. Open 9-5, Sat. 10-4. SIZE: Medium. *STOCK: British decorative arts including furniture, 1850-1960, £30-£1,000; Scandinavian decorative arts including furniture, 1900 to date, £30-£5,000; silver, mainly 19th-20th C, £30-£3,000.* LOC: Next door to Christies. PARK: Nearby - Sauchiehall St. Centre. TEL: 0141 332 4033; fax - 0141 332 5505. SER: Valuations; restorations (silver and jewellery); buys at auction (as stock). VAT: Spec.

Stenlake and McCourt - Kollectables

51 Parnie St. G1 5LU. Est. 1984. Open 10-5. SIZE: Small. *STOCK: Edwardian postcards; cigarette cards, stamps.* LOC: Directly behind Tron Theatre. PARK: Meters. TEL: 0141 552 2208. SER: Valuations (as stock). FAIRS: Scottish Philatelic Congress and others.

Strachan Antiques

40 Darnley St., Pollokshields. G41 2SE. (Alex and Lorna Strachan). Est. 1990. Open 10-5, Sun. 12-5. CL: Wed. SIZE: Warehouse. *STOCK: Furniture, Arts and Crafts, Art Nouveau, Victorian and Edwardian, £50-£5,000.* LOC: Off M8, J20 westbound, J21 eastbound. PARK: Own. TEL: 0141 429 4411. VAT: Stan/Spec.

Victoria Antiques Ltd

100 Torrisdale St. G42 8PH. Est. 1963. CL: Sat. SIZE: Large. *STOCK: General antiques, Victoriana, shipping goods.* LOC: Adjacent Queen's Park railway station. TEL: 0141 423 7216; fax - 0141 423 6497; home - 0141 423 6567/632 4372. SER: Valuations; buys at auction. VAT: Stan/Spec.

Glasgow continued

The Victorian Village

57 West Regent St. G2. Open 10-5, Sat. 10-4. LOC: Near Renfield St. PARK: Meters. TEL: 0141 332 0808. VAT: Stan/Spec. Below are listed the dealers at these premises.

Anne's Antiques

Jewellery, china, silver.

"Golden Oldies"

Jewellery. SER: Repairs; commissions.

Marjory Kerr

Jewellery, silver, clocks.

Iona & Isla McKinnon

Fine china and small furniture.

Cathy McLay "Saratoga Trunk"

Textiles, lace, jewellery. TEL: 0141 331 2707.

Putting-on-the-Ritz

Art Deco, china, jewellery, 1920's curios. TEL: 0141 332 9808.

Rosamond Rutherford

Victorian jewellery, Scottish agate, silver, Sheffield plate. TEL: 0141 332 9808.

Virginia Antique Galleries

31/35 Virginia St., (Off Argyle St). G1 1DT. (M. Robinson). Open 10-5, Sun. 12-5. SIZE: 20 dealers. *STOCK: Furniture, glass, jewellery, silver, porcelain and brass.* TEL: 0141 552 2573/8640; office - 0141 552 5840.

West of Scotland Antique Centre Ltd

Langside Lane, 539 Victoria Rd., Queen's Park. G42 8BH. (Wosac Ltd). Est. 1969. Open 9.30-5.30, Sun. 12-5. SIZE: Large - 8 dealers. *STOCK: Pine, Georgian to Edwardian, £50-£3,000.* PARK: Easy. TEL: 0141 423 7122. VAT: Stan/Spec.

Glasgow continued

Tim Wright Antiques LAPADA

147 Bath St. (T. and J. Wright). Est. 1971. Open 9.45-5, Sat. 10.30-2. SIZE: 6 showrooms. *STOCK: Furniture; European and Oriental ceramics and glass, decorative items, silver and plate, brass and copper, mirrors and prints, all £50-£6,000.* LOC: On opposite corner to Christie's. PARK: Multi-storey opposite and meters. TEL: 0141 221 0364. VAT: Mainly Spec.

Yesteryear

14 Kildrostan St., Pollokshields. G41 4LY. (Ian C. Taylor). Open 9.30-5.30, prior telephone call advisable. *STOCK: Silver, jewellery, china.* TEL: 0141 423 0099.

GRANTOWN-ON-SPEY (Morayshire)

Strathspey Gallery LAPADA

40 High St. PH26 3EH. HADA. Resident. (Franfam Ltd). Est. 1971. Open 10-1 and 2-5 (1-2 by appointment), Thurs. 10-1. SIZE: Medium. *STOCK: Furniture including early oak; collectors' ceramics and metalware; pictures including wildlife and sporting.* LOC: Town centre. PARK: Easy and behind shop. TEL: 01479 873290; home - same. SER: Valuations. VAT: Mainly Spec.

GULLANE (East Lothian)

Gullane Antiques

5 Rosebery Place. EH31 2BQ. (E.A. Lindsey). Est. 1981. Open 10.30-1 and 2.30-5. CL: Wed. SIZE: Medium. *STOCK: China and glass, 1850-1930, £5-£100; prints and watercolours, early 20th C, £25-£100; metalwork, 1900's, £5-£50.* LOC: 6 miles north of Haddington, off A1. PARK: Easy. TEL: 01620 842994.

'Old King Cole' tile panel by William Rowe from the Seymour Ward at St. Thomas's Hospital. It cost the hospital £8,000 to buy back.

From an article entitled "Doulton Lambeth Wares" by Mark Oliver of Phillips which appeared in the June 1997 issue of **Antique Collecting.**

HADDINGTON (East Lothian)

Elm House Antiques

The Sands, Church St. EH41 3EX. (Mrs I. MacDonald). Est. 1972. Open daily, appointment advisable, and Sat. 10-1 and 2-5. SIZE: Small. *STOCK: English porcelain and pottery, 18th and 19th C, £20-£600; blue and white earthenware, Scottish pottery, £20-£900; boxes, furniture, £25-£800.* LOC: Off A1, end of High St. PARK: Easy. TEL: 0162 082 3413; home - same.

Leslie and Leslie

EH41 3JJ. Open 9-1 and 2-5. CL: Sat. *STOCK: General antiques.* TEL: 01620 822241; fax - same. VAT: Stan.

HUNTLY (Aberdeenshire)

Bygones

Bogie St. (Sue and Bruce Watts). Open Thurs.-Sat. 10-4. SIZE: Medium. *STOCK: Clocks, £50-£500+; china, £5-£50; furniture and general collectables; all 19th-20th C.* LOC: Off Duke Street, towards railway station. TEL: 01466 794412. SER: Restorations (clocks).

Huntly Antiques

43 Duke St. (Mrs J. Barker). Open Mon. and Sat. 10-1 and 2-5, Thurs. 10-1, other times by appointment. SIZE: Small. *STOCK: Jewellery, china, glass and furniture, 19th-20th C, £5-£250.* LOC: Off Aberdeen/Inverness road. PARK: Easy. TEL: 01466 793307.

INCHTURE (Perthshire)

Inchmartine Fine Art

Inchmartine House. PH12 9QQ. (P.M. Stephens). Est. 1998. Open 9-5.30. *STOCK: Mainly Scottish oils and watercolours, £150-£1,500.* LOC: Take A90 Perth/Dundee road, entrance on left at Lodge. PARK: Easy. TEL: 01828 686412; home - same; fax - 01828 686748; mobile - 0402 190128. FAIRS: Buxton; Tatton Park; Northern at Harrogate; Hocker Hall. VAT: Spec.

Inchture continued

C.S. Moreton (Antiques)

Inchmartine House. PH14 9QQ. (P.M. and Mrs M. Stephens). Est. 1922. Open 9-5.30. *STOCK: Furniture, £50-£10,000; carpets and rugs, £50-£3,000; ceramics, metalware; all 16th C to 1860; old cabinet makers' tools.* LOC: Take A90 Perth/Dundee road, entrance on left at Lodge. PARK: Easy. TEL: 01828 686412; home - same; fax - 01828 686748; mobile - 0402 190128. SER: Valuations; cabinet making and repairs. FAIRS: Buxton, Tatton Park, Northern at Harrogate, Hocker Hall. VAT: Mainly Spec.

INVERNESS (Inverness-shire)

Gallery Persia

Upper Myrtlefield, Nairnside. IV1 2BX. (G. MacDonald). Open by appointment only. *STOCK: Persian, Turkoman, Afghanistan, Caucasus, Anatolian rugs and carpets, late 19th C to 1940, £500-£2,000+; quality contemporary pieces, £100+.* LOC: From A9 1st left after flyover, 1st left at roundabout, then 2.25 miles on B9006, then 1st right, 1st left. PARK: Easy. TEL: 01463 792198; home - same. SER: Valuations; restorations (cleaning and repair). FAIRS: Treetops Hotel, Aberdeen (monthly); Inverness (July); Game, Scone Palace, Perth (July).

JEDBURGH (Roxburghshire)

Mainhill Gallery

Ancrum. TD8 6XA. (Diana Bruce). Est. 1981. Open 10.30-5.30, prior telephone call advisable, or by appointment. SIZE: Medium. *STOCK: Oil paintings, watercolours, etchings, some sculpture and ceramics, 19th C to contemporary, £35-£7,000.* LOC: Just off A68, 3 miles north of Jedburgh, centre of Ancrum. PARK: Easy. TEL: 01835 830518. SER: Valuations; buys at auction. VAT: Spec.

Jedburgh continued

R. and M. Turner (Antiques Ltd) LAPADA
34-36 High St. TD8 6AG. Est. 1965. Open 9.30-5.30, Sat. 10-5. SIZE: Large. *STOCK: Furniture, clocks, porcelain, paintings, silver, jewellery, 17th-20th C and fine reproductions.* LOC: On A68 to Edinburgh. PARK: Own. TEL: 01835 863445; fax - 01835 863349. SER: Valuations; packing; shipping; interior design. VAT: Stan/Spec.

KILBARCHAN (Renfrewshire)

Gardner's The Antique Shop LAPADA
Wardend House, Kibblestone Rd. PA10 2PN. (G.D. and R.K.F. Gardner). Est. 1950. Open to Trade 7 days, retail 9-6, Sat. 10-1. SIZE: Large. *STOCK: General antiques.* LOC: 12 miles from Glasgow, at far end of Tandlehill Rd. 10 mins. from Glasgow Airport. TEL: 01505 702292.

KILLEARN, Nr. Glasgow (Stirlingshire)

Country Antiques
G63 9AJ. (Lady J. Edmonstone). Est. 1975. Open Mon.-Sat. *STOCK: Small antiques and decorative items.* Not Stocked: Reproduction. LOC: A81. In main street. PARK: Easy. TEL: Home - 01360 770215.

KILLIN (Perthshire)

Maureen H. Gauld
Cameron Buildings, Main St. FK21 8TE. Est. 1975. Open March-Oct. 10-5, Nov.-Feb. Thurs., Fri., Sat. SIZE: Medium. *STOCK: General antiques, furniture, silver and paintings, £5-£3,500.* PARK: Easy. TEL: 01567 820475; home - 01567 820605.

KILMACOLM (Renfrewshire)

Kilmacolm Antiques Ltd
Stewart Place. PA13 4AF. (H. Maclean). Est. 1973. Open 10-1 and 2.30-5.30. CL: Sun. except by appointment. SIZE: Medium. *STOCK: Furniture, 18th-19th C, £100-£8,000; objets d'art, 19th C; jewellery, £5-£5,000; paintings, £100-£5,000.* LOC: First shop on right when travelling from Bridge of Weir. PARK: Easy. TEL: 01505 873149. SER: Restorations (furniture, silver, jewellery, porcelain). FAIRS: Hopetown, Roxburghe, Edinburgh, Inverness. VAT: Stan/Spec.

KILMARNOCK (Ayrshire)

MacInnes Antiques
5c David Orr St., Bonnington. KA1 2KQ. (Mrs M. MacInnes). Est. 1973. Open by appointment. *STOCK: General antiques.* TEL: 01563 526739.

Kilmarnock continued

QS Antiques and Cabinetmakers
Moorfield Industrial Estate. KA2 0DP. (J.R. Cunningham and D.A. Johnson). Est. 1980. Open 9-5.30, Sat. 9-5. SIZE: Large. *STOCK: Furniture including stripped pine, 18th-19th C; shipping goods, architectural and collectors' items.* PARK: Easy. TEL: 01563 571071. SER: Restorations (upholstery, stripping); custom-built kitchens and furniture. VAT: Stan.

KILMICHAEL GLASSARY By Lochgilphead (Argyllshire)

Rhudle Mill
PA31 8QE. (D. Murray). Est. 1979. Open daily, weekends by appointment. SIZE: Medium. *STOCK: Furniture, 18th C to Art Deco, £30-£3,000; small items and bric-a-brac, £5-£500.* LOC: Signposted 3 miles south of Kilmartin on A816 Oban to Lochgilphead road. PARK: Easy. TEL: 01546 605284; home - same. SER: Restorations (furniture); French polishing; buys at auction.

KINCARDINE O'NEIL Nr. Aboyne (Aberdeenshire)

Amber Antiques
Stranduff Croft. AB34 5AA. (V. Watson). Est. 1982. Open by appointment only. SIZE: Small. *STOCK: Jewellery especially amber, Victorian and Edwardian, £25-£500; silver, Georgian-Edwardian, £10-£500; Oriental objets d'art, £5-£1,000; pictures, 16th-20th C, £25-£500; antiquarian books.* LOC: On North Deeside Rd. PARK: Easy. TEL: 01339 884338. SER: Valuations; buys at auction. FAIRS: Aberdeen, Inverness, Banchory, Newark.

KINGHORN (Fife)

The Pend Antiques
53 High St. KY3 9UW. Est. 1990. Open 11-5 (afternoons only in winter), Sat. 10.30-5. CL: Tues. SIZE: Large. *STOCK: Pre-1930's furniture, prints, china, glass, textiles and general collectables, £1-£750.* PARK: Easy. TEL: 01592 890207; home - 01592 890140. SER: Valuations; restorations; stripping, waxing, small repairs.

KINGSTON-ON-SPEY (Morayshire)

Collectables
Lein Rd. IV32 7NW. (J. Penman and B. Taylor). Est. 1987. Open daily and last Sun. of month, prior telephone call required. SIZE: Small. *STOCK: Militaria and jewellery, lap desks, china, collectables, small furniture, £5-£200.* LOC: On B9105. PARK: Easy. TEL: 01343 870462. SER: Valuations. FAIRS: Inverness and Aberdeen.

KINGUSSIE (Inverness-shire)

Mostly Pine

High St. PH21 1HR. Est. 1980. Open 10-5.30 (also store in Spey Street - open Sat. 10-5.30 and by appointment). *STOCK: Furniture and collectibles.* LOC: A9. TEL: 01540 661838. SER: Restorations (pine). VAT: Stan/Spec.

KINROSS (Kinross)

Miles Antiques LAPADA

Mill St. KY13 7DR. (K. and S. Miles). Est. 1979. Open 12-5, weekends by appointment. SIZE: Large. *STOCK: Furniture including decorative, Georgian, Victorian and Edwardian, £100-£5,000; china and pottery, £50-£500.* LOC: Off M90, junction 6. Take right at High St. then second left. PARK: Easy. TEL: 01577 864858; home - 01577 863881. SER: Restorations (upholstery, polishing, small repairs). VAT: Stan/Spec.

Portcullis Antiques

76 High St. KY13 7AJ. (Charles Cranston). Est. 1982. Open 2-5.30, Sat. 11-4.30, Sun. 1-4.30. CL: Mon. and Thurs. SIZE: Small. *STOCK: China and porcelain, 19th-20th C, £10-£600; small furniture, 20th C, £50-£500; brass, silver and plate, 19th-20th C, £5-£700.* LOC: Just off M90. PARK: Opposite in Avenue Rd. TEL: 01577 862276; home - same.

KIRKCUDBRIGHT (Kirkcudbrightshire)

The Antique Shop

69 St Mary St. DG6 4DU. Open 10-5. SIZE: 3 dealers. *STOCK: General antiques, collectors' items, linen and lace, kichenalia, furniture and bric-a-brac, 18th-20th C, to £1,500.*

Chapel Antiques

Chapel Farm. DG6 4NG. (A. Bradley). Est. 1981. Open 2-5 and by appointment. SIZE: Small. *STOCK: China, small and shipping furniture, silver, brass and copper, 18th-20th C, £5-£1,000.* LOC: 200yds. off A75 between Ringford and Twynholm by-passes on A762, 2.5 miles from Kirkcudbright. PARK: Easy. TEL: 01557 820281.

Osborne

41 Castle St. DG6 4JD. (R.A. Mitchell). Est. 1948. Open 9-12.30 and 1.30-5. CL: Wed. pm and Sat. pm. TEL: 01557 330441; fax - 01557 331791. VAT: Stan/Spec.

LANGHOLM (Dumfriesshire)

The Antique Shop

High St. DG13 0DH. (R. and V. Baird). Est. 1970. Open 10.30-5. CL: Wed. pm. SIZE: Small. *STOCK: China, glass, pictures, 18th-20th C; jewellery, rugs, 19th-20th C; also Trade Warehouse of furniture, shipping goods and antiquarian books.* LOC: 20 miles north of Carlisle on A7. PARK: 100yds. TEL: 0138 73 80238.

LARGS (Ayrshire)

Narducci Antiques

11 Waterside St. KA30 9LN. (G. Narducci). Open Tues., Thurs. and Sat., 2.30-5.30 or by appointment - Trade anytime. SIZE: Warehouse. *STOCK: General antiques and shipping goods.* TEL: 01475 672612; 01294 461687/467137; fax - 01294 470002. SER: Packing and shipping; road haulage (Europe). *Mainly Trade and Export.*

LENNOXTOWN (Lanarkshire)

Campsie Antiques

2 Service St. (R. Allen). Open 10-5.30, Sun. 12-4. SIZE: Small. *STOCK: Collectables.* LOC: A891. PARK: Easy. TEL: 01360 311100.

LETHAM, by Forfar (Angus)

Idvies Antiques

Idvies House. (Tim Slingsby). Est. 1988. Open from 10, Sun. from 11.30. SIZE: Small. *STOCK: Furniture, 18th-19th C, £250-£1,500; pictures, 19th C, £100-£400; smalls, 18th-19th C, £5-100.* LOC: Approximately 5 miles south-east of Forfar on B9128. PARK: Easy. TEL: 01307 818402; fax and home - 01307 818933. SER: Valuations; restorations (furniture); buys at auction (period furniture).

LINLITHGOW (West Lothian)

Heritage Antiques

222 High St. EH49 7ES. (Ann J. R. Davidson). Est. 1980. Open 10-1 and 2-5. CL: Wed. *STOCK: Jewellery, china, glass, silver, small furniture and objects.* PARK: Nearby. TEL: 01506 847460. SER: Valuations; repairs (jewellery).

Mir Russki

28 Beechwood. (Ian Bateman). Est. 1994. Open by appointment only. *STOCK: Russian silver, 18th C to 1917; Norwegian silver, 19th to early 20th C.* TEL: 01506 843973. SER: Buys at auction (Russian silver); mail order stocklist available. FAIRS: NEC and other major.

MEIGLE (Perthshire)

Herrald of Edinburgh

Kings of Kinloch. PH12 8QX. Est. 1882. Open 9.30-1 and 2-5, Sun. by appointment. SIZE: Large. *STOCK: Furniture, Persian rugs, Continental and Eastern china, brass, copper and crystal.* TEL: 01828 640273; fax - same. SER: Restorations; custom build. VAT: Stan/Spec.

Meigle Antiques Centre

Alyth Rd. PH12 8RP. (J. McGill, H. Sudron and A. Henderson). Est. 1995. Open 10-1 and 2-6 including Sun. SIZE: Large. *STOCK: Furniture, Victorian and Edwardian, £100-£5,000; china and glass, Victorian and Edwardian, £10-£1,000; metalware and collectables.* LOC: A94 from Perth or B954 from Dundee. PARK: Own large. TEL: 01828 640617. VAT: Stan/Spec

MOFFAT (Dumfriesshire)

Alton House Antiques

Alton House, DG10 9LB. Resident. (T.J. Hull). Est. 1995. Open anytime by appointment. SIZE: Small. *STOCK: Stripped pine, 18th-20th C, £5-£500; other stripped woods, 19th-20th C, £5-£300; general antiques, 19th-20th C, £5-£500.* PARK: Easy. TEL: 01683 220903; fax - same; home - 01683 220903. SER: Restorations (stripping and repairs); buys at auction. *Trade Only.*

Ram Antiques

19 High St. DG10 9HL. (Paul and Jean Gale). Open 10-1 and 2-5, Sun. 1-5. CL: Wed. SIZE: Small. *STOCK: Furniture, 19th-20th C, £300-£1,000; china and pottery, 1800-1940, silver, brass and copper, 1850-1900, £5-£500.* TEL: 01683 220405. SER: Valuations. VAT: Global/ Spec.

MONTROSE (Angus)

Harper-James LAPADA

25-27 Baltic St. DD10 8EX. Resident. (D.R. James). Est. 1991. Open 9-5, other times by appointment. SIZE: Large. *STOCK: Furniture, clocks, silver and jewellery, 1690-1910, £50-£6,000; ceramics and pottery, 1800-1945, £10-£650+; general antiques and curios, £2-£750.* LOC: From south turn right at Peel statue, then first left. PARK: Easy. TEL: 01674 671307; home - same. SER: Valuations; restorations (furniture, upholstery); French polishing; export. FAIRS: Major U.K. VAT: Stan/Spec.

NAIRN (Nairnshire)

Moray Antiques

78 High St. IV12 4AU. (Mrs Melanie Muir). Est. 1997. Open 10.30-1 and 2-5, Thurs. 10.30-1, Sat. 10.30-5. SIZE: Medium. *STOCK: Victorian silver and plate, £50-£500; Victorian glass, 1920's-1930's pottery, £50-£200; 19th C furniture, £250-£2,000.* LOC: Sign on A96, 15 miles from Inverness. PARK: Easy. TEL: 01667 455570; fax and home - 01667 454371. SER: Valuations; buys at auction.

NEWBURGH (Fife)

Newburgh Antiques

222 High St. KY14 6DZ. (Miss D.J. Fraser). Est. 1991. Open 10.30-12 and 1.30-5. CL: Mon. SIZE: Small. *STOCK: Wemyss ware, 1882-1930, £100-£2,000; Scottish watercolours and oil paintings, 1800-1950's, £100-£1,500; furniture, 1750-1900, £200-£2,000.* LOC: A913. PARK: Easy. TEL: 01337 841026; home - 01337 840725. SER: Valuations.

NEWTONMORE (Inverness-shire)

The Antique Shop

Main St. PH20 1DD. (J. Harrison). Est. 1964. Open 9.30-5.30. SIZE: Medium. *STOCK: Furniture, £20-£1,000; glass, china, silver, plate,*

Giant Pooh, with a button-up jacket and Piglet wearing a scarf. Pooh is 31in. tall. Introduced in 1997 was a range of Pooh squeezy toys, which could be purchased boxed as a group or collected separately. There is also a miniature soft toy range for the children's collecting market. (Golden Bear Products)

'Almost every adult has owned a soft, cuddly toy in their infancy and never completely forgotten the security and comfort they received from these little creatures of plush and felt.' *Constance King* investigates the world of the teddy bear. From an article entitled "Teddy Bears" which appeared in the November 1997 issue of **Antique Collecting.**

Newtonmore continued

copper, brass, secondhand books, vintage fishing tackle. LOC: On A86 opposite Mains Hotel. PARK: Easy. TEL: 01540 673272.

NORTH BERWICK (East Lothian)

Fraser Antiques

129 High St. EH39 4HB. Est. 1968. Open Sat. only 9.30-12.30 or by appointment. *STOCK: Porcelain, glass, pictures, silver, furniture and general antiques.* TEL: 01620 892722. SER: Restorations.

Kirk Ports Gallery

49A Kirk Ports. (Alan Lindsey). Open 10-5.30 and Sun. in summer 11-4.30. CL: Thurs. in winter. SIZE: Medium. *STOCK: Oil paintings, £100-£500; watercolours, £50-£300; etchings and prints, £30-£100; all 19th C to 1940.* LOC: Behind main street. PARK: Easy. TEL: 01620 894114. SER: Valuations.

North Berwick continued

Lindsey Antiques
49a Kirk Ports. (Stephen Lindsey). Est. 1993. Open 10-1 and 2-5. CL: Thurs. SIZE: Medium. *STOCK: Ceramics and glass, 1800-1935, £20-£500; furniture, 1750-1910, £150-£2,000.* LOC: Behind main street. PARK: Easy. TEL: 01620 894114. SER: Valuations. FAIRS: Inglston and Meadowbank Stadium, Edinburgh.

OBAN (Argyllshire)

The Fitzroy Gallery (formerly The McIan Gallery)
10 Argyll Sq. PA34 4AZ. Est. 1973. Open 10-5. *STOCK: Russian sculpture; contemporary paintings.* TEL: 01631 566755. SER: Restorations; framing; regular exhibitions.

Oban Antiques
35 Stevenson St. PA34 5NA. (P. and P. Baker). Est. 1970. Open 10-5, some seasonal variation. SIZE: Medium. *STOCK: Furniture and general antiques, mainly 19th to early 20th C; books, prints, jewellery, silver, ceramics and collectables, £5-£1,500.* LOC: Off George (main) St. PARK: Easy. TEL: 01631 566203.

PAISLEY (Renfrewshire)

Corrigan Antiques
Woodlands, High Calside. Open by appointment only. SIZE: Small. *STOCK: Furniture and accessories.* LOC: 5 minutes from Glasgow Airport. TEL: 0141 887 7542; fax - 0141 848 9700; mobile - 0802 631110.

Paisley Fine Books
17 Corsebar Crescent. PA2 9QA. (Mr and Mrs B. Merrifield). Est. 1985. Open by appointment. SIZE: Small. *STOCK: Books on architecture, art, antiques and collecting.* TEL: 0141 884 2661; fax - same; e-mail - bernieajc@aol.com. SER: Free book search; catalogues issued.

PERTH (Perthshire)

Ainslie's Antique Warehouse
Unit 3, Gray St. PH2 0JH. (T.S. and A. Ainslie). Open 9-5, by appointment at weekends. SIZE: Large. *STOCK: General antiques.* TEL: 01738 636825.

A.S. Deuchar and Son
10-12 South St. PH2 8PG. (A.S. and A.W.N. Deuchar). Open 10-1 and 2-5. CL: Sat. SIZE: Large. *STOCK: Victorian shipping goods, furniture, 19th C paintings, china, brass, silver and plate.* LOC: Glasgow to Aberdeen Rd., near Queen's Bridge. PARK: Easy. TEL: 01738 626297; home - 07138 551452. VAT: Stan/Spec.

Forsyth Antiques
2 St. Paul's Sq. PH1 5QW. (A. McDonald Forsyth). Est. 1961. Open 10-5. SIZE: Medium. *STOCK: Silver, 18th-19th C, £5-£1,000; jewellery, 19th-20th C, £5-£750; Monart glass, 20th C, £5-£500.* LOC: Behind St. Paul's Church, junction of High St. and Methven St. PARK: Easy. TEL: 01738 624877. SER: Valuations; buys at auction (silver). VAT: Stan/Spec.

Perth continued

Gallery One
1/2 St. Paul's Sq. PH1 5QW. (A. McDonald Forsyth). Est. 1990. Open 10-5. *STOCK: Scottish pictures, Monart glass, silver, jewellery, furniture.* LOC: Junction of High St. and Methven St. PARK: Easy. TEL: 01738 624877. SER: Valuations.

The George Street Gallery
38 George St. PH1 5JL. (S. Hardie). Open 10-1 and 2-5. CL: Wed. and Sat. pm. *STOCK: 20th C oil paintings, watercolours, etchings and prints by Scottish artists.* TEL: 01738 638953.

Hardie Antiques
25 St. John St. PH1 5SH. PADA. (T.G. Hardie). Est. 1980. Open 9.30-5, Sat. 10-4.30. SIZE: Medium. *STOCK: Jewellery and silver, 18th-20th C, £5-£5,000.* PARK: Nearby. TEL: 01738 633127; fax - 01738 552025; home - 01738 551764. SER: Valuations. VAT: Stan/Spec.

Henderson
5 North Methven St. PH1 5PN. (J.G. Henderson). Est. 1935. Open 9-5.30. CL: Wed. pm. SIZE: Small. *STOCK: Porcelain, glass, 1720-1950, £5-£500; silver, jewellery, 1800-1900, £2-£1,000; coins, medals and stamps, £1-£500.* Not Stocked: Furniture. LOC: On A9. PARK: Easy. TEL: 01738 624836; home - 01738 621923. SER: Valuations. VAT: Stan.

Ian Murray Antique Warehouse
21 Glasgow Rd. PH2 0NZ. Open 9-5, Sat. 10-1. SIZE: Large - 8 dealers. *STOCK: General antiques, Victorian, Edwardian and shipping items.* PARK: Easy. TEL: 01738 637222. VAT: Stan/Spec.

Nigel Stacy-Marks Ltd
23 George St. PH1 5JY. (Nigel and Ginny Stacy-Marks). Open 9.30-5.30. SIZE: Medium. *STOCK: Oils and watercolours, 19th-20th C, £250-£25,000; British etchings, late 19th C to mid 20th C, £100-£1,000; Oriental rugs, 20th C, £150-£5,000.* LOC: Town centre, just south of museum, behind Tay St. PARK: Nearby. TEL: 01738 626300; fax - 01738 620460. SER: Valuations; restorations; framing; regular exhibitions (catalogues on request). VAT: Stan/Spec.

Tay Street Gallery
70 Tay St. PH2 8NN. (I.C. Ingram). Est. 1972. Open Tues., Thurs. and Fri. 10-1 and 2-3.30 or by appointment. SIZE: Small. *STOCK: Furniture and related items, pictures and prints, 17th-19th C.* LOC: Overlooking River Tay. PARK: Easy. TEL: 01738 620604. VAT: Stan/Spec.

PITLOCHRY (Perthshire)

Blair Antiques
14 Bonnethill Rd. PH16 5BS. (Duncan Huie). Est. 1976. Open 9-5. CL: Thurs. pm. *STOCK: Period*

Pitlochry continued

furniture, Scottish oil paintings, silver - some provincial, curios, clocks, pottery and porcelain. LOC: Beside Scotlands Hotel, off A9 to Inverness. TEL: 01796 472624; fax - 01796 474202. SER: Valuations; buys at auction. VAT: Stan/Spec.

PITTENWEEM (Fife)

The Little Gallery

20 High St. KY10 2LA. (Dr. Ursula Ditchburn-Bosch). Est. 1988. Open 10-5, Sun. 2-5. CL: Mon. and Tues. (and Wed. in winter). SIZE: Small. *STOCK: China, 18th C to 1930's, £5-£100; small furniture, mainly Victorian, £30-£300; rustica, £5-£150; contemporary paintings, £40-£700.* LOC: From Market Sq. towards church, on right. PARK: Easy. TEL: 01333 311227; home - same. SER: Valuations.

PORTREE (Isle of Skye)

Croft Comforts Antiques

2 Wentworth St. IV51 9EJ. (Ms Fiona Middleton). Est. 1984. Open daily. CL: Tues. and Wed. Oct. to April. SIZE: Small. *STOCK: China, porcelain, curios and stoneware, 19th-20th C; furniture, 19th C and Edwardian.* PARK: Nearby. TEL: 01478 613762; fax - same. SER: Buys at auction.

PORTSOY (Banff)

Other Times Antiques

13-15 Seafield St. AB45 2QT. (D. McLean and T. Matheson). Est. 1986. Open 10-5 including Sun. CL: Wed. *STOCK: General antiques, 1700-1950.* TEL: 01261 842866. VAT: Stan/Spec.

PRESTWICK (Ayrshire)

Crossroads Antiques

7 The Cross. KA9 1AJ. (Timothy Okeeffe). Est. 1989. Open 9-5. SIZE: Medium. *STOCK: Furniture, 18th-20th C, £5-£1,000+; china and silver, 19th-20th C, £5-£500+.* PARK: Nearby. TEL: 01292 474004. SER: Valuations; buys at auction.

RAIT (Perthshire)

Rait Village Antiques Centre

PH2 7RT. LOC: Midway between Perth and Dundee, 1 mile north of A90. PARK: Easy. Below are listed the dealers at this centre:

Fair Finds

(Lynda Templeman). *Large stock of antique and early 20th C country house furnishings, pictures, rugs, silver and clocks, £50-£10,000.* TEL: 01821 670379.

Guiscard Miniatures

Open 10.30-5. CL: Thurs. *Fine miniature furniture and collectables dolls, juvenilia.* TEL: 01821 670392; fax - same. SER: Miniature furniture made to order.

Gordon Loraine Antiques

(Liane and Gordon Loraine) *Georgian, Victorian and Edwardian furniture, decorative items and collectables.* TEL: 01821 670760.

Rait continued

J. and L. Newton

Upholstered furniture, antique pine, decorative accessories, textiles and cushions. TEL: 01821 670205

Rait Antiques

Period and decorative furniture, woodworking tools. TEL: 01821 670318.

Robert Sinclair Antiques

Small furniture and collectables. TEL: 01821 670505.

Whimsical Wemyss

(Lynda Templeman and Chris Comben) *Wemyss-ware, £50-£3,000.* TEL: 01821 67039.

SALTCOATS (Ayrshire)

Narducci Antiques

57 Raise St. KA21 5JZ. (G. Narducci). Est. 1972. Open 10-1 and 2.30-5.30 or by appointment. *STOCK: General antiques and shipping goods.* TEL: 01294 461687/01475 672612; mobiles - 0831 100152/0374 102748. SER: Packing, export, shipping and European haulage. *Mainly Trade and Export.*

SELKIRK (Selkirkshire)

Heatherlie Antiques

6/8 Heatherlie Terrace. TD7 5AH. (A.F.D. Scott). Est. 1979. Open 9-12.30 and 2-5. CL: Sat. pm. SIZE: Medium. *STOCK: Furniture, £50-£5,000; pottery and porcelain, general antiques, brass, bric-a-brac and copper, £5-£250; all 19th-20th C.* LOC: Leave A7 at Selkirk market place and take Moffat/Peebles road for 1/2 mile. PARK: Easy. TEL: 01750 20114.

ST. ANDREWS (Fife)

Bygones

68 South St. KY16 9JT. (Mrs J. Guest). Open 10-4.30, Sun. 2-4.30. CL: Thurs. *STOCK: Furniture, smalls, silver, bric-a-brac.* LOC: Near town hall. PARK: Easy. TEL: 01334 475849.

A. and F. McIlreavy Rare and Interesting Books

57 South St. KY16 9QR. ABA. (Alan and Fiona McIlreavy). Est. 1977. Open 9.30-5. SIZE: Medium. *STOCK: Books, 17th-20th C; antiquarian maps and prints.* PARK: Easy. TEL: 01334 472487; home - 01334 870982. SER: Valuations. FAIRS: ABA Edinburgh and Chelsea.

Old St. Andrews Gallery

9 Albany Place. KY16 9HH. (Mr and Mrs D.R. Brown). Est. 1973. CL: 1-2 daily. SIZE: Medium. *STOCK: Golf memorabilia, 19th C, £100-£20,000; silver, jewellery especially Scottish 19th-20th C, £100-£10,000; general antiques, from 18th C, £50-£5,000.* LOC: Main street. PARK: Easy. TEL: 01334 477840. SER: Valuations; restorations (jewellery, silver); buys at auction (golf memorabilia). VAT: Stan.

St. Andrews continued

St. Andrews Fine Art

84a Market St. KY16 9PA. Open 10-1 and 2-5. *STOCK: Scottish oils, watercolours and drawings, 19th-20th C.* TEL: 01334 474080.

STANLEY (Perthshire)

Coach House Antiques Ltd

Charleston. PH1 4PN. (John Walker). Est. 1971. Open by appointment. SIZE: Medium. *STOCK: Period furniture, from 1760, from £200; decorative items, 18th-19th C, from £50; garden furniture, 19th C, from £100.* LOC: 9 miles north of Perth off A9. Take first slip road to Lungarty and Stanley, continue 2 miles through village, sign at end of road Charleston PARK: Easy. TEL: 01738 828627; home - same. SER: Valuations; restorations; buys at auction (furniture). VAT: Spec.

Gilberts

Charleston. PH1 4PN. ISVA. (Nicola Gilbert). Est. 1996. Open by appointment. SIZE: Medium. *STOCK: Decorative furniture and objects, 19th C, £50-£500; needleworks including samplers and bedspreads.* LOC: 9 miles north of Perth off A9, take first slip road to Lungarty and Stanley - continue 2 miles through village, Charleston Farm set back in fields. PARK: Easy. TEL: 01738 828627; home - same. SER: Valuations; buys at auction (decorative items).

STEWARTON (Ayrshire)

Woolfsons of James Street Ltd t/a Past & Present

3 Lainshaw St. KA3 5BY. Est. 1983. Open 9.30-5.30, Sun. 12-5.30. SIZE: Medium. *STOCK: Furniture, £100-£500; porcelain, £25-£500; bric-a-brac, £5-£50; all from 1800.* LOC: Stewarton Cross. PARK: Easy. TEL: 01560 484113. SER: Valuations; restorations (French polishing, upholstery, wood). VAT: Stan/Spec.

STIRLING (Stirlingshire)

Abbey Antiques

35 Friars St. FK8 1HA. Resident. (S. Campbell). Est. 1980. Open 10-5. SIZE: Small. *STOCK: Jewellery, £10-£5,000; silver, £5-£1,000; furniture including pine, £20-£1,000; paintings, £50-£2,500; bric-a-brac, £1-£100; coins and medals, £1-£1,000; all 18th-20th C.* LOC: Off Murray Place, part of main thoroughfare. PARK: Nearby. TEL: 01786 447840; home - 01786 470595. SER: Valuations; restorations (china, furniture, jewellery); buys at auction (paintings, furniture, jewellery).

STONEHAVEN (Kincardineshire)

Bygones & Contemporaries

16 Evan St. (L. Watt). Open 10-5.30. SIZE: Medium. *STOCK: Victoriana, collectables, small furniture, to £1,000.* LOC: Town centre. PARK: Easy. TEL: 01569 767484.

STRATHBLANE (Stirlingshire)

Whatnots

16 Milngavie Rd. G63 9EH. (F. Bruce). Est. 1965. *STOCK: Furniture, paintings, jewellery, silver and plate, clocks, small items, shipping goods, horse drawn and old vehicles.* LOC: 25 miles from Stirling and 10 miles from Glasgow. PARK: Easy. TEL: 01360 770310. VAT: Stan/Spec.

THORNHILL Nr. Dumfries (Dumfries-shire)

Thornhill Gallery

47-48 Drumlanrig St. DG3 5LJ. (A.S.B. Crawford). Est. 1984. Open 9-5.30 or by appointment. SIZE: Small. *STOCK: Fine art, glass, ceramics.* LOC: A76 in village centre. PARK: Easy. TEL: 01848 330566; home - same.

TROON (Ayrshire)

Old Troon Sporting Antiques

49 Ayr St. KA10 6EB. (R.S. Pringle). Est. 1984. CL: Wed. pm. and Sat. pm. SIZE: Medium. *STOCK: Golf items, 19th C, to £500+.* LOC: 5 minutes from A77. PARK: Easy. TEL: 01292 311822; home - 01292 313744; fax - 01292 313111. SER: Valuations; buys at auction (golf items). VAT: Stan.

ULLAPOOL (Wester Ross)

Wishing Well Antiques

Shore St. IU26 2RL. (Simon and Eileen Calder). Est. 1988. Open 10-6, including Sun. in summer. SIZE: Medium. *STOCK: China, glass, silver, pottery, furniture, country artefacts, curiosities.* LOC: Centre of village, 50 miles from Inverness. PARK: Easy. TEL: 01854 613188; home - 01854 655307. SER: Valuations; restorations; wood stripping.

UPPER LARGO (Fife)

Waverley Antiques

13 Main St. KY8 6EL. (D.V. and C.A. St. Clair). Est. 1962. Open 10.30-5.30, Sun. by appointment. SIZE: Medium. *STOCK: Pictures, furniture, china, pottery, glass and works of art.* LOC: Coast road from Leven to St. Andrews. PARK: Easy. TEL: 01333 360437; home - same. SER: Valuations. VAT: Spec.

WALKERBURN (Peebleshire)

Townhouse Antiques

EH43 6AY. (B. Brett and J. Juett). Open 10.30-4.30. CL: Wed. *STOCK: Textiles, collectables, china, furniture.* LOC: On A72, 7 miles east of Peebles. TEL: 01896 870694/870371.

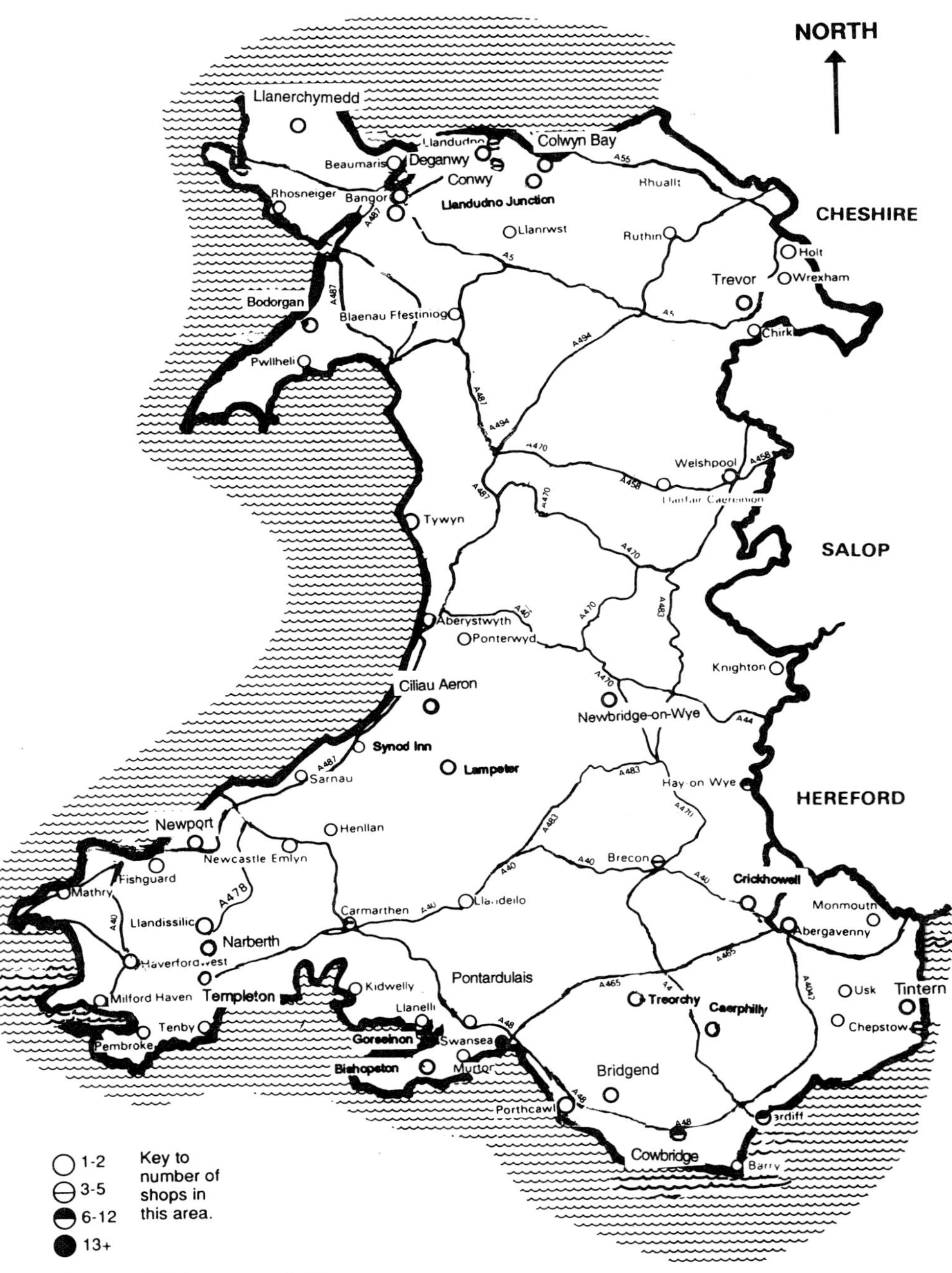

1-2
3-5
6-12
13+
Key to number of shops in this area.

Please note this is only a rough map designed to show dealers the number of shops in the various towns, and is not necessarily totally accurate.

ABERGAVENNY

Henry H. Close

36 Cross St. NP3 3AY. (Mr and Mrs H. Close). Est. 1968. Open 9-5. *STOCK: 18th-19th C furniture, porcelain, pottery, glass, brass, copper, silver, prints.* TEL: 01873 853583. VAT: Stan.

H.K. Lockyer

22 Monk St. NP7 5NP. Open 9.30-5.30. *STOCK: Antiquarian maps, prints and books.* PARK: Opposite. TEL: 01873 855825. VAT: Stan/Spec.

ABERYSTWYTH

The Furniture Cave

33 Cambrian St. SY23 1NZ. (P. David). Est. 1975. Open 9-5, Wed. 9-3, Sat. 10-4. *STOCK: Pine, 1700-1930, from £100; general antiques, Victorian and Edwardian, £30-£3,000; small items, 19th C, £10-£500.* LOC: First right off Terrace Rd., at railway station end. PARK: Nearby. TEL: 01970 611234. SER: Restorations.

Howards of Aberystwyth BADA LAPADA

10 Alexandra Rd. SY23 1LE. Open by appointment only. *STOCK: Welsh pottery including Gaudy, copper lustre, Staffordshire pottery animal and decorative figures, early pottery.* TEL: 01970 624973; fax - same; mobile - 0831 850544. FAIRS: Olympia.

BANGOR

Jones and Dyson, Ann Evans LAPADA

10 Wellfield Arcade. (E.C.P. Dyson, K. Jones and A. Evans). Est. 1994. Open Thurs. Fri. and Sat. 10-4.30. SIZE: Small. *STOCK: Late Victorian and Edwardian jewellery, £50-£3,500; furniture and porcelain.* LOC: Near High St. PARK: Easy. TEL: 01248 370898. SER: Valuations; restorations. FAIRS: NEC, Country House Events, Towy. VAT: Spec.

David Windsor Gallery

201 High St. LL57 1NU. Est. 1970. Open 10-5. CL: Wed. *STOCK: Oils and watercolours, 18th-20th C; maps, engravings, lithographs.* TEL: 01248 364639. SER: Restorations; framing; mounting. VAT: Stan/Spec.

BARRY

Flame 'n' Grate

99-100 High St. CF6 8DS. (A. Galsworthy). Open 9-5.30. *STOCK: Antique and reproduction fireplaces and surrounds.* TEL: 01446 744788.

BEAUMARIS

Castle Antiques

13 Church St. LL58 8AB. (J. and S. Jones). Open 9-5.30, including Sun. in summer. *STOCK: Oak, mahogany and upholstered furniture; pictures, silver and decorative items.* LOC: Opposite Post Office. TEL: 01248 810474.

Beaumaris continued

Museum of Childhood

1 Castle St. LL58 8AP. *STOCK: Children's toys and memorabilia collectables.* TEL: 01248 712498.

BISHOPSTON, Nr. Swansea

Maybery Antiques

1 Brandy Cove Rd. SA3 3HB. (W. Maybery). Est. 1969. Open 11 -5. CL: Mon. and Tues. *STOCK: Furniture, 18th-19th C; porcelain and pottery, 18th-20th C; paintings, general antiques, 19th-20th C.* LOC:.75 of a mile from Murton P.O. PARK: Easy. TEL: 01792 232550. SER: Valuations.

BLAENAU FFESTINIOG

The Antique Shop

Bryn Marian. LL41 3HD. (Mrs R. Roberts). Est. 1971. *STOCK: Victoriana, furniture, brass and copper, oil lamps, clocks and watches.* TEL: 01766 830629/830041.

BODORGAN

Michael Webb Fine Art LAPADA

LL62 5DN. Open by appointment only. *STOCK: Victorian and 20th C oil paintings and watercolours.* TEL: 01407 840336. SER: Valuations; restorations; framing. VAT: Spec.

BRECON

Hazel of Brecon

6 The Bulwark. LD3 7LB. (H. Hillman). Est. 1969. Open 10-5.30. CL: Wed. SIZE: Medium. *STOCK: Jewellery, 19th-20th C, £50-£4,000.* LOC: Main square, town centre. PARK: Easy. TEL: 01874 625274 (24 hr. answering service). SER: Valuations; repairs.

Maps, Prints and Books

7 The Struet. LD3 7LL. (Mr and Mrs D.G. Evans). Est. 1961. Open 9-1 and 2-5. CL: Wed. SIZE: Large. *STOCK: Books, maps, prints, 17th C, £5-£500.* LOC: A438, opposite Kwik Save. PARK: Opposite. TEL: 01874 622714. VAT: Stan.

Silvertime

6 The Bulwark. LD3 7LB. (L. Hillman). Open 10-5.30. CL: Wed. SIZE: Small. *STOCK: Silver and gold watches; antique and collectors' clocks; 19th-20th C silver and plate.* LOC: Town centre, on main square. PARK: Easy. TEL: 01874 625274 (24 hr. answering service). SER: Valuations; repairs.

BRIDGEND

Hart Antiques

Victoria Chambers, 7 Dunraven Place. CF31 1JF. (Mrs Cheryl Hart). Open 9-3, Sat. 9-5. SIZE: Small. *STOCK: Textiles, 18th to early 20th C, £20-£1,000; costume, late 18th C to 1920, £10-£600; small decorative furniture, lighting and accessories, 19th to early 20th C, £5-£500.* LOC:

Bridgend continued

Town centre, 20yds from Post Office and Cenotaph. PARK: Easy. TEL: 01656 665400; fax - same; home - 01656 646965. SER: Valuations. FAIRS: Shepton Mallet; Malvern; Carmarthen; Swansea; Thornbury; Hensol Castle; NEC; Textile Society - Armitage Centre, Manchester.

CAERPHILLY

G.J. Gittins and Son

10 Clive St. Open 9-5, Sat. 10-5. CL: Wed. *STOCK: General antiques, jewellery and shipping goods.* TEL: 01222 868835.

CARDIFF

Alexander Antiques

312 Whitchurch Rd. (J.R. Bradley). Open 10-5.30. *STOCK: Jewellery, clocks and furniture.* TEL: 01222 621824.

Back to the Wood

Old Post Office Sorting Office, West Canal Wharf. CF1 5DB. (I. Cooling). Open 9-5. *STOCK: Pine and fireplaces.* LOC: Next door to Jacobs Antique Centre. TEL: 01222 390939. SER: Restorations (fireplaces); pine stripping.

Cardiff Antiques Centre

10/12 Royal Arcade. (C. and J. Rowles). Open 10-5.30. *STOCK: Antiques and collectables.* LOC: Town centre. TEL: 01222 398891.

Charlotte's Wholesale Antiques

129 Woodville Rd., Cathays. CF2 4DZ. (P.G. Cason). Open 9.30-4. SIZE: Large and warehouse. *STOCK: Shipping goods, general antiques, period furniture.* TEL: 01222 759809/224632.

Cronin Antiques

12 Mackintosh Place, Roath. CF2 4RQ. (J. Cronin). Open 9.30-4.30. *STOCK: General antiques, silver and jewellery.* TEL: 01222 498929.

Jacobs Antique Centre

West Canal Wharf. C51 5DB. Open Wed.-Sat. 9.30-5. SIZE: Large - 80 dealers. *STOCK: General antiques, stripped pine and furniture.* LOC: 2 mins. from main railway and bus stations. PARK: 100yds. TEL: Thurs. and Sat. only 01222 390939. SER: Valuations; restorations; buys at auction.

Kings Fireplaces, Antiques and Interiors

The Old Church, Adamsdown Sq., Adamsdown. (B. Quinn). Est. 1984. SIZE: Medium. *STOCK: Period fireplaces including French marble; Victorian and Edwardian furniture.* TEL: 01222 492439. SER: Restorations (furniture and fireplaces); fireplace installations. VAT: Stan.

Llanishen Antiques

26 Crwys Rd., Cathays. CF2 4NL. (Mrs J. Boalch). Open 10.30-4.30. CL: Wed. except by appointment. *STOCK: Furniture, silver, china, glass, bric-a-brac.* TEL: 01222 397244.

Cardiff continued

Manor House Fine Arts

73 Pontcanna St., Pontcanna. CF1 9HS. (S.K. Denley-Hill). Est. 1976. Open Thurs.-Sat. 10.30-5.30, other times by appointment. SIZE: Medium. *STOCK: Watercolours, oil paintings and prints, £50-£2,000; general antiques and smalls, £10-£1,000; all 1800-1960.* LOC: Pontcanna St. is at north end of Cathedral Rd. PARK: Easy. TEL: 01222 227787. SER: Valuations; restorations; framing and mounting; buys at auction. VAT: Stan/Spec.

Past and Present

242 Whitchurch Rd., Heath. CF4 3ND. (C. and J. Rowles). Est. 1970. Open 10-5.30. Open to trade all week at rear of shop. SIZE: Medium. *STOCK: Clocks, 19th C, £50-£3,000+; furniture, 18th-19th C, £5-£1,000+; china and bric-a-brac, £5-£500.* LOC: From M4 along eastern avenue by-pass, city turn-off by University Hospital, 1st left into Whitchurch Rd. PARK: Nearby. TEL: 01222 621443/759529. SER: Valuations; buys at auction.

San Domenico Stringed Instruments

175 Kings Rd., Pontcanna. CF1 9DF. (H.W. Morgan). Open 10-4, Sat. 10-1. SIZE: Small. *STOCK: Fine violins, violas, cellos and bows, mainly 18th-19th C, £300-£20,000.* LOC: Off Cathedral Rd. or Cowbridge Rd. PARK: Easy. TEL: 01222 235881; home - 01222 777156; fax - 01222 344510. SER: Valuations; restorations; buys at auction. VAT: Stan/Spec.

CARMARTHEN

Audrey Bull

2 Jacksons Lane. Open 10-5. *STOCK: Period and Welsh country furniture, general antiques, especially jewellery and silver.* TEL: 01267 222655; home - 01834 813425. VAT: Spec.

Cwmgwili Mill

Bronwydd Arms. SA33 6HX. (M.J. Sandell). Est. 1950. Open 9-1 and 2-6, Sat. 9-1 and 2-6, Sun. by appointment. SIZE: Large. *STOCK: Furniture, oak, mahogany, pine, 18th-20th C.* PARK: Easy. TEL: 01267 231500; home - 01267 237215. VAT: Spec.

Merlins Antiques

Market Precinct. SA31 1QY. (Mrs J.R. Perry). Open 10-4.30. CL: Mon. *STOCK: Small items - porcelain, pottery, glass, silver and plate, postcards.* TEL: 01267 237728.

The Pot Board

30 King St. (Nigel and Gill Batten). Est. 1987. Open 9.30-5.30. SIZE: 5 showrooms. *STOCK: Pine furniture, mainly Victorian, £100-£1,000; chairs, mainly reproduction, £50-£300.* LOC: Town centre, near St Peter's church. PARK: Loading only and 50 yards. TEL: 01267 236623; fax - 01834 842788; home - 01834 842699. SER: Restorations (furniture, including stripping); buys at auction (pine). VAT: Spec.

CHEPSTOW

Foxgloves

St. Mary St. (Leslie Brain). Open Tues.-Sat. 10ish-5. *STOCK: Period and antique furniture; pictures, china and objet d'art.* TEL: 01291 622386.

Glance Back Bookshop

17 Upper Church St. NP6 5EX. Open 10ish-5.30 daily, Bank Holidays and Sun. (Easter to Oct.) - lunchtime to 5.30. SIZE: 8 rooms. *STOCK: Books including antiquarian; stamps, coins, tokens, medals, postcards pre-1930, banknotes, pens, military cap badges, antiquarian maps and prints.* LOC: Town centre. PARK: Easy. SER: Restorations (works of art on paper, canvas or board); framing and colouring.

Glance Gallery

17a Upper Church St. NP6 5EX. Open 10ish-5.30, Sun. in summer 1-5.30. SIZE: Large. *STOCK: Antiquarian prints and maps.* LOC: Town centre. PARK: Easy. SER: Valuations; restorations (canvas, board or paper); framing; hand-colouring.

Jones Centre

23 St. Mary St. Open 10-5. SIZE: 2 floors - several dealers. *STOCK: General antiques, furniture, china, bric-a-brac.*

Plough House Interiors

Upper Church St. NP6 5HU. (Mr and Mrs P. Jones). Est. 1972. Open 10-5, Sat. 10-4.30, Sun. by appointment. CL: Wed. SIZE: Large. *STOCK: Victorian and Edwardian furniture and shipping goods.* LOC: 2 miles from Severn Bridge and M4. PARK: Easy. TEL: 01291 625200; home - same. SER: Valuations; restorations; buys at auction. VAT: Stan/Spec.

CHIRK

Seventh Heaven

Chirk Mill. LL14 5BU. (Mr and Mrs J.J. Butler). Est. 1971. Open every day. SIZE: Large. *STOCK: Brass, iron and wooden beds including half-tester, four-poster and canopied, mainly 19th C.* LOC: B5070, below village, off A5 bypass. PARK: Easy. TEL: 01691 777622/773563; fax - 01691 777313; internet - http://www.seventh-heaven.co.uk; e-mail - requests@seventh-heaven.co.uk. VAT: Stan.

CILIAU AERON, Nr. Lampeter

K.W. Finlay Antiques

The Forge, Neuaddlwyd. SA48 8DQ. Est. 1969. Usually open but prior telephone call advisable. SIZE: Medium. *STOCK: Furniture, 18th-20th C, £50-£3,000; smalls.* Not Stocked: Militaria, jewellery. LOC: A482. PARK: Easy. TEL: 01545 570536; home - same. VAT: Stan/Spec.

COLWYN BAY

North Wales Antiques - Colwyn Bay

58 Abergele Rd. LL29 7PP. (F. Robinson). Est. 1971. Open 9-5. SIZE: Large warehouse. *STOCK: Shipping items, Victorian, early oak, mahogany and pine.* LOC: On A55. PARK: Easy. TEL: 01492 530521; evenings - 01352 720253. VAT: Stan.

CONWY

Conwy Antiques

17 Bangor Rd. LL32 8NG. (E. Calligan). Open 10-5. *STOCK: General antiques and collectables.* TEL: 01492 592461.

Paul Gibbs Antiques and Decorative Arts

25 Castle St. LL32 8AY. Open 10-5. *STOCK: Antiques and Decorative Arts, 1880-1940's; art pottery, especially major factories.* TEL: 01492 593429; fax - same.

Teapot Museum and Shop

25 Castle St. LL32 8AY. Open every day Easter to end Oct. *STOCK: Traditional and novelty teapots and tea-related items. Also permanent display of 1,000+ antique, rare and novelty teapots from 1730.* TEL: 01492 593429; fax - same.

COWBRIDGE

The Antiques Centre

Ebenezer Chapel, 48A Eastgate. SIZE: 10 stands and Sat. fleamarket. *STOCK: General antiques.* TEL: 01446 771100. SER: Valuations; restorations; buys at auction.

Bulmer's

42 Eastgate. (Hugh and Louise Bulmer). Est. 1992. Open 10-1 and 2-5.30 (by appointment 1-2), Sat.10-5.30. CL: Mon. SIZE: Small. *STOCK: Furniture, 18th C, £1,000-£2,000; ceramics, 19th C, £50-£200.* PARK: Easy. TEL: 01446 775744; home - 01656 890721. SER: Valuations; buys at auction. VAT: Stan/Spec.

Cowbridge Antique Centre

75 Eastgate. (T.C. Monaghan). Est. 1974. Open 10-5.30. SIZE: Medium. *STOCK: Furniture, 18th-19th C, £50-£1,000+; ceramics, 18th-20th C, £10-£750; collectables, 19th-20th C, £10-£500.* PARK: Easy. TEL: 01446 775841; home - same. SER: Valuations; restorations; upholstery.

Eastgate Antiques

6 High St. (Liz Herbert). Est. 1984. Open 10-1 and 2-5.30. CL: Mon. SIZE: Medium. *STOCK: Furniture, silver, jewellery, oils and watercolours, 18th C to Edwardian.* LOC: Off A48. PARK: Nearby. TEL: 01446 775111; home - 01446 773505. SER: Buys at auction (furniture). VAT: Stan/Spec.

Havard and Havard LAPADA

59 Eastgate. CF71 7EL. (Philip and Christine Havard). Est. 1992. Open 10-1 and 2-5.30, Sat.

Cowbridge continued

10-5.30. CL: Wed. and Mon. SIZE: Small. *STOCK: Oak, mahogany and walnut furniture especially provincial, £100-£5,000; metalware and samplers, £25-£1,000; all 18th-19th C.* LOC: Main street, 500 yards after lights on right. PARK: Easy. TEL: 01446 775021. SER: Valuations. FAIRS: Margam. VAT: Stan/Spec.

Renaissance Antiques

The Antique Centres, Ebenezer Chapel, 48A Eastgate. (R.W. and J.A. Barnicott). Est. 1984. Open 10-5, Sun. 2-4. SIZE: Small. *STOCK: Small furniture, Georgian, Victorian and Edwardian, £100-£3,000; brass, copper, plate, decorative ceramics, Staffordshire figures, objets d'art, 18th to 20th C, £5-£500.* Not Stocked: Coins, militaria, reproductions. LOC: Main street.

CRICKHOWELL

Gallop and Rivers Architectural Antiques

Ty'r Ash, Brecon Rd. NP8 1SF. (G. P. Gallop and R. A. Rivers). Open 9.30-5. *STOCK: Architectural items, pine and country furniture.* TEL: 01873 811084. VAT: Stan.

DEGANWY

Acorn Antiques

Castle Buildings. LL31 9EJ. (K.S. Bowers-Jones). Open 10-5. *STOCK: Ceramics, glass, furniture, pictures, brass and copper, 19th C.* TEL: 01492 584083.

FISHGUARD

Hermitage Antiquities

10 West St. SA65 9AE. (J.B. Thomas). Est. 1976. Open 10-12.30 and 2-5. CL: Wed. and Sat. pm. SIZE: Small. *STOCK: Arms, armour and militaria - full suits of armour, 16th-17th C; military long-guns, pistols, swords; cased pistol sets, military headgear, ethnographica, 16th-19th C, £50-£5,000; antiquities, jewellery, objets d'art.* LOC: 50yds. on right after leaving Square on Harbour road (West St.). PARK: 300yds. TEL: 01348 873037; home - 01348 872322. SER: Valuations; restorations (arms and armour, inlay work on wheel locks, flintlock parts re-built, woodwork repairs); buys at auction (arms and armour). VAT: Spec.

Manor House Antiques

Main St. SA65 9HG. (R.E. Davies). Open 9.15-5.30. *STOCK: General antiques especially porcelain and pottery.* TEL: 01348 873260.

GORSEINON, Nr. Swansea

Gold and Silver Shop

1 Cross St. SA1 1BA. (D. Paine). Open 9-2. *STOCK: Gold and silver, general antiques.* TEL: 01792 891874.

HAVERFORDWEST

Kent House Antiques

Kent House, Market St. SA61 1NF. (G. Fanstone and P. Thorpe). Est. 1987. Open 10-5. CL: Mon. SIZE: Medium. *STOCK: Victoriana, decorative items, hand-made rugs, £5-£500+.* LOC: Town centre. PARK: Easy. TEL: 01437 768175; home - same. SER: Valuations; restorations (furniture, some china).

Gerald Oliver Antiques

14 Albany Terrace, St. Thomas Green. SA61 1RH. Est. 1957. Open 9.30-1 and 2-5. CL: Thurs. pm. SIZE: Small. *STOCK: Furniture, pre-1890, £20-£6,000; ceramics, treen, metalwork, small silver, from £20; unusual, decorative and local interest items.* LOC: Via by-pass and up Merlins Hill to St. Thomas Green. PARK: Easy. TEL: 01437 762794. SER: Valuations. VAT: Spec.

HAY-ON-WYE

Antique Market

6 Market St. HR3 5AD. Open 10-5, Sun. 11-5. SIZE: 19 dealers. *STOCK: General antiques and collectables.* LOC: By the Butter Market. TEL: 01497 820175.

Richard Booth's Bookshop Ltd

44 Lion St. and Hay Castle. HR3 5AA. Est. 1974. Open 7 days 9-5.30, later at weekends and during summer. SIZE: Very large. *STOCK: Books, magazines, photographs, records, postcards, leather bindings.* LOC: Town centre. TEL: 01497 820322; fax - 01497 821150; Hay Castle - 01497 820503; fax - 01497 821314.

Hebbards of Hay

7 Market St. HR3 5AF. (P.E. Hebbard). Est. 1958. Open 10-5. SIZE: Small. *STOCK: Pottery and porcelain.* LOC: A438, opposite the Post Office. PARK: Own. TEL: 01497 820413.

Tamara Le Bailly Antiques

5 Market St. HR3 5AF. Open 10-5.30, but appointment advisable. CL: Tues. SIZE: Shop + trade barn. *STOCK: Decorative antiques, furniture, lighting.* PARK: Nearby. TEL: 01497 821157/820656; mobile - 0831 630883.

Lion Fine Arts

19 Lion St. HR3 5AD. (Charles and Sylvia Spencer). Est. 1986. Open 10.30-1 and 2-5, other times by appointment. CL: Tues. and Sat. p.m. SIZE: Small. *STOCK: Pottery, porcelain and glass, 18th to mid19th C, £25-£250; furniture, prints and objets d'art, £30-£900; some second-hand and antiquarian books.* LOC: Turn right from Oxford Rd. car park, then second turning left. PARK: Limited. TEL: 01497 821726; home - same.

Mark Westwood Antiquarian Books

High Town. HR3 5AE. ABA. PBFA. Est. 1976. Open 10.30-5.30, including Sundays in summer. *STOCK: Antiquarian and secondhand books on most subjects, £2-£1,000.* TEL: 01497 820068. SER: Valuations; buys at auction (antiquarian books). VAT: Stan.

HENLLAN, Nr. Newcastle Emlyn

Michael Lloyd

Dolhaidd Mansion. SA44 5TG. Est. 1987. Open by appointment. SIZE: Large. *STOCK: Country furniture, pine, general antiques.* LOC: On A484, 2 miles Newcastle Emlyn. TEL: 01559 370582. VAT: Stan/Spec. *Trade Only.*

HOLT, Nr. Wrexham

Furn Davies Partnership

Rock Cottage, Bridge St. LL13 9JG. Open Thurs., Fri. and Sat. 10-5, other times by appointment. *STOCK: Furniture, 18th-19th C, and decorative items.* TEL: 01829 270210. SER: Valuations; restorations.

KIDWELLY

Country Antiques (Wales) BADA LAPADA

Old Castle Mill. SA17 4UU. (R. and L. Bebb). Open 10-5. CL: Mon. SIZE: Large. *STOCK: Welsh furniture and folk art; Welsh clocks, pottery.* LOC: Leave bypass (A484), into centre of village, turn by Boot and Shoe public house. PARK: Easy. TEL: 01554 890534. SER: Valuations; lectures. VAT: Stan/Spec.

Kidwelly Antiques LAPADA

31 Bridge St. SA17 4UU. (R. and L. Bebb). Open 10-5. CL: Mon. SIZE: Large. *STOCK:*

Kidwelly continued

***Georgian and Victorian furniture and accessories; collectables.* LOC: Leave bypass (A484), into centre of village. PARK: Opposite shop. TEL: 01554 890328. VAT: Stan/Spec.**

KNIGHTON

Offa's Dyke Antique Centre

4 High St. LD7 1AT. (Mrs. H. Hood and I. Watkins). Est. 1985. Open 10-1 and 2-5. SIZE: Medium - 16 dealers. *STOCK: Pottery, bijouterie, 18th-19th C furniture, £5-£1,000.* LOC: Near town clock. PARK: Easy. TEL: 01547 528635; evenings - 01547 528940/560272.

Islwyn Watkins

1 High St. LD7 1AT. Est. 1978. Open 10-1 and 2.30-5, prior telephone call advisable, Mon. and Wed. by appointment. SIZE: Small. *STOCK: Pottery including studio, 18th-20th C, £25-£350; country and domestic bygones, treen, 18th-20th C, £5-£100; small country furniture, 18th-19th C, £20-£400.* Not Stocked: Jewellery, silver, militaria. LOC: By town clock. PARK: Easy. TEL: 01547 520145; home - 01547 528940. SER: Valuations.

LAMPETER

Barn Antiques

2 Market St. SA48 7DR. (N. Megicks). Est. 1980. Open 9-5.30, Wed. 9-1. SIZE: Medium. *STOCK: Pine, oak, mahogany, mainly 19th C, £50-£3,000; reproduction pine and oak.* LOC: Pedestrianised street just off town centre. PARK: Easy. TEL: 01570 423526. SER: Valuations; restorations (re-veneering, inlay work, French polishing, pine stripping and finishing). VAT: Stan.

LLANDEILO

Jim and Pat Ash

The Warehouse, 5 Station Rd. SA19 6NG. Est. 1977. Open 9.30-5. SIZE: Large. *STOCK: Victorian and antique furniture, Welsh country, oak, pine, mahogany, walnut.* LOC: 50yds. off A40. PARK: Easy. TEL: 01558 823726. SER: Valuations; shipping. VAT: Stan/Margin/Export.

LLANDUDNO

The Antique Shop

24 Vaughan St. LL30 1AH. (C.G. Lee). Est. 1938. Open 9-5.30. SIZE: Medium. *STOCK: Jewellery, silver, porcelain, glass, ivories, metal goods, from 1700; period furniture, shipping goods.* LOC: Near promenade. PARK: Easy. TEL: 01492 875575.

LLANDUDNO JUNCTION

Collinge Antiques

Old Fyffes Warehouse, Conwy Rd. LL31 9LU. (Nicky Collinge). Est. 1978. Open seven days. SIZE: Large. *STOCK: General antiques including Welsh dressers, dining, drawing and bedroom furniture, clocks, porcelain and pottery, silver, copper and brass, paintings, prints, glass and collectables, mainly Victorian and Edwardian.* LOC: Just off A55, Deganwy exit (A546). PARK: Easy. TEL: 01492 580022; fax - same. SER: Valuations; restorations including French polishing; buys at auction. VAT: Stan/Spec.

The Country Seat

35 Conwy Rd. LL31 9LU. (Steve and Helen Roberts). Open 10-4.30, Mon 10-1, Tues. 12-4 or by appointment. CL: Wed. SIZE: Small. *STOCK: Old and interesting items including paintings, pottery and porcelain, jewellery, furniture, linen, ephemera and bric-a-brac; decorative arts, 19th-20th C.* LOC: Just off A55. PARK: Easy. TEL: 01492 573256.

LLANELLI

Alice's Antiques

24 Upper Park St. SA15 3YN. (Mrs A. Davies). Est. 1940. Open 10-1 and 2-6. CL: Tues. pm. SIZE: Small. *STOCK: General antiques, 1850-1950, £5-£50; paintings, silver, Georgian and Victorian, china, metalware.* LOC: On main road in town centre. PARK: At rear. TEL: 01554 773045. SER: Valuations; buys at auction. VAT: Stan.

Llanelli continued

John Carpenter

SA14 7HA. Resident. Est. 1973. Open by appointment. *STOCK: Musical instruments, furniture, general antiques.* LOC: 5 minutes from Cross Hands. TEL: 01269 831094.

LLANERCHYMEDD (ANGLESEY)

Two Dragons Oriental Antiques

8 High St. LL71 8EA. Open by appointment. SIZE: Large warehouse. *STOCK: Chinese country furniture.* TEL: 01248 470204/470100.

LLANFAIR CAEREINION Nr. Welshpool

Heritage Restorations

Maes y Glydfa. SY21 0HD. (Jo and Fran Gluck). Est. 1970. Open 9-5. SIZE: Large. *STOCK: Pine and country furniture, £50-£2,000; some oak and architectural items, all 18th-19th C.* LOC: A458 from Welshpool. Past village, after 2 miles take first left after river bridge and caravan park, then follow signs. PARK: Easy. TEL: 01938 810384; home - same. SER: Restorations (furniture including pine stripping). VAT: Stan/Spec.

LLANGOLLEN

J. and R. Langford

12 Bridge St. LL20 8PF. (P. and M. Silverston). Est. 1960. CL: Thurs. pm. and 1-2 daily. SIZE: Medium. *STOCK: Furniture, £100-£7,000; pottery and porcelain, £50-£2,000; silver, general antiques, clocks, paintings, £20-£4,000; all 18th-20th C.* LOC: Turn right at Royal Hotel, shop on right. PARK: Easy. TEL: 01978 860182; home - 01978 860493. SER: Valuations.

Passers Buy (Marie Evans)

Oak St/Chapel St. LL20 8NR. (Mrs M. Evans). Est. 1970. Open 11-5 - always on Tues., Fri. and Sat, often on Mon., Wed. and Thurs. - prior 'phone call advisable, Sun. by appointment. SIZE: Medium. *STOCK: Furniture, Staffordshire figures, Gaudy Welsh, fairings and general antiques.* LOC: Just off A5. Junction of Chapel St. and Oak St. PARK: Easy. TEL: 01978 860861/757385. FAIRS: Anglesey (June and Oct.)

LLANRWST

Snowdonia Antiques

LL26 0EP. (J. Collins). Est. 1961. Open 9-5.30, Sun. by appointment. SIZE: Medium. *STOCK: Period furniture especially longcase clocks.* LOC: Turn off A5 just before Betws-y-Coed on to A496 for 4 miles. PARK: Easy. TEL: 01492 640789. SER: Restorations (furniture); repairs (grandfather clocks).

MATHRY

Cartrefle Antiques

SA62 5AD. (M. Hughes and Y. Chesters). Open in summer 10-5.30; in winter Wed.-Sat. 10.30-4, evenings by appointment. *STOCK: General antiques especially jewellery.* PARK: Easy. TEL: 01348 831591/837868.

MILFORD HAVEN

Milford Haven Antiques

Robert St. SA73 2HS. Est. 1968. Open 10-5. *STOCK: General antiques.* TEL: 01646 692152.

MONMOUTH

Carol Freeman Antiques

The Gallery, Nailers Lane. NP5 3SE. Open 10-5. *STOCK: General antiques and secondhand items.* TEL: 01600 772252; home - 01600 712658.

MURTON, Nr. Swansea

West Wales Antiques LAPADA

18 Manselfield Rd. SA3 3AR. (W.H. Davies). Est. 1956. Open 10-1 and 2-5. *STOCK: Porcelain, 18th C, £20-£800; Welsh porcelain, 1814-1820, £100-£3,000; dolls, 1880-1920; 18th-19th C furniture, silver, pottery, glass, jewellery and collectors' items.* LOC: M4-A4067-B4436, entrance to Gower Peninsula. TEL: 01792 234318. VAT: Stan/Spec.

NARBERTH

Peter Thomas Antiques

32 High St. SA67 7AS. Est. 1987. Open 10-4.30, Sun., Mon. and Tues. by appointment. SIZE: Medium. *STOCK: Oak and fruitwood furniture, metalwork and paintings, 16th to late 18th C, £500-£15,000.* LOC: Town centre. PARK: Easy. TEL: 01834 860671; home - same. SER: Valuations; restorations; buys at auction. VAT: Spec.

NEWBRIDGE-ON-WYE Nr. Llandrindod Wells

Allam Antiques

Old Village Hall. LD1 6HL. (Paul Allam). Est. 1985. Open 10-5, Sun. by appointment. SIZE: Medium. *STOCK: Furniture, 1700-1930, £50-£1,000; reproduction furniture, £50-£500; smalls, 19th-20th C, £1-£100.* LOC: A470. PARK: Easy. TEL: 01597 860654; home - 01597 860455. SER: Valuations; restorations; commission reproduction.

NEWCASTLE EMLYN

Castle Antiques

Market Sq. SA38 9AE. (Mr and Mrs B.G. Houser). Est. 1986. Open 9.30-5.30. SIZE: Small. *STOCK: Furniture, 1700 to 1920s, £500-£2,000; china and glass, 18th-19th C, £50-£200.* LOC: Town centre by clock tower. PARK: Castle St. TEL: 01239 710420; home - same.

Newcastle Emlyn continued

Emlyn Antiques

1 Sycamore St. SA38 9AJ. (John and Norma Birkby). Est. 1962. Open 10.30-5.30, Sun. by appointment. CL: Wed. SIZE: Medium. *STOCK: Mahogany furniture, 18th-19th C, £500-£1,000+; oils and watercolours, 19th C, £100-£500; mechanical music, 18th-20th C, £1,000-£5,000.* LOC: Main street. PARK: Nearby. TEL: 01239 711235; home and fax - 01559 362758.

John Latter Antiques

3 Market Sq. SA38 9AQ. Est. 1959. Open 10-1 and 2-5, Sun. by appointment. SIZE: Small. *STOCK: Decorative furniture, 18th-20th C, £100-£200; fabrics, 19th-20th C, £100-£200; objets de vertu, 18th-20th C, £50-£100.* LOC: Town centre by clock tower. PARK: Easy. TEL: 01239 711117; home - 01239 711500. SER: Valuations.

NEWPORT

The Carningli Centre

East St. SA42 05Y. (Ann Gent). Est. 1994. Open 10-5.30, Sat. 10.30-5.30, Wed. and Sun. by appointment only. *STOCK: Country furniture, 17th-19th C; pine, mainly 19th C, all £50-£1,000; railwayana, £10-£500; some art books.* TEL: 01239 820724. SER: Restorations (furniture); polishing.

PEMBROKE

Pembroke Antiques Centre

Wesleyan Chapel, Main St. Open 10-5. SIZE: Large. *STOCK: Pine, oak, mahogany and shipping furniture; china, rugs, paintings, Art Deco enamel signs, kitchenalia, pottery, curios and collectables.* TEL: 01646 687017.

PONTARDDULAIS, Nr. Swansea

The Emporium

112 St Teilo St. SA4 1SS. (Laura Jeremy). Est. 1992. Open 10.30-6. SIZE: Medium. *STOCK: Furniture, 1900-1950, £5-£500; Victorian metalware, collectables, bric-a-brac.* LOC: Off M4, junction 48. PARK: Easy. TEL: 01792 885185. SER: Restorations. FAIRS: Local.

PONTERWYD, Nr. Aberystwyth

Doggie Hubbard's Bookshop

Ffynnon Cadno. ABA. (C.L.B. Hubbard). Est. 1946. Open 10-5, Sun. by appointment. SIZE: Medium. *STOCK: Rare books on dogs, 16th-19th C, £50-£500; scarce books on dogs, 19th-20th C, £25-£100; other books on dogs, 20th C, £5-£25.* LOC: 1/2 mile from Ponterwyd westwards on A44. PARK: Easy. TEL: 01970 890224; home - same. SER: Valuations; buys at auction (rare dog books).

PORTHCAWL

Harlequin Antiques

Dock St. CF36 3BL. (Ann and John Ball). Est. 1974. Open 9-5. *STOCK: General antiques; textiles; early 19th to 20th C books.* TEL: 01656 785910.

PWLLHELI

Rodney Adams Antiques

Hall Place, 10 Penlan St. and 62 High St. LL53 5DH. Resident. Est. 1965. CL: Sun. except by appointment. *STOCK: Longcase clocks and period furniture.* TEL: 01758 613173; evenings - 01758 614337. VAT: Stan/Spec.

RHOSNEIGR

Fan-Fayre Antiques

High St. LL64 5UQ. Resident. (S. Richards). Est. 1976. Open summer only, winter by appointment. SIZE: Small. *STOCK: Jewellery, porcelain, silver, collectable items, 19th C, £25-£500.* LOC: 5 miles off A5 from the Holyhead Rd., on Anglesey Island. PARK: Easy. TEL: 01407 810580 (anwerphone). SER: Valuations. FAIRS: St. Martins, Birmingham; Newark and Nottinghamshire Showground.

RHUALLT, Nr. St. Asaph

Barbara Trefor Antiques

Rhuallt Hall. LL17 0TR. Est. 1967. Open by appointment any time. SIZE: Medium. *STOCK: General antiques and country furniture, £5-£5,000.* Not Stocked: Jewellery, cards and medals. LOC: On A55 take Rhuallt turning, B5429, grey stone farmhouse at end of village, close to Smithy Arms. PARK: Easy. TEL: 01745 583604.

RUTHIN

R. and S. M. Percival Antiques

Porth-y-Dwr, 65 Clwyd St. LL15 1HN. Est. 1979. Open daily, Sun. and Mon. by appointment. SIZE: Medium. *STOCK: Pine, mahogany and oak furniture and decorative smalls, 18th-19th C, £100-£1,000+.* PARK: Behind shop. TEL: 01824 704454; home - 01978 790370. SER: Valuations; buys at auction (furniture). FAIRS: Newark.

SARNAU

Ffynnon Las

SA44 6QT. (P. and G. Palmer). Est. 1971. Open at any time. SIZE: Small. *STOCK: Decorated furniture in American and European styles, 19th to early 20th C; stripped pine.* LOC: Off A487 9 miles north of Cardigan, down track. PARK: Easy. TEL: 01239 654648; home - same.

SWANSEA

James Allan

22 Park St. SA1 3DJ. (S.J. Allan). Est. 1929. Open 9.30-4.30. SIZE: Small. *STOCK: Jewellery, 1850 to date, £50-£5,000.* LOC: Off Kingsway, round corner from Mothercare. PARK: Nearby. TEL: 01792 652176. SER: Valuations. VAT: Stan.

Swansea continued

Bygone Antiques

38-39 St. Helens Rd. (C.A. Oliver). Open 9.30-5. *STOCK: China, furniture, linen and collectors' items.* TEL: 01792 468248.

Keith Chugg Antiques

Gwydr Lane, Uplands. Open 9-5.30, Sat. 9-1. *STOCK: Pianos and general antiques including furniture.* TEL: 01792 472477.

Clydach Antiques

83 High St., Clydach. SA6 5LJ. (R.T. Pulman). Open 10-5, Sat. 10-1. *STOCK: General antiques.* TEL: 01792 843209.

Philip Davies Fine Art LAPADA

130 Overland Rd., Mumbles. SA3 4EU. Open 10-5 (prior telephone call advisable). *STOCK: British oils, watercolours and prints, 1850-1950, £25-£10,000.* TEL: 01792 361766; fax - same. SER: Valuations; restorations (paintings and frames); commission sales.

Dylan's Bookshop

Salubrious Passage. SA1 3RT. (J.M. Towns). Open 10-5. *STOCK: Antiquarian books on Welsh history and topography, Anglo/Welsh literature and general books.* TEL: 01792 655255; fax - same.

Eynon Hughes Antiques

Henrietta St. (rear of 21 Walters Rd). (E. and M. Hughes). Est. 1984. Open 10.30-5.30. *STOCK: Longcase clocks, £500-£3,000; furniture, 18th-20th C, £50-£1,500; china and collectables, £5-£500.* PARK: Easy. TEL: 01792 651446; home - 01994 427253.

Anne and Colin Hulbert (Antiques and Firearms)

17 Approach Rd., Manselton. SA5 8PD. Est. 1962. CL: Sun. pm. SIZE: Small. *STOCK: Shipping goods and general antiques.* PARK: Easy. TEL: 01792 653818; home - same. SER: Valuations; buys at auction (furniture). *Trade Only.*

Edward Lawson Studio

110 Oxford St. SA1 3JJ. Est. 1981. Open Tues.-Fri. 10-3, prior telephone call advisable, or by appointment. *STOCK: Welsh topographical prints, 18th-19th C, £10-£500; Welsh maps, 17th-19th C, £15-£1,000; children's book illustrations, late 19th-early 20th C, £10-£30.* LOC: Lower Oxford Street, out of town centre towards Guildhall. PARK: Easy. TEL: 01792 643400. SER: Restoration; cleaning; framing.

Magpie Antiques

57 St. Helens Rd. SA1 4BH. (H. Hallesy). Est. 1984. Usually open 10-5. CL: Thurs. *STOCK: Ceramics including Swansea, Lllanelly and other Welsh potteries; oak and country furniture.* PARK: Opposite. TEL: 01792 648722. SER: Valuations; restorations (furniture).

Swansea continued

Kim Scurlock

25 Russell St. SA1 4HR. (B.D. and E.A. Leigh). Est. 1982. Open 10-5, Sat. 10-1. CL: Mon. SIZE: Medium. *STOCK: Victorian pine and country furniture, £25-£1,000; general antiques, china, glass and collectables; reproduction pine.* LOC: Between Walters Rd. and St. Helens Rd. PARK: Easy. TEL: 01792 643085. VAT: Stan.

Thicke Galleries LAPADA

SA2 8BG. (T.G. Thicke). Est. 1981. Open by appointment only. SIZE: Medium. *STOCK: Oils and watercolours, 19th C to early 20th C, to £8,000.* LOC: Coast road to West Swansea. PARK: Easy. TEL: 01792 207515. SER: Valuations; restorations (oils and watercolours). FAIRS: Robert Soper exhibitions; Alan Lewis; Towy; Cardiff Fine Art; Craig-y-nos. VAT: Spec.

SYNOD INN, Nr. Llandysul

Norman Williams

Trewyddel Forge, Gwenlli. SA44 6JJ. Open 10-4 (longer in summer), by appointment almost any time. SIZE: Medium. *STOCK: General antiques, furniture and decorative items, some Welsh quilts and blankets, 19th-20th C.* LOC: Between Aberaeron and Cardigan on the A487. PARK: Easy. TEL: 01545 580707; home - 01239 810330.

TEMPLETON, Nr. Narberth

Barn Court Antiques

Barn Court. SA67 7AR. (D., A. and M. Evans). Est. 1989. Open 10-5. SIZE: Medium. *STOCK: Mahogany, walnut, rosewood and oak furniture, Georgian to late Victorian, £100-£3,000; oils and watercolours, £100-£2,000; china and glass, mainly Victorian, £10-£500.* LOC: Off A40 on A478 Narberth to Tenby road. PARK: Easy. TEL: 01834 861224.

TENBY

Audrey Bull

15 Upper Frog St. SA70 7DJ. Open 9.30-5. *STOCK: Period and Welsh country furniture, general antiques, especially jewellery and silver.* TEL: 01834 843114; workshop - 01834 871873; home - 01834 813425. VAT: Spec.

Clareston Antiques

Warren St. SA70 7JS. (K. and Mrs M.J.A. Hunt). Est. 1964. Open 10-5, or by appointment. CL: Wed. SIZE: Small. *STOCK: Georgian and Victorian furniture; English and Welsh porcelain and pottery; silver and models.* LOC: Town centre, near police station. PARK: Easy. TEL: 01834 843350; home - same. SER: Valuations.

TINTERN

Tintern Antiques

The Old Bakehouse. NP6 6SE. (Dawn Floyd). Open 9.30-5.30. *STOCK: Antique jewellery and general antiques.* TEL: 01291 689705.

TREORCHY

All Old Exports Ltd.

Unit 35, Ynyswen Industrial Estate. CF42 6EP. (Steven Evans). Est. 1981. Open 9-5, Sat 10-4. SIZE: Warehouse. *STOCK: Victorian mahogany, Edwardian to 1920's oak, shipping goods.* LOC: Junction 34, M4, then A4119. PARK: Own. TEL: 01443 776410/431756; fax - 01443 776982; mobile - 0835 308567. SER: North American and Japanese market specialists; container packing and shipping. VAT: Stan/Spec.

TREVOR, Nr. Llangollen

Romantiques

Bryn Seion Chapel, Station Rd. LL20 7TP. (Miss S.E. Atkin). Est. 1994. Open 10-4 including Sun. SIZE: Large. *STOCK: Furniture, £100-£3,500; smalls, £1-£1,000.* LOC: Off A5 and A539 Llangollen road. PARK: Easy. TEL: Mobile - 0378 279614; home - 01978 752140. SER: Valuations; restorations (furniture, upholstery, clocks); buys at auction.

TYWYN

Welsh Art

(Miles Wynn Cato). Open by appointment only (also in London). *STOCK: Welsh paintings, 1550-1950; Welsh portraits of all periods and historical Welsh material.* TEL: 0171 259 0306 and 01654 711715.

USK

Castle Antiques

41 Old Market St. NP5 1AL. (S. Lockyer). Open 12-5 or by appointment. *STOCK: General antiques especially English and Welsh pottery, porcelain, blue and white transfer ware.* TEL: 01291 672424; home - 01495 785286.

WELSHPOOL

F.E. Anderson and Son LAPADA

5-6 High St. SY21 7JF. (D. and I. Anderson). Open daily. *STOCK: Furniture, 17th-19th C; mirrors, paintings and early metalware.* TEL: 01938 553340; home - 01938 590509/553324.

WREXHAM

Granny Midge's Emporium

1 Watery Rd. LL13 7NW. (Midge, Richard and Heugo Heard). Est. 1979. Open 10-5.30. SIZE: Large. *STOCK: Pine - antique, original, painted and stripped, to 1890's, £25-£3,000; decorative, garden, architectural and country items.* LOC: 5 minutes off Wrexham A483 bypass, leave at Ruthin exit, to town centre.. PARK: Own. TEL: 01978 365463. SER: Valuations; restorations (pine stripping, finishing and small repairs); buys at auction (as stock).

Index of Packers and Shippers: Exporters of Antiques (Containers)

LONDON

Anglo Pacific International plc LAPADA
Bush Industrial Estate, Standard Rd., NW10 6DF. Tel: 0181 965 0667; fax - 0181*j571*
serving worldwide destinations by land, sea or air. Free estimates and advice.

AR. GS International Transport Ltd
North London Freight Centre, York Way, Kings Cross, N1 0BB. Tel: 0171 833 3955; fax - 0171 837 8672. *Fine art and antiques removals by road transport, Europe especially Italy, door-to-door service. Documentation.*

B B F Fine Art Services Ltd
Copenhagen House, Copenhagen Place, E14 7DE. Tel: 0171 515 7005; fax - 0171 515 6001; e-mail - mailbox@bbfwwide.demon.co.uk. *Fine art packers, worldwide shippers by sea, air and road.*

Robert Boys Shipping
175D Bermondsey St., Newhams Row, SE1 3UW. Tel: 0171 357 7168; fax - 0171 357 7179. *World-wide shipping. Air and sea cargo. Specialists in fine art and furniture to Japan and part load containers to Japan (all ports) on a weekly basis. Japanese speaking staff.*

Bullens Ltd.
East Wing, The Granary, York Way. N1 0PF. Tel: 0181 347 9135. *Specialist comprehensive removal service.*

A French bisque-headed lady doll with her painted brisé fan held open before her face. It was for Parisiennes of this type, which were equipped with trunks, that many of the fans were intended. The swivel head incised with the size 'O'. c.1868. 13in. high.

From an article entitled 'Miniature Fans' by Constance King which appeared in the June 1998 issue of **Antique Collecting.**

London continued

Davies Turner Worldwide Movers Ltd.

London Headquarters : 49 Wates Way, Mitcham, CR4 4HR. Tel: 0171 622 4393; fax - 0171 720 3897; e-mail - dtwm@msn.com. *Fine art and antiques packers and shippers. Courier and finder service. Full container L.C.L. and groupage service worldwide.*

London continued

Featherstons

7 Ingate Place, SW8 3NS. Tel: 0171 720 0422; fax - 0171 720 6330. *Antiques and fine art packed and shipped or airfreighted worldwide. Security storage.*

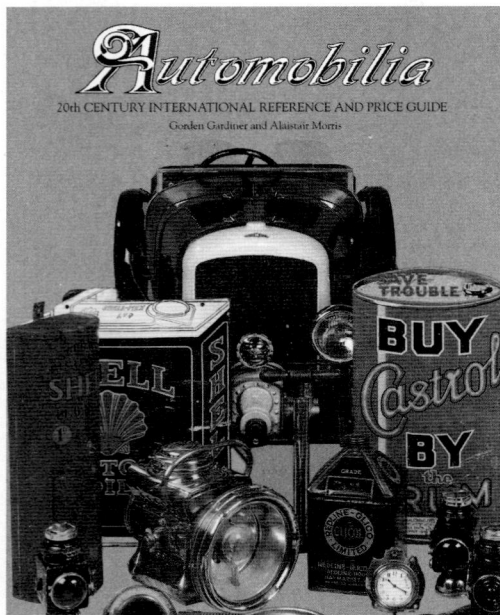

London continued

Gander and White Shipping Ltd

LAPADA

Head Office, 21 Lillie Rd., SW6 1UE. Tel: 0171 381 0571; fax - 0171 381 5428. ***Specialist packers and shippers of antiques and works of art.***

Gander and White Shipping Ltd

LAPADA

14 Mason's Yard, Duke St., St. James's, SW1Y 6BU. Tel: 0171 930 5383; fax - 0171 930 4145; cables - Gandite.

Hedleys Humpers Ltd

LAPADA

St Leonards Road, North Acton, NW10 6DJ. Tel: 0181 965 8733 (10 lines); fax - 0181 965 0249. ***Weekly door to door services to Europe, plus part load shipments by air and sea worldwide. Offices in London, Paris and New York.***

Interdean Ltd.

3/5 Cumberland Ave., NW10 7RU. Tel: 0181 961 4141; telex - 922119; fax - 0181 965 4484. *Antiques and fine art packed, shipped and airfreighted worldwide. Storage and international removals. Full container L.C.L. and groupage service worldwide.*

London continued

Interpack Worldwide plc

3 Standard Road, North Acton. NW10 6EX. Tel: 0181 965 5550; fax - 0181 453 0544. *Worldwide shipping, packing, insurance.*

Kuwahara Ltd LAPADA

6 McNicol Drive, NW10 7AW. Tel: 0181 963 1100; fax - 0181 963 0100. ***Specialist packers and shippers of antiques and works of art. Regular groupage service to Japan.***

Lockson Services Ltd LAPADA

29 Broomfield St., Limehouse, E14 6BX. Tel: 0171 515 8600 (6 lines); fax - 0171 515 4043; mobile (weekends) - 0831 621428; New York office - 201 861 3012; internet - www.lockson.co.uk; e-mail - enquiries@lockson.co.uk. ***Specialist packers and shippers of fine art and antiques by air, sea and road to the USA, Japan, Thailand, Far East, Canada and many more worldwide destinations. A complete personalised service. At all Olympia, Newark and Ardingly fairs. Offices in London and New York.***

Masterpack Ltd - Fine Art Packers & Shippers

Nationwide Building, Stanley Gardens, The Vale, W3 7SZ. Tel: 0171 262 8274; fax - 0171 262 5334. *Fine art packers and shippers. Personal service guaranteed.*

London continued

Momart Ltd
199-205 Richmond Rd., E8 3NJ. Tel: 0181 986 3624; fax - 0181 533 0122. *Fine art handling including transportation, case making and packing: import/export services, exhibition installation and storage.*

Stephen Morris Shipping plc
Barpart House, Kings Cross Freight Depot, York Way, N1 0UZ. Tel: 0171 713 0080; fax - 0171 713 0151; e-mail - stemo@aol.com. *Specialist packers and shippers of antiques and fine art worldwide. Weekly European service.*

Nelson Shipping
Unit C3, Six Bridges Trading Estate, Marlborough Grove, SE1 5JT. Tel: 0171 394 7770; fax - 0171 394 7707. *Expert export and packing service.*

Nippon Express (UK) Ltd
Unit A, Six Bridges Trading Estate, Marlborough Grove, SE1 5JT. Tel: 0171 237 8293; fax - 0171 231 4463. *Mainly Japanese imports/exports, both commercial and removals. Also import/export all other Far East countries.*

London continued

The Packing Shop
Plaza G13, 535 Kings Rd., SW10 0SZ. Tel: 0171 352 2021; fax - 0171 351 7576. *Fine art and general antiques shipped worldwide, especially United States and Europe.*

The Packing Shop
Unit L, London Stone Business Estate, Broughton St., SW8 3QR. Tel: 0171 498 3255. *Specialised service to overseas antique fairs and exhibitions. USA, Australasia and Europe regularly serviced.*

Pitt and Scott Ltd
60 Coronation Road. NW10 7PX. Tel: 0171 278 5585; fax - 0171 278 5592. *Packers and shippers of antiques and fine art. Shipping, forwarding and airfreight agents. Comprehensive service provided for visiting antique dealers. Insurance arranged.*

L.J. Roberton Ltd LAPADA
Marlborough House, Cooks Rd., Stratford, E15 2PW. Tel: 0181 519 2020; fax - 0181 519 8571.

London continued

Robinsons International LAPADA

The Gateway, Staples Corner. NW2 7AJ Tel: 0181 208 8484; fax - 0181 208 8488. ***Specialist packers and shippers of antiques and fine art worldwide. Established over 100 years.***

T. Rogers and Co. Ltd

PO Box No. 8, 1A Broughton St., SW8 3QL. Tel: 0171 622 9151; fax - 0171 627 3318. *Specialists in storage, packing, removal, shipping and forwarding antiques and works of art. Insurance.*

Trans-Euro Fine Art Division LAPADA

Drury Way, Brent Park, NW10 0JN. Tel: 0181 784 0100; fax - 0181 459 3376. ***Specialist packing and worldwide shipping services by air, sea and road. Single items, part loads or full containers. Courier and buyer services.***

Wingate and Johnston Ltd LAPADA

134 Queens Road, Peckham, SE15 2HR. Tel: 0171 732 8123; fax - 0171 732 2631. ***Specialists in the international movement of antiques and fine art for over a hundred and fifty years - services incorporate all requirements from case making to documentation and insurance. Freight groupage specialists.***

BUCKINGHAMSHIRE

Paget Shipping Ltd

Spaceregal Centre, Coln Industrial Estate, Old Bath Rd., Colnbrook, SL3 0NJ. Tel: 01753 682426; fax - 01753 686367. *Packing and shipping of antiques and works of art worldwide especially South America and Bermuda.*

CHESHIRE

The Rocking Chair Antiques

Unit 3, St. Peters Way, Warrington, WA27 7BL. Tel: 01925 652409; fax - same; mobile - 0374 492891. *Exporters and packers.*

DEVON

Barnstaple Removal and Haulage

86 Newport Road, Barnstaple. EX32 9BE. Tel: 01271 321121/321449. *Container packing and shipping worldwide.*

Bishop's Blatchpack

Kestrel Way, Sowton Industrial Estate, Exeter, EX2 7PA. Tel: 01392 420404; fax - 01392 423851. *International fine art packers and shippers.*

DORSET

Alan Franklin Transport LAPADA

26 Blackmoor Rd., Ebblake Industrial Estate, Verwood, BH31 6BB. Tel: 01202 826539; fax - 01202 827337. ***Container packing and shipping. Weekly door to door European service. Paris Office - 2 Rue Etienne Dolet, 93400 St. Ouen, Paris. Tel: 00 33140 115000; fax - 00 33140 114821. Belgian office - De Klerckstraat 41, B8300, Knokke. Tel: 00 3250 623579; fax - same.***

ESSEX

Geo. Copsey and Co. Ltd

Danes Rd., Romford. Tel: 01708 740714 or 0181 592 1003. *Worldwide packers and shippers.*

Crown Worldwide Movers

Security House, Abbey Wharf Industrial Estate, Kingsbridge Rd., Barking, IG11 0BD. Tel: 0181 591 3388; fax - 0181 594 4571. *Packers and shippers - 12 offices throughout U.K.*

GLOUCESTERSHIRE

The Removal Company - Loveday & Loveday

2 Wilkinson Rd., Cirencester, GL7 1YT. Tel: 01285 651505. *Shipping and packing.*

A.J. Williams (Shipping) LAPADA

607 Sixth Ave., Central Business Park, Hengrove, Bristol, BS14 9BZ. Tel: 01275 892166; fax - 01275 891333.

HAMPSHIRE

Cantay International LAPADA

Telford Rd., Basingstoke, RG21 6YU. Tel: 01256 465533; fax - 01256 324959. ***Specialist packers and shippers of antiques and fine art worldwide. A member of the Robinsons Group.***

Robinsons International LAPADA

16 Millbank St., Southampton, SO14 5QQ. Tel: 01703 220069; fax - 01703 331274. ***Specialist packers and shippers of antiques and fine art worldwide. Established over 100 years.***

Robinsons International LAPADA

Telford Rd., Basingstoke, RG21 6YU. Tel: 01256 465533; fax - 01256 324959. ***Specialist packers and shippers of antiques and fine art worldwide. Established over 100 years.***

KENT

Sutton Valence Antiques LAPADA

Unit 4, Haslemere Parkwood Estate, Sutton Rd., Maidstone, ME15 9NL. Tel: 01622 675332; fax - 01622 692593. ***Antique and shipping furniture. Container packing and shipping. Facilities for 20ft and 40ft containers, all documentation. Worldwide service.***

LANCASHIRE

A.M. Blackburn

14 Rainhall Crescent, Barnoldswick. Tel: 01282 815419. *Export, packers, shippers, courier service.*

Lancashire continued

Alan Butterworth (Horwich)
Tel: 01204 468094. Open by appointment. *Dealers, export packers and shippers; courier service - UK and Continent.*

Robinsons International LAPADA
32 Stanley Rd., Manchester, M45 8QXTel: 0161 766 8414; fax - 0161 767 9057. *Specialist packers and shippers of antiques and fine art worldwide. Established over 100 years.*

LEICESTERSHIRE

Richard Kimbell Ltd
The Old Bus Station, Harborough Road, Desborough. NN14 2QX. Tel: 01536 762093; fax - 01536 763263. *Container packers and shippers. Speedy despatch - competitive rates.*

MERSEYSIDE

John Mason International Ltd LAPADA
35 Wilson Rd., Huyton, Liverpool, L36 6AE. Tel: 0151 449 3938. *Specialist packer, full and part container loads, groupage service world-wide, courier and finder service.*

MIDDLESEX

Air-Sea Packing Group Ltd
Air-Sea House, Third Cross Rd., Twickenham, TW2 5EB. Tel: 0181 893 3303; fax - 0181 893 3068. *Specialist packers and shippers.*

MCN International
Unit 10 Shield Drive, West Cross Centre, Brentford TW8 8EX Tel: 0181 580 1001; fax - 0181 580 1002. *Fine interiors project management, antique and fine art shippers, incorporating Vitesse in conjunction with Federal Express.*

Sovereign International Freight Ltd
Sovereign House, 8-10 St. Dunstans Rd., Feltham, TW13 4JU. Tel: 0181 751 3131; fax - 0181 751 4517. *Heathrow Airport based shippers and packers registered to BS 5750 quality. Holders of the Queen's Award for Export and National Training Award. Specialist in antiques and the fine art trades.*

Vulcan International Services LtdLAPADA
Units 13/14, Ascot Rd., Clockhouse Lane, Feltham, TW14 8QF. Tel: 01784 244152; 01784 248183. *Fine art packers and shippers worldwide.*

OXFORDSHIRE

Cantay International LAPADA
Nuffield Way, Abingdon, OX14 1TN. Tel: 01235 552255; fax - 01235 553573. *Specialist packers and shippers of antiques and fine art worldwide. A member of the Robinsons Group.*

Cotswold Carriers
Unit 9, Worcester Rd. Industrial Estate, Chipping Norton, OX7 5XW. Tel: 01608 642856; fax - 01608 645295. *Removals, storage, shipping, door-to-door Continental deliveries.*

Oxfordshire continued

Robinsons International LAPADA
Nuffield Way, Abingdon, OX14 1TN. Tel: 01235 552255; fax - 01235 553573. *Specialist packers and shippers of antiques and fine art worldwide. Established over 100 years.*

SOMERSET

Robinsons International LAPADA
Ashmead Rd., Keynsham, Bristol. BS18 1SX. Tel: 0117 986 6266; fax - 0117 986 2723. *Specialist packers and shippers of antiques and fine art worldwide. Established over 100 years.*

SURREY

James Bourlet Inc. UK Ltd LAPADA
06 Beta Way, Thorpe Industrial Park, Crabtree Road, Egham, TW20 8RE. Tel: 01784 470000; fax - 01784 436252. *Fine art packing, freight forwarding. USA - 30-62 Revlon Avenue, Long Island City, New York NY 11101. Tel: (718) 392 9770; fax - (718) 392 2470.*

W. Ede & Co
The Edes Business Park, Restmor Way, Wallington, SM2 5AA. Tel: 0181 773 9388/9933; fax - 0181 773 9011. *Worldwide packing and shipping, complete documentation and removals service, container packing.*

SUSSEX EAST

Global Services
West St., Lewes, BN7 2NJ. Tel: 01273 475903. *Packers and shippers of antiques, arms, armour and fine works of art.*

SUSSEX WEST

Gander and White Shipping Ltd LAPADA
Newpound, Wisborough Green, Billingshurst, RH14 0AY. Tel: 01403 700044; fax - 01403 700814. *Specialist packers and shippers of fine art and antiques.*

Martells International
Queen's Road, East Grinstead, RH19 1BA. Tel: 01342 321303; fax - 01342 317522. *National and international removers, export packers and shippers.*

TYNE AND WEAR

Owen Humble (Packing and Shipping) Ltd
Clayton House, Walbottle Rd., Lemington, Newcastle-upon-Tyne, NE15 9RU. Tel: 0191 267 7220. *Worldwide service.*

WARWICKSHIRE

Crown Worldwide
Unit 9 Ratcliffe Road Industrial Estate, Ratcliffe Rd., Atherstone, CV9 1JA. Tel: 01827 714631.

WEST MIDLANDS

Thomas Blakemore Ltd - Shipping U.S.A.

The British Shop, Old Sandwell House, Sandwell Street, Walsall, WS1 3DR. Tel: 01922 721088; fax - 01922 611330; (USA - 910 434 1455; fax - 910 434 6759) *Weekly container from Birmingham to High Point, North Carolina, USA. Pick-up and pack, no minimums.*

Robinsons International LAPADA

585 Moseley Rd., Birmingham, B12 9BJ. Tel: 0121 449 4731; fax - 0121 449 9942. ***Specialist packers and shippers of antiques and fine art worldwide. Established over 100 years.***

WILTSHIRE

Martin Bros Ltd

The Old Sawmills, The Street, Kilmington, Nr Warminster. BA12 6RG. Tel: 01985 844144; fax - 01985 844113. *Specialist carriers of fine art and furniture throughout mainland UK.*

R. K. Neil Ltd - Scandinavia

Tel: 01985 844144; fax - 01985 844113. *Specialist carriers of fine art and furniture to Denmark, Sweden and Norway. Weekly door to door service.*

WORCESTERSHIRE

Simon Hall Freight

Units 5 and 6, Willersey Industrial Estate, Willersey, Nr. Broadway, WR12 7PR. Tel: 01386

Worcestershire continued

858555; fax - 01386 858501. *Specialist packers and shippers for fine art and antiques world wide. UK collections and deliveries. Humidity controlled containerised and conventional storage.*

YORKSHIRE EAST

Peter Smith t/a Boothferry Antiques

388 Wincolmlee, Hull, HU2 0QL. Tel: 01482 225220/666033. *Single items or container loads. Couriers covering north of England. Full documentation.*

SCOTLAND

Crown Worldwide Movers

Containerbase, Gartsherrie Rd., Coatbridge, Lanarkshire. ML5 2EL. Tel: 01236 449666; fax - 01236 449888. *Packers and shippers.*

Kuwahara Ltd LAPADA

33 Royal Park Terrace, Edinburgh, EH8 8JA. Tel: 0131 652 2131; fax - same. ***Specialist packers and shippers of antiques and works of art. Regular groupage service to Japan.***

WALES

Kuwahara Ltd LAPADA

54 Cathedral Rd., Cardiff, South Glam., CF1 9LL. Tel: 01222 224537; fax - 01222 229747. ***Specialist packers and shippers of antiques and works of art. Regular groupage service to Japan.***

Index of Auctioneers

LONDON

Academy Auctioneers and Valuers

Northcote House, Northcote Avenue, Ealing, W5 3UR. Tel: 0181 579 7466. *Monthly sales of antiques, collectables, works of art, furniture, paintings, ceramics, jewellery and silver. Regular general sales. Open 9-5. Valuations.*

Bloomsbury Book Auctions

3 and 4 Hardwick St., EC1R 4RY. Tel: 0171 833 2636/7 and 0171 636 1945. *Twenty-four sales per year of books, manuscripts and maps and especially disposal of academic libraries. Occasional sales of prints, posters and drawings. Sellers commission 15 % (trade 12.5%); buyers premium 15%.*

Bonhams Chelsea

65-69 Lots Rd., Chelsea, SW10 0RN. Tel: 0171 393 3900; fax - 0171 393 3906. *Regular sales of British, European and Russian Pictures including watercolours, oils, prints and frames; silver & objects of vertu; clocks; ceramics including Art Nouveau & Art Deco; furniture, carpets & objects of art; architectural including light fittings, fireplaces and garden statuary; collectors items such as toys, dolls & teddies, textiles, cameras & scientific instruments, rock & pop, rare records & entertainment sales. Viewing Mon.-Fri. 9-4.30, Sun. 11-4.*

Bonhams Knightsbridge

Montpelier St., Knightsbridge, SW7 1HH. Tel: 0171 393 3900; fax - 0171 393 3905. *Regular auctions of watercolours, Old Masters, European and modern pictures, portrait miniatures, prints, carved frames, furniture, clocks and watches, Lalique, commercial scent bottles, Oriental and contemporary ceramics, objects of art, tribal art and antiquities, silver, jewellery, objects of vertu, books and manuscripts, antique and modern guns, musical instruments, Oriental carpets and rugs. Annual theme sales to coincide with Cowes Week, The Boat Show and Crufts - pictures, sculptures and related works of art. Viewing Mon.-Fri. 9-4.30, Sun. 11-4.*

Christie's

8 King St., St.James's, SW1Y 6QT. Tel: 0171 839 9060; fax - 0171 839 1611. *Porcelain, pottery, objets d'art and miniatures, pictures including Old Masters, English, Victorian, Continental, Impressionist, Contemporary, prints, drawings,*

London continued

watercolours, Art Deco, Art Nouveau; Japanese and Chinese, Islamic and Persian works of art; glass, silver, jewellery, books, modern guns, furniture, carpets, tapestries, clocks and watches, garden statuary, photographs, Russian works of art, sculpture, wine, house sales (contents only).

Christie's South Kensington Ltd

85 Old Brompton Rd., SW7 3LD. Tel: 0171 581 7611; fax - 0171 321 3321; telex - 922061. *Sales of jewellery, silver, pictures, watercolours, drawings and prints; furniture and carpets, ceramics and works of art, printed books; costume, textiles and embroidery; toys and games, dolls, wines, Art Nouveau, Art Deco, cameras. Periodic sales of automata, mechanical music and vintage machines, motoring and aeronautical items including car mascots; Staffordshire portrait figures, pot-lids and Goss; miniatures, antiquities and cigarette and postcards.*

Forrest and Co Ltd

17-31 Gibbins Rd. Stratford, E15 2HU. Tel: 0181 534 2931. *Fortnightly general sales (Thurs.), including antiques and household furniture, china, glassware, carpets, rugs, pictures, prints, etc.*

Stanley Gibbons Auctions

399 Strand, WC2R 0LX. Tel: 0171 836 8444; fax - 0171 836 7342. *Three sales annually of philatelic material in London with Gt. Britian, British Empire and overseas stamps and postal history. Postal and telephone bidding available. Please send for a free copy of our Auction Information Pack and a sample catalogue.*

Glendining and Co

101 New Bond St., W1Y 0AS. Tel: 0171 493 2445. *Specialist auctioneers of coins and medals. Quarterly sales of coins; three sales annually of orders, decorations and medals.*

Harmers of London Stamp Auctioneers Ltd.

91 New Bond St., W1A 4EH. Tel: 0171 629 0218, fax - 0171 495 0260. *Auctions of Great Britain, British Commonwealth, Foreign countries, Airmail stamps, also postal history and literature, monthly. Fully illustrated catalogues. Valuations for sale, probate or insurance.*

London continued

Hornsey Auctions Ltd

54-56 High St., Hornsey, N8 7NX. Tel: 0181 340 5334; fax - same. *Sales weekly on Wed. at 6.30. Viewing Tues. 5-8 and Wed. from 10. Open Thurs, Fri. and Mon. 9.30-5.30 and Sat 11-4 to take in for next auction.*

Lloyds International Auction Galleries Ltd

118 Putney Bridge Rd., Putney, SW15 2NQ. Tel: 0181 788 7777. *Fortnightly sales of antique and modern furniture, china, glassware, pictures and collectables.*

Lots Road Galleries

71 Lots Rd., Chelsea, SW10 0RN. Tel: 0171 351 7771; fax - 0171 376 8349; internet - http://www.auctions-on-line.com/LotsRoad. *Auctions every Monday at 1 pm and 6 pm, approx. 600 lots of antique, traditional and decorative furniture, Oriental carpets, paintings, prints, ceramics, clocks, glass, silver, objets d'art and soft furnishings. On view 5-7 Thurs., 10-4 Fri., Sat. and Sun., all day Mon. Goods accepted Mon.-Fri. Payment by direct credit 9 days after the sale. Catalogue details and auction results by fax, phone or live auction line. Valuers, consultants and carriers. VAT registered.*

Thomas Moore Auctioneers Ltd.

217-219 High Rd., Greenwich, SE10 8NB. Tel: 0181 858 7848. *Weekly sales of porcelain, glass, silver, prints and furniture etc., mainly antique items. Periodic sales throughout the year of period antiques and objects - details on application. All sales on Thurs. at 10. Viewing Wed. 2-8 and Thurs. 9-10.*

Phillips

101 New Bond St., W1Y 0AS. Tel: 0171 629 6602; fax - 0171 629 8876; Internet - http://www.phillips-auctions.com/ *Regular sales of fine furniture, paintings, ceramics, jewellery, silver, clocks, watches, Oriental works of art, textiles, books, musical instruments, works of art, stamps, medals and decorative arts.*

Phillips Bayswater

10 Salem Rd., W2 4DL. Tel: 0171 229 9090. *Sales of furniture, porcelain and works of art each Mon. with the exception of four pre-arranged dates reserved for pianos. Sales of pictures/paintings alternate with those of collectors' items each Tues. Viewing Thurs. 5.15-7.30pm, Fri. 9-5, Sat. 9-12.30, Sun. 2-5, morning of sale. Buyers premium 15% plus VAT.*

Rippon Boswell and Co.

The Arcade, South Kensington Station, SW7 2NA. Tel: 0171 589 4242. *International specialist auctioneers of old and antique Oriental carpets. Approximately two auctions annually in London. Also in Germany, Switzerland, USA and Far East.*

London continued

Rosebery Fine Art Ltd.

The Old Railway Station, Crystal Palace Station Road, SE19 2AZ. Tel: 0181 778 4024. *Sales of antique furniture, ceramics, glass, works of art, pictures, silver, jewellery, books, toys, musical instruments, held twice a month on Tues. and Wed.*

Sotheby's

34-35 New Bond St., W1A 2AA. Tel: 0171 293 5000. *Open for free valuations Mon.-Fri. 9-5. Daily sales of paintings, drawings, watercolours, prints, books and manuscripts, European sculpture and works of art, antiquities, silver, ceramics, glass, jewellery, Oriental works of art, furniture, musical instruments, clocks and watches, vintage cars, wine, postage stamps, coins, medals, toys and dolls and other collectors' items.*

Southgate Auction Rooms

55 High St., Southgate, N14 6LD. Tel: 0181 886 7888. *Weekly Mon. sales at 5 pm of jewellery, silver, china, porcelain, paintings, furniture. Viewing Sat. 9-12 noon and from 9 on day of sale.*

BEDFORDSHIRE

Downer Ross (Auctioneers)

The Old Town Hall, Woburn, MK17 9PZ. Tel: 01525 290502. *Sales every four weeks on a Thurs.*

Wilson Peacock

The Auction Centre, 26 Newnham St., Bedford, MK40 3JR. Tel: 01234 266366. *Antiques sale first Fri. monthly. Viewing Thurs. prior 9-6. General sales every Sat. at 9.30.*

BERKSHIRE

Dreweatt Neate

Donnington Priory, Donnington, Nr. Newbury, RG14 2JE. Tel: 01635 31234; fax - 01635 522639. *Sales on the premises mainly on a weekly basis. General furnishings - fortnightly on Tues. Antique furniture - six annually. Paintings, books, prints, silver and jewellery, ceramics - three of each annually. Buyers' premium 11.75% including VAT.*

Edwards & Elliott

32 High St., Ascot, SL5 7HG. Tel: 01344 872588. *Regular sales of antique furniture, porcelain and glass; silver, plate and jewellery; oil paintings, watercolours and prints; rugs and assorted collectables at the Silver Ring Grandstand, Ascot Racecourse.*

Martin and Pole Nicholas

The Auction House, Milton Road, Wokingham, RG40 1DB. Tel: 0118 979 0460; fax - 0118 977 6166. *Sale of antiques and collectables held usually on 3rd Wed. every month at above address.*

Berkshire continued

Shiplake Fine Art Sales
(Thimbleby & Shorland) 31 Great Knollys Street, Reading, RG1 7HU. Tel: 0118 950 8611. *About six collective sales annually of antique, Victorian and all good quality modern furniture and effects, approximately 700 lots at Memorial Hall, Shiplake, Nr. Henley-on-Thames.*

Thimbleby & Shorland
31 Great Knollys St., Reading, RG1 7HU. Tel: 0118 950 8611. *Collective sales of antique and modern furniture and effects held monthly on Sat. at Reading Cattle Market. Also four specialist sales of horse-drawn vehicles, harness, horse brasses, driving sundries, whips and lamps, etc.*

BUCKINGHAMSHIRE

Amersham Auction Rooms
125 Station Road, Amersham, HP7 0AH. Tel: 01494 729292. *Weekly general and monthly selected antique sales held on Thurs. at 10.30.*

CAMBRIDGESHIRE

Cheffins, Grain and Comins
The Cambridge Saleroom, 2 Clifton Rd., Cambridge, CB1 4BW. Tel: 01223 213343 (10 lines). *Regular weekly and other specialist sales of furniture, clocks, porcelain, silver, pictures, sporting items, wine, rural and domestic bygones.*

Grounds and Co.
2 Nene Quay, Wisbech, PE13 1AG. Tel: 01945 585041/2. *Three specialist sales annually, each approximately 600 lots.*

Phillips
The Golden Rose, 17 Emmanuel Rd., Cambridge, CB1 1JW. Tel: 01223 66523. *Regular sales of good furniture, pictures, silver, jewellery, ceramics and Victoriana. Enquiries to David Fletcher.*

Wilson Peacock
The Auction Centre, 75 New Street, St Neots. PE19 1AN. Tel: 01480 474550. *General sale every Thurs. at 11. Viewing Wed. prior 9-8.*

CHESHIRE

Andrew, Hilditch and Son Ltd.
Hanover House, 1A The Square, Sandbach, CW11 0AP. Tel: 01270 767246/762048. *Quarterly sales of fine pictures and period furnishings. General and Edwardian furniture sales held weekly.*

Cheyne's
38 Hale Rd., Altrincham, WA14 2EX. Tel: 0161 941 4879. *Bi-monthly sales held at All Saints Church Hall, Hale Barns. Viewing day prior 2.30-4.30 and 6-8 and sale morning 9-10.30.*

Frank R. Marshall and Co.
Marshall House, Church Hill, Knutsford, WA16 6DH. Tel: 01565 653284. *Regular sales of antique furniture, objets d'art, silver, pewter,*

Cheshire continued

glass, porcelain, pictures, brass and copper. Fortnightly household collective sales including bric-a-brac. Specialised sales in The Knutsford Auction Salerooms.

Phillips North West
New House, 150 Christleton Rd., Chester, CH3 5TD. Tel: 01244 313936; fax - 01244 340028. 22 *salerooms countrywide including Chester.*

Peter Wilson Fine Art Auctioneers
Victoria Gallery, Market St., Nantwich, CW5 5DG. Tel: 01270 623878; fax - 01270 610508. *Bi-monthly sale on Wed. and Thurs. of fine art and antiques, Victorian and Edwardian items; viewing Sun. 2-4, Mon. and Tues. 10-4. Sales of later furnishings and household effects weekly on Thurs. at 11, viewing Wed. 10-4.*

Wright Manley
Beeston Castle Salerooms, Beeston Castle Smithfield, Tarporley, CW6 0DR. Tel: 01829 260318; fax - 01829 261208. *Fortnightly Victoriana and household sales and quarterly catalogued fine art and furniture sales.*

CORNWALL

Jefferys
The Auction Rooms, 5 Fore St., Lostwithiel, PL22 0BP. Tel: 01208 872245; fax - 01208 873260. *Sales of antique furniture, ceramics, glass, jewellery, silver and plate, pictures, prints and collectors items held on 3rd June, 5th August, 7th October and 9th December, 1998, all sales held on Wednesdays at 10 a.m.*

Lambrays
Polmorla Walk Galleries, The Platt, Wadebridge, PL27 7AE. Tel: 0120 881 3593. *Fortnightly sales of antiques and objets d'art. Illustrated catalogues issued.*

W.H. Lane & Son
Fine Art Auctioneers, 65 Morrab Rd.,Penzance, TR18 2QT. Tel: 01736 361447; fax - 01736 350097. *Six sales annually of antiques and objets d'art. Two specialist book sales annually. Six picture sales annually (specialists in the Newlyn and St. Ives Schools). Two specialist toy sales annually. Frequent house sales.*

David Lay FSVA
The Penzance Auction House, Alverton, Penzance, TR18 4RE. Tel: 01736 361414; fax - 01736 360035. *Regular sales of fine art, antiques, collectors' items, books and studio pottery. Three-weekly general household sales.*

Phillips Cornwall
Cornubia Hall, Par, PL24 2AQ. Tel: 01726 814047. *Monthly sales of antiques, Victorian and later furnishings, silver, jewellery, pictures and collectors' items.*

Cornwall continued

Pooley's

Regent Auction Rooms, Abbey St., Penzance. Tel: Salerooms - 01736 368814; office - 01736 363816. *Bi-monthly sales of antique furniture, objets d'art, silver and jewellery.*

Martyn Rowe Auctioneers and Valuers

Truro Auction Centre, Calenick St., Truro, TR1 2SG. Tel: 01872 2160020; fax - 01872 261794. *Weekly on Thurs. at 10 am - Victorian, Edwardian and general sales. Viewing morning of sale and previous Wed 2-6 pm. Antique and picture sales - every 6-8 weeks. Collectors and sporting sales - every 6-8 weeks. Quarterly sales of vintage and classic motorcycles, cars and automobilia. House, commercial, industrial and receivership sales on site or at auction centre.*

CUMBRIA

Cumbria Auction Rooms

12 Lowther St., Carlisle, CA3 8DA. Tel: 01228 25259. *Weekly sales of Victorian and later furniture and effects. Quarterly catalogue sales of antiques and works of art. Valuations.*

Mitchell's Auction Co.

The Furniture Hall, 47 Station Rd., Cockermouth, CA13 9PZ. Tel: 01900 827800; fax - 01900 828073. *Weekly (Thurs.) sales of antique, reproduction and modern furniture and effects, approximately 800 lots, starting at 9.30 am. Viewing Wed. 2.30-4.30 and throughout sale. Five fine art sales per annum, viewing Wed. prior 12-7 and prior to sale.*

James Thompson

64 Main St., Kirkby Lonsdale, LA6 2AJ. Tel: 015242 71555; fax - 015242 72939. *Monthly two day sales of silver, ceramics, general antiques. Picture sales six times a year.*

Thomson, Roddick and Laurie Ltd.

19 Crosby St., Carlisle, CA1 1DQ. Tel: 01228 28939/39636. *Bi-monthly catalogue sales of antiques and collectors' items and regular specialist sales particularly antiquarian books, silver and pictures at Dumfries and Carlisle. Monthly general furniture sales at Wigton and Annan (Dumfriesshire).*

DERBYSHIRE

Armstrong Auctions

Midland Rd., Swadllincote, DE11 0AH. Tel: 01283 217772. *Weekly general sales and periodic antique sales held in Swadlincote Auction Rooms.*

Neales

Becket Street, Derby DE1 1HW Tel: 01332 302601. *Bi-monthly specialist sales including decorative arts 1880-1960, incl. Arts & Crafts, Art Nouveau and Art Deco; paintings, drawings and prints; silver; plated ware and bijouterie; glass; European and Oriental ceramics, furniture, carpets*

Derbyshire continued

and rugs, bronzes and metalwork, clocks and barometers. Fortnightly collective sales (Tuesday) of general antique and later furnishings, shipping goods and reproduction furnishings, period and later ceramics, glass and decorative effects. Sales on the premises of the contents of town and country properties.

Noel Wheatcroft & Son

Matlock Auction Gallery, The Old Picture Palace, Dale Rd., Matlock, DE4 3LU. Tel: 01629 57460; fax - 01629 57956. *Monthly sales of antiques and general items.*

DEVON

Bearne's

St Edmund's Court, Okehampton St. Exeter EX4 1DU. Tel: 01392 422800. *Regular sales of antique furniture, works of art, silver, jewellery, collectors' items, books, clocks and watches, paintings, ceramics and glass, carpets and rugs.*

Bonhams - West Country

Dowell St., Honiton, EX14 8LX. Tel: 01404 41872; fax - 01404 43137. *Regular monthly auctions of furniture, works of art, ceramics, pictures, silver and jewellery, and collectors' items.*

Kingsbridge Auction Sales (J.A.S. Hawkins) inc. Charles Head and Son

113 Fore St., Kingsbridge, TQ7 1BG. Tel: 01548 856829. *Regular sales of antique and general household furniture and effects.*

Lyme-Bay Auction Galleries

28 Harbour Rd., Seaton. Tel: 01297 22453. *General household and antique auctions held every four to six weeks.*

Phillips

Alphin Brook Rd., Alphington, Exeter, EX2 8TH. Tel: 01392 439025; fax - 01392 410361. *Quarterly sales of antiques and fine art held at Ponderham Castle, near Exeter, to include silver, plated articles, jewellery, ceramics and glass, pictures and prints, objects and works of art, clocks and antique furniture. General sales of antique and later furniture and effects held at Alphin Brook Road Salerooms. Book sales held twice a year.*

Potbury and Sons

The Auction Rooms, Temple St., Sidmouth, EX10 8LN. Tel: 01395 515555; fax - 01395 512608. *Fortnightly sales; fine arts every two months.*

Rendells

Stone Park, Ashburton, TQ13 7RH. Tel: 01364 653017: fax - 01364 654251. *Sales every four weeks (Thurs. and Fri.) of antique and reproduction furniture, ceramics, silver, jewellery, pictures, clocks and barometers, copper and brass, miscellanea, toys and collectables. No buyers premium.*

Devon continued

Taylor's
Honiton Galleries, 205 High St., Honiton, EX14 8LF. Tel: 01404 42404. *Sales of paintings and prints, antiques, silver, books and porcelain.*

Ward and Chowen
Tavistock Auction Rooms, Market Rd., Tavistock, PL19 0BW. Tel: 01822 612603; fax - 01822 617311.

Whitton and Laing
32 Okehampton St., Exeter, EX4 1DY. Tel: 01392 252621; fax - 01392 496607. *Monthly auctions of antiques, silver and jewellery. Book auctions two or three times a year. General auctions weekly.*

DORSET

Cottees
The Market, East St., Wareham, BH20 4NR. Tel: 01929 552826; fax - 01929 554916. *Furniture and effects every two weeks.*

Hy. Duke and Son
Fine Art Salerooms, Weymouth Avenue, Dorchester, DT1 1QS. Tel: 01305 265080; fax - 01305 260101. *Regular six weekly sales including specialist sections of silver and jewellery, Oriental and English porcelain, English and Continental furniture, pictures, books and Oriental rugs. Complete valuation and advisory service, including insurance, probate and forward tax planning.*

Hy. Duke and Son
The Weymouth Auction Rooms, Nicholas St., Weymouth. Tel: 01305 761499; fax - 01305 260101. *Bi-weekly sales of Victoriana, later furniture, bric-a-brac and household effects. Valuation service for sale purposes.*

House and Son
Lansdowne House, Christchurch Rd., Bournemouth, BH1 3JW. Tel: 01202 298044. *Fortnightly sales of selected furniture, pictures, books, silver, porcelain and glass. Catalogues £2.50 including postage.*

Wm. Morey and Sons
Salerooms, St. Michaels Lane, Bridport, DT6 3RB. Tel: 01308 422078. *Antique and general sales held every three to four weeks on Thursdays.*

Phillips Auctioneers
Gild House, 70 Norwich Ave. West, Bournemouth, BH2 6AW and Long Street Salerooms, Sherborne. Tel: 01202 769352/01935 815271.

Riddetts of Bournemouth
Richmond Hill, Bournemouth Square, Bournemouth, BH2 6EJ. Tel: 01202 555686; fax - 01202 311004. *Fortnightly sales which include fine antiques, jewellery, silver, plate, pictures. Illustrated sale programme free. Catalogue subscription £40 p.a.*

Dorset continued

Southern Counties Auctioneers
The Livestock Market, Christys Lane, Shaftesbury, SP7 8PH. Tel: 01747 851735. *Monthly sales of antique furniture and effects.*

DURHAM

Denis Edkins
Auckland Auction Rooms, 58 Kingsway, Bishop Auckland, DL14 7JF. Tel: 01388 603095. *General and antique sales from time to time.*

G. Tarn Bainbridge and Son
Northern Rock House, High Row, Darlington, DL3 7QN. Tel: 01325 462633/462553. *Three to four collective sales annually and country house sales.*

Thomas Watson and Son
Northumberland St., Darlington, DL3 7HJ. Tel: 01325 462559. *Regular sales of antiques and good quality house contents.*

ESSEX

Black Horse Agencies - Ambrose
149 High Rd., Loughton, IG10 4LZ. Tel: 0181 502 3951; fax - 0181 532 0833. *Sales held monthly, contact for further details.*

Cooper Hirst Auctions
The Granary Salerooms, Victoria Rd., Chelmsford, CM2 6LH. Tel: 01245 260535. *Regular sales of antiques every 8/9 weeks and weekly Tues. sales of Victoriana, bric-a-brac etc. Catalogue subscription service available.*

Reeman Dansie Howe & Son
Head Gate Auction Rooms, 12 Head Gate, Colchester, CO3 3BT. Tel: 01206 574271. *Sales held every Wed. Viewing 9-7 Tues. prior. Bi-monthly Fine Art sales.*

Simon H. Rowland
Chelmsford Auction Rooms, 42 Mildmay Rd., Chelmsford, CM2 0DZ. Tel: 01245 354251. *Regular sales by order of the Sheriff of Essex and private vendors.*

Saffron Walden Auctions
1 Market St., Saffron Walden, CB10 1JB. Tel: 01799 513281. *Sales of antique and fine furniture, antique effects and objets d'art held every month.*

John Stacey & Sons (Leigh-on-Sea) Ltd
Leigh Auction Rooms, 86-90 Pall Mall, Leigh-on-Sea, SS9 1RG. Tel: 01702 77051. *Monthly sales of period and other furniture, works of art and collectors' items. Catalogue subscription £40.*

Stanfords
11-14 East Hill, Colchester, CO1 2QX. Tel: 01206 868070. *Weekly Tuesday sales of antique and modern furniture, china, glass, silver and decorative items at 10 a.m. Quarterly and monthly specialists sales of antique furniture and collectables - please ring for further information.*

Essex continued

G.E. Sworder and Sons

14 Cambridge Road, Stansted Mountfitchet CM24 8BZ. Tel: 01279 817778; fax - 01279 817779. *Monthly auctions of antique furniture, ceramics, silver, pictures, decorative items. Viewing Sat. prior 9-12 and Mon. prior 9-5. Weekly Thurs. at 11 auction of Victorian, Edwardian and later furniture and collectables. Viewing morning of sale and Wed. 2-5.*

Trembath Welch (incorporating J.M. Welch & Son)

Old Town Hall, Great Dunmow, CM6 1AU. Tel: 01371 873014; fax - 01371 875936. *At the Salerooms, Chequers Lane - selected antique furniture and effects sales quarterly. Sales of collectables, household furniture and antiques every two weeks. Catalogue subscription service available.*

GLOUCESTERSHIRE

Bristol Auction Rooms Ltd

St. John's Place, Apsley Rd., Clifton, Bristol, BS8 2ST. Tel: 0117 973 7201; fax - 0117 973 5671. *Six-weekly auctions of antique furniture, clocks, rugs, textiles, paintings and prints, glass, pottery, porcelain, books and ephemera, silver, objects of vertu, toys and collectables. View Sat. prior 9.30-1; day prior from 9.30-7, and on day from 9 to sale at 10.30. Fortnightly auctions of Victorian and modern household furniture and effects. View day prior to sale from 12-6 and on day from 9 until sale at 10.30. Specialist auctions and house sales held throughout the year. Catalogue subscription service. Buyers' premium.*

Bruton, Knowles

Albion Chambers, 111 Eastgate St., Gloucester, GL1 1PZ. Tel: 01452 521267. *Fine art auctioneers and valuers. House and collective sales held throughout the year. Valuations and inventories prepared.*

Corinium Galleries

25 Gloucester St., Cirencester, GL7 2DJ. Tel: 01285 659057. *Mon. auctions of postcards and small collectables every six weeks.*

Fraser Glennie and Partners

The Old Rectory, Siddington, Cirencester, GL7 6HL. Tel: 01285 659677; fax - 01285 642256. *Monthly sales of antiques, other furniture, collectors' items and musical instruments at the Bingham Hall, Cirencester.*

Mallams Fine Art Auctioneers and Valuers

26 Grosvenor St., Cheltenham, GL52 2SG. Tel: 01242 235712; fax - 01242 241943. Est. 1788. *Regular sales of furniture, ceramics, paintings, textiles, rugs and works of art, sporting, toy and collectors items.*

Gloucestershire continued

Moore, Allen and Innocent

33 Castle St., Cirencester, GL7 1QD. Tel: 01285 651831. *Monthly collective sales of over 1,000 lots of antique and other furniture and effects. Bi-annual specialist picture sales and sporting sales. Fri. at 10. Viewing day prior 10.30-8. 10% buyers premium.*

Short Graham and Co

City Chambers, 4/6 Clarence St., Gloucester, GL1 1DX. Tel: 01452 521177. *Sales of Georgian, Victorian, Edwardian and later furniture, ceramics, glass, metalwork, silver, plate, jewellery, miscellanea, collectors' items, books, pictures and outside effects every four to six weeks.*

Wotton Auction Rooms Ltd

(formerly Sandoe Luce Panes) Tabernacle Rd., Wotton-under-Edge, GL12 7EB. Tel: 01453 844733; fax - 01453 845448. *Large monthly catalogued two-day sales of 1,200-1,500 lots - all categories. Valuations.*

HAMPSHIRE

Basingstoke Auction Rooms

82-84 Sarum Hill, Basingstoke, RG21 1ST. Tel: 01256 840707. *Regular sales of antiques and fine art and fortnightly general sales. Occasional specialist sales. Catalogues available. Buyers' premium 10%.*

Hants. and Berks. Auctions

82-84 Sarum Hill, Basingstoke. Tel: 01256 840707. *Monthly sales at Heckfield Village Hall on Sat. 10.30. Viewing previous day 11-9. Sales include antiques, reproduction and household furniture, clocks, porcelain, glass, silver, pictures, etc. Occasional specialist sales. Catalogues available.*

Jacobs and Hunt

Lavant St., Petersfield, GU32 3EF. Tel: 01730 262744. *General antique sales every six to eight weeks on Fri.*

George Kidner

The Old School, The Square, Pennington, Lymington, SO41 8GN. Tel: 01590 670070; fax - 01590 675167. Emsworth Rd. - 01590 679487. *Monthly specialist sales - furniture, works of art, silver and jewellery, modern and antique guns and related items, collectors' items, oils, prints and watercolours, European ceramics and Oriental works of art. Viewing - Sat. previous 9.30-1, Mon. 9.30-4.30, Tues. 9.30-7. Also saleroom at Emsworth Rd., Lymington - Victorian, Edwardian and later furniture and effects. Viewing - day previous 9.30-7.*

May and Son

18 Bridge St., Andover, SP10 1BH. Tel: 01264 323417/363331; fax - 01264 338841. *Monthly sales of antique furniture and effects at Penton Mewsey Village Hall (Lots from private sources only). No buyers' premium.*

Hampshire continued

D.M. Nesbit and Co.
7 Clarendon Rd., Southsea, Portsmouth, PO5 2ED. Tel: 01705 864321; fax - 01705 295522. *Monthly sales of antique furniture, silver, porcelain and pictures.*

Phillips Auctioneers
54 Southampton Rd., Ringwood, BH24 1JD. Tel: 01425 473333.

Phillips Auctioneers
The Red House, Hyde St., Winchester, SO23 7DX. Tel: 01962 862515; fax - 01962 865166. *Sales of fine furniture, pictures, silver, jewellery, ceramics, metalware, clocks, rugs and works of art.*

Romsey Auction Rooms
86 The Hundred, Romsey, SO51 8BX. Tel: 01794 513331; fax - 01794 511770. *Monthly sales of antique and period furniture and effects and quarterly sales of silver, jewellery and plated items; regular toy sales.*

HEREFORDSHIRE

Russell, Baldwin and Bright
The Fine Art Saleroom, Ryelands Rd., Leominster, HR6 8NZ. Tel: 01568 611122; fax - 01568 610519. *Monthly 2-day sales of antiques and collectors' items (approx. 1,000 lots per sale). Two or three sales per month of antique and household effects.*

HERTFORDSHIRE

Brown and Merry - Tring Market Auctions
Brook Street, Tring, HP23 5EF. Tel: 0144282 6446. *Fortnightly Sat. sales of antiques and collectables held at The Market Premises, Brook St., Tring. Fine art sales held on last Fri. of alternate months.*

ISLE OF WIGHT

Shanklin Auction Rooms
79 Regent St., Shanklin, PO37 7AP. Tel: 01983 863441. *Monthly auctions of antiques and fine arts.*

Ways
The Auction House, Garfield Rd., Ryde, PO33 2PT. Tel: 01983 562255. *Five-weekly sales of antique and modern furniture, silver, copper and brass, oils, watercolours and prints, jewellery, china, clocks.*

KENT

Bracketts
Fine Art Auctioneers, Auction Hall, Pantiles, Tunbridge Wells, TN2 5QL. Tel: 01892 544500. *Fortnightly sales of antique and later furniture and effects and specialist antique sales.*

The Canterbury Auction Galleries
40 Station Rd. West, Canterbury, CT2 8AN. Tel: 01227 763337; fax - 01227 456770. *Bi-monthly auctions of Fine Art and Antiques held on Tues. at 10.30, viewing Mon. prior 10-7. Auctions of Victorian and later furniture held on the first Sat. of the month at 10, viewing Fri. prior 3-8. Valuations.*

Halifax Property Services formerly John Hogbin & Son
53 High St., Tenterden, TN30 6BG. Tel: 01580 763200. *Antique and other furniture and effects on Wednesdays, 18 sales per year.*

Hobbs Parker
Romney House, Ashford Market, Ashford, TN23 1PG. Tel: 01233 622222; fax - 01233 646642. *Monthly sales of antiques and household furniture.*

Hogben Auctioneers & Valuers
Unit C Highfield Industrial Estate, Off Warren Road, Folkestone, CT19 6DD. Tel: 01303 240808/246810; fax - 01303 246256. *Fine art saleroom - monthly sales.*

Kent continued

Ibbett, Mosely

125 High St., Sevenoaks, TN13 1UT. Tel: 01732 456731. *Antiques and objets d'art.*

Lambert and Foster Auction Sale Rooms

102 High St., Tenterden, TN30 6HU. Tel: 01580 762083. *Three offices in Kent. Monthly general sales of good quality antique furniture and effects.*

B.J. Norris

The Quest, West St., Harrietsham. ME17 1JD. Tel: 01622 859515. *Regular sales at The Agricultural Hall, Maidstone at 10. Viewing from 8 on morning of sale.*

Phillips

11 Bayle Parade, Folkestone, CT20 1SQ. Tel: 01303 245555; fax - 01303 259178. *Seventeen fine art and Victoriana sales each year.*

Phillips International Auctioneers & Valuers

49 London Rd., Sevenoaks, TN13 1AR. Tel: 01732 740310. *Alternating sales of antiques, collectors' items and Victoriana, 22 per year.*

LANCASHIRE

Acorn Auctions

PO Box 152, Salford, Manchester, M17 1BP. Tel: 0161 877 8818. *Tues. sales, approximately every 5 weeks, held at Unit 6, Block C, Astra Business Centre, Guiness Rd., Trafford Park, Manchester. 10 per year all specialising in paper collectables - postage stamps and history, manuscripts, autographs, picture and cigarette cards, books, prints, drawings and watercolours. Sales commence at 2 pm., viewing Mon. previous 10.30-6.30, and sale morning 9-1.15.*

Capes Dunn & Co Fine Art Auctioneers & Valuers

The Auction Galleries, 38 Charles St., Manchester, M1 7DB. Tel: 0161 273 1911; fax - 0161 273 3474. Est. 1826. *Catalogues of weekly specialist sales available on request. Regional office in Lytham.*

Kingsway Auction Rooms Ltd

The Galleries, Kingsway, Ansdell, Lytham St. Annes, FY8 1AB. Tel: 01253 735442. *Sales of antique, reproduction and modern furnishings and appointments held fortnightly or every three weeks on Tues. Approximately 400-600 lots commencing 9.30. Viewing Fri. 2-4, Mon. 9-7 and prior to sale. Buyers' premium 10%.*

Tony & Sons Ltd

2-8 Lynwood Rd., Blackburn, BB2 6HP. Tel: 01254 691748. *Monthly sales of antique, second-hand and modern jewellery. Valuations.*

Lancashire continued

Warren & Wignall Ltd

The Mill, Earnshaw Bridge, Leyland PR5 3PH. Tel: 01772 451430; fax - 01772 454516. *Sales of general antiques every three weeks. All sales Wed. at 10, viewing Tues. 9-7.*

LEICESTERSHIRE

Freckeltons

1 Leicester Rd., Loughborough, LE11 2AE. Tel: 01509 214564; fax - 01509 236114. *Monthly sales of general antiques.*

Gilding's Auctioneers and Valuers

Roman Way, Market Harborough, LE16 7PQ. Tel: 01858 410414. *Regular antique and Victoriana sales, with weekly general household sales.*

Heathcote Ball & Co

Castle Auction Rooms, 78 St. Nicholas Circle, Leicester, LE1 5NW. Tel: 0116 2536789; fax - 0116 2538517. *Auctions every four to six weeks.*

LINCOLNSHIRE

DDM Auctions Ltd

DDM Auction Rooms, Old Courts Road, Brigg, DN20 8JJ. Tel: 01652 650172; fax - 01652 650085. *Fine art and antique auctions held every seven weeks, also Victorian and household auctions fortnightly on a Saturday. Valuation clinic every Thursday morning. Catalogue subscription service available.*

Dowse

Foresters' Galleries, Falkland Way, Barton-upon-Humber, DN18 5RL. Tel: 01652 632335. *Monthly sales of general antiques and collectors' items.*

Eleys Auctioneers

1 Main Ridge West, Boston, PE21 6QQ. Tel: 01205 361687. *Regular antique and collectors sales.*

Escritt and Barrell

Saleroom - Dysart Rd. Office - 24 St Peter's Hill, Grantham, NG31 6QF. Tel: 01476 566991. *Three-weekly general shipping and antique sales, quarterly antique sales.*

Thomas Mawer and Son

63 Monks Rd., Lincoln, LN2 5HP. Tel: 01522 524984. *General sales fortnighly. Catalogued antique sales quarterly.*

Richardsons

Bourne Auction Rooms, Spalding Rd., Bourne, PE10 9LE. Tel: 01778 422686. *Antiques sales every month. Antique and modern sales every other Sat. Various specific sales periodically, eg silver, clocks, bygones, transport.*

Lincolnshire continued

Marilyn Swain

The Old Barracks, Sandon Rd., Grantham, NG31 9AS. Tel: 01476 568861; fax - 01476 576100. *Quarterly antiques and fine art sales. Fortnightly sales of Victorian and later general household furniture and effects.*

MERSEYSIDE

J. Kent (Auctioneers) Ltd.

2/6 Valkyrie Rd., Wallasey, L45 4RQ. Tel: 0151 638 3107; fax - same. *Weekly general sale; antiques, fine art and collectors' items on first Wed. of each month at 10. Viewing Tues. 9-6.*

Kingsley and Co. Auctioneers

3/4 The Quadrant, Hoylake, Wirral, L47 2EE. Tel: 0151 632 5821; fax - 0151 632 5823. *Sales every Tues. at 10, of antiques, fine arts, general chattels. Viewing Sat. 9-12.30, Mon. 9-5 and Tues. 9-10.*

Outhwaite and Litherland

Kingsway Galleries, Fontenoy St., Liverpool, L3 2BE. Tel: 0151 236 6561; fax - 0151 236 1070. *Victorian, Edwardian and modern furnishings - weekly Tues. General antiques and fine quality reproductions - monthly Tues. Fine art sales, including all works illustrative of the fine arts - monthly Wed. Specialist sales of books, wines, stamps etc. periodically. Members of SOFAA. Branch offices at Southport and Hoylake, Wirral.*

NORFOLK

Hugh Beck Auctions

The Cornhall, Cattle Market St., Fakenham, NR21 9AW. Tel: 01328 851557. *Weekly sales of antique and other furniture every Thurs. at 11. Country house sales as instructed.*

Clowes Nash Auctions

Norwich Livestock & Commercial Centre, Hall Rd., Norwich, NR4 6EQ. Tel: 01603 504488. *Antiques and general furniture weekly sales.*

Ewings

Market Place, Reepham, Norwich, NR10 4JJ. Tel: 01603 870473. *Periodic sales of antiques and modern furniture and effects.*

Thos. Wm. Gaze and Son

Diss Auction Rooms, Roydon Rd., Diss, IP22 3LN. Tel: 01379 650306. *Weekly catalogue sales of antiques and cottage furniture on Fri. at 11am. Periodic specialist sales including fine antiques, rural bygones, architectural, horse tack and carriages, automobilia, toys and scientific, etc.*

G.A. Key - Aylsham Salerooms

Incorporated Auctioneers, 8 Market Place, Aylsham, NR11 6EH. Tel: 01263 733195. *Three weekly sales of period, antique and Victorian furniture, silver, porcelain etc. Bi-monthly picture sales - oils, watercolours and prints etc. Six book sales annually and regular collectors' sales. Weekly sales of shipping and secondhand furniture.*

NORTHAMPTONSHIRE

Goldsmiths

15 Market Place, Oundle, PE8 4BA. Tel: 01832 272349. *Sales approximately bi-monthly.*

Heathcote Ball & Co Ltd

The Northampton Auction Galleries, Commercial St., Northampton, NN1 1PJ. Tel: 01604 622735 (office); 01604 37263 (auction). *Regular fine art and antique sales, fortnightly general sales, specialist sales. Mailing subscription £30 p.a; general sales details faxed fortnightly, £5 p.a. subscription.*

Southams

Corn Exchange, Thrapston, NN14 4JJ. Tel: 01832 734486. Est. 1900. *First Thurs. each month, viewing Wed. 9.30-8 sales of antiques and superior furniture, silver, plate, copper and brass, fine china, glass, Oriental rugs, oil paintings, watercolours and prints. 10% buyer's premium. Catalogues £2 including postage. Annual subscription £18.*

H. Wilford Ltd.

Midland Rd., Wellingborough, NN8 1NB. Tel: 01933 222760/222762. *Weekly sales of antique and modern furniture, shipping goods, jewellery etc. every Thurs. (over 1200 lots).*

NOTTINGHAMSHIRE

Arthur Johnson and Sons (Auctioneers)

The Nottingham Auction Centre, Meadow Lane, Nottingham, NG2 3GY. Tel: 0115 986 9128; fax - 0115 986 2139. *Approximately 1,000 lots weekly on Sat. at 10 am of antique and shipping furniture, silver, gold, porcelain, metalware and collectables.*

Mellors & Kirk

Gregory St., Nottingham, NG7 2NL. Tel: 0115 979 0000. *Weekly auctions of antiques, ceramics, glass, silver and jewellery on Fridays. Fine antiques and pictures every two months.*

Neales

192-194 Mansfield Rd., Nottingham, NG1 3HU. Tel: 0115 962 4141. *Bi-monthly specialist sales of paintings, drawings, prints and books; silver, jewellery, bijouterie and watches; European and Oriental ceramics and works of art, glass; furniture and decoration; clocks, barometers and mechanical music; metalwork, fabrics, needlework, carpets and rugs; collectors' toys and dolls; stamps, coins and medals, post and cigarette cards; autographs and collectors' items. Weekly collective sales (Mon.) of general antique and later furnishings, shipping goods and reproduction furnishings. Period and later ceramics, glass and decorative effects. Sales on the premises of the contents of town and country properties.*

Nottinghamshire continued

Phillips Inc. Henry Spencer and Sons - Fine Art Auctioneers

20 The Square, Retford, DN22 6XE. Tel: 01777 708633; fax - 01777 706724. *Specialist sales of furniture, carpets, ornamental items, works of art; paintings, drawings and prints; porcelain and glass, silver, jewellery and bijouterie. Non-specialist sales of furniture and effects held twice a month. Sales on the premises at town and country houses.*

Richard Watkinson and Partners

17 Northgate, Newark, NG24 1EX. Tel: 01636 77154. *Monthly sales of antique and Victorian furniture, oil paintings, silver etc. Weekly sales of early 20th C and general household furniture.*

OXFORDSHIRE

Dreweatt Neate Holloways

49 Parsons St., Banbury, OX16 8PF. Tel: 01295 253197; fax - 01295 252642. *General or specialist sales on the premises every other week. Buyers' premium 11.75% inc. VAT.*

Mallams

Fine Art Auctioneers, Bocardo House, 24A St. Michael's St., Oxford, OX1 2EB. Tel: 01865 241358. *Frequent sales of furniture, silver, paintings and works of art. House sales arranged on the premises.*

Messengers

Messengers Auction Centre, 27 Sheep St., Bicester, OX6 7JF. Tel: 01869 252901; fax - 01869 320283. *Victorian and general household sales, monthly. Antique auctions every 6-8 weeks. Bi-annual specialist sales of woodworking and other tools.*

Phillips International Fine Art Auctioneers

39 Park End St., Oxford, OX1 1JD. Tel: 01865 723524; fax - 01865 791064; internet - http://www.phillips-auctions.com. *Fortnightly sales of Victoriana and general effects. Specialist sales of fine furniture, rugs, works of art, silver, jewellery, ceramics, collectors' items and paintings throughout the year.*

Simmons and Sons

32 Bell St., Henley-on-Thames, RG9 2BH. Tel: 01491 571111; fax - 01491 579833. *Eight antique sales and eight general sales per year held at the saleroom Watcombe Manor, Ingham Lane, Watlington, Oxon. Sales start 10.30, viewing Sat. previous 9.30-12.30, previous day 10-8 and morning of sale.*

SHROPSHIRE

Halls Fine Art

Welsh Bridge Salerooms, Shrewsbury, SY3 8LA. Tel: 01743 231212; fax - 01743 271014. *Weekly household and Victoriana sales (Fri.). Monthly catalogued antique sales.*

Perry and Phillips

Auction Rooms, Old Mill Antique Centre, Mill St., Bridgnorth, WV15 5AQ. Tel: 01746 762248. *Weekly (Tues.) sales of good quality household furniture and effects. Monthly sales of antique furniture, Victoriana, china, porcelain, pictures etc. Regular specialist and house contents sales.*

SOMERSET

Aldridges of Bath

The Auction Galleries, 130-132 Walcot St., Bath, BA1 5BG. Tel: 01225 462830; fax - 01225 311319. *Weekly (Tues.) sales, broken down into specialist categories:- Antique furniture to include clocks and Oriental carpets; silver and porcelain, glass and metalware; paintings and prints; Victorian and general furniture. Viewing Sat. mornings and Mon. Catalogues available upon annual subscription. Large car park.*

Auction Centres - Mudford

Main Hall, Main Street, Mudford, Yeovil, BA21 5TE. Tel: 01935 851511. *Frequent sales - fine art and antiques, Victoriana and general, country house. Catalogues by post. Valuations. Storage and delivery.*

Clevedon Salerooms

Herbert Rd., Clevedon, BS21 7ND. Tel: 01275 876699; fax - 01275 343765. *Bi-monthly auctions of antique furniture, fine art and collectors' items. Fortnightly sales of Victorian, Edwardian and general furniture and effects. Occasional specialist sales and sales held on vendors' property. Valuations.*

Cooper & Tanner Chartered Surveyors

The Agricultural Centre, Standerwick, Frome, BA11 2QB. Tel: 01373 831010. *Weekly sales of antiques and general household chattels 10.30 am Wed. Viewing morning of sale. Haulage service.*

Gardiner Houlgate

The Old Malthouse, Comfortable Place, Upper Bristol Rd., Bath, BA1 3AJ. Tel: 01225 447933. *Regular sales of antique furniture and works of art. Frequent sales of Victorian and later furnishings. Fortnightly jewellery sales, quarterly musical instrument sales, specialist clocks and watches sales. Valuations.*

Greenslade Taylor Hunt Fine Art

Magdalene House, Church Square, Taunton, TA1 1SB. Tel: 01823 332525; fax - 01823 323923. *Weekly Wed. sales of Victorian and later furniture and household effects. Monthly, last Thurs., sales of antique furniture, metalwork, ceramics, glass, paintings and prints. Quarterly sales of silver, plate, jewellery and objects of vertu. Viewing 2 days prior 10-4.*

Somerset continued

Lawrence Fine Art Auctioneers Ltd.
South St., Crewkerne, TA18 8AB. Tel: 01460 73041; fax - 01460 74627. *Specialist auctioneers and valuers. Regular sales of antiques and fine art. General sales every Wednesday except first Wednesday of each month.*

Lawrence Fine Art Auctioneers Ltd.
The Corfield Hall, Magdalene St., Taunton, TA1 1SG. Tel: 01823 330567; fax - 01823 330596. *Three sales each month, General on first and third Tuesdays, Fine Art on the fourth Tuesday.*

The London Cigarette Card Co. Ltd
Sutton Rd., Somerton, TA11 6QP. Tel: 01458 273452; fax - 01458 273515. *Suppliers of thousands of different series of cigarette and trade cards and special albums. Publishers of catalogues, reference books and monthly magazine. Regular auctions in London and Somerset. S.A.E. for details. Showroom in West St. open Mon-Sat. or mail order.*

Mart Road Salerooms
Office - 13 The Parade, Minehead, TA24 5NL. Tel: Office - 01643 702281; saleroom - 01643 703646. *Regular sales every three weeks of antique and other furniture and effects at Mart Road Salerooms, Minehead. Occasional house clearances.*

Phillips Auctioneers - Bath
1 Old King St., Bath, BA1 2JT. Tel: 01225 310609. *Member of the Phillips Auction Group. Regular sales of antique furniture and Victoriana as well as silver and jewellery, pictures, books and fine wine, ceramics and glass and 20th C decorative items.*

Richards
The Town Hall, Axbridge, BS26 2AR. Tel: 01934 732969. *Bi-monthly sales of privately entered fine art and selected antiques of all categories and all types of collectable items. Valuations; inventories prepared.*

Tamlyn and Son
56 High St., Bridgwater, TA6 3BN. Tel: 01278 458241; fax - 01278 458242; saleroom - 01278 445251.

Wellington Salerooms
Mantle St., Wellington, TA21 8AR. Tel: 01823 664815. *Six-weekly sales of general antiques. Fortnightly sales of Victorian, Edwardian and shipping goods.*

Woodspring Auctions
Churchill Rd., Weston-super-Mare, BS23 3HD. Tel: 01934 628419. *Fortnightly sales of Edwardian and general furniture, brass, copper, glass, china and bric-a-brac.*

STAFFORDSHIRE

Bagshaws
The Estate Saleroom, High St., Uttoxeter, ST14 7HP. Tel: 01889 562811, fax - 01889 563795. *Monthly sales of Victorian and general household furniture and effects.*

John German
1 Lichfield St., Burton-on-Trent, DE14 3QZ. Tel: 01283 512244; fax - 01283 517896. *Occasional sales of major house contents; specialist fine art valuation department.*

Hall and Lloyd, Auctioneers
South St., Stafford, ST16 2DZ. Tel: 01785 58176; fax - 01785 228224. Est. 1882. *Regular fortnightly sales of antique and general household furniture and effects 1,000 or more lots every other Thurs. Special catalogued sales of antiques held regularly.*

Louis Taylor Fine Art Auctioneers
Britannia House, 10 Town Rd., Hanley, Stoke-on-Trent. ST1 2QG. Tel: 01782 214111. *Quarterly fine art sales including furniture, pictures, pottery, porcelain, silver and works of art. Specialist Royal Doulton and Beswick auctions. General Victoriana auctions held every two weeks.*

Wintertons
Lichfield Auction Centre, Fradley Park, Fradley, Lichfield, WS13 8NF. Tel: 01543 263256. *Bi-monthly sales of antiques and fine art and sales of Victorian and general furniture every 2-3 weeks.*

SUFFOLK

Abbotts Auction Rooms
Campsea Ashe, Nr. Woodbridge, IP13 0PS. Tel: 01728 746323; fax - 01728 746880. *Monthly sales of antique furniture & effects held on Wednesdays. Viewing two days prior. Sales calendar and catalogues available. Weekly sales of Victoriana & household furniture held on Mondays to coincide with livestock market. Viewing Sat. 9-11 am.*

H.A. Adnams
The Auction Room, St. Edmunds Rd. Office - 98 High St., Southwold, IP18 6DP. Tel: 01502 723292/724794.

Boardman - Fine Art Auctioneers
Station Road Corner, Haverhill, CB9 0EY. Tel: 01440 730414. *Large sales held quarterly specialising in selected fine furniture (particularly oak), clocks and paintings.*

Diamond Mills and Co. Fine Art Auctioneers
117 Hamilton Rd., Felixstowe, IP11 7BL. Tel: 01394 282281 (3 lines). Ipswich office - 01473 218600. *Periodic fine art sales. Monthly general sales. Auctions at The Orwell Hall, Orwell Rd., Felixstowe.*

Suffolk continued

Durrant's

10 New Market, Beccles, NR34 9HA. Tel: 01502 712122. *Antique and general furniture auctions every Fri. at Gresham Rd., Beccles.*

Lacy Scott and Knight Fine Art & Furniture

10 Risbygate St., Bury St. Edmunds, IP33 3AA. Tel: 01284 763531; fax - 01284 704713. *Quarterly sales of fine art including antique and decorative furniture, silver, pictures, ceramics etc. on behalf of executors and private vendors. Regular (every three weeks) sales of Victoriana and general household contents. Also quarterly sales of diecast and tinplate toys (2 of which include working steam scale models) and annual fine wine sales.*

Neal Sons and Fletcher

26 Church St., Woodbridge, IP12 1DP. Tel: 01394 382263. *Two special mixed antiques sales annually. Individual specialised sales and complete house contents sales as required. Household furniture sales on a Wednesday of each month.*

Olivers

The Saleroom, Burkitts Lane, Sudbury, CO10 6HB. Tel: 01787 880305. *Fortnightly sales of Victorian and later furniture and household effects. Regular sales of antiques and works of art. Enquiries to James Fletcher FRICS.*

Phillips East Anglia

32 Boss Hall Rd., Ipswich, IP1 5DJ. Tel: 01473 740494. *Four two-day specialist sales annually at Bury St. Edmunds. Twelve mixed sales in Ipswich.*

Suffolk Sales

The Saleroom, Church St., Clare, CO10 8PD. Tel: 01787 277993. *Sales of antiques and chattles held every three weeks on Sat. at 11 a.m., viewing Fri. 9-9 p.m, Sat. from 9 a.m.*

SURREY

Chancellors Auctions

74 London Rd., Kingston, KT2 6PX. Tel: 0181 541 4139. *Weekly sales on Thurs. One fine art and antiques sale each month. Viewing previous Tues. 2-8 and Wed. 9-5. Three general sales each month, viewing Wed. 2-8 and Thurs. 9-10.30. All sales start at 10.30.*

Clarke Gammon Fine Art Auctioneers

The Guildford Auction Rooms, Bedford Rd., Guildford, GU1 4SJ. Tel: 01483 566458; fax - 01483 563555.

Croydon Auction Rooms (Rosan and Co) (incorporating E.Reeves Auctions)

144/150 London Rd., Croydon, CR0 2TD. Tel: 0181 688 1123/4/5. *Fortnightly collective sales - 10 am Sat., viewing Fri. prior.*

Surrey continued

Ewbank Auctioneers

Burnt Common Auction Rooms, London Rd., Send, Woking, GU23 7LN. Tel: 01483 223101; fax - 01483 222171. *Monthly general and fine art sales on a Thurs., viewing Wed. 10am-9pm.*

Hamptons International

Baverstock House, 93 High St., Godalming, GU7 1AL. Tel: 01483 423567; fax - 01483 426392. *Regular (Wed. and Thurs.) fine art sales at 93 High Street, specialising in selected fine furniture, rugs, paintings and watercolours, porcelain, glass, jewellery, silver, objets d'art and books. Two sales each month of general and Victorian furniture, shipping goods and household effects, held on first and third Sat. House sales conducted on the premises when instructed. Valuations.*

Lawrences' - Auctioneers

Norfolk House, 80 High St., Bletchingley, RH1 4PA. Tel: 01883 743323; fax - 01883 744578. *Six-weekly antique and reproduction furniture and effects.*

Parkins

18 Malden Rd., Cheam, SM3 8SD. Tel: 0181 644 6633/4. *Sales of general household furniture and effects 2nd and 4th Mon. at 10. Viewing Fri. 2-4 and Sat. 10-4. Special antique sale on 1st Mon. at 10. Small antiques and collectables one Fri. evening each month at 7 pm - please telephone for details.*

Richmond and Surrey Auctions

The Old Railway Parcels Depot, Kew Road, Richmond, TW9 2NA. Tel: 0181 948 6677; fax - 0181 948 2021. Est. 1992. *Auctioneers, valuers and consultants. Sales every Thurs. 6pm.*

Wentworth Auction Galleries

21 Station Approach, Virginia Water, GU25 4DW. Tel: 01344 843711. *Antique and general sales every four to six weeks.*

P.F. Windibank Fine Art Auctioneers & Valuers

Dorking Halls, Reigate Rd., Dorking, RH4 1SG. Tel: 01306 884556/876280; fax - 01306 884669. *Antique auctions held every four to five weeks throughout the year.*

SUSSEX EAST

Burstow and Hewett

Abbey Auction Galleries and Granary Sale Rooms, Battle, TN33 0AT. Tel: 01424 772374. *Monthly sales of antique furniture, silver, jewellery, porcelain, brass, rugs etc. at the Abbey Auction Galleries. Also monthly evening sales of fine oil paintings, watercolours, prints, and engravings. At the Granary Sale Rooms - monthly sales of furniture, china, silver, brass, etc.*

Sussex East continued

Gorringe's Auction Galleries
Terminus Rd., Bexhill-on-Sea, TN39 3LR. Tel: 01424 212994; fax - 01424 224035. *Monthly sales of antique and modern furniture, metalware, European, Oriental, ceramics and glass, silver plate, plated goods, jewellery, bijouterie, objet d'art, pictures, libraries of books, etc.*

Gorringe's Auction Galleries
15 North St., Lewes, BN7 2PD. Tel: 01273 472503. *Sales approximately every six weeks of period furniture, Oriental carpets and rugs, oil paintings, watercolour drawings and prints, decorative china, glass, silver plate, jewellery etc.*

Graves, Son and Pilcher Fine Arts
Hove Street, Hove, BN3 2GL. Tel: 01273 735266; fax - 01273 723813. *Monthly sales of fine art including antique furniture, pictures, silver, Oriental carpets and rugs and ornamental items. Specialised sales of primitive art, coins, books and jewellery.*

Edgar Horn's Fine Art Auctioneers
46/50 South St., Eastbourne, BN21 4XB. Tel: 01323 410419. *Fortnightly antique and later furniture and effects sales (Tues). Six specialist antique furniture, silver and jewellery, ceramics and glass, oil paintings and watercolours and works of art sales (Wed).*

Raymond P. Inman
The Auction Galleries, 35 and 40 Temple St., Brighton, BN1 3BH. Tel: 01273 774777; fax - 01273 735660. *Monthly sales of antiques, furniture, china, brass, pictures, silver, jewellery, collectables, etc.*

Lewes Auction Rooms (Julian Dawson)
56 High St., Lewes, BN7 1XE. Tel: 01273 478221. *Antique furniture and effects every six weeks. General furniture and effects every Mon. (Salerooms - Garden Street).*

Wallis and Wallis
West Street Auction Galleries, Lewes, BN7 2NJ. Tel: 01273 480208. Est. 1928. *Nine annual sales of arms and armour, militaria, coins and medals. Specimen catalogue £4.50. Current catalogues £7. Die-cast and tin plate toys and models - catalogue £6.50. Commission bids (without charge) accepted. Valuations.*

SUSSEX WEST

John Bellman Ltd
New Pound, Wisborough Green, Billingshurst, RH14 0AY. Tel: 01403 700858; fax - 01403 700059. *Two day sale once a month - Thurs. am - ceramics and Oriental, Thurs. pm - silver, jewellery, clocks; Fri. am - furniture, Fri. pm - collectables, works of art, paintings. Viewing Mon. 9-4, Tues. 9-8, Wed. 9-4. Book sales quarterly.*

Sussex West continued

Denham's
Horsham Auction Galleries, Warnham, RH12 3RZ. Tel: 01403 255699; fax - 01403 253837. *Antique sales held monthly - good furniture of all periods, silver, jewellery, European and Oriental ceramics and collectors' items, paintings, drawings, prints and bronzes, metalware and Oriental carpets and rugs. Also monthly sales of general antiques, modern and shipping furniture. Periodic sales of books, stamps, coins and medals, arms and armour and specialist collections as advertised.*

R.H. Ellis and Sons
44/46 High St., Worthing, BN11 1LL. Tel: 01903 238999. *Monthly specialist auctions of antique, Victorian and Edwardian furniture and porcelain. Quarterly auctions of silver, watercolours, paintings, Oriental carpets and rugs.*

King & Chasemore
Midhurst Auction Rooms, West St., Midhurst, GU29 9NQ. Tel: 01730 812456; fax - 01730 814514. *General sales of antique and modern furniture and effects every six weeks.*

Phillips Fine Art Salerooms
Baffins Hall, Baffins Lane, Chichester, PO19 1UA. Tel: 01243 787548. *Sales monthly on Wed. at 10 am of antique and reproduction furniture, clocks, silver, porcelain, paintings, Persian and other carpets. Viewing day prior and Sat morning prior.*

Sotheby's Sussex
Summers Place, Billingshurst, RH14 9AD. Tel: 01403 783933; fax - 01403 785153. *Regular sales of paintings, furniture, carpets, clocks, ceramics, glass, silver, jewellery, vertu, sporting guns, medals, militaria, armour, aeronautica, toys, dolls, Oriental items and garden statuary.*

Stride and Son
Southdown House, St. John's St., Chichester, PO19 1XQ. Tel: 01243 780207; fax - 01243 786713. *Sales last Fri. monthly - antiques and general; periodic book and document sales.*

Sussex Auction Galleries
59 Perrymount Rd., Haywards Heath, RH16 3DR. Tel: 01444 414935. *Auctions of antiques and reproduction furniture and effects including ceramics, silver and jewellery, clocks, Persian rugs and Victoriana. Also regular sales of lost/found property from Sussex Police Authority and handling agents from Gatwick Airport. Annual catalogue subscription £22.*

Worthing Auction Galleries
Fleet House, Teville Gate, Worthing, BN11 1UA. Tel: 01903 205565. *Fortnightly sales alternating between antique, general, reproduction and modern furniture and china, glass, silver, plate, jewellery, objet d'art, pictures and clocks. Viewing Sat. prior 9-12 and Mon. 9-1 and 2-4 prior to sale on Tues. or We. commencing at 10 am.*

TYNE AND WEAR

Anderson and Garland

Fine Art Salerooms, Marlborough House, Marlborough Crescent, Newcastle-upon-Tyne, NE1 4EE. Tel: 0191 232 6278; fax - 0191 261 8665. *Regular sales of paintings, prints, antique furniture, silver and collectors' items.*

Anderson and Garland

Kepier Chare, Crawcrook, Ryton, NE40 4TS. Tel: 0191 413 8348. *Fortnightly sales of Victorian and later furnishings.*

Boldon Auction Galleries

24a Front St., East Boldon, NE36 0SJ. Tel: 0191 537 2630. *Quarterly antique auctions.*

Thomas N. Miller Auctioneers

Algernon Rd., Byker, Newcastle-upon-Tyne, NE6 2UN. Tel: 0191 265 8080; fax - 0191 265 5050. *Antique auctions every Tuesday and Wednesday.*

WARWICKSHIRE

Bigwood Auctioneers Ltd

The Old School, Tiddington, Stratford-upon-Avon, CV37 7AW. Tel: 01789 269415. *Monthly Victoriana sales. Monthly sales of fine furniture and works of art. Quarterly sales of wines, sporting goods and other specialist sales. Catalogues and calendars on request. Valuations for all purposes.*

Black Horse Agencies - Locke and England

18 Guy St., Leamington Spa, CV32 4RT. Tel: 01926 889100; fax - 01926 470608. *Antique furniture, porcelain, pictures, silver each month at The Salerooms Walton House, 11 The Parade, Leamington Spa. Shipping goods, Victorian and Edwardian furniture, household effects and collectables weekly. House contents sales. All sales held Thurs. 11 am. Telephone for further details or catalogues.*

John Briggs and Parsley

17 Market Street, Atherstone, CV9 1ET. Tel: 01827 718912. *Auctions on clients' instructions.*

Henley-in-Arden Auction Sales Ltd

The Estate Office, Warwick Rd., Henley-in-Arden, B95 5BH. Tel: 01564 792154. *Sales of antique and modern furniture and effects, second Sat. each month.*

Warwick and Warwick Ltd

Chalon House, Scar Bank, Millers Road, Warwick, CV34 5DB. Tel: 01926 499031; fax - 01926 491906. *Philatelic auctioneers and private treaty specialists. Stamp auctions held monthly. Post-cards, cigarette cards, autographs, ephemera, medals, militaria, coins and other collectables sold by auction periodically.*

WEST MIDLANDS

Biddle & Webb

Ladywood Middleway, Birmingham, B16 0PP. Tel: 0121 455 8042. *Fine art sales first Fri. monthly; antique sales on second Fri. monthly; silver, jewellery, medals, coins and watches on fourth Fri. monthly; toys, dolls, model railways and juvenalia sales on Fri. alternate months, all sales at 11. Weekly Tues. sales of Victoriana and collectables at 10.30.*

Fellows and Sons

Augusta House, 19 Augusta St., Hockley, Birmingham, B18 6JA. Tel: 0121 212 2131; fax - 0121 212 1249. *Auctioneers and valuers of jewels, silver, fine art.*

James and Lister Lea

1741 Warwick Rd., Knowle, B93 0LX. Tel: 01564 779187. Est. 1846. *Three sales annually of contents of country and town houses as required. All sale items are from private sources with an emphasis on the more unusual collectors' items. Buyer's premium 10% plus VAT.*

Old Hill Antiques & Auction Rooms

220 Halesowen Rd., Old Hill, Cradley Heath, B64 6HN. Tel: 01384 411121. *Auctioneers and valuers.*

Phillips Midlands

The Old House, Station Rd., Knowle, Solihull, B93 0HT. Tel: 01564 776151. *Specialised weekly sales of fine furniture and works of art; silver and jewellery; Victoriana; paintings; collectors' items; ceramics and 19th-20th C decorative arts; books. Free sales programme and subscription on request.*

Walker Barnett and Hill

Waterloo Road Salerooms, Clarence St., Wolverhampton, WV1 4JE. Tel: 01902 773531; fax - 01902 712940. *Monthly sales of fine reproduction furniture and effects on last Monday of each month at 10.30. Bailiffs/County Court auctions. Fine art and antique sales every 6/8 weeks.*

Weller and Dufty Ltd

141 Bromsgrove St., Birmingham, B5 6RQ. Tel: 0121 692 1414; fax - 0121 622 5605. *Ten sales annually, approximately every five weeks, of antique and modern firearms, edged weapons, militaria etc. Periodic sales of specialist items - military vehicles and associated military equipment. Postal bids accepted. Illustrated catalogue available.*

WILTSHIRE

Hamptons Auctioneers & Valuers

20 High St., Marlborough, SN8 1AA. Tel: 01672 516161; fax - 01672 515882. *Antique and selected quality furniture and effects sales first Wed. bi-monthly. General household sales first Wed. bi-monthly and every third Wed. monthly.*

Wiltshire continued

Swindon Auction Rooms

The Planks, Old Town, Swindon, SN3 1QP. Tel: 01793 615915. *General sales every Saturday at 10am. Antique section on first Saturday in the month.*

Woolley and Wallis

Salisbury Salerooms Ltd 51-61 Castle St., Salisbury, SP1 3SU. Tel: 01722 424500; fax - 01722 424508. *Monthly sales of antique furniture. Specialised sales of porcelain and pottery, glass and metalwork, Eastern carpets and rugs, books and maps, paintings, watercolours and prints, textiles, fans, lace, toys and dolls, musical instruments, collectables, Oriental furniture and ceramics, works of art. Quarterly sales of silver and plate, jewellery, watches, objects of art and wines. Fortnightly sales of household furniture.*

WORCESTERSHIRE

Griffiths and Co.

57 Foregate St., Worcester, WR1 1DZ. Tel: 01905 26464.

Philip Laney FRICS - Fine Art

The Portland Room, Portland Rd., Malvern, WR14 2TA. Tel: 01684 893933. *Monthly sales of antiques and collectors' items.*

Phipps and Pritchard

Bank Buildings, Kidderminster, DY10 1BU. Tel: 01562 822244 and 822187. *Regular six-weekly sales of antique furniture, watercolours and oil paintings, copper, brass, glass, china and porcelain, stamps and coins, weapons. Private house sales also conducted.*

Philip Serrell - Auctioneers & Valuers

The Malvern Sale Room, Barnards Green Rd., Malvern. Tel: 01684 892314. *Bi-monthly catalogued antique and fine art auctions. Fortnightly general sales. Specialist on the premises sales. Free sales estimates.*

YORKSHIRE EAST

Gilbert Baitson

The Edwardian Auction Galleries, Wiltshire Rd, Hull, HU4 6PG. Tel: 01482 500500; after hours - 01482 645241; fax - 01482 500501. *Sales of antique and modern furnishings every Wed. at 10.30. Viewing day prior until 8 pm.*

Dee Atkinson & Harrison - Agricultural and Fine Arts

The Exchange Saleroom, Driffield, YO25 7LJ. Tel: 01377 253151; fax - 01377 241041. *Regular bi-monthly sales of antiques, Victorian, Edwardian and quality furnishings, paintings, silver, jewellery etc. Viewing two days prior. Fortnightly household sales. Biennial collectors' toys and sporting sales.*

Yorkshire East continued

H. Evans and Sons

1 St. James's St., Hessle Rd., Hull, HU3 2DH. Tel: 01482 323033; fax - 01482 211954. *Five antiques sales annually, fortnightly general furniture and effects.*

Spencers Auctioneers and Estate Agents

The Imperial and Repository Salerooms, 18 Quay Rd., Bridlington, YO15 2AP. Tel: 01262 676724. *General auctions every Thurs. Regular sales of antiques and fine arts.*

YORKSHIRE NORTH

Bairstow Eves Fine Art

West End Rooms, The Paddock, Whitby, YO21 3AX. Tel: 01947 820033/820011. *Monthly antiques sales. 10% buyers premium including VAT.*

Boulton and Cooper Ltd

St. Michaels House, Market Place, Malton, YO17 0LR. Tel: 01653 696151. *Members of SOFAA. Alternating monthly antique sales at Malton and York. Fortnightly general sales at Pickering.*

H.C. Chapman and Son Ltd

The Auction Mart, North St., Scarborough, YO11 1DL. Tel: 01723 372424; fax - 01723 500697; internet - http://www.thesaurus.co.uk/hcchapman. *Members of SOFAA. Monthly special sales of antiques and fine art held on Tues., viewing Fri. 4-7, Sat. 10-4, Mon. 9-12. Annual catalogue subscription £45. Weekly Mon. sales of Edwardian and later furniture, household miscellanea and modern furnishings. Viewing Sat. 10-4 and Mon. from 9.*

Hutchinson-Scott

The Grange, Marton-le-Moor, Ripon, HG4 5AT. Tel: 01423 324264. *Periodic general sales plus two or three catalogue sales annually. Specialist in fine antiques and works of art.*

James Johnston

The Square, Boroughbridge, YO5 9AS. Tel: 01423 322382. *Monthly collective auction sales of antique and later furniture and effects at The Village Hall, Whixley, Nr. York and occasional private dispersal sales.*

Morphets of Harrogate

6 Albert St., Harrogate, HG1 1JL. Tel: 01423 530030; fax - 01423 500717. *Sales of antiques and works of art, interspersed with regular sales of general furniture and effects. Catalogue subscription scheme.*

Scarthingwell Auction Centre

Scarthingwell, Nr. Tadcaster, LS24 9PG. Tel: 01937 557955. *Evening antique and general sales held twice-monthly on Mon. and Tues. evenings, approx 900 lots. Viewing on prior Sun. 12-5 and from 4 on sale days.*

Yorkshire North continued

Stephenson and Son

20 Castlegate, York, YO1 1RT. Tel: 01904 625533. *Six sales annually of antique and Victorian furniture, silver and paintings.*

Summersgill Auctioneers

8 Front St., Acomb, York, YO2 3BZ. Tel: 01904 791131. *Auctions of antiques and household effects and collectors' items.*

Tennants

The Auction Centre, Leyburn, DL8 5SG. Tel: 01969 623780; fax - 01969 624281. *Minimum of three 1000 lot non-catalogue sales each month of antiques and later house contents, mainly on Sat. at 9.30, viewing Fri. 9-7. Three fine art sales each year. Catalogue subscription service. Specialist sales of collectors' items, books, etc.*

YORKSHIRE SOUTH

A.E. Dowse and Son Sheffield

Cornwall Galleries, Scotland St., Sheffield, S3 7DE. Tel: 0114 2725858; fax - 0114 2490550. *Monthly Sat. sales of antiques. Quarterly sales of diecast, tin plate and collectors' toys. Monthly sales of modern furniture and shipping goods.*

YORKSHIRE WEST

De Rome

12 New John St., Westgate, Bradford, BD1 2QY. Tel: 01274 734116/9. *Regular sales.*

Andrew Hartley Fine Arts

Victoria Hall Salerooms, Little Lane, Ilkley, LS29 8EA. Tel: 01943 816363. *Fifty sales annually including six good antique and fine art and other specialist sales.*

Phillips at Hepper House

17a East Parade, Leeds, LS1 2BH. Tel: 0113 2448011; fax - 0113 2429875. *Monthly sales of antique furniture and objets d'art and regular speciality sales of pictures, ceramics, silver and jewellery, etc.*

John H. Raby & Son

Salem Auction Rooms, 21 St. Mary's Rd., Bradford, BD8 7QL. Tel: 01274 491121. *Sales of antique furniture and pictures every four to six weeks, shipping goods and collectables every week.*

CHANNEL ISLANDS

Bonhams & Langlois Auctioneers

Westaway Chambers, Don St., St. Helier, Jersey, JE2 4TR. Tel: 01534 22441; fax - 01534 59354. *Regular antique and specialised auctions, weekly general sales (Wed).*

SCOTLAND

Christie's Scotland

164-166 Bath St., Glasgow, Lanarkshire, G2 4TB. Tel: 0141 332 8134; fax - 0141 332 5759. *Regular specialist sales of jewellery, silver, furniture, paintings, together with sales of particular Scottish interest, including golfing and football memorabilia, whisky, Wemyss Ware.*

Frasers (Auctioneers)

8a Harbour Rd., Inverness, Inverness-shire, IV1 1SY. Tel: 01463 232395; fax - 01463 233634. *Weekly sales on Wed. at 6 pm.*

Leslie and Leslie

Haddington, East Lothian, EH41 3JJ. Tel: 01620 822241; fax - same. *General auctions every three months.*

Loves Auction Rooms

52-54 Canal St., Perth, Perthshire, PH2 8LF. Tel: 01738 633337; fax - 01738 629830. *Regular sales of antique and decorative furniture, jewellery, silver and plate, ceramics, works of art, metalware, glass, pictures, clocks, mirrors, pianos, Eastern carpets and rugs, garden furniture, architectural items. Weekly Fri. sales of Victoriana and household effects at 10.30. Specialist sales of books and collectors' items. Valuations.*

Lyon and Turnbull Ltd

51 George St., Edinburgh, Midlothian, EH2 2HT. Tel: 0131 225 4627.

Macdougalls Auctioneers & Valuers

Lower Breakish, Breakish, Isle of Skye, IV42 8QA Tel: 01471 822777; fax - same. *Sales held every eight weeks of antiques and general furniture. Sales held Sat. at 2pm in Broadford Hall (10 mins. from the Skye bridge).*

McTear's

Clydeway Business Centre, 8 Elliot Place, Glasgow G3 8EP. Tel: 0141 221 4456; fax - 0141 641 5035. *Weekly Fri. sales at 10.30 of antique, reproduction and shipping furniture, jewellery, silver, porcelain and paintings. Viewing prior Thurs. 10-5.*

John Milne

9 North Silver St., Aberdeen, Aberdeenshire, AB1 1RJ. Tel: 01224 639336. *Weekly general sales, regular catalogue sales of antiques, silver, paintings, books, jewellery and collectors' items.*

Robert Paterson & Son

8 Orchard St., Paisley, Glasgow, PA1 1UZ. Tel: 0141 889 2435. *Fortnightly Tuesday sales.*

Phillips Scotland

207 Bath St., Glasgow, G2 4HD. Tel: 0141 221 8377. *Monthly general sales of Victorian and later effects; specialist sales of furniture, works of art, books, carpets, 20th C decorative arts and Scottish contemporary art throughout the year.*

Scotland continued

Phillips Scotland
65 George St., Edinburgh, Midlothian, EH2 2JL. Tel: 0131 225 2266. *Regular specialist sales of oil paintings and watercolours; furniture, Oriental carpets, clocks and works of art; silver and jewellery; books, Oriental and European ceramics and glass. Bi-annual sales of decorative arts; dolls and textiles. Fortnightly sales of Victoriana.*

L.S. Smellie and Sons Ltd.
The Furniture Market, Lower Auchingramont Rd., Hamilton, Lanarkshire, ML10 6BE. Tel: 01698 282007. *Fine antiques auctions - third Thurs. in Feb., May, Aug. and Nov. Weekly sales every Mon. at 10 am. (600 lots) household furniture, porcelain and jewellery.*

Taylor's Auction Rooms
11 Panmure Row, Montrose, Angus, DD10 8HH. Tel: 01674 672775. *Antiques sales held every second Sat.*

Thomson, Roddick & Laurie Ltd.
60 Whitesands, Dumfries, Dumfriesshire, DG1 2RS. Tel: 01387 255366. *Quarterly catalogued antique and collectors sales, sporting sales, silver and jewellery sales.*

Scotland continued

Thomson, Roddick & Laurie Ltd.
20 Murray Street, Annan, Dumfriesshire, DG12 6EG. Tel: 01461 202575. *Bi-monthly sales of household furnishing and effects.*

WALES

Dodds Property World
Victoria Auction Galleries, Mold, Clwyd, CH7 1EB. Tel: 01352 752552. *Weekly Wed. auctions of general furniture and shipping goods at 10.30am. Bi-monthly auctions of antique furniture, silver, porcelain and pictures etc. at 10.30am on Sat. Catalogues available.*

Peter Francis
Curiosity Salerooms, King St., Carmarthen, South Wales SA31 1BH. Tel: 01267 233456/7. *Antiques sales held every six weeks. Household sales at regular intervals.*

Harry Ray & Co
Lloyds Bank Chambers, Broad Street, Welshpool, SY21 7RR. Tel: 01938 552555. *Monthly country sales.*

Rennies
87 Monnow St., Monmouth, Gwent, NP5 3EW. Tel: 01600 712916. *Periodic sales of antique furniture and effects, usually on Thurs.*

Adye Mary Fedden, RA, LG, PPRWS, OBE, Hon. Litt Bath University (born Bristol, Avon, 14th August 1915), 'Circus Horses', oil on masonite board, 20in. x 24in. Signs work 'Fedden'. As a strategy to launch the publication of her biography, Mary was persuaded to mount solo shows at the Coram Gallery and Beaux Arts London in 1995; however, it has not been her practice for some years to stage such exhibitions. Many galleries have her paintings from time to time but particularly rewarding sources are Thompson's Gallery, 18 Dover Street, London W1X 3PB (tel: 0171 629 6878) and Manya Igel Fine Arts. Price guide: drawings, £500; watercolours, £400 upwards; oil paintings, £600 upwards. Such is the demand for her paintings that prices at auction have been particularly strong in recent years. For example, in 1996 at Sotheby's, a 1961 oil painting, 30in. x 24in., of fruit and flowers, sold, with buyer's premium, for £7,475. (Manya Igel Fine Arts Ltd)

From an article entitled 'Contemporary British Artists' which appeared in the June 1998 issue of **Antique Collecting.**

Services

This section has been included to enable us to list those businesses which do not sell antiques but are in associated trades, mainly restorations. The following categories are included.

Art, Books, Carpets & Rugs, Ceramics, Clocks & Barometers, Consultancy, Courier, Enamel, Engraving, Fireplaces, Framing, Furniture, Glass, Insurance & Finance, Ivory, Jewellery & Silver, Locks & Keys, Metalwork, Photography, Reproduction Stonework, Suppliers, Textilers, Tortoiseshell, Toys.

We would point out that the majority of dealers also restoreand can give advice in this field.

Below are listed the trade associations mentioned within this section.

BAFRA	-	British Antique Furniture Restorers' Assn
FTAG	-	Fine Art Trade Guild
GADAR	-	Guild of Antique Dealers & Restorers
GMC	-	Guild of Master Craftsmen
MBHI	-	Member of British Horological Institute
UKIC	-	UK Institute for Conservation
CGCG	-	Ceramic & Glass Conservation Group
BTCM	-	British Tradtional Cabinet Makers
BFMA	-	British Furniture Manufacturers Assn
BCFA	-	British Contract Furniture Assn
ASFI	-	Assn of Suppliers to Furniture Industry
GAI	-	Guild of Architectural Ironmongers
MBWCG	-	Member British Watch & Clockmakers Guild

ART

Armor Paper Conservation Ltd

Glebe Cottage, 2 The Green, Garsington, Oxon. OX44 9DF. Tel: 01865 361741; fax - 01865 361815. *Conservation and restoration of drawings, prints, watercolour paintings, documents and archive material.*

Richard Bennett

18 Kirkgate, Thirsk, Yorks North. YO7. Tel: 01845 524085; home - same. UKIC, AABPR. Est. 1979. Open by appointment. *Oil paintings cleaned and lined on the premises; gilt/gesso frames restored and repaired; framing.*

Art continued

Paul Congdon-Clelford

14 Bostock Close, Sparsholt, Winchester, Hants. SO21 2QH. Tel: 01962 776495. IPC, ABPR, FATG, GADAR. *Conservator of oil paintings and works on paper; collection and delivery.*

Claudio Moscatelli Oil Painting Restoration

46 Cambridge St., London SW1V 4QH. Tel: 0171 828 1304. Associate member Assn British Picture Restorers. *Oil paintings cleaned, relined, retouched and varnished.*

Art continued

Plowden & Smith Ltd

190 St Ann's Hill, London SW18 2RT. Tel: 0181 874 4005; fax - 0181 874 7248. *3 Royal Warrants. Full conservation and restoration service for all types of objects including outside statuary, monuments and buildings. Undertake mounting, display and exhibition. Any type of fine art problem dealt with.* VAT: Stan.

BOOKS

Brignell Bookbinders

2 Cobbles Yard, Napier St., Cambridge, Cambs. CB1 1HP. Tel: 01223 321280; fax - same. Society of Bookbinders, GMC. Est. 1982. *Book restoration, conservation, table tops, leather photo cases, journal and thesis bindings, boxes and limited editions.* VAT: Stan.

The Dummy Book Company

1 Cow Shed, Upton Grove, Tetbury, Glos. Tel: 01666 503376. TADA. (Jonathan Eaton). View by appointment. *Manufacturer of a wide range of book themed gifts, including desk accessories, storage hides and clocks. Faux book spines for use within the home or office.*

The Manor Bindery Ltd.

Calshot Rd., Fawley, Southampton, Hants. SO4 1BB. Tel: 01703 894488; fax - 01703 899418. *Manufacturers of false books, either to use as a display or for cabinet makers to apply to doors and cupboards. Also book tables, decorative objects and accessories, various decorative replica book boxes. Leather library shelf edging and range of cabinets with false book doors. Individual items made to order with a book theme.*

CARPETS & RUGS

Barin Carpets Restoration

57a New Kings Rd., London SW6 4SE. Tel: 0171 731 0546. GMC. Conservation Register Museums and Galleries Commission. *Oriental carpets, rugs, European tapestries, Aubussons expertly cleaned, restored and lined. Expert advice, free estimates.*

The Restoration Studio

Unit 11 Kolbe House, 63 Jeddo Rd., London W12 9EE. Tel: 0181 740 4977. Member Rug Restorers Assn. *Restoration, cleaning, lining and mounting of tapestries, Aubusson carpets, kilims and all kinds of needlework.*

CERAMICS

Ceramic Restorations

Unit 15 Coppull Mill, Mill Lane, Coppull, Chorley, Lancs. PR7 5AN. Tel: 01257 792835; fax - 01257 793994. (Simon Bennett and Alan Jones). *Quality restoration of all ceramics and glassware using latest technology, experienced team undertakes restorations for individuals, trade and auction houses in UK and and Europe. Free estimates, regular collections and deliveries within London area.* VAT: Stan.

Ceramics continued

China Repairers

64 Charles Lane, London NW8 7SB. Tel: 0171 722 8407. (H. Howard and V. Baron). Est. 1952. *Specialised restoration of all pottery and porcelain; restoration courses given.*

The China Repairers

1 Street Farm Workshops, Doughton, Tetbury, Glos. Tel: 0166 503551. TADA. (Mrs A. Chalmers). *Long established china restorers and, more recently, mirror and picture frame gilders. Awarded Royal Warrant.*

Porcelain Repairs

240 Stockport Rd., Cheadle Heath, Stockport, Cheshire. SK3 0LX. Tel: 0161 428 9599; fax - 0161 286 6702. CGCG, UKIC. (I. Norman and A. Jones). Est. 1970. *Highest standard restorations of European and Oriental ceramics, especially under glaze blue and white, museum repairs, carat gilding and modelling. Cracks and crazing removed without any overpainting or glazing.*

CLOCKS & BAROMETERS

Clive and Lesley Cobb

3 Pembroke Crescent, Hove, East Sussex. BN3 5DH. Tel: 01273 772649. Listed by the Conservation Unit of the Museum and Galleries Commission. Est. 1972. *Quality, sympathetic restoration of lacquer clock cases and furniture, and painted clock dials.*

Edmund Czajkowski and Son

See entry under BAFRA (Lincs.)

Martin H. Dunn

Glebe Farm, Clarke's Rd., North Killingholme, Lincs. DN40 3JQ. Tel: 01469 540901; fax - 01469 541512. Guild of Lincolnshire Craftsmen. *Clock movements and dials, brass work. Agent for several German clock movement makers.* VAT: Stan.

Richard Higgins (Conservation)

See entry under BAFRA (Shrops).

E. Hollander

1 Bennetts Castle, 89 The Street, Capel, Dorking, Surrey. RH5 5JX. Tel: 01306 713377; fax - 01306 712013. Open by appointment. *Restoration of all forms of clocks, mechanisms, cases, dials and barometers.*

Clocks and Barometers continued

A.C. Layne

48 Cecil St., Carlisle, Cumbria. CA1 1NT. Tel: 01228 545019. Open 8-11.30 and 1-4. *Repairs to antique clocks and complicated watches.*

Robert B. Loomes

3 Kings Rd., Stamford, Lincs. PE9 1HD. Tel: 01780 481319. MBWCG. Strictly by appointment. *British antique clock restoration - longcase, lantern and bracket. Dial restoration, brass and painted dials. Valuations.*

Lynton Clocks and Dials

22 Norwich St., Fakenham, Norfolk. NR21 9AE. Tel: 01328 863666; fax - 01485 518650. LBHI. MWCG. *Clock repairs and restorations. Manufacturers and restorers of vitreous enamelled dials up to 12" diameter.*

William C. Mansell

24 Connaught St., London W2. Tel: 0171 723 4154. *Specialists in repair/restoration of antique clocks and vintage watches.*

Meadows and Passmore Ltd

Medmaw House, Farningham Rd., Crowborough, East Sussex. TN6 2JP. Tel: 01892 662255; fax - 01892 662277. *Clock and barometer parts, tools and materials. Mail Order Only.*

Menim Restorations

Bow St., Langport, Somerset. Tel: 01458 252157. GMC. Est. 1830. *Specialists in English and French clocks, full cabinet making and horological service; French polishing.*

Newcombe and Son

89 Maple Rd., Penge, London SE20 8UL. Tel: 0181 778 0816. MBHI, GMC, Conservation Register of Museums and Galleries Commission. *Specialist repair and restoration of fine quality longcase, bracket and wall clocks. Barometers repaired, silvering and gilding, clock faces (including enamel) restored or repainted, brass and wooden frets, clock hands, all hand cut and finished to order, clocks bought and sold.*

Repton Clocks

Acton Cottage, 48 High St., Repton, Derbys. DE65 6GF. Tel: 01283 703657; fax - 01283 702367. MBWCMG; MBHI. Open by appointment 9-6. CL: Sat. *Antique and modern watch and clock restoration; musical box repairs; gear cutting; clocks made to order.*

Kevin Sheehan

15 Market Place, Tetbury, Glos. Tel: 01666 503099. TADA. Open 9-4.30, Sat. 10-12. *Specialist repairer of English and French 18th-19th C clocks. Written estimates given, all work guaranteed. Awarded Royal Warrant.*

Clocks and Barometers continued

Southerns

Precista House, 48/56 High St., Orpington, Kent. BR6 0JH. Tel: 01689 824318/875206; fax - 01689 870079; e-mail - 106212.3302@compuserve.com. BJA; MBWCG; Jewellery Industry Distributors Assn. *Watch and clock replacement and restoration materials; specialised tools for the horological trade.* VAT: Stan. *Trade Only.*

A.R. Webb

9 Northam Rd., Southampton, Hants. SO14 0NZ. Tel: 01703 221546. Open 9-5. *Restorer of clocks and watches.*

CONSULTANCY

Athena Antiques

59 Elvetham Rd., Fleet, Hants. Tel: 01252 615526; home - same. (Richard Briant). Est. 1975. Available seven days by appointment. *Consultancy; valuations (jewellery, silver, clocks and furniture); restorations (clocks and furniture); buys at auction on commission.* LOC: Near Fleet railway station.

John Fell-Clark LAPADA

84 Ledbury Rd., London W11 2AH. Tel: 0171 229 0224; home - same. Est. 1971. By appointment. *Valuations; restorations; consultancy and interior design; buys at auction (17th-20th C furniture and tapestries).* LOC: Off Westbourne Grove. VAT: Spec.

Geoffrey Godden

3 The Square, Findon, West Sussex. Tel: 01903 873456. *Consultant and lecturer in ceramics.*

David Pettifer Ltd

73 Glebe Place, London SW3 5JB. Tel: 0171 352 3088; fax - same. Est. 1963. Open Tues.-Thurs. 9-6. *Consultant and agent for 18th to early 19th C furniture and works of art.*

COURIER

Antique Tours

11 Farleigh Rise, Monkton Farleigh, Nr. Bradford-on-Avon, Wilts. BA15 2QP. Tel: 01225 858527 (24 hr. answerphone); mobile - 0860 489831. (C.J. Veal). Est. 1988. *Private hire chauffeur service; car tours of antique shops in the West Country, or any other area, for up to four persons; service to and from air and sea ports; packing and shipping arranged. Genealogical research also undertaken.*

The English Room

London SW1 4PY. Tel: 0171 720 6655; fax - 0171 978 2397. (Mrs Val Cridland). Est. 1985. By appointment only. *Search and courier (trade and private), London and country - shipment of goods purchased aranged.* Stan/Spec.

Courier continued

Personal Touring Services

25 Howard Rd., London SE25 5BU. Tel: 0181 656 3207; fax - same. (John and Jane Goldsmith). *Driver guided tours to major antiques fairs, multi-dealer centres and individual dealers in the UK, except Ireland. One to eight passengers can be accommodated in a choice of estate car or luxury minibus. Itineraries prepared, accommodation selected and reserved, packing and shipping arranged, airport transfers undertaken.*

Neil Robson Antiques Courier Service

10 Towrise, Sulgrave, Banbury, Oxon. OX17 2SB. Tel: 01295 760045; mobile - 0385 785447. TVADA. *Complete service for overseas buyers, throughout Britain and into Europe. Personalised itineraries covering all aspects of the trade - specialist dealers, fair, markets, auction, restorers and reproduction sources. Clients met at airport with spacious car or people carrier and accompanied throughout trip. Collection, packing, shipping and documentation of goods arranged.*

ENAMEL

Istvan Markovits - Enameller Consultant

11 Mallard Place, Strawberry Vale, Twickenham, Middx. TW1 4SW. Tel: 0181 891 1743; mobile - 0498 570770. *Badgemakers. Worldwide restorers of enamel antique jewellery. Restorers of clock faces and ceramics.*

ENGRAVING

Edward J. Woods - Hand and Machine Engravers

30 Hillborough Rd., Westcliff-on-Sea, Southend, Essex. SS0 0SA. Tel: 01702 340436. GMC. Est. 1970. *Engraving for silversmiths, polishers and platers, jewellery manufacturers; chapter rings, barometer dials, etc.* VAT: Stan.

FIREPLACES

Antiques and Restoration

Old Town Hall, Antique Village, Levenshulme, Manchester, Lancs. Tel: 0161 256 4644; mobile - 0976 985982. (Lesley Bright). Open 10-5, Sun. 11-4. *Antiques, fireplaces and restoration, also carpentry and re-claimed pine furniture.*

FRAMING

Natural Wood Framing

Eight Bells Gallery, 14 Church St., Tetbury, Glos. Tel: 01666 505070. FATG; TADA. *Bespoke framing specialising in antiques, textiles and restorations. Contemporary and sporting art stocked.*

FURNITURE

British Antique Furniture Restorers' Association (In county order)

Bedfordshire

Duncan Everitt - D.M.E. Restorations Ltd

11 Church St., Ampthill, Beds. MK45 2PL. Tel: 01525 405819; fax - 01525 756177. BAFRA.

Berkshire

Graham Childs - Alpha (Antique) Restorations

High St., Compton, Newbury, Berks. RG20 6NL. Tel: 01635 578245; mobile - 0860 575203. BAFRA. *Fine oak, walnut and mahogany. Traditional hand finishes. Veneering and inlaying Clock cases.*

Ben Norris & Co

Knowl Hill Farm, Knowl Hill, Kingsclere, Newbury, Berks. RG15 8NY. Tel: 01635 297950; fax - 01635 299851. BAFRA. *All aspects of furniture restoration including carving, gilding, copy chair making and architectural woodwork. BADA Dip. Excellent storage facilities.* VAT: Stan.

Buckinghamshire

David Hordern Restorations (Thame) Ltd.

8/9 Lea Lane, Thame Rd., Long Crendon, Aylesbury, Bucks. HP18 9RN. Tel: 01844 202213; fax - 01844 202214. BAFRA. *Boulle, cabinetwork, carving, gilding, lacquer, leather, marble, marquetry, ormolu, upholstery.*

Cambridgeshire

Ludovic Potts

Unit 1/1A, Haddenham Business Park, Station Rd., Haddenham, Ely, Cambs. CB3 3XD. Tel: 01353 741537; fax - 01353 741822. BAFRA.

Robert Williams

Osborn's Farm, 32 Church St., Willingham, Cambs. CB4 5HT. Tel: 01954 260972. BAFRA. *Boulle, carving, clockcases, inlay work, marquetry, metalwork, painted furniture, with the emphasis on carefully cleaning and retaining old patinated surfaces. Survey and condition reports undertaken.*

Cumbria

Jeremy Hall - Peter Hall & Son

Danes Rd., Staveley, Kendal, Cumbria. LA8 9PL. Tel: 01539 821633; fax - 01539 821905. BAFRA.

BAFRA continued

Derbyshire

Anthony Allen Antique Restorers

Old Wharf Workshop, Redmoor Lane, New Mills, High Peak, Derbys. SK22 3JL. Tel: 01663 745274. BAFRA. *Boulle, marquetry, walnut, oak, veneering restorations and upholstery; clock movements and clockcases.*

Devon

David Battle

Brightley Pound, Umberleigh, Devon. EX37 9AL. Tel: 01769 540483. BAFRA. *Cabinet making, restoration and conservation work; polishing, clock cases, veneer and marquetry work, wood-turning. Specialists in 17th-19th C English and Continental furniture. Collections and deliveries.*

Dan Bent

Newholt, Court Rd., Newton Ferrers, Plymouth, Devon. PL8 1DE. Tel: 01752 872831. BAFRA.

Tony Vernon

15 Follett Rd., Topsham, Devon. EX3 0JP. Tel: 01392 874635. BAFRA. *Furniture, cabinet making, upholstery, gilding, veneering, inlay and French polishing.*

Stevie Young

The Workshop, Little Pit Cottage, Clyst Lydon, Cullompton, Devon. EX15 2NF. Tel: 01884 277660. BAFRA.

Dorset

Michael Barrington

The Old Rectory, Warmwell, Dorchester, Dorset. DT2 8HQ. Tel: 01305 852104; fax - same. BAFRA. *Conservator and restorer of 17th-20th C furniture, gilding, upholstery, metalwork, music boxes and barrel pianos, automatons and rocking horses.*

Peter Binnington

Barn Studio, Botany Farm, East Lulworth, Wareham, Dorset BH20 5QH. Tel: 01929 400224; fax - 01929 400744. BAFRA. *Restoration of period furniture and interiors, gilding and verre eglomisé, decorated surfaces.*

Richard Bolton

Athelhampton House, Dorchester, Dorset. DT2 7LG. Tel: 01305 848346. BAFRA. *All aspects of furniture restoration undertaken; individual tuition given to beginners and more experienced.* LOC: A35 between Puddletown and Tolpuddle.

Peter Brazier - Court Restorations Ltd

Nash Court Farmhouse, Marnhull, Sturminster Newton, Dorset. DT10 1JZ. Tel: 01258 820255. BAFRA. *Comprehensive restoration service.*

BAFRA continued

Philip Hawkins

Glebe Workshop, Semley, Shaftesbury, Dorset. SP7 9AP. Tel: 01747 830830. BAFRA. *16th to early 18th C oak and country furniture restoration.*

S.R. Robertson

4 Burraton Yard, Poundbury Village, Dorset. Tel: 01305 257377. BAFRA.

Raymond Robertson - Tolpuddle Antique Restorers

The Stables, Southover House, Tolpuddle, Dorchester, Dorset. DT2 7HF. Tel: 01305 848739. BAFRA. *Furniture, clocks and barometers, marquetry, veneering and boulle work, lacquer, japaning and gilding.*

Essex

Clive Beardall

104b High St., Maldon, Essex. CM9 5ET. Tel: 01621 857890. BAFRA.

Dick Patterson - Forge Studio Workshops

Stour St., Manningtree, Essex. CO11 1BE. Tel: 01206 396222. BAFRA. *Carving, general restoration, copying and bespoke cabinet making.*

William A.J. Pigeon - Lomas Pigeon & Co. Ltd

The Workshops, Rear of 37 Beehive Lane, Chelmsford, Essex. CM2 9SU. Tel: 01245 353708; fax - 01245 355211. BAFRA. *Period cabinet restoration, French polishing, traditional upholstery, desk linings, rocking horses.*

Gloucestershire

Keith Bawden - Restorer of Antiques

Mews Workshops, Montpellier Retreat, Cheltenham, Glos. GL50 2XG. Tel: 01242 230320. BAFRA. *All period furniture, plus restoration of items made from wood, metals, porcelain, pottery, fabrics, leather, ivory, papier-mâché, etc.*

Peter Campion - Uedelhoven & Campion

Rear of Well House, Gretton, Cheltenham, Glos. GL54 5EP. Tel: 01242 604403. BAFRA. *Restoration and small antique furniture showroom.*

Alan Hessel

The Old Town Workshop, St. George's Close, Moreton-in-Marsh, Glos. GL56 0LP. Tel: 01608 650026; fax - same. BAFRA. *Comprehensive restoration service. English and Continental fine period furniture.*

BAFRA continued

Stephen Hill

5 Cirencester Workshops, Brewery Court, Cirencester, Glos. GL7 1JH. Tel: 01285 658817 (24 hr); fax - 01285 652554. BAFRA. *General furniture including oak, walnut, mahogany, 17th-19th C gilding, carving, upholstery, rush and cane seating. Furniture made by commission only.*

Christian Macduff Hunt - Hunt and Lomas

Village Farm Workshops, Preston Village, Cirencester, Glos. GL7 5PR. Tel: 01285 640111. BAFRA. *17th-19th C oak, mahogany, walnut, satinwood, carving.*

Donald Hunter

The Old School Room, Shipton Oliffe, Cheltenham, Glos. GL54 4JG. Tel: 01242 820755. BAFRA. *Restoration of fine antiques, cabinet making, water gilding, lacquer work, decorative finishes.*

Andrew Lelliott

6 Tetbury Hill, Avening, Tetbury, Glos. GL8 8LT. Tel: 01453 835783/832652. BAFRA. TADA. Conservation Register Museums & Galleries Commission. *Comprehensive restorations.*

Godfrey Robertson

Fourwinds, Ablington, Bibury, Cirencester, Glos. GL7 5NX. Tel: 01285 740355; fax - same. BAFRA. *General restorations, willing to work in situ if necessary.*

Angus Stewart

Sycamore Barn, Bourton Industrial Park, Bourton-on-the-Water, Cheltenham, Glos. GL54 2HQ. Tel: 01451 821611. BAFRA. *16th-18th C cabinet making, gold leafing, decorative finishes, lacquer, carving and mirror glass.*

Laurence Whitfield

The Old School, Winstone, Cirencester, Glos. GL7 7JX. Tel: 01285 821342. BAFRA.

Hampshire

Guy Bagshaw

The Old Dairy, Plain Farm, East Tisted, Alton, Hants. GU34 3RT. Tel: 01420 588362. BAFRA. *18th to early 19th C English furniture restoration. Tutored weekend courses available.*

John Hartley

The Tankerdale Workshop, The Old Forge, Village St., Sheet, Petersfield, Hants. GU32 2AQ. Tel: 01730 233792; fax - 01730 233922. BAFRA. *Comprehensive restoration and conservation service, including carving, gilding, painted furniture, lacquer, marquetry, boulle and architectural woodwork. Adviser to The National Trust.*

BAFRA continued

David C. E. Lewry

Wychelms, 66 Gorran Avenue, Rowner, Gosport, Hants. PO13 0NF. Tel: 01329 286901; fax - 01329 289964; mobile - 0385 766844. BAFRA. *17th to early 19th C furniture.*

Humphrey Sladden

Yard House, South Harting, Petersfield, Hants. GU31 5NS. Tel: 01730 825339. BAFRA.

Herefordshire

Reginald W. Dudman Antique Restorations

The Old Vicarage, Blakemere, Hereford, Herefs. HR2 9PY. Tel: 01981 500413. BAFRA.

Hertfordshire

John B. Carr - Charles Perry Restorations Ltd

Praewood Farm, Hemel Hempstead Rd., St. Albans, Herts. AL3 6AA. Tel: 01727 853487. BAFRA.

Kent

Timothy Akers - Antique Furniture Restorations

The Forge, 39 Chancery Lane, Beckenham, Kent. BR3 2NR. Tel: 0181 650 9179. BAFRA. *Restorations of 17th-19th C English furniture, longcase and bracket clocks.*

Benedict Clegg

Rear of 20 Camden Rd., Tunbridge Wells. Kent. TN1 2PT. Tel: 01892 548095. BAFRA.

Raymond Konyn Antique Restorations

The Old Wheelwright's Shop, Brasted Forge, Brasted, Westerham, Kent. TN16 1JL. Tel: 01959 563863; fax - 01959 561262. BAFRA. *Furniture, traditional upholstery, longcase and bracket clock cases, polishing, brass casting. Consultancy.*

Timothy Long Restoration

St. John's Church, London Rd., Dunton Green, Sevenoaks, Kent. TN13 2 TE. Tel: 01732 743368; fax - 01732 742206. BAFRA. *Cabinet restoration, French polishing, upholstery, brass and steel cabinet fittings.*

Bruce Luckhurst

The Little Surrenden Workshops, Ashford Rd., Bethersden, Kent. TN26 3BG. Tel: 01233 820589. BAFRA. *Conservation and restoration training plus comprehensive restoration service.*

Richard J. Marson - R.M. Restoration

Unit 8 Hilltop Meadows, Old London Rd., Knockholt, Kent. TN14 7JW. Tel: 01959 533771. BAFRA. *Period furniture, traditional upholstery, French polishing.*

BAFRA continued

Lancashire

Eric Smith - Antique Furniture Restorations

The Church, Park Rd., Darwen, Lancs. BB3 2LD. Tel: 01254 776222. BAFRA. UKIC. MA. Conservation Register Museums & Galleries Commission. *Restoration of longcase clocks and furniture. Comprehensive conservation and restoration of fine furniture.*

Lincolnshire

Michael Czajkowski - Edmund Czajkowski and Son

96 Tor-o-Moor Rd., Woodhall Spa, Lincs. LN10 6SB. Tel: 01526 352895; fax - same. BAFRA. *Furniture, clocks and barometers restored, including church clocks. Veneering, marquetry, English lacquer and boulle work, carving and gilding.*

London

Martin Body - Giltwood Restoration

7 Addington Sq., London SE5 7JZ. Tel: 0171 703 4351. BAFRA. *Specialist conservation of fine gilded furniture and frames.*

Lucinda Compton and Jane Hall - Compton Hall Restoration

Unit A, 133 Riverside Business Centre, Haldane Place, London SW18 4UQ. Tel: 0181 874 0762; fax - same. BAFRA. *Lacquer, gilding, painted furniture, paper-mâché, tôleware.*

William Cook

167 Battersea High St., London SW11 3JS. Tel: 0171 736 5329 or 01672 513017. BAFRA. *18th C and English period furniture.*

Marie Louise Crawley

39 Woodvale, London SE23 3DS. Tel: 0181 516 0002; fax - same. BAFRA. *Painted furniture, papier-mâché, tôle ware, lacquer and gilding.*

Robert H. Crawley

75 St. Mary's Rd., Ealing, London W5 5RH. Tel: 0181 566 5074. BAFRA.

Raymond Dudman - W. Thomas Ltd.

12 Warwick Place. London. W9 2PX. Tel: 0171 286 1945. BAFRA.

Brian A. Duffy - Hope & Piaget

12 and 13 Burmarsh Workshops, Marsden St., London NW5 3JA. Tel: 0171 267 6040; fax - same. BAFRA. UKIC.

Sebastian Giles Furniture

8A Junction Mews, London W2 1PN. Tel: 0171 258 3721. BAFRA.

BAFRA continued

Alun Courtney Smith

45 Windmill Rd., Brentford, Middx. TW8 0QQ. Tel: 0181 568 5249; fax - 0181 560 4017. BAFRA.

Rodrigo Titian

318 Kensal Rd., London W10 5BN. Tel: 0181 960 6247; fax - 0181 969 6126. BAFRA. *Carving, gilding, lacquer, painted furniture, French polishing.*

Clifford J. Tracy

6-40 Durnford St., London N15 5NQ. Tel: 0181 800 4773/4; fax - 0181 800 4351. BAFRA. *General restorations including boulle, marquetry, leather lining, upholstery.*

Norfolk

David Bartram

The Raveningham Centre, Beccles Rd., Raveningham, Nr. Norwich, Norfolk. NR14 6NU. Tel: 01508 548721. BAFRA. *18th-19th C English furniture, rosewood, walnut and mahogany, inlay and turning; full cabinet making service, chair copying and upholstery.*

Michael Dolling

Church Farm Barns, Glandford, Holt. Norfolk. NR25 7JR. Tel: 01263 741115. BAFRA.

Roderick Larwood

The Oaks, Station Rd., Larling, Norfolk. NR16 2QS. Tel: 01953 717937; fax - same. BAFRA. *Brass inlay, 18th to early 19th C furniture; French polishing.*

Oxfordshire

Alistair J. Frayling-Cork

2 Mill Lane, Wallingford, Oxon. OX10 0DH. Tel: 01491 826221. BAFRA. *Antique and period furniture, clock cases, ebonising, wood turning, stringed instruments and brass fittings repaired.*

Clive Payne

Unit 4, Mount Farm, Churchill, Chipping Norton. Oxon. OX7 6NP. Tel: 01608 658856; fax - same; mobile - 0410 878891. BAFRA.

Colin Piper - Conservation & Restoration

Highfield House, The Greens, Leafield, Witney, Oxon. OX8 5NP. Tel: 01993 878593. BAFRA.

Shropshire

Richard Higgins (Conservation)

The Old School, Longnor, Nr. Shrewsbury, Shrops. SY5 7PP. Tel: 01743 718162; fax - 01743 718022. BAFRA. LBHI. Conservation Register Museums and Galleries Commission. *Comprehensive restoration of all fine furniture and*

BAFRA continued

clocks, including movements and dials; specialist work to boulle, marquetry, carving, turning, cabinet and veneer work, lacquer, ormolu, metalwork, casting, glazing, polishing, upholstery, cane and rush seating. Stocks of old timber, veneers, tortoiseshell etc. held to ensure sympathetic restoration.

Somerset

Stuart Bradbury - M&S Bradbury

The Barn, Hanham Lane, Paulton, Somerset. BS18 5PF. Tel: 01761 418910. BAFRA. *All aspects of antique furniture restoration.*

Nicholas Bridges

20 Newchester Cross, Merriott. Somerset. TA16 5QJ. Tel: 01460 78345. BAFRA.

Michael Durkee

Castle House, 1 Bennetts Field Estate, Wincanton, Somerset. BA9 9DT. Tel: 01963 33884. BAFRA. *Restoration, conservation and finishing of all styles of period furniture. Boulle and inlay work.*

Alan Stacey - Boxwood Antique Restorers

Somerset. Tel: 01963 33988; fax - 01963 32555. BAFRA. Open by appointment. *Finest quality antique restoration and conservation. Wax polishing, French polishing, carving, metalwork, brass fittings, specialist cabinet making, tortoiseshell specialists (tea caddies, frames, brushes, etc.), ivory, shagreen, horn, mother of pearl, etc. Regular deliveries to London and surrounding areas.* VAT: Stan.

Robert Tandy Restoration

Unit 5 Manor Workshops, Manor Park, West End, Nailsea, Bristol, Somerset. BS19 2DD Tel: 01275 856378. BAFRA. *Furniture restoration especially 17th-19th C longcase clock cases; French polishing and traditional oil and wax finishing.* VAT : Stan.

Surrey

David J. Booth - A.E. Booth & Son

9 High St., Ewell, Surrey. KT17 1SG. Tel: 0181 393 5245. BAFRA. *Restorations and polishing, upholstery. Barometers, longcase clocks, mahogany and walnut.*

Glen Fraser-Sinclair - G. and R. Fraser-Sinclair

Hays Bridge Farm, Brickhouse Lane, South Godstone, Surrey. RH9 8JW. Tel: 01342 844112. BAFRA. *18th C furniture.*

Michael Hedgecoe LAPADA

21 Burrow Hill Green, Chobham, Surrey. GU24 8QS. Tel: 01276 858206; fax - same. BAFRA. *General restorations, cabinet work, polishing, upholstery, chair making.*

BAFRA continued

Stuart Hobbs Antique Furniture Restoration

Meath Paddock, Meath Green Lane, Horley, Surrey. RH6 8HZ. Tel: 01293 782349. GMC. BAFRA. *Full restoration service for period furniture.*

Simon Marsh

The Old Butchers Shop, High St., Bletchingly. Surrey. RH1 4PA. Tel: 01883 743350; fax - 01883 744844. BAFRA.

Timothy Morris

Unit 4a, 19 St Peters St., Croydon, Surrey. CR2 7DG. Tel: 0181 681 2992. BAFRA.

Timothy Naylor

The Workshop, 2 Chertsey Rd., Chobham, Surrey. GU24 8NB. Tel: 01276 855122. BAFRA. *Antique furniture restoration.*

David A. Sayer - Courtlands Restorations

Courtlands, Park Rd., Banstead, Surrey. SM7 3EF. Tel: 01737 352429; fax - 01737 373255. BAFRA. *Full restoration service including repairs, polishing, carving, turning, veneering, gilding. Metal parts - replacement or repair.*

East Sussex

Maxwell Black

Brookhouse Studios, Novington Lane, East Chiltington, Lewes, East Sussex. BN7 3AX. Tel: 01273 890175. BAFRA.

West Sussex

Peter G. Casebow

Pilgrims, Mill Lane, Worthing, West Sussex. BN13 3DE. Tel: 01903 264045. BAFRA. *Period furniture, turning, marquetry, inlay, fretwork, polishing.*

John Lloyd

The Old Bakehouse, The Street, Bolney, West Sussex. RH17 5PG. Tel: 01444 881988. BAFRA. *Sympathetic restoration and conservation of English and Continental furniture; traditional hand finishing, veneering, marquetry and inlay work, carving and turning, gilding, upholstery, rush/cane work, leather lining and tooling, lock repairs and keys. Antique furniture copied or designed and made to order. Regular delivery/collection service to London.*

Simon Paterson Fine Furniture Restoration

74 Double Barn, West Dean, Chichester, West Sussex. PO18 0RR. BAFRA.

Noel Pepperall

Dairy Lane Cottage, Walberton, Arundel, West Sussex. BN18 0PT. Tel: 01243 551282. BAFRA. *Gilding and painted furniture a speciality.*

BAFRA continued

Albert Plumb Furniture Restoration

31 Whyke Lane, Chichester, West Sussex. PO19 2JS. Tel: 01243 789100; fax - 01243 788468. BAFRA. *Oak, walnut, mahogany and country furniture, upholstery and cabinet making.*

Wiltshire

William Cook

High Trees House, Savernake Forest, Marlborough, Wilts. SN8 4NE. Tel: 01672 513017. BAFRA.

Worcestershire

Jeffrey Hall - Malvern Studios

56 Cowleigh Rd., Malvern, Worcs. WR14 1QD. Tel: 01684 574913; fax - 01684 569475. BAFRA

Phillip Slater

93 Hewell Rd., Barnt Green, Worcs. B45 8NL. Tel: 0121 445 4942. BAFRA.

North Yorkshire

Lucinda Compton

Manor House, Marton-le-Moor, Ripon, North Yorks. HG4 5AT. Tel: 01423 324290. BAFRA.

T. L. Phelps - Fine Furniture Restoration

8 Mornington Terrace, Harrogate, North Yorks. HG1 5DH. Tel: 01423 524604. BAFRA. *Specialist restoration and conservation services; all cabinet work, including dining tables, large items; all veneer work; architectural woodwork; traditional hand polishing, colouring and waxed finishes.*

South Yorkshire

Neil Trinder

Burrowlee House, Burrowlee Rd., Hillsborough, Sheffield, South Yorks. S19 6LX. Tel: 0114 2852428/2552972. BAFRA. *Boulle, gilding, marquetry, carving, fine furniture.*

West Yorkshire

Rodney F. Kemble

16 Crag Vale Terrace, Glusburn, Nr. Keighley, West Yorks. BD20 8QU. Tel: 01535 636954/ 633702. BAFRA. *Cabinet restorations, clock cases, traditional hand finishes and upholstery.*

Scotland

Gow Antique Restoration

Pitscandly Farm House, Forfar, by Lunanhead, Angus, Scotland. DD8 3NZ. Tel: 01307 465342. BAFRA. (Jeremy Gow). Accredited by Historical Scotland and the Museums and Galleries Commission. Appointment advisable. *17th-19th C English and Continental furniture. Specialist restoration of European furniture, marquetry.*

BAFRA continued

William Trist

135 St Leonard's St., Edinburgh, Scotland. EH8 9RB. Tel: 0131 667 7775; fax - 0131 667 4333. BAFRA.

Luigi Maria Villani

Hillhead Farm, Forres, Scotland. IV36 0RT. Tel: 01309 676247. BAFRA. *Freelance restorer of antique furniture, picture and mirror frames and objets d'art; study days, tuition and advice.*

Wales

Bryan Wigington - Antique Furniture Restoration

Pembertons, 4 Hightown, Hay-on-Wye, Powys, Wales. HR3 5AE. Tel: 01497 820545 (24 hr.) BAFRA. Est. 1961. Open any time by appointment. *Furniture conservation and restoration.* LOC: Next to Post Office.

Non-BAFRA Furniture Restorers

(In alphabetical order)

Acorns to Oak

65 Main St. Grassington, North Yorks. BD23 5AA. Tel: 01756 753045; fax - 01756 752865. *Specialists in all types of solid oak furniture.*

The Antique Restoration Centre

14 Suffolk Rd., Cheltenham, Glos. GL50 2AQ. Tel: 01242 262549. Open Mon-Fri 9.30-5. *All types of restoration - all restorers BADA qualified.*

Antiques and Restoration

See under Fireplaces.

B.P.A. Antique Restorations LAPADA

Bell Passage Antiques, 36-38 High St., Wickwar, Glos. GL12 8NP. Tel: 01454 294251; fax - same. Est. 1966. *Restorers of antique and modern furniture, specialists in French and wax polishing, picture restoration, gilding, inlay and metal work. Chair copying a speciality; traditional and modern upholstery. Work carried out on site.*

Batheaston

20 Leafield Way, Corsham, Wilts. SN13 9SW. Tel: 01225 811295; fax - 01225 810501. BFMA. BCFA. *Oak reproduction furniture made from solid kiln dried timbers, antique hand finish. Extensive range of Windsor, ladderback and country Hepplewhite chairs; refectory, gateleg and other extendable tables, Welsh dressers, sideboards and other cabinet models. Trade Only.*

Belvedere Reproductions

11 Dove St., Ipswich, Suffolk. IP4 1NG. Tel: 01473 727585; fax - 01473 253229. *Suppliers of traditionally constructed and hand polished oak and fruitwood country furniture.* VAT: Stan.

Furniture continued

Berry & Crowther
9 Whitestones Workshop, Stocksmoor, Huddersfield, West Yorks. HD4 6XQ. Tel: 01484 609800; fax - same. *Fine antique restorers and conservators; restoration with traditional methods to highest standards on fine furniture, ceramics and clocks. Insurance work approved.*

Rupert Bevan
40 Fulham High St., London SW6 3LQ. Tel: 0171 731 1919; fax - same. *Gilding, carving and painting.* VAT: Stan.

A.E. Booth & Son
Crows Nest, Edgeley Rd., Barton, Torquay, Devon. TQ2 8ND. Tel: 01803 312091. *Restorations, polishing, upholstery. Barometers, longcase, mahogany and walnut.*

Lawrence Brass
154 Sutherland Avenue, Maida Vale, London W9. Tel: 0122 585 2222. UKIC. Approved by the Museums and Galleries Commission. *Conservation and restoration of fine antiques, metal work, gilding and upholstery.*

Paul Bruce Antiques
Frobisher Rd., Ipswich, Suffolk. IP3 0HR. Tel: 01473 255400/233671; fax - 01473 233656. IADCC. *Makers of fine furniture in oak, mahogany and walnut. Restorations; valuations.* VAT: Stan.

Bruton Cast Ltd
Station Road Industrial Estate, Bruton, Somerset. BA10 0EH. Tel: 01749 813266; mobile - 0973 342047; fax - 01749 813266. *Quality Victorian replica furniture - mahogany, teak, pine.*

James Burrell
Upton Barn, Seavington St. Michael, Ilminster, Somerset. TA19 0PZ. Tel: 01460 240610. *17th-19th C furniture (English), European furniture, carving, clock cases, inlay work, marquetry, lacquerwork, upholstery.*

Cane and Able - Cane & Rush Restoration
The Plains, Ampton, Bury St. Edmunds, Suffolk. IP31 1HX. Tel: 01284 728097. *Specialist restorers of antique furniture, rush seating, antique cane.*

Catspaw Restoration
6 Oakley Wood Farm, Wallingford, Oxon. OX10 6QG. Tel: 01491 834987. (R. O. McConnell). Est. 1972. *Sympathetic restoration of antiques and decorative items.*

Clare Hall Company
The Barns, Clare Hall, Cavendish Rd., Clare, Nr. Sudbury, Suffolk. CO10 8PJ. Tel: 01787 278445; fax - 01787 278803; 01787 277510 (ansaphone). Est. 1970. *Hand-made copies of floor standing and table globes. Full cabinet making especially four poster beds; restoration of all antiques and upholstery.* VAT: Stan/Spec.

Furniture continued

Classic Reproductions
Swan Corner, Pewsey, Wilts. SN9 5HL. Tel: 01672 563333; fax - 01672 562391. *Suppliers of replica antiques from Java and manufacturers of custom designed pine furniture including tables, beds, chests, bookcases and desks.*

J.W. Crisp Antiques
1 Kingston Mews, Kingston Lane, Teddington, Middx. TW11. Tel: 0181 977 5554. (M. Murren). Open Mon-Fri 10-4 (prior phone call advisable). *Restoration of furniture and French polishing.*

EFMA
4 Northgate Close, Rottingdean, Brighton, East Sussex. BN2 7DZ. Tel: 01273 589744; fax - 01273 589745. (Anthony and Patrick Hoole). Fed. of Sussex Industries, IDDA, Inst. of Export, Inst. of Linguists. *Hand-finished reproductions in walnut, elm, myrtle, yew, mahogany, satinwood. Custom-work and bespoke polishing - 18th C, Biedermeier, Victorian, mahogany dining tables. Country furniture - distressed oak and cherry refectory, gateleg and coffee tables, Windsor chairs. Tables reproduced from old timber.* VAT: Stan.

D.S. Embling - The Cabinet Repair Shop
Woodlands Farm, Blacknest, Alton, Hants. GU34 4QB. Tel: 01252 794260. C&G London Inst. GMC; League of Professional Craftsmen. Est. 1977. *Antique and modern furniture restoration and repair including marquetry and veneering. French polishing, modern finishes. Parts made, wood turning, collection and delivery; insurance claim repairs.*

Everitt and Rogers
Dawsnest Workshop, Grove Rd., Tiptree, Essex. CO5 0JE. Tel: 01621 816508. GADAR. Est. 1969. *Expert antique furniture restoration.*

John Farbrother Furniture Restoration
Ivy House, Main St., Shipton-by-Beningbrough, York, North Yorks. YO6 1AB. Tel: 01904 470187. GADAR. Est. 1987. *All repairs undertaken, refinishing process from complete strip to reviving existing finish. French polishing, oil, wax and lacquers. Pressurised fluid application woodworm treatment.*

Fauld Town and Country Furniture (Division of I. & J.L. Brown Ltd.)
58 Commercial Rd., Hereford, Herefs. HR1 2BP. Tel: 01432 353183; fax - 01432 275338. (Ian and Joyce Brown). Est. 1972. Open 8-5, appointment advisable. *Windsor chairs, extensive range of farmhouse tables, case pieces, including dressers; all traditional reproduction.* VAT: Stan.

Furniture continued

Andrew Foott

4 Claremont Rd., Cheadle Hulme, Cheshire. SK8 6EG. Tel: 0161 485 3559. *Sympathetic restoration and conservation of antique furniture and mercurial barometers; free advice and estimates; quality items occasionally for sale.*

Georgian Cabinets Manufacturers Ltd

Unit 4 Fountayne House, 2-8 Fountayne Rd., London N15 4QL. Tel: 0181 885 1293; fax - 0181 365 1114. Est. 1964. *Manufacturers, restorers and polishers. Large stock of inlaid furniture.* LOC: Near Seven Sisters underground, Tottenham. VAT: Stan.

Melven Glander

Tel: 01284 828429. *Restoration and repair service to furniture, woodwork, clocks and period fixtures and fittings; free estimates and advice. Collection and delivery. Upholstery arranged.*

Greycroft Antiques

Greycroft, Station Rd., Errol, Perthshire, Scotland. PH2 7SN. Tel: 01821 642221; home - same. (D. and Mrs J. Pickett). Est. 1981. Open 10-5.30 or by appointment.

Mark Griffin Furniture

Byrebrook Studio, Lower Farm, North Moor, Oxon. OX8 1AU. Tel: 01865 300171; fax - 01865 883454.

Roland Haycraft

The Lamb Arcade, Wallingford, Oxon.Tel: 01491 839622. *All aspects of antique restorations; one-off reproductions and copying service. Fine furniture designed and made to traditional standards.*

B.R. Honeyborne

The Whyle Cottage, Pudleston, Leominster, Herefs. HR6 0RE. Tel: 01568 750250. Guild of Herefordshire Craftsmen. *Antique furniture restoration and restoration courses; postal service of mouldings and bracket feet.*

Michael Jeffries

3 Upper Lambridge St., Larkhall, Bath, Somerset. BA1 6RY. Tel: 01225 310417; 01225 448103. Assn. of Master Upholsterers. *Antique upholstered furniture; decorative pieces.* VAT: Stan.

Johnson Antique Restoration

43 High St., Chatteris, Cambs. PE16 6BH. Tel: 01354 692622. GADAR. *Quality French polishing, caning, basic upholstery, veneering and structural repairs. Restored antique furniture sold at antique centre.*

T. H. Kelsall (Woodcrafts)

82 Main Rd., Slyne with Hest, Lancaster, Lancs. LA2 6AU. Tel: 01524 822347. GMC, GADAR. Est. 1987. *Repair and restoration of fine antique furniture and clocks, barometers and other works. Cabinet making, carving, marquetry, inlays, veneering, turning and polishing. Replica furniture and clock cases made to order.*

E.C. Legg and Son

3 College Farm Workshops, Tetbury Rd., Cirencester, Glos. GL7 6PY. Tel: 01285 650695. Est. 1902. Open 9-5. CL: Sat. *Restoration of furniture and gilt frames; caning; re-leathering desk tops.*

David Mitchell

45 St. Michael's Rd., Bedford, Beds. MK40 2LD. Tel: 01234 359976. *Veneering, carving, turning, inlay, French polishing; oil painting restoration.*

R.V. Morgan & Co

Unit 41, 26-28 The Queensway, Ponders End, Enfield, Middx. EN3 4SA. Tel: 0181 805 0353; fax - 0181 372 9946. GADAR. Est. 1983. Open by appointment. *Inlays, veneers, turning, carving, fretwork; furniture made to order.* LOC: Off Hertford road, off A10. VAT: Stan.

M. R. Nelms

Unit 2, Trench Farm, Tilley Green, Wem, Shrops. SY4 5PJ. Tel: 01939 235463. GADAR. *Furniture, including antique and fitted, full restoration, antique boxes and clock cases a speciality.*

Nicholas J. Newman

22 Eastcroft Rd., West Ewell, Surrey. KT19 9TX. Tel: 0181 224 3347. *Comprehensive restorations including exterior woodwork and locks.*

Nigel Northeast Cabinet Makers

Furniture Workshops, Back Drove, West Winterslow, Salisbury, Wilts. SP5 1RY. Tel: 01980 862051; fax - 01980 863986. GADAR. Est. 1982. *Antique restoration and French polishing. New furniture made to order, chairs made to complete sets. Cane and rush seating; fire and flood damage service.* VAT: Stan.

Painted and Plastered

5 Long St., Tetbury, Glos. Tel: 01666 505808. TADA. (Tara Higgins). Open 10-5.30. *Hand-painted furniture and design. Pieces available at the showroom or to commission. Renovation, special paint effects, murals, trompe l'oeil and faux finishes. Finder service.*

Pinewood Furniture Studio Ltd

1 Eagle Trading Estate, Stourbridge Rd., Halesowen, West Midlands. B63 3UA. Tel: 0121 550 8228; fax - 0121 585 5611. *Manufacturers of pine furniture. Special orders undertaken.* VAT: Stan.

Plowden & Smith Ltd

See entry under Art.

Furniture continued

Nathan Polley Antique Furniture Restoration
The Barn, The Chippings, Tetbury, Glos. Tel: 01666 504997. TADA. *Fine furniture restorers and cabinet makers. Inlay work, wood turning, French polishing, waxing. Specialist in period mahogany, walnut and early oak.*

Neil Postons Restorations
29 South St., Leominster, Herefordshire. HR6 8JQ. Tel: 01568 616677; fax - same; home - 01568 770442. UKIC. Registered with the Museums and Galleries Commission. Open 8.45-5.30, Sat. and other times by appointment. *Antique and fine furniture restorations including re-construction, veneering, carving, turning, French and wax polishing, re-upholstery, rush and cane seating.*

Nicholas S. Reeve
The Old Oaks, Otley Rd., Framsden, Stowmarket, Suffolk. IP14 6HU. Tel: Mobile - 0850 817216; fax - 01473 890173. Est. 1860. *Makers of 16th-18th C oak and cherry English country period furniture.* VAT: Stan.

Riches
Wixamtree, 69 Wood Lane, Cottonend, Beds. MK45 3AP. Tel: 01234 742121. (R.J. Jennings). *Re-upholstery, repairs and re-caning.*

R.S. Rust (Replicas)
83 Main Rd., Kesgrave, Ipswich, Suffolk. IP5 1AF. Tel: 01473 623092. Est. 1977. Open Tues., Thurs., Fri. 9-5. *Replica hardwood furniture.*

David R. Solomons and Son
14 Moss Hall Grove, London N12 8PB. Tel: 0181 446 1693; works - 0181 985 6674; fax - 0181 446 9225. British Traditional Cabinet Makers. *Manufacturers of traditional furniture especially in burr/burl elm and burr/burl walnut veneers.* VAT: Stan. *Trade Only.*

Julian Stanley Woodcarving - Furniture
Unit 5 The Sitch, Longborough, Moreton-in-Marsh, Glos. GL56 0QJ. Tel: 01451 831122; fax - same. *Fine quality copies of 16th-19th C antiques - exotic carved furniture, figure carving, portrait busts (especially in lime), mirror frames and architectural pieces of all dimensions. Gilding, upholstery, painting and polishing. Work designed and made to order. No restorations.* VAT: Stan/Spec.

Thakeham Furniture
Marehill Rd., Pulborough, West Sussex. RH20 2DY. Tel: 01798 872006. (Timothy Chavasse). *Cabinet work, veneer repairs, wax and French polishing, turning, marquetry, carving, etc.*

Treen Antiques
Treen House, 72 Park Rd., Prestwich, Manchester, Lancs. M25 0FA. Tel: 0161 720 7244; fax - same; mobile - 0973 471185. GADAR, RFS, FHS, UKIC. Open by appointment. *Conservation and restoration of all antique furniture (including vernacular) and woodwork, with emphasis on preserving original finish. Research undertaken, housekeeping advice, environmental monitoring and all aspects of conservation. Furniture assessment and advice on purchase and sales. Courses in restoration work held on request. Listed in Bonham's Directory.*

Furniture continued

Barry J. Wateridge
Padouk, Portsmouth Rd., Bramshott Chase, Hindhead, Surrey. GU26 6DB. Tel: 01428 607235. *French polishing and antique furniture restorations.*

Weaver Neave and Daughter
17 Lifford St. Putney, London SW15 1NY. Tel: 0181 785 2464. *Re-caning and re-rushing of antique furniture in traditional manner with traditional materials.*

Gerald Weir Antiques
Unit 1, Riverside Industrial Park, Wherstead Rd., Ipswich, Suffolk. Tel: 01473 252606; fax - 01473 214621. Open by appointment. *Suppliers of reproduction oak furniture for European markets and decorative furniture for American markets. Trade Only.*

Jonathan Wilbye
Church Green Farm, Old Church Lane, Pateley Bridge, North Yorks. HG3 5LZ. Tel: 01423 711581. *Full restoration service including all carving, inlay, turning and polishing. Longcase clock cases a speciality.*

Peter Williams Antique Furniture Restoration
Silkmill House, 4 Charlton Rd., Tetbury, Glos. Tel: 01666 502311. TADA. *Early oak, period mahogany, walnut and country furniture. Wood-turning, French polishing and wax finish, gold tooled leather. Insurance claims. Antiques bought and sold. Established over 25 years.*

GLASS

Mill Lane Stained Glass Workshop
Lower House, Mill Lane, Longhope, Glos. GL17 0AA. Tel: 01452 831100. *Design, manufacture and installation of traditional stained glass windows, domestic and secular. Manufacture of traditional leaded lights, including historic and listed buildings. Repair and renovation work undertaken.*

Sargeant Restorations
21 The Green, Westerham, Kent. TN16 1AX. *Restoration and cleaning of chandeliers, lustres and candelabra.*

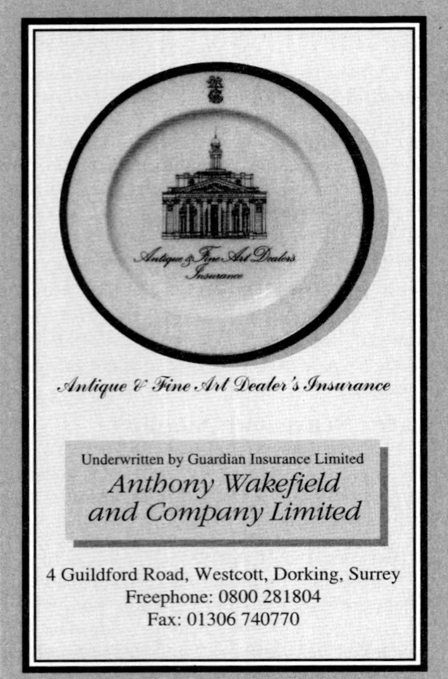

INSURANCE & FINANCE

Antique & Fine Art Finance Ltd

The Malthouse, 50 Kington St. Michael, Chippenham, Wilts. SN14 6JE. Tel: 01249 750701; fax - same. *Provision of finance facilities to the clients of antique and fine art dealers.*

The Art and Antiques Service

Scales Barn, 1 Pearces Yard, Grantchester, Cambridge, Cambs. CB3 9NZ. Tel: 01223 846699; fax - 01223 846626; mobile - 0850 932894. *Professional valuations and insurance for probate, family division. Buying specific items or total refurbishments including architectural - fireplaces, doors. Advice on building up or scaling down collections and placing items for sale.*

Lockson Insurance Consultants

29 Broomfield St, London E14 6BX. Tel: 0171 515 8600; fax - 0171 515 4866; e-mail - enquiries@lockson.co.uk; internet - www.lockson.co.uk. *Specialists in antique dealers master policy and antiquarian book dealers cover.*

Minet Ltd.

Fine Arts and Jewellery Division, 66 Prescot St., London E1 8HG. Tel: 0171 481 0707; fax - 0171 488 9786. *International insurance brokers, specialising in fine arts and jewellery.*

Insurance & Finance continued

Anthony Wakefield & Company Ltd

4 Guildford Rd., Westcott, Dorking, Surrey. RH4 2JZ. Tel: 01306 740555; fax - 01306 740770. Members IIB. *Fine art and household insurance brokers; special terms for collectors; exclusive antique and fine art dealers policy with Guardian; exclusive Connoisseur household policy with dealers/fairs extension.*

Windsor Insurance Brokers Ltd - SKS Division

160-166 Borough High St., London SE1 1JR Tel: 0171 407 7144; fax - 0171 827 9312. Lloyds Insurance Brokers. *Specialist Lloyd's brokers in antique and fine art dealers, fine art galleries, contemporary art galleries, restorers and conservators, antique centres, auctioneers and valuers "Heirloom" designed for dealers' own collections and household and all risks insurance brokers. Official brokers to LAPADA, BAFRA, The Fine Art Trade Guild, IDDA.*

IVORY

Boxwood Antique Restorers

See under Furniture - BAFRA Section Alan Stacey (Somerset).

JEWELLERY & SILVER

Goldcare

5 Bedford St., Middlesborough, Cleveland. TS1 2LL. Tel: 01642 231343. *Jewellery repair, engraving, re-stringing, stone cutting. Restoration of silver and cutlery; brass, copper, pinchbeck restoration.* VAT: Stan.

LOCKS & KEYS

Bramah Security Centres Ltd.

31 Oldbury Place, London W1M 3AP. Tel: 0171 935 7147; fax - 0171 935 2779. Open Mon.-Fri. 8.30-5. *Keys cut to old locks; old locks opened; repair of old locks; new locks made to an old design; original Bramah locks dated. Quotation provided. Overseas work undertaken.* LOC: Near Baker Street tube station. VAT: Stan.

METALWORK

Plowden & Smith Ltd

See entry under Art

Allan Reeling Metal Restoration

42 Hodge Bower, Ironbridge, Shrops. TF8 7QL. Tel: 01952 433031. *Restoration and refurbishment of metal items including cleaning, repair and polishing.*

Surrey Antique Restoration

Croydon/South London area. Tel: 0181 684 1356; fax - same. *High quality restoration of metalware, using traditional methods and materials. Over 25 years experience.*

PHOTOGRAPHY

Gerry Clist Photography LMPA

London NW6. Tel: 0171 624 0716; fax - 0171 624 9475. *Specialising in sculptures, antiques and works of art photography - studio and location.*

REPRODUCTION STONEWORK

Hampshire Gardencraft

Rake Industries, Rake, Nr. Petersfield, Hants. GU31 5DR. Tel: 01730 895182; fax - 01730 893216. *Manufacturers of antiqued garden ornaments, troughs and pots in reconstituted stone in an old Cotswold stone finish. Many designs, catalogue available.*

SUPPLIERS

C. and A.J. Barmby

140 Lavender Hill, Tonbridge, Kent. TA9 2NJ. Tel: 01732 771590. (Chris and Angela Barmby). Est. 1980. Open 9.30-4.45. *Suppliers of display stands in wire, acrylic and wood; reference books and catalogues; lamps and magnifers. Exhibitor at Alexandra Palace, Wembley, and all IACF fairs.* VAT: Stan.

Dauphin Display (Oxford) Ltd

PO Box 602, Oxford, Oxon. OX44 9LU. Tel: 01865 343542; fax - 01865 343307. (John Harrison-Banfield). Est. 1985. Open 9-5, Sat. by

Suppliers continued

appointment. Please telephone for directions. *Design and manufacture of stands, mounts, cabinets and environmental cases. Mounting service. Acrylic display stands - other materials utilised include glass, wood, metal, stone, marble, brass and bronze. Free mail order catalogue available.*

The Display Stand Company Ltd

5 Rickett St., London SW6 1RU. Tel: 0171 381 0255; fax - same. (D. Mayes). Est. 1993. Open by appointment only. *Specialist suppliers of display stands, bespoke stands for individual works of art.* VAT: Stan.

Just Bros. and Co.

Roeder House, Vale Rd., London N4 1NG. Tel: 0181 880 2505; fax - 0181 802 0062. Member British Jewellery and Giftware Federation Ltd. Open 9-5, Fri. 9-12.30. *Reproduction presentation cases, Victoriana and traditional range of quality cases - part of largest selection in Europe. Catalogue on request.*

Marshall Brass

Keeling Hall Rd., Foulsham, Norfolk. NR20 5PR. Tel: 01362 684105; fax - 01362 684280. GMC. *Suppliers of quality period replica furniture fittings in brass and iron.*

Suppliers continued

Martin and Co. Ltd

119 Camden St., Birmingham, West Midlands. B1 3DJ. Tel: 0121 233 2111; fax - 0121 236 0488. ASFI, GAI. *Cabinet hardware supplied - handles, locks, hinges, castors etc. Trade Only.*

Alan Morris Wholesale

Stonecourt, Townsend, Nympsfield, Glos. GL10 3UF. Tel: 01453 861069. (Alan Leadbetter). Est. 1969. *Display stands - coated wire, plastic, acrylic and wood for plates, cups, saucers, bowls etc; wire and disc; jewellery boxes, polishing and cleaning cloths, peelable white labels and strung tickets. Mail order available.* VAT: Stan. *Trade Only.*

Relics

35 Bridge St., Witney, Oxon. OX8. Tel: 01993 704611. (B Wiles, R. Russell and C. Walker). Est. 1987. Open 9-5. *Suppliers of furniture restoration material, brass castors, handles, locks, waxes and polish, upholstery and caning requisites, reproduction paints, stencils, etc. Mail order also.* LOC: Main road.

J. Shiner and Sons Ltd.

8 Windmill St., London W1P 1HF. Tel: 0171 636 0740; fax - 0171 580 0740. *Suppliers of brass handles, castors, locks, brass grills and leathers.*

Suffolk Brass

Thurston, Bury St. Edmunds, Suffolk. IP31 3SN. Tel: 01359 233383; fax - 01359 233384. *Period replica cabinet fittings in brass and iron. One-off castings in lost wax or sand. Catalogue £5. Trade Only.*

The Victorian Ring Box Company

North Lodge, Ardpeaton, Cove, Argyll & Bute, Scotland. G84 0NY. Tel: 01436 850261; fax - same. (R. and K.J. Young). By appointment only. *International designers, manufacturers and distributors of high quality antique style presentation boxes.*

TEXTILES

The Textile Conservancy Company Ltd

40 Crooms Hill, Greenwich, London SE10 8HD. Tel: 0181 305 1737; fax - 0181 305 1107. UKIC *Treatment of historic textiles, including cleaning, support to areas of damage, lining and providing hanging systems for wall-hangings and tapestries and treating upholstery coverings. Advice on storage and display of textiles and collection management. Free half-hour consultation on last Fri. of each month, 3-5.30, by appointment only.*

The Textile Restoration Studio

2 Talbot Rd., Bowdon, Altrincham, Cheshire. WA14 3JD. Tel: 0161 928 0020; fax - same. Conservation Register Museums and Galleries Commission. *Cleaning and repair of all antique*

Textiles continued

textiles including tapestries, samplers, canvas work, beadwork, lace, costume, ecclesiastical vestments and furnishings, dolls and fans. Mail order catalogue of specialist textile conservation materials (free with large stamped addressed envelope). Home cleaning kits for needlework and acid free tissue packs available to the trade.

TORTOISESHELL

Boxwood Antique Restorers

See under Furniture - BAFRA Section Alan Stacey (Somerset).

TOYS

Robert Mullis Rocking Horse Maker

55 Berkeley Rd., Wroughton, Swindon, Wilts. SN4 9BN. Tel: 01793 813583; fax - same. British Toymakers Guild. *Full or partial restorations of antique horses, some wooden toy restoration. Traditional methods and materials used. Collection and delivery. New rocking horses made in five sizes, commissions undertaken.*

Tobilane Designs

Newton Holme Farm, Whittington, Carnforth, Lancs. LA6 2NZ. Tel: 015242 72662; home - same. (Paul and Elaine Commander). Est. 1985. Open 10-5 including Sun. *Makers and restorers of a wide range of wooden toys including rocking horses and dolls' houses. Buys at auction (toys, teddies, dolls and rocking horses). Commissions accepted, replicas made.* LOC: B6254 3 miles south of Kirkby Lonsdale, between Whittington and Arkholme. VAT: Stan.

Fairs Calendar

Because this list is compiled in advance, alterations or cancellations to the fairs listed can occur. We strongly advise anyone wishing to attend a Fair, especially if they have to travel any distance, to telephone the organiser to confirm the details given here.

LONDON

Sunday 31st May/Wednesday 3rd June
The London Book Fair, The Hotel Russell, Russell Square, W.C.1. *(P.B.F.A. - 01763 248400)*
Thursday 4th/Sunday 14th June
The Fine Art & Antiques Fair, The Olympia, Hammersmith Road, W.14. *(P & O Events Ltd - 0171 370 8234)*
Sunday 7th June
Antique & Collectors' Fair, The Dartmouth House, 37 Charles Street (Off Berkeley Square), Mayfair, W.1. *(Adams Antiques Fairs - 0171 254 4054)*
Antiques Fair, The London Hilton on Park Lane, 22 Park Lane, W.1. *(Heritage Antiques Fairs - 0171 624 5173)*
Antique & Collectors' Fair, The Lee Valley Leisure Centre, Picketts-Lock Lane, Off Meridian Way, Edmonton, N.9. *(Jax Fairs - 01444 400570)*
The London Glass Fair, The Commonwealth Institute, Kensington High Street, W.8. *(P & A Antiques - 0181 543 5075)*
Thursday 11th/Saturday 20th June
The Grosvenor House Art & Antiques Fair, Under the Patronage of Her Majesty Queen Elizabeth The Queen Mother) The Great Room, Grosvenor House, Park Lane, W.1. *(Alison Vaissieré - 0171 495 8743)*
Thursday 11th/ Monday 15th June
The Hali International Antique Carpet & Textiles Fair, The Exhibition Halls, Olympia, Hammersmith Road, W.14. *(Hali - Mr Andy Powell - 0171 970 4690)*
Friday 12th/Sunday 14th June
Ceramics Fair, The Cumberland Hotel, Marble Arch, W.1 *(Wakefield Ceramics Fairs - 01905 776091)*
Friday 12th/Monday 15th June
The International Ceramics Fair & Seminar, The Park Lane Hotel, Piccadilly, W.1. *(Brian & Anna Haughton - 0171 734 5491)*
Saturday 13th/Sunday 14th June
Antiquarian Map & Print Fair, The Bonnington Hotel, Southampton Row, W.C.1. *(David Bannister - 01242 514287)*
Sunday 14th June
The Ephemera Society Fair, The Hotel Russell, Russell Square, W.C.1. *(Ephemera Society - 01923 829079)*
Antiques Fair, The Rembrandt Hotel, Thurloe Place, S.W.7. *(Heritage Antiques Fairs - 0171 624 5173)*
The International Map Collectors' Society's Annual Map Fair, The Forte Crest Bloomsbury, Coram Street, W.C.1. *(International Map Collectors Society - 0181 769 5041)*

London continued

Friday 19th/Sunday 21st June
The Kensington Contemporary Art & Design Show, The Kensington Town Hall, Hornton Street, W.8. *(Penman Antiques Fairs - 01444 482514)*
Saturday 20th June
Antiques Fair, The Chelsea Town Hall, King's Road, S.W.3. *(Adams Antiques Fairs - 0171 254 4054)*
Antique & Collectors' Fair, The Muswell Hill Centre, Entrance Summerland Gardens, Muswell Hill Road, N.10. *(M & S Enterprises - 0181 440 2330)*
Sunday 21st June
The ADA Antiquities Fair, The Britannia Hotel, Grosvenor Square, W.1. *(Antiquities Dealers Association - 01497 831759)*
Antique & Collectors' Fair, The Royal Horticultural Hall,Vincent Square, Victoria, S.W.1. *(Adams Antiques Fairs - 0171 254 4054)*
Antiques Fair, The Chelsea Town Hall, King's Road, S.W.3. *(Mainwarings Antique Fairs - 01225 723094)*
Antiques Fair, The London Marriott Hotel, Grosvenor Square, W.1. *(Heritage Antiques Fairs - 0171 624 5173)*
Wednesday 24th June
Antique Fair, The Crystal Palace Sports Ground, Crystal Palace, S.E.19 *(P & A Antiques - 0181 543 5075)*
Sunday 28th June
Antique & Collectors' Fair, The Harrow Leisure Centre, Christchurch Avenue, Harrow. *(Garden City Promotions - 0181 368 1902)*
Antiques Fair, The Inter-Continental London, 1 Hamilton Place, Hyde Park Corner, W.1. *(Heritage Antiques Fairs - 0171 624 5173)*
Antiques Fair, The Atkinson Morley's Hall, Copse Hill, Wimbledon, S.W.20. *(P & A Antiques - 0181 543 5075)*
Sunday 5th July
Antique & Collectors' Fair, The Dartmouth House, 37 Charles Street (Off Berkeley Square), Mayfair, W.1. *(Adams Antiques Fairs - 0171 254 4054)*
Antiques Fair, The Rembrandt Hotel, Thurloe Place, S.W.7. *(Heritage Antiques Fairs - 0171 624 5173)*
Saturday 11th July
Antiques Fair, The Chelsea Town Hall, King's Road, S.W.3. *(Adams Antiques Fairs - 0171 254 4054)*
Sunday 12th July
Antique & Collectors' Fair, The Royal Horticultural Hall,Vincent Square, Victoria, S.W.1. *(Adams Antiques Fairs - 0171 254 4054)*

London continued

Antiques Fair, The London Hilton on Park Lane, 22 Park Lane, W.1. *(Heritage Antiques Fairs - 0171 624 5173)*
Antiques Fair, The Chelsea Town Hall, King's Road, S.W.3. *(Mainwarings Antique Fairs - 01225 723094)*
Sunday 12th/Monday 13th July
The London Book Fair, The Hotel Russell, Russell Square, Bloomsbury, W.C.1. *(P.B.F.A. - 01763 248400)*
Monday 13th July
Antiquarian Map & Print Fair, The Bonnington Hotel, Southampton Row, W.C.1. *(David Bannister - 01242 514287)*
Sunday 19th July
Antique & Collectors' Fair, Kensington Town Hall, Hornton Street, Kensington, W.8. *(Adams Antiques Fairs - 0171 254 4054)*
The Ephemera Society Bazaar, The Bonnington Hotel, 92 Southampton Row, W.C.1. *(Ephemera Society - 01923 829079)*
Sunday 26th July
Antiques Fair, The Atkinson Morley's Hall, Copse Hill, Wimbledon, S.W.20. *(P & A Antiques - 0181 543 5075)*
Sunday 9th/Monday 10th August
The London Book Fair, The Hotel Russell, Russell Square, Bloomsbury, W.C.1. *(P.B.F.A. - 01763 248400)*
Monday 10th August
Antiquarian Map & Print Fair, The Bonnington Hotel, Southampton Row, W.C.1. *(David Bannister - 01242 514287)*
Thursday 13th/Sunday 16th August
The Great Antiques Fair, Earls Court 2, Earls Court Exhibition Centre, S.W.5 *(P & O Events, Linda Colban - 0121 782 2899)*
Wednesday 19th August
Antique Fair, The Crystal Palace Sports Ground, Crystal Palace, S.E.19 *(P & A Antiques - 0181 543 5075)*
Antique Fair, Sunday 23rd August
Antique & Collectors' Fair, The Royal Horticultural Hall,Vincent Square, Victoria, S.W.1. *(Adams Antiques Fairs - 0171 254 4054)*
Antiques Fair, The Atkinson Morley's Hall, Copse Hill, Wimbledon, S.W.20. *(P & A Antiques - 0181 543 5075)*
Saturday 29th August
Antiques Fair, The Chelsea Town Hall, King's Road, S.W.3. *(Adams Antiques Fairs - 0171 254 4054)*
Sunday 30th August
Antiques Fair, The Chelsea Town Hall, King's Road, S.W.3. *(Mainwarings Antique Fairs - 01225 723094)*
Monday 31st August
Antiques & Collectors Fair, The Wembley Exhibition Centre, Hall 3, Empire Way, Wembley. *(Wembley Antiques Fairs Ltd - 01702 233123)*
Sunday 6th September
Antique & Collectors' Fair, The Royal Horticultural Hall,Vincent Square, Victoria, S.W.1. *(Adams Antiques Fairs - 0171 254 4054)*
Antiques Fair, The Rembrandt Hotel, Thurloe Place, S.W.7. *(Heritage Antiques Fairs - 0171 624 5173)*
Antique & Collectors' Fair, The Lee Valley Leisure Centre, Picketts-Lock Lane, Off Meridian Way, Edmonton, N.9. *(Jax Fairs - 01444 400570)*

London continued

Thursday 10th/Sunday 20th September
The 87th Chelsea Antiques Fair, The Chelsea Old Town Hall, King's Road, S.W.3. *(Penman Antiques Fairs - 01444 482514)*
Sunday 13th September
Antique & Collectors' Fair, The Dartmouth House, 37 Charles Street (Off Berkeley Square), Mayfair, W.1. *(Adams Antiques Fairs - 0171 254 4054)*
Antiques Fair, The London Marriott Hotel, Grosvenor Square, W.1. *(Heritage Antiques Fairs - 0171 624 5173)*
Sunday 13th/Monday 14th September
The London Book Fair, The Hotel Russell, Russell Square, Bloomsbury, W.C.1. *(P.B.F.A. - 01763 248400)*
Monday 14th September
Antiquarian Map & Print Fair, The Bonnington Hotel, Southampton Row, W.C.1. *(David Bannister - 01242 514287)*
Sunday 20th September
Antique & Collectors' Fair, Kensington Town Hall, Hornton Street, Kensington, W.8. *(Adams Antiques Fairs - 0171 254 4054)*
Antiques Fair, The London Hilton on Park Lane, 22 Park Lane, W.1. *(Heritage Antiques Fairs - 0171 624 5173)*
Tuesday 22nd/Sunday 27th September
The Decorative Antiques & Textiles Fair, The Marquee, The Riverside Terraces, Battersea Park, S.W.11. *(Heritage Antiques Fairs - 0171 624 5173)*
Wednesday 23rd September
Antique Fair, The Crystal Palace Sports Ground, Crystal Palace, S.E.19 *(P & A Antiques - 0181 543 5075)*
Wednesday 23rd/ Sunday 27th September
The 20th Century British Art Fair, The Royal College of Art, Kensington Gore, S.W.7. *(Gay Hutson - 0181 742 1611)*
Saturday 26th September
Antiques Fair, The Chelsea Town Hall, King's Road, S.W.3. *(Adams Antiques Fairs - 0171 254 4054)*
Sunday 27th September
Antique & Collectors' Fair, The Royal Horticultural Hall,Vincent Square, Victoria, S.W.1. *(Adams Antiques Fairs - 0171 254 4054)*
Antique & Collectors' Fair, The Harrow Leisure Centre, Christchurch Avenue, Harrow. *(Garden City Promotions - 0181 368 1902)*
Antiques Fair, The Inter-Continental London, 1 Hamilton Place, Hyde Park Corner, W.1. *(Heritage Antiques Fairs - 0171 624 5173)*
Antiques Fair, The Atkinson Morley's Hall, Copse Hill, Wimbledon, S.W.20. *(P & A Antiques - 0181 543 5075)*
Antique & Collectors' Fair, The Great Hall, Alexandra Palace, Wood Green, N.22 *(Pig & Whistle Promotions - 0181 883 7061)*
Antiques Fair, The Chelsea Town Hall, King's Road, S.W.3. *(Mainwarings Antique Fairs - 01225 723094)*
Sunday 4th October
Antique & Collectors' Fair, The Dartmouth House, 37 Charles Street (Off Berkeley Square), Mayfair, W.1. *(Adams Antiques Fairs - 0171 254 4054)*
Antiques Fair, The London Hilton on Park Lane, 22 Park Lane, W.1. *(Heritage Antiques Fairs - 0171 624 5173)*

London continued

Antique & Collectors' Fair, The Lee Valley Leisure Centre, Picketts-Lock Lane, Off Meridian Way, Edmonton, N.9. *(Jax Fairs - 01444 400570)*

Thursday 8th/Sunday 11th October

The City of London Antiques Fair, The Honourable Artilllery Company, Armoury House, City Road, E.C.1. *(Penman Antiques Fairs - 01444 482514)*

Sunday 11th October

Antique & Collectors' Fair, The Royal Horticultural Hall,Vincent Square, Victoria, S.W.1. *(Adams Antiques Fairs - 0171 254 4054)*

Antiques Fair, The Inter-Continental London, 1 Hamilton Place, Hyde Park Corner, W.1. *(Heritage Antiques Fairs - 0171 624 5173)*

The London Glass & Ceramics Fair, The Commonwealth Institute, Kensington High Street, W.8. *(P & A Antiques - 0181 543 5075)*

Sunday 11th/Monday 12th October

The London Book Fair, The Hotel Russell, Russell Square, Bloomsbury, W.C.1. *(P.B.F.A. - 01763 248400)*

Monday 12th October

Antiquarian Map & Print Fair, The Bonnington Hotel, Southampton Row, W.C.1. *(David Bannister - 01242 514287)*

Tuesday 13th/Sunday 18th October

The LAPADA Show, The Royal College of Art, Kensington Gore, S.W.7 *(Susannah Hollamby - 0171 823 3511)*

Thursday 15th/Sunday 18th October

The City of London Art Fair, The Honourable Artilllery Company, Armoury House, City Road, E.C.1. *(Penman Antiques Fairs - 01444 482514)*

Sunday 18th October

The Ephemera Society Bazaar, The Bonnington Hotel, 92 Southampton Row, W.C.1. *(Ephemera Society - 01923 829079)*

Antiques Fair, The London Marriott Hotel, Grosvenor Square, W.1. *(Heritage Antiques Fairs - 0171 624 5173)*

Wednesday 21st October

Antique Fair, The Crystal Palace Sports Ground, Crystal Palace, S.E.19 *(P & A Antiques - 0181 543 5075)*

Sunday 25th October

Antique & Collectors' Fair, Kensington Town Hall, Hornton Street, Kensington, W.8. *(Adams Antiques Fairs - 0171 254 4054)*

The 25th International Antique Scientific & Medical Instrument Fair, The Radisson SAS Portman Hotel, Portman Square, W.1 *(Mr P Delehar - 0181 866 8659)*

Antique & Collectors' Fair, The Harrow Leisure Centre, Christchurch Avenue, Harrow. *(Garden City Promotions - 0181 368 1902)*

Antiques Fair, The Rembrandt Hotel, Thurloe Place, S.W.7. *(Heritage Antiques Fairs - 0171 624 5173)*

Antiques Fair, The Atkinson Morley's Hall, Copse Hill, Wimbledon, S.W.20. *(P & A Antiques - 0181 543 5075)*

Thursday 29th October/Sunday 1st November

The Kensington Antiques & Fine Art Fair, The Kensington Town Hall, Hornton Street, W.8. *(Penman Antiques Fairs - 01444 482514)*

Saturday 31st October

Antiques Fair, The Chelsea Town Hall, King's Road, S.W.3. *(Adams Antiques Fairs - 0171 254 4054)*

London continued

Sunday 1st November

Antique & Collectors' Fair, The Dartmouth House, 37 Charles Street (Off Berkeley Square), Mayfair, W.1. *(Adams Antiques Fairs - 0171 254 4054)*

Antiques Fair, The London Marriott Hotel, Grosvenor Square, W.1. *(Heritage Antiques Fairs - 0171 624 5173)*

Antique & Collectors' Fair, The Lee Valley Leisure Centre, Picketts-Lock Lane, Off Meridian Way, Edmonton, N.9. *(Jax Fairs - 01444 400570)*

Antiques Fair, The Chelsea Town Hall, King's Road, S.W.3. *(Mainwarings Antique Fairs - 01225 723094)*

Sunday 1st/Monday 2nd November

The London Book Fair, The Hotel Russell, Russell Square, Bloomsbury, W.C.1. *(P.B.F.A. - 01763 248400)*

Sunday 8th November

Antique & Collectors' Fair, The Royal Horticultural Hall,Vincent Square, Victoria, S.W.1. *(Adams Antiques Fairs - 0171 254 4054)*

Antiques Fair, The London Hilton on Park Lane, 22 Park Lane, W.1. *(Heritage Antiques Fairs - 0171 624 5173)*

Sunday 8th November

Decorative & Applied Arts Fair, The Commonwealth Institute, Kensington High Street, W8 *(P & A Antiques - 0181 543 5075)*

Monday 9th November

Antiquarian Map & Print Fair, The Bonnington Hotel, Southampton Row, W.C.1. *(David Bannister - 01242 514287)*

Sunday 15th November

Antiques Fair, The London Marriott Hotel, Grosvenor Square, W.1. *(Heritage Antiques Fairs - 0171 624 5173)*

Antiques Fair, The Chelsea Town Hall, King's Road, S.W.3. *(Mainwarings Antique Fairs - 01225 723094)*

Antique & Collectors' Fair, The Great Hall, Alexandra Palace, Wood Green, N.22 *(Pig & Whistle Promotions - 0181 883 7061)*

Monday 16th/Sunday 22nd November

The Fine Art & Antiques Fair, The Olympia, Hammersmith Road, W.14. *(P & O Events Ltd - 0171 370 8234)*

Wednesday 18th November

Antique Fair, The Crystal Palace Sports Ground, Crystal Palace, S.E.19 *(P & A Antiques - 0181 543 5075)*

Saturday 21st November

Antiques Fair, The Chelsea Town Hall, King's Road, S.W.3. *(Adams Antiques Fairs - 0171 254 4054)*

Sunday 22nd November

The Ephemera Society Fair, The Hotel Russell, Russell Square, W.C.1. *(Ephemera Society - 01923 829079)*

Antiques Fair, The Rembrandt Hotel, Thurloe Place, S.W.7. *(Heritage Antiques Fairs - 0171 624 5173)*

Antiques Fair, The Atkinson Morley's Hall, Copse Hill, Wimbledon, S.W.20. *(P & A Antiques - 0181 543 5075)*

Sunday 29th November

Antique & Collectors' Fair, The Harrow Leisure Centre, Christchurch Avenue, Harrow. *(Garden City Promotions - 0181 368 1902)*

Antiques Fair, The Inter-Continental London, 1 Hamilton Place, Hyde Park Corner, W.1. *(Heritage Antiques Fairs - 0171 624 5173)*

London continued

Sunday 6th December
Antique & Collectors' Fair, The Dartmouth House, 37 Charles Street (Off Berkeley Square), Mayfair, W.1. *(Adams Antiques Fairs - 0171 254 4054)*
Antiques Fair, The Rembrandt Hotel, Thurloe Place, S.W.7. *(Heritage Antiques Fairs - 0171 624 5173)*
Antique & Collectors' Fair, The Lee Valley Leisure Centre, Picketts-Lock Lane, Off Meridian Way, Edmonton, N.9. *(Jax Fairs - 01444 400570)*
Antiques Fair, The Chelsea Town Hall, King's Road, S.W.3. *(Mainwarings Antique Fairs - 01225 723094)*
Saturday 12th December
Antiques Fair, The Chelsea Town Hall, King's Road, S.W.3. *(Adams Antiques Fairs - 0171 254 4054)*
Sunday 13th December
Antique & Collectors' Fair, The Royal Horticultural Hall,Vincent Square, Victoria, S.W.1. *(Adams Antiques Fairs - 0171 254 4054)*
Antiques Fair, The London Marriott Hotel, Grosvenor Square, W.1. *(Heritage Antiques Fairs - 0171 624 5173)*
Sunday 13th/Monday 14th Dcember
The London Book Fair, The Hotel Russell, Russell Square, Bloomsbury, W.C.1. *(P.B.F.A. - 01763 248400)*
Monday 14th December
Antiquarian Map & Print Fair, The Bonnington Hotel, Southampton Row, W.C.1. *(David Bannister - 01242 514287)*
Sunday 20th December
The Ephemera Society Bazaar, The Bonnington Hotel, 92 Southampton Row, W.C.1. *(Ephemera Society - 01923 829079)*
Sunday 27th December
Antique & Collectors' Fair, The Harrow Leisure Centre, Christchurch Avenue, Harrow. *(Garden City Promotions - 0181 368 1902)*
Antiques Fair, The Atkinson Morley's Hall, Copse Hill, Wimbledon, S.W.20. *(P & A Antiques - 0181 543 5075)*
Monday 28th December
Antiques & Collectors' Fair, The Wembley Exhibition Centre, Hall 3, Empire Way, Wembley. *(Wembley Antiques Fairs Ltd - 01702 233123)*

REGIONS

Monday 1st/Tuesday 2nd June
Antiques & Collectors' Fair, The Newark & Nottinghamshire Showground, Newark, Notts. *(DMG Antiques Fairs - 01636 702326)*
Wednesday 3rd June
Antiques & Collectors' Fair, The Racecourse, Stratford On Avon, Warks. *(Antiques & Collectors' World - 01737 812989)*
Antique Fair, The Village Hall, Long Melford, Suffolk. *(Graham Turner Antiques Fairs - 01473 658224)*
Friday 5th/Sunday 7th June
The Hatfield House Antique Fair, Hatfield House, Herts. *(Bailey Fairs Ltd - 01277 214677)*
The Petersfield Antiques Fairs, The Town Hall, Petersfield, Hants. *(Gamlin Exhibition Services - 01452 862557)*

Regions continued

Saturday 6th June
Antiques & Collectors' Fair, The W.I. Hall, Frinton on Sea, Essex. *(Best of Fairs - 01787 280306)*
Antiques Fair, The Chorleywood Memorial Hall, Common Road, Chorleywood, Herts. *(Chiltern Fairs - 01753 890301)*
Saturday 6th/Sunday 7th June
Antique & Collectors' Fair, The Pavilion Gardens, Buxton, Derbys. *(Unicorn Fairs Ltd - 0161 773 7001)*
Sunday 7th June
Antiques Fair, The Old Swan Hotel, Harrogate, N. Yorks. *(Abbey Antiques Fairs - 01482 445785)*
Antiques & Collectors' Market, The Essex County Showground, Chelmsford, Essex. *(Antiques & Collectors' World - 01737 812989)*
Antique & Collectors' Fair, The New Village Hall, Copdock, Near Ipswich, Suffolk. *(Best of Fairs - 01787 280306)*
Antiques Fair, The Centre for Epilepsy, Chalfont St Peter, Bucks. *(Chiltern Fairs - 01753 890301)*
Antiques & Collectors' Fair, The Three Counties Showground, Malvern, Worcestershire. *(DMG Antiques Fairs - 01636 702326)*
Antique Fair, The Watford Grammar School, Rickmansworth Road, Watford, Herts. *(H-N Fairs - 01462 671688)*
Antique & Collectors' Fair, The Copthorne Hotel, Culverhouse Cross, Cardiff, Wales. *(David Robinson Fairs - 01222 620520)*
Antique & Collectors' Fair, The Royal Enclosure, The Racecourse, Ascot, Berks. *(Silhouette Fairs - 01635 44338)*
Antique & Collectors' Fair, The Exhibition Halls, Park Hall, Charnock Richard, Lancs. *(Unicorn Fairs Ltd - 0161 773 7001)*
Antiques Fairs, The Sandown Exhibition Centre, Sandown Park, Esher, Surrey. *(Wonder Whistle Enterprises - 0171 249 4050)*
Friday 12th/Sunday 14th June
Antiques Fair, The Bingley Hall County Showground, Stafford, Staffs. *(Bowman Antiques Fairs - 0113 284 3333)*
The Cheshire Country Antiques Fair, The Arley Hall, Near Knutsford, Cheshire. *(Cooper Antique Fairs - 01249 661111)*
The Duncombe Park Antiques Fair, Near Helmsley, North Yorks. *(Galloway Antiques Fair - 01423 522122)*
Saturday 13th/Sunday 14th June
The First Annual Shuttleworth Antiques Fair, Shuttleworth Centre, Old Warden Park, Biggleswade, Beds. *(Graham Turner Antiques Fairs - 01473 658224)*
Saturday 13th June
Antique & Collectors' Fair, The Town Hall, Clare, Suffolk. *(Best of Fairs - 01787 280306)*
Saturday 13th/Sunday 14th June
Antiques & Collectors' Fair, The Old School, Long Melford, Suffolk. *(Best of Fairs - 01787 280306)*
Sunday 14th June
Antiques & Collectors' Fair, The Oatlands Park Hotel, Weybridge, Surrey. *(Antiques & Collectors' World - 01737 812989)*

Regions continued

Antiques & Collectors' Fair, The Newmarket Racecourse, Newmarket, Suffolk. *(DMG Antiques Fairs - 01636 702326)*

Antique Fair, The Bellhouse Hotel, Oxford Road (A40), Beaconsfield, Bucks. *(Midas Fairs - 01494 674170)*

Antique & Collectors' Fair, The Exhibition Halls, Park Hall, Charnock Richard, Lancs. *(Unicorn Fairs Ltd - 0161 773 7001)*

Tuesday 16th June

Antiques & Collectors' Fair, The Suffolk Showground, Bucklesham Road, Ipswich, Suffolk. *(DMG Antiques Fairs - 01636 702326)*

Friday 19th/Sunday 21st June

Antiques Fair, The Avington Park, Winchester, Hants. *(Galloway Antiques Fairs - 01423 522122)*

Saturday 20th June

Antique & Collectors' Fair, The Church Rooms, Lavenham, Suffolk. *(Best of Fairs - 01787 280306)*

Antiques & Collectors Fair, The Pomme d'Or Hotel, St Helier, Jersey. *(Linda Brennan - 01534 639506)*

Antique & Collectors' Fair, The Salisbury Leisure Centre, The Butts, Hulse Road, Salisbury, Wilts. *(Devon County Antiques Fairs - 01363 82571)*

Saturday 20th/Sunday 21st June

Antiques & Collectors' Fair, The Sports Dome, Bentham Country Club, Near Gloucester, Glos. *(Excalibur - Julie Cannon - 0117 907 1180)*

Antiques Fair, The White Lion Hotel, Market Cross Place, Aldeburgh, Suffolk.
(Graham Turner Antiques Fairs - 01473 658224)

Sunday 21st June

Antiques Fair, The Bankfield Hotel, Bingley, W. Yorks. *(Abbey Antiques Fairs - 01482 445785)*

Antiques & Collectors' Market, The Spectrum Leisure Centre, Guildford, Surrey. *(Antiques & Collectors' World - 01737 812989)*

Antique & Collectors' Fair, The Leisure Centre, Seafront, Felixstowe, Suffolk. *(Best of Fairs - 01787 280306)*

Antique & Collectors' Fair, The Harrow Leisure Centre, Christ Church Avenue, Wealdstone, Middlesex. *(Jax Fairs - 01444 400570)*

Antique & Collectors' Fair, The Plumley Village Hall, Near Knutsford, Cheshire. *(N & B Fairs - 01565 722144)*

Antique & Collectors' Fair, The Abbey Hall, Abingdon, Oxon. *(Silhouette Fairs - 01635 44338)*

Antique & Collectors' Fair, The Exhibition Halls, Park Hall, Charnock Richard, Lancs. *(Unicorn Fairs Ltd - 0161 773 7001)*

Tuesday 23rd June

Antiques Fair, The Public Hall, Southdown Road, Harpenden, Herts. *(Chiltern Fairs - 01753 890301)*

Antiques Fairs, The Sandown Exhibition Centre, Sandown Park, Esher, Surrey. *(Wonder Whistle Enterprises - 0171 249 4050)*

Friday 26th/Sunday 28th June

The 18th/20th Century Tatton Park Fine Arts Fair, Tatton Park, Knutsford, Cheshire. *(Bailey Fairs - 01277 214677)*

Regions continued

Saturday 27th June

Antiques Fair, The Castle Hall, Hertford, Herts. *(Camfair Antiques Fairs - 01945 870160)*

Saturday 27th/Sunday 28th June

Antiques & Collectors' Fair, The Old School, Long Melford, Suffolk. *(Best of Fairs - 01787 280306)*

Sunday 28th June

Antiques Fair, The Willerby Manor, Hull, E. Yorks. *(Abbey Antiques Fairs - 01482 445785*

Antiques & Collectors' Market, The Newbury Racecourse, Newbury, Berks. *(Antiques & Collectors' World - 01737 812989)*

Antiques Fair, The Racecourse, Maidenhead Road, Windsor, Berks. *(Chiltern Fairs - 01753 890301)*

The Brunel Clock & Watch Fair, The Brunel University, Kingston Lane, Uxbridge, Middlesex. *(Mr P Dungate - 01895 834694)*

Antiques Fair, The Haberdashers Askes Girls School, Aldenham Road, Elstree, Herts. *(Harlequin Fairs - 01462 671688)*

Antique & Collectors' Fair, The Town Hall, Hungerford, Berks. *(Silhouette Fairs - 01635 44338)*

Antique & Collectors' Fair, The Exhibition Halls, Park Hall, Charnock Richard, Lancs. *(Unicorn Fairs Ltd - 0161 773 7001)*

Wednesday 1st July

Antiques & Collectors' Fair, The Racecourse, Stratford On Avon, Warks. *(Antiques & Collectors' World - 01737 812989)*

Antique Fair, The Village Hall, Long Melford, Suffolk. *(Graham Turner Antiques Fairs - 01473 658224)*

Thursday 2nd July

Antiques & Collectors' Fair, The Bingley Hall County Showground, Stafford, Staffs. *(Bowman Antiques Fairs - 0113 284 3333)*

Saturday 4th July

Antiques & Collectors' Fair, The W.I. Hall, Frinton on Sea, Essex. *(Best of Fairs - 01787 280306)*

Antique & Collectors' Fair, The Town Hall, Clare, Suffolk. *(Best of Fairs - 01787 280306)*

Antiques Fair, The Chorleywood Memorial Hall, Common Road, Chorleywood, Herts. *(Chiltern Fairs - 01753 890301)*

Saturday 4th/Sunday 5th July

Antiques Fair, The Westpoint Exhibition Centre, Clyst St Mary, Exeter, Devon. *(Devon County Antiques Fairs - 01363 82571)*

Sunday 5th July

Antiques Fair, The Old Swan Hotel, Harrogate, N. Yorks. *(Abbey Antiques Fairs - 01482 445785)*

Antiques & Collectors' Market, The East of England Showground, Peterborough, Cambs. *(Antiques & Collectors' World - 01737 812989)*

Antique & Collectors' Fair, The New Village Hall, Copdock, Near Ipswich, Suffolk. *(Best of Fairs - 01787 280306)*

Antiques Fair, The Centre for Epilepsy, Chalfont St Peter, Bucks. *(Chiltern Fairs - 01753 890301)*

Antique Fair, The Watford Grammar School, Rickmansworth Road, Watford, Herts. *(H-N Fairs - 01462 671688)*

Regions continued

Antique & Collectors' Fair, The Newhouse Country Hotel, Thornhill, Cardiff, Wales. *(David Robinson Fairs - 01222 620520)*
Antique & Collectors' Fair, The Royal Enclosure, The Racecourse, Ascot, Berks. *(Silhouette Fairs - 01635 44338)*
Antique & Collectors' Fair, The Exhibition Halls, Park Hall, Charnock Richard, Lancs. *(Unicorn Fairs Ltd - 0161 773 7001)*

Friday 10th/Sunday 12th July
The 27th Annual Edinburgh Antiques Fair, The Roxburghe Hotel, Charlotte Square, Edinburgh, Scotland. *(Galloway Antiques Fairs - 01423 522122)*

Saturday 11th July
Antique & Collectors' Fair, The Masonic Hall, Bottom of High Street, Lymington, Hants. *(Grandma's Attic Antique Fairs - 01590 677687)*

Saturday 11th/Sunday 12th July
Antiques & Collectors' Fair, The Royal Bath & West Showground, Shepton Mallet, Somerset *(DMG Antiques Fairs - 01636 702326)*
Antique & Collectors' Fair, The Pavilion Gardens, Buxton, Derbys. *(Unicorn Fairs Ltd - 0161 773 7001)*
Ceramics Fair, The Burford School, Burford, Oxfordshire. *(Wakefield Ceramics Fairs - 01905 776091)*

Sunday 12th July
Antique & Collectors' Fair, The Brockenhurst Village Hall, Highwood Road, (off Sway Road) New Forest, Brockenhurst, Hants. *(Grandma's Attic Antique Fairs - 01590 677687)*
Antique Fair, The Bellhouse Hotel, Oxford Road (A40), Beaconsfield, Bucks. *(Midas Fairs - 01494 674170)*
Antique & Collectors' Fair, The Exhibition Halls, Park Hall, Charnock Richard, Lancs. *(Unicorn Fairs Ltd - 0161 773 7001)*

Friday 17th/Sunday 19th July
Antiques Fair, The Chester Racecourse, Chester, Cheshire. *(Bailey Fairs - 01277 214677)*
Antiques Fair, Ripley Castle, Ripley, Harrogate, N. Yorks. *(Galloway Antiques Fairs - 01423 522122)*
The First Woolverstone Fine Art & Antiques Fair, Ipswich High School for Girls (in the New Sports Hall) Woolverstone, Near Ipswich, Suffolk. *(Lomax Antique Fairs - 01603 737631)*

Saturday 18th/Sunday 19th July
The North Cotswolds Antiques Fair, Stanway House, Near Winchcombe, Glos. *(Cooper Antiques Fair - 01249 661111)*
Antique & Collectors' Fair, Kingston Maurward House, The Dorset College of Agriculture & Horticulture, Dorchester, Dorset. *(Grandma's Attic Antique Fairs - 01590 677687)*

Saturday 18th July
Antique & Collectors' Fair, The Church Rooms, Lavenham, Suffolk. *(Best of Fairs - 01787 280306)*

Sunday 19th July
Antiques & Collectors' Market, The Essex County Showground, Chelmsford, Essex. *(Antiques & Collectors' World - 01737 812989)*
Antiques & Collectors' Market, The Spectrum Leisure Centre, Guildford, Surrey. *(Antiques & Collectors' World - 01737 812989)*

Regions continued

Antiques & Collectors' Fair, The Three Counties Showground, Malvern, Worcestershire. *(DMG Antiques Fairs - 01636 702326)*
Antiques Fair, The Haberdashers Askes Girls School, Aldenham Road, Elstree, Herts. *(Harlequin Fairs - 01462 671688)*
Antique & Collectors' Fair, The Copthorne Hotel, Culverhouse Cross, Cardiff, Wales. *(David Robinson Fairs - 01222 620520)*
Antique & Collectors' Fair, The Abbey Hall, Abingdon, Oxon. *(Silhouette Fairs - 01635 44338)*
Antique & Collectors' Fair, The Exhibition Halls, Park Hall, Charnock Richard, Lancs. *(Unicorn Fairs Ltd - 0161 773 7001)*

Tuesday 21st/Wednesday 22nd July
Antiques & Collectors' Fair, The South of England Showground, Ardingly, Sussex. *(DMG Antiques Fairs - 01636 702326)*

Thursday 23rd/Sunday 26th July
The 32nd Annual Snape Antiques Fair, The Maltings, Snape, Nr. Aldeburgh, Suffolk *(Anglian Arts & Antiques - 01986 872368)*

Friday 24th/Sunday 26th July
The Annual Lakes School Antiques Fair, Troutbeck Bridge, Near Windermere, Cumbria. *(Bailey Fairs - 01277 214677)*
Antiques Fair, The Bingley Hall County Showground, Stafford, Staffs. *(Bowman Antiques Fairs - 0113 284 3333)*
Antique & Collectors' Fair, The Yorkshire Showground, Harrogate, N. Yorks. *(Great Northern International Antiques & Collectors' Fairs Ltd - 01325 380077)*
The Sussex Art & Antiques Fair, The Barkham Manor, Piltdown, A272, Near Uckfield, Sussex. *(Penman Antiques Fairs - 01444 482514)*

Saturday 25th July
Antique & Collectors' Fair, The Town Hall, Clare, Suffolk. *(Best of Fairs - 01787 280306)*
Antiques Fair, The Castle Hall, Hertford, Herts. *(Camfair Antiques Fairs - 01945 870160)*
Antique & Collectors' Fair, The St Thomas' Church Hall (Top of High Street) Lymington, Hants. *(Grandma's Attic Antique Fairs - 01590 677687)*

Saturday 25th/Sunday 26th July
Antiques & Collectors' Fair, The Old School, Long Melford, Suffolk. *(Best of Fairs - 01787 280306)*

Sunday 26th July
Antiques Fair, The Willerby Manor, Hull, E. Yorks. *(Abbey Antiques Fairs - 01482 445785*
Antiques Fair, The Racecourse, Maidenhead Road, Windsor, Berks. *(Chiltern Fairs - 01753 890301)*
Antique & Collectors' Fair, The Lyndhurst Park Hotel, High Street, Lyndhurst, Hants. *(Grandma's Attic Antique Fairs - 01590 677687)*
Antique & Collectors' Fair, The Plumley Village Hall, Near Knutsford, Cheshire. *(N & B Fairs - 01565 722144)*
Antique & Collectors' Fair, The Town Hall, Hungerford, Berks. *(Silhouette Fairs - 01635 44338)*
Antique & Collectors' Fair, The Exhibition Halls, Park Hall, Charnock Richard, Lancs. *(Unicorn Fairs Ltd - 0161 773 7001)*

Regions continued

Antiques Fairs, The Sandown Exhibition Centre, Sandown Park, Esher, Surrey. *(Wonder Whistle Enterprises - 0171 249 4050)*

Tuesday 28th July

Antiques Fair, The Public Hall, Southdown Road, Harpenden, Herts. *(Chiltern Fairs - 01753 890301)*

Friday 31st July/Sunday 2nd August

Antiques Fair, Alnwick Castle, Alnwick, Northumberland. *(Galloway Antiques Fairs - 01423 522122)*

Saturday 1st August

Antiques Fair, The Chorleywood Memorial Hall, Common Road, Chorleywood, Herts. *(Chiltern Fairs - 01753 890301)*

Antique & Collectors' Fair, The Matford Centre in the Exeter Livestock Centre, Matford Park Road, Marsh Barton, Exeter, Devon. *(Devon County Antiques Fairs - 01363 82571)*

Antique & Collectors' Fair, The Masonic Hall, Bottom of High Street, Lymington, Hants. *(Grandma's Attic Antique Fairs - 01590 677687)*

Sunday 2nd August

Antiques Fair, The Old Swan Hotel, Harrogate, N. Yorks. *(Abbey Antiques Fairs - 01482 445785)*

Antiques Fair, The Centre for Epilepsy, Chalfont St Peter, Bucks. *(Chiltern Fairs - 01753 890301)*

Antiques & Collectors' Fair, The Three Counties Showground, Malvern, Worcestershire. *(DMG Antiques Fairs - 01636 702326)*

Antique & Collectors' Fair, The Winchester Guildhall, The Broadway, Winchester, Hants. *(Grandma's Attic Antique Fairs - 01590 677687)*

Antique Fair, The Watford Grammar School, Rickmansworth Road, Watford, Herts. *(H-N Fairs - 01462 671688)*

Antique & Collectors' Fair, The Friendly Hotel, Tongwynlais, Cardiff, Wales. *(David Robinson Fairs - 01222 620520)*

Antique & Collectors' Fair, The Exhibition Halls, Park Hall, Charnock Richard, Lancs. *(Unicorn Fairs Ltd - 0161 773 7001)*

Wednesday 5th August

Antiques & Collectors' Fair, The Racecourse, Stratford On Avon, Warks. *(Antiques & Collectors' World - 01737 812989)*

Antique Fair, The Village Hall, Long Melford, Suffolk. *(Graham Turner Antiques Fairs - 01473 658224)*

Thursday 6th/Sunday 9th August

The Antiques for Everyone Fair, The National Exhibition Centre, Birmingham, W. Midlands *(Centre Exhibitions - 0121 767 2760)*

Sunday 9th August

Antiques Fair, The Village Hall, Lewes Road, Ditchling, W. Sussex. *(Mr G Deakin - 01273 845 141)*

Antique Fair, The Bellhouse Hotel, Oxford Road (A40), Beaconsfield, Bucks. *(Midas Fairs - 01494 674170)*

Antique & Collectors' Fair, The Exhibition Halls, Park Hall, Charnock Richard, Lancs. *(Unicorn Fairs Ltd - 0161 773 7001)*

Monday 10th/Tuesday 11th August

Antiques & Collectors' Fair, The Newark & Nottinghamshire Showground, Newark, Notts. *(DMG Antiques Fairs - 01636 702326)*

Regions continued

Wednesday 12th/Sunday 16th August

The Annual Dublin Antiques Fair, The Burlington Hotel, Dublin, Ireland *(Bailey Fairs - 01277 214677)*

Friday 14th/Sunday 16th August

The South Cotswolds Antiques Fair, The Westonbirt School, Tetbury, Glos. *(Cooper Antique Fairs - 01249 661111)*

Saturday 15th August

Antique & Collectors' Fair, The Masonic Hall, Bottom of High Street, Lymington, Hants. *(Grandma's Attic Antique Fairs - 01590 677687)*

Sunday 16th August

Antiques & Collectors' Fair, The Newmarket Racecourse, Newmarket, Suffolk. *(DMG Antiques Fairs - 01636 702326)*

Antique & Collectors' Fair, The Brockenhurst Village Hall, Highwood Road, (off Sway Road) New Forest, Brockenhurst, Hants. *(Grandma's Attic Antique Fairs - 01590 677687)*

Antique & Collectors' Fair, The Abbey Hall, Abingdon, Oxon. *(Silhouette Fairs - 01635 44338)*

Antique & Collectors' Fair, The Exhibition Halls, Park Hall, Charnock Richard, Lancs. *(Unicorn Fairs Ltd - 0161 773 7001)*

Saturday 22nd August

Antique & Collectors' Fair, The St Thomas' Church Hall (Top of High Street) Lymington, Hants. *(Grandma's Attic Antique Fairs - 01590 677687)*

Saturday 22nd/Sunday 23rd August

The Long Melford Antiques Fair, The Village Hall, Long Melford, Suffolk. *(Graham Turner Antiques Fairs - 01473 658224)*

Sunday 23rd August

Antiques Fair, The Old Swan Hotel, Harrogate, N. Yorks. *(Abbey Antiques Fairs - 01482 445785)*

Antiques Fair, The Racecourse, Maidenhead Road, Windsor, Berks. *(Chiltern Fairs - 01753 890301)*

Antiques & Collectors' Fair, The South of England Showground, Ardingly, Sussex. *(DMG Antiques Fairs - 01636 702326)*

Antique & Collectors' Fair, The Potters Heron Hotel, (Ampfield A31 Between Romsey/Winchester), Hants. *(Grandma's Attic Antique Fairs - 01590 677687)*

Antique & Collectors' Fair, The Town Hall, Hungerford, Berks. *(Silhouette Fairs - 01635 44338)*

Antique & Collectors' Fair, The Exhibition Halls, Park Hall, Charnock Richard, Lancs. *(Unicorn Fairs Ltd - 0161 773 7001)*

Friday 28th/Saturday 29th August

The 31st Lindfield Antiques Fair, The King Edward Hall, Lindfield, Near Haywards Heath, W. Sussex. *(Ron Beech - 01273 705827)*

Friday 28th/Monday 31st August

The Annual Ilkley Antiques Fair, Kings Hall & Wintergardens, Station Road, Ilkley, North Yorks. *(Bailey Fairs - 01277 214677)*

Antiques Fair, The Naworth Castle, Brampton, Cumbria. *(Galloway Antiques Fairs - 01423 522122)*

Saturday 29th August

Antiques Fair, The Castle Hall, Hertford, Herts. *(Camfair Antiques Fairs - 01945 870160)*

Antique & Collectors' Fair, The Masonic Hall, Bottom of High Street, Lymington, Hants. *(Grandma's Attic Antique Fairs - 01590 677687)*

Regions continued

Saturday 29th/Monday 31st August
Antique & Collectors' Fair, The Pavilion Gardens, Buxton, Derbys. *(Unicorn Fairs Ltd - 0161 773 7001)*
Sunday 30th August
Antiques Fair, The Willerby Manor, Hull, E. Yorks. *(Abbey Antiques Fairs - 01482 445785*
Antiques & Collectors' Market, The Newbury Racecourse, Newbury, Berks. *(Antiques & Collectors' World - 01737 812989)*
The Midland Clock & Watch Fair, The National Motorcycle Museum, Opposite NEC, Solihull, W. Midlands *(Mr P Dungate - 01895 834694)*
Antique & Collectors' Fair, The Lyndhurst Park Hotel, High Street, Lyndhurst, Hants. *(Grandma's Attic Antique Fairs - 01590 677687)*
Antique & Collectors' Fair, The Plumley Village Hall, Near Knutsford, Cheshire. *(N & B Fairs - 01565 722144)*
Antique & Collectors' Fair, The Copthorne Hotel, Culverhouse Cross, Cardiff, Wales. *(David Robinson Fairs - 01222 620520)*
Antique & Collectors' Fair, The Exhibition Halls, Park Hall, Charnock Richard, Lancs. *(Unicorn Fairs Ltd - 0161 773 7001)*
Sunday 30th/Monday 31st August
Antiques & Collectors' Market, The Goodwood Racecourse, Near Chichester, W. Sussex. *(Antiques & Collectors' World - 01737 812989)*
Ceramics Fair, The Oatland Park Hotel, Weybridge, Surrey. *(Wakefield Ceramics Fairs - 01905 776091)*
Monday 31st August
Antiques & Collectors' Fair, The Pomme d'Or Hotel, St Helier, Jersey. *(Linda Brennan - 01534 639506)*
Antiques Fair, The Northwood College, Maxwell Road, Northwood, Middlesex. *(Chiltern Fairs - 01753 890301)*
Antique & Collectors' Fair, The Allendale Centre, Hanham Road, Wimborne, Dorset. *(Grandma's Attic Antique Fairs - 01590 677687)*
Antique & Collectors' Fair, The Community Hall, Station Road, Woodbridge, Suffolk. *(Kyson Fairs - 01473 735528)*
Antique & Collectors' Fair, The Copthorne Hotel, Culverhouse Cross, Cardiff, Wales. *(David Robinson Fairs - 01222 620520)*
Wednesday 2nd September
Antiques & Collectors' Fair, The Racecourse, Stratford On Avon, Warks. *(Antiques & Collectors' World - 01737 812989)*
Antique Fair, The Village Hall, Long Melford, Suffolk. *(Graham Turner Antiques Fairs - 01473 658224)*
Friday 4th/Sunday 6th September
The Hatfield House Antique Fair, Hatfield House, Herts. *(Bailey Fairs Ltd - 01277 214677)*
The Oxfordshire Antiques Fair, The Bloxham School, Bloxham, Near Banbury, Oxon. *(Cooper Antiques Fairs - 01249 661111)*
Antique & Collectors' Fair, The Yorkshire Showground, Harrogate, N. Yorks. *(Great Northern International Antiques & Collectors' Fairs Ltd - 01325 380077)*

Regions continued

Saturday 5th September
Antiques Fair, The Chorleywood Memorial Hall, Common Road, Chorleywood, Herts. *(Chiltern Fairs - 01753 890301)*
Antique & Collectors' Fair, The Masonic Hall, Bottom of High Street, Lymington, Hants. *(Grandma's Attic Antique Fairs - 01590 677687)*
Saturday 5th/Sunday 6th September
Antiques Fair, The Westpoint Exhibition Centre, Clyst St Mary, Exeter, Devon. *(Devon County Antiques Fairs - 01363 82571)*
Ceramics Fair, The Royal Crown Derby Museum, Derby, Derbys. *(Wakefield Ceramics Fairs - 01905 776091)*
Sunday 6th September
Antiques Fair, The Centre for Epilepsy, Chalfont St Peter, Bucks. *(Chiltern Fairs - 01753 890301)*
Antique & Collectors' Fair, The Winchester Guildhall, The Broadway, Winchester, Hants. *(Grandma's Attic Antique Fairs - 01590 677687)*
Antique Fair, The Watford Grammar School, Rickmansworth Road, Watford, Herts. *(H-N Fairs - 01462 671688)*
Antiques Fair, The Parkshot Centre, Parkshot, Near BR Station, Richmond, Surrey. *(P & A Antiques - 0181 543 5075)*
Antique & Collectors' Fair, The Royal Enclosure, The Racecourse, Ascot, Berks. *(Silhouette Fairs - 01635 44338)*
Antique & Collectors' Fair, The Exhibition Halls, Park Hall, Charnock Richard, Lancs. *(Unicorn Fairs Ltd - 0161 773 7001)*
Antiques Fairs, The Sandown Exhibition Centre, Sandown Park, Esher, Surrey. *(Wonder Whistle Enterprises - 0171 249 4050)*
Tuesday 8th September
Antiques & Collectors' Fair, The Suffolk Showground, Bucklesham Road, Ipswich, Suffolk. *(DMG Antiques Fairs - 01636 702326)*
Wednesday 9th/Sunday 13th September
The Tatton Park Antiques Fair, Tatton Park, Knutsford, Cheshire. *(Bailey Fairs - 01277 214677)*
Friday 11th/Sunday 13th September
The Cotswold Oak & Country Antiques Fair, The Chavenage House, Tetbury, Glos. *(Cooper Antique Fairs - 01249 661111)*
Antiques Fair, Fulbeck Hall, Near Grantham, Lincs. *(Galloway Antique Fairs - 01423 522122)*
The Petersfield Antiques Fairs, The Town Hall, Petersfield, Hants. *(Gamlin Exhibition Services - 01452 862557)*
Antique & Collectors' Fair, Kingston Maurward House, The Dorset College of Agriculture & Horticulture, Dorchester, Dorset. *(Grandma's Attic Antique Fairs - 01590 677687)*
Sunday 13th September
Antiques Fair, The Bankfield Hotel, Bingley, W. Yorks. *(Abbey Antiques Fairs - 01482 445785)*
Antiques & Collectors' Fair, The Oatlands Park Hotel, Weybridge, Surrey. *(Antiques & Collectors' World - 01737 812989)*
Antiques & Collectors' Market, The Essex County Showground, Chelmsford, Essex. *(Antiques & Collectors' World - 01737 812989)*

Regions continued

Antiques & Collectors' Fair, The Three Counties Showground, Malvern, Worcestershire. *(DMG Antiques Fairs - 01636 702326)*
The Brunel Clock & Watch Fair, The Brunel University, Kingston Lane, Uxbridge, Middlesex. *(Mr P Dungate - 01895 834694)*
The Furze Hill Antiques Fair, The Banqueting Centre, Margaretting, Near Chelmsford, Essex. *(Graham Turner Antiques Fairs - 01473 658224)*
Antique & Collectors' Fair, The Harrow Leisure Centre, Christ Church Avenue, Wealdstone, Middlesex. *(Jax Fairs - 01444 400570)*
Antique & Collectors' Fair, The Royal Chace Hotel, Queens Banqueting Suite, The Ridgeway, Enfield, Middlesex. *(M & S Enterprises - 0181 440 2330)*
Antique Fair, The Bellhouse Hotel, Oxford Road (A40), Beaconsfield, Bucks. *(Midas Fairs - 01494 674170)*
Antique & Collectors' Fair, The Stakis Hotel, Chepstow Road, Langstone, Newport, Wales. *(David Robinson Fairs - 01222 620520)*

Friday 18th/Sunday 20th September
Antiques Fair, The Holdenby House, Holdenby, Northants. *(Galloway Antiques Fairs - 01423 522122)*

Saturday 19th September
Antique & Collectors' Fair, The Matford Centre in the Exeter Livestock Centre, Matford Park Road, Marsh Barton, Exeter, Devon. *(Devon County Antiques Fairs - 01363 82571)*
Antique & Collectors' Fair, The Masonic Hall, Bottom of High Street, Lymington, Hants. *(Grandma's Attic Antique Fairs - 01590 677687)*
Antique & Collectors' Fair, The Muswell Hill Centre, Entrance Summerland Gardens, Muswell Hill Road, N.10. *(M & S Enterprises - 0181 440 2330)*

Sunday 20th September
Antiques Fair, The Old Swan Hotel, Harrogate, N. Yorks. *(Abbey Antiques Fairs - 01482 445785)*
Antique & Collectors' Fair, The Brockenhurst Village Hall, Highwood Road, (off Sway Road) New Forest, Brockenhurst, Hants. *(Grandma's Attic Antique Fairs - 01590 677687)*
Antiques Fair, The Haberdashers Askes Girls School, Aldenham Road, Elstree, Herts. *(Harlequin Fairs - 01462 671688)*
Antiques & Collectors' Fair, The Elliots Sports & Social Club, Rowley Lane, Elstree Way, Borehamwood, Herts. *(M & S Enterprises - 0181 440 2330)*
Antique & Collectors' Fair, The Abbey Hall, Abingdon, Oxon. *(Silhouette Fairs - 01635 44338)*
Antique & Collectors' Fair, The Exhibition Halls, Park Hall, Charnock Richard, Lancs. *(Unicorn Fairs Ltd - 0161 773 7001)*

Tuesday 22nd September
Antiques Fair, The Public Hall, Southdown Road, Harpenden, Herts. *(Chiltern Fairs - 01753 890301)*

Tuesday 22nd/Wednesday 23rd September
Antiques & Collectors' Fair, The South of England Showground, Ardingly, Sussex. *(DMG Antiques Fairs - 01636 702326)*

Thursday 24th/Sunday 27th September
Antiques Fair, Ripley Castle, Ripley, Harrogate, N. Yorks. *(Galloway Antiques Fairs - 01423 522122)*

Regions continued

Thursday 24th/Wednesday 30th September
The 48th Northern Antiques Fair, The Pavilions of Harrogate, N. Yorks *(Bailey Fairs - 01277 214677)*

Saturday 26th September
Antiques Fair, The Castle Hall, Hertford, Herts. *(Camfair Antiques Fairs - 01945 870160)*
Antique & Collectors' Fair, The St Thomas' Church Hall (Top of High Street) Lymington, Hants. *(Grandma's Attic Antique Fairs - 01590 677687)*

Saturday 26th/Sunday 27th September
Antiques & Collectors' Fair, The Royal Bath & West Showground, Shepton Mallet, Somerset *(DMG Antiques Fairs - 01636 702326)*

Sunday 27th September
Antiques Fair, The Willerby Manor, Hull, E. Yorks. *(Abbey Antiques Fairs - 01482 445785*
Antiques & Collectors' Market, The Newbury Racecourse, Newbury, Berks. *(Antiques & Collectors' World - 01737 812989)*
Antiques Fair, The Racecourse, Maidenhead Road, Windsor, Berks. *(Chiltern Fairs - 01753 890301)*
Antique & Collectors' Fair, The Lyndhurst Park Hotel, High Street, Lyndhurst, Hants. *(Grandma's Attic Antique Fairs - 01590 677687)*
Antique & Collectors' Fair, The Community Hall, Station Road, Woodbridge, Suffolk. *(Kyson Fairs - 01473 735528)*
Antique & Collectors' Fair, The Plumley Village Hall, Near Knutsford, Cheshire. *(N & B Fairs - 01565 722144)*
Antique & Collectors' Fair, The Friendly Hotel, Tongwynlais, Cardiff, Wales. *(David Robinson Fairs - 01222 620520)*
Antique & Collectors' Fair, The Town Hall, Hungerford, Berks. *(Silhouette Fairs - 01635 44338)*
Antique & Collectors' Fair, The Exhibition Halls, Park Hall, Charnock Richard, Lancs. *(Unicorn Fairs Ltd - 0161 773 7001)*

Thursday 1st/Sunday 4th October
The 31st Surrey Antique Fair, The Civic Hall, Guildford, Surrey. *(Cultural Exhibition Ltd - 01483 422562)*

Thursday 1st/Sunday 4th October
Antiques for All Seasons, The Royal Armouries Museum, Leeds, Yorks. *(Centre Exhibitions - 0121 767 2760)*

Friday 2nd/Sunday 4th October
Antiques Fair, The Bingley Hall County Showground, Stafford, Staffs. *(Bowman Antiques Fairs - 0113 284 3333)*
The NorthYorkshire Antiques Fair, Hovingham Hall, Hovingham, Yorks. *(Cooper Antique Fairs - 01249 661111)*
Antique & Collectors' Fair, The Knavesmire Exhibition Centre, The Racecourse, York, Yorks. *(Great Northern International Antique & Collectors Fairs Ltd - 01325 380077)*

Saturday 3rd October
Antiques Fair, The Chorleywood Memorial Hall, Common Road, Chorleywood, Herts. *(Chiltern Fairs - 01753 890301)*
Antique & Collectors' Fair, The Salisbury Leisure Centre, The Butts, Hulse Road, Salisbury, Wilts. *(Devon County Antiques Fairs - 01363 82571)*

Regions continued

Antique & Collectors' Fair, The Masonic Hall, Bottom of High Street, Lymington, Hants. *(Grandma's Attic Antique Fairs - 01590 677687)*

Sunday 4th October

Antiques Fair, The Old Swan Hotel, Harrogate, N. Yorks. *(Abbey Antiques Fairs - 01482 445785)*

Antiques & Collectors' Market, The Goodwood Racecourse, Near Chichester, W. Sussex. *(Antiques & Collectors' World - 01737 812989)*

Antiques Fair, The Centre for Epilepsy, Chalfont St Peter, Bucks. *(Chiltern Fairs - 01753 890301)*

The Midland Clock & Watch Fair, The National Motorcycle Museum, Opposite NEC, Solihull, W. Midlands *(Mr P Dungate - 01895 834694)*

Antique & Collectors' Fair, The Winchester Guildhall, The Broadway, Winchester, Hants. *(Grandma's Attic Antique Fairs - 01590 677687)*

Antique Fair, The Watford Grammar School, Rickmansworth Road, Watford, Herts. *(H-N Fairs - 01462 671688)*

Antiques Fair, The Parkshot Centre, Parkshot, Near BR Station, Richmond, Surrey. *(P & A Antiques - 0181 543 5075)*

Antique & Collectors' Fair, The Royal Enclosure, The Racecourse, Ascot, Berks. *(Silhouette Fairs - 01635 44338)*

Antique & Collectors' Fair, The Exhibition Halls, Park Hall, Charnock Richard, Lancs. *(Unicorn Fairs Ltd - 0161 773 7001)*

Wednesday 7th October

Antiques & Collectors' Fair, The Racecourse, Stratford On Avon, Warks. *(Antiques & Collectors' World - 01737 812989)*

Antique Fair, The Village Hall, Long Melford, Suffolk. *(Graham Turner Antiques Fairs - 01473 658224)*

Friday 9th/Sunday 11th October

The Cheshire Country Antiques Fair, The Arley Hall, Near Knutsford, Cheshire. *(Cooper Antique Fairs - 01249 661111)*

Saturday 10th October

Antique & Collectors' Fair, The Matford Centre in the Exeter Livestock Centre, Matford Park Road, Marsh Barton, Exeter, Devon. *(Devon County Antiques Fairs - 01363 82571)*

Saturday 10th/Sunday 11th October

Antique & Collectors' Fair, The Pavilion Gardens, Buxton, Derbys. *(Unicorn Fairs Ltd - 0161 773 7001)*

Ceramics Fair, The Burford School, Burford, Oxfordshire. *(Wakefield Ceramics Fairs - 01905 776091)*

Sunday 11th October

Antiques & Collectors' Fair, The Oatlands Park Hotel, Weybridge, Surrey. *(Antiques & Collectors' World - 01737 812989)*

Antiques Fair, The Village Hall, Lewes Road, Ditchling, W. Sussex. *(Mr G Deakin - 01273 845 141)*

Antiques & Collectors' Fair, The Three Counties Showground, Malvern, Worcestershire. *(DMG Antiques Fairs - 01636 702326)*

The Furze Hill Antiques Fair, The Banqueting Centre, Margaretting, Near Chelmsford, Essex. *(Graham Turner Antiques Fairs - 01473 658224)*

Antique & Collectors' Fair, The Allendale Centre, Hanham Road, Wimborne, Dorset. *(Grandma's Attic Antique Fairs - 01590 677687)*

Regions continued

Antique & Collectors' Fair, The Bushey Golf & Country Club, Banqueting Suite, The High Street, Bushey, Herts. *(M & S Enterprises - 0181 440 2330)*

Antique Fair, The Bellhouse Hotel, Oxford Road (A40), Beaconsfield, Bucks. *(Midas Fairs - 01494 674170)*

Antique & Collectors' Fair, The Stakis Hotel, Chepstow Road, Langstone, Newport, Wales. *(David Robinson Fairs - 01222 620520)*

Antique & Collectors' Fair, The Exhibition Halls, Park Hall, Charnock Richard, Lancs. *(Unicorn Fairs Ltd - 0161 773 7001)*

Thursday 15th October

Antiques Fairs, The Sandown Exhibition Centre, Sandown Park, Esher, Surrey. *(Wonder Whistle Enterprises - 0171 249 4050)*

Thursday 15th/Sunday 18th October

The Annual Decorative Antiques & Fine Arts Fair, The Pavilion Gardens, Buxton, Derbys. *(Bailey Fairs - 01277 214677)*

Friday 16th/Sunday 18th October

The Stafford County Antique Fair, The Sandon Hall, Sandon, Near Stone, Staffs. *(Cooper Antiques Fair - 01249 661111)*

Antiques Fair, The Stansted House, Rowlands Castle, Hants. *(Galloway Antiques Fairs - 01423 522122)*

Saturday 17th October

Antiques & Collectors' Fair, The Pomme d'Or Hotel, St Helier, Jersey. *(Linda Brennan - 01534 639506)*

Antiques Fair, The Dr. Challoner's Grammar School, Amersham, Bucks. *(Chiltern Fairs - 01753 890301)*

Antique & Collectors' Fair, The Muswell Hill Centre, Entrance Summerland Gardens, Muswell Hill Road, N.10. *(M & S Enterprises - 0181 440 2330)*

Saturday 17th/Sunday 18th October

The 46th Luton Antiques Fair, The Putteridge Bury House on the A505 Luton to Hitchin Road, Herts. *(Mr D Ball - 01525 210753)*

Sunday 18th October

Antiques & Collectors' Market, The Goodwood Racecourse, Near Chichester, W. Sussex. *(Antiques & Collectors' World - 01737 812989)*

Antique & Collectors' Fair, The Potters Heron Hotel, (Ampfield A31 Between Romsey/Winchester), Hants. *(Grandma's Attic Antique Fairs - 01590 677687)*

Antiques Fair, The Haberdashers Askes Girls School, Aldenham Road, Elstree, Herts. *(Harlequin Fairs - 01462 671688)*

Antique & Collectors' Fair, The Community Hall, Station Road, Woodbridge, Suffolk. *(Kyson Fairs - 01473 735528)*

Antiques & Collectors' Fair, The Wembley Park Sports & Social Club, Bridge Road, Wembley Park, Wembley, Middlesex. *(M & S Enterprises - 0181 440 2330)*

Antique & Collectors' Fair, The Abbey Hall, Abingdon, Oxon. *(Silhouette Fairs - 01635 44338)*

Antique & Collectors' Fair, The Exhibition Halls, Park Hall, Charnock Richard, Lancs. *(Unicorn Fairs Ltd - 0161 773 7001)*

Regions continued

Monday 19th/Tuesday 20th October
Antiques & Collectors' Fair, The Newark & Nottinghamshire Showground, Newark, Notts. *(DMG Antiques Fairs - 01636 702326)*
Friday 23rd/Sunday 25th October
Antiques Fair, Deene Park, Corby, Northants. *(Galloway Antique Fairs - 01423 522122)*
The 7th East Anglian Antique Dealers Fair, Langley Park School, Loddon, Norfolk. *(Lomax Antique Fairs - 01603 737631)*
Saturday 24th October
Antique & Collectors' Fair, The Masonic Hall, Bottom of High Street, Lymington, Hants. *(Grandma's Attic Antique Fairs - 01590 677687)*
Saturday 24th/Sunday 25th October
Antiques & Collectors' Fair, The Cardiff International Arena, Cardiff, S. Glamorgan, Wales. *(DMG Antiques Fairs - 01636 702326)*
Ceramics Fair, The Felbridge Hotel, East Grinstead, W. Sussex. *(Wakefield Ceramics Fairs - 01905 776091)*
Sunday 25th October
Antiques Fair, The Willerby Manor, Hull, E. Yorks. *(Abbey Antiques Fairs - 01482 445785*
Antiques & Collectors' Market, The Newbury Racecourse, Newbury, Berks. *(Antiques & Collectors' World - 01737 812989)*
Antiques Fair, The Racecourse, Maidenhead Road, Windsor, Berks. *(Chiltern Fairs - 01753 890301)*
Antiques & Collectors' Fair, The Newmarket Racecourse, Newmarket, Suffolk. *(DMG Antiques Fairs - 01636 702326)*
Antique & Collectors' Fair, The Lyndhurst Park Hotel, High Street, Lyndhurst, Hants. *(Grandma's Attic Antique Fairs - 01590 677687)*
Antique & Collectors' Fair, The Royal Chace Hotel, Queens Banqueting Suite, The Ridgeway, Enfield, Middlesex. *(M & S Enterprises - 0181 440 2330)*
Antique & Collectors' Fair, The Plumley Village Hall, Near Knutsford, Cheshire. *(N & B Fairs - 01565 722144)*
Antique & Collectors' Fair, The Town Hall, Hungerford, Berks. *(Silhouette Fairs - 01635 44338)*
Antique & Collectors' Fair, The Exhibition Halls, Park Hall, Charnock Richard, Lancs. *(Unicorn Fairs Ltd - 0161 773 7001)*
Tuesday 27th October
Antiques Fair, The Public Hall, Southdown Road, Harpenden, Herts. *(Chiltern Fairs - 01753 890301)*
Thursday 29th October
Antiques & Collectors' Fair, The Bingley Hall County Showground, Stafford, Staffs. *(Bowman Antiques Fairs - 0113 284 3333)*
Friday 30th/Saturday 31st October
Ceramics Fair, The Lady Manners School, Bakewell, Derbys. *(Wakefield Ceramics Fairs - 01905 776091)*
Friday 30th October/Sunday 1st November
Antiques Fair, The Stonyhurst College, Clitheroe, Lancs. *(Galloway Antiques Fairs - 01423 522122)*
Saturday 31st October
Antiques Fair, The Castle Hall, Hertford, Herts. *(Camfair Antiques Fairs - 01945 870160)*

Regions continued

Antique & Collectors' Fair, The St Thomas' Church Hall (Top of High Street) Lymington, Hants. *(Grandma's Attic Antique Fairs - 01590 677687)*
Antique & Collectors' Fair, The Muswell Hill Centre, Entrance Summerland Gardens, Muswell Hill Road, N.10. *(M & S Enterprises - 0181 440 2330)*
Sunday 1st November
Antiques Fair, The Old Swan Hotel, Harrogate, N. Yorks. *(Abbey Antiques Fairs - 01482 445785)*
Antiques & Collectors' Market, The Goodwood Racecourse, Near Chichester, W. Sussex. *(Antiques & Collectors' World - 01737 812989)*
Antiques Fair, The Centre for Epilepsy, Chalfont St Peter, Bucks. *(Chiltern Fairs - 01753 890301)*
Antiques & Collectors' Fair, The Three Counties Showground, Malvern, Worcestershire. *(DMG Antiques Fairs - 01636 702326)*
Antique & Collectors' Fair, The Winchester Guildhall, The Broadway, Winchester, Hants. *(Grandma's Attic Antique Fairs - 01590 677687)*
Antique Fair, The Watford Grammar School, Rickmansworth Road, Watford, Herts. *(H-N Fairs - 01462 671688)*
Antique & Collectors' Fair, The Copthorne Hotel, Culverhouse Cross, Cardiff, Wales. *(David Robinson Fairs - 01222 620520)*
Antique & Collectors' Fair, The Exhibition Halls, Park Hall, Charnock Richard, Lancs. *(Unicorn Fairs Ltd - 0161 773 7001)*
Tuesday 3rd/Wednesday 4th November
Antiques & Collectors' Fair, The South of England Showground, Ardingly, Sussex. *(DMG Antiques Fairs - 01636 702326)*
Wednesday 4th November
Antiques & Collectors Market, The Racecourse, Stratford On Avon, Warks. *(Antiques & Collectors' World - 01737 812989)*
Antique Fair, The Village Hall, Long Melford, Suffolk. *(Graham Turner Antiques Fairs - 01473 658224)*
Friday 6th/Sunday 8th November
The Hever Castle Antiques Fair, The Pavilion, Hever Castle, Near Edenbridge, Kent. *(Cooper Antiques Fairs - 01249 661111)*
The Duncombe Park Antiques Fair, Duncombe Park, Helmsley, N. Yorks. *(Galloway Antiques Fairs - 01423 522122)*
Antique & Collectors' Fair, The Yorkshire Showground, Harrogate, N. Yorks. *(Great Northern International Antiques & Collectors' Fairs Ltd - 01325 380077)*
Saturday 7th November
Antiques Fair, The Chorleywood Memorial Hall, Common Road, Chorleywood, Herts. *(Chiltern Fairs - 01753 890301)*
Antique & Collectors' Fair, The Masonic Hall, Bottom of High Street, Lymington, Hants. *(Grandma's Attic Antique Fairs - 01590 677687)*
Saturday 7th/Sunday 8th November
Antiques Fair, The Westpoint Exhibition Centre, Clyst St Mary, Exeter, Devon. *(Devon County Antiques Fairs - 01363 82571)*

Regions continued

Antique & Collectors' Fair, The Pavilion Gardens, Buxton, Derbys. *(Unicorn Fairs Ltd - 0161 773 7001)*

Ceramics Fair, The Michael Herbert Hall, Wilton, Near Salisbury, Wilts. *(Wakefield Ceramics Fairs - 01905 776091)*

Sunday 8th November

Antiques Fair, The Bankfield Hotel, Bingley, W. Yorks. *(Abbey Antiques Fairs - 01482 445785)*

Antiques & Collectors' Fair, The Oatlands Park Hotel, Weybridge, Surrey. *(Antiques & Collectors' World - 01737 812989)*

Antique & Collectors' Fair, The Brockenhurst Village Hall, Highwood Road, (off Sway Road) New Forest, Brockenhurst, Hants. *(Grandma's Attic Antique Fairs - 01590 677687)*

The Glass Collectors' Fair, The National Motorcycle Museum, Birmingham, W. Midlands. *(Patricia Hier - 01260 271975)*

Antique & Collectors' Fair, The Harrow Leisure Centre, Christ Church Avenue, Wealdstone, Middlesex. *(Jax Fairs - 01444 400570)*

Antique & Collectors' Fair, The Bushey Golf & Country Club, Banqueting Suite, The High Street, Bushey, Herts. *(M & S Enterprises - 0181 440 2330)*

Antique Fair, The Bellhouse Hotel, Oxford Road (A40), Beaconsfield, Bucks. *(Midas Fairs - 01494 674170)*

The Furze Hill Antiques Fair, The Banqueting Centre, Margaretting, Near Chelmsford, Essex. *(Graham Turner Antiques Fairs - 01473 658224)*

Antique & Collectors' Fair, The Exhibition Halls, Park Hall, Charnock Richard, Lancs. *(Unicorn Fairs Ltd - 0161 773 7001)*

Friday 13th/Sunday 15th November

The Annual Holker Hall Antiques Fair, Cart-in-Cartmel, Cumbria. *(Bailey Fairs - 01277 214677)*

The Leicester County Antiques Fair, The Prestwold Hall, Near Hoton, Loughborough, Leics. *(Cooper Antiques Fairs - 01249 661111)*

The 21st Edinburgh Winter Antiques Fair, The Roxburghe Hotel, Charlotte Square, Edinburgh, Scotland. *(Galloway Antiques Fairs - 01423 522122)*

Saturday 14th/Sunday 15th November

The Annual Woodbridge Antique Fair, The Melton Grange Hotel, Pyches Road, Woodbridge, Suffolk. *(Graham Turner Antiques Fairs - 01473 658224)*

Antique & Collectors' Fair, Kingston Maurward House, The Dorset College of Agriculture & Horticulture, Dorchester, Dorset. *(Grandma's Attic Antique Fairs - 01590 677687)*

Sunday 15th November

Antiques & Collectors' Market, The Goodwood Racecourse, Near Chichester, W. Sussex. *(Antiques & Collectors' World - 01737 812989)*

Antiques Fair, The Haberdashers Askes Girls School, Aldenham Road, Elstree, Herts. *(Harlequin Fairs - 01462 671688)*

Antique & Collectors' Fair, The Community Hall, Station Road, Woodbridge, Suffolk. *(Kyson Fairs - 01473 735528)*

Antique & Collectors' Fair, The Stakis Hotel, Chepstow Road, Langstone, Newport, Wales. *(David Robinson Fairs - 01222 620520)*

Regions continued

Antique & Collectors' Fair, The Abbey Hall, Abingdon, Oxon. *(Silhouette Fairs - 01635 44338)*

Antique & Collectors' Fair, The Exhibition Halls, Park Hall, Charnock Richard, Lancs. *(Unicorn Fairs Ltd - 0161 773 7001)*

Tuesday 17th November

Antiques & Collectors' Fair, The National Agricultural Centre, Stoneleigh, Near Kenilworth, W. Midlands. *(DMG Antiques Fairs - 01636 702326)*

Friday 20th/Sunday 22nd November

The Annual Chester Racecourse Antiques Fair, The Racecourse, Chester, Cheshire *(Bailey Fairs - 01277 214677)*

Antiques Fair, Beaulieu Stately Home, Beaulieu, Hants. *(Galloway Antique Fairs - 01423 522122)*

Saturday 21st November

Antiques Fair, The Castle Hall, Hertford, Herts. *(Camfair Antiques Fairs - 01945 870160)*

Antique & Collectors' Fair, The Muswell Hill Centre, Entrance Summerland Gardens, Muswell Hill Road, N.10. *(M & S Enterprises - 0181 440 2330)*

Saturday 21st/Sunday 22nd November

Antiques & Collectors' Fair, The Royal Bath & West Showground, Shepton Mallet, Somerset *(DMG Antiques Fairs - 01636 702326)*

The Long Melford Antiques Fair, The Village Hall, Long Melford, Suffolk. *(Graham Turner Antiques Fairs - 01473 658224)*

Sunday 22nd November

Antiques Fair, The Old Swan Hotel, Harrogate, N. Yorks. *(Abbey Antiques Fairs - 01482 445785)*

Antiques & Collectors' Market, The Newbury Racecourse, Newbury, Berks. *(Antiques & Collectors' World - 01737 812989)*

Antiques Fair, The Racecourse, Maidenhead Road, Windsor, Berks. *(Chiltern Fairs - 01753 890301)*

Antique & Collectors' Fair, The Lyndhurst Park Hotel, High Street, Lyndhurst, Hants. *(Grandma's Attic Antique Fairs - 01590 677687)*

Antique & Collectors' Fair, The Royal Chace Hotel, Queens Banqueting Suite, The Ridgeway, Enfield, Middlesex. *(M & S Enterprises - 0181 440 2330)*

Antique & Collectors' Fair, The 'Rest', Rest Bay, Porthcawl, Wales. *(David Robinson Fairs)*

Antique & Collectors' Fair, The Town Hall, Hungerford, Berks. *(Silhouette Fairs - 01635 44338)*

Antique & Collectors' Fair, The Exhibition Halls, Park Hall, Charnock Richard, Lancs. *(Unicorn Fairs Ltd - 0161 773 7001)*

Tuesday 24th November

Antiques Fair, The Public Hall, Southdown Road, Harpenden, Herts. *(Chiltern Fairs - 01753 890301)*

Wednesday 25th/Sunday 29th November

The Annual Gleneagles Antiques Fair, Gleneagles Hotel, Perthshire, Scotland *(Bailey Fairs - 01277 214677)*

Saturday 28th November

Antique & Collectors' Fair, The Matford Centre in the Exeter Livestock Centre, Matford Park Road, Marsh Barton, Exeter, Devon. *(Devon County Antiques Fairs - 01363 82571)*

Regions continued

Sunday 29th November
Antiques Fair, The Willerby Manor, Hull, E. Yorks. *(Abbey Antiques Fairs - 01482 445785*
Antiques & Collectors' Market, The Goodwood Racecourse, Near Chichester, W. Sussex. *(Antiques & Collectors' World - 01737 812989)*
Antiques Fair, The Northwood College, Maxwell Road, Northwood, Middlesex. *(Chiltern Fairs - 01753 890301)*
Antique & Collectors' Fair, The Littledown Centre, Castle Lane, (North-east of Bournemouth) Dorset. *(Grandma's Attic Antique Fairs - 01590 677687)*
Antiques & Collectors' Fair, The Elliots Sports & Social Club, Rowley Lane, Elstree Way, Borehamwood, Herts. *(M & S Enterprises - 0181 440 2330)*
Antique & Collectors' Fair, The Plumley Village Hall, Near Knutsford, Cheshire. *(N & B Fairs - 01565 722144)*
Antique & Collectors' Fair, The Exhibition Halls, Park Hall, Charnock Richard, Lancs. *(Unicorn Fairs Ltd - 0161 773 7001)*
Antiques Fairs, The Sandown Exhibition Centre, Sandown Park, Esher, Surrey. *(Wonder Whistle Enterprises - 0171 249 4050)*

Wednesday 2nd December
Antiques & Collectors Market, The Racecourse, Stratford On Avon, Warks. *(Antiques & Collectors' World - 01737 812989)*
Antique Fair, The Village Hall, Long Melford, Suffolk. *(Graham Turner Antiques Fairs - 01473 658224)*

Friday 4th/Sunday 6th December
The Scone Palace Antiques Fair, Perth, Scotland. *(Galloway Antiques Fairs - 01423 522122)*

Saturday 5th December
Antiques Fair, The Chorleywood Memorial Hall, Common Road, Chorleywood, Herts. *(Chiltern Fairs - 01753 890301)*

Saturday 5th/Sunday 6th December
Antique & Collectors' Fair, The Pavilion Gardens, Buxton, Derbys. *(Unicorn Fairs Ltd - 0161 773 7001)*

Sunday 6th December
Antiques Fair, The Old Swan Hotel, Harrogate, N. Yorks. *(Abbey Antiques Fairs - 01482 445785)*
Antiques & Collectors' Market, The Spectrum Leisure Centre, Guildford, Surrey. *(Antiques & Collectors' World - 01737 812989)*
Antiques Fair, The Centre for Epilepsy, Chalfont St Peter, Bucks. *(Chiltern Fairs - 01753 890301)*
Antiques & Collectors' Fair, The Three Counties Showground, Malvern, Worcestershire. *(DMG Antiques Fairs - 01636 702326)*
Antique & Collectors' Fair, David Lloyd Riverside Club, Christchurch Road, Ringwood, Hants. *(Grandma's Attic Antique Fairs - 01590 677687)*
Antique Fair, The Watford Grammar School, Rickmansworth Road, Watford, Herts. *(H-N Fairs - 01462 671688)*
Antique & Collectors' Fair, The Friendly Hotel, Tongwynlais, Cardiff, Wales. *(David Robinson Fairs - 01222 620520)*

Regions continued

Antique & Collectors' Fair, The Royal Enclosure, The Racecourse, Ascot, Berks. *(Silhouette Fairs - 01635 44338)*
Antique & Collectors' Fair, The Exhibition Halls, Park Hall, Charnock Richard, Lancs. *(Unicorn Fairs Ltd - 0161 773 7001)*

Monday 7th/Tuesday 8th December
Antiques & Collectors' Fair, The Newark & Nottinghamshire Showground, Newark, Notts. *(DMG Antiques Fairs - 01636 702326)*

Friday 11th/Sunday 13th December
The Haughton Tower Antiques Fair, Near Preston, Lancs *(Bailey Fairs - 01277 214677)*
Antiques Fair, The Bingley Hall County Showground, Stafford, Staffs. *(Bowman Antiques Fairs - 0113 284 3333)*

Saturday 12th December
Antiques & Collectors' Fair, The Pomme d'Or Hotel, St Helier, Jersey. *(Linda Brennan - 01534 639506)*
Antique & Collectors' Fair, The Salisbury Leisure Centre, The Butts, Hulse Road, Salisbury, Wilts. *(Devon County Antiques Fairs - 01363 82571)*

Sunday 13th December
Antiques & Collectors' Fair, The Oatlands Park Hotel, Weybridge, Surrey. *(Antiques & Collectors' World - 01737 812989)*
Antiques Fair, The Village Hall, Lewes Road, Ditchling, W. Sussex. *(Mr G Deakin - 01273 845 141)*
The Brunel Clock & Watch Fair, The Brunel University, Kingston Lane, Uxbridge, Middlesex. *(Mr P Dungate - 01895 834694)*
Antique & Collectors' Fair, The Community Hall, Station Road, Woodbridge, Suffolk. *(Kyson Fairs - 01473 735528)*
Antiques & Collectors' Fair, The Wembley Park Sports & Social Club, Bridge Road, Wembley Park, Wembley, Middlesex. *(M & S Enterprises - 0181 440 2330)*
Antique Fair, The Bellhouse Hotel, Oxford Road (A40), Beaconsfield, Bucks. *(Midas Fairs - 01494 674170)*
Antiques Fair, The Parkshot Centre, Parkshot, Near BR Station, Richmond, Surrey. *(P & A Antiques - 0181 543 5075)*
Antique & Collectors' Fair, The Abbey Hall, Abingdon, Oxon. *(Silhouette Fairs - 01635 44338)*
The Furze Hill Antiques Fair, The Banqueting Centre, Margaretting, Near Chelmsford, Essex. *(Graham Turner Antiques Fairs - 01473 658224)*
Antique & Collectors' Fair, The Exhibition Halls, Park Hall, Charnock Richard, Lancs. *(Unicorn Fairs Ltd - 0161 773 7001)*

Tuesday 15th December
Antiques Fair, The Public Hall, Southdown Road, Harpenden, Herts. *(Chiltern Fairs - 01753 890301)*

Saturday 19th December
Antiques Fair, The Castle Hall, Hertford, Herts. *(Camfair Antiques Fairs - 01945 870160)*
Antique & Collectors' Fair, The Muswell Hill Centre, Entrance Summerland Gardens, Muswell Hill Road, N.10. *(M & S Enterprises - 0181 440 2330)*

Regions continued

Saturday 19th/Sunday 20th December
The South Cotswolds Antiques Fair, The Westonbirt School, Tetbury, Glos. *(Cooper Antique Fairs - 01249 661111)*
Sunday 20th December Antiques Fair, The Bankfield Hotel, Bingley, W. Yorks. *(Abbey Antiques Fairs - 01482 445785)*
Antiques Fair, The Willerby Manor, Hull, E. Yorks. *(Abbey Antiques Fairs - 01482 445785*
Antiques Fair, The Haberdashers Askes Girls School, Aldenham Road, Elstree, Herts. *(Harlequin Fairs - 01462 671688)*
Antique & Collectors' Fair, The Exhibition Halls, Park Hall, Charnock Richard, Lancs. *(Unicorn Fairs Ltd - 0161 773 7001)*
Sunday 27th December
Antiques Fair, The Old Swan Hotel, Harrogate, N. Yorks. *(Abbey Antiques Fairs - 01482 445785)*
Antiques Fair, The Racecourse, Maidenhead Road, Windsor, Berks. *(Chiltern Fairs - 01753 890301)*
Antique & Collectors' Fair, The Bushey Golf & Country Club, Banqueting Suite, The High Street, Bushey, Herts. *(M & S Enterprises - 0181 440 2330)*
Antique & Collectors' Fair, The Plumley Village Hall, Near Knutsford, Cheshire. *(N & B Fairs - 01565 722144)*
Antique & Collectors' Fair, The Exhibition Halls, Park Hall, Charnock Richard, Lancs. *(Unicorn Fairs Ltd - 0161 773 7001)*
Monday 28th December
Antique & Collectors' Fair, The Allendale Centre, Hanham Road, Wimborne, Dorset. *(Grandma's Attic Antique Fairs - 01590 677687)*

1999 Dates

Friday 1st January
Antique & Collectors' Fair, The Winchester Guildhall, The Broadway, Winchester, Hants. *(Grandma's Attic Antique Fairs - 01590 677687)*
2nd/3rd January
Antique & Collectors' Fair, The Pavilion Gardens, Buxton, Derbys. *(Unicorn Fairs Ltd - 0161 773 7001)*
10th January
Antiques Fair, The Bankfield Hotel, Bingley, W. Yorks. *(Abbey Antiques Fairs - 01482 445785)*
17th January
The Midland Clock & Watch Fair, The National Motorcycle Museum, Opposite NEC, Solihull, W. Midlands *(Mr P Dungate - 01895 834694)*
24th January
Antiques Fair, The Old Swan Hotel, Harrogate, N. Yorks. *(Abbey Antiques Fairs - 01482 445785)*
31st January
Antiques Fair, The Willerby Manor, Hull, E. Yorks. *(Abbey Antiques Fairs - 01482 445785*
5th/7th February
The Fifth Norwich Fine Art & Antiques Fair, St Andrew's Hall, Norwich, Norfolk, *(Lomax Antiques Fairs - 01603 737631)*
14th February
The Brunel Clock & Watch Fair, The Brunel University, Kingston Lane, Uxbridge, Middlesex. *(Mr P Dungate - 01895 834694)*

Regions continued

21st February
Antiques Fair, The Old Swan Hotel, Harrogate, N. Yorks. *(Abbey Antiques Fairs - 01482 445785)*
28th February
Antiques Fair, The Willerby Manor, Hull, E. Yorks. *(Abbey Antiques Fairs - 01482 445785*
14th March
Antiques Fair, The Old Swan Hotel, Harrogate, N. Yorks. *(Abbey Antiques Fairs - 01482 445785)*
21st March
Antiques Fair, The Bankfield Hotel, Bingley, W. Yorks. *(Abbey Antiques Fairs - 01482 445785)*
28th March
Antiques Fair, The Willerby Manor, Hull, E. Yorks. *(Abbey Antiques Fairs - 01482 445785)*
The Midland Clock & Watch Fair, The National Motorcycle Museum, Opposite NEC, Solihull, W. Midlands *(Mr P Dungate - 01895 834694)*
4th/5th April
Antiques Fair, The Old Swan Hotel, Harrogate, N. Yorks. *(Abbey Antiques Fairs - 01482 445785)*
April 18th
The Brunel Clock & Watch Fair, The Brunel University, Kingston Lane, Uxbridge, Middlesex. *(Mr P Dungate - 01895 834694)*
25th April
Antiques Fair, The Willerby Manor, Hull, E. Yorks. *(Abbey Antiques Fairs - 01482 445785*
29th April - 2nd May
The Harrogate Antique & Fine Art Fair, The Harrogate International Centre, Harrogate, N. Yorks. *(Louise Walker - 01823 323363)*
2nd May
Antiques Fair, The Old Swan Hotel, Harrogate, N. Yorks. *(Abbey Antiques Fairs - 01482 445785)*
9th May
Antiques Fair, The Bankfield Hotel, Bingley, W. Yorks. *(Abbey Antiques Fairs - 01482 445785)*
22nd/24th May
The Seventh Langley Park Spring Antiques Fair, The Langley Park School, Loddon, Norfolk. *(Lomax Antiques Fair - 01603 737631)*
23rd May
Antiques Fair, The Willerby Manor, Hull, E. Yorks. *(Abbey Antiques Fairs - 01482 445785*
The Midland Clock & Watch Fair, The National Motorcycle Museum, Opposite NEC, Solihull, W. Midlands *(Mr P Dungate - 01895 834694)*
30th May
Antiques Fair, The Old Swan Hotel, Harrogate, N. Yorks. *(Abbey Antiques Fairs - 01482 445785)*
13th June
Antiques Fair, The Old Swan Hotel, Harrogate, N. Yorks. *(Abbey Antiques Fairs - 01482 445785)*
20th June, 199
Antiques Fair, The Bankfield Hotel, Bingley, W. Yorks. *(Abbey Antiques Fairs - 01482 445785)*
27th June
Antiques Fair, The Willerby Manor, Hull, E. Yorks. *(Abbey Antiques Fairs - 01482 445785*
The Brunel Clock & Watch Fair, The Brunel University, Kingston Lane, Uxbridge, Middlesex. *(Mr P Dungate - 01895 834694)*

ALPHABETICAL LIST OF TOWNS AND VILLAGES WITH THE COUNTIES UNDER WHICH THEY APPEAR IN THIS GUIDE

A
Abbots Langley, Herts.
Abbots Leigh, Somerset.
Aberdeen, Scotland.
Aberfeldy, Scotland.
Aberford, W. Yorks.
Abergavenny, Wales.
Abernyte, Scotland.
Aberystwyth, Wales.
Abinger Hammer, Surrey.
Abrid, Essex.
Accrington, Lancs.
Acle, Norfolk.
Acrise, Kent.
Addingham, W. Yorks.
Adversane, W. Sussex.
Albrighton (Neachley), Shrops.
Alcester, Warks.
Aldeburgh, Suffolk.
Alderley Edge, Cheshire.
Alderney, C I.
Alford, Scotland.
Alfreton, Derbys.
Alfriston, E. Sussex.
Allington, Lincs.
Allonby, Cumbria.
Alnwick, Northumbs.
Alresford, Hants.
Alrewas, Staffs.
Alsager, Cheshire.
Alston, Cumbria.
Altrincham, Cheshire.
Alverstoke, Hants.
Amersham, Bucks.
Ampthill, Beds.
Andoversford, Glos.
Angarrack, Cornwall.
Angmering, W. Sussex.
Antrim, Co. Antrim, N. Ireland.
Appledore, Kent.
Armagh, Co. Armagh, N. Ireland.
Arthingworth, Northants.
Arundel, W. Sussex.
Ash, Kent.
Ash Priors, Somerset.
Ash Vale, Surrey.
Ashbourne, Derbys.
Ashburton, Devon.
Ashford, Kent.
Ashtead, Surrey.
Ashton-under-Lyne, Lancs.
Aslockton, Notts.
Assington, Suffolk.
Aston Tirrold, Oxon.
Astwood Bank, Worcs.
Atcham, Shrops.
Atherstone, Warks.
Attleborough, Norfolk.
Atworth, Wilts.
Auchterarder, Scotland.
Auldearn, Scotland.
Avening, Glos.
Avoch, Scotland.
Axbridge, Somerset.
Axminster, Devon.
Aylesby, Lincs.
Aylsham, Norfolk.
Ayr, Scotland.

B
Badgworth, Somerset.
Bakewell, Derbys.
Balcombe, W. Sussex.
Balderton, Notts.
Baldock, Herts.
Balfron, Scotland.
Ballater, Scotland.
Ballyclare, Co. Antrim, N. Ireland.
Ballynahinch, Co. Down, N. Ireland.
Bampton, Devon.
Banbridge, Co. Down, N. Ireland.
Banchory, Scotland.
Bangor, Wales.
Barham, Kent.
Barkham, Berks.
Barling Magna, Essex.
Barlow, Derbys.
Barnard Castle, Durham.
Barnet, Herts.
Barnoldswick, Lancs.
Barnsley, Glos.
Barnsley, Yorks. South.
Barnstaple, Devon.
Barnt Green, Worcs.
Barnwell, Northants.
Barrhead, Scotland.
Barrington, Somerset.
Barry, Wales.
Barton, Cheshire.
Barton-on-Humber, Lincs.
Basingstoke, Hants.
Bassingbourn, Cambs.
Baston, Lincs.
Bath, Somerset.
Battle, E. Sussex.
Battlesbridge, Essex.
Bawdeswell, Norfolk.
Bawtry, S. Yorks.
Baythorne End, Essex.
Beaconsfield, Bucks.
Beaminster, Dorset.
Beattock, Scotland.
Beauly, Scotland.
Beaumaris, Wales.
Beccles, Suffolk.
Beckenham, Kent.
Bedale, N. Yorks.
Bedford, Beds.
Bedingfield, Suffolk.
Beetham, Cumbria.
Belfast, N. Ireland.
Belper, Derbys.
Bembridge, Isle of Wight.
Benenden, Kent.
Benson, Oxon.
Bentley, Suffolk.
Berkeley, Glos.
Berkhamsted, Herts.
Berwick-on-Tweed, Northumbs.
Bessacarr, S. Yorks.
Betchworth, Surrey.
Beverley, E. Yorks.
Bewdley, Worcs.
Bexhill-on-Sea, E. Sussex.
Bexleyheath, Kent.
Bicester, Oxon.
Bickerstaffe, Lancs.
Biddenden, Kent.
Bideford, Devon.
Bidford-on-Avon, Warks.

Biggleswade, Beds.
Billingham, Cleveland.
Billingshurst, W. Sussex.
Bingham, Notts.
Bingley, W. Yorks.
Birchington, Kent.
Birdbrook, Essex.
Birkenhead, Merseyside.
Birmingham, W. Mids.
Birstwith, N. Yorks.
Bishop's Castle, Shrops.
Bishop's Stortford, Herts.
Bishops Cleeve, Glos.
Bishops Waltham, Hants.
Bishopston, Wales.
Bishopswood, Somerset.
Blackburn, Lancs.
Blackmore, Essex.
Blackpool, Lancs.
Bladon, Oxon.
Blaenau Ffestiniog, Wales.
Blairgowrie, Scotland.
Blandford Forum, Dorset.
Bletchingley, Surrey.
Blewbury, Oxon.
Bloxham, Oxon.
Bloxwich, W. Mids.
Blythburgh, Suffolk.
Bodmin, Cornwall.
Bodorgan, Wales.
Bognor Regis, W. Sussex.
Bollington, Cheshire.
Bolton, Lancs.
Bolton Abbey, N. Yorks.
Bolton-by-Bowland, Lancs.
Boroughbridge, N. Yorks.
Boscastle, Cornwall.
Boston, Lincs.
Boston Spa, W. Yorks.
Botley, Hants.
Bottisham, Cambs.
Boughton, Kent.
Bourne, Lincs.
Bourne End, Bucks.
Bournemouth, Dorset.
Bourton-on-the-Water, Glos.
Bovey Tracey, Devon.
Bowness-on-Windermere, Cumbria.
Brackley, Northants.
Bradfield St. George, Suffolk.
Bradford, W. Yorks.
Bradford-on-Avon, Wilts.
Brailsford, Derbys.
Bramhall, Cheshire.
Bramley, Surrey.
Brampton, Cumbria.
Brancaster Staithe, Norfolk.
Brandsby, N. Yorks.
Branksome, Dorset.
Brasted, Kent.
Braunton, Devon.
Brecon, Wales.
Brentwood, Essex.
Brereton, Staffs.
BrewoodStaffs
Bridge of Earn, Scotland.
Bridgend, Wales.
Bridgnorth, Shrops.
Bridlington, E. Yorks.
Bridport, Dorset.
Brierfield, Lancs.
Brighton, E. Sussex.
Brinklow, Warks.
Brinkworth, Wilts.
Bristol, Glos.
Brixham, Devon.
Brixworth, Northants.
Broadstairs, Kent.
Broadway, Worcs.
Brobury, Herefs.
Brockdish, Norfolk.
Brodick and Whiting Bay, Scotland.
Bromley, Kent.
Brompton, N. Yorks.
Broseley, Shrops.
Broughton Astley, Leics.
Broxted, Essex.
Bruton, Somerset.
Buckland St. Mary, Somerset.
Budleigh Salterton, Devon.
Bungay, Suffolk.
Bures, Suffolk.
Burford, Oxon.
Burgess Hill, W. Sussex.
Burghfield Common, Berks.
Burneston, N. Yorks.
Burnham, Bucks.
Burnham Market, Norfolk.
Burnham on Crouch, Essex.
Burnham-on-Sea, Somerset.
Burnley, Lancs.
Burscough, Lancs.
Burton-on-Trent, Staffs.
Burwash, E. Sussex.
Burwell, Cambs.
Bury, Lancs.
Bury St. Edmunds, Suffolk.
Bushey, Herts.
Bushmills, Co. Antrim, N. Ireland.
Buxton, Derbys.

C

Cadnam, Hants.
Caerphilly, Wales.
Caistor, Lincs.
Callington, Cornwall.
Calne, Wilts.
Camberley, Surrey.
Camborne, Cornwall.
Cambridge, Cambs.
Cambridge, Glos.
Camelford, Cornwall.
Canonbie, Scotland.
Canterbury, Kent.
Cardiff, Wales.
Carhampton, Somerset.
Carlisle, Cumbria.
Carmarthen, Wales.
Carrefour Selous, St. Lawrence, Jersey, C.I.
Carshalton, Surrey.
Cartmel, Cumbria.
Castle Ashby, Northants.
Castle Cary, Somerset.
Castle Combe, Wilts.
Castle Douglas, Scotland.
Castletown, Isle of Man.
Cavendish, Suffolk.
Caversham, Berks.
Cawood, N. Yorks.
Ceres, Scotland.
Cerne Abbas, Dorset.
Chagford, Devon.
Chalfont St. Giles, Bucks.
Chalford, Glos.
Chalgrove, Oxon.
Chard, Somerset.
Charlton Marshall, Dorset.
Charmouth, Dorset.
Chatburn, Lancs.
Cheadle, Cheshire.
Cheadle Hulme, Cheshire.
Cheddleton, Staffs.
Chelmsford, Essex.
Cheltenham, Glos.
Chepstow, Wales.
Cherhill, Wilts.
Chertsey, Surrey.
Chesham, Bucks.
Chester, Cheshire.
Chesterfield, Derbys.
Chichester, W. Sussex.
Chiddingstone, Kent.
Chilcompton, Somerset.
Chilton, Oxon.
Chingford, Essex.
Chippenham, Wilts.
Chipping Campden, Glos.

Chipping Norton, Oxon.
Chipping Sodbury, Glos.
Chirk, Wales.
Chislehurst, Kent.
Chittering, Cambs.
Chobham, Surrey.
Chorley, Lancs.
Chorleywood, Herts.
Christchurch, Dorset.
Christian Malford, Wilts.
Church Stretton, Shrops.
Churt, Surrey.
Ciliau Aeron, Wales.
Cirencester, Glos.
Clacton-on-Sea, Essex.
Clare, Suffolk.
Claudy, Co. Londonderry, N. Ireland.
Cleobury Mortimer, Shrops.
Clevedon, Somerset.
Clitheroe, Lancs.
Clola by Mintlaw, Scotland.
Clutton, Somerset.
Coalville, Leics.
Cobham, Surrey.
Cockermouth, Cumbria.
Cockfosters, Herts.
Cocking, W. Sussex.
Codford, Wilts.
Codicote, Herts.
Codsall, Staffs.
Coggeshall, Essex.
Colchester, Essex.
Coldstream, Scotland.
Coleraine, Co. Londonderry, N. Ireland.
Coleshill, Warks.
Collessie, Scotland.
Collingham, Notts.
Colne, Lancs.
Colsterworth, Lincs.
Coltishall, Norfolk.
Colwyn Bay, Wales.
Colyton, Devon.
Comber, Co Down, N. Ireland.
Comberton, Cambs.
Congleton, Cheshire.
Consett, Durham.
Cooden, E. Sussex.
Cookstown, Co. Tyrone, N. Ireland.
Corby Hill, Cumbria.
Corringham, Essex.
Corsham, Wilts.
Costessey, Norfolk.
Coulsdon, Surrey.
Cove, Scotland.
Coventry, W. Mids.
Cowbridge, Wales.
Cowes, Isle of Wight.
Cowfold, W. Sussex.
Coxley, Somerset.
Cranborne, Dorset.
Cranbrook, Kent.
Craven Arms, Shrops.
Crawley, Hants.
Crayford, Kent.
Cremyll, Cornwall.
Crewe, Cheshire.
Crewkerne, Somerset.
Crickhowell, Wales.
Cricklade, Wilts.
Crieff, Scotland.
Cromer, Norfolk.
Crook, Durham.
Crosby Ravensworth, Cumbria.
Cross Hills, N. Yorks.
Cross in Hand, E. Sussex.
Croughton, Northants.
Crowborough, E. Sussex.
Croydon, Surrey.
Crudwell, Wilts.
Cuckfield, W. Sussex.
Culham, Oxon.
Cullompton, Devon.

D

Danbury, Essex.
Darlington, Durham.
Dartford, Kent.
Dartmouth, Devon.
Darwen, Lancs.
Datchet, Berks.
Davenham, Cheshire.
Deal, Kent.
Debenham, Suffolk.
Deddington, Oxon.
Deganwy, Wales.
Denby Dale, W. Yorks.
Denny, Scotland.
Derby, Derbys.
Desborough, Northants.
Devizes, Wilts.
Didcot, Oxon.
Dingwall, Scotland.
Disley, Cheshire.
Diss, Norfolk.
Ditchling, E. Sussex.
Doddington, Cambs.
Donaghadee, Co. Down, N. Ireland.
Doncaster, S. Yorks.
Dorchester, Dorset.
Dorchester-on-Thames, Oxon.
Dorking, Surrey.
Dornoch, Scotland.
Dorridge, W. Mids.
Douglas, Isle of Man.
Doveridge, Derbys.
Dowlish Wake, Somerset.
Downham, Kent.
Downham Market, Norfolk.
Driffield, E. Yorks.
Drimpton, Dorset.
Droitwich, Worcs.
Dronfield, Derbys.
Drumnadrochit, Scotland.
Duffield, Derbys.
Dulverton, Somerset.
Dumfries, Scotland.
Dundee, Scotland.
Dunkeld, Scotland.
Dunmow, Essex.
Dunsfold, Surrey.
Durham, Durham.
Durrington, W. Sussex.
Duxford, Cambs.

E

Eachwick, Northumbs.
Eaglescliffe, Cleveland.
Earsham, Norfolk.
Easingwold, N. Yorks.
East Budleigh, Devon.
East Grinstead, W. Sussex.
East Hagbourne, Oxon.
East Molesey, Surrey.
East Peckham, Kent.
East Pennard, Somerset.
East Rudham, Norfolk.
Eastbourne, E. Sussex.
Eastleigh, Hants.
Ebrington, Glos.
Eccleston, Lancs.
Edenbridge, Kent.
Edenfield, Lancs.
Edgware, Middx.
Edinburgh, Scotland.
Edwinstowe, Notts.
Egham, Surrey.
Elgin, Scotland.
Elie, Scotland.
Ellesmere, Shrops.
Elton, Notts.
Ely, Cambs.
Empingham, Rutland.
Emsworth, Hants.
Endmoor, Cumbria.

Enfield, Middx.
Epsom, Surrey.
Ermington, Devon.
Eversley, Hants.
Evesham, Worcs.
Ewell, Surrey.
Exeter, Devon.
Exmouth, Devon.
Exning, Suffolk.
Eye, Suffolk.

F

Fairford, Glos.
Fairlie, Scotland.
Fakenham, Norfolk.
Faldingworth, Lincs.
Falmouth, Cornwall.
Fareham, Hants.
Faringdon, Oxon.
Farnborough, Hants.
Farnham, Surrey.
Farningham, Kent.
Faversham, Kent.
Felixstowe, Suffolk.
Felsted, Essex.
Felton, Northumbs.
Feniscowles, Lancs.
Feock, Cornwall.
Fernhurst, W. Sussex.
Filey, N. Yorks.
Finchingfield, Essex.
Finedon, Northants.
Fishguard, Wales.
Fishlake, S. Yorks.
Flamborough, E. Yorks.
Flaxton, N. Yorks.
Flimwell, E. Sussex.
Flore, Northants.
Fochabers, Scotland.
Folkestone, Kent.
Fordham, Cambs.
Fordingbridge, Hants.
Forest Row, E. Sussex.
Forfar, Scotland.
Forres, Scotland.
Four Elms, Kent.
Four Oaks, W. Mids.
Fowlmere, Cambs.
Framlingham, Suffolk.
Frampton West, Lincs.
Freckleton, Lancs.
Freshford, Somerset.
Freshwater, Isle of Wight.
Freuchie, Scotland.
Frinton-on-Sea, Essex.
Friockheim, Scotland.
Frome, Somerset.

G

Gainsborough, Lincs.
Gants Hill, Essex.
Gargrave, N. Yorks.
Garstang, Lancs.
Gateshead, Tyne and Wear.
Gaydon, Warks.
Gilberdyke, E. Yorks.
Gillingham, Dorset.
Glasgow, Scotland.
Glastonbury, Somerset.
Glossop, Derbys.
Gloucester, Glos.
Godalming, Surrey.
Gorseinon, Wales.
Gosforth, Cumbria.
Gosport, Hants.
Grampound, Cornwall.
Grantham, Lincs.
Grantown-on-Spey, Scotland.
Grasmere, Cumbria.
Grassmoor, Derbys.
Gravesend, Kent.
Grays, Essex.
Great Ayton, N. Yorks.
Great Baddow, Essex.
Great Bardfield, Essex.
Great Bookham, Surrey.
Great Chesterford, Essex.
Great Harwood, Lancs.
Great Houghton, S. Yorks.
Great Malvern, Worcs.
Great Missenden, Bucks.
Great Oakley, Essex.
Great Shefford, Berks.
Great Waltham, Essex.
Greatham, Hants.
Green Hammerton, N. Yorks.
Greyabbey, Co. Down, N. Ireland.
Greystoke, Cumbria.
Grimsby, Lincs.
Grosmont, N. Yorks.
Gt. Yarmouth, Norfolk.
Guildford, Surrey.
Guilsborough, Northants.
Guisborough, Cleveland.
Gullane, Scotland.

H

Hacheston, Suffolk.
Haddenham, Bucks.
Haddington, Scotland.
Hadleigh, Suffolk.
Hadlow, Kent.
Hadlow Down, E. Sussex.
Halesowen, W. Mids.
Halesworth, Suffolk.
Halfway, Berks.
Halstead, Essex.
Hampton, Middx.
Hampton Hill, Middx.
Hampton Wick, Surrey.
Harefield, Middx.
Harlington, Beds.
Harpenden, Herts.
Harpole, Northants.
Harrietsham, Kent.
Harrogate, N. Yorks.
Harrow, Middx.
Harston, Cambs.
Hartlepool, Cleveland.
Hartley Wintney, Hants.
Harwich, Essex.
Haselbech, Northants.
Haslemere, Surrey.
Haslingden, Lancs.
Hastings, E. Sussex.
Hatherleigh, Devon.
Hatton, Warks.
Haverfordwest, Wales.
Hawes, N. Yorks.
Haworth, W. Yorks.
Hay-on-Wye, Wales.
Haydon Bridge, Northumbs.
Hayfield, Derbys.
Hayle, Cornwall.
Hayling Island, Hants.
Hazel Grove, Cheshire.
Heacham, Norfolk.
Headcorn, Kent.
Headington, Oxon.
Heanor, Derbys.
Heath and Reach, Beds.
Hebden Bridge, W. Yorks.
Helmsley, N. Yorks.
Helsby, Cheshire.
Helston, Cornwall.
Hemel Hempstead, Herts.
Hempstead, Essex.
Hemswell Cliff, Lincs.
Henfield, W. Sussex.
Henley-in-Arden, Warks.
Henllan, Wales.
Hereford, Herefs.
Hertford, Herts.
Heswall, Merseyside.
Hexham, Northumbs.
High Wycombe, Bucks.
Highbridge, Somerset.
Hinckley, Leics.
Hindhead, Surrey.
Hitchin, Herts.
Hoby, Leics.

Hodnet, Shrops.
Holbeach, Lincs.
Holkham, Norfolk.
Holmfirth, W. Yorks.
Holt, Norfolk.
Holt, Wales.
Holywood, Co. Down, N. Ireland.
Honiton, Devon.
Horam, E. Sussex.
Horncastle, Lincs.
Horndean, Hants.
Horsebridge, E. Sussex.
Horsell, Surrey.
Horsham, W. Sussex.
Horton, Berks.
Hoylake, Merseyside.
Huddersfield, W. Yorks.
Hull, E. Yorks.
Hungerford, Berks.
Hunstanton, Norfolk.
Huntercombe, Oxon.
Huntingdon, Cambs.
Huntly, Scotland.
Hursley, Hants.
Hurst, Berks.
Hurst Green, E. Sussex.
Hurstpierpoint, W. Sussex.
Hythe, Kent.

I
Ibstock, Leics.
Ickleton, Cambs.
Ilchester, Somerset.
Ilford, Essex.
Ilfracombe, Devon.
Ilkley, W. Yorks.
Ilminster, Somerset.
Inchture, Scotland.
Inverness, Scotland.
Ipswich, Suffolk.
Irby-in-the-Marsh, Lincs.
Ironbridge, Shrops.
Isleworth, Middx.
Islip, Northants.
Iver, Bucks.
Ixworth, Suffolk.

J
Jedburgh, Scotland.
Jesmond, Tyne and Wear.

K
Keighley, W. Yorks.
Kelling, Norfolk.
Kelvedon, Essex.
Kempsford, Glos.
Kendal, Cumbria.
Kenilworth, Warks.
Kentisbeare, Devon.
Kessingland, Suffolk.
Keswick, Cumbria.
Kettering, Northants.
Ketton, Lincs.
Kew, Surrey.
Kew Green, Surrey.
Kidderminster, Worcs.
Kidwelly, Wales.
Kilbarchan, Scotland.
Kilham, E. Yorks.
Killamarsh, Derbys.
Killearn, Scotland.
Killin, Scotland.
Killinghall, N. Yorks.
Kilmacolm, Scotland.
Kilmarnock, Scotland.
Kilmichael Glassary, Scotland.
Kincardine O'Neil, Scotland.
King's Langley, Herts.
King's Lynn, Norfolk.
Kinghorn, Scotland.
Kingsbridge, Devon.
Kingsley, Staffs.
Kingsthorpe, Northants.
Kingston-on-Spey, Scotland.
Kingston-upon-Thames, Surrey.
Kingswear, Devon.
Kingussie, Scotland.
Kinross, Scotland.
Kirby Wiske, N. Yorks.
Kirk Deighton, N. Yorks.
Kirkby Lonsdale, Cumbria.
Kirkby Stephen, Cumbria.
Kirkcudbright, Scotland.
Kirton, Lincs.
Kirton in Lindsey, Lincs.
Knaresborough, N. Yorks.
Knebworth, Herts.
Knighton, Wales.
Knipton, Leics.
Knowle, W. Mids.
Knutsford, Cheshire.

L
Lake, Isle of Wight.
Laleham, Surrey.
Lamberhurst, Kent.
Lampeter, Wales.
Lancaster, Lancs.
Landbeach, Cambs.
Lane End, Bucks.
Langford, Notts.
Langham, Norfolk.
Langholm, Scotland.
Langley Burrell, Wilts.
Largs, Scotland.
Lavenham, Suffolk.
Leamington Spa, Warks.
Leavenheath, Suffolk.
Lechlade, Glos.
Leckhampstead, Berks.
Ledbury, Herefs.
Leeds, W. Yorks.
Leedstown, Cornwall.
Leek, Staffs.
Leicester, Leics.
Leigh, Kent.
Leigh, Lancs.
Leigh, Staffs.
Leigh-on-Sea, Essex.
Leighton Buzzard, Beds.
Leiston, Suffolk.
Lennoxtown, Scotland.
Leominster, Herefs.
Lepton, W. Yorks.
Letham, Scotland.
Lewes, E. Sussex.
Leyburn, N. Yorks.
Lichfield, Staffs.
Limpsfield, Surrey.
Lincoln, Lincs.
Lindfield, W. Sussex.
Lingfield, Surrey.
Linlithgow, Scotland.
Lisbellaw, Co. Fermanagh, N. Ireland.
Lisburn, Co. Antrim, N. Ireland.
Liss, Hants.
Little Bedwyn, Wilts.
Little Chalfont, Bucks.
Little Downham, Cambs.
Little Haywood, Staffs.
Little Malvern, Worcs.
Littlebourne, Kent.
Littlehampton, W. Sussex.
Littleton, Cheshire.
Littleton, Somerset.
Litton Cheney, Dorset.
Liverpool, Merseyside.
Llandeilo, Wales.
Llandissilio Wales
Llandudno, Wales.
Llandudno Junction, Wales.
Llanelli, Wales.
Llanerchymedd (Anglesey), Wales.
Llanfair Caereinion, Wales.
Llangollen, Wales.

Llanrwst, Wales.
Long Buckby, Northants.
Long Clawson, Leics.
Long Eaton, Derbys.
Long Hanborough, Oxon.
Long Marston, Warks.
Long Marton, Cumbria.
Long Melford, Suffolk.
Long Preston, N. Yorks.
Long Stratton, Norfolk.
Long Sutton, Lincs.
Longridge, Lancs.
Looe, Cornwall.
Lostwithiel, Cornwall.
Loughborough, Leics.
Louth, Lincs.
Low Newton, Cumbria.
Lowestoft, Suffolk.
Lubenham, Leics.
Ludlow, Shrops.
Lurgan, Co. Armagh, N. Ireland.
Luton, Beds.
Lydford, Devon.
Lye, W. Mids.
Lymington, Hants.
Lyndhurst, Hants.
Lyneham, Wilts.
Lynton, Devon.
Lytchett Minster, Dorset.
Lytham St. Annes, Lancs.

M

Macclesfield, Cheshire.
Maidencombe, Devon.
Maidenhead, Berks.
Maidstone, Kent.
Maldon, Essex.
Malmesbury, Wilts.
Malton, N. Yorks.
Malvern Link, Worcs.
Malvern Wells, Worcs.
Manchester, Lancs.
Manfield, N. Yorks.
Manningtree, Essex.
Mansfield, Notts.
Manton, Rutland.
Mapplewell, S. Yorks.
Marazion, Cornwall.
Margate, Kent.
Market Bosworth, Leics.
Market Deeping, Lincs.
Market Drayton, Shrops.
Market Harborough, Leics.
Market Rasen, Lincs.
Market Weighton, E. Yorks.
Markington, N. Yorks.
Marlborough, Wilts.
Marlow, Bucks.
Marple Bridge, Cheshire.
Martlesham, Suffolk.
Martock, Somerset.
Masham, N. Yorks.
Matching Green, Essex.
Mathry, Wales.
Matlock, Derbys.
Meare, Somerset.
Medbourne, Leics.
Meigle, Scotland.
Melbury Osmond, Dorset.
Melksham, Wilts.
Mellor, Cheshire.
Melmerby, N. Yorks.
Menston, W. Yorks.
Merriott, Somerset.
Merstham, Surrey.
Merton, Devon.
Messingham, Lincs.
Mevagissey, Cornwall.
Middleton Village, Lancs.
Midhurst, W. Sussex.
Midsomer Norton, Somerset.
Milburn, Cumbria.
Mildenhall, Suffolk.
Milford, Surrey.
Milford Haven, Wales.
Milnthorpe, Cumbria.
Milton Keynes, Bucks.
Milton Lilbourne, Wilts.
Milverton, Somerset.
Minchinhampton, Glos.
Minety, Wilts.
Minsteracres, Northumbs.
Mirfield, W. Yorks.
Mobberley, Cheshire.
Modbury, Devon.
Moffat, Scotland.
Monkton, Devon.
Monmouth, Wales.
Montacute, Somerset.
Montrose, Scotland.
Morchard Bishop, Devon.
Morden, Surrey.
Morecambe, Lancs.
Morestead, Hants.
Moreton-in-Marsh, Glos.
Moretonhampstead, Devon.
Much Wenlock, Shrops.
Murton, Wales.

N

Nantwich, Cheshire.
Narberth, Wales.
Narborough, Leics.
Needham Market, Suffolk.
Nelson, Lancs.
Nether Stowey, Somerset.
Nettlebed, Oxon.
New Bolingbroke, Lincs.
Newark, Notts.
Newbridge-on-Wye, Wales.
Newburgh, Scotland.
Newby Bridge, Cumbria.
Newcastle Emlyn, Wales.
Newcastle-under-Lyme, Staffs.
Newcastle-upon-Tyne, Tyne and Wear.
Newhaven, E. Sussex.
Newmarket, Suffolk.
Newnham, Kent.
Newport, Essex.
Newport, Isle of Wight.
Newport, Shrops.
Newport, Wales.
Newry, Co. Down, N. Ireland.
Newton Abbot, Devon.
Newton St. Cyres, Devon.
Newton Tony, Wilts.
Newtonmore, Scotland.
Newtown, Derbys.
Newtownabbey, Co. Antrim, N. Ireland.
North Aston, Oxon.
North Berwick, Scotland.
North Cave, E. Yorks.
North Kelsey Moor, Lincs.
North Petherton, Somerset.
North Shields, Tyne and Wear.
North Walsham, Norfolk.
North Wraxall, Wilts.
Northallerton, N. Yorks.
Northampton, Northants.
Northchapel, W. Sussex.
Northfleet, Kent.
Northleach, Glos.
Norton, Glos.
Norton, N. Yorks.
Norwich, Norfolk.
Nottingham, Notts.
Nutley, E. Sussex.

O

Oadby, Leics.
Oakham, Rutland.
Oban, Scotland.
Odiham, Hants.
Okehampton, Devon.
Oldham, Lancs.
Ollerton, Notts.

Olney, Bucks.
Orford, Suffolk.
Ormskirk, Lancs.
Orpington, Kent.
Osbournby, Lincs.
Osgathorpe, Leics.
Otford, Kent.
Otley, W. Yorks.
Outwell, Cambs.
Oxford, Oxon.
Oxted, Surrey.

P

Painswick, Glos.
Paisley, Scotland.
Parkstone, Dorset.
Pateley Bridge, N. Yorks.
Patrington, E. Yorks.
Paulerspury, Northants.
Peasenhall, Suffolk.
Peel, Isle of Man.
Pembroke, Wales.
Penkridge, Staffs.
Penn, Bucks.
Penrith, Cumbria.
Penryn, Cornwall.
Penshurst, Kent.
Penzance, Cornwall.
Pershore, Worcs.
Perth, Scotland.
Peterborough, Cambs.
Petersfield, Hants.
Petts Wood, Kent.
Petworth, W. Sussex.
Pevensey, E. Sussex.
Pevensey Bay, E. Sussex.
Pickering, N. Yorks.
Pitlochry, Scotland.
Pittenweem, Scotland.
Plumley, Cheshire.
Plymouth, Devon.
Polegate, E. Sussex.
Pontarddulais, Wales.
Pontefract, W. Yorks.
Ponterwyd, Wales.
Poole, Dorset.
Portadown, Co. Armagh, N. Ireland.
Portaferry, Co. Down, N. Ireland.
Portballintrae, Co. Antrim, N. Ireland.
Porthcawl, Wales.
Portree, Scotland.
Portrush, Co. Antrim, N. Ireland.
Portslade, W. Sussex.
Portsmouth, Hants.
Portsoy, Scotland.
Portstewart, Co. Londonderry, N. Ireland.
Potterspury, Northants.
Poulton-le-Fylde, Lancs.
Poynton, Cheshire.
Preston, Lancs.
Prestwick, Scotland.
Princes Risborough, Bucks.
Puckeridge, Herts.
Puddletown, Dorset.
Pulborough, W. Sussex.
Purleigh, Essex.
Pwllheli, Wales.

Q

Queen Camel, Somerset.
Queniborough, Leics.
Quorn, Leics.

R

Radlett, Herts.
Rainford, Merseyside.
Rait, Scotland.
Ramsbury, Wilts.
Ramsey, Cambs.
Ramsgate, Kent.
Raveningham, Norfolk.
Ravensmoor, Cheshire.
Ravenstonedale, Cumbria.
Rayleigh, Essex.
Reading, Berks.
Redbourn, Herts.
Redditch, Worcs.
Redgrave, Suffolk.
Redhill, Surrey.
Reepham, Norfolk.
Reigate, Surrey.
Rhosneigr, Wales.
Rhuallt, Wales.
Richmond, Surrey.
Rickmansworth, Herts.
Ridgewell, Essex.
Ringway, Cheshire.
Ringwood, Hants.
Ripley, Derbys.
Ripley, Surrey.
Ripon, N. Yorks.
Risby, Suffolk.
Riverhead, Kent.
Rochdale, Lancs.
Rochester, Kent.
Rode, Somerset.
Rodley, Glos.
Rolvenden, Kent.
Romsey, Hants.
Ross-on-Wye, Herefs.
Rotherham, S. Yorks.
Rottingdean, E. Sussex.
Roxwell, Essex.
Royston, Herts.
Rugeley, Staffs.
Rumford, Cornwall.
Runfold, Surrey.
Rushden, Northants.
Ruskington, Lincs.
Ruthin, Wales.
Ryde, Isle of Wight.
Rye, E. Sussex.

S

Sabden, Lancs.
Saffron Walden, Essex.
Salisbury, Wilts.
Saltaire, W. Yorks.
Saltcoats, Scotland.
Samlesbury, Lancs.
Sanderstead, Surrey.
Sandgate, Kent.
Sandhurst, Berks.
Sandhurst, Kent.
Sandwich, Kent.
Sarnau, Wales.
Sawbridgeworth, Herts.
Sayers Common, W. Sussex.
Scarborough, N. Yorks.
Scarthingwell, N. Yorks.
Scarthoe, Lincs.
Scratby, Norfolk.
Scunthorpe, Lincs.
Seaford, E. Sussex.
Seaton, Devon.
Sedbergh, Cumbria.
Selkirk, Scotland.
Sellindge, Kent.
Semley, Wilts.
Settle, N. Yorks.
Sevenoaks, Kent.
Shaftesbury, Dorset.
Shaldon, Devon.
Shanklin, Isle of Wight.
Shardlow, Derbys.
Sharrington, Norfolk.
Sheffield, S. Yorks.
Shefford, Beds.
Shenfield, Essex.
Shenton, Leics.
Shepperton, Surrey.
Sherborne, Dorset.
Sherburn in Elmet, N. Yorks.
Shere, Surrey.
Sheringham, Norfolk.
Shifnal, Shrops.

Shipley, W. Yorks.
Shipston-on-Stour, Warks.
Shirley, Surrey.
Shrewsbury, Shrops.
Sible Hedingham, Essex.
Sidcup, Kent.
Siddington, Cheshire.
Sidmouth, Devon.
Sileby, Leics.
Skegness, Lincs.
Skipton, N. Yorks.
Slad, Glos.
Sleaford, Lincs.
Snainton, N. Yorks.
Snape, Suffolk.
Snodland, Kent.
Solihull, W. Mids.
Somersham, Cambs.
Somerton, Somerset.
Sonning-on-Thames, Berks.
South Brent, Devon.
South Cave, E. Yorks.
South Harting, W. Sussex.
South Molton, Devon.
South Shields, Tyne and Wear.
South Walsham, Norfolk.
Southampton, Hants.
Southborough, Kent.
Southend-on-Sea, Essex.
Southport, Merseyside.
Southwell, Notts.
Southwold, Suffolk.
Sowerby Bridge, W. Yorks.
Spalding, Lincs.
Spennithorne, N. Yorks.
St. Albans, Herts.
St. Andrews, Scotland.
St. Annes-on-Sea, Lancs.
St Aubin, Jersey, C I.
St. Austell, Cornwall.
St. Gerrans, Cornwall.
St. Helens, Isle of Wight.
St. Helier, Jersey, C I.
St. Ives, Cambs.
St. Ives, Cornwall.
St. Lawrence, Jersey, C I.
St. Leonards-on-Sea, E. Sussex.
St. Margaret's Bay, Kent.
St. Martin, Guernsey, C I.
St. Neots, Cambs.
St. Peter Port, Guernsey, C I.
St. Sampson, Guernsey, C I.
Stafford, Staffs.
Staines, Surrey.
Stalham, Norfolk.
Stamford, Lincs.
Standlake, Oxon.
Stanford-le-Hope, Essex.
Stanley, Scotland.
Stansted, Essex.
Stanton, Shrops.
Staunton Harold, Leics.
Staveley, Cumbria.
Stewarton, Scotland.
Steyning, W. Sussex.
Stickney, Lincs.
Stiffkey, Norfolk.
Stillington, N. Yorks.
Stirling, Scotland.
Stock, Essex.
Stockbridge, Hants.
Stockbury, Kent.
Stockland, Devon.
Stockport, Cheshire.
Stoke by Nayland, Suffolk.
Stoke Ferry, Norfolk.
Stoke-on-Trent, Staffs.
Stonehaven, Scotland.
Storrington, W. Sussex.
Stourbridge, W. Mids.
Stow-on-the-Wold, Glos.
Stowmarket, Suffolk.
Stradbroke, Suffolk.
Stratford-upon-Avon, Warks.
Strathblane, Scotland.
Stretton, Cheshire.
Stretton-on-Fosse, Warks.
Stretton-under-Fosse, Warks.
Stroud, Glos.
Sturminster Newton, Dorset.
Suckley, Worcs.
Sudbury, Suffolk.
Sunderland, Tyne and Wear.
Sundridge, Kent.
Sunningdale, Berks.
Surbiton, Surrey.
Sutton, Surrey.
Sutton Bridge, Lincs.
Sutton Coldfield, W. Mids.
Sutton Valence, Kent.
Sutton-on-Sea, Lincs.
Swadlincote, Derbys.
Swaffham, Norfolk.
Swafield, Norfolk.
Swanage, Dorset.
Swansea, Wales.
Swindon, Wilts.
Swinford, Leics.
Swinton, Lancs.
Synod Inn, Wales.

T

Tacolneston, Norfolk.
Taddington, Glos.
Tadley, Hants.
Tarporley, Cheshire.
Tarvin, Cheshire.
Tarvin Sands, Cheshire.
Tattenhall, Cheshire.
Tattershall, Lincs.
Taunton, Somerset.
Tavistock, Devon.
Taynton, Oxon.
Teignmouth, Devon.
Telford, Shrops.
Templeton, Wales.
Tenby, Wales.
Tenterden, Kent.
Tern Hill, Shrops.
Tetbury, Glos.
Tetsworth, Oxon.
Tewkesbury, Glos.
Teynham, Kent.
Thame, Oxon.
Thames Ditton, Surrey.
Thatcham, Berks.
Thirsk, N. Yorks.
Thorne, S. Yorks.
Thornhill, Scotland.
Thornton le Dale, N. Yorks.
Ticknall, Derbys.
Tilehurst, Berks.
Tillington, W. Sussex.
Tilston, Cheshire.
Tingewick, Bucks.
Tintern, Wales.
Tisbury, Wilts.
Titchfield, Hants.
Tiverton, Devon.
Tockwith, N. Yorks.
Toddington, Beds.
Todmorden, W. Yorks.
Tonbridge, Kent.
Topcliffe, N. Yorks.
Topsham, Devon.
Torquay, Devon.
Totnes, Devon.
Tottenhill, Norfolk.
Towcester, Northants.
Trawden, Lancs.
Tregony, Cornwall.
Treorchy, Wales.
Trevor, Wales.
Tring, Herts.
Troon, Scotland.
Truro, Cornwall.
Tunbridge Wells, Kent.
Tutbury, Staffs.

Tuxford, Notts.
Twickenham, Middx.
Twyford, Bucks.
Twyford, Hants.
Twyford, Norfolk.
Tynemouth, Tyne and Wear.
Tywardreath, Cornwall.
Tywyn, Wales.

U

Uckfield, E. Sussex.
Ullapool, Scotland.
Ulverston, Cumbria.
Upham, Hants.
Upper Boddington, Northants.
Upper Largo, Scotland.
Uppingham, Rutland.
Upton-upon-Severn, Worcs.
Usk, Wales.
Uxbridge, Middx.

V

Vale, Guernsey, C I.
Ventnor, Isle of Wight.

W

Waddington, Lincs.
Wadebridge, Cornwall.
Wadhurst, E. Sussex.
Wainfleet, Lincs.
Wakefield, W. Yorks.
Walford, Herefs.
Walkerburn, Scotland.
Wallasey, Merseyside.
Wallingford, Oxon.
Walsall, W. Mids.
Walsden, W. Yorks.
Walton-on-Thames, Surrey.
Walton-on-the-Hill and Tadworth, Surrey.
Walton-on-the-Naze, Essex.
Wansford, Cambs.
Warboys, Cambs.
Wareham, Dorset.
Wareside, Herts.
Warfield, Berks.
Wargrave, Berks.
Warminster, Wilts.
Warnham, W. Sussex.
Warrenpoint, Co. Down, N. Ireland.
Warrington, Cheshire.
Warwick, Warks.
Washington, W. Sussex.
Washington, Tyne and Wear.
Watchet, Somerset.
Watlington, Oxon.
Watton, Norfolk.
Wednesbury, W. Mids.
Weedon, Northants.
Weeford, Staffs.
Wellingborough, Northants.
Wellington, Somerset.
Wells, Somerset.
Wells-next-the-Sea, Norfolk.
Welshpool, Wales.
Wendover, Bucks.
West Auckland, Durham.
West Bridgford, Notts.
West Buckland, Somerset.
West Byfleet, Surrey.
West Deeping, Lincs.
West Haddon, Northants.
West Harptree, Somerset.
West Kirby, Merseyside.
West Malling, Kent.
West Yatton, Wilts.
Westbourne, W. Sussex.
Westbury, Wilts.
Westcliff-on-Sea, Essex.
Westerham, Kent.
Weston-Super-Mare, Somerset.
Weybridge, Surrey.
Weymouth, Dorset.
Whaley Bridge, Derbys.
Whalley, Lancs.
Whaplode, Lincs.
Wheathampstead, Herts.
Whimple, Devon.
Whitby, N. Yorks.
Whitchurch, Bucks.
Whitchurch, Shrops.
White Colne, Essex.
White Roding, Essex.
Whitefield, Lancs.
Whitehaven, Cumbria.
Whitley Bay, Tyne and Wear.
Whitstable, Kent.
Whixley, N. Yorks.
Wickham, Hants.
Wickham Market, Suffolk.
Wickwar, Glos.
Widegates, Cornwall.
Wigan, Lancs.
Willingdon, E. Sussex.
Williton, Somerset.
Wilmslow, Cheshire.
Wilstead (Wilshamstead), Beds.
Wilstone, Herts.
Wilton, Wilts.
Wimborne Minster, Dorset.
Wincanton, Somerset.
Winchcombe, Glos.
Winchester, Hants.
Windermere, Cumbria.
Windlesham, Surrey.
Windsor and Eton, Berks.
Wing, Rutland.
Wingham, Kent.
Winslow, Bucks.
Winton, Cumbria.
Wisbech, Cambs.
Withington, Glos.
Witney, Oxon.
Wittersham, Kent.
Wiveliscombe, Somerset.
Woburn, Beds.
Woking, Surrey.
Wolseley Bridge, Staffs.
Wolverhampton, W. Mids.
Woodbridge, Suffolk.
Woodbury, Devon.
Woodchurch, Kent.
Woodford Green, Essex.
Woodford Halse, Northants.
Woodhall Spa, Lincs.
Woodhouse Eaves, Leics.
Woodlesford, W. Yorks.
Woodstock, Oxon.
Woodville, Derbys.
Wooler, Northumbs.
Woolhampton, Berks.
Woolpit, Suffolk.
Woore, Shrops.
Wootton Bassett, Wilts.
Worcester, Worcs.
Workington, Cumbria.
Wortham, Suffolk.
Worthing, W. Sussex.
Wraysbury, Berks.
Wrentham, Suffolk.
Wrexham, Wales.
Writtle, Essex.
Wrotham, Kent.
Wroxham, Norfolk.
Wykeham, N. Yorks.
Wymeswold, Leics.
Wymondham, Norfolk.

Y

Yarm, Cleveland.
Yarmouth, Isle of Wight.
Yatton, Somerset.
Yazor, Herefs.
Yealmpton, Devon.
Yeaveley, Derbys.
Yeovil, Somerset.
York, N. Yorks.
Yoxall, Staffs.
Yoxford, Suffolk.

Specialist Dealers' Index

Most antique dealers in Britain sell a wide range of goods, from furniture through pottery and porcelain, to pictures, prints and clocks. Much of the interest in visiting antiques shops comes from this diversity. However, a number of dealers specialise and the following is an index to these. Most of them will stock a representative selection of the items under which they are classified.

The name of the business, together with the area of London or town and county under which the detailed entry can be found are given in the index. Again we would repeat the advice given in the introduction that, if readers are looking for a particular item, they are advised to telephone first before making a long journey.

Classifications

Antiques Centres and Markets
Antiquarian Books
Antiquities
Architectural Items
Arms & Armour
Art Deco & Art Nouveau
Barometers - see also clock dealers
Beds
Brass - see Metalware/work
Bronzes
Carpets & Rugs
Cars & Carriages
Chinese Art - see Oriental
Church Furniture & Furnishings
Clocks & Watches
Coins & Medals
Dolls & Toys
Etchings & Engravings
Fire Related Items
Frames
Furniture -
  Continental (mainly French)
  Country
  Georgian
  Oak
  Pine
Victorian
Garden Furniture, Ornaments & Statuary
Glass - see also Glass Domes & Paperweights
Glass Domes
Icons - see Russian Art
Islamic Art
Japanese Art - see Oriental
Jewellery - see Silver & Jewellery
Lighting
Maps & Prints
Metalware/work
Miniatures
Mirrors
Musical Boxes, Instruments & Literature
Nautical Instruments - see Scientific
Needlework - see Tapestries
Netsuke - see Oriental
Oil Paintings
Paperweights
Photographs & Equipment
Porcelain & Pottery
Prints - see Maps
Rugs - see Carpets
Russian/Soviet Art
Scientific Instruments
Sculpture
Shipping Goods & Period Furniture for the Trade
Silver & Jewellery
Sporting Items & Associated Memorabilia
Sporting Paintings & Prints
Stamps
Tapestries, Textiles & Needlework
Taxidermy
Tools - including Needlework & Sewing
Toys - see Dolls
Trade Dealers - see Shipping Goods
Treen
Vintage Cars - see Carriages & Cars
Watercolours
Wholesale Dealers - see Shipping Goods
Wine Related Items

Antiques Centres & Markets

Georgian Village Antiques Market, London E17.
Angel Arcade, London N1.
Camden Passage Antiques Centre, London N1.
The Fleamarket, London N1.
London Militaria Market, London N1.
The Mall Antiques Arcade, London N1.
Palmers Green Antiques Centre, London N13.
Southgate Antiques & Collectables, London N14.
Hampstead Antique and Craft Market, London NW3.
Alfies Antique Market, London NW8.
Bermondsey Antiques Market, London SE1.
Greenwich Antiques Market, London SE10.
Sydenham Antiques Centre, London SE26.
Franklin's Camberwell Antiques Market, London SE5.
Cobwebs, London SE9.
Northcote Road Antiques Market, London SW11.
Antiquarius, London SW3.
Bourbon-Hanby Antiques Centre, London SW3.
Fulham Cross Antiques, London SW6.
Magpies, London SW6.
Bond Street Antiques Centre, London W1.
Grays Antique Market, London W1.
Arbras Gallery, London W11.
The Corner Portobello Antiques Supermarket, London W11.
Crown Arcade, London W11.
Dolphin Arcade, London W11.
Grays Portobello, London W11.
The Red Lion Market (Portobello Antiques Market), London W11.
Roger's Antiques Gallery, London W11.
The Silver Fox Gallery, London W11.
Stouts Antiques Market, London W11.
World Famous Portobello Market, London W11.
The Old Cinema Antique Department Store, London W4.
Kensington Church Street Antiques Centre, London W8.
Apple Market Stalls, London WC2.
Covent Garden Flea Market, London WC2.
The London Silver Vaults, London WC2.
Ampthill Emporium, Ampthill, Beds.
The Woburn Abbey Antiques Centre, Woburn, Beds.
Barkham Antique Centre, Barkham, Berks.
Hungerford Arcade, Hungerford, Berks.
Stables Antique Centre, Reading, Berks.
Hall's Corner Antiques, Tilehurst, Berks.
Moss End Antique Centre, Warfield, Berks.
Amersham Antiques and Collectors Centre, Amersham, Bucks.
Buck House Antique Centre, Beaconsfield, Bucks.
Nightingale Antiques, Little Chalfont, Bucks.
Marlow Antique Centre, Marlow, Bucks.
Well Cottage Antiques Centre, Princes Risborough, Bucks.
Tingewick Antiques Centre, Tingewick, Bucks.
Antiques at...Wendover Antiques Centre, Wendover, Bucks.
Winslow Antiques Centre, Winslow, Bucks.
Collectors' Market, Cambridge, Cambs.
Gwydir Street Antiques Centre, Cambridge, Cambs.
The Old Bishop's Palace Antique Centre, Little Downham, Cambs.
Fitzwilliam Antiques Centre, Peterborough, Cambs.
Hyperion Antique Centre, St Ives, Cambs.
Walpole Highway Antiques Centre, Wisbech, Cambs.
Chester Drawers Antique Centre, Chester, Cheshire.
Guildhall Fair - Chester, Chester, Cheshire.
Davenham Antiques Centre & Tea Room, Davenham, Cheshire.
Arts and Antiques Centre, Knutsford, Cheshire.
E. R. Antiques Centre, Stockport, Cheshire.
Tarporley Antique Centre, Tarporley, Cheshire.
Wilmslow Antique Bazaar, Wilmslow, Cheshire.
Bodmin Antiques Centre, Bodmin, Cornwall.
Waterfront Antiques Market, Falmouth, Cornwall.
Chapel Street Antiques Market, Penzance, Cornwall.
Carlisle Antique and Craft Centre, Carlisle, Cumbria.
Cockermouth Antiques Market, Cockermouth, Cumbria.
Alfreton Antiques Centre, Alfreton, Derbys.
Bakewell Antiques and Collectors' Centre, Bakewell, Derbys.
Belper Antiques Centre, Belper, Derbys.
Matlock Antiques, Collectables and Craft Centre, Matlock, Derbys.
Memory Lane Antiques Centre, Ripley, Derbys.
The Shambles, Ashburton, Devon.
Colyton Antique Centre, Colyton, Devon.
The Antique Centre on the Quay, Exeter, Devon.
McBains of Exeter, Exeter, Devon.
The Meeting, Exeter, Devon.
Phantique, Exeter, Devon.
The Quay Gallery Antiques Emporium, Exeter, Devon.
The Antique Centre Abingdon House, Honiton, Devon.
Newton Abbot Antiques Centre, Newton Abbot, Devon.
Barbican Antiques Centre, Plymouth, Devon.
New Street Antique Centre, Plymouth, Devon.
Sidmouth Antiques and Collectors Centre, Sidmouth, Devon.
The Furniture Market, South Molton, Devon.
Mulberry House, Topsham, Devon.
Hardy's Collectables, Bournemouth, Dorset.
Bridport Antiques Centre, Bridport, Dorset.
Charmouth Antique Centre, Charmouth, Dorset.
The Old House Antiques & Collectors Centre, Christchurch, Dorset.
Colliton Antique Centre, Dorchester, Dorset.
Sherborne Antique Centre, Sherborne, Dorset.
North Quay Collector's Centre, Weymouth, Dorset.
Wimborne Antiques and Collectables Centre, Wimborne Minster, Dorset.
Battlesbridge Antique Centre, Battlesbridge, Essex.
Blackmore Antiques & Craft Centre, Blackmore, Essex.
Church Hall Farm Antique & Craft Centre, Broxted, Essex.
Trinity Antiques Centre, Colchester, Essex.
Finchingfield Antiques Centre, Finchingfield, Essex.
Kendons and Atticus Books, Grays, Essex.
Baddow Antique Centre, Great Baddow, Essex.
Townsford Mill Antiques Centre, Halstead, Essex.
Harwich Antiques Centre, Harwich, Essex.
Kelvedon Antiques, Kelvedon, Essex.
Maldon Antiques and Collectors Market, Maldon, Essex.
Saffron Walden Antiques Centre, Saffron Walden, Essex.
Walton Antique Centre, Walton-on-the-Naze, Essex.
Berkeley Antiques Market, Berkeley, Glos.
The Bristol Antiques Centre, Bristol, Glos.
St. Nicholas Markets, Bristol, Glos.
Charlton Kings Antiques Centre, Cheltenham, Glos.
Cheltenham Antique Market, Cheltenham, Glos.
Cirencester Antique Market, Cirencester, Glos.
Gloucester Antique Centre, Gloucester, Glos.
Apsley House Antiques Centre, Lechlade, Glos.
Jubilee Hall Antiques Centre, Lechlade, Glos.
Lechlade Antiques Arcade, Lechlade, Glos.
The Swan Antiques and Crafts Centre, Lechlade, Glos.
Antique Centre, Moreton-in-Marsh, Glos.
Dale House Antiques, Moreton-in-Marsh, Glos.
Windsor House Antiques Centre, Moreton-in-Marsh, Glos.
Painswick Antique Centre, Painswick, Glos.
Durham House Antiques Centre, Stow-on-the-Wold, Glos.

Fox Cottage Antiques, Stow-on-the-Wold, Glos.
The Antique and Interior Centre, Tetbury, Glos.
The Antiques Emporium, Tetbury, Glos.
Tewkesbury Antique & Curio Centre, Tewkesbury, Glos.
The Antique Centre, St. Peter Port, Guernsey, Channel Islands.
Dolphin Quay Antique Centre, Emsworth, Hants.
The Antiques Centre, Hartley Wintney, Hants.
Cedar Antiques Centre Ltd, Hartley Wintney, Hants.
Lymington Antiques Centre, Lymington, Hants.
The Folly Antiques Centre, Petersfield, Hants.
Bridge House Antique Centre, Wickham, Hants.
Samuels Spencers Antiques and Decorative Arts Emporium, Winchester, Hants.
Hereford Antique Centre, Hereford, Herefs.
Leominster Antiques Market, Leominster, Herefs.
Bushey Antique Centre, Bushey, Herts.
Hertford Antiques, Hertford, Herts.
The Herts and Essex Antiques Centre, Sawbridgeworth, Herts.
By George! Antiques Centre, St. Albans, Herts.
St. Albans Antique Market, St. Albans, Herts.
Tring Triangle Antiques Centre, Tring, Herts.
Royal Victoria Arcade, Ryde, Isle of Wight.
Beckenham Antique Market, Beckenham, Kent.
The Village Antique Centre, Brasted, Kent.
Bromley Antique Market, Bromley, Kent.
Burgate Antique Centre, Canterbury, Kent.
Rastro Antiques, Canterbury, Kent.
Cranbrook Antique Centre, Cranbrook, Kent.
Copperfields Antique & Craft Centre, Dartford, Kent.
Malthouse Arcade, Hythe, Kent.
Sandgate Antiques Centre, Sandgate, Kent.
Noah's Ark Antique Centre, Sandwich, Kent.
The Antiques Centre, Sevenoaks, Kent.
Bradbourne Gallery, Sevenoaks, Kent.
Sidcup Antique and Craft Centre, Sidcup, Kent.
Sparks Antiques Centre, Tenterden, Kent.
Tenterden Antiques Centre, Tenterden, Kent.
Barden House Antiques, Tonbridge, Kent.
Corn Exchange Antiques Centre, Tunbridge Wells, Kent.
Tunbridge Wells Antique Centre, Tunbridge Wells, Kent.
Castle Antiques Centre, Westerham, Kent.
Bolton Antique Centre, Bolton, Lancs.
Ironchurch Antiques Centre, Bolton, Lancs.
King's Mill Antique Centre, Burnley, Lancs.
Antiques and Crafts Centre, Chorley, Lancs.
The Assembly Rooms Market, Lancaster, Lancs.
G.B. Antiques Ltd, Lancaster, Lancs.
Lancaster Leisure Park Antiques Centre, Lancaster, Lancs.
The Attic Centre, Longridge, Lancs.
Antiques Village, Manchester, Lancs.
The Ginnell Gallery Antique Centre, Manchester, Lancs.
The Antique Centre, Preston, Lancs.
Preston Antique Centre, Preston, Lancs.
Walter Aspinall Antiques, Sabden, Lancs.
Oxford Street Antique Centre, Leicester, Leics.
Whitemoors Antiques and Fine Art, Shenton, Leics.
Portobello Row Antique & Collectors' Centre, Boston, Lincs.
Abbeygate Antique & Craft Centre, Grimsby, Lincs.
Astra House Antiques Centre, Hemswell Cliff, Lincs.
Hemswell Antiques Centre, Hemswell Cliff, Lincs.
Great Expectations, Horncastle, Lincs.
Lindsey Court Antiques, Horncastle, Lincs.
Irby Antiques Centre, Irby-in-the-Marsh, Lincs.
The Chapel Emporium Antique Centre, Long Sutton, Lincs.
Old Maltings Antique Centre, Louth, Lincs.
St. Martins Antiques Centre, Stamford, Lincs.
Stamford Antiques Centre, Stamford, Lincs.
Hoylake Antique Centre, Hoylake, Merseyside.
The Jay's Middx Antique Centre, Harefield, Middx.
Riverside Antiques, Harefield, Middx.
Phelps Antiques, Twickenham, Middx.
Coltishall Antiques Centre, Coltishall, Norfolk.
Fakenham Antique Centre, Fakenham, Norfolk.
Le Strange Old Barns Antiques, Arts & Craft Centre, Hunstanton, Norfolk.
The Old Granary Antiques and Collectors Centre, King's Lynn, Norfolk.
Pine and Things, King's Lynn, Norfolk.
Cloisters Antiques Fair, Norwich, Norfolk.
Norwich Antique, Collectors & Interiors Centre, Norwich, Norfolk.
Norwich Antiques Centre, Norwich, Norfolk.
St. Michael at Plea Antiques Centre, Norwich, Norfolk.
Wells Antique Centre, Wells-next-the-Sea, Norfolk.
E.K. Antiques, Finedon, Northants.
Finedon Antiques (Antiques Centre), Finedon, Northants.
The Village Antique Market, Weedon, Northants.
Antiques and Bric-a-Brac Market, Wellingborough, Northants.
Occleshaw Antiques Centre, Edwinstowe, Notts.
Castle Gate Antiques Centre, Newark, Notts.
Newark Antiques Centre, Newark, Notts.
Portland Street Antiques Centre, Newark, Notts.
Tudor Rose Antiques Centre, Newark, Notts.
Top Hat Antiques Centre, Nottingham, Notts.
Old George Inn Antique Galleries, Burford, Oxon.
Country Markets Antiques and Collectables, Chilton, Oxon.
Chipping Norton Antique Centre, Chipping Norton, Oxon.
Deddington Antiques Centre, Deddington, Oxon.
Didcot Antiques Centre, Didcot, Oxon.
Friday Street Antique Centre, Henley-on-Thames, Oxon.
Henley Antique Centre, Henley-on-Thames, Oxon.
The Oxford Antique Trading Co, Oxford, Oxon.
TheSwan at Tetsworth, Tetsworth, Oxon.
The Lamb Arcade, Wallingford, Oxon.
Le Print Antique Centre, Woodstock, Oxon.
Span Antiques, Woodstock, Oxon.
Clola Antiques Centre, Clola by Mintlaw, Scotland.
Heritage House Antiques, Glasgow, Scotland.
King's Court Antique Centre, Glasgow, Scotland.
The Victorian Village, Glasgow, Scotland.
Virginia Antique Galleries, Glasgow, Scotland.
Ian Murray Antique Warehouse, Perth, Scotland.
Rait Village Antiques Centre, Rait, Scotland.
Old Mill Antique Centre, Bridgnorth, Shrops.
Stretton Antiques Market, Church Stretton, Shrops.
Cleobury Mortimer Antique Centre, Cleobury Mortimer, Shrops.
Ironbridge Antique & Reproduction Centre, Ironbridge, Shrops.
Pepper Lane Antiques `, Ludlow, Shrops.
Amanda's Antique Centre/Flea Market Newport, Shrops.
Princess Antique Centre, Shrewsbury, Shrops.
Shrewsbury Antique Centre, Shrewsbury, Shrops.
Shrewsbury Antique Market, Shrewsbury, Shrops.
Assembly Antiques Centre, Bath, Somerset.
Bartlett Street Antique Centre, Bath, Somerset.
Bath Antiques Market, Bath, Somerset
Bath Saturday Antiques Market, Bath, Somerset.
Fountain Antiques Centre, Bath, Somerset.
Paragon Antiques and Collectors Market, Bath, Somerset.

Guildhall Antique Market, Chard, Somerset.
Octopus Antique Centre, Crewkerne, Somerset.
Oscars Antiques, Crewkerne, Somerset.
County Antiques Centre, Ilminster, Somerset.
Taunton Antiques Market - Silver Street, Taunton, Somerset.
Green Dragon Antiques Centre, Wincanton, Somerset.
The Somerset and Dorset Antique Centre, Yeovil, Somerset.
Rugeley Antique Centre, Brereton, Staffs.
The Leek Antiques Centre, Leek, Staffs.
The Tudor of Lichfield Antiques Centre, Lichfield, Staffs.
Antique Market, Newcastle-under-Lyme, Staffs.
Windmill Antiques, Stafford, Staffs.
Old Chapel Antique & Collectables Centre, Tutbury, Staffs.
Tutbury Mill Antiques Centre, Tutbury, Staffs.
Blackbrook Antiques Village, Weeford, Staffs.
Waveney Antiques Centre, Beccles, Suffolk.
Clare Antique Warehouse, Clare, Suffolk.
Long Melford Antique Centre, Long Melford, Suffolk.
The Old Town Hall Antique Centre, Needham Market, Suffolk.
The Risby Barn, Risby, Suffolk.
Snape Antiques and Collectors Centre, Snape, Suffolk.
The Emporium Antiques and Collectors Centre, Southwold, Suffolk.
Wrentham Antiques Centre, Wrentham, Suffolk.
Memories, Bramley, Surrey.
Chertsey Antiques, Chertsey, Surrey.
Dorking Antique Centre, Dorking, Surrey.
Pilgrims Antique Centre, Dorking, Surrey.
Victoria and Edward Antiques Centre, Dorking, Surrey.
The Antiques Arcade, East Molesey, Surrey.
The Sovereign Antique Centre, East Molesey, Surrey.
Bourne Mill Antiques, Farnham, Surrey.
Farnham Antique Centre, Farnham, Surrey.
Maltings Monthly Market, Farnham, Surrey.
The Antiques Centre, Guildford, Surrey.
Haslemere Antique Market, Haslemere, Surrey.
Wood's Wharf Antiques Bazaar, Haslemere, Surrey.
Kingston Antique Market, Kingston-upon-Thames, Surrey.
Antiques Centre, Oxted, Surrey.
Richmond Antiques, Richmond, Surrey.
Shere Antiques Centre, Shere, Surrey.
Fern Cottage Antiques, Thames Ditton, Surrey.
Tymes Past Antiques, Battle, E. Sussex.
Brighton Antique Wholesalers, Brighton, E. Sussex.
Brighton Flea Market, Brighton, E. Sussex.
Chateaubriand Antiques Centre, Burwash, E. Sussex.
Eastbourne Antiques Market, Eastbourne, E. Sussex.
Enterprise Collectors Market, Eastbourne, E. Sussex.
The Old Town Antiques Centre, Eastbourne, E. Sussex.
Pharoahs Antiques Centre, Eastbourne, E. Sussex.
George Street Antiques Centre, Hastings, E. Sussex.
Horsebridge Antiques Centre, Horsebridge, E. Sussex.
Church-Hill Antiques Centre, Lewes, E. Sussex.
Cliffe Antiques Centre, Lewes, E. Sussex.
The Emporium Antique Centre, Lewes, E. Sussex.
Lewes Antique Centre, Lewes, E. Sussex.
The Courtyard Antiques Market, Seaford, E. Sussex.
Seaford's "Barn Collectors' Market" and Studio Bookshop, Seaford, E. Sussex.
The Hastings Antique Centre, St. Leonards-on-Sea, E. Sussex.
Old House Antique Centre, Adversane, W. Sussex.
Tarrant Street Antique Centre, Arundel, W. Sussex.
Treasure House Antiques and Collectors Market, Arundel, W. Sussex.
Great Grooms Antique Centre, Billingshurst, W. Sussex.
Almshouses Arcade, Chichester, W. Sussex.
Chichester Antiques Centre, Chichester, W. Sussex.
Curfew Antiques Centre, Midhurst, W. Sussex.
Petworth Antique Market, Petworth, W. Sussex.
Anna Harrison Antiques Centre, Gosforth, Tyne and Wear.
Jacobs Antique Centre, Cardiff, Wales.
Jones Centre, Chepstow, Wales.
The Antiques Centre, Cowbridge, Wales.
Antique Market, Hay-on-Wye, Wales.
Offa's Dyke Antique Centre, Knighton, Wales.
Pembroke Antiques Centre, Pembroke, Wales.
Malthouse Antiques Centre, Alcester, Warks.
Bidford Antiques Centre, Bidford-on-Avon, Warks.
The Stables Antique Centre, Hatton, Warks.
Stratford Antique Centre, Stratford-upon-Avon, Warks.
The Stratford Antiques and Interiors Centre Ltd, Stratford-upon-Avon, Warks.
The Old Cornmarket Antiques Centre, Warwick, Warks.
Vintage Antiques Centre, Warwick, Warks.
The Warwick Antique Centre, Warwick, Warks.
The Birmingham Antique Centre Ltd, Birmingham, W. Mids.
Warley Antique Centre, Birmingham, W. Mids.
Regency Antique Trading Centre, Stourbridge, W. Mids.
The Marlborough Parade Antique Centre, Marlborough, Wilts.
King Street Curios, Melksham, Wilts.
Antique and Collectors Market, Salisbury, Wilts.
The Avonbridge Antiques and Collectors Market, Salisbury, Wilts.
Tubbjoys Antique Market, Wootton Bassett, Wilts.
Malvern Antiques Centre, Great Malvern, Worcs.
Antiques and Curios, Worcester, Worcs.
St. Georges Antiques, Worcester, Worcs.
The Tything Antique Centre, Worcester, Worcs.
Worcester Antiques Centre, Worcester, Worcs.
Grannie's Treasures, Hull, E. Yorks.
The Mall Antique Centre &
Geoffrey Mole Antiques, Hull, E. Yorks.
The Ginnel, Harrogate, N. Yorks.
Montpellier Mews Antique Market, Harrogate, N. Yorks.
Malton Antique Market, Malton, N. Yorks.
Scarthingwell Arcades, Scarthingwell, N. Yorks.
Drey Antique Centre, Sherburn in Elmet, N. Yorks.
The Emporium, York, N. Yorks.
York Antiques Centre, York, N. Yorks.
Treasure House Antiques Centre, Bawtry, S. Yorks.
Foster's Antique Centre, Rotherham, S. Yorks.
Court House Antique Centre, Sheffield, S. Yorks.
Sheffield Antiques Emporium
, Sheffield, S. Yorks.
Halifax Antiques Centre, Halifax, W. Yorks.
Headrow Antiques Centre, Leeds, W. Yorks.
Leeds Antiques Centre, Leeds, W. Yorks.
The Victoria Centre, Saltaire, W. Yorks.
Todmorden Antiques Centre, Todmorden, W. Yorks.
Harrington Antiques Centre, Woodlesford, W. Yorks.

Antiquarian Books

Ash Rare Books, London EC3.
J. Clarke-Hall Ltd, London EC4.
Michael Finney Antique Prints and Books, London N1.
M.E. Korn, London N10.
W. Forster, London N16.
Walford's - Nicholas Goodyer, London N5.
Fisher and Sperr, London N6.
East-Asia Co, London NW1.
The Schuster Gallery, London NW2.
P.G. de Lotz, London NW3.
Keith Fawkes, London NW3.

Barrie Marks Ltd, London NW5.
H. Baron, London NW6.
The Warwick Leadlay Gallery, London SE10.
Rogers Turner Books, London SE10.
J. A. Allen & Co. (The Horseman's Bookshop) Ltd, London SW1.
Classic Bindings, London SW1.
Christopher Edwards, London SW1.
Thomas Heneage Art Books, London SW1.
Sims, Reed Ltd, London SW1.
Hünersdorff Rare Books, London SW10.
John Thornton, London SW10.
Paul Foster's Bookshop, London SW14.
Han-Shan Tang Books, London SW15.
William Reeves Bookseller Ltd, London SW16.
Robin Greer, London SW6.
Paul Orssich, London SW8.
G. Heywood Hill Ltd, London W1.
Holland & Holland, London W1.
Maggs Bros Ltd, London W1.
Marlborough Rare Books Ltd, London W1.
The O'Shea Gallery, London W1.
Paralos Ltd, London W1.
Pickering and Chatto, London W1.
Jonathan Potter Ltd, London W1.
Bernard Quaritch Ltd (Booksellers), London W1.
Russell Rare Books, London W1.
Robert G. Sawers, London W1.
Bernard J. Shapero Rare Books, London W1.
Henry Sotheran Ltd, London W1.
Books & Things, London W11.
Demetzy Books, London W11.
D. Parikian, London W14.
Bayswater Books, London W2.
Hosains Books and Antiques, London W2.
Crawley and Asquith Ltd, London W8.
Adrian Harrington, London W8.
Atlantis Bookshop, London WC1.
Cinema Bookshop, London WC1.
Robert Frew Ltd, London WC1.
London Antiquarian Book Arcade, London WC1.
Marchmont Bookshop, London WC1.
The Museum Bookshop, London WC1.
Skoob Books Ltd, London WC1.
Skoob Two, London WC1.
Bell, Book and Radmall, London WC2.
Blackwell's, London WC2.
David Drummond at Pleasures of Past Times, London WC2.
W. and G. Foyle Ltd, London WC2.
Henry Pordes Books Ltd, London WC2.
Reg and Philip Remington, London WC2.
Bertram Rota Ltd, London WC2.
Stage Door Prints, London WC2.
Storey's Ltd, London WC2.
Tooley Adams & Co., London WC2.
Watkins Books Ltd, London WC2.
Zeno Booksellers and Publishers, London WC2.
Zwemmer, London WC2.
Marlborough Sporting Gallery and Bookshop, Hungerford, Berks.
Penn Barn, Penn, Bucks.
David Bickersteth, Bassingbourn, Cambs.
G. David, Cambridge, Cambs.
Deighton Bell and Co, Cambridge, Cambs.
Galloway and Porter Ltd, Cambridge, Cambs.
Sarah Key, Cambridge, Cambs.
Old Soke Books, Peterborough, Cambs.
Forest Books of Cheshire, Alsager, Cheshire.
Stothert - Antiquarian Books, Chester, Cheshire.
Lion Gallery and Bookshop, Knutsford, Cheshire.
New Street Books, Penzance, Cornwall.
Maurice Dodd Books, Carlisle, Cumbria.
Norman Kerr - Gatehouse Bookshop, Cartmel, Cumbria.
Peter Bain Smith (Bookseller), Cartmel, Cumbria.
Archie Miles Bookshop, Gosforth, Cumbria.
The Book House, Ravenstonedale, Cumbria.
R. F. G. Hollett and Son, Sedbergh, Cumbria.
Michael Moon, Whitehaven, Cumbria.
G.K. Hadfield, Swadlincote, Derbys.
Chantry Bookshop and Gallery, Dartmouth, Devon.
Exeter Rare Books, Exeter, Devon.
Honiton Old Bookshop, Honiton, Devon.
Geoffrey M. Woodhead, Honiton, Devon.
P.M. Pollak, South Brent, Devon.
Collards Books, Totnes, Devon.
Ancient and Modern Bookshop (including Garret's Antiques), Blandford Forum, Dorset.
PIC's Bookshop, Bridport, Dorset.
Words Etcetera, Dorchester, Dorset.
Christopher Williams Antiquarian Bookseller, Parkstone, Dorset.
Antique Map and Bookshop, Puddletown, Dorset.
The Swan Gallery, Sherborne, Dorset.
Reference Works, Swanage, Dorset.
Books Afloat, Weymouth, Dorset.
Books & Bygones, Weymouth, Dorset.
J. Shotton Antiquarian Books, Prints and Coins, Durham, Durham.
Elkin Mathews, Coggeshall, Essex.
Castle Bookshop, Colchester, Essex.
Cotham Hill Bookshop, Bristol, Glos.
A.R. Heath, Bristol, Glos.
Triangle Books (inc. John Roberts Bookshop Est. 1955), Bristol, Glos.
The Wise Owl Bookshop, Bristol, Glos.
David Bannister FRGS, Cheltenham, Glos.
Michael Rayner, Cheltenham, Glos.
Ian Hodgkins and Co. Ltd, Slad, Glos.
The Coach House Bookshop, Tetbury, Glos.
Channel Islands Galleries Ltd, St. Peter Port, Guernsey, Channel Islands.
Geoffrey P. Gavey, Vale, Guernsey, Channel Islands.
Laurence Oxley, Alresford, Hants.
Hughes and Smeeth Ltd, Lymington, Hants.
The Petersfield Bookshop, Petersfield, Hants.
H.M. Gilbert and Son, Southampton, Hants.
Peter M. Daly, Winchester, Hants.
H.M. Gilbert, Winchester, Hants.
SPCK Bookshops, Winchester, Hants.
Ross Old Book and Print Shop, Ross-on-Wye, Herefs.
H. Pordes Ltd, Cockfosters, Herts.
Wheldon and Wesley Ltd, Codicote, Herts.
Eric T. Moore, Hitchin, Herts.
Clive A. Burden, Rickmansworth, Herts.
Julia Margaret Cameron Gallery, Cowes, Isle of Wight.
Charles Dickens Bookshop, Cowes, Isle of Wight.
Ventnor Rare Books, Ventnor, Isle of Wight.
John Blench & Son, St. Helier, Jersey, Channel Islands.
The Selective Eye Gallery, St. Helier, Jersey, Channel Islands.
Thesaurus (Jersey) Ltd, St. Helier, Jersey, Channel Islands.
Graham Stead Antiques, Brasted, Kent.
The Canterbury Bookshop, Canterbury, Kent.
Chaucer Bookshop, Canterbury, Kent.
Periwinkle Press, Newnham, Kent.
Baggins Book Bazaar - The Largest Secondhand Bookshop in England, Rochester, Kent.
Baskerville Books, Tunbridge Wells, Kent.
Hall's Bookshop, Tunbridge Wells, Kent.
London House Antiques, Westerham, Kent.
Taylor-Smith, Westerham, Kent.
W.B. McCormack, Lancaster, Lancs.
Forest Books of Cheshire, Manchester, Lancs.
Gibb's Bookshop Ltd, Manchester, Lancs.
Eric J. Morten, Manchester, Lancs.
Secondhand and Rare Books, Manchester, Lancs.
Halewood and Sons, Preston, Lancs.
Preston Book Co, Preston, Lancs.
Anthony W. Laywood, Knipton, Leics
P.J. Cassidy (Books), Holbeach, Lincs
Golden Goose Books, Lincoln, Lincs.
Harlequin Gallery, Lincoln, Lincs.
Staniland (Booksellers), Stamford, Lincs.
C.K. Broadhurst and Co Ltd, Southport, Merseyside.
Ian Sheridan's Bookshop Hampton, Hampton, Middx.
Anthony C. Hall, Twickenham, Middx.
John Ives Bookseller, Twickenham, Middx.
Rita Shenton, Twickenham, Middx.
David Ferrow, Gt. Yarmouth, Norfolk.
Simon Gough Books, Holt, Norfolk.
Baron Art, Kelling, Norfolk.
J & D Clarke Book and Print Dealers, Norwich, Norfolk.
Peter Crowe, Antiquarian Book Seller, Norwich, Norfolk.
The Scientific Anglian (Bookshop), Norwich, Norfolk.
The Tombland Bookshop, Norwich, Norfolk.
R.L. Cook, Sheringham, Norfolk.
Turret House, Wymondham, Norfolk
The Old Hall Bookshop, Brackley, Northants.

The Bookstore, Northampton, Northants.
Hickey Books, Northampton, Northants.
Occultique, Northampton, Northants.
Park Gallery & Bookshop, Wellingborough, Northants.
Emerald Isle Books, Belfast, N. Ireland.
The Book Shelf, Mansfield, Notts.
N.J. Doris - 'Dorisbooks', Nottingham, Notts.
E.M. Lawson and Co, East Hagbourne, Oxon.
Richard J. Kingston, Henley-on-Thames, Oxon.
Blackwell's Rare Books, Oxford, Oxon.
Thorntons of Oxford Ltd, Oxford, Oxon.
Titles - Old and Rare Books, Oxford, Oxon.
Waterfield's, Oxford, Oxon.
Goldmark Books, Uppingham, Rutland.
Highland Antiques, Avoch, Scotland.
The McEwan Gallery, Ballater, Scotland.
McNaughtan's Bookshop, Edinburgh, Scotland.
Alan Rankin, Edinburgh, Scotland.
James Thin (Booksellers), Edinburgh, Scotland.
Marianne Simpson, Fochabers, Scotland.
Amber Antiques, Kincardine O'Neil, Scotland.
Paisley Fine Books, Paisley, Scotland.
A. and F. McIlreavy Rare and Interesting Books, St. Andrews, Scotland.
Candle Lane Books, Shrewsbury, Shrops.
George Bayntun, Bath, Somerset.
George Gregory, Bath, Somerset.
Patterson Liddle, Bath, Somerset.
Rothwell and Dunworth, Dulverton, Somerset.
Janet Clarke, Freshford, Somerset.
Steven Ferdinando, Queen Camel,, Somerset.
Sterling Books, Weston-Super-Mare, Somerset.
Mike Abrahams Books, Lichfield, Staffs.
Images - Peter Stockham, Lichfield, Staffs.
The Staffs Bookshop, Lichfield, Staffs.
Besleys Books, Beccles, Suffolk.
Trinders' Fine Tools, Clare, Suffolk.
Claude Cox at College Gateway Bookshop, Ipswich, Suffolk.
R.G. Archer, Lavenham,, Suffolk.
R.E. and G.B. Way, Newmarket, Suffolk.
Abington Books, Redgrave, Suffolk.
Vandeleur Antiquarian Books, Epsom, Surrey.
J.W. McKenzie, Ewell, Surrey.
Thomas Thorp Bookseller, Guildford, Surrey.
Charles W. Traylen, Guildford, Surrey.
Lloyds of Kew, Kew, Surrey.
A. Burton-Garbett, Morden, Surrey.
Reigate Galleries Ltd, Reigate, Surrey.
Raymond Slack FRSA & Shirley Warren, Sanderstead, Surrey.
Elizabeth Gant, Thames Ditton, Surrey.
Holleyman and Treacher Ltd, Brighton, E. Sussex.
Colin Page Antiquarian Books, Brighton, E. Sussex.
Brian Page Antiques, Brighton, E. Sussex.
Camilla's Bookshop, Eastbourne, E. Sussex.
Roderick Dew, Eastbourne, E. Sussex.
A. & T. Gibbard, Eastbourne, E. Sussex.
Premier Gallery & Bookshop, Eastbourne, E. Sussex.
Howes Bookshop, Hastings, E. Sussex.
Bow Windows Book Shop, Lewes, E. Sussex.
A. & Y. Cumming, Lewes, E. Sussex.
Fifteenth Century Bookshop, Lewes, E. Sussex.
The Book Jungle, St. Leonards-on-Sea, E. Sussex.
Lombard Gallery, Petworth, W. Sussex.
R.D. Steedman, Newcastle-upon-Tyne, Tyne and Wear.
H.K. Lockyer, Abergavenny, Wales.
Maps, Prints and Books, Brecon, Wales.
Glance Back Bookshop, Chepstow, Wales.
Richard Booth's Bookshop Ltd, Hay-on-Wye, Wales.
Mark Westwood Antiquarian Books, Hay-on-Wye, Wales.
Doggie Hubbard's Bookshop, Ponterwyd,, Wales.
Dylan's Bookshop, Swansea, Wales.
Edward Lawson Studio, Swansea, Wales.
The Stratford Bookshop, Stratford-upon-Avon, Warks.
Robert Vaughan, Stratford-upon-Avon, Warks.
Duncan M. Allsop, Warwick, Warks.
Alan Richards Brocante, Birmingham, W. Mids.
David Temperley Fine and Antiquarian Books, Birmingham, W. Mids.
Clive Farahar and Sophie Dupré - Rare Books, Autographs and Manuscripts, Calne, Wilts.
Hilmarton Manor Press, Calne, Wilts.
The Military Parade Bookshop, Marlborough, Wilts.
Heraldry Today, Ramsbury, Wilts.
The Barn Book Supply, Salisbury, Wilts.
D.M. Beach, Salisbury, Wilts.
Victoria Bookshop, Swindon, Wilts.
Clent Books, Bewdley, Worcs.
Malvern Bookshop, Great Malvern, Worcs.
Antique Map and Print Gallery, Worcester, Worcs.
The Grove Country Bookshop with Coopers of Ilkley, Bolton Abbey, N. Yorks.
The Great Ayton Bookshop, Great Ayton, N. Yorks.
Potterton Books, Thirsk, N. Yorks.
Barbican Bookshop, York, N. Yorks.
Minster Gate Bookshop, York, N. Yorks.
Ken Spelman, York, N. Yorks.
Alan Hill Books, Sheffield, Sheffield, S. Yorks.
The Toll House Bookshop, Holmfirth, W. Yorks.
The Grove Bookshop, Ilkley, W. Yorks.

Antiquities

Ian Auld, London N1.
C.J. Martin (Coins) Ltd, London N14.
Oriental Bronzes Ltd, London NW5.
Robin Symes Ltd, London SW1.
Christopher Sheppard, London SW7.
Charles Ede Ltd, London W1.
Hadji Baba Ancient Art,, London W1.
Mansour Gallery, London W1.
Seaby Antiquities, London W1.
Rupert Wace Ancient Art Ltd, London W1.
Town Hall Antiques, Woburn, Beds.
The Ancient Art Shop, Windsor and Eton, Berks.
Past Treasures Ltd, Wendover, Bucks.
Potter's Antiques and Coins, Bristol, Glos.
A. Burton-Garbett, Morden, Surrey.
Molly Alexander, Seaford, E. Sussex.
Hermitage Antiquities, Fishguard, Wales.

Architectural Items

The London Architectural Salvage & Supply Co. (LASSCo), London EC2.
Westland & Company, London EC2.
Townsends, London NW8.
The Old Cinema Antique Warehouse, London SE1.
The Junk Shop, London SE10.
Lamont Antiques Ltd, London SE10.
Thornhill Galleries Ltd. in association with A. & R. Dockerill Ltd, London SW15.
Charles Edwards, London SW6.
Fairfax Antiques and Fireplaces, London SW6.
Thornhill Galleries Ltd, London SW6.
Architectural Antiques - Bedford, Bedford, Beds.
T. Smith, Chalfont St. Giles, Bucks.
Adrian Hornsey Ltd, Twyford, Bucks.
Solopark Plc, Cambridge, Cambs.
Nostalgia Architectural Antiques, Stockport, Cheshire.
Cheshire Brick and Slate Co, Tarvin Sands, Cheshire.
The Great Northern Architectural Antique Company Ltd, Tattenhall, Cheshire.
Antique Fireplace Centre, Hartlepool, Cleveland.
Riverside Antiques, Ballynahinch, Co. Down, N. Ireland.
W.R.S. Architectural Antiques, Low Newton, Cumbria.
Havenplan's Architectural Emporium, Killamarsh, Derbys.
Ashburton Marbles, Ashburton, Devon.
Rex Antiques, Chagford, Devon.
Fagins Antiques, Exeter, Devon.
Great Western Antiques, Torquay, Devon.
Talisman, Gillingham, Dorset.
Churchgate Antiques, Sible Hedingham, Essex.
Au Temps Perdu, Bristol, Glos.
Robert Mills Architectural Antiques Ltd, Bristol, Glos.
Cox's Architectural Reclamation Yard, Moreton-in-Marsh, Glos.
Ronson's Architectural Effects, Norton, Glos.
Architectural Heritage, Taddington, Glos.

Burgess Farm Antiques, Morestead, Hants.
"Old Cottage Things", Romsey, Hants.
The Pine Cellars, Winchester, Hants.
Baileys Architectural Antiques, Ross-on-Wye, Herefs.
Bygone Times International Plc, Eccleston, Lancs.
Old Smithy, Feniscowles, Lancs.
Antique Fireplaces, Manchester, Lancs.
In-Situ Architectural Antiques, Manchester, Lancs.
Victoriana Architectural, Long Clawson, Leics.
Antique Fireplaces, Liverpool, Merseyside.
Peco, Hampton, Middx.
Crowther of Syon Lodge Ltd, Isleworth, Middx.
Architectural Heritage of Northants, Weedon, Northants.
Rococo Antiques and Interiors, Weedon, Northants.
Hallidays (Fine Antiques) Ltd, Dorchester-on-Thames, Oxon.
Aston Pine Antiques, Faringdon, Oxon.
Oxford Architectural Antiques, Faringdon, Oxon.
The Country Seat, Huntercombe, Oxon.
Dunedin Antiques Ltd, Edinburgh, Scotland.
EASY - Edinburgh & Glasgow Architectural Salvage Yards, Edinburgh, Scotland.
EASY - Edinburgh and Glasgow Architectural Salvage Yards, Glasgow, Scotland.
Architectural Antiques and Interiors, Ludlow, Shrops.
David Bridgwater, Bath, Somerset.
Source, Bath, Somerset.
Walcot Reclamation, Bath, Somerset.
Chris's Crackers, Carhampton, Somerset.
Wells Reclamation Company, Coxley, Somerset.
Castle Reclamation, Martock, Somerset.
Harrison House Antiques, North Petherton, Somerset.
J.C. Giddings, Wiveliscombe, Somerset.
Anvil Antiques Ltd, Leek, Staffs.
E.T. Webster, Blythburgh,, Suffolk.
Drummonds of Bramley Architectural Antiques Ltd, Bramley, Surrey.
Antique Buildings Ltd, Dunsfold, Surrey.
The Packhouse, Runfold, Surrey.
Antique Church Furnishings, Walton-on-Thames, Surrey.
Brighton Architectural Salvage, Brighton, E. Sussex.
Shiners Architectural Reclamation, Newcastle-upon-Tyne, Tyne and Wear.
Gallop and Rivers Architectural Antiques, Crickhowell, Wales.
The Original Choice Ltd, Birmingham, W. Mids.
Retro Products, Lye, W. Mids.
Harriet Fairfax Fireplaces and General Antiques, Langley Burrell, Wilts.
Ray Coggins Antiques, Westbury, Wilts.
Holloways, Suckley, Worcs.
Kevin Marshall's Antiques Warehouse, Hull, E. Yorks.
Old Flames, Easingwold, N. Yorks.
White House Farm Antiques, Easingwold, N. Yorks.
Robert Aagaard & Co, Knaresborough, N. Yorks.
Daleside Antiques, Markington, N. Yorks.
Andy Thornton Architectural Antiques Ltd, Halifax, W. Yorks.

Arms & Armour

London Militaria Market, London N1.
Finchley Fine Art Galleries, London N12.
Laurence Corner, London NW1.
Peter Dale Ltd, London SW1.
Spink and Son Ltd, London SW1.
Period Brass Lights, London SW7.
Blunderbuss Antiques, London W1.
Holland & Holland, London W1.
Under Two Flags, London W1.
Michael C. German, London W8.
Robert Hales Antiques Ltd, London W8.
Trafalgar Square Collectors Centre, London WC2.
T.L.O. Militaria, Windsor and Eton, Berks.
Anthony D. Goodlad, Chesterfield, Derbys.
Rex Antiques, Chagford, Devon.
Blade and Bayonet, Bournemouth, Dorset.
Boscombe Militaria, Bournemouth, Dorset.
Sterling Coins and Medals, Bournemouth, Dorset.
M. & R. Lankshear Antiques, Christchurch, Dorset.
Castle Antiques, Leigh-on-Sea, Essex.
Chris Grimes Militaria, Bristol, Glos.
Heydens Militaria, Cheltenham, Glos.
Military Curios, HQ84, Gloucester, Glos.
Mark A. Serle (Antiques and Restoration), Lechlade, Glos.
Hampton Gallery, Tetbury, Glos.
Romsey Medal and Collectors Centre, Romsey, Hants.
Trecilla Antiques, Ross-on-Wye, Herefs.
A. & R. Ritchie, St. Helier, Jersey, Channel Islands.
H.S. Greenfield and Son, Gunmakers (Est. 1805), Canterbury, Kent.
J.T. Rutherford and Son, Sandgate, Kent.
Bulldog Antiques, Manchester, Lancs.
Bus Stop Curios, Manchester, Lancs.
Garth Vincent Antique Arms and Armour, Allington, Lincs.
Antiques & Collectables, Scunthorpe, Lincs.
David Allan Antiques, Birkenhead, Merseyside.
The Old Brigade, Kingsthorpe, Northants.
Michael D. Long - Trident Arms, Nottingham, Notts.
Angus Antiques, Dundee, Scotland.
English Heritage, Bridgnorth, Shrops.
Atfield and Daughter, Ipswich, Suffolk.
One Bell, Lavenham, Suffolk.
West Street Antiques, Dorking, Surrey.
Casque and Gauntlet Militaria, Farnham, Surrey.
Mark and David Hawkins, Brighton, E. Sussex.
St. Pancras Antiques, Chichester, W. Sussex.
Michael Miller, Hurstpierpoint, W. Sussex.
Steve Johnson Medals & Militaria, Newcastle-upon-Tyne, Tyne and Wear.
Hermitage Antiquities, Fishguard, Wales.
Arbour Antiques Ltd, Stratford-upon-Avon, Warks.
James Wigington Arms and Armour, Stratford-upon-Avon, Warks.
March Medals, Birmingham, W. Mids.
Edred A.F. Gwilliam, Cricklade, Wilts.
Magpie Jewellers and Antiques and Magpie Arms & Armour, Evesham, Worcs.
Cairncross and Sons, Filey, N. Yorks.
Hanover Antiques & Collectables, Scarborough, N. Yorks.
Adamson Armoury, Skipton, N. Yorks.
Andrew Spencer Bottomley, Holmfirth, W. Yorks.
D.W. Dyson (Antique Weapons), Huddersfield, W. Yorks.

Art Deco & Art Nouveau

The Antique Trader, London N1.
Pieter Oosthuizen t/a de Verzamelaar, London N1.
Style, London N1.
Tadema Gallery, London N1.
Titus Omega, London N1.
Art Furniture, London NW1.
Beverley, London NW8.
Bizarre, London NW8.
The Gallery on Church Street, London NW8.
The Studio, London NW8.
Behind the Boxes - Art Deco, London SE26.
Cobra and Bellamy, London SW1.
Gallery '25, London SW1.
Keshishian, London SW1.
Twentieth Century, London SW12.
The Arts & Crafts Furniture Co Ltd, London SW14.
Acanthus Antiques, London SW19.
Butler and Wilson, London SW3.
David Gill, London SW3.
The Purple Shop, London SW3.
Gordon Watson Ltd, London SW3.
The Lamp Gallery, London SW6.
Editions Graphiques Gallery, London W1.
Liberty, London W1.
Mayfair Gallery, London W1.
The Facade, London W11.
Peter Farlow, London W11.
Joan Leigh, London W11.
Themes and Variations, London W11
Haslam and Whiteway, London W8.
John Jesse, London W8.
New Century, London W8.
Pruskin Gallery, London W8.
Deco Inspired, London WC2.
Morgan Stobbs, Windsor and Eton, Berks.
20th Century, Cambridge, Cambs.
Bizarre Decorative Arts North West, Altrincham, Cheshire.

Aldersey Hall Ltd, Chester, Cheshire.
Nantwich Art Deco and Decorative Arts, Nantwich, Cheshire.
Antique Furniture Warehouse, Stockport, Cheshire.
Maggie Mays, Buxton, Derbys.
Lionel Geneen Ltd, Bournemouth, Dorset.
Times Past, Coggeshall, Essex.
Bernard Weaver Antiques, Cirencester, Glos.
Greystones Antiques and Interiors, Lechlade, Glos.
Ruskin Antiques, Stow-on-the-Wold, Glos.
Alexanders, Titchfield, Hants.
Delf Stream Gallery, Sandwich, Kent.
Modern Design Classics, Westerham, Kent.
Vicary Antiques, Lancaster, Lancs.
A.S. Antique Galleries, Manchester, Lancs.
Osiris Antiques, Southport, Merseyside.
Arbiter, Wallasey, Merseyside.
Aspidistra Antiques, Finedon, Northants.
The Rendezvous Gallery, Aberdeen, Scotland.
Montresor, Edinburgh, Scotland.
Jeremy Sniders Antiques, Glasgow, Scotland.
Strachan Antiques, Glasgow, Scotland.
Rhudle Mill, Kilmichael Glassary, Scotland.
Antiques on the Square, Church Stretton, Shrops.
Expressions, Shrewsbury, Shrops.
A J Antiques, Bath, Somerset.
Tara's Hall, Hadleigh, Suffolk.
Decodream, Coulsdon, Surrey.
Dorking Emporium Antiques Centre, Dorking, Surrey.
Bits and Pieces Antiques, Farnham, Surrey.
The Gooday Gallery, Richmond, Surrey.
Cockrell Antiques, Surbiton, Surrey.
Art Deco Etc., Brighton, E. Sussex.
Oasis Antiques, Brighton, E. Sussex.
Timewarp, Brighton, E. Sussex.
Witney & Airault, Brighton, E. Sussex.
Skyline Interiors, Willingdon, E. Sussex.
Peter Hancock Antiques, Chichester, W. Sussex.
Paul Gibbs Antiques and Decorative Arts, Conwy, Wales.
Alan Richards Brocante, Birmingham, W. Mids.
Tango Art Deco, Knowle, W. Mids.
Bona Art Deco Store, Marlborough, Wilts.
Bridge House Antiques (formerly Avenue Antiques of Hull), Beverley, E. Yorks.
Muir Hewitt Art Deco Originals, Halifax, W. Yorks.

Barometers (see also clock dealers)

C.R. Frost and Son Ltd, London EC1.
Patric Capon, London N1.
Strike One (Islington) Ltd, London N5.
R.E. Rose FBHI, London SE9.
John Carlton-Smith, London SW1.
Jillings of Belgravia, London SW1.
Trevor Philip and Sons Ltd, London SW1.
The Clock Clinic Ltd, London SW15.
Aubrey Brocklehurst, London SW7.
Brian Fielden, London W1.
Ronald Phillips Ltd, London W1.
Stair and Company Ltd, London W1.
Old Father Time Clock Centre, London W11.
Raffety, London W8.
The Clock Workshop, Caversham, Berks.
Alan Walker, Halfway, Berks.
Medalcrest Ltd, Hungerford, Berks.
The Old Malthouse, Hungerford, Berks.
M.V. Tooley, CMBHI, Chesham, Bucks.
John Beazor and Sons Ltd, Cambridge, Cambs.
Doddington House Antiques, Doddington, Cambs.
T. W. Pawson - Clocks, Somersham, Cambs.
Derek and Tina Rayment Antiques, Barton, Cheshire.
Andrew Foott Antiques, Cheadle Hulme, Cheshire.
The Clock House, Hazel Grove, Cheshire.
Peter Bosson Antiques, Wilmslow, Cheshire.
Mike Read Antique Sciences, St. Ives, Cornwall.
Honiton Clock Clinic, Honiton, Devon.
Barometer World Ltd, Merton, Devon.
Alan Jones Antiques, Okehampton, Devon.
Leigh C. Extence, Shaldon, Devon.
Good Hope Antiques, Beaminster, Dorset.
M.C. Taylor, Bournemouth, Dorset.
Tom Tribe and Son, Sturminster Newton, Dorset.
Mark Marchant (Antiques), Coggeshall, Essex.
Littlebury Antiques - Littlebury Restorations Ltd, Saffron Walden, Essex.
It's About Time, Westcliff-on-Sea, Essex.
Montpellier Clocks, Cheltenham, Glos.
Saxton House Gallery, Chipping Campden, Glos.
Antony Preston Antiques Ltd, Stow-on-the-Wold, Glos.
Styles of Stow, Stow-on-the-Wold, Glos.
Vanbrugh House Antiques, Stow-on-the-Wold, Glos.
Evans and Evans, Alresford, Hants.
Clockwise, Emsworth, Hants.
Bryan Clisby Antique Clocks, Hartley Wintney, Hants.
The Clock-Work Shop, Winchester, Hants.
G.E. Marsh Antique Clocks Ltd, Winchester, Hants.
Barometer Shop, Leominster, Herefs.
Robert Horton Antiques, Hertford, Herts.
John Chawner, Birchington, Kent.
Michael Sim, Chislehurst, Kent.
Anthony Woodburn, Leigh, Kent.
De Tavener Antiques, Ramsgate, Kent.
Devron Green Antiques, Tunbridge Wells, Kent.
Marks Antiques, Westerham, Kent.
Tankerton Antiques, Whitstable, Kent.
Drop Dial Antiques, Bolton, Lancs.
Harrop Fold Clocks (F. Robinson), Bolton-by-Bowland, Lancs.
N. Bryan-Peach Antiques, Wymeswold, Leics.
Robin Fowler (Period Clocks), Aylesby, Lincs.
Claire Langley Antiques, Stamford, Lincs.
Rita Shenton, Twickenham, Middx.
Keith Lawson Antique Clocks, Scratby, Norfolk.
The Antique Galleries, Paulerspury, Northants.
Peter Wiggins, Chipping Norton, Oxon.
Gerald E. Marsh (Antique Clocks), North Aston, Oxon.
Rosemary and Time, Thame, Oxon.
Mark Shanks, Watlington, Oxon.
Craiglea Clocks, Edinburgh, Scotland.
Muirhead Moffat and Co, Glasgow, Scotland.
R.G. Cave and Sons Ltd, Ludlow, Shrops.
Dodington Antiques, Whitchurch, Shrops.
Bath Galleries, Bath, Somerset.
K & D Antique Clocks, Bath, Somerset.
David Gibson, Crewkerne, Somerset.
Bernard G. House, Wells, Somerset.
Edward A. Nowell, Wells, Somerset.
Grosvenor Clocks, Leek, Staffs.
James A. Jordan, Lichfield, Staffs.
J. de Haan & Son, Clare, Suffolk.
Ashley Antiques, Ipswich, Suffolk.
Antique Clocks by Simon Charles, Long Melford, Suffolk.
Patrick Marney, Long Melford, Suffolk.
Suthburgh Antiques, Long Melford, Suffolk.
Trident Antiques, Long Melford, Suffolk.
Horological Workshops, Guildford, Surrey.
Surrey Clock Centre, Haslemere, Surrey.
B. M. and E. Newlove, Surbiton, Surrey.
R. Saunders, Weybridge, Surrey.
Chattels Antiques, Woking, Surrey.
Chaunt House, Burwash, E. Sussex.
Baskerville Antiques, Petworth, W. Sussex.
The Grandfather Clock Shop, Shipston-on-Stour, Warks.
'Time in Hand', Shipston-on-Stour, Warks.
Summersons, Warwick, Warks.
R. Collyer, Birmingham, W. Mids.
Osborne Antiques, Sutton Coldfield, W. Mids.
P.A. Oxley Antique Clocks and Barometers, Cherhill, Wilts.
Inglenook Antiques, Ramsbury, Wilts.
Hansen Chard Antiques, Pershore, Worcs.
Time and Motion, Beverley, E. Yorks.
Lewis E. Hickson FBHI, Gilberdyke, E. Yorks.

Beds

Tobias and The Angel, London SW13.
And So To Bed Limited, London SW6.

Simon Horn Furniture Ltd, London SW6.
Hirst Antiques, London W11.
The Old Dairy, London W4.
The Pine Merchants, Great Missenden, Bucks.
And So To Bed, Keswick, Cumbria.
Staveley Antiques, Staveley, Cumbria.
The Antiques Warehouse, Buxton, Derbys.
Pugh's Farm Antiques, Monkton, Devon.
Annterior Antiques, Plymouth, Devon.
Antique Bed Shop, Halstead, Essex.
Antique Four-Poster Beds, Bristol, Glos.
Morpheus - Elgin House, Tetbury, Glos.
Chatelain Antiques and Interior Decoration, Hereford, Herefs.
Old Pine Shop, Walford, Herefs.
Harriet Ann Sleigh Beds, Benenden, Kent.
Brass Bed Shop, Canterbury, Kent.
House Things Antiques, Hinckley, Leics.
A Barn Full of Brass Beds, Louth, Lincs.
Graham Pickett Antiques, Stamford, Lincs.
Peco, Hampton, Middx.
B & T Addrison, Downham Market, Norfolk.
Rococo Antiques and Interiors, Weedon, Northants.
The Corner Cupboard, Woodford Halse, Northants.
Meadow Lane Antiques, Nottingham, Notts.
Manor Farm Antiques, Standlake, Oxon.
Swans, Oakham, Rutland.
Orlando Jones, Bath, Somerset.
Antiques Warehouse, Framlingham, Suffolk.
Goodbreys, Framlingham, Suffolk.
Sleeping Beauty Antique Beds, Brighton, E. Sussex.
The Victorian Brass Bedstead Company, Cocking, W. Sussex.
Seventh Heaven, Chirk, Wales.
Antiques and All Pine, Swindon, Wilts.
S.W. Antiques, Pershore, Worcs.
Penny Farthing Antiques, North Cave, E. Yorks.
Village Farm Antiques, Wykeham, N. Yorks.

Brass (see Metal)

Bronzes

Furniture Vault, London N1.
Julian Antiques, London N1.
Kevin Page Oriental Art, London N1.
Style, London N1.
Finchley Fine Art Galleries, London N12.
Lenson Smith, London NW8.
Tara Antiques, London NW8.
Robert Bowman, London SW1.
Victor Franses Gallery, London SW1.
M. and D. Lewis, London SW1.
Peter Nahum at The Leicester Galleries, London SW1.
Seago, London SW1.
Christine Bridge, London SW13.
Kensington Sporting Paintings Ltd, London SW20.
Anthony James and Son Ltd, London SW3.
Tulissio De Beaumont, London SW6.
Barry Davies Oriental Art, London W1.
Editions Graphiques Gallery, London W1.
Eskenazi Ltd, London W1.
William Redford, London W1.
The Sladmore Gallery of Sculpture, London W1.
Tryon & Swann Gallery, London W1.
Cohen and Pearce (Oriental Porcelain), London W11.
M. and D. Lewis, London W11.
J. Lipitch Ltd, London W11.
Graham Walpole, London W11.
David Brower Antiques, London W8.
H. and W. Deutsch Antiques, London W8.
Grosvenor Antiques Ltd, London W8.
John Jesse, London W8.
Howard Jones, London W8.
Pruskin Gallery, London W8.
Mary Wise, London W8.
Ivor and Patricia Lewis Antique and Fine Art Dealers, Peterborough, Cambs.
West End Galleries, Buxton, Derbys.
Falle Fine Art Limited, St Helier, Jersey, Channel Islands.
Falle Fine Art Limited, St Helier, Jersey, Channel Islands.
Michael Sim, Chislehurst, Kent.
Apollo Antique Galleries, Westerham, Kent.
London House Antiques, Westerham, Kent.
Modern Design Classics, Westerham, Kent.
Mary Cruz, Bath, Somerset.
Edward Cross - Fine Paintings, Weybridge, Surrey.
Richard Hagen, Broadway, Worcs.

Carpets & Rugs

Joseph Lavian, London N4.
David J. Wilkins, London NW1.
Soviet Carpet and Art Centre, London NW2.
Orientalist, London NW5.
Robert Franses and Sons, London NW8.
Belgrave Carpet Gallery Ltd, London SW1.
Victor Franses Gallery, London SW1.
S. Franses Ltd, London SW1.
Heraz (David Hartwright Ltd), London SW1.
Keshishian, London SW1.
Mayorcas Ltd, London SW1.
Rare Carpets Gallery, London SW10.
Gallery Yacou, London SW3.
Perez, London SW3.
Robert Stephenson, London SW3.
Bookham Galleries, London SW6.
Perez Antique Carpets Gallery, London SW6.
Anglo Persian Carpet Co, London SW7.
Heskia, London SW8.
Aaron Gallery, London W1.
Atlantic Bay Carpets, London W1.
Colefax and Fowler, London W1.
John Eskenazi Ltd, London W1.
Essie Carpets, London W1.
C. John (Rare Rugs) Ltd, London W1.
Alexander Juran and Co, London W1.
Kennedy Carpets, London W1.
Mayfair Carpet Gallery Ltd, London W1.
Paul Nels Ltd, London W1.
Rabi Gallery Ltd, London W1.
Shaikh and Son (Oriental Rugs) Ltd, London W1.
Vigo Carpet Gallery, London W1.
Alex Zadah Fine Oriental & European Carpets, London W1.
David Black Oriental Carpets, London W11.
Fairman Carpets Ltd, London W11.
Graham and Green, London W11.
A. Rezai Persian Carpets, London W11.
Coats Oriental Carpets, London W8.
Sinai Antiques Ltd, London W8.
Oriental Rug Gallery Ltd, Windsor and Eton, Berks.
Clive Rogers Oriental Rugs, Wraysbury, Berks.
Peter Norman Antiques and Restorations, Burwell, Cambs.
Parvis Sigaroudinia, Lisburn, Co. Antrim, N. Ireland.
J.L. Arditti, Christchurch, Dorset.
Christchurch Carpets, Christchurch, Dorset.
Hamptons, Christchurch, Dorset.
Eric Pride Oriental Rugs, Cheltenham, Glos.
Anthony Hazledine, Fairford, Glos.
Samarkand Galleries, Stow-on-the-Wold, Glos.
The Odiham Gallery, Odiham, Hants.
Oriental Rug Gallery Ltd, St. Albans, Herts.
Kashan Carpets Ltd., Brasted, Kent.
Desmond and Amanda North, East Peckham, Kent.
Rosewood Gallery, Hadlow, Kent.
Samovar Antiques, Hythe, Kent.
The Rug Gallery, Leicester, Leics.
Country and Eastern, Norwich, Norfolk.
M.D. Cannell Antiques, Raveningham, Norfolk.
Richard Purdon, Burford, Oxon.
Thames Oriental Rug Co, Henley-on-Thames, Oxon.
Christopher Legge Oriental Carpets, Oxford, Oxon.
Tattersall's, Uppingham, Rutland.
R.L. Rose Ltd, Edinburgh, Scotland.
Whytock and Reid, Edinburgh, Scotland.
Young Antiques, Edinburgh, Scotland.
R.L. Rose Ltd, Glasgow, Scotland.
C.S. Moreton (Antiques), Inchture, Scotland.
Gallery Persia, Inverness, Scotland.
Herrald of Edinburgh, Meigle, Scotland.
Nigel Stacy-Marks Ltd, Perth, Scotland.
Haliden Oriental Rug Shop, Bath, Somerset.
Bruce Tozer Rugs & Antiques, Bath, Somerset.
Michael and Amanda Lewis Oriental Carpets and Rugs, Wellington, Somerset.

The Persian Carpet Studio, Leavenheath, Suffolk.
Karel Weijand Fine Oriental Carpets, Farnham, Surrey.
Oriental Rug Gallery, Guildford, Surrey.
Dennis Woodman Oriental Carpets, Kew, Surrey.
Lindfield Galleries - David Adam, Lindfield, W. Sussex.
Majid Amini - Persian Carpet Gallery, Petworth, W. Sussex.
A.W. Hone and Son Oriental Carpets, Birmingham, W. Mids.
D & J Lines Antiques, Worcester, Worcs.
London House Oriental Rugs and Carpets, Harrogate, N. Yorks.
Omar (Harrogate) Ltd, Harrogate, N. Yorks.
The Gordon Reece Gallery, Knaresborough, N. Yorks.
Ellis's, Sheffield, S. Yorks.
The Oriental Rug Shop, Sheffield, S. Yorks.
London House Oriental Rugs and Carpets, Boston Spa, W. Yorks.

Cars & Carriages

T.L.O. Militaria, Windsor and Eton, Berks.
Finesse Fine Art, Weymouth, Dorset.
Fieldings Antiques, Haslingden, Lancs.
The Complete Automobilist, Baston, Lincs.
Whatnots, Strathblane, Scotland.
C.A.R.S. (Classic Automobilia & Regalia Specialists), Brighton, E. Sussex.

Chinese Art (see Oriental)

Church Furniture & Furnishings

The London Architectural Salvage & Supply Co. (LASSCo), London EC2.
Whiteway and Waldron Ltd, London SW6.
Havenplan's Architectural Emporium, Killamarsh, Derbys.
Robert Mills Architectural Antiques Ltd, Bristol, Glos.
Kitchenalia, Longridge, Lancs.
Antique Church Furnishings, Walton-on-Thames, Surrey.

Clocks & Watches

City Clocks, London EC1.
C.R. Frost and Son Ltd, London EC1.
Patric Capon, London N1.
Julian Antiques, London N1.
Sugar Antiques, London N1.
Strike One (Islington) Ltd, London N5.
Penny Farthing Antiques, London SE1.
North London Clock Shop Ltd, London SE25.
R.E. Rose FBHI, London SE9.
Camerer Cuss and Co, London SW1.
John Carlton-Smith, London SW1.
Charles Frodsham & Co Ltd, London SW1.
Harrods Ltd, London SW1.
Jillings of Belgravia, London SW1.
Somlo Antiques, London SW1.
The Clock Clinic Ltd, London SW15.
Norman Adams Ltd, London SW3.
Big Ben Antique Clocks, London SW6.
Gutlin Clocks and Antiques, London SW6.
Aubrey Brocklehurst, London SW7.
A. & H. Page, London SW7.
Carrington and Co. Ltd, London W1.
Garrard & Co. Ltd (The Crown Jewellers), London W1.
Mallett and Son (Antiques) Ltd, London W1.
Mallett at Bourdon House Ltd, London W1.
Pendulum of Mayfair Ltd, London W1.
Ronald Phillips Ltd, London W1.
Michael Rose - Source of the Unusual, London W1.
The Royal Arcade Watch Shop, London W1.
Central Gallery (Portobello), London W11.
Kleanthous Antiques, Stouts Antiques Market, London W11.
Mayflower Antiques, London W11.
Old Father Time Clock Centre, London W11.
The Silver Fox Gallery, London W11.
The Badger, London W5.
David Brower Antiques, London W8.
Raffety, London W8.
Roderick Antique Clocks, London W8.
Thomas Kettle Ltd, London WC2.
The London Silver Vaults, London WC2.
Pearl Cross Ltd, London WC2.
House of Clocks, Ampthill, Beds.
The Clock Workshop, Caversham, Berks.
Robert and Georgina Hastie, Hungerford, Berks.
The Old Malthouse, Hungerford, Berks.
Times Past Antiques, Windsor and Eton, Berks.
Wyrardisbury Antiques, Wraysbury, Berks.
M.V. Tooley, CMBHI, Chesham, Bucks.
Robin Unsworth Antiques, Olney, Bucks.
Tim Marshall Antiques, Tingewick, Bucks.
Peter Norman Antiques and Restorations, Burwell, Cambs.
John Beazor and Sons Ltd, Cambridge, Cambs.
Doddington House Antiques, Doddington, Cambs.
Mere Antiques, Fowlmere, Cambs.
Antique Clocks, Harston, Cambs.
T. W. Pawson - Clocks, Somersham, Cambs.
Anthony Baker Antiques, Alderley Edge, Cheshire.
Adams Antiques, Chester, Cheshire.
Veevers, Chester, Cheshire.
The Clock House, Hazel Grove, Cheshire.
Chapel Antiques, Nantwich, Cheshire.
Coppelia Antiques, Plumley, Cheshire.
Peter Bosson Antiques, Wilmslow, Cheshire.
Robert Christie Antiques, Ballyclare, Co. Antrim, N. Ireland.
Time & Tide Antiques, Portaferry, Co. Down, N. Ireland.
Paul Jennings Antiques, Angarrack, Cornwall.
Little Jem's, Penzance, Cornwall.
Saint Nicholas Galleries Ltd. (Antiques and Jewellery), Carlisle, Cumbria.
Langley Antiques, Corby Hill, Cumbria.
Calvert Antiques, Endmoor, Cumbria.
David Hill, Kirkby Stephen, Cumbria.
Lewis Antiques, Bakewell, Derbys.
Dragon Antiques, Duffield, Derbys.
Derbys Clocks, Glossop, Derbys.
Goodacre Engraving Ltd, Long Eaton, Derbys.
G.K. Hadfield, Swadlincote, Derbys.
Nimbus Antiques, Whaley Bridge, Derbys.
Moor Antiques, Ashburton, Devon.
Gold and Silver Exchange, Exeter, Devon.
John Nathan Antiques, Exeter, Devon.
Honiton Clock Clinic, Honiton, Devon.
Brian Taylor Antiques, Plymouth, Devon.

Leigh C. Extence, Shaldon, Devon.
Tempus Fugit, Shaldon, Devon.
L.G. Wootton Clocks and Watches, South Brent, Devon.
Good Hope Antiques, Beaminster, Dorset.
M.C. Taylor, Bournemouth, Dorset.
D.J. Burgess, Parkstone, Dorset.
Tom Tribe and Son, Sturminster Newton, Dorset.
Eden House Antiques, West Auckland, Durham.
Mark Marchant (Antiques), Coggeshall, Essex.
Antique Clock Repair Shoppe, Gants Hill, Essex.
W.A. Pinn and Sons, Sible Hedingham, Essex.
It's About Time, Westcliff-on-Sea, Essex.
Antique Corner with A & C Antique Clocks, Bristol, Glos.
Montpellier Clocks, Cheltenham, Glos.
Saxton House Gallery, Chipping Campden, Glos.
School House Antiques, Chipping Campden, Glos.
Arthur S. Lewis, Gloucester, Glos.
Gerard Campbell, Lechlade, Glos.
Jeffrey Formby Antiques, Moreton-in-Marsh, Glos.
Keith Harding's World of Mechanical Music, Northleach, Glos.
Colin Brand Antiques, Stow-on-the-Wold, Glos.
Styles of Stow, Stow-on-the-Wold, Glos.
Vanbrugh House Antiques, Stow-on-the-Wold, Glos.
Evans and Evans, Alresford, Hants.
Olive Antiques, Alverstoke, Hants.
Clockwise, Emsworth, Hants.
Bryan Clisby Antique Clocks, Hartley Wintney, Hants.
A.W. Porter and Son, Hartley Wintney, Hants.
Barry Papworth, Lymington, Hants.
Gaylords, Titchfield, Hants.
Twyford Antiques, Twyford, Hants.
The Clock-Work Shop, Winchester, Hants.
G.E. Marsh Antique Clocks Ltd, Winchester, Hants.
Trecilla Antiques, Ross-on-Wye, Herefs.
Howards, Baldock, Herts.
Robert Horton Antiques, Hertford, Herts.
The Clock Shop - Philip Setterfield of St. Albans, St. Albans, Herts.
Country Clocks, Tring, Herts.
John Corrin Antiques, Douglas, Isle of Man.
Jeremiah's Antiques, St Helier, Jersey, Channel Islands.
John Chawner, Birchington, Kent.
Clockshop, Boughton, Kent.
Old Manor House Antiques, Brasted, Kent.
Michael Sim, Chislehurst, Kent.
Anthony Woodburn, Leigh, Kent.
De Tavener Antiques, Ramsgate, Kent.
Michael Fitch Antiques, Sandgate, Kent.
Nancy Wilson, Sandwich, Kent.
Aaron Antiques, Snodland, Kent.
Derek Roberts Fine Antique Clocks, Music Boxes, Barometers, Tonbridge, Kent.
B. Somerset, Tonbridge, Kent.
Aaron Antiques, Tunbridge Wells, Kent.
Hadlow Antiques, Tunbridge Wells, Kent.
Pantiles Spa Antiques, Tunbridge Wells, Kent.
The Old Clock Shop, West Malling, Kent.
Marks Antiques, Westerham, Kent.
Regal Antiques, Westerham, Kent.
Tankerton Antiques, Whitstable, Kent.
Drop Dial Antiques, Bolton, Lancs.
Harrop Fold Clocks (F. Robinson), Bolton-by-Bowland, Lancs.
Fieldings Antiques, Haslingden, Lancs.
P.W. Norgrove - Antique Clocks, Haslingden, Lancs.
Boodle and Dunthorne Ltd, Manchester, Lancs.
Bulldog Antiques, Manchester, Lancs.
Brittons Jewellers and Antiques, Nelson, Lancs.
Charles Howell Jeweller, Oldham, Lancs.
H.C. Simpson and Sons Jewellers (Oldham)Ltd, Oldham, Lancs.
Hackler's Jewellers, Preston, Lancs.
Davies Antiques, Whalley, Lancs.
Lowe of Loughborough, Loughborough, Leics.
Old Timers, Swinford, Leics.
N. Bryan-Peach Antiques, Wymeswold, Leics.
Robin Fowler (Period Clocks), Aylesby, Lincs.
Grantham Clocks, Grantham, Lincs.
Wilkinson's, Grantham, Lincs.
Second Time Around, Hemswell Cliff, Lincs.
Robert Kitching, Horncastle, Lincs.
Staines Antiques, Horncastle, Lincs.
Trade Antiques, Long Sutton, Lincs.
Harwood Tate, Market Rasen, Lincs.
Beckside Antiques, Messingham, Lincs.
Pinfold Antiques, Ruskington, Lincs.
Antiques & Collectables, Scunthorpe, Lincs.
Wilkinson's, Sleaford, Lincs.
Claire Langley Antiques, Stamford, Lincs.
Kevin Whay's Clock Shop and Antiques, Hoylake, Merseyside.
Boodle and Dunthorne Ltd, Liverpool, Merseyside.
Theta Gallery, Liverpool, Merseyside.
Weldons Jewellery and Antiques, Southport, Merseyside.
Rita Shenton, Twickenham, Middx.
As Time Goes By - Antique and Exterior Clocks, Aylsham, Norfolk.
Village Clocks, Coltishall, Norfolk.
R.C. Woodhouse (Antiquarian Horologist), Hunstanton, Norfolk.
Tim Clayton Jewellery, King's Lynn, Norfolk.
Keith Lawson Antique Clocks, Scratby, Norfolk.
Parriss, Sheringham, Norfolk.
Norton Antiques, Twyford, Norfolk.
M.C. Chapman, Finedon, Northants.
Michael Jones Jeweller, Northampton, Northants.
Hazel Cottage Clocks, Eachwick, Northumbs.
Gordon Caris, Hexham, Northumbs.
David and Carole Potter Antiques, Nottingham, Notts.
Horseshoe Antiques and Gallery, Burford, Oxon.
Hubert's Antiques, Burford, Oxon.
Jonathan Howard, Chipping Norton, Oxon.
Craig Barfoot, East Hagbourne, Oxon.
Gerald E. Marsh (Antique Clocks), North Aston, Oxon.
Laurie Leigh Antiques, Oxford, Oxon.
Rosemary and Time, Thame, Oxon.
Witney Antiques, Witney, Oxon.
C. Reynolds Antiques, Oakham, Rutland.
Rutland Antique Clock Gallery, Oakham, Rutland.
John Mann Antique Clocks, Canonbie, Scotland.
Ian Burton, Denny, Scotland.
Craiglea Clocks, Edinburgh, Scotland.
Donald Ellis incorporating Bruntsfield Clocks, Edinburgh, Scotland.
John Whyte, Edinburgh, Scotland.
West End Antiques, Elgin, Scotland.
Brown's Clocks, Glasgow, Scotland.
James Forrest and Co (Jewellers) Ltd, Glasgow, Scotland.
Muirhead Moffat and Co, Glasgow, Scotland.
Mytton Antiques, Atcham, Shrops.
Bridgnorth Antiques Centre, Bridgnorth, Shrops.
R.G. Cave and Sons Ltd, Ludlow, Shrops.
The Curiosity Shop, Ludlow, Shrops.
Mitre House Antiques, Ludlow, Shrops.
Dodington Antiques, Whitchurch, Shrops.
John Hawley (MBHI) Antique Clocks, Badgworth, Somerset.
Bath Galleries, Bath, Somerset.
K & D Antique Clocks, Bath, Somerset.
Quiet Street Antiques, Bath, Somerset.
David Gibson, Crewkerne, Somerset.
J.C. White, Milverton, Somerset.
Bernard G. House, Wells, Somerset.
Edward A. Nowell, Wells, Somerset.
Edward Venn, Williton, Somerset.
Grosvenor Clocks, Leek, Staffs.
James A. Jordan, Lichfield, Staffs.
Richard Midwinter Antiques, Newcastle-under-Lyme, Staffs.
Jennifer and Raymond Norman Antiques, Eye, Suffolk.
Clock House, Leavenheath, Suffolk.
Antique Clocks by Simon Charles, Long Melford, Suffolk.
Suthburgh Antiques, Long Melford, Suffolk.
Village Clocks, Long Melford, Suffolk.
Antique Clocks by Simon Charles, Sudbury, Suffolk.
Edward Manson (Clocks), Woodbridge, Suffolk.
Suffolk House Antiques, Yoxford, Suffolk.
Simon Marsh, Bletchingley, Surrey.
Antique Clocks by Patrick Thomas, Dorking, Surrey.
Norfolk House Galleries, Dorking, Surrey.

Abbott Antiques, East Molesey, Surrey.
Roger A. Davis Antiquarian Horologist, Great Bookham, Surrey.
Horological Workshops, Guildford, Surrey.
Surrey Clock Centre, Haslemere, Surrey.
Hill Rise Antiques, Richmond, Surrey.
F. and T. Lawson Antiques, Richmond, Surrey.
B. M. and E. Newlove, Surbiton, Surrey.
S. Warrender and Co, Sutton, Surrey.
The Clock Shop Weybridge, Weybridge, Surrey.
Chattels Antiques, Woking, Surrey.
D.H. Edmonds Ltd, Brighton, E. Sussex.
Yellow Lantern Antiques Ltd, Brighton, E. Sussex.
Chaunt House, Burwash, E. Sussex.
Wm. Bruford and Son Ltd, Eastbourne, E. Sussex.
John Cowderoy Antiques, Eastbourne, E. Sussex.
Coach House Antiques, Hastings, E. Sussex.
The Old Mint House, Pevensey, E. Sussex.
Arundel Clocks, Arundel, W. Sussex.
The Clock Shop, Hurstpierpoint, W. Sussex.
Julian Antiques, Hurstpierpoint, W. Sussex.
Churchill Clocks, Midhurst, W. Sussex.
Baskerville Antiques, Petworth, W. Sussex.
J. Powell (Hove) Ltd, Portslade, W. Sussex.
Thakeham Furniture, Pulborough, W. Sussex.
Peter Smith Antiques, Sunderland, Tyne and Wear.
Silvertime, Brecon, Wales.
Past and Present, Cardiff, Wales.
Snowdonia Antiques, Llanrwst, Wales.
Rodney Adams Antiques, Pwllheli, Wales.
Eynon Hughes Antiques, Swansea, Wales.
The Grandfather Clock Shop, Shipston-on-Stour, Warks.
'Time in Hand', Shipston-on-Stour, Warks.
Summersons, Warwick, Warks.
R. Collyer, Birmingham, W. Mids.
F. Meeks & Co, Birmingham, W. Mids.
M. Allen Watch and Clockmaker, Four Oaks, W. Mids.
Osborne Antiques, Sutton Coldfield, W. Mids.
Alan M. France, Wolverhampton, W. Mids.
Avon Antiques, Bradford-on-Avon, Wilts.
Moxhams Antiques, Bradford-on-Avon, Wilts.
Trevor Waddington Antique Clocks, Bradford-on-Avon, Wilts.
P.A. Oxley Antique Clocks and Barometers, Cherhill, Wilts.
Inglenook Antiques, Ramsbury, Wilts.
Salisbury Antiques Warehouse, Salisbury, Wilts.
Chris Wadge Clocks, Salisbury, Wilts.
Allan Smith Antique Clocks, Swindon, Wilts.
Broadway Clocks, Broadway, Worcs.
Hansen Chard Antiques, Pershore, Worcs.
Time and Motion, Beverley, E. Yorks.
Lewis E. Hickson FBHI, Gilberdyke, E. Yorks.
The Old Ropery Antique Clocks, Kilham, E. Yorks.
John Pearson Antique Clock Restoration, Birstwith, N. Yorks.
Milestone Antiques, Easingwold, N. Yorks.
Haworth Antiques, Harrogate, N. Yorks.
D. Mason & Son, Harrogate, N. Yorks.
Chris Wilde Antiques, Harrogate, N. Yorks.
Brian Loomes, Pateley Bridge, N. Yorks.
D. & E.A. Shackleton Antiques, Snainton, N. Yorks.
N.J. and C.S. Dodsworth, Spennithorne, N. Yorks.
Tomlinson (Antiques) Ltd. & Period Furniture Ltd, Tockwith, N. Yorks.
Chattels Antiques, Topcliffe, N. Yorks.
Keith Stones Grandfather Clocks, Bessacarr, S. Yorks.
Fishlake Antiques, Fishlake, S. Yorks.
F S Antiques, Sheffield, S. Yorks.
Top Hat Antique Centre, Sheffield, S. Yorks.
Canterbury House, Thorne, S. Yorks.

Coins & Medals

George Rankin Coin Co. Ltd, London E2.
C.J. Martin (Coins) Ltd, London N14.
Christopher Eimer, London NW11.
Dolphin Coins, London NW3.
The Armoury of St. James's Military Antiquarians, London SW1.
Knightsbridge Coins, London SW1.
Spink and Son Ltd, London SW1.
Beaver Coin Room, London SW5.
Seaby Antiquities, London W1.
Michael Coins, London W8.
A.H. Baldwin and Sons Ltd, London WC2.
M. Bord (Gold Coin Exchange), London WC2.
Trafalgar Square Collectors Centre, London WC2.
T.L.O. Militaria, Windsor and Eton, Berks.
B.R.M. Coins, Knutsford, Cheshire.
Cookstown Antiques, Cookstown, Co. Tyrone, N. Ireland.
Souvenir Antiques, Carlisle, Cumbria.
Penrith Coin and Stamp Centre, Penrith, Cumbria.
Sterling Coins and Medals, Bournemouth, Dorset.
The Treasure Chest, Weymouth, Dorset.
Robin Finnegan (Jeweller), Darlington, Durham.
J. Shotton Antiquarian Books, Prints and Coins, Durham, Durham.
Potter's Antiques and Coins, Bristol, Glos.
Butler and Co, Cheltenham, Glos.
Military Curios, HQ84, Gloucester, Glos.
Romsey Medal and Collectors Centre, Romsey, Hants.
The Coin and Jewellery Shop, Accrington, Lancs.
Chard Coins, Blackpool, Lancs.
Gold and Silver Exchange, Gt. Yarmouth, Norfolk.
Clive Dennett Coins, Norwich, Norfolk.
Hockley Coins, Nottingham, Notts.
Val Smith Coins and Antiques, Nottingham, Notts.
Denver House Antiques and Collectables, Burford, Oxon.
The Collectors Shop, Edinburgh, Scotland.
Edinburgh Coin Shop, Edinburgh, Scotland.
A.D. Hamilton and Co, Glasgow, Scotland.
Abbey Antiques, Stirling, Scotland.
Collectors' Gallery, Shrewsbury, Shrops.
Bath Stamp and Coin Shop, Bath, Somerset.
Neate Militaria & Antiques, Sudbury, Suffolk.
St. Pancras Antiques, Chichester, W. Sussex.
Intercoin, Newcastle-upon-Tyne, Tyne and Wear.
Glance Back Bookshop, Chepstow, Wales.
Format of Birmingham Ltd, Birmingham, W. Mids.
Castle Galleries, Salisbury, Wilts.
Whitmore, Great Malvern, Worcs.
B.B.M. Jewellery and Antiques, Kidderminster, Worcs.
C.J. and A.J. Dixon Ltd, Bridlington, E. Yorks.
Coins International and Antiques International, Leeds, W. Yorks.

Dolls & Toys

Donay Antiques, London N1.
Judith Lassalle, London N1.
Relic Antiques, London N1.
Yesterday Child, London N1.
Dolly Land, London N21.
Bearly Trading Co, London SE20.
Engine 'n' Tender, London SE25.
Victoriana Dolls, London W11.
Dolls and Toys of Yesteryear at Bow House Antiques, Hungerford, Berks.
Tim Armitage, Nantwich, Cheshire.
Rosina's, Falmouth, Cornwall.
Abbey House, Derby, Derbys.
Honiton Antique Toys, Honiton, Devon.
The Vintage Toy and Train Museum Shop, Sidmouth, Devon.
Boscombe Models and Collectors Shop, Bournemouth, Dorset.
Hobby Horse Antiques, Bridport, Dorset.
Tilly's Antiques, Leigh-on-Sea, Essex.
The Doll's House, Northleach, Glos.
Park House Antiques, Stow-on-the-Wold, Glos.
Peter Pan's of Gosport, Gosport, Hants.
The Old Toy Shop, Ringwood, Hants.
The Attic, Baldock, Herts.
Bridge Antiques, Wingham, Kent.
Irving Antique Toys, Manchester, Lancs.
Swag, Preston, Lancs.
C. and K.E. Dring, Lincoln, Lincs.

Francis Bowers Chess Suppliers, Whaplode, Lincs.
Stiffkey Antiques, Stiffkey, Norfolk.
Granny's Attic, Nottingham, Notts.
Angus Antiques, Dundee, Scotland.
Now and Then (Toy Centre), Edinburgh, Scotland.
Stockbridge Antiques and Fine Art, Edinburgh, Scotland.
Pastimes Vintage Toys, Glasgow, Scotland.
Images - Peter Stockham, Lichfield, Staffs.
Jennifer and Raymond Norman Antiques, Eye, Suffolk.
Trench Puzzles, Stowmarket, Suffolk.
Childhood Memories, Farnham, Surrey.
Bears and Friends, Brighton, E. Sussex.
C.A.R.S. (Classic Automobilia & Regalia Specialists), Brighton, E. Sussex.
Paul Goble, Brighton, E. Sussex.
Sue Pearson, Brighton, E. Sussex.
Coach House Antiques, Hastings, E. Sussex.
Recollect Studios, Sayers Common, W. Sussex.
Museum of Childhood, Beaumaris, Wales.
Dolly Mixtures, Birmingham, W. Mids.
Robert Taylor, Four Oaks, W. Mids.
'Broadway Bears & Dolls', Broadway, Worcs.
Grannie's Parlour, Hull, E. Yorks.
Windmill Antiques, Thirsk, N. Yorks.
Fun Antiques, Sheffield, S. Yorks.
Collectors Old Toy Shop and Antiques, Halifax, W. Yorks.
Memory Lane, Sowerby Bridge, W. Yorks.

Etchings & Engravings

Royal Exchange Art Gallery, London EC3.
Moreton Street Gallery, London SW1.
Old Maps and Prints, London SW1.
A & C International, London SW17.
The Map House, London SW3.
Old Church Galleries, London SW3.
King's Court Galleries, London SW6.
Julie Collino, London SW7.
The Wyllie Gallery, London SW7.
Agnew's, London W1.
Editions Graphiques Gallery, London W1.
William Weston Gallery, London W1.
Justin F. Skrebowski Prints, London W11.
Foye Gallery, Luton, Beds.
The Lantern Shop Gallery, Sidmouth, Devon.
PIC's Bookshop, Bridport, Dorset.
Antique Map and Bookshop, Puddletown, Dorset.
Elizabeth Cannon Antiques, Colchester, Essex.
Talbot Court Galleries, Stow-on-the-Wold, Glos.
Oldfield Gallery, Portsmouth, Hants.
The Shanklin Gallery, Shanklin, Isle of Wight.
Peter Goodall, Ventnor, Isle of Wight.
G. and D.I. Marrin and Sons, Folkestone, Kent.
London House Antiques, Westerham, Kent.
Hammond Smith (Fine Art), Leicester, Leics.
Leics Sporting Gallery and Brown Jack Bookshop, Lubenham, Leics.
Graftons of Market Harborough, Market Harborough, Leics.
P.J. Cassidy (Books), Holbeach, Lincs.
The Coach House, Costessey, Norfolk.
TRADA, Chipping Norton, Oxon.
The Barry M. Keene Gallery, Henley-on-Thames, Oxon.
Elizabeth Harvey-Lee, North Aston, Oxon.
John Garner, Uppingham, Rutland.
The McEwan Gallery, Ballater, Scotland.
Open Eye Gallery Ltd, Edinburgh, Scotland.
Ewan Mundy Fine Art Ltd, Glasgow, Scotland.
Mainhill Gallery, Jedburgh, Scotland.
The George Street Gallery, Perth, Scotland.
Nigel Stacy-Marks Ltd, Perth, Scotland.
The Mount, Woore, Shrops.
George Gregory, Bath, Somerset.
England's Gallery, Leek, Staffs.
King's Court Galleries, Dorking, Surrey.
The Court Gallery, East Molesey, Surrey.
Limpsfield Watercolours, Limpsfield, Surrey.
Reigate Galleries Ltd, Reigate, Surrey.
Palmer Galleries, Richmond, Surrey.
Boathouse Gallery, Walton-on-Thames, Surrey.
The Witch Ball, Brighton, E. Sussex.
Faringdon Gallery, Arundel, W. Sussex.
George House Gallery, Petworth, W. Sussex.
Osborne Art and Antiques, Jesmond,, Tyne and Wear.
David Windsor Gallery, Bangor, Wales.
Ronald Carr, Salisbury, Wilts.
The Jerram Gallery, Salisbury, Wilts.
Heirloom & Howard Limited, West Yatton, Wilts.
Penoyre Antiques, Pershore, Worcs.

Fire Related Items

Westland & Company, London EC2.
House of Steel Antiques, London N1.
Julian Antiques, London N1.
Amazing Grates - Fireplaces Ltd, London N2.
The Antique Shop (Valantique), London N2.
Tsar Architectural, London N7.
Acquisitions (Fireplaces) Ltd, London NW5.
Townsends, London NW8.
Nigel A. Bartlett, London SE1.
Main Street Antiques, London SE10.
Oddiquities, London SE23.
Under Milkwood, London SE24.
Ward Antiques, London SE7.
The Fireplace, London SE9.
Nicholas Gifford-Mead, London SW1.
H.W. Poulter and Son, London SW10.
Thornhill Galleries Ltd. in association with A. & R. Dockerill Ltd, London SW15.
Mr Wandle's Workshop, London SW18.
O.F. Wilson Ltd, London SW3.
J. Crotty and Son Ltd, London SW6.
Fairfax Antiques and Fireplaces, London SW6.
Hollingshead and Co, London SW6.
Old World Trading Co, London SW6.
Thornhill Galleries Ltd, London SW6.
Ruby Buckle (Antique Fireplaces), London W2.
The Chiswick Fireplace Co., London W4.
Architectural Antiques, London W6.
Architectural Antiques - Bedford, Bedford, Beds.
Below Stairs of Hungerford, Hungerford, Berks.
The Fire Place (Hungerford) Ltd, Hungerford, Berks.
Grosvenor House Interiors, Beaconsfield, Bucks.
Ann Roberts Antiques, Congleton, Cheshire.
Pillory House, Nantwich, Cheshire.
Nostalgia Architectural Antiques, Stockport, Cheshire.
Antique Fireplaces, Tarvin, Cheshire.
Antique Fireplace Centre, Hartlepool, Cleveland.
Riverside Antiques, Ballynahinch, Co. Down, N. Ireland.
Hearth and Home, Penrith, Cumbria.
Staveley Antiques, Staveley, Cumbria
Wooden Box Antiques, Woodville, Derbys.
Ashburton Marbles, Ashburton, Devon.
Antique Fireplace Centre, Plymouth, Devon.
Antique Metals, Coggeshall, Essex.
Au Temps Perdu, Bristol, Glos.
Flame and Grate, Bristol, Glos.
Period Fireplaces, Bristol, Glos.
Cox's Architectural Reclamation Yard, Moreton-in-Marsh, Glos.
Baileys Architectural Antiques, Ross-on-Wye, Herefs.
Victorian Fireplace, Canterbury, Kent.
Old Smithy, Feniscowles, Lancs.
Antique Fireplaces, Manchester, Lancs.
Colin Blakey Fireplaces, Nelson, Lancs.
Britain's Heritage, Leicester, Leics.
David Allan Antiques, Birkenhead, Merseyside.
Antique Fireplaces, Liverpool, Merseyside.
Peco, Hampton, Middx.
Crowther of Syon Lodge Ltd, Isleworth, Middx.
Marble Hill Gallery, Twickenham, Middx.
Stiffkey Antiques, Stiffkey, Norfolk.
Rococo Antiques and Interiors, Weedon, Northants.
Mews Antique and Reproduction Fireplaces & Architectural Salvage, Belfast, N. Ireland.
Blacksmiths Forge, Balderton, Notts.
Key Antiques, Chipping Norton, Oxon.
Hallidays (Fine Antiques) Ltd, Dorchester-on-Thames, Oxon.
Aston Pine Antiques, Faringdon, Oxon.
Oxford Architectural Antiques, Faringdon, Oxon.
Burning Embers, Aberdeen, Scotland.

EASY - Edinburgh & Glasgow Architectural Salvage Yards, Edinburgh, Scotland.
T. and J. W. Neilson Ltd, Edinburgh, Scotland.
EASY - Edinburgh and Glasgow Architectural Salvage Yards, Glasgow, Scotland.
The Renaissance Furniture Store, Glasgow, Scotland.
Walcot Reclamation, Bath, Somerset.
Rickett & Co. Antiques, Shepperton, Surrey.
Brighton Architectural Salvage, Brighton, E. Sussex.
L.E. Lampard and Sons, Horsham, W. Sussex.
Shiners Architectural Reclamation, Newcastle-upon-Tyne, Tyne and Wear.
Grate Expectations (Fireplaces), Washington, Tyne and Wear.
Flame 'n' Grate, Barry, Wales.
Back to the Wood, Cardiff, Wales.
Kings Fireplaces, Antiques and Interiors, Cardiff, Wales.
The Original Choice Ltd, Birmingham, W. Mids.
Tudor House Antiques, Halesowen, W. Mids.
Old Flames, Easingwold, N. Yorks.
Robert Aagaard & Co, Knaresborough, N. Yorks.
Chimney Piece Antique Fires, Sheffield, S. Yorks.
Chapel House Fireplaces, Holmfirth, W. Yorks.

Frames

Paul Mason Gallery, London SW1.
Nigel Milne Ltd, London SW1.
Arnold Wiggins and Sons Ltd, London SW1.
Paul Mitchell Ltd, London W1.
Rollo Whately Ltd, London W1.
Daggett Gallery, London W11.
Lacy Gallery, London W11.
Justin F. Skrebowski Prints, London W11.
The Fairhurst Gallery, Norwich, Norfolk.
Rob Dixon Fine Engravings, Culham, Oxon.
Looking Glass of Bath, Bath, Somerset.
W. Greenwood (Fine Art), Burneston, N. Yorks.
Coulter Galleries, York, N. Yorks.

Furniture - Continental (mainly French)

Charlton House Antiques, London N1.
Gordon Gridley, London N1.
Janet Love Interiors, London N1.
Relic Antiques, London N1.
Tapsell Antiques, London N1.
Lenson Smith, London NW8.
Robert E. Hirschhorn, London SE5.
Didier Aaron (London)Ltd, London SW1.
Antiquités, London SW1.
Blanchard (London) Ltd, London SW1.
Ciancimino Ltd, London SW1.
Ross Hamilton Ltd, London SW1.
Hermitage Antiques plc, London SW1.
Carlton Hobbs, London SW1.
Christopher Howe, London SW1.
Jeremy Ltd, London SW1.
M. and D. Lewis, London SW1.
Rogier Antiques, London SW1.
Rupert Hastie, London SW10.
Thomas Kerr Antiques Ltd, London SW10.
McVeigh & Charpentier, London SW10.
Rendlesham Antiques, London SW10.
Simon Coleman Antiques, London SW13.
Jorgen Antiques, London SW15.
Adams Room Antiques, London SW19.
No. 12, London SW3.
Prides of London, London SW3.
O.F. Wilson Ltd, London SW3.
275 Antiques, London SW6.
313 Antiques, London SW6.
I. and J.L. Brown Ltd, London SW6.
Rupert Cavendish Antiques, London SW6.
Nicole Fabre, London SW6.
Birdie Fortescue Antiques, London SW6.
Judy Greenwood, London SW6.
Peter Hurford Antiques, London SW6.
Lewin, London SW6.
Megan Mathers Antiques, London SW6.
Sylvia Napier Ltd, London SW6.
Orrell & Brown Interiors, London SW6.
M. Pauw Antiques, London SW6.
Adrian Alan Ltd, London W1.
Konrad O. Bernheimer Ltd, London W1.
H. Blairman and Sons Ltd., London W1.
Howard Antiques, London W1.
Mallett at Bourdon House Ltd, London W1.
Partridge Fine Arts plc, London W1.
Pelham Galleries Ltd, London W1.
William Redford, London W1.
Toynbee-Clarke Interiors Ltd, London W1.
M. Turpin Ltd, London W1.
P.R. Barham, London W11.
Barham Antiques, London W11.
Canonbury, London W11.
Curá Antiques, London W11.
M. and D. Lewis, London W11.
J. Lipitch Ltd, London W11.
Daniel Mankowitz, London W11.
Robin Martin Antiques, London W11.
Oakstar Ltd, London W11.
Rostrum Antiques, London W11.
Marshall Gallery, London W14.
Claude Bornoff, London W2.
Adrian Alan Ltd, London W8.
David Brower Antiques, London W8.
Jonathan Harris, London W8.
Reindeer Antiques Ltd, London W8.
Jacob Stodel, London W8.
Pamela Teignmouth and Son, London W8.
John A. Pearson Antiques, Horton, Berks.
Youll's Antiques, Hungerford, Berks.
Csaky's Antiques, Sonning-on-Thames, Berks.
Country Furniture, Windsor and Eton, Berks.
Ulla Stafford Antiques, Windsor and Eton, Berks.
Jack Harness Antiques, Marlow, Bucks.
Phoenix Antiques, Fordham, Cambs.
Ivor and Patricia Lewis Antique and Fine Art Dealers, Peterborough, Cambs.
David H. Dickinson, Bramhall, Cheshire.
Adams Antiques, Chester, Cheshire.
Richmond Galleries, Chester, Cheshire.
Antique Furniture Warehouse, Stockport, Cheshire.
West End Galleries, Buxton, Derbys.
Merchant House Antiques, Honiton, Devon.
Pilgrim Antiques, Honiton, Devon.
Sextons, Kentisbeare, Devon.
Pugh's Farm Antiques, Monkton, Devon.
Colystock Antiques, Stockland, Devon.
Lionel Geneen Ltd, Bournemouth, Dorset.
Talisman, Gillingham, Dorset.
Georgina Ryder, Sherborne, Dorset.
Millers Antiques Kelvedon, Kelvedon, Essex.
Old Barn Antiques, Matching Green, Essex.
Gloucester House Antiques Ltd, Fairford, Glos.
Gary Wright Antiques, Moreton-in-Marsh, Glos.
Craig Carrington Antiques, Painswick, Glos.
Annarella Clark Antiques, Stow-on-the-Wold, Glos.
Antony Preston Antiques Ltd, Stow-on-the-Wold, Glos.
Geoffrey Stead, Stow-on-the-Wold, Glos.
The Decorator Source, Tetbury, Glos.
Gales Antiques, Tetbury, Glos.
Simon Seiff Antiques, Tetbury, Glos.
Artemesia, Alresford, Hants.
Cedar Antiques Limited, Hartley Wintney, Hants.
David Lazarus Antiques, Hartley Wintney, Hants.
Phoenix Green Antiques, Hartley Wintney, Hants.
Charles Wallrock - Wick Antiques, Lymington, Hants.
Millers of Chelsea Antiques Ltd, Ringwood, Hants.
I. and J.L. Brown Ltd, Hereford, Herefs.
Great Brampton House Antiques Ltd, Hereford, Herefs.
The Elizabethan Shop, Ross-on-Wye, Herefs.
Boulevard Antiques, St Aubin, Jersey, Channel Islands.
Lennox Cato, Edenbridge, Kent.
Samovar Antiques, Hythe, Kent.
Dench Antiques, Sandgate, Kent.
Henry Baines, Southborough, Kent.
Flower House Antiques, Tenterden, Kent.
Sparks Antiques, Tenterden, Kent.
Claremont Antiques, Tunbridge Wells, Kent.
Up Country, Tunbridge Wells, Kent.
Bridge Antiques, Wingham, Kent.
Park Galleries Antiques, Fine Art and Decor, Bolton, Lancs.
J. Green and Son, Queniborough,, Leics.
Robin Cox Antiques, Ketton, Lincs.

Moor Pine, North Kelsey Moor, Lincs.
Graham Pickett Antiques, Stamford, Lincs.
J. and R. Ratcliffe, Waddington, Lincs.
Ron Green, Towcester, Northants.
Helios & Co (Antiques), Weedon, Northants.
Charlotte and John Lambe, Belfast, N. Ireland.
Ashton Gower Antiques, Burford, Oxon.
Jonathan Fyson Antiques, Burford, Oxon.
Gateway Antiques, Burford, Oxon.
Bugle Antiques, Chipping Norton, Oxon.
Summers Davis Antiques Ltd, Wallingford, Oxon.
Witney Antiques, Witney, Oxon.
Swans, Oakham, Rutland.
Whytock and Reid, Edinburgh, Scotland.
Aldric Young, Edinburgh, Scotland.
Jeremy Sniders Antiques, Glasgow, Scotland.
Doveridge House of Neachley, Albrighton (Neachley), Shrops.
Hall's Antiques, Ash Priors, Somerset.
Jadis Ltd, Bath, Somerset.
Mayfly, Bath, Somerset.
Pennard House Antiques, Bath, Somerset.
East St Antiques, Crewkerne, Somerset.
Pennard House, East Pennard, Somerset.
Gilbert & Dale, Ilchester, Somerset.
The Chapel at Rode, Rode, Somerset.
Gil Adams Antiques, Debenham, Suffolk.
Dix-Sept, Framlingham, Suffolk.
Suffolk Antique Connection, Stoke by Nayland, Suffolk.
Heath-Bullocks, Godalming, Surrey.
Marryat, Richmond, Surrey.
Ripley Antiques, Ripley, Surrey.
Wych House Antiques, Woking, Surrey.
Dermot and Jill Palmer Antiques, Brighton, E. Sussex.
Ruddy Antiques, Brighton, E. Sussex.
Graham Lower, Flimwell, E. Sussex.
John Botting Antiques, Horam, E. Sussex.
Delmas, Hurst Green, E. Sussex.
Graham Price Antiques Ltd, Polegate, E. Sussex.
Julian Antiques, Hurstpierpoint, W. Sussex.
The French Room, Petworth, W. Sussex.
T.G. Wilkinson Antiques Ltd, Petworth, W. Sussex.
Sayer Antiques, Warnham, W. Sussex.
Apollo Antiques Ltd, Warwick, Warks.
Alan Richards Brocante, Birmingham, W. Mids.
L.P. Antiques (Mids) Ltd, Walsall, W. Mids.
Kimber & Son, Wolverhampton, W. Mids.
Martin-Quick Antiques, Wolverhampton, W. Mids.
Avon Antiques, Bradford-on-Avon, Wilts.
Moxhams Antiques, Bradford-on-Avon, Wilts.
St Mary's Chapel Antiques, Devizes, Wilts.
St Mary's Chapel Antiques, Devizes, Wilts.
Edward Marnier Antiques, Tisbury, Wilts.
Number 9, Warminster, Wilts.
Obelisk Antiques, Warminster, Wilts.
Norwood House Antiques, Killinghall, N. Yorks.

Furniture - Country (for 16th-17th C, see also Oak)

At the Sign of the Chest of Drawers, London N1.
Michael Lewis Antiques, London N1.
Rookery Farm Antiques, London N1.
This and That (Furniture), London NW1.
Robert E. Hirschhorn, London SE5.
Rogier Antiques, London SW1.
The Furniture Cave, London SW10.
Robert Young Antiques, London SW11.
Simon Coleman Antiques, London SW13.
Yesterday's Antiques, London SW14.
I. and J.L. Brown Ltd, London SW6.
Alistair Sampson Antiques Ltd, London W1.
M. and D. Seligmann, London W8.
Alan Hodgson, Great Shefford, Berks.
Jack Harness Antiques, Marlow, Bucks.
Tim Marshall Antiques, Tingewick, Bucks.
Simon and Penny Rumble Antiques, Chittering, Cambs.
A.P. and M.A. Haylett, Outwell, Cambs.
Olwyn Boustead Antiques, Chester, Cheshire.
Farmhouse Antiques, Chester, Cheshire.
Richmond Galleries, Chester, Cheshire.
Adams Antiques, Nantwich, Cheshire.
Antiques and Curios, Ravensmoor, Cheshire.
Oak Room, Stockport, Cheshire.
Moyallon Antiques, Portadown, Co. Armagh, N. Ireland.
Blackwater Pine Antiques, Truro, Cornwall.
Anvil Antiques, Cartmel, Cumbria.
Maggie Tallentire Antiques, Cartmel, Cumbria.
Langley Antiques, Corby Hill, Cumbria.
David Hill, Kirkby Stephen, Cumbria.
Mortlake Antiques, Kirkby Stephen, Cumbria.
Utopia Antiques Ltd, Low Newton, Cumbria.
Sandgate Antiques, Penrith, Cumbria.
Winton Hall Antiques, Winton, Cumbria.
Peter Bunting Antiques, Bakewell, Derbys.
Byethorpe Furniture (Brian Yates Antiques), Barlow, Derbys.
Rex Antiques, Chagford, Devon.
Cobweb Antiques, Cullompton, Devon.
Wickham Antiques, Honiton, Devon.
Sextons, Kentisbeare, Devon.
Pugh's Farm Antiques, Monkton, Devon.
Timepiece, Teignmouth, Devon.
Barrington Antiques, Tiverton, Devon.
The Ark Antiques & Design, Topsham Devon.
Fine Pine Antiques, Totnes, Devon.
Bryan Chew, Wimborne Minster, Dorset.
English Rose Antiques, Coggeshall, Essex.
Dean Antiques, Colchester, Essex.
Julia Bennet (Antiques), Dunmow, Essex.
Lennard Antiques, Sible Hedingham, Essex.
Denzil Verey, Barnsley, Glos.
J. and R. Bateman Antiques, Chalford, Glos.
John P. Townsend, Cheltenham, Glos.
Waterloo Antiques, Cirencester, Glos.
Woodminster Antiques, Cirencester, Glos.
Gloucester House Antiques Ltd, Fairford, Glos.
Outhouse Antiques, Kempsford, Glos.
Annarella Clark Antiques, Stow-on-the-Wold, Glos.
Keith Hockin (Antiques) Ltd, Stow-on-the-Wold, Glos.
Huntington Antiques Ltd, Stow-on-the-Wold, Glos.
The Chest of Drawers, Tetbury, Glos.
Day Antiques, Tetbury, Glos.
Fifty-One Antiques Et Cetera, Tetbury, Glos.
Gales Antiques, Tetbury, Glos.
Peter Norden Antiques, Tetbury, Glos
Simon Seiff Antiques, Tetbury, Glos.
Westwood House Antiques, Tetbury, Glos.
Airdale Antiques, Hartley Wintney, Hants.
Cedar Antiques Limited, Hartley Wintney, Hants.
Phoenix Green Antiques, Hartley Wintney, Hants.
Burgess Farm Antiques, Morestead, Hants.
Millers of Chelsea Antiques Ltd, Ringwood, Hants.
Elizabeth Viney, Stockbridge, Hants.
The Pine Cellars, Winchester, Hants.
I. and J.L. Brown Ltd, Hereford, Herefs.
The Elizabethan Shop, Ross-on-Wye, Herefs.
Singleton Antiques, Ross-on-Wye, Herefs.
M. and J. Russell, Yazor, Herefs.
Tim Wharton Antiques, Redbourn, Herts.
Dinah Stoodley & Celia Jennings, Brasted, Kent.
Michael Pearson Antiques, Canterbury, Kent.
The Pedlar's Pack, Hadlow, Kent.
Henry Baines, Southborough, Kent.
Jackson-Grant Antiques, Teynham, Kent.
Claremont Antiques, Tunbridge Wells, Kent.
Phoenix Antiques, Tunbridge Wells, Kent.
Up Country, Tunbridge Wells, Kent.
Kitchenalia, Longridge, Lancs.
Davies Antiques, Whalley, Lancs.
Richard Kimbell Ltd, Market Harborough, Leics.

Quorn Pine and Decoratives, Quorn, Leics.
Haydn Earl Antiques and Period Interiors, Louth, Lincs.
Audley House, Osbournby, Lincs.
Graham Pickett Antiques, Stamford, Lincs.
Sinclair's, Stamford, Lincs.
Holt Antique Centre, Holt, Norfolk.
Sue Miller Antiques and Collectables, Langham, Norfolk.
B.R. & J.B. Gunnett, Brixworth, Northants.
Richard Kimbell Ltd, Desborough, Northants.
Paul Hopwell Antiques, West Haddon, Northants.
Mark Seabrook Antiques, West Haddon, Northants.
Horseshoe Antiques and Gallery, Burford, Oxon.
Swan Gallery, Burford, Oxon.
Bugle Antiques, Chipping Norton, Oxon.
Key Antiques, Chipping Norton, Oxon.
The Country Store and Linen Cupboard, Deddington, Oxon.
Dorchester Antiques, Dorchester-on-Thames, Oxon.
Wychwood Antiques, Taynton, Oxon.
Windrush Antiques, Witney, Oxon.
Witney Antiques, Witney, Oxon.
Chris Baylis Country Chairs, Woodstock, Oxon.
Tim Hardie Antiques, Edinburgh, Scotland.
Ark Antiques, Bishop's Castle, Shrops.
John Clegg, Ludlow, Shrops.
G. & D. Ginger Antiques, Ludlow, Shrops.
Marcus Moore Antiques, Stanton, Shrops.
Dodington Antiques, Whitchurch, Shrops.
Lansdown Antiques, Bath, Somerset.
Acorn Antiques, Dulverton, Somerset.
Gilbert & Dale, Ilchester, Somerset.
Chez Chalon, Merriott, Somerset.
Milverton Antiques, Milverton, Somerset.
J.C. White, Milverton, Somerset.
Montacute Antiques, Montacute, Somerset.
Times Past, Somerton, Somerset.
Tilly Manor Antiques, West Harptree, Somerset.
Johnson's, Leek, Staffs.
Guillemot, Aldeburgh, Suffolk.
Dix-Sept, Framlingham, Suffolk.
Noel Mercer Antiques, Long Melford, Suffolk.
Oswald Simpson, Long Melford, Suffolk.
Peasenhall Art and Antiques Gallery, Peasenhall, Suffolk.
Suffolk Antique Connection, Stoke by Nayland, Suffolk.
Suffolk House Antiques, Yoxford, Suffolk.
Stoneycroft Farm, Betchworth, Surrey.
Cobham Galleries, Cobham, Surrey.
Christopher's Antiques, Farnham, Surrey.
Elm House Antiques, Merstham, Surrey.
Mollie Evans, Richmond, Surrey.
Anthony Welling Antiques, Ripley, Surrey.
Hadlow Down Antiques, Hadlow Down, E. Sussex.
John Bird and Annette Puttnam Antiques, Lewes, E. Sussex.
Pastorale Antiques, Lewes, E. Sussex.
Graham Price Antiques Ltd, Polegate, E. Sussex.
Park View Antiques, Wadhurst, E. Sussex.
Antiquities, Arundel, W. Sussex.
Michael Wakelin and Helen Linfield, Billingshurst, W. Sussex.
Alexander Antiques, Henfield, W. Sussex.
West Street Antiques & Presents, Midhurst, W. Sussex.
Angel Antiques, Petworth, W. Sussex.
J.C. Tutt Antiques, Petworth, W. Sussex.
Audrey Bull, Carmarthen, Wales.
Havard and Havard, Cowbridge, Wales.
Gallop and Rivers Architectural Antiques, Crickhowell, Wales.
Michael Lloyd, Henllan, Wales.
Country Antiques (Wales), Kidwelly, Wales.
Islwyn Watkins, Knighton, Wales.
Jim and Pat Ash, Llandeilo, Wales.
Collinge Antiques, Llandudno Junction, Wales.
Heritage Restorations, Llanfair Caereinion, Wales.
The Carningli Centre, Newport, Wales.
Kim Scurlock, Swansea, Wales.
Audrey Bull, Tenby, Wales.
Down Memory Lane, Atherstone, Warks.
King's Cottage Antiques, Leamington Spa, Warks.
Chadwick Antiques, Knowle, W. Mids.
L.P. Antiques (Mids) Ltd, Walsall, W. Mids.
Combe Cottage Antiques, Castle Combe, Wilts.
St Mary's Chapel Antiques, Devizes, Wilts.
Annmarie Turner Antiques, Marlborough, Wilts.
Number 9, Warminster, Wilts.
D & J Lines Antiques, Worcester, Worcs.
The Antique Pine & Country Furniture Shop, Driffield, E. Yorks.
Bill Bentley, Harrogate, N. Yorks.
Elaine Phillips Antiques Ltd, Harrogate, N. Yorks.
York Cottage Antiques, Helmsley, N. Yorks.
Northern Antiques Company, Norton, N. Yorks.
Pateley Bridge Antiques, Pateley Bridge, N. Yorks.
Roy Precious, Settle, N. Yorks.
E. Thistlethwaite, Settle, N. Yorks.
Barry Alexander Ogleby (Jnr) Antiques, Thirsk, N. Yorks.
Chattels Antiques, Topcliffe, N. Yorks.
Coach House Antiques, Whitby, N. Yorks.
Ruth Ford Antiques, York, N. Yorks.
Fishlake Antiques, Fishlake, S. Yorks.
Fagin & Co., Todmorden, W. Yorks.

Furniture - Georgian

Bookal's, London EC1.
Peter Chapman Antiques, London N1.
Dome Antiques (Exports) Ltd, London N1.
Furniture Vault, London N1.
Gordon Gridley, London N1.
Inheritance, London N1.
Regent Antiques, London N1.
Restall Brown and Clennell Ltd, London N1.
Tapsell Antiques, London N1.
Vane House Antiques, London N1.
Finchley Fine Art Galleries, London N12.
Martin Henham (Antiques), London N2.
Betty Gould and Julian Gonnermann Antiques, London N6.
W.R. Harvey & Co (Antiques) Ltd, London NW1.
G. and F. Gillingham Ltd, London NW2.
Patricia Beckman Antiques, London NW3.
David and Charles Wainwright, London NW3.
Camden Art Gallery, London NW8.
Patricia Harvey Antiques and Decoration, London NW8.
Wellington Gallery, London NW8.
The Antiques Pavilion, London SE1.
The Old Cinema Antique Warehouse, London SE1.
Tower Bridge Antiques, London SE1.
The Junk Shop, London SE10.
Relcy Antiques, London SE10.
Robert E. Hirschhorn, London SE5.
Antique Warehouse, London SE8.
Anno Domini Antiques, London SW1.
Hilary Batstone Decorative Antiques, London SW1.
John Bly, London SW1.
Ciancimino Ltd, London SW1.
General Trading Co Ltd, London SW1.
Ross Hamilton Ltd, London SW1.
Harrods Ltd, London SW1.
Hawksmoor, London SW1.
Hotspur Ltd, London SW1.
Christopher Howe, London SW1.
Humphrey-Carrasco, London SW1.
Jeremy Ltd, London SW1.
Lucy Johnson, London SW1.
Peter Jones, London SW1.
Pairs Antiques Ltd, London SW1.
William Tillman Ltd, London SW1.
Westenholz Antiques Ltd, London SW1.
Alasdair Brown Antiques, London SW10.
The Furniture Cave, London SW10.
Rupert Hastie, London SW10.
Stephen Long, London SW10.
Mallord Street Antiques, London SW10.
The Dining Room Shop, London SW13.
Joy McDonald, London SW13.
Jeremy Seale Antiques, London SW13.
Jorgen Antiques, London SW15.
H.C. Baxter and Sons, London SW16.
Adams Room Antiques, London SW19.
Norman Adams Ltd, London SW3.
Apter Fredericks Ltd, London SW3.
Richard Courtney Ltd, London SW3.
Robert Dickson and Lesley Rendall Antiques, London SW3.
Michael Foster, London SW3.
C. Fredericks and Son, London SW3.

Godson and Coles, London SW3.
Anthony James and Son Ltd, London SW3.
John Keil Ltd, London SW3.
Michael Lipitch Ltd, London SW3.
Peter Lipitch Ltd, London SW3.
Prides of London, London SW3.
Charles Saunders Antiques, London SW3.
Clifford Wright Antiques Ltd, London SW3.
Antique and Modern Furniture Ltd, London SW5.
313 Antiques, London SW6.
Bookham Galleries, London SW6.
John Clay, London SW6.
Fergus Cochrane Antiques, London SW6.
George Floyd Ltd, London SW6.
George d'Epinois, London SW6.
HRW Antiques (London) Ltd, London SW6.
Peter Hurford Antiques, London SW6.
Eric King Antiques, London SW6.
L. and E. Kreckovic, London SW6.
Michael Luther Antiques, London SW6.
Michael Marriott Ltd, London SW6.
David Martin-Taylor Antiques, London SW6.
Megan Mathers Antiques, London SW6.
Orrell & Brown Interiors, London SW6.
Ossowski, London SW6.
M. Pauw Antiques, London SW6.
Rogers & Co, London SW6.
Ferenc Toth, London SW6.
Vaughan, London SW6.
H. Blairman and Sons Ltd., London W1.
Antoine Cheneviere Fine Arts, London W1.
Colefax and Fowler, London W1.
Brian Fielden, London W1.
Fortnum and Mason plc, London W1.
Halcyon Days, London W1.
Patrick Jefferson Ltd, London W1.
Leuchars and Jefferson, London W1.
Mallett and Son (Antiques) Ltd, London W1.
Partridge Fine Arts plc, London W1.
Pendulum of Mayfair Ltd, London W1.
Ronald Phillips Ltd, London W1.
Scarisbrick and Bate Ltd, London W1.
Stair and Company Ltd, London W1.
Toynbee-Clarke Interiors Ltd, London W1.
M. Turpin Ltd, London W1.
Michael Aalders, London W11.
B. and T. Antiques, London W11.
Britannia Export Antiques, London W11.
Butchoff Antiques, London W11.
Michael Davidson, London W11.
Judy Fox, London W11.
J. Lipitch Ltd, London W11.
Daniel Mankowitz, London W11.
Robin Martin Antiques, London W11.
Terence Morse and Son Ltd, London W11.
Oakstar Ltd, London W11.
Rostrum Antiques, London W11.
Louis Stanton, London W11.
David and Charles Wainwright, London W11.
Trude Weaver, London W11.
Marshall Gallery, London W14.
J. Roger (Antiques) Ltd, London W14.
Aberdeen House Antiques, London W5.
The Badger, London W5.
Terrace Antiques, London W5.
Murray Thomson Ltd, London W6.
Eddy Bardawil, London W8.
Barnet Antiques, London W8.
Anne-Marie Cattanach, London W8.
Lewis and Lloyd, London W8.
C.H. Major (Antiques) Ltd, London W8.
Reindeer Antiques Ltd, London W8.
Brian Rolleston Antiques Ltd, London W8.
Patrick Sandberg Antiques, London W8.
Pamela Teignmouth and Son, London W8.
Fluss and Charlesworth Ltd, London W9.
Victoria Antiques, Alderney, Alderney, Channel Islands.
Robert Harman Antiques, Ampthill, Beds.
Paris Antiques, Ampthill, Beds.
Pilgrim Antiques, Ampthill, Beds.
Guy Roe Antiques, Ampthill, Beds.
S. and S. Timms Antiques Ltd, Ampthill, Beds.
David Ball Antique Furnisher, Leighton Buzzard, Beds.
Town Hall Antiques, Woburn, Beds.
John A. Pearson Antiques, Horton, Berks.
Bow House Antiques, Hungerford, Berks.
Robert and Georgina Hastie, Hungerford, Berks.
Roger King Antiques, Hungerford, Berks.
Medalcrest Ltd, Hungerford, Berks.
The Old Malthouse, Hungerford, Berks.
Widmerpool House Antiques, Maidenhead, Berks.
Cavendish Fine Arts, Sonning-on-Thames, Berks.
Csaky's Antiques, Sonning-on-Thames, Berks.
John Connell - Wargrave Antiques, Wargrave, Berks.
Eton Antiques Partnership, Windsor and Eton, Berks.
Shirley Hayden Antiques, Windsor and Eton, Berks.
Peter J. Martin, Windsor and Eton, Berks.
Ulla Stafford Antiques, Windsor and Eton, Berks.
Times Past Antiques, Windsor and Eton, Berks.
Woodage Antiques, Windsor and Eton, Berks.
The Cupboard Antiques, Amersham, Bucks.
June Elsworth - Beaconsfield Ltd, Beaconsfield, Bucks.
Grosvenor House Interiors, Beaconsfield, Bucks.
Period Furniture Showrooms, Beaconsfield, Bucks.
The Spinning Wheel, Beaconsfield, Bucks.
Fenlan, Olney, Bucks.
John Overland Antiques, Olney, Bucks.
Country Furniture Shop, Penn, Bucks.
Wendover Antiques, Wendover, Bucks.
Peter Norman Antiques and Restorations, Burwell, Cambs.
Jess Applin Antiques, Cambridge, Cambs.
John Beazor and Sons Ltd, Cambridge, Cambs.
Mere Antiques, Fowlmere, Cambs.
Quayside Antiques, St Ives, Cambs.
Anthony Baker Antiques, Alderley Edge, Cheshire.
Sara Frances Antiques, Alderley Edge, Cheshire.
Lostock Antiques, Altrincham, Cheshire.
David H. Dickinson, Bramhall, Cheshire.
Andrew Foott Antiques, Cheadle Hulme, Cheshire.
Adams Antiques, Chester, Cheshire.
Olwyn Boustead Antiques, Chester, Cheshire.
Melody's Antique Galleries, Chester, Cheshire.
Moor Hall Antiques, Chester, Cheshire.
John Titchner & Sons, Chester, Cheshire.
Glynn Interiors, Knutsford, Cheshire.
John Titchner and Sons, Littleton, Cheshire.
The Mulberry Bush, Marple Bridge, Cheshire.
David Bedale, Mobberley, Cheshire.
Chapel Antiques, Nantwich, Cheshire.
Coppelia Antiques, Plumley, Cheshire.
Hole in the Wall Antiques, Stockport, Cheshire.
Page Antiques, Stockport, Cheshire.
Marie José Burke, Tarporley, Cheshire.
Margaret Bedi Antiques, Billingham, Cleveland.
Ruby Snowden Antiques, Yarm, Cleveland.
Robert Christie Antiques, Ballyclare, Co. Antrim, N. Ireland.
Dunluce Antiques, Bushmills, Co. Antrim, N. Ireland.
MacHenry Antiques, Newtownabbey, Co. Antrim, N. Ireland.
Furney Antiques and Interiors, Donaghadee, Co. Down, N. Ireland.
Downshire House Antiques, Newry, Co. Down, N. Ireland.
McCabe's Antique Galleries, Newry, Co. Down, N. Ireland.
Time & Tide Antiques, Portaferry, Co Down, N. Ireland.
Antiques and Fine Art Gallery, Warrenpoint, Co. Down, N. Ireland.
Forge Antiques, Lisbellaw, Co. Fermanagh, N. Ireland.
K.O. Hagan, Claudy, Co. Londonderry, N. Ireland.
John Bragg Antiques, Lostwithiel, Cornwall.
Ken Ashbrook Antiques, Penzance, Cornwall.
Pydar Antiques and Pine, Truro, Cornwall.
Victoria Antiques, Wadebridge, Cornwall.
Anthemion - The Antique Shop, Cartmel, Cumbria.
Anvil Antiques, Cartmel, Cumbria.

Jennywell Hall Antiques, Crosby Ravensworth, Cumbria.
Calvert Antiques, Endmoor, Cumbria.
Haughey Antiques, Kirkby Stephen, Cumbria.
Mortlake Antiques, Kirkby Stephen, Cumbria.
Townhead Antiques, Newby Bridge, Cumbria.
Winton Hall Antiques, Winton, Cumbria.
Pamela Elsom - Antiques, Ashbourne, Derbys.
Martin and Dorothy Harper Antiques, Bakewell, Derbys.
Lewis Antiques, Bakewell, Derbys.
Water Lane Antiques, Bakewell, Derbys.
Antique Exporters U.K, Brailsford, Derbys.
The Antiques Warehouse, Buxton, Derbys.
The Penny Post Antiques, Buxton, Derbys.
Hackney House Antiques, Chesterfield, Derbys.
Ian Morris, Chesterfield, Derbys.
Dragon Antiques, Duffield, Derbys.
Wayside Antiques, Duffield, Derbys.
N. and C.A. Haslam, Grassmoor, Derbys.
Shardlow Antiques Warehouse, Shardlow, Derbys.
Sam Savage Antiques, Ticknall, Derbys.
Nimbus Antiques, Whaley Bridge, Derbys.
Wooden Box Antiques, Woodville, Derbys.
Gravelly Bank Pine Antiques, Yeaveley, Derbys.
M. W. Dunscombe Antiques, Ashburton, Devon.
Moor Antiques, Ashburton, Devon.
J. Collins and Son, Bideford, Devon.
John Prestige Antiques, Brixham, Devon.
Alison Gosling Antiques, Budleigh Salterton, Devon.
David J. Thorn, Budleigh Salterton, Devon.
Rex Antiques, Chagford, Devon.
Cullompton Old Tannery Antiques, Cullompton, Devon.
Mills Antiques, Cullompton, Devon.
Umborne Antiques, Cullompton, Devon.
Roderick Butler, Honiton, Devon.
L.J. Huggett and Son, Honiton, Devon.
Lombard Antiques, Honiton, Devon.
Merchant House Antiques, Honiton, Devon.
Pilgrim Antiques, Honiton, Devon.
Upstairs, Downstairs, Honiton, Devon.
Sextons, Kentisbeare, Devon.
W. J. Woodhams, Shaldon, Devon.
Philip Andrade, South Brent, Devon.
Extence Antiques, Teignmouth, Devon.
Bygone Days Antiques, Tiverton, Devon.
The Ark Antiques & Design, Topsham, Devon.
Past and Present, Totnes, Devon.
Anthony James Antiques, Whimple, Devon.
Colin Rhodes Antiques, Yealmpton, Devon.
Good Hope Antiques, Beaminster, Dorset.
Antiques for All, Blandford Forum, Dorset.
Strowger of Blandford, Blandford Forum, Dorset.
Lionel Geneen Ltd, Bournemouth, Dorset.
Sainsburys of Bournemouth Ltd, Bournemouth, Dorset.
Peter Stebbing, Bournemouth, Dorset.
David Mack Antiques, Branksome, Dorset.
Zona Dawson Antiques, Charlton Marshall, Dorset.
Hamptons, Christchurch, Dorset.
Tower Antiques, Cranborne, Dorset.
Michael Legg Antiques, Dorchester, Dorset.
Legg of Dorchester, Dorchester, Dorset.
Shaston Antiques, Shaftesbury, Dorset.
Dodge and Son, Sherborne, Dorset.
Heygate Browne Antiques, Sherborne, Dorset.
Piers Pisani Antiques, Sherborne, Dorset.
Brown's Antiques, Barnard Castle, Durham.
Joan and David White Antiques, Barnard Castle, Durham.
Alan Ramsey Antiques, Darlington, Durham.
Eden House Antiques, West Auckland, Durham.
Revival, Abridge, Essex.
Swan Antiques, Baythorne End, Essex.
Lindsell Chairs, Coggeshall, Essex.
Dean Antiques, Colchester, Essex.
Julia Bennet (Antiques), Dunmow, Essex.
Michael Beaumont Antiques, Hempstead, Essex.
Colton Antiques, Kelvedon, Essex.
Millers Antiques Kelvedon, Kelvedon, Essex.
Thomas Sykes Antiques, Kelvedon, Essex.
Richard Wrenn Antiques, Leigh-on-Sea, Essex.
Clive Beardall Antiques, Maldon, Essex.
Old Barn Antiques, Matching Green, Essex.
Stone Hall Antiques, Matching Green, Essex.
West Essex Antiques, Matching Green, Essex.
Brown House Antiques, Newport, Essex.
F.G. Bruschweiler (Antiques) Ltd, Rayleigh, Essex.
The Interior Design Shop, Saffron Walden, Essex.
Hedingham Antiques, Sible Hedingham, Essex.
W.A. Pinn and Sons, Sible Hedingham, Essex.
Barton House Antiques, Stanford-le-Hope, Essex.
Harris Antiques (Stansted), Stansted, Essex.
Linden House Antiques, Stansted, Essex.
White Roding Antiques, White Roding, Essex.
Andrew Lelliott, Avening, Glos.
Robin Butler, Bristol, Glos.
H.W. Keil (Cheltenham) Ltd, Cheltenham, Glos.
Latchford Antiques, Cheltenham, Glos.
Triton Gallery, Cheltenham, Glos.
Swan Antiques, Chipping Campden, Glos.
Forum Antiques, Cirencester, Glos.
Hares, Cirencester, Glos.
Rankine Taylor Antiques, Cirencester, Glos.
Patrick Waldron Antiques, Cirencester, Glos.
Waterloo Antiques, Cirencester, Glos.
Bernard Weaver Antiques, Cirencester, Glos.
Blenheim Antiques, Fairford, Glos.
Mark Carter Antiques, Fairford, Glos.
A.J. Ponsford Antiques, Gloucester, Glos.
Berry Antiques, Moreton-in-Marsh, Glos.
Europa Antiques, Moreton-in-Marsh, Glos.
Lemington House Antiques, Moreton-in-Marsh, Glos.
Elizabeth Parker, Moreton-in-Marsh, Glos.
Gary Wright Antiques, Moreton-in-Marsh, Glos.
Craig Carrington Antiques, Painswick, Glos.
Acorn Antiques, Stow-on-the-Wold, Glos.
Duncan J. Baggott, Stow-on-the-Wold, Glos.
Baggott Church Street Ltd, Stow-on-the-Wold, Glos.
Colin Brand Antiques, Stow-on-the-Wold, Glos.
Christopher Clarke Antiques Ltd, Stow-on-the-Wold, Glos.
Fosse Way Antiques, Stow-on-the-Wold, Glos.
Huntington Antiques Ltd, Stow-on-the-Wold, Glos.
Roger Lamb Antiques & Works of Art, Stow-on-the-Wold, Glos.
Antony Preston Antiques Ltd, Stow-on-the-Wold, Glos.
Priests Antiques, Stow-on-the-Wold, Glos.
Queens Parade Antiques Ltd, Stow-on-the-Wold, Glos.
Michael Rowland Antiques, Stow-on-the-Wold, Glos.
Stow Antiques, Stow-on-the-Wold, Glos.
Styles of Stow, Stow-on-the-Wold, Glos.
Vanbrugh House Antiques, Stow-on-the-Wold, Glos.
Ball and Claw Antiques, Tetbury, Glos.
Breakspeare Antiques, Tetbury, Glos.
The Chest of Drawers, Tetbury, Glos.
Gales Antiques, Tetbury, Glos.
Morpheus - Elgin House, Tetbury, Glos.
Peter Norden Antiques, Tetbury, Glos.
Porch House Antiques, Tetbury, Glos.
Berkeley Antiques, Tewkesbury, Glos.
Gainsborough House Antiques, Tewkesbury, Glos.
Prichard Antiques, Winchcombe, Glos.
Mark Blower Antiques, St. Martin, Guernsey, Channel Islands.

Grange Antiques, St. Peter Port, Guernsey, Channel Islands.
St. James's Gallery Ltd, St. Peter Port, Guernsey, Channel Islands.
Butterfly Pine, Botley, Hants.
Nicholas Abbott, Hartley Wintney, Hants.
Andwells, Hartley Wintney, Hants.
Antique House, Hartley Wintney, Hants.
Deva Antiques, Hartley Wintney, Hants.
David Lazarus Antiques, Hartley Wintney, Hants.
Millon Antiques, Hartley Wintney, Hants.
Phoenix Green Antiques, Hartley Wintney, Hants.
Lita Kaye of Lyndhurst, Lyndhurst, Hants.
Cull Antiques, Petersfield, Hants.
Millers of Chelsea Antiques Ltd, Ringwood, Hants.
L. Moody, Southampton, Hants.
Elizabeth Viney, Stockbridge, Hants.
Gasson Antiques and Interiors, Tadley, Hants.
Gaylords, Titchfield, Hants.
J.W. Blanchard Ltd, Winchester, Hants.
Burns and Graham, Winchester, Hants.
Mary Roofe Antiques, Winchester, Hants.
Great Brampton House Antiques Ltd, Hereford, Herefs.
John Nash Antiques and Interiors, Ledbury, Herefs.
Serendipity, Ledbury, Herefs.
Jeffery Hammond Antiques, Leominster, Herefs.
Anthony Butt Antiques, Baldock, Herts.
Ralph and Bruce Moss, Baldock, Herts.
The Windhill Antiquary, Bishop's Stortford, Herts.
Michael Gander, Hitchin, Herts.
Hanbury Antiques, Hitchin, Herts.
Phillips of Hitchin (Antiques) Ltd, Hitchin, Herts.
Tom Salusbury Antiques, Hitchin, Herts.
J.N. Antiques, Redbourn, Herts.
Tim Wharton Antiques, Redbourn, Herts.
John Bly, Tring, Herts.
New England House Antiques, Tring, Herts.
Collins Antiques (F.G. and C. Collins Ltd.), Wheathampstead, Herts.
Michael Armson (Antiques) Ltd, Wilstone, Herts.
John Corrin Antiques, Douglas, Isle of Man.
Stablegate Antiques, Barham, Kent.
David Barrington, Brasted, Kent.
Peter Dyke, Brasted, Kent.
Keymer Son & Co. Ltd, Brasted, Kent.
Roy Massingham Antiques, Brasted, Kent.
Tilings Antiques, Brasted, Kent.
Conquest House Antiques, Canterbury, Kent.
Chislehurst Antiques, Chislehurst, Kent.
Michael Sim, Chislehurst, Kent.
Lennox Cato, Edenbridge, Kent.
Chevertons of Edenbridge Ltd, Edenbridge, Kent.
Alan Lord Antiques, Folkestone, Kent.
Samovar Antiques, Hythe, Kent.
Deo Juvante Antiques, Rochester, Kent.
J.D. and R.M. Walters, Rolvenden, Kent.
Christopher Buck Antiques, Sandgate, Kent.
Dench Antiques, Sandgate, Kent.
Finch Antiques, Sandgate, Kent.
Michael Fitch Antiques, Sandgate, Kent.
Freeman and Lloyd Antiques, Sandgate, Kent.
James Porter Antiques, Sandwich, Kent.
Nancy Wilson, Sandwich, Kent.
Steppes Hill Farm Antiques, Stockbury, Kent.
Sutton Valence Antiques, Sutton Valence, Kent.
Flower House Antiques, Tenterden, Kent.
Garden House Antiques, Tenterden, Kent.
Sparks Antiques, Tenterden, Kent.
Jackson-Grant Antiques, Teynham, Kent.
Devron Green Antiques, Tunbridge Wells, Kent.
The Pantiles Antiques, Tunbridge Wells, Kent.
Pantiles Spa Antiques, Tunbridge Wells, Kent.
Phoenix Antiques, Tunbridge Wells, Kent.
John Thompson, Tunbridge Wells, Kent.
Up Country, Tunbridge Wells, Kent.
Rose and Crown Antiques, West Malling, Kent.
Apollo Antique Galleries, Westerham, Kent.
Brazil Antiques, Westerham, Kent.
Anthony J. Hook, Westerham, Kent.
London House Antiques, Westerham, Kent.
Marks Antiques, Westerham, Kent.
Taylor-Smith, Westerham, Kent.
Westerham House Antiques, Westerham, Kent.
Laurens Antiques, Whitstable, Kent.
Tankerton Antiques, Whitstable, Kent.
Silvesters, Wingham, Kent.
E.W. Webster, Bickerstaffe, Lancs.
Park Galleries Antiques, Fine Art and Decor, Bolton, Lancs.
Brun Lea Antiques (J. Waite Ltd), Burnley, Lancs.
K.C. Antiques, Darwen, Lancs.
P.J. Brown Antiques, Haslingden, Lancs.
The Baron Antiques, Manchester, Lancs.
Bulldog Antiques, Manchester, Lancs.
Luigino Vescovi, Morecambe, Lancs.
Brooks Antiques, Nelson, Lancs.
Alan Grice Antiques, Ormskirk, Lancs.
S.C. Falk, Rochdale, Lancs.
Old Bakehouse Antiques and Gallery, Broughton Astley, Leics.
Withers of Leicester, Hoby, Leics.
Corry's, Leicester, Leics.
Walter Moores and Son, Leicester, Leics.
Lowe of Loughborough, Loughborough, Leics.
Abbey Antiques, Market Harborough, Leics.
J. Stamp and Sons, Market Harborough, Leics.
Ken Smith Antiques Ltd, Narborough, Leics.
David E. Burrows, Osgathorpe, Leics.
J. Green and Son, Queniborough,, Leics.
Mill on the Soar Antiques Ltd, Quorn, Leics.
Paddock Antiques, Woodhouse Eaves, Leics.
Clive Underwood Antiques, Colsterworth, Lincs.
Alan Read Period Furniture, Horncastle, Lincs.
Laurence Shaw Antiques, Horncastle, Lincs.
Staines Antiques, Horncastle, Lincs.
Haydn Earl Antiques and Period Interiors, Louth, Lincs.
Harwood Tate, Market Rasen, Lincs.
Pinfold Antiques, Ruskington, Lincs.
Dawson of Stamford Ltd, Stamford, Lincs.
Claire Langley Antiques, Stamford, Lincs.
Graham Pickett Antiques, Stamford, Lincs.
St. George's Antiques, Stamford, Lincs.
St. Mary's Galleries, Stamford, Lincs.
J. and R. Ratcliffe, Waddington, Lincs.
Underwoodhall Antiques, Woodhall Spa, Lincs.
V.O.C. Antiques, Woodhall Spa, Lincs
Stefani Antiques, Liverpool, Merseyside.
Colin Stock, Rainford, Merseyside.
Decor Galleries, Southport, Merseyside.
Tony and Anne Sutcliffe Antiques, Southport, Merseyside.
Yarnall Antiques, Wallasey, Merseyside.
Helen Horswill Antiques and Decorative Arts, West Kirby, Merseyside.
Cynthia Morgan Interiors, Enfield, Middx.
Kathleen Mann - The Other Shop, Harrow, Middx.
Tobias Jellinek Antiques, Twickenham, Middx.
Ivy House Antiques, Acle, Norfolk.
A.E. Bush and Partners, Attleborough, Norfolk.
M. and A. Cringle, Burnham Market, Norfolk.
Anne Hamilton Antiques, Burnham Market, Norfolk.
Market House, Burnham Market, Norfolk.
Roger Bradbury Antiques, Coltishall, Norfolk.
A.E. Seago, Cromer, Norfolk.
Anne Hamilton Antiques, East Rudham, Norfolk.
Peter Howkins, Gt. Yarmouth, Norfolk.
Peter Robinson, Heacham, Norfolk.
Arthur Brett and Sons Ltd, Norwich, Norfolk.
Nicholas Fowle Antiques, Norwich, Norfolk.
John Howkins Antiques, Norwich,

Norfolk.
Echo Antiques, Reepham, Norfolk.
Leo Pratt and Son, South Walsham, Norfolk.
Stalham Antique Gallery, Stalham, Norfolk.
Norton Antiques, Twyford, Norfolk.
T.C.S. Brooke, Wroxham, Norfolk.
M.E. and J.E. Standley, Wymondham, Norfolk.
Berengar Antiques, Barnwell, Northants.
Simon Banks Antiques, Finedon, Northants.
M.C. Chapman, Finedon, Northants.
Robert Cheney Antiques, Finedon, Northants.
Huntershield Antiques, Flore, Northants.
Christopher Jones at Flore House, Flore, Northants.
F. and C.H. Cave, Northampton, Northants.
The Antique Galleries, Paulerspury, Northants.
Reindeer Antiques Ltd, Potterspury, Northants.
Boadens Antiques, Hexham, Northumbs.
Hallstile Antiques, Hexham, Northumbs.
Hedley's of Hexham, Hexham, Northumbs.
James Miller Antiques, Wooler, Northumbs.
E.M. Cheshire, Bingham, Notts.
Rectory Bungalow Workshop, Elton, Notts.
Meadow Lane Antiques, Nottingham, Notts.
Pegasus Antiques, Nottingham, Notts.
David and Carole Potter Antiques, Nottingham, Notts.
Strouds (of Southwell Antiques), Southwell, Notts.
Benson Antiques Centre & Gallery, Benson, Oxon.
Ashton Gower Antiques, Burford, Oxon.
Burford Antique Centre, Burford, Oxon.
Gateway Antiques, Burford, Oxon.
Hubert's Antiques, Burford, Oxon.
Anthony Nielsen Antiques, Burford, Oxon.
David Pickup, Burford, Oxon.
Swan Gallery, Burford, Oxon.
Walkers, Burford, Oxon.
Rupert Hitchcox Antiques, Chalgrove, Oxon.
Georgian House Antiques, Chipping Norton, Oxon.
Hallidays (Fine Antiques) Ltd, Dorchester-on-Thames, Oxon.
The Faringdon Antique Centre, Faringdon, Oxon.
La Chaise Antique, Faringdon, Oxon.
Richard J. Kingston, Henley-on-Thames, Oxon.
The Country Seat, Huntercombe, Oxon.
Willow Antiques and the Nettlebed Antique Merchants, Nettlebed, Oxon.
de Albuquerque Antiques, Wallingford, Oxon.
Chris and Lin O'Donnell Antiques, Wallingford, Oxon.
Mike Ottrey Antiques, Wallingford, Oxon.
Summers Davis Antiques Ltd, Wallingford, Oxon.
Cross Antiques, Watlington, Oxon.
Stephen Orton Antiques, Watlington, Oxon.
Mark Shanks, Watlington, Oxon.
Colin Greenway Antiques, Witney, Oxon.
W.R. Harvey & Co (Antiques) Ltd, Witney, Oxon.
Joan Wilkins Antiques, Witney, Oxon.
Windrush Antiques, Witney, Oxon.
Witney Antiques, Witney, Oxon.
Robin Sanders and Sons, Woodstock, Oxon.
Thistle House Antiques, Woodstock, Oxon.
Churchgate Antiques, Empingham, Rutland.
Swans, Oakham, Rutland.
T.J. Roberts, Uppingham, Rutland.
Woodman's House Antiques, Uppingham, Rutland.
Robert Bingley Antiques, Wing, Rutland.
Colin Wood (Antiques) Ltd, Aberdeen, Scotland.
Michael Young, Aberdeen, Scotland.
T.W. Beaty, Beattock, Scotland.
Coldstream Antiques, Coldstream, Scotland.
Westport Fine Art, Dundee, Scotland.
Dunkeld Interiors, Dunkeld, Scotland.
Laurance Black Ltd, Edinburgh, Scotland.
Bruntsfield Antiques, Edinburgh, Scotland.
Dunedin Antiques Ltd, Edinburgh, Scotland.
A. Essex & Co, Edinburgh, Scotland.
Georgian Antiques, Edinburgh, Scotland.
London Road Antiques, Edinburgh, Scotland.
Stockbridge Antiques and Fine Art, Edinburgh, Scotland.
Whytock and Reid, Edinburgh, Scotland.
Aldric Young, Edinburgh, Scotland.
Gow Antiques, Forfar, Scotland.
Albany Antiques, Glasgow, Scotland.
Butler's Furniture Galleries Ltd, Glasgow, Scotland.
Muirhead Moffat and Co, Glasgow, Scotland.
C.S. Moreton (Antiques), Inchture, Scotland.
Kilmacolm Antiques Ltd, Kilmacolm, Scotland.
QS Antiques and Cabinetmakers, Kilmarnock, Scotland.
Rhudle Mill, Kilmichael Glassary, Scotland.
Miles Antiques, Kinross, Scotland.
Harper-James, Montrose, Scotland.
Newburgh Antiques, Newburgh, Scotland.
Crossroads Antiques, Prestwick, Scotland.
Coach House Antiques Ltd, Stanley, Scotland.
Doveridge House of Neachley, Albrighton (Neachley), Shrops.
Mytton Antiques, Atcham, Shrops.
Longmynd Antiques, Church Stretton, Shrops.
R.G. Cave and Sons Ltd, Ludlow, Shrops.
M. and R. Taylor (Antiques), Ludlow, Shrops.
Teme Valley Antiques, Ludlow, Shrops.
Valentyne Dawes Gallery, Ludlow, Shrops.
F.C. Manser and Son Ltd, Shrewsbury, Shrops.
Marcus Moore Antiques, Stanton, Shrops.
Brian James Antiques, Telford, Shrops.
L. Onions - White Cottage Antiques, Tern Hill, Shrops.
Dodington Antiques, Whitchurch, Shrops.
Hall's Antiques, Ash Priors, Somerset.
A J Antiques, Bath, Somerset.
Alderson, Bath, Somerset.
Beau Nash Antiques, Bath, Somerset.
Lawrence Brass, Bath, Somerset.
Geoffrey Breeze, Bath, Somerset.
Mary Cruz, Bath, Somerset.
Frank Dux Antiques, Bath, Somerset.
Jadis Ltd, Bath, Somerset.
Montague Antiques, Bath, Somerset.
Quiet Street Antiques, Bath, Somerset.
T.E. Robinson, Bath, Somerset.
M.G.R. Exports, Bruton, Somerset.
Chris's Crackers, Carhampton, Somerset.
Guy Dennler Antiques, Dulverton, Somerset.
C.W.E. and R.I. Dyte Antiques, Highbridge, Somerset.
West End House Antiques, Ilminster, Somerset.
The Chapel at Rode, Rode, Somerset.
Edward A. Nowell, Wells, Somerset.
Tilly Manor Antiques, West Harptree, Somerset.
Edward Venn, Williton, Somerset.
J.C. Giddings, Wiveliscombe, Somerset.
John Hamblin, Yeovil, Somerset.
Milestone Antiques, Lichfield, Staffs.
Richard Midwinter Antiques, Newcastle-under-Lyme, Staffs.
Browse, Stafford, Staffs.
The Potteries Antique Centre, Stoke-on-Trent, Staffs.
Armson's of Yoxall Antiques, Yoxall, Staffs.
H.W. Heron and Son Ltd, Yoxall, Staffs.
Thompson's Gallery, Aldeburgh, Suffolk.
Saltgate Antiques, Beccles, Suffolk.
P. Dawson Furniture Restorers, Bentley, Suffolk.
Denzil Grant Antiques, Bradfield St. George, Suffolk.
Country House Antiques, Bungay, Suffolk.
Peppers Period Pieces, Bury St. Edmunds, Suffolk.
Cavendish Rose Antiques, Cavendish, Suffolk.
J. de Haan & Son, Clare, Suffolk.
F.D. Salter Antiques, Clare, Suffolk.
Gil Adams Antiques, Debenham, Suffolk.

C. & A.C. Bigden Antiques, Debenham, Suffolk.
Ian Collins Antiques, Debenham, Suffolk.
English and Continental Antiques, Eye, Suffolk.
Randolph, Hadleigh, Suffolk.
Ashley Antiques, Ipswich, Suffolk.
Hubbard Antiques, Ipswich, Suffolk.
J. and J. Baker, Lavenham,, Suffolk.
Warrens Antiques Warehouse, Leiston, Suffolk.
Karen Bryan Antiques, Long Melford, Suffolk.
Roger Carling and Tess Sinclair, Long Melford, Suffolk.
Charles Antiques, Long Melford, Suffolk.
Sandy Cooke Antiques, Long Melford, Suffolk.
Alexander Lyall Antiques, Long Melford, Suffolk.
Seabrook Antiques, Long Melford, Suffolk.
Suthburgh Antiques, Long Melford, Suffolk.
Martlesham Antiques, Martlesham, Suffolk.
Mary Palmer Antiques, Stradbroke, Suffolk.
Napier House Antiques, Sudbury, Suffolk.
Antique Furniture Warehouse, Woodbridge, Suffolk.
David Gibbins Antiques, Woodbridge, Suffolk.
Hamilton Antiques, Woodbridge, Suffolk.
Anthony Hurst Antiques, Woodbridge, Suffolk.
Sarah Meysey-Thompson Antiques, Woodbridge, Suffolk.
A.G. Voss, Woodbridge, Suffolk.
J.C. Heather, Woolpit, Suffolk.
Suffolk House Antiques, Yoxford, Suffolk.
John Anthony Antiques, Bletchingley, Surrey.
Simon Marsh, Bletchingley, Surrey.
Howard Blay Antiques, Dorking, Surrey.
Dolphin Square Antiques, Dorking, Surrey.
Dorking Desk Shop, Dorking, Surrey.
Dorking Emporium Antiques Centre, Dorking, Surrey.
Hantss of Dorking, Dorking, Surrey.
Harman's Antiques, Dorking, Surrey.
Holmwood Antiques, Dorking, Surrey.
The House of Bulow Antiques, Dorking, Surrey.
Mayfair Antiques, Dorking, Surrey.
Norfolk House Galleries, Dorking, Surrey.
Elaine Saunderson Antiques, Dorking, Surrey.
Surrey Antiques, Dorking, Surrey.
Thorpe and Foster Ltd, Dorking, Surrey.
West Street Antiques, Dorking, Surrey.
A. E. Booth & Son, Ewell, Surrey.
Christopher's Antiques, Farnham, Surrey.
Heytesbury Antiques, Farnham, Surrey.
Heath-Bullocks, Godalming, Surrey.
M. J. Bowdery, Hindhead, Surrey.
Oriel Antiques, Hindhead, Surrey.
Glencorse Antiques, Kingston-upon-Thames, Surrey.
Elm House Antiques, Merstham, Surrey.
Michael Andrews Antiques, Milford, Surrey.
F.G. Lawrence and Sons, Redhill, Surrey.
The Gallery, Reigate, Surrey.
Antique Mart, Richmond, Surrey.
The Chair Set - Antiques, Richmond, Surrey.
Hill Rise Antiques, Richmond, Surrey.
F. and T. Lawson Antiques, Richmond, Surrey.
Marryat, Richmond, Surrey.
Roderic Antiques, Richmond, Surrey.
J. Hartley Antiques Ltd, Ripley, Surrey.
Ripley Antiques, Ripley, Surrey.
Sage Antiques and Interiors, Ripley, Surrey.
Cockrell Antiques, Surbiton, Surrey.
B. M. and E. Newlove, Surbiton, Surrey.
Clifford and Roger Dade, Thames Ditton, Surrey.
Ian Caldwell, Walton-on-the-Hill and Tadworth, Surrey.
Church House Antiques, Weybridge, Surrey.
R. Saunders, Weybridge, Surrey.
Weybridge Antiques, Weybridge, Surrey.
Alexandria Antiques, Brighton, E. Sussex.
Brighton Antique Wholesalers, Brighton, E. Sussex.
Alan Fitchett Antiques, Brighton, E. Sussex.
Dudley Hume, Brighton, E. Sussex.
Patrick Moorhead Antiques, Brighton, E. Sussex.
Michael Norman Antiques Ltd, Brighton, E. Sussex.
Ben Ponting Antiques, Brighton, E. Sussex.
Yellow Lantern Antiques Ltd, Brighton, E. Sussex.
Dycheling Antiques, Ditchling, E. Sussex.
Aspidistra Antiques, Forest Row, E. Sussex.
Hadlow Down Antiques, Hadlow Down, E. Sussex.
John Botting Antiques, Horam, E. Sussex.
Ashcombe Coach House, Lewes, E. Sussex.
Cliffe Gallery Antiques, Lewes, E. Sussex.
The Old Mint House, Pevensey, E. Sussex.
Trade Wind, Rottingdean, E. Sussex.
Bragge and Sons, Rye, E. Sussex.
Herbert Gordon Gasson, Rye, E. Sussex.
Rye Antiques, Rye, E. Sussex.
The Old House, Seaford, E. Sussex.
Aarquebus Antiques, St. Leonards-on-Sea, E. Sussex.
Ringles Cross Antiques, Uckfield, E. Sussex.
Bygones, Angmering, W. Sussex.
Michael Wakelin and Helen Linfield, Billingshurst, W. Sussex.
Frensham House Antiques, Chichester, W. Sussex.
Gems Antiques, Chichester, W. Sussex.
David Foord-Brown Antiques, Cuckfield, W. Sussex.
Richard Usher Antiques, Cuckfield, W. Sussex.
Callingham Antiques, Northchapel, W. Sussex.
Baskerville Antiques, Petworth, W. Sussex.
J. Du Cros Antiques, Petworth, W. Sussex.
Richard Gardner Antiques, Petworth, W. Sussex.
Granville Antiques, Petworth, W. Sussex.
William Hockley Antiques, Petworth, W. Sussex.
Red Lion Antiques, Petworth, W. Sussex.
T.G. Wilkinson Antiques Ltd, Petworth, W. Sussex.
J. Powell (Hove) Ltd, Portslade, W. Sussex.
Thakeham Furniture, Pulborough, W. Sussex.
Loewenthal Antiques, Tillington, W. Sussex.
Wilsons Antiques, Worthing, W. Sussex.
Ian Sharp Antiques, Tynemouth, Tyne and Wear.
Cwmgwili Mill, Carmarthen, Wales.
K.W. Finlay Antiques, Ciliau Aeron, Wales.
Bulmer's, Cowbridge, Wales.
Cowbridge Antique Centre, Cowbridge Wales.
Havard and Havard, Cowbridge, Wales
Renaissance Antiques, Cowbridge, Wales.
Gerald Oliver Antiques, Haverfordwest, Wales.
Furn Davies Partnership, Holt, Wales.
Kidwelly Antiques, Kidwelly, Wales.
J. and R. Langford, Llangollen, Wales.
Snowdonia Antiques, Llanrwst, Wales.
Peter Thomas Antiques, Narberth, Wales.
Castle Antiques, Newcastle Emlyn, Wales.
Emlyn Antiques, Newcastle Emlyn, Wales.
Rodney Adams Antiques, Pwllheli, Wales.
Eynon Hughes Antiques, Swansea, Wales.
Barn Court Antiques, Templeton, Wales.
Clareston Antiques, Tenby, Wales.
F.E. Anderson and Son, Welshpool, Wales.
Yesterdays, Leamington Spa, Warks.
The Grandfather Clock Shop, Shipston-on-Stour, Warks.
Apollo Antiques Ltd, Warwick, Warks.
Fynewood Antiques, Warwick, Warks.
Patrick and Gillian Morley Antiques, Warwick, Warks.
James Reeve, Warwick, Warks.
Don Spencer Antiques, Warwick, Warks.
Peter Clark Antiques, Birmingham, W. Mids.
John Hubbard Antiques and Fine Art, Birmingham, W. Mids.

The Old Bakehouse, Birmingham, W. Mids.
Thomas Coulborn and Sons, Sutton Coldfield, W. Mids.
Kimber & Son, Wolverhampton, W. Mids.
Martin-Quick Antiques, Wolverhampton, W. Mids.
Avon Antiques, Bradford-on-Avon, Wilts.
Mac Humble Antiques, Bradford-on-Avon, Wilts.
Moxhams Antiques, Bradford-on-Avon, Wilts.
Paul Nash Antiques, Bradford-on-Avon, Wilts.
Town and Country Antiques, Bradford-on-Avon, Wilts.
Harley Antiques, Christian Malford, Wilts.
Matthew Eden, Corsham, Wilts.
Robin Shield Antiques, Cricklade, Wilts.
Turpin's Antiques, Little Bedwyn, Wilts.
Andrew Britten Antiques, Malmesbury, Wilts.
The Antique and Book Collector, Marlborough, Wilts.
Cook of Marlborough Fine Art Ltd, Marlborough, Wilts.
Robert Kime Antiques, Marlborough, Wilts.
Alan Jaffray, Melksham, Wilts.
Ray Best Antiques, Newton Tony, Wilts.
Derek Boston Antiques, Salisbury, Wilts.
Robert Bradley Antiques, Salisbury, Wilts.
Edward Hurst Antiques, Salisbury, Wilts.
Salisbury Antiques Warehouse, Salisbury, Wilts.
Edward Marnier Antiques, Tisbury, Wilts.
Bishopstrow Antiques, Warminster, Wilts.
Obelisk Antiques, Warminster, Wilts.
Mark Patterson Antiques, Wilton, Wilts.
A.J. Romain and Sons, Wilton, Wilts.
Barnt Green Antiques, Barnt Green, Worcs.
Fenwick and Fenwick Antiques, Broadway, Worcs.
H.W. Keil Ltd, Broadway, Worcs.
Miscellany Antiques, Great Malvern, Worcs.
Penoyre Antiques, Pershore, Worcs.
Lower House Fine Antiques, Redditch, Worcs.
Bygones by the Cathedral, Worcester, Worcs.
Bygones (Worcester), Worcester, Worcs.
Jean Hodge, Worcester, Worcs.
M. Lees and Sons, Worcester, Worcs.
Peachley Antiques, Worcester, Worcs.
Priory Antiques, Bridlington, E. Yorks.
David K. Hakeney Antiques, Hull, E. Yorks.
Houghton Hall Antiques, Market Weighton, E. Yorks.
Bennett's Antiques & Collectables, Bedale, N. Yorks.
Anthony Graham Antiques, Boroughbridge, N. Yorks.
St. James House Antiques, Boroughbridge, N. Yorks.
R.S. Wilson and Sons, Boroughbridge, N. Yorks.
Milestone Antiques, Easingwold, N. Yorks.
Elm Tree Antiques, Flaxton, N. Yorks.
Bernard Dickinson, Gargrave, N. Yorks.
R.N. Myers and Son, Gargrave, N. Yorks.
Alexander Adamson, Harrogate, N. Yorks.
Armstrong, Harrogate, N. Yorks.
Bryan Bowden, Harrogate, N. Yorks.
Derbys Antiques Ltd, Harrogate, N. Yorks.
Garth Antiques, Harrogate, N. Yorks.
Haworth Antiques, Harrogate, N. Yorks.
David Love, Harrogate, N. Yorks.
Charles Lumb and Sons Ltd, Harrogate, N. Yorks.
Walker Galleries Ltd, Harrogate, N. Yorks.
Weatherell's of Harrogate Antiques and Fine Arts, Harrogate, N. Yorks.
Chris Wilde Antiques, Harrogate, N. Yorks.
Sturman's Antiques, Hawes, N. Yorks.
Milton J. Holgate, Knaresborough, N. Yorks.
John Thompson Antiques, Knaresborough, N. Yorks.
Trade Antiques - D.D. White, Manfield, N. Yorks.
Daleside Antiques, Markington, N. Yorks.
Aura Antiques, Masham, N. Yorks.
Sigma Antiques and Fine Art, Ripon, N. Yorks.
Anderson Slater Antiques, Settle, N. Yorks.
Corn Mill Antiques, Skipton, N. Yorks.
D. & E.A. Shackleton Antiques, Snainton, N. Yorks.
N.J. and C.S. Dodsworth, Spennithorne, N. Yorks.
Barry Alexander Ogleby (Jnr) Antiques, Thirsk, N. Yorks.
B. Ogleby - St James' House Antiques, Thirsk, N. Yorks.
Tomlinson (Antiques) Ltd. & Period Furniture Ltd, Tockwith, N. Yorks.
Garth Antiques, Whixley, N. Yorks.
Robert Morrison and Son, York, N. Yorks.
Julie Goddard Antiques, Sheffield, S. Yorks.
Peter James Antiques, Sheffield, S. Yorks.
A.E. Jameson and Co, Sheffield, S. Yorks.
Top Hat Antique Centre, Sheffield, S. Yorks.
Bingley Antiques, Haworth, W. Yorks.
Coopers of Ilkley, Ilkley, W. Yorks.
Barleycote Hall Antiques, Keighley, W. Yorks.
Geary Antiques, Leeds, W. Yorks.
Windsor House Antiques (Leeds) Ltd., Leeds, W. Yorks.
Park Antiques, Menston, W. Yorks.
The Titus Gallery, Shipley, W. Yorks.

Furniture - Oak (prior to 1700)

W.R. Harvey & Co (Antiques) Ltd, London NW1.
David and Charles Wainwright, London NW3.
Robert E. Hirschhorn, London SE5.
Christopher Howe, London SW1.
Lucy Johnson, London SW1.
The Furniture Cave, London SW10.
Robert Young Antiques, London SW11.
Joy McDonald, London SW13.
Apter Fredericks Ltd, London SW3.
Joanna Booth, London SW3.
Alistair Sampson Antiques Ltd, London W1.
Louis Stanton, London W11.
David and Charles Wainwright, London W11.
Beedham Antiques Ltd, Hungerford, Berks.
Fenlan, Olney, Bucks.
Tim Marshall Antiques, Tingewick, Bucks.
Simon and Penny Rumble Antiques, Chittering, Cambs.
Melody's Antique Galleries, Chester, Cheshire.
Adams Antiques, Nantwich, Cheshire.
Pillory House, Nantwich, Cheshire.
Hole in the Wall Antiques, Stockport, Cheshire.
Oak Room, Stockport, Cheshire.
Anvil Antiques, Cartmel, Cumbria.
Maggie Tallentire Antiques, Cartmel, Cumbria.
Langley Antiques, Corby Hill, Cumbria.
Jennywell Hall Antiques, Crosby Ravensworth, Cumbria.
Kendal Studios Antiques, Kendal, Cumbria.
Shire Antiques, Newby Bridge, Cumbria.
Sandgate Antiques, Penrith, Cumbria.
Winton Hall Antiques, Winton, Cumbria.
Peter Bunting Antiques, Bakewell, Derbys.
Michael Goldstone, Bakewell, Derbys.
Richard Glass, Whaley Bridge, Derbys.
Robert Byles, Bampton, Devon.
Rex Antiques, Chagford, Devon.
Cullompton Old Tannery Antiques, Cullompton, Devon.
Wickham Antiques, Honiton, Devon.
Alan Jones Antiques, Okehampton, Devon.
Colystock Antiques, Stockland, Devon.
Colin Rhodes Antiques, Yealmpton, Devon.
Bryan Chew, Wimborne Minster, Dorset.
Brown's Antiques, Barnard Castle, Durham.
Grant's Antiques, Barnard Castle, Durham.
Julia Bennet (Antiques), Dunmow, Essex.
C. and J. Mortimer and Son, Great Chesterford, Essex.
Michael Beaumont Antiques, Hempstead, Essex.
Millers Antiques Kelvedon, Kelvedon, Essex.
Freemans Antiques, Roxwell, Essex.

Lennard Antiques, Sible Hedingham, Essex.
Andrew Lelliott, Avening, Glos.
Robin Butler, Bristol, Glos.
J. and R. Bateman Antiques, Chalford, Glos.
School House Antiques, Chipping Campden, Glos.
Swan Antiques, Chipping Campden, Glos.
William H. Stokes, Cirencester, Glos.
Woodminster Antiques, Cirencester, Glos.
Mark Carter Antiques, Fairford, Glos.
Gloucester House Antiques Ltd, Fairford, Glos.
A.J. Ponsford Antiques, Gloucester, Glos.
Lemington House Antiques, Moreton-in-Marsh, Glos.
Duncan J. Baggott, Stow-on-the-Wold, Glos.
J. and J. Caspall Antiques, Stow-on-the-Wold, Glos.
Keith Hockin (Antiques) Ltd, Stow-on-the-Wold, Glos.
Priests Antiques, Stow-on-the-Wold, Glos.
Arthur Seager Antiques, Stow-on-the-Wold, Glos.
Day Antiques, Tetbury, Glos.
Peter Norden Antiques, Tetbury, Glos.
Westwood House Antiques, Tetbury, Glos.
Quatrefoil, Fordingbridge, Hants.
Cedar Antiques Limited, Hartley Wintney, Hants.
Elizabeth Viney, Stockbridge, Hants.
P. and S.N. Eddy, Leominster, Herefs.
Hubbard Antiques, Leominster, Herefs.
The Elizabethan Shop, Ross-on-Wye, Herefs.
Singleton Antiques, Ross-on-Wye, Herefs.
M. and J. Russell, Yazor, Herefs.
Dobson's Antiques, Abbots Langley, Herts.
Tim Wharton Antiques, Redbourn, Herts.
Collins Antiques (F.G. and C. Collins Ltd.), Wheathampstead, Herts.
R. Kirby Antiques, Acrise, Kent.
Dinah Stoodley & Celia Jennings, Brasted, Kent.
Michael Pearson Antiques, Canterbury, Kent.
Douglas Bryan, Cranbrook, Kent.
Old English Oak, Sandgate, Kent.
Henry Baines, Southborough, Kent.
Jackson-Grant Antiques, Teynham, Kent.
The Baron Antiques, Manchester, Lancs.
Davies Antiques, Whalley, Lancs.
Frank Nunan Antiques, Wigan, Lancs.
Lowe of Loughborough, Loughborough, Leics.
Robin Cox Antiques, Ketton, Lincs.
Audley House, Osbournby, Lincs.
Sinclair's, Stamford, Lincs.
St. Mary's Galleries, Stamford, Lincs.
J. and R. Ratcliffe, Waddington, Lincs.
Tobias Jellinek Antiques, Twickenham, Middx.
Pearse Lukies, Aylsham, Norfolk.
Arthur Brett and Sons Ltd, Norwich, Norfolk.
Nick Goodwin Exports, Guilsborough, Northants.
Doric Antiques, Upper Boddington, Northants.
Paul Hopwell Antiques, West Haddon, Northants.
E.M. Cheshire, Bingham, Notts.
Horseshoe Antiques and Gallery, Burford, Oxon.
Anthony Nielsen Antiques, Burford, Oxon.
Swan Gallery, Burford, Oxon.
Bugle Antiques, Chipping Norton, Oxon.
Key Antiques, Chipping Norton, Oxon.
Willow Antiques and the Nettlebed Antique Merchants, Nettlebed, Oxon.
Windrush Antiques, Witney, Oxon.
Witney Antiques, Witney, Oxon.
Joan Frere Antiques, Drumnadrochit, Scotland.
Strathspey Gallery, Grantown-on-Spey, Scotland.
G. & D. Ginger Antiques, Ludlow, Shrops.
Marcus Moore Antiques, Stanton, Shrops.
L. Onions - White Cottage Antiques, Tern Hill, Shrops.
Dodington Antiques, Whitchurch, Shrops.
Stuart Interiors (Antiques) Ltd, Barrington, Somerset.
Lawrence Brass, Bath, Somerset.
Frank Dux Antiques, Bath, Somerset.
Milverton Antiques, Milverton, Somerset.
Montacute Antiques, Montacute, Somerset.
Times Past, Somerton, Somerset.
Tilly Manor Antiques, West Harptree, Somerset.
Barry M. Sainsbury, Wincanton, Somerset.
John Nicholls, Leigh, Staffs.
Richard Midwinter Antiques, Newcastle-under-Lyme, Staffs.
P. Dawson Furniture Restorers, Bentley, Suffolk.
Denzil Grant Antiques, Bradfield St. George, Suffolk.
Peppers Period Pieces, Bury St. Edmunds, Suffolk.
C. & A.C. Bigden Antiques, Debenham, Suffolk.
Ian Collins Antiques, Debenham, Suffolk.
Quercus, Debenham, Suffolk.
J. and J. Baker, Lavenham,, Suffolk.
Noel Mercer Antiques, Long Melford, Suffolk.
Seabrook Antiques, Long Melford, Suffolk.
Oswald Simpson, Long Melford, Suffolk.
Suthburgh Antiques, Long Melford, Suffolk.
Trident Antiques, Long Melford, Suffolk.
Hamilton Antiques, Woodbridge, Suffolk.
Anthony Hurst Antiques, Woodbridge, Suffolk.
Suffolk House Antiques, Yoxford, Suffolk.
Stoneycroft Farm, Betchworth, Surrey.
Howard Blay Antiques, Dorking, Surrey.
Sage Antiques and Interiors, Ripley, Surrey.
Anthony Welling Antiques, Ripley, Surrey.
B. M. and E. Newlove, Surbiton, Surrey.
R. Saunders, Weybridge, Surrey.
E. and B. White, Brighton, E. Sussex.
Graham Lower, Flimwell, E. Sussex.
Herbert Gordon Gasson, Rye, E. Sussex.
Rye Antiques, Rye, E. Sussex.
Monarch Antiques, St. Leonards-on-Sea, E. Sussex.
Park View Antiques, Wadhurst, E. Sussex.
L.E. Lampard and Sons, Horsham, W. Sussex.
Cwmgwili Mill, Carmarthen, Wales.
Peter Thomas Antiques, Narberth, Wales.
Down Memory Lane, Atherstone, Warks.
King's Cottage Antiques, Leamington Spa, Warks.
The Grandfather Clock Shop, Shipston-on-Stour, Warks.
James Reeve, Warwick, Warks.
Mac Humble Antiques, Bradford-on-Avon, Wilts.
Turpin's Antiques, Little Bedwyn, Wilts.
A.J. Romain and Sons, Wilton, Wilts.
H.W. Keil Ltd, Broadway, Worcs.
R.N. Myers and Son, Gargrave, N. Yorks.
Bill Bentley, Harrogate, N. Yorks.
Derbys Antiques Ltd, Harrogate, N. Yorks.
Elaine Phillips Antiques Ltd, Harrogate, N. Yorks.
York Cottage Antiques, Helmsley, N. Yorks.
Pateley Bridge Antiques, Pateley Bridge, N. Yorks.
Roy Precious, Settle, N. Yorks.
Barry Alexander Ogleby (Jnr) Antiques, Thirsk, N. Yorks.
Chattels Antiques, Topcliffe, N. Yorks.
Coach House Antiques, Whitby, N. Yorks.

Furniture - Pine

At the Sign of the Chest of Drawers, London N1.
Islington Antiques, London N1.
Michael Lewis Antiques, London N1.
Rookery Farm Antiques, London N1.
Home to Home, London N6.
This and That (Furniture), London NW1.
Main Street Antiques, London SE10.
Abbott Antiques and Country Pine, London SE26.
The Furniture Cave, London SW10.
Remember When, London SW13.
Yesterday's Antiques, London SW14.
Woodentops Country Furniture, London SW18.
Bishops Park Antiques, London SW6.
The Pine Mine (Crewe-Read Antiques), London SW6.
Andy's All Pine, London W14.

The Old Dairy, London W4.
Antique Pine Ltd, London W5.
Terrace Antiques, London W5.
The Pine Parlour, Ampthill, Beds.
Willow Farm Pine Centre, Harlington, Beds.
Alan Hodgson, Great Shefford, Berks.
Dee's Antique Pine, Windsor and Eton, Berks.
Bourne End Antiques Centre, Bourne End, Bucks.
T. Smith, Chalfont St. Giles, Bucks.
For Pine, Chesham, Bucks.
The Pine Merchants, Great Missenden, Bucks.
Bach Antiques, Lane End, Bucks.
Jack Harness Antiques, Marlow, Bucks.
Pine Antiques, Olney, Bucks.
Tingewick Antiques Centre, Tingewick, Bucks.
Cambridge Pine, Bottisham, Cambs.
Abbey Antiques, Ramsey, Cambs.
The Edge Antiques, Alderley Edge, Cheshire.
Richmond Galleries, Chester, Cheshire.
Pine Too, Congleton, Cheshire.
Steven Blackhurst, Crewe, Cheshire.
Chapel Antiques, Nantwich, Cheshire.
Antiques and Curios, Ravensmoor, Cheshire.
Moyallon Antiques, Portadown, Co. Armagh, N. Ireland.
Herbert Gould and Co., Holywood, Co. Down, N. Ireland.
K.O. Hagan, Claudy, Co. Londonderry, N. Ireland.
Homes, Pubs and Clubs, Coleraine, Co. Londonderry, N. Ireland.
Pine and Period Furniture, Grampound, Cornwall.
Pinewood Studios, Penzance, Cornwall.
Blackwater Pine Antiques, Truro, Cornwall.
Pydar Antiques and Pine, Truro, Cornwall.
Ben Eggleston Antiques, Long Marton, Cumbria.
Utopia Antiques Ltd, Low Newton, Cumbria.
The Barn, Buxton, Derbys.
Friargate Pine and Antiques Centre, Derby, Derbys.
Tanglewood, Derby, Derbys.
Pine Antiques Workshop, Doveridge, Derbys.
Michael Allcroft Antiques, Hayfield, Derbys.
Wooden Box Antiques, Woodville, Derbys.
Gravelly Bank Pine Antiques, Yeaveley, Derbys.
W.G. Potter and Son, Axminster, Devon.
Robert Byles, Bampton, Devon.
Petticombe Manor Antiques, Bideford, Devon.
Cobweb Antiques, Cullompton, Devon.
Cullompton Old Tannery Antiques, Cullompton, Devon.
The Old Dairy - Antiques & Bygones, Honiton, Devon.
Annterior Antiques, Plymouth, Devon.
Colystock Antiques, Stockland, Devon.
King Street Curios, Tavistock, Devon.
Timepiece, Teignmouth, Devon.
Barrington Antiques, Tiverton, Devon.
Fine Pine Antiques, Totnes, Devon.
Antiques and Furnishings, Bournemouth, Dorset.
Pine on the Green, Sherborne, Dorset.
Hay Green Antiques, Blackmore, Essex.
English Rose Antiques, Coggeshall, Essex.
Partners in Pine, Coggeshall, Essex.
Dean Antiques, Colchester, Essex.
The Stores, Great Waltham, Essex.
Churchgate Antiques, Sible Hedingham, Essex.
Fox and Pheasant Antique Pine, White Colne, Essex.
Denzil Verey, Barnsley, Glos.
Oldwoods, Bristol, Glos.
Relics - Pine Furniture, Bristol, Glos.
Bed of Roses, Cheltenham, Glos.
John P. Townsend, Cheltenham, Glos.
Campden Country Pine Antiques, Chipping Campden, Glos.
Waterloo Antiques, Cirencester, Glos.
Europa Antiques, Moreton-in-Marsh, Glos.
Ronson's Architectural Effects, Norton, Glos.
Kelly Antiques, Rodley, Glos.
Morpheus - Elgin House, Tetbury, Glos.
Berkeley Antiques, Tewkesbury, Glos.
The Pine Collection, St. Peter Port, Guernsey, Channel Islands.
Pinecrafts, Bishops Waltham, Hants.
Butterfly Pine, Botley, Hants.
C.W. Buckingham, Cadnam, Hants.
Folly Farm Antiques, Crawley, Hants.
Airdale Antiques, Hartley Wintney, Hants.
Hursley Antiques, Hursley, Hants.
Burgess Farm Antiques, Morestead, Hants.
Smith & Sons, Ringwood, Hants.
The Pine Cellars, Winchester, Hants.
Old Pine Shop, Walford, Herefs.
Dobson's Antiques, Abbots Langley, Herts.
Country Life Antiques, Bushey, Herts.
Frenches Farm Antiques, King's Langley, Herts.
Galerias Segui, Cowes, Isle of Wight.
Richard Moate Antiques and Back 2 Wood Pine Stripping, Appledore, Kent.
Harriet Ann Sleigh Beds, Benenden, Kent.
Antique and Design, Canterbury, Kent.
Pine and Things, Canterbury, Kent.
Antiques & Pine and Farningham Pine, Farningham, Kent.
Penny Lampard, Headcorn, Kent.
Traditional Pine Furniture, Hythe, Kent.
Old English Pine, Sandgate, Kent.
Claremont Antiques, Tunbridge Wells, Kent.
Treasures of Woodchurch, Woodchurch, Kent.
Ann and Peter Christian, Blackpool, Lancs.
Enloc Antiques, Colne, Lancs.
Kitchenalia, Longridge, Lancs.
House Things Antiques, Hinckley, Leics.
Victoriana Architectural, Long Clawson, Leics.
Country Pine Antiques, Market Bosworth, Leics.
Abbey Antiques, Market Harborough, Leics.
Richard Kimbell Ltd, Market Harborough, Leics.
David E. Burrows, Osgathorpe, Leics.
Quorn Pine and Decoratives, Quorn, Leics.
R. A. James Antiques, Sileby, Leics.
Robert J. Kent Antiques, Frampton West, Lincs.
Bell Antiques, Grimsby, Lincs.
Kate, Hemswell Cliff, Lincs.
Moor Pine, North Kelsey Moor, Lincs.
Andrew Thomas, Stamford, Lincs.
Richard Kimbell, Enfield, Middx.
Valtone Pine, Hampton, Middx.
B & T Addrison, Downham Market, Norfolk.
Earsham Hall Pine, Earsham, Norfolk.
Heathfield Antiques, Holt, Norfolk.
Heathfield Country Pine, Holt, Norfolk.
Holt Antique Centre, Holt, Norfolk.
M.D. Cannell Antiques, Raveningham, Norfolk.
Echo Antiques, Reepham, Norfolk.
B.R. & J.B. Gunnett, Brixworth, Northants.
Richard Kimbell Ltd, Desborough, Northants.
Nick Goodwin Exports, Guilsborough, Northants.
Laila Gray Antiques, Kingsthorpe, Northants.
The Country Pine Shop, West Haddon, Northants.
The Corner Cupboard, Woodford Halse, Northants.
Hearth and Home, Belfast, N. Ireland.
Bailiffgate Antique Pine, Alnwick, Northumbs.
Haydon Bridge Antiques, Haydon Bridge, Northumbs.
Minsteracres Pine & Oak, Minsteracres, Northumbs.
Jack Spratt Antiques, Newark, Notts.
Harlequin Antiques, Nottingham, Notts.
Aston Pine Antiques, Faringdon, Oxon.
The Faringdon Antique Centre, Faringdon, Oxon.
Times Past Antiques, Auchterarder, Scotland.
London Road Antiques, Edinburgh, Scotland.
West of Scotland Antique Centre Ltd, Glasgow, Scotland.
QS Antiques and Cabinetmakers, Kilmarnock, Scotland.
Mostly Pine, Kingussie, Scotland.
Alton House Antiques, Moffat, Scotland.
Abbey Antiques, Stirling, Scotland.
Ark Antiques, Bishop's Castle, Shrops.
St. George's Antiques, Telford, Shrops.
Country Interiors, Bath, Somerset.
Lansdown Antiques, Bath, Somerset.
Pennard House Antiques, Bath, Somerset.
Antiques and Country Pine, Crewkerne, Somerset.
East St Antiques, Crewkerne, Somerset.
Hennessy, Crewkerne, Somerset.
Pennard House, East Pennard, Somerset.

Westville House Antiques, Littleton, Somerset.
Chez Chalon, Merriott, Somerset.
Milverton Antiques, Milverton, Somerset.
Bay Tree House Antiques, Weston-Super-Mare, Somerset.
Burton Antiques, Burton-on-Trent, Staffs.
Justin Pinewood Ltd, Burton-on-Trent, Staffs.
Country Cottage Interiors, Kingsley, Staffs.
Anvil Antiques Ltd, Leek, Staffs.
Gemini Trading, Leek, Staffs.
Roger Haynes - Antiques Finder, Leek, Staffs.
Guillemot, Aldeburgh, Suffolk.
Joyce Hardy Pine and Country Furniture, Hacheston, Suffolk.
Orwell Pine Co Ltd, Ipswich, Suffolk.
Carlton Road Antiques, Lowestoft, Suffolk.
Mildenhall Antiques, Mildenhall, Suffolk.
House of Christian, Ash Vale, Surrey.
Cherub Antiques, Carshalton, Surrey.
The Pine Warehouse, Egham, Surrey.
The Packhouse, Runfold, Surrey.
Yesterdays Pine, Shere, Surrey.
Euro-Pine, Sutton, Surrey.
Antique Church Furnishings, Walton-on-Thames, Surrey.
Richard Kimbell Antiques, Windlesham, Surrey.
Hadlow Down Antiques, Hadlow Down, E. Sussex.
John Bird and Annette Puttnam Antiques, Lewes, E. Sussex.
Cliffe Gallery Antiques, Lewes, E. Sussex.
Bob Hoare Pine Antiques, Lewes, E. Sussex.
Pastorale Antiques, Lewes, E. Sussex.
Graham Price Antiques Ltd, Polegate, E. Sussex.
Ann Lingard - Rope Walk Antiques, Rye, E. Sussex.
Park View Antiques, Wadhurst, E. Sussex.
Antiquities, Arundel, W. Sussex.
Squire's Pantry Pine and Antiques, Cowfold, W. Sussex.
Red Lion Antiques, Petworth, W. Sussex.
Stewart Antiques, Petworth, W. Sussex.
Northumbria Pine, Whitley Bay, Tyne and Wear.
The Furniture Cave, Aberystwyth, Wales.
Back to the Wood, Cardiff, Wales.
Cwmgwili Mill, Carmarthen, Wales.
The Pot Board, Carmarthen, Wales.
Barn Antiques, Lampeter, Wales.
Jim and Pat Ash, Llandeilo, Wales.
Heritage Restorations, Llanfair Caereinion, Wales.
The Carningli Centre, Newport, Wales.
R. and S. M. Percival Antiques, Ruthin, Wales.
Kim Scurlock, Swansea, Wales.
Granny Midge's Emporium, Wrexham, Wales.
Cottage Pine Antiques, Brinklow, Warks.
Pine and Things, Shipston-on-Stour, Warks.
The Old Bakehouse, Birmingham, W. Mids.
Tudor House Antiques, Halesowen, W. Mids.
North Wilts Exporters, Brinkworth, Wilts.
Crudwell Furniture, Crudwell, Wilts.
Pillars Antiques, Lyneham, Wilts.
Sambourne House Antiques, Minety, Wilts.
St. James Antiques, Little Malvern, Worcs.
The Antique Pine & Country Furniture Shop, Driffield, E. Yorks.
Imperial Antiques, Hull, E. Yorks.
Pieter Plantenga, Market Weighton, E. Yorks.
L.L. Ward and Son, Brandsby, N. Yorks.
Country Pine Antiques, Brompton, N. Yorks.
Heathcote Antiques, Cross Hills, N. Yorks.
Fox's Antique Pine, Easingwold, N. Yorks.
Milestone Antiques, Easingwold, N. Yorks.
The Main Pine Co, Green Hammerton, N. Yorks.
Michael Green Traditional Interiors, Harrogate, N. Yorks.
Havelocks, Harrogate, N. Yorks.
Westway Pine, Helmsley, N. Yorks.
The Emporium, Knaresborough, N. Yorks.
Daleside Antiques, Markington, N. Yorks.
Kindon Antiques Ltd, Melmerby, N. Yorks.
Northern Antiques Company, Norton, N. Yorks.
Millgate Pine & Antiques, Thirsk, N. Yorks.
Ruth Ford Antiques, York, N. Yorks.
St. John Antiques, York, N. Yorks.
Fishlake Antiques, Fishlake, S. Yorks.
Rebecca L. Calvert t/a Farmhouse Antiques, Great Houghton, S. Yorks.
A Maze of Pine and Roses, Mapplewell, S. Yorks.
Peter James Antiques, Sheffield, S. Yorks.
Aberford Antiques Ltd, Aberford, W. Yorks.
Manor Barn, Addingham, W. Yorks.
Cottingley Antiques, Bradford, W. Yorks.
K.L.M. & Co. Antiques, Lepton, W. Yorks.
Cottage Antiques, Pontefract, W. Yorks.
Memory Lane, Sowerby Bridge, W. Yorks.
Cottage Antiques (1984) Ltd, Walsden, W. Yorks.

Furniture - Victorian (1830-1901) (also Shipping Furniture and Period Furniture to the Trade)

P. Blake - Old Cottage Antiques, London E11.
Bookal's, London EC1.
Peter Chapman Antiques, London N1.
Dome Antiques (Exports) Ltd, London N1.
Furniture Vault, London N1.
The Graham Gallery, London N1.
Inheritance, London N1.
Janet Love Interiors, London N1.
Chris Newland Antiques, London N1.
Regent Antiques, London N1.
Restall Brown and Clennell Ltd, London N1.
Marcus Ross Antiques, London N1.
Finchley Fine Art Galleries, London N12.
Betty Gould and Julian Gonnermann Antiques, London N6.
Home to Home, London N6.
Crouch End Antiques, London N8.
Solomon, London N8.
G. and F. Gillingham Ltd, London NW2.
Patricia Beckman Antiques, London NW3.
David and Charles Wainwright, London NW3.
Camden Art Gallery, London NW8.
Just Desks, London NW8.
Wellington Gallery, London NW8.
Antique Warehouse, London SE1.
The Antiques Pavilion, London SE1.
Euro Antiques Warehouse, London SE1.
Oola Boola Antiques London, London SE1.
Tower Bridge Antiques, London SE1.
The Junk Shop, London SE10.
Relcy Antiques, London SE10.
Robert Whitfield Antiques, London SE10.
Peter Allen Antiques Ltd. World Wide Antique Exporters, London SE15.
Abbott Antiques and Country Pine, London SE26.
Ward Antiques, London SE7.
Antique Warehouse, London SE8.
Hilary Batstone Decorative Antiques, London SW1.
John Bly, London SW1.
General Trading Co Ltd, London SW1.
Ross Hamilton Ltd, London SW1.
Harrods Ltd, London SW1.
Hawksmoor, London SW1.
William Hotopf Antiques, London SW1.
Christopher Howe, London SW1.
Humphrey-Carrasco, London SW1.
M. and D. Lewis, London SW1.
Pairs Antiques Ltd, London SW1.
Westenholz Antiques Ltd, London SW1.
Alasdair Brown Antiques, London SW10.
Overmantels, London SW11.
Jeremy Seale Antiques, London SW13.
A. and J. Fowle, London SW16.
Chelsea Bric-a-Brac Shop Ltd, London SW19.
Prides of London, London SW3.
Antique and Modern Furniture Ltd, London SW5.
275 Antiques, London SW6.
313 Antiques, London SW6.
John Clay, London SW6.
Fergus Cochrane Antiques, London SW6.
ChristopherEdwards, London SW6.
HRW Antiques (London) Ltd, London SW6.

Eric King Antiques, London SW6.
L. and E. Kreckovic, London SW6.
Michael Luther Antiques, London SW6.
David Martin-Taylor Antiques, London SW6.
Megan Mathers Antiques, London SW6.
Rogers & Co, London SW6.
Adrian Alan Ltd, London W1.
Fortnum and Mason plc, London W1.
Arenski, London W11.
P.R. Barham, London W11.
Barham Antiques, London W11.
Benchmark Art Furniture Ltd, London W11.
Britannia Export Antiques, London W11.
Butchoff Antiques, London W11.
Judy Fox, London W11.
Graham and Green, London W11.
M. and D. Lewis, London W11.
Terence Morse and Son Ltd, London W11.
Myriad Antiques, London W11.
David and Charles Wainwright, London W11.
Trude Weaver, London W11.
Marshall Gallery, London W14.
Craven Gallery, London W2.
Jacqueline Edge, London W2.
The Old Dairy, London W4.
Aberdeen House Antiques, London W5.
The Badger, London W5.
Terrace Antiques, London W5.
Murray Thomson Ltd, London W6.
Adrian Alan Ltd, London W8.
Haslam and Whiteway, London W8.
Lewis and Lloyd, London W8.
Pamela Teignmouth and Son, London W8.
Victoria Antiques, Alderney, Alderney, Channel Islands.
Robert Harman Antiques, Ampthill, Beds.
Paris Antiques, Ampthill, Beds.
Pilgrim Antiques, Ampthill, Beds.
Guy Roe Antiques, Ampthill, Beds.
S. and S. Timms Antiques Ltd, Ampthill, Beds.
David Ball Antique Furnisher, Leighton Buzzard, Beds.
J. Denton (Antiques), Luton, Beds.
Luton Antiques Centre, Luton, Beds.
Manor Antiques, Wilstead (Wilshamstead), Beds.
Town Hall Antiques, Woburn, Beds.
Bow House Antiques, Hungerford, Berks.
Roger King Antiques, Hungerford, Berks.
Medalcrest Ltd, Hungerford, Berks.
Hill Farm Antiques, Leckhampstead, Berks.
Widmerpool House Antiques, Maidenhead, Berks.
John Connell - Wargrave Antiques, Wargrave, Berks.
Eton Antiques Partnership, Windsor and Eton, Berks.
Shirley Hayden Antiques, Windsor and Eton, Berks.
Peter J. Martin, Windsor and Eton, Berks.
Times Past Antiques, Windsor and Eton, Berks.
Woodage Antiques, Windsor and Eton, Berks.
The Cupboard Antiques, Amersham, Bucks.
June Elsworth - Beaconsfield Ltd, Beaconsfield, Bucks.
Period Furniture Showrooms, Beaconsfield, Bucks.
The Spinning Wheel, Beaconsfield, Bucks.
Fenlan, Olney, Bucks.
John Overland Antiques, Olney, Bucks.
Robin Unsworth Antiques, Olney, Bucks.
Country Furniture Shop, Penn, Bucks.
Tingewick Antiques Centre, Tingewick, Bucks.
Adrian Hornsey Ltd, Twyford, Bucks.
Jess Applin Antiques, Cambridge, Cambs.
Comberton Antiques, Comberton, Cambs.
Mere Antiques, Fowlmere, Cambs.
Sydney House Antiques, Wansford, Cambs.
Sara Frances Antiques, Alderley Edge, Cheshire.
Lostock Antiques, Altrincham, Cheshire.
Andrew Foott Antiques, Cheadle Hulme, Cheshire.
Olwyn Boustead Antiques, Chester, Cheshire.
Moor Hall Antiques, Chester, Cheshire.
John Titchner & Sons, Chester, Cheshire.
W. Buckley Antiques Exports, Congleton, Cheshire.
Glynn Interiors, Knutsford, Cheshire.
John Titchner and Sons, Littleton, Cheshire.
The Mulberry Bush, Marple Bridge, Cheshire.
Chapel Antiques, Nantwich, Cheshire.
Coppelia Antiques, Plumley, Cheshire.
Antiques Import Export UK, Stockport, Cheshire.
Hole in the Wall Antiques, Stockport, Cheshire.
Limited Editions, Stockport, Cheshire.
Page Antiques, Stockport, Cheshire.
Margaret Bedi Antiques, Billingham, Cleveland.
The Country Antiques, Antrim, Co. Antrim, N. Ireland.
Robert Christie Antiques, Ballyclare, Co. Antrim, N. Ireland.
Dunluce Antiques, Bushmills, Co. Antrim, N. Ireland.
MacHenry Antiques, Newtownabbey, Co. Antrim, N. Ireland.
Moyallon Antiques, Portadown, Co. Armagh, N. Ireland.
Downshire House Antiques, Newry, Co. Down, N. Ireland.
McCabe's Antique Galleries, Newry, Co. Down, N. Ireland.
Time & Tide Antiques, Portaferry, Co. Down, N. Ireland.
Antiques and Fine Art Gallery, Warrenpoint, Co. Down, N. Ireland.
Forge Antiques, Lisbellaw, Co. Fermanagh, N. Ireland.
K.O. Hagan, Claudy, Co. Londonderry, N. Ireland.
John Bragg Antiques, Lostwithiel, Cornwall.
Ken Ashbrook Antiques, Penzance, Cornwall.
Pydar Antiques and Pine, Truro, Cornwall.
Victoria Antiques, Wadebridge, Cornwall.
Anthemion - The Antique Shop, Cartmel, Cumbria.
Calvert Antiques, Endmoor, Cumbria.
Haughey Antiques, Kirkby Stephen, Cumbria.
Mortlake Antiques, Kirkby Stephen, Cumbria.
Water Lane Antiques, Bakewell, Derbys.
The Antiques Warehouse, Buxton, Derbys.
Maggie Mays, Buxton, Derbys.
The Penny Post Antiques, Buxton, Derbys.
Hackney House Antiques, Chesterfield, Derbys.
Ian Morris, Chesterfield, Derbys.
Wayside Antiques, Duffield, Derbys.
N. and C.A. Haslam, Grassmoor, Derbys.
Taylor Robinson Antiques, Ripley, Derbys.
Sam Savage Antiques, Ticknall, Derbys.
Nimbus Antiques, Whaley Bridge, Derbys.
Wooden Box Antiques, Woodville, Derbys.
Gravelly Bank Pine Antiques, Yeaveley, Derbys.
M. W. Dunscombe Antiques, Ashburton, Devon.
Moor Antiques, Ashburton, Devon.
Petticombe Manor Antiques, Bideford, Devon.
John Prestige Antiques, Brixham, Devon.
Alison Gosling Antiques, Budleigh Salterton, Devon.
Mills Antiques, Cullompton, Devon.
Umborne Antiques, Cullompton, Devon.
Pennies, Exeter, Devon.
House of Antiques, Honiton, Devon.
L.J. Huggett and Son, Honiton, Devon.
Lombard Antiques, Honiton, Devon.
Merchant House Antiques, Honiton, Devon.
Upstairs, Downstairs, Honiton, Devon.
Pugh's Farm Antiques, Monkton, Devon.
W. J. Woodhams, Shaldon, Devon.
Philip Andrade, South Brent, Devon.
Bygone Days Antiques, Tiverton, Devon.
The Ark Antiques & Design, Topsham, Devon.
Great Western Antiques, Torquay, Devon.
Past and Present, Totnes, Devon.
Anthony James Antiques, Whimple, Devon.
Woodbury Antiques, Woodbury, Devon.
Colin Rhodes Antiques, Yealmpton, Devon.
Antiques for All, Blandford Forum, Dorset.

Victorian Chairman, Bournemouth, Dorset.
David Mack Antiques, Branksome, Dorset.
Zona Dawson Antiques, Charlton Marshall, Dorset.
Hamptons, Christchurch, Dorset.
Tower Antiques, Cranborne, Dorset.
Michael Legg Antiques, Dorchester, Dorset.
Shaston Antiques, Shaftesbury, Dorset.
Heygate Browne Antiques, Sherborne, Dorset.
Piers Pisani Antiques, Sherborne, Dorset.
Joan and David White Antiques, Barnard Castle, Durham.
Alan Ramsey Antiques, Darlington, Durham.
Eden House Antiques, West Auckland, Durham.
Revival, Abridge, Essex.
Swan Antiques, Baythorne End, Essex.
Hay Green Antiques, Blackmore, Essex.
Nicholas Salter Antiques, Chingford, Essex.
Argentum Antiques, Coggeshall, Essex.
Lindsell Chairs, Coggeshall, Essex.
Argyll House Antiques, Felsted, Essex.
John Burls, Great Oakley, Essex.
Michael Beaumont Antiques, Hempstead, Essex.
Flowers Antiques, Ilford, Essex.
Colton Antiques, Kelvedon, Essex.
Tilly's Antiques, Leigh-on-Sea, Essex.
Clive Beardall Antiques, Maldon, Essex.
Old Barn Antiques, Matching Green, Essex.
Stone Hall Antiques, Matching Green, Essex.
West Essex Antiques, Matching Green, Essex.
Brown House Antiques, Newport, Essex.
F.G. Bruschweiler (Antiques) Ltd, Rayleigh, Essex.
Bush Antiques, Saffron Walden, Essex.
The Interior Design Shop, Saffron Walden, Essex.
Hedingham Antiques, Sible Hedingham, Essex.
Harris Antiques (Stansted), Stansted, Essex.
Linden House Antiques, Stansted, Essex.
It's About Time, Westcliff-on-Sea, Essex.
White Roding Antiques, White Roding, Essex.
Bristol Guild of Applied Art Ltd, Bristol, Glos.
Oldwoods, Bristol, Glos.
Latchford Antiques, Cheltenham, Glos.
Past & Present, Cheltenham, Glos.
Swan Antiques, Chipping Campden, Glos.
Patrick Waldron Antiques, Cirencester, Glos.
Blenheim Antiques, Fairford, Glos.
Mark Carter Antiques, Fairford, Glos.
Berry Antiques, Moreton-in-Marsh, Glos.
Europa Antiques, Moreton-in-Marsh, Glos.
Lemington House Antiques, Moreton-in-Marsh, Glos.
Elizabeth Parker, Moreton-in-Marsh, Glos.
Gary Wright Antiques, Moreton-in-Marsh, Glos.
Acorn Antiques, Stow-on-the-Wold, Glos.
Christopher Clarke Antiques Ltd, Stow-on-the-Wold, Glos.
Queens Parade Antiques Ltd, Stow-on-the-Wold, Glos.
Styles of Stow, Stow-on-the-Wold, Glos.
Ball and Claw Antiques, Tetbury, Glos.
Balmuir House Antiques, Tetbury, Glos.
The Chest of Drawers, Tetbury, Glos.
Porch House Antiques, Tetbury, Glos.
Berkeley Antiques, Tewkesbury, Glos.
St. James's Gallery Ltd, St. Peter Port, Guernsey, Channel Islands.
Butterfly Pine, Botley, Hants.
Antique House, Hartley Wintney, Hants.
Plestor Barn Antiques, Liss, Hants.
Charles Wallrock - Wick Antiques, Lymington, Hants.
Affordable Antiques, Portsmouth, Hants.
The Gallery, Portsmouth, Hants.
L. Moody, Southampton, Hants.
Gasson Antiques and Interiors, Tadley, Hants.
Gaylords, Titchfield, Hants.
J.W. Blanchard Ltd, Winchester, Hants.
Cabbages & Kings, Winchester, Hants.
Warings of Hereford, Hereford, Herefs.
John Nash Antiques and Interiors, Ledbury, Herefs.
Serendipity, Ledbury, Herefs.
Jeffery Hammond Antiques, Leominster, Herefs.
Anthony Butt Antiques, Baldock, Herts.
Hanbury Antiques, Hitchin, Herts.
Phillips of Hitchin (Antiques) Ltd, Hitchin, Herts.
Tom Salusbury Antiques, Hitchin, Herts.
J.N. Antiques, Redbourn, Herts.
New England House Antiques, Tring, Herts.
Collins Antiques (F.G. and C. Collins Ltd.), Wheathampstead, Herts.
Michael Armson (Antiques) Ltd, Wilstone, Herts.
John Corrin Antiques, Douglas, Isle of Man.
Royal Standard Antiques, Cowes, Isle of Wight.
Hayter's, Ryde, Isle of Wight.
Stablegate Antiques, Barham, Kent.
Courtyard Antiques, Brasted, Kent.
Peter Dyke, Brasted, Kent.
Keymer Son & Co. Ltd, Brasted, Kent.
Roy Massingham Antiques, Brasted, Kent.
Graham Stead Antiques, Brasted, Kent.
Conquest House Antiques, Canterbury, Kent.
Chislehurst Antiques, Chislehurst, Kent.
The Gallery, Downham, Kent.
Chevertons of Edenbridge Ltd, Edenbridge, Kent.
Alan Lord Antiques, Folkestone, Kent.
Samovar Antiques, Hythe, Kent.
Newnham Court Antiques, Maidstone, Kent.
Northfleet Hill Antiques, Northfleet, Kent.
Deo Juvante Antiques, Rochester, Kent.
J.D. and R.M. Walters, Rolvenden, Kent.
Dench Antiques, Sandgate, Kent.
Finch Antiques, Sandgate, Kent.
Michael Fitch Antiques, Sandgate, Kent.
Steppes Hill Farm Antiques, Stockbury, Kent.
Colin Wilson Antiques, Sundridge, Kent.
Sparks Antiques, Tenterden, Kent.
Devron Green Antiques, Tunbridge Wells, Kent.
Kentdale Antiques, Tunbridge Wells, Kent.
Linden Park Antiques, Tunbridge Wells, Kent.
The Pantiles Antiques, Tunbridge Wells, Kent.
Pantiles Spa Antiques, Tunbridge Wells, Kent.
Phoenix Antiques, Tunbridge Wells, Kent.
Up Country, Tunbridge Wells, Kent.
Rose and Crown Antiques, West Malling, Kent.
Apollo Antique Galleries, Westerham, Kent.
Brazil Antiques, Westerham, Kent.
Anthony J. Hook, Westerham, Kent.
Marks Antiques, Westerham, Kent.
Taylor-Smith, Westerham, Kent.
Westerham House Antiques, Westerham, Kent.
Laurens Antiques, Whitstable, Kent.
Tankerton Antiques, Whitstable, Kent.
Silvesters, Wingham, Kent.
Charles International Antiques, Wrotham, Kent.
Brun Lea Antiques (J. Waite Ltd), Burnley, Lancs.
Folly Antiques, Clitheroe, Lancs.
Cottage Antiques, Darwen, Lancs.
K.C. Antiques, Darwen, Lancs.
L. Booth Antiques and Reproductions, Freckleton, Lancs.
P.J. Brown Antiques, Haslingden, Lancs.
The Baron Antiques, Manchester, Lancs.
Bulldog Antiques, Manchester, Lancs.
R.J. O'Brien and Son Antiques Ltd, Manchester, Lancs.
Premiere Antiques, Manchester, Lancs.
Prestwich Antiques Ltd, Manchester, Lancs.
Luigino Vescovi, Morecambe, Lancs.
Brooks Antiques, Nelson, Lancs.
The Odd Chair Company, Preston, Lancs.
House Things Antiques, Hinckley, Leics.
Withers of Leicester, Hoby, Leics.
Corry's, Leicester, Leics.
Walter Moores and Son, Leicester, Leics.
Abbey Antiques, Market Harborough, Leics.
J. Stamp and Sons, Market Harborough, Leics.

Ken Smith Antiques Ltd, Narborough, Leics.
J. Green and Son, Queniborough,, Leics.
Mill on the Soar Antiques Ltd, Quorn, Leics.
Clive Underwood Antiques, Colsterworth, Lincs.
Pilgrims Antiques Centre, Gainsborough, Lincs.
Grantham Furniture Emporium, Grantham, Lincs.
Seaview Antiques, Horncastle, Lincs.
Laurence Shaw Antiques, Horncastle, Lincs.
Staines Antiques, Horncastle, Lincs.
C. and K.E. Dring, Lincoln, Lincs.
Beckside Antiques, Messingham, Lincs.
Graham Pickett Antiques, Stamford, Lincs.
Sinclair's, Stamford, Lincs.
St. George's Antiques, Stamford, Lincs.
The Antique Shop, Sutton Bridge, Lincs.
Underwoodhall Antiques, Woodhall Spa, Lincs.
V.O.C. Antiques, Woodhall Spa, Lincs.
Stefani Antiques, Liverpool, Merseyside.
Colin Stock, Rainford, Merseyside.
Decor Galleries, Southport, Merseyside.
Tony and Anne Sutcliffe Antiques, Southport, Merseyside.
Yarnall Antiques, Wallasey, Merseyside.
Cynthia Morgan Interiors, Enfield, Middx.
Kathleen Mann - The Other Shop, Harrow, Middx.
Ivy House Antiques, Acle, Norfolk.
A.E. Bush and Partners, Attleborough, Norfolk.
Brancaster Staithe Antiques, Brancaster Staithe, Norfolk.
Brockdish Antiques, Brockdish, Norfolk.
M. and A. Cringle, Burnham Market, Norfolk.
A.E. Seago, Cromer, Norfolk.
B & T Addrison, Downham Market, Norfolk.
Peter Howkins, Gt. Yarmouth, Norfolk.
Peter Robinson, Heacham, Norfolk.
Norfolk Galleries, King's Lynn, Norfolk.
Old Coach House, Long Stratton, Norfolk.
Eric Bates and Sons, North Walsham, Norfolk.
Nicholas Fowle Antiques, Norwich, Norfolk.
John Howkins Antiques, Norwich, Norfolk.
Echo Antiques, Reepham, Norfolk.
Leo Pratt and Son, South Walsham, Norfolk.
Stalham Antique Gallery, Stalham, Norfolk.
Jubilee Antiques, Tottenhill, Norfolk.
M.E. and J.E. Standley, Wymondham, Norfolk.
Brackley Antiques, Brackley, Northants.
Simon Banks Antiques, Finedon, Northants.
Huntershield Antiques, Flore, Northants.
Christopher Jones at Flore House, Flore, Northants.
F. and C.H. Cave, Northampton, Northants.
Bryan Perkins Antiques, Wellingborough, Northants.
The Corner Cupboard, Woodford Halse, Northants.
Charlotte and John Lambe, Belfast, N. Ireland.
Haydon Bridge Antiques, Haydon Bridge, Northumbs.
Boadens Antiques, Hexham, Northumbs.
Hallstile Antiques, Hexham, Northumbs.
Hedley's of Hexham, Hexham, Northumbs.
James Miller Antiques, Wooler, Northumbs.
Blacksmiths Forge, Balderton, Notts.
Rectory Bungalow Workshop, Elton, Notts.
Fair Deal Antiques, Mansfield, Notts.
Harlequin Antiques, Nottingham, Notts.
Meadow Lane Antiques, Nottingham, Notts.
Pegasus Antiques, Nottingham, Notts.
David and Carole Potter Antiques, Nottingham, Notts.
Strouds (of Southwell Antiques), Southwell, Notts.
Benson Antiques Centre & Gallery, Benson, Oxon.
Ashton Gower Antiques, Burford, Oxon.
Burford Antique Centre, Burford, Oxon.
Gateway Antiques, Burford, Oxon.
Hubert's Antiques, Burford, Oxon.
Anthony Nielsen Antiques, Burford, Oxon.
David Pickup, Burford, Oxon.
Walkers, Burford, Oxon.
Rupert Hitchcox Antiques, Chalgrove, Oxon.
Georgian House Antiques, Chipping Norton, Oxon.
Hallidays (Fine Antiques) Ltd, Dorchester-on-Thames, Oxon.
The Faringdon Antique Centre, Faringdon, Oxon.
La Chaise Antique, Faringdon, Oxon.
Richard J. Kingston, Henley-on-Thames, Oxon.
The Country Seat, Huntercombe, Oxon.
Willow Antiques and the Nettlebed Antique Merchants, Nettlebed, Oxon.
de Albuquerque Antiques, Wallingford, Oxon.
Chris and Lin O'Donnell Antiques, Wallingford, Oxon.
Cross Antiques, Watlington, Oxon.
Stephen Orton Antiques, Watlington, Oxon.
Mark Shanks, Watlington, Oxon.
Colin Greenway Antiques, Witney, Oxon.
W.R. Harvey & Co (Antiques) Ltd, Witney, Oxon.
Joan Wilkins Antiques, Witney, Oxon.
Bees Antiques, Woodstock, Oxon.
Robin Sanders and Sons, Woodstock, Oxon.
Thistle House Antiques, Woodstock, Oxon.
Swans, Oakham, Rutland.
T.J. Roberts, Uppingham, Rutland.
Woodman's House Antiques, Uppingham, Rutland.
Robert Bingley Antiques, Wing, Rutland.
Colin Wood (Antiques) Ltd, Aberdeen, Scotland.
Michael Young, Aberdeen, Scotland.
Highland Antiques, Avoch, Scotland.
T.W. Beaty, Beattock, Scotland.
Coldstream Antiques, Coldstream, Scotland.
Westport Fine Art, Dundee, Scotland.
Dunkeld Antiques, Dunkeld, Scotland.
Dunkeld Interiors, Dunkeld, Scotland.
Laurance Black Ltd, Edinburgh, Scotland.
Bruntsfield Antiques, Edinburgh, Scotland.
Alan Day Antiques, Edinburgh, Scotland.
Dunedin Antiques Ltd, Edinburgh, Scotland.
Georgian Antiques, Edinburgh, Scotland.
Tim Hardie Antiques, Edinburgh, Scotland.
London Road Antiques, Edinburgh, Scotland.
Whytock and Reid, Edinburgh, Scotland.
Young Antiques, Edinburgh, Scotland.
Pringle Antiques, Fochabers, Scotland.
Gow Antiques, Forfar, Scotland.
Albany Antiques, Glasgow, Scotland.
Butler's Furniture Galleries Ltd, Glasgow, Scotland.
Strachan Antiques, Glasgow, Scotland.
Kilmacolm Antiques Ltd, Kilmacolm, Scotland.
QS Antiques and Cabinetmakers, Kilmarnock, Scotland.
Rhudle Mill, Kilmichael Glassary, Scotland.
Miles Antiques, Kinross, Scotland.
Meigle Antiques Centre, Meigle (Perthshire), Scotland.
Newburgh Antiques, Newburgh, Scotland.
A.S. Deuchar and Son, Perth, Scotland.
Crossroads Antiques, Prestwick, Scotland.
Doveridge House of Neachley, Albrighton (Neachley), Shrops.
Mytton Antiques, Atcham, Shrops.
Bridgnorth Antiques Centre, Bridgnorth, Shrops.
Longmynd Antiques, Church Stretton, Shrops.
Hodnet Antiques, Hodnet, Shrops.
M. and R. Taylor (Antiques), Ludlow, Shrops.
Valentyne Dawes Gallery, Ludlow, Shrops.
F.C. Manser and Son Ltd, Shrewsbury, Shrops.
Quayside Antiques, Shrewsbury, Shrops.
Brian James Antiques, Telford, Shrops.

Hall's Antiques, Ash Priors, Somerset.
A J Antiques, Bath, Somerset.
The Antiques Warehouse, Bath, Somerset.
Lawrence Brass, Bath, Somerset.
Geoffrey Breeze, Bath, Somerset.
Mary Cruz, Bath, Somerset.
Kingsley Gallery, Bath, Somerset.
Montague Antiques, Bath, Somerset.
M.G.R. Exports, Bruton, Somerset.
Chris's Crackers, Carhampton, Somerset.
Guy Dennler Antiques, Dulverton, Somerset.
C.W.E. and R.I. Dyte Antiques, Highbridge, Somerset.
West End House Antiques, Ilminster, Somerset.
The Chapel at Rode, Rode, Somerset.
Selwoods, Taunton, Somerset.
Tilly Manor Antiques, West Harptree, Somerset.
John Hamblin, Yeovil, Somerset.
Gilligans Antiques, Leek, Staffs.
Milestone Antiques, Lichfield, Staffs.
Richard Midwinter Antiques, Newcastle-under-Lyme, Staffs.
Browse, Stafford, Staffs.
Manor Court Antiques, Stoke-on-Trent, Staffs.
The Potteries Antique Centre, Stoke-on-Trent, Staffs.
H.W. Heron and Son Ltd, Yoxall, Staffs.
Thompson's Gallery, Aldeburgh, Suffolk.
Galleries Antique Warehouse, Assington, Suffolk.
Saltgate Antiques, Beccles, Suffolk.
P. Dawson Furniture Restorers, Bentley, Suffolk.
Country House Antiques, Bungay, Suffolk.
Peppers Period Pieces, Bury St. Edmunds, Suffolk.
Cavendish Rose Antiques, Cavendish, Suffolk.
J. de Haan & Son, Clare, Suffolk.
Gil Adams Antiques, Debenham, Suffolk.
C. & A.C. Bigden Antiques, Debenham, Suffolk.
English and Continental Antiques, Eye, Suffolk.
Halesworth Antiques Market, Halesworth, Suffolk.
A. Abbott Antiques, Ipswich, Suffolk.
Ashley Antiques, Ipswich, Suffolk.
The Edwardian Shop, Ipswich, Suffolk.
Hubbard Antiques, Ipswich, Suffolk.
Ixworth Antiques, Ixworth, Suffolk.
Warrens Antiques Warehouse, Leiston, Suffolk.
Karen Bryan Antiques, Long Melford, Suffolk.
Roger Carling and Tess Sinclair, Long Melford, Suffolk.
Charles Antiques, Long Melford, Suffolk.
Alexander Lyall Antiques, Long Melford, Suffolk.
Carlton Road Antiques, Lowestoft, Suffolk.
Mary Palmer Antiques, Stradbroke, Suffolk.
Napier House Antiques, Sudbury, Suffolk.
Hamilton Antiques, Woodbridge, Suffolk.
Anthony Hurst Antiques, Woodbridge, Suffolk.
Lambert's Barn, Woodbridge, Suffolk.
A.G. Voss, Woodbridge, Suffolk.
J.C. Heather, Woolpit, Suffolk.
Wrentham Antiques, Wrentham, Suffolk.
House of Christian, Ash Vale, Surrey.
Dolphin Square Antiques, Dorking, Surrey.
Dorking Desk Shop, Dorking, Surrey.
Dorking Emporium Antiques Centre, Dorking, Surrey.
Harman's Antiques, Dorking, Surrey.
Holmwood Antiques, Dorking, Surrey.
The House of Bulow Antiques, Dorking, Surrey.
Mayfair Antiques, Dorking, Surrey.
Surrey Antiques, Dorking, Surrey.
West Street Antiques, Dorking, Surrey.
A. E. Booth & Son, Ewell, Surrey.
The Antiques Warehouse, Farnham, Surrey.
Christopher's Antiques, Farnham, Surrey.
M. J. Bowdery, Hindhead, Surrey.
Oriel Antiques, Hindhead, Surrey.
Glencorse Antiques, Kingston-upon-Thames, Surrey.
I.O.U. (Interesting, Old & Unusual), Lingfield, Surrey.
Elm House Antiques, Merstham, Surrey.
Michael Andrews Antiques, Milford, Surrey.
F.G. Lawrence and Sons, Redhill, Surrey.
The Gallery, Reigate, Surrey.
Antique Mart, Richmond, Surrey.
Hill Rise Antiques, Richmond, Surrey.
Marryat, Richmond, Surrey.
Roderic Antiques, Richmond, Surrey.
Sage Antiques and Interiors, Ripley, Surrey.
Cockrell Antiques, Surbiton, Surrey.
B. M. and E. Newlove, Surbiton, Surrey.
Brocante, Weybridge, Surrey.
Church House Antiques, Weybridge, Surrey.
Olde Forge Antiques, Weybridge, Surrey.
Weybridge Antiques, Weybridge, Surrey.
Country Antiques, Windlesham, Surrey.
The Old Mint House, Bexhill-on-Sea, E. Sussex.
Alexandria Antiques, Brighton, E. Sussex.
Ashton's Antiques, Brighton, E. Sussex.
Brighton Antique Wholesalers, Brighton, E. Sussex.
Alan Fitchett Antiques, Brighton, E. Sussex.
Dudley Hume, Brighton, E. Sussex.
Patrick Moorhead Antiques, Brighton, E. Sussex.
Ben Ponting Antiques, Brighton, E. Sussex.
Ruddy Antiques, Brighton, E. Sussex.
Colonial Times, Cross in Hand, E. Sussex.
Dycheling Antiques, Ditchling, E. Sussex.
Timothy Partridge Antiques, Eastbourne, E. Sussex.
Aspidistra Antiques, Forest Row, E. Sussex.
Hadlow Down Antiques, Hadlow Down, E. Sussex.
Coach House Antiques, Hastings, E. Sussex.
John Botting Antiques, Horam, E. Sussex.
Cliffe Gallery Antiques, Lewes, E. Sussex.
The Old Mint House, Pevensey, E. Sussex.
Graham Price Antiques Ltd, Polegate, E. Sussex.
Trade Wind, Rottingdean, E. Sussex.
Rye Antiques, Rye, E. Sussex.
The Old House, Seaford, E. Sussex.
Aarquebus Antiques, St. Leonards-on-Sea, E. Sussex.
Nicholas Cole Antiques, St Leonards-on-Sea, E. Sussex.
Bygones, Angmering, W. Sussex.
W.D. Priddy Antiques, Chichester, W. Sussex.
Richard Usher Antiques, Cuckfield, W. Sussex.
Callingham Antiques, Northchapel, W. Sussex.
Baskerville Antiques, Petworth, W. Sussex.
J. Du Cros Antiques, Petworth, W. Sussex.
Richard Gardner Antiques, Petworth, W. Sussex.
Red Lion Antiques, Petworth, W. Sussex.
J. Powell (Hove) Ltd, Portslade, W. Sussex.
Wilsons Antiques, Worthing, W. Sussex.
Ian Sharp Antiques, Tynemouth, Tyne and Wear.
Cwmgwili Mill, Carmarthen, Wales.
Plough House Interiors, Chepstow, Wales.
K.W. Finlay Antiques, Ciliau Aeron, Wales.
North Wales Antiques - Colwyn Bay, Colwyn Bay, Wales.
Cowbridge Antique Centre, Cowbridge, Wales.
Havard and Havard, Cowbridge, Wales.
Renaissance Antiques, Cowbridge, Wales.
Furn Davies Partnership, Holt, Wales.
Kidwelly Antiques, Kidwelly, Wales.
Barn Antiques, Lampeter, Wales.
Collinge Antiques, Llandudno Junction, Wales.
J. and R. Langford, Llangollen, Wales.
Castle Antiques, Newcastle Emlyn, Wales.
Emlyn Antiques, Newcastle Emlyn, Wales.
R. and S. M. Percival Antiques, Ruthin, Wales.
Eynon Hughes Antiques, Swansea, Wales.
Kim Scurlock, Swansea, Wales.
Barn Court Antiques, Templeton, Wales.
Clareston Antiques, Tenby, Wales.

All Old Exports Ltd., Treorchy, Wales.
Romantiques, Trevor, Wales.
Down Memory Lane, Atherstone, Warks.
Yesterdays, Leamington Spa, Warks.
Apollo Antiques Ltd, Warwick, Warks.
Fynewood Antiques, Warwick, Warks.
John Goodwin and Sons, Warwick, Warks.
Patrick and Gillian Morley Antiques, Warwick, Warks.
James Reeve, Warwick, Warks.
Don Spencer Antiques, Warwick, Warks.
Archives, Birmingham, W. Mids.
Peter Clark Antiques, Birmingham, W. Mids.
John Hubbard Antiques and Fine Art, Birmingham, W. Mids.
The Old Bakehouse, Birmingham, W. Mids.
Nicholas Green's Antiques, Coventry, W. Mids.
Retro Products, Lye, W. Mids.
Brett Wilkins Antiques, Wednesbury, W. Mids.
Golden Oldies, Wolverhampton, W. Mids.
Kimber & Son, Wolverhampton, W. Mids.
Martin Taylor Antiques, Wolverhampton, W. Mids.
Audley House Antiques, Bradford-on-Avon, Wilts.
Mac Humble Antiques, Bradford-on-Avon, Wilts.
Calne Antiques, Calne, Wilts.
Robin Shield Antiques, Cricklade, Wilts.
Andrew Britten Antiques, Malmesbury, Wilts.
Cross Hayes Antiques, Malmesbury, Wilts.
The Antique and Book Collector, Marlborough, Wilts.
Cook of Marlborough Fine Art Ltd, Marlborough, Wilts.
Alan Jaffray, Melksham, Wilts.
Derek Boston Antiques, Salisbury, Wilts.
Salisbury Antiques Warehouse, Salisbury, Wilts.
Edward Marnier Antiques, Tisbury, Wilts.
Bishopstrow Antiques, Warminster, Wilts.
Isabella Antiques, Warminster, Wilts.
Obelisk Antiques, Warminster, Wilts.
K. and A. Welch, Warminster, Wilts.
Hingstons of Wilton, Wilton, Wilts.
Barnt Green Antiques, Barnt Green, Worcs.
Carlton Antiques, Great Malvern, Worcs.
Miscellany Antiques, Great Malvern, Worcs.
S.W. Antiques, Pershore, Worcs.
Lower House Fine Antiques, Redditch, Worcs.
M. Lees and Sons, Worcester, Worcs.
Priory Antiques, Bridlington, E. Yorks.
David K. Hakeney Antiques, Hull, E. Yorks.
Houghton Hall Antiques, Market Weighton, E. Yorks.
Penny Farthing Antiques, North Cave, E. Yorks.
The Old Copper Shop and Post House Antiques, South Cave, E. Yorks.
Bennett's Antiques & Collectables, Bedale, N. Yorks.
Anthony Graham Antiques, Boroughbridge, N. Yorks .
St. James House Antiques, Boroughbridge, N. Yorks.
R.S. Wilson and Sons, Boroughbridge, N. Yorks.
Milestone Antiques, Easingwold, N. Yorks.
Elm Tree Antiques, Flaxton, N. Yorks.
Garth Antiques, Harrogate, N. Yorks.
Haworth Antiques, Harrogate, N. Yorks.
David Love, Harrogate, N. Yorks.
Chris Wilde Antiques, Harrogate, N. Yorks.
Sturman's Antiques, Hawes, N. Yorks.
Norwood House Antiques, Killinghall, N. Yorks.
Milton J. Holgate, Knaresborough, N. Yorks.
Reflections, Knaresborough, N. Yorks.
John Thompson Antiques, Knaresborough, N. Yorks.
Trade Antiques - D.D. White, Manfield, N. Yorks.
Sigma Antiques and Fine Art, Ripon, N. Yorks.
Anderson Slater Antiques, Settle, N. Yorks.
Corn Mill Antiques, Skipton, N. Yorks.
Barry Alexander Ogleby (Jnr) Antiques, Thirsk, N. Yorks.
B. Ogleby - St James' House Antiques, Thirsk, N. Yorks.
Julie Goddard Antiques, Sheffield, S. Yorks.
Peter James Antiques, Sheffield, S. Yorks.
N.P. and A. Salt Antiques, Sheffield, S. Yorks.
Top Hat Antique Centre, Sheffield, S. Yorks.
Paul Ward Antiques, Sheffield, S. Yorks.
Aberford Antiques Ltd, Aberford, W. Yorks.
Joan's Antiques, Denby Dale, W. Yorks.
Bingley Antiques, Haworth, W. Yorks.
Barleycote Hall Antiques, Keighley, W. Yorks.
The Antique Exchange, Leeds, W. Yorks.
Geary Antiques, Leeds, W. Yorks.
Windsor House Antiques (Leeds) Ltd., Leeds, W. Yorks.
Park Antiques, Menston, W. Yorks.
The Titus Gallery, Shipley, W. Yorks.

Garden Furniture, Ornaments & Statuary

The London Architectural Salvage & Supply Co. (LASSCo), London EC2.
Westland & Company, London EC2.
Gordon Gridley, London N1.
House of Steel Antiques, London N1.
Teger Trading and Bushe Antiques, London N4.
David and Charles Wainwright, London NW3.
The Old Cinema Antique Warehouse, London SE1.
Hilary Batstone Decorative Antiques, London SW1.
Seago, London SW1.
275 Antiques, London SW6.
Charles Edwards, London SW6.
Sylvia Napier Ltd, London SW6.
M. Pauw Antiques, London SW6.
Mallett at Bourdon House Ltd, London W1.
Myriad Antiques, London W11.
Clifton Little Venice, London W9.
S & J Acquisitions, Luton, Beds.
Below Stairs of Hungerford, Hungerford, Berks.
Cheshire Brick and Slate Co, Tarvin Sands, Cheshire.
The Great Northern Architectural Antique Company Ltd, Tattenhall, Cheshire.
Haughey Antiques, Kirkby Stephen, Cumbria.
Townhead Antiques, Newby Bridge, Cumbria.
Talisman, Gillingham, Dorset.
Wiffen's Antiques, Parkstone, Dorset.
I. Westrope, Birdbrook, Essex.
Julia Bennet (Antiques), Dunmow, Essex.
Ronson's Architectural Effects, Norton, Glos.
Duncan J. Baggott, Stow-on-the-Wold, Glos.
Architectural Heritage, Taddington, Glos.
Jardinique, Greatham, Hants.
Lennox Cato, Edenbridge, Kent.
Jimmy Warren Antiques, Littlebourne, Kent.
Folly Antiques, Clitheroe, Lancs.
Crowther of Syon Lodge Ltd, Isleworth, Middx.
Reindeer Antiques Ltd, Potterspury, Northants.
The Country Seat, Huntercombe, Oxon.
Willow Antiques and the Nettlebed Antique Merchants, Nettlebed, Oxon.
John Garner, Uppingham, Rutland.
Coach House Antiques Ltd, Stanley, Scotland.
David Bridgwater, Bath, Somerset.
Mayfly, Bath, Somerset.
Source, Bath, Somerset.
Walcot Reclamation, Bath, Somerset.
Dix-Sept, Framlingham, Suffolk.
Drummonds of Bramley Architectural Antiques Ltd, Bramley, Surrey.
Heath-Bullocks, Godalming, Surrey.
Sweerts de Landas, Ripley, Surrey.
The Packhouse, Runfold, Surrey.
Brighton Architectural Salvage, Brighton, E. Sussex.
Dermot and Jill Palmer Antiques, Brighton, E. Sussex.
John Bird and Annette Puttnam Antiques, Lewes, E. Sussex.
The Old Bakehouse, Birmingham, W. Mids.
Matthew Eden, Corsham, Wilts.
Holloways, Suckley, Worcs.
White House Farm Antiques, Easingwold, N. Yorks.

Glass (see also Glass Domes & Paperweights)

Carol Ketley Antiques, London N1.
Highgate Antiques, London N6.
Wilkinson plc, London SE6.
Galerie Moderne Ltd, London SW1.
William Hotopf Antiques, London SW1.
Gerald Sattin Ltd, London SW1.
Christine Bridge, London SW13.
The Dining Room Shop, London SW13.
R.A. Barnes Antiques, London SW15.
Mark J. West - Cobb Antiques Ltd, London SW19.
W.G.T.Burne (Antique Glass) Ltd, London SW20.
Christopher Sheppard, London SW7.
H.W. Newby (A.J. & M.V. Waller), London SW8.
Thomas Goode and Co (London) Ltd, London W1.
Ronald Phillips Ltd, London W1.
Wilkinson plc, London W1.
Benchmark Art Furniture Ltd, London W11.
Patricia Harbottle, London W11.
Mercury Antiques, London W11.
E.S. Phillips and Sons, London W11.
Tomkinson Stained Glass, London W11.
Craven Gallery, London W2.
Denton Antiques, London W8.
Jeanette Hayhurst Fine Glass, London W8.
Peter Shepherd Antiques, Hurst, Berks.
Cavendish Fine Arts, Sonning-on-Thames, Berks.
Berks Antiques Co Ltd, Windsor and Eton, Berks.
Gabor Cossa Antiques, Cambridge, Cambs.
Dunluce Antiques, Bushmills, Co. Antrim, N. Ireland.
Brian R. Bolt Antiques, Portballintrae, Co. Antrim, N. Ireland.
Antiques, Marazion, Cornwall.
Brownside Coach House, Alston, Cumbria.
Elizabeth and Son, Ulverston, Cumbria.
Martin and Dorothy Harper Antiques, Bakewell, Derbys.
Mary Payton Antiques, Chagford, Devon.
A & D Antiques, Blandford Forum, Dorset.
Peter Stebbing, Bournemouth, Dorset.
Quarterjack Antiques, Sturminster Newton, Dorset.
Richard Wrenn Antiques, Leigh-on-Sea, Essex.
Robin Butler, Bristol, Glos.
Potter's Antiques and Coins, Bristol, Glos.
Latchford Antiques, Cheltenham, Glos.
Rankine Taylor Antiques, Cirencester, Glos.
Grimes House Antiques & Fine Art, Moreton-in-Marsh, Glos.
Denys Sargeant, Westerham, Kent.
Jack Moore Antiques and Stained Glass, Trawden, Lancs.
Keystone Antiques, Coalville, Leics.
Liz Allport-Lomax, Coltishall, Norfolk.
Sue Miller Antiques and Collectables, Langham, Norfolk.
Dorothy's Antiques, Sheringham, Norfolk.
Laurie Leigh Antiques, Oxford, Oxon.
Joan Wilkins Antiques, Witney, Oxon.
Bees Antiques, Woodstock, Oxon.
Fine Antique Glass, Abernyte, Scotland.
Forsyth Antiques, Perth, Scotland.
Gallery One, Perth, Scotland.
Frank Dux Antiques, Bath, Somerset.
Somervale Antiques, Midsomer Norton, Somerset.
C. and R. Scattergood, Burton-on-Trent, Staffs.
Mary Palmer Antiques, Stradbroke, Suffolk.
Pat Golding, Arundel, W. Sussex.
David R. Fileman, Steyning, W. Sussex.
Delomosne and Son Ltd, North Wraxall, Wilts.
Dragon Antiques, Harrogate, N. Yorks.
York Cottage Antiques, Helmsley, N. Yorks.

Glass Domes

"Get Stuffed", London N1.
Old Father Time Clock Centre, London W11.
John Burton Natural Craft Taxidermy, Ebrington, Glos.
Heads 'n' Tails, Wiveliscombe, Somerset.

Icons (see Russian Art)

Islamic Art

Spink and Son Ltd, London SW1.
Aaron Gallery, London W1.
Emanouel Corporation (UK) Ltd, London W1.
Hadji Baba Ancient Art, London W1.
Mansour Gallery, London W1.
Bashir Mohamed Ltd, London W1.
Axia Art Consultants Ltd, London W11.
Hosains Books and Antiques, London W2.
Clive Rogers Oriental Rugs, Wraysbury, Berks.
Dennis Woodman Oriental Carpets, Kew, Surrey.

Japanese Art (see Oriental)

Jewellery (see Silver & Jewellery)

Lighting

Carlton Davidson Antiques, London N1.
Sara Lemkow, London N1.
Turn On Lighting, London N1.
The Antique Shop (Valantique), London N2.
Winchmore Antiques, London N21.
David Malik and Son Ltd, London NW10.
B.C. Metalcrafts Ltd, London NW9.
Oddiquities, London SE23.
Wilkinson plc, London SE6.
Hilary Batstone Decorative Antiques, London SW1.
Blanchard (London) Ltd, London SW1.
Hermitage Antiques plc, London SW1.
Carlton Hobbs, London SW1.
Christopher Howe, London SW1.
Jeremy Ltd, London SW1.
Lion, Witch and Lampshade, London SW1.
Rogier Antiques, London SW1.
H.W. Poulter and Son, London SW10.
Allegra's Lighthouse Antiques, London SW19.
W.G.T.Burne (Antique Glass) Ltd, London SW20.
275 Antiques, London SW6.
313 Antiques, London SW6.
Christopher Bangs, London SW6.
Fergus Cochrane Antiques, London SW6.
J. Crotty and Son Ltd, London SW6.
Charles Edwards, London SW6.
ChristopherEdwards, London SW6.
Judy Greenwood, London SW6.
Hollingshead and Co, London SW6.
The Lamp Gallery, London SW6.
Sylvia Napier Ltd, London SW6.
Old World Trading Co, London SW6.
M. Pauw Antiques, London SW6.
Tulissio De Beaumont, London SW6.
Vaughan, London SW6.
Christopher Wray's Lighting Emporium, London SW6.
Period Brass Lights, London SW7.
W. Sitch and Co. Ltd., London W1.
Stair and Company Ltd, London W1.
M. Turpin Ltd, London W1.
Jones Antique Lighting, London W11.
Marshall Gallery, London W14.
R. Davighi, London W6.
Mrs. M.E. Crick Chandeliers, London W8.
Denton Antiques, London W8.
George and Peter Cohn, London WC1.
Manor Antiques, Wilstead (Wilshamstead), Beds.
Below Stairs of Hungerford, Hungerford, Berks.
Temple Lighting (Jeanne Temple Antiques), Milton Keynes, Bucks.
Starlight, Wansford, Cambs.
The Edge Antiques, Alderley Edge, Cheshire.
Staveley Antiques, Staveley, Cumbria.
The Lantern Shop Gallery, Sidmouth, Devon.
Antique Metals, Coggeshall, Essex.
Government House, Cheltenham, Glos.
H.W. Keil (Cheltenham) Ltd, Cheltenham, Glos.
Triton Gallery, Cheltenham, Glos.
J. and J. Caspall Antiques, Stow-on-the-Wold, Glos.
Antony Preston Antiques Ltd, Stow-on-the-Wold, Glos.
Queens Parade Antiques Ltd, Stow-on-the-Wold, Glos.
Fritz Fryer Antique Lighting, Ross-on-Wye, Herefs.
Magic Lanterns, St. Albans, Herts.
Denys Sargeant, Westerham, Kent.
Prestwich Antiques Ltd, Manchester, Lancs.
The Stiffkey Lamp Shop, Stiffkey, Norfolk.
Barclay Antiques, Headington, Oxon.
Fine Antique Glass, Abernyte, Scotland.
Berland's of Edinburgh, Edinburgh, Scotland.
Mayfly, Bath, Somerset.

Ian McCarthy, Clutton, Somerset.
Odeon Antiques, Leek, Staffs.
Post House Antiques, Bletchingley, Surrey.
Rickett & Co. Antiques, Shepperton, Surrey.
Timewarp, Brighton, E. Sussex.
Libra Antiques, Hurst Green, E. Sussex.
David R. Fileman, Steyning, W. Sussex.
The Incandescent Lighting Company, Leamington Spa, Warks.
Delomosne and Son Ltd, North Wraxall, Wilts.
Inglenook Antiques, Ramsbury, Wilts.
Lower House Fine Antiques, Redditch, Worcs.
Old Flames, Easingwold, N. Yorks.
'Bobbins' Wool, Crafts, Antiques, Whitby, N. Yorks.

Maps & Prints

Ash Rare Books, London EC3.
J. Clarke-Hall Ltd, London EC4.
Boutique Fantasque, London N1.
Michael Finney Antique Prints and Books, London N1.
Judith Lassalle, London N1.
Finbar MacDonnell, London N1.
The Totteridge Gallery, London N20.
Centaur Gallery, London N6.
The Schuster Gallery, London NW2.
John Denham Gallery, London NW6.
Gallery Kaleidoscope, London NW6.
The Warwick Leadlay Gallery, London SE10.
Addison-Ross Gallery, London SW1.
Julian Hartnoll, London SW1.
Paul Mason Gallery, London SW1.
Christopher Mendez incorporating Craddock and Barnard, London SW1.
Old Maps and Prints, London SW1.
The Parker Gallery, London SW1.
Michael Parkin Fine Art Ltd, London SW1.
Henry Sotheran Ltd, London SW1.
John Bloxham (Fine Art) Ltd, London SW11.
A & C International, London SW17.
Gallery Lingard, London SW3.
Stephanie Hoppen Ltd, London SW3.
The Map House, London SW3.
Old Church Galleries, London SW3.
20th Century Gallery, London SW6.
King's Court Galleries, London SW6.
Michael Marriott Ltd, London SW6.
Trowbridge Gallery, London SW6.
Paul Orssich, London SW8.
Lumley Cazalet Ltd, London W1.
Andrew Edmunds, London W1.
H. Fritz-Denneville Fine Arts Ltd, London W1.
The O'Shea Gallery, London W1.
Jonathan Potter Ltd, London W1.
Bernard J. Shapero Rare Books, London W1.
Stephen Somerville Ltd, London W1.
Henry Sotheran Ltd, London W1.
Norman Blackburn, London W11.
Patrick Lassalle, London W11.
Justin F. Skrebowski Prints, London W11.
Bayswater Books, London W2.
Connaught Galleries, London W2.
The Lucy B. Campbell Gallery, London W8.
Crawley and Asquith Ltd, London W8.
Adrian Harrington, London W8.
Austin/Desmond Fine Art, London WC1.
J.A.L. Franks & Co, London WC1.
Robert Frew Ltd, London WC1.
London Antiquarian Book Arcade, London WC1.
The Print Room, London WC1.
Grosvenor Prints, London WC2.
Lee Jackson, London WC2.
Stage Door Prints, London WC2.
Storey's Ltd, London WC2.
Tooley Adams & Co., London WC2.
The Witch Ball, London WC2.
Graham Gallery, Burghfield Common, Berks.
The Studio Gallery, Datchet, Berks.
Jaspers Fine Arts Ltd, Maidenhead, Berks.
Grove Gallery, Windsor and Eton, Berks.
Omniphil Prints, Chesham, Bucks.
Penn Barn, Penn, Bucks.
Medina Antiquarian Maps and Prints, Winslow, Bucks.
Benet Gallery, Cambridge, Cambs.
The Lawson Gallery, Cambridge, Cambs.
Sebastian Pearson Paintings Prints and Works of Art, Cambridge, Cambs.
Old Soke Books, Peterborough, Cambs.
J. Alan Hulme, Chester, Cheshire.
Moor Hall Antiques, Chester, Cheshire.
Richard A. Nicholson, Chester, Cheshire.
Lion Gallery and Bookshop, Knutsford, Cheshire.
Harper Fine Paintings, Poynton, Cheshire.
Phyllis Arnold Gallery Antiques, Greyabbey, Co. Down, N. Ireland.
John Maggs, Falmouth, Cornwall.
Souvenir Antiques, Carlisle, Cumbria.
Archie Miles Bookshop, Gosforth, Cumbria.
Kendal Studios Antiques, Kendal, Cumbria.
R. F. G. Hollett and Son, Sedbergh, Cumbria.
Medina Gallery, Barnstaple, Devon.
Medina Gallery, Bideford, Devon.
Mary Payton Antiques, Chagford, Devon.
Chantry Bookshop and Gallery, Dartmouth, Devon.
The Lantern Shop Gallery, Sidmouth, Devon.
Birbeck Gallery, Torquay, Devon.
The Artist Gallery, Bournemouth, Dorset.
PIC's Bookshop, Bridport, Dorset.
Words Etcetera, Dorchester, Dorset.
F. Whillock, Litton Cheney, Dorset.
Antique Map and Bookshop, Puddletown, Dorset.
The Swan Gallery, Sherborne, Dorset.
The Treasure Chest, Weymouth, Dorset.
J. Shotton Antiquarian Books, Prints and Coins, Durham, Durham.
Castle Bookshop, Colchester, Essex.
Simon Hilton, Dunmow, Essex.
Newport Gallery, Newport, Essex.
Cleeve Picture Framing, Bishops Cleeve, Glos.
Alexander Gallery, Bristol, Glos.
Cotham Hill Bookshop, Bristol, Glos.
Triangle Books (inc. John Roberts Bookshop Est. 1955), Bristol, Glos.
David Bannister FRGS, Cheltenham, Glos.
Steven D. Bartrick, Gloucester, Glos.
Kenulf Fine Arts, Stow-on-the-Wold, Glos.
Talbot Court Galleries, Stow-on-the-Wold, Glos.
Vanbrugh House Antiques, Stow-on-the-Wold, Glos.
Tetbury Gallery, Tetbury, Glos.
Channel Islands Galleries Ltd, St. Peter Port, Guernsey, Channel Islands.
Geoffrey P. Gavey, Vale, Guernsey, Channel Islands.
Laurence Oxley, Alresford, Hants.
Hughes and Smeeth Ltd, Lymington, Hants.
The Petersfield Bookshop, Petersfield, Hants.
Oldfield Gallery, Portsmouth, Hants.
Bell Fine Art, Winchester, Hants.
Printed Page, Winchester, Hants.
Brobury House Gallery, Brobury, Herefs.
Moreden Prints, Leominster, Herefs.
Ross Old Book and Print Shop, Ross-on-Wye, Herefs.
Eric T. Moore, Hitchin, Herts.
Clive A. Burden, Rickmansworth, Herts.
James of St Albans, St. Albans, Herts.
Julia Margaret Cameron Gallery, Cowes, Isle of Wight.
Galerias Segui, Cowes, Isle of Wight.
The Shanklin Gallery, Shanklin, Isle of Wight.
Ventnor Rare Books, Ventnor, Isle of Wight.
Marlborough House Antiques, Yarmouth, Isle of Wight.
John Blench & Son, St. Helier, Jersey, Channel Islands.
Grange Gallery and Fine Arts Ltd, St. Helier, Jersey, Channel Islands.
The Selective Eye Gallery, St. Helier, Jersey, Channel Islands.
Thesaurus (Jersey) Ltd, St. Helier, Jersey, Channel Islands.
The Canterbury Bookshop, Canterbury, Kent.
Chaucer Bookshop, Canterbury, Kent.
Leadenhall Gallery, Canterbury, Kent.
Cranbrook Gallery, Cranbrook, Kent.
G. and D.I. Marrin and Sons, Folkestone, Kent.
The China Locker, Lamberhurst, Kent.
Periwinkle Press, Newnham, Kent.
Langley Galleries, Rochester, Kent.
Devron Green Antiques, Tunbridge Wells, Kent.
London House Antiques, Westerham, Kent.
W.B. McCormack, Lancaster, Lancs.
Forest Books of Cheshire, Manchester, Lancs.
Halewood and Sons, Preston, Lancs.
Leics Sporting Gallery and Brown Jack Bookshop, Lubenham, Leics.
P.J. Cassidy (Books), Holbeach, Lincs.
Golden Goose Books, Lincoln, Lincs.

Harlequin Gallery, Lincoln, Lincs.
Lyver & Boydell Galleries, Liverpool, Merseyside.
The Hampton Hill Gallery, Hampton Hill, Middx.
The Coach House, Costessey, Norfolk.
David Ferrow, Gt. Yarmouth, Norfolk.
The Haven Gallery, Gt. Yarmouth, Norfolk.
Baron Art, Holt, Norfolk.
In the Picture (The Golf Collection), Holt, Norfolk.
Baron Art, Kelling, Norfolk.
J & D Clarke Book and Print Dealers, Norwich, Norfolk.
Crome Gallery and Frame Shop, Norwich, Norfolk.
Peter Crowe, Antiquarian Book Seller, Norwich, Norfolk.
Right Angle, Brackley, Northants.
Savage Fine Art, Haselbech, Northants.
The Bookstore, Northampton, Northants.
Park Gallery & Bookshop, Wellingborough, Northants.
Jane Neville Gallery, Aslockton, Notts.
TRADA, Chipping Norton, Oxon.
Rob Dixon Fine Engravings, Culham, Oxon.
The Barry M. Keene Gallery, Henley-on-Thames, Oxon.
Elizabeth Harvey-Lee, North Aston, Oxon.
Magna Gallery, Oxford, Oxon.
Sanders of Oxford Ltd, Oxford, Oxon.
Churchgate Antiques, Empingham, Rutland.
The Old House Gallery, Oakham, Rutland.
Marc Oxley Fine Art, Uppingham, Rutland.
The McEwan Gallery, Ballater, Scotland.
Calton Gallery, Edinburgh, Scotland.
The Carson Clark Gallery - Scotland's Map Heritage Centre, Edinburgh, Scotland.
Alan Rankin, Edinburgh, Scotland.
A. and F. McIlreavy Rare and Interesting Books, St. Andrews, Scotland.
The Mount, Woore, Shrops.
Andrew Dando, Bath, Somerset.
Patterson Liddle, Bath, Somerset.
Sarah Russell Rare Antiquarian Prints, Bath, Somerset.
Trimbridge Galleries, Bath, Somerset.
Michael Lewis Gallery, Bruton, Somerset.
Julian Armytage, Crewkerne, Somerset.
House of Antiquity, Nether Stowey, Somerset.
The Bournemouth Gallery Ltd, Lichfield, Staffs.
Besleys Books, Beccles, Suffolk.
Suthburgh Antiques, Long Melford, Suffolk.
Dolphin Square Antiques, Dorking, Surrey.
King's Court Galleries, Dorking, Surrey.
Vandeleur Antiquarian Books, Epsom, Surrey.
Reigate Galleries Ltd, Reigate, Surrey.
Palmer Galleries, Richmond, Surrey.
Leoframes, Brighton, E. Sussex.
The Witch Ball, Brighton, E. Sussex.
A. & T. Gibbard, Eastbourne, E. Sussex.
Murray Brown, Pevensey Bay, E. Sussex.
Ivan R. Deverall, Uckfield, E. Sussex.
Baynton-Williams, Arundel, W. Sussex.
The Antique Atlas, East Grinstead, W. Sussex.
The Antique Print Shop, East Grinstead, W. Sussex.
George House Gallery, Petworth, W. Sussex.
Julia Holmes Antique Maps and Prints, South Harting, W. Sussex.
Osborne Art and Antiques, Jesmond,, Tyne and Wear.
H.K. Lockyer, Abergavenny, Wales.
David Windsor Gallery, Bangor, Wales.
Maps, Prints and Books, Brecon, Wales.
Manor House Fine Arts, Cardiff, Wales.
Glance Back Bookshop, Chepstow, Wales.
Glance Gallery, Chepstow, Wales.
Philip Davies Fine Art, Swansea, Wales.
Edward Lawson Studio, Swansea, Wales.
Robert Vaughan, Stratford-upon-Avon, Warks.
Eastgate Fine Arts, Warwick, Warks.
Carleton Gallery, Birmingham, W. Mids.
D.M. Beach, Salisbury, Wilts.
Bracebridge Fine Art, Astwood Bank, Worcs.
Gandolfi House, Malvern Wells, Worcs.
Antique Map and Print Gallery, Worcester, Worcs.
The Grove Country Bookshop with Coopers of Ilkley, Bolton Abbey, N. Yorks.
The Great Ayton Bookshop, Great Ayton, N. Yorks.
Country Connections (Esk House Arts), Grosmont, N. Yorks.
McTague of Harrogate, Harrogate, N. Yorks.
Minster Gate Bookshop, York, N. Yorks.
Alan Hill Books, Sheffield, Sheffield, S. Yorks.
The Grove Bookshop, Ilkley, W. Yorks.
Oakwood Gallery, Leeds, W. Yorks.

Metalware/work

Heritage Antiques, London N1.
House of Steel Antiques, London N1.
Sara Lemkow, London N1.
Robert Young Antiques, London SW11.
Chelsea Bric-a-Brac Shop Ltd, London SW19.
Christopher Bangs, London SW6.
Peter Place Antiques, London SW6.
Jack Casimir Ltd, London W11.
Johnny Von Pflugh Antiques, London W11.
Graham Walpole, London W11.
Manor Antiques, Wilstead (Wilshamstead), Beds.
Christopher Sykes Antiques, Woburn, Beds.
Below Stairs of Hungerford, Hungerford, Berks.
The Fire Place (Hungerford) Ltd, Hungerford, Berks.
Turpins Antiques, Hungerford, Berks.
Berks Metal Finishers Ltd, Sandhurst, Berks.
Peter J. Martin, Windsor and Eton, Berks.
Sundial Antiques, Amersham, Bucks.
Phoenix Antiques, Fordham, Cambs.
A.P. and M.A. Haylett, Outwell, Cambs.
The Antique Shop, Chester, Cheshire.
Antiques and Curios, Ravensmoor, Cheshire.
Shire Antiques, Newby Bridge, Cumbria.
Pamela Elsom - Antiques, Ashbourne, Derbys.
Martin and Dorothy Harper Antiques, Bakewell, Derbys.
Water Lane Antiques, Bakewell, Derbys.
Roderick Butler, Honiton, Devon.
Morchard Bishop Antiques, Morchard Bishop, Devon.
Alan Jones Antiques, Okehampton, Devon.
Peter Stebbing, Bournemouth, Dorset.
J.B. Antiques, Wimborne Minster, Dorset.
Antique Metals, Coggeshall, Essex.
Richard Wrenn Antiques, Leigh-on-Sea, Essex.
William H. Stokes, Cirencester, Glos.
J. and J. Caspall Antiques, Stow-on-the-Wold, Glos.
Christopher Clarke Antiques Ltd, Stow-on-the-Wold, Glos.
Country Life Antiques, Stow-on-the-Wold, Glos.
Keith Hockin (Antiques) Ltd, Stow-on-the-Wold, Glos.
Huntington Antiques Ltd, Stow-on-the-Wold, Glos.
Arthur Seager Antiques, Stow-on-the-Wold, Glos.
Muriel Lindsay, Winchcombe, Glos.
Prichard Antiques, Winchcombe, Glos.
Cedar Antiques Limited, Hartley Wintney, Hants.
Cull Antiques, Petersfield, Hants.
Elizabeth Viney, Stockbridge, Hants.
P. and S.N. Eddy, Leominster, Herefs.
Hubbard Antiques, Leominster, Herefs.
Michael Gander, Hitchin, Herts.
Two Maids Antiques, Biddenden, Kent.
Dinah Stoodley & Celia Jennings, Brasted, Kent.
James Porter Antiques, Sandwich, Kent.
E.W. Webster, Bickerstaffe, Lancs.
House Things Antiques, Hinckley, Leics.
V.O.C. Antiques, Woodhall Spa, Lincs.
Peter Robinson, Heacham, Norfolk.
Arthur Brett and Sons Ltd, Norwich, Norfolk.
M.D. Cannell Antiques, Raveningham, Norfolk.
Huntershield Antiques, Flore, Northants.

Rococo Antiques and Interiors, Weedon, Northants.
Mark Seabrook Antiques, West Haddon, Northants.
E.M. Cheshire, Bingham, Notts.
Jonathan Fyson Antiques, Burford, Oxon.
Horseshoe Antiques and Gallery, Burford, Oxon.
Anthony Nielsen Antiques, Burford, Oxon.
Key Antiques, Chipping Norton, Oxon.
Mike Ottrey Antiques, Wallingford, Oxon.
Joan Wilkins Antiques, Witney, Oxon.
Witney Antiques, Witney, Oxon.
Unicorn Antiques, Edinburgh, Scotland.
Tim Wright Antiques, Glasgow, Scotland.
Brian and Caroline Craik Ltd, Bath, Somerset.
Source, Bath, Somerset.
Ian McCarthy, Clutton, Somerset.
Montacute Antiques, Montacute, Somerset.
Lords Antiques, Taunton, Somerset.
Bernard G. House, Wells, Somerset.
Tilly Manor Antiques, West Harptree, Somerset.
Peppers Period Pieces, Bury St. Edmunds, Suffolk.
J. and J. Baker, Lavenham,, Suffolk.
Oswald Simpson, Long Melford, Suffolk.
Suffolk House Antiques, Yoxford, Suffolk.
Anthony Welling Antiques, Ripley, Surrey.
Rickett & Co. Antiques, Shepperton, Surrey.
Wellers Restoration Centre, Eastbourne, E. Sussex.
Rye Antiques, Rye, E. Sussex.
Park View Antiques, Wadhurst, E. Sussex.
Michael Wakelin and Helen Linfield, Billingshurst, W. Sussex.
J. Du Cros Antiques, Petworth, W. Sussex.
Retro Products, Lye, W. Mids.
Avon Antiques, Bradford-on-Avon, Wilts.
Town and Country Antiques, Bradford-on-Avon, Wilts.
Combe Cottage Antiques, Castle Combe, Wilts.
Harriet Fairfax Fireplaces and General Antiques, Langley Burrell, Wilts.
Turpin's Antiques, Little Bedwyn, Wilts.
Rupert Gentle Antiques, Milton Lilbourne, Wilts.
H.W. Keil Ltd, Broadway, Worcs.
D & J Lines Antiques, Worcester, Worcs.
Bill Bentley, Harrogate, N. Yorks.
Garth Antiques, Harrogate, N. Yorks.
Charles Lumb and Sons Ltd, Harrogate, N. Yorks.
Elaine Phillips Antiques Ltd, Harrogate, N. Yorks.
York Cottage Antiques, Helmsley, N. Yorks.
Aura Antiques, Masham, N. Yorks.
E. Thistlethwaite, Settle, N. Yorks.
Garth Antiques, Whixley, N. Yorks.
Minster Antiques, York, N. Yorks.
Geary Antiques, Leeds, W. Yorks.

Miniatures

D.S. Lavender (Antiques) Ltd, London W1.
S.J. Phillips Ltd, London W1.
H. and W. Deutsch Antiques, London W8.
Wendover Antiques, Wendover, Bucks.
Simon Brett, Moreton-in-Marsh, Glos.
Michael Sim, Chislehurst, Kent.
Regal Antiques, Westerham, Kent.
Gough Bros. Art Shop and Gallery, Bognor Regis, W. Sussex.
Arden Gallery, Henley-in-Arden, Warks.

Mirrors

Julian Antiques, London N1.
Tapsell Antiques, London N1.
Anno Domini Antiques, London SW1.
Ossowski, London SW1.
Overmantels, London SW11.
Joy McDonald, London SW13.
Norman Adams Ltd, London SW3.
Anthony James and Son Ltd, London SW3.
Peter Lipitch Ltd, London SW3.
Clifford Wright Antiques Ltd, London SW3.
275 Antiques, London SW6.
House of Mirrors, London SW6.
Peter Hurford Antiques, London SW6.
P.L. James, London SW6.
Through the Looking Glass Ltd, London SW6.
Ferenc Toth, London SW6.
Brian Fielden, London W1.
Stair and Company Ltd, London W1.
M. Turpin Ltd, London W1.
Oakstar Ltd, London W11.
Valerie Howard, London W8.
Through the Looking Glass Ltd, London W8.
Woodage Antiques, Windsor and Eton, Berks.
Doddington House Antiques, Doddington, Cambs.
Cullompton Antique Mirrors, Cullompton, Devon.
Simpsons - Bespoke Carvings, Brentwood, Essex.
Triton Gallery, Cheltenham, Glos.
Stow Antiques, Stow-on-the-Wold, Glos.
Balmuir House Antiques, Tetbury, Glos.
Chatelain Antiques and Interior Decoration, Hereford, Herefs.
The Windhill Antiquary, Bishop's Stortford, Herts.
Ashton Gower Antiques, Burford, Oxon.
Tattersall's, Uppingham, Rutland.
Looking Glass of Bath, Bath, S omerset.
Quiet Street Antiques, Bath, Somerset.
Molland Antique Mirrors, Leek, Staffs.
J. de Haan & Son, Clare, Suffolk.
The Gallery, Reigate, Surrey.
Dermot and Jill Palmer Antiques, Brighton, E. Sussex.
Julian Antiques, Hurstpierpoint, W. Sussex.
Penoyre Antiques, Pershore, Worcs.
W. Greenwood (Fine Art), Burneston, N. Yorks.

Musical Instruments, Boxes & Literature

Boxes and Musical Instruments, London E8.
Vincent Freeman, London N1.
Tony Bingham, London NW3.
Otto Haas (A. and M. Rosenthal), London NW3.
Talking Machine, London NW4.
H. Baron, London NW6.
Robert Morley and Co Ltd, London SE13.
William Reeves Bookseller Ltd, London SW16.
John and Arthur Beare, London W1.
Peter Biddulph, London W1.
Pelham Galleries Ltd, London W1.
Mayflower Antiques, London W11.
Travis and Emery, London WC2.
Times Past Antiques, Windsor and Eton, Berks.
Mill Farm Antiques, Disley, Cheshire.
Bruntsfield Antiques, Edinburgh, Scotland.

Oil Paintings

Royal Exchange Art Gallery, London EC3.
Peter Chapman Antiques, London N1.
The Graham Gallery, London N1.
Inheritance, London N1.
Swan Fine Art, London N1.
Finchley Fine Art Galleries, London N12.
Martin Henham (Antiques), London N2.
Lauri Stewart - Fine Art, London N2.
The Totteridge Gallery, London N20.
Centaur Gallery, London N6.
Sandra Lummis Fine Art, London N8.
Barkes and Barkes, London NW1.
Gunter Fine Art, London NW2.
Leask Ward, London NW3.
Duncan R. Miller Fine Arts, London NW3.
Newhart (Pictures) Ltd, London NW3.
John Denham Gallery, London NW6.
Gallery Kaleidoscope, London NW6.
Camden Art Gallery, London NW8.
Nicholas Drummond/Wrawby Moor Art Gallery Ltd, London NW8.
Patricia Harvey Antiques and Decoration, London NW8.
The Greenwich Gallery, London SE10.
Relcy Antiques, London SE10.
Didier Aaron (London)Ltd, London SW1.
Ackermann & Johnson, London SW1.
Addison-Ross Gallery, London SW1.
Verner Åmell Ltd, London SW1.
Antiquus, London SW1.
Chris Beetles Ltd, London SW1.
John Bly, London SW1.
Brisigotti Antiques Ltd, London SW1.
David Carritt Limited, London SW1.
Miles Wynn Cato, London SW1.
Chaucer Fine Arts Ltd, London SW1.
Cox and Company, London SW1.
Simon Dickinson Ltd, London SW1.
Douwes Fine Art Ltd, London SW1.
Eaton Gallery, London SW1.

Frost and Reed Ltd (Est. 1808), London SW1.
Martyn Gregory Gallery, London SW1.
Ross Hamilton Ltd, London SW1.
Harrods Ltd, London SW1.
Julian Hartnoll, London SW1.
Hawksmoor, London SW1.
Hazlitt, Gooden and Fox Ltd, London SW1.
Hermitage Antiques plc, London SW1.
Carlton Hobbs, London SW1.
Christopher Hull Gallery, London SW1.
Sally Hunter Fine Art, London SW1.
Malcolm Innes Gallery, London SW1.
Derek Johns Ltd, London SW1.
MacConnal-Mason Gallery, London SW1.
The Mall Galleries, London SW1.
Paul Mason Gallery, London SW1.
Mathaf Gallery Ltd, London SW1.
Matthiesen Fine Art Ltd., London SW1.
Moreton Street Gallery, London SW1.
Guy Morrison, London SW1.
Peter Nahum at The Leicester Galleries, London SW1.
Pairs Antiques Ltd, London SW1.
Paisnel Gallery, London SW1.
The Parker Gallery, London SW1.
Michael Parkin Fine Art Ltd, London SW1.
Polak Gallery, London SW1.
Portland Gallery, London SW1.
Steven Rich & Michael Rich, London SW1.
Julian Simon Fine Art Ltd, London SW1.
Spink and Son Ltd, London SW1.
Bill Thomson - Albany Gallery, London SW1.
Trafalgar Galleries, London SW1.
Rafael Valls Ltd, London SW1.
Rafael Valls Ltd, London SW1.
Johnny Van Haeften Ltd, London SW1.
Waterman Fine Art Ltd, London SW1.
Whitford Fine Art, London SW1.
Wildenstein and Co Ltd, London SW1.
Jonathan Clark & Co, London SW10.
Collins and Hastie Ltd, London SW10.
Hollywood Road Gallery, London SW10.
Lane Fine Art Ltd, London SW10.
Offer Waterman and Co. Fine Art, London SW10.
Park Walk Gallery, London SW10.
Pawsey and Payne, London SW10.
John Bloxham (Fine Art) Ltd, London SW11.
Alton Gallery, London SW13.
New Grafton Gallery, London SW13.
A & C International, London SW17.
Ted Few, London SW17.
The David Curzon Gallery, London SW19.
Kensington Sporting Paintings Ltd, London SW20.
The Andipa Gallery, London SW3.
Campbell's of Walton Street, London SW3.
Colin Denny Ltd, London SW3.
Gallery Lingard, London SW3.
Stephanie Hoppen Ltd, London SW3.
20th Century Gallery, London SW6.
Rupert Cavendish Antiques, London SW6.
Charles Edwards, London SW6.
John Spink, London SW6.
Julie Collino, London SW7.
The Taylor Gallery, London SW7.
The Wyllie Gallery, London SW7.
Agnew's, London W1.
Konrad O. Bernheimer Ltd, London W1.
Browse and Darby Ltd, London W1.
Burlington Paintings Ltd, London W1.
P. and D. Colnaghi & Co Ltd, London W1.
Connaught Brown plc, London W1.
Editions Graphiques Gallery, London W1.
The Fine Art Society plc, London W1.
H. Fritz-Denneville Fine Arts Ltd, London W1.
Deborah Gage (Works of Art) Ltd, London W1.
Thomas Gibson Fine Art Ltd, London W1.
Richard Green, London W1.
Hahn and Son Fine Art Dealers, London W1.
The Lefevre Gallery, London W1.
Maas Gallery, London W1.
Mallett Gallery, London W1.
Marlborough Fine Art (London) Ltd, London W1.
David Messum, London W1.
Roy Miles Gallery, London W1.
John Mitchell and Son, London W1.
Noortman, London W1.
Hal O'Nians, London W1.
Partridge Fine Arts plc, London W1.
W.H. Patterson Fine Arts Ltd, London W1.
Pyms Gallery, London W1.
Stephen Somerville Ltd, London W1.
Spink Leger Pictures, London W1.
Stoppenbach and Delestre Ltd, London W1.
William Thuillier, London W1.
Tryon & Swann Gallery, London W1.
Walpole Gallery, London W1.
Waterhouse and Dodd, London W1.
The Weiss Gallery, London W1.
Wilkins and Wilkins, London W1.
Williams and Son, London W1.
Michael Aalders, London W11.
Addison Fine Art, London W11.
Arenski, London W11.
Butchoff Antiques, London W11.
Caelt Gallery, London W11.
Curá Antiques, London W11.
Charles Daggett Gallery, London W11.
Fleur de Lys Gallery, London W11.
Gavin Graham Gallery, London W11.
Lacy Gallery, London W11.
Milne and Moller, London W11.
Philp, London W11.
Piano Nobile Fine Paintings, London W11.
Justin F. Skrebowski Prints, London W11.
Stern Art Dealers, London W11.
Johnny Von Pflugh Antiques, London W11.
Stephen Garratt (Fine Paintings), London W14.
Marshall Gallery, London W14.
Manya Igel Fine Arts Ltd, London W2.
Aberdeen House Antiques, London W5.
Ealing Gallery, London W5.
Baumkotter Gallery, London W8.
Crawley and Asquith Ltd, London W8.
George Dare, London W8.
Sabin Galleries Ltd, London W8.
Austin/Desmond Fine Art, London WC1.
Baroq at Brindleys, Heath and Reach, Beds.
Foye Gallery, Luton, Beds.
Woburn Fine Arts, Woburn, Beds.
Graham Gallery, Burghfield Common, Berks.
The Studio Gallery, Datchet, Berks.
John A. Pearson Antiques, Horton, Berks.
Jaspers Fine Arts Ltd, Maidenhead, Berks.
The Coworth Gallery, Sunningdale, Berks.
Grove Gallery, Windsor and Eton, Berks.
H.S. Wellby Ltd, Haddenham, Bucks.
Penn Barn, Penn, Bucks.
Cambridge Fine Art Ltd, Cambridge, Cambs.
The Lawson Gallery, Cambridge, Cambs.
Sebastian Pearson Paintings Prints and Works of Art, Cambridge, Cambs.
Baron Fine Art, Chester, Cheshire.
Harper Fine Paintings, Poynton, Cheshire.
Margaret Bedi Antiques, Billingham, Cleveland.
T.B. and R. Jordan (Fine Paintings), Eaglescliffe, Cleveland.
Dunluce Antiques, Bushmills, Co. Antrim, N. Ireland.
Antiques and Fine Art Gallery, Warrenpoint, Co. Down, N. Ireland.
Copperhouse Gallery - W. Dyer & Sons, Hayle, Cornwall.
Tony Sanders Penzance Gallery and Antiques, Penzance, Cornwall.
Myles Varcoe, Tywardreath, Cornwall.
Peter Haworth, Beetham, Cumbria.
The Gallery, Penrith, Cumbria.
R. F. G. Hollett and Son, Sedbergh, Cumbria.
Kenneth Upchurch, Ashbourne, Derbys.
Charles H. Ward, Derby, Derbys.
J. Collins and Son, Bideford, Devon.
Medina Gallery, Bideford, Devon.
Mill Gallery, Ermington, Devon.
Honiton Fine Art, Honiton, Devon.
Skeaping Gallery, Lydford, Devon.
Gordon Hepworth Fine Art, Newton St. Cyres, Devon.
Michael Wood Fine Art, Plymouth, Devon.
Bygone Days Antiques, Tiverton, Devon.
Birbeck Gallery, Torquay, Devon.
Stour Gallery, Blandford Forum, Dorset.
Hants Gallery, Bournemouth, Dorset.
Brandler Galleries, Brentwood, Essex.
Neil Graham Gallery, Brentwood, Essex.
S. Bond and Son, Colchester, Essex.
Simon Hilton, Dunmow, Essex.
C. and J. Mortimer and Son, Great Chesterford, Essex.
John Burls, Great Oakley, Essex.

Thomas Sykes Antiques, Kelvedon, Essex.
Newport Gallery, Newport, Essex.
David Lloyd Gallery, Purleigh, Essex.
Reddings Art and Antiques, Southend-on-Sea, Essex.
Galerie Lev, Woodford Green, Essex.
Cleeve Picture Framing, Bishops Cleeve, Glos.
The Priory Gallery, Bishops Cleeve, Glos.
Alexander Gallery, Bristol, Glos.
David Howard, Cheltenham, Glos.
H.W. Keil (Cheltenham) Ltd, Cheltenham, Glos.
Manor House Gallery, Cheltenham, Glos.
Triton Gallery, Cheltenham, Glos.
School House Antiques, Chipping Campden, Glos.
P.J. Ward Fine Paintings, Cirencester, Glos.
Gerard Campbell, Lechlade, Glos.
Astley House - Fine Art, Moreton-in-Marsh, Glos.
Astley House - Fine Art, Moreton-in-Marsh, Glos.
Berry Antiques, Moreton-in-Marsh, Glos.
Grimes House Antiques & Fine Art, Moreton-in-Marsh, Glos.
Southgate Gallery, Moreton-in-Marsh, Glos.
Nina Zborowska, Painswick, Glos.
Baggott Church Street Ltd, Stow-on-the-Wold, Glos.
Cotswold Galleries, Stow-on-the-Wold, Glos.
The John Davies Gallery, Stow-on-the-Wold, Glos.
The Fosse Gallery, Stow-on-the-Wold, Glos.
Fosse Way Antiques, Stow-on-the-Wold, Glos.
Kenulf Fine Arts, Stow-on-the-Wold, Glos.
Roger Lamb Antiques & Works of Art, Stow-on-the-Wold, Glos.
Arthur Seager Antiques, Stow-on-the-Wold, Glos.
Balmuir House Antiques, Tetbury, Glos.
Tetbury Gallery, Tetbury, Glos.
Brian Sinfield - Compton Cassey Gallery, Withington, Glos.
Mark Blower Antiques, St. Martin, Guernsey, Channel Islands.
Channel Islands Galleries Ltd, St. Peter Port, Guernsey, Channel Islands.
St. James's Gallery Ltd, St. Peter Port, Guernsey, Channel Islands.
Geoffrey P. Gavey, Vale, Guernsey, Channel Islands.
Antique House, Hartley Wintney, Hants.
Corfields Ltd, Lymington, Hants.
Robert Perera Fine Art, Lymington, Hants.
The Petersfield Bookshop, Petersfield, Hants.
Lacewing Fine Art Gallery, Romsey, Hants.
Bell Fine Art, Winchester, Hants.
Webb Fine Arts, Winchester, Hants.
Countrylife Gallery, Hitchin, Herts.
Carole Thomas (Fine Arts), Hitchin, Herts.
The Shanklin Gallery, Shanklin, Isle of Wight.
Falle Fine Art Limited, St Helier, Jersey, Channel Islands.
Falle Fine Art Limited, St Helier, Jersey, Channel Islands.
Grange Gallery and Fine Arts Ltd, St. Helier, Jersey, Channel Islands.
The Selective Eye Gallery, St. Helier, Jersey, Channel Islands.
I.G.A. Old Masters Ltd, St. Lawrence, Jersey, Channel Islands.
Peter Dyke, Brasted, Kent.
Michael Sim, Chislehurst, Kent.
Francis Iles, Rochester, Kent.
Langley Galleries, Rochester, Kent.
Alexandra's Antiques, St. Margaret's Bay, Kent.
Sundridge Gallery, Sundridge, Kent.
Sparks Antiques, Tenterden, Kent.
Nicholas Bowlby, Tunbridge Wells, Kent.
Devron Green Antiques, Tunbridge Wells, Kent.
Graham Gallery, Tunbridge Wells, Kent.
Pantiles Spa Antiques, Tunbridge Wells, Kent.
Apollo Antique Galleries, Westerham, Kent.
London House Antiques, Westerham, Kent.
Charnley Fine Arts, Longridge, Lancs.
Fulda Gallery Ltd, Manchester, Lancs.
St. James Antiques, Manchester, Lancs.
Henry Donn Gallery, Whitefield, Lancs.
Corry's, Leicester, Leics.
Leics Sporting Gallery and Brown Jack Bookshop, Lubenham, Leics.
P. Stanworth (Fine Arts), Market Bosworth, Leics.
Graftons of Market Harborough, Market Harborough, Leics.
Lincoln Fine Art, Lincoln, Lincs.
Lyver & Boydell Galleries, Liverpool, Merseyside.
Ailsa Gallery, Twickenham, Middx.
The Coach House, Costessey, Norfolk.
The Haven Gallery, Gt. Yarmouth, Norfolk.
Baron Art, Holt, Norfolk.
Baron Art, Kelling, Norfolk.
The Bank House Gallery, Norwich, Norfolk.
Crome Gallery and Frame Shop, Norwich, Norfolk.
The Fairhurst Gallery, Norwich, Norfolk.
Mandell's Gallery, Norwich, Norfolk.
The Westcliffe Gallery, Sheringham, Norfolk.
Staithe Lodge Gallery, Swafield, Norfolk.
Norton Antiques, Twyford, Norfolk.
Coughton Galleries Ltd, Arthingworth, Northants.
Berengar Antiques, Barnwell, Northants.
Right Angle, Brackley, Northants.
Castle Ashby Gallery, Castle Ashby, Northants.
Savage Fine Art, Haselbech, Northants.
Dragon Antiques, Kettering, Northants.
Clark Galleries, Towcester, Northants.
Ron Green, Towcester, Northants.
Bryan Perkins Antiques, Wellingborough, Northants.
The Bell Gallery, Belfast, N. Ireland.
Haydon Bridge Antiques, Haydon Bridge, Northumbs.
Haydon Gallery, Haydon Bridge, Northumbs.
Boadens Antiques, Hexham, Northumbs.
Jane Neville Gallery, Aslockton, Notts.
Anthony Mitchell Fine Paintings, Nottingham, Notts.
Benson Antiques Centre & Gallery, Benson, Oxon.
H.C. Dickins, Bloxham, Oxon.
Horseshoe Antiques and Gallery, Burford, Oxon.
Hubert's Antiques, Burford, Oxon.
The Stone Gallery, Burford, Oxon.
Swan Gallery, Burford, Oxon.
Georgian House Antiques, Chipping Norton, Oxon.
The Country Store and Linen Cupboard, Deddington, Oxon.
Hallidays (Fine Antiques) Ltd, Dorchester-on-Thames, Oxon.
The Barry M. Keene Gallery, Henley-on-Thames, Oxon.
Thames Gallery, Henley-on-Thames, Oxon.
Churchgate Antiques, Empingham, Rutland.
Fine Art of Oakham, Oakham, Rutland.
The Old House Gallery, Oakham, Rutland.
John Garner, Uppingham, Rutland.
Marc Oxley Fine Art, Uppingham, Rutland.
Atholl Antiques, Aberdeen, Scotland.
The Rendezvous Gallery, Aberdeen, Scotland.
Colin Wood (Antiques) Ltd, Aberdeen, Scotland.
Michael Young, Aberdeen, Scotland.
Paul Hayes Gallery, Auchterarder, Scotland.
Highland Antiques, Avoch, Scotland.
The McEwan Gallery, Ballater, Scotland.
Westport Fine Art, Dundee, Scotland.
Laurance Black Ltd, Edinburgh, Scotland.
Bourne Fine Art Ltd, Edinburgh, Scotland.
Calton Gallery, Edinburgh, Scotland.
Tom Fidelo, Edinburgh, Scotland.
Malcolm Innes Gallery, Edinburgh, Scotland.
John Mathieson and Co, Edinburgh, Scotland.
Open Eye Gallery Ltd, Edinburgh, Scotland.
The Scottish Gallery, Edinburgh, Scotland.
Aldric Young, Edinburgh, Scotland.
Young Antiques, Edinburgh, Scotland.
The Roger Billcliffe Fine Art, Glasgow, Scotland.
Ewan Mundy Fine Art Ltd, Glasgow, Scotland.
Inchmartine Fine Art, Inchture, Scotland.
Mainhill Gallery, Jedburgh, Scotland.
Kilmacolm Antiques Ltd, Kilmacolm, Scotland.

Newburgh Antiques, Newburgh, Scotland.
The Fitzroy Gallery (formerly The McIan Gallery), Oban, Scotland.
Gallery One, Perth, Scotland.
The George Street Gallery, Perth, Scotland.
Nigel Stacy-Marks Ltd, Perth, Scotland.
St. Andrews Fine Art, St. Andrews, Scotland.
Abbey Antiques, Stirling, Scotland.
John Boulton Fine Art, Broseley, Shrops.
Teme Valley Antiques, Ludlow, Shrops.
Valentyne Dawes Gallery, Ludlow, Shrops.
Wenlock Fine Art, Much Wenlock, Shrops.
F.C. Manser and Son Ltd, Shrewsbury, Shrops.
Haygate Gallery, Telford, Shrops.
The Mount, Woore, Shrops.
Hall's Antiques, Ash Priors, Somerset.
Adam Gallery, Bath, Somerset.
Beau Nash Antiques, Bath, Somerset.
Mary Cruz, Bath, Somerset.
AnthonyHepworth Fine Art, Bath, Somerset.
Trimbridge Galleries, Bath, Somerset.
The Court Gallery, Nether Stowey, Somerset.
Nick Cotton Fine Art, Watchet, Somerset.
Sadler Street Gallery,, Wells, Somerset.
Tim Everett, West Buckland, Somerset.
England's Gallery, Leek, Staffs.
Richard Midwinter Antiques, Newcastle-under-Lyme, Staffs.
Thompson's Gallery, Aldeburgh, Suffolk.
The Fortescue Gallery, Ipswich, Suffolk.
J. and J. Baker, Lavenham,, Suffolk.
Charles Antiques, Long Melford, Suffolk.
Trident Antiques, Long Melford, Suffolk.
Equus Art Gallery, Newmarket, Suffolk.
Peasenhall Art and Antiques Gallery, Peasenhall, Suffolk.
The Falcon Gallery, Wortham, Suffolk.
Suffolk House Antiques, Yoxford, Suffolk.
Cider House Galleries Ltd, Bletchingley, Surrey.
Cobham Galleries, Cobham, Surrey.
The Whitgift Galleries, Croydon, Surrey.
Antique Clocks by Patrick Thomas, Dorking, Surrey.
The Court Gallery, East Molesey, Surrey.
Heytesbury Antiques, Farnham, Surrey.
Glencorse Antiques, Kingston-upon-Thames, Surrey.
Bourne Gallery Ltd, Reigate, Surrey.
The Gallery, Reigate, Surrey.
Roland Goslett Gallery, Richmond, Surrey.
F. and T. Lawson Antiques, Richmond, Surrey.
Marryat, Richmond, Surrey.
Piano Nobile Fine Paintings, Richmond, Surrey.
Cedar House Gallery, Ripley, Surrey.
Sage Antiques and Interiors, Ripley, Surrey.
B. M. and E. Newlove, Surbiton, Surrey.
Boathouse Gallery, Walton-on-Thames, Surrey.
Edward Cross - Fine Paintings, Weybridge, Surrey.
Willow Gallery, Weybridge, Surrey.
Stephen Welbourne, Brighton, E. Sussex.
John Day of Eastbourne Fine Art, Eastbourne, E. Sussex.
Premier Gallery & Bookshop, Eastbourne, E. Sussex.
Stewart Gallery, Eastbourne, E. Sussex.
Delmas, Hurst Green, E. Sussex.
Murray Brown, Pevensey Bay, E. Sussex.
E. Stacy-Marks Limited, Polegate, E. Sussex.
Molly Alexander, Seaford, E. Sussex.
Susan and Robert Botting, Billingshurst, W. Sussex.
Lannards Gallery, Billingshurst, W. Sussex.
Gough Bros. Art Shop and Gallery, Bognor Regis, W. Sussex.
The Canon Gallery, Petworth, W. Sussex.
George House Gallery, Petworth, W. Sussex.
Lombard Gallery, Petworth, W. Sussex.
T.G. Wilkinson Antiques Ltd, Petworth, W. Sussex.
Wilsons Antiques, Worthing, W. Sussex.
Anna Harrison Fine Antiques, Gosforth, Tyne and Wear.
MacDonald Fine Art, Gosforth, Tyne and Wear.
Osborne Art and Antiques, Jesmond,, Tyne and Wear.
The Dean Gallery Ltd, Newcastle-upon-Tyne, Tyne and Wear.
David Windsor Gallery, Bangor, Wales.
Michael Webb Fine Art, Bodorgan, Wales.
Manor House Fine Arts, Cardiff, Wales.
Emlyn Antiques, Newcastle Emlyn, Wales.
Philip Davies Fine Art, Swansea, Wales.
Thicke Galleries, Swansea, Wales.
Barn Court Antiques, Templeton, Wales.
Welsh Art, Tywyn, Wales.
Arden Gallery, Henley-in-Arden, Warks.
Colmore Galleries Ltd, Henley-in-Arden, Warks.
Fine-Lines (Fine Art), Shipston-on-Stour, Warks.
Astley House - Fine Art, Stretton-on-Fosse, Warks.
John Hubbard Antiques and Fine Art, Birmingham, W. Mids.
Robert Withers Antiques & Paintings, Halesowen, W. Mids.
Oldswinford Gallery, Stourbridge, W. Mids.
Driffold Gallery, Sutton Coldfield, W. Mids.
Robin Shield Antiques, Cricklade, Wilts.
D.M. Beach, Salisbury, Wilts.
The Jerram Gallery, Salisbury, Wilts.
Salisbury Antiques Warehouse, Salisbury, Wilts.
Bracebridge Fine Art, Astwood Bank, Worcs.
Richard Hagen, Broadway, Worcs.
Hay Loft Gallery, Broadway, Worcs.
Haynes Fine Art of Broadway, Broadway, Worcs.
Haynes Fine Art of Broadway Picton House Galleries, Broadway, Worcs.
John Noott Galleries, Broadway, Worcs.
Malvern Arts, Great Malvern, Worcs.
Gandolfi House, Malvern Wells, Worcs.
The Highway Gallery, Upton-upon-Severn, Worcs.
James H. Starkey Galleries, Beverley, E. Yorks.
Steven Dews Fine Art, Hull, E. Yorks.
Anthony Graham Antiques, Boroughbridge, N. Yorks .
W. Greenwood (Fine Art), Burneston, N. Yorks.
Garth Antiques, Harrogate, N. Yorks.
Sutcliffe Galleries, Harrogate, N. Yorks.
Walker Galleries Ltd, Harrogate, N. Yorks.
E. Stacy-Marks Limited, Helmsley, N. Yorks.
Reflections, Knaresborough, N. Yorks.
Thirkill Antiques, Leyburn, N. Yorks.
Gary K. Blissett, Long Preston, N. Yorks.
Talents Fine Arts Ltd, Malton, N. Yorks.
Rose Fine Art and Antiques, Ripon, N. Yorks.
Roy Precious, Settle, N. Yorks.
Richard Bennett, Thirsk, N. Yorks.
Garth Antiques, Whixley, N. Yorks.
Coulter Galleries, York, N. Yorks.
The Basement Gallery at Fulwood Antiques, Sheffield, S. Yorks.
Hibbert Brothers Ltd, Sheffield, S. Yorks.
E. Carrol, Bingley, W. Yorks.
Oakwood Gallery, Leeds, W. Yorks.
The Titus Gallery, Shipley, W. Yorks.
Todmorden Fine Art, Todmorden, W. Yorks.
Robin Taylor Fine Arts, Wakefield, W. Yorks.

Oriental Items

Nanwani and Co, London EC3.
Chancery Antiques Ltd, London N1.
Hart and Rosenberg, London N1.
Inheritance, London N1.
Japanese Gallery, London N1.
Wan Li, London N1.
Laurence Mitchell Antiques Ltd, London N1.
Kevin Page Oriental Art, London N1.
Marcus Ross Antiques, London N1.
Tapsell Antiques, London N1.
East-Asia Co, London NW1.
Leask Ward, London NW3.
Malcolm Rushton - Early Oriental Art, London NW3.
Oriental Bronzes Ltd, London NW5.

Milne Henderson, London NW6.
B.C. Metalcrafts Ltd, London NW9.
Shirley Day Ltd, London SW1.
Clare Lawrence Ltd, London SW1.
Sainsbury & Mason, London SW1.
Spink and Son Ltd, London SW1.
Ki, London SW6.
Sylvia Napier Ltd, London SW6.
Daphne Rankin and Ian Conn, London SW6.
Konrad O. Bernheimer Ltd, London W1.
Brandt Oriental Art, London W1.
Barry Davies Oriental Art, London W1.
Eskenazi Ltd, London W1.
John Eskenazi Ltd, London W1.
Robert Hall, London W1.
Gerard Hawthorn Ltd, London W1.
Roger Keverne, London W1.
Sydney L. Moss Ltd, London W1.
Nicholas S. Pitcher Oriental Art, London W1.
Jonathan Robinson, London W1.
Alistair Sampson Antiques Ltd, London W1.
Robert G. Sawers, London W1.
A & J Speelman Ltd, London W1.
Toynbee-Clarke Interiors Ltd, London W1.
Jan van Beers Oriental Art, London W1.
Linda Wrigglesworth, London W1.
Cohen and Pearce (Oriental Porcelain), London W11.
M.C.N. Antiques, London W11.
The Nanking Porcelain Co, London W11.
Edric Van Vredenburgh Ltd, London W11.
AntikWest AB, London W8.
Gregg Baker Oriental Art, London W8.
Berwald Oriental Art, London W8.
David Brower Antiques, London W8.
Coats Oriental Carpets, London W8.
Cohen & Cohen, London W8.
H. and W. Deutsch Antiques, London W8.
J.A.N. Fine Art, London W8.
Japanese Gallery, London W8.
Peter Kemp, London W8.
S. Marchant & Son, London W8.
Robert McPherson, London W8.
A.V. Santos, London W8.
Sinai Antiques Ltd, London W8.
Jorge Welsh Oriental Porcelain & Works of Art, London W8.
Clive Rogers Oriental Rugs, Wraysbury, Berks.
Glade Antiques, Marlow, Bucks.
Gabor Cossa Antiques, Cambridge, Cambs.
Highland Antiques, Stockport, Cheshire.
David L.H. Southwick Rare Art, Kingswear, Devon.
Brian Taylor Antiques, Plymouth, Devon.
Mere Antiques, Topsham, Devon.
Lionel Geneen Ltd, Bournemouth, Dorset.
Oriental Gallery, Moreton-in-Marsh, Glos.
Artique, Tetbury, Glos.
Oriental Rug Gallery Ltd, St. Albans, Herts.
Michael Sim, Chislehurst, Kent.
Mandarin Gallery - Oriental Art, Otford, Kent.
Flower House Antiques, Tenterden, Kent.
The Rug Gallery, Leicester, Leics.
M.D. Cannell Antiques, Raveningham, Norfolk.
The Country Seat, Huntercombe, Oxon.
Another World, Edinburgh, Scotland.
Albany Antiques, Glasgow, Scotland.
Amber Antiques, Kincardine O'Neil, Scotland.
Peter Wain, Market Drayton, Shrops.
F.C. Manser and Son Ltd, Shrewsbury, Shrops.
Haliden Oriental Rug Shop, Bath, Somerset.
Robin Kennedy, Richmond, Surrey.
Hyndford Antiques, Brighton, E. Sussex.
Patrick Moorhead Antiques, Brighton, E. Sussex.
Brian Page Antiques, Brighton, E. Sussex.
Gensing Antiques, St. Leonards-on-Sea, E. Sussex.
Ringles Cross Antiques, Uckfield, E. Sussex.
Two Dragons Oriental Antiques, Llanerchymedd (Anglesey), Wales.
Heirloom & Howard Limited, West Yatton, Wilts.
Paul M. Peters Antiques, Harrogate, N. Yorks.

Paperweights

Garrick D. Coleman, London W11.
Garrick D. Coleman, London W8.
Sweetbriar Gallery, Helsby, Cheshire.
Portique, Bournemouth, Dorset.
Todd and Austin Antiques of Winchester, Winchester, Hants.
The Stone Gallery, Burford, Oxon.
Antiques and Fine Art, Crieff, Scotland.
David R. Fileman, Steyning, W. Sussex.

Photographs & Equipment

Jubilee Photographica, London N1.
Vintage Cameras Ltd, London SE26.
Bayswater Books, London W2.
Classic Collection, London WC1.
Jessop Classic Photographica, London WC1.
Sweetbriar Gallery, Helsby, Cheshire.
Portique, Bournemouth, Dorset.
Todd and Austin Antiques of Winchester, Winchester, Hants.
The Stone Gallery, Burford, Oxon.
Antiques and Fine Art, Crieff, Scotland.
David R. Fileman, Steyning, W. Sussex.

Porcelain and Pottery

Hart and Rosenberg, London N1.
Diana Huntley, London N1.
Carol Ketley Antiques, London N1.
Laurence Mitchell Antiques Ltd, London N1.
Jacqueline Oosthuizen, London N1.
Finchley Fine Art Galleries, London N12.
Martin Henham (Antiques), London N2.
Highgate Antiques, London N6.
D.M. and P. Manheim (Peter Manheim) Ltd, London N6.
Klaber and Klaber, London NW3.
The Collector, London NW8.
Albert Amor Ltd, London SW1.
Galerie Moderne Ltd, London SW1.
Ross Hamilton Ltd, London SW1.
Lucy Johnson, London SW1.
Le Pavillon de Sèvres Ltd, London SW1.
M. and D. Lewis, London SW1.
Gerald Sattin Ltd, London SW1.
Stephen Long, London SW10.
Robert Young Antiques, London SW11.
The Dining Room Shop, London SW13.
R.A. Barnes Antiques, London SW15.
Jacqueline Oosthuizen, London SW3.
Rogers de Rin, London SW3.
H.W. Newby (A.J. & M.V. Waller), London SW8.
Thomas Goode and Co (London) Ltd, London W1.
Harcourt Antiques, London W1.
Brian Haughton Antiques, London W1.
Alistair Sampson Antiques Ltd, London W1.
Venners Antiques, London W1.
Judy Fox, London W11.
M. and D. Lewis, London W11.
Mercury Antiques, London W11.
The Nanking Porcelain Co, London W11.
Schredds of Portobello, London W11.
The Badger, London W5.
Harold's Place, London W5.
Tony Dixon, London W6.
Garry Atkins, London W8.
David Brower Antiques, London W8.
Davies Antiques, London W8.
Richard Dennis, London W8.
H. and W. Deutsch Antiques, London W8.
Grosvenor Antiques Ltd, London W8.
Hope and Glory, London W8.
Jonathan Horne, London W8.
Valerie Howard, London W8.
Roderick Jellicoe, London W8.
Howard Jones, London W8.
Peter Kemp, London W8.
Libra Antiques, London W8.
London Antique Gallery, London W8.
E. and H. Manners, London W8.
Oliver-Sutton Antiques, London W8.
M. and D. Seligmann, London W8.
Jean Sewell (Antiques) Ltd, London W8.
Simon Spero, London W8.
Constance Stobo, London W8.
Stockspring Antiques, London W8.
Mary Wise, London W8.
Anchor Antiques Ltd, London WC2.
Baroq at Brindleys, Heath and Reach, Beds.
Cobblers Hall Antiques, Toddington, Beds.
Cavendish Fine Arts, Sonning-on-Thames, Berks.
Berks Antiques Co Ltd, Windsor and Eton, Berks.
Ulla Stafford Antiques, Windsor and Eton, Berks.
Gabor Cossa Antiques, Cambridge, Cambs.

Cottage Antiques, Cambridge, Cambs.
Abbey Antiques, Ramsey, Cambs.
Sydney House Antiques, Wansford, Cambs.
Aldersey Hall Ltd, Chester, Cheshire.
The Antique Shop, Chester, Cheshire.
Cameo Antiques, Chester, Cheshire.
Made of Honour, Chester, Cheshire.
Watergate Antiques, Chester, Cheshire.
Little Collectables, Congleton, Cheshire.
The Mulberry Bush, Marple Bridge, Cheshire.
Imperial Antiques, Stockport, Cheshire.
Ruby Snowden Antiques, Yarm, Cleveland.
The Country Antiques, Antrim, Co. Antrim, N. Ireland.
Dunluce Antiques, Bushmills, Co. Antrim, N. Ireland.
Downshire House Antiques, Newry, Co. Down, N. Ireland.
McCabe's Antique Galleries, Newry, Co. Down, N. Ireland.
Antiques, Marazion, Cornwall.
Clock Tower Antiques, Tregony, Cornwall.
Alan Bennett, Truro, Cornwall.
Saint Nicholas Galleries Ltd. (Antiques and Jewellery), Carlisle, Cumbria.
Souvenir Antiques, Carlisle, Cumbria.
Dower House Antiques, Kendal, Cumbria.
Kendal Studios Antiques, Kendal, Cumbria.
Netherley Cottage Antiques, Milburn, Cumbria.
Jane Pollock Antiques, Penrith, Cumbria.
Kenneth Upchurch, Ashbourne, Derbys.
Selected Antiques & Collectables, Barnstaple, Devon.
David J. Thorn, Budleigh Salterton, Devon.
Mary Payton Antiques, Chagford, Devon.
The Old Brass Kettle, Moretonhampstead, Devon.
Philip Andrade, South Brent, Devon.
Charterhouse Antiques, Teignmouth, Devon.
Mere Antiques, Topsham, Devon.
Birbeck Gallery, Torquay, Devon.
Box of Porcelain, Dorchester, Dorset.
Heygate Browne Antiques, Sherborne, Dorset.
Reference Works, Swanage, Dorset.
Grant's Antiques, Barnard Castle, Durham.
Domino Antiques, Barling Magna, Essex.
Bush House, Corringham, Essex.
Argyll House Antiques, Felsted, Essex.
John Burls, Great Oakley, Essex.
Castle Antiques, Leigh-on-Sea, Essex.
Richard Wrenn Antiques, Leigh-on-Sea, Essex.
Bush Antiques, Saffron Walden, Essex.
Barton House Antiques, Stanford-le-Hope, Essex.
Harris Antiques (Stansted), Stansted, Essex.
Julian Tatham-Losh, Andoversford, Glos.
Stuart House Antiques, Chipping Campden, Glos.
Swan Antiques, Chipping Campden, Glos.
Sodbury Antiques, Chipping Sodbury,, Glos.
Woodminster Antiques, Cirencester, Glos.
Berry Antiques, Moreton-in-Marsh, Glos.
Chandlers Antiques, Moreton-in-Marsh, Glos.
Mrs M.K. Nielsen, Moreton-in-Marsh, Glos.
Acorn Antiques, Stow-on-the-Wold, Glos.
Colin Brand Antiques, Stow-on-the-Wold, Glos.
Dolphin Antiques, Tetbury, Glos.
Muriel Lindsay, Winchcombe, Glos.
Grange Antiques, St. Peter Port, Guernsey, Channel Islands.
St. James's Gallery Ltd, St. Peter Port, Guernsey, Channel Islands.
Artemesia, Alresford, Hants.
Goss and Crested China Centre and Goss Museum, Horndean, Hants.
Lita Kaye of Lyndhurst, Lyndhurst, Hants.
Lane Antiques, Stockbridge, Hants.
Tilings Antiques, Brasted, Kent.
W.W. Warner (Antiques) Ltd, Brasted, Kent.
Serendipity, Deal, Kent.
Alan Wood, Gravesend, Kent.
Amherst Antiques, Riverhead, Kent.
Kent Cottage, Rolvenden, Kent.
Delf Stream Gallery, Sandwich, Kent.
Aaron Antiques, Snodland, Kent.
Steppes Hill Farm Antiques, Stockbury, Kent.
Pantiles Spa Antiques, Tunbridge Wells, Kent.
Old Corner House Antiques, Wittersham, Kent.
Roy W. Bunn, Barnoldswick, Lancs.
Park Galleries Antiques, Fine Art and Decor, Bolton, Lancs.
Cottage Antiques, Darwen, Lancs.
Clare's Antiques and Auction Galleries, Garstang, Lancs.
Village Antiques, Manchester, Lancs.
Paddock Antiques, Woodhouse Eaves, Leics.
Staines Antiques, Horncastle, Lincs.
Underwoodhall Antiques, Woodhall Spa, Lincs.
Ivy House Antiques, Acle, Norfolk.
Liz Allport-Lomax, Coltishall, Norfolk.
Roger Bradbury Antiques, Coltishall, Norfolk.
Isabel Neal Cabinet Antiques, Coltishall, Norfolk.
Peter Robinson, Heacham, Norfolk.
Richard Scott Antiques, Holt, Norfolk.
Sue Miller Antiques and Collectables, Langham, Norfolk.
Malcolm Turner, Norwich, Norfolk.
Dorothy's Antiques, Sheringham, Norfolk.
Leo Pratt and Son, South Walsham, Norfolk.
T.C.S. Brooke, Wroxham, Norfolk.
Peter Jackson Antiques, Brackley, Northants.
R. and M. Nicholas, Towcester, Northants.
Felton Park Antiques, Felton, Northumbs.
Hedley's of Hexham, Hexham, Northumbs.
Melville Kemp Ltd, Nottingham, Notts.
David and Carole Potter Antiques, Nottingham, Notts.
Swan Gallery, Burford, Oxon.
Bees Antiques, Woodstock, Oxon.
Robin Sanders and Sons, Woodstock, Oxon.
The Old House Gallery, Oakham, Rutland.
T.J. Roberts, Uppingham, Rutland.
Steeple Antiques, Ceres, Scotland.
Laurance Black Ltd, Edinburgh, Scotland.
Bruntsfield Antiques, Edinburgh, Scotland.
Present Bygones, Edinburgh, Scotland.
Young Antiques, Edinburgh, Scotland.
Tim Wright Antiques, Glasgow, Scotland.
Strathspey Gallery, Grantown-on-Spey, Scotland.
Elm House Antiques, Haddington, Scotland.
Miles Antiques, Kinross, Scotland.
Herrald of Edinburgh, Meigle, Scotland.
Harper-James, Montrose, Scotland.
Newburgh Antiques, Newburgh, Scotland.
Micawber Antiques, Bridgnorth, Shrops.
Tudor House Antiques (Bill Dickenson), Ironbridge, Shrops.
Teme Valley Antiques, Ludlow, Shrops.
Peter Wain, Market Drayton, Shrops.
David and Sally March Antiques, Abbots Leigh, Somerset.
Andrew Dando, Bath, Somerset.
Anthony Hepworth Fine Art, Bath, Somerset.
Quiet Street Antiques, Bath, Somerset.
M. Wood, Bishopswood, Somerset.
Dowlish Wake Antiques, Dowlish Wake, Somerset.
West End House Antiques, Ilminster, Somerset.
Staplegrove Lodge Antiques, Taunton, Somerset.
Milestone Antiques, Lichfield, Staffs.
Eveline Winter, Rugeley, Staffs.
Ceramic Search - Top of the Hill, Stoke-on-Trent, Staffs.
Five Towns Antiques, Stoke-on-Trent, Staffs.
The Potteries Antique Centre, Stoke-on-Trent, Staffs.
Derby Cottage Collectables, Exning, Suffolk.
J. and J. Baker, Lavenham,, Suffolk.
Oswald Simpson, Long Melford, Suffolk.
John Read, Martlesham, Suffolk.
David Gibbins Antiques, Woodbridge, Suffolk.
Red House Antiques, Yoxford, Suffolk.
Suffolk House Antiques, Yoxford, Suffolk.
Churt Curiosity Shop, Churt, Surrey.
Decodream, Coulsdon, Surrey.
Dolphin Square Antiques, Dorking, Surrey.

Dorking Emporium Antiques Centre, Dorking, Surrey.
Church Street Antiques, Godalming, Surrey.
Susan Becker, Walton-on-Thames, Surrey.
Brocante, Weybridge, Surrey.
Patrick Moorhead Antiques, Brighton, E. Sussex.
Yellow Lantern Antiques Ltd, Brighton, E. Sussex.
Stewart Gallery, Eastbourne, E. Sussex.
Southdown Antiques, Lewes, E. Sussex.
Leonard Russell, Newhaven, E. Sussex.
Herbert Gordon Gasson, Rye, E. Sussex.
Pat Golding, Arundel, W. Sussex.
Gems Antiques, Chichester, W. Sussex.
Richard Gardner Antiques, Petworth, W. Sussex.
William Hockley Antiques, Petworth, W. Sussex.
H & S Collectables, Gosforth, Tyne and Wear.
Ian Sharp Antiques, Tynemouth, Tyne and Wear.
Howards of Aberystwyth, Aberystwyth, Wales.
Paul Gibbs Antiques and Decorative Arts, Conwy, Wales.
Bulmer's, Cowbridge, Wales.
Manor House Antiques, Fishguard, Wales.
Hebbards of Hay, Hay-on-Wye, Wales.
Islwyn Watkins, Knighton, Wales.
J. and R. Langford, Llangollen, Wales.
Passers Buy (Marie Evans), Llangollen, Wales.
West Wales Antiques, Murton, Wales.
Magpie Antiques, Swansea, Wales.
Clareston Antiques, Tenby, Wales.
Castle Antiques, Usk, Wales.
Coleshill Antiques and Interiors Ltd, Coleshill, Warks.
Janice Paull Antiques, Kenilworth, Warks.
Burman Antiques, Stratford-upon-Avon, Warks.
H. and R.L. Parry Ltd, Sutton Coldfield, W. Mids.
Pendeford House Antiques, Wolverhampton, W. Mids.
Moxhams Antiques, Bradford-on-Avon, Wilts.
Antiques - Rene Nicholls, Malmesbury, Wilts.
Heirloom & Howard Limited, West Yatton, Wilts.
Bygones by the Cathedral, Worcester, Worcs.
Bygones (Worcester), Worcester, Worcs.
John Edwards Antiques, Worcester, Worcs.
M. Lees and Sons, Worcester, Worcs.
Long Tran Antiques, Worcester, Worcs.
Worcester Antiques Centre, Worcester, Worcs.
The Crested China Co, Driffield, E. Yorks.
Alexander Adamson, Harrogate, N. Yorks.
Bryan Bowden, Harrogate, N. Yorks.
David Love, Harrogate, N. Yorks.
York Cottage Antiques, Helmsley, N. Yorks.
Country Collector, Pickering, N. Yorks.
Nanbooks, Settle, N. Yorks.
Anderson Slater Antiques, Settle, N. Yorks.
Rebecca L. Calvert t/a Farmhouse Antiques, Great Houghton, S. Yorks.
Top Hat Antique Centre, Sheffield, S. Yorks.
Muir Hewitt Art Deco Originals, Halifax, W. Yorks.

Prints (see Maps & Prints)

Rugs (see Carpets & Rugs)

Russian/Soviet Art

Soviet Carpet and Art Centre, London NW2.
Hermitage Antiques plc, London SW1.
The Andipa Gallery, London SW3.
Richardson and Kailas Icons, London SW6.
Antoine Cheneviere Fine Arts, London W1.
Roy Miles Gallery, London W1.
Wartski Ltd, London W1.
Temple Gallery, London W11.
The Mark Gallery, London W2.
Mir Russki, Linlithgow, Scotland.
The Fitzroy Gallery (formerly The McIan Gallery), Oban, Scotland.

Scientific Instruments

Finchley Fine Art Galleries, London N12.
Victor Burness Antiques and Scientific Instruments, London SE1.
Peter Laurie Antiques, London SE10.
Relcy Antiques, London SE10.
Jillings of Belgravia, London SW1.
Thomas Mercer (Chronometers) Ltd, London SW1.
Trevor Philip and Sons Ltd, London SW1.
Captain O.M. Watts, London W1.
Peter Delehar, London W11.
Mayflower Antiques, London W11.
Johnny Von Pflugh Antiques, London W11.
Gillian Gould at Ocean Leisure, London WC2.
Arthur Middleton, London WC2.
Christopher Sykes Antiques, Woburn, Beds.
Malcolm Frazer Antiques, Cheadle, Cheshire.
Time & Tide Antiques, Portaferry, Co. Down, N. Ireland.
Mike Read Antique Sciences, St. Ives, Cornwall.
Alan Jones Antiques, Plymouth, Devon.
Branksome Antiques, Branksome, Dorset.
Mayflower Antiques, Harwich, Essex.
The Chart House, Shenfield, Essex.
Chris Grimes Militaria, Bristol, Glos.
Country Life Antiques, Stow-on-the-Wold, Glos.
Barometer Shop, Leominster, Herefs.
Michael Sim, Chislehurst, Kent.
Hadlow Antiques, Tunbridge Wells, Kent.
Turret House, Wymondham, Norfolk.
Bernard G. House, Wells, Somerset.
Patrick Marney, Long Melford, Suffolk.
Roy Arnold, Needham Market, Suffolk.
Principia Arts and Sciences, Marlborough, Wilts.
Minster Antiques, York, N. Yorks.

Sculpture

Centaur Gallery, London N6.
Duncan R. Miller Fine Arts, London NW3.
Tara Antiques, London NW8.
Robert E. Hirschhorn, London SE5.
Robert Bowman, London SW1.
Chaucer Fine Arts Ltd, London SW1.
Shirley Day Ltd, London SW1.
Nicholas Gifford-Mead, London SW1.
Hazlitt, Gooden and Fox Ltd, London SW1.
Seago, London SW1.
Whitford Fine Art, London SW1.
Jonathan Clark & Co, London SW10.
Ted Few, London SW17.
Tulissio De Beaumont, London SW6.
Agnew's, London W1.
Adrian Alan Ltd, London W1.
Browse and Darby Ltd, London W1.
Lumley Cazalet Ltd, London W1.
P. and D. Colnaghi & Co Ltd, London W1.
Editions Graphiques Gallery, London W1.
Eskenazi Ltd, London W1.
The Fine Art Society plc, London W1.
Christopher Gibbs Ltd, London W1.
Patrick Jefferson Ltd, London W1.
The Sladmore Gallery of Sculpture, London W1.
Stoppenbach and Delestre Ltd, London W1.
Curá Antiques, London W11.
Hirst Antiques, London W11.
Milne and Moller, London W11.
Philp, London W11.
Piano Nobile Fine Paintings, London W11.
Edric Van Vredenburgh Ltd, London W11.
Wolseley Fine Arts Ltd, London W11.
Adrian Alan Ltd, London W8.
Simon Hilton, Dunmow, Essex.
Quatrefoil, Fordingbridge, Hants.
Lacewing Fine Art Gallery, Romsey, Hants.
Nicholas Bowlby, Tunbridge Wells, Kent.
London House Antiques, Westerham, Kent.
Robin Cox Antiques, Ketton, Lincs.
Pearse Lukies, Aylsham, Norfolk.
Arthur Brett and Sons Ltd, Norwich, Norfolk.
The Barry M. Keene Gallery, Henley-on-Thames, Oxon.
Calton Gallery, Edinburgh, Scotland.
The Roger Billcliffe Fine Art, Glasgow, Scotland.
Mainhill Gallery, Jedburgh, Scotland.
David Bridgwater, Bath, Somerset.
Bruton Gallery, Bath, Somerset.
AnthonyHepworth Fine Art, Bath, Somerset.
Tim Everett, West Buckland, Somerset.

Equus Art Gallery, Newmarket, Suffolk.
Piano Nobile Fine Paintings, Richmond, Surrey.
Apollo Antiques Ltd, Warwick, Warks.
Patrick and Gillian Morley Antiques, Warwick, Warks.
The Jerram Gallery, Salisbury, Wilts.

Shipping Goods & Period Furniture for the Trade

Regent Antiques, London N1.
Keith Skeel Antique Warehouse, London N1.
Madeline Crispin Antiques, London NW1.
Antique Trade Warehouse, London SE1.
Antique Warehouse, London SE1.
Oola Boola Antiques London, London SE1.
Penny Farthing Antiques, London SE1.
Tower Bridge Antiques, London SE1.
J.A. Fredericks and Son, London W1.
Secondhand Alley, Shefford, Beds.
Tavistock Antiques, St. Neots, Cambs.
R. Wilding, Wisbech, Cambs.
W. Buckley Antiques Exports, Congleton, Cheshire.
Paul Jennings Antiques, Angarrack, Cornwall.
Ben Eggleston Antiques, Long Marton, Cumbria.
Antique Exporters U.K, Brailsford, Derbys.
Michael Allcroft Antiques, Newtown, Derbys.
Shardlow Antiques Warehouse, Shardlow, Derbys.
John Prestige Antiques, Brixham, Devon.
Fagins Antiques, Exeter, Devon.
McBains of Exeter, Exeter, Devon.
Sextons, Kentisbeare, Devon.
Richard Dunton Antiques, Bournemouth, Dorset.
Sandy's Antiques, Bournemouth, Dorset.
Wiffen's Antiques, Parkstone, Dorset.
Alan Ramsey Antiques, Darlington, Durham.
G.T. Ratcliff Ltd, Kelvedon, Essex.
Barton House Antiques, Stanford-le-Hope, Essex.
Bristol Trade Antiques, Bristol, Glos.
Cabbages & Kings, Winchester, Hants.
Alan Lord Antiques, Folkestone, Kent.
Sutton Valence Antiques, Maidstone, Kent.
Sutton Valence Antiques, Sutton Valence, Kent.
Charles International Antiques, Wrotham, Kent.
West Lancs. Antique Exports, Burscough, Lancs.
The Antique Shop, Edenfield, Lancs.
P.J. Brown Antiques, Haslingden, Lancs.
R.J. O'Brien and Son Antiques Ltd, Manchester, Lancs.
G.G. Exports, Middleton Village, Lancs.
Tyson's Antiques, Morecambe, Lancs.
John Robinson Antiques, Wigan, Lancs.
Boulevard Antique and Shipping Centre, Leicester, Leics.
Streetwalker Antiques Warehouse, Barton-on-Humber, Lincs.
Grantham Furniture Emporium, Grantham, Lincs.
Michael Brewer, Lincoln, Lincs.
C. and K.E. Dring, Lincoln, Lincs.
Trade Antiques, Long Sutton, Lincs.
G & J Crowson, Skegness, Lincs.
Bridge Antiques, Sutton Bridge, Lincs.
Old Barn Antiques Warehouse, Sutton Bridge, Lincs.
Kensington Tower Antiques Ltd, Liverpool, Merseyside.
The Original British American Antiques, Liverpool, Merseyside.
Swainbanks Ltd, Liverpool, Merseyside.
Theta Gallery, Liverpool, Merseyside.
Molloy's Furnishers Ltd, Southport, Merseyside.
Tony and Anne Sutcliffe Antiques, Southport, Merseyside.
Sheila Hart and John Giles, Aylsham, Norfolk.
Pearse Lukies, Aylsham, Norfolk.
Old Coach House, Long Stratton, Norfolk.
John Roe Antiques, Islip, Northants.
R.E. Thompson, Long Buckby, Northants.
Bryan Perkins Antiques, Wellingborough, Northants.
T. Baker, Langford, Notts.
Fair Deal Antiques, Mansfield, Notts.
Newark Antiques Warehouse, Newark, Notts.
Meadow Lane Antiques, Nottingham, Notts.
Times Past Antiques, Auchterarder, Scotland.
Imrie Antiques, Bridge of Earn, Scotland.
Neil Livingstone, Dundee, Scotland.
George Duff Antiques, Edinburgh, Scotland.
Georgian Antiques, Edinburgh, Scotland.
Narducci Antiques, Largs, Scotland.
A.S. Deuchar and Son, Perth, Scotland.
Narducci Antiques, Saltcoats, Scotland.
Mitre House Antiques, Ludlow, Shrops.
M.G.R. Exports, Bruton, Somerset.
Pennard House, East Pennard, Somerset.
T.M. Dyte Antiques, Highbridge, Somerset.
The Treasure Chest, Highbridge, Somerset.
Harrison House Antiques, North Petherton, Somerset.
J.C. Giddings, Wiveliscombe, Somerset.
Burton Antiques, Burton-on-Trent, Staffs.
Cordelia and Perdy's Antique Junk Shop, Lichfield, Staffs.
Armson's of Yoxall Antiques, Yoxall, Staffs.
Goodbreys, Framlingham, Suffolk.
A. Abbott Antiques, Ipswich, Suffolk.
The Edwardian Shop, Ipswich, Suffolk.
Antique Furniture Warehouse, Woodbridge, Suffolk.
Laurence Tauber Antiques, Surbiton, Surrey.
Euro-Pine, Sutton, Surrey.
Bexhill Antique Exporters, Bexhill-on-Sea, E. Sussex.
The Old Mint House, Bexhill-on-Sea, E. Sussex.
Attic Antiques, Brighton, E. Sussex.
Lloyd Williams - Antique Anglo Am Warehouse, Eastbourne, E. Sussex.
The Old Mint House, Pevensey, E. Sussex.
John H. Yorke Antiques, St. Leonards-on-Sea, E. Sussex.
J. Powell (Hove) Ltd, Portslade, W. Sussex.
Peter Smith Antiques, Sunderland, Tyne and Wear.
Charlotte's Wholesale Antiques, Cardiff, Wales.
Michael Lloyd, Henllan, Wales.
Anne and Colin Hulbert (Antiques and Firearms), Swansea, Wales.
All Old Exports Ltd., Treorchy, Wales.
Smithfield Antiques, Lye, W. Mids.
Brett Wilkins Antiques, Wednesbury, W. Mids.
Martin Taylor Antiques, Wolverhampton, W. Mids.
North Wilts Exporters, Brinkworth, Wilts.
Calne Antiques, Calne, Wilts.
Harley Antiques, Christian Malford, Wilts.
Pillars Antiques, Lyneham, Wilts.
Cross Hayes Antiques, Malmesbury, Wilts.
Sambourne House Antiques, Minety, Wilts.
K. and A. Welch, Warminster, Wilts.
The Mall Antique Centre &
Geoffrey Mole Antiques, Hull, E. Yorks.
Pearson Antiques, Hull, E. Yorks.
Trade Antiques - D.D. White, Manfield, N. Yorks.
Tomlinson (Antiques) Ltd. & Period Furniture Ltd, Tockwith, N. Yorks.
Roger Appleyard Ltd, Rotherham, S. Yorks.
Philip Turnor Antiques, Rotherham, S. Yorks.
Dronfield Antiques, Sheffield, S. Yorks.
N.P. and A. Salt Antiques, Sheffield, S. Yorks.
Paul Graham Antiques, Shipley, W. Yorks.

Silver and Jewellery

George Rankin Coin Co. Ltd, London E2.
Finecraft Workshop Ltd, London EC1.
Jonathan Harris (Jewellery) Ltd, London EC1.
Hirsh Ltd, London EC1.
Joseph and Pearce Ltd, London EC1.
A.R. Ullmann Ltd, London EC1.
Nanwani and Co, London EC3.
Searle and Co Ltd, London EC3.
Eclectica, London N1.
The Graham Gallery, London N1.
Rosemary Hart, London N1.
Sherry Hatcher, London N1.
John Laurie (Antiques) Ltd, London N1.
Jacqueline Oosthuizen, London N1.
The Little Curiosity Shop, London N21.

Delieb Antiques, London NW11.
The Corner Cupboard, London NW2.
Silver Belle, London NW8.
Creek Antiques, London SE10.
Vale Stamps and Antiques, London SE3.
A.D.C. Heritage Ltd, London SW1.
J.H. Bourdon-Smith Ltd, London SW1.
Cobra and Bellamy, London SW1.
Cornucopia, London SW1.
Kenneth Davis (Works of Art) Ltd, London SW1.
Alastair Dickenson Fine Silver Ltd, London SW1.
N. and I. Franklin, London SW1.
Harvey and Gore, London SW1.
Kojis Antique Jewellery Ltd, London SW1.
Longmire Ltd (Three Royal Warrants), London SW1.
Nigel Milne Ltd, London SW1.
Gerald Sattin Ltd, London SW1.
The Silver Fund Ltd, London SW1.
James Hardy and Co, London SW3.
Stanley Leslie, London SW3.
McKenna and Co, London SW3.
Merola, London SW3.
Jacqueline Oosthuizen, London SW3.
Christine Schell, London SW3.
Gordon Watson Ltd, London SW3.
Nicholas Harris, London SW6.
M.P. Levene Ltd, London SW7.
A. & H. Page, London SW7.
Philip Antrobus Ltd, London W1.
Armour-Winston Ltd, London W1.
Asprey plc, London W1.
Paul Bennett, London W1.
Bentley & Co Ltd, London W1.
Bond Street Silver Galleries, London W1.
Boodle and Dunthorne Ltd, London W1.
John Bull (Antiques) Ltd JB Silverware, London W1.
Carrington and Co. Ltd, London W1.
Sandra Cronan Ltd, London W1.
A. B. Davis Ltd, London W1.
Demas, London W1.
Editions Graphiques Gallery, London W1.
Garrard & Co. Ltd (The Crown Jewellers), London W1.
Simon Griffin Antiques Ltd, London W1.
Hadleigh Jewellers, London W1.
Hancocks and Co, London W1.
Hennell of Bond Street Ltd. Founded 1736 (incorporating Frazer and Haws (1868) and E. Lloyd Lawrence (1830)), London W1.
Holmes Ltd, London W1.
Brand Inglis, London W1.
Johnson Walker & Tolhurst Ltd, London W1.
Lacloche Freres, London W1.
D.S. Lavender (Antiques) Ltd, London W1.
Marks Antiques, London W1.
Moira, London W1.
Richard Ogden Ltd, London W1.
S.J. Phillips Ltd, London W1.
David Richards and Sons, London W1.
Michael Rose - Source of the Unusual, London W1.
Tessiers Ltd, London W1.
Wartski Ltd, London W1.
Britannia Export Antiques, London W11.
Central Gallery (Portobello), London W11.
J. Freeman, London W11.
Kleanthous Antiques, Stouts Antiques Market, London W11
Portobello Antique Store, London W11.
Schredds of Portobello, London W11.
The Silver Fox Gallery, London W11.
Colin Smith and Gerald Robinson Antiques, London W11.
Craven Gallery, London W2.
M. McAleer, London W2.
Mary Cooke Antiques Ltd, London W8.
H. and W. Deutsch Antiques, London W8.
Green's Antique Galleries, London W8.
Hampson and Lewis, London W8.
John Jesse, London W8.
Howard Jones, London W8.
Lev (Antiques) Ltd, London W8.
Fay Lucas Gallery, London W8.
Sinai Antiques Ltd, London W8.
Nortonbury Antiques, London WC1.
Thomas Kettle Ltd, London WC2.
The London Silver Vaults, London WC2.
Pearl Cross Ltd, London WC2.
The Silver Mouse Trap, London WC2.
Styles Silver, Hungerford, Berks.
Berks Antiques Co Ltd, Windsor and Eton, Berks.
Turks Head Antiques, Windsor and Eton, Berks.
Buckies, Cambridge, Cambs.
Pembroke Antiques, Cambridge, Cambs.
Attic Gallery, Wisbech, Cambs.
D.J. Massey and Son, Alderley Edge, Cheshire.
Boodle and Dunthorne Ltd, Chester, Cheshire.
Cameo Antiques, Chester, Cheshire.
Kayes of Chester, Chester, Cheshire.
Lowe and Sons, Chester, Cheshire.
Veevers, Chester, Cheshire.
Watergate Antiques, Chester, Cheshire.
The Clock House, Hazel Grove, Cheshire.
D.J. Massey and Son, Macclesfield, Cheshire.
Highland Antiques, Stockport, Cheshire.
Imperial Antiques, Stockport, Cheshire.
A. Baker and Sons, Warrington, Cheshire.
The Country Antiques, Antrim, Co. Antrim, N. Ireland.
Dunluce Antiques, Bushmills, Co. Antrim, N. Ireland.
Brian R. Bolt Antiques, Portballintrae, Co. Antrim, N. Ireland.
Old Priory Antiques, Greyabbey, Co. Down, N. Ireland.
Cookstown Antiques, Cookstown, Co. Tyrone, N. Ireland.
Little Jem's, Penzance, Cornwall.
Alan Bennett, Truro, Cornwall.
Saint Nicholas Galleries Ltd. (Antiques and Jewellery), Carlisle, Cumbria.
Jane Pollock Antiques, Penrith, Cumbria.
Elizabeth and Son, Ulverston, Cumbria.
Mark Parkhouse Antiques and Jewellery, Barnstaple, Devon.
Timothy Coward Fine Silver, Braunton, Devon.
David J. Thorn, Budleigh Salterton, Devon.
Gold and Silver Exchange, Exeter, Devon.
Brian Mortimer, Exeter, Devon.
John Nathan Antiques, Exeter, Devon.
Boase Antiques, Exmouth, Devon.
J. Barrymore and Co, Honiton, Devon.
Otter Antiques, Honiton, Devon.
Charterhouse Antiques, Teignmouth, Devon.
Extence Antiques, Teignmouth, Devon.
A & D Antiques, Blandford Forum, Dorset.
G.B. Mussenden and Son Antiques, Jewellery and Silver, Bournemouth, Dorset.
Geo. A. Payne and Son Ltd, Bournemouth, Dorset.
R.E. Porter, Bournemouth, Dorset.
Portique, Bournemouth, Dorset.
Peter Stebbing, Bournemouth, Dorset.
Batten's Jewellers, Bridport, Dorset.
Greystoke Antiques, Sherborne, Dorset.
Henry Willis (Antique Silver), Sherborne, Dorset.
Georgian Gems Antique Jewellers, Swanage, Dorset.
Heirlooms Antique Jewellers and Silversmiths, Wareham, Dorset.
Robin Finnegan (Jeweller), Darlington, Durham.
Argentum Antiques, Coggeshall, Essex.
Elizabeth Cannon Antiques, Colchester, Essex.
Grahams of Colchester, Colchester, Essex.
J. Streamer Antiques, Leigh-on-Sea, Essex.
Richard Wrenn Antiques, Leigh-on-Sea, Essex.
Gostick Hall Antiques, Newport, Essex.
Harris Antiques (Stansted), Stansted, Essex.
Whichcraft Jewellery, Writtle, Essex.
Grey-Harris and Co, Bristol, Glos.
Kemps, Bristol, Glos.
Greens of Cheltenham Ltd, Cheltenham, Glos.
Martin and Co. Ltd, Cheltenham, Glos.
Scott-Cooper Ltd, Cheltenham, Glos.
Swan Antiques, Chipping Campden, Glos.
Sodbury Antiques, Chipping Sodbury,, Glos.
Walter Bull and Son (Cirencester) Ltd, Cirencester, Glos.
Rankine Taylor Antiques, Cirencester, Glos.
Grange Antiques, St. Peter Port, Guernsey, Channel Islands.
Olive Antiques, Alverstoke, Hants.
Squirrel Collectors Centre, Basingstoke, Hants.
A.W. Porter and Son, Hartley Wintney, Hants.
Barry Papworth, Lymington, Hants.
Meg Campbell, Southampton, Hants.
Parkhouse and Wyatt Ltd, Southampton, Hants.

Robin Howard Antiques, Titchfield, Hants.
Warings of Hereford, Hereford, Herefs.
Abbey Antiques - Fine Jewellery & Silver, Hemel Hempstead, Herts.
Bexfield Antiques, Hitchin, Herts.
Forget-me-Knot Antiques, St. Albans, Herts.
Stuart Wharton, St. Albans, Herts.
J. and H. Bell Antiques, Castletown, Isle of Man.
A. & R. Ritchie, St. Helier, Jersey, Channel Islands.
R. J. Baker, Canterbury, Kent.
Owlets, Hythe, Kent.
Amherst Antiques, Riverhead, Kent.
Kaizen International, Rochester, Kent.
Steppes Hill Farm Antiques, Stockbury, Kent.
Chapel Place Antiques, Tunbridge Wells, Kent.
Glassdrumman Antiques, Tunbridge Wells, Kent.
Pantiles Spa Antiques, Tunbridge Wells, Kent.
Andrew Smith Antiques, West Malling, Kent.
The Coin and Jewellery Shop, Accrington, Lancs.
Kenworthys Ltd, Ashton-under-Lyne, Lancs.
Ancient and Modern, Blackburn, Lancs.
Mitchell's (Lock Antiques), Blackburn, Lancs.
Chard Coins, Blackpool, Lancs.
Leigh Jewellery, Leigh, Lancs.
Snuff Box, Lytham St. Annes, Lancs.
Boodle and Dunthorne Ltd, Manchester, Lancs.
Cathedral Jewellers, Manchester, Lancs.
St. James Antiques, Manchester, Lancs.
Brittons Jewellers and Antiques, Nelson, Lancs.
Charles Howell Jeweller, Oldham, Lancs.
H.C. Simpson and Sons Jewellers (Oldham)Ltd, Oldham, Lancs.
Keystone Antiques, Coalville, Leics.
Corry's, Leicester, Leics.
Letty's Antiques, Leicester, Leics.
Stanley Hunt Jewellers, Gainsborough, Lincs.
Pilgrims Antiques Centre, Gainsborough, Lincs.
Wilkinson's, Grantham, Lincs.
Rowletts of Lincoln, Lincoln, Lincs.
James Usher and Son Ltd, Lincoln, Lincs.
Wilkinson's, Sleaford, Lincs.
Dawson of Stamford Ltd, Stamford, Lincs.
St. Mary's Galleries, Stamford, Lincs.
C. Rosenberg, Heswall, Merseyside.
Kevin Whay's Clock Shop and Antiques, Hoylake, Merseyside.
Boodle and Dunthorne Ltd, Liverpool, Merseyside.
Edward's Jewellers, Liverpool, Merseyside.
Stefani Antiques, Liverpool, Merseyside.
H.S. Walne, Southport, Merseyside.
Weldons Jewellery and Antiques, Southport, Merseyside.
Bond Street Antiques (inc. Jas. J. Briggs Est. 1820), Cromer, Norfolk.
Barry's Antiques, Gt. Yarmouth, Norfolk.
Folkes Antiques and Jewellers, Gt. Yarmouth, Norfolk.
Peter Howkins, Gt. Yarmouth, Norfolk.
Wheatleys, Gt. Yarmouth, Norfolk.
Tim Clayton Jewellery, King's Lynn, Norfolk.
Albrow and Sons Family Jewellers, Norwich, Norfolk.
Clive Dennett Coins, Norwich, Norfolk.
Leona Levine Silver Specialist, Norwich, Norfolk.
Maddermarket Antiques, Norwich, Norfolk.
Oswald Sebley, Norwich, Norfolk.
James and Ann Tillett, Norwich, Norfolk.
Thomas Tillett & Co, Norwich, Norfolk.
Parriss, Sheringham, Norfolk.
Michael Jones Jeweller, Northampton, Northants.
Sinclair's Antique Gallery, Belfast, N. Ireland.
Boadens Antiques, Hexham, Northumbs.
Melville Kemp Ltd, Nottingham, Notts.
Barclay Antiques, Headington, Oxon.
Thames Gallery, Henley-on-Thames, Oxon.
Reginald Davis Ltd, Oxford, Oxon.
Payne and Son (Goldsmiths) Ltd, Oxford, Oxon.
MGJ Jewellers Ltd., Wallingford, Oxon.
Churchgate Antiques, Empingham, Rutland.
McCalls (Aberdeen), Aberdeen, Scotland.
McCalls Limited, Aberdeen, Scotland.
Michael Young, Aberdeen, Scotland.
Joseph Bonnar, Jewellers, Edinburgh, Scotland.
Goodwin's Antiques Ltd, Edinburgh, Scotland.
Montresor, Edinburgh, Scotland.
Royal Mile Curios, Edinburgh, Scotland.
John Whyte, Edinburgh, Scotland.
West End Antiques, Elgin, Scotland.
James Forrest and Co (Jewellers) Ltd, Glasgow, Scotland.
A.D. Hamilton and Co, Glasgow, Scotland.
Jeremy Sniders Antiques, Glasgow, Scotland.
Tim Wright Antiques, Glasgow, Scotland.
Kilmacolm Antiques Ltd, Kilmacolm, Scotland.
Amber Antiques, Kincardine O'Neil, Scotland.
Mir Russki, Linlithgow, Scotland.
Harper-James, Montrose, Scotland.
Forsyth Antiques, Perth, Scotland.
Gallery One, Perth, Scotland.
Hardie Antiques, Perth, Scotland.
Old St. Andrews Gallery, St. Andrews, Scotland.
Abbey Antiques, Stirling, Scotland.
English Heritage, Bridgnorth, Shrops.
Teme Valley Antiques, Ludlow, Shrops.
Cruck House Antiques, Much Wenlock, Shrops.
Sue Dyer Antiques, Shrewsbury, Shrops.
Hutton Antiques, Shrewsbury, Shrops.
The Little Gem, Shrewsbury, Shrops.
F.C. Manser and Son Ltd, Shrewsbury, Shrops.
Abbey Galleries, Bath, Somerset.
Bladud House Antiques, Bath, Somerset.
D. and B. Dickinson, Bath, Somerset.
E.P. Mallory and Son Ltd, Bath, Somerset.
Castle Antiques, Burnham-on-Sea, Somerset.
Beach Antiques, Clevedon, Somerset.
Winston Mac (Silversmith), Bury St. Edmunds, Suffolk.
A. Abbott Antiques, Ipswich, Suffolk.
Temptations, Ashtead, Surrey.
T. M. Collins, Dorking, Surrey.
Hebeco, Dorking, Surrey.
Pauline Watson, Dorking, Surrey.
Cry for the Moon, Guildford, Surrey.
Tramp Jewellers, Guildford, Surrey.
Glydon and Guess Ltd, Kingston-upon-Thames, Surrey.
Horton's, Richmond, Surrey.
Lionel Jacobs, Richmond, Surrey.
S. Warrender and Co, Sutton, Surrey.
Church House Antiques, Weybridge, Surrey.
Not Just Silver, Weybridge, Surrey.
Harry Diamond and Son, Brighton, E. Sussex.
James Doyle Antiques, Brighton, E. Sussex.
D.H. Edmonds Ltd, Brighton, E. Sussex.
Paul Goble, Brighton, E. Sussex.
The Gold and Silversmiths of Hove, Brighton, E. Sussex.
Douglas Hall Ltd, Brighton, E. Sussex.
Hallmarks, Brighton, E. Sussex.
The House of Antiques, Brighton, E. Sussex.
Harry Mason, Brighton, E. Sussex.
S.L. Simmons, Brighton, E. Sussex.
Wm. Bruford and Son Ltd, Eastbourne, E. Sussex.
Trade Wind, Rottingdean, E. Sussex.
Rye Antiques, Rye, E. Sussex.
Aarquebus Antiques, St. Leonards-on-Sea, E. Sussex.
Peter Hancock Antiques, Chichester, W. Sussex.
Westbourne Antiques, Westbourne, W. Sussex.
Rathbone Law Antiques, Worthing, W Sussex.
Sovereign Antiques, Gateshead, Tyne and Wear.
Davidson's The Jewellers Ltd, Newcastle-upon-Tyne, Tyne and Wear.
Intercoin, Newcastle-upon-Tyne, Tyne and Wear.
Owen's Jewellers, Newcastle-upon-Tyne, Tyne and Wear.
Jones and Dyson, Ann Evans, Bangor, Wales.
Hazel of Brecon, Brecon, Wales.
Silvertime, Brecon, Wales.

Alexander Antiques, Cardiff, Wales.
Cronin Antiques, Cardiff, Wales.
Audrey Bull, Carmarthen, Wales.
Gold and Silver Shop, Gorseinon, Wales.
Cartrefle Antiques, Mathry, Wales.
James Allan, Swansea, Wales.
Audrey Bull, Tenby, Wales.
Coleshill Antiques and Interiors Ltd, Coleshill, Warks.
MPA Warwick Ltd, Gaydon, Warks.
Howards Jewellers, Stratford-upon-Avon, Warks.
Russell Lane Antiques, Warwick, Warks.
Peter Clark Antiques, Birmingham, W. Mids.
Maurice Fellows, Birmingham, W. Mids.
Rex Johnson and Sons, Birmingham, W. Mids.
Piccadilly Jewellers, Birmingham, W. Mids.
H. and R.L. Parry Ltd, Sutton Coldfield, W. Mids.
Hardwick Antiques, Walsall, W. Mids.
Nicholls Jewellers and Antiques, Walsall, W. Mids.
Cross Keys Jewellers, Devizes, Wilts.
Cross Keys Jewellers, Marlborough, Wilts.
Jonathan Green Antiques, Salisbury, Wilts.
Howards of Broadway, Broadway, Worcs.
Magpie Jewellers and Antiques and Magpie Arms & Armour, Evesham, Worcs.
B.B.M. Jewellery and Antiques, Kidderminster, Worcs.
Lower House Fine Antiques, Redditch, Worcs.
Bygones by the Cathedral, Worcester, Worcs.
Bygones (Worcester), Worcester, Worcs.
Karen Guest Antiques, Beverley, E. Yorks.
Karen Guest Antiques, Driffield, E. Yorks.
Lesley Berry Antiques, Flamborough, E. Yorks.
Country Antiques, Boroughbridge, N. Yorks.
D. Mason & Son, Harrogate, N. Yorks.
Ogden of Harrogate Ltd, Harrogate, N. Yorks.
Mary Milnthorpe and Daughters Antique Shop, Settle, N. Yorks.
Barbara Cattle, York, N. Yorks.
Golden Memories of York, York, N. Yorks.
Robert M. Himsworth, York, N. Yorks.
John Mason Jewellers Ltd, Rotherham, S. Yorks.
Canterbury House, Thorne, S. Yorks.
Geoff Neary (incorporating Fillans Antiques Ltd), Huddersfield, W. Yorks.
Jack Shaw and Co, Ilkley, W. Yorks.
Keighleys of Keighley, Keighley, W. Yorks.
Aladdin's Cave, Leeds, W. Yorks.
Coins International and Antiques International, Leeds, W. Yorks.

Sporting Items and Associated Memorabilia

Risky Business, London NW8.
Holland & Holland, London W1.
World Famous Portobello Market, London W11.
Sean Arnold Sporting Antiques, London W2.
Below Stairs of Hungerford, Hungerford, Berks.
Sir William Bentley Billiards (Antique Billiard Table Specialist Company), Hungerford, Berks.
Warboys Antiques, Warboys, Cambs.
Yesterday Tackle and Books, Bournemouth, Dorset.
John Burton Natural Craft Taxidermy, Ebrington, Glos.
Simon Brett, Moreton-in-Marsh, Glos.
Hamilton Billiards & Games Co., Knebworth, Herts.
Garden House Antiques, Tenterden, Kent.
The Spinning Wheel, Southport, Merseyside.
Manfred Schotten Antiques, Burford, Oxon.
Old St. Andrews Gallery, St. Andrews, Scotland.
Old Troon Sporting Antiques, Troon, Scotland.
Billiard Room Antiques, Chilcompton, Somerset.
The Falcon Gallery, Wortham, Suffolk.
Academy Billiard Company, West Byfleet, Surrey.
Olde Forge Antiques, Weybridge, Surrey.
Burman Antiques, Stratford-upon-Avon, Warks.
James Wigington Arms and Armour, Stratford-upon-Avon, Warks.
Grant Fine Art, Droitwich, Worcs.
Fun Antiques, Sheffield, S. Yorks.

Sporting Paintings & Prints

Swan Fine Art, London N1.
Relcy Antiques, London SE10.
Ackermann & Johnson, London SW1.
Addison-Ross Gallery, London SW1.
Frost and Reed Ltd (Est. 1808), London SW1.
Malcolm Innes Gallery, London SW1.
Paul Mason Gallery, London SW1.
Collins and Hastie Ltd, London SW10.
Kensington Sporting Paintings Ltd, London SW20.
Old Church Galleries, London SW3.
Richard Green, London W1.
Holland & Holland, London W1.
The O'Shea Gallery, London W1.
Frank T. Sabin Ltd, London W1.
Tryon & Swann Gallery, London W1.
Connaught Galleries, London W2.
Iona Antiques, London W8.
Grosvenor Prints, London WC2.
Marlborough Sporting Gallery and Bookshop, Hungerford, Berks.
Coltsfoot Gallery, Leominster, Herefs.
G. and D.I. Marrin and Sons, Folkestone, Kent.
Leics Sporting Gallery and Brown Jack Bookshop, Lubenham, Leics.
In the Picture (The Golf Collection), Holt, Norfolk.
Paul Hopwell Antiques, West Haddon, Northants.
Jane Neville Gallery, Aslockton, Notts.
Sally Mitchell's Gallery, Tuxford, Notts.
H.C. Dickins, Bloxham, Oxon.
John Garner, Uppingham, Rutland.
Paul Hayes Gallery, Auchterarder, Scotland.
Malcolm Innes Gallery, Edinburgh, Scotland.
Strathspey Gallery, Grantown-on-Spey, Scotland.
Julian Armytage, Crewkerne, Somerset.
Equus Art Gallery, Newmarket, Suffolk.
Vandeleur Antiquarian Books, Epsom, Surrey.
Julia Holmes Antique Maps and Prints, South Harting, W. Sussex.
Burman Antiques, Stratford-upon-Avon, Warks.
Country Connections (Esk House Arts), Grosmont, N. Yorks.

Stamps

Argyll Etkin Gallery, London W1.
Michael Coins, London W8.
J.A.L. Franks & Co, London WC1.
Stanley Gibbons, London WC2.
Avalon Post Card and Stamp Shop, Chester, Cheshire.
Penrith Coin and Stamp Centre, Penrith, Cumbria.
Denver House Antiques and Collectables, Burford, Oxon.
Jeremy's (Oxford Stamp Centre), Oxford, Oxon.
A.J. Saywell Ltd. (The Oxford Stamp Shop), Oxford, Oxon.
Edinburgh Coin Shop, Edinburgh, Scotland.
Collectors' Gallery, Shrewsbury, Shrops.
Bath Stamp and Coin Shop, Bath, Somerset.
Corridor Stamp Shop, Bath, Somerset.
Glance Back Bookshop, Chepstow, Wales.

Tapestries, Textiles & Needlework

Linda Gumb, London N1.
The Textile Company, London N1.
Joseph Lavian, London N4.
Robert Franses and Sons, London NW8.
Gallery of Antique Costume and Textiles, London NW8.
Hilary Batstone Decorative Antiques, London SW1.
S. Franses Ltd, London SW1.
Joss Graham, London SW1.
Heraz (David Hartwright Ltd), London SW1.
Keshishian, London SW1.
Mayorcas Ltd, London SW1.
Peta Smyth - Antique Textiles, London SW1.
Rare Carpets Gallery, London SW10.
Antiques and Things, London SW11.
The Kilim Warehouse Ltd, London SW12.
Classic Fabrics with Robin Haydock, London SW13.
Tobias and The Angel, London SW13.

Joanna Booth, London SW3.
Robert Stephenson, London SW3.
313 Antiques, London SW6.
Judy Greenwood, London SW6.
Perez Antique Carpets Gallery, London SW6.
Heskia, London SW8.
Atlantic Bay Carpets, London W1.
John Eskenazi Ltd, London W1.
C. John (Rare Rugs) Ltd, London W1.
Alexander Juran and Co, London W1.
Paul Nels Ltd, London W1.
Pelham Galleries Ltd, London W1.
Vigo Carpet Gallery, London W1.
Linda Wrigglesworth, London W1.
Alex Zadah Fine Oriental & European Carpets, London W1.
Sheila Cook, London W11.
Fairman Carpets Ltd, London W11.
David Ireland, London W11.
Daniel Mankowitz, London W11.
Coats Oriental Carpets, London W8.
Jonathan Horne, London W8.
Lunn Antiques, London WC2.
Robert and Georgina Hastie, Hungerford, Berks.
Made of Honour, Chester, Cheshire.
Martin and Dorothy Harper Antiques, Bakewell, Derbys.
The House that Moved, Exeter, Devon.
The Honiton Lace Shop, Honiton, Devon.
The Lace Shop, South Molton, Devon.
Georgina Ryder, Sherborne, Dorset.
Maureen Morris, Saffron Walden, Essex.
The Stuffed Dog Antiques, Berkeley, Glos.
Anthony Hazledine, Fairford, Glos.
Huntington Antiques Ltd, Stow-on-the-Wold, Glos.
Meg Andrews, Harpenden, Herts.
Two Maids Antiques, Biddenden, Kent.
The Lace Basket, Tenterden, Kent.
Farmhouse Antiques, Bolton-by-Bowland, Lancs.
20th Century Frocks, Lincoln, Lincs.
Jocelyn Chatterton, Louth, Lincs.
Audley House, Osbournby, Lincs.
Country and Eastern, Norwich, Norfolk.
The Barn, Collingham, Notts.
Witney Antiques, Witney, Oxon.
Clutter, Uppingham, Rutland.
Present Bygones, Edinburgh, Scotland.
Townhouse Antiques, Walkerburn, Scotland.
Antique Linens and Lace, Bath, Somerset.
Antique Textiles, Bath, Somerset.
Ann King, Bath, Somerset.
Susannah, Bath, Somerset.
Bruce Tozer Rugs & Antiques, Bath, Somerset.
Faded Elegance, Dulverton, Somerset.
Times Past, Somerton, Somerset.
Richard Midwinter Antiques, Newcastle-under-Lyme, Staffs.
Tara's Hall, Hadleigh, Suffolk.
Oswald Simpson, Long Melford, Suffolk.
Sarah Meysey-Thompson Antiques, Woodbridge, Suffolk.
Heytesbury Antiques, Farnham, Surrey.
Hart Antiques, Bridgend, Wales.
Patrick and Gillian Morley Antiques, Warwick, Warks.
Avon Antiques, Bradford-on-Avon, Wilts.
Emma Hurley Antiques and Textiles, Warminster, Wilts.
Penny Farthing Antiques, North Cave, E. Yorks.
London House Oriental Rugs and Carpets, Boston Spa, W. Yorks.
Real Macoy, Keighley, W. Yorks.
Lawn and Lace, Mirfield, W. Yorks.
Echoes, Todmorden, W. Yorks.

Taxidermy

"Get Stuffed", London N1.
Curios, London N19.
Below Stairs of Hungerford, Hungerford, Berks.
Yesterday Tackle and Books, Bournemouth, Dorset.
Castle Antiques, Leigh-on-Sea, Essex.
John Burton Natural Craft Taxidermy, Ebrington, Glos.
Heads 'n' Tails, Wiveliscombe, Somerset.
The Enchanted Aviary, Bury St. Edmunds, Suffolk.

Tools (including Needlework & Sewing)

The Old Tool Chest, London N1.
Ye Little Shoppe, Modbury, Devon.
Thomas and Pamela Hudson, Cirencester, Glos.
Mark A. Serle (Antiques and Restoration), Lechlade, Glos.
Norton Antiques, Twyford, Norfolk.
Ark Antiques, Bishop's Castle, Shrops.
David Bridgwater, Bath, Somerset.
Sheila Cooper t/a Sheila Smith Antiques, Bath, Somerset.
Peppers Period Pieces, Bury St. Edmunds, Suffolk.
Trinders' Fine Tools, Clare, Suffolk.
Roy Arnold, Needham Market, Suffolk.

Toys (see Dolls & Toys)

Trade Dealers (see Shipping Goods)

Treen

Halcyon Days, London EC3.
Robert Young Antiques, London SW11.
Halcyon Days, London W1.
M. and D. Seligmann, London W8.
Cobblers Hall Antiques, Toddington, Beds.
Phoenix Antiques, Fordham, Cambs.
A.P. and M.A. Haylett, Outwell, Cambs.
Brian R. Bolt Antiques, Portballintrae, Co. Antrim, N. Ireland.
Anvil Antiques, Cartmel, Cumbria.
Maggie Tallentire Antiques, Cartmel, Cumbria.
Mortlake Antiques, Kirkby Stephen, Cumbria.
Shire Antiques, Newby Bridge, Cumbria.
Baggott Church Street Ltd, Stow-on-the-Wold, Glos.
Huntington Antiques Ltd, Stow-on-the-Wold, Glos.
Day Antiques, Tetbury, Glos.
Prichard Antiques, Winchcombe, Glos.
Millers of Chelsea Antiques Ltd, Ringwood, Hants.
Elizabeth Viney, Stockbridge, Hants.
Mary Roofe Antiques, Winchester, Hants.
Two Maids Antiques, Biddenden, Kent.
E.W. Webster, Bickerstaffe, Lancs.
Audley House, Osbournby, Lincs.
Mark Seabrook Antiques, West Haddon, Northants.
The Barn, Collingham, Notts.
Brian and Caroline Craik Ltd, Bath, Somerset.
Foord Antiques and Restoration, Bures, Suffolk.
Peppers Period Pieces, Bury St. Edmunds, Suffolk.
J. Du Cros Antiques, Petworth, W. Sussex.
Islwyn Watkins, Knighton, Wales.
Moxhams Antiques, Bradford-on-Avon, Wilts.
Combe Cottage Antiques, Castle Combe, Wilts.
Annmarie Turner Antiques, Marlborough, Wilts.
Fenwick and Fenwick Antiques, Broadway, Worcs.
Bill Bentley, Harrogate, N. Yorks.
Michael Green Traditional Interiors, Harrogate, N. Yorks.

Vintage Cars (see Carriages & Cars)

Watercolours

Royal Exchange Art Gallery, London EC3.
Boutique Fantasque, London N1.
Michael Finney Antique Prints and Books, London N1.
Finchley Fine Art Galleries, London N12.
Lauri Stewart - Fine Art, London N2.
The Totteridge Gallery, London N20.
Centaur Gallery, London N6.
Sandra Lummis Fine Art, London N8.
Barkes and Barkes, London NW1.
Gunter Fine Art, London NW2.
Newhart (Pictures) Ltd, London NW3.
Gallery Kaleidoscope, London NW6.
The Greenwich Gallery, London SE10.
Chris Beetles Ltd, London SW1.
Miles Wynn Cato, London SW1.
Douwes Fine Art Ltd, London SW1.
Frost and Reed Ltd (Est. 1808), London SW1.
Martyn Gregory Gallery, London SW1.
Sally Hunter Fine Art, London SW1.
Moreton Street Gallery, London SW1.
Old Maps and Prints, London SW1.
Paisnel Gallery, London SW1.
Michael Parkin Fine Art Ltd, London SW1.
Polak Gallery, London SW1.
Spink and Son Ltd, London SW1.
Bill Thomson - Albany Gallery, London SW1.
Waterman Fine Art Ltd, London SW1.
Collins and Hastie Ltd, London SW10.
Hollywood Road Gallery, London SW10.
Park Walk Gallery, London SW10.
Pawsey and Payne, London SW10.
John Bloxham (Fine Art) Ltd, London SW11.

Alton Gallery, London SW13.
A & C International, London SW17.
The David Curzon Gallery, London SW19.
Campbell's of Walton Street, London SW3.
Colin Denny Ltd, London SW3.
Gallery Lingard, London SW3.
Green and Stone, London SW3.
Stephanie Hoppen Ltd, London SW3.
20th Century Gallery, London SW6.
John Spink, London SW6.
Julie Collino, London SW7.
Agnew's, London W1.
Andrew Clayton-Payne, London W1.
Connaught Brown plc, London W1.
Editions Graphiques Gallery, London W1.
The Fine Art Society plc, London W1.
Maas Gallery, London W1.
Mallett Gallery, London W1.
John Mitchell and Son, London W1.
Hal O'Nians, London W1.
Piccadilly Gallery, London W1.
Stephen Somerville Ltd, London W1.
Spink Leger Pictures, London W1.
Waterhouse and Dodd, London W1.
Charles Daggett Gallery, London W11.
Milne and Moller, London W11.
Justin F. Skrebowski Prints, London W11.
Stephen Garratt (Fine Paintings), London W14.
Ealing Gallery, London W5.
Crawley and Asquith Ltd, London W8.
George Dare, London W8.
Simon Spero, London W8.
Beryl Kendall, The English Watercolour Gallery, London W9.
Abbott and Holder, London WC1.
Sebastian D'Orsai Ltd, London WC1.
Beverley J. Pyke - Fine British Watercolours, Alderney, Channel Islands.
Baroq at Brindleys, Heath and Reach, Beds.
Charterhouse Gallery Ltd, Heath and Reach, Beds.
David Ball Antique Furnisher, Leighton Buzzard, Beds.
Foye Gallery, Luton, Beds.
Knight's Gallery, Luton, Beds.
Graham Gallery, Burghfield Common, Berks.
Marlborough Sporting Gallery and Bookshop, Hungerford, Berks.
Jaspers Fine Arts Ltd, Maidenhead, Berks.
Grove Gallery, Windsor and Eton, Berks.
J. Manley, Windsor and Eton, Berks.
Grosvenor House Interiors, Beaconsfield, Bucks.
Windmill Fine Art, High Wycombe, Bucks.
Angela Hone Watercolours, Marlow, Bucks.
Penn Barn, Penn, Bucks.
Medina Antiquarian Maps and Prints, Winslow, Bucks.
Cambridge Fine Art Ltd, Cambridge, Cambs.
Sebastian Pearson Paintings Prints and Works of Art, Cambridge, Cambs.
Baron Fine Art, Chester, Cheshire.
Richard A. Nicholson, Chester, Cheshire.
Harper Fine Paintings, Poynton, Cheshire.
Margaret Bedi Antiques, Billingham, Cleveland.
T.B. and R. Jordan (Fine Paintings), Eaglescliffe, Cleveland.
Phyllis Arnold Gallery Antiques, Greyabbey, Co. Down, N. Ireland.
Copperhouse Gallery - W. Dyer & Sons, Hayle, Cornwall.
Tony Sanders Penzance Gallery and Antiques, Penzance, Cornwall.
Myles Varcoe, Tywardreath, Cornwall.
St. Breock Gallery, Wadebridge, Cornwall.
Peter Haworth, Beetham, Cumbria.
The Gallery, Penrith, Cumbria.
Kenneth Upchurch, Ashbourne, Derbys.
Charles H. Ward, Derby, Derbys.
J. Collins and Son, Bideford, Devon.
Medina Gallery, Bideford, Devon.
Chantry Bookshop and Gallery, Dartmouth, Devon.
Mill Gallery, Ermington, Devon.
Honiton Fine Art, Honiton, Devon.
Skeaping Gallery, Lydford, Devon.
Michael Wood Fine Art, Plymouth, Devon.
Bygone Days Antiques, Tiverton, Devon.
Stour Gallery, Blandford Forum, Dorset.
Hants Gallery, Bournemouth, Dorset.
The Swan Gallery, Sherborne, Dorset.
Domino Antiques, Barling Magna, Essex.
Brandler Galleries, Brentwood, Essex.
Neil Graham Gallery, Brentwood, Essex.
S. Bond and Son, Colchester, Essex.
Richard Iles Gallery, Colchester, Essex.
Simon Hilton, Dunmow, Essex.
Newport Gallery, Newport, Essex.
David Lloyd Gallery, Purleigh, Essex.
Reddings Art and Antiques, Southend-on-Sea, Essex.
Galerie Lev, Woodford Green, Essex.
Cleeve Picture Framing, Bishops Cleeve, Glos.
The Priory Gallery, Bishops Cleeve, Glos.
Alexander Gallery, Bristol, Glos.
David Howard, Cheltenham, Glos.
The Loquens Gallery, Cheltenham, Glos.
Manor House Gallery, Cheltenham, Glos.
School House Antiques, Chipping Campden, Glos.
Astley House - Fine Art, Moreton-in-Marsh, Glos.
Nina Zborowska, Painswick, Glos.
The John Davies Gallery, Stow-on-the-Wold, Glos.
The Fosse Gallery, Stow-on-the-Wold, Glos.
Kenulf Fine Arts, Stow-on-the-Wold, Glos.
Roger Lamb Antiques & Works of Art, Stow-on-the-Wold, Glos.
Tetbury Gallery, Tetbury, Glos.
Channel Islands Galleries Ltd, St. Peter Port, Guernsey, Channel Islands.
Geoffrey P. Gavey, Vale, Guernsey, Channel Islands.
Laurence Oxley, Alresford, Hants.
Antique House, Hartley Wintney, Hants.
J. Morton Lee, Hayling Island, Hants.
Corfields Ltd, Lymington, Hants.
The Petersfield Bookshop, Petersfield, Hants.
Lacewing Fine Art Gallery, Romsey, Hants.
Bell Fine Art, Winchester, Hants.
Brobury House Gallery, Brobury, Herefs.
Coltsfoot Gallery, Leominster, Herefs.
Countrylife Gallery, Hitchin, Herts.
Carole Thomas (Fine Arts), Hitchin, Herts.
Galerias Segui, Cowes, Isle of Wight.
The Shanklin Gallery, Shanklin, Isle of Wight.
Falle Fine Art Limited, St Helier, Jersey, Channel Islands.
Falle Fine Art Limited, St Helier, Jersey, Channel Islands.
Cranbrook Gallery, Cranbrook, Kent.
Judith Peppitt, Harrietsham, Kent.
Periwinkle Press, Newnham, Kent.
Francis Iles, Rochester, Kent.
Langley Galleries, Rochester, Kent.
Sundridge Gallery, Sundridge, Kent.
Nicholas Bowlby, Tunbridge Wells, Kent.
Graham Gallery, Tunbridge Wells, Kent.
Apollo Antique Galleries, Westerham, Kent.
Old Corner House Antiques, Wittersham, Kent.
Fulda Gallery Ltd, Manchester, Lancs.
Hammond Smith (Fine Art), Leicester, Leics.
P. Stanworth (Fine Arts), Market Bosworth, Leics.
Graftons of Market Harborough, Market Harborough, Leics.
Lincoln Fine Art, Lincoln, Lincs.
Lyver & Boydell Galleries, Liverpool, Merseyside.
The Hampton Hill Gallery, Hampton Hill, Middx.
Marble Hill Gallery, Twickenham, Middx.
The Coach House, Costessey, Norfolk.
The Haven Gallery, Gt. Yarmouth, Norfolk.
Crome Gallery and Frame Shop, Norwich, Norfolk.
The Fairhurst Gallery, Norwich, Norfolk.
Mandell's Gallery, Norwich, Norfolk.
The Westcliffe Gallery, Sheringham, Norfolk.
Staithe Lodge Gallery, Swafield, Norfolk.
Norton Antiques, Twyford, Norfolk.
Coughton Galleries Ltd, Arthingworth, Northants.
Right Angle, Brackley, Northants.
Savage Fine Art, Haselbech, Northants.
Dragon Antiques, Kettering, Northants.
The Bell Gallery, Belfast, N. Ireland.
Haydon Bridge Antiques, Haydon Bridge, Northumbs.
Haydon Gallery, Haydon Bridge, Northumbs.

Anthony Mitchell Fine Paintings, Nottingham, Notts.
John Harrison Fine Art, Aston Tirrold, Oxon.
Benson Antiques Centre & Gallery, Benson, Oxon.
H.C. Dickins, Bloxham, Oxon.
The Burford Gallery, Burford, Oxon.
Horseshoe Antiques and Gallery, Burford, Oxon.
The Stone Gallery, Burford, Oxon.
Wren Gallery, Burford, Oxon.
The Country Store and Linen Cupboard, Deddington, Oxon.
The Barry M. Keene Gallery, Henley-on-Thames, Oxon.
Fine Art of Oakham, Oakham, Rutland.
The Old House Gallery, Oakham, Rutland.
Marc Oxley Fine Art, Uppingham, Rutland.
The Rendezvous Gallery, Aberdeen, Scotland.
The McEwan Gallery, Ballater, Scotland.
Calton Gallery, Edinburgh, Scotland.
Malcolm Innes Gallery, Edinburgh, Scotland.
John Mathieson and Co, Edinburgh, Scotland.
Young Antiques, Edinburgh, Scotland.
The Roger Billcliffe Fine Art, Glasgow, Scotland.
Ewan Mundy Fine Art Ltd, Glasgow, Scotland.
Inchmartine Fine Art, Inchture, Scotland.
Mainhill Gallery, Jedburgh, Scotland.
Newburgh Antiques, Newburgh, Scotland.
The George Street Gallery, Perth, Scotland.
Nigel Stacy-Marks Ltd, Perth, Scotland.
St. Andrews Fine Art, St. Andrews, Scotland.
John Boulton Fine Art, Broseley, Shrops.
Teme Valley Antiques, Ludlow, Shrops.
Cruck House Antiques, Much Wenlock, Shrops.
F.C. Manser and Son Ltd, Shrewsbury, Shrops.
Haygate Gallery, Telford, Shrops.
The Mount, Woore, Shrops.
Hall's Antiques, Ash Priors, Somerset.
Adam Gallery, Bath, Somerset.
Trimbridge Galleries, Bath, Somerset.
The Court Gallery, Nether Stowey, Somerset.
Sadler Street Gallery,, Wells, Somerset.
England's Gallery, Leek, Staffs.
Richard Midwinter Antiques, Newcastle-under-Lyme, Staffs.
Thompson's Gallery, Aldeburgh, Suffolk.
The Fortescue Gallery, Ipswich, Suffolk.
J. and J. Baker, Lavenham,, Suffolk.
Equus Art Gallery, Newmarket, Suffolk.
Peasenhall Art and Antiques Gallery, Peasenhall, Suffolk.
The Falcon Gallery, Wortham, Suffolk.
Suffolk House Antiques, Yoxford, Suffolk.
Cobham Galleries, Cobham, Surrey.
The Court Gallery, East Molesey, Surrey.
Barbara Rubenstein Fine Art, Godalming, Surrey.
Glencorse Antiques, Kingston-upon-Thames, Surrey.
Limpsfield Watercolours, Limpsfield, Surrey.
Bourne Gallery Ltd, Reigate, Surrey.
The Gallery, Reigate, Surrey.
Roland Goslett Gallery, Richmond, Surrey.
F. and T. Lawson Antiques, Richmond, Surrey.
Marryat, Richmond, Surrey.
Palmer Galleries, Richmond, Surrey.
Cedar House Gallery, Ripley, Surrey.
Sage Antiques and Interiors, Ripley, Surrey.
Margaret Melville Watercolours, Staines, Surrey.
Boathouse Gallery, Walton-on-Thames, Surrey.
Edward Cross - Fine Paintings, Weybridge, Surrey.
Stephen Welbourne, Brighton, E. Sussex.
John Day of Eastbourne Fine Art, Eastbourne, E. Sussex.
Premier Gallery & Bookshop, Eastbourne, E. Sussex.
Molly Alexander, Seaford, E. Sussex.
Faringdon Gallery, Arundel, W. Sussex.
Sussex Fine Art, Arundel, W. Sussex.
Susan and Robert Botting, Billingshurst, W. Sussex.
Lannards Gallery, Billingshurst, W. Sussex.
Gough Bros. Art Shop and Gallery, Bognor Regis, W. Sussex.
The Antique Print Shop, East Grinstead, W. Sussex.
The Canon Gallery, Petworth, W. Sussex.
George House Gallery, Petworth, W. Sussex.
Lombard Gallery, Petworth, W. Sussex.
Wilsons Antiques, Worthing, W. Sussex.
Anna Harrison Fine Antiques, Gosforth, Tyne and Wear.
MacDonald Fine Art, Gosforth, Tyne and Wear.
Osborne Art and Antiques, Jesmond,, Tyne and Wear.
The Dean Gallery Ltd, Newcastle-upon-Tyne, Tyne and Wear.
David Windsor Gallery, Bangor, Wales.
Michael Webb Fine Art, Bodorgan, Wales.
Manor House Fine Arts, Cardiff, Wales.
Emlyn Antiques, Newcastle Emlyn, Wales.
Philip Davies Fine Art, Swansea, Wales.
Thicke Galleries, Swansea, Wales.
Barn Court Antiques, Templeton, Wales.
Arden Gallery, Henley-in-Arden, Warks.
Colmore Galleries Ltd, Henley-in-Arden, Warks.
Fine-Lines (Fine Art), Shipston-on-Stour, Warks.
The Loquens Gallery, Stratford-upon-Avon, Warks.
John Hubbard Antiques and Fine Art, Birmingham, W. Mids.
The Windmill Gallery, Birmingham, W. Mids.
Robert Withers Antiques & Paintings, Halesowen, W. Mids.
Oldswinford Gallery, Stourbridge, W. Mids.
Driffold Gallery, Sutton Coldfield, W. Mids.
Audley House Antiques, Bradford-on-Avon, Wilts.
D.M. Beach, Salisbury, Wilts.
The Jerram Gallery, Salisbury, Wilts.
Richard Hagen, Broadway, Worcs.
Hay Loft Gallery, Broadway, Worcs.
Haynes Fine Art of Broadway, Broadway, Worcs.
Haynes Fine Art of Broadway Picton House Galleries, Broadway, Worcs.
John Noott Galleries, Broadway, Worcs.
Malvern Arts, Great Malvern, Worcs.
Gandolfi House, Malvern Wells, Worcs.
The Highway Gallery, Upton-upon-Severn, Worcs.
James H. Starkey Galleries, Beverley, E. Yorks.
Anthony Graham Antiques, Boroughbridge, N. Yorks .
W. Greenwood (Fine Art), Burneston, N. Yorks.
Garth Antiques, Harrogate, N. Yorks.
McTague of Harrogate, Harrogate, N. Yorks.
Walker Galleries Ltd, Harrogate, N. Yorks.
E. Stacy-Marks Limited, Helmsley, N. Yorks.
Gary K. Blissett, Long Preston, N. Yorks.
Talents Fine Arts Ltd, Malton, N. Yorks.
Rose Fine Art and Antiques, Ripon, N. Yorks.
Richard Bennett, Thirsk, N. Yorks.
Garth Antiques, Whixley, N. Yorks.
Coulter Galleries, York, N. Yorks.
The Basement Gallery at Fulwood Antiques, Sheffield, S. Yorks.
E. Carrol, Bingley, W. Yorks.
The Titus Gallery, Shipley, W. Yorks.
Robin Taylor Fine Arts, Wakefield, W. Yorks.

Wholesale Dealers (see Shipping Goods)

Wine Related Items

The Hugh Johnson Collection, London SW1.
Patricia Harbottle, London W11.
Christopher Sykes Antiques, Woburn, Beds.
Bacchus Antiques - In the Service of Wine, Cartmel, Cumbria.
Bell Antiques, Bourton-on-the-Water, Glos.
Robin Butler, Bristol, Glos.
Neil Willcox, Twickenham, Middx.
Bacchus Gallery, Petworth, W. Sussex.

Dealers' Index

In order to facilitate reference to dealers both the names of the individuals and their business names are indexed separately, i.e. the name of their shop or business, as well as the town and county under which they appear. Thus A E Jones and C Smith of High Street Antiques will be indexed under

Jones, A E, Town, County
Smith, C, Town, County
and High Street Antiques, Town, County

A

B

C

D

E

F

G

H

I

J

K

M

N

O

P

S

T

U

STOP PRESS

LONDON W1

Paul Champkins BADA

41 Dover Street, W1X 3RB. Open by appointment. SIZE: Small. *STOCK: Chinese, Korean and Japanese art, £1,000-£100,000.* LOC: Off Piccadilly. PARK: Short stay. SER: Valuations; restorations. FAIRS: Grosvenor House. TEL: 0171 495 4600; fax - 01235 751 206. VAT: Spec.

LONDON EC1

La Maison BADA

410 St. John Street, EC1V 4NJ. (Guillaume and Louise Bacon). Open 10-6, Sun. by appointment. SIZE: Large. *STOCK: Beds, French antiques - armoires, mirrors, chandeliers, garden ornaments, etc.* LOC: 1 min. walk from Angel tube station. PARK: Easy. SER: Restorations. TEL: 0171 837 6522; fax - same. VAT: Stan.

FOR A NEW OR SUBSTANTIALLY ALTERED ENTRY USE THIS FORM

Please complete and return this form; there is no charge

NAME OF SHOP ....

ADDRESS OF SHOP ....

....
full address including actual county (not postal area)

Name (or names) and initials of proprietor(s) ....
(Mr/Mrs/Miss/or title)

Previous trading address (if applicable) ....

....

State whether 'Trade Only' (Yes or No) ....

BADA (Yes or No) .... LAPADA (Yes or No) ....

Year Established .... Resident on premises (Yes or No) ....

OPENING HOURS: (One entry, e.g. '9.30—5.30' if open all day or part day.
Two entries, e.g. '9.30—1.00, 2,00—5.30' if closed for lunch)

Please put 'CLOSED' and 'BY APPT.' where applicable

	Morning	Afternoon
Sunday	....	....
Monday	....	....
Tuesday	....	....
Wednesday	....	....
Thursday	....	....
Friday	....	....
Saturday	....	....

SIZE OF SHOWROOM

Small (up to 600 sq.ft.) ....

Medium (600 to 1,500 sq.ft.) ....

Large (over 1,500 sq.ft.) ....

HOW TO GET TO YOUR SHOP (BUSINESS)

Brief helpful details from the nearest well-known road:

....

....

....

....

OF WHAT DOES YOUR STOCK CHIEFLY CONSIST?

(A) Please list in order of importance	(B) Approximate period or date of stock	(C) Indication of price range of stock eg £50–£100 or £5–£25
1. (Principal stock)		
2.		
3.		

IS PARKING ***OUTSIDE*** **YOUR SHOP (BUSINESS)** Easy (Yes or No) ....

TELEPHONE NUMBER: Business ....

Home ....
(only if customers can ring for appointments outside business hours)

V.A.T. scheme operated — Standard/Special/Both ....

SERVICES OFFERED:

Valuations (Yes or No) ....

Restorations (Yes or No) ....

Type of work ....

Buying specific items at auction for a commission (Yes or No) ....

Type of item ....

FAIRS:

At which fairs (if any) do you normally exhibit? ....

....

....

CERTIFICATION:

The information given above is accurate and you may publish it in the Guide. I understand that this entry is entirely free.

Signed ....

Date ....

ENGLISH COUNTY BOUNDARIES

Map showing county boundaries of England. For county boundary details of Northern Ireland, Scotland and Wales see maps at start of relevant sections.

SCOTLAND
NORTHUMBERLAND
TYNE & WEAR
ISLE OF MAN
CUMBRIA
DURHAM
CLEVELAND
NORTH YORKSHIRE
LANCASHIRE
WEST YORKSHIRE
East Yorkshire
MERSEYSIDE
SOUTH YORKSHIRE
CHESHIRE
DERBYSHIRE
NOTTINGHAMSHIRE
STAFFORDSHIRE
LINCOLNSHIRE
SHROPSHIRE
LEICESTERSHIRE
WEST MIDLANDS
RUTLAND
WALES
NORFOLK
HEREFORD
WORCESTER
WARWICKSHIRE
NORTHAMPTONSHIRE
CAMBRIDGESHIRE
BEDFORDSHIRE
GLOUCESTERSHIRE
OXFORDSHIRE
BUCKINGHAMSHIRE
SUFFOLK
HERTFORDSHIRE
ESSEX
BERKSHIRE
GREATER LONDON
WILTSHIRE
SOMERSET
SURREY
HAMPSHIRE
KENT
DORSET
WEST SUSSEX
EAST SUSSEX
ISLE OF WIGHT